A NORTON CRITICAL EDITION

Alexis de Tocqueville
DEMOCRACY IN AMERICA

AN ANNOTATED TEXT
BACKGROUNDS
INTERPRETATIONS

Edited by

ISAAC KRAMNICK

CORNELL UNIVERSITY

W. W. NORTON & COMPANY

New York • London

W. W. Norton & Company has been independent since its founding in 1923, when William Warder Norton and Mary D. Herter Norton first published lectures delivered at the People's Institute, the adult education division of New York City's Cooper Union. The Nortons soon expanded their program beyond the Institute, publishing books by celebrated academics from America and abroad. By mid-century, the two major pillars of Norton's publishing program—trade books and college texts—were firmly established. In the 1950s, the Norton family transferred control of the company to its employees, and today—with a staff of four hundred and a comparable number of trade, college, and professional titles published each year—W. W. Norton & Company stands as the largest and oldest publishing house owned wholly by its employees.

The text of this book is composed in Fairfield Medium
with the display set in Bernhard Modern.

Series design by Antonina Krass.
Composition by PennSet, Inc.
Manufacturing by the Courier Companies—Westford Division.
Production manager: Benjamin Reynolds.

Library of Congress Cataloging-in-Publication Data
Tocqueville, Alexis de, 1805–1859.
  [De la démocratie en Amérique. English]
  Democracy in America : an annotated text backgrounds interpretations /
Alexis de Tocqueville ; edited by Isaac Kramnick.— 1st ed.
     p.   cm.—(Norton critical edition)
  Includes bibliographical references.

  ISBN 978-0-393-92986-7 (pbk.)

  1. United States—Politics and government. 2. United States—Social
conditions—To 1865. 3. Democracy—United States. 4. United States—
History—1815–1861. I. Kramnick, Isaac. II. Title.
JK216.T713 2008
320.973—dc22

                                                           2007027404

W. W. Norton & Company, Inc., 500 Fifth Avenue, New York, NY 10110-0017
www.wwnorton.com

W. W. Norton & Company Ltd., Castle House,
75/76 Wells Street, London W1T 3QT

1   2   3   4   5   6   7   8   9   0

FOR MY GRANDCHILDREN

May their generation finally realize democracy in America

Contents

Introduction

I

Few "Great Books" have been so universally canonized as Alexis de Tocqueville's *Democracy in America*. Even fewer have made it into the very heart of a nation's civic discourse and public culture as has Tocqueville's study of nineteenth-century America. Tocqueville and his book are everywhere in America: in presidential and congressional speeches; in newspaper editorials and op-ed pieces; in academic symposia, Sunday supplements and sermons; in high school and college classrooms (60,000 copies are sold to college students alone each year); on radio and TV commentary; even unto the use of Tocqueville as a poster boy for charitable giving. United Way chapters across the United States have since 1972 enrolled anyone who donates $10,000 or more to the giant charity into the "Alexis de Tocqueville Society," noting in their literature that "Tocqueville's most important observation was that Americans helped each other in time of need."[1]

One reason Tocqueville is a favorite of the chattering classes is that, as the fabled *New York Times* journalist James Reston observed, "his observations are still as fresh as this morning's newspapers."[2] Moreover, it's easy for virtually anyone in public life to quote some Tocqueville, since, as the *Washington Post* offered in 1984, "citing Tocqueville is a bit like citing the Bible; you can find about anything in it to support your argument."[3] Not that all who invoke Tocqueville have necessarily read his nearly 900-page book. The humorist Russell Baker, in fact, has suggested that "of all the great unread writers I believe Tocqueville to be the most quoted."[4]

But many, of course, do read Tocqueville and read him through, convinced that *Democracy in America* is truly a timeless classic. On this there is an amazing consensus uniting liberals and conservatives, as two of the essays below indicate. For the liberal professor and journalist Max Lerner, *Democracy in America* "is the greatest book ever written on America"; for the conservative academic Edward Banfield, it is "the greatest book ever written by anyone about America."

If imitation is a sign of canonical respect, then Tocqueville has his devoted acolytes, and they have repeated his epic trek across America and like him offered reflections on America. In 1981, the 150th an-

---

1. United Way, National Alexis de Tocqueville Society Awards brochure.
2. *New York Times*, 2 July 1986.
3. *Washington Post*, 6 November 1984.
4. *New York Times*, 23 November 1976.

niversary of the visit, the journalist Richard Reeves duplicated Tocqueville's trip and offered thoughts about Ronald Reagan's America in his cleverly titled *American Journey: Traveling with Tocqueville in Search of Democracy in America*. Much more ambitious was the TV network C-Span's nine-month traipse across the country in 1997 and 1998 to visit and broadcast live from the exact places on the exact dates that Tocqueville had visited them in his equivalent nine months from May 1831 to February 1832. This produced many hours of television and a book, *Traveling Tocqueville's America*. In the book's preface the network explained its fascination with Tocqueville. It had been shaped by the countless speeches they had broadcast over their first twenty years in which "political figures, presidents and congressmen, liberals and conservatives" all cited Tocqueville's *Democracy in America*.[5] More recently, in 2005, to honor the bicentennial of Tocqueville's birth, Bernard-Henri Lévy, the very embodiment today of "the French intellectual," retraced Tocqueville's journey as well. His *American Vertigo: Traveling America in the Footsteps of Tocqueville* put the nineteenth-century French visitor to Jacksonian America once again at the center of public chatter in the United States and France.

II

Alexis de Tocqueville was born on July 29, 1805, to parents who were provincial nobility from Northern France near the Channel coast. Tutored at home until he was fifteen, he spent three years at a lycée before studying law in Paris from ages eighteen to twenty-two. In 1827 Tocqueville was appointed to a minor judicial position at Versailles, where he met Gustave de Beaumont, another judicial functionary, who later, as Tocqueville's close friend, accompanied him to America.

In his legal studies and while working in Versailles, Tocqueville read widely in the classics of European social and political thought as well as in French and English constitutional history. In these years he also saw firsthand the clash of reactionary aristocratic ideals represented by Charles X, the brother of Louis XVI, who had come to the French throne in 1824, with the revolutionary democratic ferver of the 1830 Paris barricades, which led Charles to abdicate. If Tocqueville faulted the excesses of both camps, he was no more a partisan of Louis-Philippe, the Citizen-King, who wrapped himself in the tricolor of the Revolution instead of the Bourbon Lily, and his bourgeois monarchy that followed with its commercial and financial sponsorship.

It was in the context of his studies and the tumultuous interactions of French democratic, aristocratic, and monarchic ideals that Tocqueville came up with the idea of asking the French Ministry of the Interior to send him and Beaumont to America to study prisons and penitentiaries. The Ministry authorized the study but refused to provide funds, which proved no great problem for the two well-connected

---

5. Anne Bentzel, *Traveling Tocqueville's America: Retracing the 17-State Tour That Inspired Alexis de Tocqueville's political classic Democracy in America* (Baltimore, 1998), p. ix.

young men, who sailed for America on April 2, 1831. They clearly had more in mind than simply a study of prisons. As the twenty-five-year-old Tocqueville and the twenty-eight-year-old Beaumont told friends on their departure, they wanted to write a book on "all the mechanisms of this vast American society" that would, they hoped, be a "great work which would make our reputation some day."[6] Indeed, it did.

Their journey from Le Havre to Newport, Rhode Island, took five and a half weeks, with their arrival on the 9th of May. They remained in the United States until February 20, 1832, nine and a half months later. They did manage to see America's major prisons, starting with Sing Sing, "up the river" from New York, but that was by no means all they saw. By every conceivable conveyance—coach, canoe, steamer, donkey, and horse—they covered more than 7,000 miles of America, spending 271 days in the United States and 15 in Canada. From Newport and Boston in the East to Wisconsin and Michigan in the West, from Louisiana in the South to Canada in the North, the two Frenchmen traveled with their guns and their notebooks. They were wined and dined by the great and important, and they spent long periods in lonely isolation, sometimes gravely ill. Tocqueville read whatever he could lay his hands on, and the two interviewed presidents and embittered Native Americans. As Beaumont tells it, Tocqueville was always observing, always writing:

> Tocqueville . . . when traveling never rested. . . . Rest was foreign to his nature, and whether his body was actively employed or not, his mind was always at work. . . . It never occurred to him to consider an excursion as an amusement, or conversation as relaxation. For Tocqueville the most agreeable conversation was that which was the most useful. The bad day was the day lost or ill-spent. The smallest loss of time was unpleasant to him.[7]

Upon his return to France it took Tocqueville over eight years to write the entire book that would, as he hoped, make his reputation. After he and Beaumont published *Du Système pénitentiare aux États-unis* in 1833, Tocqueville published his *Democracy in America* in two installments, two volumes as Part I in 1835, and two more volumes as Part II in 1840. He was quickly translated into English by a young English friend, Henry Reeve, whose American editions of *Democracy in America*, published in 1838 and 1841 provide the text for this Norton Critical Edition.

His fellow Frenchmen immediately saw the importance of Tocqueville's achievement. The statesman-intellectual Royer-Collard wrote that "since Montesquieu there has been nothing like *Democracy in America*." In his review, reproduced below, Sainte-Beuve insists that "we would have to go back a long way to find a book of scientific and political observations that has so awakened and rewarded the atten-

---

6. Quoted in James T. Schleifer, *The Making of Tocqueville's Democracy in America* (Chapel Hill, 1980), p. 3.
7. Quoted in Matthew J. Mancini, *Alexis de Tocqueville* (New York, 1994), p. 15.

tion of our philosophers." In another review Rossi wrote: "no impartial reader can fail to admire on each page the purity of form, the subtle power of observation, the shrewd judgment, the ingenuity, the simple, lively style, both assured and gracious . . . . His workmanship is exquisite." No wonder, then, that his publisher is said to have told Tocqueville "well, it seems you've written a masterpiece."[8] In England, the great John Stuart Mill noted in his 1835 review that Tocqueville's work

> has at once taken its rank among the most remarkable productions of our time; and is a book with which, both for its facts and its speculations, all who would understand, or who would be called upon to exercise influence over their age, are bound to be familiar. It will contribute to give to the political speculations of our time a new character . . . .

Tocqueville had to be particularly pleased with the book's reception in America. As early as 1836 *The North American Review* hailed *Democracy in America* "as by far the most philosophical, ingenious, and instructive, which has been produced in Europe on the subject of America." A year later *The United States Democratic Review* wrote that Tocqueville's book was "decidedly the most remarkable and really valuable work that has ever yet appeared upon this country from the hand of a foreigner." No longer, wrote *The Knickerbocker* in 1838, did America seem "an enigma to all the world for he has put into the hands of the European public a key to our long-concealed mysteries."

III

"The dominant idea in the book," Tocqueville wrote a friend in 1835, in a letter reprinted below, the "idea which embraces all the others" is the "irresistible future" that is democracy, the inevitable and divinely inspired triumph of democratic ideals over aristocratic. The future was set: "society was tending every day more and more towards equality." America has put to rest the fears of intellectuals who ever since Plato had assumed that the word democracy was "synonymous with destruction, spoilation and murder." America proved that in a democratic government and in a society of equals property was "respected, liberty preserved and religion honored." Even if poetry and other elevated productions of the mind might languish in a democracy like America with its "blending of social ranks,"

> it yet has a nobility of its own; and that after all it may be God's will to spread a moderate amount of happiness over all men, instead of heaping a large sum upon a few by allowing only a small minority to approach perfection.

What particularly struck Tocqueville, himself then a functionary of the French state, was the absence of public power in America, no clear-cut set of government officials with directive administrative au-

8. Quoted in André Jardin, *Tocqueville: A Biography* (Baltimore, 1998), p. 224.

thority. In letters home he wrote that "in spite of anxiously searching for the government, one can find it nowhere." There was no army, no taxation, no central government; "the executive power is nothing." What he found was "the spectacle of a society marching along all alone, without guide or support." What made it all work was not the administrative state, so familiar to Europeans, but "the cooperation of individual wills."

Tocqueville worried that a self-governing political system absent the steadying influence of a professional administrative class, let alone the entrenched privileges of traditional elites, might produce a new tyranny, the democratic tyranny of the majority, a concern in *Democracy in America* that has riveted its readers from the 1830s to this day. *The Knickerbocker*, so full of praise for the Frenchman unraveling the American puzzle, faulted his picture of the despotism of public opinion in America, rebuking him for the claim that he knew "no country in which there is so little independence of mind and freedom of discussion, as in America." John Stuart Mill, whose *On Liberty* later revisited similar themes, insisted in 1840 that Tocqueville's description of the insignificance of individuals before growing mass tyranny confused the effects of democracy with "the tendencies of modern commercial society." Some early reviewers and some contemporary scholars wonder whether Tocqueville's worries were fueled by the narrow circle of elites he talked with and the overly Federalist and Whig orientation of the books and tracts he read while in America. Still, "the tyranny of the majority" remains the signature theme most identified with Tocqueville and his *Democracy in America*.

The text explores aspects of American life that blunt the potential for majority tyranny. The entire legal system, especially the role in politics of lawyers, all schooled in and committed to the importance of precedent and continuity, is a brake on runaway democracy. The spirit of localism, pride in local self-government, as well as the significant role of religion in American social life, far greater, Tocqueville contends, than elsewhere, bring a self-restraint and a suspicion of central government meddling that tempers the likelihood of the tyranny of the majority. By far the most powerful antidote to the potential excesses of democracy that Tocqueville finds in America is the country's irrepressible "spirit of association."

"Americans of all ages, all stations in life, and all types of disposition," Tocqueville writes, "are forever forming associations." These may be commercial, religious, moral, cultural, or simply fraternal groupings, but, he concludes, "nothing, in my view, deserves more attention" than this American inclination to create voluntary associations. It produces a richly textured intermediate level of associational civil society standing between individuals and the state, inhibiting centralized tyranny just as the nobility and the clergy did under the ancien régime. Schools of civic engagement, mutual trust and obligation, these myriads of social networks and reciprocal communities constitute what the contemporary American scholar Robert Putnam labels a nation's "social capital." In his *Bowling Alone: The Collapse and Revival of American Community,* Putnam anoints Tocqueville "the patron saint of contemporary social capitalists" as he laments the late-twentieth-century decline of the rich associational life that Tocqueville saw as so uniquely American.[9] No wonder then that contemporary communitarian critics of excessive American individualism and self-centeredness look to Tocqueville as their prophetic voice and to *Democracy in America* as their sacred text.

Alongside and vying with their associational zeal Tocqueville finds nineteenth-century Americans obsessively focused on self, constantly striving, relentlessly driven by personal ambition and a passion for wealth. Tocqueville saw greed and exploitation as central to the enslavement of Southern blacks and to the gradual extermination of the aboriginal American population, which in the revealing parlance of the age he sometimes labeled "savages." Americans, Tocqueville observed, believed in the equality and brotherhood of all men, yet violated natural law and the laws of humanity by brutalizing Blacks and removing Indians. Nat Turner's Rebellion, the very year of Tocqueville's visit to America, convinced him that a cataclysmic war between the races was inevitable in the South, which is evident in his 1835 comment to John Quincy Adams, below, about other slave uprisings.

Tocqueville saw the American Indian as particularly victimized by American acquisitiveness and the "grasping search for gain." The greed of settlers and their restless urge to subdue and improve "the untouched splendor of America" doomed America's aboriginal peoples to ultimate extermination. In a moving letter to his mother written on Christmas Day 1831, Tocqueville described how Americans had deceived and humiliated Indians in order to appropriate their land. Unlike the Spanish, the Americans do not as a matter of policy wantonly slaughter all natives, he wrote, but with their manipulative treaties they used ostensibly more civilized and humane legal methods to rid the land of the once proud tribes. "In a hundred years," he wrote his mother, there will be "not even a single man belonging to the most remarkable of the Indian races."

IV

His book on America established Tocqueville's reputation, as he had hoped it would. The year after Volume II appeared he was made a member of the Académie Française, an honor reserved for the forty most eminent artists and intellectuals in all France. It launched him on a career in public affairs as well. In the 1840s and early 1850s Tocqueville was active in French national politics, elected repeatedly to the Chamber of Deputies from the family seat near Cherbourg, and he even served for a short time as France's foreign minister.

His specialty as a parliamentarian was foreign affairs, and he sought to abolish slavery in France's colonies even as he supported French colonialism in Algeria, describing it as progressive and civilizing. Dur-

9. Robert D. Putnam, *Bowling Alone: The Collapse and Revival of American Community* (New York, 2000), p. 292.

ing the revolutionary upheavals of 1848, Tocqueville denounced the socialist ideas and policies of Louis Blanc in speeches to the Chamber of Deputies. Four years later, he parted company with his former admirer and sponsor Louis Napoleon when that President of the Republic took the title Emperor Napoleon III.

Tocqueville returned to writing after leaving politics and in 1856 published his other remarkable work, *The Ancien Régime and the Revolution*, a study of the emergence of a centralized state in France from the end of the feudal era through the politics of the French Revolution. He died at the age of 54, a victim of tuberculosis, in 1859, the year his friend John Stuart Mill published *On Liberty*, the book so often linked to *Democracy in America*.

It took over a century for Tocqueville's reputation to achieve the prominence it now has in American life. With the exception of Henry Adams, who saw the Frenchman's writings as the "gospel of my private religion,"[1] few paid much attention to him, until there was a bit of notice with the centennial of *Democracy in America* in the 1930s. The Nisbet and Kloppenberg selections below chronicle the spectacular Tocqueville renaissance in America after World War II and during the long cold war. He has never achieved such canonical status in his native France. On college campuses, consensus historians, professors of American Studies, and social scientists who were seeking a unique American civic culture that immunized her against European totalitarianism rediscovered *Democracy in America*, and they assigned it. The text's protean quality and the ease with which its meaning and relevance can be shaped and used across the political spectrum made it available for quotation by all varieties of politicians and pundits. No wonder that the Frenchman's words are more likely to be heard in the American public square today than Jefferson's or Lincoln's, which improbably and paradoxically makes him more than they America's public philosopher.

What better proof of this surprising stature than a survey by the *New York Times* to determine how the trauma of September 11, 2001, had left its mark "on how American history is written and taught" five years later. The only text cited by the many scholars interviewed in September 2006 is *Democracy in America*. A historian explains how he now assigns "Tocqueville's writing about tyranny of the majority in [his] course" to help his students understand why after the attack "civil liberties would take a beating" in America.[2] Several weeks after the anniversary of 9/11 Tocqueville was still on the American public mind in an even more unexpected setting. In a *New York Times* review of a book on the history of gambling in America, which claimed that 54 million people visited casinos in America in 2004, the reviewer finished with the obligatory Tocqueville quote, even on this esoteric topic. The review ends: "Tocqueville, as always, got it exactly right.

---

1. Quoted in Michael Kammen, *Alexis de Tocqueville and Democracy in America* (Washington, D.C., 1998), p. 10.
2. *New York Times*, 6 September 2006.

'Those who live in the midst of democratic fluctuations have always before their eyes the image of chance,' he wrote, 'and they end by liking all undertakings in which chance plays a part.' "[3] What an achievement, this canonic and iconic place in American life, for a visitor who spent nine and a half months in the country!

I would like to thank W. W. Norton's Carol Bemis and Ann Shin for the idea of this book and Elana Beale for all her wonderful help in putting it together. Thanks also, once again, to Michael Busch for his invaluable assistance and to Susan Tarrow for her splendid translations from French to English.

3. *New York Times,* 6 October 2006.

A Note on the Text

The text reproduced here with no changes is the first American print-ing of the complete *Democracy in America* in 1841, translated from the French by Henry Reeve. The one exception is that the "American Editor," John C. Spencer, who added his own notes to the text, wrote prefaces to each of Tocqueville's two volumes, which have been moved to the Backgrounds section of this Norton Critical Edition. Tocque-ville's footnotes are indicated, as they were then, by various printer's marks. Henry Reeve's footnotes are labeled *Translator's Note*. The notes added by the editor of this Norton Critical Edition are num-bered and found at the end of the text.

A Note on the Text

The Text of
DEMOCRACY IN AMERICA

DEMOCRACY IN AMERICA.

BY

ALEXIS DE TOCQUEVILLE,

MEMBER OF THE INSTITUTE OF FRANCE, AND OF THE CHAMBER
OF DEPUTIES, ETC., ETC.

TRANSLATED BY HENRY REEVE, ESQ.

WITH AN ORIGINAL PREFACE AND NOTES BY

JOHN C. SPENCER,

COUNSELLOR AT LAW

FOURTH EDITION,
REVISED AND CORRECTED FROM THE EIGHTH PARIS EDITION.

IN TWO VOLUMES.

VOL. I

NEW YORK:

J. & H. G. LANGLEY, 57 CHATHAM STREET.

PHILADELPHIA:—THOMAS, COWPERTHWAITE, & CO.

BOSTON:—C. C. LITTLE & J. BROWN.

1841.

Table of Contents

CHAPTER XVIII.

Introduction.

Among the novel objects that attracted my attention during my stay in the United States, nothing struck me more forcibly than the general equality of conditions. I readily discovered the prodigious influence which this primary fact exercises on the whole course of society, by giving a certain direction to public opinion, and a certain tenor to the laws; by imparting new maxims to the governing powers, and peculiar habits to the governed.

I speedily perceived that the influence of this fact extends far beyond the political character and the laws of the country, and that it has no less empire over civil society than over the government; it creates opinions, engenders sentiments, suggests the ordinary practices of life, and modifies whatever it does not produce.

The more I advanced in the study of American society, the more I perceived that the equality of conditions is the fundamental fact from which all others seem to be derived, and the central point at which all my observations constantly terminated.

I then turned my thoughts to our own hemisphere, where I imagined that I discerned something analogous to the spectacle which the New World presented to me. I observed that the equality of conditions is daily advancing toward those extreme limits which it seems to have reached in the United States; and that the democracy which governs the American communities, appears to be rapidly rising into power in Europe.

I hence conceived the idea of the book which is now before the reader.

It is evident to all alike that a great democratic revolution is going on among us; but there are two opinions as to its nature and consequences. To some it appears to be a novel accident, which as such may still be checked; to others it seems irresistible, because it is the most uniform, the most ancient, and the most permanent tendency which is to be found in history.

Let us recollect the situation of France seven hundred years ago, when the territory was divided among a small number of families, who were the owners of the soil and the rulers of the inhabitants; the right of governing descended with the family inheritance from generation to generation; force was the only means by which man could act on man; and landed property was the sole source of power.

Soon, however, the political power of the clergy was founded, and began to exert itself; the clergy opened its ranks to all classes, to the poor and the rich, the villain and the lord; equality penetrated into the government through the church, and the being who, as a serf, must have vegetated in perpetual bondage, took his place as a priest in the midst of nobles, and not unfrequently above the heads of kings.

The different relations of men became more complicated and more numerous, as society gradually became more stable and more civilized. Thence the want of civil laws was felt; and the order of legal functionaries soon rose from the obscurity of the tribunals and their dusty chambers, to appear at the court of the monarch, by the side of the feudal barons in their ermine and their mail.

While the kings were ruining themselves by their great enterprises, and the nobles exhausting their resources by private wars, the lower orders were enriching themselves by commerce. The influence of money began to be perceptible in state affairs. The transactions of business opened a new road to power, and the financier rose to a station of political influence in which he was at once flattered and despised.

Gradually the spread of mental acquirements, and the increasing taste for literature and art, opened chances of success to talent; science became the means of government, intelligence led to social power, and the man of letters took a part in the affairs of the state.

The value attached to the privileges of birth, decreased in the exact proportion in which new paths were struck out to advancement. In the eleventh century nobility was beyond all price; in the thirteenth it might be purchased; it was conferred for the first time in 1270; and equality was thus introduced into the government by the aristocracy itself.

In the course of these seven hundred years, it sometimes happened that, in order to resist the authority of the crown or to diminish the power of their rivals, the nobles granted a certain share of political rights to the people. Or, more frequently, the king permitted the lower orders to enjoy a degree of power, with the intention of repressing the aristocracy.

In France the kings have always been the most active and the most constant of levellers. When they were strong and ambitious, they spared no pains to raise the people to the level of the nobles; when they were temperate or weak, they allowed the people to rise above themselves. Some assisted the democracy by their talents, others by their vices. Louis XI. and Louis XIV. reduced every rank beneath the throne to the same subjection; Louis XV. descended, himself and all his court, into the dust.[1]

As soon as land was held on any other than a feudal tenure, and personal property began in its turn to confer influence and power, every improvement which was introduced in commerce or manufacture, was a fresh element of the equality of conditions. Henceforward every new discovery, every new want which it engendered, and every new desire which craved satisfaction, was a step toward the universal level. The taste for luxury, the love of war, the sway of fashion, the most superficial, as well as the deepest passions of the human heart, co-operated to enrich the poor and to empoverish the rich.

From the time when the exercise of the intellect became the source of strength and of wealth, it is impossible not to consider every addition to science, every fresh truth, and every new idea, as a germe of power placed within the reach of the people. Poetry, eloquence, and memory, the grace of wit, the glow of imagination, the depth of thought, and all the gifts which are bestowed by Providence with an equal hand, turned to the advantage of the democracy; and even when they were in the possession of its adversaries, they still served its cause by throwing into relief the natural greatness of man; its conquests spread, therefore, with those of civilization and knowledge; and literature became an arsenal, where the poorest and weakest could always find weapons to their hand.

In perusing the pages of our history, we shall scarcely meet with a single great event, in the lapse of seven hundred years, which has not turned to the advantage of equality.

The crusades[2] and the wars of the English[3] decimated the nobles, and divided their possessions; the erection of communes introduced an element of democratic liberty into the bosom of feudal monarchy; the invention of firearms equalized the villain and the noble on the field of battle; printing opened the same resources to the minds of all classes; the post was organized so as to bring the same information to the door of the poor man's cottage and to the gate of the palace; and protestantism proclaimed that all men are alike able to find the road to heaven. The discovery of America offered a thousand new paths to fortune, and placed riches and power within the reach of the adventurous and the obscure.

If we examine what has happened in France at intervals of fifty years, beginning with the eleventh century, we shall invariably perceive that a twofold revolution has taken place in the state of society. The noble has gone down on the social ladder, and the *roturier*[4] has gone up; the one descends as the other rises. Every half-century brings them nearer to each other, and they will very shortly meet.

Nor is this phenomenon at all peculiar to France. Whithersoever we turn our eyes, we shall discover the same continual revolution throughout the whole of Christendom.

The various occurrences of national existence have everywhere turned to the advantage of democracy; all men have aided it by their exertions: those who have intentionally laboured in its cause, and those who have served it unwittingly—those who have fought for it, and those who have declared themselves its opponents—have all been driven along in the same track, have all laboured to one end, some ignorantly, and some unwillingly; all have been blind instruments in the hands of God.

The gradual development of the equality of conditions is, therefore, a providential fact, and it possesses all the characteristics of a divine decree: it is universal, it is durable, it constantly eludes all human interference, and all events as well as all men contribute to its progress.

Would it, then, be wise to imagine that a social impulse which dates from so far back, can be checked by the efforts of a generation? Is it credible that the democracy which has annihilated the feudal system, and vanquished kings, will respect the citizen and the capitalist? Will it stop now that it has grown so strong and its adversaries so weak?

None can say which way we are going, for all terms of comparison are wanting: the equality of conditions is more complete in the Christian countries of the present day, than it has been at any time, or in any part of the world; so that the extent of what already exists prevents us from foreseeing what may be yet to come.

The whole book which is here offered to the public, has been written under the impression of a kind of religious dread, produced in the author's mind by the contemplation of so irresistible a revolution, which has advanced for centuries in spite of such amazing obstacles, and which is still proceeding in the midst of the ruins it has made.

It is not necessary that God himself should speak in order to disclose to us the unquestionable signs of his will; we can discern them in the habitual course of nature, and in the invariable tendency of events; I know, without a special revelation, that the planets move in the orbits traced by the Creator's finger.

If the men of our time were led by attentive observation and by sincere reflection, to acknowledge that the gradual and progressive development of social equality is at once the past and future of their history, this solitary truth would confer the sacred character of a divine decree upon the change. To attempt to check democracy would be in that case to resist the will of God; and the nations would then be constrained to make the best of the social lot awarded to them by Providence.

The Christian nations of our age seem to me to present a most alarming spectacle; the impulse which is bearing them along is so strong that it cannot be stopped, but it is not yet so rapid that it cannot be guided: their fate is in their hands; yet a little while and it may be so no longer.

The first duty which is at this time imposed upon those who direct our affairs is to educate the democracy; to warm its faith, if that be possible; to purify its morals; to direct its energies; to substitute a knowledge of business for its inexperience, and an acquaintance with its true interests for its blind propensities; to adapt its government to time and place, and to modify it in compliance with the occurrences and the actors of the age.

A new science of politics is indispensable to a new world.

This, however, is what we think of least; launched in the middle of a rapid stream, we obstinately fix our eyes on the ruins which may still be described upon the shore we have left, while the current sweeps us along, and drives us backward toward the gulf.

In no country in Europe has the great social revolution which I have been describing, made such rapid progress as in France; but it has always been borne on by chance. The heads of the state have never had any forethought for its exigences, and its victories have been obtained without their consent or without their knowledge. The most powerful, the most intelligent, and the most moral classes of the nation have never attempted to connect themselves with it in order to guide it. The people have consequently been abandoned to its wild propensities, and it has grown up like those outcasts who receive their education in the public streets, and who are unacquainted with aught but the vices and wretchedness of society. The existence of a democracy was seemingly unknown, when, on a sudden, it took possession of the supreme power. Everything was then submitted to its caprices; it was worshipped as the idol of strength; until, when it was enfeebled by its own excesses, the legislator conceived the rash project of annihilating its power, instead of instructing it and correcting its vices; no attempt was made to fit it to govern, but all were bent on excluding it from the government.

The consequence of this has been that the democratic revolution has been effected only in the material parts of society, without that concomitant change in laws, ideas, customs, and manners, which was necessary to render such a revolution beneficial. We have gotten a democracy, but without the conditions which lessen its vices, and render its natural advantages more prominent; and although we already perceive the evils it brings, we are ignorant of the benefits it may confer.

While the power of the crown, supported by the aristocracy, peaceably governed the nations of Europe, society possessed, in the midst of its wretchedness, several different advantages which can now scarcely be appreciated or conceived.

The power of a part of his subjects was an insurmountable barrier to the tyranny of the prince; and the monarch who felt the almost divine character which he enjoyed in the eyes of the multitude, derived a motive for the just use of his power from the respect which he inspired.

High as they were placed above the people, the nobles could not but take that calm and benevolent interest in its fate which the shepherd feels toward his flock; and without acknowledging the poor as their equals, they watched over the destiny of those whose welfare Providence had intrusted to their care.

The people, never having conceived the idea of a social condition different from its own, and entertaining no expectation of ever ranking with its chiefs, received benefits from them without discussing their rights. It grew attached to them when they were clement and just, but it submitted without resistance or servility to their exactions, as to the inevitable visitations of the arm of God. Custom, and the manners of the time, had moreover created a species of law in the midst of violence, and established certain limits to oppression.

As the noble never suspected that any one would attempt to deprive him of the privileges which he believed to be legitimate, and as the serf looked upon his own inferiority as a consequence of the immutable order of nature, it is easy to imagine that a mutual exchange of good-will took place between two classes so differently gifted by fate. Inequality and wretchedness were then to be found in society; but the souls of neither rank of men were degraded.

Men are are not corrupted by the exercise of power or debased by the habit of obedience; but by the exercise of power which they believe to be illegal, and by obedience to a rule which they consider to be usurped and oppressive.

On one side were wealth, strength, and leisure, accompanied by the refinement of luxury, the elegance of taste, the pleasures of wit, and the religion of art. On the other were labor, and a rude ignorance; but in the midst of this coarse and ignorant multitude, it was not uncommon to meet with energetic passions, generous sentiments, profound religious convictions, and independent virtues.

The body of a state thus organized, might boast of its stability, its power, and above all, of its glory.

But the scene is now changed, and gradually the two ranks mingle; the divisions which once severed mankind, are lowered; property is divided, power is held in common, the light of intelligence spreads, and the capacities of all classes are equally cultivated; the state becomes democratic, and the empire of democracy is slowly and peaceably introduced into the institutions and manners of the nation.

I can conceive a society in which all men would profess an equal attachment and respect for the laws of which they are the common authors; in which the authority of the state would be respected as necessary, though not as divine; and the loyalty of the subject to the chief magistrate would not be a passion, but a quiet and rational persuasion. Every individual being in the possession of rights which he is sure to retain, a kind of manly reliance and reciprocal courtesy would arise between all classes, alike removed from pride and meanness.

The people, well acquainted with its true interests, would allow, that in order to profit by the advantages of society, it is necessary to satisfy its demands. In this state of things, the voluntary association of the citizens might supply the individual exertions of the nobles, and the community would be alike protected from anarchy and from oppression.

I admit that in a democratic state thus constituted, society will not be stationary; but the impulses of the social body may be regulated and directed forward; if there be less splendour than in the halls of an aristocracy, the contrast of misery will be less frequent also; the pleasures of enjoyment may be less excessive, but those of comfort will be more general; the sciences may be less perfectly cultivated, but ignorance will be less common; the impetuosity of the feelings will be repressed, and the habits of the nation softened; there will be more vices and fewer crimes.

In the absence of enthusiasm and of an ardent faith, great sacrifices may be obtained from the members of a commonwealth by an appeal to their understandings and their experience: each individual will feel the same necessity for uniting with his fellow-citizens to protect his own weakness; and as he knows that if they are to assist he must co-operate, he will readily perceive that his personal interest is identified with the interest of the community.

The nation, taken as a whole, will be less brilliant, less glorious, and perhaps less strong; but the majority of the citizens will enjoy a greater degree of prosperity, and the people will remain quiet, not because it despairs of melioration, but because it is conscious of the advantages of its condition.

If all the consequences of this state of things were not good or useful, society would at least have appropriated all such as were useful and good; and having once and for ever renounced the social advantages of aristocracy, mankind would enter into possession of all the benefits which democracy can afford.

But here it may be asked what we have adopted in the place of those institutions, those ideas, and those customs of our forefathers which we have abandoned.

The spell of royalty is broken, but it has not been succeeded by the majesty of the laws; the people have learned to despise all authority. But fear now extorts a larger tribute of obedience than that which was formerly paid by reverence and by love.

I perceive that we have destroyed those independent beings which were able to cope with tyranny single-handed; but it is the government that has inherited the privileges of which families, corporations, and individuals, have been deprived; the weakness of the whole community has, therefore, succeeded to that influence of a small body of citizens, which, if it was sometimes oppressive, was often conservative.

The division of property has lessened the distance which separated the rich from the poor; but it would seem that the nearer they draw to each other, the greater is their mutual hatred, and the more vehement the envy and the dread with which they resist each other's claims to power; the notion of right is alike insensible to both classes, and force affords to both the only argument for the present, and the only guarantee for the future.

The poor man retains the prejudices of his forefathers without their faith, and their ignorance without their virtues; he has adopted the doctrine of self-interest as the rule of his actions, without understanding the science which controls it, and his egotism is no less blind than his devotedness was formerly.

If society is tranquil, it is not because it relies upon its strength and its well-being, but because it knows its weakness and its infirmities: a single effort may cost it its life; everybody feels the evil, but no one has courage or energy enough to seek the cure; the desires, the regret, the sorrows, and the joys of the time, produce nothing that is visible or permanent, like the passions of old men which terminate in impotence.

We have, then, abandoned whatever advantages the old state of things afforded, without receiving any compensation from our present condition; having destroyed an aristocracy, we seem inclined to survey its ruins with complacency, and to fix our abode in the midst of them.

The phenomena which the intellectual world presents are not less deplorable. The democracy of France, checked in its course or abandoned to its lawless passions, has overthrown whatever crossed its path, and has shaken all that it has not destroyed. Its control over society has not been gradually introduced, or peaceably established, but it has constantly advanced in the midst of disorder, and the agitation of a conflict. In the heat of the struggle each partisan is hurried beyond the limits of his opinions by the opinions and the excesses of his opponents, until he loses sight of the end of his exertions, and holds a language which disguises his real sentiments or secret instincts. Hence arises the strange confusion which we are beholding.

I cannot recall to my mind a passage in history more worthy of sorrow and of pity than the scenes which are happening under our eyes; it is as if the natural bond which unites the opinions of man to his tastes, and his actions to his principles, was now broken; the sympathy which has always been acknowledged between the feelings and the ideas of mankind, appears to be dissolved, and all the laws of moral analogy to be abolished.

Zealous Christians may be found among us, whose minds are nurtured in the love and knowledge of a future life, and who readily espouse the cause of human liberty, as the source of all moral greatness. Christianity, which has declared that all men are equal in the sight of God, will not refuse to acknowledge that all citizens are equal in the eye of the law. But, by a singular concourse of events, religion is entangled in those institutions which democracy assails, and it is not unfrequently brought to reject the equality it loves, and to curse that cause of liberty as a foe, which it might hallow by its alliance.

By the side of these religious men I discern others whose looks are turned to the earth more than to heaven; they are the partisans of liberty, not only as the source of the noblest virtues, but more especially as the root of all solid advantages; and they sincerely desire to extend its sway, and to impart its blessings to mankind. It is natural that they should hasten to invoke the assistance of religion, for they must know that liberty cannot be established without morality, nor morality without faith; but they have seen religion in the ranks of their adversaries, and they inquire no farther; some of them attack it openly, and the remainder are afraid to defend it.

In former ages slavery has been advocated by the venal and slavishminded, while the independent and the warm-hearted were struggling without hope to save the liberties of mankind. But men of high and generous characters are now to be met with, whose opinions are at variance with their inclinations, and who praise that servility which they have themselves never known. Others, on the contrary, speak in the name of liberty as if they were able to feel its sanctity and its majesty, and loudly claim for humanity those rights which they have always disowned.

There are virtuous and peaceful individuals whose pure morality, quiet habits, affluence, and talents, fit them to be the leaders of the surrounding population; their love of their country is sincere, and they are prepared to make the greatest sacrifices to its welfare, but they confound the abuses of civilization with its benefits, and the idea of evil is inseparable in their minds from that of novelty.

Not far from this class is another party, whose object is to materialise mankind, to hit upon what is expedient without heeding what is just; to acquire knowledge without faith, and prosperity apart from virtue; assuming the title of the champions of modern civilization, and placing themselves in a station which they usurp with insolence, and from which they are driven by their own unworthiness.

Where are we then?

The religionists are the enemies of liberty, and the friends of liberty attack religion; the high-minded and the noble advocate subjection, and the meanest and most servile minds preach independence; honest and enlightened citizens are opposed to all progress, while men without patriotism and without principles, are the apostles of civiliation and of intelligence.

Has such been the fate of the centuries which have preceded our own? and has man always inhabited a world, like the present, where nothing is linked together, where virtue is without genius, and genius without honour; where the love of order is confounded with a taste for oppression, and the holy rites of freedom with a contempt of law; where the light thrown by conscience on human actions is dim, and where nothing seems to be any longer forbidden or allowed, honorable or shameful, false or true?

I cannot, however, believe that the Creator made man to leave him in an endless struggle with the intellectual miseries which surround us. God destines a calmer and a more certain future to the communities of Europe; I am unacquainted with his designs, but I shall not cease to believe in them because I cannot fathom them, and I had rather mistrust my own capacity than his justice.

There is a country in the world where the great revolution which I am speaking of seems nearly to have reached its natural limits; it has been effected with ease and simplicity, say rather that this country has attained the consequences of the democratic revolution which we are undergoing, without having experienced the revolution itself.

The emigrants who fixed themselves on the shores of America in the beginning of the seventeenth century, severed the democratic principle from all the principles which repressed it in the old communities of Europe, and transplanted it unalloyed to the New World. It has there been allowed to spread in perfect freedom, and to put forth its consequences in the laws by influencing the manners of the country.

It appears to me beyond a doubt, that sooner or later we shall arrive, like the Americans, at an almost complete equality of conditions. But I do not conclude from this, that we shall ever be necessarily led to draw the same political consequences which the Americans have derived from a similar social organization. I am far from supposing that they have chosen the only form of government which a democracy may adopt; but the identity of the efficient cause of laws and manners in the two countries is sufficient to account for the immense interest we have in becoming acquainted with its effects in each of them.

It is not, then, merely to satisfy a legitimate curiosity that I have examined America; my wish has been to find instruction by which we may ourselves profit. Whoever should imagine that I have intended to write a panegyric would be strangely mistaken, and on reading this book, he will perceive that such was not my design: nor has it been my object to advocate any form of government in particular, for I am of opinion that absolute excellence is rarely to be found in any legislation; I have not even affected to discuss whether the social revolution, which I believe to be irresistible, is advantageous or prejudicial to mankind; I have acknowledged this revolution as a fact already accomplished or on the eve of its accomplishment; and I have selected the nation, from among those which have undergone it, in which its development has been the most peaceful and the most complete, in order to discern its natural consequences, and, if it be possible, to distinguish the means by which it may be rendered profitable. I confess that in America I saw more than America; I sought the image of democracy itself, with its inclinations, its character, its prejudices, and its passions, in order to learn what we have to fear or to hope from its progress.

In the first part of this work I have attempted to show the tendency given to the laws by the democracy of America, which is abandoned almost without restraint to its instinctive propensities; and to exhibit the course it prescribes to the government, and the influence it exercises on affairs. I have sought to discover the evils and the advantages which it produces. I have examined the precautions used by the Americans to direct it, as well as those which they have not adopted, and I have undertaken to point out the causes which enable it to govern society.

It was my intention to depict, in a second part, the influence which the equality of conditions and the rule of democracy exercise on the civil society, the habits, the ideas, and the manners of the Americans; I begin, however, to feel less ardour for the accomplishment of this project, since the excellent work of my friend and travelling companion M. de Beaumont has been given to the world.* I do not know whether I have succeeded in making known what I saw in America, but I am certain that such has been my sincere desire, and that I have never, knowingly, moulded facts to ideas, instead of ideas to facts.

Whenever a point could be established by the aid of written documents, I have had recourse to the original text, and to the most authentic and approved works.† I have cited my authorities in the notes, and any one may refer to them. Whenever an opinion, a political custom, or a remark on the manners of the country was concerned, I endeavoured to consult the most enlightened men I met with. If the point in question was important or doubtful, I was not satisfied with one testimony, but I formed my opinion on the evidence of several witnesses. Here the reader must necessarily believe me upon my word. I could frequently have quoted names which are either known to him, or which deserve to be so, in proof of what I advance; but I have carefully abstained from this practice. A stranger frequently hears important truths at the fireside of his host, which the latter would perhaps conceal even from the ear of friendship; he consoles himself with his guest, for the silence to which he is restricted, and the shortness of the traveller's stay takes away all fear of his indiscretion. I carefully noted every conversation of this nature as soon as it occurred, but

---

* This work is entitled, Marie, ou l'Esclavage aux Etats-Unis.
† Legislative and administrative documents have been furnished me with a degree of politeness which I shall always remember with gratitude. Among the American functionaries who thus favoured my inquiries I am proud to name Mr. Edward Livingston, then Secretary of State, and late American minister at Paris. During my stay at the session of Congress, Mr. Livingston was kind enough to furnish me with the greater part of the documents I possess relative to the federal government. Mr. Livingston is one of those rare individuals whom one loves, respects, and admires, from their writings, and to whom one is happy to incur the debt of gratitude on farther acquaintance.

these notes will never leave my writing-case; I had rather injure the success of my statements than add my name to the list of those strangers who repay the generous hospitality they have received by subsequent chagrin and annoyance.

I am aware that, notwithstanding my care, nothing will be easier than to criticise this book, if any one ever chooses to criticise it.

Those readers who may examine it closely will discover the fundamental idea which connects the several parts together. But the diversity of the subjects I have had to treat is exceedingly great, and it will not be difficult to oppose an isolated fact to the body of facts which I quote, or an isolated idea to the body of ideas I put forth. I hope to be read in the spirit which has guided my labours, and that my book may be judged by the general impression it leaves, as I have formed my own judgement not on any single reason, but upon the mass of evidence.

It must not be forgotten that the author who wishes to be understood is obliged to push all his ideas to their utmost theoretical consequences, and often to the verge of what is false or impracticable; for if it be necessary sometimes to quit the rules of logic in active life, such is not the case in discourse, and a man finds that almost as many difficulties spring from inconsistency of language, as usually arise from consistency of conduct.

I conclude by pointing out myself what many readers will consider the principal defect of the work. This book is written to favour no particular views, and in composing it I have entertained no design of serving or attacking any party: I have undertaken not to see differently, but to look farther than parties, and while they are busied for the morrow, I have turned my thoughts to the future.

DEMOCRACY IN AMERICA.

FIRST PART.

Chapter I.

EXTERIOR FORM OF NORTH AMERICA.

North America divided into two vast regions, one inclining toward the Pole, the other toward the Equator—Valley of the Mississippi—Traces of the Revolutions of the Globe.—Shore of the Atlantic Ocean, where the English Colonies were founded.—Difference in the Appearance of North and of South America at the Time of their Discovery.—Forests of North America.—Prairies.—Wandering Tribes of Natives.—Their outward Appearance, Manners, and Language.—Traces of an unknown people.

North America presents in its external form certain general features, which it is easy to discriminate at the first glance.

A sort of methodical order seems to have regulated the separation of land and water, mountains and valleys. A simple but grand arrangement is discoverable amid the confusion of objects and the prodigious variety of scenes.

This continent is divided, almost equally, into two vast regions, one of which is bounded, on the north by the arctic pole, and by the two great oceans on the east and west. It stretches toward the south, forming a triangle, whose irregular sides meet at length below the great lakes of Canada.

The second region begins where the other terminates, and includes all the remainder of the continent.

The one slopes gently toward the pole, the other toward the equator.

The territory comprehended in the first region descends toward the north with so imperceptible a slope that it may almost be said to form a level plain. Within the bounds of this immense tract of country there are neither high mountains nor deep valleys. Streams meander through it irregularly; great rivers mix their currents, separate and meet again, disperse and form vast marshes, losing all trace of their channels in the labyrinth of waters they have themselves created; and thus, at length, after innumerable windings, fall into the polar seas. The great lakes which bound this first region are not walled in, like most of those in the Old World, between hills and rocks. Their banks are flat, and rise but a few feet above the level of their waters; each of them thus forming a vast bowl filled to the brim. The slightest change in the structure of the globe would cause their waters to rush either toward the pole or to the tropical sea.

The second region is more varied on its surface, and better suited for the habitation of man. Two long chains of mountains divide it from one extreme to the other; the Allegany ridge takes the form of the shores of the Atlantic ocean; the other is parallel with the Pacific.

The space which lies between these two chains of mountains contains 1,341,649 square miles.* Its surface is therefore about six times as great as that of France.

This vast territory, however, forms a single valley, one side of which descends gradually from the rounded summits of the Alleganies, while the other rises in an uninterrupted course toward the tops of the Rocky mountains.

At the bottom of the valley flows an immense river, into which the various streams issuing from the mountains fall from all parts. In memory of their native land, the French formerly called this river the St. Louis. The Indians, in their pompous language, have named it the Father of Waters, or the Mississippi.

The Mississippi takes its source above the limit of the two great regions of which I have spoken, not far from the highest point of the table-land where they unite. Near the same spot rises another river,† which empties itself into the polar seas. The course of the Mississippi is at first devious: it winds several times toward the north, whence it rose; and, at length, after having been delayed in lakes and marshes, it flows slowly onward to the south.

*   Darby's "View of the United States."
†   Mackenzie's river.

Sometimes quietly gliding along the argillaceous bed which nature has assigned to it; sometimes swollen by storms, the Mississippi waters 2,500 miles in its course.* At the distance of 1,364 miles from its mouth this river attains an average depth of fifteen feet; and it is navigated by vessels of 300 tuns burden for a course of nearly 500 miles. Fifty-seven large navigable rivers contribute to swell the waters of the Mississippi; among others the Missouri, which traverses a space of 2,500 miles; the Arkansas of 1,300 miles; the Red river 1,000 miles; four whose course is from 800 to 1,000 miles in length, viz: the Illinois, the St. Peter's, the St. Francis, and the Moingona; beside a countless multitude of rivulets which unite from all parts their tributary streams.

The valley which is watered by the Mississippi seems formed to be the bed of this mighty river, which like a god of antiquity dispenses both good and evil in its course. On the shores of the stream nature displays an inexhaustible fertility; in proportion as you recede from its banks, the powers of vegetation languish, the soil becomes poor, and the plants that survive have a sickly growth. Nowhere have the great convulsions of the globe left more evident traces than in the valley of the Mississippi: the whole aspect of the country shows the powerful effects of water, both by its fertility and by its barrenness. The waters of the primeval ocean accumulated enormous beds of vegetable mould in the valley, which they levelled as they retired. Upon the right shore of the river are seen immense plains, as smooth as if the husbandman had passed over them with his roller. As you approach the mountains, the soil becomes more and more unequal and steril; the ground is, as it were, pierced in a thousand places by primitive rocks, which appear like the bones of a skeleton whose flesh is partly consumed. The surface of the earth is covered with a granitic sand, and huge irregular masses of stone, among which a few plants force their growth, and give the appearance of a green field covered with the ruins of a vast edifice. These stones and this sand discover, on examination, a perfect analogy with those which compose the arid and broken summits of the Rocky mountains. The flood of waters which washed the soil to the bottom of the valley, afterward carried away portions of the rocks themselves; and these, dashed and bruised against the neighbouring cliffs, were left scattered like wrecks at their feet.†

The valley of the Mississippi is, upon the whole, the most magnificent dwelling-place prepared by God for man's abode; and yet it may be said that at present it is but a mighty desert.

On the eastern side of the Alleganies, between the base of these mountains and the Atlantic ocean, lies a long ridge of rocks and sand, which the sea appears to have left behind as it retired. The mean breadth of this territory does not exceed one hundred miles; but it is about nine hundred miles in length. This part of the American continent has a soil which offers every obstacle to the husbandman, and its vegetation is scanty and unvaried.

* Warden's "Description of the United States."
† See Appendix A.

Upon this inhospitable coast the first united efforts of human industry were made. This tongue of arid land was the cradle of those English colonies which were destined one day to become the United States of America. The centre of power still remains there; while in the backward states the true elements of the great people, to whom the future control of the continent belongs, are secretly springing up.

When the Europeans first landed on the shores of the Antilles, and afterward on the coast of South America, they thought themselves transported into those fabulous regions of which poets had sung. The sea sparkled with phosphoric light, and the extraordinary transparency of its waters discovered to the view of the navigator all that had hitherto been hidden in the deep abyss.* Here and there appeared little islands perfumed with odoriferous plants, and resembling baskets of flowers, floating on the tranquil surface of the ocean. Every object which met the sight, in this enchanting region, seemed prepared to satisfy the wants, or contribute to the pleasures of man. Almost all the trees were loaded with nourishing fruits, and those which were useless as food, delighted the eye by the brilliancy and variety of their colours. In groves of fragrant lemon-trees, wild figs, flowering myrtles, acacias, and oleanders, which were hung with festoons of various climbing-plants, covered with flowers, a multitude of birds unknown in Europe displayed their bright plumage, glittering with purple and azure, and mingled their warbling in the harmony of a world teeming with life and motion.†

Underneath this brilliant exterior death was concealed. The air of these climates had so enervating an influence that man, completely absorbed by the present enjoyment, was rendered regardless of the future.

North America appeared under a very different aspect: there, everything was grave, serious, and solemn; it seemed created to be the domain of intelligence, as the south was that of sensual delight. A turbulent and foggy ocean washed its shores. It was girded round by a belt of granitic rocks, or by wide plains of sand. The foliage of its woods was dark and gloomy; for they were composed of firs, larches, evergreen oaks, wild olive-trees, and laurels.

Beyond this outer belt lay the thick shades of the central forests, where the largest trees which are produced in the two hemispheres grow side by side. The plane, the catalpa, the sugar-maple, and the Virginian poplar, mingled their branches with those of the oak, the beech, and the lime.

In these, as in the forests of the Old World, destruction was perpetually going on. The ruins of vegetation were heaped upon each other;

---

* Malte Brun tells us (vol. v., p. 726) that the water of the Caribbean sea is so transparent, that corals and fish are discernible at a depth of sixty fathoms. The ship seemed to float in the air, the navigator became giddy as his eye penetrated through the crystal flood, and beheld submarine gardens, or beds of shells, or gilded fishes gliding among tufts and thickets of seaweed.

† See Appendix B.

but there was no labouring hand to remove them, and their decay was not rapid enough to make room for the continual work of reproduction. Climbing-plants, grasses, and other herbs, forced their way through the mass of dying trees; they crept along their bending trunks, found nourishment in their dusty cavities, and a passage beneath the lifeless bark. Thus decay gave its assistance to life, and their respective productions were mingled together. The depths of these forests were gloomy and obscure, and a thousand rivulets, undirected in their course by human industry, preserved in them a constant moisture. It was rare to meet with flowers, wild fruits, or birds, beneath their shades. The fall of a tree overthrown by age, the rushing torrent of a cataract, the lowing of the buffalo, and the howling of the wind, were the only sounds which broke the silence of nature.

To the east of the great river the woods almost disappeared; in their stead were seen prairies of immense extent. Whether nature in her infinite variety had denied the germes of trees to these fertile plains, or whether they had once been covered with forests, subsequently destroyed by the hand of man, is a question which neither tradition nor scientific research has been able to resolve.

These immense deserts were not, however, devoid of human inhabitants. Some wandering tribes had been for ages scattered among the forest shades or the green pastures of the prairie. From the mouth of the St. Lawrence to the Delta of the Mississippi, and from the Atlantic to the Pacific ocean, these savages possessed certain points of resemblance which bore witness of their common origin: but at the same time they differed from all other known races of men:* they were neither white like the Europeans, nor yellow like most of the Asiatics, nor black like the negroes. Their skin was reddish brown, their hair long and shining, their lips thin, and their cheek-bones very prominent. The languages spoken by the North American tribes were various as far as regarded their words, but they were subject to the same grammatical rules. Those rules differed in several points from such as had been observed to govern the origin of language.

The idiom of the Americans seemed to be the product of new combinations, and bespoke an effort of the understanding, of which the Indians of our days would be incapable.†

The social state of these tribes differed also in many respects from all that was seen in the Old World. They seemed to have multiplied freely in the midst of their deserts, without coming in contact with other races more civilized than their own.

Accordingly, they exhibited none of those indistinct, incoherent no-

---

* With the progress of discovery, some resemblance has been found to exist between the physical conformation, the language, and the habits of the Indians of North America, and those of the Tongous, Mantchous, Moguls, Tartars, and other wandering tribes of Asia. The land occupied by these tribes is not very distant from Behring's strait; which allows of the supposition, that at a remote period they gave inhabitants to the desert continent of America. But this is a point which has not yet been clearly elucidated by science. See Malte Brun, vol. v.; the works of Humboldt; Fischer, "Conjecture sur l'Origine des Américains"; Adair, "History of the American Indians."

† See Appendix C.

tions of right and wrong, none of that deep corruption of manners that is usually joined with ignorance and rudeness among nations which, after advancing to civilization, have relapsed into a state of barbarism. The Indian was indebted to no one but himself; his virtues, his vices, and his prejudices, were his own work; he had grown up in the wild independence of his nature.

If, in polished countries, the lowest of the people are rude and uncivil, it is not merely because they are poor and ignorant, but that, being so, they are in daily contact with rich and enlightened men. The sight of their own hard lot and of their weakness, which are daily contrasted with the happiness and power of some of their fellow-creatures, excites in their hearts at the same time the sentiments of anger and of fear: the consciousness of their inferiority and of their dependance irritates while it humiliates them. This state of mind displays itself in their manners and language; they are at once insolent and servile. The truth of this is easily proved by observation; the people are more rude in aristocratic countries than elsewhere; in opulent cities than in rural districts. In those places where the rich and powerful are assembled together, the weak and the indigent feel themselves oppressed by their inferior condition. Unable to perceive a single chance of regaining their equality, they give up to despair, and allow themselves to fall below the dignity of human nature.

This unfortunate effect of the disparity of conditions is not observable in savage life; the Indians, although they are ignorant and poor, are equal and free.

At the period when Europeans first came among them, the natives of North America were ignorant of the value of riches, and indifferent to the enjoyments which civilized man procures to himself by their means. Nevertheless, there was nothing coarse in their demeanour; they practised an habitual reserve, and a kind of aristocratic politeness.

Mild and hospitable when at peace, though merciless in war beyond any known degree of human ferocity, the Indian would expose himself to die of hunger in order to succour the stranger who asked admittance by night at the door of his hut—yet he could tear in pieces with his hands the still quivering limbs of his prisoner. The famous republics of antiquity never gave examples of more unshaken courage, more haughty spirits, or more intractable love of independence, than were hidden in former times among the wild forests of the New World.* The Europeans produced no great impression when they landed upon the shores of North America: their presence engendered neither envy nor fear. What influence could they possess over such men as we have described? The Indian could live without wants, suf-

---

* We learn from President Jefferson's "Notes upon Virginia," p. 148, that among the Iroquois, when attacked by a superior force, aged men refused to fly, or to survive the destruction of their country; and they braved death like the ancient Romans when their capital was sacked by the Gauls. Farther on, p. 160, he tells us that there is no example of an Indian, who, having fallen into the hands of his enemies, begged for his life; on the contrary, the captive sought to obtain death at the hands of his conquerors by the use of insult and provocation.

fer without complaint, and pour out his death-song at the stake.* Like all the other members of the great human family, these savages believed in the existence of a better world, and adored, under different names, God, the Creator of the universe. Their notions on the great intellectual truths were, in general, simple and philosophical.†

Although we have here traced the character of a primitive people, yet it cannot be doubted that another people, more civilized and more advanced in all respects, had preceded it in the same regions.

An obscure tradition, which prevailed among the Indians to the north of the Atlantic, informs us that these very tribes formerly dwelt on the west side of the Mississippi. Along the banks of the Ohio, and throughout the central valley, there are frequently found, at this day, *tumuli* raised by the hands of men. On exploring these heaps of earth to their centre, it is usual to meet with human bones, strange instruments, arms and utensils of all kinds, made of a metal, or destined for purposes, unknown to the present race.

The Indians of our time are unable to give any information relative to the history of this unknown people. Neither did those who lived three hundred years ago, when America was first discovered, leave any accounts from which even an hypothesis could be formed. Tradition— that perishable, yet ever-renewed monument of the pristine world— throws no light upon the subject. It is an undoubted fact, however, that in this part of the globe thousands of our fellow-beings had lived. When they came hither, what was their origin, their destiny, their history, and how they perished, no one can tell.

How strange does it appear that nations have existed, and afterward so completely disappeared from the earth, that the remembrance of their very names is effaced: their languages are lost; their glory is vanished like a sound without an echo; but perhaps there is not one which has not left behind it a tomb in memory of its passage. The most durable monument of human labour is that which recalls the wretchedness and nothingness of man.

Although the vast country which we have been describing was inhabited by many indigenous tribes, it may justly be said, at the time of its discovery by Europeans, to have formed one great desert. The Indians occupied, without possessing it. It is by agricultural labour that man appropriates the soil, and the early inhabitants of North America lived by the produce of the chase. Their implacable prejudices, their uncontrolled passions, their vices, and still more perhaps their savage virtues, consigned them to inevitable destruction. The ruin of these nations began from the day when Europeans landed on their shores: it has proceeded ever since, and we are now seeing the completion of it. They seemed to have been placed by Providence amid the riches of

---

* See "Histoire de la Louisiane," by Lepage Dupratz; Charlevoix, "Histoire de la Nouvelle France"; "Lettres du Rev. G. Hecwelder"; "Transactions of the American Philosophical Society," v. i.; Jefferson's "Notes on Virginia," pp. 135–190. What is said by Jefferson is of especial weight, on account of the personal merit of the writer, and of the matter-of-fact age in which he lived.

† See Appendix D.

the New World to enjoy them for a season, and then surrender them. Those coasts, so admirably adapted for commerce and industry; those wide and deep rivers; that inexhaustible valley of the Mississippi; the whole continent, in short, seemed prepared to be the abode of a great nation, yet unborn.

In that land the great experiment was to be made by civilized man, of the attempt to construct society upon a new basis; and it was there, for the first time, that theories hitherto unknown, or deemed impracticable, were to exhibit a spectacle for which the world had not been prepared by the history of the past.

Chapter II.

ORIGIN OF THE ANGLO-AMERICANS, AND ITS IMPORTANCE, IN RELATION TO THEIR FUTURE CONDITION.

Utility of knowing the Origin of Nations in order to understand their social Condition and their Laws.—America the only Country in which the Starting-Point of a great People has been clearly observable.—In what respects all who emigrated to British America were similar.—In what they differed.—Remark applicable to all the Europeans who established themselves on the shores of the New World.—Colonization of Virginia.—Colonization of New England.—Original Character of the first Inhabitants of New England.—Their Arrival.—Their first Laws.—Their social Contract.—Penal Code borrowed from the Hebrew Legislation.—Religious Fervour.—Republican Spirit.—Intimate Union of the Spirit of Religion with the Spirit of Liberty.

After the birth of a human being, his early years are obscurely spent in the toils or pleasures of childhood. As he grows up, the world receives him, when his manhood begins, and he enters into contact with his fellows. He is then studied for the first time, and it is imagined that the germe of the vices and the virtues of his maturer years is then formed.

This, if I am not mistaken, is a great error. We must begin higher up; we must watch the infant in his mother's arms; we must see the first images which the external world casts upon the dark mirror of his mind; the first occurrences which he beholds; we must hear the first words which awaken the sleeping powers of thought, and stand by his earliest efforts, if we would understand the prejudices, the habits, and the passions, which will rule his life. The entire man is, so to speak, to be seen in the cradle of the child.

The growth of nations presents something analogous to this; they all bear some marks of their origin; and the circumstances which accompanied their birth and contributed to their rise, affect the whole term of their being.

If we were able to go back to the elements of states, and to examine the oldest monuments of their history, I doubt not that we should discover the primary cause of the prejudices, the habits, the ruling passions, and in short of all that constitutes what is called the national character: we should then find the explanation of certain customs which now seem at variance with prevailing manners, of such laws as conflict with established principles, and of such incoherent opinions as are here and there to be met with in society, like those fragments of broken chains which we sometimes see hanging from the vault of an edifice, and supporting nothing. This might explain the destinies of certain nations which seem borne along by an unknown force to ends of which they themselves are ignorant. But hitherto facts have been wanting to researches of this kind: the spirit of inquiry has only come upon communities in their latter days; and when they at length turned their attention to contemplate their origin, time had already obscured it, or ignorance and pride adorned it with truth-concealing fables.

America is the only country in which it has been possible to study the natural and tranquil growth of society, and where the influence exercised on the future condition of states by their origin is clearly distinguishable.

At the period when the peoples of Europe landed in the New World, their national characteristics were already completely formed; each of them had a physiognomy of its own; and as they had already attained that stage of civilization at which men are led to study themselves, they have transmitted to us a faithful picture of their opinions, their manners, and their laws. The men of the sixteenth century are almost as well known to us as our contemporaries. America consequently exhibits in the broad light of day the phenomena which the ignorance or rudeness of earlier ages conceals from our researches. Near enough to the time when the states of America were founded to be accurately acquainted with their elements, and sufficiently removed from that period to judge of some of their results. The men of our own day seem destined to see farther than their predecessors into the series of human events. Providence has given us a torch which our forefathers did not possess, and has allowed us to discern fundamental causes in the history of the world which the obscurity of the past concealed from them.

If we carefully examine the social and political state of America after having studied its history, we shall remain perfectly convinced that not an opinion, not a custom, not a law, I may even say not an event, is upon record which the origin of that people will not explain. The readers of this book will find the germe of all that is to follow in the present chapter, and the key to almost the whole work.

The emigrants who came at different periods to occupy the territory now covered by the American Union, differed from each other in many respects; their aim was not the same, and they governed themselves on different principles.

These men had, however, certain features in common, and they were all placed in an analogous situation. The tie of language is perhaps the strongest and most durable that can unite mankind. All the emigrants spoke the same tongue; they were all offsets from the same people. Born in a country which had been agitated for centuries by the struggles of faction, and in which all parties had been obliged in their turn to place themselves under the protection of the laws, their political education had been perfected in this rude school, and they were more conversant with the notions of right, and the principles of true freedom, than the greater part of their European contemporaries. At the period of the first emigrations, the parish system, that fruitful germe of free institutions, was deeply rooted in the habits of the English; and with it the doctrine of the sovereignty of the people had been introduced even into the bosom of the monarchy of the house of Tudor.[1]

The religious quarrels which have agitated the Christian world were then rife. England had plunged into the new order of things with headlong vehemence. The character of its inhabitants, which had always been sedate and reflecting, became argumentative and austere. General information had been increased by intellectual debate, and the mind had received a deeper cultivation. While religion was the topic of discussion, the morals of the people were reformed. All these national features are more or less discoverable in the physiognomy of those adventurers who came to seek a new home on the opposite shores of the Atlantic.

Another remark, to which we shall hereafter have occasion to recur, is applicable not only to the English, but to the French, the Spaniards, and all the Europeans who successively established themselves in the New World. All these European colonies contained the elements, if not the development, of a complete democracy. Two causes led to this result. It may safely be advanced, that on leaving the mother-country the emigrants had in general no notion of superiority over one another. The happy and the powerful do not go into exile, and there are no surer guarantees of equality among men than poverty and misfortune. It happened, however, on several occasions that persons of rank were driven to America by political and religious quarrels. Laws were made to establish a gradation of ranks; but it was soon found that the soil of America was entirely opposed to a territorial aristocracy. To bring that refractory land into cultivation, the constant and interested exertions of the owner himself were necessary; and when the ground was prepared, its produce was found to be insufficient to enrich a master and a farmer at the same time. The land was then naturally broken up into small portions, which the proprietor cultivated for himself. Land is the basis of an aristocracy, which clings to the soil that supports it; for it is not by privileges alone, nor by birth, but by landed property handed down from generation to generation, that an aristocracy is constituted. A nation may present immense fortunes and extreme wretchedness; but unless those fortunes are territorial, there is no aristocracy, but simply the class of the rich and that of the poor.

All the British colonies had then a great degree of similarity at the epoch of their settlement. All of them, from their first beginning, seemed destined to behold the growth, not of the aristocratic liberty of their mother-country, but of that freedom of the middle and lower orders of which the history of the world has as yet furnished no complete example.

In this general uniformity several striking differences were however discernible, which it is necessary to point out. Two branches may be distinguished in the Anglo-American family, which have hitherto grown up without entirely commingling; the one in the south, the other in the north.

Virginia received the first English colony; the emigrants[2] took possession of it in 1607. The idea that mines of gold and silver are the sources of national wealth, was at that time singularly prevalent in Europe; a fatal delusion, which has done more to empoverish the nations which adopted it, and has cost more lives in America, than the united influence of war and bad laws. The men sent to Virginia* were seekers of gold, adventurers without resources and without character, whose turbulent and restless spirits endangered the infant colony† and rendered its progress uncertain. The artisans and agriculturists arrived afterward; and although they were a more moral and orderly race of men, they were in nowise above the level of the inferior classes in England.‡ No lofty conceptions, no intellectual system directed the foundation of these new settlements. The colony was scarcely established when slavery was introduced,§ and this was the main circumstance which has exercised so prodigious an influence on the character, the laws, and all the future prospects of the south.

Slavery, as we shall afterward show, dishonours labour; it introduces idleness into society, and, with idleness, ignorance and pride, luxury and distress. It enervates the powers of the mind, and benumbs the activity of man. The influence of slavery, united to the English character, explains the manners and the social condition of the southern states.

In the north, the same English foundation was modified by the most opposite shades of character; and here I may be allowed to enter into some details. The two or three main ideas which constitute the basis of the social theory of the United States were first combined in the northern British colonies, more generally denominated the states of New England.‖ The principles of New England spread at first to the neighbouring states; they then passed successively to the more distant ones; and at length they imbued the whole confederation. They now extend their influence beyond its limits over the whole American

---

* The charter granted by the crown of England, in 1609, stipulated, among other conditions, that the adventurers should pay to the crown a fifth of the produce of all gold and silver mines. See Marshall's "Life of Washington," vol. i., pp. 18–66.

† A large portion of the adventurers, says Stith (History of Virginia), were unprincipled young men of family, whom their parents were glad to ship off, discharged servants, fraudulent bankrupts, or debauchees; and others of the same class, people more apt to pillage and destroy than to assist the settlement, were the seditious chiefs who easily led this band into every kind of extravagance and excess. See for the history of Virginia the following works:—
"History of Virginia, from the first Settlements in the year 1624," by Smith.
"History of Virginia," by William Stith.
"History of Virginia, from the earliest Period," by Beverley.

‡ It was not till some time later that a certain number of rich English capitalists came to fix themselves in the colony.

§ Slavery was introduced about the year 1620, by a Dutch vessel, which landed twenty negroes on the banks of the river James. See Chalmer.

‖ The states of New England are those situated to the east of the Hudson; they are now six in number: 1. Connecticut; 2. Rhode Island; 3. Massachusetts; 4. Vermont; 5. New Hampshire; 6. Maine.

world. The civilization of New England has been like a beacon lit upon a hill, which, after it has diffused its warmth around, tinges the distant horizon with its glow.

The foundation of New England was a novel spectacle, and all the circumstances attending it were singular and original. The large majority of colonies have been first inhabited either by men without education and without resources, driven by their poverty and their misconduct from the land which gave them birth, or by speculators and adventurers greedy of gain. Some settlements cannot even boast so honourable an origin; St. Domingo was founded by buccaneers; and, at the present day, the criminal courts of England supply the population of Australia.

The settlers who established themselves on the shores of New England all belonged to the more independent classes of their native country. Their union on the soil of America at once presented the singular phenomenon of a society containing neither lords nor common people, neither rich nor poor. These men possessed, in proportion to their number, a greater mass of intelligence than is to be found in any European nation of our own time. All, without a single exception, had received a good education, and many of them were known in Europe for their talents and their acquirements. The other colonies had been founded by adventurers without family; the emigrants of New England brought with them the best elements of order and morality, they landed in the desert accompanied by their wives and children. But what most especially distinguished them was the aim of their undertaking. They had not been obliged by necessity to leave their country, the social position they abandoned was one to be regretted, and their means of subsistence were certain. Nor did they cross the Atlantic to improve their situation, or to increase their wealth; the call which summoned them from the comforts of their homes was purely intellectual; and in facing the inevitable sufferings of exile, their object was the triumph of an idea.

The emigrants, or, as they deservedly styled themselves, the pilgrims, belonged to that English sect, the austerity of whose principles had acquired for them the name of puritans. Puritanism was not merely a religious doctrine, but it corresponded in many points with the most absolute democratic and republican theories. It was this tendency which had aroused its most dangerous adversaries. Persecuted by the government of the mother-country, and disgusted by the habits of a society opposed to the rigour of their own principles, the puritans went forth to seek some rude and unfrequented part of the world, where they could live according to their own opinions, and worship God in freedom.

A few quotations will throw more light upon the spirit of these pious adventurers than all we can say of them. Nathaniel Morton,* the historian of the first years of the settlement, thus opens his subject:—

* "New England's Memorial," p. 13, Boston, 1826. See also "Hutchinson's History," vol. ii., p. 440.

"GENTLE READER: I have for some length of time looked upon it as a duty incumbent, especially on the immediate successors of those that have had so large experience of those many memorable and signal demonstrations of God's goodness, viz, the first beginners of this plantation in New England, to commit to writing his gracious dispensations on that behalf; having so many inducements thereunto, not onely otherwise, but so plentifully in the sacred Scriptures: that so, what we have seen, and what our fathers have told us (Psalm lxxviii. 3, 4), we may not hide from our children, showing to the generations to come the praises of the Lord; that especially the seed of Abraham his servant, and the children of Jacob his chosen (Psalm cv. 5, 6), may remember his marvellous works in the beginning and progress of the planting of New England, his wonders and the judgements of his mouth; how that God brought a vine into this wilderness; that he cast out the heathen and planted it; that he made room for it, and caused it to take deep root; and it filled the land (Psalm lxxx. 8, 9). And not onely so, but also that he hath guided his people by his strength to his holy habitation, and planted them in the mountain of his inheritance in respect of precious gospel enjoyments: and that as especially God may have the glory of all unto whom it is most due; so also some rays of glory may reach the names of those blessed saints, that were the main instruments and the beginning of this happy enterprise."

It is impossible to read this opening paragraph without an involuntary feeling of religious awe; it breathes the very savour of gospel antiquity. The sincerity of the author heightens his power of language. The band, which to his eyes was a mere party of adventures, gone forth to seek their fortune beyond seas, appears to the reader as the germe of a great nation wafted by Providence to a predestined shore.

The author thus continues his narrative of the departure of the first pilgrims:—

"So they left that goodly and pleasant city of Leyden, which had been their resting-place for above eleven years; but they knew that they were pilgrims and strangers here below, and looked not much on these things, but lifted up their eyes to Heaven, their dearest country, where God hath prepared for them a city (Heb. xi. 16), and therein quieted their spirits. When they came to Delfs-Haven they found the ship and all things ready; and such of their friends as could not come with them, followed after them, and sundry came from Amsterdam to see them shipt, and to take their leaves of them. One night was spent with little sleep with the most, but with friendly entertainment and Christian discourse, and other real expressions of true Christian love. The next day they went on board, and their friends with them, where truly doleful was the sight of that sad and mournful parting, to hear what sighs and sobs and prayers did sound among them; what tears did gush from every eye, and pithy speeches pierced each other's heart, that sundry of the Dutch strangers that stood on the key as spectators could not refrain from tears. But the tide (which stays for no man) calling them away that were thus loath to depart, their reverend pastor falling down on his knees, and they all with him, with watery cheeks commended them with most fervent prayers unto the Lord and his blessing; and then, with mutual embraces and many tears, they took their leaves one of another, which proved to be the last leave to many of them."

The emigrants were about 150 in number, including the women and the children. Their object was to plant a colony on the shores of the Hudson; but after having been driven about for some time in the Atlantic ocean, they were forced to land on that arid coast of New England which is now the site of the town of Plymouth. The rock is still shown on which the pilgrims disembarked.*

"But before we pass on," continues our historian, "let the reader with me make a pause, and seriously consider this poor people's present condition, the more to be raised up to admiration of God's goodness toward them in their preservation: for being now passed the vast ocean, and a sea of troubles before them in expectation, they had now no friends to welcome them, no inns to entertain or refresh them, no houses, or much less towns to repair unto to seek for succour; and for the season it was winter, and they that know the winters of the country know them to be sharp and violent, subject to cruel and fierce storms, dangerous to travel to known places, much more to search unknown coasts. Besides, what could they see but a hideous and desolate wilderness, full of wilde beasts, and wilde men ? and what multitudes of them there were, they then knew not: for which way soever they turned their eyes (save upward to Heaven) they could have but little solace or content in respect of any outward object; for summer being ended, all things stand in appearance with a weather-beaten face, and the whole country full of woods and thickets represented a wild and savage hue; if they looked behind them, there was the mighty ocean which they had passed, and was now as a main bar or gulph to separate them from all the civil parts of the world."

It must not be imagined that the piety of the puritans was of a merely speculative kind, or that it took no cognizance of the course of worldly affairs. Puritanism, as I have already remarked, was scarcely less a political than a religious doctrine. No sooner had the emigrants landed on the barren coast, described by Nathaniel Morton, than their first care was to constitute a society, by passing the following act:†—

"IN THE NAME OF GOD, AMEN! We, whose names are underwritten, the loyal subjects of our dread sovereign lord King James, &c., &c., having undertaken for the glory of God and advancement of the Christian faith, and the honour of our king and country, a voyage to plant the first colony in the northern parts of Virginia: do by these presents

---

* This rock is become an object of veneration in the United States. I have seen bits of it carefully preserved in several towns of the Union. Does not this sufficiently show that all human power and greatness is in the soul of man? Here is a stone which the feet of a few outcasts pressed for an instant, and this stone becomes famous; it is treasured by a great nation, its very dust is shared as a relic; and what is become of the gateways of a thousand palaces?
† "New England Memorial," p. 37.

solemnly and mutually, in the presence of God and one another, covenant and combine ourselves together into a civil body politic, for our better ordering and preservation, and furtherance of the ends aforesaid: and by virtue hereof do enact, constitute, and frame, such just and equal laws, ordinances, acts, constitutions, and officers, from time to time, as shall be thought most meet and convenient for the general good of the colony: unto which we promise all due submission and obedience," &c.*

This happened in 1620, and from that time forward the emigration went on. The religious and political passions which ravished the British empire during the whole reign of Charles I.,[3] drove fresh crowds of sectarians every year to the shores of America. In England the stronghold of puritanism was in the middle classes, and it was from the middle classes that the majority of the emigrants came. The population of New England increased rapidly; and while the hierarchy of rank despotically classed the inhabitants of the mother-country, the colony continued to present the novel spectacle of a community homogeneous in all its parts. A democracy, more perfect than any which antiquity had dreamed of, started in full size and panoply from the midst of an ancient feudal society.

The English government was not dissatisfied with an emigration which removed the elements of fresh discord and of future revolutions. On the contrary, everything was done to encourage it, and little attention was paid to the destiny of those who sought a shelter from the rigour of their country's laws on the soil of America. It seemed as if New England was a region given up to the dreams of fancy, and the unrestrained experiments of innovators.

The English colonies (and this is one of the main causes of their prosperity) have always enjoyed more internal freedom and more political independence than the colonies of other nations; but this principle of liberty was nowhere more extensively applied than in the states of New England.

It was generally allowed at that period that the territories of the New World belonged to that European nation which had been the first to discover them. Nearly the whole coast of North America thus became a British possession toward the end of the sixteenth century. The means used by the English government to people these new domains were of several kinds: the king sometimes appointed a governor of his own choice, who ruled a portion of the New World in the name and under the immediate orders of the crown;† this is the colonial system adopted by the other countries of Europe. Sometimes grants of certain tracts were made by the crown to an individual or to a company,‡ in which case all the civil and political power fell into the hands of one

---

* The emigrants who founded the state of Rhode Island in 1638, those who landed at New Haven in 1637, the first settlers in Connecticut in 1639, and the founders of Providence in 1640, began in like manner by drawing up a social contract, which was submitted to the approval of all the interested parties. See "Pitkin's History," pp. 42, 47.

† This was the case in the state of New York.

‡ Maryland, the Carolinas, Pennsylvania, and New Jersey, were in this situation. See Pitkin's History, vol. i., pp. 11–31.

or more persons, who, under the inspection and control of the crown, sold the lands and governed the inhabitants. Lastly, a third system consisted in allowing a certain number of emigrants to constitute a political society under the protection of the mother-country, and to govern themselves in whatever was not contrary to her laws. This mode of colonization, so remarkably favourable to liberty, was adopted only in New England.*

In 1628,† a charter of this kind was granted by Charles I. to the emigrants who went to form the colony of Massachusetts But, in general, charters were not given to the colonies of New England till they had acquired a certain existence. Plymouth, Providence, New Haven, the state of Connecticut, and that of Rhode Island,‡ were founded without the co-operation, and almost without the knowledge of the mother-country. The new settlers did not derive their incorporation from the head of the empire, although they did not deny its supremacy; they constituted a society of their own accord, and it was not till thirty or forty years afterward, under Charles II.,⁴ that their existence was legally recognised by a royal charter.

This frequently renders it difficult to detect the link which connected the emigrants with the land of their forefathers, in studying the earliest historical and legislative records of New England. They perpetually exercised the rights of sovereignty; they named their magistrates, concluded peace or declared war, made police regulations, and enacted laws, as if their allegiance was due only to God.§ Nothing can be more curious, and at the same time more instructive than the legislation of that period; it is there that the solution of the great social problem which the United States now present to the world is to be found.

Among these documents we shall notice as especially characteristic, the code of laws promulgated by the little state of Connecticut in 1650.‖

The legislators of Connecticut¶ begin with the penal laws, and, strange to say, they borrow their provisions from the text of holy writ.

---

* See the work entitled, *"Historical Collection of State Papers and other Authentic Documents intended as Materials for a History of the United States of America,"* by Ebenezer Hazard, Philadelphia, 1792, for a great number of documents relating to the commencement of the colonies, which are valuable from their contents and their authenticity; among them are the various charters granted by the king of England and the first acts of the local governments.

  See also the analysis of all these charters given by Mr. Story, judge of the supreme court of the United States, in the introduction to his Commentary on the Constitution of the United States. It results from these documents that the principles of representative government and the external forms of political liberty were introduced into all the colonies at their origin. These principles were more fully acted upon in the North than in the South, but they existed everywhere.

† See Pitkin's History, p. 35. See the History of the Colony of Massachusetts Bay by Hutchinson, vol. i., p. 9.

‡ See Pitkin's History, pp. 42, 47.

§ The inhabitants of Massachusetts had deviated from the forms which are preserved in the criminal and civil procedure of England: in 1650 the decrees of justice were not yet headed by the royal style. See Hutchinson, vol. i., p. 452.

‖ Code of 1650, p. 28. Hartford, 1830.

¶ See also in Hutchinson's History, vol. i., pp. 435, 456, the analysis of the penal code adopted in 1648, by the colony of Massachusetts: this code is drawn up on the same principles as that of Connecticut.

"Whoever shall worship any other God than the Lord," says the preamble of the code, "shall surely be put to death." This is followed by ten or twelve enactments of the same kind, copied verbatim from the books of Exodus, Leviticus, and Deuteronomy. Blasphemy, sorcery, adultery,* and rape, were punished with death; an outrage offered by a son to his parents, was to be expiated by the same penalty. The legislation of a rude and half-civilized people was thus transferred to an enlightened and moral community. The consequence was, that the punishment of death was never more frequently prescribed by the statute, and never more rarely enforced toward the guilty.

The chief care of the legislators, in this body of penal laws, was the maintenance of orderly conduct and good morals in the community: they constantly invaded the domain of conscience, and there was scarcely a sin which they did not subject to magisterial censure. The reader is aware of the rigor with which these laws punished rape and adultery; intercourse between unmarried persons was likewise severely repressed. The judge was empowered to inflict a pecuniary penalty, a whipping, or marriage,† on the misdemeanants; and if the records of the old courts of New Haven may be believed, prosecutions of this kind were not infrequent. We find a sentence bearing date the first of May, 1660, inflicting a fine and a reprimand on a young woman who was accused of using improper language, and of allowing herself to be kissed.‡ The code of 1650 abounds in preventive measures. It punishes idleness and drunkenness with severity.§ Innkeepers are forbidden to furnish more than a certain quantity of liquor to each consumer; and simple lying, whenever it may be injurious,‖ is checked by a fine or a flogging. In other places, the legislator, entirely forgetting the great principles of religious toleration which he had himself upheld in Europe, renders attendance on divine service compulsory,¶ and goes so far as to visit with severe punishment,< and even with death, the Christians who chose to worship God according to a ritual

---

* Adultery was also punished with death by the law of Massachusetts; and Hutchinson, vol. i., p. 441, says that several persons actually suffered for this crime. He quotes a curious anecdote on this subject, which occurred in the year 1663. A married woman had had criminal intercourse with a young man; her husband died, and she married the lover. Several years had elapsed, when the public began to suspect the previous intercourse of this couple; they were thrown into prison, put upon trial, and very narrowly escaped capital punishment.

† Code of 1650, p. 48. It seems sometimes to have happened that the judge superadded these punishments to each other, as is seen in a sentence pronounced in 1643 (New Haven Antiquities, p. 114) by which Margaret Bedford, convicted of loose conduct, was condemned to be whipped, and afterward to marry Nicolas Jemmings her accomplice.

‡ New Haven Antiquities, p. 104. See also Hutchinson's History for several causes equally extraordinary.

§ Code of 1650, pp. 50, 57.

‖ Ibid, p. 64.

¶ Ibid, p. 44.

< This was not peculiar to Connecticut. See for instance the law which, on the 13th of September, 1644, banished the ana-baptists from the state of Massachusetts. (Historical Collection of State Papers, vol. i., p. 538.) See also the law against the quakers, passed on the 14th of October, 1656. "Whereas," says the preamble, "an accursed race of heretics called quakers has sprung up," &c. The clauses of the statute inflict a heavy fine on all captains of ships who should import quakers into the country. The quakers who may be found there shall be whipped and imprisoned with hard labour. Those members of the sect who should defend their opinions shall be first fined, then imprisoned, and finally driven out of the province. (Historical Collection of State Papers, vol. i., p. 630.)

differing from his own.* Sometimes indeed, the zeal of his enactments induces him to descend to the most frivolous particulars: thus a law is to be found in the same code which prohibits the use of tobacco.† It must not be forgotten that these fantastical and vexatious laws were not imposed by authority, but that they were freely voted by all the persons interested, and that the manners of the community were even more austere and more puritanical than the laws. In 1649 a solemn association was formed in Boston to check the worldly luxury of long hair.‡

These errors are no doubt discreditable to the human reason; they attest the inferiority of our nature, which is incapable of laying firm hold upon what is true and just, and is often reduced to the alternative of two excesses. In strict connexion with this penal legislation, which bears such striking marks of a narrow sectarian spirit, and of those religious passions which had been warmed by persecution, and were still fermenting among the people, a body of political laws is to be found, which, though written two hundred years ago, is still ahead of the liberties of our age.

The general principles which are the groundwork of modern constitutions—principles which were imperfectly known in Europe, and not completely triumphant even in Great Britain, in the seventeenth century—were all recognised and determined by the laws of New England: the intervention of the people in public affairs, the free voting of taxes, the responsibility of authorities, personal liberty, and trial by jury, were all positively established without discussion.

From these fruitful principles, consequences have been derived and applications have been made such as no nation in Europe has yet ventured to attempt.

In Connecticut the electoral body consisted, from its origin, of the whole number of citizens; and this is readily to be understood,§ when we recollect that this people enjoyed an almost perfect equality of fortune, and a still greater uniformity of capacity.‖ In Connecticut, at this period, all the executive functionaries were elected, including the governor of the state.¶ The citizens above the age of sixteen were obliged to bear arms; they formed a national militia, which appointed its own officers, and was to hold itself at all times in readiness to march for the defence of the country.<

In the laws of Connecticut, as well as in all those of New England, we find the germe and gradual development of that township independence, which is the life and mainspring of American liberty at the present day. The political existence of the majority of the nations

---

* By the penal law of Massachusetts, any catholic priest who should set foot in the colony after having been once driven out of it, was liable to capital punishment.

† Code of 1650, p. 96.

‡ New England's Memorial, p. 316. See Appendix E.

§ Constitution of 1638, p. 17.

‖ In 1641 the general assembly of Rhode Island unanimously declared that the government of the state was a democracy, and that the power was vested in the body of free citizens, who alone had the right to make the laws and to watch their execution. Code of 1650, p. 70.

¶ Pitkin's History, p. 47.

< Constitution of 1638, p. 12.

of Europe commenced in the superior ranks of society, and was gradually and always imperfectly communicated to the different members
of the social body. In America, on the other hand, it may be said that
the township was organized before the county, the county before the
state, the state before the Union.

In New England, townships were completely and definitively constituted as early as 1650. The independence of the township was the nucleus around which the local interests, passions, rights, and duties,
collected and clung. It gave scope to the activity of a real political life,
most thoroughly democratic and republican. The colonies still recognised the supremacy of the mother-country; monarchy was still the
law of the state; but the republic was already established in every
township.

The towns named their own magistrates of every kind, rated themselves, and levied their own taxes.* In the townships of New England
the law of representation was not adopted, but the affairs of the community were discussed, as at Athens, in the market-place, by a general
assembly of the citizens.

In studying the laws which were promulgated at this first era of the
American republics, it is impossible not to be struck by the remarkable
acquaintance with the science of government, and the advanced theory of legislation, which they display. The ideas there formed of the
duties of society toward its members, are evidently much loftier and
more comprehensive than those of the European legislators at that
time: obligations were there imposed which were elsewhere slighted.
In the states of New England, from the first, the condition of the poor
was provided for;† strict measures were taken for the maintenance of
roads, and surveyors were appointed to attend to them;‡ registers were
established in every parish, in which the results of public deliberations, and the births, deaths, and marriages of the citizens were entered;§ clerks were directed to keep these registers;‖ officers were
charged with the administration of vacant inheritances, and with the
arbitration of litigated landmarks; and many others were created
whose chief functions were the maintenance of public order in the
community.¶ The law enters into a thousand useful provisions for a
number of social wants which are at present very inadequately felt in
France.

But it is by the attention it pays to public education that the original
character of American civilization is at once placed in the clearest
light. "It being," says the law, "one chief project of Satan to keep men
from the knowledge of the Scripture by persuading from the use of
tongues, to the end that learning may not be buried in the graves of
our forefathers, in church and commonwealth, the Lord assisting our

---

* Code of 1650, p. 80.
† Code of 1650, p. 78.
‡ Code of 1750, p. 94.
§ See Hutchinson's History, vol. i., p. 455.
‖ Ibid, p. 86.
¶ Ibid, p. 40.

endeavours, . . ."* Here follow clauses establishing schools in every township, and obliging the inhabitants, under pain of heavy fines, to support them. Schools of a superior kind were founded in the same manner in the more populous districts. The municipal authorities were bound to enforce the sending of children to school by their parents; they were empowered to inflict fines upon all who refused compliance; and in cases of continued resistance, society assumed the place of the parent, took possession of the child, and deprived the father of those natural rights which he used to so bad a purpose. The reader will undoubtedly have remarked the preamble of these enactments: in America, religion is the road to knowledge, and the observance of the divine laws leads man to civil freedom.

If, after having cast a rapid glance over the state of American society in 1650, we turn to the condition of Europe, and more especially to that of the continent, at the same period, we cannot fail to be struck with astonishment. On the continent of Europe, at the beginning of the seventeenth century, absolute monarchy had everywhere triumphed over the ruins of the oligarchical and feudal liberties of the middle ages. Never were the notions of right more completely confounded than in the midst of the splendour and literature of Europe; never was there less political activity among the people; never were the principles of true freedom less widely circulated; and at that very time, those principles, which were scorned or unknown by the nations of Europe, were proclaimed in the deserts of the New World, and were accepted as the future creed of a great people. The boldest theories of the human reason were put into practice by a community so humble, that not a statesman condescended to attend to it; and a legislation without precedent was produced off-hand by the imagination of the citizens. In the bosom of this obscure democracy, which had as yet brought forth neither generals, nor philosophers, nor authors, a man might stand up in the face of a free people, and pronounce amid general acclamations the following fine definition of liberty:†—

"Nor would I have you to mistake in the point of your own liberty. There is a liberty of corrupt nature, which is affected both by men and beasts to do what they list; and this liberty is inconsistent with authority, impatient of all restraint; by this liberty, *'sumus omnes deteriores:'* 't is the grand enemy of truth and peace, and all the ordinance of God are bent against it. But there is a civil, a moral, a federal liberty, which is the proper end and object of authority; it is a liberty for that only which is just and good: for this liberty you are to stand with the hazard of your very lives, and whatsoever crosses it, is not authority, but a distemper thereof. This liberty is maintained in a way of subjection to authority; and the authority set over you will, in all administrations for

---

* Code of 1650, p. 90.
† Mather's Magnalia Christi Americana, vol. ii., p. 13. This speech was made by Winthrop; he was accused of having committed arbitrary actions during his magistracy, but after having made the speech of which the above is a fragment, he was acquitted by acclamation, and from that time forward he was always re-elected governor of the state. See Marshall, vol. i., p. 166.

your good, be quietly submitted unto by all but such as have a disposition to shake off the yoke and lose their true liberty, by their murmuring at the honour and power of authority."

The remarks I have made will suffice to display the character of Anglo-American civilization in its true light. It is the result (and this should be constantly present to the mind) of two distinct elements, which in other places have been in frequent hostility, but which in America have been admirably incorporated and combined with one another. I allude to the spirit of religion and the spirit of liberty.

The settlers of New England were at the same time ardent sectarians and daring innovators. Narrow as the limits of some of their religious opinions were, they were entirely free from political prejudices.

Hence arose two tendencies, distinct but not opposite, which are constantly discernible in the manners as well as in the laws of the country.

It might be imagined that men who sacrificed their friends, their family, and their native land, to a religious conviction, were absorbed in the pursuit of the intellectual advantages which they purchased at so dear a rate. The energy, however, with which they strove for the acquirements of wealth, moral enjoyment, and the comforts as well as the liberties of the world, was scarcely inferior to that with which they devoted themselves to Heaven.

Political principles, and all human laws and institutions were moulded and altered at their pleasure; the barriers of the society in which they were born were broken down before them; the old principles which had governed the world for ages were no more; a path without a turn, and a field without a horizon, were opened to the exploring and ardent curiosity of man: but at the limits of the political world he checks his researches, he discreetly lays aside the use of his most formidable faculties, he no longer consents to doubt or to innovate, but carefully abstaining from raising the curtain of the sanctuary, he yields with submissive respect to truths which he will not discuss.

Thus in the moral world, everything is classed, adapted, decided, and foreseen; in the political world everything is agitated, uncertain, and disputed: in the one is a passive, though a voluntary obedience; in the other an independence, scornful of experience and jealous of authority.

These two tendencies, apparently so discrepant, are far from conflicting; they advance together, and mutually support each other.

Religion perceives that civil liberty affords a noble exercise to the faculties of man, and that the political world is a field prepared by the Creator for the efforts of the intelligence. Contented with the freedom and the power which it enjoys in its own sphere, and with the place which it occupies, the empire of religion is never more surely established than when it reigns in the hearts of men unsupported by aught beside its native strength.

Religion is no less the companion of liberty in all its battles and its triumphs; the cradle of its infancy, and the divine source of its claims.

The safeguard of morality is religion, and morality is the best security of law as well as the surest pledge of freedom.*

REASONS OF CERTAIN ANOMALIES WHICH THE LAWS AND CUSTOMS OF THE ANGLO-AMERICANS PRESENT.

Remains of aristocratic Institutions in the midst of a complete Democracy— Why?—Distinction carefully to be drawn between what is of Puritanical and what is of English Origin.

The reader is cautioned not to draw too general or too absolute an inference from what has been said. The social condition, the religion, and the manners of the first emigrants undoubtedly exercised an immense influence on the destiny of their new country. Nevertheless it was not in their power to found a state of things originating solely in themselves: no man can entirely shake off the influence of the past; and the settlers, unintentionally or involuntarily, mingled habits and notions derived from their education and from the traditions of their country, with those habits and notions which were exclusively their own. To form a judgement on the Anglo-Americans of the present day, it is therefore necessary carefully to distinguish what is of puritanical from what is of English origin.

Laws and customs are frequently to be met with in the United States which contrast strongly with all that surrounds them. These laws seem to be drawn up in a spirit contrary to the prevailing tenor of the American legislation; and these customs are no less opposed to the general tone of society. If the English colonies had been founded in an age of darkness, or if their origin was already lost in the lapse of years, the problem would be insoluble.

I shall quote a single example to illustrate what I advance.

The civil and criminal procedure of the Americans has only two means of action—committal or bail. The first measure taken by the magistrate is to exact security from the defendant, or, in case of refusal, to incarcerate him: the ground of the accusation, and the importance of the charges against him are then discussed.

It is evident that a legislation of this kind is hostile to the poor man, and favourable only to the rich. The poor man has not always a security to produce, even in a civil cause: and if he is obliged to wait for justice in prison, he is speedily reduced to distress. The wealthy individual, on the contrary, always escapes imprisonment in civil causes; nay, more, he may readily elude the punishment which awaits him for a delinquency, by breaking his bail. So that all the penalties of the law are, for him, reducible to fines.† Nothing can be more aristocratic than this system of legislation. Yet in America it is the poor who make the law, and they usually reserve the greatest social advantages to themselves. The explanation of the phenomenon is to be found in England; the laws of which I speak are English,‡ and the Americans

---

* See Appendix F.
† Crimes no doubt exist for which bail is inadmissible, but they are few in number.
‡ See Blackstone; and Delolme, book i., chap x

have retained them, however repugnant they may be to the tenor of their legislation, and the mass of their ideas.

Next to its habits, the thing which a nation is least apt to change is its civil legislation. Civil laws are only familiarly known to legal men, whose direct interest it is to maintain them as they are, whether good or bad, simply because they themselves are conversant with them. The body of the nation is scarcely acquainted with them: it merely perceives their action in particular cases; but it has some difficulty in seizing their tendency, and obeys them without reflection.

I have quoted one instance where it would have been easy to adduce a great number of others.

The surface of American society is, if I may use the expression, covered with a layer of democracy, from beneath which the old aristocratic colours sometimes peep.

Chapter III.

SOCIAL CONDITION OF THE ANGLO-AMERICANS.

A social condition is commonly the result of circumstances, sometimes of laws, oftener still of these two causes united; but wherever it exists, it may justly be considered as the source of almost all the laws, the usages, and the ideas, which regulate the conduct of nations; whatever it does not produce, it modifies.

It is, therefore, necessary, if we would become acquainted with the legislation and the manners of a nation, to begin by the study of its social condition.

THE STRIKING CHARACTERISTIC OF THE SOCIAL CONDITION OF THE
ANGLO-AMERICANS IS ITS ESSENTIAL DEMOCRACY.

The first Emigrants of New England—Their Equality—Aristocratic Laws introduced in the South—Period of the Revolution—Change in the Law of Descent—Effects produced by this Change—Democracy carried to its utmost Limits in the new States of the West—Equality of Education.

Many important observations suggest themselves upon the social condition of the Anglo-Americans; but there is one which takes precedence of all the rest. The social condition of the Americans is eminently democratic; this was its character at the foundation of the colonies, and is still more strongly marked at the present day.

I have stated in the preceding chapter that great equality existed among the emigrants who settled on the shores of New England. The germe of aristocracy was never planted in that part of the Union. The only influence which obtained there was that of intellect; the people were used to reverence certain names as the emblems of knowledge and virtue. Some of their fellow-citizens acquired a power over the rest which might truly have been called aristocratic, if it had been capable of invariable transmission from father to son.

This was the state of things to the east of the Hudson: to the south-west of that river, and in the direction of the Floridas, the case was different. In most of the states situated to the southwest of the Hudson some great English proprietors had settled, who had imported with them aristocratic principles and the English law of descent. I have explained the reasons why it was impossible ever to establish a powerful aristocracy in America; these reasons existed with less force to the southwest of the Hudson. In the south, one man, aided by slaves, could cultivate a great extent of country: it was therefore common to see rich landed proprietors. But their influence was not altogether aristocratic as that term is understood in Europe, since they possessed no privileges; and the cultivation of their estates being carried on by slaves, they had no tenants depending on them, and consequently no patronage. Still, the great proprietors south of the Hudson constituted a superior class, having ideas and tastes of its own, and forming the centre of political action. This kind of aristocracy sympathized with the body of the people, whose passions and interests it easily embraced; but it was too weak and too short-lived to excite either love or hatred for itself. This was the class which headed the insurrection in the south, and furnished the best leaders of the American revolution.[1]

At the period of which we are now speaking, society was shaken to its centre; the people, in whose name the struggle had taken place, conceived the desire of exercising the authority which it had acquired; its democratic tendencies were awakened; and having thrown off the yoke of the mother-country, it aspired to independence of every kind. The influence of individuals gradually ceased to be felt, and custom and law united together to produce the same result.

But the law of descent was the last step to equality. I am surprised that ancient and modern jurists have not attributed to this law a greater influence on human affairs.* It is true that these laws belong to civil affairs: but they ought nevertheless to be placed at the head of all political institutions; for, while political laws are only the symbol of a nation's condition, they exercise an incredible influence upon its social state. They have, moreover, a sure and uniform manner of operating upon society, affecting, as it were, generations yet unborn.

Through their means man acquires a kind of preternatural power over the future lot of his fellow-creatures. When the legislator has once regulated the law of inheritance, he may rest from his labour. The machine once put in motion will go on for ages, and advance, as if self-guided, toward a given point. When framed in a particular manner, this law unites, draws together, and vests property and power in a few hands: its tendency is clearly aristocratic. On opposite principles

---

* I understand by the law of descent all those laws whose principal object it is to regulate the distribution of property after the death of its owner. The law of entail is of this number; it certainly prevents the owner from disposing of his possessions before his death; but this is solely with a view of preserving them entire for the heir. The principal object, therefore, of the law of entail is to regulate the descent of property after the death of its owner; its other provisions are merely means to this end.

its action is still more rapid; it divides, distributes, and disperses both property and power. Alarmed by the rapidity of its progress, those who despair of arresting its motion endeavour to obstruct by difficulties and impediments; they vainly seek to counteract its effect by contrary efforts: but it gradually reduces or destroys every obstacle, until by its incessant activity the bulwarks of the influence of wealth are ground down to the fine and shifting sand which is the basis of democracy. When the law of inheritance permits, still more when it decrees, the equal division of a father's property among all his children, its effects are of two kinds: it is important to distinguish them from each other, although they tend to the same end.

In virtue of the law of partible inheritance, the death of every proprietor brings about a kind of revolution in property: not only do his possessions change hands, but their very nature is altered; since they are parcelled into shares, which become smaller and smaller at each division. This is the direct, and, as it were, the physical effect of the law. It follows, then, that in countries where equality of inheritance is established by law, property, and especially landed property, must have a tendency to perpetual diminution. The effects, however, of such legislation would only be perceptible after a lapse of time, if the law was abandoned to its own working; for supposing a family to consist of two children (and in a country peopled as France is, the average number is not above three), these children, sharing among them the fortune of both parents, would not be poorer than their father or mother.

But the law of equal division exercises its influence not merely upon the property itself, but it affects the minds of the heirs, and brings their passions into play. These indirect consequences tend powerfully to the destruction of large fortunes, and especially of large domains.

Among the nations whose law of descent is founded upon the right of primogeniture, landed estates often pass from generation to generation without undergoing division. The consequence of which is, that family feeling is to a certain degree incorporated with the estate. The family represents the estate, the estate the family; whose name, together with its origin, its glory, its power, and its virtues, is thus perpetuated in an imperishable memorial of the past, and a sure pledge of the future.

When the equal partition of property is established by law, the intimate connexion is destroyed between family feeling and the preservation of the paternal estate; the property ceases to represent the family; for, as it must inevitably be divided after one or two generations, it has evidently a constant tendency to diminish, and must in the end be completely dispersed. The sons of the great landed proprietor, if they are few in number, or if fortune befriend them, may indeed entertain the hope of being as wealthy as their father, but not that of possessing the same property as he did; their riches must necessarily be composed of elements different from his.

Now, from the moment when you divest the land-owner of that interest in the preservation of his estate which he derives from association, from tradition, and from family pride, you may be certain that sooner or later he will dispose of it; for there is a strong pecuniary interest in favour of selling, as floating capital produces higher interest than real property, and is more readily available to gratify the passions of the moment.

Great landed estates which have once been divided, never come together again; for the small proprietor draws from his land a better revenue in proportion, than the large owner does from his; and of course he sells it at a higher rate.* The calculations of gain, therefore, which decided the rich man to sell his domain, will still more powerfully influence him against buying small estates to unite them into a large one.

What is called family pride is often founded upon an illusion of self-love. A man wishes to perpetuate and immortalize himself, as it were, in his great-grandchildren. Where the *esprit de famille* ceases to act, individual selfishness comes into play. When the idea of family becomes vague, indeterminate, and uncertain, a man thinks of his present convenience; he provides for the establishment of the succeeding generation, and no more.

Either a man gives up the idea of perpetuating his family, or at any rate he seeks to accomplish it by other means than that of a landed estate.

Thus not only does the law of partible inheritance render it difficult for families to preserve their ancestral domains entire, but it deprives them of the inclination to attempt it, and compels them in some measure to co-operate with the law in their own extinction.

The law of equal distribution proceeds by two methods: by acting upon things, it acts upon persons; by influencing persons, it affects things. By these means the law succeeds in striking at the root of landed property, and dispersing rapidly both families and fortunes.†

Most certainly is it not for us, Frenchmen of the nineteenth century, who daily behold the political and social changes which the law of partition is bringing to pass, to question its influence. It is perpetually conspicuous in our country, overthrowing the walls of our dwellings and removing the landmarks of our fields. But although it has produced great effects in France, much still remains for it to do. Our recollections, opinions, and habits, present powerful obstacles to its progress.

In the United States it has nearly completed its work of destruction, and there we can best study its results. The English laws concerning

---

* I do not mean to say that the small proprietor cultivates his land better, but he cultivates it with more ardour and care; so that he makes up by his labour for his want of skill.

† Land being the most stable kind of property, we find, from time to time, rich individuals who are disposed to make great sacrifices in order to obtain it, and who willingly forfeit a considerable part of their income to make sure of the rest. But these are accidental cases. The preference for landed property is no longer found habitually in any class but among the poor. The small land-owner, who has less information, less imagination, and fewer passions, than the great one, is generally occupied with the desire of increasing his estate; and it often happens that by inheritance, by marriage, or by the chances of trade, he is gradually furnished with the means. Thus, to balance the tendency which leads men to divide their estates, there exists another, which incites them to add to them. This tendency, which is sufficient to prevent estates from being divided *ad infinitum*, is not strong enough to create great territorial possessions, certainly not to keep them up in the same family.

the transmission of property were abolished in almost all the states at the time of the revolution. The law of entail was so modified as not to interrupt the free circulation of property.* The first having passed away, estates began to be parcelled out; and the change became more and more rapid with the progress of time. At this moment, after a lapse of little more than sixty years, the aspect of society is totally altered; the families of the great landed proprietors are almost all commingled with the general mass. In the state of New York, which formerly contained many of these, there are but two who still keep their heads above the stream; and they must shortly disappear. The sons of these opulent citizens have become merchants, lawyers, or physicians. Most of them have lapsed into obscurity. The last trace of hereditary ranks and distinctions is destroyed—the law of partition has reduced all to one level.

I do not mean that there is any deficiency of wealthy individuals in the United States; I know of no country, indeed, where the love of money has taken stronger hold on the affections of men, and where a profounder contempt is expressed for the theory of the permanent equality of property. But wealth circulates with inconceivable rapidity, and experience shows that it is rare to find two succeeding generations in the full enjoyment of it.

This picture, which may perhaps be thought overcharged, still gives a very imperfect idea of what is taking place in the new states of the west and southwest. At the end of the last century a few bold adventurers began to penetrate into the valleys of the Mississippi, and the mass of the population very soon began to move in that direction: communities unheard of till then were seen to emerge from their wilds: states, whose names were not in existence a few years before, claimed their place in the American Union; and in the western settlements we may behold democracy arrived at its utmost extreme. In these states, founded off hand, and as it were by chance, the inhabitants are but of yesterday. Scarcely known to one another, the nearest neighbours are ignorant of each other's history. In this part of the American continent, therefore, the population has not experienced the influence of great names and great wealth, nor even that of the natural aristocracy of knowledge and virtue. None are there to wield that respectable power which men willingly grant to the remembrance of a life spent in doing good before their eyes. The new states of the west are already inhabited; but society has no existence among them.

It is not only the fortunes of men which are equal in America; even their aquirements partake in some degree of the same uniformity. I do not believe there is a country in the world where, in proportion to the population, there are so few uninstructed, and at the same time so few learned individuals. Primary instruction is within the reach of everybody; superior instruction is scarcely to be obtained by any. This is not surprising; it is in fact the necessary consequence of what we have ad-

* See Appendix G.

vanced above. Almost all the Americans are in easy circumstances, and can therefore obtain the first elements of human knowledge.

In America there are comparatively few who are rich enough to live without a profession. Every profession requires an apprenticeship, which limits the time of instruction to the early years of life. At fifteen they enter upon their calling, and thus their education ends at the age when ours begins. Whatever is done afterward, is with a view to some special and lucrative object; a science is taken up as a matter of business, and the only branch of it which is attended to is such as admits of an immediate practical application.

[This paragraph does not fairly render the meaning of the author. The original French is as follows:

"En Amérique il y a peu de riches; presque tous les Américains ont donc besoin d'exercer une profession. Or, toute profession exige un apprentissage. Les Américains ne peuvent donc donner à la culture générale de l'intelligence que les premières années de la vie: à quinze ans, ils entrent dans une carrère: ainsi leur education finit le plus souvent à l'époque où la nôtre commence."

What is meant by the remark, that "at fifteen they enter upon a career, and thus their education is very often finished at the epoch when ours commences," is not clearly perceived. Our professional men enter upon their course of preparation for their respective professions, wholly between eighteen and twenty-one years of age. Apprentices to trades are bound out, ordinarily, at fourteen, but what general education they receive is after that period. Previously, they have acquired the mere elements of reading, writing, and arithmetic. But it is supposed there is nothing peculiar to America, in the age at which apprenticeship commences. In England, they commence at the same age, and it is believed that the same thing occurs throughout Europe. It is feared that the author has not here expressed himself with his usual clearness and precision.—*American Editor.*]

In America most of the rich men were formerly poor: most of those who now enjoy leisure were absorbed in business during their youth; the consequence of which is, that when they might have had a taste for study they had no time for it, and when the time is at their disposal they have no longer the inclination.

There is no class, then, in America in which the taste for intellectual pleasures is transmitted with hereditary fortune and leisure, and by which the labours of the intellect are held in honour. Accordingly there is an equal want of the desire and the power of application to these objects.

A middling standard is fixed in America for human knowledge. All approach as near to it as they can; some as they rise, others as they descend. Of course, an immense multitude of persons are to be found who entertain the same number of ideas on religion, history, science, political economy, legislation, and government. The gifts of intellect proceed directly from God, and man cannot prevent their unequal distribution. But in consequence of the state of things which we have here represented, it happens, that although the capacities of men are widely different, as the Creator has doubtless intended they should be, they are submitted to the same method of treatment.

In America the aristocratic element has always been feeble from its birth; and if at the present day it is not actually destroyed, it is at any rate so completely disabled that we can scarcely assign to it any degree of influence in the course of affairs.

The democratic principle, on the contrary, has gained so much strength by time, by events, and by legislation, as to have become not only predominant but all-powerful. There is no family or corporate authority, and it is rare to find even the influence of individual character enjoy any durability.

America, then, exhibits in her social state a most extraordinary phenomenon. Men are there seen on a greater equality in point of fortune and intellect, or in other words, more equal in their strength, than in any other country of the world, or, in any age of which history has preserved the remembrance.

POLITICAL CONSEQUENCES OF THE SOCIAL CONDITION OF THE ANGLO-AMERICANS.

The political consequences of such a social condition as this are easily deducible.

It is impossible to believe that equality will not eventually find its way into the political world as it does everywhere else. To conceive of men remaining for ever unequal upon one single point, yet equal on all others, is impossible; they must come in the end to be equal upon all.

Now I know of only two methods of establishing equality in the political world: every citizen must be put in possession of his rights, or rights must be granted to no one. For nations which have arrived at the same stage of social existence as the Anglo-Americans, it is therefore very difficult to discover a medium between the sovereignty of all and the absolute power of one man: and it would be vain to deny that the social condition which I have been describing is equally liable to each of these consequences.

There is, in fact, a manly and lawful passion for equality, which excites men to wish all to be powerful and honoured. This passion tends to elevate the humble to the rank of the great; but there exists also in the human heart a depraved taste for equality, which impels the weak to attempt to lower the powerful to their own level, and reduces men to prefer equality in slavery to inequality with freedom. Not that those nations whose social condition is democratic naturally despise liberty; on the contrary, they have an instinctive love of it. But liberty is not the chief and constant object of their desires; equality is their idol: they make rapid and sudden efforts to obtain liberty, and if they miss their aim, resign themselves to their disappointment; but nothing can satisfy them except equality, and rather than lose it they resolve to perish.

On the other hand, in a state where the citizens are nearly on an equality, it becomes difficult for them to preserve their independence against the aggressions of power. No one among them being strong enough to engage singly in the struggle with advantage, nothing but a general combination can protect their liberty: and such a union is not always to be found.

From the same social position, then, nations may derive one or the other of two great political results; these results are extremely different from each other, but they may both proceed from the same cause.

The Anglo-Americans, are the first who, having been exposed to this formidable alternative, have been happy enough to escape the dominion of absolute power. They have been allowed by their circumstances, their origin, their intelligence, and especially by their moral feeling, to establish and maintain the sovereignty of the people.

Chapter IV.

THE PRINCIPLE OF THE SOVEREIGNTY OF THE PEOPLE IN AMERICA.

It predominates over the whole of Society in America.—Application made of this Principle by the Americans even before their Revolution.—Development given to it by that Revolution.—Gradual and irresistible Extension of the elective Qualification.

Whenever the political laws of the United States are to be discussed, it is with the doctrine of the sovereignty of the people that we must begin.

The principle of the sovereignty of the people, which is to be found, more or less, at the bottom of almost all human institutions, generally remains concealed from view. It is obeyed without being recognised, or if for a moment it be brought to light, it is hastily cast back into the gloom of the sanctuary.

"The will of the nation" is one of those expressions which have been most profusely abused by the wily and the despotic of every age. To the eyes of some it has been represented by the venal suffrages of a few of the satellites of power; to others, by the votes of a timid or an interested minority; and some have even discovered it in the silence of a people, on the supposition that the fact of submission established the right of command.

In America, the principle of the sovereignty of the people is not either barren or concealed, as it is with some other nations; it is recognised by the customs and proclaimed by the laws; it spreads freely, and arrives without impediment at its most remote consequences. If there be a country in the world where the doctrine of the sovereignty of the people can be fairly appreciated, where it can be studied in its application to the affairs of society, and where its dangers and its advantages may be foreseen, that country is assuredly America.

I have already observed that, from their origin, the sovereignty of the people was the fundamental principle of the greater number of the

British colonies in America. It was far, however, from then exercising as much influence on the government of society as it now does. Two obstacles, the one external, the other internal, checked its invasive progress.

It could not ostensibly disclose itself in the laws of the colonies which were still constrained to obey the mother-country; it was therefore obliged to spread secretly, and to gain ground in the provincial assemblies, and especially in the townships.

American society was not yet prepared to adopt it with all its consequences. The intelligence of New England, and the wealth of the country to the south of the Hudson (as I have shown in the preceding chapter), long exercised a sort of aristocratic influence, which tended to limit the exercise of social authority within the hands of a few. The public functionaries were not universally elected, and the citizens were not all of them electors. The electoral franchise was everywhere placed within certain limits, and made dependant on a certain qualification, which was exceedingly low in the north, and more considerable in the south.

The American revolution broke out, and the doctrine of the sovereignty of the people, which had been nurtured in the townships, took possession of the state: every class was enlisted in its cause; battles were fought, and victories obtained for it; until it became the law of laws.

A scarcely less rapid change was effected in the interior of society, where the law of descent completed the abolition of local influences.

At the very time when this consequence of the laws and of the revolution became apparent to every eye, victory was irrevocably pronounced in favour of the democratic cause. All power was, in fact, in its hands, and resistance was no longer possible. The higher orders submitted without a murmur and without a struggle to an evil which was thenceforth inevitable. The ordinary fate of falling powers awaited them; each of their several members followed his own interest; and as it was impossible to wring the power from the hands of a people which they did not detest sufficiently to brave, their only aim was to secure its good-will at any price. The most democratic laws were consequently voted by the very men whose interests they impaired: and thus, although the higher classes did not excite the passions of the people against their order, they accelerated the triumph of the new state of things; so that, by a singular change, the democratic impulse was found to be most irresistible in the very states where the aristocracy had the firmest hold.

The state of Maryland, which had been founded by men of rank, was the first to proclaim universal suffrage,* and to introduce the most democratic forms into the conduct of its government.

When a nation modifies the elective qualification, it may easily be foreseen that sooner or later that qualification will be entirely abolished. There is no more invariable rule in the history of society: the farther electoral rights are extended, the more is felt the need of ex-

* See the amendments made to the constitution of Maryland in 1801 and 1809.

tending them; for after each concession the strength of the democracy increases, and its demands increase with its strength. The ambition of those who are below the appointed rate is irritated in exact proportion to the great number of those who are above it. The exception at last becomes the rule, concession follows concession, and no stop can be made short of universal suffrage.

At the present day the principle of the sovereignty of the people has acquired, in the United States, all the practical development which the imagination can conceive. It is unencumbered by those fictions which have been thrown over it in other countries, and it appears in every possible form according to the exigency of the occasion. Sometimes the laws are made by the people in a body, as at Athens; and sometimes its representatives, chosen by universal suffrage, transact business in its name, and almost under its immediate control.

In some countries a power exists which, though it is in a degree foreign to the social body, directs it, and forces it to pursue a certain track. In others the ruling force is divided, being partly within and partly without the ranks of the people. But nothing of the kind is to be seen in the United States; there society governs itself for itself. All power centres in its bosom; and scarcely an individual is to be met with who would venture to conceive, or, still more, to express, the idea of seeking it elsewhere. The nation participates in the making of its laws by the choice of its legislators, and in the execution of them by the choice of the agents of the executive government; it may almost be said to govern itself, so feeble and so restricted is the share left to the administration, so little do the authorities forget their popular origin and the power from which they emanate.*

Chapter V.

NECESSITY OF EXAMINING THE CONDITION OF THE STATES BEFORE THAT OF THE UNION AT LARGE.

It is proposed to examine in the following chapter, what is the form of government established in America on the principle of the sovereignty of the people; what are its resources, its hinderances, its advantages, and its dangers. The first difficulty which presents itself arises from the complex nature of the constitution of the United States, which consists of two distinct social structures, connected, and, as it were, encased, one within the other; two governments, completely separate, and almost independent, the one fulfilling the ordinary duties, and responding to the daily and indefinite calls of a community, the other circumscribed within certain limits, and only exercising an exceptional authority over the general interests of the country. In short, there are twenty-four small sovereign nations, whose agglomer-

* See Appendix H.

ation constitutes the body of the Union. To examine the Union before we have studied the states, would be to adopt a method filled with obstacles. The Federal government of the United States was the last which was adopted; and it is in fact nothing more than a modification or a summary of those republican principles which were current in the whole community before it existed, and independently of its existence. Moreover, the federal government is, as I have just observed, the exception; the government of the states is the rule. The author who should attempt to exhibit the picture as a whole, before he had explained its details, would necessarily fall into obscurity and repetition.

The great political principles which govern American society at this day, undoubtedly took their origin and their growth in the state. It is therefore necessary to become acquainted with the state in order to possess a clew to the remainder. The states which at present compose the American Union, all present the same features as far as regards the external aspect of their institutions. Their political or administrative existence is centred in three foci of action, which may not inaptly be compared to the different nervous centres which convey motion to the human body. The township is the lowest in order, then the county, and lastly the state; and I propose to devote the following chapter to the examination of these three divisions.

THE AMERICAN SYSTEM OF TOWNSHIPS AND MUNICIPAL BODIES. *

Why the Author begins the Examination of the political Institutions with the Township—Its existence in all Nations.—Difficulty of establishing and preserving Independence.—Its Importance.—Why the Author has selected the township System of New England as the main Object of his Inquiry.

It is not undesignedly that I begin this subject with the township. The village or township is the only association which is so perfectly natural, that wherever a number of men are collected, it seems to constitute itself.

The town, or tithing, as the smallest division of a community, must necessarily exist in all nations, whatever their laws and customs may be: if man makes monarchies, and establishes republics, the first association of mankind seems constituted by the hand of God. But although the existence of the township is coeval with that of man, its liberties are not the less rarely respected and easily destroyed. A nation

* [It is by this periphrasis that I attempt to render the French expressions "*Commune*" and "*Systeme Communal.*" I am not aware that any English word precisely corresponds to the general term of the original. In France every association of human dwellings forms a *commune*, and every commune is governed by a *maire* and a *conseil municipal*. In other words, the *mancipium* or municipal privilege, which belongs in England to chartered corporations alone, is alike extended to every commune into which the cantons and departments of France were divided at the revolution. Thence the different application of the expression, which is general in one country and restricted in the other. In America, the counties of the northern states are divided into townships, those of the southern into parishes; beside which, municipal bodies, bearing the name of corporations, exist in the cities. I shall apply these several expressions to render the term *commune*. The word "parish," now commonly used in England, belongs exclusively to the ecclesiastical division; it denotes the limits over which a *person's* (*persona ecclesia* or perhaps *parochianus*) rights extend.—*Translator's Note.*]

is always able to establish great political assemblies, because it habitu-ally contains a certain number of individuals fitted by their talents, if not by their habits, for the direction of affairs. The township is, on the contrary, composed of coarser materials, which are less easily fash-ioned by the legislator. The difficulties which attend the consolidation of its independence rather augment than diminish with the increasing enlightenment of the people. A highly-civilized community spurns the attempts of a local independence, is disgusted at its numerous blunders, and is apt to despair of success before the experiment is completed. Again, no immunities are so ill-protected from the en-croachments of the supreme power as those of municipal bodies in general: they are unable to struggle, single-handed, against a strong or an enterprising government, and they cannot defend their cause with success unless it be identified with the customs of the nation and sup-ported by public opinion. Thus, until the independence of townships is amalgamated with the manners of a people, it is easily destroyed; and it is only after a long existence in the laws that it can be thus amalgamated. Municipal freedom eludes the exertions of man; it is rarely created; but it is, as it were, secretly and spontaneously engen-dered in the midst of a semi-barbarous state of society. The constant action of the laws and the national habits, peculiar circumstances, and above all, time, may consolidate it; but there is certainly no na-tion on the continent of Europe which has experienced its advan-tages. Nevertheless, local assemblies of citizens constitute the strength of free nations. Municipal institutions are to liberty what primary schools are to science; they bring it within the people's reach, they teach men how to use and how to enjoy it. A nation may establish a system of free government, but without the spirit of mu-nicipal institutions it cannot have the spirit of liberty. The transient passions, and the interests of an hour, or the chance of circum-stances, may have created the external forms of independence; but the despotic tendency which has been repelled will, sooner or later, inevitably reappear on the surface.

In order to explain to the reader the general principles on which the political organizations of the counties and townships of the United States rest, I have thought it expedient to choose one of the states of New England as an example, to examine the mechanism of its consti-tution, and then to cast a general glance over the country.

The township and the county are not organized in the same manner in every part of the Union; it is, however, easy to perceive that the same principles have guided the formation of both of them throughout the Union. I am inclined to believe that these principles have been carried farther in New England than elsewhere, and consequently that they offer greater facilities to the observations of a stranger.

The institutions of New England form a complete and regular whole; they have received the sanction of time, they have the support of the laws, and the still stronger support of the manners of the com-munity, over which they exercise the most prodigious influence; they consequently deserve our attention on every account.

LIMITS OF THE TOWNSHIP.

The township of New England is a division which stands between the *commune* and the *canton* of France, and which corresponds in general to the English tithing, or town. Its average population is from two to three thousand;* so that, on the one hand, the interests of the inhabitants are not likely to conflict, and, on the other, men capable of conducting its affairs are always to be found among its citizens.

AUTHORITIES OF THE TOWNSHIP IN NEW ENGLAND.

The People the Source of all Power here as Elsewhere—Manages its own Affairs—No Corporation.—The greater part of the Authority vested in the Hands of the Selectmen.—How the Selectmen act.—Town-Meeting.—Enumeration of the public Officers of the Township—Obligatory and remunerated Functions.

In the township, as well as everywhere else, the people is the only source of power; but in no stage of government does the body of citizens exercise a more immediate influence. In America, the people is a master whose exigences demand obedience to the utmost limits of possibility.

In New England the majority acts by representatives in the conduct of the public business of the state; but if such an arrangement be necessary in general affairs, in the township, where the legislative and administrative action of the government is in more immediate contact with the subject, the system of representation is not adopted. There is no corporation; but the body of electors, after having designated its magistrates, directs them in everything that exceeds the simple and ordinary executive business of the state.†

This state of things is so contrary to our ideas, and so different from our customs, that it is necessary for me to adduce some examples to explain it thoroughly.

The public duties in the township are extremely numerous and minutely divided, as we shall see farther on; but the large proportion of administrative power is vested in the hands of a small number of individuals called "the selectmen."‡

The general laws of the state impose a certain number of obligations on the selectmen, which they may fulfil without the authorization of the body they govern, but which they can only neglect on their own responsibility. The law of the state obliges them, for instance, to draw up

---

* In 1830, there were 305 townships in the state of Masschusetts, and 610,014 inhabitants; which gives an average of about 2,000 inhabitants to each township.

† The same rules are not applicable to the great towns, which generally have a mayor, and a corporation divided into two bodies; this, however, is an exception which requires the sanction of a law. See the act of 22d February, 1822, for appointing the authorities of the city of Boston. It frequently happens that small towns as well as cities are subject to a peculiar administration. In 1832, 104 townships in the state of New York were governed in this manner.—*Williams's Register.*

‡ Three selectmen are appointed in the small townships, and nine in the large ones, See "The Town Officer," p. 186. See also the principal laws of the state of Massachusetts relative to the selectmen:—

Act of the 20th February, 1786, vol. i., p. 219; 24th February, 1796, vol. i., p. 488, 7th March, 1801, vol. ii., p. 45; 16th June, 1795, vol. i., p. 475; 12th March, 1808, vol, ii., p. 186; 28th February, 1787, vol. i., p. 302; 22d June, 1797, vol. i., p. 539.

the list of electors in their townships; and if they omit this part of their functions, they are guilty of a misdemeanor. In all the affairs, however, which are determined by the town-meeting, the selectmen are the organs of the popular mandate, as in France the maire executes the decree of the municipal council. They usually act upon their own responsibility, and merely put in practice principles which have been previously recognised by the majority. But if any change is to be introduced in the existing state of things, or if they wish to undertake any new enterprise, they are obliged to refer to the source of their power. If, for instance, a school is to be established, the selectmen convoke the whole body of electors on a certain day at an appointed place; they explain the urgency of the case; they give their opinion on the means of satisfying it, on the probable expense, and the site which seems to be most favourable. The meeting is consulted on these several points; it adopts the principle, marks out the site, votes the rate, and confides the execution of its resolution to the selectmen.

The selectmen have alone the right of calling a town-meeting; but they may be requested to do so: if the citizens are desirous of submitting a new project to the assent of the township, they may demand a general convocation of the inhabitants; the selectmen are obliged to comply, but they have only the right of presiding at the meeting.*

The selectmen are elected every year in the month of April or of May. The town-meeting chooses at the same time a number of municipal magistrates, who are intrusted with important administrative functions. The assessors rate the township; the collectors receive the rate. A constable is appointed to keep the peace, to watch the streets, and to forward the execution of the laws; the town-clerk records all the town votes, orders, grants, births, deaths, and marriages; the treasurer keeps the funds; the overseer of the poor performs the difficult task of superintending the action of the poor laws; committee-men are appointed to attend to the schools and to public instruction; and the road-surveyors, who take care of the greater and lesser thoroughfares of the township, complete the list of the principal functionaries. They are, however, still farther subdivided; and among the municipal officers are to be found parish commissioners, who audit the expenses of public worship; different classes of inspectors, some of whom are to direct the citizens in case of fire; tithing-men, listers, haywards, chimney-viewers, fence-viewers to maintain the bounds of property, timber-measurers, and sealers of weights and measures.†

There are nineteen principal offices in a township. Every inhabitant is constrained, on pain of being fined, to undertake these different functions; which, however, are almost all paid, in order that the poorer citizens may be able to give up their time without loss. In general the American system is not to grant a fixed salary to its functionaries.

---

* See laws of Massachusetts, vol. i., p. 150. Act of the 25th March, 1786.
† All these magistrates actually exist; their different functions are all detailed in a book called, "The Town Officer," by Isaac Goodwin, Worcester, 1827; and in the Collection of the General Laws of Massachusetts, 3 vols., Boston, 1823.

Every service has its price, and they are remunerated in proportion to
what they have done.

EXISTENCE OF THE TOWNSHIP.

Every one the best Judge of his own Interest.—Corollary of the Principle of the
Sovereignty of the People.—Application of these Doctrines in the Townships of
America.—The Township of New England is Sovereign in that which concerns it-
self alone; subject to the State in all other Matters.—Bond of Township and the
State.—In France the Government lends its Agents to the *Commune.*—In Amer-
ica the Reverse occurs.

I have already observed, that the principle of the sovereignty of the
people governs the whole political system of the Anglo-Americans.
Every page of this book will afford new instances of the same doctrine.
In the nations by which the sovereignty of the people is recognised,
every individual possesses an equal share of power, and participates
alike in the government of the state. Every individual is therefore supposed to be as well informed, as virtuous, and as strong, as any of his
fellow-citizens. He obeys the government, not because he is inferior to
the authorities which conduct it, or that he is less capable than his
neighbour of governing himself, but because he acknowledges the
utility of an association with his fellow-men, and because he knows
that no such association can exist without a regulating force. If he be
a subject in all that concerns the mutual relations of citizens, he is
free and responsible to God alone for all that concerns himself. Hence
arises the maxim that every one is the best and the sole judge of his
own private interest, and that society has no right to control a man's
actions, unless they are prejudicial to the common weal, or unless the
common weal demands his co-operation. This doctrine is universally
admitted in the United States. I shall hereafter examine the general
influence which it exercises on the ordinary actions of life: I am now
speaking of the nature of municipal bodies.

The township, taken as a whole, and in relation to the government
of the country, may be looked upon as an individual to whom the theory I have just alluded to is applied. Municipal independence is therefore a natural consequence of the principle of the sovereignty of the
people in the United States: all the American republics recognise it
more or less; but circumstances have peculiarly favoured its growth in
New England.

In this part of the Union the impulsion of political activity was given
in the townships; and it may almost be said that each of them originally formed an independent nation. When the kings of England asserted their supremacy, they were contented to assume the central
power of the state. The townships of New England remained as they
were before; and although they are now subject to the state, they were
at first scarcely dependant upon it. It is important to remember that
they have not been invested with privileges, but that they seem, on the
contrary, to have surrendered a portion of their independence to the
state. The townships are only subordinate to the state in those inter-

ests which I shall term *social*, as they are common to all the citizens. They are independent in all that concerns themselves; and among the inhabitants of New England I believe that not a man is to be found who would acknowledge that the state has any right to interfere in their local interests. The towns of New England buy and sell, prosecute or are indicted, augment or diminish their rates, without the slightest opposition on the part of the administrative authority of the state.

They are bound, however, to comply with the demands of the community. If the state is in need of money, a town can neither give nor withhold the supplies. If the state projects a road, the township cannot refuse to let it cross its territory; if a police regulation is made by the state, it must be enforced by the town. A uniform system of instruction is organized all over the country, and every town is bound to establish the schools which the law ordains. In speaking of the administration of the United States, I shall have occasion to point out the means by which the townships are compelled to obey in these different cases: I here merely show the existence of the obligation. Strict as this obligation is, the government of the state imposes it in principle only, and in its performance the township resumes all its independent rights. Thus, taxes are voted by the state, but they are assessed and collected by the township; the existence of a school is obligatory, but the township builds, pays, and superintends it. In France the state collector receives the local imposts; in America the town collector receives the taxes of the state. Thus the French government lends its agents to the commune; in America, the township is the agent of the government. The fact alone shows the extent of the differences which exist between the two nations.

PUBLIC SPIRIT OF THE TOWNSHIPS OF NEW ENGLAND.

How the Township of New England wins the Affections of its Inhabitants—Difficulty of creating local public Spirit in Europe—The Rights and Duties of the American Township favorable to it.—Characteristics of Home in the United States.—Manifestations of public Spirit in New England.—Its happy Effects.

In America, not only do municipal bodies exist, but they are kept alive and supported by public spirit. The township of New England possesses two advantages which infallibly secure the attentive interest of mankind, namely, independence and authority. Its sphere is indeed small and limited, but within that sphere its action is unrestrained; and its independence would give to it a real importance, even if its extent and population did not ensure it.

It is to be remembered that the affections of men are generally turned only where there is strength. Patriotism is not durable in a conquered nation. The New Englander is attached to his township, not only because he was born in it, but because it constitutes a strong and free social body of which he is a member, and whose government claims and deserves the exercise of his sagacity. In Europe the absence of local public spirit is a frequent subject of regret to those who are in power; every one agrees that there is no surer guarantee of order and tranquility, and yet nothing is more difficult to create. If the municipal bodies were made powerful and independent, the authorities of the nation might be disunited, and the peace of the country endangered. Yet, without power and independence, a town may contain good subjects, but it can have no active citizens. Another important fact is, that the township of New England is so constituted as to excite the warmest of human affections, without arousing the ambitious passions of the heart of man. The officers of the county are not elected, and their authority is very limited. Even the state is only a second-rate community, whose tranquil and obscure administration offers no inducement sufficient to draw men away from the circle of their interests into the turmoil of public affairs. The federal government confers power and honour on the men who conduct it; but these individuals can never be very numerous. The high station of the presidency can only be reached at an advanced period of life; and the other federal functionaries are generally men who have been favoured by fortune, or distinguished in some other career. Such cannot be the permanent aim of the ambitious. But the township serves as a centre for the desire of public esteem, the want of exciting interests, and the taste for authority and popularity, in the midst of the ordinary relations of life: and the passions which commonly embroil society, change their character when they find a vent so near the domestic hearth and the family circle.

In the American states power has been disseminated with admirable skill, for the purpose of interesting the greatest possible number of persons in the common weal. Independently of the electors who are from time to time called into action, the body politic is divided into innumerable functionaries and officers, who all, in their several spheres, represent the same powerful corporation in whose name they act. The local administration thus affords an unfailing source of profit and interest to a vast number of individuals.

The American system, which divides the local authority among so many citizens, does not scruple to multiply the functions of the town officers. For in the United States it is believed, and with truth, that patriotism is a kind of devotion which is strengthened by ritual observance. In this manner the activity of the township is continually perceptible; it is daily manifested in the fulfilment of a duty, or the exercise of right; and a constant though gentle motion is thus kept up in society which animates without disturbing it.

The American attaches himself to his home, as the mountaineer clings to his hills, because the characteristic features of his country are there more distinctly marked than elsewhere. The existence of the townships of New England is in general a happy one. Their government is suited to their tastes, and chosen by themselves. In the midst of the profound peace and general comfort which reign in America, the commotions of municipal discord are infrequent. The conduct of local business is easy. The political education of the people has long been complete; say rather that it was complete when the people first set foot upon the soil. In New England no tradition exists of a distinction of ranks; no portion of the community is tempted to oppress the remainder; and the abuses which may injure isolated individuals are forgotten in the general contentment which prevails. If the government is defective (and it would no doubt be easy to point out its deficiencies), the fact that it really emanates from those it governs, and that it acts, either ill or well, casts the protecting spell of a parental pride over its faults. No term of comparison disturbs the satisfaction of the citizen: England formerly governed the mass of the colonies, but the people was always sovereign in the township, where its rule is not only an ancient, but a primitive state.

The native of New England is attached to his township because it is independent and free: his co-operation in its affairs ensures his attachment to its interest; the well-being it affords him secures his affection; and its welfare is the aim of his ambition and of his future exertions; he takes a part in every occurrence in the place; he practices the art of government in the small sphere within his reach; he accustoms himself to those forms which can alone ensure the steady progress of liberty; he imbibes their spirit; he acquires a taste for order, comprehends the union of the balance of powers, and collects clear practical notions on the nature of his duties and the extent of his rights.

THE COUNTIES OF NEW ENGLAND.

The division of the counties in America has considerable analogy with that of the arrondissements of France. The limits of the counties are arbitrarily laid down, and the various districts which they contain have no necessary connexion, no common traditional or natural sympathy; their object is simply to facilitate the administration of public affairs.

The extent of the township was too small to contain a system of judicial institutions; each county has, however, a court of justice,* a sheriff to execute its decrees, and a prison for criminals. There are certain wants which are felt alike by all the townships of a county; it is therefore natural that they should be satisfied by a central authority. In the state of Massachusetts this authority is vested in the hands of several magistrates who are appointed by the governor of the state, with the advice† of his council.‡ The officers of the county have only a limited and occasional authority, which is applicable to certain predetermined cases. The state and the townships possess all the power requisite to conduct public business. The budget of the county is only drawn up by its officers and is voted by the legislature.§ There is no assembly which directly or indirectly represents the county; it has, therefore, properly speaking, no political existence.

---

* See the act of 14th February, 1821. Laws of Massachusetts, vol. i., p. 551.
† See the act of 20th February, 1819. Laws of Massachusetts, vol. ii., p. 494.
‡ The council of the governor is an elective body.
§ See the act of 2d November, 1791. Laws of Massachusetts, vol. i., p. 61.

A twofold tendency may be discerned in the American constitutions, which impels the legislator to centralize the legislative, and to disperse the executive power. The township of New England has in itself an indestructible element of independence; but this distinct existence could only be fictitiously introduced into the county, where its utility had not been felt. All the townships united have but one representation, which is the state, the centre of the national authority: beyond the action of the township and that of the nation, nothing can be said to exist but the influence of individual exertion.

ADMINISTRATION IN NEW ENGLAND.

Administration not perceived in America.—Why?—The Europeans believe that Liberty is promoted by depriving the social Authority of some of its Rights; the Americans, by dividing its Exercise.—Almost all the Administration confined to the Township, and divided among the town Officers.—No trace of an administrative Hierarchy to be perceived either in the Township, or above it.—The Reason of this. How it happens that the Administration of the State is uniform.—Who is empowered to enforce the Obedience of the Township and the County to the Law.—The introduction of judicial Power into the Administration.—Consequence of the Extension of the elective Principle to all Functionaries.—The Justice of the Peace in New England.—By whom Appointed.—County Officer.—Ensures the Administration of the Townships.—Court of Sessions.—Its Action.—Right of Inspection and Indictment disseminated like the other administrative Functions.—Informers encouraged by the division of Fines.

Nothing is more striking to a European traveller in the United States than the absence of what we term government, or the administration. Written laws exist in America, and one sees that they are daily executed; but although everything is in motion, the hand which gives the impulse to the social machine can nowhere be discovered. Nevertheless, as all people are obliged to have recourse to certain grammatical forms, which are the foundation of human language, in order to express their thoughts; so all communities are obliged to secure their existence by submitting to a certain portion of authority, without which they fall a prey to anarchy. This authority may be distributed in several ways, but it must always exist somewhere.

There are two methods of diminishing the force of authority in a nation.

The first is to weaken the supreme power in its very principle, by forbidding or preventing society from acting in its own defence under certain circumstances. To weaken authority in this manner is what is generally termed in Europe to lay the foundations of freedom.

The second manner of diminishing the influence of authority does not consist in stripping society of any of its rights, nor in paralysing its efforts, but in distributing the exercise of its privileges among various hands, and in multiplying functionaries, to each of whom the degree of power necessary for him to perform his duty is intrusted. There may be nations in whom this distribution of social powers might lead to anarchy; but in itself it is not anarchical. The action of authority is indeed thus rendered less irresistible, and less perilous, but it is not totally suppressed.

The revolution of the United States was the result of a mature and deliberate taste for freedom, not of a vague or ill-defined craving for independence. It contracted no alliance with the turbulent passions of anarchy; but its course was marked, on the contrary, by an attachment to whatever was lawful and orderly.

It was never assumed in the United States that the citizen of a free country has a right to do whatever he pleases: on the contrary, social obligations were there imposed upon him more various than anywhere else; no idea was ever entertained of attacking the principles, or of contesting the rights of society; but the exercise of its authority was divided, to the end that the office might be powerful and the officer insignificant, and that the community should be at once regulated and free. In no country in the world does the law hold so absolute a language as in America; and in no country is the right of applying it vested in so many hands. The administrative power in the United States presents nothing either central or hierarchical in its constitution, which accounts for its passing unperceived. The power exists, but its representative is not to be discerned.

We have already seen that the independent townships of New England protect their own private interests; and the municipal magistrates are the persons to whom the execution of the laws of the state is most frequently intrusted.* Beside the general laws, the state sometimes passes general police regulations; but more commonly the townships and town officers, conjointly with the justices of the peace, regulate the minor details of social life, according to the necessities of the different localities, and promulgate such enactments as concern the health of the community, and the peace as well as morality of the citizens.† Lastly, these municipal magistrates provide of their own accord and without any delegated powers, for those unforeseen emergencies which frequently occur in society.‡

It results from what we have said, that in the state of Massachusetts the administrative authority is almost entirely restricted to the township,§ but that it is distributed among a great number of individuals. In the French commune there is properly but one official functionary, namely, the maire; and in New England we have seen that there are nineteen. These nineteen functionaries do not in general depend upon one another. The law carefully prescribes a circle of action to each of

* See "The Town Officer," especially at the words SELECTMEN, ASSESSORS, COLLECTORS, SCHOOLS, SURVEYORS OF HIGHWAYS. I take one example in a thousand: the state prohibits travelling on a Sunday; the tything-men, who are town-officers, are especially charged to keep watch and to execute the law. See the laws of Massachusetts, vol. i., p 410.
    The selectmen draw up the lists of electors for the election of the governor, and transmit the result of the ballot to the secretary of the state. See act of 24th Feb. 1796; Ib., vol. i., p. 488.
† Thus, for instance, the selectmen authorize the construction of drains, point out the proper sites for slaughter-houses and other trades which are a nuisance to the neighbourhood. See the act of 7th June, 1785; Laws of Massachusetts, vol. i., p. 193.
‡ The selectmen take measures for the security of the public in case of contagious disease, conjointly with the justices of the peace. See the act of 22d June, 1797; vol. i., p. 539.
§ I say almost, for there are various circumstances in the annals of a township which are regulated by the justice of the peace in his individual capacity, or by the justices of the peace, assembled in the chief town of the county; thus licenses are granted by the justices. See the act of 28th Feb., 1787; vol. i., p. 297.

these magistrates; and within that circle they have an entire right to
perform their functions independently of any other authority. Above
the township scarcely any trace of a series of official dignities is to be
found. It sometimes happens that the county officers alter a decision
of the townships, or town magistrates,* but in general the authorities
of the county have no right to interfere with the authorities of the
township,† except in such matters as concern the county.

The magistrates of the township, as well as those of the county, are
bound to communicate their acts to the central government in a very
small number of predetermined cases.‡ But the central government is
not represented by an individual whose business it is to publish police
regulations and ordinances enforcing the execution of the laws; to
keep up a regular communication with the officers of the township
and the county; to inspect their conduct, to direct their actions, or to
reprimand their faults. There is no point which serves as a centre to
the radii of the administration.

What, then, is the uniform plan on which the government is conducted, and how is the compliance of the counties and their magistrates, or the townships and their officers, enforced? In the states of
New England the legislative authority embraces more subjects than it
does in France; the legislator penetrates to the very core of the administration; the law descends to the most minute details; the same enactment prescribes the principle and the method of its application, and
thus imposes a multitude of strict and rigorously defined obligations
on the secondary functionaries of the state. The consequence of this
is, that if all the secondary functionaries of the administration conform to the law, society in all its branches proceeds with the greatest
uniformity; the difficulty remains of compelling the secondary functionaries of the administration to conform to the law. It may be affirmed that, in general, society has only two methods of enforcing the
execution of the laws at its disposal; a discretionary power may be intrusted to a superior functionary of directing all the others, and of
cashiering them in case of disobedience; or the courts of justice may
be authorized to inflict judicial penalties on the offender: but these
two methods are not always available.

The right of directing a civil officer pre-supposes that of cashiering
him if he does not obey orders, and of rewarding him by promotion if
he fulfils his duties with propriety. But an elected magistrate can neither be cashiered nor promoted. All elective functions are inalienable

---

* Thus licenses are only granted to such persons as can produce a certificate of good conduct
from the selectmen. If the selectmen refuse to give the certificate, the party may appeal to
the justices assembled in the court of sessions; and they may grant the license. See the act of
12th March, 1808; vol. ii., p. 186.
    The townships have the right to make by-laws, and to enforce them by fines which are
fixed by law; but these by-laws must be approved by the court of sessions. See the act of
23d March, 1786; vol. i., p. 254.
† In Massachusetts the county-magistrates are frequently called upon to investigate the acts of
the town-magistrates; but it will be shown farther on that this investigation is a consequence, not of their administrative, but of their judicial power.
‡ The town committees of schools are obliged to make an annual report to the secretary of the
state on the condition of the school. See the act of 10th March, 1827; vol. iii., p. 183.

until their term is expired. In fact, the elected magistrate has nothing either to expect or to fear from his constituents; and when all public offices are filled by ballot, there can be no series of official dignities, because the double right of commanding and of enforcing obedience can never be vested in the same individual, and because the power of issuing an order can never be joined to that of inflicting a punishment or bestowing a reward.

The communities therefore in which the secondary functionaries of the government are elected, are perforce obliged to make great use of judicial penalties as a means of administration. This is not evident at first sight; for those in power are apt to look upon the institution of elective functionaries as one concession, and the subjection of the elective magistrate to the judges of the land as another. They are equally averse to both these innovations; and as they are more pressingly solicited to grant the former than the latter, they accede to the election of the magistrate, and leave him independent of the judicial power. Nevertheless, the second of these measures is the only thing that can possibly counterbalance the first; and it will be found that an elective authority which is not subject to judicial power will, sooner or later, either elude all control or be destroyed. The courts of justice are the only possible medium between the central power and the administrative bodies; they alone can compel the elected functionary to obey, without violating the rights of the elector. The extension of judicial power in the political world ought therefore to be in the exact ratio of the extension of elective offices; if these two institutions do not go hand in hand, the state must fall into anarchy or into subjection.

It has always been remarked that habits of legal business do not render men apt to the exercise of administrative authority. The Americans have borrowed from the English, their fathers, the idea of an institution which is unknown upon the continent of Europe: I allude to that of justices of the peace.

The justice of the peace is a sort of *mezzo termine* between the magistrate and the man of the world, between the civil officer and the judge. A justice of the peace is a well-informed citizen, though he is not necessarily versed in the knowledge of the laws. His office simply obliges him to execute the police regulations of society; a task in which good sense and integrity are of more avail than legal science. The justice introduces into the administration a certain taste for established forms and publicity, which renders him a most unserviceable instrument of despotism; and, on the other hand, he is not blinded by those superstitions which render legal officers unfit members of a government. The Americans have adopted the system of English justices of the peace, but they have deprived it of that aristocratic character which is discernible in the mother-country. The governor of Massachusetts* appoints a certain number of justices of the peace in every county, whose functions last seven years.† He farther designates

---

* We shall hereafter learn what a governor is: I shall content myself with remarking in this place, that he represents the executive power of the whole state.
† See the constitution of Massachusetts, chap. ii., §1; chap. iii., §3.

three individuals from among the whole body of justices, who form in each county what is called the court of sessions. The justices take a personal share in public business; they are sometimes intrusted with administrative functions in conjunction with elected officers;* they sometimes constitute a tribunal, before which the magistrates summarily prosecute a refractory citizen, or the citizens inform against the abuses of the magistrate. But it is in the court of sessions that they exercise their most important functions. This court meets twice a year in the county town; in Massachusetts it is empowered to enforce the obedience of the greater number† of public officers.‡ It must be observed that in the state of Massachusetts the court of sessions is at the same time an administrative body, properly so called, and a political tribunal. It has been asserted that the county is a purely administrative division. The court of sessions presides over that small number of affairs which, as they concern several townships, or all the townships of the county in common, cannot be intrusted to any one of them in particular.§ In all that concerns county business, the duties of the court of sessions are therefore purely administrative; and if in its investigations it occasionally borrows the forms of judicial procedure, it is only with a view to its own information,|| or as a guarantee to the community over which it presides. But when the administration of the township is brought before it, it almost always acts as a judicial body, and in some few cases as an administrative assembly.

The first difficulty is to procure the obedience of an authority so entirely independent of the general laws of the state as the township is. We have stated that assessors are annually named by the town-meetings, to levy the taxes. If a township attempts to evade the payment of the taxes by neglecting to name its assessors, the court of sessions condemns it to a heavy penalty.¶ The fine is levied on each of the inhabitants; and the sheriff of the county, who is an officer of justice, executes the mandate. Thus it is that in the United States the authority of the government is mysteriously concealed under the forms of a judicial sentence; and its influence is at the same time fortified by

---

* Thus, for example, a stranger arrives in a township from a country where a contagious disease prevails, and he falls ill. Two justices of the peace can, with the assent of the selectmen, order the sheriff of the county to remove and take care of him. Act of 22d June, 1797; vol. i., p. 540.

In general the justices interfere in all the important acts of the administration, and give them a semi-judicial character.

† I say *the greater number* because certain administrative misdemeanors are brought before the ordinary tribunals. If, for instance, a township refuses to make the necessary expenditure for its schools, or to name a school-committee, it is liable to a heavy fine. But this penalty is pronounced by the supreme judicial court or the court of common pleas. See the act of 10th March, 1827; laws of Massachusetts, vol. iii., p. 190. Or when a township neglects to provide the necessary war-stores. Act of 21st February, 1822; *Id.*, vol. ii., p. 670.

‡ In their individual capacity, the justices of the peace take a part in the business of the counties and townships. The more important acts of the municipal government are rarely decided upon without the co-operation of one of their body.

§ These affairs may be brought under the following heads: 1. The erection of prisons and courts of justice. 2. The county budget, which is afterward voted by the state. 3. The assessment of the taxes so voted. 4. Grants of certain patents. 5. The laying down and repairs of the county roads.

|| Thus, when a road is under consideration, almost all difficulties are disposed of by the aid of the jury.

¶ See the act of 20th February, 1786; laws of Massachusetts, vol. i., p. 217.

that irresistible power with which men have invested the formalities of law.

These proceedings are easy to follow, and to understand. The demands made upon a township are in general plain and accurately defined; they consist in a simple fact without any complication, or in a principle without its application in detail.* But the difficulty increases when it is not the obedience of the township, but that of the town officers, which is to be enforced. All the reprehensible actions of which a public functionary may be guilty are reducible to the following heads:—

He may execute the law without energy or zeal;

He may neglect to execute the law;

He may do what the law enjoins him not to do.

The last two violations of duty can alone come under the cognizance of a tribunal; a positive and appreciable fact is the indispensable foundation of an action at law. Thus, if the selectmen omit to fulfil the legal formalities usual at town elections, they may be condemned to pay a fine;† but when the public officer performs his duty without ability, and when he obeys the letter of the law without zeal or energy, he is at least beyond the reach of judicial interference. The court of sessions, even when it is invested with its administrative powers, is in this case unable to compel him to a more satisfactory obedience. The fear of removal is the only check to these quasi offences; and as the court of sessions does not originate the town authorities, it cannot remove functionaries whom it does not appoint. Moreover, a perpetual investigation would be necessary to convict the subordinate officer of negligence or lukewarmness; and the court of sessions sits but twice a year, and then only judges such offences as are brought before its notice. The only security for that active and enlightened obedience, which a court of justice cannot impose upon public officers, lies in the possibility of their arbitrary removal. In France this security is sought for in powers exercised by the heads of the administration; in America it is sought for in the principle of election.

Thus, to recapitulate in a few words what I have been showing:—

If a public officer in New England commits a crime in the exercise of his functions, the ordinary courts of justice are always called upon to pass sentence upon him.

If he commits a fault in his official capacity, a purely administrative tribunal is empowered to punish him; and, if the affair is important or urgent, the judge supplies the omission of the functionary.‡

---

* There is an indirect method of enforcing the obedience of a township. Suppose that the funds which the law demands for the maintenance of the roads have not been voted; the town-surveyor is then authorized, *ex officio*, to levy the supplies. As he is personally responsible to private individuals for the state of the roads, and indictable before the court of sessions, he is sure to employ the extraordinary right which the law gives him against the township. Thus by threatening the officer, the court of sessions exacts compliance from the town. See the act of 5th March, 1787; laws of Massachusetts, vol. i., p. 305.

† Laws of Massachusetts, vol. ii., p. 45.

‡ If, for instance, a township persists in refusing to name its assessors, the court of sessions nominates them; and the magistrates thus appointed are invested with the same authority as elected officers. See the quoted above, 20th February, 1787.

Lastly, if the same individual is guilty of one of those intangible offences, of which human justice has no cognizance, he annually appears before a tribunal from which there is no appeal, which can at once reduce him to insignificance, and deprive him of his charge. This system undoubtedly possesses great advantages, but its execution is attended with a practical difficulty which it is important to point out.

I have already observed that the administrative tribunal, which is called the court of sessions, has no right of inspection over the town officers. It can only interfere when the conduct of a magistrate is specially brought under its notice; and this is the delicate part of the system. The Americans of New England are unacquainted with the office of public prosecutor in the court of sessions,* and it may readily be perceived that it could not have been established without difficulty. If an accusing magistrate had merely been appointed in the chief town of each county, and if he had been unassisted by agents in the townships, he would not have been better acquainted with what was going on in the county than the members of the court of sessions. But to appoint agents in each township would have been to centre in his person the most formidable of powers, that of a judicial administration. Moreover, laws are the children of habit, and nothing of the kind exists in the legislation of England. The Americans have therefore divided the officers of inspection and of prosecution as well as all the other functions of the administration. Grand-jurors are bound by the law to apprize the court to which they belong of all the misdemeanors which may have been committed in their county.† There are certain great offences which are officially prosecuted by the state;‡ but more frequently the task of punishing delinquents devolves upon the fiscal officer, whose province it is to receive the fine; thus the treasurer of the township is charged with the prosecution of such administrative offences as fall under his notice. But a more especial appeal is made by American legislation to the private interest of the citizen,§ and this great principle is constantly to be met with in studying the laws of the United States. American legislators are more apt to give men credit for intelligence than for honesty; and they rely not a little on personal cupidity for the execution of the laws. When an individual is really and sensibly injured by an administrative abuse, it is natural that his personal interest should induce him to prosecute: But if a legal formality be required, which, however advantageous to the community, is of small importance to individuals, plaintiffs may be less easily found; and thus, by a tacit agreement, the laws might fall into disuse. Reduced by their system to this extremity, the Americans are obliged to

---

* I say the court of sessions, because in common courts there is a magistrate who exercises some of the functions of a public prosecutor.

† The grand-jurors are, for instance, bound to inform the court of the bad state of the roads. Laws of Massachusetts, vol. i., p. 308.

‡ If, for instance, the treasurer of the county holds back his account. Laws of Massachusetts, vol. i., p. 406.

§ Thus, if a private individual breaks down or wounded in consequence of the badness of a road, he can sue the township or the county for damages at the sessions Laws of Massachusetts, vol. i., p. 309.

encourage informers by bestowing on them a portion of the penalty in certain cases;* and to ensure the execution of the laws by the dangerous expedient of degrading the morals of the people.

The only administrative authority above the county magistrates is, properly speaking, that of the government.

GENERAL REMARKS ON THE ADMINISTRATION OF THE UNITED STATES.

Difference of the States of the Union in their Systems of Administration.—Activity and Perfection of the local Authorities decreases toward the South.—Power of the Magistrates increases; that of the Elector diminishes.—Administration passes from the Township to the County.—States of New York, Ohio, Pennsylvania.—Principles of Administration applicable to the whole Union.—Election of public Officers, and Inalienability of their Functions.—Absence of Gradation of Ranks.—Introduction of judicial Resources into the Administration.

I have already premised that after having examined the constitution of the township and the county of New England in detail, I should take a general view of the remainder of the Union. Townships and a local activity exist in every state; but in no part of the confederation is a township to be met with precisely similar to those in New England. The more we descend toward the south, the less active does the business of the township or parish become; the number of magistrates, of functions, and of rights, decreases; the population exercises a less immediate influence on affairs; town-meetings are less frequent, and the subjects of debates less numerous. The power of the elected magistrate is augmented, and that of the elector diminished, while the public spirit of the local communities is less awakened and less influential.†

These differences may be perceived to a certain extent in the state of New York; they are very sensible in Pennsylvania; but they become less striking as we advance to the northwest. The majority of the emigrants who settle in the northwestern states are natives of New England, and they carry the habits of their mother-country with them into that which they adopt. A township in Ohio is by no means dissimilar from a township in Massachusetts.

We have seen that in Massachusetts the principal part of the public

---

* In cases of invasion or insurrection, if the town officers neglect to furnish the necessary stores and ammunition for the militia, the township may be condemned to a fine of from two to five hundred dollars. It may readily be imagined that in such a case it might happen that no one cared to prosecute; hence the law adds that all the citizens may indict offences of this kind, and that half the fine shall belong to the plaintiff. See the act of 6th March, 1810; vol. ii., p. 236. The same clause is frequently to be met with in the laws of Massachusetts. Not only are private individuals thus incited to prosecute public officers, but the public officers are encouraged in the same manner to bring the disobedience of private individuals to justice. If a citizen refuses to perform the work which has been assigned to him upon a road, the road-surveyor may prosecute him, and he receives half the penalty for himself. See the laws above quoted, vol. i., p. 308.

† For details see Revised Statutes of the state of New York, part I., chap. xi., vol. i., pp. 336–364, entitled, "Of the Powers, Duties, and Privileges of Towns."

See in the digest of the laws of Pennsylvania, the words, ASSESSORS, COLLECTOR, CONSTABLES, OVERSEER OF THE POOR, SUPERVISORS OF HIGHWAYS; and in the acts of a general nature of the state of Ohio, the act of 25th February, 1834, relating to townships, p. 412; beside the peculiar dispositions relating to divers town officers, such as township's clerk, trustees, overseers of the poor, fence-viewers, appraisers of property, township's treasurer, constables, supervisor of highways.

administration lies in the township. It forms the common centre of
the interests and affections of the citizens. But this ceases to be the
case as we descend to states in which knowledge is less generally diffused, and where the township consequently offers fewer guarantees
of a wise and active administration. As we leave New England, therefore, we find that the importance of the town is gradually transferred
to the county, which becomes the centre of administration, and the
intermediate power between the government and the citizen. In Massachusetts the business of the town is conducted by the court of sessions, which is composed of a *quorum* named by the governor and his
council; but the county has no representative assembly, and its expenditure is voted by the national legislature. In the great state of New
York, on the contrary, and in those of Ohio and Pennsylvania, the inhabitants of each county choose a certain number of representatives,
who constitute the assembly of the county.* The county assembly has
the right of taxing the inhabitants to a certain extent; and in this respect it enjoys the privileges of a real legislative body: at the same time
it exercises an executive power in the county, frequently directs the
administration of the townships, and restricts their authority within
much narrower bounds than in Massachusetts.

Such are the principal differences which the systems of county and
town administration present in the federal states. Were it my intention
to examine the provisions of American law minutely, I should have to
point out still farther differences in the executive details of the several
communities. But what I have already said may suffice to show the
general principles on which the administration of the United States
rests. These principles are differently applied; their consequences are
more or less numerous in various localities; but they are always substantially the same. The laws differ, and their outward features
change, but their character does not vary. If the township and the
county are not everywhere constituted in the same manner, it is at
least true that in the United States the county and the township are
always based upon the same principle, namely, that every one is the
best judge of what concerns himself alone, and the person most able
to supply his private wants. The township and the county are therefore
bound to take care of their special interests: the state governs, but it
does not interfere with their administration. Exceptions to this rule
may be met with, but not a contrary principle.

The first consequence of this doctrine has been to cause all the
magistrates to be chosen either by, or at least from among the citizens.
As the officers are everywhere elected or appointed for a certain period, it has been impossible to establish the rules of a dependant series
of authorities; there are almost as many independent functionaries as

---

* See the Revised Statutes of the state of New York, Part I. chap. xi., vol. i., p. 410. *Idem.* chap.
xii., p. 366: also in the Acts of the State of Ohio, an act relating to county commissioners,
25th February, 1824, p. 263. See the Digest of the Laws of Pennsylvania, at the words,
COUNTY-RATES AND LEVIES, p. 170.

In the state of New York, each township elects a representative, who has a share in the administration of the county as well as in that of the township.

there are functions, and the executive power is disseminated in a multitude of hands. Hence arose the indispensable necessity of introducing the control of the courts of justice over the administration, and the system of pecuniary penalties, by which the secondary bodies and their representatives are constrained to obey the laws. The system obtains from one end of the Union to the other. The power of punishing the misconduct of public officers, or of performing the part of the executive, in urgent cases, has not, however, been bestowed on the same judges in all the states. The Anglo-Americans derived the institution of justices of the peace from a common source; but although it exists in all the states, it is not always turned to the same use. The justices of the peace everywhere participate in the administration of the townships and the counties,* either as public officers or as the judges of public misdemeanors, but in most of the states the more important classes of public offences come under the cognizance of the ordinary tribunals.

The election of public officers, or the inalienability of their functions, the absence of a gradation of powers, and the introduction of a judicial control over the secondary branches of the administration, are the universal characteristics of the American system from Maine to the Floridas. In some states (and that of New York has advanced most in this direction) traces of a centralized administration begin to be discernible. In the state of New York the officers of the central government exercise, in certain cases, a sort of inspection or control over the secondary bodies.† At other times they constitute a court of appeal for the decision of affairs.‡ In the state of New York judicial penalties are less used than in other parts as a means of administration; and the right of prosecuting the offences of public officers is vested in fewer

---

* In some of the southern states the county-courts are charged with all the details of the administration. See the Statutes of the State of Tennessee, *arts.* JUDICIARY, TAXES, &c.

† For instance, the direction of public instruction centres in the hands of the government. The legislature names the members of the university, who are denominated regents; the governor and lieutenant-governor of the state are necessarily of the number. Revised Statutes, vol. i., p. 455. The regents of the university annually visit the colleges and academies, and make their report to the legislature. Their superintendence is not inefficient, for several reasons: the colleges in order to become corporations stand in need of a charter, which is only granted on the recommendation of the regents: every year funds are distributed by the state for the encouragement of learning, and the regents are the distributors of this money. See chap. xv., "Public Instruction," Revised Statutes, vol. i., p. 455.

The school commissioners are obliged to send an annual report to the superintendent of the state. *Idem,* p. 448.

A similar report is annually made to the same person on the number and condition of the poor. *Idem,* p. 631.

‡ If any one conceives himself to be wronged by the school commissioners (who are town-officers), he can appeal to the superintendent of the primary schools, whose decision is final. Revised Statutes, vol. i., p. 487.

Provisions similar to those above cited are to be met with from time to time in the laws of the state of New York: but in general these attempts at centralization are weak and unproductive. The great authorities of the state have the right of watching and controlling the subordinate agents, without that of rewarding or punishing them. The same individual is never empowered to give an order and to punish disobedience; he has therefore the right of commanding, without the means of exacting compliance. In 1830 the superintendent of schools complained in his annual report addressed to the legislature, that several school commissioners had neglected, notwithstanding his application, to furnish him with the accounts which were due. He added, that if this omission continued, he should be obliged to prosecute them, as the law directs, before the proper tribunals.

hands.* The same tendency is faintly observable in some other states;† but in general the prominent feature of the administration in the United States is its excessive local independence.

OF THE STATE

I have described the townships and the administration: it now remains for me to speak of the state and government. This is ground I may pass over rapidly, without fear of being misunderstood; for all I have to say is to be found in written forms of the various constitutions, which are easily to be procured.‡ These constitutions rest upon a simple and rational theory; their forms have been adopted by all constitutional nations, and are become familiar to us.

In this place, therefore, it is only necessary for me to give a short analysis; I shall endeavour afterward to pass judgement upon what I now describe.

LEGISLATIVE POWER OF THE STATE.

Division of the Legislative Body into two Houses.—Senate.—House of Representatives.—Different functions of these two Bodies.

The legislative power of the state is vested in two assemblies, the first of which generally bears the name of the senate.

The senate is commonly a legislative body; but it sometimes becomes an executive and judicial one. It takes a part in the government in several ways, according to the constitution of the different states,§ but it is in the nomination of public functionaries that it most commonly assumes an executive power. It partakes of judicial power in the trial of certain political offences, and sometimes also in the decision of certain civil cases.‖ The number of its members is always small. The other branch of the legislature, which is usually called the house of representatives, has no share whatever in the administration, and only takes a part in the judicial power inasmuch as it impeaches public functionaries before the senate.

The members of the two houses are nearly everywhere subject to the same conditions of election. They are chosen in the same manner, and by the same citizens.

The only difference which exists between them is, that the term for which the senate is chosen, is in general longer than that of the house of representatives. The latter seldom remain in office longer than a year; the former usually sit two or three years.

By granting to the senators the privilege of being chosen for several

---

* Thus the district-attorney is directed to recover all fines below the sum of fifty dollars, unless such a right has been specially awarded to another magistrate. Revised Statutes, vol. i., p. 383.
† Several traces of centralization may be discovered in Massachusetts; for instance, the committees of the town-schools are directed to make an annual report to the secretary of state. See Laws of Massachusetts, vol. i., p. 367.
‡ See the Constitution of New York.
§ In Massachusetts the Senate is not invested with any administrative functions.
‖ As in the state of New York.

years, and being renewed seriatim, the law takes care to preserve in the legislative body a nucleus of men already accustomed to public business, and capable of exercising a salutary influence upon the junior members.

The Americans, plainly, did not desire, by this separation of the legislative body into two branches, to make one house hereditary and the other elective; one aristocratic and the other democratic. It was not their object to create in the one a bulwark to power, while the other represented the interests and passions of the people, The only advantages which result from the present constitution of the United States, are, the division of the legislative power, and the consequent check upon political assemblies; with the creation of a tribunal of appeal for the revision of the laws.

Time and experience, however, have convinced the Americans that if these are its only advantages, the division of the legislative power is still a principle of the greatest necessity. Pennsylvania was the only one of the United States which at first attempted to establish a single house of assembly; and Franklin[1] himself was so far carried away by the necessary consequences of the principle of the sovereignty of the people, as to have concurred in the measure; but the Pennsylvanians were soon obliged to change the law, and to create two houses. Thus the principle of the division of the legislative power was finally established, and its necessity may henceforward be regarded as a demonstrated truth.

This theory, which was nearly unknown to the republics of antiquity—which was introduced into the world almost by accident, like so many other great truths—and misunderstood by several modern nations, is at length become an axiom in the political science of the present age.

THE EXECUTIVE POWER OF THE STATE.

Office of Governor in an American State.—The Place he occupies in relation to the Legislature.—His Rights and his Duties.—His Dependance on the People.

The executive power of the state may with truth be said to be *represented* by the governor, although he enjoys but a portion of its rights. The supreme magistrate, under the title of governor, is the official moderator and counsellor of the legislature. He is armed with a suspensive veto, which allows him to stop, or at least to retard, its movements at pleasure. He lays the wants of the country before the legislative body, and points out the means which he thinks may be usefully employed in providing for them; he is the natural executor of its decrees in all the undertakings which interest the nation at large.* In the absence of the legislature, the governor is bound to take all necessary steps to guard the state against violent shocks and unforeseen dangers.

---

* Practically speaking, it is not always the governor who executes the plans of the legislature; it often happens that the letter, in voting a measure, names special agents to superintend the execution of it.

The whole military power of the state is at the disposal of the governor. He is the commander of the militia and head of the armed force. When the authority, which is by general consent awarded to the laws, is disregarded, the governor puts himself at the head of the armed force of the state, to quell resistance and to restore order.

Lastly, the governor takes no share in the administration of townships and counties, except it be indirectly in the nomination of justices of the peace, which nomination he has not the power to revoke.*

The governor is an elected magistrate, and is generally chosen for one or two years only; so that he always continues to be strictly dependant on the majority who returned him.

POLITICAL EFFECTS OF THE SYSTEM OF LOCAL ADMINISTRATION IN THE UNITED STATES.

Necessary Distinction between the general Centralization of Government, and the Centralization of the local Administration.—Local Administration not centralized in the United States; great general Centralization of the Government.—Some bad Consequences resulting to the United States from the local Administration.—Administrative Advantages attending this Order of things.—The Power which conducts the Government is less regular, less enlightened, less learned, but much greater than in Europe.—Political Advantages of this Order of things.—In the United States the Interest of the Country are everywhere kept in View.—Support given to the Government by the Community.—Provincial Institutions more necessary in Proportion as the social Condition becomes more democratic.—Reason of this.

Centralization is become a word of general and daily use, without any precise meaning being attached to it. Nevertheless, there exist two distinct kinds of centralization, which it is necessary to discriminate with accuracy.

Certain interests are common to all parts of a nation, such as the enactment of its general laws, and the maintenance of its foreign relations. Other interests are peculiar to certain parts of the nation; such, for instance, as the business of different townships. When the power which directs the general interests is centred in one place, or in the same persons, it constitutes a central government. The power of directing partial or local interests, when brought together, in like manner constitutes what may be termed a central administration.

Upon some points these two kinds of centralization coalesce; but by classifying the objects which fall more particularly within the province of each of them, they may easily be distinguished.

It is evident that a central government acquires immense power when united to administrative centralization. Thus combined, it accustoms men to set their own will habitually and completely aside; to submit, not only for once or upon one point, but in every respect, and at all times. Not only, therefore, does this union of power subdue them by force, but it affects them in the ordinary habits of life, and influences each individual, first separately, and then collectively.

---

* In some of the states the justices of the peace are not nominated by the governor.

These two kinds of centralization mutually assist and attract each other: but they must not be supposed to be inseparable. It is impossible to imagine a more completely central government than that which existed in France under Louis XIV.; when the same individual was the author and the interpreter of the laws, and being the representative of France at home and abroad, he was justified in asserting that the state was identified with his person. Nevertheless, the administration was much less centralized under Louis XIV., than it is at the present day.

In England the centralization of the government is carried to great perfection; the state has the compact vigor of a man, and by the sole act of its will it puts immense engines in motion, and wields or collects the efforts of its authority. Indeed, I cannot conceive that a nation can enjoy a secure or prosperous existence without a powerful centralization of government. But I am of opinion that a central administration enervates the nations in which it exists by incessantly diminishing their public spirit. If such an administration succeeds in condensing at a given moment on a given point all the disposable resources of a people, it impairs at least the renewal of those resources. It may ensure a victory in the hour of strife, but it gradually relaxes the sinews of strength. It may contribute admirably to the transient greatness of a man, but it cannot ensure the durable prosperity of a people.

If we pay proper attention, we shall find that whenever it is said that a state cannot act because it has no central point, it is the centralization of the government in which it is deficient. It is frequently asserted, and we are prepared to assent to the proposition, that the German empire was never able to bring all its powers into action. But the reason was, that the state has never been able to enforce obedience to its general laws, because the several members of that great body always claimed the right, or found the means, of refusing their co-operation to the representatives of the common authority, even in the affairs which concerned the mass of the people; in other words, because there was no centralization of government. The same remark is applicable to the middle ages; the cause of all the confusion of feudal society was that the control, not only of local but of general interests, was divided among a thousand hands, and broken up in a thousand different ways: the absence of a central government prevented the nations of Europe from advancing with energy in any straightforward course.

We have shown that in the United States no central administration, and no dependant series of public functionaries exist. Local authority has been carried to lengths which no European nation could endure without great inconvenience, and which have even produced some disadvantageous consequences in America. But in the United States the centralization of the government is complete; and it would be easy to prove that the national power is more compact than it has ever been in the old monarchies of Europe. Not only is there but one legislative body in each state; not only does there exist but one source of political authority; but numerous district assemblies and county courts have in general been avoided, lest they should be tempted to exceed their administrative duties and interfere with the government. In America the legislature of each state is supreme: nothing can impede its authority; neither privileges, nor local immunities, nor personal influence, nor even the empire of reason, since it represents that majority which claims to be the sole organ of reason. Its own determination is, therefore, the only limit to its action. In juxtaposition to it, and under its immediate control, is the representative of the executive power, whose duty it is to constrain the refractory to submit by superior force. The only symptom of weakness lies in certain details of the action of the government. The American republics have no standing armies to intimidate a discontented minority; but as no minority has as yet been reduced to declare open war, the necessity of an army has not been felt. The state usually employs the officers of the township or the county, to deal with the citizens. Thus, for instance, in New England the assessor fixes the rate of taxes; the collector receives them; the town treasurer transmits the amount to the public treasury; and the disputes which may arise are brought before the ordinary courts of justice. This method of collecting taxes is slow as well as inconvenient, and it would prove a perpetual hinderance to a government whose pecuniary demands were large. In general it is desirable that in whatever materially affects its existence, the government should be served by officers of its own, appointed by itself, removable at pleasure, and accustomed to rapid methods of proceeding. But it will always be easy for the central government, organized as it is in America, to introduce new and more efficacious modes of action proportioned to its wants.

The absence of a central government will not, then, as has often been asserted, prove the destruction of the republics of the New World; far from supposing that the American governments are not sufficiently centralized, I shall prove hereafter that they are too much so. The legislative bodies daily encroach upon the authority of the government, and their tendency, like that of the French convention,[2] is to appropriate it entirely to themselves. Under these circumstances the social power is constantly changing hands, because it is subordinate to the power of the people, which is too apt to forget the maxims of wisdom and of foresight in the consciousness of its strength: hence arises its danger; and thus its vigor, and not its impotence, will probably be the cause of its ultimate destruction.

The system of local administration produces several different effects in America. The Americans seem to me to have outstepped the limits of sound policy, in isolating the administration of the government; for order, even in second-rate affairs, is a matter of national importance.* As the state has no administrative functionaries of its own, stationed

---

* The authority which represents the state ought not, I think, to waive the right of inspecting the local administration, even when it does not interfere more actively. Suppose, for instance, that an agent of the government was stationed at some appointed spot, in the county, to prosecute the misdemeanors of the town and county officers, would not a more uniform order be the result, without in any way compromising the independence of the township? Nothing of the kind, however, exists in America; there is nothing above the county courts, which have, as it were, only an accidental cognizance of the offences they are meant to repress.

on different parts of its territory, to whom it can give a common impulse, the consequence is that it rarely attempts to issue any general police regulations. The want of these regulations is severely felt, and is frequently observed by Europeans. The appearance of disorder which prevails on the surface, leads them at first to imagine that society is in a state of anarchy; nor do they perceive their mistake till they have gone deeper into the subject. Certain undertakings are of importance to the whole state; but they cannot be put in execution, because there is no national administration to direct them. Abandoned to the exertions of the towns or counties, under the care of elected or temporary agents, they lead to no result, or at least to no durable benefit.

The partisans of centralization in Europe maintain that the government directs the affairs of each locality better than the citizens could do it for themselves: this may be true when the central power is enlightened, and when the local districts are ignorant; when it is as alert as they are slow; when it is accustomed to act, and they to obey. Indeed, it is evident that this double tendency must augment with the increase of centralization, and that the readiness of the one, and the incapacity of the others, must become more and more prominent. But I deny that such is the case when the people is as enlightened, as awake to its interests, and as accustomed to reflect on them, as the Americans are. I am persuaded, on the contrary, that in this case the collective strength of the citizens will always conduce more efficaciously to the public welfare than the authority of the government. It is difficult to point out with certainty the means of arousing a sleeping population, and of giving it passions and knowledge which it does not possess; it is, I am well aware, an arduous task to persuade men to busy themselves about their own affairs; and it would frequently be easier to interest them in the punctilios of court etiquette than in the repairs of their common dwelling. But whenever a central administration affects to supersede the persons most interested, I am inclined to suppose that it is either misled, or desirous to mislead. However enlightened and however skillful a central power may be, it cannot of itself embrace all the details of the existence of a great nation. Such vigilance exceeds the powers of man. And when it attempts to create and set in motion so many complicated springs, it must submit to a very imperfect result, or consume itself in bootless efforts.

Centralization succeeds more easily, indeed, in subjecting the external actions of men to a certain uniformity, which at last commands our regard, independently of the objects to which it is applied, like

---

[This note seems to have been written without reference to the provision existing, it is believed, in every state of the Union, by which a local officer is appointed in each county, to conduct all public prosecutions at the expense of the state. And in each county, a grand-jury is assembled three or four times at least in every year, to which all who are aggrieved have free access, and where every complaint, particularly those against public officers which has the least color of truth, is sure to be heard and investigated.

Such an agent as the author suggests would soon come to be considered a public informer, the most odious of all characters in the United States; and he would lose all efficiency and strength. With the provision above mentioned, there is little danger that a citizen, oppressed by a public officer, would find any difficulty in becoming his own informer, and inducing a rigid inquiry into the alleged misconduct.—*American Editor*.]

those devotees who worship the statue and forget the deity it represents. Centralization imparts without difficulty an admirable regularity to the routine of business; rules the details of the social police with sagacity; represses the smallest disorder and the most petty misdemeanors; maintains society in a *statu quo*, alike secure from improvement and decline; and perpetuates a drowsy precision in the conduct of affairs, which is hailed by the heads of the administration as a sign of perfect order and public tranquility;* in short, it excels more in prevention than in action. Its force deserts it when society is to be disturbed or accelerated in its course; and if once the cooperation of private citizens is necessary to the furtherance of its measures, the secret of its impotence is disclosed. Even while it invokes their assistance, it is on the condition that they shall act exactly as much as the government chooses, and exactly in the manner it appoints. They are to take charge of the details, without aspiring to guide the system; they are to work in a dark and subordinate sphere, and only to judge the acts in which they have themselves co-operated, by their results. These, however, are not conditions on which the alliance of the human will is to be obtained; its carriage must be free, and its actions responsible, or (such is the constitution of man) the citizen had rather remain a passive spectator than a dependant actor in schemes with which he is unacquainted.

It is undeniable, that the want of those uniform regulations which control the conduct of every inhabitant of France is not unfrequently felt in the United States. Gross instances of social indifference and neglect are to be met with; and from time to time disgraceful blemishes are seen, in complete contrast with the surrounding civilization. Useful undertakings, which cannot succeed without perpetual attention and rigorous exactitude, are very frequently abandoned in the end; for in America, as well as in other countries, the people is subject to sudden impulses and momentary exertions. The European who is accustomed to find a functionary always at hand to interfere with all he undertakes, has some difficulty in accustoming himself to the complex mechanism of the administration of the townships. In general it may be affirmed that the lesser details of the police, which render life easy and comfortable, are neglected in America; but that the essential guarantees of man in society are as strong there as elsewhere. In America the power which conducts the government is far less regular, less enlightened, and less learned, but a hundredfold more authoritative, than in Europe. In no country in the world do the citizens make such exertions for the common weal; and I am acquainted with no people which has established schools as numerous and as efficacious, places of public worship better suited to the wants of the inhabitants,

---

* China appears to me to present the most perfect instance of that species of well-being which a completely central administration may furnish to the nations among which it exists. Travellers assure us that the Chinese have peace without happiness, industry without improvement, stability without strength, and public order without public morality. The condition of society is always tolerable, never excellent. I am convinced that, when China is opened to European observation, it will be found to contain the most perfect model of a central administration which exists in the universe.

or roads kept in better repair. Uniformity or permanence of design, the minute arrangement of details,* and the perfection of an ingenious administration, must not be sought for in the United States; but it will be easy to find, on the other hand, the symptoms of a power, which, if it is somewhat barbarous, is at least robust; and of an existence, which is checkered with accidents indeed, but cheered at the same time by animation and effort.

Granting for an instant that the villages and counties of the United States would be more usefully governed by a remote authority, which they had never seen, than by functionaries taken from the midst of them—admitting, for the sake of argument, that the country would be more secure, and the resources of society better employed, if the whole administration centred in a single arm, still the *political* advantages which the Americans derive from their system would induce me to prefer it to the contrary plan. It profits me but little, after all, that a vigilant authority protects the tranquility of my pleasures, and constantly averts all danger from my path, without my care or my concern, if this same authority is the absolute mistress of my liberty and of my life, and if it so monopolizes all the energy of existence, that when it languishes everything languishes around it, that when it sleeps everything must sleep, that when it dies the state itself must perish.

In certain countries of Europe the natives consider themselves as a kind of settlers, indifferent to the fate of the spot upon which they live. The greatest changes are effected without their concurrence and (unless chance may have apprized them of the event) without their knowledge; nay more, the citizen is unconcerned as to the condition of his village, the police of his street, the repairs of the church or the parsonage; for he looks upon all these things as unconnected with himself, and as the property of a powerful stranger whom he calls the government. He has only a life-interest in these possessions, and he entertains no notions of ownership or of improvement. This want of interest in his own affairs goes so far, that if his own safety or that of his children is endangered, instead of trying to avert the peril, he will fold his arms, and wait till the nation comes to his assistance. This same individual who has so completely sacrificed his own free will, has

---

* A writer of talent, who, in the comparison which he has drawn between the finances of France and those of the United States, has proved that ingenuity cannot always supply the place of a knowledge of facts, very justly reproaches the Americans for the sort of confusion which exists in the accounts of the expenditure in the townships; and after giving the model of a departmental budget in France, he adds: "We are indebted to centralization, that admirable invention of a great man, for the uniform order and method which prevail alike in all the municipal budgets, from the largest town to the humblest commune." Whatever may be my admiration of this result, when I see the communes of France, with their excellent system of accounts, plunged in the grossest ignorance of their true interests, and abandoned to so incorrigible an apathy that they seem to vegetate rather than to live; when, on the other hand, I observe the activity, the information, and the spirit of enterprise which keeps society in perpetual labour, in those American townships whose budgets are drawn up with small method and with still less uniformity, I am struck by the spectacle; for to my mind the end of a good government is to ensure the welfare of a people, and not to establish order and regularity in the midst of its misery and its distress. I am therefore led to suppose that the prosperity of the American townships and the apparent confusion of their accounts, the distress of the French communes and the perfection of their budget, may be attributable to the same cause. At any rate I am suspicious of a benefit which is united to so many evils, and I am not averse to an evil which is compensated by so many benefits.

no natural propensity to obedience; he cowers, it is true, before the pettiest officer; but he braves the law with the spirit of a conquered foe as soon as its superior force is removed: his oscillations between servitude and license are perpetual. When a nation has arrived at this state, it must either change its customs and its laws, or perish: the source of public virtue is dry; and though it may contain subjects, the race of citizens is extinct. Such communities are a natural prey to foreign conquest; and if they do not disappear from the scene of life, it is because they are surrounded by other nations similar or inferior to themselves; it is because the instinctive feeling of their country's claims still exists in their hearts; and because an involuntary pride in the name it bears, or a vague reminiscence of its by-gone fame, suffices to give them the impulse of self-preservation.

Nor can the prodigious exertions made by certain people in the defence of a country, in which they may almost be said to have lived as aliens, be adduced in favour of such a system; for it will be found that in these cases their main incitement was religion. The permanence, the glory, and the prosperity of the nation, were become parts of their faith; and in defending the country they inhabited, they defended that holy city of which they were all citizens. The Turkish tribes have never taken an active share in the conduct of the affairs of society, but they accomplished stupendous enterprises as long as the victories of the sultans were the triumphs of the Mohammedan faith.[3] In the present age they are in rapid decay, because their religion is departing, and despotism only remains. Montesquieu,[4] who attributed to absolute power an authority peculiar to itself, did it, as I conceive, undeserved honour; for despotism, taken by itself, can produce no durable results. On close inspection we shall find that religion, and not fear, has ever been the cause of the long-lived prosperity of absolute governments. Whatever exertions may be made, no true power can be founded among men which does not depend upon the free union of their inclinations; and patriotism and religion are the only two motives in the world which can permanently direct the whole of a body politic to one end.

Laws cannot succeed in rekindling the ardour of an extinguished faith; but men may be interested in the fate of their country by the laws. By this influence, the vague impulse of patriotism, which never abandons the human heart, may be directed and revived: and if it be connected with the thoughts, the passions and daily habits of life, it may be consolidated into a durable and rational sentiment. Let it not be said that the time for the experiment is already past; for the old age of nations is not like the old age of men, and every fresh generation is a new people ready for the care of the legislator.

It is not the *administrative*, but the *political* effects of the local system that I most admire in America. In the United States the interests of the country are everywhere kept in view; they are an object of solicitude to the people of the whole Union, and every citizen is as warmly attached to them as if they were his own. He takes pride in the glory of his nation; he boasts of its success, to which he conceives himself to have contributed; and he rejoices in the general prosperity by which he profits. The feeling he entertains toward the state is analogous to that which unites him to his family, and it is by a kind of egotism that he interests himself in the welfare of his country.

The European generally submits to a public officer because he represents a superior force; but to an American he represents a right. In America it may be said that no one renders obedience to man, but to justice and to law. If the opinion which the citizen entertains of himself is exaggerated, it is at least salutary; he unhesitatingly confides in his own powers, which appear to him to be all-sufficient. When a private individual meditates an undertaking, however directly connected it may be with the welfare of society, he never thinks of soliciting the co-operation of the government: but he publishes his plan, offers to execute it himself, courts the assistance of other individuals, and struggles manfully against all obstacles. Undoubtedly he is often less successful than the state might have been in his position; but in the end, the sum of these private undertaking far exceeds all that the government could effect.

As the administrative authority is within the reach of the citizens, whom it in some degree represents, it excites neither their jealously nor their hatred: as its resources are limited, every one feels that he must not rely solely on its assistance. Thus when the administration thinks fit to interfere, it is not abandoned to itself as in Europe; the duties of the private citizens are not supposed to have lapsed because the state assists in their fulfilment; but every one is ready, on the contrary, to guide and to support it. This action of individual exertions, joined to that of the public authorities, frequently performs what the most energetic central administration would be unable to execute. It would be easy to adduce several facts in proof of what I advance, but I had rather give only one, with which I am more thoroughly acquainted.* In America, the means which the authorities have at their disposal for the discovery of crimes and the arrest of criminals are few. A state police does not exist, and passports are unknown. The criminal police of the United States cannot be compared to that of France; the magistrates and public prosecutors are not numerous, and the examinations of prisoners are rapid and oral. Nevertheless in no country does crime more rarely elude punishment. The reason is that every one conceives himself to be interested in furnishing evidence of the act committed, and in stopping the delinquent. During my stay in the United States, I saw the spontaneous formation of committees for the pursuit and prosecution of a man who had committed a great crime in a certain county. In Europe a criminal is an unhappy being, who is struggling for his life against the ministers of justice, while the population is merely a spectator of the conflict: in America he is looked upon as an enemy of the human race, and the whole of mankind is against him.

I believe that provincial institutions are useful to all nations, but

* See Appendix I.

nowhere do they appear to me to be more indispensable than among a democratic people. In an aristocracy, order can always be maintained in the midst of liberty; and as the rulers have a great deal to lose, order is to them a firstrate consideration. In like manner an aristocracy protects the people from the excesses of despotism, because it always possesses an organized power ready to resist a despot. But a democracy without provincial institutions has no security against these evils. How can a populace, unaccustomed to freedom in small concerns, learn to use it temperately in great affairs? What resistance can be offered to tyranny in a country where every private individual is impotent, and where the citizens are united by no common tie? Those who dread the license of the mob, and those who fear the rule of absolute power, ought alike to desire the progressive growth of provincial liberties.

On the other hand, I am convinced that democratic nations are most exposed to fall beneath the yoke of a central administration, for several reasons, among which is the following:—

The constant tendency of these nations is to concentrate all the strength of the government in the hands of the only power which directly represents the people: because, beyond the people nothing is to be perceived but a mass of equal individuals confounded together. But when the same power is already in possession of all the attributes of the government, it can scarcely refrain from penetrating into the details of the administration; and an opportunity of doing so is sure to present itself in the end, as was the case in France. In the French revolution[5] there were two impulses in opposite directions, which must never be confounded; the one was favourable to liberty, the other to despotism. Under the ancient monarchy the king was the sole author of the laws; and below the power of the sovereign, certain vestiges of provincial institutions half-destroyed, were still distinguishable. These provincial institutions were incoherent, ill-compacted, and frequently absurd; in the hands of the aristocracy they had sometimes been converted into instruments of oppression. The revolution declared itself the enemy of royalty and of provincial institutions at the same time; it confounded all that had preceded it—despotic power and the checks to its abuses—in an indiscriminate hatred; and its tendency was at once to republicanism and to centralization. This double character of the French revolution is a fact which has been adroitly handled by the friends of absolute power. Can they be accused of laboring in the cause of despotism, when they are defending of the revolution?* In this manner popularity may be conciliated with hostility to the rights of the people, and the secret slave of tyranny may be the professed admirer of freedom.

I have visited the two nations in which the system of provincial liberty has been most perfectly established, and I have listened to the opinions of different parties in those countries. In America I met with men who secretly aspired to destroy the democratic institutions of the

* See Appendix K.

Union; in England I found others who attacked the aristocracy openly; but I know of no one who does not regard provincial independence as a great benefit. In both countries I have heard a thousand different causes assigned for the evils of the state; but the local system was never mentioned among them. I have heard citizens attribute the power and prosperity of their country to a multitude of reasons: but they *all* placed the advantages of local institutions in the foremost rank.

Am I to suppose that when men who are naturally so divided on religious opinions, and on political theories, agree on one point, (and that, one of which they have daily experience) they are all in error? The only nations which deny the utility of provincial liberties are those which have fewest of them; in other words, those who are unacquainted with the institution are the only persons who pass a censure upon it.

Chapter VI.

JUDICIAL POWER IN THE UNITED STATES, AND ITS INFLUENCE ON POLITICAL SOCIETY.

The Anglo-Americans have retained the Characteristics of judicial Power which are common to all Nations.—They have, however, made it a powerful political Organ. How.—In what the judicial System of the Anglo-Americans differs from that of all other Nations.—Why the American Judges have the Right of declaring the Laws to be Unconstitutional.—How they use this Right.—Precautions taken by the Legislator to prevent its Abuse.

I have thought it essential to devote a separate chapter to the judicial authorities of the United States, lest their great political importance should be lessened in the reader's eyes by a merely incidental mention of them. Confederations have existed in other countries beside America; and republics have not been established on the shores of the New World alone: the representative system of government has been adopted in several states of Europe; but I am not aware that any nation of the globe has hitherto organized a judicial power on the principle adopted by the Americans. The judicial organization of the United States is the institution which the stranger has the greatest difficulty in understanding. He hears the authority of a judge invoked in the political occurrences of every day, and he naturally concludes that in the United States the judges are important political functionaries: nevertheless, when he examines the nature of the tribunals, they offer nothing which is contrary to the usual habits and privileges of those bodies; and the magistrates seem to him to interfere in public affairs by chance, but by a chance which recurs every day.

When the parliament of Paris remonstrated, or refused to enregister an edict, or when it summoned a functionary accused of malversation to its bar, its political influence as a judicial body was clearly visible;

but nothing of the kind is to be seen in the United States. The Americans have retained all the ordinary characteristics of judicial authority, and have carefully restricted its action to the ordinary circle of its functions.

The first characteristic of judicial power in all nations is the duty of arbitration. But rights must be contested in order to warrant the interference of a tribunal; and an action must be brought to obtain the decision of a judge. As long, therefore, as a law is uncontested, the judicial authority is not called upon to discuss it, and it may exist without being perceived. When a judge in a given case attacks a law relating to that case, he extends the circle of his customary duties, without however stepping beyond it; since he is in some measure obliged to decide upon the law, in order to decide the case. But if he pronounces upon a law without resting upon a case, he clearly steps beyond his sphere, and invades that of the legislative authority.

The second characteristic of judicial power is, that it pronounces on special cases, and not upon general principles. If a judge in deciding a particular point destroys a general principle, by passing a judgment which tends to reject all the inferences from that principle, and consequently to annul it, he remains within the ordinary limits of his functions. But if he directly attacks a general principle without having a particular case in view, he leaves the circle in which all nations have agreed to confine his authority; he assumes a more important, and perhaps a more useful influence than that of the magistrate, but he ceases to represent the judicial power.

The third characteristic of the judicial power is its inability to act unless it is appealed to, or until it has taken cognizance of an affair. This characteristic is less general than the other two; but notwithstanding the exceptions, I think it may be regarded as essential. The judicial power is by its nature devoid of action; it must be put in motion in order to produce a result. When it is called upon to repress a crime, it punishes the criminal; when a wrong is to be redressed, it is ready to redress it; when an act requires interpretation, it is prepared to interpret it; but it does not pursue criminals, hunt out wrongs, or examine into evidence of its own accord. A judicial functionary who should open proceedings, and usurp the censorship of the laws, would in some measure do violence to the passive nature of his authority.

The Americans have retained these three distinguishing characteristics of the judicial power; an American judge can only pronounce a decision when litigation has arisen, he is only conversant with special cases, and he cannot act until the cause has been duly brought before the court. His position is therefore perfectly similar to that of the magistrate of other nations; and he is nevertheless invested with immense political power. If the sphere of his authority and his means of action are the same as those of other judges, it may be asked whence he derives a power which they do not possess. The cause of this difference lies in the simple fact that the Americans have acknowledged the right of the judges to found their decisions on the constitution, rather than on the laws. In other words, they have left them at liberty not to apply such laws as may appear to them to be unconstitutional.

I am aware that a similar right has been claimed—but claimed in vain—by courts of justice in other countries; but in America it is recognised by all the authorities; and not a party, nor so much as an individual is found to contest it. This fact can only be explained by the principles of the American constitution. In France the constitution is (or at least is supposed to be) immutable; and the received theory is that no power has the right of changing any part of it. In England, the parliament has an acknowledged right to modify the constitution; as, therefore, the constitution may undergo perpetual changes, it does not in reality exist; the parliament is at once a legislative and a constituent assembly. The political theories of America are more simple and more rational. An American constitution is not supposed to be immutable as in France; nor is it susceptible of modification by the ordinary powers of society as in England. It constitutes a detached whole, which, as it represents the determination of the whole people, is no less binding on the legislator than on the private citizen, but which may be altered by the will of the people in predetermined cases, according to established rules. In America the constitution may, therefore, vary, but as long as it exists it is the origin of all authority, and the sole vehicle of the predominating force.*

It is easy to perceive in what manner these differences must act upon the position and the rights of the judicial bodies in the three countries I have cited. If in France the tribunals were authorized to disobey the laws on the ground of their being opposed to the constitution, the supreme power would in fact be placed in their hands, since they alone would have the right of interpreting a constitution, the clauses of which can be modified by no authority. They would, therefore, take the place of the nation, and exercise as absolute a sway over society as the inherent weakness of judicial power would allow them to do. Undoubtedly, as the French judges are incompetent to declare a law to be unconstitutional, the power of changing the constitution is indirectly given to the legislative body, since no legal barrier would oppose the alterations which it might prescribe. But it is better to grant the power of changing the constitution of the people to men who represent (however imperfectly) the will of the people, than to men who represent no one but themselves.

It would be still more unreasonable to invest the English judges with the right of resisting the decisions of the legislative body, since the parliament which makes the laws also makes the constitution; and consequently a law emanating from the three powers of the state, can in no case be unconstitutional. But neither of these remarks is applicable to America.†

In the United States the constitution governs the legislator as much as the private citizen: as it is the first of laws, it cannot be modified by

---

* See Appendix L.
† See Appendix M.

a law; and it is therefore just that the tribunals should obey the constitution in preference to any law. This condition is essential to the power of the judicature; for to select that legal obligation by which he is most strictly bound, is the natural right of every magistrate.

In France the constitution is also the first of laws, and the judges have the same right to take it as the ground of their decisions; but were they to exercise this right, they must perforce encroach on rights more sacred than their own, namely, on those of society, in whose name they are acting. In this case the state motive clearly prevails over the motives of an individual. In America, where the nation can always reduce its magistrates to obedience by changing its constitution, no danger of this kind is to be feared. Upon this point therefore the political and the logical reason agree, and the people as well as the judges preserve their privileges.

Whenever a law which the judge holds to be unconstitutional is argued in a tribunal of the United States, he may refuse to admit it as a rule; this power is the only one which is peculiar to the American magistrate, but it gives rise to immense political influence. Few laws can escape the searching analysis; for there are few which are not prejudicial to some private interest or other, and none which may not be brought before a court of justice by the choice of parties, or by the necessity of the case. But from the time that a judge has refused to apply any given law in a case, that law loses a portion of its moral sanction. The persons to whose interest it is prejudicial, learn that means exist of evading its authority; and similar suits are multiplied, until it becomes powerless. One of two alternatives must then be resorted to: the people must alter the constitution, or the legislature must repeal the law.

The political power which the Americans have intrusted to their courts of justice is therefore immense; but the evils of this power are considerably diminished, by the obligation which has been imposed of attacking the laws through the courts of justice alone. If the judge had been empowered to contest the laws on the ground of theoretical generalities; if he had been enabled to open an attack or to pass a censure on the legislator, he would have played a prominent part in the political sphere; and as the champion or the antagonist of a party, he would have arrayed the hostile passions of the nation in the conflict. But when a judge contests a law, applied to some particular case in an obscure proceeding, the importance of his attack is concealed from the public gaze; his decision bears upon the interest of an individual, and if the law is slighted, it is only collaterally. Moreover, although it be censured, it is not abolished; its moral force may be diminished, but its cogency is by no means suspended; and its final destruction can only be accomplished by the reiterated attacks of judicial functionaries. It will readily be understood that by connecting the censorship of the laws with the private interests of members of the community, and by intimately uniting the prosecution of the law with the prosecution of an individual, the legislation is protected from wanton assailants, and from the daily aggressions of party spirit. The errors of the legislator are exposed whenever their evil consequences are most felt; and it is always a positive and appreciable fact which serves as the basis of a prosecution.

I am inclined to believe this practice of the American courts to be at once the most favourable to liberty as well as to public order. If the judge could only attack the legislator openly and directly, he would sometimes be afraid to oppose any resistance to his will; and at other moments party spirit might encourage him to brave it every day. The laws would consequently be attacked when the power from which they emanate is weak, and obeyed when it is strong. That is to say, when it would be useful to respect them, they would be contested; and when it would be easy to convert them into an instrument of oppression, they would be respected. But the American judge is brought into the political arena independently of his own will. He only judges the law because he is obliged to judge a case. The political question which he is called upon to resolve is connected with the interest of the parties, and he cannot refuse to decide it without abdicating the duties of his post. He performs his functions as a citizen by fulfilling the strict duties which belong to his profession as a magistrate. It is true that upon this system the judicial censorship which is exercised by the courts of justice over the legislation cannot extend to all laws indiscriminately, inasmuch as some of them can never give rise to that precise species of contestation which is termed a lawsuit; and even when such a contestation is possible, it may happen that no one cares to bring it before a court of justice. The Americans have often felt this disadvantage, but they have left the remedy incomplete, lest they should give it efficacy which might in some cases prove dangerous. Within these limits, the power vested in the American courts of justice of pronouncing a statute to be unconstitutional, forms one of the most powerful barriers which have ever been devised against the tyranny of political assemblies.

OTHER POWERS GRANTED TO THE AMERICAN JUDGES.

In the United States all the Citizens have the Right of indicting the public Functionaries before the ordinary Tribunals.—How they use this Right.—Art. 75 of the An VIII.—The Americans and the English cannot understand the Purport of this Clause.

It is perfectly natural that in a free country like America all the citizens should have the right of indicting public functionaries before the ordinary tribunals, and that all the judges should have the power of punishing public offences. The right granted to the courts of justice, of judging the agents of the executive government, when they have violated the laws, is so natural a one that it cannot be looked upon as an extraordinary privilege. Nor do the springs of government appear to me to be weakened in the United States by the custom which renders all public officers responsible to the judges of the land. The Americans seem, on the contrary, to have increased by this means that respect which is due to the authorities, and at the same time to have rendered those who are in power more scrupulous of offending public opinion.

I was struck by the small number of political trials which occur in the United States; but I have no difficulty in accounting for this circumstance. A lawsuit, of whatever nature it may be, is always a difficult and expensive undertaking. It is easy to attack a public man in a journal, but the motives which can warrant an action at law must be serious. A solid ground of complaint must therefore exist, to induce an individual to prosecute a public officer, and public officers are careful not to furnish these grounds of complaint, when they are afraid of being prosecuted.

This does not depend upon the republican form of the American institutions, for the same facts present themselves in England. These two nations do not regard the impeachment of the principal officers of state as a sufficient guarantee of their independence. But they hold that the right of minor prosecutions, which are within the reach of the whole community, is a better pledge of freedom than those great judicial actions which are rarely employed until it is too late.

In the middle ages, when it was very difficult to overtake offenders, the judges inflicted the most dreadful tortures on the few who were arrested, which by no means diminished the number of crimes. It has since been discovered that when justice is more certain and more mild, it is at the same time more efficacious. The English and the Americans hold that tyranny and oppression are to be treated like any other crime, by lessening the penalty and facilitating conviction.

In the year VIII. of the French republic, a constitution was drawn up in which the following clause was introduced: "Art. 75. All the agents of the government below the rank of ministers can only be prosecuted for offences relating to their several functions by virtue of a decree of the conseil d'etat; in which case the prosecution takes place before the ordinary tribunals." This clause survived the "Constitution de l'an VIII.," and it is still maintained in spite of the just complaints of the nation. I have always found the utmost difficulty in explaining its meaning to Englishmen or Americans. They were at once led to conclude that the conseil d'etat[1] in France was a great tribunal, established in the centre of the kingdom, which exercised a preliminary and somewhat tyrannical jurisdiction in all political causes. But when I told them that the conseil d'etat was not a judicial body, in the common sense of the term, but an administrative council composed of men dependant on the crown—so that the king, after having ordered one of his servants, called a prefect, to commit an injustice, has the power of commanding another of his servants, called a councillor of state, to prevent the former from being punished—when I demonstrated to them that the citizen who had been injured by the order of the sovereign is obliged to solicit from the sovereign permission to obtain redress, they refused to credit so flagrant an abuse, and were tempted to accuse me of falsehood or of ignorance. It frequently happened before the revolution that a parliament issued a warrant against a public officer who had committed an offence; and sometimes the proceedings were annulled by the authority of the crown. Despotism then displayed itself openly, and obedience was extorted by force.

We have then retrogaded from the point which our forefathers had reached, since we allow things to pass under the colour of justice and the sanction of the law, which violence alone could impose upon them.

Chapter VII.

POLITICAL JURISDICTION IN THE UNITED STATES.

Definition of political Jurisdiction.—What is understood by political Jurisdiction in France, in England, and in the United States.—In America the political Judge can only pass Sentence on public Officers.—He more frequently passes a Sentence of Removal from Office than a Penalty.—Political Jurisdiction, as it Exists in the United States, is, notwithstanding its Mildness, and perhaps in Consequence of that Mildness, a most powerful Instrument in the Hands of the Majority.

I understand, by political jurisdiction, that temporary right of pronouncing a legal decision with which a political body may be invested.

In absolute governments no utility can accrue from the introduction of extraordinary forms of procedure; the prince, in whose name an offender is prosecuted, is as much the sovereign of the courts of justice as of everything else, and the idea which is entertained of his power is of itself a sufficient security. The only thing he has to fear is, that the external formalities of justice may be neglected, and that his authority may be dishonoured, from a wish to render it more absolute. But in most free countries, in which the majority can never exercise the same influence upon the tribunals as an absolute monarch, the judicial power has occasionally been vested for a time in the representatives of society. It has been thought better to introduce a temporary confusion between the functions of the different authorities, than to violate the necessary principle of the unity of government.

England, France, and the United States, have established this political jurisdiction in their laws; and it is curious to examine the different use which these three great nations have made of the principle. In England and in France the house of lords and the chambre des pairs constitute the highest criminal court of their respective nations; and although they do not habitually try all political offences, they are competent to try them all. Another political body enjoys the right of impeachment before the house of lords: the only difference which exists between the two countries in this respect is, that in England the commons may impeach whomsoever they please before the lords, while in France the deputies can only employ this mode of prosecution against the ministers of the crown.

In both countries the upper house may make use of all the existing penal laws of the nation to punish the delinquents.

In the United States, as well as in Europe, one branch of the legislature is authorized to impeach, and another to judge: the house of representatives arraigns the offender, and the senate awards his sentence. But the senate can only try such persons as are brought before it by the house of representatives, and those persons must belong to the class of public functionaries. Thus the jurisdiction of the senate is less extensive than that of the peers of France, while the right of impeachment by the representatives is more general than that of the deputies. But the great difference which exists between Europe and America is, that in Europe political tribunals are empowered to inflict all the dispositions of the penal code, while in America, when they have deprived the offender of his official rank, and have declared him incapable of filling any political office for the future, their jurisdiction terminates and that of the ordinary tribunals begins.

Suppose, for instance, that the president of the United States has committed the crime of high treason; the house of representatives impeaches him, and the senate degrades him; he must then be tried by a jury, which alone can deprive him of his liberty or his life. This accurately illustrates the subject we are treating. The political jurisdiction which is established by the laws of Europe is intended to try great offenders, whatever may be their birth, their rank, or their powers in the state; and to this end all the privileges of the courts of justice are temporarily extended to a great political assembly. The legislator is then transformed into a magistrate: he is called upon to admit, to distinguish, and to punish the offence; and as he exercises all the authority of a judge, the law restricts him to the observance of all the duties of that high office, and of all the formalities of justice. When a public functionary is impeached before an English or a French political tribunal, and is found guilty, the sentence deprives him *ipso facto* of his functions, and it may pronounce him to be incapable of resuming them or any others for the future. But in this case the political interdict is a consequence of the sentence, and not the sentence itself. In Europe the sentence of a political tribunal is therefore to be regarded as a judicial verdict, rather than as an administrative measure. In the United States the contrary takes place; and although the decision of the senate is judicial in its form, since the senators are obliged to comply with the practices and formalities of a court of justice; although it is judicial in respect to the motives on which it is founded, since the senate is in general obliged to take an offence at common law as the basis of its sentence; nevertheless the object of the proceeding is purely administrative.

If it had been the intention of the American legislator to invest a political body with great judicial authority, its action would not have been limited to the circle of public functionaries, since the most dangerous enemies of the state may be in the possession of no functions at all; and this is especially true in republics, where party favour is the first of authorities, and where the strength of many a leader is increased by his exercising no legal power. If it had been the intention of the American legislator to give society the means of repressing state offences by exemplary punishment, according to the practice of ordinary justice, the resources of the penal code would all have been placed at the disposal of the political tribunals. But the weapon with which they are intrusted is an imperfect one, and it can never reach the most dangerous offenders; since men who aim at the entire subversion of the laws are not likely to murmur at a political interdict.

The main object of the political jurisdiction which obtains in the United States is, therefore, to deprive the citizen of an authority which he has used amiss, and to prevent him from ever acquiring it again. This is evidently an administrative measure sanctioned by the formalities of a judicial investigation. In this matter the Americans have created a mixed system: they have surrounded the act which removes a public functionary with the securities of a political trial; and they have deprived all political condemnations of their severest penalties. Every link of the system may easily be traced from this point; we at once perceive why the American constitutions subject all the civil functionaries to the jurisdiction of the senate, while the military, whose crimes are nevertheless more formidable, are exempted from that tribunal. In the civil service none of the American functionaries can be said to be removeable; the places which some of them occupy are inalienable, and the others derive their rights from a power which cannot be abrogated. It is therefore necessary to try them all in order to deprive them of their authority. But military officers are dependant on the chief magistrate of the state, who is himself a civil functionary; and the decision which condemns him is a blow upon them all.

If we now compare the American and European systems, we shall meet with differences no less striking in the different effects which each of them produces or may produce. In France and in England the jurisdiction of political bodies is looked upon as an extraordinary resource, which is only to be employed in order to rescue society from unwonted dangers. It is not to be denied that these tribunals, as they are constituted in Europe, are apt to violate the conservative principle of the balance of power in the state, and to threaten incessantly the lives and liberties of the subject. The same political jurisdiction in the United States is only indirectly hostile to the balance of power; it cannot menace the lives of the citizens, and it does not hover, as in Europe, over the heads of the community, since those only who have beforehand submitted to its authority upon accepting office are exposed to its severity. It is at the same time less formidable and less efficacious; indeed, it has not been considered by the legislators of the United States as a remedy for the more violent evils of society, but as an ordinary means of conducting the government. In this respect it probably exercises more real influence on the social body in America than in Europe. We must not be misled by the apparent mildness of the American legislation in all that relates to political jurisdiction. It is to be observed, in the first place, that in the United States the tribunal which passes sentence is composed of the same elements, and subject to the same influences, as the body which impeaches the offender, and that this uniformity gives an almost irresistible impulse to the vindictive passions of parties. If political judges in the United States cannot inflict such heavy penalties as those of Europe, there is the less chance of their acquitting a prisoner; and the conviction, if it is less formidable, is more certain. The principal object of the political tribunals of Europe is to punish the offender; the purpose of those in America is to deprive him of his authority. A political condemnation in the United States may, therefore, be looked upon as a preventive measure; and there is no reason for restricting the judges to the exact definitions of criminal law. Nothing can be more alarming than the excessive latitude with which political offences are described in the laws of America. Article II., section iv., of the constitution of the United States runs thus: "The president, vice-president, and all the civil officers of the United States shall be removed from office on impeachment for, and conviction of, treason, bribery, *or other high crimes and misdemeanors.*" Many of the constitutions of the states are even less explicit. "Public officers," says the constitution of Massachusetts,* "shall be impeached for misconduct or mal-administration." The constitution of Virginia declares that all the civil officers who shall have offended against the state by mal-administration, corruption, or other high crimes, may be impeached by the house of delegates: in some constitutions no offences are specified, in order to subject the public functionaries to an unlimited responsibility.† But I will venture to affirm, that it is precisely their mildness which renders the American laws most formidable in this respect. We have shown that in Europe the removal of a functionary and his political interdiction are consequences of the penalty he is to undergo, and that in America they constitute the penalty itself. The result is, that in Europe political tribunals are invested with rights which they are afraid to use, and that the fear of punishing too much hinders them from punishing at all. But in America no one hesitates to inflict a penalty from which humanity does not recoil. To condemn a political opponent to death, in order to deprive him of his power, is to commit what all the world would execrate as a horrible assassination; but to declare that opponent unworthy to exercise that authority, to deprive him of it, and to leave him uninjured in life and liberty, may appear to be the fair issue of the struggle. But this sentence, which it is so easy to pronounce, is not the less fatally severe to the majority of those upon whom it is inflicted. Great criminals may undoubtedly brave its intangible rigor, but ordinary offenders will dread it as a condemnation which destroys their position in the world, casts a blight upon their honour, and condemns them to a shameful inactivity worse than death. The influence exercised in the United States upon the progress of society by the jurisdiction of political bodies may not appear to be formidable, but it is only the more immense. It does not act directly upon the governed, but it renders the majority more absolute over those who govern; it does not confer an unbounded authority on the legislator which can only be exerted at some momentous crisis, but it establishes a temperate and regular influence, which is at all times available. If the power

---

* Chapter I., sect. ii., §8.
† See the constitutions of Illinois, Maine, Connecticut, and Georgia.

is decreased, it can, on the other hand, be more conveniently employed, and more easily abused. By preventing political tribunals from inflicting judicial punishments, the Americans seem to have eluded the worst consequences of legislative tyranny, rather than tyranny itself; and I am not sure that political jurisdiction, as it is constituted in the United States, is not the most formidable which has ever been placed in the rude grasp of a popular majority. When the American republics begin to degenerate, it will be easy to verify the truth of this observation, by remarking whether the number of political impeachments augments.*

Chapter VIII.

THE FEDERAL CONSTITUTION.

I have hitherto considered each state as a separate whole, and I have explained the different springs which the people sets in motion, and the different means of action which it employs. But all the states which I have considered as independent are forced to submit, in certain cases, to the supreme authority of the Union. The time is now come for me to examine the partial sovereignty which has been conceded to the Union, and to cast a rapid glance over the federal constitution.†

HISTORY OF THE FEDERAL CONSTITUTION.

Origin of the first Union.—Its Weakness.—Congress appeals to the constituent Authority.—Interval of two Years between the Appeal and the Promulgation of the new Constitution.

The thirteen colonies[1] which simultaneously threw off the yoke of England toward the end of the last century, possessed, as I have already observed, the same religion, the same language, the same customs, and almost the same laws; they were struggling against a common enemy; and these reasons were sufficiently strong to unite them one to another, and to consolidate them into one nation. But as each of them had enjoyed a separate existence, and a government within its own control, the peculiar interests and customs which resulted from this system, were opposed to a compact and intimate union, which would have absorbed the individual importance of each in the general importance of all. Hence arose two opposite tendencies, the one prompting the Anglo-Americans to unite, the other to divide their strength. As long as the war with the mother-country lasted, the principle of union[2] was kept alive by necessity; and although the laws which constituted it were defective, the common tie subsisted in spite

* See Appendix N.
† See the constitution of the United States.

of their imperfections.* But no sooner was peace concluded than the faults of the legislation became manifest, and the state seemed to be suddenly dissolved. Each colony became an independent republic, and assumed an absolute sovereignty. The federal government, condemned to impotence by its constitution, and no longer sustained by the presence of a common danger, saw the outrages offered to its flag by the great nations of Europe, while it was scarcely able to maintain its ground against the Indian tribes, and to pay the interest of the debt which had been contracted during the war of independence. It was already on the verge of destruction, when it officially proclaimed its inability to conduct the government, and appealed to the constituent authority of the nation.†

If America ever approached (for however brief a time) that lofty pinnacle of glory to which the proud fancy of its inhabitants is wont to point, it was at the solemn moment at which the power of the nation abdicated, as it were, the empire of the land. All ages have furnished the spectacle of a people struggling with energy to win its independence; and the efforts of the Americans in throwing off the English yoke, have been considerably exaggerated. Separated from their enemies by three thousand miles of ocean, and backed by a powerful ally, the success of the United States may be more justly attributed to their geographical position, than to the valor of their armies, or the patriotism of their citizens. It would be ridiculous to compare the American war to the wars of the French revolution, or the efforts of the Americans to those of the French, who, when they were attacked by the whole of Europe, without credit and without allies, were still capable of opposing a twentieth part of their population to their foes, and of bearing the torch of revolution beyond their frontiers while they stifled its devouring flame within the bosom of their country. But it is a novelty in the history of society to see a great people turn a calm and scrutinizing eye upon itself when apprized by the legislature that the wheels of government had stopped; to see it carefully examine the extent of the evil, and patiently wait for two whole years until a remedy was discovered, which it voluntarily adopted without having wrung a tear or a drop of blood from mankind. At the time when the inadequacy of the first constitution was discovered, America possessed the double advantage of that calm which had succeeded the effervescence of the revolution, and of those great men who had led the revolution to a successful issue. The assembly which accepted the task of composing the second constitution was small;‡ but George Washington[3] was its president, and it contained the choicest talents and the noblest hearts which had ever appeared in the New World. This national commission, after long and mature deliberation, offered to the

---

* See the articles of the first confederation formed in 1778. This constitution was not adopted by all the states until 1781. See also the analysis given of this constitution in the Federalist, from No. 15 to No. 22, inclusive, and Story's "Commentary on the Constitution of the United States," pp. 85–115.

† Congress made this declaration on the 21st of February, 1787.

‡ It consisted of fifty-five members: Washington, Madison, Hamilton, and the two Morrises, were among the number.

acceptance of the people the body of general laws which still rules the Union. All the states adopted it successively.* The new federal government commenced its functions in 1789, after an interregnum of two years. The revolution of America terminated when that of France began.

SUMMARY OF THE FEDERAL CONSTITUTION.

Division of Authority between the federal Government and the States.—The Government of the States is the Rule: the federal Government the Exception.

The first question which awaited the Americans was intricate, and by no means easy of solution; the object was so to divide the authority of the different states which composed the Union, that each of them should continue to govern itself in all that concerned its internal prosperity, while the entire nation, represented by the Union, should continue to form a compact body, and to provide for the exigencies of the people. It was as impossible to determine beforehand, with any degree of accuracy, the share of authority which each of the two governments was to enjoy, as to foresee all the incidents in the existence of a nation.

The obligations and the claims of the federal government were simple and easily definable, because the Union had been formed with the express purpose of meeting the general exigencies of the people; but the claims and obligations of the states were, on the other hand, complicated and various, because those governments penetrated into all the details of social life. The attributes of the federal government were, therefore, carefully enumerated, and all that was not included among them was declared to constitute a part of the privileges of the several governments of the states. Thus the government of the states remained the rule, and that of the confederation became the exception.†

But as it was foreseen that, in practice, questions might arise as to the exact limits of this exceptional authority, and that it would be dangerous to submit these questions to the decision of the ordinary courts of justice, established in the states by the states themselves, a high federal court was created,‡ which was destined, among other functions, to maintain the balance of power which had been established by the constitution between the two rival governments.§

---

* It was not adopted by the legislative bodies, but representatives were elected by the people for this sole purpose; and the new constitution was discussed at length in each of these assemblies.

† See the amendment to the federal constitution; Federalist, No. 32. Story, p. 711. Kent's Commentaries, vol. i., p. 364.

It is to be observed, that whenever the *exclusive* right of regulating certain matters is not reserved to congress by the constitution, the states may take up the affair, until it is brought before the national assembly. For instance, congress has the right of making a general law of bankruptcy, which, however, it neglects to do. Each state is then at liberty to make a law for itself. This point, however, has been established by discussion in the law-courts, and may be said to belong more properly to jurisprudence.

‡ The action of this court is indirect, as we shall hereafter show.

§ It is thus that the Federalist, No. 45, explains the division of supremacy between the union and the states: "The powers delegated by the constitution to the federal government are few and defined. Those which are to remain in the state governments are numerous and indefinite. The former will be exercised principally on external objects, as war, peace, negotiation, and foreign commerce. The powers reserved to the several states will extend to all the objects

PREROGATIVE OF THE FEDERAL GOVERNMENT.

Power of declaring War, making Peace, and levying general Taxes vested in the Federal Government.—What Part of the internal Policy of the Country it may direct.—The Government of the Union in some respects more central than the King's Government in the old French Monarchy.

The external relations of a people may be compared to those of private individuals, and they cannot be advantageously maintained without the agency of the single head of a government. The exclusive right of making peace and war, of concluding treaties of commerce, of raising armies, and equipping fleets, was therefore granted to the Union.* The necessity of a national government was less imperiously felt in the conduct of the internal affairs of society; but there are certain general interests which can only be attended to with advantage by a general authority. The Union was invested with the power of controlling the monetary system, of directing the post-office, and of opening the great roads which were to establish communication between the different parts of the country.† The independence of the government of each state was formally recognised in its sphere; nevertheless the federal government was authorized to interfere in the internal affairs of the states‡ in a few predetermined cases, in which an indiscreet abuse of their independence might compromise the security of the Union at large. Thus, while the power of modifying and changing their legislation at pleasure was preserved in all the republics, they were forbidden to enact *ex post facto* laws, or to create a class of nobles in their community.§ Lastly, as it was necessary that the federal government should be able to fulfil its engagements, it was endowed with an unlimited power of levying taxes.‖

In examining the balance of power as established by the federal constitution; in remarking on the one hand the portion of sovereignty which has been reserved to the several states, and on the other the share of power which the Union has assumed, it is evident that the federal legislators entertained the clearest and most accurate notions

---

which, in the ordinary course of affairs, concern the internal order and prosperity of the state."

I shall often have occasion to quote the Federalist in this work. When the bill which has since become the constitution of the United States was submitted to the approval of the people, and the discussions were still pending, three men, who had already acquired a portion of that celebrity which they have since enjoyed, John Jay, Hamilton, and Madison, formed an association with the intention of explaining to the nation the advantages of the measure which was proposed. With this view they published a series of articles in the shape of a journal, which now form a complete treatise. They entitled their journal, "The Federalist," a name which has been retained in the work. The Federalist is an excellent book, which ought to be familiar to the statesmen of all countries, although it especially concerns America.

* See constitution, sect. 8. Federalist, Nos. 41 and 42. Kent's Commentaries, vol. i., p. 207. Story, pp. 358–382; 409–426.

† Several other privileges of the same kind exist, such as that which empowers the Union to legislate on bankruptcy, to grant patents, and other matters in which its intervention is clearly necessary.

‡ Even in these cases its interference is indirect. The union interferes by means of the tribunals, as will be hereafter shown.

§ Federal Constitution, sect. 10, art. 1.

‖ Constitution, sect. 8, 9, and 10. Federalist, Nos. 30–36 inclusive, and 41–44. Kent's Commentaries, vol. i., pp. 207 and 381. Story, pp. 329 and 514.

on the nature of the centralization of government. The United States form not only a republic, but a confederation; nevertheless the authority of the nation is more central than it was in several of the monarchies of Europe when the American constitution was formed. Take, for instance, the two following examples:—

Thirteen supreme courts of justice existed in France, which, generally speaking, had the right of interpreting the law without appeal; and those provinces, styled *pays d'états*, were authorized to refuse their assent to an impost which had been levied by the sovereign who represented the nation.

In the Union there is but one tribunal to interpret, as there is one legislature to make the laws; and an impost voted by the representatives of the nation is binding upon all the citizens.

In these two essential points, therefore, the Union exercises more central authority than the French monarchy possessed, although the Union is only an assemblage of confederate republics.

In Spain certain provinces had the right of establishing a system of customhouse duties peculiar to themselves, although that privilege belongs, by its very nature, to the national sovereignty. In America the congress alone has the right of regulating the commercial relations of the states. The government of the confederation is therefore more centralized in this respect than the kingdom of Spain. It is true that the power of the crown in France or in Spain was always able to obtain by force whatever the constitution of the country denied, and that the ultimate result was consequently the same; but I am here discussing the theory of the constitution.

FEDERAL POWERS.

After having settled the limits within which the federal government was to act, the next point was to determine the powers which it was to exert.

LEGISLATIVE POWERS.

Division of the legislative Body into two Branches.—Difference in the Manner of forming the two Houses.—The Principle of the Independence of the States predominates in the Formation of the Senate.—The Principle of the Sovereignty of the Nation in the Composition of the House of Representatives.—Singular Effects of the Fact that a Constitution can only be Logical in the early Stages of a Nation.

The plan which had been laid down beforehand for the constitution of the several states was followed, in many points, in the organization of the powers of the Union. The federal legislature of the Union was composed of a senate and a house of representatives. A spirit of conciliation prescribed the observance of distinct principles in the formation of each of these two assemblies. I have already shown that two contrary interests were opposed to each other in the establishment of the federal constitution. These two interests had given rise to two opinions. It was the wish of one party to convert the Union into a league of independent states, or a sort of congress, at which the representatives of the several peoples would meet to discuss certain points of their common interests. The other party desired to unite the inhabitants of the American colonies into one sole nation, and to establish a government, which should act as the sole representative of the nation, as far as the limited sphere of its authority would permit. The practical consequences of these two theories were exceedingly different.

The question was, whether a league was to be established instead of a national government; whether the majority of the states, instead of the majority of the inhabitants of the Union, was to give the law: for every state, the small as well as the great, then retained the character of an independent power, and entered the Union upon a footing of perfect equality. If, on the contrary, the inhabitants of the United States were to be considered as belonging to one and the same nation, it was natural that the majority of the citizens of the Union should prescribe the law. Of course the lesser states could not subscribe to the application of this doctrine without, in fact, abdicating their existence in relation to the sovereignty of the confederation; since they would have passed from the condition of a co-equal and co-legislative authority, to that of an insignificant fraction of a great people. The former system would have invested them with an excessive authority, the latter would have annulled their influence altogether. Under these circumstances, the result was, that the strict rules of logic were evaded, as is usually the case when interests are opposed to arguments. A middle course was hit upon by the legislators, which brought together by force two systems theoretically irreconcilable.

The principle of the independence of the states prevailed in the formation of the senate, and that of the sovereignty of the nation predominated in the composition of the house of representatives. It was decided that each state should send two senators to congress, and a number of representatives proportioned to its population.* It results from this arrangement that the state of New York has at the present day forty representatives, and only two senators; the staté of Delaware has two senators, and only one representative; the state of Delaware is therefore equal to the state of New York in the senate, while the latter has forty times the influence of the former in the house of representatives. Thus, if the minority of the nation preponderates in the senate, it may paralyze the decisions of the majority represented in the other house, which is contrary to the spirit of constitutional government.

The facts show how rare and how difficult it is rationally and logically to combine all the several parts of legislation. In the course of

---

* Every ten years congress fixes anew the number of representatives which each state is to furnish. The total number was 69 in 1789, and 240 in 1833. (See American Almanac, 1834, p. 194.)

The constitution decided that there should not be more than one representative for every 30,000 persons; but no minimum was fixed upon. The congress has not thought fit to augment the number of representatives in proportion to the increase of population. The first act which was passed on the subject (14th of April 1792: see Laws of the United States, by Story, vol. i., p. 235) decided that there should be one representative for every 33,000 inhabitants. The last act, which was passed in 1822, fixes the proportion at one for 48,000. The population represented is composed of all the freemen and of three fifths of the slaves.

time different interests arise, and different principles are sanctioned by the same people; and when a general constitution is to be established, these interests and principles are so many natural obstacles to the rigorous application of any political system, with all its consequences. The early stages of national existence are the only periods at which it is possible to maintain the complete logic of legislation; and when we perceive a nation in the enjoyment of this advantage, before we hasten to conclude that it is wise, we should do well to remember that it is young. When the federal constitution was formed, the interest of independence for the separate states, and the interest of union for the whole people, were the only two conflicting interests which existed among the Anglo-Americans; and a compromise was necessarily made between them.

It is, however, just to acknowledge that this part of the constitution has not hitherto produced those evils which might have been feared. All the states are young and contiguous; their customs, their ideas, and their wants, are not dissimilar; and the differences which result from their size or inferiority do not suffice to set their interests at variance. The small states have consequently never been induced to league themselves together in the senate to oppose the designs of the larger ones; and indeed there is so irresistible an authority in the legitimate expression of the will of a people, that the senate could offer but a feeble opposition to the vote of the majority of the house of representatives.

It must not be forgotten, on the other hand, that it was not in the power of the American legislators to reduce to a single nation the people for whom they were making laws. The object of the federal constitution was not to destroy the independence of the states, but to restrain it. By acknowledging the real authority of these secondary communities (and it was impossible to deprive them of it), they disavowed beforehand the habitual use of constraint in enforcing the decisions of the majority. Upon this principle the introduction of the influence of the states into the mechanism of the federal government was by no means to be wondered at; since it only attested the existence of an acknowledged power, which was to be humoured, and not forcibly checked.

A FARTHER DIFFERENCE BETWEEN THE SENATE AND THE HOUSE OF REPRESENTATIVES.

The Senate named by the provincial Legislature—the Representatives, by the People.—Double Election of the Former—Single Election of the Latter.—Term of the different Offices.—Peculiar Functions of each House.

The senate not only differs from the other house in the principle which it represents, but also in the mode of its election, in the term for which it is chosen, and in the nature of its functions. The house of representatives is named by the people, the senate by the legislators of each state; the former is directly elected; the latter is elected by an elected body; the term for which the representatives are chosen is only two years, that of the senators is six. The functions of the house of representatives are purely legislative, and the only share it takes in the judicial power is in the impeachment of public officers. The senate co-operates in the work of legislation, and tries those political offences which the house of representatives submits to its decision. It also acts as the great executive council of the nation; the treaties which are concluded by the president must be ratified by the senate; and the appointments he may make must be definitively approved by the same body.*

THE EXECUTIVE POWER.†

Dependance of the President.—He is Elective and Responsible.—He is Free to act in his own Sphere under the Inspection, but not under the Direction, of the Senate.—His Salary fixed at his Entry into Office.—Suspensive Veto.

The American legislators undertook a difficult task in attempting to create an executive power dependant on the majority of the people, and nevertheless sufficiently strong to act without restraint in its own sphere. It was indispensable to the maintenance of the republican form of government that the representative of the executive power should be subject to the will of the nation.

The president is an elective magistrate. His honour, his property, his liberty, and his life, are the securities which the people has for the temperate use of his power. But in the exercise of his authority he cannot be said to be perfectly independent; the senate takes cognizance of his relations with foreign powers, and of the distribution of public appointments, so that he can neither be bribed, nor can he employ the means of corruption. The legislators of the Union acknowledged that the executive power would be incompetent to fulfil its task with dignity and utility, unless it enjoyed a greater degree of stability and of strength than had been granted to it in the separate states.

The president is chosen for four years, and he may be re-elected; so that the chances of a prolonged administration may inspire him with hopeful undertakings for the public good, and with the means of carrying them into execution. The president was made the sole representative of the executive power of the Union; and care was taken not to render his decisions subordinate to the vote of a council—a dangerous measure, which tends at the same time to clog the action of the government and to diminish its responsibility. The senate has the right of annulling certain acts of the president; but it cannot compel him to take any steps, nor does it participate in the exercise of the executive power.

The action of the legislature on the executive power may be direct; and we have just shown that the Americans carefully obviated this influence; but it may, on the other hand, be indirect. Public assemblies

---

* See the Federalist, Nos. 52–66, inclusive. Story, pp. 199–314. Constitution of the United States, sections 2 and 3.
† See the Federalist, Nos. 67–77. Constitution of the United States, art. 2. Story, pp. 115; 515–780. Kent's Commentaries, p. 255.

which have the power of depriving an officer of state of his salary, encroach upon his independence; and as they are free to make the laws, it is to be feared lest they should gradually appropriate to themselves a portion of that authority which the constitution had vested in his hands. This dependance of the executive power is one of the defects inherent in republican constitutions. The Americans have not been able to counteract the tendency which legislative assemblies have to get possession of the government, but they have rendered this propensity less irresistible. The salary of the president is fixed, at the time of his entering upon office, for the whole period of his magistracy. The president is moreover provided with a suspensive veto, which allows him to oppose the passing of such laws as might destroy the portion of independence which the constitution awards him. The struggle between the president and the legislature must always be an unequal one, since the latter is certain of bearing down all resistance by persevering in its plans; but the suspensive veto forces it at least to reconsider the matter, and, if the motion be persisted in, it must then be backed by a majority of two-thirds of the whole house. The veto is, in fact, a sort of appeal to the people. The executive power, which, without this security, might have been secretly oppressed, adopts this means of pleading its cause and stating its motives. But if the legislature is certain of overpowering all resistance by persevering in its plans, I reply, that in the constitutions of all nations, of whatever kind they may be, a certain point exists at which the legislator is obliged to have recourse to the good sense and the virtue of his fellow-citizens. This point is more prominent and more discoverable in republics, while it is more remote and more carefully concealed in monarchies, but it always exists somewhere. There is no country in the world in which everything can be provided for by the laws, or in which political institutions can prove a substitute for common sense and public morality.

DIFFERENCES BETWEEN THE POSITION OF THE PRESIDENT OF THE UNITED STATES AND THAT OF A CONSTITUTIONAL KING OF FRANCE.

Executive Power in the United States as Limited and as Partial as the Supremacy which it Represents.—Executive Power in France as Universal as the Supremacy it Represents.—The King a Branch of the Legislature.—The President the mere Executor of the Law.—Other Differences resulting from the Duration of the two Powers.—The President checked in the Exercise of the executive Authority.—The King Independent in its Exercise—Notwithstanding these Discrepances, France is more akin to a Republic than the Union to a Monarchy.—Comparison of the Number of public Officers depending upon the executive Power in the two Countries.

The executive power has so important an influence on the destinies of nations that I am inclined to pause for an instant at this portion of my subject, in order more clearly to explain the part it sustains in America. In order to form an accurate idea of the position of the president of the United States, it may not be irrelevant to compare it to that of one of the constitutional kings of Europe. In this comparison I shall pay but little attention to the external signs of power, which are more apt to deceive the eye of the observer than to guide his researches. When a monarchy is being gradually transformed into a republic, the executive power retains the titles, the honours, the etiquette, and even the funds of royalty, long after its authority has disappeared. The English, after having cut off the head of one king, and expelled another from his throne, were accustomed to accost the successors of those princes upon their knees. On the other hand, when a republic falls under the sway of a single individual, the demeanour of the sovereign is simple and unpretending, as if his authority was not yet paramount. When the emperors exercised an unlimited control over the fortunes and the lives of their fellow-citizens, it was customary to call them Cesar in conversation, and they were in the habit of supping without formality at their friends' houses. It is therefore necessary to look below the surface.

The sovereignty of the United States is shared between the Union and the states, while in France it is undivided and compact: hence arises the first and the most notable differences which exists between the president of the United States and the king of France. In the United States the executive power is as limited and partial as the sovereignty of the Union in whose name it acts; in France it is as universal as the authority of the state. The Americans have a federal, and the French a national government.

The first cause of inferiority results from the nature of things, but it is not the only one; the second in importance is as follows: sovereignty may be defined to be the right of making laws: in France, the king really exercises a portion of the sovereign power, since the laws have no weight till he has given his assent to them; he is moreover the executor of all they ordain. The president is also the executor of the laws, but he does not really co-operate in their formation, since the refusal of his assent does not annul them. He is therefore merely to be considered as the agent of the sovereign power. But not only does the king of France exercise a portion of the sovereign power, he also contributes to the nomination of the legislature, which exercises the other portion. He has the privilege of appointing the members of one chamber, and of dissolving the other at his pleasure; whereas the president of the United States has no share in the formation of the legislative body, and cannot dissolve any part of it. The king has the same right of bringing forward measures as the chambers; a right which the president does not possess. The king is represented in each assembly by his ministers, who explain his intentions, support his opinions, and maintain the principles of the government. The president and his ministers are alike excluded from congress; so that his influence and his opinions can only penetrate indirectly into that great body. The king of France is therefore on an equal footing with the legislature, which can no more act without him, than he can without it. The president exercises an authority inferior to, and depending upon, that of the legislature.

Even in the exercise of the executive power, properly so called, the point upon which his position seems to be almost analogous to that of the king of France—the president labours under several causes of inferiority. The authority of the king, in France, has, in in the first place, the advantage of duration over that of the president: and durability is one of the chief elements of strength; nothing is either loved or feared but what is likely to endure. The president of the United States is a magistrate elected for four years. The king, in France, is an hereditary sovereign.

In the exercise of the executive power the president of the United States is constantly subject to a jealous scrutiny. He may make, but he cannot conclude a treaty; he may designate, but he cannot appoint, a public officer.* The king of France is absolute in the sphere of the executive power.

The president of the United States is responsible for his actions; but the person of the king is declared inviolable by the French charter.

Nevertheless, the supremacy of public opinion is no less above the head of the one than of the other. This power is less definite, less evident, and less sanctioned by the laws in France than in America, but in fact it exists. In America it acts by elections and decrees; in France it proceeds by revolutions: but notwithstanding the different constitutions of these two countries, public opinion is the predominant authority in both of them. The fundamental principle of legislation—a principle essentially republican—is the same in both countries, although its consequences may be different, and its results more or less extensive. Whence I am led to conclude, that France with its king is nearer akin to a republic, than the Union with its president is to a monarchy.

In what I have been saying I have only touched upon the main points of distinction; and if I could have entered into details, the contrast would have been rendered still more striking.

I have remarked that the authority of the president in the United States is only exercised within the limits of a partial sovereignty, while that of the king, in France, is undivided. I might have gone on to show that the power of the king's government in France exceeds its natural limits, however extensive they may be, and penetrates in a thousand different ways into the administration of private interests. Among the examples of this influence may be quoted that which results from the great number of public functionaries, who all derive their appointments from the government. This number now exceeds all previous limits; it amounts to 138,000† nominations, each of which may be considered as an element of power. The president of the United States has not the exclusive right of making any public appointments, and their whole number scarcely exceeds 12,000.‡

---

* The constitution had left it doubtful whether the president was obliged to consult the senate in the removal as well as in the appointment of federal officers. The Federalist (No. 77) seemed to establish the affirmative; but in 1789, congress formally decided that as the president was responsible for his actions, he ought not to be forced to employ agents who had forfeited his esteem. See Kent's Commentaries, vol. i., p. 289.

† The sums annually paid by the state to these officers amount to 200,000,000 francs (eight millions sterling).

‡ This number is extracted from the "National Calendar," for 1833. The National Calendar is an American almanac which contains the names of all the federal officers.

[Those who are desirous of tracing the question respecting the power of the president to remove every executive officer of the government without the sanction of the senate, will find some light upon it by referring to 5th Marshall's Life of Washington, p. 196: 5 Sergeant and Rawle's Reports (Pennsylvania), 451. Report of a committee of the senate in 1822, in Niles's Register of 29th August in that year. It is certainly very extraordinary that such a vast power, and one so extensively affecting the whole administration of the government, should rest on such slight foundations, as an *inference* from an act of congress, providing, that when the secretary of the treasury should be removed by the president, his assistant should discharge the duties of the office. How congress could confer the power, even by a direct act, is not perceived. It must be a necessary implication from the words of the constitution, or it does not exist. It has been repeatedly denied in and out of congress, and must be considered, as yet, an unsettled question.—*American Editor*.]

ACCIDENTAL CAUSES WHICH MAY INCREASE THE INFLUENCE OF THE
EXECUTIVE GOVERNMENT.

External security of the Union.—Army of six thousand Men.—Few Ships.—The President has no Opportunity of Exercising his great Prerogatives.—In the Prerogatives he Exercises he is weak.

If the executive power is feebler in America than in France, the cause is more attributable to the circumstances than to the laws of the country.

It is chiefly in its foreign relations that the executive power of a nation is called upon to exert its skill and vigor. If the existence of the Union were perpetually threatened, and its chief interest were in daily connexion with those of other powerful nations, the executive government would assume an increased importance in proportion to the measures expected of it, and those which it would carry into effect. The president of the United States is the commander-in-chief of the army, but of an army composed of only six thousand men; he commands the fleet, but the fleet reckons but few sail; he conducts the foreign relations of the Union, but the United States are a nation without neighbours. Separated from the rest of the world by the ocean, and too weak as yet to aim at the dominion of the seas, they have no enemies, and their interests rarely come into contact with those of any other nation of the globe.

The practical part of a government must not be judged by the theory of its constitution. The president of the United States is in the possession of almost royal prerogatives, which he has no opportunity of exercising; and those privileges which he can at present use are very circumscribed: the laws allow him to possess a degree of influence which circumstances do not permit him to employ.

On the other hand, the great strength of the royal prerogative in France, arises from circumstances far more than from the laws. There the executive government is constantly struggling against prodigious obstacles, and exerting all its energies to repress them; so that it increases by the extent of its achievements, and by the importance of the events it controls, without, for that reason, modifying its constitution. If the laws had made it as feeble and as circumscribed

It results from this comparison that the king of France has eleven times as many places at his disposal as the president, although the population of France is not much more than double that of the union.

as it is in the Union, its influence would very soon become much greater.

WHY THE PRESIDENT OF THE UNITED STATES DOES NOT REQUIRE THE MAJORITY OF THE TWO HOUSES IN ORDER TO CARRY ON THE GOVERNMENT.

It is an established axiom in Europe that a constitutional king cannot persevere in a system of government which is opposed by the two other branches of the legislature. But several presidents of the United States have been known to lose the majority in the legislative body, without being obliged to abandon the supreme power, and without inflicting a serious evil upon society. I have heard this fact quoted as an instance of the independence and power of executive government in America: a moment's reflection will convince us, on the contrary, that it is a proof of its extreme weakness.

A king in Europe requires the support of the legislature to enable him to perform the duties imposed upon him by the constitution, because those duties are enormous. A constitutional king in Europe is not merely the executor of the law, but the execution of its provisions devolves so completely upon him, that he has the power of paralyzing its influence if it opposes his designs. He requires the assistance of the legislative assemblies to make the law, but those assemblies stand in need of his aid to execute it: these two authorities cannot subsist without each other, and the mechanism of government is stopped as soon as they are at variance.

In America the president cannot prevent any law from being passed, nor can he evade the obligation of enforcing it. His sincere and zealous co-operation is no doubt useful, but it is not indispensable in the carrying on of public affairs. All his important acts are directly or indirectly submitted to the legislature; and where he is independent of it he can do but little. It is therefore his weakness, and not his power, which enables him to remain in opposition to congress. In Europe, harmony must reign between the crown and the other branches of the legislature, because a collision between them may prove serious; in America, this harmony is not indispensable, because such a collision is impossible.

ELECTION OF THE PRESIDENT.

Dangers of the elective System increase in Proportion to the Extent of the Prerogative.—This System possible in America because no powerful executive Authority is required.—What Circumstances are favourable to the elective System.—Why the Election of the President does not cause a Deviation from the Principles of the Government.—Influence of the Election of the President on secondary Functionaries.

The dangers of the system of election applied to the head of the executive government of a great people, have been sufficiently exemplified by experience and by history; and the remarks I am about to make refer to America alone. These dangers may be more or less formidable in proportion to the place which the executive power occupies, and to the importance it possesses in the state; and they may vary according to the mode of election, and the circumstances in which the electors are placed. The most weighty argument against the election of a chief-magistrate is, that it offers so splendid a lure to private ambition, and is so apt to inflame men in the pursuit of power, that when legitimate means are wanting, force may not unfrequently seize what right denies.

It is clear that the greater the privileges of the executive authority are, the greater is the temptation; the more the ambition of the candidate is excited, the more warmly are their interests espoused by a throng of partisans who hope to share the power when their patron has won the prize. The dangers of the elective system increase, therefore, in the exact ratio of the influence exercised by the executive power in the affairs of state. The revolutions of Poland are not solely attributable to the elective system in general, but to the fact that the elected magistrate was the head of a powerful monarchy. Before we can discuss the absolute advantages of the elective system, we must make preliminary inquiries as to whether the geographical position, the laws, the habits, the manners, and the opinions of the people among whom it is to be introduced, will admit of the establishment of a weak and dependant executive government; for to attempt to render the representative of the state a powerful sovereign, and at the same time elective, is, in my opinion, to entertain two incompatible designs. To reduce hereditary royalty to the condition of an elective authority, the only means that I am acquainted with are to circumscribe its sphere of action beforehand, gradually to diminish its prerogatives, and to accustom the people to live without its protection. Nothing, however, is farther from the designs of the republicans of Europe than this course: as many of them only owe their hatred of tyranny to the sufferings which they have personally undergone, the extent of the executive power does not excite their hostility, and they only attack its origin without perceiving how nearly the two things are connected.

Hitherto no citizen has shown any disposition to expose his honour and his life, in order to become the president of the United States; because the power of that office is temporary, limited, and subordinate. The prize of fortune must be great to encourage adventurers in so desperate a game. No candidate has as yet been able to arouse the dangerous enthusiasm or the passionate sympathies of the people in his favour, for the very simple reason, that when he is at the head of the government he has but little power, but little wealth, and but little glory to share among his friends; and his influence in the state is too small for the success or the ruin of a faction to depend upon the elevation of an individual to power.

The great advantage of hereditary monarchies is, that as the private interest of a family is always intimately connected with the interests of the state, the executive government is never suspended for a single instant; and if the affairs of a monarchy are not better conducted than those of a republic, at least there is always some one to conduct them, well or ill, according to his capacity. In elective states, on the contrary, the wheels of government cease to act, as it were of their own accord, at the approach of an election, and even for some time previous to that event. The laws may indeed accelerate the operation of the election, which may be conducted with such simplicity and rapidity that the seat of power will never be left vacant; but, notwithstanding these precautions, a break necessarily occurs in the minds of the people.

At the approach of an election the head of the executive government is wholly occupied by the coming struggle; his future plans are doubtful; he can undertake nothing new, and he will only prosecute with indifference those designs which another will perhaps terminate. "I am so near the time of my retirement from office," said President Jefferson[4] on the 21st of January, 1809 (six weeks before the election), "that I feel no passion, I take no part, I express no sentiment. It appears to me just to leave to my successor the commencement of those measures which he will have to prosecute, and for which he will be responsible."

On the other hand, the eyes of the nation are centred on a single point; all are watching the gradual birth of so important an event. The wider the influence of the executive power extends, the greater and the more necessary is its constant action, the more fatal is the term of suspense; and a nation which is accustomed to the government, or, still more, one used to the administrative protection of a powerful executive authority, would be infallibly convulsed by an election of this kind. In the United States the action of the government may be slackened with impunity, because it is always weak and circumscribed.

One of the principal vices of the elective system is, that it always introduces a certain degree of instability into the internal and external policy of the state. But this disadvantage is less sensibly felt if the share of power vested in the elected magistrate is small. In Rome the principles of the government underwent no variation, although the consuls were changed every year, because the senate, which was an hereditary assembly, possessed the directing authority. If the elective system were adopted in Europe, the condition of most of the monarchial states would be changed at every new election. In America the president exercises a certain influence on state affairs, but he does not conduct them; the preponderating power is vested in the representatives of the whole nation. The political maxims of the country depend therefore on the mass of the people, not on the president alone; and consequently in America the elective system has no very prejudicial influence on the fixed principles of the government. But the want of fixed principles is an evil so inherent in the elective system, that it is still extremely perceptible in the narrow sphere to which the authority of the president extends.

The Americans have admitted that the head of the executive power, who has to bear the whole responsibility of the duties he is called upon to fulfil, ought to be empowered to choose his own agents, and to remove them at pleasure: the legislative bodies watch the conduct of the president more than they direct it. The consequence of this arrangement is, that at every new election the fate of all the federal public officers is in suspense. Mr. Quincy Adams, on his entry into office, discharged the majority of the individuals who had been appointed by his predecessor; and I am not aware that General Jackson allowed a single removable functionary employed in the federal service to retain his place beyond the first year which succeeded his election. It is sometimes made a subject of complaint, that in the constitutional monarchies of Europe the fate of the humbler servants of an administration depends upon that of the ministers. But in elective governments this evil is far greater. In a constitutional monarchy successive ministries are rapidly formed; but as the principal representative of the executive power does not change, the spirit of innovation is kept within bounds; the changes which take place are in the details rather than in the principles of the administrative system; but to substitute one system for another, as is done in America every four years by law, is to cause a sort of revolution. As to the misfortunes which may fall upon individuals in consequence of this state of things, it must be allowed that the uncertain situation of the public officers is less fraught with evil consequences in America than elsewhere. It is so easy to acquire an independent position in the United States, that the public officer who loses his place may be deprived of the comforts of life, but not of the means of subsistence.

I remarked at the beginning of this chapter that the dangers of the elective system applied to the head of the state, are augmented or decreased by the peculiar circumstances of the people which adopts it. However the functions of the executive power may be restricted, it must always exercise a great influence upon the foreign policy of the country, for a negotiation cannot be opened or successfully carried on otherwise than by a single agent. The more precarious and the more perilous the position of a people becomes, the more absolute is the want of a fixed and consistent external policy, and the more dangerous does the elective system of the chief magistrate become. The policy of the Americans in relation to the whole world is exceedingly simple; and it may almost be said that no country stands in need of them, nor do they require the co-operation of any other people. Their independence is never threatened. In their present condition, therefore, the functions of the executive power are no less limited by circumstances than by the laws; and the president may frequently change his line of policy without involving the state in difficulty or destruction.

Whatever the prerogatives of the executive power may be, the period which immediately precedes an election, and the moment of its duration, must always be considered as a national crisis, which is perilous in proportion to the internal embarrassments and the external dangers of the country. Few of the nations of Europe could escape the calamities of anarchy or of conquest, every time they might have to elect a new sovereign. In America society is so constituted that it can stand without assistance upon its own basis; nothing is to be feared from the pressure of external dangers; and the election of the president is a cause of agitation, but not of ruin.

MODE OF ELECTION.

Skill of the American Legislators shown in the Mode of Election adopted by them.—Creation of a special electoral Body.—Separate Votes of these Electors.—Case in which the House of Representatives is called upon to choose the President.—Results of the twelve Elections which have taken Place since the Constitution has been established.

Beside the dangers which are inherent in the system, many other difficulties may arise from the mode of election, which may be obviated by the precaution of the legislator. When a people met in arms on some public spot to choose its head, it was exposed to all the chances of civil war resulting from so martial a mode of proceeding, beside the dangers of the elective system in itself. The Polish laws, which subjected the election of the sovereign to the veto of a single individual, suggested the murder of that individual, or prepared the way to anarchy.

In the examination of the institutions, and the political as well as the social condition of the United States, we are struck by the admirable harmony of the gifts of fortune and the efforts of man. That nation possessed two of the main causes of internal peace; it was a new country, but it was inhabited by a people grown old in the exercise of freedom. America had no hostile neighbours to dread; and the American legislators, profiting by these favourable circumstances, created a weak and subordinate executive power, which could without danger be made elective.

It then only remained for them to choose the least dangerous of the various modes of election; and the rules which they laid down upon this point admirably complete the securities which the physical and political constitution of the country already afforded. Their object was to find the mode of election which would best express the choice of the people with the least possible excitement and suspense. It was admitted in the first place that the *simple* majority should be decisive; but the difficulty was to obtain this majority without an interval of delay which it was most important to avoid. It rarely happens that an individual can at once collect the majority of the suffrages of a great people; and this difficulty is enhanced in a republic of confederate states, where local influences are apt to preponderate. The means by which it was proposed to obviate this second obstacle was to delegate the electoral powers of the nation to a body of representatives. This mode of election rendered a majority more probable; for the fewer the electors are, the greater is the chance of their coming to a final decision. It also offered an additional probability of a judicious choice. It then remained to be decided whether this right of election was to be intrusted to the legislative body, the habitual representative assembly of the nation, or whether an electoral assembly should be formed for the express purpose of proceeding to the nomination of a president. The Americans chose the latter alternative, from a belief that the individuals who were returned to make the laws were incompetent to represent the wishes of the nation in the election of its chief magistrate;

and that as they are chosen for more than a year, the constituency they represented might have changed its opinion in that time. It was thought that if the legislature was empowered to elect the head of the executive power, its members would, for some time before the election, be exposed to the manœuvres of corruption, and the tricks of intrigue; whereas, the special electors would, like a jury, remain mixed up with the crowd till the day of action, when they would appear for the sole purpose of giving their votes.

It was therefore established that every state should name a certain number of electors,* who in their turn should elect the president; and as it had been observed that the assemblies to which the choice of a chief magistrate had been intrusted in elective countries, inevitably became the centres of passion and of cabal; that they sometimes usurped an authority which did not belong to them: and that their proceedings, or the uncertainty which resulted from them, were sometimes prolonged so much as to endanger the welfare of the state, it was determined that the electors should all vote upon the same day, without being convoked to the same place.† This double election rendered a majority probable, though not certain; for it was possible that as many differences might exist between the electors as between their constituents. In this case it was necessary to have recourse to one of three measures; either to appoint new electors, or to consult a second time those already appointed, or to defer the election to another authority. The first two of these alternatives, independently of the uncertainty of their results, were likely to delay the final decision, and to perpetuate an agitation which must always be accompanied with danger. The third expedient was therefore adopted, and it was agreed that the votes should be transmitted sealed to the president of the senate, and that they should be opened and counted in the presence of the senate and the house of representatives. If none of the candidates has a majority, the house of representatives then proceeds immediately to elect the president; but with the condition that it must fix upon one of the three candidates who have the highest numbers.‡

Thus it is only in case of an event which cannot often happen, and which can never be foreseen, that the election is intrusted to the ordinary representatives of the nation; and even then they are obliged to choose a citizen who has already been designated by a powerful minority of the special electors. It is by this happy expedient that the respect which is due to the popular voice is combined with the utmost celerity of execution and those precautions which the peace of the country demands. But the decision of the question by the house of

---

* As many as it sends members to congress. The number of electors at the election of 1833 was 288. (See the National Calendar, 1833.)

† The electors of the same state assemble, but they transmit to the central government the list of their individual votes, and not the mere result of the vote of the majority.

‡ In this case it is the majority of the states, and not the majority of the members, which decides the question; so that New York has not more influence in the debate than Rhode Island. Thus the citizens of the Union are first consulted as members of one and the same community; and, if they cannot agree, recourse is had to the division of the states, each of which has a separate and independent vote. This is one of the singularities of the federal constitution which can only be explained by the jar of conflicting interests.

representatives does not necessarily offer an immediate solution of the difficulty, for the majority of that assembly may still be doubtful, and in this case the constitution prescribes no remedy. Nevertheless, by restricting the number of candidates to three, and by referring the matter to the judgment of an enlightened public body, it has smoothed all the obstacles* which are not inherent in the elective system.

In the forty-four years which have elapsed since the promulgation of the federal constitution, the United States have twelve times chosen a president. Ten of these elections took place simultaneously by the votes of the special electors in the different states. The houses of representatives has only twice exercised its conditional privilege of deciding in cases of uncertainty: the first time was at the election of Mr. Jefferson in 1801; the second was in 1825, when Mr. John Quincy Adams was chosen.

CRISIS OF THE ELECTION.

The Election may be considered as a national Crisis.—Why?—Passions of the People.—Anxiety of the President.—Calm which succeeds the Agitation of the Election.

I have shown what the circumstances are which favoured the adoption of the elective system in the United States, and what precautions were taken by the legislators to obviate its dangers. The Americans are accustomed to all kinds of elections; and they know by experience the utmost degree of excitement which is compatible with security. The vast extent of the country, and the dissemination of the inhabitants, render a collision between parties less probable and less dangerous there than elsewhere. The political circumstances under which the elections have hitherto been carried on, have presented no real embarrassments to the nation.

Nevertheless, the epoch of the election of a president of the United States may be considered as a crisis in the affairs of the nation. The influence which he exercises on public business is no doubt feeble and indirect; but the choice of the president, which is of small importance to each individual citizen, concerns the citizens collectively; and however trifling an interest may be, it assumes a great degree of importance as soon as it becomes general. The president possesses but few means of rewarding his supporters in comparison to the kings of Europe; but the places which are at his disposal are sufficiently numerous to interest, directly or indirectly, several thousand electors in his success. Moreover, political parties in the United States, as well as elsewhere, are led to rally around an individual, in order to acquire a more tangible shape in the eyes of the crowd, and the name of the candidate for the presidency is put forward as the symbol and personification of their theories. For these reasons parties are strongly interested in gaining the election, not so much with a view to the triumph of their principles under the auspices of the president elected, as to

* Jefferson, in 1801, was not elected until the thirty-sixth time of balloting.

show, by the majority which returned him, the strength of the supporters of those principles.

For a long while before the appointed time is at hand, the election
becomes the most important and the all-engrossing topic of discussion. The ardor of faction is redoubled; and all the artificial passions
which the imagination can create in the bosom of a happy and peaceful land are agitated and brought to light. The president, on the other
hand, is absorbed by the cares of self-defence. He no longer governs
for the interest of the state, but for that of his re-election; he does
homage to the majority, and instead of checking its passions, as his
duty commands him to do, he frequently courts its worst caprices. As
the election draws near, the activity of intrigue and the agitation of the
populace increase; the citizens are divided into several camps, each of
which assumes the name of its favourite candidate; the whole nation
glows with feverish excitement; the election is the daily theme of the
public papers, the subject of private conversation, the end of every
thought and every action, the sole interest of the present. As soon as
the choice is determined, this ardor is dispelled; and as a calmer season returns, the current of the state, which has nearly broken its
banks, sinks to its usual level; but who can refrain from astonishment
at the cause of the storm?

RE-ELECTION OF THE PRESIDENT.

When the Head of the executive Power is Re-eligible, it is the State which is the
Source of Intrigue and Corruption.—The desire of being re-elected, the chief
Aim of a President of the United States.—Disadvantage of the System peculiar to
America.—The natural Evil of Democracy is that it subordinates all Authority to
the slightest Desires of the Majority.—The Re-election of the President encour-
ages this Evil.

It may be asked whether the legislators of the United States did
right or wrong in allowing the re-election of the president. It seems at
first sight contrary to all reason to prevent the head of the executive
power from being elected a second time. The influence which the talents and the character of a single individual may exercise upon the
fate of a whole people, especially in critical circumstances or arduous
times, is well known: a law preventing the re-election of the chief
magistrate would deprive the citizens of the surest pledge of the prosperity and the security of the commonwealth; and, by a singular inconsistency, a man would be excluded from the government at the very
time when he had shown his ability in conducting its affairs.

But if these arguments are strong, perhaps still more powerful reasons may be advanced against them. Intrigue and corruption are the
natural defects of elective government; but when the head of the state
can be re-elected, these evils rise to a great height, and compromise
the very existence of the country. When a simple candidate seeks to
rise by intrigue, his manœuvres must necessarily be limited to a narrow sphere; but when the chief magistrate enters the lists, he borrows
the strength of the government for his own purposes. In the former
case the feeble resources of an individual are in action; in the latter,

the state itself, with all its immense influence, is busied in the work of corruption and cabal. The private citizen, who employs the most immoral practices to acquire power, can only act in a manner indirectly prejudicial to the public prosperity. But if the representative of the executive descends into the lists, the cares of government dwindle into second-rate importance, and the success of his election is his first concern. All laws and negotiations are then to him nothing more than electioneering schemes; places become the reward of services rendered, not to the nation, but to its chief; and the influence of the government, if not injurious to the country, is at least no longer beneficial to the community for which it was created.

It is impossible to consider the ordinary course of affairs in the United States without perceiving that the desire of being re-elected is the chief aim of the president; that his whole administration, and even his most indifferent measures, tend to this object; and that, as the crisis approaches, his personal interest takes the place of his interest in the public good. The principle of re-eligibility renders the corrupt influence of elective governments still more extensive and pernicious. It tends to degrade the political morality of the people, and to substitute adroitness for patriotism.

In America it exercises a still more fatal influence on the sources of national existence. Every government seems to be afflicted by some evil inherent in its nature, and the genius of the legislator is shown in eluding its attacks. A state may survive the influence of a host of bad laws, and the mischief they cause is frequently exaggerated; but a law which encourages the growth of the canker within must prove fatal in the end, although its bad consequences may not be immediately perceived.

The principle of destruction in absolute monarchies lies in the excessive and unreasonable extension of the prerogative of the crown; and a measure tending to remove the constitutional provisions which counterbalance this influence would be radically bad, even if its consequences should long appear to be imperceptible. By a parity of reasoning, in countries governed by a democracy, where the people is perpetually drawing all authority to itself, the laws which increase or accelerate its action are the direct assailants of the very principle of the government.

The greatest proof of the ability of the American legislators is, that they clearly discerned this truth, and that they had the courage to act up to it. They conceived that a certain authority above the body of the people was necessary, which should enjoy a degree of independence, without however being entirely beyond the popular control; an authority which would be forced to comply with the *permanent* determinations of the majority, but which would be able to resist its caprices, and to refuse its most dangerous demands. To this end they centred the whole executive power of the nation in a single arm; they granted extensive prerogatives to the president, and they armed him with the veto to resist the encroachments of the legislature.

But by introducing the principle of re-election they partly destroyed their work; and they rendered the president but little inclined to exert the great power they had vested in his hands. If ineligible a second time, the president would be far from independent of the people, for his responsibility would not be lessened; but the favour of the people would not be so necessary to him as to induce him to court it by humouring its desires. If re-eligible (and this is more especially true at the present day, when political morality is relaxed, and when great men are rare), the president of the United States becomes an easy tool in the hands of the majority. He adopts its likings and its animosities, he hastens to anticipate its wishes, he forestalls its complaints, he yields to its idlest cravings, and instead of guiding it, as the legislature intended that he should do, he is ever ready to follow its bidding. Thus, in order not to deprive the state of the talents of an individual, those talents have been rendered almost useless, and to reserve an expedient for extraordinary perils the country has been exposed to daily dangers.

[The question of the propriety of leaving the president re-eligible, is one of that class which probably must for ever remain undecided. The author himself at page 125[98], gives a strong reason for re-eligibility, "so that the chance of a prolonged administration may inspire him with hopeful undertakings for the public good, and with the means of carrying them into execution,"—considerations of great weight. There is an important fact bearing upon this question, which should be stated in connexion with it. President Washington established the practice of declining a third election, and every one of his successors, either from a sense of its propriety or from apprehensions of the force of public opinion, has followed the example. So that it has become as much a part of the constitution, that no citizen can be a third time elected president, as it were expressed in that instrument in words. This may perhaps be considered a fair adjustment of objections on either side. Those against a continued and perpetual re-eligibility are certainly met: while the arguments in favour of an opportunity to prolong an administration under circumstances that may justify it, are allowed their due weight. One effect of this practical interpolation of the constitution unquestionably is, to increase the chances of a president's being once re-elected; as men will be more disposed to acquiesce in a measure that thus practically excludes the individual from ever again entering the field of competition.—*American Editor.*]

FEDERAL COURTS.*

Political Importance of the Judiciary in the United States.—Difficulty of treating this Subject.—Utility of judicial Power in Confederations.—What Tribunals could be introduced into the Union.—Necessity of establishing federal Courts of Justice.—Organization of the national Judiciary.—The Supreme Court.—In what it differs from all known Tribunals.

I have inquired into the legislative and executive power of the Union, and the judicial power now remains to be examined; but in this

* See chapter vi., entitled, "Judicial Power in the United States." This chapter explains the general principles of the American theory of judicial institutions. See also the federal constitution, art. 3. See the Federalist, Nos. 78–83, inclusive: and a work entitled, "Constitutional Law, being a View of the Practice and Jurisdiction of the Courts of the United States," by Thomas Sergeant. See Story, pp. 134, 162, 489, 511, 581, 668; and the organic law of the 24th September, 1789, in the collection of the laws of the United States, by Story, vol. i., p. 53.

place I cannot conceal my fears from the reader. Judicial institutions exercise a great influence on the condition of the Anglo-Americans, and they occupy a prominent place among what are properly called political institutions: in this respect they are peculiarly deserving of our attention. But I am at a loss to explain the political action of the American tribunals without entering into some technical details on their constitution and their forms of proceeding; and I know not how to descend to these minutiæ without wearying the curiosity of the reader by the natural aridity of the subject, or without risking to fall into obscurity through a desire to be succinct. I can scarcely hope to escape these various evils; for if I appear too prolix to a man of the world, a lawyer may on the other hand complain of my brevity. But these are the natural disadvantages of my subject, and more especially of the point which I am about to discuss.

The great difficulty was, not to devise the constitution of the federal government, but to find out a method of enforcing its laws. Governments have in general but two means of overcoming the opposition of the people they govern, viz, the physical force which is at their own disposal, and the moral force which they derive from the decisions of the courts of justice.

A government which should have no other means of exacting obedience than open war, must be very near its ruin; for one of two alternatives would then probably occur: if its authority was small, and its character temperate, it would not resort to violence till the last extremity, and it would connive at a number of partial acts of insubordination, in which case the state would gradually fall into anarchy; if it was enterprising and powerful, it would perpetually have recourse to its physical strength, and would speedily degenerate into a military despotism. So that its activity would not be less prejudicial to the community than its inaction.

The great end of justice is to substitute the notion of right for that of violence; and to place a legal barrier between the power of the government and the use of physical force. The authority which is awarded to the intervention of a court of justice by the general opinion of mankind is so surprisingly great, that it clings to the mere formalities of justice, and gives a bodily influence to the shadow of the law. The moral force which courts of justice possess renders the introduction of physical force exceedingly rare, and it is very frequently substituted for it; but if the latter proves to be indispensable, its power is doubled by the association of the idea of law.

A federal government stands in greater need of the support of judicial institutions than any other, because it is naturally weak, and exposed to formidable opposition.* If it were always obliged to resort to violence in the first instance, it could not fulfil its task. The Union,

---

* Federal laws are those which most require courts of justice, and those at the same time which have most rarely established them. The reason is that confederations have usually been formed by independent states, which entertained no real intention of obeying the central government, and which very readily ceded the right of commanding to the federal executive, and very prudently reserved the right of non-compliance to themselves.

therefore, required a national judiciary to enforce the obedience of the citizens to the laws, and to repel the attacks which might be directed against them. The question then remained what tribunals were to exercise these privileges; were they to be intrusted to the courts of justice which were already organized in every state? or was it necessary to create federal courts? It may easily be proved that the Union could not adapt the judicial power of the states to its wants. The separation of the judiciary from the administrative power of the state, no doubt affects the security of every citizen, and the liberty of all. But it is no less important to the existence of the nation that these several powers should have the same origin, should follow the same principles, and act in the same sphere; in a word, that they should be correlative and homogeneous. No one, I presume, ever suggested the advantage of trying offences committed in France, by a foreign court of justice, in order to ensure the impartiality of the judges. The Americans form one people in relation to their federal government; but in the bosom of this people divers political bodies have been allowed to subsist, which are dependant on the national government in a few points, and independent in all the rest—which have all a distinct origin, maxims peculiar to themselves, and special means of carrying on their affairs. To intrust the execution of the laws of the Union to tribunals instituted by these political bodies, would be to allow foreign judges to preside over the nation. Nay more, not only is each state foreign to the Union at large, but it is in perpetual opposition to the common interests, since whatever authority the Union loses turns to the advantage of the states. Thus to enforce the laws of the Union by means of the tribunals of the states, would be to allow not only foreign, but partial judges to preside over the nation.

But the number, still more than the mere character, of the tribunals of the states rendered them unfit for the service of the nation. When the federal constitution was formed, there were already thirteen courts of justice in the United States which decided causes without appeal. That number is now increased to twenty-four. To suppose that a state can subsist, when its fundamental laws may be subjected to four-and-twenty different interpretations at the same time, is to advance a proposition alike contrary to reason and to experience.

The American legislators therefore agreed to create a federal judiciary power to apply the laws of the Union, and to determine certain questions affecting general interests, which were carefully determined beforehand. The entire judicial power of the Union was centred in one tribunal, which was denominated the supreme court of the United States. But, to facilitate the expedition of business, inferior courts were appended to it, which were empowered to decide causes of small importance without appeal, and with appeal causes of more magnitude. The members of the supreme court are named neither by the people nor the legislature, but by the president of the United States, acting with the advice of the senate. In order to render them independent of the other authorities, their office was made inalienable; and it was determined that their salary, when once fixed, should not be altered by the legislature.* It was easy to proclaim the principle of a federal judiciary, but difficulties multiplied when the extent of its jurisdiction was to be determined.

MEANS OF DETERMINING THE JURISDICTION OF THE FEDERAL COURTS.

Difficulty of determining the Jurisdictions of separate courts of Justice in Confederation.—The Courts of the Union obtained the Right of fixing their own Jurisdiction.—In what Respect this Rule attacks the Portion of Sovereignty reserved to the several States.—The Sovereignty of these States restricted by the Laws, and the Interpretation of the Laws.—Consequently, the Danger of the several States is more apparent than real.

As the constitution of the United States recognised two distinct powers, in presence of each other, represented in a judicial point of view by two distinct classes of courts of justice, the utmost care which could be taken in defining their separate jurisdictions would have been insufficient to prevent frequent collisions between those tribunals. The question then arose, to whom the right of deciding the competency of each court was to be referred.

In nations which constitute a single body politic, when a question is debated between two courts relating to their mutual jurisdiction, a third tribunal is generally within reach to decide the difference; and this is effected without difficulty, because in these nations the questions of judicial competency have no connexion with the privileges of the national supremacy. But it was impossible to create an arbiter between a superior court of the Union and the superior court of a separate state, which would not belong to one of these two classes. It was therefore necessary to allow one of these courts to judge its own cause, and to take or to retain cognizance of the point which was contested. To grant this privilege to the different courts of the states, would have been to destroy the sovereignty of the Union *de facto,* after having established it *de jure;* for the interpretation of the constitution would soon have restored that portion of independence to the states of which the terms of that act deprived them. The object of the creation of a federal tribunal was to prevent the courts of the states from deciding questions affecting the national interests in their own department, and so to form a uniform body of jurisprudence for the interpretation of the laws of the Union. This end would not have been accomplished if the courts of the several states had been competent to decide upon

---

* The union was divided into districts, in each of which a resident federal judge was appointed, and the court in which he presided was termed a "district court." Each of the judges of the supreme court annually visits a certain portion of the Republic, in order to try the most important causes upon the spot; the court presided over by this magistrate is styled a "circuit court." Lastly, all the most serious cases of litigation are brought before the supreme court, which holds a solemn session once a year, at which all the judges of the circuit courts must attend. The jury was introduced into the federal courts in the same manner, and in the same cases as into the courts of the states.

It will be observed that no analogy exists between the supreme court of the United States and the French cour de cassation, since the latter only hears appeals. The supreme court decides upon the evidence of the fact, as well as upon the law of the case, whereas the cour de cassation does not pronounce a decision of its own, but refers the cause to the arbitration of another tribunal. See the law of the 24th September, 1789, laws of the United States, by Story, vol. i., p. 53.

cases in their separate capacities, from which they were obliged to abstain as federal tribunals. The supreme court of the United States was therefore invested with the right of determining all questions of jurisdiction.*

This was a severe blow upon the independence of the states, which was thus restricted not only by the laws, but by the interpretation of them; by one limit which was known, and by another which was dubious; by a rule which was certain, and a rule which was arbitrary. It is true the constitution had laid down the precise limits of the federal supremacy, but whenever this supremacy is contested by one of the states, a federal tribunal decides the question. Nevertheless, the dangers with which the independence of the states was threatened by this mode of proceeding are less serious than they appeared to be. We shall see hereafter that in America the real strength of the country is vested in the provincial far more than in the federal government. The federal judges are conscious of the relative weakness of the power in whose name they act, and they are more inclined to abandon a right of jurisdiction in cases where it is justly their own, than to assert a privilege to which they have no legal claim.

DIFFERENT CASES OF JURISDICTION.

The Matter and the Party are the first Conditions of the federal Jurisdiction.—Suits in which Ambassadors are engaged.—Suits of the Union.—Of a separate State.— By whom tried.—Causes resulting from the Laws of the Union. Why judged by the federal Tribunals.—Causes relating to the Non-performance of Contracts tried by the federal Courts.—Consequences of this Arrangement.

After having appointed the means of fixing the competency of the federal courts, the legislators of the Union defined the cases which should come within their jurisdiction. It was established, on the one hand, that certain parties must always be brought before the federal courts, without any regard to the special nature of the cause; and, on the other, that certain causes must always be brought before the same courts, without any regard to the quality of the parties in the suit. These distinctions were therefore admitted to be the bases of the federal jurisdiction.

Ambassadors are the representatives of nations in a state of amity with the Union, and whatever concerns these personages concerns in some degree the whole Union. When an ambassador is a party in a suit, that suit affects the welfare of the nation, and a federal tribunal is naturally called upon to decide it.

The Union itself may be involved in legal proceedings, and in this case it would be alike contrary to the customs of all nations, and to

---

* In order to diminish the number of these suits, it was decided that in a great many federal causes, the courts of the states should be empowered to decide conjointly with those of the Union, the losing party having then a right of appeal to the supreme court of the United States. The supreme court of Virginia contested the right of the supreme court of the United States to judge an appeal from its decisions, but unsuccessfully. See Kent's Commentaries, vol. i., pp. 300, 370, et seq.; Story's Commentaries, p. 646; and "The Organic Law of the United States," vol. i., p. 35.

common sense, to appeal to a tribunal representing any other sovereignty than its own; the federal courts, therefore, take cognizance of these affairs.

When two parties belonging to two different states are engaged in a suit, the case cannot with propriety be brought before a court of either state. The surest expedient is to select a tribunal like that of the Union, which can excite the suspicions of neither party, and which offers the most natural as well as the most certain remedy.

When the two parties are not private individuals, but states, an important political consideration is added to the same motive of equity. The quality of the parties, in this case, gives a national importance to all their disputes; and the most trifling litigation of the states may be said to involve the peace of the whole Union.*

The nature of the cause frequently prescribes the rule of competency. Thus all the questions which concern maritime commerce evidently fall under the cognizance of the federal tribunals.† Almost all these questions are connected with the interpretation of the law of nations; and in this respect they essentially interest the Union in relation to foreign powers. Moreover, as the sea is not included within the limits of any peculiar jurisdiction, the national courts only can hear causes which originate in maritime affairs.

The constitution comprises under one head almost all the cases which by their very nature come within the limits of the federal courts. The rule which it lays down is simple, but pregnant with an entire system of ideas, and with a vast multitude of facts. It declares that the judicial power of the supreme court shall extend to all cases in law and equity *arising under the laws of the United States.*

Two examples will put the intentions of the legislator in the clearest light:—

The constitution prohibits the states from making laws on the value and circulation of money: if, notwithstanding this prohibition, a state passes a law of this kind, with which the interested parties refuse to comply because it is contrary to the constitution, the case must come before a federal court, because it arises under the laws of the United States. Again, if difficulties arise in the levying of import duties which have been voted by congress, the federal court must decide the case, because it arises under the interpretation of a law of the United States.

This rule is in perfect accordance with the fundamental principles of the federal constitution. The Union as it was established in 1789, possesses, it is true, a limited supremacy; but it was intended that

---

* The constitution also says that the federal courts shall decide "controversies between a state and the citizens of another state." And here a most important question of a constitutional nature arose, which was, whether the jurisdiction given by the constitution in cases in which a state is a party, extended to suits brought *against* a state as well as *by* it, or was exclusively confined to the latter. This question was most elaborately considered in the case of *Chisholme* v. *Georgia*, and was decided by the majority of the supreme court in the affirmative. The decision created general alarm among the states, and an amendment was proposed and ratified by which the power was entirely taken away so far as it regards suits brought *against* a state. See Story's Commentaries, p. 624, or in the large edition, §1677.
† As, for instance, all cases of piracy.

within its limits it should form one and the same people.* Within those limits the Union is sovereign. When this point is established and admitted, the inference is easy; for if it be acknowledged that the United States constitute one and the same people within the bounds prescribed by their constitution, it is impossible to refuse them the rights which belong to other nations. But it has been allowed, from the origin of society, that every nation has the right of deciding by its own courts those questions which concern the execution of its own laws. To this it is answered, that the Union is in so singular a position, that in relation to some matters it constitutes a people, and that in relation to all the rest it is a nonentity. But the inference to be drawn is, that in the laws relating to these matters the Union possesses all the rights of absolute sovereignty. The difficulty is to know what these matters are; and when once it is resolved (and we have shown how it was resolved, in speaking of the means of determining the jurisdiction of the federal courts), no farther doubt can arise; for as soon as it is established that a suit is federal, that is to say, that it belongs to the share of sovereignty reserved by the constitution to the Union, the natural consequence is that it should come within the jurisdiction of a federal court.

Whenever the laws of the United States are attacked, or whenever they are resorted to in self-defence, the federal courts must be appealed to. Thus the jurisdiction of the tribunals of the Union extends and narrows its limits exactly in the same ratio as the sovereignty of the Union augments or decreases. We have shown that the principal aim of the legislators of 1789 was to divide the sovereign authority into two parts. In the one they placed the control of all the general interests of the Union, in the other the control of the special interests of its component states. Their chief solicitude was to arm the federal government with sufficient power to enable it to resist, within its sphere, the encroachments of the several states. As for these communities, the principle of independence within certain limits of their own was adopted in their behalf; and they were concealed from the inspection, and protected from the control, of the central government. In speaking of the division of authority, I observed that this latter principle had not always been held sacred, since the states are prevented from passing certain laws, which apparently belong to their own particular sphere of interest. When a state of the Union passes a law of this kind, the citizens who are injured by its execution can appeal to the federal courts.

[The remark of the author, that whenever the laws of the United States are attacked, or whenever they are resorted to in self-defence, the federal courts *must be* appealed to, which is more strongly expressed in the original, is erroneous and calculated to mislead on a point of some importance.

---

* This principle was in some measure restricted by the introduction of the several states as independent powers into the senate, and by allowing them to vote separately in the house of representatives when the president is elected by that body; but these are exceptions, and the contrary principle is the rule.

By the grant of power to the courts of the United States to decide certain cases, the powers of the state courts are not suspended, but are exercised concurrently, subject to an appeal to the courts of the United States. But if the decision of the state court is *in favour* of the right, title, or privilege claimed under a treaty or under a law of congress, no appeal lies to the federal courts. The appeal is given only when the decision is *against* the claimant under the treaty or law. See 3d, Cranch, 268. 1 Wheaton, 304.— *American Editor.*]

Thus the jurisdiction of the general courts extends not only to all the cases which arise under the laws of the Union, but also to those which arise under laws made by the several states in opposition to the constitution. The states are prohibited from making *ex-post-facto* laws in criminal cases; and any person condemned by virtue of a law of this kind can appeal to the judicial power of the Union. The states are likewise prohibited from making laws which may have a tendency to impair the obligations of contracts.* If a citizen thinks that an obligation of this kind is impaired by a law passed in his state, he may refuse to obey it, and may appeal to the federal courts.†

This provision appears to me to be the most serious attack upon the independence of the states. The rights awarded to the federal government for purposes of obvious national importance are definite and easily comprehensible; but those with which this last clause invests it are not either clearly appreciable or accurately defined. For there are vast numbers of political laws which influence the obligations of contracts, which may thus furnish an easy pretext for the aggressions of the central authority.

---

* It is perfectly clear, says Mr. Story (Commentaries, p. 503, or in the large edition §1379), that any law which enlarges, abridges, or in any manner changes the intention of the parties, resulting from the stipulations in the contract, necessarily impairs it. He gives in the same place a very long and careful definition of what is understood by a contract in federal jurisprudence. A grant made by the state to a private individual, and accepted by him, is a contract, and cannot be revoked by any future law. A charter granted by the state to a company is a contract, and equally binding to the state as to the grantee. The clause of the constitution here referred to ensures, therefore, the existence of a great part of acquired rights, but not of all. Property may legally be held, though it may not have passed into the possessor's hands by means of a contract; and its possession is an acquired right, not guarantied by the federal constitution.

† A remarkable instance of this is given by Mr. Story (p. 508, or in the large edition §1388). "Dartmouth college in New Hampshire had been founded by a charter granted to certain individuals before the American revolution, and its trustees formed a corporation under this charter. The legislature of New Hampshire had, without the consent of this corporation, passed an act changing the organization of the original provincial charter of the college, and transferring all the rights, privileges, and franchises from the old charter trustees to new trustees appointed under the act. The constitutionality of the act was contested, and after solemn arguments, it was deliberately held by the supreme court that the provincial charter was a contract within the meaning of the constitution (art. i., sect. 10), and that the amendatory act was utterly void, as impairing the obligation of that charter. The college was deemed, like other colleges of private foundation, to be a private eleemosynary institution, endowed by its charter with a capacity to take property unconnected with the government. Its funds were bestowed upon the faith of the charter, and those funds consisted entirely of private donations. It is true that the uses were in some sense public, that is, for the general benefit, and not for the mere benefit of the corporators; but this did not make the corporation a public corporation. It was a private institution for general charity. It was not distinguishable in principle from a private donation, vested in private trustees, for a public charity, or for a particular purpose of beneficence. And the state itself, if it had bestowed funds upon a charity of the same nature, could not resume those funds."

[The fears of the author respecting the danger to the independence of the states of that provision of the constitution, which gives to the federal courts the authority of deciding when a state law impairs the obligation of a contract, are deemed quite unfounded. The citizens of every state have a deep interest in preserving the obligation of the contracts entered into by them in other states: indeed without such a controlling power, "commerce among the several states" could not exist. The existence of this common arbiter is of the last importance to the continuance of the Union itself, for if there were no peaceable means of enforcing the obligations of contracts, independent of all state authority, the states themselves would inevitably come in collision in their efforts to protect their respective citizens from the consequences of the legislation of another state.

M. De Tocqueville's observation, that the rights with which the clause in question invests the federal government "are not clearly appreciable or accurately defined," proceeds upon a mistaken view of the clause itself. It relates to the *obligation* of a contract, and forbids any act by which that obligation is impaired. To American lawyers, this seems to be as precise and definite as any rule can be made by human language. The distinction between the *right* to the fruits of a contract, and the time, tribunal, and manner, in which that right is to be enforced, seems very palpable. At all events, since the decision of the supreme court of the United States in those cases in which this clause has been discussed, no difficulty is found, practically, in understanding the exact limits of the prohibition.

The next observation of the author, that "there are vast numbers of political laws which influence the obligations of contracts, which may thus furnish an easy pretext for the aggressions of the central authority," is rather obscure. Is it intended that political laws may be passed by the central authority, influencing the obligation of a contract, and thus the contracts themselves be destroyed? The answer to this would be, that the question would not arise under the clause forbidding laws, impairing the obligation of contracts, for that clause applies only to the states and not to the federal government.

If it be intended, that the states may find it necessary to pass political laws, which affect contracts, and that under the pretence of vindicating the obligation of contracts, the central authority may make aggressions on the states and annul their political laws:—the answer is, that the motive to the adoption of the clause was to reach laws of every description, political as well as all others, and that it was the abuse by the states of what may be called political laws, viz: acts confiscating demands of foreign creditors, that gave rise to the prohibition. The settled doctrine now is, that states may pass laws in respect to the making of contracts, may prescribe what contracts shall be made, and how, but that they cannot impair any that are already made.

The writer of this note is unwilling to dismiss the subject, without remarking upon what he must think a fundamental error of the author, which is exhibited in the passage commented on, as well as in other passages:—and that is, in supposing the judiciary of the United States, and particularly the supreme court, to be a part of the *political* federal government, and as the ready instrument to execute its designs upon the state authorities. Although the judges are in form commissioned by the United States, yet in fact, they are appointed by the delegates of the state, in the senate of the United States, concurrently with, and acting upon, the nomination of the president. If the legislature of each state in the Union were to elect a judge of the supreme court, he would not be less a political offi-

cer of the United States than he now is. In truth, the judiciary have no political duties to perform; they are arbiters chosen by the federal and state
governments, jointly, and when appointed, as independent of the one as of
the other. They cannot be removed without the consent of the states represented in the senate, and they can be removed without the consent of
the president, and against his wishes. Such is the theory of the constitution. And it has been felt practically, in the rejection by the senate of persons nominated as judges, by a president of the same political party with a
majority of the senators. Two instances of this kind occurred during the
administration of Mr. Jefferson.

If it be alleged that they are exposed to the influence of the executive of
the United States, by the expectation of offices in his gift, the answer is,
that judges of state courts are equally exposed to the same influence—that
all state officers, from the highest to the lowest, are in the same predicament; and that this circumstance does not, therefore, deprive them of the
character of impartial and independent arbiters.

These observations receive confirmation from every recent decision of
the supreme court of the United States, in which certain laws of individual states have been sustained, in cases where, to say the least, it was very
questionable whether they did not infringe the provisions of the constitution, and where a disposition to construe those provisions broadly and extensively, would have found very plausible grounds to indulge itself in
annulling the state laws referred to. See the cases of *City of New York,* vs.
Miln, 11th *Peters,* 103. *Briscor* vs. *the Bank of the Commonwealth of Kentucky, ib.* 257. *Charles River Bridge* vs. *Warren Bridge, ib.* 420.—*American
Editor.*]

PROCEDURE OF THE FEDERAL COURTS.

Natural Weakness of the judiciary Power in Confederations.—Legislators ought to
strive as much as possible to bring private Individuals, and not States, before the
federal Courts.—How the Americans have succeeded in this.—Direct Prosecution of private Individuals in the federal Courts.—Indirect Prosecution of the
States which violate the Laws of the Union.—The Decrees of the Supreme Court
enervate but do not destroy the provincial Laws.

I have shown what the privileges of the federal courts are, and it is
no less important to point out the manner in which they are exercised.
The irresistible authority of justice in countries in which the sovereignty is undivided, is derived from the fact that the tribunals of those
countries represent the entire nation at issue with the individual
against whom their decree is directed; and the idea of power is thus
introduced to corroborate the idea of right. But this is not always the
case in countries in which the sovereignty is divided: in them the judicial power is more frequently opposed to a fraction of the nation than
to an isolated individual, and its moral authority and physical strength
are consequently diminished. In federal states the power of the judge
is naturally decreased, and that of the justiciable parties is augmented.
The aim of the legislator in confederate states ought therefore to be,
to render the position of the courts of justice analogous to that which
they occupy in countries where the sovereignty is undivided; in other
words, his efforts ought constantly to tend to maintain the judicial

power of the confederation as the representative of the nation, and the justiciable party as the representative of an individual interest.

Every government, whatever may be its constitution, requires the means of constraining its subjects to discharge their obligations, and of protecting its privileges from their assaults. As far as the direct action of the government on the community is concerned, the constitution of the United States contrived, by a master-stroke of policy, that the federal courts, acting in the name of the laws, should only take cognizance of parties in an individual capacity. For, as it had been declared that the Union consisted of one and the same people within the limits laid down by the constitution, the inference was that the government created by this constitution, and acting within these limits, was invested with all the privileges of a national government, one of the principal of which is the right of transmitting its injunctions directly to the private citizen. When, for instance, the Union votes an impost, it does not apply to the states for the levying of it, but to every American citizen, in proportion to his assessment. The supreme court, which is empowered to enforce the execution of this law of the Union, exerts its influence not upon a refractory state, but upon the private taxpayer; and, like the judicial power of other nations, it is opposed to the person of an individual. It is to be observed that the Union chose its own antagonist; and as that antagonist is feeble, he is naturally worsted.

But the difficulty increases when the proceedings are not brought forward *by* but *against* the Union. The constitution recognises the legislative power of the state; and a law so enacted may impair the privileges of the Union, in which case a collision is unavoidable between that body and the state which has passed the law; and it only remains to select the least dangerous remedy, which is very clearly deducible from the general principles I have before established.*

It may be conceived that, in the case under consideration, the Union might have sued the state before a federal court, which would have annulled the act; and by this means it would have adopted a natural course of proceeding: but the judicial power would have been placed in open hostility to the state, and it was desirable to avoid this predicament as much as possible. The Americans hold that it is nearly impossible that a new law should not impair the interests of some private individual by its provisions: these private interests are assumed by the American legislators as the ground of attack against such measures as may be prejudicial to the Union, and it is to these cases that the protection of the supreme court is extended.

Suppose a state vends a certain portion of its territory to a company, and that a year afterward it passes a law by which the territory is otherwise disposed of, and that clause of the constitution, which prohibits laws impairing the obligation of contracts, is violated. When the purchaser under the second act appears to take possession, the possessor under the first act brings his action before the tribunals of the

* See chapter vi., on judicial power in America.

Union, and causes the title of the claimant to be pronounced null and void.* Thus, in point of fact, the judicial power of the Union is contesting the claims of the sovereignty of a state; but it only acts indirectly and upon a special application of detail: it attacks the law in its consequences, not in its principle, and it rather weakens than destroys it.

The last hypothesis that remained was that each state formed a corporation enjoying a separate existence and distinct civil rights, and that it could therefore sue or be sued before a tribunal. Thus a state could bring an action against another state. In this instance the Union was not called upon to contest a provincial law but to try a suit in which a state was a party. This suit was perfectly similar to any other cause, except that the quality of the parties was different; and here the danger pointed out at the beginning of this chapter exists with less chance of being avoided. The inherent disadvantage of the very essence of federal constitutions is, that they engender parties in the bosom of the nation which present powerful obstacles to the free course of justice.

HIGH RANK OF THE SUPREME COURTS AMONG THE GREAT POWERS OF THE STATE.

No Nation ever constituted so great a judicial Power as the Americans.—Extent of its Prerogative.—Its political Influence.—The Tranquility and the very Existence of the Union depend on the Discretion of the seven federal Judges.

When we have successfully examined in detail the organization of the supreme court, and the entire prerogatives which it exercises, we shall readily admit that a more imposing judicial power was never constituted by any people. The supreme court is placed at the head of all known tribunals, both by the nature of its rights and the class of justiciable parties which it controls.

In all the civilized countries of Europe, the government has always shown the greatest repugnance to allow the cases to which it was itself a party to be decided by the ordinary course of justice. This repugnance naturally attains its utmost height in an absolute government; and, on the other hand, the privileges of the courts of justice are extended with the increasing liberties of the people; but no European nation has at present held that all judicial controversies, without regard to their origin, can be decided by the judges of common law.

In America this theory has been actually put in practice; and the supreme court of the United States is the sole tribunal of the nation. Its power extends to all the cases arising under laws and treaties made by the executive and legislative authorities, to all cases of admiralty and maritime jurisdiction, and in general to all points which affect the law of nations. It may even be affirmed that, although its constitution is essentially judicial, its prerogatives are almost entirely political. Its sole object is to enforce the execution of the laws of the Union; and the Union only regulates the relations of the government with the cit-

* See Kent's Commentaries, vol. i., p. 387.

izens, and of the nation with foreign powers: the relations of citizens among themselves are almost exclusively regulated by the sovereignty of the states.

A second and still greater cause of the preponderance of this court may be adduced. In the nations of Europe the courts of justice are only called upon to try the controversies of private individuals; but the supreme court of the United States summons sovereign powers to its bar. When the clerk of the court advances on the steps of the tribunal, and simply says, "The state of New York *versus* the state of Ohio," it is impossible not to feel that the court which he addresses is no ordinary body; and when it is recollected that one of these parties represents one million, and the other two millions of men, one is struck by the responsibility of the seven judges whose decision is about to satisfy or to disappoint so large a number of their fellow-citizens.

The peace, the prosperity, and the very existence of the Union, are invested in the hands of the seven judges. Without their active co-operation the constitution would be a dead letter: the executive appeals to them for assistance against the encroachments of the legislative powers; the legislature demands their protection from the designs of the executive; they defend the Union from the disobedience of the states, the states from the exaggerated claims of the Union, the public interest against the interests of private citizens, and the conservative spirit of order against the fleeting innovations of democracy. Their power is enormous, but it is clothed in the authority of public opinion. They are the all-powerful guardians of a people which respects law; but they would be impotent against popular neglect or popular contempt. The force of public opinion is the most intractable of agents, because its exact limits cannot be defined; and it is not less dangerous to exceed, than to remain below the boundary prescribed.

The federal judges must not only be good citizens, and men possessed of that information and integrity which are indispensable to magistrates, but they must be statesmen—politicians, not unread in the signs of the times, not afraid to brave the obstacles which can be subdued, nor slow to turn aside such encroaching elements as may threaten the supremacy of the Union and the obedience which is due to the laws.

The president, who exercises a limited power, may err without causing great mischief in the state. Congress may decide amiss without destroying the Union, because the electoral body in which congress originates may cause it to retract its decision by changing its members. But if the supreme court is ever composed of imprudent men or bad citizens, the Union may be plunged into anarchy or civil war.

The real cause of this danger, however, does not lie in the constitution of the tribunal, but in the very nature of federal governments. We have observed that in confederate peoples it is especially necessary to consolidate the judicial authority, because in no other nations do those independent persons who are able to cope with the social body, exist in greater power or in a better condition to resist the physical strength of the government. But the more a power requires to be strengthened, the more extensive and independent it must be made; and the dangers which its abuse may create are heightened by its independence and its strength. The source of the evil is not, therefore, in the constitution of the power, but in the constitution of those states which render its existence necessary.

IN WHAT RESPECTS THE FEDERAL CONSTITUTION IS SUPERIOR TO THAT OF THE STATES.

In what respects the Constitution of the Union can be compared to that of the States.—Superiority of the Constitution of the Union attributable to the Wisdom of the federal Legislators.—Legislature of the Union less dependant on the People than that of the States.—Executive Power more independent in its Sphere.—Judicial Power less subjected to the Inclinations of the Majority.—Practical Consequences of these Facts.—The Dangers inherent in a democratic Government eluded by the federal Legislators, and increased by the Legislators of the States.

The federal constitution differs essentially from that of the states in the ends which it is intended to accomplish; but in the means by which these ends are promoted, a greater analogy exists between them. The objects of the governments are different, but their forms are the same; and in this special point of view there is some advantage in comparing them together.

I am of opinion that the federal constitution is superior to all the constitutions of the states, for several reasons.

The present constitution of the Union was formed at a later period than those of the majority of the states, and it may have derived some meliorations from past experience. But we shall be led to acknowledge that this is only a secondary cause of its superiority, when we recollect that eleven new states have been added to the American confederation since the promulgation of the federal constitution, and that these new republics have always rather exaggerated than avoided the defects which existed in the former constitutions.

The chief cause of the superiority of the federal constitution lay in the character of the legislators who composed it. At the time when it was formed the dangers of the confederation were imminent, and its ruin seemed inevitable. In this extremity the people chose the men who most deserved the esteem, rather than those who had gained the affections of the country. I have already observed, that distinguished as almost all the legislators of the Union were for their intelligence, they were still more so for their patriotism. They had all been nurtured at a time when the spirit of liberty was braced by a continual struggle against a powerful and predominant authority. When the contest was terminated, while the excited passions of the populace persisted in warring with dangers which had ceased to threaten them, these men stopped short in their career; they cast a calmer and more penetrating look upon the country which was now their own; they perceived that the war of independence was definitely ended, and that the only dangers which America had to fear were those which might result from the abuse of the freedom she had won. They had the courage to say what they believed to be true, because they were animated by a warm and sincere love of liberty; and they ventured to propose restrictions, because they were resolutely opposed to destruction.*

The greater number of the constitutions of the states assign one year for the duration of the house of representatives, and two years for that of the senate; so that members of the legislative body are constantly and narrowly tied down by the slightest desires of their constituents. The legislators of the Union were of opinion that this excessive dependance of the legislature tended to alter the nature of the main consequences of the representative system, since it vested the source not only of authority, but of government, in the people. They increased the length of the time for which the representatives were returned, in order to give them freer scope for the exercise of their own judgment.

The federal constitution, as well as the constitutions of the different states, divided the legislative body into two branches. But in the states these two branches were composed of the same elements and elected in the same manner. The consequence was that the passions and inclinations of the populace were as rapidly and as energetically represented in one chamber as in the other, and that laws were made with all the characteristics of violence and precipitation. By the federal constitution the two houses originate in like manner in the choice of the people; but the conditions of eligibility and the mode of election were changed, to the end that if, as is the case in certain nations, one branch of the legislature represents the same interests as the other, it may at least represent a superior degree of intelligence and discretion. A mature age was made one of the conditions of the senatorial dignity, and the upper house was chosen by an elected assembly of a limited number of members.

To concentrate the whole social force in the hands of the legislative body is the natural tendency of democracies; for as this is the power

---

* At this time Alexander Hamilton, who was one of the principal founders of the constitution, ventured to express the following sentiments in the Federalist, No. 71: "There are some who would be inclined to regard the servile pliancy of the executive to a prevailing current, either in the community or in the legislature, as its best recommendation. But such men entertain very crude notions, as well of the purposes for which government was instituted, as of the true means by which the public happiness may be promoted. The republican principle demands that the deliberative sense of the community should govern the conduct of those to whom they intrust the management of their affairs; but it does not require an unqualified complaisance to every sudden breeze of passion, or to every transient impulse which the people may receive from the arts of men who flatter their prejudice to betray their interests. It is a just observation that the people commonly *intend* the *public good*. This often applies to their very errors. But their good sense would despise the adulator who should pretend that they would always *reason right* about the *means* of promoting it. They know from experience that they sometimes err; and the wonder is that they so seldom err as they do, beset, as they continually are, by the wiles of parasites and sycophants; by the snares of the ambitious, the avaricious, the desperate; by the artifices of men who possess their confidence more than they deserve it; and of those who seek to possess rather than to deserve it. When occasions present themselves in which the interests of the people are at variance with their inclinations, it is the duty of persons whom they have appointed to be the guardians of those interests, to withstand the temporary delusion, in order to give them time and opportunity for more cool and sedate reflection. Instances might be cited in which a conduct of this kind has saved the people from very fatal consequences of their own mistakes, and has procured lasting monuments of their gratitude to the men who had courage and magnanimity enough to serve at the peril of their displeasure."

which emanates the most directly from the people, it is made to participate most fully in the preponderating authority of the multitude, and it is naturally led to monopolise every species of influence. This concentration is at once prejudicial to a well-conducted administration, and favourable to the despotism of the majority. The legislators of the states frequently yielded to these democratic propensities, which were invariably and courageously resisted by the founders of the Union.

In the states the executive power is vested in the hands of a magistrate, who is apparently placed upon a level with the legislature, but who is in reality nothing more than the blind agent and the passive instrument of its decisions. He can derive no influence from the duration of his functions, which terminate with the revolving year, or from the exercise of prerogatives which can scarcely be said to exist. The legislature can condemn him to inaction by intrusting the execution of the laws to special committees of its own members, and can annul his temporary dignity by depriving him of his salary. The federal constitution vests all the privileges and all the responsibility of the executive power in a single individual. The duration of the presidency is fixed at four years; the salary of the individual who fills that office cannot be altered during the term of his functions; he is protected by a body of official dependants, and armed with a suspensive veto. In short, every effort was made to confer a strong and independent position upon the executive authority, within the limits which had been prescribed to it.

In the constitution of all the states the judicial power is that which remains the most independent of the legislative authority: nevertheless, in all the states the legislature has reserved to itself the right of regulating the emoluments of the judges, a practice which necessarily subjects these magistrates to its immediate influence. In some states the judges are only temporarily appointed, which deprives them of a great portion of their power and their freedom. In others the legislative and judicial powers are entirely confounded: thus the senate of New York, for instance, constitutes in certain cases the superior court of the state. The federal constitution, on the other hand, carefully separates the judicial authority from all external influences: and it provides for the independence of the judges, by declaring that their salary shall not be altered, and that their functions shall be inalienable.

[It is not universally correct, as supposed by the author, that the state legislatures can deprive their governor of his salary at pleasure. In the constitution of New York it is provided, that the governor "shall receive for his services a compensation which shall neither be increased nor diminished during the term for which he shall have been elected;" and similar provisions are believed to exist in other states.

Nor is the remark strictly correct, that the federal constitution "provides for the independence of the judges, by declaring that their salary shall not be *altered*." The provision of the constitution is, that they shall, "at stated times, receive for their services a compensation which shall not be diminished during their continuance in office."—*American Editor.*]

The practical consequences of these different systems may easily be perceived. An attentive observer will soon remark that the business of the Union is incomparably better conducted than that of any individual state. The conduct of the federal government is more fair and more temperate than that of the states; its designs are more fraught with wisdom, its projects are more durable and more skilfully combined, its measures are put into execution with more vigor and consistency.

I recapitulate the substance of this chapter in a few words:—

The existence of democracies is threatened by two dangers, viz: the complete subjection of the legislative body to the caprices of the electoral body; and the concentration of all the powers of the government in the legislative authority.

The growth of these evils has been encouraged by the policy of the legislators of the states; but it has been resisted by the legislators of the Union by every means which lay within their control.

CHARACTERISTICS WHICH DISTINGUISH THE FEDERAL CONSTITUTION OF THE UNITED STATES OF AMERICA FROM ALL OTHER FEDERAL CONSTITUTIONS.

American Union appears to resemble all other Confederations.—Nevertheless its Effects are different.—Reason of this.—Distinctions between the Union and all other Confederations.—The American Government not a Federal, but an imperfect national Government.

The United States of America do not afford either the first or the only instance of confederate states, several of which have existed in modern Europe, without adverting to those of antiquity. Switzerland, the Germanic empire, and the republic of the United Provinces, either have been or still are confederations. In studying the constitutions of these different countries, the politician is surprised to observe that the powers with which they invested the federal government are nearly identical with the privileges awarded by the American constitution to the government of the United States. They confer upon the central power the same rights of making peace and war, of raising money and troops, and of providing for the general exigencies and the common interests of the nation. Nevertheless the federal government of these different peoples has always been as remarkable for its weakness and inefficiency as that of the Union is for its vigorous and enterprising spirit. Again, the first American confederation perished through the excessive weakness of its government; and this weak government was, notwithstanding, in possession of rights even more extensive than those of the federal government of the present day. But the more recent constitution of the United States contains certain principles which exercise a most important influence, although they do not at once strike the observer.

This constitution, which may at first sight be confounded with the federal constitutions which preceded it, rests upon a novel theory, which may be considered as a great invention in modern political science. In all the confederations which had been formed before the American constitution of 1789, the allied states agreed to obey the injunctions of a federal government: but they reserved to themselves the right of ordaining and enforcing the execution of the laws of the Union. The American states which combined in 1789 agreed that the federal government should not only dictate the laws, but that it should execute its own enactments. In both cases the right is the same, but the exercise of the right is different; and this alteration produced the most momentous consequences.

In all the confederations which had been formed before the American Union, the federal government demanded its supplies at the hands of the separate governments; and if the measure it prescribed was onerous to any one of those bodies, means were found to evade its claims: if the state was powerful, it had recourse to arms; if it was weak, it connived at the resistance which the law of the Union, its sovereign, met with, and resorted to inaction under the plea of inability. Under these circumstances one of two alternatives has invariably occurred: either the most preponderant of the allied peoples has assumed the privileges of the federal authority, and ruled all the other states in its name,* or the federal government has been abandoned by its natural supporters, anarchy has arisen between the confederates, and the Union has lost all power of action.†

In America the subjects of the Union are not states, but private citizens: the national government levies a tax, not upon the state of Massachusetts, but upon each inhabitant of Massachusetts. All former confederate governments presided over communities, but that of the Union rules individuals; its force is not borrowed, but self-derived; and it is served by its own civil and military officers, by its own army, and its own courts of justice. It cannot be doubted that the spirit of the nation, the passions of the multitude, and the provincial prejudices of each state, tend singularly to diminish the authority of a federal authority thus constituted, and to facilitate the means of resistance to its mandates; but the comparative weakness of a restricted sovereignty is an evil inherent in the federal system. In America, each state has fewer opportunities of resistance, and fewer temptations to non-compliance; nor can such a design be put in execution (if indeed it be entertained), without an open violation of the laws of the Union, a direct interruption of the ordinary course of justice, and a bold declaration of revolt; in a word, without a decisive step, which men hesitate to adopt.

In all former confederations, the privileges of the Union furnished more elements of discord than of power, since they multiplied the claims of the nation without augmenting the means of enforcing

---

* This was the case in Greece, when Philip undertook to execute the decree of the Amphictyons; in the Low Countries, where the province of Holland always gave the law; and in our own time in the Germanic confederation, in which Austria and Prussia assume a great degree of influence over the whole country, in the name of the Diet.
† Such has always been the situation of the Swiss confederation, which would have perished ages ago but for the mutual jealousies of its neighbours.

them: and in accordance with this fact it may be remarked, that the real weakness of federal governments has almost always been in the exact ratio of their nominal power. Such is not the case with the American Union, in which, as in ordinary governments, the federal government has the means of enforcing all it is empowered to demand.

The human understanding more easily invents new things than new words, and we are thence constrained to employ a multitude of improper and inadequate expressions. When several nations form a permanent league, and establish a supreme authority, which, although it has not the same influence over the members of the community as a national government, acts upon each of the confederate states in a body, this government, which is so essentially different from all others, is denominated a federal one. Another form of society is afterward discovered, in which several peoples are fused into one and the same nation with regard to certain common interests, although they remain distinct, or at least only confederate, with regard to all their other concerns. In this case the central power acts directly upon those whom it governs, whom it rules, and whom it judges, in the same manner as, but in a more limited circle than, a national government. Here the term of federal government is clearly no longer applicable to a state of things which must be styled an incomplete national government: a form of government has been found out which is neither exactly national nor federal; but no farther progress has been made, and the new word which will one day designate this novel invention does not yet exist.

The absence of this new species of confederation has been the cause which has brought all unions to civil war, to subjection, or to a stagnant apathy; and the peoples which formed these leagues have been either too dull to discern, or too pusillanimous to apply this great remedy. The American confederation perished by the same defects.

But the confederate states of America had been long accustomed to form a portion of one empire before they had won their independence: they had not contracted the habit of governing themselves, and their national prejudices had not taken deep root in their minds. Superior to the rest of the world in political knowledge, and sharing that knowledge equally among themselves, they were little agitated by the passions which generally oppose the extension of federal authority in a nation, and those passions were checked by the wisdom of the chief citizens.

The Americans applied the remedy with prudent firmness as soon as they were conscious of the evil; they amended their laws, and they saved their country.

ADVANTAGES OF THE FEDERAL SYSTEM IN GENERAL, AND ITS SPECIAL UTILITY IN AMERICA.

Happiness and Freedom of small Nations.—Power of great Nations.—Great Empires favourable to the Growth of Civilization.—Strength often the first Element of national Prosperity.—Aim of the federal System to unite the twofold Advantages resulting from a small and from a large Territory.—Advantages derived by the United States from this System.—The Law adapts itself to the Exigencies of the Population; Population does not conform to the Exigencies of the Law.— Activity, Melioration, Love, and Enjoyment of Freedom in the American Communities.—Public Spirit of the Union the abstract of provincial Patriotism.— Principles and Things circulate freely over the Territory of the United States.—The Union is happy and free as a little Nation, and respected as a great Empire.

In small nations the scrutiny of society penetrates into every part, and the spirit of improvement enters into the most trifling details; as the ambition of the people is necessarily checked by its weakness, all the efforts and resources of the citizens are turned to the internal benefit of the community, and are not likely to evaporate in the fleeting breath of glory. The desires of every individual are limited, because extraordinary faculties are rarely to be met with. The gifts of an equal fortune render the various conditions of life uniform; and the manners of the inhabitants are orderly and simple. Thus, if we estimate the gradations of popular morality and enlightenment, we shall generally find that in small nations there are more persons in easy circumstances, a more numerous population, and a more tranquil state of society than in great empires.

When tyranny is established in the bosom of a small nation, it is more galling than elsewhere, because as it acts within a narrow circle, every point of that circle is subject to its direct influence. It supplies the place of those great designs which it cannot entertain, by a violent or an exasperating interference in a multitude of minute details; and it leaves the political world to which it properly belongs, to meddle with the arrangements of domestic life. Tastes as well as actions are to be regulated at its pleasure; and the families of the citizens as well as the affairs of the state are to be governed by its decisions. This invasion of rights occurs, however, but seldom, and freedom is in truth the natural state of small communities. The temptations which the government offers to ambition are too weak, and the resources of private individuals are too slender, for the sovereign power easily to fall within the grasp of a single citizen: and should such an event have occurred, the subjects of the state can without difficulty overthrow the tyrant and his oppression by a simultaneous effort.

Small nations have therefore ever been the cradles of political liberty: and the fact that many of them have lost their immunities by extending their dominion, shows that the freedom they enjoyed was more a consequence of their inferior size than of the character of the people.

The history of the world affords no instance of a great nation retaining the form of a republican government for a long series of years,* and this had led to the conclusion that such a state of things is impracticable. For my own part, I cannot but censure the imprudence of attempting to limit the possible, and to judge the future, on the part of a being who is hourly deceived by the most palpable realities of life,

---

* I do not speak of a confederation of small republics but of a great consolidated republic.

and who is constantly taken by surprise in the circumstances with which he is most familiar. But it may be advanced with confidence that the existence of a great republic will always be exposed to far greater perils than that of a small one.

All the passions which are most fatal to republican institutions spread with an increasing territory, while the virtues which maintain their dignity do not augment in the same proportion. The ambition of the citizens increases with the power of the state; the strength of parties, with the importance of the ends they have in view; but that devotion to the common weal, which is the surest check on destructive passions, is not stronger in a large than in a small republic. It might, indeed, be proved without difficulty that it is less powerful and less sincere. The arrogance of wealth and the dejection of wretchedness, capital cities of unwonted extent, a lax morality, a vulgar egotism, and a great confusion of interests, are the dangers which almost invariably arise from the magnitude of states. But several of these evils are scarcely prejudicial to a monarchy, and some of them contribute to maintain its existence. In monarchial states the strength of the government is its own; it may use, but it does not depend on, the community: and the authority of the prince is proportioned to the prosperity of the nation: but the only security which a republican government possesses against these evils lies in the support of the majority. This support is not, however, proportionably greater in a large republic than it is in a small one; and thus while the means of attack perpetually increase both in number and in influence, the power of resistance remains the same; or it may rather be said to diminish, since the propensities and interests of the people are diversified by the increase of the population, and the difficulty of forming a compact majority is constantly augmented. It has been observed, moreover, that the intensity of human passions is heightened, not only by the importance of the end which they propose to attain, but by the multitude of individuals who are animated by them at the same time. Every one has had occasion to remark that his emotions in the midst of a sympathizing crowd are far greater than those which he would have felt in solitude. In great republics the impetus of political passion is irresistible, not only because it aims it gigantic purposes, but because it is felt and shared by millions of men at the same time.

It may therefore be asserted as a general proposition, that nothing is more opposed to the well-being and the freedom of man than vast empires. Nevertheless it is important to acknowledge the peculiar advantages of great states. For the very reason which renders the desire of power more intense in these communities than among ordinary men, the love of glory is also more prominent in the hearts of a class of citizens, who regard the applause of a great people as a reward worthy of their exertions, and an elevating encouragement to man. If we would learn why it is that great nations contribute more powerfully to the spread of human improvement than small states, we shall discover an adequate cause in the rapid and energetic circulation of ideas, and in those great cities which are the intellectual centres where all the rays of human genius are reflected and combined. To this it may be added that most important discoveries demand a display of national power which the government of a small state is unable to make; in great nations the government entertains a greater number of general notions, and is more completely disengaged from the routine of precedent and the egotism of local prejudice; its designs are conceived with more talent, and executed with more boldness.

In time of peace the well-being of small nations is undoubtedly more general and more complete; but they are apt to suffer more acutely from the calamities of war than those of great empires whose distant frontiers may for ages avert the presence of the danger from the mass of the people, which is more frequently afflicted than ruined by the evil.

But in this matter, as in many others, the argument derived from the necessity of the case predominates over all others. If none but small nations existed, I do not doubt that mankind would be more happy and more free; but the existence of great nations is unavoidable. This consideration introduces the element of physical strength as a condition of national prosperity.

It profits a people but little to be affluent and free, if it is perpetually exposed to be pillaged or subjugated; the number of its manufactures and the extent of its commerce are of small advantage, if another nation has the empire of the seas and gives the law in all the markets of the globe. Small nations are often empoverished, not because they are small, but because they are weak; and great empires prosper less because they are great than because they are strong. Physical strength is therefore one of the first conditions of the happiness and even of the existence of nations. Hence it occurs, that unless very peculiar circumstances intervene, small nations are always united to large empires in the end, either by force or by their own consent; yet I am unacquainted with a more deplorable spectacle than that of a people unable either to defend or to maintain its independence.

The federal system was created with the intention of combining the different advantages which result from the greater and the lesser extent of nations; and a single glance over the United States of America suffices to discover the advantages which they have derived from its adoption.

In great centralized nations the legislator is obliged to impart a character of uniformity to the laws, which does not always suit the diversity of customs and of districts; as he takes no cognizance of special cases, he can only proceed upon general principles; and the population is obliged to conform to the exigencies of the legislation, since the legislation cannot adapt itself to the exigencies and customs of the population; which is the cause of endless trouble and misery. This disadvantage does not exist in confederations; congress regulates the principal measures of the national government, and all the details of the administration are reserved to the provincial legislatures. It is impossible to imagine how much this division of sovereignty contributes to the well-being of each of the states which compose the Union. In these small communities, which are never agitated by the desire of aggrandizement or the cares of self-defence, all public authority and private energy is employed in internal melioration. The central government of each state, which is in immediate juxtaposition to the citizens, is daily apprized of the wants which arise in society; and new projects are proposed every year, which are discussed either at town-meetings or by the legislature of the state, and which are transmitted by the press to stimulate the zeal and to excite the interest of the citizens. This spirit of melioration is constantly alive in the American republics, without compromising their tranquility; the ambition of power yields to the less refined and less dangerous love of comfort. It is generally believed in America that the existence and the permanence of the republican form of government in the New World depend upon the existence and the permanence of the federal system; and it is not unusual to attribute a large share of the misfortunes which have befallen the new states of South America to the injudicious erection of great republics, instead of a divided and confederate sovereignty.

It is incontestably true that the love and the habits of republican government in the United States were engendered in the townships and in the provincial assemblies. In a small state, like that of Connecticut for instance, where cutting a canal or laying down a road is a momentous political question, where the state has no army to pay and no wars to carry on, and where much wealth and much honour cannot be bestowed upon the chief citizens, no form of government can be more natural or more appropriate than that of a republic. But it is this same republican spirit, it is these manners and customs of a free people, which are engendered and nurtured in the different states, to be afterward applied to the country at large. The public spirit of the Union is, so to speak, nothing more than an abstract of the patriotic zeal of the provinces. Every citizen of the United States transfuses his attachment to his little republic into the common store of American patriotism. In defending the Union, he defends the increasing prosperity of his own district, the right of conducting its affairs, and the hope of causing measures of improvement to be adopted which may be favourable to his own interests; and these are motives which are wont to stir men more readily than the general interests of the country and the glory of the nation.

On the other hand, if the temper and the manners of the inhabitants especially fitted them to promote the welfare of a great republic, the federal system smoothed the obstacles which they might have encountered. The confederation of all the American states presents none of the ordinary disadvantages resulting from great agglomerations of men. The Union is a great republic in extent, but the paucity of objects for which its government provides assimilates it to a small state. Its acts are important, but they are rare. As the sovereignty of the Union is limited and incomplete, its exercise is not incompatible with liberty; for it does not excite those insatiable desires of fame and power which have proved so fatal to great republics. As there is no common centre to the country, vast capital cities, colossal wealth, abject poverty, and sudden revolutions are alike unknown; and political passion, instead of spreading over the land like a torrent of desolation, spends its strength against the interests and the individual passions of every state.

Nevertheless, all commodities and ideas circulate throughout the Union as freely as in a country inhabited by one people. Nothing checks the spirit of enterprise. The government avails itself of the assistance of all who have talents or knowledge to serve it. Within the frontiers of the Union the profoundest peace prevails, as within the heart of some great empire; abroad, it ranks with the most powerful nations of the earth: two thousand miles of coast are open to the commerce of the world; and as it possesses the keys of the globe, its flag is respected in the most remote seas. The Union is as happy and as free as a small people, and as glorious and as strong as a great nation.

WHY THE FEDERAL SYSTEM IS NOT ADAPTED TO ALL PEOPLES, AND HOW THE ANGLO-AMERICANS WERE ENABLED TO ADOPT IT.

Every federal System contains defects which baffle the efforts of the Legislator.—The federal System is complex.—It demands a daily Exercise of Discretion on the Part of the Citizens.—Practical knowledge of Government common among the Americans.—Relative weakness of the Government of the Union, another defect inherent in the federal System.—The Americans have diminished without remedying it.—The Sovereignty of the separate States apparently weaker, but really stronger, than that of the Union.—Why.—Natural causes of Union must exist between confederate Peoples beside the Laws.—What these Causes are among the Anglo-Americans.—Maine and Georgia, separated by a Distance of a thousand Miles, more naturally united than Normandy and Britany.⁵—War, the main Peril of Confederations.—This proved even by the Example of the United States.—The Union has no great Wars to fear.—Why.—Dangers to which Europeans would be exposed if they adopted the federal System of the Americans.

When a legislator succeeds, after persevering efforts, in exercising an indirect influence upon the destiny of nations, his genius is lauded by mankind, while in point of fact, the geographical position of the country which he is unable to change, a social condition which arose without his co-operation, manners and opinions which he cannot trace to their source, and an origin with which he is unacquainted, exercise so irresistible an influence over the courses of society, that he is himself borne away by the current, after an ineffectual resistance. Like the navigator, he may direct the vessel which bears him along, but he can neither change its structure, nor raise the winds, nor lull the waters which swell beneath him.

I have shown the advantages which the Americans derive from their federal system; it remains for me to point out the circumstances which render that system practicable, as its benefits are not to be enjoyed by all nations. The incidental defects of the federal system which originate in the laws may be corrected by the skill of the legislator, but there are farther evils inherent in the system which cannot be counteracted by the peoples which adopt it. These nations must therefore find the strength necessary to support the natural imperfections of their government.

The most prominent evil of all federal systems is the very complex nature of the means they employ. Two sovereignties are necessarily in the presence of each other. The legislator may simplify and equalize the action of these two sovereignties, by limiting each of them to a sphere of authority accurately defined; but he cannot combine them into one, or prevent them from running into collision at certain points. The federal system therefore rests upon a theory which is necessarily complicated, and which demands the daily exercise of a considerable share of discretion on the part of those it governs.

A proposition must be plain to be adopted by the understanding of a people. A false notion which is clear and precise will always meet with a greater number of adherents in the world than a true principle which is obscure or involved. Hence it arises that parties, which are like small communities in the heart of the nation, invariably adopt some principle or some name as a symbol, which very inadequately represents the end they have in view and the means which are at their disposal, but without which they could neither act nor subsist. The governments which are founded upon a single principle or a single feeling which is easily defined, are perhaps not the best, but they are unquestionably the strongest and the most durable in the world.

In examining the constitution of the United States, which is the most perfect federal constitution that ever existed, one is startled, on the other hand, at the variety of information and the excellence of discretion which it presupposes in the people whom it is meant to govern. The government of the Union depends entirely upon legal fictions; the Union is an ideal nation which only exists in the mind, and whose limits and extent can only be discerned by the understanding.

When once the general theory is comprehended, numerous difficulties remain to be solved in its application; for the sovereignty of the Union is so involved in that of the states, that it is impossible to distinguish its boundaries at the first glance. The whole structure of the government is artificial and conventional; and it would be ill-adapted to a people which has not been long accustomed to conduct its own affairs, or to one in which the science of politics has not descended to the humblest classes of society. I have never been more struck by the good sense and the practical judgment of the Americans than in the ingenious devices by which they elude the numberless difficulties resulting from their federal constitution. I scarcely ever met with a plain American citizen who could not distinguish, with surprising facility, the obligations created by the laws of congress from those created by the laws of his own state; and who, after having discriminated between the matters which come under the cognizance of the Union, and those which the local legislature is competent to regulate, could not point out the exact limit of the several jurisdictions of the federal courts and the tribunals of the state.

The constitution of the United States is like those exquisite productions of human industry which ensure wealth and renown to their inventors, but which are profitless in any other hands. This truth is exemplified by the condition of Mexico at the present time. The Mexicans were desirous of establishing a federal system, and they took the federal constitution of their neighbours the Anglo-Americans as their model, and copied it with considerable accuracy.* But although they had borrowed the letter of the law, they were unable to create or to introduce the spirit and the sense which gave it life. They were involved in ceaseless embarrassments between the mechanism of their double government; the sovereignty of the states and that of the Union perpetually exceeded their respective privileges, and entered into collision; and to the present day Mexico is alternately the victim of anarchy and the slave of military despotism.

The second and the most fatal of all the defects I have alluded to, and that which I believe to be inherent in the federal system, is the relative weakness of the government of the Union. The principle upon which all confederations rest is that of a divided sovereignty. The legislator may render this partition less perceptible, he may even conceal it for a time from the public eye, but he cannot prevent it from existing; and a divided sovereignty must always be less powerful than an entire supremacy. The reader has seen in the remarks I have made on the constitution of the United States, that the Americans have displayed singular ingenuity in combining the restriction of the power of the Union within the narrow limits of the federal government, with the semblance, and to a certain extent with the force of a national government. By this means the legislators of the Union have succeeded in diminishing, though not in counteracting, the natural danger of confederations.

It has been remarked that the American government does not apply itself to the states, but that it immediately transmits its injunctions to the citizens, and compels them as isolated individuals to comply with its demands. But if the federal law were to clash with the interests and prejudices of a state, it might be feared that all the citizens of that state would conceive themselves to be interested in the cause of a single individual who should refuse to obey. If all the citizens of the state were aggrieved at the same time and in the same manner by the authority of the Union, the federal government would vainly attempt to subdue them individually; they would instinctively unite in the common defense, and they would derive a ready-prepared organization from the share of sovereignty which the institution of their state allows them to enjoy. Fiction would give way to reality, and an organized portion of the territory might then contest the central authority.

The same observation holds good with regard to the federal jurisdiction. If the courts of the Union violated an important law of a state in a private case, the real, if not the apparent contest would arise between the aggrieved state, represented by a citizen, and the Union, represented by its courts of justice.†

---

* See the Mexican constitution of 1824.
† For instance, the Union possesses by the constitution the right of selling unoccupied lands for its own profit. Supposing that the state of Ohio should claim the same right in behalf of certain territories lying within its boundaries, upon the plea that the constitution refers to

He would have but a partial knowledge of the world who should imagine that it is possible, by the aid of legal fictions, to prevent men from finding out and employing those means of gratifying their passions which have been left open to them; and it may be doubted whether the American legislators, when they rendered a collision between the two sovereignties less probable, destroyed the causes of such a misfortune. But it may even be affirmed that they were unable to ensure the preponderance of the federal element in a case of this kind. The Union is possessed of money and of troops, but the affections and the prejudices of the people are in the bosom of the states. The sovereignty of the Union is an abstract being, which is connected with but few external objects; the sovereignty of the states is hourly perceptible, easily understood, constantly active; and if the former is of recent creation, the latter is coeval with the people itself. The sovereignty of the Union is factitious, that of the states is natural, and derives its existence from its own simple influence, like the authority of a parent. The supreme power of the nation only affects a few of the chief interests of society; it represents an immense but remote country, and claims a feeling of patriotism which is vague and ill-defined; but the authority of the states controls every individual citizen at every hour and in all circumstances; it protects his property, his freedom, and his life; and when we recollect the traditions, the customs, the prejudices of local and familiar attachment with which it is connected, we cannot doubt the superiority of a power which is interwoven with every circumstance that renders the love of one's native country instinctive to the human heart.

Since legislators are unable to obviate such dangerous collisions as

---

those lands alone which do not belong to the jurisdiction of any particular state, and consequently should choose to dispose of them itself, the litigation would be carried on in the names of the purchasers from the state of Ohio, and the purchasers from the Union, and not in the names of Ohio and the Union. But what would become of this legal fiction if the federal purchaser was confirmed in his right by the courts of the Union, while the other competitor was ordered to retain possession by the tribunals of the state of Ohio?

[The difficulty supposed by the author in this note is imaginary. The question of title to the lands in the case put, must depend upon the constitution, treaties, and laws of the United States; and a decision in the state court adverse to the claim or title set up under those laws, must, by the very words of the constitution and of the judiciary act, be subject to review by the supreme court of the United States, whose decision is final.

The remarks in the text of this page upon the relative weakness of the government of the Union, are equally applicable to any form of republican or democratic government, and are not peculiar to a federal system. Under the circumstances supposed by the author, of all the citizens of a state, or a large majority of them, aggrieved at the same time and in the same manner, by the operation of any law, the same difficulty would arise in executing the laws of the state as those of the Union. Indeed, such instances of the total inefficacy of state laws, are not wanting. The fact is, that all republics depend on the willingness of the people to execute the laws. If they will not enforce them, there is, so far, an end to the government, for it possesses no power adequate to the control of the physical power of the people.

Not only in theory, but in fact, a republican government must be administered by the people themselves. They, and they alone, must execute the laws. And hence, the first principle in such governments, that on which all others depend, and without which no other can exist, is and must be, obedience to the existing laws at all times and under all circumstances. It is the vital condition of the social compact. He who claims a dispensing power for himself, by which he suspends the operation of the law in his own case, is worse than a usurper, for he not only tramples under foot the constitution of his country, but violates the reciprocal pledge which he has given to his fellow-citizens, and has received from them, that he will abide by the laws constitutionally enacted; upon the strength of which pledge, his own personal rights and acquisitions are protected by the rest of the community.—*American Editor*.]

occur between the two sovereignties which co-exist in the federal system, their first object must be, not only to dissuade the confederate states from warfare, but to encourage such institutions as may promote the maintenance of peace. Hence it results that the federal compact cannot be lasting unless there exists in the communities which are leagued together, a certain number of inducements to union which render their common dependance agreeable, and the task of the government light; and that system cannot succeed without the presence of favorable circumstances added to the influence of good laws. All the peoples which have ever formed a confederation have been held together by a certain number of common interests, which served as the intellectual ties of association.

But the sentiments and the principles of man must be taken into consideration as well as his immediate interest. A certain uniformity of civilization is not less necessary to the durability of a confederation, than a uniformity of interests in the states which compose it. In Switzerland the difference which exists between the canton of Uri and the canton of Vaud[6] is equal to that between the fifteenth and the nineteenth centuries; and, properly speaking, Switzerland has never possessed a federal government. The union between these two cantons only subsists upon the map; and their discrepances would soon be perceived if an attempt were made by a central authority to prescribe the same laws to the whole territory.

One of the circumstances which most powerfully contribute to support the federal government in America, is that the states have not only similar interests, a common origin, and a common tongue, but that they are also arrived at the same stage of civilization; which almost always renders a union feasible. I do not know of any European nation, how small soever it may be, which does not present less uniformity in its different provinces than the American people, which occupies a territory as extensive as one half of Europe. The distance from the state of Maine to that of Georgia is reckoned at about one thousand miles; but the difference between the civilization of Maine and that of Georgia is slighter than the difference between the habits of Normandy and those of Britany. Maine and Georgia, which are placed at the opposite extremities of a great empire, are consequently in the natural possession of more real inducements to form a confederation than Normandy and Britany, which are only separated by a bridge.

The geographical position of the country contributed to increase the facilities which the American legislators derived from the manners and customs of the inhabitants; and it is to this circumstance that the adoption and the maintenance of the federal system are mainly attributable.

The most important occurrence which can mark the annals of a people is the breaking out of a war. In war a people struggles with the energy of a single man against foreign nations, in the defence of its very existence. The skill of a government, the good sense of the community, and the natural fondness which men entertain for their country, may suffice to maintain peace in the interior of a district, and to favour its internal prosperity; but a nation can only carry on a great war at the cost of more numerous and more painful sacrifices; and to suppose that a great number of men will of their own accord comply with the exigencies of the state, is to betray an ignorance of mankind. All the peoples which have been obliged to sustain a long and serious warfare have consequently been led to augment the power of their government. Those which have not succeeded in this attempt have been subjugated. A long war almost always places nations in the wretched alternative of being abandoned to ruin by defeat, or to despotism by success. War therefore renders the symptoms of the weakness of a government most palpable and most alarming; and I have shown that the inherent defect of federal governments is that of being weak.

The federal system is not only deficient in every kind of centralized administration, but the central government itself is imperfectly organized, which is invariably an influential cause of inferiority when the nation is opposed to other countries which are themselves governed by a single authority. In the federal constitution of the United States, by which the central government possesses more real force, this evil is still extremely sensible. An example will illustrate the case to the reader.

The constitution confers upon congress the right of "calling forth militia to execute the laws of the Union, suppress insurrections, and repel invasions;" and another article declares that the president of the United States is the commander-in-chief of the militia. In the war of 1812,[7] the president ordered the militia of the northern states to march to the frontiers; but Connecticut and Massachusetts, whose interests were impaired by the war, refused to obey the command. They argued that the constitution authorizes the federal government to call forth the militia in cases of insurrection or invasion, but that in the present instance, there was neither invasion nor insurrection. They added, that the same constitution which conferred upon the Union the right of calling forth the militia, reserved to the states that of naming the officers; and that consequently (as they understood the clause) no officer of the Union had any right to command the militia, even during war, except the president in person: and in this case they were ordered to join an army commanded by another individual. These absurd and pernicious doctrines received the sanction not only of the governors and legislative bodies, but also of the courts of justice in both states; and the federal government was constrained to raise elsewhere the troops which it required.*

---

* Kent's Commentaries, vol. i., p. 244. I have selected an example which relates to a time posterior to the promulgation of the present constitution. If I had gone back to the days of the confederation, I might have given still more striking instances. The whole nation was at that time in a state of enthusiastic excitement; the revolution was represented by a man who was the idol of the people; but at that very period congress had, to say the truth, no resources at all at its disposal. Troops and supplies were perpetually wanting. The best devised projects failed in the execution, and the Union, which was constantly on the verge of destruction, was saved by the weakness of its enemies far more than by its own strength.

The only safeguard which the American Union, with all the relative perfection of its laws, possesses against the dissolution which would be produced by a great war, lies in its probable exemption from that calamity. Placed in the centre of an immense continent, which offers a boundless field for human industry, the Union is almost as much insulated from the world as if its frontiers were girt by the ocean. Canada contains only a million of inhabitants, and its population is divided into two inimical nations. The rigor of the climate limits the extension of its territory, and shuts up its ports during the six months of winter. From Canada to the Gulf of Mexico a few savage tribes are to be met with, which retire, perishing in their retreat, before six thousand soldiers. To the south, the union has a point of contact with the empire of Mexico; and it is thence that serious hostilities may one day be expected to arise. But for a long while to come, the uncivilized state of the Mexican community, the depravity of its morals, and its extreme poverty, will prevent that country from ranking high among nations. As for the powers of Europe, they are too distant to be formidable.*

The great advantage of the United States does not, then, consist in a federal constitution which allows them to carry on great wars, but in a geographical position, which renders such enterprises improbable.

No one can be more inclined than I am myself to appreciate the advantages of the federal system, which I hold to be one of the combinations most favourable to the prosperity and freedom of man. I envy the lot of those nations which have been enabled to adopt it; but I cannot believe that any confederate peoples could maintain a long or an equal contest with a nation of similar strength in which the government should be centralized. A people which should divide its sovereignty into fractional powers, in the presence of the great military monarchies of Europe, would, in my opinion, by that very act, abdicate its power, and perhaps its existence and its name. But such is the admirable position of the New World, that man has no other enemy than himself; and that in order to be happy and to be free, it suffices to seek the gifts of prosperity and the knowledge of freedom.

Chapter IX.

I have hitherto examined the institutions of the United States; I have passed their legislation in review, and I have depicted the present characteristics of political society in that country. But a sovereign power exists above these institutions and beyond these characteristic features, which may destroy or modify them at its pleasure; I mean that of the people. It remains to be shown in what manner this power, which regulates the laws, acts: its propensities and its passions remain to be pointed out, as well as the secret springs which retard, accelerate, or direct its irresistable course; and the effects of its unbounded authority, with the destiny which is probably reserved for it.

* Appendix O.

WHY THE PEOPLE MAY STRICTLY BE SAID TO GOVERN IN THE UNITED STATES.

In America the people appoints the legislative and the executive power, and furnishes the jurors who punish all offences against the laws. The American institutions are democratic, not only in their principle but in all their consequences; and the people elects its representatives *directly*, and for the most part *annually*, in order to ensure their dependence. The people is therefore the real directing power; and although the form of government is representative, it is evident that the opinions, the prejudices, the interests, and even the passions of the community are hindered by no durable obstacles from exercising a perpetual influence on society. In the United States the majority governs in the name of the people, as is the case in all the countries in which the people is supreme. This majority is principally composed of peaceable citizens, who, either by inclination or by interest, are sincerely desirous of the welfare of their country. But they are surrounded by the incessant agitation of parties, which attempt to gain their co-operation and to avail themselves of their support.

Chapter X.

PARTIES IN THE UNITED STATES.

Great Division to be made between Parties.—Parties which are to each other as rival Nations.—Parties properly so called.—Difference between great and small Parties.—Epochs which produce them.—Their Characteristics.—America has had great Parties.—They are extinct.—Federalists[1]—Republicans[2]—Defeat of the Federalists.—Difficulty of creating Parties in the United States.—What is done with this Intention.—Aristocratic and democratic Character to be met with in all Parties.—Struggle of General Jackson[3] against the Bank.

A great division must be made between parties. Some countries are so large that the different populations which inhabit them have contradictory interests, although they are the subjects of the same government; and they may thence be in a perpetual state of opposition. In this case the different fractions of the people may more properly be considered as distinct nations than as mere parties; and if a civil war breaks out, the struggle is carried on by rival peoples rather than by factions in the state.

But when the citizens entertain different opinions upon subjects which affect the whole country alike, such for instance, as the principles upon which the government is to be conducted, then distinctions arise which may correctly be styled parties. Parties are a necessary evil in free governments; but they have not at all times the same character and the same propensities.

At certain periods a nation may be oppressed by such insupportable evils as to conceive the design of effecting a total change in its political constitution; at other times the mischief lies still deeper, and the existence of society itself is endangered. Such are the times of great revolutions and of great parties. But between these epochs of misery and of confusion there are periods during which human society seems to rest, and mankind to make a pause. This pause is, indeed, only apparent; for time does not stop its course for nations any more than for men; they are all advancing toward a goal with which they are unacquainted; and we only imagine them to be stationary when their progress escapes our observation; as men who are going at a foot pace seem to be standing still to those who run.

But however this may be, there are certain epochs at which the changes that take place in the social and political constitution of nations are so slow and so insensible, that men imagine their present condition to be a final state; and the human mind, believing itself to be firmly based upon certain foundations, does not extend its researches beyond the horizon which it describes. These are the times of small parties and of intrigue.

The political parties which I style great are those which cling to principles more than to consequences; to general, and not to especial cases; to ideas, and not to men. These parties are usually distinguished by a nobler character, by more generous passions, more genuine convictions, and a more bold and open conduct than the others. In them, private interest, which always plays the chief part in political passions, is more studiously veiled under the pretext of the public good; and it may even be sometimes concealed from the eyes of the very person whom it excites and impels.

Minor parties are, on the other hand, generally deficient in political faith. As they are not sustained or dignified by a lofty purpose, they ostensibly display the egotism of their character in their actions. They glow with a factitious zeal; their language is vehement, but their conduct is timid and irresolute. The means they employ are as wretched as the end at which they aim. Hence it arises that when a calm state of things succeeds a violent revolution, the leaders of society seem suddenly to disappear, and the powers of the human mind to lie concealed. Society is convulsed by great parties, by minor ones it is agitated; it is torn by the former, by the latter it is degraded; and if these sometimes save it by a salutary perturbation, those invariably disturb it to no good end.

America has already lost the great parties which once divided the nation; and if her happiness is considerably increased, her morality has suffered by their extinction. When the war of independence was terminated, and the foundations of the new government were to be laid down, the nation was divided between two opinions—two opinions which are as old as the world, and which are perpetually to be met with under all the forms and all the names which have ever obtained in free communities—the one tending to limit, the other to extend indefinitely, the power of the people. The conflict of these two opinions never assumed that degree of violence in America which it has frequently displayed elsewhere. Both parties of the Americans were in fact agreed upon the most essential points; and neither of them had to destroy a traditionary constitution, or to overthrow the structure of society, in order to ensure its own triumph. In neither of them, consequently, were a great number of private interests affected by success or by defeat; but moral principles of a high order, such as the love of equality and of independence, were concerned in the struggle, and they sufficed to kindle violent passions.

The party which desired to limit the power of the people, endeavoured to apply its doctrines more especially to the constitution of the Union, whence it derived its name of *federal*. The other party, which affected to be more exclusively attached to the cause of liberty, took that of *republican*. America is the land of democracy, and the federalists were always in a minority; but they reckoned on their side almost all the great men who had been called forth by the war of independence, and their moral influence was very considerable. Their cause was, moreover, favoured by circumstances. The ruin of the confederation had impressed the people with a dread of anarchy, and the federalists did not fail to profit by this transient disposition of the multitude. For ten or twelve years they were at the head of affairs, and they were able to apply some, though not all, of their principles; for the hostile current was becoming from day to day too violent to be checked or stemmed. In 1801 the republicans got possession of the government: Thomas Jefferson was named president; and he increased the influence of their party by the weight of his celebrity, the greatness of his talents, and the immense extent of his popularity.

The means by which the federalists had maintained their position were artificial, and their resources were temporary: it was by the virtues or the talents of their leaders that they had risen to power. When the republicans attained to that lofty station, their opponents were overwhelmed by utter defeat. An immense majority declared itself against the retiring party, and the federalists found themselves in so small a minority, that they at once despaired of their future success. From that moment the republican or democratic party has proceeded from conquest to conquest, until it has acquired absolute supremacy in the country. The federalists, perceiving that they were vanquished without resource, and isolated in the midst of the nation, fell into two divisions, of which one joined the victorious republicans, and the other abandoned its rallying point and its name. Many years have already elapsed since they ceased to exist as a party.

The accession of the federalists to power was, in my opinion, one of the most fortunate incidents which accompanied the formation of the great American Union: they resisted the inevitable propensities of their age and of their country. But whether their theories were good or bad, they had the defect of being inapplicable, as a system, to the society which they professed to govern; and that which occurred under the auspices of Jefferson must therefore have taken place sooner or later. But their government gave the new republic time to acquire a certain stability, and afterward to support the rapid growth of the very doctrines which they had combated. A considerable number of their principles were in point of fact imbodied in the political creed of their opponents; and the federal constitution, which subsists at the present day, is a lasting monument of their patriotism and their wisdom.

Great political parties are not, then, to be met with in the United States at the present time. Parties, indeed, may be found which threaten the future tranquillity of the Union; but there are none which seem to contest the present form of government, or the present course of society. The parties by which the Union is menaced do not rest upon abstract principles, but upon temporal interests. These interests disseminated in the provinces of so vast an empire, may be said to constitute rival nations rather than parties. Thus, upon a recent occasion, the north contended for the system of commercial prohibition, and the south took up arms in favour of free trade, simply because the north is a manufacturing, and the south an agricultural district; and that the restrictive system which was profitable to the one, was prejudicial to the other.

In the absence of great parties, the United States abound with lesser controversies; and public opinion is divided into a thousand minute shades of difference upon questions of very little moment. The pains which are taken to create parties are inconceivable, and at the present day it is no easy task. In the United States there is no religious animosity, because all religion is respected, and no sect is predominant; there is no jealousy of rank, because the people is everything, and none can contest its authority; lastly, there is no public misery to serve as a means of agitation, because the physical position of the country opens so wide a field to industry, that man is able to accomplish the most surprising undertakings with his own native resources. Nevertheless, ambitious men are interested in the creation of parties, since it is difficult to eject a person from authority upon the mere ground that his place is coveted by others. The skill of the actors in the political world lies, therefore, in the art of creating parties. A political aspirant in the United States begins by discriminating his own interest, and by calculating upon those interests which may be collected around, and amalgamated with it: he then contrives to discover some doctrine or some principle which may suit the purposes of this new association, and which he adopts in order to bring forward his party and to secure its popularity: just as the *imprimatur* of a king was in former days incorporated with the volume which it authorized, but to which it nowise belonged. When these preliminaries are terminated, the new party is ushered into the political world.

All the domestic controversies of the Americans at first appear to a stranger to be so incomprehensible and so puerile, that he is at a loss whether to pity a people which takes such arrant trifles in good earnest, or to envy that happiness which enables it to discuss them. But when he comes to study the secret propensities which govern the factions of America, he easily perceives that the greater part of them are more or less connected with one or the other of those two divisions which have always existed in free communities. The deeper we penetrate into the workings of these parties, the more do we perceive that the object of the one is to limit, and that of the other to extend, the popular authority. I do not assert that the ostensible end, or even that the secret aim, of American parties is to promote the rule of aristocracy or democracy in the country, but I affirm that aristocratic or democratic passions may easily be detected at the bottom of all parties, and that, although they escape a superficial observation, they are the main point and the very soul of every faction in the United States.

To quote a recent example: when the president attacked the bank,[4] the country was excited and parties were formed; the well-informed classes rallied round the bank, the common people round the president. But it must not be imagined that the people had formed a rational opinion upon a question which offers so many difficulties to the most experienced statesmen. The bank is a great establishment which enjoys an independent existence, and the people, accustomed to make and unmake whatsoever it pleases, is startled to meet with this obstacle to its authority. In the midst of the perpetual fluctuation of society, the community is irritated by so permanent an institution, and is led to attack it, in order to see whether it can be shaken and controlled, like all the other institutions of the country.

REMAINS OF THE ARISTOCRATIC PARTY IN THE UNITED STATES.

Secret Opposition of wealthy Individuals to Democracy.—Their retirement.—Their taste for exclusive Pleasures and for Luxury at Home.—Their Simplicity Abroad.—Their affected Condescension toward the People.

It sometimes happens in a people among which various opinions prevail, that the balance of the several parties is lost, and one of them obtains an irresistible preponderance, overpowers all obstacles, harasses its opponents, and appropriates all the resources of society to its own purposes. The vanquished citizens despair of success, and they conceal their dissatisfaction in silence and in a general apathy. The nation seems to be governed by a single principle, and the prevailing party assumes the credit of having restored peace and unanimity to the country. But this apparent unanimity is merely a cloak to alarming dissensions and perpetual opposition.

This is precisely what occurred in America; when the democratic party got the upper hand, it took exclusive possession of the conduct of affairs, and from that time the laws and the customs of society have been adapted to its caprices. At the present day the more affluent classes of society are so entirely removed from the direction of political affairs in the United States, that wealth, far from conferring a right to the exercise of power, is rather an obstacle than a means of attaining to it. The wealthy members of the community abandon the lists, through unwillingness to contend, and frequently to contend in vain, against the poorest classes of their fellow-citizens. They concentrate all their enjoyments in the privacy of their homes, where they occupy a rank which cannot be assumed in public; and they constitute a private society in the state, which has its own tastes and its own pleasures. They submit to this state of things as an irremediable evil, but they are careful not to show that they are galled by its continuance; it is even not uncommon to hear them laud the delights of a republican government, and the advantages of democratic institutions when they are in public. Next to hating their enemies, men are most inclined to flatter them.

Mark, for instance, that opulent citizen, who is as anxious as a Jew of the middle ages to conceal his wealth. His dress is plain, his demeanor unassuming; but the interior of his dwelling glitters with luxury, and none but a few chosen guests whom he haughtily styles his equals, are allowed to penetrate into this sanctuary. No European noble is more exclusive in his pleasures, or more jealous of the smallest advantages which his privileged station confers upon him. But the very same individual crosses the city to reach a dark counting-house in the centre of traffic, where every one may accost him who pleases. If he meets his cobbler upon the way, they stop and converse; the two citizens discuss the affairs of the state in which they have an equal interest, and they shake hands before they part.

But beneath this artificial enthusiasm, and these obsequious attentions to the preponderating power, it is easy to perceive that the wealthy members of the community entertain a hearty distaste to the democratic institutions of their country. The populace is at once the object of their scorn and of their fears. If the maladministration of the democracy ever brings about a revolutionary crisis, and if monarchical institutions ever become practicable in the United States, the truth of what I advance will become obvious.

The two chief weapons which parties use in order to ensure success, are the *public press*, and the formation of *associations*.

Chapter XI.

LIBERTY OF THE PRESS IN THE UNITED STATES.

Difficulty of restraining the Liberty of the Press.—Particular reasons which some Nations have to cherish this Liberty.—The Liberty of the Press a necessary Consequence of the Sovereignty of the People as it is understood in America.—Violent Language of the periodical Press in the United States.—Propensities of the periodical Press.—Illustrated by the United States.—Opinion of the Americans upon the Repression of the Abuse of the Liberty of the Press by judicial Prosecutions.—Reasons for which the Press is less powerful in America than in France.

The influence of the liberty of the press does not affect political opinions alone, but it extends to all the opinions of men, and it modifies customs as well as laws. In another part of this work I shall attempt to determine the degree of influence which the liberty of the press has exercised upon civil society in the United States, and to point out the direction which it has given to the ideas, as well as the tone which it has imparted to the character and the feelings of the Anglo-Americans, but at present I purpose simply to examine the effects produced by the liberty of the press in the political world.

I confess that I do not entertain that firm and complete attachment to the liberty of the press, which things that are supremely good in their very nature are wont to excite in the mind; and I approve of it more from a recollection of the evils it prevents, than from a consideration of the advantages it ensures.

If any one can point out an intermediate, and yet a tenable position, between the complete independence and the entire subjection of the public expression of opinion, I should perhaps be inclined to adopt it; but the difficulty is to discover this position. If it is your intention to correct the abuses of unlicensed printing, and to restore the use of orderly language, you may in the first instance try the offender by a jury; but if the jury acquits him, the opinion which was that of a single individual becomes the opinion of the country at large. Too much and too little has therefore hitherto been done; if you proceed, you must bring the delinquent before permanent magistrates; but even here the cause must be heard before it can be decided; and the very principles which no book would have ventured to avow are blazoned forth in the pleadings, and what was obscurely hinted at in a single composition is then repeated in a multitude of other publications. The language in which a thought is imbodied is the mere carcase of the thought, and not the idea itself; tribunals may condemn the form, but the sense and spirit of the work is too subtile for their authority: too much has still been done to recede, too little to attain your end: you must therefore proceed. If you establish a censorship of the press, the tongue of the public speaker will still make itself heard, and you have only increased the mischief. The powers of thought do not rely, like the powers of physical strength, upon the number of their mechanical agents, nor can a host of authors be reckoned like the troops which compose an army; on the contrary, the authority of a principle is often increased by the smallness of the number of men by whom it is expressed. The words of a strong-minded man, which penetrate amid the passions of a listening assembly, have more weight than the vociferations of a thousand orators; and if it be allowed to speak freely in any public place, the consequence is the same as if free speaking was allowed in every village. The liberty of discourse must therefore be destroyed as well as the liberty of the press; this is the necessary term of your efforts; but if your object was to repress the abuses of liberty, they have brought you to the feet of a despot. You have been led from the extreme of independence to the extreme of subjection, without meeting with a single tenable position for shelter or repose.

There are certain nations which have peculiar reasons for cherishing the press, independently of the general motives which I have just pointed out. For in certain countries which profess to enjoy the privileges of freedom, every individual agent of the government may violate the laws with impunity, since those whom he oppresses cannot prosecute him before the courts of justice. In this case the liberty of the press is not merely a guarantee, but it is the only guarantee of their liberty and their security which the citizens possess. If the rulers of these nations proposed to abolish the independence of the press, the people would be justified in saying: "Give us the right of prosecuting your offences before the ordinary tribunals, and perhaps we may then waive our right of appeal to the tribunal of public opinion."

But in the countries in which the doctrine of the sovereignty of the people ostensibly prevails, the censorship of the press is not only dangerous, but it is absurd. When the right of every citizen to co-operate in the government of society is acknowledged, every citizen must be presumed to possess the power of discriminating between the different opinions of his cotemporaries, and of appreciating the different facts from which inferences may be drawn. The sovereignty of the people and the liberty of the press may therefore be looked upon as correlative institutions; just as the censorship of the press and universal suffrage are two things which are irreconcileably opposed, and which cannot long be retained among the institutions of the same people. Not a single individual of the twelve millions who inhabit the territory of the United States has as yet dared to propose any restrictions to the liberty of the press. The first newspaper over which I cast my eyes, upon my arrival in America, contained the following article:—

> "In all this affair, the language of Jackson has been that of a heartless despot, solely occupied with the preservation of his own authority. Ambition is his crime, and it will be his punishment too: intrigue is his native element, and intrigue will confound his tricks, and will deprive him of his power; he governs by means of corruption, and his immoral practices will redound to his shame and confusion. His conduct in the political arena has been that of a shameless and lawless gamester. He succeeded at the time, but the hour of retribution approaches, and he will be obliged to disgorge his winnings, to throw aside his false dice, and to end his days in some retirement, where he may curse his madness at his leisure; for repentance is a virtue with which his heart is likely to remain for ever unacquainted."

It is not uncommonly imagined in France, that the virulence of the press originates in the uncertain social condition, in the political excitement, and the general sense of consequent evil which prevail in that country; and it is therefore supposed that as soon as society has resumed a certain degree of composure, the press will abandon its present vehemence. I am inclined to think that the above causes explain the reason of the extraordinary ascendency it has acquired over the nation, but that they do not exercise much influence upon the tone of its language. The periodical press appears to me to be actuated by passions and propensities independent of the circumstances in which it is placed; and the present position of America corroborates this opinion

America is perhaps, at this moment, the country of the whole world which contains the fewest germes of revolution; but the press is not less destructive in its principles than in France, and it displays the same violence without the same reasons for indignation. In America, as in France, it constitutes a singular power, so strangely composed of mingled good and evil, that it is at the same time indispensable to the existence of freedom, and nearly incompatible with the maintenance of public order. Its power is certainly much greater in France than in the United States; though nothing is more rare in the latter country than to hear of a prosecution having been instituted against it. The reason of this is perfectly simple; the Americans having once admitted the doctrine of sovereignty of the people, apply it with perfect consistency. It was never their intention to found a permanent state of things with elements which undergo daily modifications; and there is consequently nothing criminal in an attack upon the existing laws, provided it be not attended with a violent infraction of them. They are moreover of opinion that courts of justice are unable to check the abuses of the press; and that as the subtilty of human language perpetually eludes the severity of judicial analysis, offences of this nature are apt to escape the hand which attempts to apprehend them. They hold that to act with efficacy upon the press, it would be necessary to find a tribunal, not only devoted to the existing order of things, but capable of surmounting the influence of public opinion; a tribunal which should conduct its proceedings without publicity, which should pronounce its decrees without assigning its motives and punish the intentions even more than the language of an author. Whosoever should have the power of creating and maintaining a tribunal of this kind, would waste his time in prosecuting the liberty of the press; for he would be the supreme master of the whole community, and he would be as free to rid himself of the authors as of their writings. In this question, therefore, there is no medium between servitude and extreme license; in order to enjoy the inestimable benefits which the liberty of the press ensures, it is necessary to submit to the inevitable evils which it engenders. To expect to acquire the former, and to escape the latter, is to cherish one of those illusions which commonly mislead nations in their times of sickness, when, tired with faction and exhausted by effort, they attempt to combine hostile opinions and contrary principles upon the same soil.

The small influence of the American journals is attributable to several reasons, among which are the following:—

The liberty of writing, like all other liberty, is most formidable when it is a novelty; for a people which has never been accustomed to co-operate in the conduct of state affairs, places implicit confidence in the first tribune who arouses its attention. The Anglo-Americans have enjoyed this liberty ever since the foundation of the settlements; moreover, the press cannot create human passions by its own power, however skilfully it may kindle them where they exist. In America politics are discussed with animation and a varied activity, but they rarely touch those deep passions which are excited whenever the positive interest of a part of the community is impaired: but in the United States the interests of the community are in a most prosperous condition. A single glance upon a French and an American newspaper is sufficient to show the difference which exists between the two nations on this head. In France the space allotted to commercial advertisements is very limited, and the intelligence is not considerable, but the most essential part of the journal is that which contains the discussion of the politics of the day. In America three quarters of the enormous sheet which is set before the reader are filled with advertisements, and the remainder is frequently occupied by political intelligence or trivial anecdotes: it is only from time to time that one finds a corner devoted to passionate discussions like those with which the journalists of France are wont to indulge their readers.

It has been demonstrated by observation, and discovered by the innate sagacity of the pettiest as well as the greatest of despots, that the influence of a power is increased in proportion as its direction is rendered more central. In France the press combines a twofold centralization: almost all its power is centered in the same spot, and vested in the same hands, for its organs are far from numerous. The influence of a public press thus constituted, upon a skeptical nation, must be unbounded. It is an enemy with which a government may sign an occasional truce, but which it is difficult to resist for any length of time.

Neither of these kinds of centralization exists in America. The United States have no metropolis; the intelligence as well as the power of the country is dispersed abroad, and instead of radiating from a point, they cross each other in every direction; the Americans have established no central control over the expression of opinion, any more than over the conduct of business. These are circumstances which do not depend on human foresight; but it is owing to the laws of the Union that there are no licenses to be granted to the printers, no securities demanded from editors, as in France, and no stamp duty as in France and England. The consequence of this is that nothing is easier than to set up a newspaper, and a small number of readers suffices to defray the expenses of the editor.

The number of periodical and occasional publications which appear in the United States actually surpasses belief. The most enlightened Americans attribute the subordinate influence of the press to this excessive dissemination; and it is adopted as an axiom of political science in that country, that the only way to neutralize the effect of public journals is to multiply them indefinitely. I cannot conceive why a truth which is so self-evident has not already been more generally admitted in Europe; it is comprehensible that the persons who hope to bring about revolutions, by means of the press, should be desirous of confining its action to a few powerful organs; but it is perfectly incredible that the partisans of the existing state of things, and the natural supporters of the laws, should attempt to diminish the influence of the press by concentrating its authority. The governments of Europe seem to treat the press with the courtesy of the knights of old; they are anxious to furnish it with the same central power which they have found to be so trusty a weapon, in order to enhance the glory of their resistance to its attacks.

In America there is scarcely a hamlet which has not its own newspaper. It may readily be imagined that neither discipline nor unity of design can be communicated to so multifarious a host, and each one is consequently led to fight under his own standard. All the political journals of the United States are indeed arrayed on the side of the administration or against it; but they attack and defend it in a thousand different ways. They cannot succeed in forming those great currents of opinion which overwhelm the most solid obstacles. This division of the influence of the press produces a variety of other consequences which are scarcely less remarkable. The facility with which journals can be established induces a multitude of individuals to take a part in them; but as the extent of competition precludes the possibility of considerable profit, the most distinguished classes of society are rarely led to engage in these undertakings. But such is the number of the public prints, that even if they were a source of wealth, writers of ability could not be found to direct them all. The journalists of the United States are usually placed in a very humble position, with a scanty education, and a vulgar turn of mind. The will of the majority is the most general of laws, and it establishes certain habits which form the characteristics of each peculiar class of society; thus it dictates the etiquette practised at courts and the etiquette of the bar. The characteristics of the French journalist consist in a violent, but frequently an eloquent and lofty manner of discussing the politics of the day; and the exceptions to this habitual practice are only occasional. The characteristics of the American journalist consist in an open and coarse appeal to the passions of the populace; and he habitually abandons the principles of political science to assail the characters of individuals, to track them into private life, and disclose all their weaknesses and errors.

Nothing can be more deplorable than this abuse of the powers of thought; I shall have occasion to point out hereafter the influence of the newspapers upon the taste and the morality of the American people, but my present subject exclusively concerns the political world. It cannot be denied that the effects of this extreme license of the press tend indirectly to the maintenance of public order. The individuals who are already in possession of a high station in the esteem of their fellow-citizens, are afraid to write in the newspapers, and they are thus deprived of the most powerful instrument which they can use to excite the passions of the multitude to their own advantage.*

The personal opinions of the editors have no kind of weight in the eyes of the public: the only use of a journal is, that it imparts the knowledge of certain facts, and it is only by altering or distorting those facts, that a journalist can contribute to the support of his own views.

But although the press is limited to these resources, its influence in America is immense. It is the power which impels the circulation of political life through all the districts of that vast territory. Its eye is constantly open to detect the secret springs of political designs, and to

---

* They only write in the papers when they choose to address the people in their own name; as, for instance, when they are called upon to repel calumnious imputations, and to correct a mis-statement of facts.

summon the leaders of all parties to the bar of public opinion. It rallies the interests of the community round certain principles, and it draws up the creed which factions adopt; for it affords a means of intercourse between parties which hear, and which address each other, without ever having been in immediate contact. When a great number of the organs of the press adopt the same line of conduct, their influence becomes irresistible; and public opinion, when it is perpetually assailed from the same side, eventually yields to the attack. In the United States each separate journal exercises but little authority: but the power of the periodical press is only second to that of the people.*

The Opinions which are established in the United States under the Empire of the Liberty of the Press, are frequently more firmly rooted than those which are formed elsewhere under the Sanction of a Censor.

In the United States the democracy perpetually raises fresh individuals to the conduct of public affairs; and the measures of the administration are consequently seldom regulated by the strict rules of consistency or of order. But the general principles of the government are more stable, and the opinions most prevalent in society are generally more durable than in many other countries. When once the Americans have taken up an idea, whether it be well or ill-founded, nothing is more difficult than to eradicate it from their minds. The same tenacity of opinion has been observed in England, where, for the last century, greater freedom of conscience, and more invincible prejudices have existed, than in all the other countries of Europe. I attribute this consequence to a cause which may at first sight appear to have a very opposite tendency, namely, to the liberty of the press. The nations among which this liberty exists are as apt to cling to their opinions from pride as from conviction. They cherish them because they hold them to be just, and because they exercised their own free will in choosing them; and they maintain them, not only because they are true, but because they are their own. Several other reasons conduce to the same end.

It was remarked by a man of genius,[1] that "ignorance lies at the two ends of knowledge." Perhaps it would have been more correct to say that absolute convictions are to be met with at the two extremities, and that doubt lies in the middle; for the human intellect may be considered in three distinct states, which frequently succeed one another.

A man believes implicitly, because he adopts a proposition without inquiry. He doubts as soon as he is assailed by the objections which his inquiries may have aroused. But he frequently succeeds in satisfying these doubts, and then he begins to believe afresh: he no longer lays hold on a truth in its most shadowy and uncertain form, but he sees it clearly before him, and he advances onward by the light it gives him.†

* See Appendix P.
† It may, however, be doubted whether this rational and self-guiding conviction arouses as much fervour or enthusiastic devotedness in men as their first dogmatical belief.

When the liberty of the press acts upon men who are in the first of these three states, it does not immediately disturb their habit of believing implicitly without investigation, but it constantly modifies the objects of their intuitive convictions. The human mind continues to discern but one point upon the whole intellectual horizon, and that point is in continual motion. Such are the symptoms of sudden revolutions, and of the misfortunes that are sure to befall those generations which abruptly adopt the unconditional freedom of the press.

The circle of novel ideas is, however, soon terminated; the torch of experience is upon them, and the doubt and mistrust which their uncertainty produces, become universal. We may rest assured that the majority of mankind will either believe they know not wherefore, or will not know what to believe. Few are the beings who can ever hope to attain that state of rational and independent conviction which true knowledge can beget, in defiance of the attacks of doubt.

It has been remarked that in times of great religious fervor, men sometimes change their religious opinions; whereas, in times of general skepticism every one clings to his own persuasion. The same thing takes place in politics under the liberty of the press. In countries where all the theories of social science have been contested in their turn, the citizens who have adopted one of them, stick to it, not so much because they are assured of its excellence, as because they are not convinced of the superiority of any other. In the present age men are not very ready to die in defence of their opinions, but they are rarely inclined to change them; and there are fewer martyrs as well as fewer apostates.

Another still more valid reason may yet be adduced: when no abstract opinions are looked upon as certain, men cling to the mere propensities and external interests of their position, which are naturally more tangible and more permanent than any opinions in the world.

It is not a question of easy solution whether the aristocracy or the democracy is most fit to govern a country. But it is certain that democracy annoys one part of the community, and that aristocracy oppresses another part. When the question is reduced to the simple expression of the struggle between poverty and wealth, the tendency of each side of the dispute becomes perfectly evident without farther controversy.

Chapter XII.

POLITICAL ASSOCIATIONS IN THE UNITED STATES.

Daily use which the Anglo-Americans make of the Right of Association.—Three kinds of political Association.—In what Manner the Americans apply the representative System to Association.—Dangers resulting to the State.—Great Convention of 1831 relative to the Tariff. Legislative Character of this Convention. Why the unlimited Exercise of the Right of Association is less dangerous in the United States than elsewhere. Why it may be looked upon as necessary. Utility of Associations in a democratic People.

In no country in the world has the principle of association been more successfully used, or more unsparingly applied to a multitude of different objects, than in America. Beside the permanent associations which are established by law under the names of townships, cities, and counties, a vast number of others are formed and maintained by the agency of private individuals.

The citizen of the United States is taught from his earliest infancy to rely upon his own exertions, in order to resist the evils and the difficulties of life; he looks upon the social authority with an eye of mistrust and anxiety, and he only claims its assistance when he is quite unable to shift without it. This habit may even be traced in the schools of the rising generation, where the children in their games are wont to submit to rules which they have themselves established, and to punish misdemeanors which they have themselves defined. The same spirit pervades every act of social life. If a stoppage occurs in a thoroughfare, and the circulation of the public is hindered, the neighbours immediately constitute a deliberative body; and this extemporaneous assembly gives rise to an executive power, which remedies the inconvenience, before anybody has thought of recurring to an authority superior to that of the persons immediately concerned. If the public pleasures are concerned, an association is formed to provide for the splendour and the regularity of the entertainment. Societies are formed to resist enemies which are exclusively of a moral nature, and to diminish the vice of intemperance: in the United States associations are established to promote public order, commerce, industry, morality, and religion; for there is no end which the human will, seconded by the collective exertions of individuals, despairs of attaining.

I shall hereafter have occasion to show the effects of association upon the course of society, and I must confine myself for the present to the political world. When once the right of association is recognized, the citizens may employ it in several different ways.

An association consists simply in the public assent which a number of individuals give to certain doctrines; and in the engagement which they contract to promote the spread of those doctrines by their exertions. The right of associating with these views is very analogous to the liberty of unlicensed writing; but societies thus formed possess more authority than the press. When an opinion is represented by a society, it necessarily assumes a more exact and explicit form. It numbers its partisans, and compromises their welfare in its cause; they, on the other hand, become acquainted with each other, and their zeal is increased by their number. An association unites the efforts of minds which have a tendency to diverge, in one single channel, and urges them vigorously toward one single end which it points out.

The second degree in the right of association is the power of meeting. When an association is allowed to establish centres of action at certain important points in the country, its activity is increased, and its influence extended. Men have the opportunity of seeing each other; means of execution are more readily combined; and opinions are maintained with a degree of warmth and energy which written language cannot approach.

Lastly, in the exercise of the right of political association, there is a third degree: the partisans of an opinion may unite in electoral bodies, and choose delegates to represent them in a central assembly. This is, properly speaking, the application of the representative system to a party.

Thus, in the first instance, a society is formed between individuals professing the same opinion, and the tie which keeps it together is of a purely intellectual nature: in the second case, small assemblies are formed which only represent a fraction of the party. Lastly, in the third case, they constitute a separate nation in the midst of the nation, a government within the government. Their delegates, like the real delegates of the majority, represent the entire collective force of their party; and they enjoy a certain degree of that national dignity and great influence which belong to the chosen representatives of the people. It is true that they have not the right of making the laws; but they have the power of attacking those which are in being, and of drawing up before hand those which they may afterward cause to be adopted.

If, in a people which is imperfectly accustomed to the exercise of freedom, or which is exposed to violent political passions, a deliberating minority, which confines itself to the contemplation of future laws, be placed in juxtaposition to the legislative majority, I cannot but believe that public tranquility incurs very great risks in that nation. There is doubtless a very wide difference between proving that one law is in itself better than another, and proving that the former ought to be substituted for the latter. But the imagination of the populace is very apt to overlook this difference, which is so apparent in the minds of thinking men. It sometimes happens that a nation is divided into two nearly equal parties, each of which affects to represent the majority. If, in immediate contiguity to the directing power, another power be established, which exercises almost as much moral authority as the former, it is not to be believed that it will long be content to speak without acting; or that it will always be restrained by the abstract consideration of the nature of associations, which are meant to direct, but not to enforce opinions, to suggest but not to make the laws.

The more we consider the independence of the press in its principal consequences, the more are we convinced that it is the chief, and, so to speak, the constitutive element of freedom in the modern world. A nation which is determined to remain free, is therefore right in demanding the unrestrained exercise of this independence. But the *unrestrained* liberty of political association cannot be entirely assimilated to the liberty of the press. The one is at the same time less necessary and more dangerous than the other. A nation may confine it within certain limits without forfeiting any part of its self-control; and it may sometimes be obliged to do so in order to maintain its own authority.

In America the liberty of association for political purposes is unbounded. An example will show in the clearest light to what an extent this privilege is tolerated.

The question of the tariff, or of free trade, produced a great manifestation of party feeling in America; the tariff was not only a subject of debate as a matter of opinion, but it exercised a favourable or a prejudicial influence upon several very powerful interests of the states. The north attributed a great portion of its prosperity, and the south all its sufferings, to this system. Insomuch, that for a long time the tariff was the sole source of the political animosities which agitated the union.

In 1831, when the dispute was raging with the utmost virulence, a private citizen of Massachusetts proposed to all the enemies of the tariff, by means of the public prints, to send delegates to Philadelphia in order to consult together upon the means which were most fitted to promote the freedom of trade. This proposal circulated in a few days from Maine to New Orleans by the power of the printing press: the opponents of the tariff adopted it with enthusiasm; meetings were formed on all sides, and delegates were named. The majority of these individuals were well known, and some of them had earned a considerable degree of celebrity. South Carolina alone, which afterward took up arms in the same cause, sent sixty-three delegates. On the 1st October, 1831, this assembly, which, according to the American custom, had taken the name of a convention, met at Philadelphia; it consisted of more than two hundred members. Its debates were public, and they at once assumed a legislative character; the extent of the powers of congress, the theories of free trade, and the different clauses of the tariff, were discussed in turn. At the end of ten days' deliberation the convention broke up, after having published an address to the American people, in which it is declared:—

I. That congress had not the right of making a tariff, and that the existing tariff was unconstitutional;

II. That the prohibition of free trade was prejudicial to the interests of all nations, and to that of the American people in particular.

It must be acknowledged that the unrestrained liberty of political association has not hitherto produced, in the United States, those fatal consequences which might perhaps be expected from it elsewhere. The right of association was imported from England, and it has always existed in America. So that the exercise of this privilege is now amalgamated with the manners and customs of the people. At the present time, the liberty of association is become a necessary guarantee against the tyranny of the majority. In the United States, as soon as a party has become preponderant, all the public authority passes under its control; its private supporters occupy all the places, and have all the force of the administration at their disposal. As the most distinguished partisans of the other side of the question are unable to surmount the obstacles which exclude them from power, they require some means of establishing themselves upon their own basis, and of opposing the moral authority of the minority to the physical power which domineers over it. Thus, a dangerous expedient is used to obviate a still more formidable danger.

The omnipotence of the majority appears to me to present such extreme perils to the American republics, that the dangerous measure which is used to repress it, seems to be more advantageous than prejudicial. And here I am about to advance a proposition which may remind the reader of what I said before in speaking of municipal freedom. There are no countries in which associations are more needed, to prevent the despotism of faction, or the arbitrary power of a prince, than those which are democratically constituted. In aristocratic nations, the body of the nobles and the more opulent part of the community are in themselves natural associations, which act as checks upon the abuses of power. In countries in which those associations do not exist, if private individuals are unable to create an artificial and a temporary substitute for them, I can imagine no permanent protection against the most galling tyranny; and a great people may be oppressed by a small faction, or by a single individual, with impunity.

The meeting of a great political convention, (for there are conventions of all kinds), which may frequently become a necessary measure, is always a serious occurrence, even in America, and one which is never looked forward to by the judicious friends of the country, without alarm. This was very perceptible in the convention of 1831, at which the exertions of all the most distinguished members of the assembly tended to moderate its language, and to restrain the subjects which it treated within certain limits. It is probable, in fact, that the convention of 1831 exercised a very great influence upon the minds of the malecontents, and prepared them for the open revolt against the commercial laws of the Union, which took place in 1832.

It cannot be denied that the unrestrained liberty of association for political purposes, is the privilege which a people is longest in learning how to exercise. If it does not throw the nation into anarchy, it perpetually augments the chances of that calamity. On one point, however, this perilous liberty offers a security against dangers of another kind; in countries where associations are free, secret societies are unknown. In America there are numerous factions, but no conspiracies.

Different ways in which the Right of Association is understood in Europe and in the United States.—Different use which is made of it.

The most natural privilege of man, next to the right of acting for himself, is that of combining his exertions with those of his fellow-creatures, and of acting in common with them. I am therefore led to conclude, that the right of association is almost as inalienable as the right of personal liberty. No legislator can attack it without impairing the very foundations of society. Nevertheless, if the liberty of association is a fruitful source of advantages and prosperity to some nations, it may be perverted or carried to excess by others, and the element of life may be changed into an element of destruction. A comparison of the different methods which associations pursue, in those countries in which they are managed with discretion, as well as in those where liberty degenerates into license, may perhaps be thought useful both to governments and to parties. The greater part of Europeans look upon an association as a weapon which is to be hastily fashioned, and immediately tried in the conflict. A society is formed for discussion, but the idea of impending action prevails in the minds of those who constitute it: it is, in fact, an army; and the time given to parley, serves to reckon up the strength and to animate the courage of the host, after which they direct their march against the enemy. Resources which lie within the bounds of the law may suggest themselves to the persons who compose it, as means, but never as the only means, of success.

Such, however, is not the manner in which the right of association is understood in the United States. In America, the citizens who form the minority associate, in order, in the first place, to show their numerical strength, and so to diminish the moral authority of the majority; and, in the second place, to stimulate competition, and to discover those arguments which are most fitted to act upon the majority; for they always entertain hopes of drawing over their opponents to their own side, and of afterward disposing of the supreme power in their name. Political associations in the United States are therefore peaceable in their intentions, and strictly legal in the means which they employ; and they assert with perfect truth, that they only aim at success by lawful expedients.

The difference which exists between the Americans and ourselves depends on several causes. In Europe there are numerous parties so diametrically opposed to the majority, that they can never hope to acquire its support, and at the same time they think that they are sufficiently strong in themselves to struggle and to defend their cause. When a party of this kind forms an association, its object is, not to conquer, but to fight. In America, the individuals who hold opinions very much opposed to those of the majority, are no sort of impediment to its power; and all other parties hope to win it over to their own principles in the end. The exercise of the right of association becomes dangerous in proportion to the impossibility which excludes great parties from acquiring the majority. In a country like the United States, in which the differences of opinion are mere differences of hue, the right of association may remain unrestrained without evil consequences. The inexperience of many of the European nations in the enjoyment of liberty, leads them only to look upon the liberty of association as a right of attacking the government. The first notion which presents itself to a party, as well as to an individual, when it has acquired a consciousness of its own strength, is that of violence: the notion of persuasion arises at a later period, and is only derived from experience. The English, who are divided into parties which differ most essentially from each other, rarely abuse the right of association, because they have long been accustomed to exercise it. In France, the passion for war is so intense that there is no undertaking so mad, or so injurious to the welfare of the state, that a man does not consider himself honoured in defending it, at the risk of his life.

But perhaps the most powerful of the causes which tend to mitigate the excesses of political association in the United States is universal suffrage. In countries in which universal suffrage exists, the majority is never doubtful, because neither party can pretend to represent that portion of the community which has not voted. The associations which are formed are aware, as well as the nation at large, that they do not represent the majority: this is, indeed, a condition inseparable from their existence; for if they did represent the preponderating power, they would change the law instead of soliciting its reform. The consequence of this is, that the moral influence of the government which they attack is very much increased, and their own power is very much enfeebled.

In Europe there are few associations which do not affect to represent the majority, or which do not believe that they represent it. This conviction or this pretension tends to augment their force amazingly, and contributes no less to legalize their measures. Violence may seem to be excusable in defence of the cause of oppressed right. Thus it is, in the vast labyrinth of human laws, that extreme liberty sometimes corrects abuses of license, and that extreme democracy obviates the dangers of democratic government. In Europe, associations consider themselves, in some degree, as the legislative and executive councils of the people, which is unable to speak for itself. In America, where they only represent a minority of the nation, they argue and they petition.

The means which the associations of Europe employ, are in accordance with the end which they propose to obtain. As the principal aim of these bodies is to act, and not to debate, to fight rather than to persuade, they are naturally led to adopt a form of organization which differs from the ordinary customs of civil bodies, and which assumes the habits and the maxims of military life. They centralize the direction of their resources as much as possible, and they intrust the power of the whole party to a very small number of leaders.

The members of these associations reply to a watchword, like soldiers on duty: they profess the doctrine of passive obedience; say rather, that in uniting together they at once abjure the exercise of their own judgment and free will; and the tyrannical control, which these societies exercise, is often far more insupportable than the authority possessed over society by the government which they attack. Their moral force is much diminished by these excesses, and they lose the powerful interest which is always excited by a struggle between oppressors and the oppressed. The man who in given cases consents to obey his fellows with servility, and who submits his activity, and even his opinions, to their control, can have no claim to rank as a free citizen.

The Americans have also established certain forms of government which are applied to their associations, but these are invariably borrowed from the forms of the civil administration. The independence of each individual is formally recognised; the tendency of the members of the association points, as it does in the body of the community, toward the same end, but they are not obliged to follow the same track. No one abjures the exercise of his reason and his free will; but every one exerts that reason and that will for the benefit of a common undertaking.

Chapter XIII.

GOVERNMENT OF THE DEMOCRACY IN AMERICA.

I am well aware of the difficulties which attend this part of my subject; but although every expression which I am about to make use of may clash, upon some one point, with the feelings of the different parties which divide my country, I shall speak my opinion with the most perfect openness.

In Europe we are at a loss how to judge the true character and the more permanent propensities of democracy, because in Europe two conflicting principles exist, and we do not know what to attribute to the principles themselves, and what to refer to the passions which they bring into collision. Such, however, is not the case in America; there the people reigns without any obstacle, and it has no perils to dread, and no injuries to avenge. In America, democracy is swayed by its own free propensities; its course is natural, and its activity is unrestrained: the United States consequently afford the most favourable opportunity of studying its real character. And to no people can this inquiry be more vitally interesting than to the French nation, which is blindly driven onward by a daily and irresistible impulse, toward a state of things which may prove either despotic or republican, but which will assuredly be democratic.

UNIVERSAL SUFFRAGE.

I have already observed that universal suffrage has been adopted in all the states of the Union: it consequently occurs among different populations which occupy very different positions in the scale of society. I have had opportunities of observing its effects in different localities, and among races of men who are nearly strangers to each other by their language, their religion, and their manner of life; in Louisiana as well as in New England, in Georgia and in Canada. I have remarked that universal suffrage is far from producing in America either all the good or all the evil consequences which are assigned to it in Europe, and that its effects differ very widely from those which are usually attributed to it.

CHOICE OF THE PEOPLE, AND INSTINCTIVE PREFERENCES OF THE AMERICAN DEMOCRACY.

In the United States the most talented Individuals are rarely placed at the Head of Affairs.—Reasons of this Peculiarity.—The Envy which prevails in the lower Orders of France against the higher Classes, is not a French, but a purely democratic Sentiment.—For what Reason the most distinguished Men in America frequently seclude themselves from public Affairs.

Many people in Europe are apt to believe without saying it, or to say without believing it, that one of the great advantages of universal suffrage is, that it intrusts the direction of public affairs to men who are worthy of the public confidence. They admit that the people is unable to govern for itself, but they aver that it is always sincerely disposed to promote the welfare of the state, and that it instinctively designates those persons who are animated by the same good wishes, and who are the most fit to wield the supreme authority. I confess that the observations I made in America by no means coincide with these opinions. On my arrival in the United States I was surprised to find so much distinguished talent among the subjects, and so little among the heads of the government. It is a well-authenticated fact, that at the present day the most talented men in the United States are very rarely placed at the head of affairs; and it must be acknowledged that such has been the result, in proportion as democracy has outstepped all its former limits. The race of American statesmen has evidently dwindled most remarkably in the course of the last fifty years.

Several causes may be assigned to this phenomenon. It is impossible, notwithstanding the most strenuous exertions, to raise the intelligence of the people above a certain level. Whatever may be the facilities of acquiring information, whatever may be the profusion of easy methods and of cheap science, the human mind can never be instructed and educated without devoting a considerable space of time to those objects.

The greater or the lesser possibility of subsisting without labour is therefore the necessary boundary of intellectual improvement. This boundary is more remote in some countries, and more restricted in others; but it must exist somewhere as long as the people is constrained to work in order to procure the means of physical subsistence, that is to say, as long as it retains its popular character. It is therefore quite as difficult to imagine a state in which all the citizens should be very well-informed, as a state in which they should all be wealthy; these two difficulties may be looked upon as correlative. It may very readily be admitted that the mass of the citizens are sincerely disposed to promote the welfare of their country; nay more, it may even be allowed that the lower classes are less apt to be swayed by considerations of personal interest than the higher orders; but it is always more or less impossible for them to discern the best means of attaining the end, which they desire with sincerity. Long and patient observation, joined to a multitude of different notions, is required to form a just estimate of the character of a single individual; and can it be supposed that the vulgar have the power of succeeding in an inquiry which misleads the penetration of genius itself? The people has neither the time nor the means which are essential to the prosecution of an investigation of this kind; its conclusions are hastily formed from a superficial inspection of the more prominent features of a question. Hence it often assents to the clamour of a mountebank, who knows the secret of stimulating its tastes; while its truest friends frequently fail in their exertions.

Moreover, the democracy is not only deficient in that soundness of judgment which is necessary to select men really deserving of its confidence, but it has neither the desire nor the inclination to find them out. It cannot be denied that democratic institutions have a very strong tendency to promote the feeling of envy in the human heart; not so much because they afford to every one the means of rising to the level of any of his fellow-citizens, as because those means perpetually disappoint the persons who employ them. Democratic institutions awaken and foster a passion for equality which they can never entirely satisfy. This complete equality eludes the grasp of the people at the very moment when it thinks to hold it fast, and "flies," as Pascal says, "with eternal flight;" the people is excited in the pursuit of an advantage, which is the more precious because it is not sufficiently remote to be unknown, or sufficiently near to be enjoyed. The lower orders are agitated by the chance of success, they are irritated by its uncertainty; and they pass from the enthusiasm of pursuit to the exhaustion of ill-success, and lastly to the acrimony of disappointment. Whatever transcends their own limits appears to be an obstacle to their desires, and there is no kind of superiority, however legitimate it may be, which is not irksome in their sight.

It has been supposed that the secret instinct, which leads the lower orders to remove their superiors as much as possible from the direction of public affairs, is peculiar to France. This, however, is an error; the propensity to which I allude is not inherent in any particular nation, but in democratic institutions in general; and although it may have been heightened by peculiar political circumstances, it owes its origin to a higher cause.

In the United States, the people is not disposed to hate the superior classes of society; but it is not very favourably inclined toward them, and it carefully excludes them from the exercise of authority. It does not entertain any dread of distinguished talents, but it is rarely captivated by them; and it awards its approbation very sparingly to such as have risen without the popular support.

While the natural propensities of democracy induce the people to reject the most distinguished citizens as its rulers, these individuals are no less apt to retire from a political career, in which it is almost impossible to retain their independence, or to advance without degrading themselves. This opinion has been very candidly set forth by Chancellor Kent,[1] who says, in speaking with great eulogium of that part of the constitution which empowers the executive to nominate the judges: "It is indeed probable that the men who are best fitted to discharge the duties of this high office would have too much reserve in their manners, and too much austerity in their principles, for them to be returned by the majority at an election where universal suffrage is adopted." Such were the opinions which were printed without contradiction in America in the year 1830!

I hold it to be sufficiently demonstrated, that universal suffrage is by no means a guarantee of the wisdom of the popular choice; and that whatever its advantages may be, this is not one of them.

CAUSES WHICH MAY PARTLY CORRECT THESE TENDENCIES OF THE
DEMOCRACY.

Contrary Effects produced on Peoples as well as on Individuals by great Dangers.—
Why so many distinguished Men stood at the Head of Affairs in America fifty
Years ago.—Influence which the Intelligence and the Manners of the People ex-
ercise upon its Choice.—Example of New England.—States of the Southwest.[2]—
Influence of certain Laws upon the Choice of the People.—Election by an
elected Body.—Its Effects upon the Composition of the Senate.

When a state is threatened by serious dangers, the people frequently succeeds in selecting the citizens who are the most able to
save it. It has been observed that man rarely retains his customary
level in presence of very critical circumstances; he rises above, or he
sinks below, his usual condition, and the same thing occurs in nations
at large. Extreme perils sometimes quench the energy of a people instead of stimulating it; they excite without directing its passions; and
instead of clearing, they confuse its powers of perception. The Jews
deluged the smoking ruins of their temple with the carnage of the
remnant of their host. But it is more common, both in the case of nations and in that of individuals, to find extraordinary virtues arising
from the very imminence of the danger. Great characters are then
thrown into relief, as the edifices which are concealed by the gloom of
night, are illuminated by the glare of a conflagration. At those dangerous times genius no longer abstains from presenting itself in the
arena; and the people, alarmed by the perils of its situation, buries its
envious passions in a short oblivion. Great names may then be drawn
from the urn of an election.

I have already observed that the American statesmen of the present
day are very inferior to those who stood at the head of affairs fifty
years ago. This is as much a consequence of the circumstances, as of
the laws of the country. When America was struggling in the high
cause of independence to throw off the yoke of another country, and
when it was about to usher a new nation into the world, the spirits of
its inhabitants were roused to the height which their great efforts required. In this general excitement, the most distinguished men were
ready to forestall the wants of the community, and the people clung to
them for support, and placed them at its head. But events of this magnitude are rare; and it is from an inspection of the ordinary course of
affairs that our judgement must be formed.

If passing occurrences sometimes act as checks upon the passions
of democracy, the intelligence and the manners of the community exercise an influence which is not less powerful, and far more permanent. This is extremely perceptible in the United States.

In New England the education and the liberties of the communities
were engendered by the moral and religious principles of their
founders. Where society has acquired a sufficient degree of stability to
enable it to hold certain maxims and to retain fixed habits, the lower
orders are accustomed to respect intellectual superiority, and to submit to it without complaint, although they set at nought all those priv-

ileges which wealth and birth have introduced among mankind. The democracy in New England consequently makes a more judicious choice than it does elsewhere.

But as we descend toward the south, to those states in which the constitution of society is more modern and less strong, where instruction is less general, and where the principles of morality, of religion, and of liberty, are less happily combined, we perceive that the talents and the virtues of those who are in authority become more and more rare.

Lastly, when we arrive at the new southwestern states, in which the constitution of society dates but from yesterday, and presents an agglomeration of adventurers and speculators, we are amazed at the persons who are invested with public authority, and we are led to ask by what force, independent of the legislation and of the men who direct it, the state can be protected, and society be made to flourish.

There are certain laws of a democratic nature which contribute, nevertheless, to correct, in some measure, the dangerous tendencies of democracy. On entering the house of representatives at Washington, one is struck by the vulgar demeanour of that great assembly. The eye frequently does not discover a man of celebrity within its walls. Its members are almost all obscure individuals, whose names present no associations to the mind: they are mostly village-lawyers, men in trade, or even persons belonging to the lower classes of society. In a country in which education is very general, it is said that the representatives of the people do not always know how to write correctly.

At a few yards' distance from this spot is the door of the senate, which contains within a small space a large proportion of the celebrated men of America. Scarcely an individual is to be perceived in it who does not recall the idea of an active and illustrious career: the senate is composed of eloquent advocates, distinguished generals, wise magistrates, and statesmen of note, whose language would at all times do honour to the most remarkable parliamentary debates of Europe.

What then is the cause of this strange contrast, and why are the most able citizens to be found in one assembly rather than in the other? Why is the former body remarkable for its vulgarity and its poverty of talent, while the latter seems to enjoy a monopoly of intelligence and of sound judgement? Both of these assemblies emanate from the people; both of them are chosen by universal suffrage; and no voice has hitherto been heard to assert, in America, that the senate is hostile to the interests of the people. From what cause, then, does so startling a difference arise? The only reason which appears to me adequately to account for it is, that the house of representatives is elected by the populace directly, and that of the senate is elected by elected bodies. The whole body of the citizens names the legislature of each state, and the federal constitution converts these legislatures into so many electoral bodies, which return the members of the senate. The senators are elected by an indirect application of universal suffrage; for the legislatures which name them are not aristocratic or privileged bodies which exercise the electoral franchise in their own right; but they are chosen by the totality of the citizens; they are generally elected every year, and new members may constantly be chosen, who will employ their electoral rights in conformity with the wishes of the public. But this transmission of the popular authority through an assembly of chosen men, operates an important change in it, by refining its discretion and improving the forms which it adopts. Men who are chosen in this manner, accurately represent the majority of the nation which governs them; but they represent the elevated thoughts which are current in the community, the generous propensities which prompt its nobler actions, rather than the petty passions which disturb, or the vices which disgrace it.

The time may be already anticipated at which the American republics will be obliged to introduce the plan of election by an elected body more frequently into their system of representation, or they will incur no small risk of perishing miserably among the shoals of democracy.

And here I have no scruple in confessing that I look upon this peculiar system of election as the only means of bringing the exercise of political power to the level of all classes of the people. Those thinkers who regard this institution as the exclusive weapon of a party, and those who fear, on the other hand, to make use of it, seem to me to fall into as great an error in the one case as in the other.

INFLUENCE WHICH THE AMERICAN DEMOCRACY HAS EXERCISED ON THE LAWS RELATING TO ELECTIONS.

When Elections are rare, they expose the State to a violent Crisis.—When they are frequent, they keep up a degree of feverish Excitement.—The Americans have preferred the second of these two Evils.—Mutability of the Laws.—Opinions of Hamilton[3] and Jefferson on this Subject.

When elections recur at long intervals, the state is exposed to violent agitation every time they take place. Parties exert themselves to the utmost in order to gain a prize which is so rarely within their reach; and as the evil is almost irremediable for the the candidates who fail, the consequence of their disappointed ambition may prove most disastrous: if, on the other hand, the legal struggle can be repeated within a short space of time, the defeated parties take patience.

When elections occur frequently, this recurrence keeps society in a perpetual state of feverish excitement, and imparts a continual instability to public affairs.

Thus, on the one hand, the state is exposed to the perils of a revolution, on the other, to perpetual mutability; the former system threatens the very existence of the government, the latter is an obstacle to all steady and consistent policy. The Americans have preferred the second of these evils to the first; but they were led to this conclusion by their instinct much more than by their reason; for a taste for variety is one of the characteristic passions of democracy. An extraordinary mutability has, by this means, been introduced into their legislation.

Many of the Americans consider the instability of their laws as a

necessary consequence of a system whose general results are beneficial. But no one in the United States affects to deny the fact of this instability, or to contend that it is not a great evil.

Hamilton, after having demonstrated the utility of a power which
might prevent, or which might at least impede, the promulgation of
bad laws, adds: "It may perhaps be said that the power of preventing
bad laws includes that of preventing good ones, and may be used to
the one purpose as well as to the other. But this objection will have
but little weight with those who can properly estimate the mischiefs of
that inconstancy and mutability in the laws which form the greatest
blemish in the character and genius of our government."—(Federalist,
No. 73.)

And again, in No 62 of the same work, he observes: "The facility
and excess of law-making seem to be the diseases to which our governments are most liable. . . . The mischievous effects of the mutability in
the public councils arising from a rapid succession of new members,
would fill a volume; every new election in the states is found to change
one half of the representatives. From this change of men must proceed a change of opinions and of measures which forfeits the respect
and confidence of other nations, poisons the blessings of liberty itself,
and diminishes the attachment and reverence of the people toward a
political system which betrays so many marks of infirmity."

Jefferson himself, the greatest democrat whom the democracy of
America has as yet produced, pointed out the same evils.

"The instability of our laws," he said in a letter to Madison,[4] "is really a very serious inconvenience. I think we ought to have obviated it
by deciding that a whole year should always be allowed to elapse between the bringing in of a bill and the final passing of it. It should
afterward be discussed and put to the vote without the possibility of
making any alteration in it; and if the circumstances of the case required a more speedy decision, the question should not be decided by
a simple majority, but by a majority of at least two thirds of both
houses."

PUBLIC OFFICERS UNDER THE CONTROL OF THE DEMOCRACY IN AMERICA.

Simple Exterior of the American public Officers.—No official Costume.—All public
Officers are remunerated.—Political Consequences of this System.—No public
Career exists in America.—Result of this.

Public officers in the United States are commingled with the crowd
of citizens; they have neither palaces, nor guards, nor ceremonial costumes. This simple exterior of the persons in authority is connected,
not only with the peculiarities of the American character, but with the
fundamental principles of that society. In the estimation of the democracy, a government is not a benefit, but a necessary evil. A certain degree of power must be granted to public officers, for they would be of
no use without it. But the ostensible semblance of authority is by no
means indispensable to the conduct of affairs; and it is needlessly offensive to the susceptibility of the public. The public officers them-

selves are well aware that they only enjoy the superiority over their fellow-citizens, which they derive from their authority, upon condition of putting themselves on a level with the whole community by their manners. A public officer in the United States is uniformly civil, accessible to all the world, attentive to all requests, and obliging in all his replies. I was pleased by these characteristics of a democratic government; and I was struck by the manly independence of the citizens, who respect the office more than the officer, and who are less attached to the emblems of authority than to the man who bears them.

I am inclined to believe that the influence which costumes really exercise, in an age like that in which we live, has been a good deal exaggerated. I never perceived that a public officer in America was the less respected while he was in the discharge of his duties because his own merit was set off by no adventitious signs. On the other hand, it is very doubtful whether a peculiar dress contributes to the respect which public characters ought to have for their own position, at least when they are not otherwise inclined to respect it. When a magistrate (and in France such instances are not rare), indulges his trivial wit at the expense of a prisoner, or derides a predicament in which a culprit is placed, it would be well to deprive him of his robes of office, to see whether he would recall some portion of the natural dignity of mankind when he is reduced to the apparel of a private citizen.

A democracy may, however, allow a certain show of magisterial pomp, and clothe its officers in silks and gold, without seriously compromising its principles. Privileges of this kind are transitory; they belong to the place, and are distinct from the individual: but if public officers are not uniformly remunerated by the state, the public charges must be intrusted to men of opulence and independence, who constitute the basis of an aristocracy; and if the people still retains its right of election, that election can only be made from a certain class of citizens.

When a democratic republic renders offices which had formerly been remunerated, gratuitous, it may safely be believed that that state is advancing to monarchical institutions; and when a monarchy begins to remunerate such officers as had hitherto been unpaid, it is a sure sign that it is approaching toward a despotic or a republican form of government. The substitution of paid for unpaid functionaries is of itself, in my opinion, sufficient to constitute a serious revolution.

I look upon the entire absence of gratuitous functionaries in America as one of the most prominent signs of the absolute dominion which democracy exercises in that country. All public services, of whatsoever nature they may be, are paid; so that every one has not merely a right, but also the means of performing them. Although, in democratic states, all the citizens are qualified to occupy stations in the government, all are not tempted to try for them. The number and the capacities of the candidates are more apt to restrict the choice of electors than the conditions of the candidateship.

In nations in which the principle of election extends to every place in the state, no political career can, properly speaking, be said to exist.

Men are promoted as if by chance to the rank which they enjoy, and they are by no means sure of retaining it. The consequence is that in tranquil times public functions offer but few lures to ambition. In the United States the persons who engage in the perplexities of political life are individuals of very moderate pretensions. The pursuit of wealth generally diverts men of great talents and of great passions from the pursuit of power; and it very frequently happens that a man does not undertake to direct the fortune of the state until he has discovered his incompetence to conduct his own affairs. The vast number of very ordinary men who occupy public stations is quite as attributable to these causes as to the bad choice of the democracy. In the United States, I am not sure that the people would return the men of superior abilities who might solicit its support, but it is certain that men of this description do not come forward.

ARBITRARY POWER OF MAGISTRATES* UNDER THE RULE OF THE AMERICAN DEMOCRACY.

For what Reason the arbitrary Power of Magistrates is greater in absolute Monarchies and in democratic Republics that it is in limited Monarchies.—Arbitrary Power of the Magistrates in New England.

In two different kinds of government the magistrates exercise a considerable degree of arbitrary power; namely, under the absolute government of a single individual, and under that of a democracy.

This identical result proceeds from causes which are nearly analogous.

In despotic states the fortune of no citizen is secure; and public officers are not more safe than private individuals. The sovereign, who has under his control the lives, the property, and sometimes the honour of the men whom he employs, does not scruple to allow them a great latitude of action, because he is convinced that they will not use it to his prejudice. In despotic states the sovereign is so attached to the exercise of his power, that he dislikes the constraint even of his own regulations; and he is well pleased that his agents should follow a somewhat fortuitous line of conduct, provided he be certain that their actions will never counteract his desires.

In democracies, as the majority has every year the right of depriving the officers whom it has appointed of their power, it has no reason to fear abuse of their authority. As the people is always able to signify its wishes to those who conduct the government, it prefers leaving them to make their own exertions, to prescribing an invariable rule of conduct which would at once fetter their activity and the popular authority.

It may even be observed, on attentive consideration, that under the rule of a democracy the arbitrary power of the magistrate must be still greater than in despotic states. In the latter, the sovereign has the

---

* I here used the word *magistrates* in the widest sense in which it can be taken; I apply it to all the officers to whom the execution of the laws is intrusted.

power of punishing all the faults with which he becomes acquainted, but it would be vain for him to hope to become acquainted with all those which are committed. In the former the sovereign power is not only supreme, but it is universally present. The American functionaries are, in point of fact, much more independent in the sphere of action which the law traces out for them, than any public officer in Europe. Very frequently the object which they are to accomplish is simply pointed out to them, and the choice of the means is left to their own discretion.

In New England, for instance, the selectmen of each township are bound to draw up the list of persons who are to serve on the jury; the only rule which is laid down to guide them in their choice is that they are to select citizens possessing the elective franchise and enjoying a fair reputation.* In France the lives and liberties of the subjects would be thought to be in danger, if a public officer of any kind was intrusted with so formidable a right. In New England, the same magistrates are empowered to post the names of habitual drunkards in public houses, and to prohibit the inhabitants of a town from supplying them with liquor.† A censorial power of this excessive kind would be revolting to the population of the most absolute monarchies; here, however, it is submitted to without difficulty.

Nowhere has so much been left by the law to the arbitrary determination of the magistrate as in democratic republics, because this arbitrary power is unattended by any alarming consequences. It may even be asserted that the freedom of the magistrate increases as the elective franchise is extended, and as the duration of the time of office is shortened. Hence arises the great difficulty which attends the conversion of a democratic republic into a monarchy. The magistrate ceases to be elective, but he retains the rights and the habits of an elected officer, which lead directly to despotism.

It is only in limited monarchies that the law which prescribes the sphere in which public officers are to act, superintends all their measures. The cause of this may be easily detected. In limited monarchies the power is divided between the king and the people, both of whom are interested in the stability of the magistrate. The king does not venture to place the public officers under the control of the people, lest they should be tempted to betray his interests; on the other hand, the people fears lest the magistrates should serve to oppress the liberties of the country, if they were entirely dependant upon the crown: they cannot therefore be said to depend on either the one or the other. The same cause which induces the king and the people to render public officers independent, suggests the necessity of such securities as may prevent their independence from encroaching upon the authority of the former and the liberties of the latter. They consequently agree as to the necessity of restricting the functionary to a line of conduct laid

---

* See the net of 27th February, 1813. General Collection of the Laws of Massachusetts, vol. ii., p. 331. It should be added that the jurors are afterward drawn from these lists by lot.
† See the act of 28th February, 1787. General Collection of the Laws of Massachusetts, vol. i., p. 302.

down beforehand, and they are interested in confining him by certain regulations which he cannot evade.

[The observations respecting the arbitary powers of magistrates are practically among the most erroneous in the work. The author seems to have confounded the idea of magistrates being *independent* with their being arbitrary. Yet he had just before spoken of their dependance on popular election as a reason why there was no apprehension of the abuse of their authority. The independence then to which he alludes must be an immunity from responsibility to any other department. But it is a fundamental principle of our system, that all officers are liable to criminal prosecution "whenever they act partially or oppressively from a malicious or corrupt motive." See 15 Wendell's Reports, 278. That our magistrates are independent when they do not act partially or oppressively is very true, and it is to be hoped, is equally true in every form of government. There would seem, therefore, not to be such a degree of independence as necessarily to produce arbitrariness. The author supposes that magistrates are more arbitrary in a despotism and in a democracy than in a limited monarchy. And yet, the limits of independence and of responsibility existing in the United States are borrowed from and identical with those established in England—the most prominent instance of a limited monarchy. See the authorities referred to in the case in Wendell's Reports, before quoted. Discretion in the execution of various ministerial duties, and in the awarding of punishment by judicial officers, is indispensable in every system of government, from the utter impossibility of "laying down beforehand a line of conduct" (as the author expresses it) in such cases. The very instances of discretionary power to which he refers, and which he considers *arbitrary*, exist in England. There, the persons from whom juries are to be formed for the trial of causes civil and criminal, are selected by the sheriffs, who are appointed by the crown—a power, certainly more liable to abuse in their hands, than in those of selectmen or other town-officers, chosen annually by the people. The other power referred to, that of posting the names of habitual drunkards, and forbidding their being supplied with liquor, is but a reiteration of the principles contained in the English statute of 32 Geo. III. ch. 45, respecting idle and disorderly persons. Indeed, it may be said with great confidence, that there is not an instance of discretionary power being vested in American magistrates which does not find its prototype in the English laws. The whole argument of the author, on this point therefore, would seem to fail.—*American Editor.*]

INSTABILITY OF THE ADMINISTRATION IN THE UNITED STATES.

In America the public Acts of a Community frequently leave fewer Traces than the Occurrences of a Family—Newspapers the only historical Remains.—Instability of the Administration prejudicial to the Art of Government.

The authority which public men possess in America is so brief, and they are so soon commingled with the ever-changing population of the country, that the acts of a community frequently leave fewer traces than the occurrences of a private family. The public administration is, so to speak, oral and traditionary. But little is committed to writing, and that little is wafted away for ever, like the leaves of the sibyl, by the smallest breeze.

The only historical remains in the United States are the news-papers; but if a number be wanting, the chain of time is broken, and the present is severed from the past. I am convinced that in fifty years it will be more difficult to collect authentic documents concerning the social condition of the Americans at the present day, than it is to find remains of the administration of France during the middle ages; and if the United States were ever invaded by barbarians, it would be neces-sary to have recourse to the history of other nations, in order to learn anything of the people which now inhabits them.

The instability of the administration has penetrated into the habits of the people: it even appears to suit the general taste, and no one cares for what occurred before his time. No methodical system is pur-sued; no archives is formed; and no documents are brought together when it would be very easy to do so. Where they exist little store is set upon them; and I have among my papers several original public docu-ments which were given to me in answer to some of my inquiries. In America society seems to live from hand to mouth, like an army in the field. Nevertheless, the art of administration may undoubtedly be ranked as a science, and no sciences can be improved, if the discover-ies and observations of successive generations are not connected to-gether in the order in which they occur. One man, in the short space of his life, remarks a fact; another conceives an idea; the former in-vents a means of execution, the latter reduces a truth to a fixed propo-sition; and mankind gathers the fruits of individual experience upon its way, and gradually forms the sciences. But the persons who con-duct the administration in America can seldom afford any instruction to each other; and when they assume the direction of society, they simply possess those attainments which are most widely disseminated in the community, and no experience peculiar to themselves. Democ-racy, carried to its farthest limits, is therefore prejudicial to the art of government; and for this reason it is better adapted to a people already versed in the conduct of an administration, than to a nation which is uninitiated in public affairs.

This remark, indeed, is not exclusively applicable to the science of administration. Although a democratic government is founded upon a very simple and natural principle, it always presupposes the existence of a high degree of culture and enlightenment in society.* At the first glance it may be imagined to belong to the earliest ages of the world; but maturer observation will convince us that it could only come last in the succession of human history.

[These remarks upon the "instability of administration" in America, are partly correct, but partly erroneous. It is certainly true that our public men are not educated to the business of government; even our diplomatists are selected with very little reference to their experience in that department. But the universal attention that is paid by the intelligent, to the measures of government and to the discussions to which they give rise, is in itself no

---

* It is needless to observe, that I speak here of the democratic form of government as applied to a people, not merely to a tribe.

slight preparation for the ordinary duties of legislation. And, indeed, this the author subsequently seems to admit. As to there being "no archives formed" of public documents, the author is certainly mistaken. The journals of congress, the journals of state legislatures, the public documents transmitted to and originating in those bodies, are carefully preserved and disseminated through the nation: and they furnish in themselves the materials of a full and accurate history. Our great defect, doubtless, is in the want of statistical information. Excepting the annual reports of the state of our commerce, made by the secretary of the treasury, under a law, and excepting the census which is taken every ten years under the authority of congress, and those taken by the states, we have no official statistics. It is supposed that the author had this species of information in his mind when he alluded to the general deficiency of our archives.—*American Editor.*]

CHARGES LEVIED BY THE STATE UNDER THE RULE OF THE AMERICAN DEMOCRACY.

In all Communities Citizens divisible into three Classes—Habits of each of these Classes in the Direction of public Finances.—Why public Expenditures must tend to increase when the People governs.—What renders the Extravagance of a Democracy less to be feared in America.—Public Expenditure under a Democracy.

Before we can affirm whether a democratic form of government is economical or not, we must establish a suitable standard of comparison. The question would be one of easy solution if we were to attempt to draw a parallel between a democratic republic and an absolute monarchy. The public expenditure would be found to be more considerable under the former than under the latter; such is the case with all free states compared to those which are not so. It is certain that despotism ruins individuals by preventing them from producing wealth, much more than by depriving them of the wealth they have produced: it dries up the source of riches, while it usually respects acquired property. Freedom, on the contrary, engenders far more benefits than it destroys; and the nations which are favoured by free institutions, invariably find that their resources increase even more rapidly than their taxes.

My present object is to compare free nations to each other; and to point out the influence of democracy upon the finances of a state.

Communities, as well as organic bodies, are subject to certain fixed rules in their formation which they cannot evade. They are composed of certain elements which are common to them at all times and under all circumstances. The people may always be mentally divided into three distinct classes. The first of these classes consists of the wealthy; the second, of those who are in easy circumstances; and the third is composed of those who have little or no property, and who subsist more especially by the work which they perform for the two superior orders. The proportion of the individuals who are included in these three divisions may vary according to the condition of society; but the divisions themselves can never be obliterated.

It is evident that each of these classes will exercise an influence, peculiar to its own propensities, upon the administration of the finances of the state. If the first of the three exclusively possesses the legislative power, it is probable that it will not be sparing of the public funds, because the taxes which are levied on a large fortune only tend to diminish the sum of superfluous enjoyment, and are, in point of fact, but little felt. If the second class has the power of making the laws, it will certainly not be lavish of taxes, because nothing is so onerous as a large impost which is levied upon a small income. The government of the middle classes appears to me to be the most economical, though perhaps not the most enlightened, and certainly not the most generous, of free governments.

But let us now suppose that the legislative authority is vested in the lowest orders: there are two striking reasons which show that the tendency of the expenditure will be to increase, not to diminish.

As the great majority of those who create the laws are possessed of no property upon which taxes can be imposed, all the money which is spent for the community appears to be spent to their advantage, at no cost of their own; and those who are possessed of some little property readily find means of regulating the taxes so that they are burdensome to the wealthy and profitable to the poor, although the rich are unable to take the same advantage when they are in possession of the government.

In countries in which the poor* should be exclusively invested with the power of making the laws, no great economy of public expenditure ought to be expected; that expenditure will always be considerable; either because the taxes do not weigh upon those who levy them, or because they are levied in such a manner as not to weigh upon those classes. In other words, the government of the democracy is the only one under which the power which lays on taxes escapes the payment of them.

It may be objected (but the argument has no real weight) that the true interest of the people is indissolubly connected with that of the wealthier portion of the community, since it cannot but suffer by the severe measures to which it resorts. But is it not the true interest of kings to render their subjects happy; and the true interest of nobles to admit recruits into their order on suitable grounds? If remote advantages had power to prevail over the passions and the exigencies of the moment, no such thing as a tyrannical sovereign or an exclusive aristocracy could ever exist.

Again, it may be objected that the poor are never invested with the sole power of making the laws; but I reply, that wherever universal suffrage has been established, the majority of the community unquestionably exercises the legislative authority, and if it be proved that the poor always constitute the majority, it may be added, with perfect truth, that in the countries in which they possess the elective fran-

---

* The word *poor* is used here, and throughout the remainder of this chapter, in a relative and not in an absolute sense. Poor men in America would often appear rich in comparison with the poor of Europe; but they may with propriety be styled poor in comparison with their more affluent countrymen.

chise, they possess the sole power of making laws. But it is certain that in all the nations of the world the greater number has always consisted of those persons who hold no property, or of those whose property is insufficient to exempt them from the necessity of working in order to procure an easy subsistence. Universal suffrage does therefore in point of fact invest the poor with the government of society.

The disastrous influence which popular authority may sometimes exercise upon the finances of a state, was very clearly seen in some of the democratic republics of antiquity, in which the public treasure was exhausted in order to relieve indigent citizens, or to supply the games and theatrical amusements of the populace. It is true that the representative system was then very imperfectly known, and that, at the present time, the influence of popular passions is less felt in the conduct of public affairs; but it may be believed that the delegate will in the end conform to the principles of his constituents, and favour their propensities as much as their interests.

The extravagance of democracy is, however, less to be dreaded in proportion as the people acquires a share of property, because on the one hand the contributions of the rich are then less needed, and on the other, it is more difficult to lay on taxes which do not affect the interests of the lower classes. On this account universal suffrage would be less dangerous in France than in England, because in the latter country the property on which taxes may be levied is vested in fewer hands. America, where the great majority of the citizens is possessed of some fortune, is in a still more favourable position than France.

There are still farther causes which may increase the sum of public expenditures in democratic countries. When the aristocracy governs, the individuals who conduct the affairs of state are exempted, by their own station in society, from every kind of privation: they are contented with their position; power and renown are the objects for which they strive; and, as they are placed far above the obscurer throng of citizens, they do not always distinctly perceive how the wellbeing of the mass of the people ought to redound to their own honour. They are not, indeed, callous to the sufferings of the poor, but they cannot feel those miseries as acutely as if they were themselves partakers of them. Provided that the people appear to submit to its lot, the rulers are satisfied, and they demand nothing farther from the government. An aristocracy is more intent upon the means of maintaining its influence, than upon the means of improving its condition.

When, on the contrary, the people is invested with the supreme authority, the perpetual sense of their own miseries impels the rulers of society to seek for perpetual meliorations. A thousand different objects are subjected to improvement; the most trivial details are sought out as susceptible of amendment; and those changes which are accompanied with considerable expense, are more especially advocated, since the object is to render the condition of the poor more tolerable, who cannot pay for themselves.

Moreover, all democratic communities are agitated by an ill-defined excitement, and by a kind of feverish impatience, that engenders a multitude of innovations, almost all of which are attended with expense.

In monarchies and aristocracies, the natural taste which the rulers have for power and for renown, is stimulated by the promptings of ambition, and they are frequently incited by these temptations to very costly undertakings. In democracies, where the rulers labour under privations, they can only be courted by such means as improve their wellbeing, and these improvements cannot take place without a sacrifice of money. When a people begins to reflect upon its situation, it discovers a multitude of wants to which it had not before been subject, and to satisfy these exigencies, recourse must be had to the coffers of the state. Hence it arises, that the public charges increase in proportion as civilization spreads, and that the imposts are augmented as knowledge pervades the community.

The last cause which frequently renders a democratic government dearer than any other is, that a democracy does not always succeed in moderating its expenditure, because it does not understand the art of being economical. As the designs which it entertains are frequently changed, and the agents of those designs are more frequently removed, its undertakings are often ill-conducted or left unfinished: in the former case the state spends sums out of all proportion to the end which it proposes to accomplish; in the second, the expense itself is unprofitable.

TENDENCIES OF THE AMERICAN DEMOCRACY AS REGARDS THE SALARIES OF PUBLIC OFFICERS.

In Democracies those who establish high Salaries have no Chance of profiting by them.—Tendency of the American Democracy to increase the Salaries of subordinate Officers, and to lower those of the more important Functionaries.— Reason of this.—Comparative Statement of the Salaries of public Officers in the United States and in France.

There is a powerful reason which usually induces democracies to economize upon the salaries of public officers. As the number of citizens who dispense the remuneration is extremely large in democratic countries, so the number of persons who can hope to be benefited by the receipt of it is comparatively small. In aristocratic countries, on the contrary, the individuals who appoint high salaries, have almost always a vague hope of profiting by them. These appointments may be looked upon as a capital which they create for their own use, or at least, as a resource for their children.

It must, however, be allowed that a democratic state is most parsimonious toward its principal agents. In America the secondary officers are much better paid, and the dignitaries of the administration much worse than they are elsewhere.

These opposite effects result from the same cause: the people fixes the salaries of the public officers in both cases; and the scale of remuneration is determined by the consideration of its own wants. It is held to be fair that the servants of the public should be placed in the same easy circumstances as the public itself;* but when the question turns upon the salaries of the great officers of state, this rule fails, and chance alone can guide the popular decision. The poor have no adequate conceptions of the wants which the higher classes of society may feel. The sum which is scanty to the rich, appears enormous to the poor man, whose wants do not extend beyond the necessaries of life: and in his estimation the governor of a state, with his two or three hundred a year, is a very fortunate and enviable being.† If you undertake to convince him that the representative of a great people ought to be able to maintain some show of splendour in the eyes of foreign nations, he will perhaps assent to your meaning; but when he reflects on his own humble dwelling, and on the hard-earned produce of his wearisome toil, he remembers all that he could do with a salary which you say is insufficient, and he is startled or almost frightened at the sight of such uncommon wealth. Besides, the secondary public officer is almost on a level with the people, while the others are raised above it. The former may therefore excite his interest, but the latter begins to arouse his envy.

This is very clearly seen in the United States, where the salaries seem to decrease as the authority of those who receive them augments.‡

Under the rule of an aristocracy it frequently happens, on the contrary, that while the high officers are receiving munificent salaries, the inferior ones have not more than enough to procure the necessaries of life. The reason of this fact is easily discoverable from causes very analogous to those to which I have just alluded. If a democracy is unable to conceive the pleasures of the rich, or to see them without envy, an aristocracy is slow to understand, or, to speak more correctly, is unacquainted with the privations of the poor. The poor man is not (if we

---

* The easy circumstances in which secondary functionaries are placed in the United States, result also from another cause, which is independent of the general tendencies of democracy: every kind of private business is very lucrative, and the state would not be served at all if it did not pay its servants. The country is in the position of a commercial undertaking, which is obliged to sustain an expensive competition, notwithstanding its taste for economy.
† The state of Ohio, which contains a million of inhabitants, gives its governor a salary of only $1,200 (260*l*) a year.
‡ To render this assertion perfectly evident, it will suffice to examine the scale of salaries of the agents of the federal government. I have added the salaries attached to the corresponding officers in France, to complete the comparison:—

UNITED STATES. Treasury Department.		FRANCE. Ministère des Finances.	
Messenger . . . .$ 700	150*l*.	Huissier, 1,500 fr. . . . . .60*l*.	
Clerk with lowest salary . .1,000	217	Clerk with lowest salary, 1,000 to 1,800 fr. . . . . .40 to 72	
Clerk with highest salary . .1,600	347	Clerk with highest salary, 3,200 to 3,600 fr. . . . . . .128 to 144	
Chief clerk 2,000	434	Secrétaire-general, 20,000 fr. 800	
Secretary of state 6,000	1,300	The minister, 80,000 fr. 3,200	
The president 25,000	5,400	The king, 12,000,000 fr. 480,000	

I have perhaps done wrong in selecting France as my standard of comparison. In France the democratic tendencies of the nation exercise an ever-increasing influence upon the government, and the chambers show a disposition to raise the lowest salaries and to lower the principal ones. Thus the minister of finance, who received 160,000 fr. under the empire, receives 80,000 fr., in 1835; the directeurs-généraux of finance, who then received 50,000 fr. now receive only 20,000 fr.

use the term aright) the fellow of the rich one; but he is a being of another species. An aristocracy is therefore apt to care but little for the fate of its subordinate agents: and their salaries are only raised when they refuse to perform their service for too scanty a remuneration.

It is the parsimonious conduct of democracy toward its principal officers, which has countenanced a supposition of far more economical propensities than any which it really possesses. It is true that it scarcely allows the means of honorable subsistence to the individuals who conduct its affairs; but enormous sums are lavished to meet the exigencies or to facilitate the enjoyments of the people.* The money raised by taxation may be better employed, but it is not saved. In general, democracy gives largely to the community, and very sparingly to those who govern it. The reverse is the case in the aristocratic countries, where the money of the state is expended to the profit of the persons who are at the head of affairs.

DIFFICULTY OF DISTINGUISHING THE CAUSES WHICH CONTRIBUTE TO THE ECONOMY OF THE AMERICAN GOVERNMENT.

We are liable to frequent errors in the research of those facts which exercise a serious influence upon the fate of mankind, since nothing is more difficult than to appreciate their real value. One people is naturally inconsistent and enthusiastic; another is sober and calculating; and these characteristics originate in their physical constitution, or in remote causes with which we are unacquainted.

There are nations which are fond of parade and the bustle of festivity, and which do not regret the costly gayeties of an hour. Others, on the contrary, are attached to more retiring pleasures, and seem almost ashamed of appearing to be pleased. In some countries the highest value is set upon the beauty of public edifices; in others the productions of art are treated with indifference, and everything which is unproductive is looked down upon with contempt. In some renown, in others money, is the ruling passion.

Independently of the laws, all these causes concur to exercise a very powerful influence upon the conduct of the finances of the state. If the Americans never spend the money of the people in galas, it is not only because the imposition of taxes is under the control of the people, but because the people takes no delight in public rejoicings. If they repudiate all ornament from their architecture, and set no store on any but the more practical and homely advantages, it is not only because they live under democratic institutions, but because they are a commercial nation. The habits of private life are continued in public; and we ought carefully to distinguish that economy which depends

---

* See the American budgets for the cost of indigent citizens and gratuitous instruction. In 1831, 50,000*l*. were spent in the state of New York for the maintenance of the poor; and at least 200,000*l*. were devoted to gratuitous instruction. (Williams's New York Annual Register, 1832, pp. 205, 243.) The state of New York contained only 1,900,000 inhabitants in the year 1830; which is not more than double the amount of population in the department du Nord in France.

upon their institutions, from that which is the natural result of their manners and customs.

WHETHER THE EXPENDITURE OF THE UNITED STATES CAN BE COMPARED TO THAT OF FRANCE.

Two Points to be established in order to estimate the Extent of the public Charges, viz: the national Wealth, and the Rate of Taxation.—The Wealth and the Charges of France not accurately known.—Why the Wealth and Charges of the Union cannot be accurately known.—Researchers of the Author with a View to discover the Amount of Taxation in Pennsylvania.—General Symptoms which may serve to indicate the Amount of the public Charges in a given Nation.—Result of this Investigation for the Union.

Many attempts have recently been made in France to compare the public expenditure of that country with the expenditure of the United States; all these attempts have, however, been unattended by success; and a few words will suffice to show that they could not have had a satisfactory result.

In order to estimate the amount of the public charges of a people, two preliminaries are indispensable: it is necessary, in the first place, to know the wealth of that people; and in the second, to learn what portion of that wealth is devoted to the expenditure of the state. To show the amount of taxation without showing the resources which are destined to meet the demand, is to undertake a futile labour; for it is not the expenditure, but the relation of the expenditure to the revenue, which it is desirable to know.

The same rate of taxation which may easily be supported by a wealthy contributor, will reduce a poor one to extreme misery. The wealth of nations is composed of several distinct elements, of which population is the first, real property the second, and personal property the third. The first of these three elements may be discovered without difficulty. Among civilized nations it is easy to obtain an accurate census of the inhabitants; but the two others cannot be determined with so much facility. It is difficult to take an exact account of all the lands in a country which are under cultivation, with their natural or their acquired value; and it is still more impossible to estimate the entire personal property which is at the disposal of a nation, and which eludes the strictest analysis by the diversity and number of shapes under which it may occur. And, indeed, we find that the most ancient civilized nations of Europe, including even those in which the administration is most central, have not succeeded, as yet, in determining the exact condition of their wealth.

In America the attempt has never been made; for how would such an investigation be possible in a country where society has not yet settled into habits of regularity and tranquillity; where the national government is not assisted by a multitude of agents whose exertions it can command, and direct to one sole end; and where statistics are not studied, because no one is able to collect the necessary documents, or can find time to peruse them? Thus the primary elements of the calculations which have been made in France, cannot be obtained in the Union; the relative wealth of the two countries is unknown: the property of the former is not accurately determined, and no means exist of computing that of the latter.

I consent therefore, for the sake of the discussion, to abandon this necessary term of the comparison, and I confine myself to a computation of the actual amount of taxation, without investigating the relation which subsists between the taxation and the revenue. But the reader will perceive that my task has not been facilitated by the limits which I here lay down for my researches.

It cannot be doubted that the central administration of France, assisted by all the public officers who are at its disposal, might determine with exactitude the amount of the direct and indirect taxes levied upon the citizens. But this investigation, which no private individual can undertake, has not hitherto been completed by the French government, or, at least, its results have not been made public. We are acquainted with the sum total of the state; we know the amount of the departmental expenditure; but the expenses of the communal divisions have not been computed, and the amount of the public expenses of France is unknown.

If we now turn to America, we shall perceive that the difficulties are multiplied and enhanced. The Union publishes an exact return of the amount of its expenditure; the budgets of the four-and-twenty states furnish similar returns of their revenues; but the expenses incident to the affairs of the counties and the townships are unknown.*

The authority of the federal government cannot oblige the provincial governments to throw any light upon this point; and even if these governments were inclined to afford their simultaneous co-operation, it may be doubted whether they possess the means of procuring a satisfactory answer. Independently of the natural difficulties of the task, the political organization of the country would act as a hinderance to the success of their efforts. The county and town magistrates are not appointed by the authorities of the state, and they are not subjected to their control. It is therefore very allowable to suppose, that if the state

---

* The Americans, as we have seen, have four separate budgets; the Union, the states, the counties, and the townships, having each severally their own. During my stay in America I made every endeavour to discover the amount of the public expenditure in the townships and counties of the principal states of the Union, and I readily obtained the budget of the larger townships, but I found it quite impossible to procure that of the smaller ones. I possess, however, some documents relating to county expenses, which, although incomplete, are still curious. I have to thank Mr. Richards, mayor of Philadelphia, for the budgets of thirteen of the counties of Pennsylvania, viz: Lebanon, Centre, Franklin, Fayette, Montgomery, Luzerne, Dauphin, Butler, Allegany, Columbia, Northampton, Northumberland, and Philadelphia, for the year 1830. Their population at that time consisted of 493,207 inhabitants. On looking at the map of Pennsylvania, it will be seen that these thirteen counties are scattered in every direction, and so generally affected by the causes which usually influence the condition of a country, that they may easily be supposed to furnish a correct average of the financial state of the counties of Pennsylvania in general; and thus, upon reckoning that the expenses of these counties amounted in the year 1830, to about 72,330*l.*, or nearly 3s. for each inhabitant, and calculating that each of them contributed in the same year about *10s. 2d.* toward the Union, and about 3s. to the state of Pennsylvania, it appears that they each contributed as their share of all the public expenses (except those of the townships), the sum of 16s. 2d. This calculation is doubly incomplete, as it applies only to a single year and to one part of the public charges; but it has at least the merit of not being conjectural.

was desirous of obtaining the returns which we require, its designs would be counteracted by the neglect of those subordinate officers whom it would be obliged to employ.* It is, in point of fact, useless to inquire what the Americans might do to forward this inquiry, since it is certain that they have hitherto done nothing at all. There does not exist a single individual at the present day, in America or in Europe, who can inform us what each citizen of the Union annually contributes to the public charges of the nation.†

Hence we must conclude, that it is no less difficult to compare the social expenditure, than it is to estimate the relative wealth of France and of America. I will even add, that it would be dangerous to attempt this comparison; for when statistics are not founded upon computations which are strictly accurate, they mislead instead of guiding aright. The mind is easily imposed upon by the false affectation of exactitude, which prevails even in the mis-statements of the science,

---

* Those who have attempted to draw a comparison between the expenses of France and America, have at once perceived that no such comparison could be drawn between the total expenditure of the two countries; but they have endeavoured to contrast detached portions of this expenditure. It may readily be shown that this second system is not at all less defective than the first.

If I attempt to compare the French budget with the budget of the Union, it must be remembered that the latter embraces much fewer objects than the central government of the former country, and that the expenditure must consequently be much smaller. If I contrast the budgets of the departments to those of the states which constitute the Union, it must be observed, that as the power and control exercised by the states is much greater than that which is exercised by the departments, their expenditure is also more considerable. As for the budgets of the counties, nothing of the kind occurs in the French system of finance; and it is, again, doubtful whether the corresponding expenses should be referred to the budget of the state or to those of the municipal divisions.

Municipal expenses exist in both countries, but they are not always analogous. In America the townships discharge a variety of offices which are reserved in France to the departments or the state. It may, moreover, be asked, what is to be understood by the municipal expenses of America. The organization of the municipal bodies or townships differs in the several states: Are we to be guided by what occurs in New England or in Georgia, in Pennsylvania or in the state of Illinois?

A kind of analogy may very readily be perceived between certain budgets in the two countries; but as the elements of which they are composed always differ more or less, no fair comparison can be instituted between them.

† Even if we knew the exact pecuniary contribution of every French and American citizen to the coffers of the state, we should only come at a portion of the truth. Governments not only demand supplies of money, but they call for personal services, which may be looked upon as equivalent to a given sum. When a state raises an army, beside the pay of the troops which is furnished by the entire nation, each soldier must give up his time, the value of which depends on the use he might make of it if he were not in the service. The same remark applies to the militia: the citizen who is in the militia devotes a certain portion of valuable time to the maintenance of the public peace, and he does in reality surrender to the state those earnings which he is prevented from gaining. Many other instances might be cited in addition to these. The governments of France and America both levy taxes of this kind, which weigh upon the citizens; but who can estimate with accuracy their relative amount in the two countries?

This, however, is not the last of the difficulties which prevent us from comparing the expenditure of the Union with that of France. The French government contracts certain obligations which do not exist in America, and vice versa. The French government pays the clergy; in America the voluntary principle prevails. In America there is a legal provision for the poor; in France they are abandoned to the charity of the public. The French public officers are paid by a fixed salary: in America they are allowed certain perquisites. In France contributions in kind take place on very few roads: in America upon almost all the thoroughfares: in the former country the roads are free to all travellers: in the latter turnpikes abound. All these differences in manner in which contributions are levied in the two countries, enhance the difficulty of comparing their expenditure; for there are certain expenses which the citizens would not be subjected to, or which would at any rate be much less considerable, if the state did not take upon itself to act in the name of the public.

and adopts with confidence the errors which are apparelled in the forms of mathematical truth.

We abandon, therefore, our numerical investigation, with the hope of meeting with data of another kind. In the absence of positive documents, we may form an opinion as to the proportion which the taxation of a people bears to its real prosperity, by observing whether its external appearance is flourishing; whether, after having discharged the calls of the state, the poor man retains the means of subsistence, and the rich the means of enjoyment; and whether both classes are contented with their position, seeking however to meliorate it by perpetual exertions, so that industry is never in want of capital, nor capital unemployed by industry. The observer who draws his inferences from these signs will, undoubtedly, be led to the conclusion, that the American of the United States contributes a much smaller portion of his income to the state than the citizen of France. Nor, indeed, can the result be otherwise.

A portion of the French debt is the consequence of two successive invasions; and the Union has no similar calamity to fear. A nation placed upon the continent of Europe is obliged to maintain a large standing army; the isolated position of the Union enables it to have only 6,000 soldiers. The French have a fleet of 300 sail; the Americans have 52 vessels.* How, then, can the inhabitant of the Union be called upon to contribute as largely as the inhabitant of France? No parallel can be drawn between the finances of two countries so differently situated.

It is by examining what actually takes place in the Union, and not by comparing the Union with France, that we may discover whether the American government is really economical. On casting my eyes over the different republics which form the confederation, I perceive that their governments lack perseverance in their undertakings, and that they exercise no steady control over the men whom they employ. Whence I naturally infer, that they must often spend the money of the people to no purpose, or consume more of it than is really necessary to their undertakings. Great efforts are made, in accordance with the democratic origin of society, to satisfy the exigencies of the lower orders, to open the career of power to their endeavours, and to diffuse knowledge and comfort among them. The poor are maintained, immense sums are annually devoted to public instruction, all services whatsoever are remunerated, and the most subordinate agents are liberally paid. If this kind of government appears to me to be useful and rational, I am nevertheless constrained to admit that it is expensive.

Wherever the poor direct public affairs and dispose of the national resources, it appears certain, that as they profit by the expenditure of the state, they are apt to augment that expenditure.

I conclude therefore, without having recourse to inaccurate computations, and without hazarding a comparison which might prove in-

---

* See the details in the budget of the French minister of marine; and for America, the National Calendar of 1833, v. 228

correct, that the democratic government of the Americans is not a cheap government, as is sometimes asserted: and I have no hesitation in predicting, that if the people of the United States is ever involved in serious difficulties, its taxation will speedily be increased to the rate of that which prevails in the greater part of the aristocracies and the monarchies of Europe.

CORRUPTION AND VICES OF THE RULERS IN A DEMOCRACY, AND CONSEQUENT EFFECTS UPON PUBLIC MORALITY.

In Aristocracies Rulers sometimes endeavour to corrupt the People.—In Democracies Rulers frequently show themselves to be corrupt.—In the former their Vices are directly prejudicial to the Morality of the People.—In the latter their indirect Influence is still more permicious.

A distinction must be made, when the aristocratic and the democratic principles mutually inveigh against each other, as tending to facilitate corruption. In aristocratic governments the individuals who are placed at the head of affairs are rich men, who are solely desirous of power. In democracies statesmen are poor, and they have their fortunes to make. The consequence is, that in aristocratic states the rulers are rarely accessible to corruption, and have very little craving for money; while the reverse is the case in democratic nations.

But in aristocracies, as those who are desirous of arriving at the head of affairs are possessed of considerable wealth, and as the number of persons by whose assistance they may rise is comparatively small, the government is, if I may use the expression, put up to a sort of auction. In democracies, on the contrary, those who are covetous of power are very seldom wealthy, and the number of citizens who confer that power is extremely great. Perhaps in democracies the number of men who might be bought is by no means smaller, but buyers are rarely to be met with; and, besides, it would be necessary to buy so many persons at once, that the attempt is rendered nugatory.

Many of the men who have been in the administration in France during the last forty years, have been accused of making their fortunes at the expense of the state or of its allies; a reproach which was rarely addressed to the public characters of the ancient monarchy. But in France the practice of bribing electors is almost unknown, while it is notoriously and publicly carried on in England. In the United States I never heard a man accused of spending his wealth in corrupting the populace; but I have often heard the probity of public officers questioned; still more frequently have I heard their success attributed to low intrigues and immoral practices.

If, then, the men who conduct the government of an aristocracy sometimes endeavour to corrupt the people, the heads of a democracy are themselves corrupt. In the former case the morality of the people is directly assailed; in the latter, an indirect influence is exercised upon the people, which is still more to be dreaded.

As the rulers of democratic nations are almost always exposed to the suspicion of dishonourable conduct, they in some measure lend the authority of the government to the base practices of which they are accused. They thus afford an example which must prove discouraging to the struggles of virtuous independence, and must foster the secret calculations of a vicious ambition. If it be asserted that evil passions are displayed in all ranks of society; that they ascend the throne by hereditary right; and that despicable characters are to be met with at the head of aristocratic nations as well as in the sphere of a democracy; this objection has but little weight in my estimation. The corruption of men who have casually risen to power has a course and vulgar infection in it, which renders it contagious to the multitude. On the contrary, there is a kind of aristocratic refinement, and an air of grandeur in the depravity of the great, which frequently prevents it from spreading abroad.

The people can never penetrate the perplexing labyrinth of court intrigue, and it will always have difficulty in detecting the turpitude which lurks under elegant manners, refined tastes, and graceful language. But to pillage the public purse, and to vend the favours of the state, are arts which the meanest villain may comprehend, and hope to practice in his turn.

In reality it is far less prejudicial to be a witness to the immorality of the great, than to that immorality which leads to greatness. In a democracy, private citizens see a man of their own rank in life, who rises from that obscure position, and who becomes possessed of riches and of power in a few years: the spectacle excites their surprise and their envy: and they are led to inquire how the person who was yesterday their equal, is to-day their ruler. To attribute his rise to his talents or his virtues is unpleasant; for it is tacitly to acknowledge that they are themselves less virtuous and less talented than he was. They are therefore led (and not unfrequently their conjecture is a correct one), to impute his success mainly to some of his defects; and an odious mixture is thus formed of the ideas of turpitude and power, unworthiness and success, utility and dishonour.

EFFORTS OF WHICH A DEMOCRACY IS CAPABLE.

The Union has only had one struggle hitherto for its Existence.—Enthusiasm at the Commencement of the War.—Indifference toward its Close.—Difficulty of establishing a military Conscription or impressment of Seamen in America.—Why a democratic People is less capable of sustained Effort than another.

I here warn the reader that I speak of a government which implicitly follows the real desires of the people, and not of a government which simply commands in its name. Nothing is so irresistible as a tyrannical power commanding in the name of the people, because, while it exercises that moral influence which belongs to the decisions of the majority, it acts at the same time with the promptitude and the tenacity of a single man.

It is difficult to say what degree of exertion a democratic government may be capable of making, at a crisis in the history of the nation.

But no great democratic republic has hitherto existed in the world. To style the oligarchy which ruled over France in 1793, by that name, would be to offer an insult to the republican form of government. The United States afford the first example of the kind.

The American Union has now subsisted for half a century, in the course of which time its existence has only once been attacked, namely, during the war of independence. At the commencement of that long war, various occurrences took place which betokened an extraordinary zeal for the service of the country.* But as the contest was prolonged, symptoms of private egotism began to show themselves. No money was poured into the public treasury; few recruits could be raised to join the army; the people wished to acquire independence, but was very ill disposed to undergo the privations by which alone it could be obtained. "Tax laws," says Hamilton in the Federalist (No. 12), "have in vain been multiplied; new methods to enforce the collection have in vain been tried; the public expectation has been uniformly disappointed; and the treasuries of the states have remained empty. The popular system of administration inherent in the nature of popular government, coinciding with the real scarcity of money incident to a languid and mutilated state of trade, has hitherto defeated every experiment for extensive collections, and has at length taught the different legislatures the folly of attempting them."

The United States have not had any serious war to carry on since that period. In order, therefore, to appreciate the sacrifices which democratic nations may impose upon themselves, we must wait until the American people is obliged to put half its entire income at the disposal of the government, as was done by the English; or until it sends forth a twentieth part of its population to the field of battle, as was done by France.

In America the use of conscription is unknown, and men are induced to enlist by bounties. The notions and habits of the people of the United States are so opposed to compulsory enlistment, that I do not imagine that it can ever be sanctioned by the laws. What is termed the conscription in France is assuredly the heaviest tax upon the population of that country; yet how could a great continental war be carried on without it? The Americans have not adopted the British impressment of seamen, and they have nothing which corresponds to the French system of maritime conscription; the navy, as well as the merchant service, is supplied by voluntary engagement. But it is not easy to conceive how a people can sustain a great maritime war, without having recourse to one or the other of these two systems. Indeed, the Union, which has fought with some honour upon the seas, has never possessed a very numerous fleet, and the equipment of the small number of American vessels has always been excessively expensive.

---

* One of the most singular of these occurrences was the resolution which the Americans took of temporarily abandoning the use of tea. Those who know that men usually cling more to their habits than to their life, will doubtless admire this great and obscure sacrifice which was made by a whole people.

[The remark that "in America the use of conscription is unknown, and men are induced to enlist by bounties," is not exactly correct. During the last war with Great Britain, the state of New York, in October, 1814 (see the laws of that session, p. 15), passed an act to raise troops for the defence of the state, in which the whole body of the militia were directed to be classed, and each class to furnish one soldier, so as to make up the whole number of 12,000 directed to be raised. In case of the refusal of a class to furnish a man, one was to be detached from them by ballot, and was compelled to procure a substitute or serve personally. The intervention of peace rendered proceedings under the act unnecessary, and we have not, therefore, the light of experience to form an opinion whether such a plan of raising a military force is practicable. Other states passed similar laws. The system of classing was borrowed from the practice of the revolution.—*American Editor.*]

I have heard American statesmen confess that the Union will have great difficulty in maintaining its rank on the seas, without adopting the system of impressment or of maritime conscription; but the difficulty is to induce the people, which exercises the supreme authority, to submit to impressment or any compulsory system.

It is incontestable, that in times of danger a free people displays far more energy than one which is not so. But I incline to believe, that this is more especially the case in those free nations in which the democratic element preponderates. Democracy appears to me to be much better adapted for the peaceful conduct of society, or for an occasional effort of remarkable vigor, than for the hardy and prolonged endurance of the storms which beset the political existence of nations. The reason is very evident; it is enthusiasm which prompts men to expose themselves to dangers and privations; but they will not support them long without reflection. There is more calculation, even in the impulses of bravery, than is generally attributed to them; and although the first efforts are suggested by passion, perseverance is maintained by a distinct regard of the purpose in view. A portion of what we value is exposed, in order to save the remainder.

But it is this distinct perception of the future, founded upon a sound judgement and an enlightened experience, which is most frequently wanting in democracies. The populace is more apt to feel than to reason; and if its present sufferings are great, it is to be feared that the still greater sufferings attendant upon defeat will be forgotten.

Another cause tends to render the efforts of a democratic government less persevering than those of an aristocracy. Not only are the lower classes less awakened than the higher orders to the good or evil chances of the future, but they are liable to suffer far more acutely from present privations. The noble exposes his life, indeed, but the chance of glory is equal to the chance of harm. If he sacrifices a large portion of his income to the state, he deprives himself for a time of the pleasure of affluence; but to the poor man death is embellished by no pomp or renown; and the imposts which are irksome to the rich are fatal to him.

This relative impotence of democratic republics is, perhaps, the greatest obstacle to the foundation of a republic of this kind in Europe. In order that such a state should subsist in one country of the Old World, it would be necessary that similar institutions should be introduced into all the other nations.

I am of opinion that a democratic government tends in the end to increase the real strength of society; but it can never combine, upon a single point and at a given time, so much power as an aristocracy or a monarchy. If a democratic country remained during a whole century subject to a republican government, it would probably at the end of that period be more populous and more prosperous than the neighbouring despotic states. But it would have incurred the risk of being conquered much oftener than they would in that lapse of years.

SELF-CONTROL OF THE AMERICAN DEMOCRACY.

The American People acquiesces slowly, or frequently does not acquiesce in what is beneficial to its Interests.—The faults of the American Democracy are for the most part reparable.

The difficulty which a democracy has in conquering the passions, and in subduing the exigencies of the moment, with a view to the future, is conspicuous in the most trivial occurrences in the United States. The people which is surrounded by flatterers, has great difficulty in surmounting its inclinations; and whenever it is solicited to undergo a privation or any kind of inconvenience, even to attain an end which is sanctioned by its own rational conviction, it almost always refused to comply at first. The deference of the Americans to the laws has been very justly applauded; but it must be added, that in America the legislation is made by the people and for the people. Consequently, in the United States, the law favours those classes which are most interested in evading it elsewhere. It may therefore be supposed that an offensive law, which should not be acknowledged to be one of immediate utility, would either not be enacted or would not be obeyed.

In America there is no law against fraudulent bankruptcies; not because they are few, but because there are a great number of bankruptcies. The dread of being prosecuted as a bankrupt acts with more intensity upon the mind of the majority of the people, than the fear of being involved in losses or ruin by the failure of other parties; and a sort of guilty tolerance is extended by the public conscience, to an offence which every one condemns in his individual capacity. In the new states of the southwest, the citizens generally take justice into their own hands, and murders are of very frequent occurrence. This arises from the rude manners and the ignorance of the inhabitants of those deserts, who do not perceive the utility of investing the law with adequate force, and who prefer duels to prosecutions.

Some one observed to me one day, in Philadelphia, that almost all crimes in America are caused by the abuse of intoxicating liquors, which the lower classes can procure in great abundance from their excessive cheapness.—"How comes it," said I, "that you do not put a duty upon brandy?"—"Our legislators," rejoined my informant, "have frequently thought of this expedient; but the task of putting it in operation is a difficult one: a revolt might be apprehended; and the members who should vote for a law of this kind would be sure of losing their seats."—"Whence I am to infer," I replied, "that the drinking population constitutes the majority in your country, and that temperance is somewhat unpopular."

When these things are pointed out to the American statesmen, they content themselves with assuring you that time will operate the necessary change, and that the experience of evil will teach the people its true interests. This is frequently true: although a democracy is more liable to error than a monarch or a body of nobles, the chances of its regaining the right path, when once it has acknowledged its mistake, are greater also; because it is rarely embarrassed by internal interests, which conflict with those of the majority, and resist the authority of reason. But a democracy can only obtain truth as the result of experience; and many nations may forfeit their existence, while they are awaiting the consequences of their errors.

The great privilege of the Americans does not simply consist in their being more enlightened than other nations, but in their being able to repair the faults they may commit. To which it must be added, that a democracy cannot derive substantial benefit from past experience, unless it be arrived at a certain pitch of knowledge and civilization. There are tribes and peoples whose education has been so vicious, and whose character presents so strange a mixture of passion, of ignorance, and of erroneous notions upon all subjects, that they are unable to discern the cause of their own wretchedness, and they fall a sacrifice to ills with which they are unacquainted.

I have crossed vast tracts of country that were formerly inhabited by powerful Indian nations which are now extinct; I have myself passed some time in the midst of mutilated tribes, which see the daily decline of their numerical strength, and of the glory of their independence; and I have heard these Indians themselves anticipate the impending doom of their race. Every European can perceive means which would rescue these unfortunate beings from inevitable destruction. They alone are insensible to the expedient; they feel the wo which year after year heaps upon their heads, but they will perish to a man without accepting the remedy. It would be necessary to employ force to induce them to submit to the protection and the constraint of civilization.

The incessant revolutions which have convulsed the South American provinces for the last quarter of a century have frequently been adverted to with astonishment, and expectations have been expressed that those nations would speedily return to their *natural state*. But can it be affirmed that the turmoil of revolution is not actually the most natural state of the South American Spaniards at the present time? In that country society is plunged into difficulties from which all its efforts are insufficient to rescue it. The inhabitants of that fair portion of the western hemisphere seem obstinately bent on pursuing the work of inward havoc. If they fall into a momentary repose from the effects of exhaustion, that repose prepares them for a fresh state of phrensy. When I consider their condition, which alternates between misery and crime, I should be inclined to believe that despotism itself would be a benefit to them, if it were possible that the words despotism and benefit could ever be united in my mind.

CONDUCT OF FOREIGN AFFAIRS BY THE AMERICAN DEMOCRACY.

Direction given to the foreign Policy of the United States by Washington and Jefferson.—Almost all the defects inherent in democratic Institutions are brought to light in the Conduct of foreign Affairs.—Their advantages are less perceptible.

We have seen that the federal constitution intrusts the permanent direction of the external interests of the nation to the president and the senate;* which tends in some degree to detach the general foreign policy of the Union from the control of the people. It cannot therefore be asserted, with truth, that the external affairs of state are conducted by the democracy.

The policy of America owes its rise to Washington, and after him to Jefferson, who established those principles which it observes at the present day. Washington said, in the admirable letter which he addressed to his fellow-citizens, and which may be looked upon as his political bequest to the country:—

"The great rule of conduct for us in regard to foreign nations is, in extending our commercial relations, to have with them as little *political* connexion as possible. So far as we have already formed engagements, let them be fulfilled with perfect good faith. Here let us stop.

"Europe has a set of primary interests, which to us have none, or a very remote relation. Hence, she must be engaged in frequent controversies, the causes of which are essentially foreign to our concerns. Hence, therefore, it must be unwise in us to implicate ourselves, by artificial ties, in the ordinary vicissitudes of her politics, or the ordinary combinations and collisions of her friendships or enmities.

"Our detached and distant situation invites and enables us to pursue a different course. If we remain one people, under an efficient government, the period is not far off when we may defy material injury from external annoyance; when we may take such an attitude as will cause the neutrality we may at any time resolve upon to be scrupulously respected; when belligerent nations, under the impossibility of making acquisitions upon us, will not lightly hazard the giving us provocation; when we may choose peace or war, as our interest, guided by justice, shall counsel.

"Why forego the advantages of so peculiar a situation? Why quit our own to stand upon foreign ground? Why, by interweaving our destiny with that of any part of Europe, entangle our peace and prosperity in the toils of European ambition, rivalship, interest, humor, or caprice?

---

* "The president," says the constitution, art. ii., sect. 2, § 2, "shall have power, by and with the advice and consent of the senate, to make treaties, provided two thirds of the senators present concur." The reader is reminded that the senators are returned for a term of six years, and that they are chosen by the legislature of each state.

"It is our true policy to steer clear of permanent alliances with any portion of the foreign world; so far, I mean, as we are now at liberty to do it; for let me not be understood as capable of patronising infidelity to existing engagements. I hold the maxim no less applicable to public than to private affairs, that honesty is always the best policy. I repeat it, therefore, let those engagements be observed in their genuine sense; but in my opinion it is unnecessary, and would be unwise, to extend them.

"Taking care always to keep ourselves, by suitable establishments, in a respectable defensive posture, we may safely trust to temporary alliances for extraordinary emergencies."

In a previous part of the same letter, Washington makes the following admirable and just remark: "The nation which indulges toward another an habitual hatred, or an habitual fondness is, in some degree, a slave. It is a slave to its animosity or its affection, either of which is sufficient to lead it astray from its duty and its interest."

The political conduct of Washington was always guided by these maxims. He succeeded in maintaining his country in a state of peace, while all the other nations of the globe were at war; and he laid it down as a fundamental doctrine, that the true interest of the Americans consisted in a perfect neutrality with regard to the internal dissensions of the European powers.

Jefferson went still farther, and introduced a maxim into the policy of the Union, which affirms, that "the Americans ought never to solicit any privileges from foreign nations, in order not to be obliged to grant similar privileges themselves."

These two principles, which were so plain and so just as to be adapted to the capacity of the populace, have greatly simplified the foreign policy of the United States. As the Union takes no part in the affairs of Europe, it has, properly speaking, no foreign interests to discuss, since it has at present no powerful neighbours on the American continent. The country is as much removed from the passions of the Old World by its position, as by the line of policy which it has chosen; and it is neither called upon to repudiate nor to espouse the conflicting interests of Europe; while the dissensions of the New World are still concealed within the bosom of the future.

The Union is free from all pre-existing obligations; and it is consequently enabled to profit by the experience of the old nations of Europe, without being obliged, as they are, to make the best of the past, and to adapt it to their present circumstances; or to accept that immense inheritance which they derive from their forefathers—an inheritance of glory mingled with calamities, and of alliances conflicting with national antipathies. The foreign policy of the United States is reduced by its very nature to await the chances of the future history of the nation; and for the present it consists more in abstaining from interference than in exerting its activity.

It is therefore very difficult to ascertain, at present, what degree of sagacity the American democracy will display in the conduct of the foreign policy of the country; and upon this point its adversaries, as well as its advocates, must suspend their judgement. As for myself, I have no hesitation in avowing my conviction, that it is most especially in the conduct of foreign relations, that democratic governments appear to me to be decidedly inferior to governments carried on upon different principles. Experience, instruction, and habit, may almost always succeed in creating a species of practical discretion in democracies, and that science of the daily occurrences of life which is called good sense. Good sense may suffice to direct the ordinary course of society; and among a people whose education has been provided for, the advantages of democratic liberty in the internal affairs of the country may more than compensate for the evils inherent in a democratic government. But such is not always the case in the mutual relations of foreign nations.

Foreign politics demand scarcely any of those qualities which a democracy possesses; and they require, on the contrary, the perfect use of almost all those faculties in which it is deficient. Democracy is favourable to the increase of the internal resources of a state; it tends to diffuse a moderate independence; it promotes the growth of public spirit, and fortifies the respect which is entertained for law in all classes of society: and these are advantages which only exercise an indirect influence over the relations which one people bears to another. But a democracy is unable to regulate the details of an important undertaking, to persevere in a design, and to work out its execution in the presence of serious obstacles. It cannot combine its measures with secrecy, and will not await their consequences with patience. These are qualities which more especially belong to an individual or to an aristocracy; and they are precisely the means by which an individual people attains a predominant position.

If, on the contrary, we observe the natural defects of aristocracy, we shall find that their influence is comparatively innoxious in the direction of the external affairs of a state. The capital fault of which aristocratic bodies may be accused, is that they are more apt to contrive their own advantage than that of the mass of the people. In foreign politics it is rare for the interest of the aristocracy to be in any way distinct from that of the people.

The propensity which democracies have to obey the impulse of passion rather than the suggestions of prudence, and to abandon a mature design for the gratification of a momentary caprice, was very clearly seen in America on the breaking out of the French revolution. It was then as evident to the simplest capacity as it is at the present time, that the interests of the Americans forbade them to take any part in the contest which was about to deluge Europe with blood, but which could by no means injure the welfare of their own country. Nevertheless the sympathies of the people declared themselves with so much violence in behalf of France, that nothing but the inflexible character of Washington, and the immense popularity which he enjoyed, could have prevented the Americans from declaring war against England. And even then, the exertions, which the austere reason of that great man made to repress the generous but imprudent passions of his fellow-citizens, very nearly deprived him of the sole recompense which he had ever claimed—that of his country's love. The majority then reprobated the line of policy which he adopted, and which has since been unanimously approved by the nation.*

If the constitution and the favour of the public had not intrusted the direction of the foreign affairs of the country to Washington, it is certain that the American nation would at that time have taken the very measures which it now condemns.

Almost all the nations which have exercised a powerful influence upon the destinies of the world, by conceiving, following up, and executing vast designs—from the Romans to the English—have been governed by aristocratic institutions. Nor will this be a subject of wonder when we recollect that nothing in the world has so absolute a fixity of purpose as an aristocracy. The mass of the people may be led astray by ignorance or passion; the mind of a king may be biased, and his perseverance in his designs may be shaken—beside which a king is not immortal; but an aristocratic body is too numerous to be led astray by the blandishments of intrigue, and yet not numerous enough to yield readily to the intoxicating influence of unreflecting passion: it has the energy of a firm and enlightened individual, added to the power which it derives from its perpetuity.

Chapter XIV.

WHAT THE REAL ADVANTAGES ARE WHICH AMERICAN SOCIETY DERIVES FROM THE GOVERNMENT OF THE DEMOCRACY.

Before I enter upon the subject of the present chapter, I am induced to remind the reader of what I have more than once adverted to in the course of this book. The political institutions of the United States appear to me to be one of the forms of government which a democracy may adopt: but I do not regard the American constitution as the best, or as the only one which a democratic people may establish. In showing the advantages which the Americans derive from the government of democracy, I am therefore very far from meaning, or from believing, that similar advantages can be obtained only from the same laws.

---

* See the fifth volume of Marshall's Life of Washington. "In a government constituted like that of the United States," he says, "it is impossible for the chief magistrate, however firm he may be, to oppose for any length of time the torrents of popular opinion: and the prevalent opinion of that day seemed to incline to war. In fact, in the session of congress held at the time, it was frequently seen that Washington had lost the majority in the house of representatives." The violence of the language used against him in public was extreme, and in a political meeting they did not scruple to compare him indirectly to the treacherous Arnold. "By the opposition," says Marshall, "the friends of the administration were declared to be an aristocratic and corrupt faction, who, from a desire to introduce monarchy, were hostile to France, and under the influence of Britain; that they were a paper nobility, whose extreme sensibility at every measure which threatened the funds, induced a tame submission to injuries and insults, which the interests and honour of the nation required them to resist."

GENERAL TENDENCY OF THE LAWS UNDER THE RULE OF THE AMERICAN
DEMOCRACY, AND HABITS OF THOSE WHO APPLY THEM.

Defects of a democratic Government easy to be discovered.—Its Advantages only to
be discerned by long Observation.—Democracy in America often inexpert, but
the general Tendency of the Laws advantageous.—In the American Democracy
public Officers have no permanent Interests distinct from those of the Majority.—Result of this State of Things.

The defects and the weaknesses of a democratic government may
very readily be discovered; they are demonstrated by the most flagrant
instances, while its beneficial influence is less perceptibly exercised. A
single glance suffices to detect its evil consequences, but its good
qualities can only be discerned by long observation. The laws of the
American democracy are frequently defective or incomplete; they
sometimes attack vested rights, or give a sanction to others which are
dangerous to the community; but even if they were good, the frequent
changes which they undergo would be an evil. How comes it, then,
that the American republics prosper, and maintain their position?

In the consideration of laws, a distinction must be carefully observed between the end at which they aim, and the means by which
they are directed to that end; between their absolute and their relative
excellence. If it be the intention of the legislator to favour the interests
of the minority at the expense of the majority, and if the measures he
takes are so combined as to accomplish the object he has in view with
the least possible expense of time and exertion, the law may be well
drawn up, although its purpose be bad; and the more efficacious it is,
the greater is the mischief which it causes.

Democratic laws generally tend to promote the welfare of the greatest possible number; for they emanate from a majority of the citizens,
who are subject to error, but who cannot have an interest opposed to
their own advantage. The laws of an aristocracy tend, on the contrary,
to concentrate wealth and power in the hands of the minority, because
an aristocracy, by its very nature, constitutes a minority. It may therefore be asserted, as a general proposition, that the purpose of a
democracy, in the conduct of its legislation, is useful to a greater number of citizens than that of an aristocracy. This is, however, the sum
total of its advantages.

Aristocracies are infinitely more expert in the science of legislation
than democracies ever can be. They are possessed of a self-control
which protects them from the errors of a temporary excitement; and
they form lasting designs which they mature with the assistance of
favourable opportunities. Aristocratic government proceeds with the
dexterity of art; it understands how to make the collective force of all
its laws converge at the same time to a given point. Such is not the
case with democracies, whose laws are almost always ineffective or in-
opportune. The means of democracy are therefore more imperfect
than those of aristocracy, and the measures which it unwittingly
adopts are frequently opposed to its own cause; but the object it has in
view is more useful.

Let us now imagine a community so organized by nature, or by its constitution, that it can support the transitory action of bad laws, and that it can await, without destruction, the general tendency of the legislation: we shall then be able to conceive that a democratic government, notwithstanding its defects, will be most fitted to conduce to the prosperity of this community. This is precisely what has occurred in the United States; and I repeat, what I have before remarked, that the great advantage of the Americans consists in their being able to commit faults which they may afterward repair.

An analogous observation may be made respecting public officers. It is easy to perceive that the American democracy frequently errs in the choice of the individuals to whom it intrusts the power of the administration; but it is more difficult to say why the state prospers under their rule. In the first place it is to be remarked, that if in a democratic state the governors have less honesty and less capacity than elsewhere, the governed on the other hand are more enlightened and more attentive to their interests. As the people in democracies is more incessantly vigilant in its affairs, and more jealous of its rights, it prevents its representatives from abandoning that general line of conduct which its own interest prescribes. In the second place, it must be remembered that if the democratic magistrate is more apt to misuse his power, he possesses it for a shorter period of time. But there is yet another reason which is still more general and conclusive. It is no doubt of importance to the welfare of nations that they should be governed by men of talents and virtue; but it is perhaps still more important than the interests of those men should not differ from the interests of the community at large; for if such were the case, virtues of a high order might become useless, and talents might be turned to a bad account.

I say that it is important that the interests of the persons in authority should not conflict with or oppose the interests of the community at large; but I do not insist upon their having the same interests as the *whole* population, because I am not aware that such a state of things ever existed in any country.

No political form has hitherto been discovered, which is equally favourable to the prosperity and the development of all the classes into which society is divided. These classes continue to form, as it were, a certain number of distinct nations in the same nation; and experience has shown that it is no less dangerous to place the fate of these classes exclusively in the hands of any one of them, than it is to make one people the arbiter of the destiny of another. When the rich alone govern, the interest of the poor is always endangered; and when the poor make the laws, that of the rich incurs very serious risks. The advantage of democracy does not consist, therefore, as has sometimes been asserted, in favouring the prosperity of all, but simply in contributing to the well-being of the greatest possible number.

The men who are intrusted with the direction of public affairs in the United States, are frequently inferior, both in point of capacity and of morality, to those whom aristocratic institutions would raise to power. But their interest is identified and confounded with that of the majority of their fellow-citizens. They may frequently be faithless, and frequently mistake; but they will never systematically adopt a line of conduct opposed to the will of the majority; and it is impossible that they should give a dangerous or an exclusive tendency to the government.

The mal-administration of a democratic magistrate is a mere isolated fact, which only occurs during the short period for which he is elected. Corruption and incapacity do not act as common interests, which may connect men permanently with one another. A corrupt or an incapable magistrate will not concert his measures with another magistrate, simply because that individual is as corrupt and as incapable as himself; and these two men will never unite their endeavors to promote the corruption and inaptitude of their remote posterity. The ambition and the manœuvres of the one will serve, on the contrary, to unmask the other. The vices of a magistrate, in democratic states, are usually peculiar to his own person.

But under aristocratic governments public men are swayed by the interest of their order, which, if it is sometimes confounded with the interests of the majority, is very frequently distinct from them. This interest is the common and lasting bond which unites them together; it induces them to coalesce, and to combine their efforts in order to attain an end which does not always ensure the greatest happiness of the greatest number; and it serves not only to connect the persons in authority, but to unite them to a considerable portion of the community, since a numerous body of citizens belongs to the aristocracy, without being invested with official functions. The aristocratic magistrate is therefore constantly supported by a portion of the community, as well as by the government of which he is a member.

The common purpose which connects the interest of the magistrates in aristocracies, with that of a portion of their contemporaries, identifies it with that of future generations; their influence belongs to the future as much as to the present. The aristocratic magistrate is urged at the same time toward the same point, by the passions of the community, by his own, and I may almost add, by those of his posterity. Is it, then, wonderful that he does not resist such repeated impulses? And, indeed, aristocracies are often carried away by the spirit of their order without being corrupted by it; and they unconsciously fashion society to their own ends, and prepare it for their own descendants.

The English aristocracy is perhaps the most liberal which ever existed, and no body of men has ever, uninterruptedly, furnished so many honorable and enlightened individuals to the government of a country. It cannot, however, escape observation, that in the legislation of England the good of the poor has been sacrificed to the advantage of the rich, and the rights of the majority to the privileges of the few. The consequence is, that England, at the present day, combines the extremes of fortune in the bosom of her society; and her perils and calamities are almost equal to her power and her renown.

In the United States, where the public officers have no interests to promote connected with their caste, the general and constant influence of the government is beneficial, although the individuals who conduct it are frequently unskilful and sometimes contemptible. There is, indeed, a secret tendency in democratic institutions to render the exertions of the citizens subservient to the prosperity of the community, notwithstanding their private vices and mistakes; while in aristocratic institutions there is a secret propensity, which, notwithstanding the talents and the virtue of those who conduct the government, leads them to contribute to the evils which oppress their fellow-creatures. In aristocratic governments public men may frequently do injuries which they do not intend; and in democratic states they produce advantages which they never thought of.

PUBLIC SPIRIT IN THE UNITED STATES.

Patriotism of Instinct.—Patriotism of Reflection.—Their different Characteristics.—Nations ought to strive to acquire the second when the first has disappeared.—Efforts of the Americans to acquire it.—Interest of the Individual intimately connected with that of the Country.

There is one sort of patriotic attachment which principally arises from that instinctive, disinterested, and undefinable feeling which connects the affections of man with his birthplace. This natural fondness is united to a taste for ancient customs, and to a reverence for ancestral traditions of the past; those who cherish it love their country as they love the mansion of their fathers. They enjoy the tranquility which it affords them; they cling to the peaceful habits which they have contracted within its bosom; they are attached to the reminiscences which it awakens, and they are even pleased by the state of obedience in which they are placed. This patriotism is sometimes stimulated by religious enthusiasm, and then it is capable of making the most prodigious efforts. It is in itself a kind of religion: it does not reason, but it acts from the impulse of faith and of sentiment. By some nations the monarch has been regarded as a personification of the country; and the fervour of patriotism being converted into the fervour of loyalty, they took a sympathetic pride in his conquests, and gloried in his power. At one time, under the ancient monarchy, the French felt a sort of satisfaction in the sense of their dependance upon the arbitrary pleasure of their king, and they were wont to say with pride: "We are the subjects of the most powerful king in the world."

But, like all instinctive passions, this kind of patriotism is more apt to prompt transient exertion than to supply the motives of continuous endeavour. It may save the state in critical circumstances, but it will not unfrequently allow the nation to decline in the midst of peace. While the manners of a people are simple, and its faith unshaken, while society is steadily based upon traditional institutions, whose legitimacy has never been contested, this instinctive patriotism is wont to endure.

But there is another species of attachment to a country which is more rational than the one we have been describing. It is perhaps less generous and less ardent, but it is more fruitful and more lasting; it is coeval with the spread of knowledge, it is nurtured by the laws, it grows by the exercise of civil rights, and in the end, it is confounded with the personal interest of the citizen. A man comprehends the influence which the prosperity of his country has upon his own welfare; he is aware that the laws authorize him to contribute his assistance to that prosperity, and he labours to promote it as a portion of his interest in the first place, and as a portion of his right in the second.

But epochs sometimes occur, in the course of the existence of a nation, at which the ancient customs of a people are changed, public morality destroyed, religious belief disturbed, and the spell of tradition broken, while the diffusion of knowledge is yet imperfect, and the civil rights of the community are ill secured, or confined within very narrow limits. The country then assumes a dim and dubious shape in the eyes of the citizens; they no longer behold it in the soil which they inhabit, for that soil is to them a dull inanimate clod; nor in the usages of their forefathers, which they have been taught to look upon as a debasing yoke; nor in religion, for of that they doubt; nor in the laws, which do not originate in their own authority; nor in the legislator, whom they fear and despise. The country is lost to their senses, they can neither discover it under its own, nor under borrowed features, and they intrench themselves within the dull precincts of a narrow egotism. They are emancipated from prejudice, without having acknowledged the empire of reason; they are animated neither by the instinctive patriotism of monarchical subjects, nor by the thinking patriotism of republican citizens; but they have stopped half-way between the two, in the midst of confusion and of distress.

In this predicament, to retreat is impossible; for a people cannot restore the vivacity of its earlier times, any more than a man can return to the innocence and the bloom of childhood: such things may be regretted, but they cannot be renewed. The only thing, then, which remains to be done, is to proceed, and to accelerate the union of private with public interests, since the period of disinterested patriotism is gone by for ever.

I am certainly very far from averring, that, in order to obtain this result, the exercise of political rights should be immediately granted to all the members of the community. But I maintain that the most powerful, and perhaps the only means of interesting men in the welfare of their country, which we still possess, is to make them partakers in the government. At the present time civic zeal seems to me to be inseparable from the exercise of political rights; and I hold that the number of citizens will be found to augment or decrease in Europe in proportion as those rights are extended.

In the United States, the inhabitants were thrown but as yesterday upon the soil which they now occupy, and they brought neither customs nor traditions with them there; they meet each other for the first time with no previous acquaintance; in short, the instinctive love of their country can scarcely exist in their minds; but every one takes as zealous an interest in the affairs of his township, his country, and of the whole state, as if they were his own, because every one, in his sphere, takes an active part in the government of society.

The lower orders in the United States are alive to the perception of the influence exercised by the general prosperity upon their own welfare; and simple as this observation is, it is one which is but too rarely made by the people. But in America the people regard this prosperity as the result of its own exertions; the citizen looks upon the fortune of the public as his private interest, and he cooperates in its success, not so much from a sense of pride or of duty, as from what I shall venture to term cupidity.

It is unnecessary to study the institutions and the history of the Americans in order to discover the truth of this remark, for their manners render it sufficiently evident. As the American participates in all that is done in his country, he thinks himself obliged to defend whatever may be censured; for it is not only his country which is attacked upon these occasions, but it is himself. The consequence is, that his national pride resorts to a thousand artifices, and to all the petty tricks of individual vanity.

Nothing is more embarrassing in the ordinary intercourse of life than this irritable patriotism of the Americans. A stranger may be well inclined to praise many of the institutions of their country, but he begs permission to blame some of the peculiarities which he observes—a permission which is however inexorably refused. America is therefore a free country, in which, lest anybody should be hurt by your remarks, you are not allowed to speak freely of private individuals or of the state; of the citizens or of the authorities; of public or of private undertakings; or, in short, of anything at all, except it be of the climate and the soil; and even then Americans will be found ready to defend either the one or the other, as if they had been contrived by the inhabitants of the country.

In our times, option must be made between the patriotism of all and the government of a few; for the force and activity which the first confers, are irreconcilable with the guarantees of tranquility which the second furnishes.

NOTION OF RIGHTS IN THE UNITED STATES.

No great People without a Notion of Rights.—How the Notion of Rights can be given to a People.—Respect of Rights in the United States.—Whence it arises.

After the idea of virtue, I am acquainted with no higher principle than that of right; or, to speak more accurately, these two ideas are commingled in one. The idea of right is simply that of virtue introduced into the political world. It is the idea of right which enabled men to define anarchy and tyranny; and which taught them to remain independent without arrogance, as well as to obey without servility. The man who submits to violence is debased by his compliance; but when he obeys the mandate of one who possesses that right of authority which he acknowledges in a fellow-creature, he rises in some measure above the person who delivers the command. There are no great men without virtue, and there are no great nations—it may also be added that there would be no society—without the notion of rights; for what is the condition of a mass of rational and intelligent beings who are only united together by the bond of force?

I am persuaded that the only means which we possess at the present time of inculcating the notion of rights, and of rendering it, as it were, palpable to the senses, is to invest all the members of the community with the peaceful exercise of certain rights: this is very clearly seen in children, who are men without the strength and the experience of manhood. When a child begins to move in the midst of the objects which surround him, he is instinctively led to turn everything which he can lay his hands upon to his own purpose; he has no notion of the property of others; but as he gradually learns the value of things, and begins to perceive that he may in his turn be deprived of his possessions he becomes more circumspect, and he observes those rights in others which he wishes to have respected in himself. The principle which the child derives from the possession of his toys, is taught to the man by the objects which he may call his own. In America those complaints against property in general, which are so frequent in Europe, are never heard, because in America there are no paupers; and as every one has property of his own to defend, every one recognises the principle upon which he holds it.

The same thing occurs in the political world. In America the lowest classes have conceived a very high notion of political rights, because they exercise those rights; and they refrain from attacking those of other people, in order to ensure their own from attack. While in Europe the same classes sometimes recalcitrate even against the supreme power, the American submits without a murmur to the authority of the pettiest magistrate.

This truth is exemplified by the most trivial details of national peculiarities. In France very few pleasures are exclusively reserved for the higher classes; the poor are admitted wherever the rich are received; and they consequently behave with propriety, and respect whatever contributes to the enjoyments in which they themselves participate. In England, where wealth has a monopoly of amusement as well as of power, complaints are made that whenever the poor happen to steal into the enclosures which are reserved for the pleasures of the rich, they commit acts of wanton mischief: can this be wondered at, since care has been taken that they should have nothing to lose?

The government of the democracy brings the notion of political rights to the level of the humblest citizens, just as the dissemination of wealth brings the notion of property within the reach of all the members of the community; and I confess that, to my mind, this is one of its greatest advantages. I do not assert that it is easy to teach men to exercise political rights; but I maintain that when it is possible, the effects which result from it are highly important: and I add that if there ever was a time at which such an attempt ought to be made, that time is our own. It is clear that the influence of religious belief is shaken, and that the notion of divine rights is declining; it is evident that public morality is vitiated, and the notion of moral rights is also disappearing: these are general symptoms of the substitution of argument for faith, and of calculation for the impulses of sentiment. If, in the midst of this general disruption, you do not succeed in connecting the notion of rights with that of personal interest, which is the only immutable point in the human heart, what means will you have of governing the world except by fear? When I am told that since the laws are weak and the populace is wild, since passions are excited and the authority of virtue is paralyzed, no measures must be taken to increase the rights of the democracy; I reply, that it is for these very reasons that some measures of the kind must be taken; and I am persuaded that governments are still more interested in taking them than society at large, because governments are liable to be destroyed, and society cannot perish.

I am not, however, inclined to exaggerate the example which America furnishes. In those states the people was invested with political rights at a time when they could scarcely be abused, for the citizens were few in number and simple in their manners. As they have increased, the Americans have not augmented the power of the democracy, but they have, if I may use the expression, extended its dominions.

It cannot be doubted that the moment at which political rights are granted to a people that had before been without them, is a very critical, though it be a very necessary one. A child may kill before he is aware of the value of life; and he may deprive another person of his property before he is aware that his own may be taken away from him. The lower orders, when first they are invested with political rights, stand in relation to those rights, in the same position as a child does to the whole of nature, and the celebrated adage may then be applied to them, *Homo, puer robustus.*[1] This truth may even be perceived in America. The states in which the citizens have enjoyed their rights longest are those in which they make the best use of them.

It cannot be repeated too often that nothing is more fertile in prodigies than the art of being free; but there is nothing more arduous than the apprenticeship of liberty. Such is not the case with despotic institutions; despotism often promises to make amends for a thousand previous ills; it supports the right, it protects the oppressed, and it maintains public order. The nation is lulled by the temporary prosperity which accures to it, until it is roused to a sense of its own misery. Liberty, on the contrary, is generally established in the midst of agitation, it is perfected by civil discord, and its benefits cannot be appreciated until it is already old.

RESPECT FOR THE LAW IN THE UNITED STATES.

Respect of the Americans for the Law.—Parental Affection which they entertain for it.—Personal Interest of every one to increase the Authority of the Law.

It is not always feasible to consult the whole people, either directly or indirectly, in the formation of the law; but it cannot be denied that when such a measure is possible, the authority of the law is very much augmented. This popular origin, which impairs the excellence and the wisdom of legislation, contributes prodigiously to increase its power. There is an amazing strength in the expression of the determination of a whole people; and when it declares itself, the imagination of those who are most inclined to contest it, is overawed by its authority. The truth of this fact is very well known by parties; and they consequently strive to make out a majority whenever they can. If they have not the greater numbers of voters on their side, they assert that the true majority abstained from voting; and if they are foiled even there, they have recourse to the body of those persons who had no votes to give.

In the United States, except slaves, servants, and paupers in the receipt of relief from the townships, there is no class of persons who do not exercise the elective franchise, and who do not contribute indirectly to make the laws. Those who design to attack the laws must consequently either modify the opinion of the nation or trample upon its decision.

A second reason, which is still more weighty, may be farther adduced: in the United States every one is personally interested in enforcing the obedience of the whole community to the law; for as the minority may shortly rally the majority to its principles, it is interested in professing that respect for the decrees of the legislator, which it may soon have occasion to claim for its own. However irksome an enactment may be, the citizen of the United States complies with it, not only because it is the work of the majority, but because it originates in his own authority; and he regards it as a contract to which he is himself a party.

In the United States, then, that numerous and turbulent multitude does not exist, which always looks upon the law as its natural enemy, and accordingly surveys it with fear and with distrust. It is impossible, on the other hand, not to perceive that all classes display the utmost reliance upon the legislation of their country, and that they are attached to it by a kind of parental affection.

I am wrong, however, in saying all classes; for as in America the European scale of authority is inverted, the wealthy are there placed in a position analogous to that of the poor in the Old World, and it is the opulent classes which frequently look upon the law with suspicion. I have already observed that the advantage of democracy is not, as has been sometimes asserted, that it protects the interests of the whole community, but simply that it protects those of the majority. In the United States, where the poor rule, the rich have always some reason to dread the abuses of their power. This natural anxiety of the rich may produce a sullen dissatisfaction, but society is not disturbed by it; for the same reason which induces the rich to withhold their confidence in the legislative authority, makes them obey its mandates; their wealth, which prevents them from making the law, prevents them from withstanding it. Among civilized nations revolts are rarely excited except by such persons as have nothing to lose by them; and if the laws of a democracy are not always worthy of respect, at least they always obtain it: for those who usually infringe the laws have no excuse for not complying with the enactments they have themselves made, and by which they are themselves benefited, while the citizens whose interests might be promoted by the infraction of them, are induced, by their character and their station, to submit to the decisions of the legislature, whatever they may be. Beside which, the people in America obeys the law not only because it emanates from the popular authority, but because that authority may modify it in any points which may prove vexatory; a law is observed because it is a self-imposed evil in the first place, and an evil of transient duration in the second.

ACTIVITY WHICH PERVADES ALL THE BRANCHES OF THE BODY POLITIC IN THE UNITED STATES; INFLUENCE WHICH IT EXERCISES UPON SOCIETY.

More difficult to conceive the political Activity which pervades the United States than the Freedom and Equality which reign here.—The great Activity which perpetually agitates the legislative Bodies is only an Episode to the general Activity.—Difficult for an American to confine himself to his own Business.—Political Agitation extends to all social Intercourse.—Commercial Activity of the Americans partly attributable to this Cause.—Indirect Advantages which Society derives from a democratic Government.

On passing from a country in which free institutions are established to one where they do not exist, the traveller is struck by the change; in the former all is bustle and activity, in the latter everything is calm and motionless. In the one, melioration and progress are the general topics of inquiry; in the other, it seems as if the community only aspired to repose in the enjoyment of the advantages which it has acquired. Nevertheless, the country which exerts itself so strenuously to promote its welfare is generally more wealthy and more prosperous than that which appears to be so contented with its lot; and when we compare them together, we can scarcely conceive how so many new wants are daily felt in the former, while so few seem to occur in the latter.

If this remark is applicable to those free countries in which monarchical and aristocratic institutions subsist, it is still more striking with regard to democratic republics. In these states it is not only a portion of the people which is busied with the melioration of its social condition, but the whole community is engaged in the task; and it is not the exigencies and the convenience of a single class for which a provision is to be made, but the exigencies and the convenience of all ranks of life.

It is not impossible to conceive the surpassing liberty which the Americans enjoy; some idea may likewise be formed of the extreme equality which subsists among them; but the political activity which pervades the United States must be seen in order to be understood. No sooner do you set foot upon the American soil than you are stunned by a kind of tumult; a confused clamour is heard on every side; and a thousand simultaneous voices demand the immediate satisfaction of their social wants. Everything is in motion around you; here, the people of one quarter of a town are met to decide upon the building of a church; there, the election of a representative is going on; a little farther, the delegates of a district are posting to the town in order to consult upon some local improvements; or in another place the labourers of a village quit their ploughs to deliberate upon the project of a road or a public school. Meetings are called for the sole purpose of declaring their disapprobation of the line of conduct pursued by the government; while in other assemblies the citizens salute the authorities of the day as the fathers of their country. Societies are formed which regard drunkenness as the principal cause of the evils under which the state labours, and which solemnly bind themselves to give a constant example of temperance.*

The great political agitation of the American legislative bodies, which is the only kind of excitement that attracts the attention of foreign countries, is a mere episode or a sort of continuation of that universal movement which originates in the lowest classes of the people and extends successively to all the ranks of society. It is impossible to spend more efforts in the pursuit of enjoyment.

The cares of political life engross a most prominent place in the occupation of a citizen in the United States; and almost the only pleasure of which an American has any idea, is to take a part in the government, and to discuss the part he has taken. This feeling pervades the most trifling habits of life; even the women frequently attend public meetings, and listen to political harangues as a recreation after their household labours. Debating clubs are to a certain extent a substitute for theatrical entertainments: an American cannot converse, but he can discuss; and when he attempts to talk he falls into a dissertation. He speaks to you as if he were addressing a meeting; and if he should warm in the course of the discussion, he will infallibly say "gentlemen," to the person with whom he is conversing.

In some countries the inhabitants display a certain repugnance to avail themselves of the political privileges with which the law invests them; it would seem that they set too high a value upon their time to spend it on the interests of the community; and they prefer to withdraw within the exact limits of a wholesome egotism, marked out by four sunk fences and a quickset hedge. But if an American were condemned to confine his activity to his own affairs, he would be robbed of one half of his existence; he would feel an immense void in the life which he is accustomed to lead, and his wretchedness would be unbearable.† I am persuaded that if ever a despotic government is established in America, it will find it more difficult to surmount the habits which free institutions have engendered, than to conquer the attachment of the citizens to freedom.

This ceaseless agitation which democratic government has intro-

---

* At the time of my stay in the United States the temperance societies already consisted of more than 270,000 members; and their effect had been to diminish the consumption of fermented liquors by 500,000 gallons per annum in the state of Pennsylvania alone.
† The same remark was made at Rome under the first Cesars. Montesquieu somewhere alludes to the excessive despondency of certain Roman citizens who, after the excitement of political life, were all at once flung back into the stagnation of private life.

duced into the political world, influences all social intercourse. I am not sure that upon the whole this is not the greatest advantage of democracy; and I am much less inclined to applaud it for what it does, than for what it causes to be done.

It is incontestable that the people frequently conducts public business very ill; but it is impossible that the lower orders should take a part in public business without extending the circle of their ideas, and without quitting the ordinary routine of their mental acquirements. The humblest individual who is called upon to cooperate in the government of society, acquires a certain degree of self-respect; and as he possesses authority, he can command the services of minds much more enlightened than his own. He is canvassed by a multitude of applicants, who seek to deceive him in a thousand different ways, but who instruct him by their deceit. He takes a part in political undertakings which did not originate in his own conception, but which give him a taste for undertakings of the kind. New meliorations are daily pointed out in the property which he holds in common with others, and this gives him the desire of improving that property which is more peculiarly his own. He is perhaps neither happier nor better than those who came before him, but he is better informed and more active. I have no doubt that the democratic institutions of the United States, joined to the physical constitution of the country, are the cause (not the direct, as is so often asserted, but the indirect cause) of the prodigious commercial activity of the inhabitants. It is not engendered by the laws, but the people learns how to promote it by the experience derived from legislation.

When the opponents of democracy assert that a single individual performs the duties which he undertakes much better than the government of the community, it appears to me that they are perfectly right. The government of an individual, supposing an equality of instruction on either side, is more consistent, more persevering, and more accurate than that of a multitude, and it is much better qualified judiciously to discriminate the characters of the men it employs. If any deny what I advance, they have certainly never seen a democratic government, or have formed their opinion upon very partial evidence. It is true that even when local circumstances and the disposition of the people allow democratic institutions to subsist, they never display a regular and methodical system of government. Democratic liberty is far from accomplishing all the projects it undertakes, with the skill of an adroit despotism. It frequently abandons them before they have borne their fruits, or risks them when the consequences may prove dangerous; but in the end it produces more than any absolute government, and if it do fewer things well, it does a great number of things. Under its sway, the transactions of the public administration are not nearly so important as what is done by private exertion. Democracy does not confer the most skilful kind of government upon the people, but it produces that which the most skilful governments are frequently unable to awaken, namely, an all-pervading and restless activity, a superabundant force, and an energy which is inseparable from it, and which may, under favourable circumstances, beget the most amazing benefits. These are the true advantages of democracy.

In the present age, when the destinies of Christendom seem to be in suspense, some hasten to assail democracy as its foe while it is yet in its early growth; and others are ready with their vows of adoration for this new deity which is springing forth from chaos: but both parties are very imperfectly acquainted with the object of their hatred or of their desires; they strike in the dark, and distribute their blows by mere chance.

We must first understand what the purport of society and the aim of government are held to be. If it be your intention to confer a certain elevation upon the human mind, and to teach it to regard the things of this world with generous feelings; to inspire men with a scorn of mere temporal advantage; to give birth to living convictions, and to keep alive the spirit of honorable devotedness; if you hold it to be a good thing to refine the habits, to embellish the manners, to cultivate the arts of a nation, and to promote the love of poetry, of beauty, and of renown; if you would constitute a people not unfitted to act with power upon all other nations; nor unprepared for those high enterprises, which, whatever be the result of its efforts, will leave a name for ever famous in time—if you believe such to be the principal object of society, you must avoid the government of democracy, which would be a very uncertain guide to the end you have in view.

But if you hold it to be expedient to divert the moral and intellectual activity of man to the production of comfort, and to the acquirement of the necessaries of life; if a clear understanding be more profitable to men than genius; if your object be not to stimulate the virtues of heroism, but to create habits of peace; if you had rather behold vices than crimes, and are content to meet with fewer noble deeds, provided offences be diminished in the same proportion; if, instead of living in the midst of a brilliant state of society, you are contented to have prosperity around you; if, in short, you are of opinion that the principal object of a government is not to confer the greatest possible share of power and of glory upon the body of the nation, but to ensure the greatest degree of enjoyment, and the least degree of misery, to each of the individuals who compose it—if such be your desires, you can have no surer means of satisfying them than by equalizing the condition of men, and establishing democratic institutions.

But if the time be past at which such a choice was possible, and if some superhuman power impel us toward one or the other of these two governments without consulting our wishes, let us at least endeavour to make the best of that which is allotted to us; and let us so inquire into its good and its evil propensities as to be able to foster the former, and repress the latter to the utmost.

Chapter XV.

UNLIMITED POWER OF THE MAJORITY IN THE UNITED STATES, AND ITS CONSEQUENCES.

Natural Strength of the Majority in Democracies.—Most of the American Constitutions have increased this Strength by artificial Means.—How this has been done—Pledged Delegates.—Moral Power of the Majority.—Opinion as to its Infallibility—Respect for its Rights, how augmented in the United States.

The very essence of democratic government consists in the absolute sovereignty of the majority: for there is nothing in democratic states which is capable of resisting it. Most of the American constitutions have sought to increase this natural strength of the majority by artificial means.*

The legislature is, of all political institutions, the one which is most easily swayed by the wishes of the majority. The Americans determined that the members of the legislature should be elected by the people immediately, and for a very brief term, in order to subject them, not only to the general convictions, but even to the daily passions of their constituents. The members of both houses are taken from the same class in society, and are nominated in the same manner; so that the modifications of the legislative bodies are almost as rapid and quite as irresistible as those of a single assembly. It is to a legislature thus constituted, that almost all the authority of the government has been intrusted.

But while the law increased the strength of those authorities which of themselves were strong, it enfeebled more and more those which were naturally weak. It deprived the representatives of the executive of all stability and independence; and by subjecting them completely to the caprices of the legislature, it robbed them completely of the slender influence which the nature of a democratic government might have allowed them to retain. In several states the judicial power was also submitted to the elective discretion of the majority; and in all them its existence was made to depend on the pleasure of the legislative authority, since the representatives were empowered annually to regulate the stipend of the judges.

Custom, however, has done even more than law. A proceeding which will in the end set all the guarantees of representative government at naught, is becoming more and more general in the United States: it frequently happens that the electors, who choose a delegate, point out a certain line of conduct to him, and impose upon him a certain number of positive obligations which he is pledged to fulfil. With the exception of the tumult, this comes to the same thing as if the majority of the populace held its deliberations in the market-place.

---

* We observed in examining the federal constitution that the efforts of the legislators of the Union had been diametrically opposed to the present tendency. The consequence has been that the federal government is more independent in its sphere than that of the states. But the federal government scarcely ever interferes in any but external affairs; and the governments of the states are in reality the authorities which direct society in America.

Several other circumstances concur in rendering the power of the majority in America, not only preponderant, but irresistible. The moral authority of the majority is partly based upon the notion, that there is more intelligence and more wisdom in a great number of men collected together than in a single individual, and that the quantity of legislators is more important than their quality. The theory of equality is in fact applied to the intellect of man; and human pride is thus assailed in its last retreat, by a doctrine which the minority hesitate to admit, and in which they very slowly concur. Like all other powers, and perhaps more than all other powers, the authority of the many requires the sanction of time; at first it enforces obedience by constraint; but its laws are not respected until they have long been maintained.

The right of governing society, which the majority supposes itself to derive from its superior intelligence, was introduced into the United States by the first settlers; and this idea, which would be sufficient of itself to create a free nation, has now been amalgamated with the manners of the people, and the minor incidents of social intercourse.

The French, under the old monarchy, held it for a maxim (which is still a fundamental principle of the English constitution), that the king could do no wrong; and if he did wrong, the blame was imputed to his advisers. This notion was highly favorable to habits of obedience; and it enabled the subject to complain of the law, without ceasing to love and honour the lawgiver. The Americans entertain the same opinion with respect to the majority.

The moral power of the majority is founded upon yet another principle, which is, that the interests of the many are to be preferred to those of the few. It will readily be perceived that the respect here professed for the rights of the majority must naturally increase or diminish according to the state of parties. When a nation is divided into several irreconcilable factions, the privilege of the majority is often overlooked, because it is intolerable to comply with its demands.

If there existed in America a class of citizens whom the legislating majority sought to deprive of exclusive privileges, which they had possessed for ages, and to bring down from an elevated station to the level of the ranks of the multitude, it is probable that the minority would be less ready to comply with its laws. But as the United States were colonized by men holding an equal rank among themselves, there is as yet no natural or permanent source of dissension between the interests of its different inhabitants.

There are certain communities in which the persons who constitute the minority can never hope to draw over the majority to their side, because they must then give up the very point which is at issue between them. Thus, an aristocracy can never become a majority while it retains its exclusive privileges, and it cannot cede its privileges without ceasing to be an aristocracy.

In the United States, political questions cannot be taken up in so general and absolute a manner; and all parties are willing to recognise the rights of the majority, because they all hope to turn those rights to their own advantage at some future time. The majority therefore in that country exercises a prodigious actual authority, and a moral influence which is scarcely less preponderant; no obstacles exist which can impede, or so much as retard its progress, or which can induce it to heed the complaints of those whom it crushes upon its path. This state of things is fatal in itself and dangerous for the future.

HOW THE UNLIMITED POWER OF THE MAJORITY INCREASES, IN AMERICA, THE INSTABILITY OF LEGISLATION AND THE ADMINISTRATION INHERENT IN DEMOCRACY.

The Americans increase the mutability of the Laws which is inherent in Democracy by changing the Legislature every Year, and by vesting it with unbounded Authority.—The same Effect is produced upon the Administration.—In America social Melioration is conducted more energetically, but less perseveringly than in Europe.

I have already spoken of the natural defects of democratic institutions, and they all of them increase in the exact ratio of the power of the majority. To begin with the most evident of them all; the mutability of the laws is an evil inherent in democratic government, because it is natural to democracies to raise men to power in very rapid succession. But this evil is more or less sensible in proportion to the authority and the means of action which the legislature possesses.

In America the authority exercised by the legislative bodies is supreme; nothing prevents them from accomplishing their wishes with celerity, and with irresistible power, while they are supplied by new representatives every year. That is to say, the circumstances which contribute most powerfully to democratic instability, and which admit of the free application of caprice to every object in the state, are here in full operation. In conformity with this principle, America is, at the present day, the country in the world where laws last the shortest time. Almost all the American constitutions have been amended within the course of thirty years: there is, therefore, not a single American state which has not modified the principles of its legislation in that lapse of time.* As for the laws themselves, a single glance upon the archives of the different states of the Union suffices to convince one, that in America the activity of the legislator never slackens. Not that the American democracy is naturally less stable than any other, but that it is allowed to follow its capricious propensities in the formation of the laws.

The omnipotence of the majority and the rapid as well as absolute manner in which its decisions are executed in the United States, have not only the effect of rendering the law unstable, but they exercise the

* The legislative acts promulgated by the state of Massachusetts alone, from the year 1780 to the present time, already fill three stout volumes: and it must not be forgotten that the collection to which I allude was published in 1823, when many old laws which had fallen into disuse were omitted. The state of Massachusetts, which is not more populous than a department of France, may be considered as the most stable, the most consistent, and the most sagacious in its undertakings of the whole Union.

same influence upon the execution of the law and the conduct of the public administration. As the majority is the only power which it is important to court, all its projects are taken up with the greatest ardour; but no sooner is its attention distracted, than all this ardour ceases; while in the free states of Europe, the administration is at once independent and secure, so that the projects of the legislature are put into execution, although its immediate attention may be directed to other objects.

In America certain meliorations are undertaken with much more zeal and activity than elsewhere; in Europe the same ends are promoted by much less social effort, more continuously applied.

Some years ago several pious individuals undertook to meliorate the condition of the prisons. The public was excited by the statements which they put forward, and the regeneration of criminals became a very popular undertaking. New prisons were built; and, for the first time, the idea of reforming as well as of punishing the delinquent, formed a part of prison discipline. But this happy alteration, in which the public had taken so hearty an interest, and which the exertions of the citizens had irresistibly accelerated, could not be completed in a moment. While the new penitentiaries were being erected (and it was the pleasure of the majority they should be terminated with all possible celerity), the old prisons existed, which still contained a great number of offenders. These jails became more unwholesome and more corrupt in proportion as the new establishments were beautified and improved, forming a contrast which may readily be understood. The majority was so eagerly employed in founding the new prisons, that those which already existed, were forgotten; and as the general attention was diverted to a novel object, the care which had hitherto been bestowed upon the others ceased. The salutary regulations of discipline were first relaxed, and afterward broken; so that in the immediate neighbourhood of a prison, which bore witness to the mild and enlightened spirit of our time, dungeons might be met with, which reminded the visiter of the barbarity of the middle ages.

TYRANNY OF THE MAJORITY.

How the Principle of the Sovereignty of the People is to be understood.—Impossibility of conceiving a mixed Government.—The sovereign Power must centre somewhere.—Precautions to be taken to control its Action.—These Precautions have not been taken in the United States.—Consequences.

I hold it to be an impious and an execrable maxim that, politically speaking, a people has a right to do whatsoever it pleases; and yet I have asserted that all authority originates in the will of the majority. Am I, then, in contradiction with myself?

A general law—which bears the name of justice—has been made and sanctioned, not only by a majority of this or that people, but by a majority of mankind. The rights of every people are consequently confined within the limits of what is just. A nation may be considered in the light of a jury which is empowered to represent society at large, and to apply the great and general law of justice. Ought such a jury, which represents society, to have more power than the society in which the laws it applies originate?

When I refuse to obey an unjust law, I do not contest the right which the majority has of commanding, but I simply appeal from the sovereignty of the people to the sovereignty of mankind. It has been asserted that a people can never entirely outstep the boundaries of justice and of reason in those affairs which are more peculiarly its own; and that consequently full power may fearlessly be given to the majority by which it is represented. But this language is that of a slave.

A majority taken collectively may be regarded as a being whose opinions, and most frequently whose interests, are opposed to those of another being, which is styled a minority. If it be admitted that a man, possessing absolute power, may misuse that power by wronging his adversaries, why should a majority not be liable to the same reproach? Men are not apt to change their characters by agglomeration; nor does their patience in the presence of obstacles increase with the consciousness of their strength.* And for these reasons I can never willingly invest any number of my fellow-creatures with that unlimited authority which I should refuse to any one of them.

I do not think that it is possible to combine several principles in the same government, so as at the same time to maintain freedom, and really to oppose them to one another. The form of government which is usually termed *mixed* has always appeared to me to be a mere chimera. Accurately speaking, there is no such thing as a mixed government (with the meaning usually given to that word), because in all communities some one principle of action may be discovered, which preponderates over the others. England in the last century, which has been more especially cited as an example of this form of government, was in point of fact an essentially aristocratic state, although it comprised very powerful elements of democracy: for the laws and customs of the country were such, that the aristocracy could not but preponderate in the end, and subject the direction of public affairs to its own will. The error arose from too much attention being paid to the actual struggle which was going on between the nobles and the people, without considering the probable issue of the contest, which was in reality the important point. When a community really has a mixed government, that is to say, when it is equally divided between two adverse principles, it must either pass through a revolution, or fall into complete dissolution.

I am therefore of opinion that some one social power must always be made to predominate over the others; but I think that liberty is endangered when this power is checked by no obstacles which may retard its course, and force it to moderate its own vehemence.

Unlimited power is in itself a bad and dangerous thing; human be-

---

* No one will assert that a people cannot forcibly wrong another people: but parties may be looked upon as lesser nations within a greater one, and they are aliens to each other: if therefore it be admitted that a nation can act tyrannically toward another nation, it cannot be denied that a party may do the same toward another party.

ings are not competent to exercise it with discretion; and God alone can be omnipotent, because his wisdom and his justice are always equal to his power. But no power upon earth is so worthy of honor for itself, or of reverential obedience to the rights which it represents, that I would consent to admit its uncontrolled and all-predominant authority. When I see that the right and the means of absolute command are conferred on a people or upon a king, upon an aristocracy or a democracy, a monarchy or a republic, I recognise the germe of tyranny, and I journey onward to a land of more hopeful institutions.

In my opinion the main evil of the present democratic institutions of the United States does not arise, as is often asserted in Europe, from their weakness, but from their overpowering strength; and I am not so much alarmed at the excessive liberty which reigns in that country, as at the very inadequate securities which exist against tyranny.

When an individual or a party is wronged in the United States, to whom can he apply for redress? If to public opinion, public opinion constitutes the majority; if to the legislature, it represents the majority, and implicitly obeys its instructions; if to the executive power, it is appointed by the majority and is a passive tool in its hands; the public troops consist of the majority under arms; the jury is the majority invested with the right of hearing judicial cases; and in certain states even the judges are elected by the majority. However iniquitous or absurd the evil of which you complain may be, you must submit to it as well as you can.*

If, on the other hand, a legislative power could be so constituted as to represent the majority without necessarily being the slave of its pas-

---

* A striking instance of the excesses which may be occasioned by the despotism of the majority occurred at Baltimore in the year 1812. At that time the war was very popular in Baltimore. A journal which had taken the other side of the question excited the indignation of the inhabitants by its opposition. The populace assembled, broke the printing-presses, and attacked the houses of the newspaper editors. The militia was called out, but no one obeyed the call; and the only means of saving the poor wretches who were threatened by the phrensy of the mob, was to throw them into prison as common malefactors. But even this precaution was ineffectual; the mob collected again during the night; the magistrates again made a vain attempt to call out the militia; the prison was forced, one of the newspaper editors was killed upon the spot, and the others were left for dead: the guilty parties were acquitted by the jury when they were brought to trial.

I said one day to an inhabitant of Pennsylvania: "Be so good as to explain to me how it happens, that in a state founded by quakers, and celebrated for its toleration, freed blacks are not allowed to exercise civil rights. They pay the taxes: is it not fair that they should have a vote."

"You insult us," replied my informant, "if you imagine that our legislators could have omitted so gross an act of injustice and intolerance."

What, then, the blacks possess the right of voting in this country?"

"Without the smallest doubt."

"How comes it, then, that at the polling-booth this morning I did not perceive a single negro in the whole meeting?"

"This is not the fault of the law; the negroes have an undisputed right of voting; but they voluntarily abstain from making their appearance."

"A very pretty piece of modesty on their parts," rejoined I.

"Why, the truth is, that they are not disinclined to vote, but they are afraid of being maltreated; in this country the law is sometimes unable to maintain its authority without the support of the majority. But in this case the majority entertains very strong prejudices against the blacks, and the magistrates are unable to protect them in the exercise of their legal privileges."

"What, then, the majority claims the right not only of making the laws, but of breaking the laws it has made?"

sions; an executive, so as to retain a certain degree of uncontrolled authority; and a judiciary, so as to remain independent of the two other powers; a government would be formed which would still be democratic, without incurring any risk of tyrannical abuse.

I do not say that tyrannical abuses frequently occur in America at the present day; but I maintain that no sure barrier is established against them, and that the causes which mitigate the government are to be found in the circumstances and the manners of the country more than in its laws.

EFFECTS OF THE UNLIMITED POWER OF THE MAJORITY UPON THE ARBITRARY AUTHORITY OF THE AMERICAN PUBLIC OFFICERS.

Liberty left by the American Laws to public Officers within a certain Sphere.—Their Power.

A distinction must be drawn between tyranny and arbitrary power. Tyranny may be exercised by means of the law, and in that case it is not arbitrary: arbitrary power may be exercised for the good of the community at large, in which case it is not tyrannical. Tyranny usually employs arbitrary means, but, if necessary, it can rule without them.

In the United States the unbounded power of the majority, which is favourable to the legal despotism of the legislature, is likewise favourable to the arbitrary authority of the magistrates. The majority has an entire control over the law when it is made and when it is executed; and as it possesses an equal authority over those who are in power, and the community at large, it considers public officers as its passive agents, and readily confides the task of serving its designs to their vigilance. The details of their office and the privileges which they are to enjoy are rarely defined beforehand; but the majority treats them as a master does his servants, when they are always at work in his sight, and he has the power of directing or reprimanding them at every instant.

In general the American functionaries are far more independent than the French civil officers, within the sphere which is prescribed to them. Sometimes, even, they are allowed by the popular authority to exceed those bounds; and as they are protected by the opinion, and backed by the co-operation of the majority, they venture upon such manifestations of their power as astonish a European. By this means habits are formed in the heart of a free country which may some day prove fatal to its liberties.

POWER EXERCISED BY THE MAJORITY IN AMERICA UPON PUBLIC OPINION.

In America, when the Majority has once irrevocably decided a Question, all Discussion ceases.—Reason of this.—Moral Power exercised by the Majority upon Opinion.—Democratic Republics have deprived Despotism of its physical Instruments.—Their Despotism sways the Minds of Men.

It is in the examination of the display of public opinion in the United States, that we clearly perceive how far the power of the majority surpasses all the powers with which we are acquainted in Europe. Intellectual principles exercise an influence which is so invisible and often so inappreciable, that they baffle the toils of oppression. At the present time the most absolute monarchs in Europe are unable to prevent certain notions, which are opposed to their authority, from circulating in secret throughout their dominions, and even in their courts. Such is not the case in America; so long as the majority is still undecided, discussion is carried on; but as soon as its decision is irrevocably pronounced, a submissive silence is observed; and the friends, as well as the opponents of the measure, unite in assenting to its propriety. The reason of this is perfectly clear: no monarch is so absolute as to combine all the powers of society in his own hands, and to conquer all opposition, with the energy of a majority, which is invested with the right of making and of executing the laws.

The authority of a king is purely physical, and it controls the actions of the subject without subduing his private will; but the majority possesses a power which is physical and moral at the same time; it acts upon the will as well as upon the actions of men, and it represses not only all contest, but all controversy.

I know no country in which there is so little true independence of mind and freedom of discussion as in America. In any constitutional state in Europe every sort of religious and political theory may be advocated and propagated abroad; for there is no country in Europe so subdued by any single authority, as not to contain citizens who are ready to protect the man who raises his voice in the cause of truth, from the consequences of his hardihood. If he is unfortunate enough to live under an absolute government, the people is upon his side; if he inhabits a free country, he may find a shelter behind the authority of the throne, if he require one. The aristocratic part of society supports him in some countries, and the democracy in others. But in a nation where democratic institutions exist, organized like those of the United States, there is but one sole authority, one single element of strength and of success, with nothing beyond it.

In America, the majority raises very formidable barriers to the liberty of opinion: within these barriers an author may write whatever he pleases, but he will repent it if he ever step beyond them. Not that he is exposed to the terrors of an auto-da-fé,[1] but he is tormented by the slights and persecutions of daily obloquy. His political career is closed for ever, since he has offended the only authority which is able to promote his success. Every sort of compensation, even that of celebrity, is refused to him. Before he published his opinions, he imagined that he held them in common with many others; but no sooner has he declared them openly, than he is loudly censured by his overbearing opponents, while those who think, without having the courage to speak, like him, abandon him in silence. He yields at length, oppressed by the daily efforts he has been making, and he subsides into silence as if he was tormented by remorse for having spoken the truth.

Fetters and headsmen were the coarse instruments which tyranny formerly employed; but the civilization of our age has refined the arts of despotism, which seemed however to have been sufficiently perfected before. The excesses of monarchical power had devised a variety of physical means of oppression; the democratic republics of the present day have rendered it as entirely an affair of the mind, as that will which it is intended to coerce. Under the absolute sway of an individual despot, the body was attacked in order to subdue the soul; and the soul escaped the blows which were directed against it, and rose superior to the attempt; but such is not the course adopted by tyranny in democratic republics; there the body is left free, and the soul is enslaved. The sovereign can no longer say, "You shall think as I do on pain of death;" but he says, "You are free to think differently from me, and to retain your life, your property, and all that you possess; but if such be your determination, you are henceforth an alien among your people. You may retain your civil rights, but they will be useless to you, for you will never be chosen by your fellow-citizens, if you solicit their suffrages; and they will affect to scorn you, if you solicit their esteem. You will remain among men, but you will be deprived of the rights of mankind. Your fellow-creatures will shun you like an impure being; and those who are most persuaded of your innocence will abandon you too, lest they should be shunned in their turn. Go in peace! I have given you your life, but it is an existence incomparably worse than death."

Absolute monarchies have thrown an odium upon despotism; let us beware lest democratic republics should restore oppression, and should render it less odious and less degrading in the eyes of the many, by making it still more onerous to the few.

Works have been published in the proudest nations of the Old World, expressly intended to censure the vices and deride the follies of the time; Labruyère[2] inhabited the palace of Louis XIV. when he composed his chapter upon the Great, and Molière[3] criticised the courtiers in the very pieces which were acted before the court. But the ruling power in the United States is not to be made game of; the smallest reproach irritates its sensibility, and the slightest joke which has any foundation in truth renders it indignant; from the style of its language to the more solid virtues of its character, everything must be made the subject of encomium. No writer, whatever be his eminence, can escape from this tribute of adulation to his fellow-citizens. The majority lives in the perpetual exercise of self-applause; and there are certain truths which the Americans can only learn from strangers or from experience.

If great writers have not at present existed in America, the reason is very simply given in these facts; there can be no literary genius without freedom of opinion, and freedom of opinion does not exist in America. The inquisition[4] has never been able to prevent a vast number of anti-religious books from circulating in Spain. The empire of the majority succeeds much better in the United States, since it actually removes the wish of publishing them. Unbelievers are to be met with in America, but, to say the truth, there is no public organ of infidelity. Attempts have been made by some governments to protect the morality of nations by prohibiting licentious books. In the United States no one is punished for this sort of works, but no one is induced to write them; not because all the citizens are immaculate in their manners, but because the majority of the community is decent and orderly.

In these cases the advantages derived from the exercise of this power are unquestionable; and I am simply discussing the nature of the power itself. This irresistible authority is a constant fact, and its beneficent exercise is an accidental occurrence.

EFFECTS OF THE TYRANNY OF THE MAJORITY UPON THE NATIONAL CHARACTER OF THE AMERICANS.

Effects of the Tyranny of the Majority more sensibly felt hitherto in the Manners than in the Conduct of Society.—They check the development of leading Characters.—Democratic Republics, organized like the United States, bring the Practice of courting favour within the reach of the many.—Proofs of this Spirit in the United States.—Why there is more Patriotism in the People than in those who govern in its name.

The tendencies which I have just alluded to are as yet very slightly perceptible in political society; but they already begin to exercise an unfavourable influence upon the national character of the Americans. I am inclined to attribute the singular paucity of distinguished political characters to the ever-increasing activity of the despotism of the majority in the United States.

When the American revolution broke out, they arose in great numbers; for public opinion then served, not to tyrannize over, but to direct the exertions of individuals. Those celebrated men took a full part in the general agitation of mind common at that period, and they attained a high degree of personal fame, which was reflected back upon the nation, but which was by no means borrowed from it.

In absolute governments, the great nobles who are nearest to the throne flatter the passions of the sovereign, and voluntarily truckle to his caprices. But the mass of the nation does not degrade itself by servitude; if often submits from weakness, from habit, or from ignorance, and sometimes from loyalty. Some nations have been known to sacrifice their own desires to those of the sovereign with pleasure and with pride; thus exhibiting a sort of independence in the very act of submission. These peoples are miserable, but they are not degraded. There is a great difference between doing what one does not approve, and feigning to approve what one does; the one is the necessary case of a weak person, the other befits the temper of a lacquey.

In free countries, where every one is more or less called upon to give his opinion in the affairs of state; in democratic republics, where public life is incessantly commingled with domestic affairs, where the sovereign authority is accessible on every side, and where its attention can almost always be attracted by vociferation, more persons are to be met with who speculate upon its foibles, and live at the cost of its passions, than in absolute monarchies. Not because men are naturally worse in these states than elsewhere, but the temptation is stronger, and of easier access at the same time. The result is a far more extensive debasement of the characters of citizens.

Democratic republics extend the practice of currying favour with the many, and they introduce it into a great number of classes at once: this is one of the most serious reproaches that can be addressed to them. In democratic states organized on the principles of the American republics, this is more especially the case, where the authority of the majority is so absolute and so irresistible, that a man must give up his rights as a citizen, and almost abjure his quality as a human being, if he intends to stray from the track which it lays down.

In that immense crowd which throngs the avenues to power in the United States, I found very few men who displayed any of that manly candour, and that masculine independence of opinion, which frequently distinguished the Americans in former times, and which constitute the leading feature in distinguished characters wheresoever they may be found. It seems, at first sight, as if all the minds of the Americans were formed upon one model, so accurately do they correspond in their manner of judging. A stranger does, indeed, sometimes meet with Americans who dissent from these rigorous formularies; with men who deplore the defects of the laws, the mutability and the ignorance of democracy; who even go so far as to observe the evil tendencies which impair the national character, and to point out such remedies as it might be possible to apply; but no one is there to hear these things beside yourself, and you, to whom these secret reflections are confided, are a stranger and a bird of passage. They are very ready to communicate truths which are useless to you, but they continue to hold a different language in public.

If ever these lines are read in America, I am well assured of two things: in the first place, that all who peruse them will raise their voices to condemn me; and in the second place, that very many of them will acquit me at the bottom of their conscience.

[The author's views upon what he terms the tyranny of the majority, the despotism of public opinion in the United States, have already excited some remarks in this country, and will probably give occasion to more. As stated in the preface to this edition, the editor does not conceive himself called upon to discuss the speculative opinions of the author, and supposes he will best discharge his duty by confining his observations to what he deems errors of fact or law. But in reference to this particular subject, it seems due to the author to remark, that he visited the United States at a particular time, when a successful political chieftain had succeeded in establishing his party in power, as it seemed, firmly and permanently; when the preponderance of that party was immense, and when there seemed little prospect of any change. He may have met with men, who sank under the astonishing popularity of General Jackson, who despaired of the republic, and who therefore shrank from the expression of their opinions. It must be confessed, however, that the author is obnoxious to the charge which has been made, of the want of perspicuity and distinctness in this part of his work. He does not mean that the press was silent, for he has himself not only noticed, but furnished proof of the great free-dom, not to say licentiousness, with which it assailed the character of the president, and the measures of his administration.

He does not mean to represent the opponents of the dominant party as having thrown down their weapons of warfare, for his book shows throughout his knowledge of the existence of an active and able party, constantly opposing and harassing the administration.

But, after a careful perusal of the chapters on this subject, the editor is inclined to the opinion, that M. De Tocqueville intends to speak of the *tyranny of the party* in excluding from public employment all those who do not adopt the *Shibboleth* of the majority. The language at pp. 286, 287[214–15], which he puts in the mouth of a majority, and his observa-tions immediately preceding this note, seem to furnish the key to his meaning; although it must be admitted that there are other passages to which a wider construction may be given. Perhaps they may be reconciled by the idea that the author considers the acts and opinions of the domi-nant party as the just and true expression of public opinion. And hence, when he speaks of the intolerance of public opinion, he means the exclu-siveness of the party, which, for the time being, may be predominant. He had seen men of acknowledged competency removed from office, or ex-cluded from it, wholly on the ground of their entertaining opinions hostile to those of the dominant party, or majority. And he had seen this system extended to the very lowest officers of the government, and applied by the electors in their choice of all officers of all descriptions; and this he deemed persecution—tyranny—despotism. But he surely is mistaken in representing the effect of this system of terror as stifling all complaint, si-lencing all opposition, and inducing "enemies and friends to yoke them-selves alike to the triumphant car of the majority." He mistook a temporary state of parties for a permanent and ordinary result, and he was carried away by the immense majority that then supported the administration, to the belief of a universal acquiescence. Without intending here to speak of the merits or demerits of those who represented that majority, it is proper to remark, that the great change which, has taken place since the period when the author wrote, in the political condition of the very persons who he supposed then wielded the terrors of disfranchisement against their op-ponents, in itself furnishes a full and complete demonstration of the error of his opinions respecting the "true independence of mind and freedom of discussion" in America. For without such discussion to enlighten the minds of the people, and without a stern independence of the rewards and threats of those in power, the change alluded to could not have occured.

There is reason to complain not only of the ambiguity, but of the style of exaggeration which pervades all the remarks of the author on this sub-ject—so different for the well considered and nicely adjusted language employed by him on all other topics. Thus, p. 282[211], he implies that there is no means of redress afforded even by the judiciary, for a wrong committed by the majority. His error is, *first*, in supposing the jury to con-stitute the judicial power; *second*, overlooking what he has himself else-where so well described, the independence of the judiciary and its means of controlling the action of a majority in a state or in the federal govern-ment; and *thirdly*, in omitting the proper consideration of the frequent changes of popular sentiment by which the majority of yesterday becomes the minority of to-day, and its acts of injustice are reversed.

Certain it is that the instances which he cites at this page, do not establish his position respecting the disposition of the majority. The riot at Baltimore was, like other riots in England and in France, the result of popular phrensy excited to madness by conduct of the most provoking character. The majority in the state of Maryland and throughout the United States, highly disapproved the acts of violence committed on the occasion. The acquittal by a jury of those arraigned for the murder of Gen. Lingan, proves only that there was not sufficient evidence to identify the accused, or that the jury was governed by passion. It is not perceived how the majority of the people are answerable for the verdicts rendered. The guilty have often been erroneously acquitted in all countries, and in France particularly, recent instances are not wanting of acquittals, especially in prosecutions for political offences, against clear and indisputable testimony. And it was entirely fortuitous that the jury was composed of men whose sympathies were with the rioters and murderers, if the fact was so. It not unfrequently happens that a jury taken from lists furnished years perhaps, and always a long time, before the trial, are decidedly hostile to the temporary prevailing sentiments of their city, county, or state.

As to the other instance, if the inhabitant of Pennsylvania intended to intimate to our author, that a coloured voter would be in personal jeopardy for venturing to appear at the polls to exercise his right, it must be said in truth, that the incident was local and peculiar, and contrary to what is annually seen throughout the states where coloured persons are permitted to vote, who exercise that privilege with as full immunity from injury or oppression, as any white citizen. And, after all, it is believed that the state of feeling intimated by the informant of our author, is but an indication of dislike to a *caste* degraded by servitude and ignorance; and it is not perceived how it proves the despotism of a majority over the freedom and independence of opinion. If it be true, it proves a detestable tyranny over *acts*, over the exercise of an acknowledged right. The apprehensions of a mob committing violence deterred the coloured voters from approaching the polls. Are instances unknown in England or even in France, of peaceable subjects being prevented by mobs or the fear of them, from the exercise of a right, from the discharge of a duty? And are they evidences of the despotism of a majority in those countries?—*American Editor.*]

I have heard of patriotism in the United States, and it is a virtue which may be found among the people, but never among the leaders of the people. This may be explained by analogy; despotism debases the oppressed, much more than the oppressor; in absolute monarchies the king has often great virtues, but the courtiers are invariably servile. It is true that the American courtiers do not say, "sire," or "your majesty"—a distinction without a difference. They are for ever talking of the natural intelligence of the populace they serve; they do not debate the question as to which of the virtues of their master are preeminently worthy of admiration; for they assure him that he possesses all the virtues under heaven without having acquired them, or without caring to acquire them: they do not give him their daughters and their wives to be raised at his pleasure to the rank of his concubines, but, by sacrificing their opinions, they prostitute themselves. Moralists and philosophers in America are not obliged to conceal their opinions under the veil of allegory; but, before they venture upon a harsh truth, they say: "We are aware that the people which we are addressing is too

superior to all the weaknesses of human nature to lose the command
of its temper for an instant; and we should not hold this language if
we were not speaking to men, whom their virtues and their intelligence render more worthy of freedom than all the rest of the world."
   It would have been impossible for the sycophants of Louis XIV. to
flatter more dexterously. For my part, I am persuaded that in all governments, whatever their nature may be, servility will cower to force,
and adulation will cling to power. The only means of preventing men
from degrading themselves, is to invest no one with that unlimited authority which is the surest method of debasing them.

THE GREATEST DANGERS OF THE AMERICAN REPUBLICS PROCEED FROM
THE UNLIMITED POWER OF THE MAJORITY.

Democratic Republics liable to perish from a misuse of their Power, and not by Impotence.—The Governments of the American Republics are more Centralized
and more Energetic than those of the Monarchies of Europe.—Dangers resulting
from this.—Opinions of Hamilton and Jefferson upon this Point.

Governments usually fall a sacrifice to impotence or to tyranny. In
the former case their power escapes from them: it is wrested from
their grasp in the latter. Many observers who have noticed the anarchy
of democratic states, have imagined that the government of those
states was naturally weak and impotent. The truth is, that when once
hostilities are begun between parties, the government loses its control
over society. But I do not think that a democratic power is naturally
without resources: say rather, that it is almost always by the abuse of
its force, and the misemployment of its resources, that a democratic
government fails. Anarchy is almost always produced by its tyranny or
its mistakes, but not by its want of strength.
   It is important not to confound stability with force, or the greatness
of a thing with its duration. In democratic republics, the power which
directs* society is not stable; for it often changes hands and assumes
a new direction. But whichever way it turns, its force is almost irresistible. The governments of the American republics appear to me to
be as much centralized as those of the absolute monarchies of Europe,
and more energetic than they are. I do not, therefore, imagine that
they will perish from weakness.†
   If ever the free institutions of America are destroyed, that event may
be attributed to the unlimited authority of the majority, which may at
some future time urge the minorities to desperation, and oblige them
to have recourse to physical force. Anarchy will then be the result, but
it will have been brought about by despotism.
   Mr. Hamilton expresses the same opinion in the Federalist, No. 51.
"It is of great importance in a republic not only to guard the society

---

* This power may be centred in an assembly, in which case it will be strong without being stable; or it may be centred in an individual, in which case it will be less strong, but more stable.
† I presume that it is scarcely necessary to remind the reader here, as well as throughout the
remainder of this chapter, that I am speaking not of the federal government, but of the several governments of each state which the majority controls at its pleasure.

against the oppression of its rulers, but to guard one part of the society against the injustice of the other part. Justice is the end of government. It is the end of civil society. It ever has been, and ever will be pursued until it be obtained, or until liberty be lost in the pursuit. In a society, under the forms of which the stronger faction can readily unite and oppress the weaker, anarchy may as truly be said to reign as in a state of nature, where the weaker individual is not secured against the violence of the stronger: and as in the latter state even the stronger individuals are prompted by the uncertainty of their condition to submit to a government which may protect the weak as well as themselves, so in the former state will the more powerful factions be gradually induced by a like motive to wish for a government which will protect all parties, the weaker as well as the more powerful. It can be little doubted, that if the state of Rhode Island was separated from the confederacy and left to itself, the insecurity of rights under the popular form of government within such narrow limits, would be displayed by such reiterated oppressions of the factious majorities, that some power altogether independent of the people would soon be called for by the voice of the very factions whose misrule had proved the necessity of it."

Jefferson has also thus expressed himself in a letter to Madison:* "The executive power in our government is not the only, perhaps not even the principal object of my solicitude. The tyranny of the legislature is really the danger most to be feared, and will continue to be so for many years to come. The tyranny of the executive power will come in its turn, but at a more distant period."

I am glad to cite the opinion of Jefferson upon this subject rather than that of another, because I consider him to be the most powerful advocate democracy has ever sent forth.

Chapter XVI.

CAUSES WHICH MITIGATE THE TYRANNY OF THE MAJORITY IN THE UNITED STATES.

ABSENCE OF CENTRAL ADMINISTRATION.

The national Majority does not pretend to conduct all Business.—Is obliged to employ the town and county Magistrates to execute its supreme Decisions.

I have already pointed out the distinction which is to be made between a centralized government and a centralized administration. The former exists in America, but the latter is nearly unknown there. If the directing power of the American communities had both these instruments of government at its disposal, and united the habit of executing

---

* 15th March, 1789.

its own commands to the right of commanding; if, after having established the general principles of government, it descended to the details of public business; and if, having regulated the great interests of the country, it would penetrate into the privacy of individual interest, freedom would soon be banished from the New World.

But in the United States the majority, which so frequently displays the tastes and the propensities of a despot, is still destitute of the more perfect instruments of tyranny.

In the American republics the activity of the central government has never as yet been extended beyond a limited number of objects sufficiently prominent to call forth its attention. The secondary affairs of society have never been regulated by its authority; and nothing has hitherto betrayed its desire of interfering in them. The majority is become more and more absolute, but it has not increased the prerogatives of the central government; those great prerogatives have been confined to a certain sphere; and although the despotism of the majority may be galling upon one point, it cannot be said to extend to all. However the predominant party in the nation may be carried away by its passions; however ardent it may be in the pursuit of its projects, it cannot oblige all the citizens to comply with its desires in the same manner, and at the same time, throughout the country. When the central government which represents that majority has issued a decree, it must intrust the execution of its will to agents, over whom it frequently has no control, and whom it cannot perpetually direct. The townships, municipal bodies, and counties, may therefore be looked upon as concealed breakwaters, which check or part the tide of popular excitement. If an oppressive law were passed, the liberties of the people would still be protected by the means by which that law would be put in execution: the majority cannot descend to the details, and (as I will venture to style them) the puerilities of administrative tyranny. Nor does the people entertain that full consciousness of its authority, which would prompt it to interfere in these matters; it knows the extent of its natural powers, but it is unacquainted with the increased resources which the art of government might furnish.

This point deserves attention; for if a democratic republic, similar to that of the United States, were ever founded in a country where the power of a single individual had previously subsisted, and the effects of a centralized administration had sunk deep into the habits and the laws of the people, I do not hesitate to assert, that in that country a more insufferable despotism would prevail than any which now exists in the absolute monarchies of Europe; or indeed than any which could be found on this side the confines of Asia.

THE PROFESSION OF THE LAW IN THE UNITED STATES SERVES TO COUNTERPOISE THE DEMOCRACY.

Utility of discriminating the natural Propensities of the Members of the legal Profession.—These Men called upon to act a prominent Part in future Society.—In what Manner the peculiar Pursuits of Lawyers give an aristocratic turn to their Ideas.—Accidental Causes which may check this Tendency.—Ease with which the Aristocracy coalesces with legal Men.—Use of Lawyers to a Despot.—The Profession of the Law constitutes the only aristocratic Element with which the natural Elements of Democracy will combine.—Peculiar Causes which tend to give an aristocratic turn of Mind to the English and American Lawyer.—The Aristocracy of America is on the Bench and at the Bar.—Influence of Lawyers upon American Society.—Their peculiar magisterial Habits affect the Legislature, the Administration, and even the People.

In visiting the Americans and in studying their laws, we perceive that the authority they have intrusted to members of the legal profession, and the influence which these individuals exercise in the government, is the most powerful existing security against the excesses of democracy.

This effect seems to me to result from a general cause which it is useful to investigate, since it may produce analogous consequences elsewhere.

The members of the legal profession have taken an important part in all the vicissitudes of political society in Europe during the last five hundred years. At one time they have been the instruments of those who were invested with political authority, and at another they have succeeded in converting political authorities into their instrument. In the middle ages they afforded a powerful support to the crown; and since that period they have exerted themselves to the utmost to limit the royal prerogative. In England they have contracted a close alliance with the aristocracy; in France they have proved to be the most dangerous enemies of that class. It is my object to inquire whether, under all these circumstances, the members of the legal profession have been swayed by sudden and momentary impulses; or whether they have been impelled by principles which are inherent in their pursuits, and which will always recur in history. I am incited to this investigation by reflecting that this particular class of men will most likely play a prominent part in that order of things to which the events of our time are giving birth.

Men who have more especially devoted themselves to legal pursuits, derive from those occupations certain habits of order, a taste for formalities, and a kind of instinctive regard for the regular connexion of ideas, which naturally render them very hostile to the revolutionary spirit and the unreflecting passions of the multitude.

The special information which lawyers derive from their studies, ensures them a separate station in society; and they constitute a sort of privileged body in the scale of intelligence. This notion of their superiority perpetually recurs to them in the practice of their profession: they are the masters of a science which is necessary, but which is not very generally known: they serve as arbiters between the citizens; and the habit of directing the blind passions of parties in litigation to their purpose, inspires them with a certain contempt for the judgement of the multitude. To this it may be added, that they naturally constitute *a body*; not by any previous understanding, or by an agreement which directs them to a common end; but the analogy of their studies and the uniformity of their proceedings connect their minds together, as much as a common interest would combine their endeavours.

A portion of the tastes and of the habits of the aristocracy may consequently be discovered in the characters of men in the profession of the law. They participate in the same instinctive love of order and of formalities; and they entertain the same repugnance to the actions of the multitude, and the same secret contempt of the government of the people. I do not mean to say that the natural propensities of lawyers are sufficiently strong to sway them irresistibly; for they, like most other men, are governed by their private interests and the advantages of the moment.

In a state of society in which the members of the legal profession are prevented from holding that rank in the political world which they enjoy in private life, we may rest assured that they will be the foremost agents of revolution. But it must then be inquired whether the cause which induces them to innovate and to destroy is accidental, or whether it belongs to some lasting purpose which they entertain. It is true that lawyers mainly contributed to the overthrow of the French monarchy in 1789; but it remains to be seen whether they acted thus because they had studied the laws, or because they were prohibited from co-operating in the work of legislation.

Five hundred years ago the English nobles headed the people, and spoke in its name; at the present time, the aristocracy supports the throne, and defends the royal prerogative. But aristocracy has, notwithstanding this, its peculiar instincts and propensities. We must be careful not to confound isolated members of a body with the body itself. In all free governments, of whatsoever form they may be, members of the legal profession will be found at the head of all parties. The same remark is also applicable to the aristocracy; for almost all the democratic convulsions which have agitated the world have been directed by nobles.

A privileged body can never satisfy the ambition of all its members; it has always more talents and more passions than it can find places to content and to employ; so that a considerable number of individuals are usually to be met with, who are inclined to attack those very privileges, which they find it impossible to turn to their own account.

I do not, then, assert that all the members of the legal profession are at all times the friends of order and the opponents of innovation, but merely that most of them usually are so. In a community in which lawyers are allowed to occupy, without opposition, that high station which naturally belongs to them, their general spirit will be eminently conservative and anti-democratic. When an aristocracy excludes the leaders of that profession from its ranks, it excites enemies which are the more formidable to its security as they are independent of the nobility by their industrious pursuits; and they feel themselves to be its equal in point of intelligence, although they enjoy less opulence and less power. But whenever an aristocracy consents to impart some of its privileges to these same individuals, the two classes coalesce very readily, and assume, as it were, the consistency of a single order of family interests.

I am, in like manner, inclined to believe that a monarch will always be able to convert legal practitioners into the most serviceable instruments of his authority. There is a far greater affinity between this class of individuals and the executive power, than there is between them and the people; just as there is a greater natural affinity between the nobles and the monarch, than between the nobles and the people, although the higher orders of society have occasionally resisted the prerogative of the crown in concert with the lower classes.

Lawyers are attached to public order beyond every other consideration, and the best security of public order is authority. It must not be forgotten, that if they prize the free institutions of their country much, they nevertheless value the legality of those institutions far more; they are less afraid of tyranny than of arbitrary power; and provided that the legislature take upon itself to deprive men of their independence, they are not dissatisfied. (a)

I am therefore convinced that the prince who, in presence of an encroaching democracy, should endeavour to impair the judicial authority in his dominions, and to diminish the political influence of lawyers, would commit a great mistake. He would let slip the substance of authority to grasp at the shadow. He would act more wisely in introducing men connected with the law into the government; and if he intrusted them with the conduct of a despotic power, bearing some marks of violence, that power would most likely assume the external features of justice and of legality in their hands.

The government of democracy is favourable to the political power of lawyers; for when the wealthy, the noble, and the prince, are excluded from the government, they are sure to occupy the highest stations in their own right, as it were, since they are the only men of information and sagacity, beyond the sphere of the people, who can be the object of the popular choice. If, then, they are led by their tastes to combine with the aristocracy, and to support the crown, they are naturally brought into contact with the people by their interests. They like the government of democracy, without participating in its propensities, and without imitating its weaknesses; whence they derive a twofold authority from it and over it. The people in democratic states does not mistrust the members of the legal profession, because it is well known that they are interested in serving the popular cause; and it listens to them without irritation, because it does not attribute to them any sinister designs. The object of lawyers is not, indeed, to overthrow the institutions of democracy, but they constantly endeavour to give it an impulse which diverts it from its real tendency, by means which are

---

(a) This translation does not accurately convey the meaning of M. de Tocqueville's expression. He says: "Ils craignent moins la tyrannie que l'arbitraire, et pourvu que le législateur se charge lui-même d'enlever aux hommes leur indépendance, ils sont à peu pres content."
The more correct rendering would be: "They fear tyranny less than arbitrary sway, and provided it is the legislator himself who undertakes to deprive men of their independence, they are almost content."—*Reviser.*

foreign to its nature. Lawyers belong to the people by birth and interest, to the aristocracy by habit and by taste, and they may be looked
upon as the natural bond and connecting link of the two great classes
of society.

The profession of the law is the only aristocratic element which can
be amalgamated without violence with the natural elements of democracy, and which can be advantageously and permanently combined
with them. I am not unacquainted with the defects which are inherent
in the character of that body of men; but without this admixture of
lawyer-like sobriety with the democratic principle, I question whether
democratic institutions could long be maintained; and I cannot believe that a republic could subsist at the present time, if the influence
of lawyers in public business did not increase in proportion to the
power of the people.

This aristocratic character, which I hold to be common to the legal
profession, is much more distinctly marked in the United States and
in England than in any other country. This proceeds not only from the
legal studies of the English and American lawyers, but from the nature
of the legislation, and the position which those persons occupy, in the
two countries. The English and the Americans have retained the law
of precedents; that is to say, they continue to found their legal opinions and the decisions of their courts upon the opinions and decisions
of their forefathers. In the mind of an English or American lawyer, a
taste and a reverence for what is old are almost always united to a love
of regular and lawful proceedings.

This predisposition has another effect upon the character of the legal profession and upon the general course of society. The English and
American lawyers investigate what has been done; the French advocate inquiries what should have been done: the former produces
precedents; the latter reasons. A French observer is surprised to hear
how often an English or an American lawyer quotes the opinions of
others, and how little he alludes to his own; while the reverse occurs
in France. There, the most trifling litigation is never conducted without the introduction of an entire system of ideas peculiar to the counsel employed; and the fundamental principles of law are discussed in
order to obtain a perch of land by the decision of the court. This abnegation of his own opinion, and this implicit deference to the opinion
of his forefathers, which are common to the English and American
lawyer, this subjection of thought which he is obliged to profess, necessarily give him more timid habits and more sluggish inclinations in
England and America than in France.

The French codes are often difficult of comprehension, but they can
be read by every one; nothing, on the other hand, can be more impenetrable to the uninitiated than a legislation founded upon precedents.
The indispensable want of legal assistance which is felt in England and
in the United States, and the high opinion which is generally entertained of the ability of the legal profession, tend to separate it more and
more from the people, and to place it in a distinct class. The French
lawyer is simply a man extensively acquainted with the statues of his

country; but the English or American lawyer resembles the hierophants of Egypt, for, like them, he is the sole interpreter of an occult science.

[The remark that English and American lawyers found their opinions and their decisions upon those of their forefathers, is calculated to excite surprise in an American reader, who supposes that *law*, as a prescribed rule of action, can only be ascertained in cases where the statutes are silent, by reference to the decisions of courts. On the continent, and particularly in France, as the writer of this note learned from the conversation of M. De Tocqueville, the judicial tribunals do not deem themselves bound by any precedents, or by any decisions of their predecessors or of the appellate tribunals. They respect such decisions as the opinions of distinguished men, and they pay no higher regard to their own previous adjucations of any case. It is not easy to perceive how the law can acquire any stability under such a system, or how any individual can ascertain his rights, without a lawsuit. This note should not be concluded without a single remark upon what the author calls an implicit deference to the opinions of our forefathers, and abnegation of our own opinions. The common law consists of principles founded on the common sense of mankind, and adapted to the circumstances of man in civilized society. When these principles are once settled by competent authority, or rather *declared* by such authority, they are supposed to express the common sense and the common justice of the community; and it requires but a moderate share of modesty for any one entertaining a different view of them, to consider that the disinterested and intelligent judges who have declared them, are more likely to be right than he is. Perfection, even in the law, he does not consider attainable by human beings, and the greatest approximation to it is all he expects or desires. Besides, there are very few cases of positive and abstract rule, where it is of any consequence which, of any two or more modifications of it, should be adopted. The great point is, that there should be *a rule* by which conduct may be regulated. Thus, whether in mercantile transactions notice of a default by a principal shall be given to an endorser, or a guarantor, and when and how such notice shall be given, are not so important in themselves, as it is that there should be some rule to which merchants may adapt themselves and their transactions. Statutes cannot, or at least do not, prescribe the rules in a large majority of cases. If then they are not drawn from the decisions of courts, they will not exist, and men will be wholly at a loss for a guide in the most important trans-actions of business. Hence the deference paid to legal decisions. But this is not implicit, as the author supposes. The course of reasoning by which the courts have come to their conclusions, is often assailed by the advocate and shown to be fallacious, and the instances are not unfrequent of courts disregarding prior decisions and overruling them when not fairly deducible from sound reason.

Again, the principles of the common law are flexible, and adapt themselves to changes in society, and a well-known maxim in our system, that when the reason of the law ceases, the law itself ceases, has overthrown many an antiquated rule. Within these limits, it is conceived there is range enough for the exercise of all the reason of the advocate and the judge, without unsettling everything and depriving the conduct of human affairs of all guidance from human authority;—and the talents of our lawyers and courts find sufficient exercise in applying the principles of one case to the facts of another.—*American Editor.*]

The station which lawyers occupy in England and America, exercises no less an influence upon their habits and their opinions. The English aristocracy, which has taken care to attract to its sphere whatever is at all analogous to itself, has conferred a high degree of importance and of authority upon the members of the legal profession. In English society lawyers do not occupy the first rank, but they are contented with the station assigned to them; they constitute, as it were, the younger branch of the English aristocracy, and they are attached to their elder brothers, although they do not enjoy all their privileges. The English lawyers consequently mingle the tastes and the ideas of the aristocratic circles in which they move, with the aristocratic interests of their profession.

And indeed the lawyer-like character which I am endeavouring to depict, is most distinctly to be met with in England: there laws are esteemed not so much because they are good, as because they are old; and if it be necessary to modify them in any respect, or to adapt them to the changes which time operates in society, recourse is had to the most inconceivable contrivances in order to uphold the traditionary fabric, and to maintain that nothing has been done which does not square with the intentions, and complete the labours, of former generations. The very individuals who conduct these changes disclaim all intention of innovation, and they had rather resort to absurd expedients than plead guilty of so great a crime. This spirit more especially appertains to the English lawyers; they seem indifferent to the real meaning of what they treat, and they direct all their attention to the letter, seeming inclined to infringe the rules of common sense and of humanity, rather than to swerve one tittle from the law. The English legislation may be compared to the stock of an old tree, upon which lawyers have engrafted the most various shoots, with the hope, that, although their fruits may differ, their foliage at least will be confounded with the venerable trunk which supports them all.

In America there are no nobles or literary men, and the people is apt to mistrust the wealthy; lawyers consequently form the highest political class, and the most cultivated circle of society. They have therefore nothing to gain by innovation, which adds a conservative interest to their natural taste for public order. If I were asked where I place the American aristocracy, I should reply without hesitation, that it is not composed of the rich, who are united together by no common tie, but that it occupies the judicial bench and the bar.

The more we reflect upon all that occurs in the United States, the more shall we be persuaded that the lawyers, as a body, form the most powerful, if not the only counterpoise to the democratic element. In that country we perceive how eminently the legal profession is qualified by its powers, and even by its defects, to neutralize the vices which are inherent in popular government. When the American people is intoxicated by passion, or carried away by the impetuosity of its ideas, it is checked and stopped by the almost invisible influence of its legal counsellors, who secretly oppose their aristocratic propensities to its democratic instincts, their superstitious attachment to what is antique to its love of novelty, their narrow views to its immense designs, and their habitual procrastination to its ardent impatience.

The courts of justice are the most visible organs by which the legal profession is enabled to control the democracy. The judge is a lawyer, who, independently of the taste for regularity and order which he has contracted in the study of legislation, derives an additional love of stability from his own inalienable functions. His legal attainments have already raised him to a distinguished rank among his fellow-citizens; his political power completes the distinction of his station, and gives him the inclinations natural to privileged classes.

Armed with the power of declaring the laws to be unconstitutional,[*] the American magistrate perpetually interferes in political affairs. He cannot force the people to make laws, but at least he can oblige it not to disobey its own enactments, or to act inconsistently with its own principles. I am aware that a secret tendency to diminish the judicial power exists in the United States; and by most of the constitutions of the several states, the government can, upon the demand of the two houses of the legislature, remove the judges from their station. By some other constitutions the members of the tribunals are elected, and they are even subjected to frequent re-elections. I venture to predict that these innovations will sooner or later be attended with fatal consequences; and that it will be found out at some future period, that the attack which is made upon the judicial power has affected the democratic republic itself.

It must not, however, be supposed that the legal spirit of which I have been speaking has been confined in the United States to the courts of justice; it extends far beyond them. As the lawyers constitute the only enlightened class which the people does not mistrust, they are naturally called upon to occupy most of the public stations. They fill the legislative assemblies, and they conduct the administration; they consequently exercise a powerful influence upon the formation of the law, and upon its execution. The lawyers are, however, obliged to yield to the current of public opinion, which is too strong for them to resist it; but it is easy to find indications of what their conduct would be, if they were free to act as they chose. The Americans, who have made such copious innovations in their political legislation, have introduced very sparing alterations in their civil laws, and that with great difficulty, although those laws are frequently repugnant to their social condition. The reason of this is, that in matters of civil law the majority is obliged to defer to the authority of the legal profession, and that the American lawyers are disinclined to innovate when they are left to their own choice.

It is curious for a Frenchman, accustomed to a very different state of things, to hear the perpetual complaints which are made in the United States, against the stationary propensities of legal men, and their prejudices in favour of existing institutions.

The influence of the legal habits which are common in America ex-

---

* See chapter vi., p. 101, on the judicial power in the United States.

tends beyond the limits I have just pointed out. Scarcely any question arises in the United States which does not become, sooner or later, a subject of judicial debate; hence all parties are obliged to borrow the ideas, and even the language, usual in judicial proceedings, in their daily controversies. As most public men are, or have been, legal practitioners, they introduce the customs and technicalities of their profession into the affairs of the country. The jury extends this habitude to all classes. The language of the law thus becomes, in some measure, a vulgar tongue; the spirit of the law, which is produced in the schools and courts of justice, gradually penetrates beyond their walls into the bosom of society, where it descends to the lowest classes, so that the whole people contracts the habits and the tastes of the magistrate. The lawyers of the United States form a party which is but little feared and scarcely perceived, which has no badge peculiar to itself, which adapts itself with great flexibility to the exigencies of the time, and accommodates itself to all the movements of the social body: but this party extends over the whole community, and it penetrates into all classes of society; it acts upon the country imperceptibly, but it finally fashions it to suit its purposes.

TRIAL BY JURY IN THE UNITED STATES CONSIDERED AS A POLITICAL INSTITUTION.

Trial by Jury, which is one of the Instruments of the Sovereignty of the People, deserves to be compared with the other Laws which establish that Sovereignty.—Composition of the Jury in the United States.—Effect of Trial by Jury upon the national Character.—It educates the People.—It tends to establish the Authority of the Magistrates, and to extend a knowledge of Law among the People.

Since I have been led by my subject to recur to the administration of justice in the United States, I will not pass over this point without advertising to the institution of the jury. Trial by jury may be considered in two separate points of view: as a judicial, and as a political institution. If it entered into my present purpose to inquire how far trial by jury (more especially in civil cases) contributes to ensure the best administration of justice, I admit that its utility might be contested. As the jury was first introduced at a time when society was in an uncivilized state, and when courts of justice were merely called upon to decide on the evidence of facts, it is not an easy task to adapt it to the wants of a highly civilized community, when the mutual relations of men are multiplied to a surprising extent, and have assumed the enlightened and intellectual character of the age.*

My present object is to consider the jury as a political institution; and any other course would divert me from my subject. Of trial by jury,

---

* The investigation of trial by jury as a judicial institution, and the appreciation of its effects in the United States, together with the advantages the Americans have derived from it, would suffice to form a book, and a book upon a very useful and curious subject. The state of Louisiana would in particular afford the curious phenomenon of a French and English legislation, as well as a French and English population, which are gradually combining with each other. See the "Digeste des Lois de la Louisiane," in two volumes; and the "Traité sur les Regles des Actions civiles," printed in French and English at New Orleans in 1830.

considered as a judicial institution, I shall here say but very few words. When the English adopted trial by jury they were a semi-barbarous people; they are become, in course of time, one of the most enlightened nations of the earth; and their attachment to this institution seems to have increased with their increasing cultivation. They soon spread beyond their insular boundaries to every corner of the habitable globe; some have formed colonies, others independent states; the mother-country has maintained its monarchical constitution; many of its offspring have founded powerful republics; but wherever the English have been, they have boasted of the privilege of trial by jury.* They have established it, or hastened to re-establish it, in all their settlements. A judicial institution which obtains the suffrages of a great people for so long a series of ages, which is zealously renewed at every epoch of civilization, in all the climates of the earth, and under every form of human government, cannot be contrary to the spirit of justice.†

I turn, however, from this part of the subject. To look upon the jury as a mere judicial institution, is to confine our attention to a very narrow view of it; for, however great its influence may be upon the decisions of the law-courts, that influence is very subordinate to the powerful effects which it produces on the destinies of the community at large. The jury is above all a political institution, and it must be regarded in this light in order to be duly appreciated.

By the jury, I mean a certain number of citizens chosen indiscriminately, and invested with a temporary right of judging. Trial by jury, as applied to the repression of crime, appears to me to introduce an eminently republican element into the government, upon the following grounds:—

---

* All the English and American jurists are unanimous upon this head. Mr. Story, judge of the supreme court of the United States, speaks, in his treatise on the federal constitution, of the advantages of trial by jury in civil cases: "The inestimable privilege of a trial by jury in civil cases—a privilege scarcely inferior to that in criminal cases, which is counted by all persons to be essential to political and civil liberty". . . (Story, book iii., ch. xxxviii.)

† If it were our province to point out the utility of the jury as a judicial institution in this place, much might be said, and the following arguments might be brought forward among others:—

By introducing the jury into the business of the courts you are enabled to diminish the number of judges; which is a very great advantage. When judges are very numerous, death is perpetually thinning the ranks of the judicial functionaries, and laying places vacant for new comers. The ambition of the magistrates is therefore continually excited, and they are naturally made dependant upon the will of the majority, or the individual who fills up vacant appointments: the officers of the courts then rise like the officers of an army. This state of things is entirely contrary to the sound administration of justice, and to the intentions of the legislator. The office of a judge is made inalienable in order that he may remain independent; but of what advantage is it that his independence is protected, if he be tempted to sacrifice it of his own accord? When judges are very numerous, many of them must necessarily be incapable of performing their important duties; for a great magistrate is a man of no common powers: and I am inclined to believe that a half-enlightened tribunal is the worst of all instruments for attaining those objects which it is the purpose of courts of justice to accomplish. For my own part, I had rather submit the decision of a case to ignorant jurors directed by a skilful judge, than to judges, a majority of whom are imperfectly acquainted with jurisprudence and with the laws.

[I venture to remind the reader, lest this note should appear somewhat redundant to an English eye, that the jury is an institution which has only been naturalized in France within the present century; that it is even now exclusively applied to those criminal causes which come before the courts of assize, or to the prosecutions of the public press; and that the judges and counsellors of the numerous local tribunals of France—forming a body of many thousand judicial functionaries—try all civil causes, appeals from criminal causes, and minor offences, without the jury.—*Translator's Note.*]

The institution of the jury may be aristocratic or democratic, according to the class of society from which the jurors are selected; but it always preserves its republican character, inasmuch as it places the real direction of society in the hands of the governed, or of a portion of the governed, instead of leaving it under the authority of the government. Force is never more than a transient element of success; and after force comes the notion of right. A government which should only be able to crush its enemies upon a field of battle, would very soon be destroyed. The true sanction of political laws is to be found in penal legislation, and if that sanction be wanting, the law will sooner or later lose its cogency. He who punishes infractions of the law is therefore the real master of society. Now, the institution of the jury raises the people itself, or at least a class of citizens, to the bench of judicial authority. The institution of the jury consequently invests the people, or that class of citizens, with the direction of society.*

In England the jury is returned from the aristocratic portion of the nation,† the aristocracy makes the laws, applies the laws, and punishes all infractions of the laws; everything is established upon a consistent footing, and England may with truth be said to constitute an aristocratic republic. In the United States the same system is applied to the whole people. Every American citizen is qualified to be an elector, a juror, and is eligible to office.‡ The system of the jury, as it is understood in America, appears to me to be as direct and as extreme a consequence of the sovereignty of the people, as universal suffrage. These institutions are two instruments of equal power, which contribute to the supremacy of the majority. All the sovereigns who have chosen to govern by their own authority, and to direct society instead of obeying its direction, have destroyed or enfeebled the institution of the jury. The monarchs of the house of Tudor sent to prison jurors who refused to convict, and Napoleon¹ caused them to be returned by his agents.

However clear most of these truths may seem to be, they do not command universal assent, and in France, at least, the institution of trial by jury is still very imperfectly understood. If the question arise as to the proper qualification of jurors, it is confined to a discussion of

---

* An important remark must however be made. Trial by jury does unquestionably invest the people with a general control over the actions of citizens, but it does not furnish means of exercising this control in all cases, or with an absolute authority. When an absolute monarch has the right of trying offences by his representatives, the fate of the prisoner is, as it were, decided beforehand. But even if the people were predisposed to convict, the composition and the non-responsibility of the jury would still afford some chances favourable to the protection of innocence.

† [In France, the qualification of the jurors is the same as the electoral qualification, namely, the payment of 200 francs per annum in direct taxes; they are chosen by lot. In England, they are returned by the sheriff; the qualifications of jurors were raised to 10*l*. per annum in England, and 6*l*. in Wales, of freehold land or copyhold, by the statute W. and M., c. 24: leaseholders for a time determinable upon life or lives, of the clear yearly value of 20*l*. per annum over and above the rent reserved, are qualified to serve on juries; and jurors in the courts of Westminster and city of London must be householders, and possessed of real and personal estates of the value of 100*l*. The qualifications, however, prescribed in different statutes, vary according to the object for which the jury is impannelled. See Blackstone's Commentaries, b. iii., c. 23—*Translator's Note.*]

‡ See Appendix Q.

the intelligence and knowledge of the citizens who may be returned, as if the jury was merely a judicial institution. This appears to me to be the least part of the subject. The jury is pre-eminently a political institution; it must be regarded as one form of the sovereignty of the people; when that sovereignty is repudiated, it must be rejected; or it must be adapted to the laws by which that sovereignty is established. The jury is that portion of the nation to which the execution of the laws is intrusted, as the houses of parliament constitute that part of the nation which makes the laws; and in order that society may be governed with consistency and uniformity, the list of citizens qualified to serve on juries must increase and diminish with the list of electors. This I hold to be the point of view most worthy of the attention of the legislator; and all that remains is merely accessory.

I am so entirely convinced that the jury is pre-eminently a political institution, that I still consider it in this light when it is applied in civil causes. Laws are always unstable unless they are founded upon the manners of a nation: manners are the only durable and resisting power in a people. When the jury is reserved for criminal offences, the people only sees its occasional action in certain particular cases; the ordinary course of life goes on without its interference, and it is considered as an instrument, but not as the only instrument, of obtaining justice. This is true *a fortiori* when the jury is only applied to certain criminal causes.

When, on the contrary, the influence of the jury is extended to civil causes, its application is constantly palpable; it affects all the interests of the community; every one co-operates in its work: it thus penetrates into all the usages of life, it fashions the human mind to its peculiar forms, and is gradually associated with the idea of justice itself.

The institution of the jury, if confined to criminal causes, is always in danger; but when once it is introduced into civil proceedings, it defies the aggressions of time and of man. If it had been as easy to remove the jury from the manners as from the laws of England, it would have perished under Henry VIII. and Elizabeth; and the civil jury did in reality, at that period, save the liberties of the country. In whatever manner the jury be applied, it cannot fail to exercise a powerful influence upon the national character; but this influence is prodigiously increased when it is introduced into civil causes. The jury, and more especially the civil jury, serves to communicate the spirit of the judges to the minds of all the citizens; and this spirit, with the habits which attend it, is the soundest preparation for free institutions. It imbues all classes with a respect for the thing judged, and with the notion of right. If these two elements be removed, the love of independence is reduced to a mere destructive passion. It teaches men to practise equity; every man learns to judge his neighbour as he would himself be judged: and this is especially true of the jury in civil causes; for, while the number of persons who have reason to apprehend a criminal prosecution is small, every one is liable to have a civil action brought against him. The jury teaches every man not to recoil before the responsibility of his own actions, and impresses him with that manly confidence without which political virtue cannot exist. It invests each citizen with a kind of magistracy; it makes them all feel the duties which they are bound to discharge toward society; and the part which they take in the government. By obliging men to turn their attention to affairs which are not exclusively their own, it rubs off that individual egotism which is the rust of society.

The jury contributes most powerfully to form the judgement, and to increase the natural intelligence of a people; and this is, in my opinion, its greatest advantage. It may be regarded as a gratuitous public school ever open, in which every juror learns to exercise his rights, enters into daily communication with the most learned and enlightened members of the upper classes, and becomes practically acquainted with the laws of his country, which are brought within the reach of his capacity by the efforts of the bar, the advice of the judge, and even by the passions of the parties. I think that the practical intelligence and political good sense of the Americans are mainly attributable to the long use which they have made of the jury in civil causes.

I do not know whether the jury is useful to those who are in litigation; but I am certain it is highly beneficial to those who decide the litigation; and I look upon it as one of the most efficacious means for the education of the people, which society can employ.

What I have hitherto said applies to all nations; but the remark I am now about to make is peculiar to the Americans and to democratic peoples. I have already observed that in democracies the members of the legal profession, and the magistrates, constitute the only aristocratic body which can check the irregularities of the people. This aristocracy is invested with no physical power; but it exercises its conservative influence upon the minds of men: and the most abundant source of its authority is the institution of the civil jury. In criminal causes, when society is armed against a single individual, the jury is apt to look upon the judge as the passive instrument of social power, and to mistrust his advice. Moreover, criminal causes are entirely founded upon the evidence of facts which common sense can readily appreciate; upon this ground the judge and the jury are equal. Such, however, is not the case in civil causes; then the judge appears as a disinterested arbiter between the conflicting passions of the parties. The jurors look up to him with confidence, and listen to him with respect, for in this instance their intelligence is completely under the control of his learning. It is the judge who sums up the various arguments with which their memory has been wearied out, and who guides them through the devious course of the proceedings; he points their attention to the exact question of fact, which they are called upon to solve, and he puts the answer to the question of law into their mouths. His influence upon their verdict is almost unlimited.

If I am called upon to explain why I am but little moved by the arguments derived from the ignorance of jurors in civil causes, I reply, that in these proceedings, whenever the question to be solved is not a mere question of fact, the jury has only the semblance of a judicial body. The jury sanctions the decisions of the judge; they, by the authority of society which they represent, and he, by that of reason and of law.*

In England and in America the judges exercise an influence upon criminal trials which the French judges have never possessed. The reason of this difference may easily be discovered; the English and American magistrates establish their authority in civil causes, and only transfer it afterward to tribunals of another kind, where that authority was not acquired. In some cases (and they are frequently the most important ones), the American judges have the right of deciding causes, alone.† Upon these occasions they are, accidentally, placed in the position which the French judges habitually occupy: but they are still surrounded by the reminiscence of the jury, and their judgement has almost as much authority as the voice of the community at large, represented by that institution. Their influence extends beyond the limits of the courts; in the recreations of private life as well as in the turmoil of public business, abroad and in the legislative assemblies, the American judge is constantly surrounded by men who are accustomed to regard his intelligence as superior to their own; and after having exercised his power in the decision of causes, he continues to influence the habits of thought, and the characters of the individuals who took a part in his judgement.

[The remark in the text, that "in some cases, and they are frequently the most important ones, the American judges have the right of deciding causes alone," and the author's note, that "the federal judges decide, upon their own authority, almost all the questions most important to the country," seem to require explanation in consequence of their connexion with the context in which the author is speaking of the trial by jury. They seem to imply that there are some cases which ought to be tried by jury, that are decided by the judges. It is believed that the learned author, although a distinguished advocate in France never thoroughly comprehended the grand divisions of our complicated system of law, in civil cases. First, is the distinction between cases in equity and those in which the rules of the common law govern. Those in equity are always decided by the judge or judges, who may, however, send questions of fact to be tried in the common law courts by a jury. But as a general rule this is entirely in the discretion of the equity judge. Second, in cases at common law, there are questions of fact and questions of law:—the former are invariably tried by a jury, the latter, whether presented in the course of a jury trial, or by pleading, in which the facts are admitted, are always decided by the judges.

Third, cases of admiralty jurisdiction, and proceedings in rem of an analogous nature, are decided by the judges without the intervention of a jury. The cases in this last class fall within the peculiar jurisdiction of the federal courts, and with this exception, the federal judges do not decide upon their own authority any questions, which, if presented in the state courts, would not also be decided by the judges of those courts. The supreme court of the United States, from the nature of its institution as almost wholly an appellant court, is called on to decide merely questions

---

* See Appendix R.
† The federal judges decide upon their own authority almost all the questions most important to the country.

of law, and in no case can that court decide a question of fact, unless it arises in suits peculiar to equity or admiralty jurisdiction. Indeed the author's original note is more correct than the translation. It is as follows: "Les juges fédéraux tranchent presque toujours seuls les questions qui touchent de plus près au *gouvernement* du pays." And it is very true that the supreme court of the United States, in particular, decides those questions which most nearly affect the *government* of the country, because those are the very questions which arise upon the constitutionality of the laws of congress and of the several states, the final and conclusive determination of which is vested in that tribunal.—*American Editor.*]

The jury, then, which seems to restrict the rights of magistracy, does in reality consolidate its power; and in no country are the judges so powerful as there where the people partakes their privileges. It is more especially by means of the jury in civil causes that the American magistrates imbue all classes of society with the spirit of their profession. Thus the jury, which is the most energetic means of making the people rule, is also the most efficacious means of teaching it to rule well.

Chapter XVII.

PRINCIPAL CAUSES WHICH TEND TO MAINTAIN THE DEMOCRATIC REPUBLIC IN THE UNITED STATES.

A democratic republic subsists in the United States; and the principal object of this book has been to account for the fact of its existence. Several of the causes which contribute to maintain the institutions of America have been voluntarily passed by, or only hinted at, as I was borne along by my subject. Others I have been unable to discuss; and those on which I have dwelt most, are, as it were, buried in the details of the former part of this work.

I think, therefore, that before I proceed to speak of the future, I cannot do better than collect within a small compass the reasons which best explain the present. In this retrospective chapter I shall be succinct; for I shall take care to remind the reader very summarily of what he already knows; and I shall only select the most prominent of those facts which I have not yet pointed out.

All the causes which contribute to the maintenance of the democratic republic in the United States are reducible to three heads:

I. The peculiar and accidental situation in which Providence has placed the Americans.

II. The laws.

III. The manners and customs of the people.

ACCIDENTAL OR PROVIDENTIAL CAUSES WHICH CONTRIBUTE TO THE MAINTENANCE OF THE DEMOCRATIC REPUBLIC IN THE UNITED STATES.

The Union has no Neighbours.—No Metropolis.—The Americans have had the Chances of Birth in their Favour.—America an empty Country.—How this Circumstance contributes powerfully to the Maintenance of the democratic Republic in America.—How the American Wilds are Peopled.—Avidity of the Anglo-Americans in taking Possession of the Solitudes of the New World.—Influence of physical Prosperity upon the political Opinions of the Americans.

A thousand circumstances, independent of the will of man, concur to facilitate the maintenance of a democratic republic in the United States. Some of these peculiarities are known, the others may easily be pointed out; but I shall confine myself to the most prominent among them.

The Americans have no neighbours, and consequently they have no great wars, or financial crises, or inroads, or conquests to dread; they require neither great taxes, nor great armies, nor great generals; and they have nothing to fear from a scourge which is more formidable to republics than all these evils combined, namely, military glory. It is impossible to deny the inconceivable influence which military glory exercises upon the spirit of a nation. General Jackson, whom the Americans have twice elected to be the head of their government, is a man of a violent temper and mediocre talents; no one circumstance in the whole course of his career ever proved that he is qualified to govern a free people; and indeed the majority of the enlightened classes of the Union has always been opposed to him. But he was raised to the presidency, and has been maintained in that lofty station, solely by the recollection of a victory which he gained, twenty years ago, under the walls of New Orleans; a victory[1] which was, however, a very ordinary achievement, and which could only be remembered in a country where battles are rare. Now the people who is thus carried away by the illusions of glory, is unquestionably the most cold and calculating, the most unmilitary (if I may use the expression), and the most prosaic of all the peoples of the earth.

America has no great capital city,* whose influence is directly or indirectly felt over the whole extent of the country, which I hold to be one of the first causes of the maintenance of republican institutions in the United States. In cities, men cannot be prevented from concerting

---

* The United States have no metropolis; but they already contain several very large cities. Philadelphia reckoned 161,000 inhabitants and New York 202,000, in the year 1830. The lower orders which inhabit these cities constitute a rabble even more formidable than the populace of European towns. They consist of freed blacks in the first place, who are condemned by the laws and by public opinion, to an hereditary state of misery and degradation. They also contain a multitude of Europeans who have been driven to the shores of the New World by their misfortunes or their misconduct; and these men inoculate the United States with all our vices, without bringing with them any of those interests which counteract their baneful influence. As inhabitants of a country where they have no civil rights, they are ready to turn all the passions which agitate the community to their own advantage; thus, within the last few months serious riots have broken out in Philadelphia and in New York. Disturbances of this kind are unknown in the rest of the country, which is nowise alarmed by them, because the population of the cities has hitherto exercised neither power nor influence over the rural districts.

Nevertheless, I look upon the size of certain American cities, and especially on the nature of their population, as a real danger which threatens the future security of the democratic republics of the New World: and I venture to predict that they will perish from this circumstance, unless the government succeed in creating an armed force, which, while it remains under the control of the majority of the nation, will be independent of the town population, and able to repress its excesses.

together, and from awakening a mutual excitement which prompts sudden and passionate resolutions. Cities may be looked upon as large assemblies, of which all the inhabitants are members; their populace exercises a prodigious influence upon the magistrates, and frequently executes its own wishes without their intervention.

To subject the provinces to the metropolis, is therefore not only to place the destiny of the empire in the bands of a portion of the community, which may be reprobated as unjust, but to place it in the hands of a populace acting under its own impulses, which must be avoided as dangerous. The preponderance of capital cities is therefore a serious blow upon the representative system; and it exposes modern republics to the same defect as the republics of antiquity, which all perished from not being acquainted with that system.

It would be easy for me to adduce a great number of secondary causes which have contributed to establish, and which concur to maintain, the democratic republic of the United States. But I discern two principal circumstances among these favourable elements, which I hasten to point out. I have already observed that the origin of the American settlements may be looked upon as the first and most efficacious cause, to which the present prosperity of the United States may be attributed. The Americans had the chances of birth in their favour; and their forefathers imported that equality of conditions into the country, whence the democratic republic has very naturally taken its rise. Nor was this all they did; for beside this republican condition of society, the early settlers bequeathed to their descendants those customs, manners, and opinions, which contribute most to the success of a republican form of government. When I reflect upon the consequences of this primary circumstance, methinks I see the destiny of America imbodied in the first puritan who landed on those shores, just as the human race was represented by the first man.

The chief circumstance which has favoured the establishment and the maintenance of a democratic republic in the United States, is the nature of the territory which the Americans inhabit. Their ancestors gave them the love of equality and of freedom: but God himself gave them the means of remaining equal and free, by placing them upon a boundless continent, which is open to their exertions. General prosperity is favourable to the stability of all governments, but more particularly of a democratic constitution, which depends upon the disposition of the majority, and more particularly of that portion of the community which is most exposed to feel the pressure of want. When the people rules, it must be rendered happy, or it will overturn the state: and misery is apt to stimulate it to those excesses to which ambition rouses kings. The physical causes, independent of the laws, which contribute to promote general prosperity, are more numerous in America than they have ever been in any other country in the world, at any other period of history. In the United States, not only is legislation democratic, but nature herself favours the cause of the people.

In what part of human tradition can be found anything at all similar to that which is occurring under our eyes in North America? The celebrated communities of antiquity were all founded in the midst of hostile nations, which they were obliged to subjugate before they could flourish in their place. Even the moderns have found, in some parts of South America, vast regions inhabited by a people of inferior civilization, but which occupied and cultivated the soil. To found their new states, it was necessary to extirpate or to subdue a numerous population, until civilization has been made to blush for their success. But North America was only inhabited by wandering tribes, who took no thought of the natural riches of the soil: and that vast country was still, properly speaking, an empty continent, a desert land awaiting its inhabitants.

Everything is extraordinary in America, the social condition of the inhabitants, as well as the laws; but the soil upon which these institutions are founded is more extraordinary than all the rest. When man was first placed upon the earth by the Creator, that earth was inexhaustible in its youth; but man was weak and ignorant: and when he had learned to explore the treasures which it contained, hosts of his fellow-creatures covered its surface, and he was obliged to earn an asylum for repose and for freedom by the sword. At that same period North America was discovered, as if it had been kept in reserve by the Deity, and had just risen from beneath the waters of the deluge.

That continent still presents, as it did in the primeval time, rivers which rise from never-failing sources, green and moist solitudes, and fields which the ploughshare of the husbandman has never turned. In this state it is offered to man, not in the barbarous and isolated condition of the early ages, but to a being who is already in possession of the most potent secrets of the natural world, who is united to his fellow-men, and instructed by the experience of fifty centuries. At this very time thirteen millions of civilized Europeans are peaceably spreading over those fertile plains, with whose resources and whose extent they are not yet accurately acquainted. Three or four thousand soldiers drive the wandering races of the aborigines before them; these are followed by the pioneers, who pierce the woods, scare off the beasts of prey, explore the courses of the inland streams, and make ready the triumphal procession of civilization across the waste.

The favourable influence of the temporal prosperity of America upon the institutions of that country has been so often described by others, and adverted to by myself, that I shall not enlarge upon it beyond the addition of a few facts. An erroneous notion is generally entertained, that the deserts of America are peopled by European emigrants, who annually disembark upon the coasts of the New World, while the American population increases and multiplies upon the soil which its forefathers tilled. The European settler, however, usually arrives in the United States without friends, and sometimes without resources; in order to subsist he is obliged to work for hire, and he rarely proceeds beyond that belt of industrious population which adjoins the ocean. The desert cannot be explored without capital or credit, and the body must be accustomed to the rigours of a new climate before it can be exposed to the chances of forest life. It is the

Americans themselves who daily quit the spots which gave them birth, to acquire extensive domains in a remote country. Thus the European leaves his cottage for the transatlantic shores; and the American, who is born on that very coast, plunges in the wilds of central America. This double emigration is incessant: it begins in the remotest parts of Europe, it crosses the Atlantic ocean, and it advances over the solitudes of the New World. Millions of men are marching at once toward the same horizon; their language, their religion, their manners differ, their object is the same. The gifts of fortune are promised in the west, and to the west they bend their course.

No event can be compared with this continuous removal of the human race, except perhaps those irruptions which preceded the fall of the Roman empire. Then, as well as now, generations of men were impelled forward in the same direction to meet and struggle on the same spot; but the designs of Providence were not the same; then, every new comer was the harbinger of destruction and of death; now, every adventurer brings with him the elements of prosperity and of life. The future still conceals from us the ulterior consequences of this emigration of the American toward the west; but we can hardly apprehend its more immediate results. As a portion of the inhabitants annually leave the states in which they were born, the population of these states increases very slowly, although they have long been established: thus in Connecticut, which only contains 59 inhabitants to the square mile, the population has not been increased by more than one quarter in forty years, while that of England has been augmented by one third in the lapse of the same period. The European emigrant always lands, therefore, in a country which is but half full, and where hands are in request: he becomes a workman in easy circumstances; his son goes to seek his fortune in unpeopled regions, and he becomes a rich landowner. The former amasses the capital which the latter invests, and the stranger as well as the native is unacquainted with want.

The laws of the United States are extremely favourable to the division of property; but a cause which is more powerful than the laws prevents property from being divided to excess.* This is very perceptible in the states which are beginning to be thickly peopled; Massachusetts is the most populous part of the Union, but it contains only 80 inhabitants to the square mile, which is much less than in France, where 162 are reckoned to the same extent of country. But in Massachusetts estates are very rarely divided; the eldest son takes the land, and the others go to seek their fortune in the desert. The law has abolished the right of primogeniture, but circumstances have concurred to re-establish it under a form of which none can complain, and by which no just rights are impaired.

A single fact will suffice to show the prodigious number of individuals who leave New England, in this manner, to settle themselves in the wilds. We were assured in 1830, that thirty-six of the members of con-

---

* In New England the estates are exceeding small, but they are rarely subjected to farther division.

gress were born in the little state of Connecticut. The population of Connecticut, which constitutes only one forty-third part of that of the United States, thus furnished one eight of the whole body of representatives. The state of Connecticut, however, only sends five delegates to congress; and the thirty-one others sit for the new western states. If these thirty-one individuals had remained in Connecticut, it is probable that instead of becoming rich landowners they would have remained humble labourers, that they would have lived in obscurity without being able to rise into public life, and that, far from becoming useful members of the legislature, they might have been unruly citizens.

These reflections do not escape the observation of the Americans any more than of ourselves. "It cannot be doubted," says Chancellor Kent in his Treatise on American Law, "that the division of landed estates must produce great evils when it is carried to such excess that each parcel of land is insufficient to support a family; but these disadvantages have never been felt in the United States, and many generations must elapse before they can be felt. The extent of our inhabited territory, the abundance of adjacent land, and the continual stream of emigration flowing from the shores of the Atlantic toward the interior of the country, suffice as yet, and will long suffice, to prevent the parcelling out of estates."

It is difficult to describe the rapacity with which the American rushes forward to secure the immense booty which fortune proffers to him. In the pursuit, he fearlessly braves the arrow of the Indian and the distempers of the forest; he is unimpressed by the silence of the woods; the approach of beasts of prey does not disturb him; for he is goaded onward by a passion more intense than the love of life. Before him lies a boundless continent, and he urges onward as if time pressed, and he was afraid of finding no room for his exertions. I have spoken of the emigration from the older states, but how shall I describe that which takes place from the more recent ones? Fifty years have scarcely elapsed since that of Ohio was founded; the greater part of its inhabitants were not born within its confines; its capital has only been built thirty years, and its territory is still covered by an immense extent of uncultivated fields; nevertheless, the population of Ohio is already proceeding westward, and most of the settlers who descend to the fertile savannahs of Illinois are citizens of Ohio. These men left their first country to improve their condition; they quit their resting-place to meliorate it still more; fortune awaits them everywhere, but happiness they cannot attain. The desire of prosperity has become an ardent and restless passion in their minds, which grows by what it gains. They early broke the ties which bound them to their natal earth, and they have contracted no fresh ones on their way. Emigration was at first necessary to them as a means of subsistence; and it soon becomes a sort of game of chance, which they pursue for the emotions it excites, as much as for the gain it procures.

Sometimes the progress of man is so rapid that the desert reappears behind him. The woods stoop to give him a passage, and spring up again when he has passed. It is not uncommon in crossing the new states of the west to meet with deserted dwellings in the midst of the wilds; the traveller frequently discovers the vestiges of a log-house in the most solitary retreats, which bear witness to the power, and no less to the inconstancy of man. In these abandoned fields, and over those ruins of a day, the primeval forest soon scatters a fresh vegetation; the beasts resume the haunts which were once their own; and nature covers the traces of man's path with branches and with flowers, which obliterate his evanescent track.

I remember that in crossing one of the woodland districts which still cover the state of New York, I reached the shore of a lake, which was embosomed with forests coeval with the world. A small island, covered with woods, whose thick foliage concealed its banks, rose from the centre of the waters. Upon the shores of the lake no object attested the presence of man, except a column of smoke which might be seen on the horizon rising from the tops of the trees to the clouds, and seeming to hang from heaven rather than to be mounting to the sky. An Indian shallop was hauled up on the sand, which tempted me to visit the islet that had at first attracted my attention, and in a few minutes I set foot upon its banks. The whole island formed one of those delicious solitudes of the New World, which almost lead civilized man to regret the haunts of the savage. A luxuriant vegetation bore witness to the incomparable fruitfulness of the soil. The deep silence, which is common to the wilds of North America, was only broken by the hoarse cooing of the wood-pigeon and the tapping of the woodpecker upon the bark of trees. I was far from supposing that this spot had ever been inhabited, so completely did nature seem to be left to her own caprices; but when I reached the centre of the isle I thought that I discovered some traces of man. I then proceeded to examine the surrounding objects with care, and I soon perceived that an European had undoubtedly been led to seek a refuge in this retreat. Yet what changes had taken place in the scene of his labours! The logs which he had hastily hewn to build himself a shed had sprouted afresh; the very props were intertwined with living verdure, and his cabin was transformed into a bower. In the midst of these shrubs a few stones were to be seen, blackened with fire and sprinkled with thin ashes; here the hearth had no doubt been, and the chimney in falling had covered it with rubbish. I stood for some time in silent admiration of the exuberance of nature and the littleness of man; and when I was obliged to leave that enchanting solitude, I exclaimed with melancholy, "Are ruins, then, already here?"

In Europe we are wont to look upon a restless disposition, an unbounded desire of riches, and an excessive love of independence, as propensities very formidable to society. Yet these are the very elements which ensure a long and peaceful duration to the republics of America. Without these unquiet passions the population would collect in certain spots, and would soon be subject to wants like those of the Old World, which it is difficult to satisfy; for such is the present good fortune of the New World, that the vices of its inhabitants are scarcely less favourable to society than their virtues. These circumstances exercise a great influence on the estimation in which human actions are held in the two hemispheres. The Americans frequently term what we should call cupidity a laudable industry; and they blame as faint-heartedness what we consider to be the virtue of moderate desires.

In France simple tastes, orderly manners, domestic affections, and the attachment which men feel to the place of their birth, are looked upon as great guarantees of the tranquility and happiness of the state. But in America nothing seems to be more prejudicial to society than these virtues. The French Canadians, who have faithfully preserved the traditions of their pristine manners, are already embarrassed for room upon their small territory; and this little community, which has so recently begun to exist, will shortly be a prey to the calamities incident to old nations. In Canada the most enlightened, patriotic, and humane inhabitants, make extraordinary efforts to render the people dissatisfied with those simple enjoyments which still content it. There the seductions of wealth are vaunted with as much zeal, as the charms of an honest but limited income in the Old World; and more exertions are made to excite the passions of the citizens there than to calm them elsewhere. If we listen to the eulogies, we shall hear that nothing is more praiseworthy than to exchange the pure and homely pleasures which even the poor man tastes in his own country, for the dull delights of prosperity under a foreign sky; to leave the patrimonial hearth, and the turf beneath which his forefathers sleep; in short, to abandon the living and the dead in quest of fortune.

At the present time America presents a field for human effort, far more extensive than any sum of labour which can be applied to work it. In America, too much knowledge cannot be diffused; for all knowledge, while it may serve him who possesses it, turns also to the advantage of those who are without it. New wants are not to be feared, since they can be satisfied without difficulty; the growth of human passions need not be dreaded, since all passions may find an easy and a legitimate object: nor can men be put in possession of too much freedom, since they are scarcely ever tempted to misuse their liberties.

The American republics of the present day are like companies of adventurers, formed to explore in common the waste lands of the New World, and busied in a flourishing trade. The passions which agitate the Americans most deeply, are not their political, but their commercial passions; or, to speak more correctly, they introduce the habits they contract in business into their political life. They love order, without which affairs do not prosper; and they set an especial value upon a regular conduct, which is the foundation of a solid business: they prefer the good sense which amasses large fortunes, to that enterprising spirit which frequently dissipates them; general ideas alarm their minds, which are accustomed to positive calculations; and they hold practice in more honour than theory.

It is in America that one learns to understand the influence which physical prosperity exercises over political actions, and even over opinions which ought to acknowledge no sway but that of reason; and it is more especially among strangers that this truth is perceptible. Most of the European emigrants to the New World carry with them that wild love of independence and of change, which our calamities are so apt to engender. I sometimes met with Europeans, in the United States, who had been obliged to leave their own country on account of their political opinions. They all astonished me by the language they held; but one of them surprised me more than all the rest. As I was crossing one of the most remote districts of Pennsylvania, I was benighted, and obliged to beg for hospitality at the gate of a wealthy planter, who was a Frenchman by birth. He bade me sit down beside his fire, and we began to talk with that freedom which befits persons who meet in the backwoods, two thousand leagues from their native country. I was aware that my host had been a great leveller and an ardent demagogue, forty years ago, and that his name was not unknown to fame. I was therefore not a little surprised to hear him discuss the rights of property as an economist or a landowner might have done: he spoke of the necessary gradations which fortune establishes among men, of obedience to established laws, of the influence of good morals in commonwealths, and of the support which religious opinions give to order and to freedom; he even went so far as to quote an evangelical authority in corroboration of one of his political tenets.

I listened, and marvelled at the feebleness of human reason. A proposition is true or false, but no art can prove it to be one or the other, in the midst of the uncertainties of science and the conflicting lessons of experience, until a new incident disperses the clouds of doubt; I was poor, I become rich; and I am not to expect that prosperity will act upon my conduct, and leave my judgement free: my opinions change with my fortune, and the happy circumstances which I turn to my advantage, furnish me with that decisive argument which was before wanting.

[The sentence beginning "I was poor, I become rich," &c., struck the editor, on perusal, as obscure, if not contradictory. The original seems more explicit, and justice to the author seems to require that it should be presented to the reader. "J'étais pauvre, me voici riche; du moins, si le bien-être, en agissant sur ma conduite, laissait mon jugement en liberté! Mais non, mes opinions sont en effet changées avec ma fortune, et, dans l'événement heureux dont je profite, j'ai réellement découvert la raison déterminante qui jusque-là m'avait manqué."—*American Editor.*]

The influence of prosperity acts still more freely upon the American than upon strangers. The American has always seen the connexion of public order and public prosperity, intimately united as they are, go on before his eyes; he does not conceive that one can subsist without the other; he has therefore nothing to forget; nor has he, like so many Europeans, to unlearn the lessons of his early education.

INFLUENCE OF THE LAWS UPON THE MAINTENANCE OF THE DEMOCRATIC REPUBLIC IN THE UNITED STATES.

Three principal Causes of the Maintenance of the democratic Republic—Federal Constitutions—Municipal Institutions.—Judicial Power.

The principal aim of this book has been to make known the laws of the United States; if this purpose has been accomplished, the reader is already enabled to judge for himself which are the laws that really tend to maintain the democratic republic, and which endanger its existence. If I have not succeeded in explaining this in the whole course of my work, I cannot hope to do so within the limits of a single chapter. It is not my intention to retrace the path I have already pursued; and a very few lines will suffice to recapitulate what I have previously explained.

Three circumstances seem to me to contribute most powerfully to the maintenance of the democratic republic in the United States.

The first is that federal form of government which the Americans have adopted, and which enables the Union to combine the power of a great empire with the security of a small state;—

The second consists in those municipal institutions which limit the despotism of the majority, and at the same time impart a taste for freedom, and a knowledge of the art of being free, to the people;—

The third is to be met with in the constitution of the judicial power. I have shown in what manner the courts of justice serve to repress the excesses of democracy; and how they check and direct the impulses of the majority, without stopping its activity.

INFLUENCE OF MANNERS UPON THE MAINTENANCE OF THE DEMOCRATIC REPUBLIC IN THE UNITED STATES.

I have previously remarked that the manners of the people may be considered as one of the general causes to which the maintenance of a democratic republic in the United States is attributable. I here use the word *manners*, with the meaning which the ancients attached to the word *mores*; for I apply it not only to manners, in their proper sense of what constitutes the character of social intercourse, but I extend it to the various notions and opinions current among men, and to the mass of those ideas which constitute their character of mind. I comprise, therefore, under this term the whole moral and intellectual condition of a people. My intention is not to draw a picture of American manners, but simply to point out such features of them as are favourable to the maintenance of political institutions.

RELIGION CONSIDERED AS A POLITICAL INSTITUTION, WHICH POWERFULLY CONTRIBUTES TO THE MAINTENANCE OF THE DEMOCRATIC REPUBLIC AMONG THE AMERICANS.

North America peopled by Men who professed a democratic and republican Christianity.—Arrival of the Catholics.—For what Reason the Catholics form the most democratic and the most republican Class at the present Time.

Every religion is to be found in juxtaposition to a political opinion, which is connected with it by affinity. If the human mind be left to follow its own bent, it will regulate the temporal and spiritual institutions of society upon one uniform principle; and man will endeavour, if I may use the expression, to harmonize the state in which he lives upon earth, with the state he believes to await him in heaven.

The greatest part of British America was peopled by men who, after having shaken off the authority of the pope, acknowledged no other religious supremacy: they brought with them into the New World a form of Christianity, which I cannot better describe, than by styling it a democratic and republican religion. This sect contributed powerfully to the establishment of a democracy and a republic; and from the earliest settlement of the emigrants, politics and religion contracted an alliance which has never been dissolved.

About fifty years ago Ireland began to pour a catholic population into the United States; on the other hand, the catholics of America made proselytes, and at the present moment more than a million of Christians, professing the truths of the church of Rome, are to be met with in the Union. These catholics are faithful to the observances of their religion; they are fervent and zealous in the support and belief of their doctrines. Nevertheless they constitute the most republican and the most democratic class of citizens which exists in the United States; and although this fact may surprise the observer at first, the cause by which it is occasioned may easily be discovered upon reflection.

I think that the catholic religion has erroneously been looked upon as the natural enemy of democracy. Among the various sects of Christians, catholicism seems to me, on the contrary, to be one of those which are most favourable to the equality of conditions. In the catholic church, the religious community is composed of only two elements; the priest and the people. The priest alone rises above the rank of his flock, and all below him are equal.

On doctrinal points the catholic faith places all human capacities upon the same level; it subjects the wise and the ignorant, the man of genius and the vulgar crowd, to the details of the same creed; it imposes the same observances upon the rich and needy, it inflicts the same austerities upon the strong and the weak, it listens to no compromises with mortal man, but reducing all the human race to the same standard, it confounds all the distinctions of society at the foot of the same altar, even as they are confounded in the sight of God. If catholicism predisposes the faithful to obedience, it certainly does not prepare them for inequality; but the contrary may be said of protestantism, which generally tends to make men independent, more than to render them equal.

Catholicism is like an absolute monarchy; if the sovereign be removed, all the other classes of society are more equal than they are in republics. It has not unfrequently occurred that the catholic priest has left the service of the altar to mix with the governing powers of society, and to make his place among the civil gradations of men. This religious influence has sometimes been used to secure the interests of that political state of things to which he belonged. At other times catholics have taken the side of aristocracy from a spirit of religion.

But no sooner is the priesthood entirely separated from the government, as is the case in the United States, than it is found that no class of men are more naturally disposed than the catholics to transfuse the doctrine of the equality of conditions into the political world. If then, the catholic citizens of the United States are not forcibly led by the nature of their tenets to adopt democratic and republican principles, at least they are not necessarily opposed to them; and their social position, as well as their limited number, obliges them to adopt these opinions. Most of the catholics are poor, and they have no chance of taking a part in the government unless it be open to all the citizens. They constitute a minority, and all rights must be respected in order to ensure to them the free exercise of their own privileges. These two causes induce them, unconsciously, to adopt political doctrines which they would perhaps support with less zeal if they were rich and preponderant.

The catholic clergy of the United States has never attempted to oppose this political tendency; but it seeks rather to justify its results. The priests in America have divided the intellectual world into two parts: in the one they place the doctrines of revealed religion, which command their assent; in the other they leave those truths, which they believe to have been freely left open to the researches of political inquiry. Thus the catholics of the United States are at the same time the most faithful believers and the most zealous citizens.

It may be asserted that in the United States no religious doctrine displays the slightest hostility to democratic and republican institutions. The clergy of all the different sects hold the same language; their opinions are consonant to the laws, and the human intellect flows onward in one sole current.

I happened to be staying in one of the largest towns in the Union, when I was invited to attend a public meeting which had been called for the purpose of assisting the Poles, and of sending them supplies of arms and money. I found two or three thousand persons collected in a vast hall which had been prepared to receive them. In a short time a priest in his ecclesiastical robes advanced to the front of the hustings: the spectators rose, and stood uncovered, while he spoke in the following terms:—

"Almighty God! the God of armies! Thou who didst strengthen the hearts and guide the arms of our fathers when they were fighting for the sacred rights of national independence; thou who didst make them triumph over a hateful oppression, and hast granted to our people the benefits of liberty and peace; turn, O Lord, a favourable eye upon the other hemisphere; pitifully look down upon that heroic nation which is even now struggling as we did in the former time, and for the same rights which we defended with our blood. Thou, who didst create man in the likeness of the same image, let no tyranny mar thy work, and establish inequality upon the earth. Almighty God! do thou watch over the destiny of the Poles, and render them worthy to be free. May thy wisdom direct their councils, and may they strength sustain their arms! Shed forth thy terror over their enemies; scatter the powers which take counsel against them; and vouchsafe that the injustice which the world has beheld for fifty years, be not consummated in our time. O Lord, who holdest alike the hearts of nations and of men in thy powerful hand, raise up allies to the sacred cause of right; arouse the French nation from the apathy in which its rulers retain it, that it go forth again to fight for the liberties of the world.

"Lord, turn not thou thy face from us, and grant that we may always be the most religious as well as the freest people of the earth. Almighty God, hear our supplications this day. Save the Poles, we beseech thee, in the name of thy well-beloved Son, our Lord Jesus Christ, who died upon the cross for the salvation of men. Amen."

The whole meeting responded "Amen!" with devotion.

INDIRECT INFLUENCE OF RELIGIOUS OPINIONS UPON POLITICAL SOCIETY IN THE UNITED STATES.

Christain Morality common to all Sects.—Influence of Religion upon the Manners of the Americans.—Respect for the marriage Tie.—In what manner Religion confines the Imagination of the Americans within certain Limits, and checks the Passion of Innovation.—Opinion of the Americans on the political Utility of Religion.—Their Exertions to extend and secure its Predominance.

I have just shown what the direct influence of religion upon politics is in the United States; but its indirect influence appears to me to be still more considerable, and it never instructs the Americans more fully in the art of being free than when it says nothing of freedom.

The sects which exist in the United States are innumerable. They all differ in respect to the worship which is due from man to his Creator; but they all agree in respect to the duties which are due from man to man. Each sect adores the Deity in its own peculiar manner; but all the sects preach the same moral law in the name of God. If it be of the slightest importance to man, as an individual, that his religion should be true, the case of society is not the same. Society has no future life to hope for or to fear; and provided the citizens profess a religion, the peculiar tenets of that religion are of very little importance to its interests. Moreover, almost all the sects of the United States are comprised within the great unity of Christianity, and Christian morality is everywhere the same.

It may be believed without unfairness, that a certain number of Americans pursue a peculiar form of worship, from habit more than from conviction. In the United States the sovereign authority is religious, and consequently hypocrisy must be common; but there is no country in the whole world in which the Christian religion retains a greater influence over the souls of men than in America; and there can be no greater proof of its utility, and of its conformity to human nature, than that its influence is most powerfully felt over the most enlightened and free nation of the earth.

I have remarked that the members of the American clergy in general, without even excepting those who do not admit religious liberty, are all in favour of civil freedom; but they do not support any particular political system. They keep aloof from parties, and from public affairs. In the United States religion exercises but little influence upon the laws, and upon the details of public opinion; but it directs the manners of the community, and by regulating domestic life, it regulates the state.

I do not question that the great austerity of manners which is observable in the United States, arises, in the first instance, from religious faith. Religion is often unable to restrain man from the numberless temptations of fortune; nor can it check that passion for gain which every incident of his life contributes to arouse; but its influence over the mind of woman is supreme, and women are the protectors of morals. There is certainly no country in the world where the tie of marriage is so much respected as in America, or where conjugal happiness is more highly or worthily appreciated. In Europe almost all the disturbances of society arise from the irregularities of domestic life. To despise the natural bonds and legitimate pleasures of home, is to contract a taste for excesses, a restlessness of heart, and the evil of fluctuating desires. Agitated by the tumultuous passions which frequently disturb his dwelling, the European is galled by the obedience which the legislative powers of the state exact. But when the American retires from the turmoil of public life to the bosom of his family, he finds in it the image of order and of peace. There his pleasures are simple and natural, his joys are innocent and calm; and as he finds that an orderly life is the surest path to happiness, he accustoms himself without difficulty to moderate his opinions as well as his tastes. While the European endeavours to forget his domestic troubles by agitating society, the American derives from his own home that love of order, which he afterward carries with him into public affairs.

In the United States the influence of religion is not confined to the manners, but it extends to the intelligence of the people. Among the Anglo-Americans, there are some who profess the doctrines of Christianity from a sincere belief in them, and others who do the same because they are afraid to be suspected of unbelief. Christianity, therefore, reigns without any obstacle, by universal consent; the consequence is, as I have before observed, that every principle of the moral world is fixed and determinate, although the political world is abandoned to the debates and the experiments of men. Thus the human mind is never left to wander across a boundless field; and, whatever may be its pretensions, it is checked from time to time by barriers which it cannot surmount. Before it can perpetrate innovation, certain primal and immutable principles are laid down, and the boldest conceptions of human device are subjected to certain forms which retard and stop their completion.

The imagination of the Americans, even in its greatest flights, is circumspect and undecided; its impulses are checked, and its works unfinished. These habits of restraint recur in political society, and are

singularly favourable both to the tranquility of the peop
durability of the institutions it has established. Nature
stances concurred to make the inhabitants of the United
men, as is sufficiently attested by the enterprising spirit
they seek for fortune. If the minds of the Americans were
trammels, they would very shortly become the most darin
and the most implacable disputants in the world. But the
ists of America are obliged to profess an ostensible respec
tian morality and equity, which does not easily permit the
the laws that oppose their designs; nor would they find it
mount the scruples of their partisans, even if they were
over their own. Hitherto no one, in the United States, has
vance the maxim, that everything is permissible with a vie
terests of society; an impious adage, which seems to
invented in an age of freedom, to shelter all the tyrants of
Thus while the law permits the Americans to do what the
ligion prevents them from conceiving, and forbids them
what is rash or unjust.

Religion in America takes no direct part in the governn
ety, but it must nevertheless be regarded as the foremost o
cal institutions of that country; for if it does not impart
freedom, it facilitates the use of free institutions. Indeed,
same point of view that the inhabitants of the United S
selves look upon religious belief. I do not know whether a
icans have a sincere faith in their religion; for who can
human heart? but I am certain that they hold it to be indis
the maintenance of republican institutions. This opinion
liar to a class of citizens or to a party, but it belongs to th
tion, and to every rank of society.

In the United States, if a political character attacks a se
not prevent even the partisans of that very sect, from supp
but if he attacks all the sects together, every one abandor
he remains alone.

While I was in America, a witness, who happened to be
assizes of the county of Chester (state of New York), decla
did not believe in the existence of God or in the immort
soul. The judge refused to admit his evidence, on the grou
witness had destroyed beforehand all the confidence of t
what he was about to say.* The newspapers related the f
any farther comment.

* The New York Spectator of August 23d, 1831, relates the fact in the follow
court of common pleas of Chester county (New York), a few days since rej
who declared his disbelief in the existence of God. The presiding judge rer
had not before been aware that there was a man living who did not believe
of God; that this belief constituted the sanction of all testimony in a court
that he knew of no cause in a Christian country, where a witness had been p
tify without such belief."

[The instance given by the author, of a person offered as a witness having b
the ground that he did not believe in the existence of a God seems to be addu
ther his assertion that the Americans hold religion to be indispensable to the
republican institutions—or his assertion, that if a man attacks all the sects

.ericans combine the notions of Christianity and of liberty so
ay in their minds, that it is impossible to make them conceive
e without the other; and with them this conviction does not
g from that barren traditionary faith which seems to vegetate in
soul rather than to live.

I have known of societies formed by the Americans to send out ministers of the gospel into the new western states, to found schools and
churches there, lest religion should be suffered to die away in those
remote settlements, and the rising states be less fitted to enjoy free institutions than the people from which they emanated. I met with
wealthy New Englanders who abandoned the country in which they
were born, in order to lay the foundations of Christianity and of freedom on the banks of the Missouri or in the prairies of Illinois. Thus
religious zeal is perpetually stimulated in the United States by the duties of patriotism. These men do not act from an exclusive consideration of the promises of a future life; eternity is only one motive of their
devotion to the cause; and if you converse with these missionaries of
Christian civilization, you will be surprised to find how much value
they set upon the goods of this world, and that you meet with a politician where you expected to find a priest. They will tell you that "all the
American republics are collectively involved with each other; if the republics of the west were to fall into anarchy, or to be mastered by a
despot, the republican institutions which now flourish upon the
shores of the Atlantic ocean would be in great peril. It is therefore our
interest that the new states should be religious, in order to maintain
our liberties."

Such are the opinions of the Americans: and if any hold that the religious spirit which I admire is the very thing most amiss in America,
and that the only element wanting to the freedom and happiness of
the human race is to believe in some blind cosmogony, or to assert
with Cabanis[2] the secretion of thought by the brain, I can only reply,
that those who hold this language have never been in America, and
that they have never seen a religious or a free nation. When they return from their expedition, we shall hear what they have to say.

There are persons in France who look upon republican institutions
as a temporary means of power, of wealth and distinction; men who
are the condottieri of liberty, and who fight for their own advantage,
whatever be the colours they wear: it is not to these that I address myself. But there are others who look forward to the republican form of
government as a tranquil and lasting state, toward which modern society is daily impelled by the ideas and manners of the time, and who

---

one abandons him and he remains alone. But it is questionable how far the fact quoted
proves either of these positions. The rule which prescribes as a qualification for a witness the
belief in a Supreme Being who will punish falsehood, without which he is deemed wholly incompetent to testify, is established for the protection of personal rights, and not to compel
the adoption of any system of religious belief. It came with all our fundamental principles
from England as a part of the common law which the colonists brought with them. It is supposed to prevail in every country in Christendom, whatever may be the form of its government; and the only doubt that arises respecting its existence in France, is created by our
author's apparent surprise at finding such a rule in America.—American Editor.]

sincerely desire to prepare men to be free. When these men attack religious opinions, they obey the dictates of their passions to the prejudice of their interests. Despotism may govern without faith, but liberty cannot. Religion is much more necessary in the republic which they set forth in glowing colours, than in the monarchy which they attack; and it is more needed in democratic republics than in any others. How is it possible that society should escape destruction if the moral tie be not strengthened in proportion as the political tie is relaxed? and what can be done with a people which is its own master, if it be not submissive to the Divinity?

PRINCIPAL CAUSES WHICH RENDER RELIGION POWERFUL IN AMERICA.

Care taken by the Americans to separate the Church from the State.—The Laws, public Opinion, and even the Exertions of the Clergy concur to promote this end.—Influence of Religion upon the Mind, in the United States, attributable to this Cause.—Reason of this.—What is the natural State of Men with regard to Religion at the present Time.—What are the peculiar and incidental Causes which prevent Men, in certain Countries, from arriving at this State.

The philosophers of the eighteenth century explained the gradual decay of religious faith in a very simple manner. Religious zeal, said they, must necessarily fail, the more generally liberty is established and knowledge diffused. Unfortunately, facts are by no means in accordance with their theory. There are certain populations in Europe whose unbelief is only equalled by their ignorance and their debasement, while in America one of the freest and most enlightened nations in the world fulfils all the outward duties of religion with fervour.

Upon my arrival in the United States, the religious aspect of the country was the first thing that struck my attention; and the longer I stayed there, the more did I perceive the great political consequences resulting from this state of things, to which I was unaccustomed. In France I had almost always seen the spirit of religion and the spirit of freedom pursuing courses diametrically opposed to each other; but in America I found that they were intimately united, and that they reigned in common over the same country. My desire to discover the causes of this phenomenon increased from day to day. In order to satisfy it, I questioned the members of all the different sects; and I more especially sought the society of the clergy, who are the depositaries of the different persuasions, and who are more especially interested in their duration. As a member of the Roman catholic church I was more particularly brought into contact with several of its priests, with whom I became intimately acquainted. To each of these men I expressed my astonishment and I explained my doubts: I found that they differed upon matters of detail alone; and that they mainly attributed the peaceful dominion of religion in their country, to the separation of church and state. I do not hesitate to affirm that during my stay in America, I did not meet with a single individual, of the clergy or of the laity, who was not of the same opinion upon this point.

This led me to examine more attentively than I had hitherto done, the station which the American clergy occupy in political society. I learned with surprise that they filled no public appointments;* not one of them is to be met with in the administration, and they are not even represented in the legislative assemblies. In several states† the law excludes them from political life; public opinion in all. And when I came to inquire into the prevailing spirit of the clergy, I found that most of its members seemed to retire of their own accord from the exercise of power, and that they made it the pride of their profession to abstain from politics.

I heard them inveigh against ambition and deceit, under whatever political opinions these vices might chance to lurk; but I learned from their discourses that men are not guilty in the eye of God for any opinions concerning political government, which they may profess with sincerity, any more than they are for their mistakes in building a house or in driving a furrow. I perceived that these ministers of the gospel eschewed all parties, with the anxiety attendant upon personal interest. These facts convinced me that what I had been told was true; and it then became my object to investigate their causes, and to inquire how it happened that the real authority of religion was increased by a state of things which diminished its apparent force: these causes did not long escape my researches.

The short space of threescore years can never content the imagination of man; nor can the imperfect joys of this world satisfy his heart. Man alone, of all created beings, displays a natural contempt of existence, and yet a boundless desire to exist; he scorns life, but he dreads annihilation. These different feelings incessantly urge his soul to the contemplation of a future state, and religion directs his musings thither. Religion, then, is simply another form of hope; and it is no less natural to the human heart than hope itself. Men cannot abandon their religious faith without a kind of aberration of intellect, and a sort of violent distortion of their true natures; but they are invincibly brought back to more pious sentiments; for unbelief is an accident, and faith is the only permanent state of mankind. If we only consider religious institutions in a purely human point of view, they may be said to derive an inexhaustible element of strength from man himself, since they belong to one of the constituent principles of human nature.

I am aware that at certain times religion may strengthen this influence, which originates in itself, by the artificial power of the laws, and by the support of those temporal institutions which direct society. Religions, intimately united to the governments of the earth, have been known to exercise a sovereign authority derived from the twofold

---

* Unless this term be applied to the functions which many of them fill in the schools. Almost all education is intrusted to the clergy.
† See the constitution of New York, art. 7, § 4:—
    "And whereas, the ministers of the gospel are, by their profession, dedicated to the service of God and the care of souls, and ought not to be diverted from the great duties of their functions; therefore no minister of the gospel, or priest of any denomination whatsoever, shall, at any time hereafter, under any pretence or description whatever, be eligible to, or capable of holding any civil or military office or place within this state."
    See also the constitutions of North Carolina, art. 31. Virginia. South Carolina, art. 1, § 23. Kentucky, art. 2, § 26. Tennessee, art. 8, § 1. Louisiana, art. 2, § 22.

source of terror and of faith; but when a religion contracts an alliance of this nature, I do not hesitate to affirm that it commits the same error, as a man who should sacrifice his future to his present welfare; and in obtaining a power to which it has no claim, it risks that authority which is rightfully its own. When a religion founds its empire upon the desire of immortality which lives in every human heart, it may aspire to universal dominion: but when it connects itself with a government, it must necessarily adopt maxims which are only applicable to certain nations. Thus, in forming an alliance with a political power, religion augments its authority over a few, and forfeits the hope of reigning over all.

As long as a religion rests upon those sentiments which are the consolation of all affliction, it may attract the affections of mankind. But if it be mixed up with the bitter passions of the world, it may be constrained to defend allies whom its interests, and not the principles of love, have given to it; or to repel as antagonists men who are still attached to its own spirit, however opposed they may be to the powers to which it is allied. The church cannot share the temporal power of the state, without being the object of a portion of that animosity which the latter excites.

The political powers which seem to be most firmly established have frequently no better guarantee for their duration, than the opinions of a generation, the interests of the time, or the life of an individual. A law may modify the social condition which seems to be most fixed and determinate; and with the social condition everything else must change. The powers of society are more or less fugitive, like the years which we spend upon the earth; they succeed each other with rapidity like the fleeting cares of life; and no government has ever yet been founded upon an invariable disposition of the human heart, or upon an imperishable interest.

As long as religion is sustained by those feelings, propensities, and passions, which are found to occur under the same forms, at all the different periods of history, it may defy the efforts of time; or at least it can only be destroyed by another religion. But when religion clings to the interests of the world, it becomes almost as fragile a thing as the powers of earth. It is the only one of them all which can hope for immortality; but if it be connected with their ephemeral authority, it shares their fortunes, and may fall with those transient passions which supported them for a day. The alliance which religion contracts with political powers must needs be onerous to itself; since it does not require their assistance to live, and by giving them its assistance it may be exposed to decay.

The danger which I have just pointed out always exists, but it is not always equally visible. In some ages governments seem to be imperishable, in others the existence of society appears to be more precarious than the life of man. Some constitutions plunge the citizens into a lethargic somnolence, and others rouse them to feverish excitement. When government appears to be so strong, and laws so stable, men do not perceive the dangers which may accrue from a union of church and state. When governments display so much inconstancy, the danger is self-evident, but it is no longer possible to avoid it; to be effectual, measures must be taken to discover its approach.

In proportion as a nation assumes a democratic condition of society, and as communities display democratic propensities, it becomes more and more dangerous to connect religion with political institutions; for the time is coming when authority will be bandied from hand to hand, when political theories will succeed each other, and when men, laws, and constitutions, will disappear or be modified from day to day, and this not for a season only, but unceasingly. Agitation and mutability are inherent in the nature of democratic republics, just as stagnation and inertness are the law of absolute monarchies.

If the Americans, who change the head of the government once in four years, who elect new legislators every two years, and renew the provincial officers every twelvemonth; if the Americans, who have abandoned the political world, to the attempts of innovators, had not placed religion beyond their reach, where could it abide in the ebb and flow of human opinions? where would that respect which belongs to it be paid, amid the struggles of faction? and what would become of its immortality in the midst of perpetual decay? The American clergy were the first to perceive this truth, and to act in conformity with it. They saw that they must renounce their religious influence, if they were to strive for political power; and they chose to give up the support of the state, rather than to share its vicissitudes.

In America, religion is perhaps less powerful than it has been at certain periods in the history of certain peoples; but its influence is more lasting. It restricts itself to its own resources, but of those none can deprive it: its circle is limited to certain principles, but those principles are entirely its own, and under its undisputed control.

On every side in Europe we hear voices complaining of the absence of religious faith, and inquiring the means of restoring to religion some remnant of its pristine authority. It seems to me that we must first attentively consider what ought to be *the natural state* of men with regard to religion, at the present time; and when we know what we have to hope and to fear, we may discern the end to which our efforts ought to be directed.

The two great dangers which threaten the existence of religions are schism and indifference. In ages of fervent devotion, men sometimes abandon their religion, but they only shake it off in order to adopt another. Their faith changes the objects to which it is directed, but it suffers no decline. The old religion, then, excites enthusiastic attachment or bitter enmity in either party; some leave it with anger, others cling to it with increased devotedness, and although persuasions differ, irreligion is unknown. Such, however, is not the case when a religious belief is secretly undermined by doctrines which may be termed negative, since they deny the truth of one religion without affirming that of any other. Prodigious revolutions then take place in the human mind, without the apparent co-operation of the passions of man, and almost without his knowledge. Men lose the objects of their fondest hopes, as if through forgetfulness. They are carried away by an imperceptible current which they have not the courage to stem, but which they follow with regret, since it bears them from a faith they love, to a skepticism that plunges them into despair.

In ages which answer to this description, men desert their religious opinions from lukewarmness rather than from dislike; they do not reject them, but the sentiments by which they were once fostered disappear. But if the unbeliever does not admit religion to be true, he still considers it useful. Regarding religious institutions in a human point of view, he acknowledges their influence upon manners and legislation. He admits that they may serve to make men live in peace with one another, and to prepare them gently for the hour of death. He regrets the faith which he has lost; and as he is deprived of a treasure which he has learned to estimate at its full value, he scruples to take it from those who still possess it.

On the other hand, those who continue to believe, are not afraid openly to avow their faith. They look upon those who do not share their persuasion as more worthy of pity than of opposition; and they are aware, that to acquire the esteem of the unbelieving, they are not obliged to follow their example. They are hostile to no one in the world; and as they do not consider the society in which they live as an arena in which religion is bound to face its thousand deadly foes, they love their contemporaries, while they condemn their weaknesses, and lament their errors.

As those who do not believe, conceal their incredulity; and as those who believe, display their faith, public opinion pronounces itself in favour of religion: love, support, and honour, are bestowed upon it, and it is only by searching the human soul, that we can detect the wounds which it has received. The mass of mankind, who are never without the feeling of religion, do not perceive anything at variance with the established faith. The instinctive desire of a future life brings the crowd about the altar, and opens the hearts of men to the precepts and consolations of religion.

But this picture is not applicable to us; for there are men among us who have ceased to believe in Christianity, without adopting any other religion; others who are in the perplexities of doubt, and who already affect not to believe; and others, again, who are afraid to avow that Christian faith which they still cherish in secret.

Amid these lukewarm partisans and ardent antagonists, a small number of believers exist, who are ready to brave all obstacles, and to scorn all dangers, in defence of their faith. They have done violence to human weakness, in order to rise superior to public opinion. Excited by the effort they have made, they scarcely know where to stop; and as they know that the first use which the French made of independence, was to attack religion, they look upon their contemporaries with dread, and they recoil in alarm from the liberty which their fellow-citizens are seeking to obtain. As unbelief appears to them to be a novelty, they comprise all that is new in one indiscriminate animosity. They are at war with their age and country, and they look upon every opinion which is put forth there as the necessary enemy of the faith.

Such is not the natural state of men with regard to religion at the present day; and some extraordinary or incidental cause must be at work in France, to prevent the human mind from following its original propensities, and to drive it beyond the limits at which it ought naturally to stop.

I am intimately convinced that this extraordinary and incidental cause is the close connexion of politics and religion. The unbelievers of Europe attack the Christians as their political opponents, rather than as their religious adversaries; they hate the Christian religion as the opinion of a party, much more than as an error of belief; and they reject the clergy less because they are the representatives of the Divinity, than because they are the allies of authority.

In Europe, Christianity has been intimately united to the powers of the earth. Those powers are now in decay, and it is, as it were, buried under their ruins. The living body of religion has been bound down to the dead corpse of superannuated polity; cut the bonds which restrain it, and that which is alive will rise once more. I know not what could restore the Christian church of Europe to the energy of its earlier days; that power belongs to God alone; but it may be the effect of human policy to leave the faith in all the full exercise of the strength which it still retains.

HOW THE INSTRUCTION, THE HABITS, AND THE PRACTICAL EXPERIENCE OF THE AMERICANS PROMOTE THE SUCCESS OF THEIR DEMOCRATIC INSTITUTIONS.

What is to be understood by the Instruction of the American People.—The human Mind is more superficially instructed in the United States than in Europe.—No one completely uninstructed.—Reason of this.—Rapidity with which Opinions are diffused even in the uncultivated States of the West.—Practical Experience more serviceable to the Americans than Book-learning.

I have but little to add to what I have already said, concerning the influence which the instruction and the habits of the Americans exercise upon the maintenance of their political institutions.

America has hitherto produced very few writers of distinction; it possesses no great historians, and not a single eminent poet. The inhabitants of that country look upon what are properly styled literary pursuits with a kind of disapprobation; and there are towns of very second rate importance in Europe, in which more literary works are annually published, than in the twenty-four states of the Union put together. The spirit of the Americans is averse to general ideas; and it does not seek theoretical discoveries. Neither politics nor manufactures direct them to these occupations; and although new laws are perpetually enacted in the United States, no great writers have hitherto inquired into the principles of their legislation. The Americans have lawyers and commentators, but no jurists; and they furnish examples rather than lessons to the world. The same observation applies to the mechanical arts. In America, the inventions of Europe are adopted with sagacity; they are perfected, and adapted with admirable skill to the wants of the country. Manufactures exist, but the science of manufacture is not cultivated; and they have good workmen, but very few inventors. Fulton[3] was obliged to proffer his services to foreign nations for a long time before he was able to devote them to his own country.

[The remark that in America "there are very good workmen but very few inventors," will excite surprise in this country. The inventive character of Fulton he seems to admit, but would apparently deprive us of the credit of his name, by the remark that he was obliged to proffer his services to foreign nations for a long time. He might have added, that those proffers were disregarded and neglected, and that it was finally in his own country that he found the aid necessary to put in execution his great project. If there be patronage extended by the citizens of the United States to any one thing in preference to another, it is to the results of inventive genius. Surely Franklin, Rittenhouse, and Perkins, have been heard of by our author; and he must have heard something of that wonderful invention, the cotton-gin of Whitney, and of the machines for making cards to comb wool. The original machines of Fulton for the application of steam have been constantly improving, so that there is scarcely a vestige of them remaining. But to sum up the whole in one word, can it be possible that our author did not visit the patent office at Washington? Whatever may be said of the *utility* of nine tenths of the inventions of which the descriptions and models are there deposited, no one who has ever seen that depository, or who has read a description of its contents, can doubt that they furnish the most incontestible evidence of extraordinary inventive genius—a genius that has excited the astonishment of other European travellers.—*American Editor.*]

The observer who is desirous of forming an opinion on the state of instruction among the Anglo-Americans, must consider the same object from two different points of view. If he only singles out the learned, he will be astonished to find how rare they are; but if he counts the ignorant, the American people will appear to be the most enlightened community in the world. The whole population, as I observed in another place, is situated between these two extremes.

In New England, every citizen receives the elementary notions of human knowledge; he is moreover taught the doctrines and the evidences of his religion, the history of his country, and the leading features of its constitution. In the states of Connecticut and Massachusetts, it is extremely rare to find a man imperfectly acquainted with all these things, and a person wholly ignorant of them is a sort of phenomenon.

When I compare the Greek and Roman republics with these American states; the manuscript libraries of the former, and their rude population, with the innumerable journals and the enlightened people of the latter; when I remember all the attempts which are made to judge the modern republics by the assistance of those of antiquity, and to infer what will happen in our time from what took place two thousand years ago, I am tempted to burn my books, in order to apply none but novel ideas to so novel a condition of society.

What I have said of New England must not, however, be applied indiscriminately to the whole Union: as we advance toward the west or the south, the instruction of the people diminishes. In the states which are adjacent to the Gulf of Mexico,[4] a certain number of individuals may be found, as in our own countries, who are devoid of the rudiments of instruction. But there is not a single district in the United States sunk in complete ignorance; and for a very simple reason; the peoples of Europe started from the darkness of a barbarous condition, to advance toward the light of civilization; their progress has been unequal; some of them have improved apace, while others have loitered in their course, and some have stopped, and are still sleeping upon the way.

Such has not been the case in the United States. The Anglo-Americans settled in a state of civilization, upon that territory which their descendants occupy; they had not to begin to learn, and it was sufficient not to forget. Now the children of these same Americans are the persons who, year by year, transport their dwellings into the wilds: and with their dwellings their acquired information and their esteem for knowledge. Education has taught them the utility of instruction, and has enabled them to transmit that instruction to their posterity. In the United States society has no infancy, but it is borne in man's estate.

The Americans never use the word "peasant," because they have no idea of the peculiar class which that term denotes; the ignorance of more remote ages, the simplicity of rural life, and the rusticity of the villager, have not been preserved among them; and they are alike unacquainted with the virtues, the vices, the coarse habits, and the simple graces of an early stage of civilization. At the extreme borders of the confederate states, upon the confines of society and of the wilderness, a population of bold adventurers have taken up their abode, who pierce the solitudes of the American woods, and seek a country there, in order to escape that poverty which awaited them in their native provinces. As soon as the pioneer arrives upon the spot which is to serve him for a retreat, he fells a few trees and builds a log-house. Nothing can offer a more miserable aspect than these isolated dwellings. The traveller who approaches one of them toward nightfall, sees the flicker of the hearth-flame through the chinks in the walls; and at night, if the wind rises, he hears the roof of boughs shake to and fro in the midst of the great forest trees. Who would not suppose that this poor hut is the asylum of rudeness and ignorance? Yet no sort of comparison can be drawn between the pioneer and the dwelling which shelters him. Everything about him is primitive and unformed, but he is himself the result of the labour and the experience of eighteen centuries. He wears the dress, and he speaks the language of cities; he is acquainted with the past, curious of the future, and ready for argument upon the present; he is, in short, a highly civilized being, who consents, for a time, to inhabit the back-woods, and who penetrates into the wilds of a New World with the Bible, an axe, and a file of newspapers.

It is difficult to imagine the incredible rapidity with which public opinion circulates in the midst of these deserts.* I do not think that so much intellectual intercourse takes place in the most enlightened and populous districts of France.† It cannot be doubted that in the United States, the instruction of the people powerfully contributes to the support of a democratic republic; and such must always be the case, I believe, where instruction which awakens the understanding, is not separated from moral education which amends the heart. But I by no means exaggerate this benefit, and I am still farther from thinking, as so many people do think in Europe, that men can be instantaneously made citizens by teaching them to read and write. True information is mainly derived from experience, and if the Americans had not been gradually accustomed to govern themselves, their book-learning would not assist them much at the present day.

I have lived a great deal with the people in the United States, and I cannot express how much I admire their experience and their good sense. An American should never be allowed to speak of Europe; for he will then probably display a vast deal of presumption and very foolish pride. He will take up with those crude and vague notions which are so useful to the ignorant all over the world. But if you question him respecting his own country, the cloud which dimmed his intelligence will immediately disperse; his language will become as clear and as precise as his thoughts. He will inform you what his rights are, and by what means he exercises them; he will be able to point out the customs which obtain in the political world. You will find that he is well acquainted with the rules of the administration, and that he is familiar with the mechanism of the laws. The citizen of the United States does not acquire his practical science and his positive notions from books; the instruction he has acquired may have prepared him for receiving those ideas, but it did not furnish them. The American learns to know the laws by participating in the act of legislation; and he takes a lesson in the forms of government, from governing. The great work of society is ever going on beneath his eyes, and, as it were, under his hands.

In the United States politics are the end and aim of education; in

---

* I travelled along a portion of the frontier of the United States in a sort of cart which was termed the mail. We passed, day and night, with great rapidity along roads which were scarcely marked out, through immense forests; when the gloom of the woods became impenetrable, the coachman lighted branches of fir and we journeyed along by the light they cast. From time to time we came to a hut in the midst of the forest, which was a postoffice. The mail dropped an enormous bundle of letters at the door of this isolated dwelling, and we pursued our way at full gallop, leaving the inhabitants of the neighbouring log-houses to send for their share of the treasure.

† In 1832, each inhabitant of Michigan paid a sum equivalent to 1 franc 22 centimes (French money) to the postoffice revenue; and each inhabitant of the Floridas paid 1 fr. 5 cent. (See National Calendar, 1833, p. 244) In the same year each inhabitant of the department du Nord, paid 1 fr. 4 cent. to the revenue of the French postoffice. (See the Compte rendu de l'Administration des Finances, 1833, p. 623.) Now the state of Michigan only contained at that time 7 inhabitants per square league; and Florida only 5; the instruction and the commercial activity of these districts are inferior to those of most of the states in the Union; while the department du Nord, which contains 3,400 inhabitants per square league, is one of the most enlightened and manufacturing parts of France.

Europe its principal object is to fit men for private life. The interference of the citizens in public affairs is too rare an occurence for it to be anticipated beforehand. Upon casting a glance over society in the two hemispheres, these differences are indicated even by its external aspect.

In Europe we frequently introduce the ideas and the habits of private life into public affairs; and as we pass at once from the domestic circle to the government of the state, we may frequently be heard to discuss the great interests of society in the same manner in which we converse with our friends. The Americans, on the other hand, transfuse the habits of public life into their manners in private; and in their country the jury is introduced into the games of schoolboys, and parliamentary forms are observed in the order of a feast.

THE LAWS CONTRIBUTE MORE TO THE MAINTENANCE OF THE DEMOCRATIC REPUBLIC IN THE UNITED STATES THAN THE PHYSICAL CIRCUMSTANCES OF THE COUNTRY, AND THE MANNERS MORE THAN THE LAWS.

All the Nations of America have a democratic State of Society.—Yet democratic Institutions subsist only among the Anglo-Americans.—The Spaniards of South America, equally favoured by physical Causes as the Anglo-Americans, unable to maintain a democratic Republic.—Mexico, which has adopted the Constitution of the United States, in the same Predicament.—The Anglo-Americans of the West less able to maintain it than those of the East.—Reason of these different Results.

I have remarked that the maintenance of democratic institutions in the United States is attributable to the circumstances, the laws, and the manners of that country.* Most Europeans are only acquainted with the first of these three causes, and they are apt to give it a preponderating importance which it does not really possess.

It is true that the Anglo-Americans settled in the New World in a state of social equality; the low-born and the noble were not to be found among them; and professional prejudices were always as entirely unknown as the prejudices of birth. Thus, as the condition of society was democratic, the empire of democracy was established without difficulty. But this circumstance is by no means peculiar to the United States; almost all the transatlantic colonies were founded by men equal among themselves, or who became so by inhabiting them. In no one part of the New World have Europeans been able to create an aristocracy. Nevertheless democratic institutions prosper nowhere but in the United States.

The American Union has no enemies to contend with; it stands in the wilds like an island in the ocean. But the Spaniards of South America were no less isolated by nature; yet their position has not relieved them from the charge of standing armies. They make war upon each other when they have no foreign enemies to oppose; and the Anglo-American democracy is the only one which has hitherto been able to maintain itself in peace.

---

* I remind the reader of the general signification which I give to the word *manners*, namely, the moral and intellectual characteristics of social man taken collectively.

The territory of the Union presents a boundless field to human activity, and inexhaustible materials for industry and labour. The passion of wealth takes the place of ambition, and the warmth of faction is mitigated by a sense of prosperity. But in what portion of the globe shall we meet with more fertile plains, with mightier rivers, or with more unexplored and inexhaustible riches, than in South America?

Nevertheless South America has been unable to maintain democratic institutions. If the welfare of nations depended on their being placed in a remote position, with an unbounded space of habitable territory before them, the Spaniards of South America would have no reason to complain of their fate. And although they might enjoy less prosperity than the inhabitants of the United States, their lot might still be such as to excite the envy of some nations in Europe. There are, however, no nations upon the face of the earth more miserable than those of South America.

Thus, not only are physical causes inadequate to produce results analogous to those which occur in North America, but they are unable to raise the population of South America above the level of European states, where they act in a contrary direction. Physical causes do not therefore affect the destiny of nations so much as has been supposed.

I have met with men in New England who were on the point of leaving a country, where they might have remained in easy circumstances, to go to seek their fortune in the wilds. Not far from that district I found a French population in Canada which was closely crowded on a narrow territory, although the same wilds were at hand; and while the emigrant from the United States purchased an extensive estate with the earnings of a short term of labour, the Canadian paid as much for land as he would have done in France. Nature offers the solitudes of the New World to Europeans; but they are not always acquainted with the means of turning her gifts to account. Other peoples of America have the same physical conditions of prosperity as the Anglo-Americans, but without their laws and their manners; and these peoples are wretched. The laws and manners of the Anglo-Americans are therefore that efficient cause of their greatness which is the object of my inquiry.

I am far from supposing that the American laws are pre-eminently good in themselves; I do not hold them to be applicable to all democratic peoples; and several of them seem to me to be dangerous, even in the United States. Nevertheless, it cannot be denied that the American legislation, taken collectively, is extremely well adapted to the genius of the people and the nature of the country which it is intended to govern. The American laws are therefore good, and to them must be attributed a large portion of the success which attends the government of democracy in America: but I do not believe them to be the principal cause of that success; and if they seem to me to have more influence upon the social happiness of the Americans than the nature of the country, on the other hand there is reason to believe that their effect is still inferior to that produced by the manners of the people.

The federal laws undoubtedly constitute the most important part of

the legislation of the United States. Mexico, which is not less fortunately situated than the Anglo-American Union, has adopted these
same laws, but is unable to accustom itself to the government of
democracy. Some other cause is therefore at work independently of
those physical circumstances and peculiar laws which enable the
democracy to rule in the United States.

Another still more striking proof may be adduced. Almost all the inhabitants of the territory of the Union are the descendants of a common stock; they speak the same language, they worship God in the
same manner, they are affected by the same physical causes, and they
obey the same laws. Whence, then, do their characteristic differences
arise? Why, in the eastern states of the Union, does the republican
government display vigor and regularity, and proceed with mature deliberation? Whence does it derive the wisdom and durability which
mark its acts, while in the western states, on the contrary, society
seems to be ruled by the powers of chance? There, public business is
conducted with an irregularity, and a passionate and feverish excitement, which does not announce a long or sure duration.

I am no longer comparing the Anglo-American states to foreign nations; but I am contrasting them with each other, and endeavouring to
discover why they are so unlike. The arguments which are derived
from the nature of the country and the difference of legislation, are
here all set aside. Recourse must be had to some other cause; and
what other cause can there be except the manners of the people?

It is in the eastern states that the Anglo-Americans have been
longest accustomed to the government of democracy, and that they
have adopted the habits and conceived the notions most favourable to
its maintenance. Democracy has gradually penetrated into their customs, their opinions, and the forms of social intercourse; it is to be
found in all the details of daily life equally as in the laws. In the eastern states the instruction and practical education of the people have
been most perfected, and religion has been most thoroughly amalgamated with liberty. Now these habits, opinions, customs, and convictions, are precisely the constituent elements of that which I have
denominated manners.

In the western states, on the contrary, a portion of the same advantages is still wanting. Many of the Americans of the west were born
in the woods, and they mix the ideas and the customs of savage life
with the civilization of their parents. Their passions are more intense;
their religious morality less authoritative; and their convictions are
less secure. The inhabitants exercise no sort of control over their
fellow-citizens, for they are scarcely acquainted with each other. The
nations of the west display, to a certain extent, the inexperience and
the rude habits of a people in its infancy; for although they are composed of old elements, their assemblage is of recent date.

The manners of the Americans of the United States are, then, the
real cause which renders that people the only one of the American nations that is able to support a democratic government; and it is the influence of manners which produces the different degrees of order and

of prosperity, that may be distinguished in the several Anglo-American democracies. Thus the effect which the geographical position of a country may have upon the duration of democratic institutions is exaggerated in Europe. Too much importance is attributed to legislation, too little to manners. These three great causes serve, no doubt, to regulate and direct the American democracy; but if they were to be classed in their proper order, I should say that the physical circumstances are less efficient than the laws, and the laws very subordinate to the manners of the people. I am convinced that the most advantageous situation and the best possible laws cannot maintain a constitution in spite of the manners of a country: while the latter may turn the most unfavourable positions and the worst laws to some advantage. The importance of manners is a common truth to which study and experience incessantly direct our attention. It may be regarded as a central point in the range of human observation, and the common termination of all inquiry. So seriously do I insist upon this head, that if I have hitherto failed in making the reader feel the important influence which I attribute to the practical experience, the habits, the opinions, in short, to the manners of the Americans, upon the maintenance of their institutions, I have failed in the principal object of my work.

WHETHER LAWS AND MANNERS ARE SUFFICIENT TO MAINTAIN DEMOCRATIC INSTITUTIONS IN OTHER COUNTRIES BESIDE AMERICA.

The Anglo-Americans, if transported into Europe, would be obliged to modify their Laws.—Distinction to be made between democratic Institutions and American Institutions.—Democratic Laws may be conceived better than, or at least different from, those which the American Democracy has adopted.—The Example of America only proves that it is possible to regulate Democracy by the assistance of Manners and Legislation.

I have asserted that the success of democratic institutions in the United States is more intimately connected with the laws themselves, and the manners of the people, than with the nature of the country. But does it follow that the same causes would of themselves produce the same results, if they were put into operation elsewhere; and if the country is no adequate substitute for laws and manners, can laws and manners in their turn prove a substitute for a country? It will readily be understood that the necessary elements of a reply to this question are wanting: other peoples are to be found in the New World beside the Anglo-Americans, and as these peoples are affected by the same physical circumstances as the latter, they may fairly be compared together. But there are no nations out of America which have adopted the same laws and manners, being destitute of the physical advantages peculiar to the Anglo-Americans. No standard of comparison therefore exists, and we can only hazard an opinion upon this subject.

It appears to me in the first place, that a careful distinction must be made between the institutions of the United States and democratic institutions in general. When I reflect upon the state of Europe, its mighty nations, its populous cities, its formidable armies, and the complex nature of its politics, I cannot suppose that even the Anglo-Americans, if they were transported to our hemisphere, with their ideas, their religion, and their manners, could exist without considerably altering their laws. But a democratic nation may be imagined, organized differently from the American people. It is not impossible to conceive a government really established upon the will of the majority; but in which the majority, repressing its natural propensity to equality, should consent, with a view to the order and the stability of the state, to invest a family or an individual with all the prerogatives of the executive. A democratic society might exist, in which the forces of the nation would be more centralized than they are in the United States; the people would exercise a less direct and less irresistible influence upon public affairs, and yet every citizen invested with certain rights, would participate, within his sphere, in the conduct of the government. The observations I made among the Anglo-Americans induce me to believe that democratic institutions of this kind, prudently introduced into society, so as gradually to mix with the habits and to be interfused with the opinions of the people, might subsist in other countries beside America. If the laws of the United States were the only imaginable democratic laws, or the most perfect which it is possible to conceive, I should admit that the success of those institutions affords no proof of the success of democratic institutions in general, in a country less favoured by natural circumstances. But as the laws of America appear to me to be defective in several respects, and as I can readily imagine others of the same general nature, the peculiar advantages of that country do not prove that democratic institutions cannot succeed in a nation less favoured by circumstances, if ruled by better laws.

If human nature were different in America from what it is elsewhere; or if the social condition of the Americans engendered habits and opinions among them different from those which originate in the same social condition in the Old World, the American democracies would afford no means of predicting what may occur in other democracies. If the Americans displayed the same propensities as all other democratic nations, and if their legislators had relied upon the nature of the country and the favour of circumstances to restrain those propensities within due limits, the prosperity of the United States would be exclusively attributable to physical causes, and it would afford no encouragement to a people inclined to imitate their example, without sharing their natural advantages. But neither of these suppositions is borne out by facts.

In America the same passions are to be met with as in Europe; some originating in human nature, others in the democratic condition of society. Thus in the United States I found that restlessness of heart which is natural to men, when all ranks are nearly equal and the chances of elevation are the same to all. I found the democratic feeling of envy expressed under a thousand different forms. I remarked that the people frequently displayed, in the conduct of affairs, a consummate mixture of ignorance and presumption; and I inferred that in

America, men are liable to the same failings and the same absurdities as among ourselves. But upon examining the state of society more attentively, I speedily discovered that the Americans had made great and successful efforts to counteract these imperfections of human nature, and to correct the natural defects of democracy. Their divers municipal laws appeared to me to be a means of restraining the ambition of the citizens within a narrow sphere, and of turning those same passions, which might have worked havoc in the state, to the good of the township or the parish. The American legislators have succeeded to a certain extent in opposing the notion of rights, to the feelings of envy; the permanence of the religious world, to the continual shifting of politics; the experience of the people, to its theoretical ignorance; and its practical knowledge of business, to the impatience of its desires.

The Americans, then, have not relied upon the nature of their country, to counterpoise those dangers which originate in their constitution and in their political laws. To evils which are common to all democratic peoples, they have applied remedies which none but themselves had ever thought of before; and although they were the first to make the experiment, they have succeeded in it.

The manners and laws of the Americans are not the only ones which may suit a democratic people; but the Americans have shown that it would be wrong to despair of regulating democracy by the aid of manners and of laws. If other nations should borrow this general and pregnant idea from the Americans, without however intending to imitate them in the peculiar application which they have made of it; if they should attempt to fit themselves for that social condition, which it seems to be the will of Providence to impose upon the generations of this age, and so to escape from the despotism or the anarchy which threatens them; what reason is there to suppose that their efforts would not be crowned with success? The organization and the establishment of democracy in Christendom, is the great political problem of the time. The Americans unquestionably, have not resolved this problem, but they furnish useful data to those who undertake the task.

IMPORTANCE OF WHAT PRECEDES WITH RESPECT TO THE STATE OF EUROPE.

It may readily be discovered with what intention I undertook the foregoing inquiries. The question here discussed is interesting not only to the United States, but to the whole world; it concerns, not a nation, but all mankind. If those nations whose social condition is democratic could only remain free as long as they are inhabitants of the wilds, we could not but despair of the future destiny of the human race; for democracy is rapidly acquiring a more extended sway, and the wilds are gradually peopled with men. If it were true that laws and manners are insufficient to maintain democratic institutions, what refuge would remain open to the notions except the despotism of a single individual? I am aware that there are many worthy persons at the present time who are not alarmed at this latter alternative, and who are so tired of liberty as to be glad of repose, far from those storms by which it is attended. But these individuals are ill acquainted with the haven to which they are bound. They are so deluded by their recollections, as to judge the tendency of absolute power by what it was formerly, and not by what it might become at the present time.

If absolute power were re-established among the democratic nations of Europe, I am persuaded that it would assume a new form, and appear under features unknown to our forefathers. There was a time in Europe, when the laws and the consent of the people had invested princes with almost unlimited authority; but they scarcely ever availed themselves of it. I do not speak of the prerogatives of the nobility, of the authority of supreme courts of justice, of corporations and their chartered rights, or of provincial privileges, which served to break the blows of the sovereign authority, and to maintain a spirit of resistance in the nation. Independently of these political institutions—which, however opposed they might be to personal liberty, served to keep alive the love of freedom in the mind of the public, and which may be esteemed to have been useful in this respect—the manners and opinions of the nation confined the royal authority within barriers which were not less powerful, although they were less conspicuous. Religion, the affections of the people, the benevolence of the prince, the sense of honour, family pride, provincial prejudices, custom, and public opinion, limited the power of kings, and restrained their authority within an invisible circle. The constitution of nations was despotic at that time, but their manners were free. Princes had the right, but they had neither the means nor the desire, of doing whatever they pleased.

But what now remains of those barriers which formerly arrested the aggressions of tyranny? Since religion has lost its empire over the souls of men, the most prominent boundary which divided good from evil is overthrown: the very elements of the moral world are indeterminate; the princes and the peoples of the earth are guided by chance, and none can define the natural limits of despotism and the bounds of license. Long revolutions have for ever destroyed the respect which surrounded the rulers of the state; and since they have been relieved from the burden of public esteem, princes may henceforward surrender themselves without fear to the seductions of arbitrary power.

When kings find that the hearts of their subjects are turned toward them, they are clement, because they are conscious of their strength; and they are chary of the affection of their people, because the affection of their people is the bulwark of the throne. A mutual interchange of good will then takes place between the prince and the people, which resembles the gracious intercourse of domestic society. The subjects may murmur at the sovereign's decree, but they are grieved to displease him; and the sovereign chastises his subjects with the light hand of parental affection.

But when once the spell of royalty is broken in the tumult of revolution; when successive monarchs have occupied the throne, and alternately displayed to the people the weakness of right, and the harshness of power, the sovereign is no longer regarded by any as the father of the state, and he is feared by all as its master. If he be weak, he is despised; if he be strong, he is detested. He is himself full of animosity and alarm; he finds that he is a stranger in his own country, and he treats his subjects like conquered enemies.

When the provinces and the towns formed so many different nations in the midst of their common country, each of them had a will of its own, which was opposed to the general spirit of subjection; but now that all the parts of the same empire, after having lost their immunities, their customs, their prejudices, their traditions, and their names, are subjected and accustomed to the same laws, it is not more difficult to oppress them collectively, than it was formerly to oppress them singly.

While the nobles enjoyed their power, and indeed long after that power was lost, the honour of aristocracy conferred an extraordinary degree of force upon their personal opposition. They afforded instances of men who, notwithstanding their weakness, still entertained a high opinion of their personal value, and dared to cope single-handed with the efforts of the public authority. But at the present day, when all ranks are more and more confounded, when the individual disappears in the throng, and is easily lost in the midst of a common obscurity, when the honour of monarchy has almost lost its empire without being succeeded by public virtue, and when nothing can enable man to rise above himself, who shall say at what point the exigencies of power and servility of weakness will stop?

As long as family feeling was kept alive, the antagonist of oppression was never alone; he looked about him, and found his clients, his hereditary friends, and his kinsfolk. If this support was wanting, he was sustained by his ancestors and animated by his posterity. But when patrimonial estates are divided, and when a few years suffice to confound the distinctions of a race, where can family feeling be found? What force can there be in the customs of a country which has changed, and is still perpetually changing its aspect; in which every act of tyranny has a precedent, and every crime an example; in which there is nothing so old that its antiquity can save it from destruction, and nothing so unparalleled that its novelty can prevent it from being done? What resistance can be offered by manners of so pliant a make, that they have already often yielded? What strength can even public opinion have retained, when no twenty persons are connected by a common tie; when not a man, nor a family, nor chartered corporation, nor class, nor free institution, has the power of representing that opinion; and when every citizen—being equally weak, equally poor, and equally dependant—has only his personal impotence to oppose to the organized force of the government?

The annals of France furnish nothing analogous to the condition in which that country might then be thrown. But it may more aptly be assimilated to the times of old, and to those hideous eras of Roman oppression, when the manners of the people were corrupted, their traditions obliterated, their habits destroyed, their opinions shaken, and freedom, expelled from the laws, could find no refuge in the land;

when nothing protected the citizens, and the citizens no longer protected themselves; when human nature was the sport of man, and princes wearied out the clemency of Heaven before they exhausted the patience of their subjects. Those who hope to revive the monarchy of Henry IV.[5], or of Louis XIV., appear to me to be afflicted with mental blindness; and when I consider the present condition of several European nations—a condition to which all the others tend—I am led to believe that they will soon be left with no other alternative than democratic liberty, or the tyranny of the Cesars.

And, indeed, it is deserving of consideration, whether men are to be entirely emancipated, or entirely enslaved; whether their rights are to be made equal, or wholly taken away from them. If the rulers of society were reduced either gradually to raise the crowd to their own level, or to sink the citizens below that of humanity, would not the doubts of many be resolved, the consciences of many be healed, and the community prepared to make great sacrifices with little difficulty? In that case, the gradual growth of democratic manners and institution should be regarded, not as the best, but as the only means of preserving freedom; and without liking the government of democracy, it might be adopted as the most applicable and the fairest remedy for the present ills of society.

It is difficult to associate a people in the work of government; but it is still more difficult to supply it with experience, and to inspire it with the feelings which it requires in order to govern well. I grant that the caprices of democracy are perpetual; its instruments are rude, its laws imperfect. But if it were true that soon no just medium would exist between the empire of democracy and the dominion of a single arm, should we not rather incline toward the former, than submit voluntarily to the latter? And if complete equality be our fate, is it not better to be levelled by free institutions than by despotic power?

Those who, after having read this book, should imagine that my intention in writing it has been to propose the laws and manners of the Anglo-Americans for the imitation of all democratic peoples, would commit a very great mistake; they must have paid more attention to the form than to the substance of my ideas. My aim has been to show, by the example of America, that laws, and especially manners, may exist, which will allow a democratic people to remain free. But I am very far from thinking that we ought to follow the example of the American democracy, and copy the means which it has employed to attain its ends; for I am well aware of the influence which the nature of a country and its political precedents exercise upon a constitution; and I should regard it as a great misfortune for mankind, if liberty were to exist, all over the world, under the same forms.

But I am of opinion that if we do not succeed in gradually introducing democratic institutions into France, and if we despair of imparting to the citizens those ideas and sentiments which first prepare them for freedom, and afterward allow them to enjoy it, there will be no independence at all, either for the middling classes or the nobility, for the poor or for the rich, but an equal tyranny over all; and I fore-

see that if the peaceable empire of the majority be not founded among us in time, we shall sooner or later arrive at the unlimited authority of a single despot.

Chapter XVIII.

THE PRESENT AND PROBABLE FUTURE CONDITION OF THE THREE RACES WHICH INHABIT THE TERRITORY OF THE UNITED STATES.

The principal part of the task which I had imposed upon myself is now performed: I have shown, as far as I was able, the laws and the manners of the American democracy. Here I might stop; but the reader would perhaps feel that I had not satisfied his expectations.

The absolute supremacy of democracy is not all that we meet with in America; the inhabitants of the New World may be considered from more than one point of view. In the course of this work my subject has often led me to speak of the Indians and the negroes; but I have never been able to stop in order to show what places these two races occupy, in the midst of the democratic people whom I was engaged in describing. I have mentioned in what spirit, and according to what laws, the Anglo-American Union was formed; but I could only glance at the dangers which menace that confederation, while it was equally impossible for me to give a detailed account of its chances of duration, independently of its laws and manners. When speaking of the United republican States, I hazarded no conjectures upon the permanence of republican forms in the New World; and when making frequent allusion to the commercial activity which reigns in the Union, I was unable to inquire into the future condition of the Americans as a commercial people.

These topics are collaterally connected with my subject, without forming a part of it; they are American, without being democratic; and to portray democracy has been my principal aim. It was therefore necessary to postpone these questions, which I now take up as the proper termination of my work.

The territory now occupied or claimed by the American Union spreads from the shores of the Atlantic to those of the Pacific ocean. On the east and west its limits are those of the continent itself. On the south it advances nearly to the tropic, and it extends upward to the icy regions of the north.*

The human beings who are scattered over this space do not form, as in Europe, so many branches of the same stock. Three races naturally distinct, and I might almost say hostile to each other, are discoverable among them at the first glance. Almost insurmountable barriers had been raised between them by education and by law, as well as by their origin and outward characteristics; but fortune has brought them to-

---

* See the map [on the cover of this volume—*Editor*].

gether on the same soil, where, although they are mixed, they do not amalgamate, and each race fulfils its destiny apart.

Among these widely differing families of men, the first which attracts attention, the superior in intelligence, in power, and in enjoyment, is the white or European, the MAN pre-eminent; and in subordinate grades, the negro and the Indian. These two unhappy races have nothing in common; neither birth, nor features, nor language, nor habits. Their only resemblance lies in their misfortunes. Both of them occupy an inferior rank in the country they inhabit; both suffer from tyranny; and if their wrongs are not the same, they originate at any rate with the same authors.

If we reasoned from what passes in the world, we should almost say that the European is to the other races of mankind, what man is to the lower animals;—he makes them subservient to his use; and when he cannot subdue, he destroys them. Oppression has at one stroke deprived the descendants of the Africans of almost all the priveleges of humanity. The negro of the United States has lost all remembrance of his country; the language which his forefathers spoke is never heard around him; he abjured their religion and forgot their customs when he ceased to belong to Africa, without acquiring any claim to European privileges. But he remains half-way between the two communities; sold by the one, repulsed by the other; finding not a spot in the universe to call by the name of country, except the faint image of a home which the shelter of his master's roof affords.

The negro has no family; woman is merely the temporary companion of his pleasures, and his children are upon an equality with himself from the moment of their birth. Am I to call it a proof of God's mercy, or a visitation of his wrath, that man in certain states appears to be insensible to his extreme wretchedness, and almost affects with a depraved taste the cause of his misfortunes? The negro, who is plunged in this abyss of evils, scarcely feels his own calamitous situation. Violence made him a slave, and the habit of servitude gives him the thoughts and desires of a slave; he admires his tyrants more than he hates them, and finds his joy and his pride in the servile imitation of those who oppress him: his understanding is degraded to the level of his soul.

The negro enters upon slavery as soon as he is born; nay, he may have been purchased in the womb, and have begun his slavery before he began his existence. Equally devoid of wants and of enjoyment, and useless to himself, he learns, with his first notions of existence, that he is the property of another who has an interest in preserving his life, and that the care of it does not devolve upon himself; even the power of thought appears to him a useless gift of Providence, and he quietly enjoys the privileges of his debasement.

If he becomes free, independence is often felt by him to be a heavier burden than slavery; for having learned, in the course of his life, to submit to everything except reason, he is too much unacquainted with her dictates to obey them. A thousand new desires beset him, and he is destitute of the knowledge and energy necessary to resist them:

these are masters which it is necessary to contend with, and he has learned only to submit and obey. In short, he sinks to such a depth of wretchedness, that while servitude brutalizes, liberty destroys him.

Oppression has been no less fatal to the Indian than to the negro race, but its effects are different. Before the arrival of the white men in the New World, the inhabitants of North America lived quietly in their woods, enduring the vicissitudes, and practising the virtues and vices common to savage nations. The Europeans, having dispersed the Indian tribes and driven them into the deserts, condemned them to a wandering life full of inexpressible sufferings.

Savage nations are only controlled by opinion and by custom. When the North American Indians had lost their sentiment of attachment to their country; when their families were dispersed, their traditions obscured, and the chain of their recollections broken; when all their habits were changed, and their wants increased beyond measure, European tyranny rendered them more disorderly and less civilized than they were before. The moral and physical condition of these tribes continually grew worse, and they became more barbarous as they became more wretched. Nevertheless the Europeans have not been able to metamorphose the character of the Indians; and though they have had power to destroy them, they have never been able to make them submit to the rules of civilized society.

The lot of the negro is placed on the extreme limit of servitude, while that of the Indian lies on the uttermost verge of liberty; and slavery does not produce more fatal effects upon the first, than independence upon the second. The negro has lost all property in his own person, and he cannot dispose of his existence without committing a sort of fraud: but the savage is his own master as soon as he is able to act; parental authority is scarcely known to him; he has never bent his will to that of any of his kind, nor learned the difference between voluntary obedience and a shameful subjection; and the very name of law is unknown to him. To be free, with him, signifies to escape from all the shackles of society. As he delights in this barbarous independence, and would rather perish than sacrifice the least part of it, civilization has little power over him.

The negro makes a thousand fruitless efforts to insinuate himself among men who repulse him; he conforms to the taste of his oppressors, adopts their opinions, and hopes by imitating them to form a part of their community. Having been told from infancy that his race is naturally inferior to that of the whites, he assents to the proposition, and is ashamed of his own nature. In each of his features he discovers a trace of slavery, and, if it were in his power, he would willingly rid himself of everything that makes him what he is.

The Indian, on the contrary, has his imagination inflated with the pretended nobility of his origin, and lives and dies in the midst of these dreams of pride. Far from desiring to conform his habits to ours, he loves his savage life as the distinguishing mark of his race, and he repels every advance to civilization, less perhaps from the hatred which he entertains for it, than from a dread of resembling the Europeans.* While he has nothing to oppose to our perfection in the arts but the resources of the desert, to our tactics nothing but undisciplined courage; while our well-digested plans are met by the spontaneous instincts of savage life, who can wonder if he fails in this unequal contest?

The negro, who earnestly desires to mingle his race with that of the European, cannot effect it; while the Indian, who might succeed to a certain extent, disdains to make the attempt. The servility of the one dooms him to slavery, the pride of the other to death.

I remember that while I was travelling through the forests which still cover the state of Alabama, I arrived one day at the log-house of a pioneer. I did not wish to penetrate into the dwelling of the American, but retired to rest myself for a while on the margin of a spring, which was not far off, in the woods. While I was in this place (which was in the neighbourhood of the Creek territory), an Indian woman appeared, followed by a negress, and holding by the hand a little white girl of five or six years old, whom I took to be the daughter of the pioneer. A sort of barbarous luxury set off the costume of the Indian; rings of metal were hanging from her nostrils and ears; her hair, which was adorned with glass beads, fell loosely upon her shoulders; and I saw that she was not married, for she still wore the necklace of shells which the bride always deposites on the nuptial couch. The negress was clad in squalid European garments.

They all three came and seated themselves upon the banks of the fountain; and the young Indian, taking the child in her arms, lavished upon her such fond caresses as mothers give; while the negress endeavoured by various little artifices to attract the attention of the young creole. The child displayed in her slightest gestures a consciousness of superiority which formed a strange contrast with her infantine weakness; as if she received the attentions of her companions with a sort of condescension.

The negress was seated on the ground before her mistress, watching her smallest desires, and apparently divided between strong affection

---

* The native of North America retains his opinions and the most insignificant of his habits with a degree of tenacity which has no parallel in history. For more than two hundred years the wandering tribes of North America have had daily intercourse with the whites, and they have never derived from them either a custom or an idea. Yet the Europeans have exercised a powerful influence over the savages: they have made them more licentious, but not more European. In the summer of 1831, I happened to be beyond Lake Michigan, at a place called Green Bay, which serves as the extreme frontier between the United States and the Indians on the northwestern side. Here I became acquainted with an American officer, Major H., who after talking to me at length on the inflexibility of the Indian character, related the following fact: "I formerly knew a young Indian," said he, "who had been educated at a college in New England, where he had greatly distinguished himself, and had acquired the external appearance of a member of civilized society. When the war broke out between ourselves and the English, in 1810, I saw this young man again; he was serving in our army at the head of the warriors of his tribe; for the Indians were admitted among the ranks of the Americans, upon condition that they would abstain from their horrible custom of scalping their victims. On the evening of the battle of * * *, C. came and sat himself down by the fire of our bivouac. I asked him what had been his fortune that day: he related his exploits; and growing warm and animated by the recollection of them, he concluded by suddenly opening the breast of his coat, saying, 'You must not betray me—see here!' And I actually beheld," said the major, "between his body and his shirt, the skin and hair of an English head still dripping with gore."

for the child and servile fear; while the savage displayed, in the midst of her tenderness, an air of freedom and of pride which was almost ferocious. I had approached the group, and I contemplated them in silence; but my curiosity was probably displeasing to the Indian woman, for she suddenly rose, pushed the child roughly from her, and giving me an angry look, plunged into the thicket.

I had often chanced to see individuals met together in the same place, who belonged to the three races of men which people North America. I had perceived from many different results the preponderance of the whites. But in the picture which I have just been describing there was something peculiarly touching; a bond of affection here united the oppressors with the oppressed, and the effort of Nature to bring them together rendered still more striking the immense distance placed between them by prejudice and by law.

THE PRESENT AND PROBABLE FUTURE CONDITION OF THE INDIAN TRIBES WHICH INHABIT THE TERRITORY POSSESSED BY THE UNION.

Gradual disappearance of the native Tribes.—Manner in which it takes place.—
Miseries accompanying the forced Migrations of the Indians.—The Savages of North America had only two ways of escaping Destruction; War or Civilization.—
They are no longer able to make War.—Reasons why they refused to become civilized when it was in their Power, and why they cannot become so now that they desire it.—Instance of the Creek and Cherokees.—Policy of the particular States toward these Indians.—Policy of the federal Government.

None of the Indian tribes which formerly inhabited the territory of New England—the Narragansets, the Mohicans, the Pequots—have any existence but in the recollection of man. The Lenapes, who received William Penn[1] a hundred and fifty years ago upon the banks of the Delaware, have disappeared; and I myself met with the last of the Iroquois, who were begging alms. The nations I have mentioned formerly covered the country to the seacoast; but a traveller at the present day must penetrate more than a hundred leagues into the interior of the continent to find an Indian. Not only have these wild tribes receded, but they are destroyed;* and as they give way or perish, an immense and increasing people fills their place. There is no instance upon record of so prodigious a growth, or so rapid a destruction; the manner in which the latter change takes place is not difficult to describe.

When the Indians were the sole inhabitants of the wilds whence they have been expelled, their wants were few. Their arms were of their own manufacture, their only drink was the water of the brook, and their clothes consisted of the skin of animals, whose flesh furnished them with food.

The Europeans introduced among the savages of North America firearms, ardent spirits, and iron: they taught them to exchange for manufactured stuffs the rough garments which had previously satis-

---

* In the thirteen original states, there are only 6,273 Indians remaining. (See Legislative Documents, 20th congress, No. 117, p. 90)

fied their untutored simplicity. Having acquired new tastes, without the arts by which they could be gratified, the Indians were obliged to have recourse to the workmanship of the whites; but in return for their productions the savage had nothing to offer except the rich furs which still abounded in his woods. Hence the chase became necessary, not merely to provide for his subsistence, but in order to procure the only objects of barter which he could furnish to Europe.* While the wants of the natives were thus increasing, their resources continued to diminish.

From the moment when a European settlement is formed in the neighborhood of the territory occupied by the Indians, the beasts of chase takes the alarm.† Thousands of savages, wandering in the forest and destitute of any fixed dwelling, did not disturb them; but as soon as the continuous sounds of European labour are heard in the neighbourhood, they begin to flee away, and retire to the west, where their instinct teaches them that they will find deserts of immeasurable extent. "The buffalo is constantly receding," say Messrs. Clarke and Cass in their Report of the year 1829; "a few years since they approached the base of the Allegany; and a few years hence they may even be rare upon the immense plains which extend to the base of the Rocky mountains." I have been assured that this effect of the approach of the whites is often felt at two hundred leagues' distance from the frontier. Their influence is thus exerted over tribes whose name is unknown to them, and who suffer the evils of usurpation long before they are acquainted with the authors of their distress.‡

Bold adventures soon penetrate into the country the Indians have deserted, and when they have advanced about fifteen or twenty leagues from the extreme frontiers of the whites, they begin to build

---

* Messrs. Clarke and Cass, in their report to congress, the 4th February, 1829, p. 23, expressed themselves thus: "The time when the Indians generally could supply themselves with food and clothing, without any of the articles of civilized life, has long since passed away. The more remote tribes, beyond the Mississippi, who live where immense herds of buffalo are yet to be found, and who follow those animals in their periodical migrations, could more easily than any others recur to the habits of their ancestors, and live without the white man or any of his manufactures. But the buffalo is constantly receding. The smaller animals, the bear, the deer, the beaver, the otter, the muskrat, & c., principally minister to the comfort and support of the Indians; and these cannot be taken without guns, ammunition, and traps.

"Among the northwestern Indians particularly, the labour of supplying a family with food in excessive. Day after day is spent by the hunter without success, and during this interval his family must subsist upon bark or roots, or perish. Want and misery are around them and among them. Many die every winter from actual starvation."

The Indians will not live as Europeans live; and yet they can neither subsist without them, nor exactly after the fashion of their fathers. This is demonstrated by a fact which I likewise give upon official authority. Some Indians of a tribe on the banks of Lake Superior had killed a European; the American government interdicted all traffic with the tribe to which the guilty parties belonged, until they were delivered up to justice. This measure had the desired effect.

† "Five years ago," says Volney in his Tableaux des Etats Unis, p. 370, "in going from Vincennes to Kaskaskia, a territory which now forms part of the state of Illinois, but which at the time I mention was completely wild (1797), you could not cross a prairie without seeing herds of from four to five hundred buffaloes. There are now none remaining; they swam across the Mississippi to escape from the hunters, and more particularly from the bells of the American cows."

‡ The truth of what I here advance may be easily proved by consulting the tabular statement of Indian tribes inhabiting the United States, and their territories. (Legislative Documents, 20th congress, No. 117, pp. 90–105.) It is there shown that the tribes of America are rapidly decreasing, although the Europeans are still at a considerable distance from them.

habitations for civilized beings in the midst of the wilderness. This is done without difficulty, as the territory of a hunting-nation is ill defined; it is the common property of the tribe, and belongs to no one in particular, so that individual interest are not concerned in the protection of any part of it.

A few European families, settled in different situations at a considerable distance from each other, soon drive away the wild animals which remain between their places of abode. The Indians, who had previously lived in a sort of abundance, then find it difficult to subsist, and still more difficult to procure the articles of barter which they stand in need of.

To drive away their game is to deprive them of the means of existence, as effectually as if the fields of our agriculturists were stricken with barrenness; and they are reduced, like famished wolves, to prowl through the forsaken woods in quest of prey. Their instinctive love of their country attaches them to the soil which gave them birth,* even after it has ceased to yield anything but misery and death. At length they are compelled to acquiesce, and to depart: they follow the traces of the elk, the buffalo, and the beaver, and are guided by those wild animals in the choice of their future country. Properly speaking, therefore, it is not the Europeans who drive away the native inhabitants of America; it is famine which compels them to recede; a happy distinction which had escaped the casuists of former times, and for which we are indebted to modern discovery.

It is impossible to conceive the extent of the sufferings which attend these forced emigrations. They are undertaken by a people already exhausted and reduced; and the countries to which the new-comers betake themselves are inhabited by other tribes which receive them with jealous hostility. Hunger is in the rear, war awaits them, and misery besets them on all sides. In the hope of escaping from such a host of enemies, they separate, and each individual endeavours to procure the means of supporting his existence in solitude and secresy, living in the immensity of the desert like an outcast in civilized society. The social tie, which distress had long since weakened, is then dissolved; they have lost their country, and their people soon deserts them; their very families are obliterated; the names they bore in common are forgotten, their language perishes, and all the traces of their origin disappear. Their nation has ceased to exist, except in the recollection of the antiquaries of America and a few of the learned of Europe.

I should be sorry to have my reader suppose that I am colouring the picture too highly: I saw with my own eyes several of the cases of misery which I have been describing; and I was the witness of sufferings which I have not the power to portray.

---

* "The Indians," says Messrs. Clarke and Cass in their report to congress, p. 15, "are attached to their country by the same feelings which bind us to ours; and, besides, there are certain superstitious notions connected with the alienation of what the Great Spirit gave to their ancestors, which operate strongly upon the tribes who have made few or no cessions, but which are gradually weakened as our intercourse with them is extended. 'We will not sell the spot which contains the bones of our fathers,' is almost always the first answer to a proposition for a sale."

At the end of the year 1831, while I was on the left bank of the Mississippi, at a place named by Europeans Memphis, there arrived a numerous band of Choctaws[2] (or Chactas, as they are called by the French in Louisiana). These savages had left their country, and were endeavouring to gain the right bank of the Mississippi, where they hoped to find an asylum which had been promised them by the American government. It was then in the middle of winter, and the cold was unusually severe; the snow had frozen hard upon the ground, and the river was drifting huge masses of ice. The Indians had their families with them; and they brought in their train the wounded and the sick, with children newly born, and old men upon the verge of death. They possessed neither tents nor wagons, but only their arms and some provisions. I saw them embark to pass the mighty river, and never will that solemn spectacle fade from my remembrance. No cry, no sob was heard among the assembled crowd: all were silent. Their calamities were of ancient date, and they knew them to be irremediable. The Indians had all stepped into the bark which was to carry them across, but their dogs remained upon the bank. As soon as these animals perceived that their masters were finally leaving the shore, they set up a dismal howl, and, plunging all together into the icy waters of the Mississippi, they swam after the boat.

The ejectment of the Indians very often takes place at the present day, in a regular, and, as it were, a legal manner. When the European population begins to approach the limit of the desert inhabited by a savage tribe, the government of the United States usually despatches envoys to them, who assemble the Indians in a large plain, and having first eaten and drunk with them, accost them in the following manner: "What have you to do in the land of your fathers? Before long you must dig up their bones in order to live. In what respect is the country you inhabit better than another? Are there no woods, marshes, or prairies, except where you dwell? And can you live nowhere but under your own sun? Beyond those mountains which you see at the horizon, beyond the lake which bounds your territory on the west, there lie vast countries where beasts of chase are found in great abundance; sell your land to us, and go to live happily in those solitudes." After holding this language, they spread before the eyes of the Indians firearms, woollen garments, kegs of brandy, glass necklaces, bracelets of tinsel, ear-rings, and looking-glasses.* If, when they have beheld all these riches, they still hesitate, it is insinuated that they have not the means

---

* See in the legislative documents of congress (Doc. 117), the narrative of what takes place on these occasions. This curious passage is from the abovementioned report, made to congress by Messrs. Clarke and Cass in February, 1829. Mr. Cass is now secretary of war.

"The Indians," says the report, "reach the treaty-ground poor, and almost naked. Large quantities of goods are taken there by the traders, and are seen and examined by the Indians. The women and children become importunate to have their wants supplied, and their influence is soon exerted to induce a sale. Their improvidence is habitual and unconquerable. The gratification of his immediate wants and desires is the ruling passion of an Indian: the expectation of future advantages seldom produces much effect. The experience of the past is lost, and the prospects of the future disregarded. It would be utterly hopeless to demand a cession of land unless the means were at hand of gratifying their immediate wants; and when their condition and circumstances are fairly considered, it ought not to surprise us that they are so anxious to relieve themselves."

of refusing their required consent, and that the government itself will not long have the power of protecting them in their rights. What are they to do? Half convinced, and half compelled, they go to inhabit new deserts, where the importunate whites will not let them remain ten years in tranquility. In this manner do the Americans obtain at a very low price whole provinces, which the richest sovereigns of Europe could not purchase.*

These are great evils, and it must be added that they appear to me to be irremediable. I believe that the Indian nations of North America are doomed to perish; and that whenever the Europeans shall be established on the shores of the Pacific ocean, that race of men will be no more.† The Indians had only the two alternatives of war or civilization; in other words, they must either have destroyed the Europeans or become their equals.

At the first settlement of the colonies they might have found it possible, by uniting their forces, to deliver themselves from the small bodies of strangers who landed on their continent.‡ They several times attempted to do it, and were on the point of succeeding; but the disproportion of their resources, at the present day, when compared with those of the whites, is too great to allow such an enterprise to be thought of. Nevertheless, there do arise from time to time among the Indians men of penetration, who foresee the final destiny which awaits the native population, and who exert themselves to unite all the tribes in common hostility to the Europeans; but their efforts are unavailing. Those tribes which are in the neighbourhood of the whites, are too much weakened to offer an effectual resistance; while the others, giving way to that childish carelessness of the morrow which characterizes savage life, wait for the near approach of danger before they prepare to meet it: some are unable, the others are unwilling to exert themselves.

---

* On the 19th of May, 1830, Mr. Edward Everett affirmed before the house of representatives, that the Americans had already acquired by *treaty*, to the east and west of the Mississippi, 230,000,000 of acres. In 1808, the Osages gave up 48,000,000 acres for an annual payment of 1,000 dollars. In 1818, the Quapaws yielded up 29,000,000 acres for 4,000 dollars. They reserved for themselves a territory of 1,000,000 acres for a hunting-ground. A solemn oath was taken that it should be respected: but before long it was invaded like the rest.

Mr. Bell, in his "Report of the Committee on Indian Affairs," February 24th, 1830, has these words: "To pay an Indian tribe what their ancient hunting-grounds are worth to them, after the game is fled or destroyed, as a mode of appropriating wild lands claimed by Indians, has been found more convenient, and certainly it is more agreeable to the forms of justice, as well as more merciful, than to assert the possession of them by the sword. Thus the practice of buying Indian titles is but the substitute which humanity and expediency have imposed, in place of the sword, in arriving at the actual enjoyment of property claimed by the right of discovery, and sanctioned by the natural superiority allowed to the claims of civilized communities, over those of savage tribes. Up to the present time, so invariable has been the operation of certain causes, first in diminishing the value of forest lands to the Indians, and secondly in disposing them to sell readily, that the plan of buying their right of occupancy has never threatened to retard, in any perceptible degree, the prosperity of any of the states." (Legislative documents, 21st congress, No. 227, p. 6.)

† This seems, indeed, to be the opinion of almost all American statesmen. "Judging of the future by the past," says Mr. Cass, "we cannot err in anticipating a progressive diminution of their numbers, and their eventual extinction, unless our border should become stationary, and they be removed beyond it, or unless some radical change should take place in the principles of our intercourse with them, which it is easier to hope for than to expect."

‡ Among other warlike enterprises, there was one of the Wampanoags, and other confederate tribes, under Metacom in 1675, against the colonists of New England; the English were also engaged in war in Virginia in 1622.

It is easy to foresee that the Indians will never conform to civilization; or that it will be too late, whenever they may be inclined to make the experiment.

Civilization is the result of a long social process which takes place in the same spot, and is handed down from one generation to another, each one profiting by the experience of the last. Of all nations, those submit to civilization with the most difficulty, which habitually live by the chase. Pastoral tribes, indeed, often change their place of abode; but they follow a regular order in their migrations, and often return again to their old stations, while the dwelling of the hunter varies with that of the animals he pursues.

Several attempts have been made to diffuse knowledge among the Indians, without controlling their wandering propensities; by the Jesuits in Canada, and by the puritans in New England;* but none of these endeavours were crowned by any lasting success. Civilization began in the cabin, but it soon retired to expire in the woods; the great error of these legislators of the Indians was their not understanding, that in order to succeed in civilizing a people, it is first necessary to fix it; which cannot be done without inducing it to cultivate the soil: the Indians ought in the first place to have been accustomed to agriculture. But not only are they destitute of this indispensable preliminary to civilization, they would even have great difficulty in acquiring it. Men who have once abandoned themselves to the restless and adventurous life of the hunter, feel an insurmountable disgust for the constant and regular labour which tillage requires. We see this proved in the bosom of our own society; but it is far more visible among peoples whose partiality for the chase is a part of their national character.

Independently of this general difficulty, there is another which applies peculiarly to the Indians; they consider labour not merely as an evil, but as a disgrace; so that their pride prevents them from becoming civilized, as much as their indolence.†

There is no Indian so wretched as not to retain, under his hut of bark, a lofty idea of his personal worth; he considers the cares of industry and labour as degrading occupations; he compares the husbandman to the ox which traces the furrow; and even in our most ingenious handicraft, he can see nothing but the labour of slaves. Not that he is devoid of admiration for the power and intellectual greatness of the whites; but although the result of our efforts surprises him, he contemns the means by which we obtain it; and while he acknowledges our ascendency, he still believes in his superiority. War and hunting are the only pursuits which appear to him worthy to be the occupations of a man.‡ The Indian, in the dreary solitude of his

---

* See the "Histoire de la Nouvelle France," by Charlevoix, and the work entitled "Lettres Edifiantes."

† "In all the tribes," says Volney in his "Tableau des Etats Unis," p. 423, "there still exists a generation of old warriors, who cannot forbear, when they see their countrymen using the hoe, from exclaiming against the degradation of ancient manners, and asserting that the savages owe their decline to these innovations; adding, that they have only to return to their primitive habits, in order to recover their power and their glory."

‡ The following description occurs in an official document: "Until a young man has been en-

woods, cherishes the same ideas, the same opinions, as the noble of
the middle ages in his castle, and he only requires to become a conqueror to complete the resemblance: thus, however strange it may
seem, it is in the forests of the New World, and not among the Europeans who people its coasts, that the ancient prejudices of Europe are
still in existence.

More than once, in the course of this work, I have endeavoured to
explain the prodigious influence which the social condition appears to
exercise upon the laws and the manners of men; and I beg to add a
few words on the same subject. When I perceive the resemblance
which exists between the political institutions of our ancestors, the
Germans, and of the wandering tribes of North America: between the
customs described by Tacitus,[3] and those of which I have sometimes
been a witness, I cannot help thinking that the same cause has
brought about the same results in both hemispheres; and that in the
midst of the apparent diversity of human affairs, a certain number of
primary facts may be discovered, from which all the others are derived. In what we usually call the German institutions, then, I am inclined only to perceive barbarian habits; and the opinions of savages,
in what we style feudal principles.

However strongly the vices and prejudices of the North American
Indians may be opposed to their becoming agricultural and civilized,
necessity sometimes obliges them to it. Several of the southern nations, and among others the Cherokees and the Creeks,* were surrounded by Europeans, who had landed on the shores of the Atlantic,
and who, either descending the Ohio or proceeding up the Mississippi, arrived simultaneously upon their borders. These tribes have not
been driven from place to place, like their northern brethren; but they
have been gradually enclosed within narrow limits, like the game
within the thicket before the huntsmen plunge into the interior. The
Indians, who were thus placed between civilization and death, found
themselves obliged to live by ignominious labour like the whites. They
took to agriculture, and without entirely forsaking their old habits or

---

gaged with an enemy, and has performed some acts of valour, he gains no consideration, but
is regarded nearly as a woman. In their great war-dances all the warriors in succession strike
the post, as it is called, and recount their exploits. On these occasions their auditory consists
of the kinsmen, friends, and comrades of the narrator. The profound impression which his
discourse produces on them is manifested by the silent attention it receives, and by the loud
shouts which hail its termination. The young man who finds himself at such a meeting without anything to recount, is very unhappy: and instances have sometimes occurred of young
warriors whose passions had been thus inflamed, quitting the war-dance suddenly, and going
off alone to seek for trophies which they might exhibit, and adventures which they might be
allowed to relate."
* These nations are now swallowed up in the states of Georgia, Tennessee, Alabama, and Mississippi. There were formerly in the south four great nations (remnants of which still exist),
the Choctaws, the Chickasaws, the Creeks, and the Cherokees. The remnants of these four
nations amounted in 1830, to about 75,000 individuals. It is computed that there are now
remaining in the territory occupied or claimed by the Anglo-American Union about 300,000
Indians. (See proceedings of the Indian board in the city of New York.) The official documents supplied to congress make the number amount to 313,130. The reader who is curious
to know the names and numerical strength of all the tribes which inhabit the Anglo-
American territory, should consult the documents I refer to. (Legislative Documents, 20th
congress, No. 117, pp. 90–105.)

manners, sacrificed only as much as was necessary to their existence.

The Cherokees went farther: they created a written language; established a permanent form of government; and as everything proceeds rapidly in the New World, before they had all of them clothes, they set up a newspaper.*

The growth of European habits has been remarkably accelerated among these Indians by the mixed race which has sprung up.† Deriving intelligence from the father's side, without entirely losing the savage customs of the mother, the half-blood forms the natural link between civilization and barbarism. Wherever this race has multiplied, the savage state has become modified, and a great change has taken place in the manners of the people.‡

The success of the Cherokees proves that the Indians are capable of civilization, but it does not prove that they will succeed in it. The difficulty which the Indians find in submitting to civilization proceeds from the influence of a general cause, which it is almost impossible for them to escape. An attentive survey of history demonstrates that, in general, barbarous nations have raised themselves to civilization by degrees, and by their own efforts. Whenever they derived knowledge from a foreign people, they stood toward it in the relation of conquerors, and not of a conquered nation. When the conquered nation is enlightened, and the conquerors are half savage, as in the case of the invasion of Rome by the northern nations, or that of China by the Moguls, the power which victory bestows upon the barbarian is sufficient to keep up his importance among civilized men, and permit him to rank as their equal, until he becomes their rival: the one has might on his side, the other has intelligence; the former admires the knowledge and the arts of the conquered, the latter envies the power of the conquerors. The barbarians at length admit civilized man into their palaces, and he in turn opens his schools to the barbarians. But when the side on which the physical force lies, also possesses an intellectual

---

* I brought back with me to France, one or two copies of this singular publication.
† See in the report of the committee on Indian affairs, 21st congress, No. 227, p. 23, the reasons for the multiplication of Indians of mixed blood among the Cherokees. The principal cause dates from the war of independence. Many Anglo-Americans of Georgia, having taken the side of England, were obliged to retreat among the Indians, where they married.
‡ Unhappily the mixed race has been less numerous and less influential in North America than in any other country. The American continent was peopled by two great nations of Europe, the French and the English. The former were not slow in connecting themselves with the daughters of the natives; but there was an unfortunate affinity between the Indian character and their own: instead of giving the tastes and habits of civilized life to the savages, the French too often grew passionately fond of the state of wild freedom they found them in. They became the most dangerous of the inhabitants of the desert, and won the friendship of the Indian by exaggerating his vices and his virtues. M. de Senonville, the governor of Canada, wrote thus to Louis XIV., in 1685: "It has long been believed that in order to civilize the savages we ought to draw them nearer to us, but there is every reason to suppose we have been mistaken. Those which have been brought into contact with us have not become French, and the French who have lived among them are changed into savages, affecting to live and dress like them." (History of New France, by Charlevoix, vol. ii., p. 345.) The Englishman, on the contrary, continuing obstinately attached to the customs and the most insignificant habits of his forefathers, has remained in the midst of the American solitudes just what he was in the bosom of European cities; he would not allow of any communication with savages whom he despised, and avoided with care the union of his race with theirs. Thus, while the French exercised no salutary influence over the Indians, the English have always remained alien from them.

preponderance, the conquered party seldom becomes civilized; it re-treats, or is destroyed. It may therefore be said, in a general way, that savages go forth in arms to seek knowledge, but that they do not re-ceive it when it comes to them.

If the Indian tribes which now inhabit the heart of the continent could summon up energy enough to attempt to civilize themselves, they might possibly succeed. Superior already to the barbarous nations which surround them, they would gradually gain strength and experi-ence; and when the Europeans should appear upon their borders, they would be in a state, if not to maintain their independence, at least to assert their right to the soil, and to incorporate themselves with the conquerors. But it is the misfortune of Indians to be brought into con-tact with a civilized people, which is also (it may be owned) the most avaricious nation on the globe, while they are still semi-barbarian: to find despots in their instructers, and to receive knowledge from the hand of oppression. Living in the freedom of the woods, the North American Indian was destitute, but he had no feeling of inferiority to-ward any one; as soon, however, as he desires to penetrate into the so-cial scale of the whites, he takes the lowest rank in society, for he enters ignorant and poor within the pale of science and wealth. After having led a life of agitation, beset with evils and dangers, but at the same time filled with proud emotions,* he is obliged to submit to a wearisome, obscure, and degraded state, and to gain the bread which nourishes him by hard and ignoble labour; such are in his eyes the only results of which civilization can boast: and even this much he is not sure to obtain.

When the Indians undertake to imitate their European neighbours, and to till the earth like the settlers, they are immediately exposed to a very formidable competition. The white man is skilled in the craft of agriculture; the Indian is a rough beginner in an art with which he is unacquainted. The former reaps abundant crops without difficulty, the latter meets with a thousand obstacles in raising the fruits of the earth.

---

* There is in the adventurous life of the hunter a certain irresistible charm which seizes the heart of man, and carries him away in spite of reason and experience. This is plainly shown by the memoirs of Tanner. Tanner is a European who was carried away at the age of six by the Indians, and has remained thirty years with them in the woods. Nothing can be con-ceived more appalling than the miseries which he describes. He tells us of tribes without a chief, families without a nation to call their own, men in a state of isolation, wrecks of pow-erful tribes wandering at random amid the ice and snow and desolate solitudes of Canada. Hunger and cold pursue them; every day their life is in jeopardy. Among these men, manners have lost their empire, traditions are without power. They become more and more savage. Tanner shared in all these miseries; he was aware of his European origin; he was not kept away from the whites by force; on the contrary, he came every year to trade with them, en-tered their dwellings, and saw their enjoyments; he knew that whenever he chose to return to civilized life, he was perfectly able to do so—and he remained thirty years in the deserts. When he came into civilized society, he declared that the rude existence which he described had a secret charm for him which he was unable to define: he returned to it again and again: at length he abandoned it with poignant regret; and when he was at length fixed among the whites, several of his children refused to share his tranquil and easy situation. I saw Tanner myself at the lower end of Lake Superior; he seemed to me to be more like a savage than a civilized being. His book is written without either taste or order; but he gives, even uncon-sciously, a lively picture of the prejudices, the passions, the vices, and, above all, of the des-titution in which he lived.

The Europeans is placed among a population whose wants he knows and partakes. The savage is isolated in the midst of a hostile people, with whose manners, language, and laws, he is imperfectly acquainted, but without whose assistance he cannot live. He can only procure the materials of comfort by bartering his commodities against the goods of the European, for the assistance of his countrymen is wholly insufficient to supply his wants. When the Indian wishes to sell the produce of his labour, he cannot always meet with a purchaser, while the European readily finds a market; and the former can only produce at a considerable cost, that which the latter vends at a very low rate. Thus the Indian has no sooner escaped those evils to which barbarous nations are exposed, than he is subjected to the still greater miseries of civilized communities; and he finds it scarcely less difficult to live in the midst of our abundance, than in the depth of his own wilderness.

He has not yet lost the habits of his erratic life; the traditions of his fathers and his passion for the chase are still alive within him. The wild enjoyments which formerly animated him in the woods painfully excite his troubled imagination; and his former privations appear to be less keen, his former perils less appalling. He contrasts the independence which he possessed among his equals with the servile position which he occupies in civilized society. On the other hand, the solitudes which were so long his free home are still at hand; a few hours' march will bring him back to them once more. The whites offer him a sum, which seems to him to be considerable, for the ground which he has begun to clear. This money of the Europeans may possibly furnish him with the means of a happy and peaceful subsistence in remote regions; and he quits the plough, resumes his native arms, and returns to the wilderness for ever.* The condition of the Creeks and Cherokees, to which I have already alluded, sufficiently corroborates the truth of this deplorable picture.

---

* The destructive influence of highly civilized nations upon others which are less so, has been exemplified by the Europeans themselves. About a century ago the French founded the town of Vincennes upon the Wabash, in the middle of the desert; and they lived there in great plenty, until the arrival of the American settlers, who first ruined the previous inhabitants by their competition, and afterward purchased their lands at a very low rate. At the time when M. de Volney, from whom I borrow these details, passed through Vincennes, the number of the French was reduced to a hundred individuals, most of whom were about to pass over to Louisiana or to Canada. These French settlers were worthy people, but idle and uninstructed: they had contracted many of the habits of savages. The Americans, who were perhaps their inferiors in a moral point of view, were immeasurably superior to them in intelligence: they were industrious, well-informed, rich, and accustomed to govern their own community.

I myself saw in Canada, where the intellectual difference between the two races is less striking, that the English are the masters of commerce and manufacture in the Canadian country, that they spread on all sides, and confine the French within limits which scarcely suffice to contain them. In like manner, in Louisiana, almost all activity in commerce and manufacture centres in the hands of the Anglo-Americans.

But the case of Texas is still more striking: the state of Texas is a part of Mexico, and lies upon the frontier between that country and the United States. In the course of the last few years the Anglo-Americans have penetrated into this province, which is still thinly peopled; they purchase land, they produce the commodities of the country, and supplant the original population. It may easily be foreseen that if Mexico takes no steps to check this change, the province of Texas will very shortly cease to belong to that government.

If the different degrees—comparatively so light—which exist in European civilization, produce results of such magnitude, the consequences which must ensue from the collision of the most perfect European civilization with Indian savages may readily be conceived.

The Indians in the little which they have done, have unquestionably displayed as much natural genius as the peoples of Europe in their most important designs; but nations as well as men require time to learn, whatever may be their intelligence and their zeal. While the savages were engaged in the work of civilization, the Europeans continued to surround them on every side, and to confine them within narrower limits; the two races gradually met, and they are now in immediate juxtaposition to each other. The Indian is already superior to his barbarous parent, but he is still very far below his white neighbour. With their resources and acquired knowledge, the Europeans soon appropriated to themselves most of the advantages which the natives might have derived from the possession of the soil: they have settled in the country, they have purchased land at a very low rate or have occupied it by force, and the Indians have been ruined by a competition which they had not the means of resisting. They were isolated in their own country, and their race only constituted a colony of troublesome aliens in the midst of a numerous and domineering people.*

Washington said in one of his messages to congress, "We are more enlightened and powerful than the Indian nations, we are therefore bound in honour to treat them with kindness and even with generosity." But this virtuous and high-minded policy has not been followed. The rapacity of the settlers is usually backed by the tyranny of the government. Although the Cherokees and the Creeks are established upon the territory which they inhabited before the settlement of the Europeans, and although the Americans have frequently treated with them as with foreign nations, the surrounding states have not consented to acknowledge them as independent peoples, and attempts have been made to subject these children of the woods to Anglo-American magistrates, laws, and customs.† Destitution had driven these unfortunate Indians to civilization, and oppression now drives them back to their former condition; many of them abandon the soil

---

* See in the legislative documents (21st congress, No. 89), instances of excesses of every kind committed by the whites upon the territory of the Indians, either in taking possession of a part of their lands, until compelled to retire by the troops of congress, or carrying off their cattle, burning their houses, cutting down their corn, and doing violence to their persons.

It appears, nevertheless, from all those documents, that the claims of the natives are constantly protected by the government from the abuse of force. The Union has a representative agent continually employed to reside among the Indians; and the report of the Cherokee agent, which is among the documents I have referred to, is almost always favourable to the Indians. "The intrusion of whites," he says, "upon the lands of the Cherokee would cause ruin to the poor, helpless, and inoffensive inhabitants." And he farther remarks upon the attempt of the state of Georgia to establish a division line for the purpose of limiting the boundaries of the Cherokees, that the line drawn having been made by the whites, and entirely upon *exparte* evidence of their several rights, was of no validity whatever.

† In 1829 the state of Alabama divided the Creek territory into counties, and subjected the Indian population to the power of European magistrates.

In 1830 the state of Mississippi assimilated the Choctaws and Chickasaws to the white population, and declared that any of them that should take the title of chief would be punished by a fine of 1,000 dollars and a year's imprisonment. When these laws were enforced upon the Choctaws who inhabited that district, the tribes assembled, their chief communicated to them the intentions of the whites, and read to them some of the laws to which it was intended that they should submit; and they unanimously declared that it was better at once to retreat again into the wilds.

which they had begun to clear, and return to their savage course of life.

If we consider the tyrannical measures which have been adopted by the legislatures of the southern states, the conduct of their governors, and the decrees of their courts of justice, we shall be convinced that the entire expulsion of the Indians is the final result to which the efforts of their policy are directed. The Americans of that part of the Union look with jealousy upon the aborigines,* they are aware that these tribes have not yet lost the traditions of savage life, and before civilization has permanently fixed them to the soil, it is intended to force them to recede by reducing them to despair. The Creeks and Cherokees, oppressed by the several states, have appealed to the central government, which is by no means insensible to their misfortunes, and is sincerely desirous of saving the remnant of the natives, and of maintaining them in the free possession of that territory which the Union is pledged to respect.† But the several states oppose so formidable a resistance to the execution of this design, that the government is obliged to consent to the extirpation of a few barbarous tribes in order not to endanger the safety of the American Union.

But the federal government, which is not able to protect the Indians, would fain mitigate the hardships of their lot; and, with this intention, proposals have been made to transport them into more remote regions at the public cost.

Between the 33d and 37th degrees of north latitude, a vast tract of country lies, which has taken the name of Arkansas, from the principal river that waters its extent. It is bounded on the one side by the confines of Mexico, on the other by the Mississippi. Numberless streams cross it in every direction; the climate is mild, and the soil productive, but it is only inhabited by a few wandering hordes of savages. The government of the Union wishes to transport the broken remnants of the indigenous population of the south, to the portion of this country which is nearest to Mexico, and at a great distance from the American settlements.

We were assured, toward the end of the year 1831, that 10,000 Indians had already gone to the shores of the Arkansas; and fresh detachments were constantly following them; but congress has been unable to excite a unanimous determination in those whom it is disposed to protect. Some, indeed, are willing to quit the seat of oppression, but the most enlightened members of the community refuse to abandon their recent dwellings and their springing crops; they are of opinion that the work of civilization, once interrupted, will never be resumed; they fear

* The Georgians, who are so much annoyed by the proximity of the Indians, inhabit a territory which does not at present contain more than seven inhabitants to the square mile. In France there are one hundred and sixty-two inhabitants to the same extent of country.

† In 1818 congress appointed commissioners to visit the Arkansas territory accompanied by a deputation of Creeks, Choctaws, and Chickasaws. This expedition was commanded by Messrs, Kennerly, M'Coy, Wash Hood, and John Bell. See the different reports of the commissioners, and their journal, in the documents of congress, No. 87, house of representatives.

that those domestic habits which have been so recently contracted, may be irrecoverably lost in the midst of a country which is still barbarous, and where nothing is prepared for the subsistence of an agricultural people; they know that their entrance into those wilds will be opposed by inimical hordes, and that they have lost the energy of barbarians, without acquiring the resources of civilization to resist their attacks. Moreover the Indians readily discover that the settlement which is proposed to them is merely a temporary expedient. Who can assure them that they will at length be allowed to dwell in peace in their new retreat? The United States pledge themselves to the observance of the obligation; but the territory which they at present occupy was formerly secured to them by the most solemn oaths of Anglo-American faith.* The American government does not indeed rob them of their lands, but it allows perpetual incursions to be made on them. In a few years the same white population which now flocks around them, will track them to the solitudes of the Arkansas; they will then be exposed to the same evils without the same remedies; and as the limits of the earth will at last fail them, their only refuge is the grave.

The Union treats the Indians with less cupidity and rigour than the policy of the several states, but the two governments are alike destitute of good faith. The states extend what they are pleased to term the benefits of their laws to the Indians, with a belief that the tribes will recede rather than submit; and the central government, which promises a permanent refuge to these unhappy beings, is well aware of its inability to secure it to them.†

Thus the tyranny of the states obliges the savages to retire, the Union, by its promises and resources, facilitates their retreat; and these measures tend to precisely the same end.‡ "By the will of our Father in heaven, the governor of the whole world," said the Chero-

---

* The fifth article of the treaty made with the Creeks in August, 1790, is in the following words: "The United States solemnly guaranty to the Creek nation all their land within the limits of the United States."

The seventh article of the treaty concluded in 1791 with the Cherokees says: "The United States solemnly guaranty to the Cherokee nation all their lands not hereby ceded." The following article declared that if any citizen of the United States or other settler not of the Indian race, should establish himself upon the territory of the Cherokees, the United States would withdraw their protection from that individual, and give him up to be punished as the Cherokee nation should think fit.

† This does not prevent them from promising in the most solemn manner to do so. See the letter of the president addressed to the Creek Indians, 23d March, 1829. ("Proceedings of the Indian Board, in the City of New York," p. 5.) "Beyond the great river Mississippi, where a part of your nation has gone, your father has provided a country large enough for all of you, and he advises you to remove to it. There your white brothers will not trouble you; they will have no claim to the land, and you can live upon it, you and all your children, as long as the grass grows or the water runs, in peace and plenty. *It will be yours for ever.*"

The secretary of war, in a letter written to the Cherokees, April 18th, 1829 (see the same work, page 6), declares to them that they cannot expect to retain possession of the land, at the time occupied by them, but gives them the most positive assurance of uninterrupted peace if they would remove beyond the Mississippi: as if the power which could not grant them protection then, would be able to afford it them hereafter!

‡ To obtain a correct idea of the policy pursued by the several states and the Union with respect to the Indians, it is necessary to consult, 1st, "The laws of the colonial and state governments relating to the Indian inhabitants." (See the legislative documents, 21st congress, No. 319.) 2d, "The laws of the Union on the same subject, and especially that of March 30th, 1802." (See Story's Laws of the United States.) 3d, "The report of Mr. Cass, secretary of war, relative to Indian affairs, November 29th, 1823.

kees in their petition to congress,* "the red man of America has become small, and the white man great and renowned. When the ancestors of the people of these United States first came to the shores of America, they found the red man strong: though he was ignorant and savage, yet he received them kindly, and gave them dry land to rest their weary feet. They met in peace, and shook hands in token of friendship. Whatever the white man wanted and asked of the Indian, the latter willingly gave. At that time the Indian was the lord, and the white man the suppliant. But now the scene has changed. The strength of the red man has become weakness. As his neighbours increased in numbers, his power became less and less, and now, of the many and powerful tribes who once covered these United States, only a few are to be seen—a few whom a sweeping pestilence had left. The northern tribes, who were once so numerous and powerful, are now nearly extinct. Thus it has happened to the red man of America. Shall we, who are remnants, share the same fate?

"The land on which we stand we have received as an inheritance from our fathers who possessed it from time immemorial, as a gift from our common Father in heaven. They bequeathed it to us as their children, and we have sacredly kept it, as containing their remains. This right of inheritance we have never ceded, nor ever forfeited. Permit us to ask what better right can the people have to a country than the right of inheritance and immemorial peaceable possession? We know it is said of late by the state of Georgia and by the executive of the United States, that we have forfeited this right; but we think it is said gratuitously. At what time have we made the forfeit? What great crime have we committed, whereby we must for ever be divested of our country and rights? Was it when we were hostile to the United States, and took part with the king of Great Britain, during the struggle for independence? If so, why was not this forfeiture declared in the first treaty which followed that war? Why was not such an article as the following inserted in the treaty: 'The United States give peace to the Cherokees, but for the part they took in the last war, declare them to be but tenants at will, to be removed when the convenience of the states, within whose chartered limits they live, shall require it'? That was the proper time to assume such a possession. But it was not thought of, nor would our forefathers have agreed to any treaty, whose tendency was to deprive them of their rights and their country."

Such is the language of the Indians: their assertions are true, their forebodings inevitable. From whichever side we consider the destinies of the aborigines of North America, their calamities appear to be irremediable: if they continue barbarous, they are forced to retire: if they attempt to civilize their manners, the contact of a more civilized community subjects them to oppression and destitution. They perish if they continue to wander from waste to waste, and if they attempt to settle, they still must perish; the assistance of Europeans is necessary to instruct them, but the approach of Europeans corrupts and repels

* December 18th, 1829.

them into savage life; they refuse to change their habits as long as their solitudes are their own, and it is too late to change them when they are constrained to submit.

The Spaniards pursued the Indians with blood-hounds, like wild beasts; they sacked the New World with no more temper or compassion than a city taken by storm: but destruction must cease, and phrensy be stayed; the remnant of the Indian population, which had escaped the massacre, mixed with its conquerors and adopted in the end their religion and their manners.* The conduct of the Americans of the United States toward the aborigines is characterized, on the other hand, by a singular attachment to the formalities of law. Provided that the Indians retain their barbarous condition, the Americans take no part in their affairs: they treat them as independent nations, and do not possess themselves of their hunting grounds without a treaty of purchase: and if an Indian nation happens to be so encroached upon as to be unable to subsist upon its territory, they afford it brotherly assistance in transporting it to a grave sufficiently remote from the land of its fathers.

The Spaniards were unable to exterminate the Indian race by those unparalleled atrocities which brand them with indelible shame, nor did they even succeed in wholly depriving it of its rights; but the Americans of the United States have accomplished this twofold purpose with singular felicity; tranquilly, legally, philanthropically, without shedding blood, and without violating a single great principle of morality in the eyes of the world.† It is impossible to destroy men with more respect for the laws of humanity.

SITUATION OF THE BLACK POPULATION IN THE UNITED STATES, AND DANGERS WITH WHICH ITS PRESENCE THREATENS THE WHITES.

Why it is more difficult to abolish Slavery, and to efface all Vestiges of it among the Moderns, than it was among the Ancients.—In the United States the prejudices of the Whites against the Blacks seem to increase in Proportion as Slavery is abolished.—Situation of the Negroes in the Northern and Southern States.—Why the Americans abolish Slavery.—Servitude, which debases the Slave, empoverishes the Master.—Contrast between the left and the right Bank of the Ohio.—To what attributable.—The black Race, as well as Slavery, recedes toward the South.—Explanation of this Fact.—Difficulties attendant upon the Abolition of Slavery in the South.—Dangers to come.—General Anxiety.—Foundation of a black Colony in Africa.—Why the Americans of the South increase the Hardships of Slavery, while they are distressed at its Continuance.

---

* The honour of this result is, however, by no means due to the Spaniards. If the Indian tribes had not been tillers of the ground at the time of the arrival of the Europeans, they would unquestionably have been destroyed in South as well as in North America.

† See among other documents, the report made by Mr. Bell in the name of the committee on Indian affairs, Feb. 24th, 1830, in which it is most logically established and most learnedly proved, that "the fundamental principle, that the Indians had no right by virtue of their ancient possession either of will or sovereignty, has never been abandoned either expressly or by implication."

In perusing this report, which is evidently drawn up by an able hand, one is astonished at the facility with which the author gets rid of all arguments founded upon reason and natural right, which he designates as abstract and theoretical principles. The more I contemplate the difference between civilized and uncivilized man with regard to the principles of justice, the more I observe that the former contests the justice of those rights, which the latter simply violates.

The Indians will perish in the same isolated condition in which they have lived; but the destiny of the negroes is in some measure inter-woven with that of the Europeans. These two races are attached to each other without intermingling; and they are alike unable entirely to separate or to combine. The most formidable of all the ills which threaten the future existence of the United States, arises from the presence of a black population upon its territory; and in contemplating the causes of the present embarrassments or of the future dangers of the United States, the observer is invariably led to consider this as a primary fact.

The permanent evils to which mankind is subjected are usually pro-duced by the vehement or the increasing efforts of men; but there is one calamity which penetrated furtively into the world, and which was at first scarcely distinguishable amid the ordinary abuses of power: it originated with an individual whose name history has not preserved; it was wafted like some accursed germe upon a portion of the soil, but it afterward nurtured itself, grew without effort, and spreads naturally with the society to which it belongs. I need scarcely add that this calamity is slavery. Christianity suppressed slavery, but the Christians of the sixteenth century re-established it—as an exception, indeed, to their social system, and restricted to one of the races of mankind; but the wound thus inflicted upon humanity, though less extensive, was at the same time rendered far more difficult of cure.

It is important to make an accurate distinction between slavery itself, and its consequences. The immediate evils which are produced by slav-ery were very nearly the same in antiquity as they are among the mod-erns; but the consequences of these evils were different. The slave, among the ancients, belonged to the same race as his master, and he was often the superior of the two in education* and instruction. Free-dom was the only distinction between them; and when freedom was conferred, they were easily confounded together. The ancients, then, had a very simple means of avoiding slavery and its evil consequences, which was that of affranchisement; and they succeeded as soon as they adopted this measure generally. Not but, in ancient states, the vestiges of servitude subsisted for some time after servitude itself was abolished. There is a natural prejudice which prompts men to despise whomso-ever has been their inferior, long after he is become their equal; and the real inequality which is produced by fortune or by law, is always succeeded by an imaginary inequality which is implanted in the man-ners of the people. Nevertheless, this secondary consequence of slavery was limited to a certain term among the ancients; for the freedman bore so entire a resemblance to those born free, that it soon became impossible to distinguish him from among them.

The greatest difficulty in antiquity was that of altering the law; among the moderns it is that of altering the manners; and, as far as we

---

* It is well known that several of the most distinguished authors of antiquity, and among them Æsop and Terence, were or had been slaves. Slaves were not always taken from barbarous nations, and the chances of war reduced highly civilized men to servitude.

are concerned, the real obstacles begin where those of the ancients left off. This arises from the circumstance that, among the moderns, the abstract and transient fact of slavery is fatally united to the physical and permanent fact of colour. The tradition of slavery dishonours the race, and the peculiarity of the race perpetuates the tradition of slavery. No African has ever voluntarily emigrated to the shores of the New World; whence it must be inferred, that all the blacks who are now to be found in that hemisphere are either slaves or freedmen. Thus the negro transmits the eternal mark of his ignominy to all his descendants; and although the law may abolish slavery, God alone can obliterate the traces of its existence.

The modern slave differs from his master not only in his condition, but in his origin. You may set the negro free, but you cannot make him otherwise than an alien to the European. Nor is this all; we scarcely acknowledge the common features of mankind in this child of debasement whom slavery has brought among us. His physiognomy is to our eyes hideous, his understanding weak, his tastes low; and we are almost inclined to look upon him as a being intermediate between man and the brutes.* The moderns, then, after they have abolished slavery, have three prejudices to contend against, which are less easy to attack, and far less easy to conquer, than the mere fact of servitude: the prejudice of the master, the prejudice of the race, and the prejudice of colour.

It is difficult for us, who have had the good fortune to be born among men like ourselves by nature, and equal to ourselves by law, to conceive the irreconcilable differences which separate the negro from the European in America. But we may derive some faint notion of them from analogy. France was formerly a country in which numerous distinctions of rank existed, that had been created by the legislation. Nothing can be more fictitious than a purely legal inferiority; nothing more contrary to the instinct of mankind than these permanent divisions which had been established between beings evidently similar. Nevertheless these divisions subsisted for ages; they still subsist in many places; and on all sides they have left imaginary vestiges, which time alone can efface. If it be so difficult to root out an inequality which solely originates in the law, how are those distinctions to be destroyed which seem to be founded upon the immutable laws of nature herself? When I remember the extreme difficulty with which aristocratic bodies, of whatever nature they may be, are commingled with the mass of the people; and the exceeding care which they take to preserve the ideal boundaries of their caste inviolate, I despair of seeing an aristocracy disappear which is founded upon visible and indelible signs. Those who hope that the Europeans will ever mix with the negroes, appear to me to delude themselves; and I am not led to any such conclusion by my own reason, or by the evidence of facts.

---

* To induce the whites to abandon the opinion they have conceived of the moral and intellectual inferiority of their former slaves, the negroes must change; but as long as this opinion subsists, to change is impossible.

Hitherto, wherever the whites have been the most powerful, they have maintained the blacks in a subordinate or a servile position; wherever the negroes have been strongest, they have destroyed the whites; such has been the only course of events which has ever taken place between the two races.

I see that in a certain portion of the territory of the United States at the present day, the legal barrier which separated the two races is tending to fall away, but not that which exists in the manners of the country; slavery recedes, but the prejudice to which it has given birth remains stationary. Whosoever has inhabited the United States, must have perceived, that in those parts of the Union in which the negroes are no longer slaves, they have in nowise drawn nearer to the whites. On the contrary, the prejudice of the race appears to be stronger in the states which have abolished slavery, than in those where it still exists; and nowhere is it so intolerant as in those states where servitude has never been known.

It is true, that in the north of the Union, marriages may be legally contracted between negroes and whites, but public opinion would stigmatize a man who should connect himself with a negress as infamous, and it would be difficult to meet with a single instance of such a union. The electoral franchise has been conferred upon the negroes in almost all the states in which slavery has been abolished; but if they come forward to vote, their lives are in danger. If oppressed, they may bring an action at law, but they will find none but whites among their judges; and although they may legally serve as jurors, prejudice repulses them from that office. The same schools do not receive the child of the black and of the European. In the theatres, gold cannot procure a seat for the servile race beside their former masters; in the hospitals they lie apart; and although they are allowed to invoke the same Divinity as the whites, it must be at a different altar, and in their own churches with their own clergy. The gates of heaven are not closed against these unhappy beings; but their inferiority is continued to the very confines of the other world. When the negro is defunct, his bones are cast aside, and the distinction of condition prevails even in the equality of death. The negro is free, but he can share neither the rights, nor the pleasures, nor the labour, nor the afflictions, nor the tomb of him whose equal he has been declared to be; and he cannot meet him upon fair terms in life or in death.

In the south, where slavery still exists, the negroes are less carefully kept apart; they sometimes share the labour and the recreations of the whites; the whites consent to intermix with them to a certain extent, and although the legislation treats them more harshly, the habits of the people are more tolerant and compassionate. In the south the master is not afraid to raise his slave to his own standing, because he knows that he can in a moment reduce him to the dust at pleasure. In the north, the white no longer distinctly perceives the barrier which separates him from the degraded race, and he shuns the negro with the more pertinacity, because he fears lest they should some day be confounded together.

Among the Americans of the south, nature sometimes reasserts her rights, and restores a transient equality between the blacks and the whites; but in the north, pride restrains the most imperious of human passions. The American of the northern states would perhaps allow the negress to share his licentious pleasures, if the laws of his country did not declare that she may aspire to be the legitimate partner of his bed; but he recoils with horror from her who might become his wife.

Thus it is, in the United States, that the prejudice which repels the negroes seems to increase in proportion as they are emancipated, and inequality is sanctioned by the manners while it is effaced from the laws of the country. But if the relative position of the two races which inhabit the United States, is such as I have described, it may be asked why the Americans have abolished slavery in the north of the Union, why they maintain it in the south, and why they aggravate its hardships there? The answer is easily given. It is not for the good of the negroes, but for that of the whites, that measures are taken to abolish slavery in the United States.

The first negroes were imported into Virginia about the year 1621.* In America, therefore, as well as in the rest of the globe, slavery originated in the south. Thence it spread from one settlement to another; but the number of slaves diminished toward the northern states, and the negro population was always very limited in New England.†

A century had scarcely elapsed since the foundation of the colonies, when the attention of the planters was struck by the extraordinary fact, that the provinces which were comparatively destitute of slaves, increased in population, in wealth, and in prosperity, more rapidly than those which contained the greatest number of negroes. In the former, however, the inhabitants were obliged to cultivate the soil themselves, or by hired labourers; in the latter, they were furnished with hands for which they paid no wages; yet, although labour and expense were on the one side, and ease with economy on the other, the former were in possession of the most advantageous system. This consequence seemed to be the more difficult to explain, since the settlers, who all belonged to the same European race, had the same habits, the same civilization, the same laws, and their shades of difference were extremely slight.

Time, however, continued to advance; and the Anglo-Americans, spreading beyond the coasts of the Atlantic ocean, penetrated farther and farther into the solitudes of the west; they met with a new soil and

---

* See Beverley's History of Virginia. See also in Jefferson's Memoirs some curious details concerning the introduction of negroes into Virginia, and the first act which prohibited the importation of them in 1778.

† The number of slaves was less considerable in the north, but the advantages resulting from slavery were not more contested there than in the south. In 1740, the legislature of the state of New York declared that the direct importation of slaves ought to be encouraged as much as possible, and smuggling severely punished, in order not to discourage the fair trader. (Kent's Commentaries, vol. ii., p. 206.) Curious researches, by Belknap, upon slavery in New England, are to be found in the Historical Collection of Massachusetts, vol. iv., p. 193. It appears that negroes were introduced there in 1630, but that the legislation and manners of the people were opposed to slavery from the first; see also, in the same work, the manner in which public opinion, and afterward the laws, finally put an end to slavery.

an unwonted climate; the obstacles which opposed them were of the most various character; their races intermingled, the inhabitants of the south went up toward the north, those of the north descended to the south; but in the midst of all these causes, the same result recurred at every step; and in general, the colonies in which there were no slaves became more populous and more rich than those in which slavery flourished. The more progress was made, the more was it shown that slavery, which is so cruel to the slave, is prejudicial to the master.

But this truth was most satisfactorily demonstrated when civilization reached the banks of the Ohio. The stream which the Indians had distinguished by the name of Ohio, or Beautiful river, waters one of the most magnificent valleys which have ever been made the abode of man. Undulating lands extend upon both shores of the Ohio, whose soil affords inexhaustible treasures to the labourer; on either bank the air is wholesome and the climate mild; and each of them forms the extreme frontier of a vast state: that which follows the numerous windings of the Ohio upon the left is called Kentucky; that upon the right bears the name of the river. These two states only differ in a single respect; Kentucky has admitted slavery, but the state of Ohio has prohibited the existence of slaves within its borders.*

Thus the traveller who floats down the current of the Ohio, to the spot where that river falls into the Mississippi, may be said to sail between liberty and servitude; and a transient inspection of the surrounding objects will convince him which of the two is most favourable to mankind.

Upon the left bank of the stream the population is rare; from time to time one descries a troop of slaves loitering in the half-desert fields; the primeval forest recurs at every turn; society seems to be asleep, man to be idle, and nature alone offers a scene of activity and of life.

From the right bank, on the contrary, a confused hum is heard, which proclaims the presence of industry; the fields are covered with abundant harvests; the elegance of the dwellings announces the taste and activity of the labourer; and man appears to be in the enjoyment of that wealth and contentment which are the reward of labour.†

The state of Kentucky was founded in 1775, the state of Ohio only twelve years later; but twelve years are more in America than half a century in Europe, and, at the present day, the population of Ohio exceeds that of Kentucky by 250,000 souls.‡ These opposite consequences of slavery and freedom may readily be understood; and they suffice to explain many of the differences which we remark between the civilization of antiquity and that of our own time.

---

* Not only is slavery prohibited in Ohio, but no free negroes are allowed to enter the territory of that state, or to hold property in it. See the statutes of Ohio.

† The activity of Ohio is not confined to individuals, but the undertakings of the state are surprisingly great: a canal has been established between Lake Erie and the Ohio, by means of which the valley of the Mississippi communicates with the river of the north, and the European commodities which arrive at New York, may be forwarded by water to New Orleans across five hundred leagues of continent.

‡ The exact numbers given by the census of 1830 were: Kentucky, 688,844; Ohio, 937,679.

Upon the left bank of the Ohio labour is confounded with the idea of slavery, upon the right bank it is identified with that of prosperity and improvement; on the one side it is degraded, on the other it is honoured; on the former territory no white labourers can be found, for they would be afraid of assimilating themselves to the negroes; on the latter no one is idle, for the white population extends its activity and its intelligence to every kind of employment. Thus the men whose task it is to cultivate the rich soil of Kentucky are ignorant and lukewarm; while those who are active and enlightened either do nothing, or pass over into the state of Ohio, where they may work without dishonour.

It is true that in Kentucky the planters are not obliged to pay wages to the slaves whom they employ; but they derive small profits from their labour, while the wages paid to free workmen would be returned with interest in the value of their services. The free workman is paid, but he does his work quicker than the slave; and rapidity of execution is one of the great elements of economy. The white sells his services, but they are only purchased at the times at which they may be useful; the black can claim no remuneration for his toil, but the expense of his maintenance is perpetual; he must be supported in his old age as well as in the prime of manhood, in his profitless infancy as well as in the productive years of youth. Payment must equally be made in order to obtain the services of either class of men; the free workman receives his wages in money; the slave in education, in food, in care, and in clothing. The money which a master spends in the maintenance of his slaves, goes gradually and in detail, so that it is scarcely perceived; the salary of the free workman is paid in a round sum, which appears only to enrich the individual who receives it; but in the end the slave has cost more than the free servant, and his labour is less productive.*

The influence of slavery extends still farther; it affects the character of the master, and imparts a peculiar tendency to his ideas and his tastes. Upon both banks of the Ohio, the character of the inhabitants is enterprising and energetic; but this vigour is very differently exercised in the two states. The white inhabitant of Ohio, who is obliged to subsist by his own exertions, regards temporal prosperity as the principal aim of his existence; and as the country which he occupies presents inexhaustible resources to his industry, and ever-varying lures to his activity, his acquisitive ardour surpasses the ordinary limits of human cupidity: he is tormented by the desire of wealth, and he boldly enters upon every path which fortune opens to him; he becomes a

---

* Independently of these causes which, wherever free workmen abound, render their labour more productive and more economical than that of slaves, another cause may be pointed out which is peculiar to the United States; the sugar-cane has hitherto been cultivated with success only upon the banks of the Mississippi, near the mouth of that river in the gulf of Mexico. In Louisiana the cultivation of the sugar-cane is exceedingly lucrative; nowhere does a labourer earn so much by his work: and, as there is always a certain relation between the cost of production and the value of the produce, the price of slaves is very high in Louisiana. But Louisiana is one of the confederate states, and slaves may be carried thither from all parts of the Union; the price given for slaves in New Orleans consequently raises the value of slaves in all the other markets. The consequence of this is, that in the countries where the land is less productive, the cost of slave labour is still very considerable, which gives an additional advantage to the competition of free labour.

sailor, pioneer, an artisan, or a labourer, with the same indifference, and he supports, with equal constancy, the fatigues and the dangers incidental to these various professions; the resources of his intelligence are astonishing, and his avidity in the pursuit of gain amounts to a species of heroism.

But the Kentuckian scorns not only labour, but all the undertakings which labour promotes; as he lives in an idle independence, his tastes are those of an idle man; money loses a portion of its value in his eyes; he covets wealth much less than pleasure and excitement; and the energy which his neighbour devotes to gain, turns with him to a passionate love of field sports and military exercises; he delights in violent bodily exertion, he is familiar with the use of arms, and is accustomed from a very early age to expose his life in single combat. Thus slavery not only prevents the whites from becoming opulent, but even from desiring to become so.

As the same causes have been continually producing opposite effects for the last two centuries in the British colonies of North America, they have established a very striking difference between the commercial capacity of the inhabitants of the south and those of the north. At the present day, it is only the northern states which are in possession of shipping, manufactures, railroads, and canals. This difference is perceptible not only in comparing the north with the south, but in comparing the several southern states. Almost all the individuals who carry on commercial operations, or who endeavour to turn slave-labour to account in the most southern districts of the Union, have emigrated from the north. The natives of the northern states are constantly spreading over that portion of the American territory, where they have less to fear from competition; they discover resources there, which escaped the notice of the inhabitants; and, as they comply with a system which they do not approve, they succeed in turning it to better advantage than those who first founded, and who still maintain it.

Were I inclined to continue this parallel, I could easily prove that almost all the differences, which may be remarked between the characters of the Americans in the southern and in the northern states, have originated in slavery; but this would divert me from my subject, and my present intention is not to point out all the consequences of servitude, but those effects which it has produced upon the prosperity of the countries which have admitted it.

The influence of slavery upon the production of wealth must have been very imperfectly known in antiquity, as slavery then obtained throughout the civilized world, and the nations which were unacquainted with it were barbarous. And indeed Christianity only abolished slavery by advocating the claims of the slave; at the present time it may be attacked in the name of the master; and, upon this point, interest is reconciled with morality.

As these truths became apparent in the United States, slavery receded before the progress of experience. Servitude had begun in the south, and had thence spread toward the north; but it now retires again. Freedom, which started from the north, now descends uninterruptedly toward the south. Among the great states, Pennsylvania now constitutes the extreme limit of slavery to the north; but even within those limits the slave-system is shaken; Maryland, which is immediately below Pennsylvania, is preparing for its abolition; and Virginia, which comes next to Maryland, is already discussing its utility and its dangers.*

No great change takes place in human institutions, without involving among its causes the law of inheritance. When the law of primogeniture obtained in the south, each family was represented by a wealthy individual, who was neither compelled nor induced to labour; and he was surrounded, as by parasitic plants, by the other members of his family, who were then excluded by law from sharing the common inheritance, and who led the same kind of life as himself. The very same thing then occurred in all the families of the south that still happens in the wealthy families of some countries in Europe, namely, that the younger sons remain in the same state of idleness as their elder brother, without being as rich as he is. This identical result seems to be produced in Europe and in America by wholly analogous causes. In the south of the United States, the whole race of whites formed an aristocratic body, which was headed by a certain number of privileged individuals, whose wealth was permanent, and whose leisure was hereditary. These leaders of the American nobility kept alive the traditional prejudices of the white race in the body of which they were the representatives, and maintained the honour of inactive life. This aristocracy contained many who were poor, but none who would work; its members preferred want to labour; consequently no competition was set on foot against negro labourers and slaves, and whatever opinion might be entertained as to the utility of their efforts, it was indispensable to employ them, since there was no one else to work.

No sooner was the law of primogeniture abolished than fortunes began to diminish, and all the families of the country were simultaneously reduced to a state in which labour became necessary to procure the means of subsistence: several of them have since entirely disappeared; and all of them learned to look forward to the time at which it would be necessary for every one to provide for his own wants. Wealthy individuals are still to be met with, but they no longer constitute a compact and hereditary body, nor have they been able to adopt a line of conduct in which they could persevere, and which they could infuse into all ranks of society. The prejudice which stigmatized labour was in the first place abandoned by common consent; the number of needy men was increased, and the needy were allowed to gain a laborious subsistence without blushing for their exertions. Thus one of the

---

* A peculiar reason contributes to detach the two last-mentioned states from the cause of slavery. The former wealth of this part of the Union was principally derived from the cultivation of tobacco. This cultivation is specially carried on by slaves; but within the last few years the market-price of tobacco has diminished, while the value of the slaves remains the same. Thus the ratio between the cost of production and the value of the produce is changed. The natives of Maryland and Virginia are therefore more disposed than they were thirty years ago, to give up slave labour in the cultivation of tobacco, or to give up slavery and tobacco at the same time.

most immediate consequences of the partible quality of estates has been to create a class of free labourers. As soon as a competition was set on foot between the free labourer and the slave, the inferiority of the latter became manifest, and slavery was attacked in its fundamental principle, which is, the interest of the master.

As slavery recedes, the black population follows its retrograde course, and returns with it to those tropical regions from which it originally came. However singular this fact may at first appear to be, it may readily be explained. Although the Americans abolish the principle of slavery, they do not set their slaves free. To illustrate this remark I will quote the example of the state of New York. In 1788, the state of New York prohibited the sale of slaves within its limits; which was an indirect method of prohibiting the importation of blacks. Thenceforward the number of negroes could only increase according to the ratio of the natural increase of population. But eight years later a more decisive measure was taken, and it was enacted that all children born of slave parents after the 4th of July, 1799, should be free. No increase could then take place, and although slaves still existed, slavery might be said to be abolished.

From the time at which a northern state prohibited the importation of slaves, no slaves were brought from the south to be sold in its markets. On the other hand, as the sale of slaves was forbidden in that state, an owner was no longer able to get rid of his slave (who thus became a burdensome possession) otherwise than by transporting him to the south. But when a northern state declared that the son of the slave should be born free, the slave lost a large portion of his market value, since his posterity was no longer included in the bargain, and the owner had then a strong interest in transporting him to the south. Thus the same law prevents the slaves of the south from coming to the northern states, and drives those of the north to the south.

The want of free hands is felt in a state in proportion as the number of slaves decreases. But in proportion as labour is performed by free hands, slave-labour becomes less productive; and the slave is then a useless or an onerous possession, whom it is important to export to those southern states where the same competition is not to be feared. Thus the abolition of slavery does not set the slave free, but it merely transfers him from one master to another, and from the north to the south.

The emancipated negroes, and those born after the abolition of slavery, do not, indeed, migrate from the north to the south; but their situation with regard to the Europeans is not unlike that of the aborigines of America; they remain half civilized, and deprived of their rights in the midst of a population which is far superior to them in wealth and in knowledge; where they are exposed to the tyranny of the laws,* and the intolerance of the people. On some accounts they are still more to be pitied than the Indians, since they are haunted by the

---

* The states in which slavery is abolished usually do what they can to render their territory disagreeable to the negroes as a place of residence; and as a kind of emulation exists between the different states in this respect, the unhappy blacks can only choose the least of the evils which beset them.

reminiscence of slavery, and they cannot claim possession of a single portion of the soil: many of them perish miserably,* and the rest congregate in the great towns, where they perform the meanest offices, and lead a wretched and precarious existence.

But even if the number of negroes continued to increase as rapidly as when they were still in a state of slavery, as the number of whites augments with twofold rapidity since the abolition of slavery, the blacks would soon be, as it were, lost in the midst of a strange population.

A district which is cultivated by slaves is in general more scantily peopled than a district cultivated by free labour: moreover, America is still a new country, and a state is therefore not half peopled at the time when it abolishes slavery. No sooner is an end put to slavery, than the want of free labour is felt, and a crowd of enterprising adventurers immediately arrive from all parts of the country, who hasten to profit by the fresh resources which are then opened to industry. The soil is soon divided among them, and a family of white settlers takes possession of each tract of country. Beside which, European emigration is exclusively directed to the free states; for what would be the fate of a poor emigrant who crosses the Atlantic in search of ease and happiness, if he were to land in a country where labour is stigmatized as degrading?

Thus the white population grows by its natural increase, and at the same time by the immense influx of emigrants; while the black population receives no emigrants, and is upon its decline. The proportion which existed between the two races is soon inverted. The negroes constitute a scanty remnant, a poor tribe of vagrants, which is lost in the midst of an immense people in full possession of the land; and the presence of the blacks is only marked by the injustice and the hardships of which they are the unhappy victims.

In several of the western states the negro race never made its appearance; and in all the northern states it is rapidly declining. Thus the great question of its future condition is confined within a narrow circle, where it becomes less formidable, though not more easy of solution.

The more we descend toward the south, the more difficult does it become to abolish slavery with advantage: and this arises from several physical causes, which it is important to point out.

The first of these causes is the climate: it is well known that in proportion as Europeans approach the tropics, they suffer more from labour. Many of the Americans even assert, that within a certain latitude the exertions which a negro can make without danger are fatal to them;† but I do not think that this opinion, which is so favourable to the indolence of the inhabitants of southern regions, is confirmed by

---

* There is a very great difference between the mortality of the blacks and of the whites in the states in which slavery is abolished; from 1820 to 1831 only one out of forty-two individuals of the white population died in Philadelphia; but one negro out of twenty-one individuals of the black population died in the same space of time. The mortality is by no means so great among the negroes who are still slaves. (See Emmerson's Medical Statistics, p. 28.)

† This is true of the spots in which rice is cultivated: rice-grounds, which are unwholesome in all countries, are particularly dangerous in those regions which are exposed to the beams of a tropical sun. Europeans would not find it easy to cultivate the soil in that part of the New World if it must necessarily be made to produce rice; but may they not subsist without rice-grounds?

experience. The southern parts of the Union are not hotter than the south of Italy and of Spain;* and it may be asked why the European cannot work as well there as in the two latter countries. If slavery has been abolished in Italy and in Spain without causing the destruction of the masters, why should not the same thing take place in the Union? I cannot believe that Nature has prohibited the Europeans in Georgia and the Floridas, under pain of death, from raising the means of subsistence from the soil; but their labour would unquestionably be more irksome and less productive† to them than to the inhabitants of New England. As the free workman thus loses a portion of his superiority over the slave in the southern states, there are fewer inducements to abolish slavery.

All the plants of Europe grow in the northern parts of the Union; the south has special productions of its own. It has been observed that slave labour is a very expensive method of cultivating corn. The farmer of corn-land in a country where slavery is unknown, habitually retains a small number of labourers in his service, and at seed-time and harvest he hires several additional hands, who only live at his cost for a short period. But the agriculturist in a slave state is obliged to keep a large number of slaves the whole year round, in order to sow his fields and to gather in his crops, although their services are only required for a few weeks; but slaves are unable to wait till they are hired, and to subsist by their own labour in the meantime like free labourers; in order to have their services, they must be bought. Slavery, independently of its general disadvantages, is therefore still more inapplicable to countries in which corn is cultivated than to those which produce crops of a different kind.

The cultivation of tobacco, of cotton, and especially of the sugar-cane, demands on the other hand, unremitting attention: and women and children are employed in it, whose services are of but little use in the cultivation of wheat. Thus slavery is naturally more fitted to the countries from which these productions are derived.

Tobacco, cotton, and the sugar-cane, are exclusively grown in the south, and they form one of the principal sources of the wealth of those states. If slavery were abolished, the inhabitants of the south would be constrained to adopt one of two alternatives: they must either change their system of cultivation, and then they would come into competition with the more active and more experienced inhabitants of the north; or, if they continued to cultivate the same produce without slave labour, they would have to support the competition of the other states of the south, which might still retain their slaves. Thus, peculiar reasons for maintaining slavery exist in the south which do not operate in the north.

---

* These states are nearer to the equator than Italy and Spain, but the temperature of the continent of America is very much lower than that of Europe.

† The Spanish government formerly caused a certain number of peasants from the Azores to be transported into a district of Louisiana called Attakapas, by way of experiment. These settlers still cultivate the soil without the assistance of slaves, but their industry is so languid as scarcely to supply their most necessary wants.

But there is yet another motive which is more cogent than all the others; the south might indeed, rigorously speaking, abolish slavery, but how should it rid its territory of the black population? Slaves and slavery are driven from the north by the same law, but this twofold result cannot be hoped for in the south.

The arguments which I have adduced to show that slavery is more natural and more advantageous in the south than in the north, sufficiently prove that the number of slaves must be far greater in the former districts. It was to the southern settlements that the first Africans were brought, and it is there that the greatest number of them have always been imported. As we advance toward the south, the prejudice which sanctions idleness increases in power. In the states nearest to the tropics there is not a single white labourer; the negroes are consequently much more numerous in the south than in the north. And, as I have already observed, this disproportion increases daily, since the negroes are transferred to one part of the Union as soon as slavery is abolished in the other. Thus the black population augments in the south, not only by its natural fecundity, but by the compulsory emigration of the negroes from the north; and the African race has causes of increase in the south very analogous to those which so powerfully accelerate the growth of the European race in the north.

In the state of Maine there is one negro in three hundred inhabitants; in Massachusetts, one in one hundred; in New York, two in one hundred; in Pennsylvania, three in the same number; in Maryland, thirty-four; in Virginia, forty-two; and, lastly, in South Carolina fifty-five per cent.* Such was the proportion of the black population to the whites in the year 1830. But this proportion is perpetually changing, as it constantly decreases in the north and augments in the south.

It is evident that the most southern states of the Union cannot abolish slavery without incurring very great dangers, which the north had no reason to apprehend when it emancipated its black population. We have already shown the system by which the northern states secure the transition from slavery to freedom, by keeping the present generation in chains, and setting their descendants free; by this means the negroes are gradually introduced into society; and while the men who might abuse their freedom are kept in a state of servitude, those who are emancipated may learn the art of being free before they become their own masters. But it would be difficult to apply this method in the south. To declare that all the negroes born after a certain period shall be free, is to introduce the principle and the notion of liberty into the heart of slavery; the blacks, whom the law thus maintains in a state of

---

* We find it asserted in an American work, entitled, "Letters on the Colonization Society," by Mr. Carey, 1833, that "for the last forty years the black race has increased more rapidly than the white race in the state of South Carolina; and that if we take the average population of the five states of the south into which slaves were first introduced, viz, Maryland, Virginia, South Carolina, North Carolina, and Georgia, we shall find that from 1790 to 1830, the whites have augmented in the proportion of 80 to 100, and the blacks in that of 112 to 100."
In the United States, 1830, the population of the two races stood as follows:—
States where slavery is abolished, 6,565,434 whites; 120,520 blacks. Slave states, 3,960,814 whites; 2,208,102 blacks.

slavery from which their children are delivered, are astonished at so unequal a fate, and their astonishment is only the prelude to their impatience and irritation. Thenceforward slavery loses in their eyes, that kind of moral power which it derived from time and habit; it is reduced to a mere palpable abuse of force. The northern states had nothing to fear from the contrast, because in them the blacks were few in number, and the white population was very considerable. But if this faint dawn of freedom were to show two millions of men their true position, the oppressors would have reason to tremble. After having effranchised the children of their slaves, the Europeans of the southern states would very shortly be obliged to extend the same benefit to the whole black population.

In the north, as I have already remarked, a twofold migration ensues upon the abolition of slavery, or even precedes that event when circumstances have rendered it probable; the slaves quit the country to be transported southward; and the whites of the northern states as well as the emigrants from Europe hasten to fill up their place. But these two causes cannot operate in the same manner in the southern states. On the one hand, the mass of slaves is too great for any expectation of their ever being removed from the country to be entertained; and on the other hand, the Europeans and the Anglo-Americans of the north are afraid to come to inhabit a country, in which labour has not yet been reinstated in its rightful honours. Besides, they very justly look upon the states in which the proportion of the negroes equals or exceeds that of the whites, as exposed to very great dangers; and they refrain from turning their activity in that direction.

Thus the inhabitants of the south would not be able, like their northern countrymen, to initiate the slaves gradually into a state of freedom, by abolishing slavery; they have no means of perceptibly diminishing the black population, and they would remain unsupported to repress its excesses. So that in the course of a few years, a great people of free negroes would exist in the heart of a white nation of equal size.

The same abuses of power which still maintain slavery, would then become the source of the most alarming perils, which the white population of the south might have to apprehend. At the present time the descendants of the Europeans are the sole owners of the land; the absolute masters of all labour; and the only persons who are possessed of wealth, knowledge, and arms. The black is destitute of all these advantages, but he subsists without them because he is a slave. If he were free, and obliged to provide for his own subsistence, would it be possible for him to remain without these things and to support life? Or would not the very instruments of the present superiority of the white, while slavery exists, expose him to a thousand dangers if it were abolished?

As long as the negro remains a slave, he may be kept in a condition not very far removed from that of the brutes; but, with his liberty, he cannot but acquire a degree of instruction which will enable him to appreciate his misfortunes, and to discern a remedy for them. Moreover, there exists a singular principle of relative justice which is very firmly implanted in the human heart. Men are much more forcibly struck by those inequalities which exist within the circle of the same class, than with those which may be remarked between different classes. It is more easy for them to admit slavery, than to allow several millions of citizens to exist under a load of eternal infamy and hereditary wretchedness. In the north the population of freed negroes feels these hardships and resents these indignities; but its members and its powers are small, while in the south it would be numerous and strong.

As soon as it is admitted that the whites and the emancipated blacks are placed upon the same territory in the situation of two alien communities, it will readily be understood that there are but two alternatives for the future; the negroes and the whites must either wholly part of wholly mingle. I have already expressed the conviction which I entertain as to the latter event.* I do not imagine that the white and the black races will ever live in any country upon an equal footing. But I believe the difficulty to be still greater in the United States than elsewhere. An isolated individual may surmount the prejudices of religion, of his country, or of his race, and if this individual is a king he may effect surprising changes in society; but a whole people cannot rise, as it were, above itself. A despot who should subject the Americans and their former slaves to the same yoke, might perhaps succeed in commingling their races; but as long as the American democracy remains at the head of affairs, no one will undertake so difficult a task; and it may be foreseen that the freer the white population of the United States becomes, the more isolated will it remain.†

I have previously observed that the mixed race is the true bond of union between the Europeans and the Indians; just so the mulattoes are the true means of transition between the white and the negro; so that wherever mulattoes abound, the intermixture of the two races is not impossible. In some parts of America, the European and the negro races are so crossed by one another, that it is rare to meet with a man who is entirely black or entirely white: when they are arrived at this point, the two races may really be said to be combined; or rather to have been absorbed in a third race, which is connected with both, without being identical with either.

Of all the Europeans the English are those who have mixed least with the negroes. More mulattoes are to be seen in the south of the Union than in the north, but still they are infinitely more scarce than in any other European colony: Mulattoes are by no means numerous in the United States; they have no force peculiar to themselves, and

---

* This opinion is sanctioned by authorities infinitely weightier than anything that I can say; thus, for instance, it is stated in the Memoirs of Jefferson (as collected by M. Conseil), "Nothing is more clearly written in the book of destiny than the emancipation of the blacks; and it is equally certain that the two races will never live in a state of equal freedom under the same government, so insurmountable are the barriers which nature, habit, and opinions, have established between them."

† If the British West India planters had governed themselves, they would assuredly not have passed the slave emancipation bill which the mother-country has recently imposed upon them.

when quarrels originating in differences of colour take place, they generally side with the whites, just as the lacqueys of the great in Europe assume the contemptuous airs of nobility to the lower orders.

The pride of origin, which is natural to the English, is singularly augmented by the personal pride which democratic liberty fosters among the Americans: the white citizen of the United States is proud of his race, and proud of himself. But if the whites and the negroes do not intermingle in the north of the Union, how should they mix in the south? Can it be supposed for an instant, that an American of the southern states, placed, as he must for ever be, between the white man with all his physical and moral superiority, and the negro, will ever think of preferring the latter? The Americans of the southern states have two powerful passions which will always keep them aloof; the first is the fear of being assimilated to the negroes, their former slaves; and the second, the dread of sinking below the whites, their neighbours.

If I were called upon to predict what will probably occur at some future time, I should say, that the abolition of slavery in the south, will, in the common course of things, increase the repugnance of the white population for the men of colour. I found this opinion upon the analogous observation which I already had occasion to make in the north. I there remarked, that the white inhabitants of the north avoid the negroes with increasing care, in proportion as the legal barriers of separation are removed by the legislature; and why should not the same result take place in the south? In the north, the whites are deterred from intermingling with the blacks by the fear of an imaginary danger; in the south, where the danger would be real, I cannot imagine that the fear would be less general.

If, on the one hand, it be admitted (and the fact is unquestionable), that the coloured population perpetually accumulates in the extreme south, and that it increases more rapidly than that of the whites; and if, on the other hand, it be allowed that it is impossible to foresee a time at which the whites and the blacks will be so intermingled as to derive the same benefits from society; must it not be inferred, that the blacks and the whites will, sooner or later, come to open strife in the southern states of the Union? But if it be asked what the issue of the struggle is likely to be, it will readily be understood, that we are here left to form a very vague surmise of the truth. The human mind may succeed in tracing a wide circle, as it were, which includes the course of future events; but within that circle a thousand various chances and circumstances may direct it in as many different ways; and in every picture of the future there is a dim spot, which the eye of the understanding cannot penetrate. It appears, however, to be extremely probable, that in the West India islands the white race is destined to be subdued, and the black population to share the same fate upon the continent.

In the West India islands the white planters are surrounded by an immense black population; on the continent, the blacks are placed between the ocean and an innumerable people, which already extends over them in a dense mass from the icy confines of Canada to the frontiers of Virginia, and from the banks of the Missouri to the shores of the Atlantic. If the white citizens of North America remain united, it cannot be supposed that the negroes will escape the destruction with which they are menaced; they must be subdued by want or by the sword. But the black population which is accumulated along the coast of the gulf of Mexico, has a chance of success, if the American Union is dissolved when the struggle between the two races begins. If the federal tie were broken, the citizens of the south would be wrong to rely upon any lasting succour from their northern countrymen. The latter are well aware that the danger can never reach them; and unless they are constrained to march to the assistance of the south by a positive obligation, it may be foreseen that the sympathy of colour will be insufficient to stimulate their exertions.

Yet, at whatever period the strife may break out, the whites of the south, even if they are abandoned to their own resources, will enter the lists with an immense superiority of knowledge and of the means of warfare: but the blacks will have numerical strength and the energy of despair upon their side; and these are powerful resources to men who have taken up arms. The fate of the white population of the southern states will, perhaps, be similar to that of the Moors[4] in Spain. After having occupied the land for centuries, it will perhaps be forced to retire to the country whence its ancestors came, and to abandon to the negroes the possession of a territory, which Providence seems to have more peculiarly destined for them, since they can subsist and labour in it more easily than the whites.

The danger of a conflict between the white and the black inhabitants of the southern states of the Union—a danger which, however remote it may be, is inevitable—perpetually haunts the imagination of the Americans. The inhabitants of the north make it a common topic of conversation, although they have no direct injury to fear from the struggle; but they vainly endeavour to devise some means of obviating the misfortunes which they foresee. In the southern states the subject is not discussed: the planter does not allude to the future in conversing with strangers; the citizen does not communicate his apprehensions to his friends; he seeks to conceal them from himself: but there is something more alarming in the tacit forebodings of the south, than in the clamorous fears of the northern states.

This all-pervading disquietude has giving birth to an undertaking which is but little known, but which may have the effect of changing the fate of a portion of the human race. From apprehension of the dangers which I have just been describing, a certain number of American citizens have formed a society for the purpose of exporting to the coast of Guinea, at their own expense, such free negroes as may be willing to escape from the oppression to which they are subject.[*]

---

[*] This society assumed the name of "The Society for the Colonization of the Blacks." See its annual reports; and more particularly the fifteenth. See also the pamphlet, to which allusion has already been made, entitled, "Letters on the Colonization Society, and on its probable Results," by Mr. Carey, Philadelphia, April, 1833.

In 1820, the society to which I allude formed a settlement in Africa, upon the 7th degree of north latitude, which bears the name of Liberia. The most recent intelligence informs us that two thousand five hundred negroes are collected there; they have introduced the democratic institutions of America into the country of their fore-fathers; and Liberia has a representative system of government, negro-jurymen, negro-magistrates, and negro-priests; churches have been built, newspapers established, and, by a singular change in the vicissi-tudes of the world, white men are prohibited from sojourning within the settlement.*

This is indeed a strange caprice of fortune. Two hundred years have now elapsed since the inhabitants of Europe undertook to tear the ne-gro from his family and his home, in order to transport him to the shores of North America; at the present day, the European settlers are engaged in sending back the descendants of those very negroes to the continent from which they were originally taken; and the barbarous Africans have been brought into contact with civilization in the midst of bondage, and have become acquainted with free political institu-tions in slavery. Up to the present time Africa has been closed against the arts and sciences of the whites; but the inventions of Europe will perhaps penetrate into those regions, now that they are introduced by Africans themselves. The settlement of Liberia is founded upon a lofty and a most fruitful idea; but whatever may be its results with regard to the continent of Africa, it can afford no remedy to the New World.

In twelve years the Colonization society has transported two thou-sand five hundred negroes to Africa; in the same space of time about seven hundred thousand blacks were born in the United States. If the colony of Liberia were so situated as to be able to receive thousands of new inhabitants every year, and if the negroes were in a state to be sent thither with advantage; if the Union were to supply the society with annual subsidies,† and to transport the negroes to Africa in ves-sels of the state, it would be still unable to counterpoise the natural increase of population among the blacks; and as it would not remove as many men in a year as are born upon its territory within the same space of time, it would fail in suspending the growth of the evil which is daily increasing in the states.‡ The negro race will never leave those shores of the American continent, to which it was brought by the pas-

---

* This last regulation was laid down by the founders of the settlement; they apprehended that a state of things might arise in Africa, similar to that which exists on the frontiers of the United States, and that if the negroes, like the Indians, were brought into collision with a people more enlightened than themselves, they would be destroyed before they could be civ-ilized.

† Nor would these be the only difficulties attendant upon the undertaking; if the Union under-took to buy up the negroes now in America, in order to transport them to Africa, the price of slaves, increasing with their scarcity, would soon become enormous; and the states of the north would never consent to expend such great sums, for a purpose which would procure such small advantages to themselves. If the Union took possession of the slaves in the south-ern states by force, or at a rate determined by law, an insurmountable resistance would arise in that part of the country. Both alternatives are equally impossible.

‡ In 1830 there were in the United States 2,010,327 slaves and 319,439 free blacks, in all 2,329,766 negroes, which formed about one fifth of the total population of the United States at that time.

sions and the vices of Europeans; and it will not disappear from the New World as long as it continues to exist. The inhabitants of the United States may retard the calamities which they apprehend, but they cannot now destroy their efficient cause.

I am obliged to confess that I do not regard the abolition of slavery as a means of warding off the struggle of the two races in the United States. The negroes may long remain slaves without complaining; but if they are once raised to the level of freemen, they will soon revolt at being deprived of all their civil rights; and as they cannot become the equals of the whites, they will speedily declare themselves as enemies. In the north everything contributed to facilitate the emancipation of the slaves; and slavery was abolished, without placing the free negroes in a position which could become formidable, since their number was too small for them ever to claim the exercise of their rights. But such is not the case in the south. The question of slavery was a question of commerce and manufacture for the slave-owners in the north; for those of the south, it is a question of life and death. God forbid that I should seek to justify the principle of negro slavery, as has been done by some American writers! But I only observe that all the countries which formerly adopted that execrable principle are not equally able to abandon it at the present time.

When I contemplate the condition of the south, I can only discover two alternatives which may be adopted by the white inhabitants of those states; viz, either to emancipate the negroes, and to intermingle with them; or, remaining isolated from them, to keep them in a state of slavery as long as possible. All intermediate measures seem to me likely to terminate, and that shortly, in the most horrible of civil wars, and perhaps in the extirpation of one or other of the two races. Such is the view which the Americans of the south take of the question, and they act consistently with it. As they are determined not to mingle with the negroes, they refuse to emancipate them.

Not that the inhabitants of the south regard slavery as necessary to the wealth of the planter; for on this point many of them agree with their northern countrymen in freely admitting that slavery is prejudicial to their interests; but they are convinced that, however preducial it may be, they hold their lives upon no other tenure. The instruction which is now diffused in the south has convinced the inhabitants that slavery is injurious to the slave-owner, but it has also shown them, more clearly than before, that no means exist of getting rid of its bad consequences. Hence arises a singular contrast; the more the utility of slavery is contested, the more firmly is it established in the laws; and while the principle of servitude is gradually abolished in the north, that self-same principle gives rise to more and more rigorous consequences in the south.

The legislation of the southern states, with regard to slaves, presents at the present day such unparalleled atrocities, as suffice to show how radically the laws of humanity have been perverted, and to betray the desperate position of the community in which that legislation has been promulgated. The Americans of this portion of the

Union have not, indeed, augmented the hardships of slavery; they have, on the contrary, bettered the physical condition of the slaves. The only means by which the ancients maintained slavery were fetters and death; the Americans of the south of the Union have discovered more intellectual securities for the duration of their power. They have employed their despotism and their violence against the human mind. In antiquity, precautions were taken to prevent the slave from breaking his chains; at the present day measures are adopted to deprive him even of the desire of freedom. The ancients kept the bodies of their slaves in bondage, but they placed no restraint upon the mind and no check upon education; and they acted consistently with their established principle, since a natural termination of slavery then existed, and one day or other the slave might be set free, and become the equal of his master. But the Americans of the south, who do not admit that the negroes can ever be commingled with themselves, have forbidden them to be taught to read or to write, under severe penalties; and as they will not raise them to their own level, they sink them as nearly as possible to that of the brutes.

The hope of liberty had always been allowed to the slave to cheer the hardships of his condition. But the Americans of the south are well aware that emancipation cannot be dangerous, when the freed man can never be assimilated to his former master. To give a man his freedom, and to leave him in wretchedness and ignominy, is nothing less than to prepare a future chief for a revolt of the slaves. Moreover, it has long been remarked, that the presence of a free negro vaguely agitates the minds of his less fortunate brethren, and conveys to them a dim notion of their rights. The Americans of the south have consequently taken measures to prevent slave-owners from emancipating their slaves in most cases; not indeed by a positive prohibition, but by subjecting that step to various forms which it is difficult to comply with.

I happened to meet with an old man, in the south of the Union, who had lived in illicit intercourse with one of his negresses, and had had several children by her, who were born the slaves of their father. He had indeed frequently thought of bequeathing to them at least their liberty; but years had elapsed without his being able to surmount the legal obstacles to their emancipation, and in the meanwhile his old age was come, and he was about to die. He pictured to himself his sons dragged from market to market, and passing from the authority of a parent to the rod of the stranger, until these horrid anticipations worked his expiring imagination into phrensy. When I saw him he was a prey to all the anguish of despair, and he made me feel how awful is the retribution of Nature upon those who have broken her laws.

These evils are unquestionably great; but they are the necessary and foreseen consequences of the very principle of modern slavery. When the Europeans chose their slaves from a race differing from their own, which many of them considered as inferior to the other races of mankind, and which they all repelled with horror from any notion of intimate connexion, they must have believed that slavery would last for ever; since there is no intermediate state which can be durable, between the excessive inequality produced by servitude, and the complete equality which originates in independence. The Europeans did imperfectly feel this truth, but without acknowledging it even to themselves. Whenever they have had to do with negroes, their conduct has either been dictated by their interest and their pride, or by their compassion. They first violated every right of humanity by their treatment of the negro; and they afterward informed him that those rights were precious and inviolable. They affected to open their ranks to the slaves, but the negroes who attempted to penetrate into the community were driven back with scorn; and they have incautiously and involuntarily been led to admit of freedom instead of slavery, without having the courage to be wholly iniquitous, or wholly just. (a)

If it be impossible to anticipate a period at which the Americans of the south will mingle their blood with that of the negroes, can they allow their slaves to become free without compromising their own security? And if they are obliged to keep that race in bondage, in order to save their own families, may they not be excused for availing themselves of the means best adapted to that end? The events which are taking place in the southern states of the Union, appear to be at once the most horrible and the most natural results of slavery. When I see the order of nature overthrown, and when I hear the cry of humanity in its vain struggle against the laws, my indignation does not light upon the men of our own time who are the instruments of these outrages; but I reserve my execration for those who, after a thousand years of freedom, brought back slavery into the world once more.

Whatever may be the efforts of the Americans of the south to maintain slavery, they will not always succeed. Slavery, which is now confined to a single tract of the civilized earth, which is attacked by Christianity as unjust, and by political economy as prejudical, and which is now contrasted with democratic liberties and the information of our age, cannot survive. By the choice of the master or the will of the slave, it will cease; and in either case great calamities may be expected to ensue. If liberty be refused to the negroes of the south, they will in the end seize it for themselves by force; if it be given, they will abuse it ere long.

WHAT ARE THE CHANCES IN FAVOUR OF THE DURATION OF THE AMERICAN UNION, AND WHAT DANGERS THREATEN IT.

Reasons why the preponderating Force lies in the States rather than in the Union—The Union will only last as long as all the States choose to belong to it.—Causes which tend to keep them united.—Utility of the Union to resist foreign Enemies, and to prevent the Existence of Foreigners in America.—No natural Barriers between the several States.—No conflicting Interests to divide them.—Reciprocal Interests of the Northern, Southern, and Western States.—Intellectual ties of Union.—Uniformity of Opinions.—Dangers of the Union resulting from the dif-

(a) In the original, "Voulant la servitude, ils se sont laissé entrainer, malgré eux ou à leur insu, vers la liberté."

"Desiring servitude, they have suffered themselves, involuntarily or ignorantly, to be drawn toward liberty."—*Reviser.*

ferent Characters and the Passions of its Citizens.—Character of the Citizens in the South and in the North.—The rapid growth of the Union one of its greatest Dangers.—Progress of the Population to the Northwest.—Power gravitates in the same Direction.—Passions originating from sudden turns of Fortune.—Whether the existing Government of the Union tends to gain strength, or to lose it.—Various signs of its Decrease.—Internal Improvement.—Waste Lands.—Indians.—The Bank.—The Tariff.—General Jackson.

The maintenance of the existing institutions of the several states depends in some measure upon the maintenance of the Union itself. It is therefore important in the first instance to inquire into the probable fate of the Union. One point may indeed be assumed at once; if the present confederation were dissolved, it appears to me to be incontestable that the states of which it is now composed would not return to their original isolated condition; but that several Unions would then be formed in the place of one. It is not my intention to inquire into the principles upon which these new Unions would probably be established, but merely to show what the causes are which may effect the dismemberment of the existing confederation.

With this object I shall be obliged to retrace some of the steps which I have already taken, and to revert to topics which I have before discussed. I am aware that the reader may accuse me of repetition, but the importance of the matter which still remains to be treated is my excuse; I had rather say too much, than say too little to be thoroughly understood, and I prefer injuring the author to slighting the subject.

The legislators who formed the constitution of 1789, endeavoured to confer a distinct and preponderating authority upon the federal power. But they were confined by the conditions of the task which they had undertaken to perform. They were not appointed to constitute the government of a single people, but to regulate the association of several states; and, whatever their inclinations might be, they could not but divide the exercise of sovereignty in the end.

In order to understand the consequences of this division, it is necessary to make a short distinction between the affairs of government. There are some objects which are national by their very nature, that is to say, which affect the nation as a body, and can only be intrusted to the man or the assembly of men who most completely represent the entire nation. Among these may be reckoned war and diplomacy. There are other objects which are provincial by their very nature, that is to say, which only affect certain localities, and which can only be properly treated in that locality. Such, for instance, is the budget of municipality. Lastly, there are certain objects of a mixed nature, which are national inasmuch as they affect all the citizens who compose the nation, and which are provincial inasmuch as it is not necessary that the nation itself should provide for them all. Such are the rights which regulate the civil and political condition of the citizens. No society can exist without civil and political rights. These rights therefore interest all the citizens alike; but it is not always necessary to the existence and the prosperity of the nation that these rights should be uniform, nor, consequently, that they should be regulated by the central authority.

There are, then, two distinct categories of objects which are submitted to the direction of the sovereign power; and these categories occur in all well-constituted communities, whatever the basis of the political constitution may otherwise be. Between these two extremes, the objects which I have termed mixed may be considered to lie. As these objects are neither exclusively national nor entirely provincial, they may be attained by a national or by a provincial government, according to the agreement of the contracting parties, without in any way impairing the contract of association.

The sovereign power is usually formed by the union of separate individuals, who compose a people; and individual powers or collective forces, each representing a very small portion of the sovereign authority, are the sole elements which are subjected to the general government of their choice. In this case the general government is more naturally called upon to regulate, not only those affairs which are of essential national importance, but those which are of a more local interest; and the local governments are reduced to that small share of sovereign authority which is indispensable to their prosperity.

But sometimes the sovereign authority is composed of preorganized political bodies, by virtue of circumstances anterior to their union; and in this case the provincial governments assume the control, not only of those affairs which more peculiarly belong to their province, but of all, or of a part of the mixed affairs to which allusion has been made. For the confederate nations which were independent sovereign states before their Union, and which still represent a very considerable share of the sovereign power, have only consented to cede to the general government the exercise of those rights which are indispensable to the Union.

When the national government, independently of the prerogatives inherit in its nature, is invested with the right of regulating the affairs which relate partly to the general and partly to the local interest, it possesses a preponderating influence. Not only are its own rights extensive, but all the rights which it does not possess exist by its sufferance, and it may be apprehended that the provincial governments may be deprived of their natural and necessary prerogatives by its influence.

When, on the other hand, the provincial governments are invested with the power of regulating those same affairs of mixed interest, an opposite tendency prevails in society. The preponderating force resides in the province, not in the nation; and it may be apprehended that the national government may in the end be stripped of the privileges which are necessary to its existence.

Independent nations have therefore a natural tendency to centralization, and confederations to dismemberment.

It now only remains for us to apply these general principles to the American Union. The several states were necessarily possessed of the right of regulating all exclusively provincial affairs. Moreover these same states retained the rights of determining the civil and political competency of the citizens, of regulating the reciprocal relations of the members of the community, and of dispensing justice; rights which are of a general nature, but which do not necessarily appertain to the national government. We have shown that the government of the Union is invested with the power of acting in the name of the whole nation, in those cases in which the nation has to appear as a single and undivided power; as, for instance, in foreign relations, and in offering a common resistance to a common enemy; in short, in conducting those affairs which I have styled exclusively national.

In this division of the rights of sovereignty, the share of the Union seems at first sight to be more considerable than that of the states; but a more attentive investigation shows it to be less so. The undertakings of the government of the Union are more vast, but their influence is more rarely felt. Those of the provincial government are comparatively small, but they are incessant, and they serve to keep alive the authority which they represent. The government of the Union watches the general interests of the country; but the general interests of a people have a very unquestionable influence upon individual happiness; while provincial interests produce a most immediate effect upon the welfare of the inhabitants. The Union secures the independence and the greatness of the nation, which do not immediately affect private citizens; but the several states maintain the liberty, regulate the rights, protect the fortune, and secure the life and the whole future prosperity of every citizen.

The federal government is very far removed from its subjects, while the provincial governments are within the reach of them all, and are ready to attend to the smallest appeal. The central government has upon its side the passions of a few superior men who aspire to conduct it; but upon the side of the provincial governments are the interests of all those second-rate individuals who can only hope to obtain power within their own state, and who nevertheless exercise the largest share of authority over the people because they are placed nearest to its level.

The Americans have therefore much more to hope and to fear from the states than from the Union; and, in conformity with the natural tendency of the human mind, they are more likely to attach themselves to the former than to the latter. In this respect their habits and feeling harmonize with their interests.

When a compact nation divides its sovereignty, and adopts a confederate form of government, the traditions, the customs, and the manners of the people are for a long time at variance with their legislation; and the former tend to give a degree of influence to the central government which the latter forbids. When a number of confederate states unite to form a single nation, the same causes operate in an opposite direction. I have no doubt that if France were to become a confederate republic like that of the United States, the government would at first display more energy than that of the Union; and if the Union were to alter its constitution to a monarchy like that of France, I think that the American government would be a long time in acquiring the force which now rules the latter nation. When the national existence of the Anglo-Americans began, their provincial existence was already of long standing; necessary relations were established between the townships and the individual citizens of the same states; and they were accustomed to consider some objects as common to them all, and to conduct other affairs as exclusively relating to their own special interests.

The Union is a vast body, which presents no definite object to patriotic feeling. The forms and limits of the state are distinct and circumscribed; since it represents a certain number of objects which are familiar to the citizens and beloved by all. It is identified with the very soil, with the right of property and the domestic affections, with the recollections of the past, the labours of the present, and the hopes of the future. Patriotism, then, which is frequently a mere extension of individual egotism, is still directed to the state, and is not excited by the Union. Thus the tendency of the interests, the habits, and the feelings of the people is to centre political activity in the states, in preference to the Union.

It is easy to estimate the different forces of the two governments, by remarking the manner in which they fulfil their respective functions. Whenever the government of a state has occasion to address an individual or an assembly of individuals, its language is clear and imperative; and such is also the tone of the federal government in its intercourse with individuals; but no sooner has it anything to do with a state, than it begins to parley, to explain its motives and to justify its conduct, to argue, to advise, and in short, anything but to command. If doubts are raised as to the limits of the constitutional powers of each government, the provincial government prefers its claims with boldness, and takes prompt and energetic steps to support it. In the meanwhile the government of the Union reasons, it appeals to the interests, to the good sense, to the glory of the nation; it temporizes, it negotiates, and does not consent to act until it is reduced to the last extremity. At first sight it might readily be imagined that it is the provincial government which is armed with the authority of the nation, and that congress represents a single state.

The federal government is, therefore, notwithstanding the precautions of those who founded it, naturally so weak, that it more peculiarly requires the free consent of the governed to enable it to subsist. It is easy to perceive that its object is to enable the states to realize with facility their determination of remaining united; and, as long as this preliminary consideration exists, its authority is great, temperate, and effective. The constitution fits the government to control individuals, and easily to surmount such obstacles as they may be inclined to offer, but it was by no means established with a view to the possible separation of one or more of the states from the Union.

If the sovereignty of the Union were to engage in a struggle with that of the states at the present day, its defeat may be confidently predicted; and it is not probable that such a struggle would be seriously undertaken. As often as steady resistance is offered to the federal government, it will be found to yield. Experience has hitherto shown that whenever a state has demanded anything with perseverance and resolution, it has invariably succeeded; and that if a separate government has distinctly refused to act, it was left to do as it thought fit.*

But even if the government of the Union had any strength inherent in itself, the physical situation of the country would render the exercise of that strength very difficult.† The United States cover an immense territory; they are separated from each other by great distances; and the population is disseminated over the surface of a country which is still half a wilderness. If the Union were to undertake to enforce the allegiance of the confederate states by military means, it would be in a position very analogous to that of England at the time of the war of independence.

However strong a government may be, it cannot easily escape from the consequences of a principle which it has once admitted as the foundation of its constitution. The Union was formed by the voluntary agreement of the states; and, in uniting together, they have not forfeited their nationality, nor have they been reduced to the condition of one and the same people. If one of the states chose to withdraw its name from the compact, it would be difficult to disprove its right of doing so; and the federal government would have no means of maintaining its claims directly, either by force or by right. In order to enable the federal government easily to conquer the resistance which may be offered to it by any one of its subjects, it would be necessary that one or more of them should be especially interested in the existence of the Union, as has frequently been the case in the history of confederations.

If it be supposed that among the states which are united by the federal tie, there are some which exclusively enjoy the principal advantages of union, or whose prosperity depends on the duration of that union, it is unquestionable that they will always be ready to support the central government in enforcing the obedience of the others. But the government would then be exerting a force not derived from itself, but from a principle contrary to its nature. States form confederations in order to derive equal advantages from their union; and in the case just alluded to, the federal government would derive its power from the unequal distribution of those benefits among the states.

If one of the confederate states have acquired a preponderance sufficiently great to enable it to take exclusive possession of the central authority, it will consider the other states as subject provinces, and it will cause its own supremacy to be respected under the borrowed name of the sovereignty of the Union. Great things may then be done in the name of the federal government, but in reality that government will have ceased to exist.* In both these cases, the power which acts in

---

* See the conduct of the northern states in the war of 1812. "During that war," says Jefferson in a letter to General Lafayette, "four of the eastern states were only attached to the Union, like so many inanimate bodies to living men."

† The profound peace of the Union affords no pretext for a standing army; and without a standing army a government is not prepared to profit by a favourable opportunity to conquer resistance, and take the sovereign power by surprise.

the name of the confederation becomes stronger, the more it abandons the natural state and the acknowledged principles of confederations.

In America the existing Union is advantageous to all the states, but it is not indispensable to any one of them. Several of them might break the federal tie without compromising the welfare of the others, although their own prosperity would be lessened. As the existence and the happiness of none of the states are wholly dependant on the present constitution, they would none of them be disposed to make great personal sacrifices to maintain it. On the other hand, there is no state which seems, hitherto, to have its ambition much interested in the maintenance of the existing Union. They certainly do not all exercise the same influence in the federal councils, but no one of them can hope to domineer over the rest, or to treat them as its inferiors or as its subjects.

It appears to me unquestionable, that if any portion of the Union seriously desired to separate itself from the other states, they would not be able, nor indeed would they attempt, to prevent it; and that the present Union will only last as long as the states which compose it choose to continue members of the confederation. If this point be admitted, the question becomes less difficult; and our object is not to inquire whether the states of the existing Union are capable of separating, but whether they will choose to remain united.

[The remarks respecting the inability of the federal government to retain within the Union any state that may choose "to withdraw its name from the contract," ought not to pass through an American edition of this work, without the expression of a dissent by the editor from the opinion of the author. The laws of the United States must remain in force in a revolted state, until repealed by congress; the customs and postages must be collected; the courts of the United States must sit, and must decide the causes submitted to them; as has been very happily explained by the author, the courts act upon individuals. If their judgements are resisted, the executive arm must interpose, and if the state authorities aid in the resistance, the military power of the whole Union must be invoked to overcome it. So long as the laws affecting the citizens of such a state remain, and so long as there remain any officers of the general government to enforce them, these results must follow not only theoretically but actually. The author probably formed the opinions which are the subject of these remarks, at the commencement of the controversy with South Carolina respecting the tariff. And when they were written and published, he had not learned the result of that controversy, in which the supremacy of the Union and its laws was triumphant. There was doubtless great reluctance in adopting the necessary measures to collect the customs, and to bring every legal question that could possibly arise out of the controversy, before the judiciary of the United States, but they were finally adopted, and were not the less successful for being the result of deliberation and of necessity. Out of that controversy have arisen some advantages of a permanent character, produced by

* Thus the province of Holland in the republic of the Low Countries, and the emperor in the Germanic Confederation, have sometimes put themselves in the place of the Union, and have employed the federal authority to their own advantage.

the legislation with it required. There were defects in the laws regulating the manner of bringing from the state courts into those of the United States, a cause involving the constitutionality of acts of congress or of the states, through which the federal authority might be evaded. Those defects were remedied by the legislation referred to; and it is now more emphatically and universally true, than when the author wrote, that the acts of the general government operate through the judiciary, upon individual citizens, and not upon the states.—*American Editor.*]

Among the various reasons which tend to render the existing Union useful to the Americans, two principal causes are peculiarly evident to the observer. Although the Americans are, as it were, alone upon their continent, their commerce makes them the neighbours of all the nations with which they trade. Notwithstanding their apparent isolation, the Americans require a certain degree of strength, which they cannot retain otherwise than by remaining united to each other. If the states were to split, they would not only diminish the strength which they are now able to display toward foreign nations, but they would soon create foreign powers upon their own territory. A system of inland custom-houses would then be established; the valleys would be divided by imaginary boundary lines; the courses of the rivers would be confined by territorial distinctions; and a multitude of hinderances would prevent the Americans from exploring the whole of that vast continent which Providence has allotted to them for a dominion. At present they have no invasion to fear, and consequently no standing armies to maintain, no taxes to levy. If the Union were dissolved, all these burdensome measures might ere long be required. The Americans are then very powerfully interested in the maintenance of their Union. On the other hand, it is almost impossible to discover any sort of material interest which might at present tempt a portion of the Union to separate from the other states.

When we cast our eyes upon the map of the United States, we perceive the chain of the Allegany mountains, running from the northeast to the southwest, and crossing nearly one thousand miles of country; and we are led to imagine that the design of Providence was to raise, between the valley of the Mississippi and the coasts of the Atlantic ocean, one of those natural barriers which break the mutual intercourse of men, and form the necessary limits of different states. But the average height of the Alleganies does not exceed 2,500 feet; their greatest elevation is not above 4,000 feet; their rounded summits, and the spacious valleys, which they conceal within their passes, are of easy access from several sides. Beside which, the principal rivers that fall into the Atlantic ocean, the Hudson, the Susquehannah, and the Potomac, take their rise beyond the Alleganies, in an open district, which borders upon the valley of the Mississippi. These streams quit this tract of country,* make their way through the barrier which would seem to turn them westward, and as they wind through the mountains, they open an easy and natural passage to man.

* See Darby's View of the United States, pp. 64, 79.

No natural barrier exists in the regions which are now inhabited by the Anglo-Americans; the Alleganies are so far from serving as a boundary to separate nations, that they do not even serve as a frontier to the states. New York, Pennsylvania, and Virginia, comprise them within their borders, and extend as much to the west as to the east of the line.

The territory now occupied by the twenty-four states of the Union, and the three great districts which have not yet acquired the rank of states, although they already contain inhabitants, covers a surface of 1,002,600 square miles,* which is about equal to five times the extent of France. Within these limits the qualities of the soil, the temperature, and the produce of the country, are extremely various. The vast extent of territory occupied by the Anglo-American republics has given rise to doubts as to the maintenance of the Union. Here a distinction must be made; contrary interests sometimes arise in the different provinces of a vast empire, which often terminate in open dissensions; and the extent of the country is then most prejudicial to the power of the state. But if the inhabitants of these vast regions are not divided by contrary interests, the extent of the territory may be favourable to their prosperity; for the unity of the government promotes the interchange of the different productions of the soil, and increases their value by facilitating their consumption.

It is indeed easy to discover different interests in the different parts of the Union, but I am unacquainted with any which are hostile to each other. The southern states are almost exclusively agricultural: the northern states are more peculiarly commercial and manufacturing: the states of the west are at the same time agricultural and manufacturing. In the south the crops consist of tobacco, of rice, of cotton, and of sugar; in the north and the west, of wheat and maize: these are different sources of wealth; but union is the means by which these sources are opened to all, and rendered equally advantageous to the several districts.

The north, which ships the produce of the Anglo-Americans to all parts of the world, and brings back the produce of the globe to the Union, is evidently interested in maintaining the confederation in its present condition, in order that the number of American producers and consumers may remain as large as possible. The north is the most natural agent of communication between the south and the west of the Union on the one hand, and the rest of the world upon the other; the north is therefore interested in the union and prosperity of the south and the west, in order that they may continue to furnish raw materials for its manufactures, and cargoes for its shipping.

The south and the west, on their side, are still more directly interested in the preservation of the Union, and the prosperity of the north.

---

* See Darby's View of the United States, p. 435. [In Carey & Lea's Geography of America, the United States are said to form an area of 2,076,400 square miles.—*Translator's Note.*]

[The discrepance between Darby's estimate of the area of the United States given by the author, and that stated by the translator, is not easily accounted for. In Bradford's comprehensive Atlas, a work generally of great accuracy, it is said that "as claimed by this country, the territory of the United States extends from 25° to 54° north latitude, and from 67° 49' to 125° west longitude, over an area of about 2,200,000 square miles."—*American Editor.*]

The produce of the south is for the most part exported beyond seas; the south and the west consequently stand in need of the commercial resources of the north. They are likewise interested in the maintenance of a powerful fleet by the Union, to protect them efficaciously. The south and the west have no vessels, but they cannot refuse a willing subsidy to defray the expenses of the navy; for if the fleets of Europe were to blockade the ports of the south and the delta of the Mississippi, what would become of the rice of the Carolinas, the tobacco of Virginia, and the sugar and cotton which grow in the valley of the Mississippi? Every portion of the federal budget does therefore contribute to the maintenance of material interests which are common to all the confederate states.

Independently of this commercial utility, the south and the west of the Union derive great political advantages from their connexion with the north. The south contains an enormous slave population; a population which is already alarming, and still more formidable for the future. The states of the west lie in the remoter parts of a single valley; and all the rivers which intersect their territory rise in the Rocky mountains or in the Alleganies, and fall into the Mississippi, which bears them onward to the gulf of Mexico. The western states are consequently entirely cut off, by their position, from the traditions of Europe and the civilization of the Old World. The inhabitants of the south, then, are induced to support the Union in order to avail themselves of its protection against the blacks; and the inhabitants of the west, in order not to be excluded from a free communication with the rest of the globe, and shut up in the wilds of central America. The north cannot but desire the maintenance of the Union, in order to remain, as it now is, the connecting link between that vast body and the other parts of the world.

The temporal interests of all the several parts of the Union are, then, intimately connected; and the same assertion holds true respecting those opinions and sentiments which may be termed the immaterial interests of men.

The inhabitants of the United States talk a great deal of their attachment to their country; but I confess that I do not rely upon that calculating patriotism which is founded upon interest, and which a change in the interests at stake may obliterate. Nor do I attach much importance to the language of the Americans, when they manifest, in their daily conversation, the intention of maintaining the federal system adopted by their forefathers. A government retains its sway over a great number of citizens, far less by the voluntary and rational consent of the multitude, than by that instinctive and, to a certain extent, involuntary agreement, which results from similarity of feelings and resemblances of opinion. I will never admit that men constitute a social body, simply because they obey the same head and the same laws. Society can only exist when a great number of men consider a great number of things in the same point of view; when they hold the same opinions upon many subjects, and when the same occurrences suggest the same thoughts and impressions to their minds.

The observer who examines the present condition of the United States upon this principle, will readily discover, that although the citizens are divided into twenty-four distinct sovereignties, they nevertheless constitute a single people; and he may perhaps be led to think that the state of the Anglo-American Union is more truly a state of society, than that of certain nations of Europe which live under the same legislation and the same prince.

Although the Anglo-Americans have several religious sects, they all regard religion in the same manner. They are not always agreed upon the measures which are most conducive to good government, and they vary upon some of the forms of government which it is expedient to adopt; but they are unanimous upon the general principles which ought to rule human society. From Maine to the Floridas, and from the Missouri to the Atlantic ocean, the people is held to be the legitimate source of all power. The same notions are entertained respecting liberty and equality, the liberty of the press, the right of association, the jury, and the responsibility of the agents of government.

If we turn from their political and religious opinions to the moral and philosophical principles which regulate the daily actions of life, and govern their conduct, we shall still find the same uniformity. The Anglo-Americans* acknowledge the absolute moral authority of the reason of the community, as they acknowledge the political authority of the mass of citizens; and they hold that public opinion is the surest arbiter of what is lawful or forbidden, true or false. The majority of them believe that a man will be led to do what is just and good by following his own interests, rightly understood. They hold that every man is born in possession of the right of self-government, and that no one has the right of constraining his fellow-creatures to be happy. They have all a lively faith in the perfectibility of man; they are of opinion that the effects of the diffusion of knowledge must necessarily be advantageous, and the consequences of ignorance fatal; they all consider society as a body in a state of improvement, humanity as a changing scene, in which nothing is, or ought to be, permanent; and they admit that what appears to them to be good to-day may be superseded by something better to-morrow. I do not give all these opinions as true, but I quote them as characteristic of the Americans.

The Anglo-Americans are not only united together by those common opinions, but they are separated from all other nations by a common feeling of pride. For the last fifty years no pains have been spared to convince the inhabitants of the United States that they constitute the only religious, enlightened, and free people. They perceive that, for the present, their own democratic institutions succeed, while those of other countries fail; hence they conceive an overweening opinion of their superiority, and they are not very remote from believing themselves to belong to a distinct race of mankind.

---

* It is scarcely necessary for me to observe that by the expression *Anglo-Americans*, I only mean to designate the great majority of the nation; for a certain number of isolated individuals are of course to be met with holding very different opinions.

The dangers which threaten the American Union do not originate in the diversity of interests or of opinions; but in the various characters and passions of the Americans. The men who inhabit the vast territory of the United States are almost all the issue of a common stock; but the effects of the climate, and more especially of slavery, have gradually introduced very striking differences between the British settler of the southern states, and the British settler of the north. In Europe it is generally believed that slavery has rendered the interests of one part of the Union contrary to those of another part; but I by no means remarked this to be the case; slavery has not created interests in the south contrary to those of the north, but it has modified the character and changed the habits of the natives of the south.

I have already explained the influence which slavery has exercised upon the commercial ability of the Americans in the south; and this same influence equally extends to their manners. The slave is a servant who never remonstrates, and who submits to everything without complaint. He may sometimes assassinate, but he never withstands, his master. In the south there are no families so poor as not to have slaves. The citizen of the southern states of the Union is invested with a sort of domestic dictatorship from his earliest years; the first notion he acquires in life is, that he is born to command, and the first habit he contracts is that of being obeyed without resistance. His education tends, then, to give him the character of a supercilious and a hasty man; irascible, violent, and ardent in his desires, impatient of obstacles, but easily discouraged if he cannot succeed upon his first attempt.

The American of the northern states is surrounded by no slaves in his childhood; he is even unattended by free servants; and is usually obliged to provide for his own wants. No sooner does he enter the world than the idea of necessity assails him on every side: he soon learns to know exactly the natural limit of his authority; he never expects to subdue those who withstand him, by force; and he knows that the surest means of obtaining the support of his fellow-creatures, is to win their favour. He therefore becomes patient, reflecting, tolerant, slow to act, and persevering in his designs.

In the southern states the more immediate wants of life are always supplied; the inhabitants of those parts are not busied in the material cares of life, which are always provided for by others; and their imagination is diverted to more captivating and less definite objects. The American of the south is fond of grandeur, luxury, and renown, of gayety, of pleasure, and above all of idleness; nothing obliges him to exert himself in order to subsist; and as he has no necessary occupations, he gives way to indolence, and does not even attempt what would be useful.

But the equality of fortunes, and the absence of slavery in the north, plunge the inhabitants in those same cares of daily life which are disdained by the white population of the south. They are taught from infancy to combat want; and to place comfort above all the pleasures of the intellect or the heart. The imagination is extinguished by the trivial details of life; and the ideas become less numerous and less general, but far more practical and more precise. As prosperity is the sole aim of exertion, it is excellently well attained; nature and mankind are turned to the best pecuniary advantage; and society is dexterously made to contribute to the welfare of each of its members, while individual egotism is the source of general happiness.

The citizen of the north has not only experience, but knowledge: nevertheless he sets but little value upon the pleasures of knowledge; he esteems it as the means of obtaining a certain end, and he is only anxious to seize its more lucrative applications. The citizen of the south is more given to act upon impulse; he is more clever, more frank, more generous, more intellectual, and more brilliant. The former, with a greater degree of activity, of common sense, of information, and of general aptitude, has the characteristic good and evil qualities of the middle classes. The latter has the tastes, the prejudices, the weaknesses, and the magnanimity of all aristocracies.

If two men are united in society, who have the same interests, and to a certain extent the same opinions, but different characters, different acquirements, and a different style of civilization, it is probable that these men will not agree. The same remark is applicable to a society of nations.

Slavery then does not attack the American Union directly in its interests, but indirectly in its manners.

The states which gave their assent to the federal contract in 1790 were thirteen in number; the Union now consists of twenty-four members. The population which amounted to nearly four millions in 1790, had more than tripled in the space of forty years; and in 1830 it amounted to nearly thirteen millions.* Changes of such magnitude cannot take place without some danger.

A society of nations, as well as a society of individuals, derives its principal changes of duration from the wisdom of its members, their individual weakness, and their limited number. The Americans who quit the coasts of the Atlantic ocean to plunge into the western wilderness, are adventurers impatient of restraint, greedy of wealth, and frequently men expelled from the states in which they were born. When they arrive in the deserts, they are unknown to each other; and they have neither traditions, family feeling, nor the force of example to check their excesses. The empire of the laws is feeble among them; that of morality is still more powerless. The settlers who are constantly peopling the valley of the Mississippi are, then, in every respect very inferior to the Americans who inhabit the older parts of the Union. Nevertheless, they already exercise a great influence in its councils; and they arrive at the government of the commonwealth before they have learned to govern themselves.†

The greater the individual weakness of each of the contracting parties, the greater are the chances of the duration of the contract; for

---

* Census of 1790 . . . . . 3,929,328.
    do. 1830 . . . . . 12,856,165.
† This indeed is only a temporary danger. I have no doubt that in time society will assume as much stability and regularity in the west, as it has already done upon the coast of the Atlantic ocean.

their safety is then dependant upon their union. When, in 1790, the most populous of the American republics did not contain 500,000 inhabitants,* each of them felt its own insignificance as an independent people, and this feeling rendered compliance with the federal authority more easy. But when one of the confederate states reckons, like the state of New York, two millions of inhabitants, and covers an extent of territory equal in surface to a quarter of France,† it feels its own strength: and although it may continue to support the Union as advantageous to its prosperity, it no longer regards that body as necessary to its existence; and, as it continues to belong to the federal compact, it soon aims at preponderance in the federal assemblies. The probable unanimity of the states is diminished as their number increases. At present the interests of the different parts of the Union are not at variance; but who is able to foresee the multifarious changes of the future, in a country in which towns are founded from day to day, and states almost from year to year?

Since the first settlement of the British colonies, the number of inhabitants has about doubled every twenty-two years. I perceive no causes which are likely to check this progressive increase of the Anglo-American population for the next hundred years; and before that space of time has elapsed, I believe that the territories and dependancies of the United States will be covered by more than a hundred millions of inhabitants, and divided into forty states.‡ I admit that these hundred millions of men have no hostile interests; I suppose on the contrary, that they are all equally interested in the maintenance of the Union; but I am still of opinion, that where there are a hundred millions of men, and forty distinct nations unequally strong, the continuance of the federal government can only be a fortunate accident.

Whatever faith I may have in the perfectibility of man, until human nature is altered, and men wholly transformed, I shall refuse to believe in the duration of a government which is called upon to hold together forty different peoples, disseminated over a territory equal to one half of Europe in extent; to avoid all rivalry, ambition, and struggles, between them; and to direct their independent activity to the accomplishment of the same designs.

But the greatest peril to which the Union is exposed by its increase, arises from the continual changes which take place in the position of its internal strength. The distance from Lake Superior to the gulf of

---

* Pennsylvania contained 431,373 inhabitants in 1790.
† The area of the state of New York is about 46,000 square miles. See Carey & Lea's American Geography, p. 142.
‡ If the population continues to double every twenty-two years, as it has done for the last two hundred years, the number of inhabitants in the United States in 1852, will be twenty millions; in 1874, forty-eight millions; and in 1896, ninety-six millions. This may still be the case even if the lands on the western slope of the Rocky mountains should be found to be unfit for cultivation. The territory which is already occupied can easily contain this number of inhabitants. One hundred millions of men disseminated over the surface of the twenty-four states, and the three dependancies, which constitute the Union, would give only 762 inhabitants to the square league, this would be far below the mean population of France, which is 1,063 to the square league; or of England, which is 1,457; and it would even be below the population of Switzerland, for that country, notwithstanding its lakes and mountains, contains 783 inhabitants to the square league. (See Maltebrun, vol. vi., p. 92.)

Mexico extends from the 47th to the 30th degree of latitude, a distance of more than twelve hundred miles, as the bird flies. The frontier of the United States winds along the whole of this immense line; sometimes falling within its limits, but more frequently extending far beyond it, into the waste. It has been calculated that the whites advance every year a mean distance of seventeen miles along the whole of this vast boundary.* Obstacles, such as an unproductive district, a lake, or an Indian nation unexpectedly encountered, are sometimes met with. The advancing column then halts for a while; its two extremities fall back upon themselves, and as soon as they are reunited they proceed onward. This gradual and continuous progress of the European race toward the Rocky mountains, has the solemnity of a providential event; it is like a deluge of men rising unabatedly, and daily driven onward by the hand of God.

Within this first line of conquering settlers, towns are built, and vast states founded. In 1790 there were only a few thousand pioneers sprinkled along the valleys of the Mississippi; and at the present day these valleys contain as many inhabitants as were to be found in the whole Union in 1790. Their population amounts to nearly four millions.† The city of Washington was founded in 1800, in the very centre of the Union; but such are the changes which have taken place, that it now stands at one of the extremities; and the delegates of the most remote western states are already obliged to perform a journey as long as that from Vienna to Paris.‡

All the states are borne onward at the same time in the path of fortune, but of course they do not all increase and prosper in the same proportion. In the north of the Union detached branches of the Allegany chain, extending as far as the Atlantic ocean, form spacious roads and ports, which are constantly accessible to vessels of the greatest burden. But from the Potomac to the mouth of the Mississippi, the coast is sandy and flat. In this part of the Union the mouths of almost all the rivers are obstructed; and the few harbours which exist among these lagunes, afford much shallower water to vessels, and much fewer commercial advantages than those of the north.

This first natural cause of inferiority is united to another cause proceeding from the laws. We have already seen that slavery, which is abolished in the north, still exists in the south; and I have pointed out its fatal consequences upon the prosperity of the planter himself.

The north is therefore superior to the south both in commerce§ and manufacture; the natural consequence of which is the more rapid increase of population and of wealth within its borders. The states situ-

---

* See Legislative Documents, 20th congress, No. 117, p. 105.
† 3,672,317; census 1830.
‡ The distance from Jefferson, the capital of the state of Missouri, to Washington is 1,019 miles. (American Almanac, 1831, p. 48.)
§ The following statements will suffice to show the difference which exists between the commerce of the south and that of the north:—
    In 1829, the tunnage of all the merchant-vessels belonging to Virginia, the two Carolinas, and Georgia (the four great southern states), amounted to only 5,243 tuns. In the same year the tunnage of the vessels of the state of Massachusetts alone amounted to 17,322 tuns.

ate upon the shores of the Atlantic ocean are already half-peopled. Most of the land is held by an owner; and these districts cannot therefore receive so many emigrants as the western states, where a boundless field is still open to their exertions. The valley of the Mississippi is far more fertile than the coast of the Atlantic ocean. This reason, added to all the others, contributes to drive the Europeans westward— a fact which may be rigorously demonstrated by figures. It is found that the sum total of the population of all the United States has about tripled in the course of forty years. But in the recent states adjacent to the Mississippi, the population has increased thirty-one fold within the same space of time.[*]

The relative position of the central federal power is continually displaced. Forty years ago the majority of the citizens of the Union was established upon the coast of the Atlantic, in the environs of the spot upon which Washington now stands; but the great body of the people is now advancing inland and to the north, so that in twenty years the majority will unquestionably be on the western side of the Alleganies. If the Union goes on to subsist, the basin of the Mississippi is evidently marked out, by its fertility and its extent, as the future centre of the federal government. In thirty or forty years, that tract of country will have assumed the rank which naturally belongs to it. It is easy to calculate that its population, compared to that of the coast of the Atlantic, will be, in round numbers, as 40 to 11. In a few years the states which founded the Union will lose the direction of its policy, and the population of the valleys of the Mississippi will preponderate in the federal assemblies.

This constant gravitation of the federal power and influence toward the northwest, is shown every ten years, when a general census of the population is made, and the number of delegates which each state sends to congress is settled afresh.[†] In 1790 Virginia had nineteen representatives in congress. This number continued to increase until the year 1813, when it reached to twenty-three: from that time it began to decrease, and in 1833, Virginia elected only twenty-one repre-

---

(See Legislative Documents, 21st congress, 2d session, No. 140, p. 244.) Thus the state of Massachusetts has three times as much shipping as the four abovementioned states. Nevertheless the area of the state of Massachusetts is only 7,335 square miles, and its population amounts to 610,014 inhabitants; while the area of the four other states I have quoted is 210,000 square miles, and their population 3,047,767. Thus the area of the state of Massachusetts forms only one thirtieth part of the area of the four states; and its population is five times smaller than theirs. (See Darby's View of the United States.) Slavery is prejudicial to the commercial prosperity of the south in several different ways; by diminishing the spirit of enterprise among the whites, and by preventing them from meeting with as numerous a class of sailors as they require. Sailors are usually taken from the lowest ranks of the population. But in the southern states these lowest ranks are composed of slaves, and it is very difficult to employ them at sea. They are unable to serve as well as a white crew, and apprehensions would always be entertained of their mutinying in the middle of the ocean, or of their escaping in the foreign countries at which they might touch.

[*] Darby's view of the United States, p. 444.

[†] It may be seen that in the course of the last ten years (1820–30) the population of one district, as for instance, the state of Delaware, has increased in the proportion of 5 per cent.; while that of another, as the territory of Michigan, has increased 250 per cent. Thus the population of Virginia has augmented 13 per cent., and that of the border state of Ohio 61 per cent., in the same space of time. The general table of these changes, which is given in the National Calendar, displays a striking picture of the unequal fortunes of the different states.

sentatives.* During the same period the state of New York advanced in the contrary direction; in 1790, it had ten representatives in congress; in 1813, twenty-seven; in 1823, thirty-four; and in 1833, forty. The state of Ohio had only one representative in 1803, and in 1833, it had already nineteen.

It is difficult to imagine a durable union of a people which is rich and strong, with one which is poor and weak, even if it were proved that the strength and wealth of the one are not the causes of the weakness and poverty of the other. But union is still more difficult to maintain at a time at which one party is losing strength, and the other is gaining it. This rapid and disproportionate increase of certain states threatens the independence of the others. New York might, perhaps, succeed with its two millions of inhabitants and its forty representatives, in dictating to the other states in congress. But even if the more powerful states make no attempt to bear down the lesser ones, the danger still exists; for there is almost as much in the possibility of the act as in the act itself. The weak generally mistrust the justice and the reason of the strong. The states which increase less rapidly than the others, look upon those which are more favoured by fortune, with envy and suspicion. Hence arise the deep-seated uneasiness and ill-defined agitation which are observable in the south, and which form so striking a contrast to the confidence and prosperity which are common to other parts of the Union. I am inclined to think that the hostile measures taken by the southern provinces upon a recent occasion, are attributable to no other cause. The inhabitants of the southern states are, of all the Americans, those who are most interested in the maintenance of the Union; they would assuredly suffer most from being left to themselves; and yet they are the only citizens who threaten to break the tie of confederation. But it is easy to perceive that the south, which has given four presidents, Washington, Jefferson, Madison, and Monroe, to the Union; which perceives that it is losing its federal influence, and that the number of its representatives in congress is diminishing from year to year, while those of the northern and western states are increasing; the south, which is peopled with ardent and irascible beings, is becoming more and more irritated and alarmed. The citizens

---

* It has just been said that in the course of the last term the population of Virginia has increased 13 per cent.; and it is necessary to explain how the number of representatives of a state may decrease, when the population of that state, far from diminishing, is actually upon the increase. I take the state of Virginia, to which I have already alluded, as my term of comparison. The number of representatives of Virginia in 1823 was proportionate to the total number of the representatives of the Union, and to the relation which its population bore to that of the whole Union; in 1833, the number of representatives of Virginia was likewise proportionate to the total number of the representatives of the Union, and to the relation which its population, augmented in the course of ten years, bore to the augmented population of the Union in the same space of time. The new number of Virginian representatives will then be to the old number, on the one hand, as the new number of all the representatives is to the old number; and, on the other hand, as the augmentation of the population of Virginia is to that of the whole population of the country. Thus, if the increase of the population of the lesser country be to that of the greater in an exact inverse ratio of the proportion between the new and the old numbers of all the representatives, the number of the representatives of Virginia will remain stationary; and if the increase of the Virginia population be to that of the whole Union in a feebler ratio than the new number of representatives of the Union to the old number, the number of the representatives of Virginia must decrease.

reflect upon their present position and remember their past influence, with the melancholy uneasiness of men who suspect oppression: if they discover a law of the Union which is not unequivocally favourable to their interests, they protest against it as an abuse of force; and if their ardent remonstrances are not listened to, they threaten to quit an association which loads them with burdens while it deprives them of their due profits. "The tariff," said the inhabitants of Carolina in 1832, "enriches the north, and ruins the south; for if this were not the case, to what can we attribute the continually increasing power and wealth of the north, with its inclement skies and arid soil; while the south, which may be styled the garden of America, is rapidly declining."*

If the changes which I have described were gradual, so that each generation at least might have time to disappear with the order of things under which it had lived, the danger would be less; but the progress of society in America is precipitate, and almost revolutionary. The same citizen may have lived to see his state take the lead in the Union, and afterward become powerless in the federal assemblies; and an Anglo-American republic has been known to grow as rapidly as a man, passing from birth and infancy to maturity in the course of thirty years. It must not be imagined, however, that the states which lose their preponderance, also lose their population or their riches; no stop is put to their prosperity, and they even go on to increase more rapidly than any kingdom in Europe.† But they believe themselves to be empoverished because their wealth does not augment as rapidly as that of their neighbours; and they think that their power is lost, because they suddenly come into collision with a power greater than their own:‡ Thus they are more hurt in their feelings and their passions, than in their interests. But this is amply sufficient to endanger the maintenance of the union. If kings and peoples had only had their true interests in view, ever since the beginning of the world, the name of war would scarcely be known among mankind.

Thus the prosperity of the United States is the source of the most serious dangers that threaten them, since it tends to create in some of the confederate states that over-excitement which accompanies a rapid increase of fortune; and to awaken in others, those feelings of envy, mistrust, and regret, which usually attend upon the loss of it. The Americans contemplate this extraordinary and hasty progress with exultation; but they would be wiser to consider it with sorrow and

---

* See the report of its committee to the convention, which proclaimed the nullification of the tariff in South Carolina.

† The population of a country assuredly constitutes the first element of its wealth. In the ten years (1820–30) during which Virginia lost two of its representatives in congress, its population increased in the proportion of 13-7 per cent.; that of Carolina in the proportion of 15 per cent.; and that of Georgia 51-5 per cent. (See the American Almanac, 1832, p. 152.) But the population of Russia, which increases more rapidly than that of any other European country, only augments in ten years at the rate of 9-5 per cent.; of France at the rate of 7 per cent.; and of Europe in general at the rate of 4-7 per cent. (See Maltebrun, vol. vi., p. 95.)

‡ It must be admitted, however, that the depreciation which has taken place in the value of tobacco, during the last fifty years, has notably diminished the opulence of the southern planters but this circumstance is as independent of the will of their northern brethren, as it is of their own.

alarm. The Americans of the United States must inevitably become one of the greatest nations in the world; their offset will cover almost the whole of North America; the continent which they inhabit is their dominion, and it cannot escape them. What urges them to take possession of it so soon? Riches, power, and renown, cannot fail to be theirs at some future time; but they rush upon their fortune as if but a moment remained for them to make it their own.

I think I have demonstrated, that the existence of the present confederation depends entirely on the continued assent of all the confederates; and, starting from this principle, I have inquired into the causes which may induce any of the states to separate from the others. The Union may, however, perish in two different ways: one of the confederate states may choose to retire from the compact, and so forcibly sever the federal tie; and it is to this supposition that most of the remarks which I have made apply: or the authority of the federal government may be progressively intrenched on by the simultaneous tendency of the united republics to resume their independence. The central power, successively stripped of all its prerogatives, and reduced to impotence by tacit consent, would become incompetent to fulfil its purpose; and the second Union would perish, like the first, by a sort of senile inaptitude. The gradual weakening of the federal tie, which may finally lead to the dissolution of the Union, is a distinct circumstance, that may produce a variety of minor consequences before it operates so violent a change. The confederation might still subsist, although its government were reduced to such a degree of inanition as to paralyze the nation, to cause internal anarchy, and to check the general prosperity of the country.

After having investigated the causes which may induce the Anglo-Americans to disunite, it is important to inquire whether, if the Union continues to subsist, their government will extend or contract its sphere of action, and whether it will become more energetic or more weak.

The Americans are evidently disposed to look upon their future condition with alarm. They perceive that in most of the nations of the world, the exercise of the rights of sovereignty tends to fall under the control of a few individuals, and they are dismayed by the idea that such will also be the case in their own country. Even the statesmen feel, or affect to feel, these fears; for, in America, centralization is by no means popular, and there is no surer means of courting the majority, than by inveighing against the encroachments of the central power. The Americans do not perceive that the countries in which this alarming tendency to centralization exists, are inhabited by a single people; while the fact of the Union being composed of different confederate communities, is sufficient to baffle all the inferences which might be drawn from analogous circumstances. I confess that I am inclined to consider the fears of a great number of Americans as purely imaginary; and far from participating in their dread of the consolidation of power in the hands of the Union, I think that the federal government is visibly losing strength.

To prove this assertion I shall not have recourse to any remote occurrences, but to circumstances which I have myself observed, and which belong to our own time.

An attentive examination of what is going on in the United States, will easily convince us that two opposite tendencies exist in that country, like two distinct currents flowing in contrary directions in the same channel. The Union has now existed for forty-five years, and in the course of that time a vast number of provincial prejudices, which were at first hostile to its power, have died away. The patriotic feeling which attached each of the Americans to his own native state is become less exclusive; and the different parts of the Union have become more intimately connected the better they have become acquainted with each other. The post,* that great instrument of intellectual intercourse, now reaches into the backwoods; and steamboats have established daily means of communication between the different points of the coast. An inland navigation of unexampled rapidity conveys commodities up and down the rivers of the country.† And to these facilities of nature and art may be added those restless cravings, that busy-mindedness, and love of pelf, which are constantly urging the American into active life, and bringing him into contact with his fellow-citizens. He crosses the country in every direction; he visits all the various populations of the land; and there is not a province in France, in which the natives are so well known to each other as the thirteen millions of men who cover the territory of the United States.

But while the Americans intermingle, they grow in resemblance of each other; the differences resulting from their climate, their origin, and their institutions; diminish; and they all draw nearer and nearer to the common type. Every year, thousands of men leave the north to settle in different parts of the Union: they bring with them their faith, their opinions, and their manners; and as they are more enlightened than the men among whom they are about to dwell, they soon rise to the head of affairs, and they adapt society to their own advantage. This continual emigration of the north to the south is peculiarly favourable to the fusion of all the different provincial characters into one national character. The civilization of the north appears to be the common standard, to which the whole nation will one day be assimilated.

The commercial ties which unite the confederate states are strengthened by the increasing manufactures of the Americans; and the union which began to exist in their opinions, gradually forms a part of their habits: the course of time has swept away the bugbear thoughts which haunted the imaginations of the citizens in 1789. The federal power is not become oppressive; it has not destroyed the independence of the states; it has not subjected the confederates to

---

* In 1832, the district of Michigan, which only contains 31,639 inhabitants, and is still an almost unexplored wilderness, possessed 940 miles of mail-roads. The territory of Arkansas, which is still more uncultivated, was already intersected by 1,938 miles of mail-roads. (See report of the general postoffice, 30th November, 1833.) The postage of newspapers alone in the whole Union amounted to 254,796 dollars.
† In the course of ten years, from 1821 to 1831, 271 steamboats have been launched upon the rivers which water the valley of the Mississippi alone. In 1829, 259 steamboats existed in the United States. (See Legislative Documents, No. 140, p. 274.)

monarchical institutions; and the Union has not rendered the lesser states dependant upon the larger ones; but the confederation has continued to increase in population, in wealth, and in power. I am therefore convinced that the natural obstacles to the continuance of the American Union are not so powerful at the present time as they were in 1789; and that the enemies of the Union are not so numerous.

Nevertheless, a careful examination of the history of the United States for the last forty-five years, will readily convince us that the federal power is declining; nor is it difficult to explain the causes of this phenomenon. When the constitution of 1789 was promulgated, the nation was a prey to anarchy; the Union, which succeeded this confusion, excited much dread and much animosity; but it was warmly supported because it satisfied an imperious want. Thus, although it was more attacked than it is now, the federal power soon reached the maximum of its authority, as is usually the case with a government which triumphs after having braced its strength by the struggle. At that time the interpretation of the constitution seemed to extend, rather than to repress, the federal sovereignity; and the Union offered, in several respects, the appearance of a single and undivided people, directed in its foreign and internal policy by a single government. But to attain this point the people had risen, to a certain extent, above itself.

The constitution had not destroyed the distinct sovereignty of the states; and all communities, of whatever nature they may be, are impelled by a secret propensity to assert their independence. This propensity is still more decided in a country like America, in which every village forms a sort of republic accustomed to conduct its own affairs It therefore cost the states an effort to submit to the federal supremacy; and all efforts, however successful they may be, necessarily subside with the causes in which they originated.

As the federal government consolidated its authority, America resumed its rank among the nations, peace returned to its frontiers, and public credit was restored; confusion was succeeded by a fixed state of things which was favourable to the full and free exercise of industrious enterprise. It was this very prosperity which made the Americans forget the cause to which it was attributable; and when once the danger was passed, the energy and the patriotism which had enabled them to brave it, disappeared from among them. No sooner were they delivered from the cares which oppressed them, than they easily returned to their ordinary habits, and gave themselves up without resistance to their natural inclinations. When a powerful government no longer appeared to be necessary, they once more began to think it irksome. The Union encouraged a general prosperity, and the states were not inclined to abandon the Union; but they desired to render the action of the power which represented that body as light as possible. The general principle of union was adopted, but in every minor detail there was an actual tendency to independence. The principle of confederation was every day more easily admitted and more rarely applied; so that the federal government brought about its own decline, while it was creating order and peace.

As soon as this tendency of public opinion began to be manifested externally, the leaders of parties, who live by the passions of the people, began to work it to their own advantage. The position of the federal government then became exceedingly critical. Its enemies were in possession of the popular favour; and they obtained the right of conducting its policy by pledging themselves to lessen its influence. From that time forward, the government of the Union has invariably been obliged to recede, as often as it has attempted to enter the lists with the government of the states. And whenever an interpretation of the terms of the federal constitution has been called for, that interpretation has most frequently been opposed to the Union, and favourable to the states.

The constitution invested the federal government with the right of providing for the interests of the nation; and it had been held that no other authority was so fit to superintend the "internal improvements" which affected the prosperity of the whole Union; such, for instance, as the cutting of canals. But the states were alarmed at a power, distinct from their own, which could thus dispose of a portion of their territory and they were afraid that the central government would, by this means, acquire a formidable extent of patronage within their own confines, and exercise a degree of influence which they intended to reserve exclusively to their own agents. The democratic party, which has constantly been opposed to the increase of the federal authority, then accused the congress of usurpation, and the chief magistrate of ambition. The central government was intimidated by the opposition; and it soon acknowledged its error, promising exactly to confine its influence, for the future, within the circle which was prescribed to it.

The constitution confers upon the Union the right of treating with foreign nations. The Indian tribes, which border upon the frontiers of the United States, had usually been regarded in this light. As long as these savages consented to retire before the civilized settlers, the federal right was not contested; but as soon as an Indian tribe attempted to fix its dwelling upon a given spot, the adjacent states claimed possession of the lands and the rights of sovereignty over the natives. The central government soon recognised both these claims; and after it had concluded treaties with the Indians as independent nations, it gave them up as subjects to the legislative tyranny of the states.*

Some of the states which had been founded upon the coast of the Atlantic, extended indefinitely to the west, into wild regions, where no European had ever penetrated. The states whose confines were irrevocably fixed, looked with a jealous eye upon the unbounded regions which the future would enable their neighbours to explore. The latter then agreed, with a view to conciliate the others, and to facilitate the act of union, to lay down their own boundaries, and to abandon all the territory which lay beyond those limits to the confederation at large.*

---

* See in the legislative documents already quoted in speaking of the Indians, the letter of the president of the United States to the Cherokees, his correspondence on this subject with his agents, and his messages to congress.

Thenceforward the federal government became the owner of all the uncultivated lands which lie beyond the borders of the thirteen states first confederated. It was invested with the right of parceling and selling them, and the sums derived from this source were exclusively reserved to the public treasury of the Union, in order to furnish supplies for purchasing tracts of country from the Indians, for opening roads to the remote settlements, and for accelerating the increase of civilization as much as possible. New states have, however, been formed in the course of time, in the midst of those wilds which were formerly ceded by the inhabitants of the shores of the Atlantic. Congress has gone on to sell, for the profit of the nation at large, the uncultivated lands which those new states contained. But the latter at length asserted that, as they were now fully constituted, they ought to enjoy the exclusive right of converting the produce of these sales to their own use. As their remonstrances became more and more threatening, congress thought fit to deprive the Union of a portion of the privileges which it had hitherto enjoyed; and at the end of 1832 it passed a law by which the greatest part of the revenue derived from the sale of lands was made over to the new western republics, although the lands themselves were not ceded to them.†

[The remark of the author, that "whenever an interpretation of the terms of the federal constitution has been called for, that interpretation has most frequently been opposed to the Union, and favourable to the states" requires considerable qualification. The instances which the author cites, are those of *legislative* interpretations, not those made by the judiciary. It may be questioned whether any of those cited by him are fair instances of *interpretation*. Although the then president and many of his friends doubted or denied the power of congress over many of the subjects mentioned by the author, yet the omission to exercise the powers thus questioned, did not proceed wholly from doubts of the constitutional authority. It must be remembered that all these questions affected local interests of the states or districts represented in congress, and the author has elsewhere shown the tendency of the local feeling to overcome all regard for the abstract interest of the Union. Hence many members have voted on these questions without reference to the constitutional question, and indeed without entertaining any doubt of their power. These instances may afford proof that the federal power is declining, as the author contends, but they do not prove any actual interpretation of the constitution. And so numerous and various are the circumstances to influence the decision of a legislative body like the congress of the United States, that the people do not regard them as sound and authoritative expositions of the true sense of the constitution, except perhaps in those very few cases, where there has been a constant and uninterrupted practice from the organization of the government. The judiciary is looked to as the only authentic expounder of the constitution, and until a law of congress has passed that

---

* The first act of cession was made by the state of New York in 1780; Virginia, Massachusetts, Connecticut, South and North Carolina, followed this example at different times, and lastly, the act of cession of Georgia was made as recently as 1802.
† It is true that the president refused his assent to this law; but he completely adopted it in principle. See message of 8th December, 1833.

ordeal, its constitutionality is open to question: of which our history furnishes many examples. . . . . There are errors in some of the instances given by our author, which would materially mislead, if not corrected. That in relation to the Indians proceeds upon the assumption that the United States claimed some rights over Indians or the territory occupied by them, inconsistent with the claims of the states. But this is a mistake. As to their lands, the United States never pretended to any right in them, except such as was granted by the cessions of the states. The principle universally acknowledged in the courts of the United States and of the several states, is, that by the treaty with Great Britain in which the independence of the colonies was acknowledged, the states became severally and individually independent, and as such succeeded to the rights of the crown of England to and over the lands within the boundaries of the respective states. The right of the crown in these lands was the absolute ownership, subject only to the rights of occupancy by the Indians so long as they remained a tribe. This right devolved to each state by the treaty which established their independence, and the United States have never questioned it. See 6th Cranch, 87; 8th Wheaton, 502, 884; 17th John's Reports, 231. On the other hand, the right of holding treaties with the Indians has universally been conceded to the United States. The right of a state to the lands occupied by the Indians, within the boundaries of such state, does not in the least conflict with the right of holding treaties on national subjects by the United States with those Indians. With respect to Indians residing in any territory *without* the boundaries of any state, or on lands ceded to the United States, the case is different; the United States are in such cases the proprietors of the soil, subject to the Indian right of occupancy, and when that right is extinguished the proprietorship becomes absolute. It will be seen, then, that in relation to the Indians and their lands, no question could arise respecting the interpretation of the constitution. The observation that "as soon as an Indian tribe attempted to fix its dwelling upon a given spot, the adjacent states claimed possession of the lands, and the rights of sovereignty over the natives"—is a strange compound of error and of truth. As above remarked, the Indian right of occupancy has ever been recognised by the states, with the exception of the case referred to by the author, in which Georgia claimed the right to possess certain lands occupied by the Cherokees. This was anomalous, and grew out of treaties and cessions, the details of which are too numerous and complicated for the limits of a note. But in no other cases have the states ever claimed the possession of lands occupied by Indians, without having previously extinguished their right by purchase.

As to the rights of sovereignty over the natives, the principle admitted in the United States is that all persons within the territorial limits of a state are and of necessity must be, subject to the jurisdiction of its laws. While the Indian tribes were numerous, distinct, and separate, from the whites, and possessed a government of their own, the state authorities, from considerations of policy, abstained from the exercise of criminal jurisdiction for offences committed by the Indians among themselves, although for offences against the whites they were subjected to the operation of the state laws. But as these tribes diminished in numbers, as those who remained among them became enervated by bad habits, and ceased to exercise any effectual government, humanity demanded that the power of the states should be interposed to protect the miserable remnants from the violence and outrage of each other. The first recorded instance of interposition in such a case was in 1821, when an Indian of the Seneca tribe in the state of New York was tried and convicted of murder on a squaw of the tribe. The courts declared their competency to take cognizance of such offences, and the legislature confirmed the declarations by a law.——Another instance of what the author calls interpretation of the constitution against the general government, is given by him in the proposed act of 1832, which passed both houses of congress, but was vetoed by the president, by which as he says, "the greatest part of the revenue derived from the sale of lands, was made over to the new western republics." But this act was not founded on any doubt of the title of the United States to the lands in question, or of its constitutional power over them, and cannot be cited as any evidence of the interpretation of the constitution. An error of fact in this statement ought to be corrected. The bill to which the author refers, is doubtless that usually called Mr. Clay's land bill. Instead of making over the greatest part of the revenue to the new states, it appropriated twelve and a half per cent. to them, in addition to five per cent. which had been originally granted for the purpose of making roads. See Niles's Register, vol. 42, p. 355.—*American Editor.*]

The slightest observation in the United States enables one to appreciate the advantages which the country derives from the bank. These advantages are of several kinds, but one of them is peculiarly striking to the stranger. The bank-notes of the United States are taken upon the borders of the desert for the same value as at Philadelphia, where the bank conducts its operations.*

The bank of the United States is nevertheless an object of great animosity. Its directors have proclaimed their hostility to the president; and they are accused, not without some show of probability, of having abused their influence to thwart his election. The president therefore attacks the establishment which they represent, with all the warmth of personal enmity; and he is encouraged in the pursuit of his revenge by the conviction that he is supported by the secret propensities of the majority. The bank may be regarded as the great monetary tie of the Union, just as congress is the great legislative tie; and the same passions which tend to render the states independent of the central power, contribute to the overthrow of the bank.

The bank of the United States always holds a great number of the notes issued by the provincial banks, which it can at any time oblige them to convert into cash. It has itself nothing to fear from a similar demand, as the extent of its resources enables it to meet all claims. But the existence of the provincial banks is thus threatened, and their operations are restricted, since they are only able to issue a quantity of notes duly proportioned to their capital. They submit with impatience to this salutary control. The newspapers which they have bought over, and the president, whose interest renders him their instrument, attack the bank with the greatest vehemence. They rouse the local passions, and the blind democratic instinct of the country to aid their cause;

---

* The present bank of the United States was established in 1816, with a capital of 35,000,000 dollars; its charter expires in 1836. Last year congress passed a law to renew it, but the president put his veto upon the bill. The struggle is still going on with great violence on either side, and the speedy fall of the bank may easily be foreseen.

and they assert that the bank-directors form a permanent aristocratic body, whose influence must ultimately be felt in the government, and must affect those principles of equality upon which society rests in America.

The contest between the bank and its opponents is only an incident in the great struggle which is going on in America between the provinces and the central power; between the spirit of democratic independence, and the spirit of gradation and subordination. I do not mean that the enemies of the bank are identically the same individuals, who, on other points, attack the federal government; but I assert that the attacks directed against the bank of the United States, originate in the same propensities which militate against the federal government; and that the very numerous opponents of the former afford a deplorable symptom of the decreasing support of the latter.

The Union has never displayed so much weakness as in the celebrated question of the tariff.* The wars of the French revolution and of 1812 had created manufacturing establishments in the north of the Union, by cutting off all free communication between America and Europe. When peace was concluded, and the channel of intercourse reopened, by which the produce of Europe was transmitted to the New World, the Americans thought fit to establish a system of import duties, for the twofold purpose of protecting their incipient manufactures, and of paying off the amount of the debt contracted during the war. The southern states, which have no manufactures to encourage, and which are exclusively agricultural, soon complained of this measure. Such were the simple facts, and I do not pretend to examine in this place whether their complaints were well founded or unjust.

As early as the year 1820, South Carolina declared, in a petition to Congress, that the tariff was "unconstitutional, oppressive, and unjust." And the states of Georgia, Virginia, North Carolina, Alabama, and Mississippi, subsequently remonstrated against it with more or less vigour. But Congress, far from lending an ear to these complaints, raised the scale of tariff duties in the years 1824 and 1828, and recognised anew the principle on which it was founded. A doctrine was then proclaimed, or rather revived, in the south, which took the name of nullification.

I have shown in the proper place that the object of the federal constitution was not to form a league, but to create a national government. The Americans of the United States form a sole and undivided people, in all the cases which are specified by that constitution; and upon these points the will of the nation is expressed, as it is in all constitutional nations, by the voice of the majority. When the majority has pronounced its decision, it is the duty of the minority to submit. Such is the sound legal doctrine, and the only one which agrees with the text of the constitution, and the known intention of those who framed it.

---

* See principally for the details of this affair, the legislative documents, 22d congress, 2d session, No. 30.

The partisans of nullification in the south maintain, on the contrary, that the intention of the Americans in uniting was not to reduce themselves to the condition of one and the same people; that they meant to constitute a league of independent states; and that each state, consequently, retains its entire sovereignty, if not *de facto*, at least *de jure*; and has the right of putting its own construction upon the laws of congress, and of suspending their execution within the limits of its own territory, if they are held to be unconstitutional or unjust.

The entire doctrine of nullification is comprised in a sentence uttered by Vice-President Calhoun,[5] the head of that party in the south, before the senate of the United States, in the year 1833: "The constitution is a compact to which the states were parties in their sovereign capacity; now, whenever a contract is entered into by parties which acknowledge no tribunal above their authority to decide in the last resort, each of them has a right to judge for itself in relation to the nature, extent, and obligations of the instrument." It is evident that a similar doctrine destroys the very basis of the federal constitution, and brings back all the evils of the old confederation, from which the Americans were supposed to have had a safe deliverance.

When South Carolina perceived that Congress turned a deaf ear to its remonstrances, it threatened to apply the doctrine of nullification to the federal tariff bill. Congress persisted in its former system; and at length the storm broke out. In the course of 1832 the citizens of South Carolina* named a national convention, to consult upon the extraordinary measures which they were called upon to take; and on the 24th November of the same year, this convention promulgated a law, under the form of a decree, which annulled the federal law of the tariff, forbade the levy of the imposts which that law commands, and refused to recognise the appeal which might be made to the federal courts of law.† This decree was only to be put into execution in the ensuing month of February, and it was intimated, that if Congress modified the tariff before that period, South Carolina might be induced to proceed no farther with her menaces; and a vague desire was afterward expressed of submitting the question to an extraordinary assembly of all the confederate states.

In the meantime South Carolina armed her militia, and prepared for war. But congress, which had slighted its suppliant subjects, lis-

---

* That is to say, the majority of the people; for the opposite party, called the Union party, always formed a very strong and active minority. Carolina may contain about 47,000 electors; 30,000 were in favour of nullification, and 17,000 opposed to it.

† This decree was preceded by a report of the committee by which it was framed, containing the explanation of the motives and object of the law. The following passage occurs in it, p. 34: "When the rights reserved by the constitution to the different states are deliberately violated, it is the duty and the right of those states to interfere, in order to check the progress of the evil, to resist usurpation, and to maintain, within their respective limits, those powers and privileges which belong to them as *independent sovereign states*. If they were destitute of this right, they would not be sovereign. South Carolina declares that she acknowledges no tribunal upon earth above her authority. She has indeed entered into a solemn compact of union with the other states: but she demands, and will exercise, the right of putting her own construction upon it; and when this compact is violated by her sister states, and by the government which they have created, she is determined to avail herself of the unquestionable right of judging what is the extent of the infraction, and what are the measures best fitted to obtain justice."

tened to their complaints as soon as they were found to have taken up arms.* A law was passed, by which the tariff duties were to be progressively reduced for ten years, until they were brought so low as not to exceed the amount of supplies necessary to the government.† Thus congress completely abandoned the principle of the tariff; and substituted a mere fiscal impost for a system of protective duties.‡ The government of the Union, in order to conceal its defeat, had recourse to an expedient which is very much in vogue with feeble governments. It yielded the point *de facto*, but it remained inflexible upon the principles in question; and while congress was altering the tariff law, it passed another bill, by which the president was invested with extraordinary powers, enabling him to overcome by force a resistance which was then no longer to be apprehended.

But South Carolina did not consent to leave the Union in the enjoyment of these scanty trophies of success: the same national convention which annulled the tariff bill, met again, and accepted the proffered concession: but at the same time it declared its unabated perseverance in the doctrine of nullification; and to prove what it said, it annulled the law investing the president with extraordinary powers, although it was very certain that the clauses of that law would never be carried into effect.

Almost all the controversies of which I have been speaking have taken place under the presidency of General Jackson; and it cannot be denied that in the question of the tariff he has supported the claims of the Union with vigour and with skill. I am however of opinion that the conduct of the individual who now represents the federal government, may be reckoned as one of the dangers which threaten its continuance.

Some persons in Europe have formed an opinion of the possible influence of General Jackson upon the affairs of his country, which appears highly extravagant to those who have seen more of the subject. We have been told that General Jackson has won sundry battles, that he is an energetic man, prone by nature and by habit to the use of force, covetous of power, and a despot by taste. All this may perhaps be true; but the inferences which have been drawn from these truths are exceedingly erroneous. It has been imagined that General Jackson is bent on establishing a dictatorship in America, on introducing a military spirit, and on giving a degree of influence to the central authority which cannot but be dangerous to provincial liberties. But in America, the time for similar undertakings, and the age for men of this kind, is not yet come; if General Jackson had entertained a hope of exercising his authority in this manner, he would infallibly have forfeited his political station, and compromised his life; accordingly he has not been so imprudent as to make any such attempt.

---

* Congress was finally decided to take this step by the conduct of the powerful state of Virginia, whose legislature offered to serve as a mediator between the Union and South Carolina. Hitherto the latter state had appeared to be entirely abandoned even by the states which had joined in her remonstrances.

† This law was passed on the 2d March, 1833.

‡ This bill was brought in by Mr. Clay, and it passed in four days through both houses of congress, by an immense majority.

Far from wishing to extend the federal power, the president belongs to the party which is desirous of limiting that power to the bare and precise letter of the constitution, and which never puts a construction upon that act, favourable to the government of the Union; far from standing forth as the champion of centralization, General Jackson is the agent of all the jealousies of the states; and he was placed in the lofty station he occupies, by the passions of the people which are most opposed to the central government. It is by perpetually flattering these passions, that he maintains his station and his popularity. General Jackson is the slave of the majority: he yields to its wishes, its propensities, and its demands; say rather, that he anticipates and forestalls them.

Whenever the governments of the states come into collision with that of the Union, the president is generally the first to question his own rights: he almost always outstrips the legislature; and when the extent of the federal power is controverted, he takes part, as it were, against himself; he conceals his official interests, and extinguishes his own natural inclinations. Not indeed that he is naturally weak or hostile to the Union; for when the majority decided against the claims of the partisans of nullification, he put himself at its head, asserted the doctrines which the nation held, distinctly and energetically, and was the first to recommend forcible measures; but General Jackson appears to me, if I may use the American expressions, to be a federalist by taste, and a republican by calculation.

General Jackson stoops to gain the favour of the majority: but when he feels that his popularity is secure, he overthrows all obstacles in the pursuit of the objects which the community approves, or of those which it does not look upon with a jealous eye. He is supported by a power with which his predecessors were unacquainted; and he tramples on his personal enemies wherever they cross his path, with a facility which no former president ever enjoyed; he takes upon himself the responsibility of measures which no one, before him, would have ventured to attempt; he even treats the national representatives with disdain approaching to insult; he puts his veto upon the laws of congress, and frequently neglects to reply to that powerful body. He is a favourite who sometimes treats his master roughly. The power of General Jackson perpetually increases; but that of the president declines: in his hands the federal government is strong, but it will pass enfeebled into the hands of his successor.

I am strangely mistaken if the federal government of the United States be not constantly losing strength, retiring gradually from public affairs, and narrowing its circle of action more and more. It is naturally feeble, but it now abandons even its pretensions to strength. On the other hand, I thought that I remarked a more lively sense of independence, and a more decided attachment to provincial government, in the states. The Union is to subsist, but to subsist as a shadow; it is to be strong in certain cases, and weak in all others; in time of warfare, it is to be able to concentrate all the forces of the nation and all the resources of the country in its hands; and in time of peace its existence is to be scarcely perceptible: as if this alternate debility and vigour were natural or possible.

I do not foresee anything for the present which may be able to check this general impulse of public opinion: the causes in which it originated do not cease to operate with the same effect. The change will therefore go on, and it may be predicted that, unless some extraordinary event occurs, the government of the Union will grow weaker and weaker every day.

I think, however, that the period is still remote, at which the federal power will be entirely extinguished by its inability to protect itself and to maintain peace in the country. The Union is sanctioned by the manners and desires of the people; its results are palpable, its benefits visible. When it is perceived that the weakness of the federal government compromises the existence of the Union, I do not doubt that a reaction will take place with a view to increase its strength.

The government of the United States is, of all the federal governments which have hitherto been established, the one which is most naturally destined to act. As long as it is only indirectly assailed by the interpretation of its laws, and as long as its substance is not seriously altered, a change of opinion, an internal crisis, or a war, may restore all the vigour which it requires. The point which I have been most anxious to put in a clear light is simply this; many people, especially in France, imagine that a change of opinion is going on in the United States, which is favourable to a centralization of power in the hands of the president and the congress. I hold that a contrary tendency may distinctly be observed. So far is the federal government from acquiring strength, and from threatening the sovereignty of the states, as it grows older, that I maintain it to be growing weaker and weaker, and that the sovereignty of the Union alone is in danger. Such are the facts which the present time discloses. The future conceals the final result of this tendency, and the events which may check, retard, or accelerate, the changes I have described; but I do not affect to be able to remove the veil which hides them from our sight.

OF THE REPUBLICAN INSTITUTIONS OF THE UNITED STATES, AND WHAT THEIR CHANCES OF DURATION ARE.

The Union is Accidental—The republican Institutions have more prospect of Permanence.—A Republic for the Present the natural State of the Anglo-Americans.—Reason of this.—In order to destroy it, all the Laws must be changed at the same Time, and a great Alteration take place in Manners.—Difficulties experienced by the Americans in creating in Aristocracy.

The dismemberment of the Union, by the introduction of war into the heart of those states which are now confederate, with standing armies, a dictatorship, and a heavy taxation, might eventually compromise the fate of the republican institutions. But we ought not to confound the future prospects of the republic with those of the Union. The Union is an accident, which will last only so long as circumstances are favourable to its existence; but a republican form of government seems to me to be the natural state of the Americans; which nothing but the continued action of hostile causes, always acting in the same direction, could change into a monarchy. The Union exists principally in the law which formed it; one revolution, one change in public opinion, might destroy it for ever; but the republic has a much deeper foundation to rest upon.

What is understood by republican government in the United States, is the slow and quiet action of society upon itself. It is a regular state of things really founded upon the enlightened will of the people. It is a conciliatory government under which resolutions are allowed time to ripen; and in which they are deliberately discussed, and executed with mature judgement. The republicans in the United States set a high value upon morality, respect religious belief, and acknowledge the existence of rights. They profess to think that a people ought to be moral, religious, and temperate, in proportion as it is free. What is called the republic in the United States, is the tranquil rule of the majority, which, after having had time to examine itself, and to give proof of its existence, is the common source of all the powers of the state. But the power of the majority is not of itself unlimited. In the moral world humanity, justice, and reason, enjoy an undisputed supremacy; in the political world vested rights are treated with no less deference. The majority recognises these two barriers; and if it now and then overstep them, it is because, like individuals, it has passions, and like them, it is prone to do what is wrong, while it discerns what is right.

But the demagogues of Europe have made strange discoveries. A republic is not, according to them, the rule of the majority, as has hitherto been thought, but the rule of those who are strenuous partisans of the majority. It is not the people who preponderates in this kind of government, but those who best know what is for the good of the people. A happy distinction, which allows men to act in the name of nations without consulting them, and to claim their gratitude while their rights are spurned. A republican government, moreover, is the only one which claims the right of doing whatever it chooses, and despising what men have hitherto respected, from the highest moral obligations to the vulgar rules of common sense. It had been supposed, until our time, that despotism was odious, under whatever form it appeared. But it is a discovery of modern days that there are such things as legitimate tyranny and holy injustice, provided they are exercised in the name of the people.

The ideas which the Americans have adopted respecting the republican form of government, render it easy for them to live under it, and ensure its duration. If, in their country, this form be often practically bad, at least it is theoretically good; and, in the end, the people always acts in conformity to it.

It was impossible, at the foundation of the states, and it would still be difficult, to establish a central administration in America. The inhabitants are dispersed over too great a space, and separated by too many natural obstacles, for one man to undertake to direct the details of their existence. America is therefore pre-eminently the country of provincial and municipal government. To this cause, which was plainly felt by all the Europeans of the New World, the Anglo-Americans added several others peculiar to themselves.

At the time of the settlement of the North American colonies, municipal liberty had already penetrated into the laws as well as the manners of the English, and the emigrants adopted it, not only as a necessary thing, but as a benefit which they knew how to appreciate. We have already seen the manner in which the colonies were founded: every province, and almost every district, was peopled separately by men who were strangers to each other, or who associated with very different purposes. The English settlers in the United States, therefore, early perceived that they were divided into a great number of small and distinct communities which belonged to no common centre; and that it was needful for each of these little communities to take care of its own affairs, since there did not appear to be any central authority which was naturally bound and easily enabled to provide for them. Thus, the nature of the country, the manner in which the British colonies were founded, the habits of the first emigrants, in short everything, united to promote, in an extraordinary degree, municipal and provincial liberties.

In the United States, therefore, the mass of the institutions of the country is essentially republican; and in order permanently to destroy the laws which form the basis of the republic, it would be necessary to abolish all the laws at once. At the present day, it would be even more difficult for a party to succeed in founding a monarchy in the United States, than for a set of men to proclaim that France should henceforward be a republic. Royalty would not find a system of legislation prepared for it beforehand; and a monarchy would then exist, really surrounded by republican institutions. The monarchical principle would likewise have great difficulty in penetrating into the manners of the Americans.

In the United States, the sovereignty of the people is not an isolated doctrine bearing no relation to the prevailing manners and ideas of the people: it may, on the contrary, be regarded as the last link of a chain of opinions which binds the whole Anglo-American world. That Providence has given to every human being the degree of reason necessary to direct himself in the affairs which interest him exclusively; such is the grand maxim upon which civil and political society rests in the United States. The father of a family applies it to his children; the master to his servants; the township to its officers; the province to its townships; the state to the provinces; the Union to the states; and when extended to the nation, it becomes the doctrine of the sovereignty of the people.

Thus, in the United States the fundamental principle of the republic is the same which governs the greater part of human actions; republican notions insinuate themselves into all the ideas, opinions, and habits of the Americans, while they are formally recognised by the legislation: and before this legislation can be altered, the whole community must undergo very serious changes. In the United States, even the religion of most of the citizens is republican, since it submits the truths of the other world to private judgement: as in politics the care of its temporal interests is abandoned to the good sense of the people. Thus every man is allowed freely to take that road which he thinks will lead him to heaven; just as the law permits every citizen to have the right of choosing his government.

It is evident that nothing but a long series of events, all having the same tendency, can substitute for this combination of laws, opinions, and manners, a mass of opposite opinions, manners, and laws.

If republican principles are to perish in America, they can only yield after a laborious social process, often interrupted, and as often resumed; they will have many apparent revivals, and will not become totally extinct until an entirely new people shall have succeeded to that which now exists. Now, it must be admitted that there is no symptom or presage of the approach of such a revolution. There is nothing more striking to a person newly arrived in the United States, than the kind of tumultuous agitation in which he finds political society. The laws are incessantly changing, and at first sight it seems impossible that a people so variable in its desires should avoid adopting, within a short space of time, a completely new form of government. Such apprehensions are, however, premature; the instability which affects political institutions is of two kinds, which ought not to be confounded: the first, which modifies secondary laws, is not incompatible with a very settled state of society; the other shakes the very foundations of the constitution, and attacks the fundamental principles of legislation; this species of instability is always followed by troubles and revolutions, and the nation which suffers under it, is in a state of violent transition.

Experience shows that these two kinds of legislative instability have no necessary connexion; for they have been found united or separate, according to times and circumstances. The first is common in the United States, but not the second: the Americans often change their laws, but the foundation of the constitution is respected.

In our days the republican principle rules in America, as the monarchical principle did in France under Louis XIV. The French of that period were not only friends of the monarchy, but they thought it impossible to put anything in its place; they received it as we receive the rays of the sun and the return of the seasons. Among them the royal power had neither advocates nor opponents. In like manner does the republican government exist in America, without contention or opposition; without proofs and arguments, by a tacit agreement, a sort of *consensus universalis*. It is, however, my opinion, that, by changing their administrative forms as often as they do, the inhabitants of the United States compromise the future stability of their government.

It may be apprehended that men, perpetually thwarted in their designs by the mutability of legislation, will learn to look upon republican institutions as an inconvenient form of society; the evil resulting from the instability of the secondary enactments, might then raise a doubt as to the nature of the fundamental principles of the constitution, and indirectly bring about a revolution; but this epoch is still very remote.

[It has been objected by an American review, that our author is mistaken in charging our laws with instability, and in answer to the charge, the permanence of our fundamental political institutions has been contrasted with the revolutions in France. But the objection proceeds upon a mistake of the author's meaning, which at this page is very clearly expressed. He refers to the instability which modifies *secondary laws*, and not to that which shakes the foundations of the constitution. The distinction is equally sound and philosophic, and those in the least acquainted with the history of our legislation, must bear witness to the truth of the author's remarks. The frequent revisions of the statutes of the states rendered necessary by the multitude, variety, and often the contradiction of the enactments, furnish abundant evidence of this instability.—*American Editor.*]

It may, however, be foreseen, even now, that when the Americans lose their republican institutions, they will speedily arrive at a despotic government, without a long interval of limited monarchy. Montesquieu remarked, that nothing is more absolute than the authority of a prince who immediately succeeds a republic, since the powers which had fearlessly been intrusted to an elected magistrate are then transferred to an hereditary sovereign. This is true in general, but it is more peculiarly applicable to a democratic republic. In the United States, the magistrates are not elected by a particular class of citizens, but by the majority of the nation; they are the immediate representatives of the passions of the multitude; and as they are wholly dependant upon its pleasure, they excite neither hatred nor fear: hence, as I have already shown, very little care has been taken to limit their influence, and they are left in possession of a vast deal of arbitrary power. This state of things has engendered habits which would outlive itself; the American magistrate would retain his power, but he would cease to be responsible for the exercise of it; and it is impossible to say what bounds could then be set to tyranny.

Some of our European politicians expect to see an aristocracy arise in America, and they already predict the exact period at which it will be able to assume the reins of government. I have previously observed, and I repeat my assertion, that the present tendency of American society appears to me to become more and more democratic. Nevertheless, I do not assert that the Americans will not, at some future time, restrict the circle of political rights in their country, or confiscate those rights to the advantage of a single individual; but I cannot imagine that they will ever bestow the exclusive exercise of them upon a privileged class of citizens, or, in other words, that they will ever found an aristocracy.

An aristocratic body is composed of a certain number of citizens, who, without being very far removed from the mass of the people, are, nevertheless, permanently stationed above it: a body which it is easy to touch, and difficult to strike; with which the people are in daily contact, but with which they can never combine. Nothing can be imagined more contrary to nature and to the secret propensities of the human heart, than a subjection of this kind; and men, who are left to follow their own bent, will always prefer the arbitrary power of a king to the regular administration of an aristocracy. Aristocratic institutions cannot subsist without laying down the inequality of men as a fundamental principle, as a part and parcel of the legislation, affecting the condition of the human family as much as it affects that of society; but these are things so repugnant to natural equity that they can only be extorted from men by constraint.

I do not think a single people can be quoted, since human society began to exist, which has, by its own free will and by its own exertions, created an aristocracy within its own bosom. All the aristocracies of the middle ages were founded by military conquest: the conqueror was the noble, the vanquished became the serf. Inequality was then imposed by force; and after it had been introduced into the manners of the country, it maintained its own authority, and was sanctioned by the legislation. Communities have existed which were aristocratic from their earliest origin, owing to circumstances anterior to that event, and which became more democratic in each succeeding age. Such was the destiny of the Romans, and of the Barbarians after them. But a people, having taken its rise in civilization and democracy, which should gradually establish an inequality of conditions until it arrived at inviolable privileges and exclusive castes, would be a novelty in the world; and nothing intimates that America is likely to furnish so singular an example.

REFLECTIONS ON THE CAUSES OF THE COMMERCIAL PROSPERITY OF THE UNITED STATES.

The Americans destined by Nature to be a great maritime People—Extent of their Coasts.—Depth of their Ports.—Size of their Rivers.—The commercial Superiority of the Anglo-Americans less attributable, however, to physical Circumstances than to moral intellectual Causes.—Reason of this Opinion.—Future Destiny of the Anglo-Americans as a commercial Nation.—The Dissolution of the Union would not check the maritime Vigour of the States.—Reason of this.—Anglo-Americans will naturally supply the Wants of the Inhabitants of South America.—They will become, like the English, the Factors of a great Portion of the World.

The coast of the United States, from the bay of Fundy to the Sabine river in the gulf of Mexico, is more than two thousand miles in extent. These shores form an unbroken line, and they are all subject to the same government. No nation in the world possesses vaster, deeper, or more secure ports for shipping than the Americans.

The inhabitants of the United States constitute a great civilized people, which fortune has placed in the midst of an uncultivated country, at a distance of three thousand miles from the central point of civilization. America consequently stands in daily need of European trade. The Americans will, no doubt, ultimately succeed in producing or manufacturing at home most of the articles which they require; but the two continents can never be independent of each other, so numerous are the natural ties which exist between their wants, their ideas, their habits, and their manners.

The Union produces peculiar commodities which are now become necessary to us, but which cannot be cultivated, or can only be raised at an enormous expense, upon the soil of Europe. The Americans only consume a small portion of this produce, and they are willing to sell us the rest. Europe is therefore the market of America, as America is the market of Europe; and maritime commerce is no less necessary to enable the inhabitants of the United States to transport their raw materials to the ports of Europe, than it is to enable us to supply them with our manufactured produce. The United States were therefore necessarily reduced to the alternative of increasing the business of other maritime nations to a great extent, if they had themselves declined to enter into commerce, as the Spaniards of Mexico have hitherto done; or, in the second place, of becoming one of the first trading powers of the globe.

The Anglo-Americans have always displayed a very decided taste for the sea. The declaration of independence broke the commercial restrictions which united them to England, and gave a fresh and powerful stimulus to their maritime genius. Ever since that time, the shipping of the Union has increased in almost the same rapid proportion as the number of its inhabitants. The Americans themselves now transport to their own shores nine tenths of the European produce which they consume.* And they also bring three quarters of the exports of the New World to the European consumer.† The ships of the United States fill the docks of Havre and of Liverpool; while the number of English and French vessels which are to be seen at New York is comparatively small.‡

Thus, not only does the American merchant face competition in his own country, but he even supports that of foreign nations in their own ports with success. This is readily explained by the fact that the vessels of the United States can cross the seas at a cheaper rate than any other vessels in the world. As long as the mercantile shipping of the United States preserves this superiority, it will not only retain what it has acquired, but it will constantly increase in prosperity.

It is difficult to say for what reason the Americans can trade at a

---

* The total value of goods imported during the year which ended on the 30th September, 1832, was 101,129,266 dollars. The value of the cargoes of foreign vessels did not amount to 10,731,039 dollars, or about one tenth of the entire sum.

† The value of goods exported during the same year amounted to 87,176,943 dollars; the value of goods exported by foreign vessels amounted to 21,036,183 dollars, or about one quarter of the whole sum. (Williams's Register, 1833, p. 398.)

‡ The tunnage of the vessels which entered all the ports of the Union in the years 1829, 1830, and 1831, amounted to 3,307,719 tuns, of which 544,571 tuns were foreign vessels; they stood therefore to the American vessels in a ratio of about 16 to 100. (National Calendar, 1833, p. 304.) The tunnage of the English vessels which entered the ports of London, Liverpool, and Hull, in the years 1820, 1826, and 1831, amounted to 443,800 tuns. The foreign vessels which entered the same ports during the same years, amounted to 159,431 tuns. The ratio between them was therefore about 36 to 100. (Companion to the Almanac, 1834, p. 169.) In the year 1832 the ratio between the foreign and British ships which entered the ports of Great Britain was 29 to 100.

lower rate than other nations; and one is at first led to attribute this circumstance to the physical or natural advantages which are within their reach; but this supposition is erroneous. The American vessels cost almost as much to build as our own;* they are not better built, and they generally last for a shorter time. The pay of the American sailor is more considerable than the pay on board European ships; which is proved by the great number of Europeans who are to be met with in the merchant-vessels of the United States. But I am of opinion that the true cause of their superiority must not be sought for in physical advantages, but that it is wholly attributable to their moral and intellectual qualities.

The following comparison will illustrate my meaning. During the campaigns of the revolution the French introduced a new system of tactics into the art of war, which perplexed the oldest generals, and very nearly destroyed the most ancient monarchies in Europe. They undertook (what had never been before attempted) to make shift without a number of things which had always been held to be indispensable in warfare; they required novel exertions on the part of their troops, which no civilized nations had ever thought of; they achieved great actions in an incredibly short space of time; and they risked human life without hesitation, to obtain the object in view. The French had less money and fewer men than their enemies; their resources were infinitely inferior; nevertheless they were constantly victorious, until their adversaries chose to imitate their example.

The Americans have introduced a similar system into their commercial speculations; and they do for cheapness what the French did for conquest. The European sailor navigates with prudence; he only sets sail when the weather is favourable; if an unforseen accident befalls him, he puts into port; at night he furls a portion of his canvass; and when the whitening billows intimate the vicinity of land, he checks his way, and takes observation of the sun. But the American neglects these precautions and braves these dangers. He weighs anchor in the midst of tempestuous gales; by night and by day he spreads his sheets to the wind; he repairs as he goes along such damage as his vessel may have sustained from the storm; and when he at last approaches the term of his voyage, he darts onward to the shore as if he already described a port. The Americans are often shipwrecked, but no trader crosses the seas so rapidly. And as they perform the same distance in a shorter time, they can perform it at a cheaper rate.

The European touches several times at different ports in the course of a long voyage; he loses a good deal of precious time in making the harbour, or in waiting for a favourable wind to leave it; and he pays daily dues to be allowed to remain there. The American starts from Boston to go to purchase tea in China: he arrives at Canton, stays there a few days, and then returns. In less than two years he has sailed as far as the entire circumference of the globe, and he has seen land

---

* Materials are, generally speaking, less expensive in America than in Europe, but the price of labour is much higher.

but once. It is true that during a voyage of eight or ten months he has drunk brackish water, and lived upon salt meat; that he has been in a continual contest with the sea, with disease, and with the tedium of monotony; but, upon his return, he can sell a pound of his tea for a halfpenny less than the English merchant, and his purpose is accomplished.

I cannot better explain my meaning than by saying that the Americans affect a sort of heroism in their manner of trading. But the European merchant will always find it very difficult to imitate his American competitor, who, in adopting the system which I have just described, follows not only a calculation of his gain, but an impulse of his nature.

The inhabitants of the United States are subject to all the wants and all the desires which result from an advanced stage of civilization; but as they are not surrounded by a community admirably adapted, like that of Europe, to satisfy their wants, they are often obliged to procure for themselves the various articles which education and habit have rendered necessaries. In America it sometimes happens that the same individual tills his field, builds his dwelling, contrives his tools, makes his shoes, and weaves the coarse stuff of which his dress is composed. This circumstance is prejudicial to the excellence of the work: but it powerfully contributes to awaken the intelligence of the workman. Nothing tends to materialize man, and to deprive his work of the faintest trace of mind, more than the extreme division of labour. In a country like America, where men devoted to special occupations are rare, a long apprenticeship cannot be required from any one who embraces a profession. The Americans therefore change their means of gaining a livelihood very readily; and they suit their occupations to the exigencies of the moment, in the manner most profitable to themselves. Men are to be met with who have successively been barristers, farmers, merchants, ministers of the gospel, and physicians. If the American be less perfect in each craft than the European, at least there is scarcely any trade with which he is utterly unacquainted. His capacity is more general, and the circle of his intelligence is enlarged.

The inhabitants of the United States are never fettered by the axioms of their profession; they escape from all the prejudices of their present station; they are not more attached to one line of operation than to another; they are not more prone to employ an old method than a new one; they have no rooted habits, and they easily shake off the influence which the habits of other nations might exercise upon their minds, from a conviction that their country is unlike any other, and that its situation is without a precedent in the world. America is a land of wonders, in which everything is in constant motion, and every movement seems an improvement. The idea of novelty is there indissolubly connected with the idea of melioration. No natural boundary seems to be set to the efforts of man; and what is not yet done is only what he has not yet attempted to do.

This perpetual change which goes on in the United States, these frequent vicissitudes of fortune, accompanied by such unforeseen fluctuations in private and in public wealth, serve to keep the minds of the citizens in a perpetual state of feverish agitation, which admirably invigorates their exertions, and keeps them in a state of excitement above the ordinary level of mankind. The whole life of an American is passed like a game of chance, a revolutionary crisis, or a battle. As the same causes are continually in operation throughout the country, they ultimately impart an irresistible impulse to the national character. The American, taken as a chance specimen of his countrymen, must then be a man of singular warmth in his desires, enterprising, fond of adventure, and above all of innovation. The same bent is manifest in all that he does; he introduces it into his political laws, his religious doctrines, his theories of social economy, and his domestic occupations; he bears it with him in the depth of the back woods, as well as in the business of the city. It is the same passion, applied to maritime commerce, which makes him the cheapest and the quickest trader in the world.

As long as the sailors of the United States retain these inspiriting advantages, and the practical superiority which they derive from them, they will not only continue to supply the wants of the producers and consumers of their own country, but they will tend more and more to become, like the English, the factors of all other peoples.* This prediction has already begun to be realized; we perceive that the American traders are introducing themselves as intermediate agents in the commerce of several European nations;† and America will offer a still wider field to their enterprise.

The great colonies which were founded in South America by the Spaniards and the Portuguese have since become empires. Civil war and oppression now lay waste those extensive regions. Population does not increase, and the thinly-scattered inhabitants are too much absorbed in the cares of self-defence even to attempt any melioration of their condition. Such, however, will not always be the case. Europe has succeeded by her own efforts in piercing the gloom of the middle ages; South America has the same Christian laws and Christian manners as we have; she contains all the germes of civilization which have grown amid the nations of Europe or their offsets, added to the advantages to be derived from our example; why then should she always remain uncivilized? It is clear that the question is simply one of time; at some future period, which may be more or less remote, the inhabitants of South America will constitute flourishing and enlightened nations.

But when the Spaniards and Portuguese of South America begin to feel the wants common to all civilized nations, they will still be unable to satisfy those wants for themselves; as the youngest children of civilization, they must perforce admit the superiority of their elder

---

* It must not be supposed that English vessels are exclusively employed in transporting foreign produce into England, or British produce to foreign countries: at the present day the merchant shipping of England may be regarded in the light of a vast system of public conveyances, ready to serve all the producers of the world, and to open communications between all peoples. The maritime genius of the Americans prompts them to enter into competition with the English.

† Part of the commerce of the Mediterranean is already carried on by American vessels.

brethren. They will be agriculturists long before they succeed in manufactures or commerce, and they will require the mediation of strangers to exchange their produce beyond seas for those articles for which a demand will begin to be felt.

It is unquestionable that the Americans of the north will one day supply the wants of the Americans of the south. Nature has placed them in contiguity; and has furnished the former with every means of knowing and appreciating those demands, of establishing a permanent connexion with those states, and of gradually filling their markets. The merchant of the United States could only forfeit these natural advantages if he were very inferior to the merchant of Europe; to whom he is, on the contrary, superior in several respects. The Americans of the United States already exercise a very considerable moral influence upon all the peoples of the New World. They are the source of intelligence, and all the nations which inhabit the same continent are already accustomed to consider them as the most enlightened, the most powerful, and the most wealthy members of the great American family. All eyes are therefore turned toward the Union; and the states of which that body is composed are the models which the other communities try to imitate to the best of their power: it is from the United States that they borrow their political principles and their laws.

The Americans of the United States stand in precisely the same position with regard to the peoples of South America as their fathers, the English, occupy with regard to the Italians, the Spaniards, the Portuguese, and all those nations of Europe, which receive their articles of daily consumption from England, because they are less advanced in civilization and trade. England is at this time the natural emporium of almost all the nations which are within its reach; the American Union will perform the same part in the other hemisphere; and every community which is founded, or which prospers in the New World, is founded and prospers to the advantage of the Anglo-Americans.

If the Union were to be dissolved, the commerce of the states which now compose it, would undoubtedly be checked for a time; but this consequence would be less perceptible than is generally supposed. It is evident that whatever may happen, the commercial states will remain united. They are all contiguous to each other; they have identically the same opinions, interests, and manners; and they are alone competent to form a very great maritime power. Even if the south of the Union were to become independent of the north, it would still require the service of those states. I have already observed that the south is not a commercial country, and nothing intimates that it is likely to become so. The Americans of the south of the United States will therefore be obliged, for a long time to come, to have recourse to strangers to export their produce, and to supply them with the commodities which are requisite to satisfy their wants. But the northern states are undoubtedly able to act as their intermediate agents cheaper than any other merchants. They will therefore retain that employment, for cheapness is the sovereign law of commerce. National claims and national prejudices cannot resist the influence of cheapness. Nothing can be more virulent than the hatred which exists between the Americans of the United States and the English. But notwithstanding these inimical feelings, the Americans derive the greater part of their manufactured commodities from England, because England supplies them at a cheaper rate than any other nation. Thus the increasing prosperity of America turns, notwithstanding the grudges of the Americans, to the advantage of British manufactures.

Reason shows and experience proves that no commercial prosperity can be durable if it cannot be united, in case of need, to naval force. This truth is as well understood in the United States as it can be anywhere else: the Americans are already able to make their flag respected; in a few years they will be able to make it feared. I am convinced that the dismemberment of the Union would not have the effect of diminishing the naval power of the Americans, but that it would powerfully contribute to increase it. At the present time the commercial states are connected with others which have not the same interests, and which frequently yield an unwilling consent to the increase of a maritime power by which they are only indirectly benefited. If, on the contrary, the commercial states of the Union formed one independent nation, commerce would become the foremost of their national interests; they would consequently be willing to make very great sacrifices to protect their shipping, and nothing would prevent them from pursuing their designs upon this point.

Nations, as well as men, almost always betray the most prominent features of their future destiny in their earliest years. When I contemplate the ardour with which the Anglo-Americans prosecute commercial enterprise, the advantages which befriend them, and the success of their undertakings, I cannot refrain from believing that they will one day become the first maritime power of the globe. They are born to rule the seas, as the Romans were to conquer the world.

CONCLUSION.

I have now nearly reached the close of my inquiry: hitherto, in speaking of the future destiny of the United States, I have endeavoured to divide my subject into distinct portions, in order to study each of them with more attention. My present object is to embrace the whole from one single point; the remarks I shall make will be less detailed, but they will be more sure. I shall perceive each object less distinctly, but I shall descry the principal facts with more certainty. A traveller, who has just left the walls of an immense city, climbs the neighbouring hill; as he goes farther off he loses sight of the men whom he has so recently quitted; their dwellings are confused in a dense mass; he can no longer distinguish the public squares, and he can scarcely trace out the great thoroughfares; but his eye has less difficulty in following the boundaries of the city, and for the first time he sees the shape of the vast whole. Such is the future destiny of the

British race in North America to my eye; the details of the stupendous picture are overhung with shade, but I conceive a clear idea of the entire subject.

The territory now occupied or possessed by the United States of America forms about one-twentieth part of the habitable earth. But extensive as these confines are, it must not be supposed that the Anglo-American race will always remain within them; indeed, it has already far overstepped them.

There was once a time at which we also might have created a great French nation in the American wilds, to counterbalance the influence of the English upon the destinies of the New World. France formerly possessed a territory in North America, scarcely less extensive than the whole of Europe. The three greatest rivers of that continent then flowed within her dominions. The Indian tribes which dwelt between the mouth of the St. Lawrence and the delta of the Mississippi were unaccustomed to any tongue but ours; and all the European settlements scattered over that immense region recalled the traditions of our country. Louisbourg, Montmorency, Duquesne, Saint-Louis, Vincennes, New Orleans, (for such were the names they bore), are words dear to France and familiar to our ears.

But a concourse of circumstances, which it would be tedious to enumerate,* have deprived us of this magnificent inheritance. Wherever the French settlers were numerically weak and partially established, they have disappeared; those who remain are collected on a small extent of country, and are now subject to other laws. The 400,000 French inhabitants of Lower Canada constitute, at the present time, the remnant of an old nation lost in the midst of a new people. A foreign population is increasing around them unceasingly and on all sides, which already penetrates among the ancient masters of the country, predominates in their cities, and corrupts their language. This population is identical with that of the United States; it is therefore with truth that I asserted that the British race is not confined within the frontiers of the Union, since it already extends to the northeast.

To the northwest nothing is to be met with but a few insignificant Russian settlements; but to the southwest, Mexico presents a barrier to the Anglo-Americans. Thus, the Spaniards and the Anglo-Americans are, properly speaking, the only two races which divide the possession of the New World. The limits of separation between them have been settled by a treaty; but although the conditions of that treaty are exceedingly favourable to the Anglo-Americans, I do not doubt that they will shortly infringe this arrangement. Vast provinces, extending beyond the frontiers of the Union toward Mexico, are still destitute of inhabitants. The natives of the United States will forestall

---

* The foremost of these circumstances is, that nations which are accustomed to free institutions and municipal government are better able than any others to found prosperous colonies. The habit of thinking and governing for oneself is indispensable in a new country, where success necessarily depends, in a great measure, upon the individual exertions of the settlers.

the rightful occupants of these solitary regions. They will take possession of the soil, and establish social institutions, so that when the legal owner arrives at length, he will find the wilderness under cultivation, and strangers quietly settled in the midst of his inheritance.

The lands of the New World belong to the first occupant, and they are the natural reward of the swiftest pioneer. Even the countries which are already peopled will have some difficulty in securing themselves from this invasion. I have already alluded to what is taking place in the province of Texas. The inhabitants of the United States are perpetually migrating to Texas, where they purchase land; and although they conform to the laws of the country, they are gradually founding the empire of their own language and their own manners. The province of Texas is still part of the Mexican dominions, but it will soon contain no Mexicans: the same thing has occurred whenever the Anglo-Americans have come into contact with populations of a different origin.

[The prophetic accuracy of the author, in relation to the present actual condition of Texas, exhibits the sound and clear perception with which he surveyed our institutions and character.—*American Editor.*]

It cannot be denied that the British race has acquired an amazing preponderance over all the other European faces in the New World; and that it is very superior to them in civilization, in industry, and in power. As long as it is only surrounded by desert or thinly-peopled countries, as long as it encounters no dense populations upon its route, through which it cannot work its way, it will assuredly continue to spread. The lines marked out by treaties will not stop it; but it will everywhere transgress these imaginary barriers.

The geographical position of the British race in the New World is peculiarly favourable to its rapid increase. Above its northern frontiers the icy regions of the pole extend; and a few degrees below its southern confines lies the burning climate of the equator. The Anglo-Americans are therefore placed in the most temperate and habitable zone of the continent.

It is generally supposed that the prodigious increase of population in the United States is posterior to their declaration of independence. But this is an error: the population increased as rapidly under the colonial system as it does at the present day; that is to say, it doubled in about twenty-two years. But this proportion, which is now applied to millions, was then applied to thousands, or inhabitants; and the same fact which was scarcely noticeable a century ago, is now evident to every observer.

The British subjects in Canada, who are dependant on a king, augment and spread almost as rapidly as the British settlers of the United States, who live under a republican government. During the war of independence, which lasted eight years, the population continued to increase without intermission in the same ratio. Although powerful Indian nations allied with the English existed, at that time, upon the western frontiers, the emigration westward was never checked. While the enemy laid waste the shores of the Atlantic, Kentucky, the western parts of Pennyslvania, and the states of Vermont and of Maine were filling with inhabitants. Nor did the unsettled state of the constitution, which succeeded the war, prevent the increase of the population, or stop its progress across the wilds. Thus, the difference of laws, the various conditions of peace and war, of order and of anarchy, have exercised no perceptible influence upon the gradual development of the Anglo-Americans. This may be readily understood: for the fact is, that no causes are sufficiently general to exercise a simultaneous influence over the whole of so extensive a territory. One portion of the country always offers a sure retreat from the calamities which afflict another part; and however great may be the evil, the remedy which is at hand is greater still.

It must not, then, be imagined that the impulse of the British race in the New World can be arrested. The dismemberment of the Union, and the hostilities which might ensue, the abolition of republican institutions, and the tyrannical government which might succeed it, may retard this impulse, but they cannot prevent it from ultimately fulfilling the destinies to which that race is reserved. No power upon earth can close upon the emigrants that fertile wilderness which offers resources to all industry and a refuge from all want. Future events, of whatever nature they may be, will not deprive the Americans of their climate or of their inland seas, of their great rivers or of their exuberant soil. Nor will bad laws, revolutions, and anarchy, be able to obliterate that love of prosperity and that spirit of enterprise which seem to be the distinctive characteristics of their race, or to extinguish that knowledge which guides them on their way.

Thus, in the midst of the uncertain future, one event at least is sure. At a period which may be said to be near (for we are speaking of the life of a nation), the Anglo-Americans will alone cover the immense space contained between the polar regions and the tropics, extending from the coasts of the Atlantic to the shores of the Pacific ocean. The territory which will probably be occupied by the Anglo-Americans at some future time, may be computed to equal three quarters of Europe in extent.* The climate of the Union is upon the whole preferable to that of Europe, and its natural advantages are not less great; it is therefore evident that its population will at some future time be proportionate to our own. Europe, divided as it is between so many different nations, and torn as it had been by incessant wars and the barbarous manners of the Middle Ages, has notwithstanding attained a population of 410 inhabitants to the square league.† What cause can prevent the United States from having as numerous a population in time?

Many ages must elapse before the divers offsets of the British race in America cease to present the same homogeneous characteristics: and the time cannot be foreseen at which a permanent inequality of

---

* The United States already extend over a territory equal to one half of Europe. The area of Europe is 500,000 square leagues, and its population 205,000,000 of inhabitants. (Maltebrun, liv. 114, vol. vi., p. 4.)
† See Maltebrun, liv. 116, vol. vi., p. 92.

conditions will be established in the New World. Whatever differences may arise, from peace or from war, from freedom or oppression, from prosperity or want, between the destinies of the different descendants of the great Anglo-American family, they will at least preserve an analogous social condition, and they will hold in common the customs and the opinions to which that social condition has given birth.

In the Middle Ages, the tie of religion was sufficiently powerful to imbue all the different populations of Europe with the same civilization. The British of the New World have a thousand other reciprocal ties; and they live at a time when the tendency to equality is general among mankind. The Middle Ages were a period when everything was broken up; when each people, each province, each city, and each family, had a strong tendency to maintain its distinct individuality. At the present time an opposite tendency seems to prevail, and the nations seem to be advancing to unity. Our means of intellectual intercourse unite the most remote parts of the earth; and it is impossible for men to remain strangers to each other, or to be ignorant of the events which are taking place in any corner of the globe. The consequence is, that there is less difference, at the present day, between the Europeans and their descendants in the New World, than there was between certain towns in the thirteenth century, which were only separated by a river. If this tendency to assimilation brings foreign nations closer to each other, it must *a fortiori* prevent the descendants of the same people from becoming aliens to each other.

The time will therefore come when one hundred and fifty millions of men will be living in North America,* equal in condition, the progeny of one race, owing their origin to the same cause, and preserving the same civilization, the same language, the same religion, the same habits, the same manners, and imbued with the same opinions, propagated under the same forms. The rest is uncertain, but this is certain; and it is a fact new to the world—a fact fraught with such portentous consequences as to battle the efforts even of the imagination.

There are, at the present time, two great nations in the world, which seem to tend toward the same end, although they started from different points; I allude to the Russians and the Americans. Both of them have grown up unnoticed; and while the attention of mankind was directed elsewhere, they have suddenly assumed a most prominent place among the nations; and the world learned their existence and their greatness at almost the same time.

All other nations seem to have nearly reached their natural limits, and only to be charged with the maintenance of their power: but these are still in the act of growth;† all the others are stopped, or continue to advance with extreme difficulty; these are proceeding with ease and with celerity along a path to which the human eye can assign no term.

---

* This would be a population proportionate to that of Europe, taken at a mean rate of 410 inhabitants to the square league.

† Russia is the country in the Old World in which population increases most rapidly in proportion.

The American struggles against the natural obstacles which oppose him; the adversaries of the Russian are men: the former combats the wilderness and savage life; the latter, civilization with all its weapons and its arts; the conquests of the one are therefore gained by the ploughshare; those of the other, by the sword. The Anglo-American relies upon personal interest to accomplish his ends, and gives free scope to the unguided exertions and common sense of the citizens; the Russian centres all the authority of society in a single arm: the principal instrument of the former is freedom; of the latter, servitude. Their starting-point is different, and their courses are not the same; yet each of them seems to be marked out by the will of Heaven to sway the destinies of half the globe.

Appendix

APPENDIX A

For information concerning all the countries of the West which have not been visited by Europeans, consult the account of two expeditions undertaken at the expense of congress by Major Long. This traveller particularly mentions, on the subject of the great American desert, that a line may be drawn nearly parallel to the 20th degree of longitude* (meridian of Washington), beginning from the Red river and ending at the river Platte. From this imaginary line to the Rocky mountains, which bound the valley of the Mississippi on the west, lie immense plains, which are almost entirely covered with sand, incapable of cultivation, or scattered over with masses of granite. In summer these plains are quite destitute of water, and nothing is to be seen on them but herds of buffaloes and wild horses. Some hordes of Indians are also found there, but in no great number.

Major Long was told that in travelling northward from the river Platte, you find the same desert lying constantly on the left; but he was unable to ascertain the truth of this report. (Long's Expedition, vol. ii. p. 361.)

However worthy of confidence may be the narrative of Major Long, it must be remembered that he only passed through the country of which he speaks, without deviating widely from the line which he had traced out for his journey.

APPENDIX B.

South America, in the regions between the tropics, produces an incredible profusion of climbing-plants, of which the Flora of the Antilles alone presents us with forty different species.

Among the most graceful of these shrubs is the passion-flower, which, according to Descourtiz, grows with such luxuriance in the Antilles, as to climb trees by means of the tendrils with which it is provided, and form moving bowers of rich and elegant festoons, decorated with blue and purple flowers, and fragrant with perfume. (VOL. i., p. 265.)

---

* The 20th degree of longitude according to the meridian of Washington, agrees very nearly with the 97th degree on the meridian of Greenwich.

The *mimosa scandens* (acacia à grandes gousses) is a creeper of enormous and rapid growth, which climbs from tree to tree, and sometimes covers more than half a league. (Vol. iii., p. 227.)

APPENDIX C.

The languages which are spoken by the Indians of America, from the Pole to Cape Horn, are said to be all formed upon the same model, and subject to the same grammatical rules; whence it may fairly be concluded that all the Indian nations sprang from the same stock.

Each tribe of the American continent speaks a different dialect; but the number of languages, properly so called, is very small, a fact which tends to prove that the nations of the New World had not a very remote origin.

Moreover, the languages of America have a great degree of regularity; from which it seems probable that the tribes which employ them had not undergone any great revolutions, or been incorporated, voluntary or by constraint, with foreign nations. For it is generally the union of several languages into one which produces grammatical irregularities.

It is not long since the American languages, especially those of the north, first attracted the serious attention of philologists, when the discovery was made that this idiom of a barbarous people was the product of a complicated system of ideas and very learned combinations. These languages were found to be very rich, and great pains had been taken at their formation to render them agreeable to the ear.

The grammatical system of the Americans differs from all others in several points, but especially in the following:—

Some nations in Europe, among others the Germans, have the power of combining at pleasure different expressions, and thus giving a complex sense to certain words. The Indians have given a most surprising extension to this power, so as to arrive at the means of connecting a great number of ideas with a single term. This will be easily understood with the help of an example quoted by Mr. Duponceau, in the Memoirs of the Philosophical Society of America.

"A Delaware woman playing with a cat, or a young dog," says this writer, 'is heard to pronounce the word *kuligatschis*; which is thus composed: *k* is the sign of the second person, and signifies 'thou' or 'thy'; *uli* is a part of the word *wulit*, which signifies 'beautiful,' 'pretty'; *gat* is another fragment of the word *wichgat*, which means 'paw'; and lastly, *schis* is a diminutive giving the idea of smallness. Thus is one word the Indian woman has expressed, 'Thy pretty little paw.' "

Take another example of the felicity with which the savages of America, have composed their words. A young man of Delaware is called *pilape*. This word is formed from *pilsit*, chaste, innocent; and *lenape*, man; viz, man in his purity and innocence.

This facility of combining words is most remarkable in the strange formation of their verbs. The most complex action is often expressed by a single verb, which serves to convey all the shades of an idea by the modification of its construction.

Those who may wish to examine more in detail this subject, which I have only glanced at superficially, should read:—

1. The correspondence of Mr. Duponceau and the Rev. Mr. Hecwelder relative to the Indian languages; which is to be found in the first volume of the Memoirs of the Philosophical Society of America, published at Philadelphia, 1819, by Abraham Small; vol. i., pp. 356–464.

2. The grammar of the Delaware or Lenape language by Geiberger, and the preface of Mr. Duponceau. All these are in the same collection, vol. iii.

3. An excellent account of these works, which is at the end of the 6th volume of the American Encyclopedia.

APPENDIX D.

See in Charlevoix, vol. i., p. 235, the history of the first war which the French inhabitants of Canada carried on, in 1610, against the Iroquois. The latter, armed with bows and arrows, offered a desperate resistance to the French and their allies. Charlevoix is not a great painter, yet he exhibits clearly enough, in this narrative, the contrast between the European manners and those of savages, as well as the different way in which the two races of men understood the sense of honour.

When the French, says he, seized upon the beaver-skins which covered the Indians who had fallen, the Hurons, their allies, were greatly offended at this proceeding; but without hesitation they set to work in their usual manner, inflicting horrid cruelties upon the prisoners, and devouring one of those who had been killed, which made the Frenchmen shudder. The barbarians prided themselves upon a scrupulousness which they were surprised at not finding in our nation; and could not understand that there was less to reprehend in the stripping of dead bodies, than in the devouring of their flesh like wild beasts.

Charlevoix in another place (vol. i., p. 230) thus describes the first torture of which Champlain was an eyewitness, and the return of the Hurons into their own village.

"Having proceeded about eight leagues," says he, "our allies halted: and having singled out one of their captives, they reproached him with all the cruelties which he had practised upon the warriors of their nation who had fallen into his hands, and told him that he might expect to be treated in like manner; adding, that if he had any spirit he would prove it by singing. He immediately chanted forth his death-song, and then his war-song, and all the songs he knew, 'but in a very mournful strain,' says Champlain, who was not then aware that all savage music has a melancholy character. The tortures which succeeded, accompanied by all the horrors which we shall mention hereafter, terrified the French, who made every effort to put a stop to them, but in vain. The following night one of the Hurons having dreamed that they were pursued, the retreat was changed to a real flight, and the savages never stopped until they were out of the reach of danger.

The moment they perceived the cabins of their own village, they cut themselves long sticks, to which they fastened the scalps which had fallen to their share, and carried them in triumph. At this sight, the women swam to the canoes, where they received the bloody scalps from the hands of their husbands, and tied them round their necks.

The warriors offered one of these horrible trophies to Champlain; they also presented him with some bows and arrows—the only spoils of the Iroquois which they had ventured to seize—entreating him to show them to the king of France.

Champlain lived a whole winter quite alone among these barbarians, without being under any alarm for his person or property.

APPENDIX E.

Although the puritanical strictness which presided over the establishment of the English colonies in America is now much relaxed, remarkable traces of it are still found in their habits and their laws. In 1792, at the very time when the anti-Christian republic of France began its ephemeral existence, the legislative body of Massachusetts promulgated the following law, to compel the citizens to observe the sabbath. We give the preamble and the principal articles of this law, which is worthy of the reader's attention.

"Whereas," says the legislator, "the observation of the Sunday is an affair of public interest; inasmuch as it produces a necessary suspension of labour, leads men to reflect upon the duties of life and the errors to which human nature is liable, and provides for the public and private worship of God the creator and governor of the universe, and for the performance of such acts of charity as are the ornament and comfort of Christian societies:—

"Whereas, irreligious or light-minded persons, forgetting the duties which the sabbath imposes, and the benefits which these duties confer on society, are known to profane its sanctity, by following their pleasures or their affairs; this way of acting being contrary to their own interest as Christians, and calculated to annoy those who do not follow their example; being also of great injury to society at large, by spreading a taste for dissipation and dissolute manners;—

"Be it enacted and ordained by the governor, council, and representatives convened in general court of assembly, that all and every person and persons shall, on that day, carefully apply themselves to the duties of religion and piety; that no tradesman or laborer shall exercise his ordinary calling, and that no game or recreation shall be used on the Lord's day, upon pain of forfeiting ten shillings;—

"That no one shall travel on that day, or any part thereof, under pain of forfeiting twenty shillings; that no vessel shall leave a harbour of the colony; that no persons shall keep outside the meetinghouse during the time of public worship, or profane the time by playing or talking, on penalty of five shillings.

"Public-houses shall not entertain any other than strangers or lodgers, under a penalty of five shillings for every person found drinking or abiding therein.

"Any person in health who, without sufficient reason, shall omit to worship God in public during three months, shall be condemned to a fine of ten shillings.

"Any person guilty of misbehaviour in a place of public worship shall be fined from five to forty shillings.

"These laws are to be enforced by the tithing-men of each township, who have authority to visit public-houses on the Sunday. The innkeeper who shall refuse them admittance shall be fined forty shillings for such offence.

"The tithing-men are to stop travellers, and to require of them their reason for being on the road on Sunday: any one refusing to answer shall be sentenced to pay a fine not exceeding five pounds sterling. If the reason given by the traveller be not deemed by the tithing-men sufficient, he may bring the traveller before the justice of the peace of the district." (*Law of the 8th March, 1792: General Laws of Massachusetts*, vol. i., p. 410.)

"On the 11th March, 1797, a new law increased the amount of fines, half of which was to be given to the informer. (*Same collection,* vol. ii., p. 525.)

On the 16th February, 1816, a new law confirmed these measures. (*Same collection,* vol. ii., p. 405.)

Similar enactments exist in the laws of the state of New York, revised in 1827 and 1828. (See *Revised Statutes,* part i., chapter 20, p. 675.) In these it is declared that no one is allowed on the sabbath to sport, to fish, play at games, or to frequent houses where liquor is sold. No one can travel except in case of necessity.

And this is not the only trace which the religious strictness and austere manners of the first emigrants have left behind them in the American laws.

In the revised statutes of the state of New York, vol. i., p. 662, is the following clause:—

"Whoever shall win or lose in the space of twenty-four hours, by gaming or betting, the sum of twenty-five dollars, shall be found guilty of a misdemeanor, and, upon conviction, shall be condemned to pay a fine equal to at least five times the value of the sum lost or won; which will be paid to the inspector of the poor of the township. He that loses twenty-five dollars or more, may bring an action to recover them; and if he neglects to do so, the inspector of the poor may prosecute the winner, and oblige him to pay into the poor's box both the sum he has gained and three times as much beside."

The laws we quote from are of recent date; but they are unintelligible without going back to the very origin of the colonies. I have no doubt that in our days the penal part of these laws is very rarely applied. Laws preserve their inflexibility long after the manners of a nation have yielded to the influence of time. It is still true, however, that nothing strikes a foreigner on his arrival in America more forcibly than the regard to the sabbath.

There is one, in particular, of the large American cities, in which all social movements begin to be suspended even on Saturday evening. You traverse its streets at the hour at which you expect men in the middle of life to be engaged in business, and young people in pleasure; and you meet with solitude and silence. Not only have all ceased to work, but they appear to have ceased to exist. Neither the movements of industry are heard, nor the accents of joy, nor even the confused murmur which arises from the midst of a great city. Chains are hung across the streets in the neighbourhood of the churches; the half-closed shutters of the houses scarcely admit a ray of sun into the dwellings of the citizens. Now and then you perceive a solitary individual, who glides silently along the deserted streets and lanes.

Next day, at early dawn, the rolling of carriages, the noise of hammers, the cries of the population, begin to make themselves heard again. The city is awake. An eager crowd hastens toward the resort of commerce and industry; everything around you bespeaks motion, bustle, hurry. A feverish activity succeeds to the lethargic stupor of yesterday: you might almost suppose that they had but one day to acquire wealth and to enjoy it.

APPENDIX F.

It is unnecessary for me to say, that in the chapter which has just been read, I have not had the intention of giving a history of America. My only object was to enable the reader to appreciate the influence which the opinions and manners of the first emigrants had exercised upon the fate of the different colonies and of the Union in general. I have therefore confined myself to the quotation of a few detached fragments.

I do not know whether I am deceived, but it appears to me that by pursuing the path which I have merely pointed out, it would be easy to present such pictures of the American republics as would not be unworthy the attention of the public, and could not fail to suggest to the statesman matter for reflection.

Not being able to devote myself to this labour, I am anxious to render it easy to others; and, for this purpose, I subjoin a short catalogue and analysis of the works which seem to me the most important to consult.

At the head of the general documents, which it would be advantageous to examine, I place the work entitled An Historical Collection of State Papers, and other authentic Documents, intended as Materials for a History of the United States of America, by Ebenezer Hasard. The first volume of this compilation, which was printed at Philadelphia in 1792, contains a literal copy of all the charters granted by the crown of England to the emigrants, as well as the principal acts of the colonial governments, during the commencement of their existence. Among other authentic documents, we here find a great many relating to the affairs of New England and Virginia during this period. The second volume is almost entirely devoted to the acts of the confederation of 1643. This federal compact, which was entered into by the colonies of New England with the view of resisting the Indians, was the first instance of union afforded by the Anglo-Americans. There were besides many other confederations of the same nature, before the famous one of 1776, which brought about the independence of the colonies.

Each colony has, besides, its own historic monuments, some of which are extremely curious; beginning with Virginia, the state which was first peopled. The earliest historian of Virginia was its founder, Capt. John Smith. Capt. Smith has left us an octavo volume, entitled, The generall Historie of Virginia and New England, by Captain John Smith, sometymes Governour in those Countryes, and Admirall of New England; printed at London in 1627. The work is adorned with curious maps and engravings of the time when it appeared; the narrative extends from the year 1584 to 1626. Smith's work is highly and deservedly esteemed. The author was one of the most celebrated adventurers of a period of remarkable adventure; his book breathes that ardour for discovery, that spirit of enterprise which characterized the men of his time, when the manners of chivalry were united to zeal for commerce, and made subservient to the acquisition of wealth.

But Capt. Smith is remarkable for uniting, to the virtues which characterized his contemporaries, several qualities to which they were generally strangers: his style is simple and concise, his narratives bear the stamp of truth, and his descriptions are free from false ornament.

This author throws most valuable light upon the state and condition of the Indians at the time when North America was first discovered.

The second historian to consult is Beverley, who commences his narrative with the year 1585, and ends it with 1700. The first part of his book contains historical documents, properly so called, relative to the infancy of the colony. The second affords a most curious picture of the state of the Indians at this remote period. The third conveys very clear ideas concerning the manners, social condition, laws, and political customs of the Virginians in the author's lifetime.

Beverley was a native of Virginia, which occasions him to say at the beginning of his book that he entreats his readers not to exercise their critical severity upon it, since, having been born in the Indies, he does not aspire to purity of language. Notwithstanding this colonial modesty, the author shows throughout his book the impatience with which he endures the supremacy of the mother-country. In this work of Beverley are also found numerous traces of that spirit of civil liberty which animated the English colonies of America at the time when he wrote. He also shows the dissensions which existed among them and retarded their independence. Beverley detests his catholic neighbours of Maryland even more than he hates the English government: his style is simple, his narrative interesting and apparently trustworthy.

I saw in America another work which ought to be consulted, entitled, The History of Virginia, by William Stith. This book affords some curious details, but I thought it long and diffuse.

The most ancient as well as the best document to be consulted on the history of Carolina is a work in small quarto, entitled, The History of Carolina, by John Lawson, printed at London in 1718. This work contains, in the first part, a journey of discovery in the west of Carolina; the account of which, given in the form of a journal, is in general confused and superficial; but it contains a very striking description of the mortality caused among the savages of that time, both by the small-pox and the immoderate use of brandy; and with a curious picture of the corruption of manners prevalent among them, which was increased by the presence of Europeans. The second part of Lawson's book is taken up with a description of the physical condition of Carolina, and its productions. In the third part, the author gives an interesting account of the manners, customs, and government of the Indians at that period. There is a good deal of talent and originality in this part of the work.

Lawson concludes his history with a copy of the charter granted to the Carolinas in the reign of Charles II. The general tone of this work is light, and often licentious, forming a perfect contrast to the solemn style of the works published at the same period in New England. Lawson's history is extremely scarce in America, and cannot be procured in Europe. There is, however, a copy of it in the royal library at Paris.

From the southern extremity of the United States I pass at once to the northern limit; as the intermediate space was not peopled till a later period.

I must first point out a very curious compilation, entitled, Collection of the Massachusetts Historical Society, printed for the first time at Boston in 1792, and reprinted in 1806. The collection of which I speak, and which is continued to the present day, contains a great number of very valuable documents relating to the history of the different states of New England. Among them are letters which have never been published, and authentic pieces which had been buried in provincial archives. The whole work of Gookin concerning the Indians is inserted there.

I have mentioned several times, in the chapter to which this note relates, the work of Nathaniel Norton, entitled New England's Memorial; sufficiently perhaps to prove that it deserves the attention of those who would be conversant with the history of New England. This book is in 8vo, and was reprinted at Boston in 1826.

The most valuable and important authority which exists upon the history of New England is the work of the Rev. Cotton Mather entitled Magnalia Christi Americana, or the Ecclesiastical History of New England, 1620–1698, 2 vols. 8vo, reprinted at Hartford, United States, in 1820.*

The author divided his work into seven books. The first presents the history of the events which prepared and brought about the establishment of New England. The second contains the lives of the first governors and chief magistrates who presided over the country. The third is devoted to the lives and labours of the evangelical ministers who during the same period had the care of souls. In the fourth the author relates the institution and progress of the University of Cambridge (Massachusetts). In the fifth he describes the principles and the discipline of the Church of New England. The sixth is taken up in retracing certain facts, which, in the opinion of Mather, prove the merciful interposition of Providence in behalf of the inhabitants of New England. Lastly, in the seventh, the author gives an account of the heresies and the troubles to which the Church of New England was exposed. Cotton Mather was an evangelical minister who was born at Boston, and passed his life there. His narratives are distinguished by the same ardour and religious zeal which led to the foundation of the colonies of New England. Traces of bad taste sometimes occur in his manner of writing; but he interests, because he is full of enthusiasm. He is often intolerant, still oftener credulous, but he never betrays an intention to deceive. Sometimes his book contains fine passages, and true and profound reflections, such as the following:—

"Before the arrival of the puritans," says he (vol. i., chap. iv.) "there were more than a few attempts of the English to people and improve the parts of New England which were to the northward of New Plymouth; but the designs of those attempts being aimed no higher than the advancement of some worldly interests, a constant series of disasters has confounded them, until there was a plantation erected upon the nobler designs of Christianity: and that plantation, though it has had more adversaries than perhaps any one upon earth, yet, having obtained help from God, it continues to this day."

Mather occasionally relieves the austerity of his descriptions with images full of tender feeling: after having spoken of an English lady whose religious ardor had brought her to America with her husband, and who soon after sank under the fatigues and privations of exile, he adds, "As for her virtuous husband, Isaac Johnson,

He tried
To live without her, liked it not, and died."—(VOL I.)

Mather's work gives an admirable picture of the time and country which he describes. In his account of the motives which led the puritans to seek an asylum beyond seas, he says:—

"The God of heaven served, as it were, a summons upon the spirits of his people in the English nation, stirring up the spirits of thousands which never saw the faces of each other, with a most unanimous inclination to leave the pleasant accommodations of their native country, and go over a terrible ocean, into a more terrible desert, for the pure enjoyment of all his ordinances. It is now reasonable that, before we pass any farther, the reasons of this undertaking should be more exactly made known unto posterity, especially unto the posterity of those that were the undertakers, lest they come at length to forget and neglect the true interest of New England. Wherefore I shall now transcribe some of them from a manuscript wherein they were then tendered unto consideration.

* A folio edition of this work was published in London in 1702.

"General Considerations for the Plantation of New England.

"First, it will be a service unto the church of great consequence, to carry the gospel unto those parts of the world, and raise a bulwark against the kingdom of antichrist, which the Jesuits labour to rear up in all parts of the world.

"Secondly, all other churches of Europe have been brought under desolations; and it may be feared that the like judgements are coming upon us; and who knows but God hath provided this place to be a refuge for many whom he means to save out of the general destruction.

"Thirdly, the land grows weary of her inhabitants, inasmuch that man, which is the most precious of all creatures, is here more vile and base than the earth he treads upon; children, neighbours, and friends, especially the poor, are counted the greatest burdens, which, if things were right, would be the chiefest of earthly blessings.

"Fourthly, we are grown to that intemperance in all excess of riot, as no mean estate almost will suffice a man to keep sail with his equals, and he that fails in it must live in scorn and contempt; hence it comes to pass, that all arts and trades are carried in that deceitful manner and unrighteous course, as it is almost impossible for a good upright man to maintain his constant charge and live comfortably in them.

"Fifthly, the schools of learning and religion are so corrupted, as (beside the unsupportable charge of education) most children, even the best, wittiest, and of the fairest hopes, are perverted, corrupted, and utterly overthrown by the multitude of evil examples and licentious behaviours in these seminaries.

"Sixthly, the whole earth is the Lord's garden, and he hath given it to the sons of Adam, to be tilled and improved by them: why then should we stand starving here for places of habitation, and in the mean time suffer whole countries, as profitable for the use of man, to lie waste without any improvement?

Seventhly, what can be a better or nobler work, and more worthy of a Christian, than to erect and support a reformed particular church in its infancy, and unite our forces with such a company of faithful people, as by timely assistance may grow stronger and prosper; but for want of it, may be put to great hazards, if not be wholly ruined.

"Eighthly, if any such as are known to be godly, and live in wealth and prosperity here, shall forsake all this to join with this reformed church, and with it run the hazard of a hard and mean condition, it will be an example of great use, both for the removing of scandal, and to give more life unto the faith of God's people in their prayers for the plantation, and also to encourage others to join the more willingly in it."

Farther on, when he declares the principles of the church of New England with respect to morals, Mather inveighs with violence against the custom of drinking healths at table, which he denounces as a pagan and abominable practice. He proscribes with the same rigor all ornaments for the hair used by the female sex, as well as their custom of having the arms and neck uncovered.

In another part of his work he relates several instances of witchcraft which had alarmed New England. It is plain that the visible action of the devil in the affairs of this world appeared to him an incontestable and evident fact.

This work of Cotton Mather displays in many places, the spirit of civil liberty and political independence which characterized the times in which he lived. Their principles respecting government are discoverable at every page. Thus, for instance, the inhabitants of Massachusetts, in the year 1630, ten years after the foundation of Plymouth, are found to have devoted 400*l*. sterling to the establishment of the University of Cambridge. In passing from the general documents relative to the history of New England, to those which describe the several states comprised within its limits, I ought first to notice The History of the Colony of Massachusetts, by Hutchinson, Lieutenant-Governor of the Massachusetts Province, 2 vols., 8vo.

The history of Hutchinson, which I have several times quoted in the chapter to which this note relates, commences in the year 1628 and ends in 1750. Throughout the work there is a striking air of truth and the greatest simplicity of style; it is full of minute details.

The best history to consult concerning Connecticut is that of Benjamin Trumbull, entitled, A Complete History of Connecticut, Civil and Ecclesiastical, 1630–1764; 2 vols., 8vo., printed in 1818, at New Haven. This history contains a clear and calm account of all the events which happened in Connecticut during the period given in the title. The author drew from the best sources; and his narrative bears the stamp of truth. All that he says of the early days of Connecticut is extremely curious. See especially the constitution of 1639, vol. i., ch. vi., p. 100; and also the penal laws of Connecticut, vol. i., ch. vii., p. 123.

The History of New Hampshire, by Jeremy Belknap, is a work held in merited estimation. It was printed at Boston in 1792, in two vols., 8vo. The third chapter of the first volume is particularly worthy of attention for the valuable details it affords on the political and religious principles of the puritans, on the causes of their emigration, and on their laws. The following curious quotation is given from a sermon delivered in 1663: "It concerneth New England always to remember that they are a plantation religious, not a plantation of trade. The profession of the purity of doctrine, worship, and discipline, is written on her forehead. Let merchants, and such as are increasing cent. per cent. remember this, that worldly gain was not the end and design of the people of New England, but religion. And if any man among us make religion as twelve, and the world as thirteen, such an one hath not the true spirit of a true New Englishman." The reader of Belknap will find in his work more general ideas, and more strength of thought, than are to be met with in the American historians even to the present day.

Among the central states which deserve our attention for their remote origin, New York and Pennsylvania are the foremost. The best history we have of the former is entitled A History of New York, by William Smith, printed in London in 1757. Smith gives us important details of the wars between the French and English in American. His is the best account of the famous confederation of the Iroquois.

With respect to Pennsylvania, I cannot do better than point out the work of Proud, entitled the History of Pennsylvania, from the original Institution and Settlement of that Province, under the first Proprietor and Governor, William Penn, in 1681, till after the year 1742; by Robert Proud; 2 vols., 8vo., printed at Philadelphia in 1797. This work is deserving of the especial attention of the reader; it contains a mass of curious documents concerning Penn, the doctrine of the Quakers, and the character, manners, and customs of the first inhabitants of Pennsylvania.

APPENDIX G.

We read in Jefferson's Memoirs as follows:—

"At the time of the first settlement of the English in Virginia, when land was had for little or nothing, some provident persons having obtained large grants of it, and being desirious of maintaining the splendor of their families, entailed their property upon their descendants. The transmission of these estates from generation to generation, to men who bore the same name, had the effect of raising up a distinct class of families, who, possessing by law the privilege of perpetuating their wealth, formed by these means a sort of patrician order, distinguished by the grandeur and luxury of their establishments. From this order it was that the king usually chose his counsellors of state."*

In the United States, the principal clauses of the English law respecting descent have been universally rejected. The first rule that we follow, says Mr. Kent, touching inheritance, is the following: If a man dies intestate, his property goes to his heirs in a direct line. If he has but one heir or heiress, he or she succeeds to the whole. If there are several heirs of the same degree, they divide the inheritance equally among them, without distinction of sex.

This rule was prescribed for the first time in the state of New York by a statute of the 23d of February, 1786. (See Revised Statutes, vol. iii., Appendix, p. 48.) It has since then been adopted in the revised statutes of the same state. At the present day this law holds good throughout the whole of the United States, with the exception of the state of Vermont, where the male heir inherits a double portion; Kent's Commentaries, vol. iv., p. 370. Mr. Kent, in the same work, vol. iv., p. 1–22, gives an historical account of American legislation on the subject of entail; by this we learn that previous to the revolution the colonies followed the English law of entail. Estates tail were abolished in Virginia in 1776, on a motion of Mr. Jefferson. They were suppressed in New York in 1786; and have since been abolished in North Carolina, Kentucky, Tennessee, Georgia, and Missouri. In Vermont, Indiana, Illinois, South Carolina, and Louisiana, entail was never introduced. Those States which thought proper to preserve the English law of entail, modified it in such a way as to deprive it of its most aristocratic tendencies. "Our general principles on the subject of government," says Mr. Kent, "tend to favour the free circulation of property."

It cannot fail to strike the French reader who studies the law of inheritance, that on these questions the French legislation is infinitely more democratic even than the American.

The American law makes an equal division of the father's property, but only in the case of his will not being known; "for every man," says the law, "in the state of New York (Revised Statutes, vol. iii. Appendix, p. 51), has entire liberty, power, and authority, to dispose of his property by will, to leave it entire, or divided in favour of any persons he chooses as his heirs, provided he do not leave it to a political body or any corporation." The French law obliges the testator to divide his property equally, or nearly so, among his heirs.

Most of the American republics still admit of entails, under certain restrictions; but the French law prohibits entail in all cases.

---

* This passage is extracted and translated from M. Conseil's work upon the Life of Jefferson, entitled, "*Mélanges Politiques et Philosophiques de Jefferson.*"

If the social condition of the Americans is more democratic than that of the French, the laws of the latter are the most democratic of the two. This may be explained more easily than at first appears to be the case. In France, democracy is still occupied in the work of destruction; in America it reigns quietly over the ruins it has made.

APPENDIX H.

SUMMARY OF THE QUALIFICATIONS OF VOTERS IN THE UNITED STATES.

All the states agree in granting the right of voting at the age of twenty one. In all of them it is necessary to have resided for a certain time in the district where the vote is given. This period varies from three months to two years.

As to the qualification; in the state of Massachusetts it is necessary to have an income of three pounds sterling or a capital of sixty pounds.

In Rhode Island a man must possess landed property to the amount of 133 dollars.

In Connecticut he must have a property which gives an income of seventeen dollars. A year of service in the militia also gives the elective privilege.

In New Jersey, an elector must have a property of fifty pounds a year.

In South Carolina and Maryland, the elector must possess fifty acres of land.

In Tennessee, he must possess some property.

In the states of Mississippi, Ohio, Georgia, Virginia, Pennsylvania, Delaware, New York, the only necessary qualification for voting is that of paying the taxes; and in most of the states, to serve in the militia is equivalent to the payment of taxes.

In Maine and New Hampshire any man can vote who is not on the pauper list.

Lastly, in the states of Missouri, Alabama, Illinois, Louisiana, Indiana, Kentucky, and Vermont, the conditions of voting have no reference to the property of the elector.

I believe there is no other state beside that of North Carolina in which different conditions are applied to the voting for the senate and the electing the house of representatives. The electors of the former, in this case, should possess in property fifty acres of land; to vote for the latter, nothing more is required than to pay taxes.

APPENDIX I.

The small number of custom-house officers employed in the United States compared with the extent of the coast renders smuggling very easy; notwithstanding which it is less practised than elsewhere, because everybody endeavours to suppress it. In America there is no police for the prevention of fires, and such accidents are more frequent than in Europe; but in general they are more speedily extinguished, because the surrounding population is prompt in lending assistance.

APPENDIX K.

It is incorrect to assert that centralization was produced by the French revolution: the revolution brought it to perfection, but did not create it.

The mania for centralization and government regulations dates from the time when jurists began to take a share in the government, in the time of Philippe-le-Bel; ever since which period they have been on the increase. In the year 1775, M. de Malesherbes, speaking in the name of the Cour des Aides, said to Louis XIV.*

". . . Every corporation and every community of citizens, retained the right of administering its own affairs; a right which not only forms part of the primitive constitution of the kingdom, but has a still higher origin; for it is the right of nature and of reason. Nevertheless, your subjects, sire, have been deprived of it; and we cannot refrain from saying that in this respect your government has fallen into puerile extremes. From the time when powerful ministers made it a political principle to prevent the convocation of a national assembly, one consequence has succeeded another, until the deliberations of the inhabitants of a village are declared null when they have not been authorized by the intendant. Of course, if the community has an expensive undertaking to carry through, it must remain under the control of the sub-delegate of the intendant, and consequently follow the plan he proposes, employ his favourite workman, pay them according to his pleasure; and if an action at law is deemed necessary, the intendant's permission must be obtained. The cause must be pleaded before this first tribunal, previous to its being carried into a public court; and if the opinion of the intendant is opposed to that of the inhabitants, or if their adversary enjoys his favour, the community is deprived of the power of defending its rights. Such are the means, sire, which have been exerted to extinguish the municipal spirit in France; and to stifle, if possible, the opinions of the citizens. The nation may be said to lie under an interdict, and to be in wardship under guardians."

What could be said more to the purpose at the present day, when the revolution has achieved what are called its victories in centralization.

In 1789, Jefferson wrote from Paris to one of his friends: "There is no country where the mania for over-governing has taken deeper root than in France, or been the source of greater mischief." Letter to Madison, 28th August, 1789.

The fact is that for several centuries past the central power of France, has done everything it could to extend central administration; it has acknowledged no other limits than its own strength. The central power to which the revolution gave birth made more rapid advances than any of its predecessors, because it was stronger and wiser than they had been; Louis XIV. committed the welfare of such communities to the caprice of an intendant; Napoleon left them to that of the minister. The same principle governed both, though its consequences were more or less remote.

APPENDIX L.

This immutability of the constitution of France is a necessary consequence of the laws of that country.

To begin with the most important of all the laws, that which decides the order of succession to the throne; what can be more immutable in its principle than a political order founded upon the natural succession of father to son? In 1814 Louis XVIII. had established the perpetual law of hereditary succession in favour of his own family. The individuals who regulated

---

* See "Mémoires pour servir à l'Histoire du Droit Public de la France en matière d'Impôts," p. 654, printed at Brussels in 1779.

the consequences of the revolution of 1830 followed his example; they merely established the perpetuity of the law in favour of another family. In this respect they imitated the Chancellor Meaupou, who, when he erected the new parliament upon the ruins of the old, took care to declare in the same ordinance that the rights of the new magistrates should be as inalienable as those of their predecessors had been.

The laws of 1830, like those of 1814, point out no way of changing the constitution; and it is evident that the ordinary means of legislation are insufficient for this purpose. As the king, peers, and deputies, all derive their authority from the constitution, these three powers united cannot alter a law by virtue of which alone they govern. Out of the pale of the constitution, they are nothing; where, then, could they take their stand to effect a change in its provisions? The alternative is clear; either their efforts are powerless against the charter, which continues to exist in spite of them, in which case they only reign in the name of the charter; or, they succeed in changing the charter, and then the law by which they existed being annulled, they themselves cease to exist. By destroying the charter they destroy themselves

This is much more evident in the laws of 1830 than in those of 1814. In 1814, the royal prerogative took its stand above and beyond the constitution; but in 1830, it was avowedly created by, and dependant on, the constitution.

A part therefore of the French constitution is immutable, because it is united to the destiny of a family; and the body of the constitution is equally immutable, because there appear to be no legal means of changing it.

These remarks are not applicable to England. That country having no written constitution, who can assert when its constitution is changed?

APPENDIX M.

The most esteemed authors who have written upon the English constitution agree with each other in establishing the omnipotence of the parliament.

Delolme says: "It is a fundamental principle with the English lawyers, that parliament can do everything except making a woman a man, or a man a woman."

Blackstone expresses himself more in detail if not more energetically, than Dololme, in the following terms:—

"The power and jurisdiction of parliament, says Sir Edward Coke (4 Inst. 36), is so transcendant and absolute, that it cannot be confined, either for causes or persons within any bounds. And of this high court, he adds, may be truly said, 'Si antiquitatem spectes, est vetustissima; si dignitatem, est honoratissima; si jurisdictionem, est capacissima.' It hath sovereign and uncontrollable authority in making, confirming, enlarging, restraining, abrogating, repealing, reviving and expounding of laws, concerning matters of all possible denominations; ecclesiastical or temporal; civil, military, maritime, or criminal; this being the place where that absolute despotic power which must, in all governments, reside somewhere, is intrusted by the constitution of these kingdoms. All mischiefs and grievances, operations and remedies, that transcend the ordinary course of the laws, are within the reach of this extraordinary tribunal. It can regulate or new-model the succession to the crown; as was done in the reigns of Henry VIII. and William III. It can alter the established religion of the land; as was done in a variety of instances in the reigns of King Henry VIII. and his three children. It can change and create afresh even the constitution of the kingdom, and of the parliaments themselves; as was done by the act of union and the several statutes for triennial and septennial elections. It can, in short, do everything that is not naturally impossible to be done; and, therefore, some have not scrupled to call its power, by a figure rather too bold, the omnipotence of parliament."

APPENDIX N.

There is no question upon which the American constitutions agree more fully than upon that of political jurisdiction. All the constitutions which take cognizance of this matter, give to the house of delegates the exclusive right of impeachment; excepting only the constitution of North Carolina which grants the same privilege to grand-juries. (Article 23.)

Almost all the constitutions give the exclusive right of pronouncing sentence to the senate, or to the assembly which occupies its place.

The only punishments which the political tribunals can inflict are removal and the interdiction of public functions for the future. There is no other constitution but that of Virginia (p. 152), which enables them to inflict every kind of punishment.

The crimes which are subject to political jurisdiction, are, in the federal constitution (section 4, art. 1); in that of Indiana (art. 3, paragraphs 23 and 24); of New York (art. 5); of Delaware (art. 5); high treason, bribery, and other high crimes or offences.

In the constitution of Massachusetts (chap. 1, section 2); that of North Carolina (art. 23); of Virginia (p. 252), misconduct and maladministration.

In the constitution of New Hampshire (p. 105) corruption, intrigue, and maladministration

In Vermont (chap. ii. art. 24), maladministration.

In South Carolina (art. 5); Kentucky (art. 5); Tennessee (art. 4); Ohio (art. 1, § 23, 24); Louisiana (art. 5); Mississippi (art. 5); Alabama (art. 6); Pennsylvania (art. 4); crimes committed in the non-performance of official duties.

In the states of Illinois, Georgia, Maine, and Connecticut, no particular offences are specified.

APPENDIX O.

It is true that the powers of Europe may carry on maritime wars with the Union; but there is always greater facility and less danger in supporting a maritime than a continental war. Maritime warfare only requires one species of effort. A commercial people which consents to furnish its government with the necessary funds, is sure to possess a fleet. And it is far easier to induce a nation to part with its money, almost unconsciously, than to reconcile it to sacrifices of men and personal efforts. Moreover, defeat by sea rarely compromises the existence or independence of the people which endures it.

As for continental wars, it is evident that the nations of Europe cannot be formidable in this way to the American Union. It would be very difficult to transport and maintain in America more than 25,000 soldiers; an army which may be considered to represent a nation of 2,000,000 of men. The most populous nation of Europe contending in this way against the

Union, is in the position of a nation of 2,000,000 of inhabitants at war with one of 12,000,000. Add to this, that America has all its resources within reach, while the European is at 4,000 miles distance from his; and that the immensity of the American continent would of itself present an insurmountable obstacle to its conquest.

APPENDIX P.

The first American journal appeared in April, 1704, and was published at Boston. See collection of the Historical Society of Massachusetts, vol. vi., p. 66.

It would be a mistake to suppose that the periodical press has always been entirely free in the American colonies: an attempt was made to establish something analogous to a censorship and preliminary security. Consult the Legislative Documents of Massachusetts of the 14th of January, 1722.

The committee appointed by the general assembly (the legislative body of the province), for the purpose of examining into circumstances connected with a paper entitled "The New England Courier," expresses its opinion that "the tendency of the said journal is to turn religion into derision, and bring it into contempt; that it mentions the sacred writers in a profane and irreligious manner; that it puts malicious interpretations upon the conduct of the ministers of the gospel; and that the government of his majesty is insulted, and the peace and tranquility of the province disturbed by the said journal. The committee is consequently of opinion that the printer and publisher, James Franklin, should be forbidden to print and publish the said journal or any other work in future, without having previously submitted it to the secretary of the province; and that the justices of the peace for the county of Suffolk should be commissioned to require bail of the said James Franklin for his good conduct during the ensuing year."

The suggestion of the committee was adopted and passed into a law, but the effect of it was null, for the journal eluded the prohibition by putting the name of Benjamin Franklin instead of James Franklin at the bottom of its columns, and this manœuvre was supported by public opinion.

APPENDIX Q.

The federal constitution has introduced the jury into the tribunals of the Union in the same way as the states had introduced it into their own several courts: but as it has not established any fixed rules for the choice of jurors, the federal courts select them from the ordinary jury-list which each state makes for itself. The laws of the states must therefore be examined for the theory of the formation of juries. See Story's Commentaries on the Constitution, B. iii., chap. 38, pp. 654–659; Sergeant's Constitutional Law, p. 165. See also the federal laws, of the years 1789, 1800, and 1802, upon the subject.

For the purpose of thoroughly understanding the American principles with respect to the formation of juries, I examined the laws of states at a distance from one another, and the following observations were the result of my inquiries.

In America all the citizens who exercise the elective franchise have the right of serving upon a jury. The great state of New York, however, has made a slight difference between the two privileges, but in a spirit contrary to that of the laws of France; for in the state of New York there are fewer persons eligible as jurymen than there are electors. It may be said in general that the right of forming part of a jury, like that of electing representatives, is open to all the citizens: the exercise of this right, however, is not put indiscriminately into any hands.

Every year a body of municipal or county magistrates—called *selectmen* in New England, *supervisors* in New York, *trustees* in Ohio, and *sheriffs of the parish* in Louisiana—choose for each county a certain number of citizens who have the right of serving as jurymen, and who are supposed to be capable of exercising their functions. These magistrates, being themselves elective, excite no distrust: their powers, like those of most republican magistrates, are very extensive and very arbitrary, and they frequently make use of them to remove unworthy or incompetent jurymen.

The names of the jurymen thus chosen are transmitted to the county court; and the jury who have to decide any affair are drawn by lot from the whole list of names.

The Americans have contrived in every way to make the common people eligible to the jury, and to render the service as little onerous as possible. The sessions are held in the chief town of every county; and the jury are indemnified for their attendance either by the state or the parties concerned. They receive in general a dollar per day, beside their travelling expenses. In America the being placed upon the jury is looked upon as a burden but it is a burden which is very supportable. See Brevard's Digest of the Public Statute Law of South Carolina, vol. i., pp. 446 and 454, vol. ii., pp. 218 and 338; The General Laws of Massachusetts, revised and published by Authority of the Legislature, v. ii., pp. 187 and 331; The Revised Statutes of the State of New York, vol. ii., pp. 411, 643, 717, 720; The Statute Law of the State of Tennessee, vol. i., p. 209; Acts of the State of Ohio, pp. 95 and 210; and Digeste Général des Actes de la Législature de la Louisiane.

APPENDIX R.

If we attentively examine the constitution of the jury as introduced into civil proceedings in England, we shall readily perceive that the jurors are under the immediate control of the judge. It is true that the verdict of the jury, in civil as well as in criminal cases, comprises the question of fact and the question of right in the same reply; thus, a house is claimed by Peter as having been purchased by him: this is the fact to be decided. The defendant puts in a plea of incompetency on the part of the vendor: this is the legal question to be resolved.

But the jury do not enjoy the same character of infallibility in civil cases, according to the practice of the English courts, as they do in criminal cases. The judge may refuse to receive the verdict; and even after the first trial has taken place, a second or new trial may be awarded by the court. See Blackstone's Commentaries, book iii., ch. 24.

END OF VOL. I.

DEMOCRACY IN AMERICA.

BY

ALEXIS DE TOCQUEVILLE,

MEMBER OF THE INSTITUTE OF FRANCE, AND OF THE CHAMBER
OF DEPUTIES, ETC., ETC.

TRANSLATED BY HENRY REEVE, ESQ.

WITH AN ORIGINAL PREFACE AND NOTES BY

JOHN C. SPENCER,

COUNSELLOR AT LAW

FOURTH EDITION,

REVISED AND CORRECTED FROM THE EIGHTH PARIS EDITION.

IN TWO VOLUMES.

VOL. II.

NEW YORK:

J. & H. G. LANGLEY, 57 CHATHAM STREET.

PHILADELPHIA:—THOMAS, COWPERTHWAITE, & CO.

BOSTON:—C. C. LITTLE & J. BROWN.

1841.

Table of Contents

of

The Second Volume.

371

THIRD BOOK.

Democracy in America

FIRST BOOK.
INFLUENCE OF DEMOCRACY ON THE PROGRESS OF OPINION IN THE UNITED STATES.

Chapter I.

PHILOSOPHICAL METHOD AMONG THE AMERICANS.

I think that in no country in the civilized world is less attention paid to philosophy than in the United States. The Americans have no philosophical school of their own; and they care but little for all the schools into which Europe is divided, the very names of which are scarcely known to them.

Nevertheless it is easy to perceive that almost all the inhabitants of the United States conduct their understanding in the same manner, and govern it by the same rules; that is to say, that without ever having taken the trouble to define the rules of a philosophical method, they are in possession of one, common to the whole people.

To evade the bondage of system and habit, of family-maxims, class-opinions, and, in some degree, of national prejudices; to accept tradition only as a means of information, and existing facts only as a lesson used in doing otherwise and doing better; to seek the reason of things for oneself, and in oneself alone; to tend to results without being bound to means, and to aim at the substance through the form;—such are the principal characteristics of what I shall call the philosophical method of the Americans.

But if I go further, and if I seek among these characteristics that which predominates over and includes almost all the rest, I discover, that in most of the operations of the mind, each American appeals to the individual exercise of his own understanding alone.

America is therefore one of the countries in the world where philosophy is least studied, and where the precepts of Descartes[1] are best applied. Nor is this surprising. The Americans do not read the works of Descartes, because their social condition deters them from speculative studies, but they follow his maxims, because this very social condition naturally disposes their understanding to adopt them.

378

In the midst of the continual movement which agitates a democratic community, the tie which unites one generation to another is relaxed or broken; every man readily loses the trace of the ideas of his forefathers or takes no care about them.

Nor can men living in this state of society derive their belief from the opinions of the class to which they belong; for, so to speak, there are no longer any clases, or those which still exist are composed of such mobile elements, that their body can never exercise a real control over its members.

As to the influence which the intelligence of one man has on that of another, it must necessarily be very limited in a country where the citizens, placed on the footing of a general similitude, are all closely seen by each other; and where, as no signs of incontestable greatness or superiority are perceived in any one of them, they are constantly brought back to their own reason as the most obvious and proximate source of truth. It is not only confidence in this or that man which is then destroyed, but the taste for trusting the *ipse dixit* of any man whatsoever. Every one shuts himself up in his own breast, and affects from that point to judge the world.

The practice which obtains among the Americans of fixing the standard of their judgement in themselves alone, leads them to other habits of mind. As they perceive that they succeed in resolving without assistance all the little difficulties which their practical life presents, they readily conclude that every thing in the world may be explained, and that nothing in it transcends the limits of the understanding. Thus they fall to denying what they cannot comprehend; which leaves them but little faith for whatever is extraordinary, and an almost insurmountable distaste for whatever is supernatural. As it is on their own testimony that they are accustomed to rely, they like to discern the object which engages their attention with extreme clearness; they therefore strip off as much as possible all that covers it, they rid themselves of whatever separates them from it, they remove whatever conceals it from sight, in order to view it more closely and in the broad light of day. This disposition of the mind soon leads them to contemn forms, which they regard as useless and inconvenient veils placed between them and the truth.

The Americans then have not required to extract their philosophical method from books; they have found it in themselves. The same thing may be remarked in what has taken place in Europe.

This same method has only been established and made popular in Europe in proportion as the condition of society has become more equal, and men have grown more like each other. Let us consider for a moment the connexion of the periods in which this change may be traced.

In the sixteenth century the Reformers subjected some of the dogmas of the ancient faith to the scrutiny of private judgement; but they still withheld from it the discussion of all the rest. In the seventeenth century, Bacon[2] in the natural sciences, and Descartes in the study of philosophy in the strict sense of the term, abolished recognised formulas, destroyed the empire of tradition, and overthrew the authority of the schools. The philosophers of the eighteenth century, generalizing at length the same principle, undertook to submit to the private judgement of each man all the objects of his belief.

Who does not perceive that Luther,[3] Descartes, and Voltaire[4] employed the same method, and that they differed only in the greater or less use which they professed should be made of it? Why did the Reformers confine themselves so closely within the circle of religious ideas? Why did Descartes, choosing only to apply his method to certain matters, though he had made it fit to be applied to all, declare that men might judge for themselves in matters philosophical but not in matters political? How happened it that in the eighteenth century those general applications were all at once drawn from this same method, which Descartes and his predecessors had either not perceived or had rejected? To what, lastly, is the fact to be attributed, that at this period the method we are speaking of suddenly emerged from the schools, to penetrate into society and become the common standard of intelligence; and that, after it had become popular among the French, it has been ostensibly adopted or secretly followed by all the nations of Europe?

The philosophical method here designated may have been engendered in the sixteenth century—it may have been more accurately defined and more extensively applied in the seventeenth; but neither in the one nor in the other could it be commonly adopted. Political laws, the condition of society, and the habits of mind which are derived from these causes, were as yet opposed to it.

It was discovered at a time when men were beginning to equalize and assimilate their conditions. It could only be generally followed in ages when those conditions had at length become nearly equal, and men nearly alike.

The philosophical method of the eighteenth century is then not only French, but it is democratic; and this explains why it was so readily admitted throughout Europe, where it has contributed so powerfully to change the face of society. It is not because the French have changed their former opinions, and altered their former manners, that they have convulsed the world; but because they were the first to generalize and bring to light a philosophical method, by the assistance of which it became easy to attack all that was old and to open a path to all that was new.

If it be asked why, at the present day, this same method is more rigorously followed and more frequently applied by the French than by the Americans, although the principle of equality be no less complete, and of more ancient date, among the latter people, the fact may be attributed to two circumstances, which it is essential to have clearly understood in the first instance.

It must never be forgotten that religion gave birth to Anglo-American society. In the United States religion is therefore commingled with all the habits of the nation and all the feelings of patriotism; whence it derives a peculiar force. To this powerful reason, another of no less intensity may be added: in America religion has, as it were, laid down its own limits. Religious institutions have remained wholly distinct from political institutions, so that former laws have been easily changed while former belief has remained unshaken. Christianity has therefore retained a strong hold on the public mind in America; and, I would more particularly remark, that its sway is not only that of a philosophical doctrine which has been adopted upon inquiry, but of a religion which is believed without discussion. In the United States, Christian sects are infinitely diversified and perpetually modified; but Christianity itself is a fact so irresistably established, that no one undertakes either to attack or to defend it. The Americans, having admitted the principal doctrines of the Christian religion without inquiry, are obliged to accept in like manner a great number of moral truths originating in it and connected with it. Hence the activity of individual analysis is restrained within narrow limits, and many of the most important of human opinions are removed from the range of its influence.

The second circumstance to which I have alluded is the following: the social condition and the constitution of the Americans are democratic, but they have not had a democratic revolution. They arrived upon the soil they occupy in nearly the condition in which we see them at the present day; and this is of very considerable importance.

There are no revolutions which do not shake existing belief, enervate authority, and throw doubts over commonly received ideas. The effect of all revolutions is therefore, more or less, to surrender men to their own guidance, and to open to the mind of every man a void and almost unlimited range of speculation. When equality of conditions succeeds a protracted conflict between the different classes of which the elder society was composed, envy, hatred and uncharitableness, pride and exaggerated self-confidence are apt to seize upon the human heart, and plant their sway there for a time. This, independently of equality itself, tends powerfully to divide men—to lead them to mistrust the judgement of others, and to seek the light of truth nowhere but in their own understandings. Every one then attempts to be his own sufficient guide, and makes it his boast to form his own opinions on all subjects. Men are no longer bound together by ideas, but by interests; and it would seem as if human opinions were reduced to a sort of intellectual dust, scattered on every side, unable to collect, unable to cohere.

Thus, that independence of mind which equality supposes to exist, is never so great, nor ever appears so excessive, as at the time when equality is beginning to establish itself, and in the course of that painful labour by which it is established. That sort of intellectual freedom which equality may give, ought therefore to be very carefully distinguished from the anarchy which revolution brings. Each of these two things must be severally considered, in order not to conceive exaggerated hopes or fears of the future.

I believe that the men who will live under the new forms of society will make frequent use of their private judgement; but I am far from thinking that they will often abuse it. This is attributable to a cause of more general application to all democratic countries, and which, in the long run, must needs restrain in them the independence of individual speculation within fixed, and sometimes narrow, limits.

I shall proceed to point out this cause in the next chapter.

Chapter II.

OF THE PRINCIPAL SOURCE OF BELIEF AMONG DEMOCRATIC NATIONS.

At different periods dogmatical belief is more or less abundant. It arises in different ways, and it may change its object or its form; but under no circumstances will dogmatical belief cease to exist, or, in other words, men will never cease to entertain some implicit opinions without trying them by actual discussion. If every one undertook to form his own opinions, and to seek for truth by isolated paths struck out by himself alone, it is not to be supposed that any considerable number of men would ever unite in any common belief.

But obviously without such common belief no society can prosper— say rather no society does subsist; for without ideas held in common, there is no common action, and without common action, there may still be men, but there is no social body. In order that society should exist, and, *a fortiori*, that a society should prosper, it is required that all the minds of the citizens should be rallied and held together by certain predominant ideas; and this cannot be the case, unless each of them sometimes draws his opinions from the common source, and consents to accept certain matters of belief at the hands of the community.

If I now consider man in his isolated capacity, I find that dogmatical belief is not less indispensable to him in order to live alone, than it is to enable him to co-operate with his fellow creatures. If man were forced to demonstrate to himself all the truths of which he makes daily use, his task would never end. He would exhaust his strength in preparatory exercises, without advancing beyond them. As, from the shortness of his life, he has not the time, nor, from the limits of his intelligence, the capacity, to accomplish this, he is reduced to take upon trust a number of facts and opinions which he has not had either the time or the power to verify himself, but which men of greater ability have sought out, or which the world adopts. On this groundwork he raises for himself the structure of his own thoughts; nor is he led to proceed in this manner by choice, so much as he is constrained by the inflexible law of his condition.

There is no philosopher of such great parts in the world, but that he believes a million of things on the faith of other people, and supposes a great many more truths than he demonstrates.

This is not only necessary but desirable. A man who should undertake to inquire into everything for himself, could devote to each thing but little time and attention. His task would keep his mind in perpetual unrest, which would prevent him from penetrating to the depth of any truth, or of grappling his mind indissolubly to any conviction. His intellect would be at once independent and powerless. He must therefore make his choice from among the various objects of human belief, and he must adopt many opinions without discussion, in order to search the better into that smaller number which he sets apart for investigation. It is true, that whoever receives an opinion on the word of another, does so far enslave his mind; but it is a salutary servitude which allows him to make a good use of freedom.

A principle of authority must then always occur, under all circumstances, in some part or other of the moral and intellectual world. Its place is variable, but a place it necessarily has. The independence of individual minds may be greater or it may be less: unbounded it cannot be. Thus the question is, not to know whether any intellectual authority exists in the ages of democracy, but simply where it resides and by what standard it is to be measured.

I have shown in the preceding chapter how the equality of conditions leads men to entertain a sort of instinctive incredulity of the supernatural, and a very lofty and often exaggerated opinion of the human understanding. The men who live at a period of social equality are not therefore easily led to place that intellectual authority to which they bow either beyond or above humanity. They commonly seek for the sources of truth in themselves, or in those who are like themselves. This would be enough to prove that at such periods no new religion could be established, and that all schemes for such a purpose would be not only impious but absurd and irrational. It may be foreseen that a democratic people will not easily give credence to divine missions; that they will turn modern prophets to a ready jest; and that they will seek to discover the chief arbiter of their belief within, and not beyond the limits of their kind.

When the ranks of society are unequal, and men unlike each other in condition, there are some individuals invested with all the power of superior intelligence, learning, and enlightenment, while the multitude is sunk in ignorance and prejudice. Men living at these aristocratic periods are therefore naturally induced to shape their opinions by the superior standard of a person or a class of persons, while they are averse to recognise the infallibility of the mass of the people.

The contrary takes place in ages of equality. The nearer the citizens are drawn to the common level of an equal and similar condition, the less prone does each man become to place implicit faith in a certain man or a certain class of men. But his readiness to believe the multitude increases, and opinion is more than ever mistress of the world. Not only is common opinion the only guide which private judgement retains among a democratic people, but among such a people it possesses a power infinitely beyond what it has elsewhere. At periods of equality men have no faith in one another, by reason of their common resemblance; but this very resemblance gives them almost unbounded confidence in the judgement of the public; for it would not seem probable, as they are all endowed with equal means of judging, but that the greater truth should go with the greater number.

When the inhabitant of a democratic country compares himself individually with all those about him, he feels with pride that he is the equal of any one of them; but when he comes to survey the totality of his fellows, and to place himself in contrast to so huge a body, he is instantly overwhelmed by the sense of his own insignificance and weakness.

The same equality which renders him independent of each of his fellow-citizens, taken severally, exposes him alone and unprotected to the influence of the greater number.

The public has therefore among a democratic people a singular power, of which aristocratic nations could never so much as conceive an idea; for it does not persuade to certain opinions, but it enforces them, and infuses them into the faculties by a sort of enormous pressure of the minds of all upon the reason of each.

In the United States the majority undertakes to supply a multitude of ready-made opinions for the use of individuals, who are thus relieved from the necessity of forming opinions of their own. Every body there adopts great numbers of theories on philosophy, morals, and politics, without inquiry, upon public trust; and if we look to it very narrowly, it will be perceived that religion herself holds her sway there, much less as a doctrine of revelation than as a commonly received opinion.

The fact that the political laws of the Americans are such that the majority rules the community with sovereign sway, materially increases the power which that majority naturally exercises over the mind. For nothing is more customary in man than to recognise superior wisdom in the person of his oppressor. This political omnipotence of the majority in the United States doubtless augments the influence which public opinion would obtain without it over the mind of each member of the community; but the foundations of that influence do not rest upon it. They must be sought for in the principle of equality itself, not in the more or less popular institutions which men living under that condition may give themselves. The intellectual dominion of the greater number would probably be less absolute among a democratic people governed by a king than in the sphere of a pure democracy, but it will always be extremely absolute; and by whatever political laws men are governed in the ages of equality, it may be foreseen that faith in public opinion will become a species of religion there, and the majority its ministering prophet.

Thus intellectual authority will be different, but it will not be diminished; and far from thinking that it will disappear, I augur that it may readily acquire too much preponderance, and confine the action of private judgement within narrower limits than are suited either to the greatness or the happiness of the human race. In the principle of equality I very clearly discern two tendencies; the one leading the mind of every man to untried thoughts, the other inclined to prohibit him from thinking at all. And I perceive how, under the dominion of certain laws, democracy would extinguish that liberty of the mind to which a democratic social condition is favorable; so that, after having broken all the bondage once imposed on it by ranks or by men, the human mind would be closely fettered to the general will of the greatest number.

If the absolute power of a majority were to be substituted by democratic nations, for all the different powers which checked or retarded overmuch the energy of individual minds, the evil would only have changed its symptoms. Men would not have found the means of independent life; they would simply have invented (no easy task) a new dress for servitude. There is—and I cannot repeat it too often—there is in this matter for profound reflection for those who look on freedom as a holy thing, and who hate not only the despot, but despotism. For myself, when I feel the hand of power lie heavy on my brow, I care but little to know who oppresses me; and I am not the more disposed to pass beneath the yoke, because it is held out to me by the arms of a million men.

Chapter III.

WHY THE AMERICANS DISPLAY MORE READINESS AND MORE TASTE FOR GENERAL IDEAS THAN THEIR FOREFATHERS THE ENGLISH.

The Deity does not regard the human race collectively. He surveys at one glance and severally all the beings of whom mankind is composed, and he discerns in each man the resemblances which assimilate him to all his fellows, and the differences which distinguish him from them. God therefore, stands in no need of general ideas;* that is to say, he is never sensible of the necessity of collecting a considerable number of analogous objects under the same form for greater convenience in thinking.

Such is, however, not the case with man. If the human mind were to attempt to examine and pass a judgement on all the individual cases before it, the immensity of detail would soon lead it astray and bewilder its discernment: in this strait, man has recourse to an imperfect but a necessary expedient, which at once assists and demonstrates his weakness.

Having superficially considered a certain number of objects, and re-

---

* [I have followed the author in what I conceive to be the misuse of the term "general ideas," which, in the restricted sense here given it, will be more familiar to the reader of Condillac, than to the student of metaphysical writers of a more accurate style and of more enlarged conceptions. What is meant by the term here, is simply the result of that inductive process by which the human or finite understanding collects and classifies its impressions for greater convenience in thinking. It may safely be asserted that the Divine Mind does not require inductions to arrive at general ideas; but some inconvenience may arise from the apparent confusion under one term of the mere *nominal* species or collective notions derived by man from experience, with the general or universal ideas of real essences existing as principles in the Divine intelligence. It is therefore necessary to add that the term is not used in the latter sense in this place; but in a subsequent chapter it is applied, with a more correct and extensive signification, to the fundamental conceptions of religion and morality.—*Translator's Note.*]

marked their resemblance, he assigns to them a common name, sets them apart, and proceeds onward.

General ideas are no proof of the strength, but rather of the insufficiency of the human intellect; for there are in nature no beings exactly alike, no things precisely identical, nor any rules indiscrimmately and alike applicable to several objects at once. The chief merit of general ideas is, that they enable the human mind to pass a rapid judgement on a great many objects at once; but, on the other hand, the notions they convey are never otherwise than incomplete, and they always cause the mind to lose as much in accuracy as it gains in comprehensiveness.

As social bodies advance in civilization, they acquire the knowledge of new facts, and they daily lay hold almost unconsciously of some particular truths. The more truths of this kind a man apprehends, the more general ideas, is he naturally led to conceive. A multitude of particular facts cannot be seen separately, without at last discovering the common tie which connects them. Several individuals lead to the perception of the species; several species to that of the genus. Hence the habit and the taste for general ideas will always be greatest among a people of ancient cultivation and extensive knowledge.

But there are other reasons which impel men to generalize their ideas, or which restrain them from it.

The Americans are much more addicted to the use of general ideas than the English, and entertain a much greater relish for them: this appears very singular at first sight, when it is remembered that the two nations have the same origin, that they lived for centuries under the same laws, and that they still incessantly interchange their opinions and their manners. This contrast becomes much more striking still, if we fix our eyes on our own part of the world, and compare together the two most enlightened nations which inhabit it. It would seem as if the mind of the English could only tear itself reluctantly and painfully away from the observation of particular facts, to rise from them to their causes; and that it only generalizes in spite of itself. Among the French, on the contrary, the taste for general ideas would seem to have grown to so ardent a passion, that it must be satisfied on every occasion. I am informed, every morning when I wake, that some general and eternal law has just been discovered, which I never heard mentioned before. There is not a mediocre scribbler who does not try his hand at discovering truths applicable to a great kingdom, and who is very ill-pleased with himself if he does not succeed in compressing the human race into the compass of an article.

So great a dissimilarity between two very enlightened nations surprises me. If I again turn my attention to England, and observe the events which have occurred there in the last half century, I think I may affirm that a taste for general ideas increases in that country in proportion as its ancient constitution is weakened.

The state of civilization is therefore insufficient by itself to explain what suggests to the human mind the love of general ideas, or diverts it from them.

When the conditions of men are very unequal, and inequality itself is the permanent state of society, individual men gradually become so dissimilar, that each class assumes the aspect of a distinct race: only one of these classes is ever in view at the same instant; and losing sight of that general tie which binds them all within the vast bosom of mankind, the observation invariably rests not on man, but on certain men. Those who live in this aristocratic state of society never, therefore, conceive very general ideas respecting themselves, and that is enough to imbue them with an habitual distrust of such ideas, and an instinctive aversion to them.

He, on the contrary, who inhabits a democratic country, sees around him on every hand, men differing but little from each other; he cannot turn his mind to any one portion of mankind, without expanding and dilating his thought till it embraces the whole. All the truths which are applicable to each of his fellow-citizens and fellowmen. Having contracted the habit of generalizing his ideas in the study which engages him most, and interests him more than others, he transfers the same habit to all his pursuits; and thus it is that the craving to discover general laws in everything, to include a great number of objects under the same formula, and to explain a mass of facts by a single cause, becomes an ardent, and sometimes an undiscerning, passion in the human mind.

Nothing shows the truth of this proposition more clearly than the opinions of the ancients respecting their slaves. The most profound and capacious minds of Rome and Greece were never able to reach the idea, at once so general and so simple, of the common likeness of men, and of the common birthright of each to freedom: they strove to prove that slavery was in the order of nature, and that it would always exist. Nay more, everything shows that those of the ancients who had passed from the servile to the free condition, many of whom have left us excellent writings, did themselves regard servitude in no other light.

All the great writers of antiquity belonged to the aristocracy of masters, or at least they saw that aristocracy established and uncontested before their eyes. Their minds, after having been expanded in several directions, were barred from further progress in this one; and the advent of Jesus Christ upon earth was required to teach that all the members of the human race are by nature equal and alike.

In the ages of equality all men are independent of each other, isolated and weak. The movements of the multitude are not permanently guided by the will of any individuals: at such times humanity seems always to advance of itself. In order therefore to explain what is passing in the world, man is driven to seek for some great causes, which, acting in the same manner on all our fellow-creatures, thus impel them all involuntarily to pursue the same track. This again naturally leads the human mind to conceive general ideas and superinduces a taste for them.

I have already shown in what way the equality of conditions leads every man to investigate truth for himself. It may readily be perceived that a method of this kind must insensibly beget a tendency to general ideas in the human mind. When I repudiate the traditions of rank, profession, and birth, when I escape from the authority of example, to seek out, by the single effort of my reason, the path to be followed, I am inclined to derive the motives of my opinions from human nature itself; which leads me necessarily, and almost unconsciously, to adopt a great number of very general notions.

All that I have here said explains the reasons for which the English display much less readiness and taste for the generalization of ideas than their American progeny, and still less again than their French neighbours; and likewise the reason for which the English of the present day display more of these qualities than their forefathers did.

The English have long been a very enlightened and a very aristocratic nation; their enlightened condition urged them constantly to generalize, and their aristocratic habits confined them to particularize. Hence arose that philosophy, at once bold and timid, broad and narrow, which has hitherto prevailed in England, and which still obstructs and stagnates in so many minds in that country.

Independently of the causes I have pointed out in what goes before, others may be discerned, less apparent but no less efficacious, which engender among almost every democratic people a taste, and frequently a passion, for general ideas. An accurate distinction must be taken between ideas of this kind. Some are the result of slow, minute and conscientious labour of the mind, and these extend the sphere of human knowledge; others spring up at once from the first rapid exercise of the wits, and beget none but very superficial and very uncertain notions.

Men who live in ages of equality have a great deal of curiosity and very little leisure; their life is so practical, so confused, so excited, so active, that but little time remains to them for thought. Such men are prone to general ideas because they spare them the trouble of studying particulars; they contain, if I may so speak, a great deal in a little compass, and give in a little time a great return. If then, upon a brief and inattentive investigation, a common relation is thought to be detected between certain objects, inquiry is not pushed any further; and without examining in detail how far these different objects differ or agree, they are hastily arranged under one formulary, in order to pass to another subject.

One of the distinguishing characteristics of a democratic period is the taste all men have at such times for easy success and present enjoyment. This occurs in the pursuits of the intellect as well as in all others. Most of those who live at a time of equality are full of an ambition at once aspiring and relaxed: they would fain succeed brilliantly and at once, but they would be dispensed from great efforts to obtain success. These conflicting tendencies lead straight to the research of general ideas, by aid of which they flatter themselves that they can figure very importantly at a small expense, and draw the attention of the public with very little trouble.

And I know not whether they be wrong in thinking thus. For their readers are as much averse to investigating anything to the bottom as they can be themselves; and what is generally sought in the productions of the mind is easy pleasure and information without labour.

If aristocratic nations do not make sufficient use of general ideas, and frequently treat them with inconsiderate disdain, it is true, on the other hand, that a democratic people is ever ready to carry ideas of this kind to excess, and to espouse them with injudicious warmth.

Chapter IV.

WHY THE AMERICANS HAVE NEVER BEEN SO EAGER AS THE FRENCH FOR GENERAL IDEAS IN POLITICAL MATTERS.

I observed in the last chapter, that the Americans show a less decided taste for general ideas than the French; this is more especially true in political matters.

Although the Americans infuse into their legislation infinitely more general ideas than the English, and although they pay much more attention than the latter people to the adjustment of the practice of affairs to theory, no political bodies in the United States have ever shown so warm an attachment to general ideas as the Constituent Assembly and the Convention[1] in France. At no time has the American people laid hold on ideas of this kind with the passionate energy of the French people in the eighteenth century, or displayed the same blind confidence in the value and absolute truth of any theory.

This difference between the Americans and the French originates in several causes, but principally in the following one. The Americans form a democratic people, which has always itself directed public affairs. The French are a democratic people, who, for a long time, could only speculate on the best manner of conducting them. The social condition of France led that people to conceive very general ideas on the subject of government, while its political constitution prevented it from correcting those ideas by experiment, and from gradually detecting their insufficiency; whereas in America the two things constantly balance and correct each other.

It may seem, at first sight, that this is very much opposed to what I have said before, that democratic nations derive their love of theory from the excitement of their active life. A more attentive examination will show that there is nothing contradictory in the proposition.

Men living in democratic countries eagerly lay hold of general ideas because they have but little leisure, and because these ideas spare them the trouble of studying particulars. This is true; but it is only to be understood to apply to those matters which are not the necessary and habitual subjects of their thoughts. Mercantile men will take up very eagerly, and without any very close scrutiny, all the general ideas on philosophy, politics, science, or the arts, which may be presented to them; but for such as relate to commerce, they will not receive them without inquiry, or adopt them without reserve. The same thing applies to statesmen with regard to general ideas in politics.

If then there be a subject upon which a democratic people is peculiarly liable to abandon itself, blindly and extravagantly, to general ideas, the best corrective that can be used will be to make that subject a part of the daily practical occupation of that people. The people will then be compelled to enter upon its details, and the details will teach them the weak points of the theory. This remedy may frequently be a painful one, but its effect is certain.

Thus it happens, that the democratic institutions which compel every citizen to take a practical part in the government, moderate that excessive taste for general theories in politics, which the principle of equality suggests.

Chapter V.

OF THE MANNER IN WHICH RELIGION IN THE UNITED STATES AVAILS ITSELF OF DEMOCRATIC TENDENCIES.

I have laid it down in a preceding chapter that men cannot do without dogmatical belief; and even that it is very much to be desired that such belief should exist among them. I now add, that of all the kinds of dogmatical belief, the most desirable appears to me to be dogmatical belief in matters of religion; and this is a very clear inference, even from no higher considerations than the interests of this world.

There is hardly any human action, however particular a character be assigned to it, which does not originate in some very general idea men have conceived of the Deity, of His relation to mankind, of the nature of their own souls, and of their duties to their fellow-creatures. Nor can anything prevent these ideas from being the common spring from which everything else emanates.

Men are therefore immeasurably interested in acquiring fixed ideas of God, of the soul, and of their common duties to their Creator and to their fellow-men; for doubt on these first principles would abandon all their actions to the impulse of chance, and would condemn them to live, to a certain extent, powerless and undisciplined.

This is then the subject on which it is most important for each of us to entertain fixed ideas; and unhappily it is also the subject on which it is most difficult for each of us, left to himself, to settle his opinions by the sole force of his reason. None but minds singularly free from the ordinary anxieties of life—minds at once penetrating, subtle, and trained by thinking—can, even with the assistance of much time and care, sound the depth of these most necessary truths. And, indeed, we see that these philosophers are themselves almost always enshrouded in uncertainties; that at every step the natural light which illuminates their path grows dimmer and less secure; and that, in spite of all their efforts, they have as yet only discovered a small number of conflicting notions, on which the mind of man has been tossed about for thousands of years, without either laying a firmer grasp on truth, or finding novelty even in its errors. Studies of this nature are far above the average capacity of men; and even if the majority of mankind were capable of such pursuits, it is evident that leisure to cultivate them would still be wanting.

Fixed ideas of God and human nature are indispensable to the daily practice of men's lives; but the practice of their lives prevents them from acquiring such ideas.

The difficulty appears to me to be without a parallel. Among the sciences there are some which are useful to the mass of mankind, and which are within its reach; others can only be approached by the few, and are not cultivated by the many, who require nothing beyond their more remote applications: but the daily practice of the science I speak of is indispensable to all, although the study of it is inaccessible to the far greater number.

General ideas respecting God and human nature are therefore the ideas above all others which it is most suitable to withdraw from the habitual action of private judgement, and in which there is most to gain and least to lose by recognising a principle of authority.

The first object and one of the principal advantages of religions is to furnish to each of these fundamental questions a solution which is at once clear, precise, intelligible to the mass of mankind, and lasting. There are religions which are very false and very absurd; but it may be affirmed, that any religion which remains within the circle I have just traced, without aspiring to go beyond it, (as many religions have attempted to do, for the purpose of inclosing on every side the free progress of the human mind,) imposes a salutary restraint on the intellect; and it must be admitted, that, if it do not save men in another world, such religion is at least very conducive to their happiness and their greatness in this.

This is more especially true of men living in free countries. When the religion of a people is destroyed, doubt gets hold of the highest portions of the intellect, and half paralyses all the rest of its powers. Every man accustoms himself to entertain none but confused and changing notions on the subjects most interesting to his fellow-creatures and himself. His opinions are ill-defended and easily abandoned; and despairing of ever resolving, by himself, the hardest problems of the destiny of man, he ignobly submits to think no more about them.

Such a condition cannot but enervate the soul, relax the springs of the will, and prepare a people for servitude. Nor does it only happen, in such a case, that they allow their freedom to be wrested from them; they frequently themselves surrender it. When there is no longer any principle of authority in religion any more than in politics, men are speedily frightened at the aspect of this unbounded independence. The constant agitation of all surrounding things alarms and exhausts them. As everything is at sea in the sphere of the intellect, they determine at least that the mechanism of society should be firm and fixed; and as they cannot resume their ancient belief, they assume a master.

For my own part, I doubt whether man can ever support at the same time complete religious independence and entire public freedom. And I am inclined to think, that if faith be wanting in him, he must serve; and if he be free, he must believe.

Perhaps, however, this great utility of religions is still more obvious among nations where equality of conditions prevails than among others. It must be acknowledged that equality, which brings great benefits into the world, nevertheless suggests to men (as will be shown hereafter) some very dangerous propensities. It tends to isolate them from each other, to concentrate every man's attention upon himself; and it lays open the soul to an inordinate love of material gratification.

The greatest advantage of religion is to inspire diametrically contrary principles. There is no religion which does not place the object of man's desires above and beyond the treasures of earth, and which does not naturally raise his soul to regions far above those of the senses. Nor is there any which does not impose on man some sort of duties to his kind, and thus draw him at times from the contemplation of himself. This occurs in religions the most false and dangerous.

Religious nations are therefore naturally strong on the very point on which democratic nations are weak; which shows of what importance it is for men to preserve their religion as their conditions become more equal.

I have neither the right nor the intention of examining the supernatural means which God employs to infuse religious belief into the heart of man. I am at this moment considering religions in a purely human point of view: my object is to inquire by what means they may most easily retain their sway in the democratic ages upon which we are entering.

It has been shown that, at times of general cultivation and equality, the human mind does not consent to adopt dogmatical opinions without reluctance, and feels their necessity acutely in spiritual matters only. This proves, in the first place, that at such times religions ought, more cautiously than at any other, to confine themselves within their own precincts; for in seeking to extend their power beyond religious matters, they incur a risk of not being believed at all. The circle within which they seek to bound the human intellect ought therefore to be carefully traced, and beyond its verge the mind should be left in entire freedom to its own guidance.

Mohammed professed to derive from Heaven, and he has inserted in the Koran, not only a body of religious doctrines, but political maxims, civil and criminal laws, and theories of science. The Gospel, on the contrary, only speaks of the general relations of men to God and to each other—beyond which it inculcates and imposes no point of faith. This alone, besides a thousand other reasons, would suffice to prove that the former of these religions will never long predominate in a cultivated and democratic age, while the latter is destined to retain its sway at these as at all other periods.

But in continuation of this branch of the subject, I find that in order for religions to maintain their authority, humanly speaking, in democratic ages, they not only must confine themselves strictly within the circle of spiritual matters: their power also depends very much on the nature of the belief they inculcate, on the external forms they assume, and on the obligations they impose.

The preceding observation, that equality leads men to very general and very extensive notions, is principally to be understood as applied to the question of religion. Men living in a similar and equal condition in the world readily conceive the idea of the one God, governing every man by the same laws, and granting to every man future happiness on the same conditions. The idea of the unity of mankind constantly leads them back to the idea of the unity of the Creator; while, on the contrary in a state of society, where men are broken up into very unequal ranks, they are apt to devise as many deities as there are nations, castes, classes, or families, and to trace a thousand private roads to Heaven.

It cannot be denied that Christianity itself has felt, to a certain extent, the influence which social and political conditions exercise on religious opinions.

At the epoch at which the Christian religion appeared upon earth, Providence, by whom the world was doubtless prepared for its coming, had gathered a large portion of the human race, like an immense flock, under the sceptre of the Cæsars. The men of whom this multitude was composed were distinguished by numerous differences; but they had thus much in common, that they all obeyed the same laws, and that every subject was so weak and insignificant in relation to the imperial potentate, that all appeared equal when their condition was contrasted with his.

This novel and peculiar state of mankind necessarily predisposed men to listen to the general truths which Christianity teaches, and may serve to explain the facility and rapidity with which they then penetrated into the human mind.

The counterpart of this state of things was exhibited after the destruction of the Empire. The Roman World, being then as it were shattered into a thousand fragments, each nation resumed its pristine individuality. An infinite scale of ranks very soon grew up in the bosom of these nations; the different races were more sharply defined, and each nation was divided by castes into several peoples. In the midst of this common effort, which seemed to be urging human society to the greatest conceivable amount of voluntary subdivision, Christianity did not lose sight of the leading general ideas which it had brought into the world. But it appeared, nevertheless, to lend itself, as much as was possible, to those new tendencies to which the fractional distribution of mankind have given birth. Men continued to worship an only God, the Creator and Preserver of all things; but every people, every city, and, so to speak, every man, thought to obtain some distinct privilege, and win the favor of an especial patron at the foot of the throne of Grace. Unable to subdivide the Deity, they multiplied and improperly enhanced the importance of the divine agents. The homage due to saints and angels became an almost idolatrous worship among the majority of the Christian world; and apprehensions might be entertained for a moment lest the religion of Christ should retrograde toward the superstitions which it had subdued.

It seems evident, that the more the barriers are removed which separate nation from nation among mankind, and citizen from citizen among a people, the stronger is the bent of the human mind, as if by its own impulse, toward the idea of an only and all-powerful Being, dispensing equal laws in the same manner to every man. In democratic ages then it is more particularly important not to allow the homage paid to secondary agents to be confounded with the worship due to the Creator alone.

Another truth is no less clear—that religions ought to assume fewer external observances in democratic periods than at any others.

In speaking of philosophical method among the Americans, I have shown that nothing is more repugnant to the human mind in an age of equality than the idea of subjection to forms. Men living at such times are impatient of figures; to their eyes symbols appear to be the puerile artifice which is used to conceal or to set off truths, which should more naturally be bared to the light of open day: they are unmoved by ceremonial observances, and they are predisposed to attach a secondary importance to the details of public worship.

Those whose care it is to regulate the external forms of religion in a democratic age should pay a close attention to these natural propensities of the human mind, in order not unnecessarily to run counter to them.

I firmly believe in the necessity of forms, which fix the human mind in the contemplation of abstract truths, and stimulate its ardor in the pursuit of them, while they invigorate its powers of retaining them steadfastly. Nor do I suppose that it is possible to maintain a religion without external observances; but, on the other hand, I am persuaded, that, in the ages upon which we are entering, it would be peculiarly dangerous to multiply them beyond measure; and that they ought rather to be limited to as much as is absolutely necessary to perpetuate the doctrine itself, which is the substance of religions of which the ritual is only the form.* A religion which should become more minute, more peremptory, and more surcharged with small observances at a time in which men are becoming more equal, would soon find itself reduced to a band of fanatical zealots in the midst of an infidel people.

I anticipate the objection, that as all religions have general and eternal truths for their object, they cannot thus shape themselves to the shifting spirit of every age, without forfeiting their claim to certainty in the eyes of mankind.

To this I reply again, that the principal opinions which constitute belief, and which theologians call articles of faith, must be very carefully distinguished from the accessories connected with them Reli-

---

* In all religions there are some ceremonies which are inherent in the substance of the faith itself, and in these nothing should on any account be changed. This is especially the case with Roman Catholicism, in which the doctrine and the form are frequently so closely united as to form one point of belief.

gions are obliged to hold fast to the former, whatever be the peculiar spirit of the age; but they should take good care not to bind themselves in the same manner to the latter, at a time when everything is in transition, and when the mind, accustomed to the moving pageant of human affairs, reluctantly endures the attempt to fix it to any given point. The fixity of external and secondary things can only afford a chance of duration when civil society is itself fixed; under any other circumstances I hold it to be perilous.

We shall have occasion to see that, of all the passions which originate in, or are fostered by, equality, there is one which it renders peculiarly intense, and which it infuses at the same time into the heart of every man: I mean the love of well-being. The taste for well-being is the prominent and indelible feature of democratic ages.

It may be believed that a religion which should undertake to destroy so deep-seated a passion, would meet its own destruction thence in the end; and if it attempted to wean men entirely from the contemplation of the good things of this world, in order to devote their faculties exclusively to the thought of another, it may be foreseen that the soul would at length escape from its grasp, to plunge into the exclusive enjoyment of present and material pleasures.

The chief concern of religions is to purify, to regulate, and to restrain the excessive and exclusive taste for well-being which men feel at periods of equality; but they would err in attempting to control it completely or to eradicate it. They will not succeed in curing men of the love of riches; but they may still persuade men to enrich themselves by none but honest means.

This brings me to a final consideration, which comprises, as it were, all the others. The more the conditions of men are equalized and assimilated to each other, the more important is it for religions, while they carefully abstain from the daily turmoil of secular affairs, not needlessly to run counter to the ideas which generally prevail, and the permanent interests which exist in the mass of the people. For as public opinion grows to be more and more evidently the first and most irresistible of existing powers, the religious principle has no external support strong enough to enable it long to resist its attacks. This is not less true of a democratic people, ruled by a despot, than in a republic. In ages of equality, kings may often command obedience, but the majority always commands belief: to the majority therefore deference is to be paid in whatsoever is not contrary to the faith.

I showed in my former volumes how the American clergy stand aloof from secular affairs. This is the most obvious, but is not the only, example of their self-restraint. In America religion is a distinct sphere, in which the priest is sovereign, but out of which he takes care never to go. Within its limits he is the master of the mind; beyond them, he leaves men to themselves, and surrenders them to the independence and instability which belong to their nature and their age. I have seen no country in which Christianity is clothed with fewer forms, figures and observances than in the United States; or where it presents more distinct, more simple, or more general notions to the mind. Although the

Christians of America are divided into a multitude of sects, they all look upon their religion in the same light. This applies to Roman Catholicism as well as to the other forms of belief. There are no Romish priests who show less taste for the minute individual observances, for extraordinary or peculiar means of salvation, or who cling more to the spirit, and less to the letter, of the law, than the Roman Catholic priests of the United States. Nowhere is that doctrine of the Church, which prohibits the worship reserved to God alone from being offered to the Saints, more clearly inculcated or more generally followed. Yet the Roman Catholics of America are very submissive and very sincere.

Another remark is applicable to the clergy of every communion. The American ministers of the Gospel do not attempt to draw or to fix all the thoughts of man upon the life to come; they are willing to surrender a portion of his heart to the cares of the present; seeming to consider the goods of this world as important, although as secondary, objects. If they take no part themselves in productive labour, they are at least interested in its progression and ready to applaud its results; and while they never cease to point to the other world as the great object of the hopes and fears of the believer, they do not forbid him honestly to court prosperity in this. Far from attempting to show that these things are distinct and contrary to one another, they study rather to find out on what point they are most nearly and closely connected.

All the American clergy know and respect the intellectual supremacy exercised by the majority: they never sustain any but necessary conflicts with it. They take no share in the altercations of parties, but they readily adopt the general opinions of their country and their age; and they allow themselves to be borne away without opposition in the current of feeling and opinion by which everything around them is carried along. They endeavour to amend their contemporaries, but they do not quit fellowship with them. Public opinion is therefore never hostile to them: it rather supports and protects them; and their belief owes its authority at the same time to the strength which is its own, and to that which they borrow from the opinions of the majority.

Thus it is, that by respecting all democratic tendencies not absolutely contrary to herself, and by making use of several of them for her own purposes, Religion sustains an advantageous struggle with that spirit of individual independence which is her most dangerous antagonist.

Chapter VI.

OF THE PROGRESS OF ROMAN CATHOLICISM IN THE UNITED STATES.

America is the most democratic country in the world, and it is at the same time (according to reports worthy of belief,) the country in which the Roman Catholic religion makes most progress. At first sight this is surprising.

Two things must here be accurately distinguished: equality inclines men to wish to form their own opinions; but, on the other hand, it imbues them with the taste and the idea of unity, simplicity, and impartiality in the power which governs society. Men living in democratic ages are therefore very prone to shake off all religious authority; but if they consent to subject themselves to any authority of this kind, they choose at least that it should be single and uniform. Religious powers not radiating from a common centre are naturally repugnant to their minds; and they almost as readily conceive that there should be no religion, as that there should be several.

At the present time, more than in any preceding one, Roman Catholics are seen to lapse into infidelity, and Protestants to be converted to Roman Catholicism. If the Roman Catholic faith be considered within the pale of the Church, it would seem to be losing ground; without that pale, to be gaining it. Nor is this circumstance difficult of explanation. The men of our days are naturally little disposed to believe; but, as soon as they have any religion, they immediately find in themselves a latent propensity which urges them unconsciously toward Catholicism. Many of the doctrines and the practices of the Romish church astonish them; but they feel a secret admiration for its discipline, and its great unity attracts them. If Catholicism could at length withdraw itself from the political animosities to which it has given rise, I have hardly any doubt but that the same spirit of the age, which appears to be so opposed to it, would become so favourable as to admit of its great and sudden advancement.

One of the most ordinary weaknesses of the human intellect is to seek to reconcile contrary principles, and to purchase peace at the expense of logic. Thus there have ever been, and will ever be, men who, after having submitted some portion of their religious belief to the principle of authority, will seek to exempt several other parts of their faith from its influence, and to keep their minds floating at random between liberty and obedience. But I am inclined to believe that the number of these thinkers will be less in democratic than in other ages; and that our posterity will tend more and more to a single division into two parts—some relinquishing Christianity entirely, and others returning to the bosom of the Church of Rome.

Chapter VII.

OF THE CAUSE OF A LEANING TO PANTHEISM AMONG DEMOCRATIC NATIONS.

I shall take occasion hereafter to show under what form the preponderating taste of a democratic people for very general ideas manifests itself in politics; but I would point out, at the present stage of my work, its principal effect on philosophy.

It cannot be denied that pantheism[1] has made great progress in our age. The writings of a part of Europe bear visible marks of it: the Germans introduce it into philosophy, and the French into literature. Most of the works of imagination published in France contain some opinions or some tinge caught from pantheistical doctrines, or they disclose some tendency to such doctrines in their authors. This appears to me not only to proceed from an accidental, but from a permanent cause.

When the conditions of society are becoming more equal, and each individual man becomes more like all the rest, more weak and more insignificant, a habit grows up of ceasing to notice the citizens to consider only the people, and of overlooking individuals to think only of their kind. At such times the human mind seeks to embrace a multitude of different objects at once; and it constantly strives to succeed in connecting a variety of consequences with a single cause. The idea of unity so possesses itself of man, and is sought for by him so universally, that if he thinks he has found it, he readily yields himself up to repose in that belief. Nor does he content himself with the discovery that nothing is in the world but a creation and a Creator; still embarrassed by this primary division of things, he seeks to expand and to simplify his conception by including God and the Universe in one great Whole.

If there be a philosophical system which teaches that all things material and immaterial, visible and invisible, which the world contains, are only to be considered as the several parts of an immense Being, which alone remains unchanged amid the continual change and ceaseless transformation of all that constitutes it, we may readily infer that such a system, although it destroy the individuality of man—nay, rather because it destroys that individuality—will have secret charms for men living in democracies. All their habits of thought prepare them to conceive it, and predispose them to adopt it. It naturally attracts and fixes their imagination; it fosters the pride, while it soothes the indolence, of their minds.

Among the different systems by whose aid Philosophy endeavours to explain the Universe, I believe pantheism to be one of those most fitted to seduce the human mind in democratic ages. Against it, all who abide in their attachment to the true greatness of man, should struggle and combine.

Chapter VIII.

THE PRINCIPLE OF EQUALITY SUGGESTS TO THE AMERICANS THE IDEA OF THE INDEFINITE PERFECTIBILITY OF MAN.

Equality suggests to the human mind several ideas which would not have originated from any other source, and it modifies almost all those previously entertained. I take as an example the idea of human perfectibility, because it is one of the principal notions that the intellect can conceive, and because it constitutes of itself a great philosophical theory, which is every instant to be traced by its consequences in the practice of human affairs.

Although man has many points of resemblance with the brute creation, one characteristic is peculiar to himself—he improves; they are incapable of improvement. Mankind could not fail to discover this difference from its earliest period. The idea of perfectibility is therefore as old as the world: equality did not give birth to it, although it has imparted to it a novel character.

When the citizens of a community are classed according to their rank, their profession or their birth, and when all men are constrained to follow the career which happens to open before them, every one thinks that the utmost limits of human power are to be discerned in proximity to himself, and none seeks any longer to resist the inevitable law of his destiny. Not indeed that an aristocratic people absolutely contests man's faculty of self-improvement, but they do not hold it to be indefinite; amelioration they conceive, but not change: they imagine that the future condition of society may be better, but not essentially different; and while they admit that mankind has made vast strides in improvement, and may still have some to make, they assign to it beforehand certain impassable limits.

Thus they do not presume that they have arrived at the supreme good or at absolute truth, (what people or what man was ever wild enough to imagine it?) but they cherish a persuasion that they have pretty nearly reached that degree of greatness and knowledge which our imperfect nature admits of; and, as nothing moves about them, they are willing to fancy that every thing is in its fit place. Then it is that the legislator affects to lay down eternal laws; that kings and nations will raise none but imperishable monuments; and that the present generation undertakes to spare generations to come the care of regulating their destinies.

In proportion as castes disappear and the classes of society approximate—as manners, customs and laws vary, from the tumultuous intercourse of men—as new facts arise—as new truths are brought to light—as ancient opinions are dissipated and others take their place—the image of an ideal perfection, for ever on the wing, presents itself to the human mind. Continual changes are then every instant occurring under the observation of every man: the position of some is rendered worse; and he learns but too well, that no people and no individual, how enlightened soever they may be, can lay claim to infallibility;—the condition of others is improved; whence he infers that man is endowed with an indefinite faculty of improvement. His reverses teach him that none may hope to have discovered absolute good—his success stimulates him to the never-ending pursuit of it. Thus, for ever seeking—for ever falling, to rise again—often disappointed, but not discouraged—he tends unceasingly toward that unmeasured greatness so indistinctly visible at the end of the long track which humanity has yet to tread.

It can hardly be believed how many facts naturally flow from the philosophical theory of the indefinite perfectibility of man, or how strong an influence it exercises even on men who, living entirely for the purposes of action and not of thought, seem to conform their actions to it, without knowing anything about it.

I accost an American sailor, and I inquire why the ships of his country are built so as to last but for a short time; he answers without hesitation that the rat of navigation is every day making such rapid progress, that the finest vessel would become almost useless if it lasted beyond a certain number of years. In these words, which fell accidentally and on a particular subject from a man of rude attainments, I recognise the general and systematic idea upon which a great people directs all its concerns.

Aristocratic nations are naturally too apt to narrow the scope of human perfectibility; democratic nations to expand it beyond compass.

Chapter IX.

THE EXAMPLE OF THE AMERICANS DOES NOT PROVE THAT A DEMOCRATIC PEOPLE CAN HAVE NO APTITUDE AND NO TASTE FOR SCIENCE, LITERATURE, OR ART.

It must be acknowledged that among few of the civilized nations of our time have the higher sciences made less progress than in the United States; and in few have great artists, fine poets, or celebrated writers been more rare. Many Europeans, struck by this fact, have looked upon it as a natural and inevitable result of equality; and they have supposed that if a democratic state of society and democratic institutions were ever to prevail over the whole earth, the human mind would gradually find its beacon-lights grow dim, and men would relapse into a period of darkness.

To reason thus is, I think, to confound several ideas which it is important to divide and to examine separately: it is to mingle, unintentionally, what is democratic with what is only American.

The religion professed by the first emigrants, and bequeathed by them to their descendants, simple in its form of worship, austere and almost harsh in its principles, and hostile to external symbols and to ceremonial pomp, is naturally unfavourable to the fine arts, and only yields a reluctant sufferance to the pleasures of literature. The Americans are a very old and a very enlightened people, who have fallen upon a new and unbounded country, where they may extend themselves at pleasure, and which they may fertilize without difficulty. This state of things is without a parallel in the history of the world. In America then every one finds facilities, unknown elsewhere, for making or increasing his fortune. The spirit of gain is always on the stretch, and the human mind, constantly diverted from the pleasures of imagination and the labours of the intellect, is there swayed by no impulse but the pursuit of wealth. Not only are manufacturing and commercial classes to be found in the United States, as they are in all other countries; but, what never occurred elsewhere, the whole community is simultaneously engaged in productive industry and commerce.

I am convinced that if the Americans had been alone in the world, with the freedom and the knowledge acquired by their forefathers, and the passions which are their own, they would not have been slow to discover that progress cannot long he made in the application of the sciences without cultivating the theory of them; that all the arts are perfected by one another; and, however absorbed they might have been by the pursuit of the principal object of their desires, they would speedily have admitted, that it is necessary to turn aside from it occasionally, in order the better to attain it in the end.

The taste for the pleasures of the mind is moreover so natural to the heart of civilized man, that among the polite nations, which are least disposed to give themselves up to these pursuits, a certain number of citizens are always to be found who take part in them. This intellectual craving, when once felt, would very soon have been satisfied.

But at the very time when the Americans were naturally inclined to require nothing of science but its special applications to the useful arts and the means of rendering life comfortable, learned and literary Europe was engaged in exploring the common sources of truth, and in improving at the same time all that can minister to the pleasures or satisfy the wants of man.

At the head of the enlightened nations of the Old World the inhabitants of the United States more particularly distinguished one, to which they were closely united by a common origin and by kindred habits. Among this people they found distinguished men of science, artists of skill, writers of eminence, and they were enabled to enjoy the treasures of the intellect without requiring to labour in amassing them. I cannot consent to separate America from Europe, in spite of the ocean which intervenes. I consider the people of the United States as that portion of the English people which is commissioned to explore the wilds of the New World; while the rest of the nation, enjoying more leisure and less harassed by the drudgery of life, may devote its energies to thought, and enlarge in all directions the empire of the mind.

The position of the Americans is therefore quite exceptional, and it may be believed that no democratic people will ever be placed in a similar one. Their strictly Puritanical origin—their exclusively commercial habits—even the country they inhabit, which seems to divert their minds from the pursuit of science, literature, and the arts—the proximity of Europe, which allows them to neglect these pursuits without relapsing into barbarism—a thousand special causes, of which I have only been able to point out the most important—have singularly concurred to fix the mind of the American upon purely practical objects. His passions, his wants, his education, and everything about him seem to unite in drawing the native of the United States earthward: his religion alone bids him turn, from time to time, a transient and distracted glance to heaven. Let us cease then to view all democratic nations under the mask of the American people, and let us attempt to survey them at length with their own proper features.

It is possible to conceive a people not subdivided into any castes or scale of ranks; in which the law, recognising no privileges, should divide inherited property into equal shares; but which, at the same time, should be without knowledge and without freedom. Nor is this an empty hypothesis: a despot may find that it is his interest to render his subjects equal and to leave them ignorant, in order more easily to keep them slaves. Not only would a democratic people of this kind show neither aptitude nor taste for science, literature, or art, but it would probably never arrive at the possession of them. The law of descent would of itself provide for the destruction of fortunes at each succeeding generation; and new fortunes would be acquired by none. The poor man, without either knowledge or freedom, would not so much as conceive the idea of raising himself to wealth; and the rich man would allow himself to be degraded to poverty, without a notion of self-defence. Between these two members of the community complete and invincible equality would soon be established.

No one would then have time or taste to devote himself to the pursuits or pleasures of the intellect; but all men would remain paralysed by a state of common ignorance and equal servitude. When I conceive a democratic society of this kind, I fancy myself in one of those low, close, and gloomy abodes, where the light which breaks in from without soon faints and fades away. A sudden heaviness overpowers me, and I grope through the surrounding darkness, to find the aperture which will restore me to daylight and the air.

But all this is not applicable to men already enlightened, who retain their freedom, after having abolished from among them those peculiar and hereditary rights which perpetuated the tenure of property in the hands of certain individuals or certain bodies.

When men living in a democratic state of society are enlightened, they readily discover that they are confined and fixed within no limits which constrain them to take up with their present fortune. They all therefore conceive the idea of increasing it; if they are free they all attempt it, but all do not succeed in the same manner. The Legislature, it is true, no longer grants privileges, but they are bestowed by nature. As natural inequality is very great, fortunes become unequal as soon as every man exerts all his faculties to get rich.

The law of descent prevents the establishment of wealthy families; but it does not prevent the existence of wealthy individuals. It constantly brings back the members of the community to a common level, from which they as constantly escape: and the inequality of fortunes augments in proportion as knowledge is diffused and liberty increased.

A sect[1] which arose in our time, and was celebrated for its talents and its extravagance, proposed to concentrate all property in the hands of a central power, whose function it should afterward be to parcel it out to individuals, according to their capacity. This would have been a method of escaping from that complete and eternal equality which seems to threaten democratic society. But it would be a simpler and less dangerous remedy to grant no privilege to any, giving to all equal cultivation and equal independence, and leaving every one to determine his own position. Natural inequality will very soon make way for itself, and wealth will spontaneously pass into the hands of the most capable.

Free and democratic communities, then, will always contain a considerable number of people enjoying opulence or competency. The wealthy will not be so closely linked to each other as the members of the former aristocratic class of society: their propensities will be different, and they will scarcely ever enjoy leisure as secure or as complete: but they will be far more numerous than those who belonged to that class of society could ever be. These persons will not be strictly confined to the cares of practical life, and they will still be able, though in different degrees, to indulge in the pursuits and pleasures of the intellect. In those pleasures they will indulge: for if it be true that the human mind leans on one side to the narrow, the practical, and the useful, it naturally rises on the other to the infinite, the spiritual, and the beautiful. Physical wants confine it to the earth; but, as soon as the tie is loosened, it will unbend itself again.

Not only will the number of those who can take an interest in the productions of the mind be enlarged, but the taste for intellectual enjoyment will descend, step by step, even to those who, in aristocratic societies, seem to have neither time nor ability to indulge in them. When hereditary wealth, the privileges of rank, and the prerogatives of birth have ceased to be, and when every man derives his strength from himself alone, it becomes evident that the chief cause of disparity between the fortunes of men is the mind. Whatever tends to invigorate, to extend, or to adorn the mind, instantly rises to great value. The utility of knowledge becomes singularly conspicuous even to the eyes of the multitude: those who have no taste for its charms set store upon its results, and make some efforts to acquire it.

In free and enlightened democratic ages, there is nothing to separate men from each other or to retain them in their peculiar sphere: they rise or sink with extreme rapidity. All classes live in perpetual intercourse from their great proximity to each other. They communicate and intermingle every day—they imitate and envy one another: this suggests to the people many ideas, notions, and desires which it would never have entertained if the distinctions of rank had been fixed and society at rest. In such nations the servant never considers himself as an entire stranger to the pleasures and toils of his master, nor the poor man to those of the rich; the rural population assimilates itself to that of the towns, and the provinces to the capital. No one easily allows himself to be reduced to the mere material cares of life; and the humblest artisan casts at times an eager and a furtive glance into the higher regions of the intellect. People do not read with the same notions or in the same manner as they do in an aristocratic community; but the circle of readers is unceasingly expanded, till it includes all the citizens.

As soon as the multitude begins to take an interest in the labors of the mind, it finds out that to excel in some of them is a powerful method of acquiring fame, power, or wealth. The restless ambition which equality begets instantly takes this direction as it does all others. The number of those who cultivate science, letters, and the arts, becomes immense. The intellectual world starts into prodigious activity: every one endeavors to open for himself a path there, and to draw the eyes of the public after him. Something analogous occurs to what happens in society in the United States politically considered. What is done, is often imperfect, but the attempts are innumerable; and although the results of individual effort are commonly very small, the total amount is always very large.

It is therefore not true to assert that men living in democratic ages are naturally indifferent to science, literature, and the arts: only it must be acknowledged that they cultivate them after their own fashion, and bring to the task their own peculiar qualifications and deficiencies.

Chapter X.

WHY THE AMERICANS ARE MORE ADDICTED TO PRACTICAL THAN TO THEORETICAL SCIENCE.

If a democratic state of society and democratic institutions do not stop the career of the human mind, they incontestably guide it in one direction in preference to another. Their effects, thus circumscribed, are still exceedingly great; and I trust I may be pardoned if I pause for a moment to survey them.

We had occasion, in speaking of the philosophical method of the American people, to make several remarks, which must here be turned to account.

Equality begets in man the desire of judging of everything for himself: it gives him, in all things, a taste for the tangible and the real, a contempt for tradition and for forms. These general tendencies are principally discernible in the peculiar subject of this chapter.

Those who cultivate the sciences among a democratic people are always afraid of losing their way in visionary speculation. They mistrust systems; they adhere closely to facts and the study of facts with their own senses. As they do not easily defer to the mere name of any fellow-man, they are never inclined to rest upon any man's authority; but, on the contrary, they are unremitting in their efforts to point out the weaker points of their neighbour's opinions. Scientific precedents have very little weight with them; they are never long detained by the subtilty of the schools, nor ready to accept big words for sterling coin; they penetrate, as far as they can, into the principal parts of the subject which engages them, and they expound them in the vernacular tongue. Scientific pursuits then follow a freer and a safer course, but a less lofty one.

The mind may, as it appears to me, divide science into three parts.

The first comprises the most theoretical principles, and those more abstract notions, whose application is either unknown or very remote.

The second is composed of those general truths, which still belong to pure theory, but lead nevertheless by a straight and short road to practical results.

Methods of application and means of execution make up the third.

Each of these different portions of science may be separately cultivated, although reason and experience show that none of them can prosper long, if it be absolutely cut off from the two others.

In America the purely practical part of science is admirably understood, and careful attention is paid to the theoretical portion which is immediately requisite to application. On this head the Americans always display a clear, free, original, and inventive power of mind. But hardly any one in the United States devotes himself to the essentially theoretical and abstract portion of human knowledge. In this respect the Americans carry to excess a tendency which is, I think, discernible, though in a less degree, among all democratic nations.

Nothing is more necessary to the culture of the higher sciences, or of the more elevated departments of science, than meditation; and nothing is less suited to meditation than the structure of democratic society. We do not find there, as among an aristocratic people, one class which clings to a state of repose because it is well off; and another, which does not venture to stir because it despairs of improving its condition. Every one is actively in motion: some in quest of power, others of gain. In the midst of this universal tumult—this incessant conflict of jarring interests—this continual stride of men, after fortune—where is that calm to be found which is necessary for the deeper combinations of the intellect? How can the mind dwell upon any single point, when everything whirls around it, and man himself is swept and beaten onward by the heady current which rolls all things in its course?

But the permanent agitation which subsists in the bosom of a peaceable and established democracy, must be distinguished from the tumultuous and revolutionary movements which almost always attend the birth and growth of democratic society. When a violent revolution occurs among a highly civilized people, it cannot fail to give a sudden impulse to their feelings and their opinions. This is more particularly true of democratic revolutions, which stir up all the classes of which a people is composed, and beget, at the same time, inordinate ambition in the breast of every member of the community. The French made most surprising advances in the exact sciences at the very time at which they were finishing the destruction of the remains of their former feudal society; yet this sudden fecundity is not to be attributed to democracy, but to the unexampled revolution which attended its growth. What happened at that period was a special incident, and it would be unwise to regard it as the test of a general principle.

Great revolutions are not more common among democratic than among other nations: I am even inclined to believe that they are less so. But there prevails among those populations a small distressing motion—a sort of incessant jostling of men, which annoys and disturbs the mind, without exciting or elevating it.

Men who live in democratic communities not only seldom indulge in meditation, but they naturally entertain very little esteem for it. A democratic state of society and democratic institutions plunge the greater part of men in constant active life; and the habits of mind which are suited to an active life, are not always suited to a contemplative one. The man of action is frequently obliged to content himself with the best he can get, because he would never accomplish his purpose if he chose to carry every detail to perfection. He has perpetually occasion to rely on ideas which he has not had leisure to search to the bottom; for he is much more frequently aided by the opportunity of an idea than by its strict accuracy; and, in the long run, he risks less in making use of some false principles, than in spending his time in establishing all his principles on the basis of truth. The world is not led by long or learned demonstrations: a rapid glance at particular incidents, the daily study of the fleeting passions of the multitude, the accidents of the time, and the art of turning them to account, decide all its affairs.

In the ages in which active life is the condition of almost every one, men are therefore generally led to attach an excessive value to the rapid bursts and superficial conceptions of the intellect; and, on the other hand, to depreciate below their true standard its slower and deeper labours. This opinion of the public influences the judgement of the men who cultivate the sciences; they are persuaded that they may succeed in those pursuits without meditation, or deterred from such pursuits as demand it.

There are several methods of studying the sciences. Among a multitude of men you will find a selfish, mercantile, and trading taste for the discoveries of the mind, which must not be confounded with that disinterested passion which is kindled in the heart of the few. A desire to utilize knowledge is one thing; the pure desire to know is another. I do not doubt that in a few minds and far between, an ardent, inexhaustible love of truth springs up, self-supported, and living in ceaseless fruition without ever attaining the satisfaction which it seeks. This ardent love it is—this proud, disinterested love of what is true—which raises men to the abstract sources of truth, to draw their mother-knowledge thence.

If Pascal had had nothing in view but some large gain, or even if he had been stimulated by the love of fame alone, I cannot conceive that he would ever have been able to rally all the powers of his mind, as he did, for the better discovery of the most hidden things of the Creator. When I see him, as it were, tear his soul from the midst of all the cares of life to devote it wholly to these researches, and, prematurely snapping the links which bind the frame to life, die of old age before forty, I stand amazed, and I perceive that no ordinary cause is at work to produce efforts so extraordinary.

The future will prove whether these passions, at once so rare and so productive, come into being and into growth as easily in the midst of democratic as in aristocratic communities. For myself, I confess that I am slow to believe it.

In aristocratic society, the class which gives the tone to opinion, and has the supreme guidance of affairs, being permanently and hereditarily placed above the multitude, naturally conceives a lofty idea of itself and of man. It loves to invent for him noble pleasures, to carve out splendid objects for his ambition. Aristocracies often commit very tyrannical and very inhuman actions; but they rarely entertain grovelling thoughts; and they show a kind of haughty contempt of little pleasures, even while they indulge in them. The effect is greatly to raise the general pitch of society. In aristocratic ages vast ideas are commonly entertained of the dignity, the power, and the greatness of man. These opinions exert their influence on those who cultivate the sciences, as well as on the rest of the community. They facilitate the natural impulse of the mind to the highest regions of thought, and they naturally prepare it to conceive a sublime—nay, almost a divine— love of truth.

Men of science at such periods are consequently carried away by theory; and it even happens that they frequently conceive an inconsiderate contempt for the practical part of learning. "Archimedes,"[1] says Plutarch,[2] "was of so lofty a spirit, that he never condescended to write any treatise on the manner of constructing all these engines of offence and defence. And as he held this science of inventing and putting together engines, and all arts generally speaking which tended to any useful end in practice, to be vile, low, and mercenary, he spent his talents and his studious hours in writing of those things only whose beauty and subtilty had in them no admixture of necessity." Such is the aristocratic aim of science: in democratic nations it cannot be the same.

The greater part of the men who constitute these nations are extremely eager in the pursuit of actual and physical gratification. As they are always dissatisfied with the position which they occupy, and are always free to leave it, they think of nothing but the means of changing their fortune, or of increasing it. To minds thus predisposed, every new method which leads by a shorter road to wealth, every machine which spares labour, every instrument which diminishes the cost of production, every discovery which facilitates pleasures or augments them, seems to be the grandest effort of the human intellect. It is chiefly from these motives that a democratic people addicts itself to scientific pursuits—that it understands, and that it respects them. In aristocratic ages, science is more particularly called upon to furnish gratification to the mind; in democracies, to the body.

You may be sure that the more a nation is democratic, enlightened, and free, the greater will be the number of these interested promoters of scientific genius, and the more will discoveries immediately applicable to productive industry confer gain, fame, and even power on their authors. For in democracies the working-class takes a part in public affairs; and public honours, as well as pecuniary remuneration, may be awarded to those who deserve them.

In a community thus organized it may easily be conceived that the human mind may be led insensibly to the neglect of theory; and that it is urged, on the contrary, with unparalleled vehemence to the applications of science, or at least to that portion of theoretical science which is necessary to those who make such applications. In vain will some innate propensity raise the mind toward the loftier spheres of the intellect; interest draws it down to the middle zone. There it may develop all its energy and restless activity, there it may engender all its wonders. These very Americans, who have not discovered one of the general laws of mechanics, have introduced into navigation an engine[3] which changes the aspect of the world.

Assuredly I do not contend that the democratic nations of our time are destined to witness the extinction of the transcendent luminaries of man's intelligence, nor even that no new lights will ever start into existence. At the age at which the world has now arrived, and among so many cultivated nations, perpetually excited by the fever of productive industry, the bonds which connect the different parts of science together cannot fail to strike the observation; and the taste for practical science itself, if it be enlightened, ought to lead men not to neglect theory. In the midst of such numberless attempted applications of so many experiments, repeated every day, it is almost impossible that general laws should not frequently be brought to light; so that great discoveries would be frequent, though great inventors be rare.

I believe, moreover, in the high calling of scientific minds. If the democratic principle does not, on the one hand, induce men to cultivate science for its own sake, on the other it enormously increases the number of those who do cultivate it. Nor is it credible that, from among so great a multitude, no speculative genius should from time to time arise, inflamed by the love of truth alone. Such an one, we may be sure, would dive into the deepest mysteries of nature, whatever be the spirit of his country or his age. He requires no assistance in his course—enough that he be not checked in it.

All that I mean to say is this:—permanent inequality of conditions leads men to confine themselves to the arrogant and sterile research of abstract truths; while the social condition and the institutions of democracy prepare them to seek the immediate and useful practical results of the sciences. This tendency is natural and inevitable: it is curious to be acquainted with it, and it may be necessary to point it out.

If those who are called upon to guide the nations of our time clearly discerned from afar off these new tendencies, which will soon be irresistible, they would understand that, possessing education and freedom, men living in democratic ages cannot fail to improve the industrial part of science; and that henceforward all the efforts of the constituted authorities ought to be directed to support the highest branches of learning, and to foster the nobler passion for science itself. In the present age the human mind must be coerced into theoretical studies; it runs of its own accord to practical applications; and, instead of perpetually referring it to the minute examination of secondary effects, it is well to divert it from them sometimes, in order to raise it up to the contemplation of primary causes.

Because the civilization of ancient Rome perished in consequence of the invasion of the Barbarians, we are perhaps too apt to think that civilization cannot perish in any other manner. If the light by which we are guided is ever extinguished, it will dwindle by degrees, and expire of itself. By dint of close adherence to mere applications, principles would be lost sight of; and when the principles were wholly forgotten, the methods derived from them would be ill pursued. New methods could no longer be invented, and men would continue to apply, without intelligence and without art, scientific processes no longer understood.

When Europeans first arrived in China, three hundred years ago, they found that almost all the arts had reached a certain degree of perfection there; and they were surprised that a people which had attained this point, should not have gone beyond it. At a later period they discovered some traces of the higher branches of science which were lost. The nation was absorbed in productive industry; the greater part of its scientific processes had been preserved, but science itself no longer existed there. This served to explain the strangely motionless state in which they found the minds of this people. The Chinese, in following the track of their forefathers, had forgotten the reasons by which the latter had been guided. They still used the formula, without asking for its meaning; they retained the instrument, but they no longer possessed the art of altering or renewing it. The Chinese, then, had lost the power of change; for them to improve was impossible. They were compelled, at all times and in all points, to imitate their predecessors, lest they should stray into utter darkness, by deviating for an instant from the path already laid down for them. The source of human knowledge was all but dry; and though the stream still ran on, it could neither swell its waters, nor alter its channel.

Notwithstanding this, China had subsisted peaceably for centuries. The invaders who had conquered the country assumed the manners of the inhabitants, and order prevailed there. A sort of physical prosperity was everywhere discernible: revolutions were rare, and war was, so to speak, unknown.

It is then a fallacy to flatter ourselves with the reflection, that the Barbarians are still far from us; for if there be some nations which allow civilization to be torn from their grasp, there are others who trample it themselves under their feet.

Chapter XI.

CONCERNING THE SPIRIT IN WHICH THE AMERICANS CULTIVATE THE ARTS.

It would be to waste the time of my readers and my own, if I strove to demonstrate how the general mediocrity of fortunes, the absence of superfluous wealth, the universal desire of comfort, and the constant efforts by which every one attempts to procure it, make the taste for the useful predominate over the love of the beautiful in the heart of man. Democratic nations, among which all these things exist, will therefore cultivate the arts which serve to render life easy, in preference to those whose object is to adorn it. They will habitually prefer the useful to the beautiful, and they will require that the beautiful should be useful.

But I propose to go further; and after having pointed out this first feature, to sketch several others.

It commonly happens that in the ages of privilege the practice of almost all the arts becomes a privilege; and that every profession is a separate walk upon which it is not allowable for every one to enter. Even when productive industry is free, the fixed character which belongs to aristocratic nations gradually segregates all the persons who practise the same art, till they form a distinct class, always composed of the same families, whose members are all known to each other, and among whom a public opinion of their own, and a species of corporate pride soon spring up. In a class or guild of this kind, each artisan has not only his fortune to make, but his reputation to preserve. He is not exclusively swayed by his own interest, or even by that of his customer, but by that of the body to which he belongs; and the interest of that body is, that each artisan should produce the best possible workmanship. In aristocratic ages, the object of the arts is therefore to manufacture as well as possible—not with the greatest dispatch, or at the lowest rate.

When, on the contrary, every profession is open to all—when a multitude of persons are constantly embracing and abandoning it—and when its several members are strangers to each other, indifferent and from their numbers hardly seen among themselves; the social tie is destroyed, and each workman, standing alone, endeavours simply to gain the greatest possible quantity of money at the least possible cost. The will of the customer is then his only limit. But at the same time a corresponding revolution takes place in the customer also. In countries in which riches as well as power are concentrated and retained in the hands of the few, the use of the greater part of this world's goods belongs to a small number of individuals, who are always the same. Necessity, public opinion, or moderate desires exclude all others from the enjoyment of them. As this aristocratic class remains fixed at the pinnacle of greatness on which it stands, without diminution or increase, it is always acted upon by the same wants and affected by them in the same manner. The men of whom it is composed naturally derive from their superior and hereditary position a taste for what is extremely well-made and lasting. This affects the general way of thinking of the nation in relation to the arts. It often occurs, among such a people, that even the peasant will rather go without the objects he covets, than procure them in a state of imperfection. In aristocracies, then, the handicraftsmen work for only a limited number of very fastidious customers: the profit they hope to make depends principally on the perfection of their workmanship.

Such is no longer the case when, all privileges being abolished, ranks are intermingled, and men are for ever rising or sinking upon the ladder of society. Among a democratic people a number of citizens always exist whose patrimony is divided and decreasing. They have contracted, under more prosperous circumstances, certain wants, which remain after the means of satisfying such wants are gone; and they are anxiously looking out for some surreptitious method of providing for them. On the other hand, there are always in democracies a large number of men whose fortune is upon the increase, but whose desires grow much faster than their fortunes; and who gloat upon the gifts of wealth in anticipation, long before they have means to command them. Such men are eager to find some short cut to these gratifications, already almost within their reach. From the combination of these two causes the result is, that in democracies there are always a multitude of individuals whose wants are above their means, and who are very willing to take up with imperfect satisfaction, rather than abandon the object of their desires.

The artisan readily understands these passions, for he himself partakes in them: in an aristocracy he would seek to sell his workmanship at a high price to the few; he now conceives that the more expeditious way of getting rich is to sell them at a low price to all. But there are only two ways of lowering the price of commodities. The first is to discover some better, shorter, and more ingenious method of producing them: the second is to manufacture a larger quantity of goods, nearly similar, but of less value. Among a democratic population, all the intellectual faculties of the workman are directed to these two objects: he strives to invent methods which may enable him not only to work better, but quicker and cheaper; or, if he cannot succeed in that, to diminish the intrinsic qualities of the thing he makes, without rendering it wholly unfit for the use for which it is intended. When none but the wealthy had watches, they were almost all very good ones: few are now made which are worth much, but every body has one in his pocket. Thus the democratic principle not only tends to direct the human mind to the useful arts, but it induces the artisan to produce with great rapidity a quantity of imperfect commodities, and the consumer to content himself with these commodities.

Not that in democracies the arts are incapable of producing very commendable works, if such be required. This may occasionally be the case, if customers appear who are ready to pay for time and trouble. In this rivalry of every kind of industry—in the midst of this immense competition and these countless experiments, some excellent workmen are formed who reach the utmost limits of their craft. But they have rarely an opportunity of displaying what they can do; they are scrupulously sparing of their powers; they remain in a state of accomplished mediocrity, which condemns itself, and, though it be very well able to shoot beyond the mark before it, aims only at what it hits. In aristocracies, on the contrary, workmen always do all they can; and when they stop, it is because they have reached the limit of their attainments.

When I arrive in a country where I find some of the finest productions of the arts, I learn from this fact nothing of the social condition or of the political constitution of the country. But if I perceive that the productions of the arts are generally of an inferior quality, very abundant and very cheap, I am convinced that, among the people where this occurs, privilege is on the decline, and that ranks are beginning to intermingle and will soon be confounded together.

The handicraftsmen of democratic ages endeavour not only to bring their useful productions within the reach of the whole community, but they strive to give to all their commodities attractive qualities which they do not in reality possess. In the confusion of all ranks every one hopes to appear what he is not, and makes great exertions to succeed in this object. This sentiment indeed, which is but too natural to the heart of man, does not originate in the democratic principle; but that principle applies it to material objects. To mimic virtue is of every age; but the hypocrisy of luxury belongs more particularly to the ages of democracy.

To satisfy these new cravings of human vanity, the arts have recourse to every species of imposture: and these devices sometimes go so far as to defeat their own purpose. Imitation-diamonds are now made which may be easily mistaken for real ones; as soon as the art of fabricating false diamonds shall have reached so high a degree of perfection that they cannot be distinguished from real ones, it is probable that both one and the other will be abandoned, and become mere pebbles again.

This leads me to speak of those arts which are called the fine arts, by way of distinction. I do not believe that it is a necessary effect of a democratic social condition and of democratic institutions to diminish the number of men who cultivate the fine arts; but these causes exert a very powerful influence on the manner in which these arts are cultivated. Many of those who had already contracted a taste for the fine arts are impoverished; on the other hand, many of those who are not yet rich begin to conceive that taste, at least by imitation; and the number of consumers increases, but opulent and fastidious consumers become more scarce. Something analogous to what I have already pointed out in the useful arts then takes place in the fine arts; the productions of artists are more numerous, but the merit of each production is diminished. No longer able to soar to what is great, they cultivate what is pretty and elegant; and appearance is more attended to than reality.

In aristocracies a few great pictures are produced; in democratic countries, a vast number of insignificant ones. In the former, statues are raised of bronze; in the latter, they are modelled in plaster.

When I arrived for the first time at New York, by that part of the Atlantic Ocean which is called the Narrows, I was surprised to perceive along the shore, at some distance from the city, a considerable number of little palaces of white marble, several of which were built after the models of ancient architecture. When I went the next day to inspect more closely the buildings which had particularly attracted my notice, I found that its walls were of whitewashed brick, and its columns of painted wood. All the edifices which I had admired the night before were of the same kind.

The social condition and the institutions of democracy impart, moreover, certain peculiar tendencies to all the imitative arts which it is easy to point out. They frequently withdraw them from the delineation of the soul to fix them exclusively on that of the body: and they substitute the representation of motion and sensation for that of sentiment and thought: in a word, they put the Real in the place of the Ideal.

I doubt whether Raphael[1] studied the minutest intricacies of the mechanism of the human body as thoroughly as the draftsmen of our own time.* He did not attach the same importance to rigorous accuracy on this point as they do, because he aspired to surpass nature. He sought to make man something which should be superior to man, and to embellish beauty's self. David[2] and his scholars were, on the contrary, as good anatomists as they were good painters. They wonderfully depicted the models which they had before their eyes, but they rarely imagined anything beyond them: they followed nature with fidelity; while Raphael sought for something better than nature. They have left us an exact portraiture of man; but he discloses in his works a glimpse of the Divinity.

This remark as to the manner of treating a subject is no less applicable to the choice of it. The painters of the middle ages generally sought far above themselves, and away from their own time, for

---

* [I trust I may be allowed to enter a protest against an opinion which some readers will perhaps agree with me in thinking a mistaken one. Whoever has examined the accurate study, the close fidelity to nature, and the profound scientific knowledge of Raphael and of almost all the great masters of art, in their drawings, (where the means by which their perfect works were achieved are more easily discernible than amidst the total splendour of those works themselves,) will, I think, prefer them to the crude design or the pedantic modelling of more recent times. Nor has the industry of the elder artists in these details ever been surpassed. For instance, in the series of sketches for Raphael's finest works, one represents the skeletons of the whole group, in perfect and not unmeaning osteology; a second reproduces the same group *fleshed* with complete anatomical science; in a third, the artist proceeds to put drapery on his figures. To compare the drawing of Raphael with that of David, is to compare the science of a surgeon with that of a butcher. The former penetrated by his art into the hidden beauty and truth of nature: the latter dragged nature to the easel, and deprived her at once of life, truth, and freedom.

I would be understood to confine this remark to the illustration here, as I think, inappropriately selected; for of the general influence of democracy on the choice of subjects, on the range of art, on the spirit, faith, and education of artists, and, last though not least, on the sympathy of the public, the passage above gives a very true analysis. The pictures of Ostade, Teniers, and Paul Potter belong as truly to the burghers of Holland, as those of Raphael and Michael Angelo to the aristocracy of the Church, or those of Titian and Velasquez, Rubens and Vandyke, to the courts and palaces of Europe—*Translator's Note.*]

mighty subjects, which left to their imagination an unbounded range. Our painters frequently employ their talents in the exact imitation of the details of private life, which they have always before their eyes; and they are for ever copying trivial objects, the originals of which are only too abundant in nature.

Chapter XII.

WHY THE AMERICANS RAISE SOME MONUMENTS SO INSIGNIFICANT, AND OTHERS SO IMPORTANT.

I have just observed, that in democratic ages monuments of the arts tend to become more numerous and less important. I now hasten to point out the exception to this rule.

In a democratic community individuals are very powerless; but the state which represents them all, and contains them all in its grasp, is very powerful. Nowhere do citizens appear so insignificant as in a democratic nation; nowhere does the nation itself appear greater, or does the mind more easily take in a wide general survey of it. In democratic communities the imagination is compressed when men consider themselves; it expands indefinitely when they think of the State. Hence it is that the same men who live on a small scale in narrow dwellings, frequently aspire to gigantic splendor in the erection of their public monuments.

The Americans have traced out the circuit of an immense city on the site which they intended to make their capital, but which, up to the present time, is hardly more densely peopled than Pontoise,[1] though, according to them, it will one day contain a million of inhabitants. They have already rooted up trees for ten miles round, lest they should interfere with the future citizens of this imaginary metropolis. They have erected a magnificent palace for Congress in the centre of the city, and have given it the pompous name of the Capitol.

The several States of the Union are every day planning and erecting for themselves prodigious undertakings, which would astonish the engineers of the great European nations.

Thus democracy not only leads men to a vast number of inconsiderable productions; it also leads them to raise some monuments on the largest scale: but between these two extremes there is a blank. A few scattered remains of enormous buildings can therefore teach us nothing of the social condition and the institutions of the people by whom they were raised. I may add, though the remark leads me to step out of my subject, that they do not make us better acquainted with its greatness, its civilization, and its real prosperity. Whensoever a power of any kind shall be able to make a whole people co-operate in a single undertaking, that power, with little knowledge and a great deal of time, will succeed in obtaining something enormous from the co-operation of efforts so multiplied. But this does not lead to the conclusion that the people was very happy, very enlightened, or even very strong.

The Spaniards found the city of Mexico full of magnificent temples and vast palaces; but that did not prevent Cortes[2] from conquering the Mexican empire with six hundred foot soldiers and sixteen horses.

If the Romans had been better acquainted with the laws of hydraulics, they would not have constructed all the aqueducts which surround the ruins of their cities—they would have made a better use of their power and their wealth. If they had invented the steam engine, perhaps they would not have extended to the extremities of their empire those long artificial roads which are called Roman Roads. These things are at once the splendid memorials of their ignorance and of their greatness.

A people which should leave no other vestige of its track than a few leaden pipes in the earth, and a few iron rods upon its surface, might have been more the master of Nature than the Romans.

Chapter XIII.

LITERARY CHARACTERISTICS OF DEMOCRATIC AGES.

When a traveller goes into a bookseller's shop in the United States, and examines the American books upon the shelves, the number of works appears extremely great; while that of known authors appears, on the contrary, to be extremely small. He will first meet with a number of elementary treatises, destined to teach the rudiments of human knowledge. Most of these books are written in Europe; the Americans reprint them, adapting them to their own country. Next comes an enormous quantity of religious works, Bibles, sermons, edifying anecdotes, controversial divinity, and reports of charitable societies; lastly, appears the long catalogue of political pamphlets. In America, parties do not write books to combat each other's opinions, but pamphlets which are circulated for a day with incredible rapidity, and then expire.

In the midst of all these obscure productions of the human brain, are to be found the more remarkable works of that small number of authors, whose names are, or ought to be, known to Europeans.

Although America is perhaps in our days the civilized country in which literature is least attended to, a large number of persons are nevertheless to be found there who take an interest in the productions of the mind, and who make them, if not the study of their lives, at least the charm of their leisure hours. But England supplies these readers with the larger portion of the books which they require. Almost all important English books are republished in the United States. The literary genius of Great Britain still darts its rays into the recesses of the forests of the New World. There is hardly a pioneer's hut which does not contain a few odd volumes of Shakspere. I remember that I read the feudal play of Henry V. for the first time in a log house.

Not only do the Americans constantly draw upon the treasures of English literature, but it may be said with truth that they find the literature of England growing on their own soil. The larger part of that small number of men in the United States who are engaged in the composition of literary works are English in substance, and still more so in form. Thus they transport into the midst of democracy the ideas and literary fashion which are current among the aristocratic nations they have taken for their model. They paint with colours borrowed from foreign manners; and as they hardly ever represent the country they were born in as it really is, they are seldom popular there.

The citizens of the United States are themselves so convinced that it is not for them that books are published, that before they can make up their minds upon the merit of one of their authors, they generally wait till his fame has been ratified in England, just as in pictures the author of an original is held to be entitled to judge of the merit of a copy.

The inhabitants of the United States have then at present, properly speaking, no literature. The only authors whom I acknowledge as American are the journalists. They indeed are not great writers, but they speak the language of their countrymen, and make themselves heard by them. Other authors are aliens; they are to the Americans what the imitators of the Greeks and Romans were to us at the revival of learning, an object of curiosity, not of general sympathy. They amuse the mind, but they do not act upon the manners of the people.

I have already said that this state of things is very far from originating in democracy alone, and that the causes of it must be sought for in several peculiar circumstances independent of the democratic principle. If the Americans, retaining the same laws and social condition, had had a different origin, and had been transported into another country, I do not question that they would have had a literature. Even as they now are, I am convinced that they will ultimately have one; but its character will be different from that which marks the American literary productions of our time, and that character will be peculiarly its own. Nor is it impossible to trace this character beforehand.

I suppose an aristocratic people among whom letters are cultivated; the labours of the mind, as well as the affairs of state, are conducted by a ruling class in society. The literary as well as the political career is almost entirely confined to this class, or to those nearest to it in rank. These premises suffice to give me a key to all the rest.

When a small number of the same men are engaged at the same time upon the same objects, they easily concert with one another, and agree upon certain leading rules which are to govern them each and all. If the object which attracts the attention of these men is literature, the productions of the mind will soon be subjected by them to precise canons, from which it will no longer be allowable to depart. If these men occupy an hereditary position in the country, they will be naturally inclined, not only to adopt a certain number of fixed rules for themselves, but to follow those which their forefathers laid down for their own guidance; their code will be at once strict and traditional. As they are not necessarily engrossed by the cares of daily life—as they have never been so, any more than their fathers were before them—they have learned to take an interest, for several generations back, in the labours of the mind. They have learned to understand literature as an art, to love it in the end for its own sake, and to feel a scholar-like satisfaction in seeing men conform to its rules. Nor is this all: the men of whom I speak began and will end their lives in easy or in affluent circumstances; hence they have naturally conceived a taste for choice gratifications, and a love of refined and delicate pleasures. Nay more, a kind of indolence of mind and heart, which they frequently contract in the midst of this long and peaceful enjoyment of so much welfare, leads them to put aside, even from their pleasures, whatever might be too startling or too acute. They had rather be amused, than intensely excited; they wish to be interested, but not to be carried away.

Now let us fancy a great number of literary performances executed by the men, or for the men, whom I have just described, and we shall readily conceive a style of literature in which everything will be regular and pre-arranged. The slightest work will be carefully touched in its least details; art and labour will be conspicuous in everything; each kind of writing will have rules of its own, from which it will not be allowed to swerve, and which distinguish it from all others. Style will be thought of almost as much importance as thought; and the form will be no less considered than the matter: the diction will be polished, measured, and uniform. The tone of the mind will be always dignified, seldom very animated; and writers will care more to perfect what they produce, than to multiply their productions. It will sometimes happen, that the members of the literary class, always living among themselves and writing for themselves alone, will lose sight of the rest of the world, which will infect them with a false and laboured style; they will lay down minute literary rules for their exclusive use, which will insensibly lead them to deviate from common sense, and finally to transgress the bounds of nature. By dint of striving after a mode of parlance different from the vulgar, they will arrive at a sort of aristocratic jargon, which is hardly less remote from pure language than is the coarse dialect of the people. Such are the natural perils of literature among aristocracies. Every aristocracy which keeps itself entirely aloof from the people becomes impotent—a fact which is as true in literature as it is in politics.*

Let us now turn the picture and consider the other side of it: let us transport ourselves into the midst of a democracy, not unprepared by ancient traditions and present culture to partake in the pleasures of the mind. Ranks are there intermingled and confounded; knowledge and power are both infinitely subdivided, and, if I may use the expres-

---

* All this is especially true of the aristocratic countries which have been long and peacefully subject to a monarchical government. When liberty prevails in an aristocracy, the higher ranks are constantly obliged to make use of the lower classes; and when they use, they approach them. This frequently introduces something of a democratic spirit into an aristocratic community. There springs up, moreover, in a privileged body, governing with energy and an habitually bold policy, a taste for stir and excitement, which must infallibly affect all literary performances.

sion, scattered on every side. Here then is a motley multitude, whose intellectual wants are to be supplied. These new votaries of the pleasures of the mind have not all received the same education; they do not possess the same degree of culture as their fathers, nor any resemblance to them—nay, they perpetually differ from themselves, for they live in a state of incessant change of place, feelings, and fortunes. The mind of each member of the community is therefore unattached to that of his fellow-citizens by tradition or by common habits; and they have never had the power, the inclination, nor the time to concert together. It is however from the bosom of this heterogeneous and agitated mass that authors spring; and from the same source their profits and their fame are distributed.

I can without difficulty understand that, under these circumstances, I must expect to meet in the literature of such a people with but few of those strict conventional rules which are admitted by readers and by writers in aristocratic ages. If it should happen that the men of some one period were agreed upon any such rules, that would prove nothing for the following period; for, among democratic nations, each new generation is a new people. Among such nations, then, literature will not easily be subjected to strict rules, and it is impossible that any such rules should ever be permanent.

In democracies it is by no means the case that all the men who cultivate literature have received a literary education; and most of those who have some tinge of bellesletters, are either engaged in politics, or in a profession which only allows them to taste occasionally and by stealth the pleasures of the mind. These pleasures, therefore, do not constitute the principal charm of their lives; but they are considered as a transient and necessary recreation amid the serious labours of life. Such men can never acquire a sufficiently intimate knowledge of the art of literature to appreciate its more delicate beauties; and the minor shades of expression must escape them. As the time they can devote to letters is very short, they seek to make the best use of the whole of it. They prefer books which may be easily procured, quickly read, and which require no learned researches to be understood. They ask for beauties, self-proffered, and easily enjoyed; above all, they must have what is unexpected and new. Accustomed to the struggle, the crosses, and the monotony of practical life, they require rapid emotions, startling passages—truths or errors brilliant enough to rouse them up, and to plunge them at once, as if by violence, into the midst of a subject.

Why should I say more? or who does not understand what is about to follow, before I have expressed it? Taken as a whole, literature in democratic ages can never present, as it does in the periods of aristocracy, an aspect of order, regularity, science, and art; its form will, on the contrary, ordinarily be slighted, sometimes despised. Style will frequently be fantastic, incorrect, over-burdened, and, loose—almost always vehement and bold. Authors will aim at rapidity of execution, more than at perfection of detail. Small productions will be more common than bulky books: there will be more wit than erudition, more imagination than profundity; and literary performances will bear marks of an untutored and rude vigour of thought—frequently of great variety and singular fecundity. The object of authors will be to astonish rather than to please, and to stir the passions more than to charm the taste.

Here and there, indeed, writers will doubtless occur who will choose a different track, and who will, if they are gifted with superior abilities, succeed in finding readers, in spite of their defects or their better qualities; but these exceptions will be rare, and even the authors who shall so depart from the received practice in the main subject of their works, will always relapse into it in some lesser details.

I have just depicted two extreme conditions: the transition by which a nation passes from the former to the latter is not sudden but gradual, and marked with shades of very various intensity. In the passage which conducts a lettered people from the one to the other, there is almost always a moment at which the literary genius of democratic nations has its confluence with that of aristocracies, and both seek to establish their joint sway over the human mind. Such epochs are transient, but very brilliant: they are fertile without exuberance, and animated without confusion. The French literature of the eighteenth century may serve as an example.

I should say more than I mean, if I were to assert that the literature of a nation is always subordinate to its social condition and its political constitution. I am aware that, independently of these causes, there are several others which confer certain characteristics on literary productions; but these appear to me to be the chief. The relations which exist between the social and political condition of a people and the genius of its authors are always very numerous: whoever knows the one, is never completely ignorant of the other.

Chapter XIV.

THE TRADE OF LITERATURE.

Democracy not only infuses a taste for letters among the trading classes, but introduces a trading spirit into literature.

In aristocracies, readers are fastidious and few in number; in democracies, they are far more numerous and far less difficult to please. The consequence is, that among aristocratic nations no one can hope to succeed without immense exertions, and that these exertions may bestow a great deal of fame, but can never earn much money; while among democratic nations, a writer may flatter himself that he will obtain at a cheap rate a meager reputation and a large fortune. For this purpose he need not be admired, it is enough that he is liked.

The ever-increasing crowd of readers, and their continual craving for something new, insures the sale of books which nobody much esteems.

In democratic periods the public frequently treat authors as kings do their courtiers; they enrich and they despise them. What more is needed by the venal souls which are born in courts, or which are worthy to live there?

Democratic literature is always infested with a tribe of writers who look upon letters as a mere trade; and for some few great authors who adorn it, you may reckon thousands of idea-mongers.

Chapter XV.

THE STUDY OF GREEK AND LATIN LITERATURE PECULIARLY USEFUL IN DEMOCRATIC COMMUNITIES.

What was called the People in the most democratic republics of antiquity, was very unlike what we designate by that term. In Athens, all the citizens took part in public affairs; but there were only twenty thousand citizens to more than three hundred and fifty thousand inhabitants. All the rest were slaves, and discharged the greater part of those duties which belong at the present day to the lower or even to the middle classes. Athens then, with her universal suffrage, was after all merely an aristocratic republic in which all the nobles had an equal right to the government.

The struggle between the patricians and plebeians of Rome must be considered in the same light: it was simply an intestine feud between the elder and younger branches of the same family. All the citizens belonging, in fact, to the aristocracy, and partaking of its character.

It is moreover to be remarked, that among the ancients, books were always scarce and dear; and that very great difficulties impeded their publication and circulation. These circumstances concentrated literary tastes and habits among a small number of men, who formed a small literary aristocracy out of the choicer spirits of the great political aristocracy. Accordingly nothing goes to prove that literature was ever treated as a trade among the Greeks and Romans.

These peoples, which not only constituted aristocracies, but very polished and free nations, of course imparted to their literary productions the defects and the merits which characterize the literature of aristocratic ages. And indeed a very superficial survey of the literary remains of the ancients will suffice to convince us, that if those were sometimes deficient in variety or fertility in their subjects, or in boldness, vivacity, or power of generalization in their thoughts, they always displayed exquisite care and skill in their details. Nothing in their works seems to be done hastily or at random: every line is written for the eye of the connoisseur, and is shaped after some conception of ideal beauty. No literature places those fine qualities, in which the writers of democracies are naturally deficient, in bolder relief than that of the ancients: no literature, therefore, ought to be more studied in democratic ages. This study is better suited than any other to combat the literary defects inherent in those ages: as for their more praiseworthy literary qualities, they will spring up of their own accord, without its being necessary to learn to acquire them.

It is important that this point should be clearly understood. A particular study may be useful to the literature of a people, without being appropriate to its social and political wants. If men were to persist in teaching nothing but the literature of the dead languages in a community where every one is habitually led to make vehement exertions to augment or to maintain his fortune, the result would be a very polished, but a very dangerous, race of citizens. For as their social and political condition would give them every day a sense of wants, which their education would never teach them to supply, they would perturb the state, in the name of the Greeks and Romans, instead of enriching it by their productive industry.

It is evident, that in democratic communities the interest of individuals, as well as the security of the commonwealth, demands that the education of the greater number should be scientific, commercial, and industrial, rather than literary. Greek and Latin should not be taught in all schools; but it is important that those who by their natural disposition or their fortune are destined to cultivate letters or prepared to relish them, should find schools where a complete knowledge of ancient literature may be acquired, and where the true scholar may be formed. A few excellent universities would do more toward the attainment of this object than a vast number of bad grammar-schools, where superfluous matters, badly learned, stand in the way of sound instruction in necessary studies.

All who aspire to literary excellence in democratic nations, ought frequently to refresh themselves at the springs of ancient literature: there is no more wholesome course for the mind. Not that I hold the literary productions of the ancients to be irreproachable; but I think that they have some especial merits, admirably calculated to counterbalance our peculiar defects. They are a prop on the side on which we are in most danger of falling.

Chapter XVI.

THE EFFECT OF DEMOCRACY ON LANGUAGE.

If the reader has rightly understood what I have already said on the subject of literature in general, he will have no difficulty in comprehending that species of influence which a democratic social condition and democratic institutions may exercise over language itself, which is the chief instrument of thought.

American authors may truly be said to live more in England than in their own country; since they constantly study the English writers, and take them every day for their models. But such is not the case with the bulk of the population, which is more immediately subjected to the peculiar causes acting upon the United States. It is not then to the written, but to the spoken language that attention must be paid, if we would detect the modifications which the idiom of an aristocratic people may undergo when it becomes the language of a democracy.

Englishmen of education, and more competent judges than I can be myself of the nicer shades of expression, have frequently assured me that the language of the educated classes in the United States is notably different from that of the educated classes in Great Britain. They complain, not only that the Americans have brought into use a number of new words—the difference and the distance between the two countries might suffice to explain that much—but that these new words are more especially taken from the jargon of parties, the mechanical arts, or the language of trade. They assert, in addition to this, that old English words are often used by the Americans in new acceptations; and lastly, that the inhabitants of the United States frequently intermingle their phraseology in the strangest manner, and sometimes place words together which are always kept apart in the language of the mother country. These remarks, which were made to me at various times by persons who appeared to be worthy of credit, led me to reflect upon the subject; and my reflections brought me, by theoretical reasoning, to the same point at which my informants had arrived by practical observation.

In aristocracies, language must naturally partake of that state of repose in which every thing remains. Few new words are coined, because few new things are made; and even if new things were made, they would be designated by known words, whose meaning has been determined by tradition. If it happens that the human mind bestirs itself at length, or is roused by light breaking in from without, the novel expressions which are introduced are characterized by a degree of learning, intelligence, and philosophy which shows that they do not originate in a democracy. After the fall of Constantinople[1] had turned the tide of science and literature toward the west, the French language was almost immediately invaded by a multitude of new words, which had all Greek or Latin roots. An erudite neologism then sprang up in France, which was confined to the educated classes, and which produced no sensible effect, or at least a very gradual one, upon the people.

All the nations of Europe successively exhibited the same change. Milton[2] alone introduced more than six hundred words into the English language, almost all derived from the Latin, the Greek, or the Hebrew.* The constant agitation which prevails in a democratic com-

---

* [I am at a loss to conceive whence the author drew so startling, and probably erroneous, an assertion. Certainly as the 'fabbro della lingua materna,' Milton must occupy a rank second to that of the great poets and divines of the reigns of Elizabeth and James. Nor indeed is the example very happily chosen, since Milton's prose writings were addressed to a pamphlet-reading people, among whom that same principle which founded the democracies of New England, had made very extensive progress. I imagine Montaigne to be a perfect example of M. de Tocqueville's meaning; his style was learned to his contemporaries, and antiquated before the best age of French literature. But happily for modern English, it has retained much more of its affinity to the language of those who were princes of learning in the early time,

munity tends unceasingly, on the contrary, to change the character of the language, as it does the aspect of affairs. In the midst of this general stir and competition of minds, a great number of new ideas are formed, old ideas are lost, or reappear, or are subdivided into an infinite variety of minor shades. The consequence is, that many words must fall into desuetude, and others must be brought into use.

Democratic nations love change for its own sake; and this is seen in their language as much as in their politics. Even when they do not need to change words, they sometimes feel a wish to transform them.

The genius of a democratic people is not only shown by the great number of words they bring into use, but also by the nature of the ideas these new words represent. Among such a people the majority lays down the law in language as well as in everything else: its prevailing spirit is as manifest in that as in other respects. But the majority is more engaged in business than in study—in political and commercial interests, than in philosophical speculation or literary pursuits. Most of the words coined or adopted for its use will therefore bear the mark of these habits; they will mainly serve to express the wants of business, the passions of party, or the details of the public administration. In these departments the language will constantly spread, while on the other hand it will gradually lose ground in metaphysics and theology.

As to the source from which democratic nations are wont to derive their new expressions, and the manner in which they go to work to coin them, both may easily be described. Men living in democratic countries know but little of the language which was spoken at Athens and at Rome, and they do not care to dive into the lore of antiquity to find the expression they happen to want. If they have sometimes recourse to learned etymologies, vanity will induce them to search at the roots of the dead languages; but erudition does not naturally furnish them with its resources. The most ignorant, it sometimes happens, will use them most. The eminently democratic desire to get above their own sphere will often lead them to seek to dignify a vulgar profession by a Greek or Latin name. The lower the calling is, and the more remote from learning, the more pompous and erudite is its appellation. Thus the French rope-dancers have transformed themselves into "Acrobates" and "Funambules."

In the absence of knowledge of the dead languages, democratic nations are apt to borrow words from living tongues; for their mutual intercourse becomes perpetual, and the inhabitants of different countries imitate each other the more readily as they grow more like each other every day.

But it is principally upon their own languages that democratic na-

---

than the French diction of the eighteenth and nineteenth centuries preserves to that of the sixteenth and seventeenth; probably owing to the greater fixedness of our aristocratic national character.

"If," says Dr. Johnson, "the language of theology were extracted from Hooker and the translation of the Bible; the terms of natural knowledge from Bacon; the phrases of policy, war, and navigation from Raleigh; the dialect of poetry and fiction from Spenser and Sidney; and the diction of common life from Shakespere, few ideas would be lost to mankind for want of English words in which they might be expressed."—*Translator's Note.*]

tions attempt to perpetrate innovations. From time to time they resume forgotten expressions in their vocabulary, which they restore to use; or they borrow from some particular class of the community a term peculiar to it, which they introduce with a figurative meaning into the language of daily life. Many expressions which originally belonged to the technical language of a profession or a party, are thus drawn into general circulation.

The most common expedient employed by democratic nations to make an innovation in language consists in giving some unwonted meaning to an expression already in use. This method is very simple, prompt, and convenient; no learning is required to use it aright, and ignorance itself rather facilitates the practice; but that practice is most dangerous to the language. When a democratic people doubles the meaning of a word in this way, they sometimes render the signification which it retains as ambiguous as that which it acquires. An author begins by a slight deflection of a known expression from its primitive meaning, and he adapts it, thus modified, as well as he can to his subject. A second writer twists the sense of the expression in another way; a third takes possession of it for another purpose; and as there is no common appeal to the sentence of a permanent tribunal which may definitely settle the signification of the word, it remains in an ambiguous condition. The consequence is, that writers hardly ever appear to dwell upon a single thought, but they always seem to point their aim at a knot of ideas, leaving the reader to judge which of them has been hit.

This is a deplorable consequence of democracy. I had rather that the language should be made hideous with words imported from the Chinese, the Tartars, or the Hurons, than that the meaning of a word in our own language should become indeterminate. Harmony and uniformity are only secondary beauties in composition: many of these things are conventional, and, strictly speaking, it is possible to forego them; but without clear phraseology there is no good language.

The principle of equality necessarily introduces several other changes into language.

In aristocratic ages, when each nation tends to stand aloof from all others, and likes to have distinct characteristics of its own, it often happens that several peoples which have a common origin become nevertheless estranged from each other; so that, without ceasing to understand the same language, they no longer all speak it in the same manner. In these ages each nation is divided into a certain number of classes, which see but little of each other and do not intermingle. Each of these classes contracts, and invariably retains, habits of mind peculiar to itself, and adopts by choice certain words and certain terms, which afterward pass from generation to generation, like their estates. The same idiom then comprises a language of the poor and a language of the rich—a language of the citizen and a language of the nobility—a learned language and a vulgar one. The deeper the divisions, and the more impassable the barriers of society become, the more must this be the case. I would lay a wager, that among the castes of India there are amazing variations of language, and that there is almost as much difference between the language of the Paria and that of the Brahmin as there is in their dress.

When on the contrary, men, being no longer restrained by ranks, meet on terms of constant intercourse—when castes are destroyed, and the classes of society are recruited and intermixed with each other, all the words of a language are mingled. Those which are unsuitable to the greater number perish: the remainder form a common store, whence every one chooses pretty nearly at random. Almost all the different dialects which divided the idioms of European nations are manifestly declining: there is no *patois* in the New World, and it is disappearing every day from the old countries.

The influence of this revolution in social conditions is as much felt in style as it is in phraseology. Not only does every one use the same words, but a habit springs up of using them without discrimination. The rules which style had set up are almost abolished: the line ceases to be drawn between expressions which seem by their very nature vulgar, and others which appear to be refined. Persons springing from different ranks of society carry the terms and expressions they are accustomed to use with them, into whatever circumstances they may pass; thus the origin of words is lost like the origin of individuals, and there is as much confusion in language as there is in society.

I am aware that in the classification of words there are rules which do not belong to one form of society any more than to another, but which are derived from the nature of things. Some expressions and phrases are vulgar, because the ideas they are meant to express are low in themselves; others are of a higher character, because the objects they are intended to designate are naturally elevated. No intermixture of ranks will ever efface these differences. But the principle of equality cannot fail to root out whatever is merely conventional and arbitrary in the forms of thought. Perhaps the necessary classification which I pointed out in the last sentence will always be less respected by a democratic people than by any other, because among such a people there are no men who are permanently disposed by education, culture, and leisure to study the natural laws of language, and who cause those laws to be respected by their own observance of them.

I shall not quit this topic without touching on a feature of democratic languages, which is perhaps more characteristic of them than any other. It has already been shown that democratic nations have a taste, and sometimes a passion, for general ideas, and that this arises from their peculiar merits and defects. This liking for general ideas is displayed in democratic languages by the continual use of generic terms or abstract expressions, and by the manner in which they are employed. This is the great merit and the great imperfection of these languages.

Democratic nations are passionately addicted to generic terms or abstract expressions, because these modes of speech enlarge thought, and assist the operations of the mind by enabling it to include several objects in a small compass. A French democratic writer will be apt to say *capacités* in the abstract for men of capacity, and without particularizing the objects to which their capacity is applied: he will talk about *actualités* to designate in one word the things passing before his eyes at the instant; and he will comprehend under the term *éventualités* whatever may happen in the universe, dating from the moment at which he speaks. Democratic writers are perpetually coining words of this kind, in which they sublimate into further abstraction the abstract terms of the language. Nay more, to render their mode of speech more succinct, they personify the subject of these abstract terms, and make it act like a real entity. Thus they would say in French, *La force des choses veut que les capacités gouvernent.**

I cannot better illustrate what I mean than by my own example. I have frequently used the word EQUALITY in an absolute sense—nay, I have personified equality in several places; thus I have said that equality does such and such things, or refrains from doing others. It may be affirmed that the writers of the age of Louis XIV. would not have used these expressions: they would never have thought of using the word equality without applying it to some particular object; and they would rather have renounced the term altogether than have consented to make a living personage of it.

These abstract terms which abound in democratic languages, and which are used on every occasion without attaching them to any particular fact, enlarge and obscure the thoughts they are intended to convey; they render the mode of speech more succinct, and the idea contained in it less clear. But with regard to language, democratic nations prefer obscurity to labour.

I know not indeed whether this loose style has not some secret charm for those who speak and write among these nations. As the men who live there are frequently left to the efforts of their individual powers of mind, they are almost always a prey to doubt: and as their situation in life is for ever changing, they are never held fast to any of their opinions by the certain tenure of their fortunes. Men living in democratic countries are, then, apt to entertain unsettled ideas, and they require loose expressions to convey them. As they never know

---

* [As a further illustration of this observation, which I have only been able to exemplify by retaining the phrase of the original, I may be allowed to advert to the relative conditions of the French and English languages in this respect. The French (whether it be from their democratic social condition or from their national vivacity) have acquired a habit of dealing familiarly with general propositions, conveyed in very loose terms. The English (whether it be from their aristocratic manners, or from their national sobriety of character) have retained much more of the positive and the concrete forms in their language. We have not arrived at that stage of democracy at which abstract ideas are enounced, upon a very superficial acquaintance, as absolute propositions, or personified till they are made to play the part of living agents. The innovations which the author points out in the text as having befallen the French language since the time of Louis XIV., are still, I think, inadmissible into the pure English. Hence arose the chief difficulty of rendering into our tongue forms of speech so repugnant to the positive genius of the language: for *égalité* I have generally written *the principle of equality*; and I have endeavoured, whenever it could be done without abridging the author's meaning, to connect each abstract term with its appropriate object. There is perhaps a tendency in the age to disregard these distinctions, and to Gallicize or generalize our forms of expression; but if I were required to point out the class of authors who have done most to vitiate the language in this respect, I should have no hesitation in fixing upon the democratic writers in the late Westminster Review.—*Translator's Note.*]

whether the idea they express today will be appropriate to the new position they may occupy tomorrow, they naturally acquire a liking for abstract terms. An abstract term is like a box with a false bottom; you may put in it what ideas you please, and take them out again without being observed.

Among all nations, generic and abstract terms form the basis of language. I do not, therefore, affect to expel these terms from democratic languages; I simply remark, that men have an especial tendency, in the ages of democracy, to multiply words of this kind—to take them always by themselves in their most abstract acceptation, and to use them on all occasions, even when the nature of the discourse does not require them.

Chapter XVII.

OF SOME OF THE SOURCES OF POETRY AMONG DEMOCRATIC NATIONS.

Various different significations have been given to the word Poetry. It would weary my readers if I were to lead them into a discussion as to which of these definitions ought to be selected: I prefer telling them at once that which I have chosen. In my opinion, Poetry is the search and the delineation of the Ideal.

The Poet is he who, by suppressing a part of what exists, by adding some imaginary touches to the picture, and by combining certain real circumstances, but which do not in fact concurrently happen, completes and extends the work of nature. Thus the object of poetry is not to represent what is true, but to adorn it, and to present to the mind some loftier imagery. Verse, regarded as the ideal beauty of language, may be eminently poetical; but verse does not, of itself, constitute poetry.

I now proceed to inquire whether, among the actions, the sentiments, and the opinions of democratic nations, there are any which lead to a conception of ideal beauty, and which may for this reason be considered as natural sources of poetry.

It must, in the first place, be acknowledged that the taste for ideal beauty, and the pleasure derived from the expression of it, are never so intense or so diffused among a democratic as among an aristocratic people. In aristocratic nations it sometimes happens that the body goes on to act as it were spontaneously, while the higher faculties are bound and burdened by repose. Among these nations the people will very often display poetic tastes, and sometimes allow their fancy to range beyond and above what surrounds them.

But in democracies the love of physical gratification, the notion of bettering one's condition, the excitement of competition, the charm of anticipated success, are so many spurs to urge men onward in the active professions they have embraced, without allowing them to deviate for an instant from the track. The main stress of the faculties is to this point. The imagination is not extinct; but its chief function is to devise what may be useful, and to represent what is real.

The principle of equality not only diverts men from the description of ideal beauty—it also diminishes the number of objects to be described.

Aristocracy, by maintaining society in a fixed position, is favourable to the solidity and duration of positive religions, as well as to the stability of political institutions. It not only keeps the human mind within a certain sphere of belief, but it predisposes the mind to adopt one faith rather than another. An aristocratic people will always be prone to place intermediate powers between God and man. In this respect it may be said that the aristocratic element is favourable to poetry. When the universe is peopled with supernatural creatures, not palpable to the senses but discovered by the mind, the imagination ranges freely, and poets, finding a thousand subjects to delineate, also find a countless audience to take an interest in their productions.

In democratic ages it sometimes happens, on the contrary, that men are as much afloat in matters of belief as they are in their laws. Scepticism then draws the imagination of poets back to earth, and confines them to the real and visible world. Even when the principle of equality does not disturb religious belief, it tends to simplify it, and to divert attention from secondary agents, to fix it principally on the Supreme Power.

Aristocracy naturally leads the human mind to the contemplation of the past, and fixes it there. Democracy, on the contrary, gives men a sort of instinctive distaste for what is ancient. In this respect aristocracy is far more favourable to poetry; for things commonly grow larger and more obscure as they are more remote; and for this twofold reason they are better suited to the delineation of the ideal.

After having deprived poetry of the past, the principle of equality robs it in part of the present. Among aristocratic nations there are a certain number of privileged personages, whose situation is, as it were, without and above the condition of man; to these, power, wealth, fame, wit, refinement, and distinction in all things appear peculiarly to belong. The crowd never sees them very closely, or does not watch them in minute details; and little is needed to make the description of such men poetical. On the other hand, among the same people, you will meet with classes so ignorant, low, and enslaved, that they are no less fit objects for poetry from the excess of their rudeness and wretchedness, than the former are from their greatness and refinement. Besides, as the different classes of which an aristocratic community is composed are widely separated, and imperfectly acquainted with each other, the imagination may always represent them with some addition to, or some subtraction from, what they really are.

In democratic communities, where men are all insignificant and very much alike, each man instantly sees all his fellows when he surveys himself.

The poets of democratic ages can never, therefore, take any man in particular as the subject of a piece; for an object of slender importance, which is distinctly seen on all sides, will never lend itself to an ideal conception.

Thus the principle of equality, in proportion as it has established itself in the world, has dried up most of the old springs of poetry. Let us now attempt to show what new ones it may disclose.

When scepticism had depopulated heaven, and the progress of equality had reduced each individual to smaller and better known proportions, the poets, not yet aware of what they could substitute for the great themes which were departing together with the aristocracy, turned their eyes to inanimate nature. As they lost sight of gods and heroes, they set themselves to describe streams and mountains. Thence originated, in the last century, that kind of poetry which has been called, by way of distinction, the descriptive. Some have thought that this sort of delineation, embellished with all the physical and inanimate objects which cover the earth, was the kind of poetry peculiar to democratic ages; but I believe this to be an error, and that it only belongs to a period of transition.

I am persuaded that in the end democracy diverts the imagination from all that is external to man, and fixes it on man alone. Democratic nations may amuse themselves for a while with considering the productions of nature; but they are only excited in reality by a survey of themselves. Here, and here alone, the true sources of poetry among such nations are to be found; and it may be believed that the poets who shall neglect to draw their inspiration hence, will lose all sway over the minds which they would enchant, and will be left in the end with none but unimpassioned spectators of their transports.

I have shown how the ideas of progression and of the indefinite perfectibility of the human race belong to democratic ages. Democratic nations care but little for what has been, but they are haunted by visions of what will be: in this direction their unbounded imagination grows and dilates beyond all measure. Here then is the widest range open to the genius of poets, which allows them to remove their performances to a sufficient distance from the eye. Democracy shuts the past against the poet, but opens the future before him.

As all the citizens who compose a democratic community are nearly equal and alike, the poet cannot dwell upon any one of them; but the nation itself invites the exercise of his powers. The general similitude of individuals, which renders any one of them taken separately an improper subject of poetry, allows poets to include them all in the same imagery, and to take a general survey of the people itself. Democratic nations have a clearer perception than any others of their own aspect; and an aspect so imposing is admirably fitted to the delineation of the ideal.

I readily admit that the Americans have no poets; I cannot allow that they have no poetic ideas. In Europe people talk a great deal of the wilds of America, but the Americans themselves never think about them: they are insensible to the wonders of inanimate nature, and they may be said not to perceive the mighty forests which surround them till they fall beneath the hatchet. Their eyes are fixed upon another sight: the American people views its own march across these wilds—drying swamps, turning the course of rivers, peopling solitudes, and subduing nature. This magnificent image of themselves does not meet the gaze of the Americans at intervals only; it may be said to haunt every one of them in his least as well as in his most important actions, and to be always fitting before his mind.

Nothing conceivable is so petty, so insipid, so crowded with paltry interests, in one word so anti-poetic, as the life of a man in the United States. But among the thoughts which it suggests, there is always one which is full of poetry, and that is the hidden nerve which gives vigour to the frame.

In aristocratic ages each people, as well as each individual, is prone to stand separate and aloof from all others. In democratic ages, the extreme fluctuations of men and the impatience of their desires keep them perpetually on the move; so that the inhabitants of different countries intermingle, see, listen to, and borrow from each other's stores. It is not only then the members of the same community who grow more alike; communities are themselves assimilated to one another, and the whole assemblage presents to the eye of the spectator one vast democracy, each citizen of which is a people. This displays the aspect of mankind for the first time in the broadest light. All that belongs to the existence of the human race taken as a whole, to its vicissitudes and to its future, becomes an abundant mine of poetry.

The poets who lived in aristocratic ages have been eminently successful in their delineations of certain incidents in the life of a people or a man; but none of them ever ventured to include within his performances the destinies of mankind—a task which poets writing in democratic ages may attempt.

At that same time at which every man, raising his eyes above his country, begins at length to discern mankind at large, the Divinity is more and more manifest to the human mind in full and entire majesty. If in democratic ages faith in positive religions be often shaken, and the belief in intermediate agents, by whatever name they are called, be overcast; on the other hand men are disposed to conceive a far broader idea of Providence itself, and its interference in human affairs assumes a new and more imposing appearance to their eyes. Looking at the human race as one great whole, they easily conceive that its destinies are regulated by the same design; and in the actions of every individual they are led to acknowledge a trace of that universal and eternal plan on which God rules our race. This consideration may be taken as another prolific source of poetry which is opened in democratic ages.

Democratic poets will always appear trivial and frigid if they seek to invest gods, demons, or angels with corporeal forms, and if they attempt to draw them down from heaven to dispute the supremacy of earth. But if they strive to connect the great events they commemorate with the general providential designs which govern the universe, and, without showing the finger of the Supreme Governor reveal the thoughts of the Supreme Mind, their works will be admired and understood, for the imagination of their contemporaries takes this direction of its own accord.

It may be foreseen in like manner that poets living in democratic ages will prefer the delineation of passions and ideas to that of persons and achievements. The language, the dress, and the daily actions of men in democracies are repugnant to ideal conceptions. These things are not poetical in themselves; and if it were otherwise, they would cease to be so, because they are too familiar to all those to whom the poet would speak of them. This forces the poet constantly to search below the external surface which is palpable to the senses, in order to read the inner soul: and nothing lends itself more to the declineation of the Ideal than the scrutiny of the hidden depths in the immaterial nature of man. I need not to ramble over earth and sky to discover a wondrous object woven of contrasts, of greatness and littleness infinite, of intense gloom and of amazing brightness—capable at once of exciting pity, admiration, terror, contempt. I find that object in myself. Man springs out of nothing, crosses Time, and disappears for ever in the bosom of God: he is seen but for a moment, staggering on the verge of the two abysses, and there he is lost.

If man were wholly ignorant of himself, he would have no poetry in him; for it is impossible to describe what the mind does not conceive. If man clearly discerned his own nature, his imagination would remain idle, and would have nothing to add to the picture. But the nature of man is sufficiently disclosed for him to apprehend something of himself; and sufficiently obscure for all the rest to be plunged in thick darkness, in which he gropes for ever—and for ever in vain—to lay hold on some completer notion of his being.

Among a democratic people poetry will not be fed with legendary lays or the memorials of old traditions. The poet will not attempt to people the universe with supernatural beings in whom his readers and his own fancy have ceased to believe; nor will he present virtues and vices in the mask of frigid personification, which are better received under their own features. All these resources fail him; but Man remains, and the poet needs no more. The destinies of mankind—man himself, taken aloof from his age and his country, and standing in the presence of Nature and of God, with his passions, his doubts, his rare prosperities and inconceivable wretchedness—will become the chief, if not the sole theme of poetry among these nations.

Experience may confirm this assertion, if we consider the productions of the greatest poets who have appeared since the world has been turned to democracy. The authors of our age who have so admirably delineated the features of Childe Harold,[1] René,[2] and Jocelyn,[3] did not seek to record the actions of an individual, but to enlarge and to throw light on some of the obscurer recesses of the human heart.

Such are the poems of democracy. The principle of equality does not then destroy all the subjects of poetry: it renders them less numerous, but more vast.

Chapter XVIII.

OF THE INFLATED STYLE OF AMERICAN WRITERS AND ORATORS.

I have frequently remarked that the Americans, who generally treat of business in clear, plain language, devoid of all ornament, and so extremely simple as to be often coarse, are apt to become inflated as soon as they attempt a more poetical diction. They then vent their pomposity from one end of an harangue to the other; and to hear them lavish imagery on every occasion, one might fancy that they never spoke of anything with simplicity.

The English are more rarely given to a similar failing. The cause of this may be pointed out without much difficulty. In democratic communities each citizen is habitually engaged in the contemplation of a very puny object, namely, himself. If he ever raises his looks higher, he then perceives nothing but the immense form of society at large, or the still more imposing aspect of mankind. His ideas are all either extremely minute and clear, or extremely general and vague: what lies between is an open void.

When he has been drawn out of his own sphere, therefore, he always expects that some amazing object will be offered to his attention; and it is on these terms alone that he consents to tear himself for an instant from the petty complicated cares which form the charm and the excitement of his life.

This appears to me sufficiently to explain why men in democracies, whose concerns are in general so paltry, call upon their poets for conceptions so vast and descriptions so unlimited.

The authors, on their part, do not fail to obey a propensity of which they themselves partake; they perpetually inflate their imaginations, and expanding them beyond all bounds, they not unfrequently abandon the great in order to reach the gigantic. By these means they hope to attract the observation of the multitude, and to fix it easily upon themselves: nor are their hopes disappointed; for as the multitude seeks for nothing in poetry but subjects of very vast dimensions, it has neither the time to measure with accuracy the proportions of all the subjects set before it, nor a taste sufficiently correct to perceive at once in what respect they are out of proportion. The author and the public at once vitiate one another.

We have just seen, that among democratic nations, the sources of poetry are grand, but not abundant. They are soon exhausted: and poets, not finding the elements of the Ideal in what is real and true, abandon them entirely and create monsters. I do not fear that the poetry of democratic nations will prove too insipid, or that it will fly too near the ground; I rather apprehend that it will be for ever losing itself in the clouds, and that it will range at last to purely imaginary regions. I fear that the productions of democratic poets may often be surcharged with immense and incoherent imagery, with exaggerated descriptions and strange creations; and that the fantastic beings of their brain may sometimes make us regret the world of reality.

Chapter XIX.

SOME OBSERVATIONS ON THE DRAMA AMONG DEMOCRATIC NATIONS.

When the revolution which subverts the social and political state of an aristocratic people begins to penetrate into literature, it generally first manifests itself in the drama, and it always remains conspicuous there.

The spectator of a dramatic piece is, to a certain extent, taken by surprise by the impression it conveys. He has no time to refer to his memory or to consult those more able to judge than himself. It does not occur to him to resist the new literary tendencies which begin to be felt by him; he yields to them before he knows what they are.

Authors are very prompt in discovering which way the taste of the public is thus secretly inclined. They shape their productions accordingly; and the literature of the stage, after having served to indicate the approaching literary revolution, speedily completes its accomplishment. If you would judge beforehand of the literature of a people which is lapsing into democracy, study its dramatic productions.

The literature of the stage, moreover, even among aristocratic nations, constitutes the most democratic part of their literature. No kind of literary gratification is so much within the reach of the multitude as that which is derived from theatrical representations. Neither preparation nor study is required to enjoy them: they lay hold on you in the midst of your prejudices and your ignorance. When the yet untutored love of the pleasures of the mind begins to affect a class of the community, it instantly draws them to the stage. The theatres of aristocratic nations have always been filled with spectators not belonging to the aristocracy. At the theatre alone the higher ranks mix with the middle and the lower classes; there alone do the former consent to listen to the opinion of the latter, or at least to allow them to give an opinion at all. At the theatre, men of cultivation and of literary attainments have always had more difficulty than elsewhere in making their taste prevail over that of the people, and in preventing themselves from being carried away by the latter. The pit has frequently made laws for the boxes.

If it be difficult for an aristocracy to prevent the people from getting the upper hand in the theatre, it will readily be understood that the people will be supreme there when democratic principles have crept into the laws and manners—when ranks are intermixed—when minds, as well as fortunes, are brought more nearly together—and when the upper class has lost, with its hereditary wealth, its power, its precedents, and its leisure. The tastes and propensities natural to democratic nations, in respect to literature, will therefore first be discernible in the drama, and it may be foreseen that they will break out there with vehemence. In written productions, the literary canons of aristocracy will be gently, gradually, and, so to speak, legally modified; at the theatre they will be riotously overthrown.

The drama brings out most of the good qualities, and almost all the defects, inherent in democratic literature. Democratic peoples hold erudition very cheap, and care but little for what occurred at Rome and Athens; they want to hear something which concerns themselves, and the delineation of the present age is what they demand.

When the heroes and the manners of antiquity are frequently brought upon the stage, and dramatic authors faithfully observe the rules of antiquated precedent, that is enough to warrant a conclusion that the democratic classes have not yet got the upper hand in the theatres.

Racine[1] makes a very humble apology in the preface to the Britannicus for having disposed of Junia among the Vestals, who, according to Aulus Gellius, he says, "admitted no one below six years of age nor above ten." We may be sure that he would neither have accused himself of the offence, nor defended himself from censure, if he had written for our contemporaries.

A fact of this kind not only illustrates the state of literature at the time when it occurred, but also that of society itself. A democratic stage does not prove that the nation is in a state of democracy, for, as we have just seen, even in aristocracies it may happen that democratic tastes affect the drama; but when the spirit of aristocracy reigns exclusively on the stage, the fact irrefragably demonstrates that the whole of society is aristocratic; and it may be boldly inferred that the same lettered and learned class, which sways the dramatic writers, commands the people and governs the country.

The refined tastes and the arrogant bearing of an aristocracy will rarely fail to lead it, when it manages the stage, to make a kind of selection in human nature. Some of the conditions of society claim its chief interest; and the scenes which delineate their manners are preferred upon the stage. Certain virtues and even certain vices are thought more particularly to deserve to figure there; and they are applauded while all others are excluded. Upon the stage, as well as elsewhere, an aristocratic audience will only meet personages of quality, and share the emotions of kings. The same thing applies to style: an aristocracy is apt to impose upon dramatic authors certain modes of expression which give the key in which everything is to be delivered. By these means the stage frequently comes to delineate only one side of man, or sometimes even to represent what is not to be met with in human nature at all—to rise above nature and to go beyond it.

In democratic communities the spectators have no such partialities, and they rarely display any such antipathies: they like to see upon the stage that medley of conditions, of feelings, and of opinions, which occurs before their eyes. The drama becomes more striking, more common, and more true. Sometimes, however, those who write for the stage in democracies also transgress the bounds of human nature— but it is on a different side from their predecessors. By seeking to represent in minute detail the little singularities of the moment and the peculiar characteristics of certain personages, they forget to portray the general features of the race.

When the democratic classes rule the stage, they introduce as much license in the manner of treating subjects as in the choice of them. As the love of the drama is, of all literary tastes, that which is most natural to democratic nations, the number of authors and of spectators, as well as of theatrical representations, is constantly increasing among these communities. A multitude composed of elements so different and scattered in so many different places, cannot acknowledge the same rules or submit to the same laws. No concurrence is possible among judges so numerous, who know not when they may meet again; and therefore each pronounces his own sentence on the piece. If the effect of democracy is generally to question the authority of all literary rules and conventions, on the stage it abolishes them altogether, and puts in their place nothing but the whim of each author and of each public.

The drama also displays in an especial manner the truth of what I have said before in speaking more generally of style and art in democratic literature. In reading the criticisms which were occasioned by the dramatic productions of the age of Louis XIV., one is surprised to remark the great stress which the public laid on the probability of the plot, and the importance which was attached to the perfect consistency of the characters, and to their doing nothing which could not be easily explained and understood. The value which was set upon the forms of language at that period, and the paltry strife about words with which dramatic authors were assailed, are no less surprising. It would seem that the men of the age of Louis XIV. attached very exaggerated importance to those details, which may be perceived in the study, but which escape attention on the stage. For, after all, the principal object of a dramatic piece is to be performed, and its chief merit is to affect the audience. But the audience and the readers in that age were the same: on quitting the theatre they called up the author for judgement to their own firesides.

In democracies, dramatic pieces are listened to, but not read. Most of those who frequent the amusements of the stage do not go there to seek the pleasures of the mind, but the keen emotions of the heart. They do not expect to hear a fine literary work, but to see a play; and provided the author writes the language of his country correctly enough to be understood, and that his characters excite curiosity and awaken sympathy, the audience are satisfied. They ask no more of fiction, and immediately return to real life. Accuracy of style is therefore less required, because the attentive observance of its rules is less perceptible on the stage.

As for the probability of the plot, it is incompatible with perpetual novelty, surprise, and rapidity of invention. It is therefore neglected, and the public excuses the neglect. You may be sure that if you succeed in bringing your audience into the presence of something that affects them, they will not care by what road you brought them there: and they will never reproach you for having excited their emotions in spite of dramatic rules.

The Americans very broadly display all the different propensities which I have here described when they go to the theatres; but it must be acknowledged that as yet a very small number of them go to theatres at all. Although play-goers and plays have prodigiously increased in the United States in the last forty years, the population indulges in this kind of amusement with the greatest reserve. This is attributable to peculiar causes, which the reader is already acquainted with, and of which a few words will suffice to remind him.

The Puritans who founded the American republics were not only enemies to amusements, but they professed an especial abhorrence for the stage. They considered it as an abominable pastime; and as long as their principles prevailed with undivided sway, scenic performances were wholly unknown among them. These opinions of the first fathers of the colony have left very deep marks on the minds of their descendants.

The extreme regularity of habits and the great strictness of manners which are observable in the United States, have as yet opposed additional obstacles to the growth of dramatic art. There are no dramatic subjects in a country which has witnessed no great political catastrophes, and in which love invariably leads by a straight and easy road to matrimony. People who spend every day in the week in making money, and the Sunday in going to church, have nothing to invite the Muse of Comedy.

A single fact suffices to show that the stage is not very popular in the United States. The Americans, whose laws allow of the utmost freedom and even license of language in all other respects, have nevertheless subjected their dramatic authors to a sort of censorship. Theatrical performances can only take place by permission of the municipal authorities. This may serve to show how much communities are like individuals; they surrender themselves unscrupulously to their ruling passions, and afterward take the greatest care not to yield too much to the vehemence of tastes which they do not possess.

No portion of literature is connected by closer or more numerous ties with the present condition of society than the drama. The drama of one period can never be suited to the following age, if in the interval an important revolution has changed the manners and the laws of the nation.

The great authors of a preceding age may be read; but pieces written for a different public will not be followed. The dramatic authors of the past live only in books. The traditional taste of certain individuals, vanity, fashion, or the genius of an actor may sustain or resuscitate for a time the aristocratic drama among a democracy; but it will speedily fall away of itself—not overthrown, but abandoned.

Chapter XX.

CHARACTERISTICS OF HISTORIANS IN DEMOCRATIC AGES

Historians who write in aristocratic ages are wont to refer all occurrences to the particular will or temper of certain individuals; and they are apt to attribute the most important revolutions to very slight accidents. They trace out the smallest causes with sagacity, and frequently leave the greatest unperceived.

Historians who live in democratic ages exhibit precisely opposite characteristics. Most of them attribute hardly any influence to the individual over the destiny of the race, nor to citizens over the fate of a people; but, on the other hand, they assign great general causes to all petty incidents. These contrary tendencies explain each other.

When the historian of aristocratic ages surveys the theatre of the world, he at once perceives a very small number of prominent actors, who manage the whole piece. These great personages, who occupy the front of the stage, arrest the observation, and fix it on themselves; and while the historian is bent on penetrating the secret motives which make them speak and act, the rest escape his memory. The importance of the things which some men are seen to do, gives him an exaggerated estimate of the influence which one man may possess; and naturally leads him to think, that in order to explain the impulses of the multitude, it is necessary to refer them to the particular influence of some one individual.

When, on the contrary, all the citizens are independent of one another, and each of them is individually weak, no one is seen to exert a great, or still less, a lasting power, over the community. At first sight, individuals appear to be absolutely devoid of any influence over it; and society would seem to advance alone by the free and voluntary concurrence of all the men who compose it. This naturally prompts the mind to search for that general reason which operates upon so many men's faculties at the same time, and turns them simultaneously in the same direction.

I am very well convinced, that even among democratic nations, the genius, the vices, or the virtues of certain individuals retard or accelerate the natural current of a people's history; but causes of this secondary and fortuitous nature are infinitely more various, more concealed, more complex, less powerful, and consequently less easy to trace in periods of equality than in ages of aristocracy, when the task of the historian is simply to detach from the mass of general events the particular influences of one man or of a few men. In the former case the historian is soon wearied by the toil; his mind loses itself in this labyrinth; and, in his inability clearly to discern or conspicuously to point out the influence of individuals, he denies their existence. He prefers talking about the characteristics of race, the physical conformation of the country, or the genius of civilization—which abridges his own labours, and satisfies his reader far better at less cost.

M. de Lafayette[1] says somewhere in his Memoirs, that the exaggerated system of general causes affords surprising consolations to second-rate statesmen. I will add, that its effects are not less consolatory to second-rate historians; it can always furnish a few mighty reasons to extricate them from the most difficult part of their work, and it indulges the indolence or incapacity of their minds, while it confers upon them the honours of deep thinking.

For myself, I am of opinion that at all times one great portion of the events of this world is attributable to general facts, and another to special influences. These two kinds of causes are always in operation; their proportion only varies. General facts serve to explain more things in democratic than in aristocratic ages, and fewer things are then assignable to special influences. At periods of aristocracy the reverse takes place: special influences are stronger, general causes weaker—unless indeed we consider as a general cause the fact itself of the inequality of conditions, which allows some individuals to baffle the natural tendencies of all the rest.

The historians who seek to describe what occurs in democratic societies are right, therefore, in assigning much to general causes, and in devoting their chief attention to discover them; but they are wrong in wholly denying the special influence of individuals, because they cannot easily trace or follow it.

The historians who live in democratic ages are not only prone to assign a great cause to every incident, but they are also given to connect incidents together, so as to deduce a system from them. In aristocratic ages, as the attention of historians is constantly drawn to individuals, the connexion of events escapes them; or rather, they do not believe in any such connexion. To them the clew of history seems every instant crossed and broken by the step of man In democratic ages, on the contrary, as the historian sees much more of actions than of actors, he may easily establish some kind of sequency and methodical order among the former.

Ancient literature, which is so rich in fine historical compositions, does not contain a single great historical system, while the poorest of modern literatures abound with them. It would appear that the ancient historians did not make sufficient use of those general theories which our historical writers are ever ready to carry to excess.

Those who write in democratic ages have another more dangerous tendency. When the traces of individual action upon nations are lost, it often happens that the world goes on to move, though the moving agent is no longer discoverable. As it becomes extremely difficult to discern and to analyze the reasons which, acting separately on the volition of each member of the community, concur in the end to produce movement in the whole mass, men are led to believe that this movement is involuntary, and that societies unconsciously obey some superior force ruling over them. But even when the general fact which governs the private volition of all individuals is supposed to be discovered upon the earth, the principle of human free will is not secure. A cause sufficiently extensive to affect millions of men at once, and sufficiently strong to bend them all together in the same direction, may well seem irresistible: having seen that mankind do yield to it, the mind is close upon the inference that mankind cannot resist it.

Historians who live in democratic ages, then, not only deny that the few have any power of acting upon the destiny of a people, but they deprive the people themselves of the power of modifying their own condition, and they subject them either to an inflexible Providence, or to some blind necessity. According to them each nation is indissolubly bound by its position, its origin, its precedents, and its character, to a certain lot, which no efforts can ever change. They involve generation in generation, and thus, going back from age to age, and from necessity to necessity, up to the origin of the world, they forge a close and enormous chain, which girds and binds the human race. To their minds it is not enough to show what events have occurred: they would fain show that events could not have occurred otherwise. They take a nation arrived at a certain stage of its history, and they affirm that it could not but follow the track which brought it thither. It is easier to make such an assertion, than to show by what means the nation might have adopted a better course.

In reading the historians of aristocratic ages, and especially those of antiquity, it would seem that, to be master of his lot, and to govern his fellow-creatures, man requires only to be master of himself. In perusing the historical volumes which our age has produced, it would seem that man is utterly powerless over himself and over all around him. The historians of antiquity taught how to command: those of our time teach only how to obey; in their writings the author often appears great, but humanity is always diminutive.

If this doctrine of necessity, which is so attractive to those who write history in democratic ages, passes from authors to their readers, till it infects the whole mass of the community and gets possession of the public mind, it will soon paralyze the activity of modern society, and reduce Christians to the level of the Turks.

I would moreover observe, that such principles are peculiarly dangerous at the period at which we are arrived. Our contemporaries are but too prone to doubt of the human free will, because each of them feels himself confined on every side by his own weakness; but they are still willing to acknowledge the strength and independence of men united in society. Let not this principle be lost sight of; for the great object in our time is to raise the faculties of men, not to complete their prostration.

Chapter XXI.

OF PARLIAMENTARY ELOQUENCE IN THE UNITED STATES.

Among aristocratic nations all the members of the community are connected with, and dependent upon, each other; the graduated scale of different ranks acts as a tie, which keeps every one in his proper place, and the whole body in subordination: Something of the same kind always occurs in the political assemblies of these nations. Parties naturally range themselves under certain leaders, whom they obey by a sort of instinct, which is only the result of habits contracted elsewhere. They carry the manners of general society into lesser assemblage.

In democratic countries it often happens that a great number of citizens are tending to the same point; but each one only moves thither, or at least flatters himself that he moves, of his own accord. Accustomed to regulate his doings by personal impulse alone, he does not willingly submit to dictation from without. This taste and habit of independence accompany him into the councils of the nation. If he consents to connect himself with other men in the prosecution of the same purpose, at least he chooses to remain free to contribute to the common success after his own fashion. Hence it is that in democratic countries parties are so impatient of control, and are never manageable except in moments of great public danger. Even then, the authority of leaders, which under such circumstances may be able to make men act or speak, hardly ever reaches the extent of making them keep silence.

Among aristocratic nations the members of political assemblies are at the same time members of the aristocracy. Each of them enjoys high established rank in his own right, and the position which he occupies in the assembly is often less important in his eyes than that which he fills in the country. This consoles him for playing no part in the discussion of public affairs, and restrains him from too eagerly attempting to play an insignificant one.

In America, it generally happens that a representative only becomes somebody from his position in the assembly. He is therefore perpetually haunted by a craving to acquire importance there, and he feels a petulant desire to be constantly obtruding his opinions upon the House. His own vanity is not the only stimulant which urges him on in his course, but that of his constituents, and the continual necessity of propitiating them. Among aristocratic nations, a member of the legislature is rarely in strict dependance upon his constituents: he is frequently to them a sort of unavoidable representative; sometimes they are themselves strictly dependant upon him; and if, at length, they reject him, he may easily get elected elsewhere, or, retiring from public life, he may still enjoy the pleasures of splendid idleness. In a democratic country, like the United States, a representative has hardly ever a lasting hold on the minds of his constituents. However small an electoral body may be, the fluctuations of democracy are constantly changing its aspect: it must therefore be courted unceasingly. He is never sure of his supporters, and, if they forsake him, he is left without a resource; for his natural position is not sufficiently elevated for him to be easily known to those not close to him; and, with the complete state of independence prevailing among the people, he cannot hope that his friends or the government will send him down to be returned by an electoral body unacquainted with him. The seeds of his fortune are, therefore, sown in his own neighborhood: from that nook of earth he must start, to raise himself to the command of a people and to influence the destinies of the world. Thus it is natural, that in democratic countries, the members of political assemblies think more of their constituents than of their party, while in aristocracies they think more of their party than of their constituents.

But what ought to be said to gratify constituents is not always what ought to be said in order to serve the party to which representatives profess to belong. The general interest of a party frequently demands that members belonging to it should not speak on great questions which they understand imperfectly; that they should speak but little on those minor questions which impede the greater ones; lastly, and for the most part, that they should not speak at all. To keep silence is the most useful service that an indifferent spokesman can render to the commonwealth.

Constituents, however, do not think so. The population of a district sends a representative to take a part in the government of a country, because they entertain a very lofty notion of his merits. As men appear greater in proportion to the littleness of the objects by which they are surrounded, it may be assumed, that the opinion entertained of the delegate will be so much the higher as talents are more rare among his constituents. It will therefore frequently happen, that the less constituents have to expect from their representative, the more will they anticipate from him; and, however incompetent he may be, they will not fail to call upon him for signal exertions, corresponding to the rank they have conferred upon him.

Independently of his position as a legislator of the state, electors also regard their representative as the natural patron of the constituency in the legislature; they almost consider him as the proxy of each of his supporters, and they flatter themselves that he will not be less zealous in defence of their private interests than those of the country. Thus electors are well assured beforehand that the representative of their choice will be an orator; that he will speak often if he can, and that in case he is forced to refrain, he will strive at any rate to compress into his less frequent orations an inquiry into all the great questions of state, combined with a statement of all the petty grievances they have themselves to complain of; so that, though he be not able to come forward frequently, he should on each occasion prove what he is capable of doing; and that, instead of perpetually lavishing his powers, he should occasionally condense them in a small compass, so as to furnish a sort of complete and brilliant epitome of his constituents and of himself. On these terms they will vote for him at the next election.

These conditions drive worthy men of humble abilities to despair; who, knowing their own powers, would never voluntarily have come forward. But thus urged on, the representative begins to speak, to the great alarm of his friends; and rushing imprudently into the midst of the most celebrated orators, he perplexes the debate and wearies the House.

All laws which tend to make the representative more dependant on the elector, not only affect the conduct of the legislators, as I have remarked elsewhere, but also their language. They exercise a simultaneous influence on affairs themselves, and on the manner in which affairs are discussed.

There is hardly a member of Congress who can make up his mind to go home without having dispatched at least one speech to his constituents; nor who will endure any interruption until he has introduced into his harangue whatever useful suggestions may be made touching the six-and-twenty States of which the Union is composed, and especially the district which he represents. He therefore presents to the mind of his auditors a succession of great general truths (which he himself only comprehends, and expresses, confusedly,) and of petty minutiæ, which he is but too able to discover and to point out. The consequence is that the debates of that great assembly are frequently vague and perplexed, and that they seem rather to drag their slow length along, than to advance toward a distinct object. Some such state of things will, I believe, always arise in the public assemblies of democracies.

Propitious circumstances and good laws might succeed in drawing to the legislature of a democratic people men very superior to those who are returned by the Americans to Congress; but nothing will ever prevent the men of slender abilities who sit there from obtruding themselves with complacency, and in all ways, upon the public. The evil does not appear to me to be susceptible of entire cure, because it not only originates in the tactics of that Assembly, but in its constitution and in that of the country. The inhabitants of the United States seem themselves to consider the matter in this light; and they show their long experience of parliamentary life, not by abstaining from making bad speeches, but by courageously submitting to hear them made. They are resigned to it, as to an evil which they know to be inevitable.

We have shown the petty side of political debates in democratic assemblies—let us now exhibit the more imposing one. The proceedings within the Parliament of England for the last one hundred and fifty years have never occasioned any great sensation out of that country; the opinions and feelings expressed by the speakers have never awakened much sympathy, even among the nations placed nearest to the great arena of British liberty; whereas Europe was excited by the very first debates which took place in the small colonial assemblies of America, at the time of the revolution.

This was attributable not only to particular and fortuitous circumstances, but to general and lasting causes. I can conceive nothing more admirable or more powerful than a great orator debating on great questions of state in a democratic assembly. As no particular class is ever represented there by men commissioned to defend its own interests, it is always to the whole nation, and in the name of the whole nation, that the orator speaks. This expands his thoughts, and heightens his power of language. As precedents have there but little weight—as there are no longer any privileges attached to certain property, nor any rights inherited in certain bodies or in certain individuals, the mind must have recourse to general truths derived from human nature to resolve the particular question under discussion. Hence the political debates of a democratic people, however small it may be, have a degree of breadth which frequently renders them attractive to mankind. All men are interested by them, because they treat of *man*, who is everywhere the same.

Among the greatest aristocratic nations, on the contrary, the most general questions are almost always argued on some special grounds derived from the practice of a particular time, or the rights of a particular class; which interest that class alone, or at most the people among whom that class happens to exist.

It is owing to this, as much as to the greatness of the French people, and the favourable disposition of the nations who listen to them, that the great effect which the French political debates sometimes produce in the world, must be attributed. The orators of France frequently speak to mankind, even when they are addressing their countrymen only.

SECOND BOOK.

INFLUENCE OF DEMOCRACY ON THE FEELINGS OF THE AMERICANS.

Chapter I.

WHY DEMOCRATIC NATIONS SHOW A MORE ARDENT AND ENDURING LOVE OF EQUALITY THAN OF LIBERTY.

The first and most intense passion which is engendered by the equality of conditions is, I need hardly say, the love of that same equality. My readers will therefore not be surprised that I speak of it before all others.

Everybody has remarked, that in our time, and especially in France, this passion for equality is every day gaining ground in the human heart. It has been said a hundred times that our contemporaries are far more ardently and tenaciously attached to equality than to freedom; but, as I do not find that the causes of the fact have been sufficiently analyzed, I shall endeavour to point them out.

It is possible to imagine an extreme point at which freedom and equality would meet and be confounded together. Let us suppose that all the members of the community take a part in the government, and that each one of them has an equal right to take a part in it. As none is different from his fellows, none can exercise a tyrannical power: men will be perfectly free, because they will all be entirely equal; and they will all be perfectly equal, because they will be entirely free. To this ideal state democratic nations tend. Such is the completest form that equality can assume upon earth; but there are a thousand others which, without being equally perfect, are not less cherished by those nations.

The principle of equality may be established in civil society, without prevailing in the political world. Equal rights may exist of indulging in the same pleasures, of entering the same professions, of frequenting the same places—in a word, of living in the same manner and seeking wealth by the same means, although all men do not take an equal share in the government.

A kind of equality may even be established in the political world, though there should be no political freedom there. A man may be the equal of all his countrymen save one, who is the master of all without distinction, and who selects equally from among them all the agents of his power.

Several other combinations might be easily imagined, by which very great equality would be united to institutions more or less free, or even to institutions wholly without freedom.

Although men cannot become absolutely equal unless they be entirely free, and consequently equality, pushed to its furthest extent, may be confounded with freedom, yet there is good reason for distinguishing the one from the other. The taste which men have for liberty, and that which they feel for equality, are, in fact, two different things; and I am not afraid to add, that, among democratic nations, they are two unequal things.

Upon close inspection, it will be seen that there is in every age some peculiar and preponderating fact with which all others are connected; this fact almost always gives birth to some pregnant idea or some ruling passion, which attracts to itself, and bears away in its course, all the feelings and opinions of the time: it is like a great stream, toward which each of the surrounding rivulets seem to flow.

Freedom has appeared in the world at different times and under various forms; it has not been exclusively bound to any social condition, and it is not confined to democracies. Freedom cannot, therefore, form the distinguishing characteristic of democratic ages. The peculiar and preponderating fact which marks those ages as its own is the equality of conditions; the ruling passion of men in those periods is the love of this equality. Ask not what singular charm the men of democratic ages find in being equal, or what special reasons they may have for clinging so tenaciously to equality rather than to the other advantages which society holds out to them equality is the distinguishing characteristic of the age they live in; that, of itself, is enough to explain that they prefer it to all the rest.

But independently of this reason there are several others, which will at all times habitually lead men to prefer equality to freedom.

If a people could ever succeed in destroying, or even in diminishing, the equality which prevails in its own body, this could only be accomplished by long and laborious efforts. Its social condition must be modified, its laws abolished, its opinions superseded, its habits changed, its manners corrupted. But political liberty is more easily lost; to neglect to hold it fast, is to allow it to escape.

Men therefore not only cling to equality because it is dear to them; they also adhere to it because they think it will last for ever.

That political freedom may compromise in its excesses the tranquillity, the property, the lives of individuals, is obvious to the narrowest and most unthinking minds. But, on the contrary, none but attentive and clear-sighted men perceive the perils with which equality threatens us, and they commonly avoid pointing them out. They know that the calamities they apprehend are remote, and flatter themselves that they will only fall upon future generations, for which the present generations takes but little thought. The evils which freedom sometimes brings with it are immediate; they are apparent to all, and all are more or less affected by them. The evils which extreme equality may produce are slowly disclosed; they creep gradually into the social frame; they are only seen at intervals, and at the moment at which they become most violent, habit already causes them to be no longer felt.

The advantages which freedom brings are only shown by length of time; and it is always easy to mistake the cause in which they originate. The advantages of equality are instantaneous, and they may constantly be traced from their source.

Political liberty bestows exalted pleasures, from time to time, upon a certain number of citizens. Equality every day confers a number of small enjoyments on every man. The charms of equality are every instant felt, and are within the reach of all: the noblest hearts are not insensible to them, and the most vulgar souls exult in them. The passion which equality engenders must therefore be at once strong and general. Men cannot enjoy political liberty unpurchased by some sacrifices, and they never obtain it without great exertions. But the pleasures of equality are self-proffered: each of the petty incidents of life seems to occasion them, and in order to taste them nothing is required but to live.

Democratic nations are at all times fond of equality, but there are certain epochs at which the passion they entertain for it swells to the height of fury. This occurs at the moment when the old social system, long menaced, completes its own destruction after a last intestine struggle, and when the barriers of rank are at length thrown down. At such times men pounce upon equality as their booty, and they cling to it as to some precious treasure which they fear to lose. The passion for equality penetrates on every side into men's hearts, expands there, and fills them entirely. Tell them not that by this blind surrender of themselves to an exclusive passion, they risk their dearest interests: they are deaf. Show them not freedom escaping from their grasp, while they are looking another way: they are blind—or rather, they can discern but one sole object to be desired in the universe.

What I have said is applicable to all democratic nations: what I am about to say concerns the French alone. Among most modern nations, and especially among all those of the continent of Europe, the taste and the idea of freedom only began to exist and to extend itself at the time when social conditions were tending to equality, and as a consequence of that very equality. Absolute kings were the most efficient levellers of ranks among their subjects. Among these nations equality preceded freedom: equality was therefore a fact of some standing, when freedom was still a novelty: the one had already created customs, opinions, and laws belonging to it, when the other, alone and for the first time, came into actual existence. Thus the latter was still only an affair of opinion and of taste, while the former had already crept into the habits of the people, possessed itself of their manners, and given a particular turn to the smallest actions in their lives. Can it be wondered that the men of our own time prefer the one to the other?

I think that democratic communities have a natural taste for freedom: left to themselves, they will seek it, cherish it, and view any privation of it with regret. But for equality, their passion is ardent, insatiable, incessant, invincible: they call for equality in freedom; if they cannot obtain that, they still call for equality in slavery. They will endure poverty, servitude, barbarism—but they will not endure aristocracy.

This is true at all times, and especially true in our own. All men and all powers seeking to cope with this irresistible passion, will be overthrown and destroyed by it. In our age, freedom cannot be established without it, and despotism itself cannot reign without its support.

Chapter II.

OF INDIVIDUALISM* IN DEMOCRATIC COUNTRIES.

I have shown how it is that in ages of equality every man seeks for his opinions within himself: I am now about to show how it is that, in the same ages, all his feelings are turned toward himself alone. *Individualism* is a novel expression to which a novel idea has given birth. Our fathers were only acquainted with egotism. Egotism is a passionate and exaggerated love of self, which leads a man to connect everything with his own person, and to prefer himself to everything in the world. Individualism is a mature and calm feeling, which disposes each member of the community to sever himself from the mass of his fellow-creatures, and to draw apart with his family and his friends; so that, after he has thus formed a little circle of his own, he willingly leaves society at large to itself. Egotism originates in blind instinct: individualism proceeds from erroneous judgement more than from depraved feelings; it originates as much in the deficiencies of the mind as in the perversity of the heart.

---

* [I adopt the expression of the original, however strange it may seem to the English ear, partly because it illustrates the remark on the introduction of general terms into democratic language which was made in a preceding chapter, and partly because I know of no English word exactly equivalent to the expression. The chapter itself defines the meaning attached to it by the author.—*Translator's Note.*]

Egotism blights the germ of all virtue: individualism, at first, only saps the virtues of public life; but, in the long run, it attacks and destroys all others, and is at length absorbed in downright egotism. Egotism is a vice as old as the world, which does not belong to one form of society more than to another: individualism is of democratic origin, and it threatens to spread in the same ratio as the equality of conditions.

Among aristocratic nations, as families remain for centuries in the same condition, often on the same spot, all generations become as it were contemporaneous. A man almost always knows his forefathers, and respects them: he thinks he already sees his remote descendants, and he loves them. He willingly imposes duties on himself toward the former and the latter; and he will frequently sacrifice his personal gratifications to those who went before and to those who will come after him.

Aristocratic institutions have, moreover, the effect of closely binding every man to several of his fellow-citizens. As the classes of an aristocratic people are strongly marked and permanent, each of them is regarded by its own members as a sort of lesser country, more tangible and more cherished than the country at large. As in aristocratic communities all the citizens occupy fixed positions, one above the other, the result is that each of them always sees a man above himself whose patronage is necessary to him, and below himself another man whose co-operation he may claim.

Men living in aristocratic ages are therefore almost always closely attached to something placed out of their own sphere, and they are often disposed to forget themselves. It is true that in those ages the notion of human fellowship is faint, and that men seldom think of sacrificing themselves for mankind; but they often sacrifice themselves for other men. In democratic ages, on the contrary, when the duties of each individual to the race are much more clear, devoted service to any one man becomes more rare; the bond of human affection is extended, but it is relaxed.

Among democratic nations new families are constantly springing up, others are constantly falling away, and all that remain change their condition; the woof of time is every instant broken, and the track of generations effaced. Those who went before are soon forgotten; of those who will come after no one has any idea: the interest of man is confined to those in close propinquity to himself.

As each class approximates to other classes, and intermingles with them, its members become indifferent and as strangers to one another. Aristocracy had made a chain of all the members of the community, from the peasant to the king: democracy breaks that chain, and severs every link of it.

As social conditions become more equal, the number of persons increases who, although they are neither rich enough nor powerful enough to exercise any great influence over their fellow-creatures, have nevertheless acquired or retained sufficient education and fortune to satisfy their own wants. They owe nothing to any man, they expect nothing from any man; they acquire the habit of always considering themselves as standing alone, and they are apt to imagine that their whole destiny is in their own hands.

Thus not only does democracy make every man forget his ancestors, but it hides his descendants, and separates his contemporaries, from him; it throws him back for ever upon himself alone, and threatens in the end to confine him entirely within the solitude of his own heart.

Chapter III.

INDIVIDUALISM STRONGER AT THE CLOSE OF A DEMOCRATIC REVOLUTION THAN AT OTHER PERIODS.

The period when the construction of democratic society upon the ruins of an aristocracy has just been completed, is especially that at which this separation of men from one another, and the egotism resulting from it, most forcibly strike the observation. Democratic communities not only contain a large number of independent citizens, but they are constantly filled with men who, having entered but yesterday upon their independent condition, are intoxicated with their new power. They entertain a presumptuous confidence in their strength, and as they do not suppose that they can henceforward ever have occasion to claim the assistance of their fellow-creatures, they do not scruple to show that they care for nobody but themselves.

An aristocracy seldom yields without a protracted struggle, in the course of which implacable animosities are kindled between the different classes of society. These passions survive the victory, and traces of them may be observed in the midst of the democratic confusion which ensues.

Those members of the community who were at the top of the late gradations of rank cannot immediately forget their former greatness; they will long regard themselves as aliens in the midst of the newly composed society. They look upon all those whom this state of society has made their equals as oppressors, whose destiny can excite no sympathy; they have lost sight of their former equals, and feel no longer bound by a common interest to their fate: each of them, standing aloof, thinks that he is reduced to care for himself alone. Those, on the contrary, who were formerly at the foot of the social scale, and who have been brought up to the common level by a sudden revolution, cannot enjoy their newly acquired independence without secret uneasiness; and if they meet with some of their former superiors on the same footing as themselves, they stand aloof from them with an expression of triumph and of fear.

It is, then, commonly at the outset of democratic society that citizens are most disposed to live apart. Democracy leads men not to draw near to their fellow-creatures; but democratic revolutions lead them to shun each other, and perpetuate in a state of equality the animosities which the state of inequality engendered.

The great advantage of the Americans is that they have arrived at a state of democracy without having to endure a democratic revolution; and that they are born equal, instead of becoming so.

Chapter IV.

THAT THE AMERICANS COMBAT THE EFFECTS OF INDIVIDUALISM BY FREE INSTITUTIONS.

Despotism, which is of a very timorous nature, is never more secure of continuance than when it can keep men asunder; and all its influence is commonly exerted for that purpose. No vice of the human heart is so acceptable to it as egotism: a despot easily forgives his subjects for not loving him, provided they do not love each other. He does not ask them to assist him in governing the state; it is enough that they do not aspire to govern it themselves. He stigmatizes as turbulent and unruly spirits those who would combine their exertions to promote the prosperity of the community; and, perverting the natural meaning of words, he applauds as good citizens those who have no sympathy for any but themselves.

Thus the vices which despotism engenders are precisely those which equality fosters. These two things mutually and perniciously complete and assist each other. Equality places men side by side, unconnected by any common tie; despotism raises barriers to keep them asunder: the former predisposes them not to consider their fellow-creatures, the latter makes general indifference a sort of public virtue.

Despotism then, which is at all times dangerous, is more particularly to be feared in democratic ages. It is easy to see that in those same ages men stand most in need of freedom. When the members of a community are forced to attend to public affairs, they are necessarily drawn from the circle of their own interests, and snatched at times from self-observation. As soon as a man begins to treat of public affairs in public, he begins to perceive that he is not so independent of his fellow-men as he had at first imagined, and that, in order to obtain their support, he must often lend them his co-operation.

When the public is supreme, there is no man who does not feel the value of public good will, or who does not endeavour to court it by drawing to himself the esteem and affection of those among whom he is to live. Many of the passions which congeal and keep asunder human hearts, are then obliged to retire and hide below the surface. Pride must be dissembled; disdain dares not break out; egotism fears its own self. Under a free government, as most public offices are elective, the men, whose elevated minds or aspiring hopes are too closely circumscribed in private life, constantly feel that they cannot do without the population that surrounds them. Men learn at such times to think of their fellow-men from ambitious motives; and they frequently find it, in a manner, their interest to forget themselves.

I may here be met by an objection derived from electioneering intrigues, the meannesses of candidates, and the calumnies of their opponents. These are opportunities for animosity, which occur the oftener, the more frequent elections become. Such evils are doubtless great, but they are transient; whereas the benefits which attend them remain. The desire of being elected may lead some men for a time to violent hostility; but this same desire leads all men in the long run mutually to support each other; and, if it happens that an election accidentally severs two friends, the electoral system brings a multitude of citizens permanently together, who would always have remained unknown to each other. Freedom engenders private animosities, but despotism gives birth to general indifference.

The Americans have combated by free institutions the tendency of equality to keep men asunder, and they have subdued it. The legislators of America did not suppose that a general representation of the whole nation would suffice to ward off a disorder at once so natural to the frame of democratic society, and so fatal: they also thought that it would be well to infuse political life into each portion of the territory, in order to multiply to an infinite extent opportunities of acting in concert, for all the members of the community, and to make them constantly feel their mutual dependance on each other. The plan was a wise one. The general affairs of a country only engage the attention of leading politicians, who assemble from time to time in the same places; and as they often lose sight of each other afterward, no lasting ties are established between them. But if the object be to have the local affairs of a district conducted by the men who reside there, the same persons are always in contact, and they are, in a manner, forced to be acquainted, and to adapt themselves to one another.

It is difficult to draw a man out of his own circle to interest him in the destiny of the state; because he does not clearly understand what influence the destiny of the state can have upon his own lot. But if it be proposed to make a road cross the end of his estate, he will see at a glance that there is a connexion between this small public affair and his greatest private affairs; and he will discover, without its being shown to him, the close tie which unites private to general interest. Thus, far more may be done by entrusting to the citizens the administration of minor affairs than by surrendering to them the control of important ones, toward interesting them in the public welfare, and convincing them that they constantly stand in need one of the other in order to provide for it. A brilliant achievement may win for you the favour of a people at one stroke; but to earn the love and respect of the population which surrounds you, a long succession of little services rendered and of obscure good deeds—a constant habit of kindness, and an established reputation for disinterestedness—will be required. Local freedom, then, which leads a great number of citizens to value the affection of their neighbours and of their kindred, perpetually brings men together, and forces them to help one another, in spite of the propensities which sever them.

In the United States the more opulent citizens take great care not to stand aloof from the people; on the contrary, they constantly keep on easy terms with the lower classes: they listen to them, they speak to them every day. They know that the rich in democracies always stand in need of the poor; and that in democratic ages you attach a poor man to you more by your manner than by benefits conferred. The magnitude of such benefits, which sets off the difference of conditions, causes a secret irritation to those who reap advantage from them; but the charm of simplicity of manners is almost irresistible: their affability carries men away, and even their want of polish is not always displeasing. This truth does not take root at once in the minds of the rich. They generally resist it as long as the democratic revolution lasts, and they do not acknowledge it immediately after that revolution is accomplished. They are very ready to do good to the people, but they still choose to keep them at arm's length; they think that is sufficient, but they are mistaken. They might spend fortunes thus without warming the hearts of the population around them;—that population does not ask them for the sacrifice of their money, but of their pride.

It would seem as if every imagination in the United States were upon the stretch to invent means of increasing the wealth and satisfying the wants of the public. The best informed inhabitants of each district constantly use their information to discover new truths which may augment the general prosperity; and, if they have made any such discoveries, they eagerly surrender them to the mass of the people.

When the vices and weaknesses, frequently exhibited by those who govern in America, are closely examined, the prosperity of the people occasions—but improperly occasions—surprise. Elected magistrates do not make the American democracy flourish; it flourishes because the magistrates are elective.

It would be unjust to suppose that the patriotism and the zeal which every American displays for the welfare of his fellow-citizens are wholly insincere. Although private interest directs the greater part of human actions in the United States, as well as elsewhere, it does not regulate them all. I must say that I have often seen Americans make great and real sacrifices to the public welfare; and I have remarked a hundred instances in which they hardly ever failed to lend faithful support to each other. The free institutions which the inhabitants of the United States possess, and the political rights of which they make so much use, remind every citizen, and in a thousand ways, that he lives in society. They every instant impress upon his mind the notion that it is the duty as well as the interest of men to make themselves useful to their fellow-creatures; and as he sees no particular ground of animosity to them, since he is never either their master or their slave, his heart readily leans to the side of kindness. Men attend to the interests of the public, first by necessity, afterward, by choice: what was intentional becomes an instinct; and by dint of working for the good of one's fellow-citizens, the habit and the taste for serving them is at length acquired.

Many people in France consider equality of conditions as one evil, and political freedom as a second. When they are obliged to yield to the former, they strive at least to escape from the latter. But I contend, that in order to combat the evils which equality may produce, there is only one effectual remedy—namely, political freedom.

Chapter V.

OF THE USE WHICH THE AMERICANS MAKE OF PUBLIC ASSOCIATIONS IN CIVIL LIFE.

I do not propose to speak of those political associations by the aid of which men endeavour to defend themselves against the despotic influence of a majority, or against the aggressions of regal power. That subject I have already treated. If each citizen did not learn, in proportion as he individually becomes more feeble and consequently more incapable of preserving his freedom single handed, to combine with his fellow-citizens for the purpose of defending it, it is clear that tyranny would unavoidably increase together with equality.

Those associations only which are formed in civil life, without reference to political objects, are here adverted to. The political associations which exist in the United States are only a single feature in the midst of the immense assemblage of associations in that country. Americans of all ages, all conditions, and all dispositions, constantly form associations. They have not only commercial and manufacturing companies, in which all take part, but associations of a thousand other kinds—religious, moral, serious, futile, extensive or restricted, enormous or diminutive. The Americans make associations to give entertainments, to found establishments for education, to build inns, to construct churches, to diffuse books, to send missionaries to the antipodes; and in this manner they found hospitals, prisons, and schools. If it be proposed to advance some truth, or to foster some feeling by the encouragement of a great example, they form a society. Wherever, at the head of some new undertaking, you see the government in France, or a man of rank in England, in the United States you will be sure to find an association.

I met with several kinds of associations in America, of which I confess I had no previous notion; and I have often admired the extreme skill with which the inhabitants of the United States succeed in proposing a common object to the exertions of a great many men, and in getting them voluntarily to pursue it.

I have since travelled over England, whence the Americans have taken some of their laws and many of their customs; and it seemed to me that the principle of association was by no means so constantly or so adroitly used in that country. The English often perform great things singly; whereas the Americans form associations for the smallest undertakings. It is evident that the former people consider association as a powerful means of action, but the latter seem to regard it as the only means they have of acting.

Thus the most democratic country on the face of the earth is that in which men have in our time carried to the highest perfection the art of pursuing in common the object of their common desires, and have applied this new science to the greatest number of purposes. Is this the result of accident? or is there in reality any necessary connexion between the principle of association and that of equality?

Aristocratic communities always contain, among a multitude of persons who by themselves are powerless, a small number of powerful and wealthy citizens, each of whom can achieve great undertakings single-handed. In aristocratic societies men do not need to combine in order to act, because they are strongly held together. Every wealthy and powerful citizen constitutes the head of a permanent and compulsory association, composed of all those who are dependant upon him, or whom he makes subservient to the execution of his designs.

Among democratic nations, on the contrary, all the citizens are independent and feeble; they can do hardly anything by themselves, and none of them can oblige his fellow-men to lend him their assistance. They all, therefore, fall into a state incapacity, if they do not learn voluntarily to help each other. If men living in democratic countries had no right and no inclination to associate for political purposes, their independence would be in great jeopardy; but they might long preserve their wealth and their cultivation: whereas if they never acquired the habit of forming associations in ordinary life, civilization itself would be endangered. A people among which individuals should lose the power of achieving great things single-handed, without acquiring the means of producing them by united exertions, would soon relapse into barbarism.

Unhappily, the same social condition which renders associations so necessary to democratic nations, renders their formation more difficult among those nations than among all others. When several members of an aristocracy agree to combine, they easily succeed in doing so: as each of them brings great strength to the partnership, the number of its members may be very limited; and when the members of an association are limited in number, they may easily become mutually acquainted, understand each other, and establish fixed regulations. The same opportunities do not occur among democratic nations, where the associated members must always be very numerous for their association to have any power.

I am aware that many of my countrymen are not in the least embarrassed by this difficulty. They contend that the more enfeebled and incompetent the citizens become, the more able and active the Government ought to be rendered, in order that society at large may execute what individuals can no longer accomplish. They believe this answers the whole difficulty, but I think they are mistaken.

A Government might perform the part of some of the largest American companies; and several States, members of the Union, have already attempted it: but what political power could ever carry on the vast multitude of lesser undertakings which the American citizens perform every day, with the assistance of the principle of association? It is easy to foresee that the time is drawing near when man will be less and less able to produce, of himself alone, the commonest necessaries of life. The task of the governing power will therefore perpetually increase, and its very efforts will extend it every day. The more it stands in the place of associations, the more will individuals, losing the notion of combining together, require its assistance: these are causes and effects which unceasingly engender each other. Will the administration of the country ultimately assume the management of all the manufactures, which no single citizen is able to carry on? And if a time at length arrives, when, in consequence of the extreme subdivision of landed property, the soil is split into an infinite number of parcels, so that it can only be cultivated by companies of husbandmen, will it be necessary that the head of the government should leave the helm of state to follow the plough? The morals and the intelligence of a democratic people would be as much endangered as its business and manufactures, if the government ever wholly usurped the place of private companies.

Feelings and opinions are recruited, the heart is enlarged, and the human mind is developed by no other means than by the reciprocal influence of men upon each other. I have shown that these influences are almost null in democratic countries; they must therefore be artificially created, and this can only be accomplished by associations.

When the members of an aristocratic community adopt a new opinion, or conceive a new sentiment, they give it a station, as it were, beside themselves, upon the lofty platform where they stand; and opinions or sentiments so conspicuous to the eyes of the multitude are easily introduced into the minds or hearts of all around. In democratic countries the governing power alone is naturally in a condition to act in this manner; but it is easy to see that its action is always inadequate, and often dangerous. A government can no more be competent to keep alive and to renew the circulation of opinions and feelings among a great people, than to manage all the speculations of productive industry. No sooner does a government attempt to go beyond its political sphere and to enter upon this new track, than it exercises, even unintentionally, an insupportable tyranny; for a government can only dictate strict rules, the opinions which it favours are rigidly enforced, and it is never easy to discriminate between its advice and its commands. Worse still will be the case if the government really believes itself interested in preventing all circulation of ideas; it will then stand motionless, and oppressed by the heaviness of voluntary torpor. Governments therefore should not be the only active powers: associations ought, in democratic nations, to stand in lieu of those powerful private individuals whom the equality of conditions has swept away.

As soon as several of the inhabitants of the United States have taken up an opinion or a feeling which they wish to promote in the world, they look out for mutual assistance; and as soon as they have found each other out, they combine. From that moment they are no longer isolated men, but a power seen from afar, whose actions serve for an example, and whose language is listened to. The first time I heard in the United States that a hundred thousand men had bound

themselves publicly to abstain from spirituous liquors, it appeared to
me more like a joke than a serious engagement; and I did not at once
perceive why these temperate citizens could not content themselves
with drinking water by their own firesides. I at last understood that
these hundred thousand Americans, alarmed by the progress of drunkenness around them, had made up their minds to patronise temperance. They acted just in the same way as a man of high rank who
should dress very plainly, in order to inspire the humbler orders with a
contempt of luxury. It is probable, that if these hundred thousand men
had lived in France, each of them would singly have memorialized the
government to watch the public houses all over the kingdom.

Nothing, in my opinion, is more deserving of our attention than the
intellectual and moral associations of America. The political and industrial associations of that country strike us forcibly; but the others
elude our observation, or if we discover them, we understand them
imperfectly, because we have hardly ever seen anything of the kind. It
must, however, be acknowledged that they are as necessary to the
American people as the former, and perhaps more so.

In democratic countries the science of association is the mother of
science; the progress of all the rest depends upon the progress it has
made.

Among the laws which rule human societies there is one which
seems to be more precise and clear than all others. If men are to remain civilized, or to become so, the art of associating together must
grow and improve, in the same ratio in which the equality of conditions is increased.

Chapter VI.

OF THE RELATION BETWEEN PUBLIC ASSOCIATIONS AND NEWSPAPERS.

When men are no longer united among themselves by firm and lasting ties, it is impossible to obtain the co-operation of any great number of them, unless you can persuade every man whose concurrence
you require that his private interest obliges him voluntarily to unite his
exertions to the exertions of all the rest. This can only be habitually
and conveniently effected by means of a newspaper; nothing but a
newspaper can drop the same thought into a thousand minds at the
same moment. A newspaper is an adviser who does not require to be
sought, but who comes of his own accord, and talks to you briefly
every day of the common weal, without distracting you from your private affairs.

Newspapers therefore become more necessary in proportion as men
become more equal, and individualism more to be feared. To suppose
that they only serve to protect freedom would be to diminish their importance: they maintain civilization. I shall not deny that in democratic countries newspapers frequently lead the citizens to launch

together in very ill-digested schemes; but if there were no newspapers there would be no common activity. The evil which they produce is therefore much less than that which they cure.

The effect of a newspaper is not only to suggest the same purpose to a great number of persons, but also to furnish means for executing in common the designs which they may have singly conceived. The principal citizens who inhabit an aristocratic country discern each other from afar; and if they wish to unite their forces, they move toward each other, drawing a multitude of men after them. It frequently happens, on the contrary, in democratic countries, that a great number of men who wish or who want to combine cannot accomplish it, because as they are very insignificant and lost amid the crowd, they cannot see, and know not where to find, one another. A newspaper then takes up the notion or the feeling which had occurred simultaneously, but singly, to each of them. All are then immediately guided toward this beacon; and these wandering minds, which had long sought each other in darkness, at length meet and unite.

The newspaper brought them together, and the newspaper is still necessary to keep them united. In order that an association among a democratic people should have any power, it must be a numerous body. The persons of whom it is composed are therefore scattered over a wide extent, and each of them is detained in the place of his domicil by the narrowness of his income, or by the small unremitting exertions by which he earns it. Means then must be found to converse every day without seeing each other, and to take steps in common without having met. Thus hardly any democratic association can do without newspapers.

There is consequently a necessary connexion between public associations and newspapers: newspapers make associations, and associations make newspapers; and if it has been correctly advanced that associations will increase in number as the conditions of men become more equal, it is not less certain that the number of newspapers increases in proportion to that of associations. Thus it is in America that we find at the same time the greatest number of associations and of newspapers.

This connexion between the number of newspapers and that of associations, leads us to the discovery of a further connexion between the state of the periodical press and the form of the administration in a country; and shows that the number of newspapers must diminish or increase among a democratic people, in proportion as its administration is more or less centralized. For, among democratic nations, the exercise of local powers cannot be entrusted to the principal members of the community, as in aristocracies. Those powers must either be abolished, or placed in the hands of very large numbers of men, who then in fact constitute an association permanently established by law, for the purpose of administering the affairs of a certain extent of territory; and they require a journal, to bring to them every day, in the midst of their own minor concerns, some intelligence of the state of their public weal. The more numerous local powers are, the greater is the number of men in whom they are vested by law; and, as this want is hourly felt, the more profusely do newspapers abound.

The extraordinary subdivision of administrative power has much more to do with the enormous number of American newspapers, than the great political freedom of the country and the absolute liberty of the press. If all the inhabitants of the Union had the suffrage—but a suffrage which should only extend to the choice of their legislators in Congress—they would require but few newspapers, because they would only have to act together on a few very important, but very rare, occasions. But within the pale of the great association of the nation, lesser associations have been established by law in every county, every city, and indeed in every village, for the purposes of local administration. The laws of the country thus compel every American to co-operate every day of his life with some of his fellow-citizens for a common purpose, and each one of them requires a newspaper to inform him what all the others are doing.

I am of opinion that a democratic people,* without any national representative assemblies, but with a great number of small local powers, would have in the end more newspapers than another people governed by a centralized administration and an elective legislation. What best explains to me the enormous circulation of the daily press in the United States, is that among the Americans I find the utmost national freedom combined with local freedom of every kind.

There is a prevailing opinion in France and England that the circulation of newspapers would be indefinitely increased by removing the taxes which have been laid upon the press. This is a very exaggerated estimate of the effects of such a reform. Newspapers increase in numbers, not only according to their cheapness, but according to the more or less frequent want which a great number of men may feel for intercommunication and combination.

In like manner I should attribute the increasing influence of the daily press to causes more general than those by which it is commonly explained. A newspaper can only subsist on the condition of publishing sentiments or principles common to a large number of men. A newspaper therefore always represents an association which is composed of its habitual readers. This association may be more or less defined, more or less restricted, more or less numerous; but the fact that the newspaper keeps alive, is a proof that at least the germ of such an association exists in the minds of its readers.

This leads me to a last reflection, with which I shall conclude this chapter. The more equal the conditions of men become, and the less strong men individually are, the more easily do they give way to the current of the multitude, and the more difficult is it for them to adhere by themselves to an opinion which the multitude discard. A newspaper represents an association; it may be said to address each of

---

* I say a *democratic people*: the administration of an aristocratic people may be the reverse of centralized, and yet the want of newspapers be little felt, because local powers are then vested in the hands of a very small number of men, who either act apart, or who know each other and can easily meet and come to an understanding.

its readers in the name of all the others, and to exert its influence over them in proportion to their individual weakness. The power of the newspaper press must therefore increase as the social conditions of men become more equal.

Chapter VII.

CONNEXION OF CIVIL AND POLITICAL ASSOCIATIONS.

There is only one country on the face of the earth where the citizens enjoy unlimited freedom of association for political purposes. This same country is the only one in the world where the continual exercise of the right of association has been introduced into civil life, and where all the advantages which civilization can confer are procured by means of it.

In all the countries where political associations are prohibited, civil associations are rare. It is hardly probable that this is the result of accident; but the inference should rather be, that there is a natural, and perhaps a necessary, connexion between these two kinds of associations.

Certain men happen to have a common interest in some concern, either a commercial undertaking is to be managed, or some speculation in manufactures to be tried; they meet, they combine, and thus by degrees they become familiar with the principle of association. The greater is the multiplicity of small affairs, the more do men, even without knowing it, acquire facility in prosecuting great undertakings in common.

Civil associations, therefore, facilitate political association: but on the other hand, political association singularly strengthens and improves associations for civil purposes. In civil life every man may, strictly speaking, fancy that he can provide for his own wants; in politics, he can fancy no such thing. When a people, then, have any knowledge of public life, the notion of association, and the wish to coalesce, present themselves every day to the minds of the whole community: whatever natural repugnance may restrain men from acting in concert, they will always be ready to combine for the sake of a party. Thus political life makes the love and practice of association more general; it imparts a desire of union, and teaches the means of combination to numbers of men who would have always lived apart.

Politics not only give birth to numerous associations, but to associations of great extent. In civil life it seldom happens that any one interest draws a very large number of men to act in concert; much skill is required to bring such an interest into existence: but in politics opportunities present themselves every day. Now it is solely in great associations that the general value of the principle of association is displayed. Citizens who are individually powerless, do not very clearly anticipate the strength which they may acquire by uniting together; it must be shown to them in order to be understood. Hence it is often easier to collect a multitude for a public purpose than a few persons; a thousand citizens do not see what interest they have in combining together—ten thousand will be perfectly aware of it. In politics men combine for great undertakings; and the use they make of the principle of association in important affairs practically teaches them that it is their interest to help each other in those of less moment. A political association draws a number of individuals at the same time out of their own circle; however they may be naturally kept asunder by age, mind, and fortune, it places them nearer together and brings them into contact. Once met, they can always meet again.

Men can embark in few civil partnerships without risking a portion of their possessions; this is the case with all manufacturing and trading companies. When men are as yet but little versed in the art of association, and are unacquainted with its principal rules, they are afraid, when first they combine in this manner, of buying their experience dear. They therefore prefer depriving themselves of a powerful instrument of success, to running the risks which attend the use of it. They are, however, less reluctant to join political associations, which appear to them to be without danger, because they adventure no money in them. But they cannot belong to these associations for any length of time without finding out how order is maintained among a large number of men, and by what contrivance they are made to advance, harmoniously and methodically, to the same object. Thus they learn to surrender their own will to that of all the rest, and to make their own exertions subordinate to the common impulse—things which it is not less necessary to know in civil than in political associations. Political associations may therefore be considered as large free-schools, where all the members of the community go to learn the general theory of association.

But even if political association did not directly contribute to the progress of civil association, to destroy the former would be to impair the latter. When citizens can only meet in public for certain purposes, they regard such meetings as a strange proceeding of rare occurrence, and they rarely think at all about it. When they are allowed to meet freely for all purposes, they ultimately look upon public association as the universal, or in a manner the sole, means which men can employ to accomplish the different purposes they may have in view. Every new want instantly revives the notion. The art of association then becomes, as I have said before, the mother of action, studied and applied by all.

When some kinds of associations are prohibited and others allowed, it is difficult to distinguish the former from the latter beforehand. In this state of doubt men abstain from them altogether, and a sort of public opinion passes current, which tends to cause any association whatsoever to be regarded as a bold and almost an illicit enterprise.*

---

* This is more especially true when the executive government has a discretionary power of allowing or prohibiting associations. When certain associations are simply prohibited by law, and the courts of justice have to punish infringements of that law, the evil is far less considerable. Then every citizen knows beforehand pretty nearly what he has to expect. He judges

It is therefore chimerical to suppose that the spirit of association, when it is repressed on some one point, will nevertheless display the same vigor on all others; and that if men be allowed to prosecute certain undertakings in common, that is quite enough for them eagerly to set about them. When the members of a community are allowed and accustomed to combine for all purposes, they will combine as readily for the lesser as for the more important ones; but if they are only allowed to combine for small affairs, they will be neither inclined nor able to effect it. It is in vain that you will leave them entirely free to prosecute their business on joint-stock account: they will hardly care to avail themselves of the rights you have granted to them; and, after having exhausted your strength in vain efforts to put down prohibited associations, you will be surprised that you cannot persuade men to form the associations you encourage.

I do not say that there can be no civil associations in a country where political association is prohibited; for men can never live in society without embarking in some common undertakings; but I maintain that in such a country civil associations will always be few in number, feebly planned, unskilfully managed, that they will never form any vast designs, or that they will fail in the execution of them.

This naturally leads me to think that freedom of association in political matters is not so dangerous to public tranquility as is supposed; and that possibly, after having agitated society for some time, it may strengthen the State in the end. In democratic countries political associations are, so to speak, the only powerful persons who aspire to rule the State. Accordingly, the governments of our time look upon associations of this kind just as sovereigns in the middle ages regarded the great vassals of the crown: they entertain a sort of instinctive abhorrence of them, and they combat them on all occasions. They bear, on the contrary, a natural good-will to civil associations, because they readily discover that, instead of directing the minds of the community to public affairs, these institutions serve to divert them from such reflections; and that, by engaging them more and more in the pursuit of objects which cannot be attained without public tranquility, they deter them from revolutions. But these governments do not attend to the fact, that political associations tend amazingly to multiply and facilitate those of a civil character, and that in avoiding a dangerous evil they deprive themselves of an efficacious remedy.

When you see the Americans freely and constantly forming associations for the purpose of promoting some political principle, of raising

---

himself before he is judged by the law, and, abstaining from prohibited associations, he embarks in those which are legally sanctioned. It is by these restrictions that all free nations have always admitted that the right of association might be limited. But if the legislature should invest a man with a power of ascertaining beforehand which associations are dangerous and which are useful, and should authorise him to destroy all associations in the bud or to allow them to be formed, as nobody would be able to foresee in what cases associations might be established and in what cases they would be put down, the spirit of association would be entirely paralyzed. The former of these laws would only assail certain associations; the latter would apply to society itself, and inflict an injury upon it. I can conceive that a regular government may have recourse to the former, but I do not concede that any government has the right of enacting the latter.

one man to the head of affairs, or of wresting power from another, you have some difficulty in understanding that men so independent do not constantly fall into the abuse of freedom. If, on the other hand, you survey the infinite number of trading companies which are in operation in the United States, and perceive that the Americans are on every side unceasingly engaged in the execution of important and difficult plans, which the slightest revolution would throw into confusion, you will readily comprehend why people so well employed are by no means tempted to perturb the State, nor to destroy that public tranquility by which they all profit.

Is it enough to observe these things separately, or should we not discover the hidden tie which connects them? In their political associations, the Americans of all conditions, minds, and ages, daily acquire a general taste for association, and grow accustomed to the use of it. There they meet together in large numbers, they converse, they listen to each other, and they are mutually stimulated to all sorts of undertakings. They afterward transfer to civil life the notions they have thus acquired, and make them subservient to a thousand purposes. Thus it is by the enjoyment of a dangerous freedom that the Americans learn the art of rendering the dangers of freedom less formidable.

If a certain moment in the existence of a nation be selected, it is easy to prove that political associations perturb the State, and paralyze productive industry: but take the whole life of a people, and it may perhaps be easy to demonstrate that freedom of association in political matters is favourable to the prosperity and even to the tranquility of the community.

I said in the former part of this work, "The unrestrained liberty of political associations cannot be entirely assimilated to the liberty of the press. The one is at the same time less necessary and more dangerous than the other. A nation may confine it within certain limits without ceasing to be mistress of itself; and it may sometimes be obliged to do so in order to maintain its own authority." And further on I added: "It cannot be denied that the unrestrained liberty of association for political purposes is the last degree of liberty which a people is fit for. If it does not throw them into anarchy, it perpetually brings them, as it were, to the verge of it." Thus I do not think that a nation is always at liberty to invest its citizens with an absolute right of association for political purposes; and I doubt whether, in any country or in any age, it be wise to set no limits to freedom of association.

A certain nation, it is said, could not maintain tranquility in the community, cause the laws to be respected, or establish a lasting government, if the right of association were not confined within narrow limits. These blessings are doubtless invaluable; and I can imagine that, to acquire or to preserve them, a nation may impose upon itself severe temporary restrictions: but still it is well that the nation should know at what price these blessings are purchased. I can understand that it may be advisable to cut off a man's arm in order to save his life; but it would be ridiculous to assert that he will be as dexterous as he was before he lost it.

Chapter VIII.

THE AMERICANS COMBAT INDIVIDUALISM BY THE PRINCIPLE OF INTEREST RIGHTLY UNDERSTOOD.

When the world was managed by a few rich and powerful individuals, these persons loved to entertain a lofty idea of the duties of man. They were fond of professing that it is praiseworthy to forget oneself, and that good should be done without hope of reward, as it is by the Deity himself. Such were the standard opinions of that time in morals.

I doubt whether men were more virtuous in aristocratic ages than in others; but they were incessantly talking of the beauties of virtue, and its utility was only studied in secret. But since the imagination takes less lofty flights and every man's thoughts are centered in himself, moralists are alarmed by this idea of self-sacrifice, and they no longer venture to present it to the human mind. They therefore content themselves with inquiring whether the personal advantage of each member of the community does not consist in working for the good of all; and when they have hit upon some point on which private interest and public interest meet and amalgamate, they are eager to bring it into notice. Observations of this kind are gradually multiplied: what was only a single remark becomes a general principle; and it is held as a truth that man serves himself in serving his fellow-creatures, and that his private interest is to do good.

I have already shown, in several parts of this work, by what means the inhabitants of the United States almost always manage to combine their own advantage with that of their fellow-citizens: my present purpose is to point out the general rule which enables them to do so. In the United States hardly anybody talks of the beauty of virtue; but they maintain that virtue is useful, and prove it every day. The American moralists do not profess that men ought to sacrifice themselves for their fellow-creatures *because* it is noble to make such sacrifices; but they boldly aver that such sacrifices are as necessary to him who imposes them upon himself, as to him for whose sake they are made.

They have found out that in their country and their age man is brought home to himself by an irresistible force; and losing all hope of stopping that force, they turn all their thoughts to the direction of it. They therefore do not deny that every man may follow his own interest; but they endeavour to prove that it is the interest of every man to be virtuous. I shall not here enter into the reasons they allege, which would divert me from my subject: suffice it to say that they have convinced their fellow-countrymen.

Montaigne[1] said long ago, "Were I not to follow the straight road for its straightness, I should follow it for having found by experience that in the end it is commonly the happiest and most useful track." The doctrine of interest rightly understood is not then new, but among the Americans of our time it finds universal acceptance: it has become popular there; you may trace it at the bottom of all their actions, you will remark it in all they say. It is as often to be met with on the lips of the poor man as of the rich. In Europe the principle of interest is much grosser than it is in America, but at the same time it is less common, and especially it is less avowed; among us men still constantly feign great abnegation which they no longer feel.

The Americans, on the contrary, are fond of explaining almost all the actions of their lives by the principle of interest rightly understood; they show with complacency how an enlightened regard for themselves constantly prompts them to assist each other, and inclines them willingly to sacrifice a portion of their time and property to the welfare of the State. In this respect I think they frequently fail to do themselves justice; for in the United States, as well as elsewhere, people are sometimes seen to give way to those disinterested and spontaneous impulses which are natural to man: but the Americans seldom allow that they yield to emotions of this kind; they are more anxious to do honour to their philosophy than to themselves.

I might here pause, without attempting to pass a judgement on what I have described. The extreme difficulty of the subject would be my excuse, but I shall not avail myself of it; and I had rather that my readers, clearly perceiving my object, should refuse to follow me, than that I should leave them in suspense.

The principle of interest rightly understood is not a lofty one, but it is clear and sure. It does not aim at mighty objects, but it attains without excessive exertion all those at which it aims. As it lies within the reach of all capacities, every one can without difficulty apprehend and retain it. By its admirable conformity to human weaknesses, it easily obtains great dominion; nor is that dominion precarious, since the principle checks one personal interest by another, and uses, to direct the passions, the very same instrument which excites them.

The principle of interest rightly understood produces no great acts of self-sacrifice, but it suggests daily small acts of self-denial. By itself it cannot suffice to make a man virtuous, but it disciplines a number of citizens in habits of regularity, temperance, moderation, foresight, self-command; and, if it does not lead men straight to virtue by the will, it gradually draws them in that direction by their habits. If the principle of interest rightly understood were to sway the whole moral world, extraordinary virtues would doubtless be more rare; but I think that gross depravity would then also be less common. The principle of interest rightly understood perhaps prevents some men from rising far above the level of mankind; but a great number of other men, who were falling far below it, are caught and restrained by it. Observe some few individuals, they are lowered by it; survey mankind, it is raised.

I am not afraid to say, that the principle of interest rightly understood appears to me the best suited of all philosophical theories to the wants of the men of our time, and that I regard it as their chief remaining security against themselves. Toward it, therefore, the minds of the moralists of our age should turn; even should they judge it to be incomplete, it must nevertheless be adopted as necessary.

I do not think upon the whole that there is more egotism among us

than in America; the only difference is, that there it is enlightened—
here it is not. Every American will sacrifice a portion of his private interests to preserve the rest; we would fain preserve the whole, and
oftentimes the whole is lost. Every body I see about me seems bent on
teaching his contemporaries, by precept and example, that what is
useful is never wrong. Will nobody undertake to make them understand how what is right may be useful?

No power upon earth can prevent the increasing equality of conditions from inclining the human mind to seek out what is useful, or
from leading every member of the community to be wrapped up in
himself. It must therefore be expected that personal interest will become more than ever the principal, if not the sole, spring of men's actions; but it remains to be seen how each man will understand his
personal interest. If the members of a community, as they become
more equal, become more ignorant and coarse, it is difficult to foresee
to what pitch of stupid excesses their egotism may lead them; and no
one can foretel into what disgrace and wretchedness they would
plunge themselves, lest they should have to sacrifice something of
their own well-being to the prosperity of their fellow-creatures.

I do not think that the system of interest, as it is professed in America, is, in all its parts, self-evident; but it contains a great number of
truths so evident, that men, if they are but educated, cannot fail to see
them. Educate, then, at any rate; for the age of implicit self-sacrifice
and instinctive virtues is already flitting far away from us, and the time
is fast approaching when freedom, public peace, and social order itself
will not be able to exist without education.

Chapter IX.

THAT THE AMERICANS APPLY THE PRINCIPLE OF INTEREST RIGHTLY
UNDERSTOOD TO RELIGIOUS MATTERS.

If the principle of interest rightly understood had nothing but the
present world in view, it would be very insufficient; for there are many
sacrifices which can only find their recompense in another; and whatever ingenuity may be put forth to demonstrate the utility of virtue, it
will never be an easy task to make that man live aright who has no
thoughts of dying.

It is therefore necessary to ascertain whether the principle of interest rightly understood is easily compatible with religious belief. The
philosophers who inculcate this system of morals tell men, that to be
happy in this life they must watch their own passions and steadily control their excess; that lasting happiness can only be secured by renouncing a thousand transient gratifications; and that a man must
perpetually triumph over himself, in order to secure his own advantage. The founders of almost all religious have held the same language. The track they point out to man is the same, only that the goal

is more remote; instead of placing in this world the reward of the sacrifices they impose, they transport it to another.

Nevertheless I cannot believe that all those who practise virtue from religious motives are only actuated by the hope of a recompense. I have known zealous Christians who constantly forgot themselves, to work with greater ardour for the happiness of their fellow-men; and I have heard them declare that all they did was only to earn the blessings of a future state. I cannot but think that they deceive themselves: I respect them too much to believe them.

Christianity indeed teaches that a man must prefer his neighbour to himself, in order to gain eternal life; but Christianity also teaches that men ought to benefit their fellow-creatures for the love of God. A sublime expression! Man searching by his intellect into the Divine conception, and seeing that order is the purpose of God, freely combines to prosecute the great design; and while he sacrifices his personal interests to this consummate order of all created things, expects no other recompense than the pleasure of contemplating it.

I do not believe that interest is the sole motive of religious men; but I believe that interest is the principal means which religions themselves employ to govern men, and I do not question that in this way they strike into the multitude and become popular. It is not easy clearly to perceive why the principle of interest rightly understood should keep men aloof from religious opinions; and it seems to me more easy to show why it should draw men to them. Let it be supposed that, in order to attain happiness in this world, a man combats his instinct on all occasions and deliberately calculates every action of his life; that, instead of yielding blindly to the impetuosity of first desires, he has learned the art of resisting them, and that he has accustomed himself to sacrifice without an effort the pleasure of a moment to the lasting interest of his whole life. If such a man believes in the religion which he professes, it will cost him but little to submit to the restrictions it may impose. Reason herself counsels him to obey, and habit has prepared him to endure them. If he should have conceived any doubts as to the object of his hopes, still he will not easily allow himself to be stopped by them; and he will decide that it is wise to risk some of the advantages of this world, in order to preserve his rights to the great inheritance promised him in another. "To be mistaken in believing that the Christian religion is true," says Pascal, "is no great loss to any one; but how dreadful to be mistaken in believing it to be false!"

The Americans do not affect a brutal indifference to a future state; they affect no puerile pride in despising perils which they hope to escape from. They therefore profess their religion without shame and without weakness; but there generally is, even in their zeal, something so indescribably tranquil, methodical, and deliberate, that it would seem as if the head, far more than the heart, brought them to the foot of the altar.

The Americans not only follow their religion from interest, but they often place in this world the interest which makes them follow it. In the middle ages the clergy spoke of nothing but a future state; they hardly cared to prove that a sincere Christian may be a happy man here below. But the American preachers are constantly referring to the earth; and it is only with great difficulty that they can divert their attention from it. To touch their congregations, they always show them how favourable religious opinions are to freedom and public tranquility; and it is often difficult to ascertain from their discourses whether the principal object of religion is to procure eternal felicity in the other world, or prosperity in this.

Chapter X.

OF THE TASTE FOR PHYSICAL WELL-BEING IN AMERICA.

In America the passion for physical well-being is not always exclusive, but it is general; and if all do not feel it in the same manner, yet it is felt by all. Carefully to satisfy all, even the least wants of the body, and to provide the little conveniences of life, is uppermost in every mind. Something of an analogous character is more and more apparent in Europe. Among the causes which produce these similar consequences in both hemispheres, several are so connected with my subject as to deserve notice.

When riches are hereditarily fixed in families, there are a great number of men who enjoy the comforts of life without feeling an exclusive taste for those comforts. The heart of man is not so much caught by the undisturbed possession of anything valuable, as by the desire, as yet imperfectly satisfied, of possessing it, and by the incessant dread of losing it.

In aristocratic communities, the wealthy, never having experienced a condition different from their own, entertain no fear of changing it; the existence of such conditions hardly occurs to them. The comforts of life are not to them the end of life, but simply a way of living; they regard them as existence itself;—enjoyed, but scarcely thought of.

As the natural and instinctive taste which all men feel for being well off is thus satisfied without trouble and without apprehension, their faculties are turned elsewhere, and cling to more arduous and more lofty undertakings, which excite and engross their minds.

Hence it is that, in the midst of physical gratifications, the members of an aristocracy often display a haughty contempt of these very enjoyments, and exhibit singular powers of endurance under the privation of them. All the revolutions which have ever shaken or destroyed aristocracies, have shown how easily men accustomed to superfluous luxuries can do without the necessaries of life; whereas men who have toiled to acquire a competency can hardly live after they have lost it.

If I turn my observation from the upper to the lower classes, I find analogous effects produced by opposite causes.

Among a nation where aristocracy predominates in society, and keeps it stationary, the people in the end get as much accustomed to poverty, as the rich to their opulence. The latter bestow no anxiety on their physical comforts, because they enjoy them without an effort; the former do not think of things which they despair of obtaining, and which they hardly know enough of to desire them. In communities of this kind, the imagination of the poor is driven to seek another world; the miseries of real life enclose it around, but it escapes from their control, and flies to seek its pleasures far beyond.

When, on the contrary, the distinctions of rank are confounded together and privileges are destroyed—when hereditary property is subdivided, and education and freedom widely diffused, the desire of acquiring the comforts of the world haunts the imagination of the poor, and the dread of losing them that of the rich. Many scanty fortunes spring up: those who possess them have a sufficient share of physical gratifications to conceive a taste for these pleasures—not enough to satisfy it. They never procure them without exertion, and they never indulge in them without apprehension. They are therefore always straining to pursue or to retain gratifications so delightful, so imperfect, so fugitive.

If I were to inquire what passion is most natural to men who are stimulated and circumscribed by the obscurity of their birth or the mediocrity of their fortune, I could discover none more peculiarly appropriate to their condition than this love of physical prosperity. The passion for physical comforts is essentially a passion of the middle classes: with those classes it grows and spreads, with them it preponderates. From them it mounts into the higher orders of society, and descends into the mass of the people.

I never met in America with any citizen so poor as not to cast a glance of hope and envy on the enjoyments of the rich, or whose imagination did not possess itself by anticipation of those good things which fate still obstinately withheld from him.

On the other hand, I never perceived among the wealthier inhabitants of the United States that proud contempt of physical gratifications which is sometimes to be met with even in the most opulent and dissolute aristocracies. Most of these wealthy persons were once poor: they have felt the sting of want; they were long a prey to adverse fortunes; and now that the victory is won, the passions which accompanied the contest have survived it: their minds are, as it were, intoxicated by the small enjoyments which they have pursued for forty years.

Not but that in the United States, as elsewhere, there are a certain number of wealthy persons, who, having come into their property by inheritance, possess, without exertion, an opulence they have not earned. But even these men are not less devotedly attached to the pleasures of material life. The love of well-being is now become the predominant taste of the nation; the great current of man's passions runs in that channel, and sweeps everything along in its course.

Chapter XI.

PECULIAR EFFECTS OF THE LOVE OF PHYSICAL GRATIFICATIONS IN DEMOCRATIC AGES.

It may be supposed, from what has just been said, that the love of physical gratifications must constantly urge the Americans to irregularities in morals, disturb the peace of families, and threaten the security of society at large. Such is not the case: the passion for physical gratifications produces in democracies effects very different from those which it occasions in aristocratic nations.

It sometimes happens that, wearied with public affairs and sated with opulence, amid the ruins of religious belief and the decline of the State, the heart of an aristocracy may by degrees be seduced to the pursuit of sensual enjoyments only. At other times the power of the monarch or the weakness of the people, without stripping the nobility of their fortune, compels them to stand aloof from the administration of affairs, and while the road to mighty enterprise is closed, abandons them to the inquietude of their own desires; they then fall back heavily upon themselves, and seek in the pleasures of the body oblivion of their former greatness.

When the members of an aristocratic body are thus exclusively devoted to the pursuit of physical gratifications, they commonly concentrate in that direction all the energy which they derive from their long experience of power. Such men are not satisfied with the pursuit of comfort; they require sumptuous depravity and splendid corruption. The worship they pay the senses is a gorgeous one; and they seem to vie with each other in the art of degrading their own natures. The stronger, the more famous, and the more free an aristocracy has been, the more depraved will it then become; and however brilliant may have been the lustre of its virtues, I dare predict that they will always be surpassed by the splendour of its vices.

The taste for physical gratifications leads a democratic people into no such excesses. The love of well-being is there displayed as a tenacious, exclusive, universal passion; but its range is confined. To build enormous palaces, to conquer or to mimic nature, to ransack the world in order to gratify the passions of a man, is not thought of: but to add a few roods of land to your field, to plant an orchard, to enlarge a dwelling, to be always making life more comfortable and convenient, to avoid trouble, and to satisfy the smallest wants without effort and almost without cost. These are small objects, but the soul clings to them; it dwells upon them closely, and day by day, till they at last shut out the rest of the world, and sometimes intervene between itself and Heaven.

This, it may be said, can only be applicable to those members of the community who are in humble circumstances; wealthier individuals will display tastes akin to those which belonged to them in aristocratic ages. I contest the proposition: in point of physical gratifications, the most opulent members of a democracy will not display tastes very different from those of the people; whether it be that, springing from the people, they really share those tastes, or that they esteem it a duty to submit to them. In democratic society the sensuality of the public has taken a moderate and tranquil course, to which all are bound to conform: it is as difficult to depart from the common rule by one's vices as by one's virtues. Rich men who live amid democratic nations are therefore more intent on providing for their smallest wants, than for their extraordinary enjoyments; they gratify a number of petty desires, without indulging in any great irregularities of passion: thus they are more apt to become enervated than debauched.

The especial taste which the men of democratic ages entertain for physical enjoyments is not naturally opposed to the principles of public order; nay, it often stands in need of order that it may be gratified. Nor is it adverse to regularity of morals, for good morals contribute to public tranquillity and are favourable to industry. It may even be frequently combined with a species of religious morality: men wish to be as well off as they can in this world, without foregoing their chance of another.

Some physical gratifications cannot be indulged in without crime; from such they strictly abstain. The enjoyment of others is sanctioned by religion and morality; to these the heart, the imagination and life itself, are unreservedly given up; till, in snatching at these lesser gifts, men lose sight of those more precious possessions which constitute the glory and the greatness of mankind.

The reproach I address to the principle of equality, is not that it leads men away in the pursuit of forbidden enjoyments, but that it absorbs them wholly in quest of those which are allowed. By these means, a kind of virtuous materialism may ultimately be established in the world, which would not corrupt, but enervate the soul, and noiselessly unbend its springs of action.

Chapter XII.

CAUSES OF FANATICAL ENTHUSIASM IN SOME AMERICANS.

Although the desire of acquiring the good things of this world is the prevailing passion of the American people, certain momentary outbreaks occur, when their souls seem suddenly to burst the bonds of matter by which they are restrained, and to soar impetuously toward Heaven.

In all the States of the Union, but especially in the half-peopled country of the far West, wandering preachers may be met with who hawk about the word of God from place to place. Whole families—old men, women, and children, cross rough passes and untrodden wilds, coming from a great distance to join a camp-meeting, where they totally forget for several days and nights, in listening to these discourses, the cares of business and even the most urgent wants of the body.

Here and there, in the midst of American society, you meet with men, full of a fanatical and almost wild enthusiasm, which hardly exists in Europe. From time to time strange sects arise, which endeavour to strike out extraordinary paths to eternal happiness. Religious insanity is very common in the United States.

Nor ought these facts to surprise us. It was not man who implanted in himself the taste for what is infinite, and the love of what is immortal: these lofty instincts are not the offspring of his capricious will; their steadfast foundation is fixed in human nature, and they exist in spite of his efforts. He may cross and distort them—destroy them he cannot.

The soul has wants which must be satisfied; and whatever pains be taken to divert it from itself, it soon grows weary, restless, and disquieted amid the enjoyments of sense. If ever the faculties of the great majority of mankind were exclusively bent upon the pursuit of material objects, it might be anticipated that an amazing reaction would take place in the souls of some men. They would drift at large in the world of spirits, for fear of remaining shackled by the close bondage of the body.

It is not then wonderful if, in the midst of a community whose thoughts tend earthward, a small number of individuals are to be found who turn their looks to Heaven. I should be surprised if mysticism did not soon make some advance among a people solely engaged in promoting its own worldly welfare.

It is said that the deserts of the Thebaid[1] were peopled by the persecutions of the Emperors and the massacres of the Circus; I should rather say that it was by the luxuries of Rome and the Epicurean philosophy of Greece.[2]

If their social condition, their present circumstances, and their laws did not confine the minds of the Americans so closely to the pursuit of worldly welfare, it is probable that they would display more reserve and more experience whenever their attention is turned to things immaterial, and that they would check themselves without difficulty. But they feel imprisoned within bounds, which they will apparently never be allowed to pass. As soon as they have passed these bounds, their minds know not where to fix themselves, and they often rush unrestrained beyond the range of common sense.

Chapter XIII.

CAUSES OF THE RESTLESS SPIRIT OF THE AMERICANS IN THE MIDST OF THEIR PROSPERITY.

In certain remote corners of the Old World you may still sometimes stumble upon a small district which seems to have been forgotten amid the general tumult, and to have remained stationary while everything around it was in motion. The inhabitants are for the most part extremely ignorant and poor; they take no part in the business of the country, and they are frequently oppressed by the government; yet their countenances are generally placid, and their spirits light.

In America I saw the freest and most enlightened men, placed in the happiest circumstances which the world affords: it seemed to me as if a cloud habitually hung upon their brow, and I thought them serious and almost sad even in their pleasures.

The chief reason of this contrast is that the former do not think of the ills they endure—the latter are for ever brooding over advantages they do not possess. It is strange to see with what feverish ardour the Americans pursue their own welfare; and to watch the vague dread that constantly torments them lest they should not have chosen the shortest path which may lead to it.

A native of the United States clings to this world's goods as if he were certain never to die; and he is so hasty in grasping at all within his reach, that one would suppose he was constantly afraid of not living long enough to enjoy them. He clutches everything, he holds nothing fast, but soon loosens his grasp to pursue fresh gratifications.

In the United States a man builds a house to spend his latter years in it, and he sells it before the roof is on: he plants a garden, and lets it just as the trees are coming into bearing: he brings a field into tillage, and leaves other men to gather the crops: he embraces a profession, and gives it up: he settles in a place, which he soon afterward leaves, to carry his changeable longings elsewhere. If his private affairs leave him any leisure, he instantly plunges into the vortex of politics; and if at the end of a year of unremitting labor he finds he has a few days' vacation, his eager curiosity whirls him over the vast extent of the United States, and he will travel fifteen hundred miles in a few days, to shake off his happiness. Death at length overtakes him, but it is before he is weary of his bootless chase of that complete felicity which is for ever on the wing.

At first sight there is something surprising in this strange unrest of so many happy men, restless in the midst of abundance. The spectacle itself is however as old as the world; the novelty is to see a whole people furnish an exemplification of it.

Their taste for physical gratifications must be regarded as the original source of that secret inquietude which the actions of the Americans betray, and of that inconstancy of which they afford fresh examples every day. He who has set his heart exclusively upon the pursuit of worldly welfare is always in a hurry, for he has but a limited time at his disposal to reach it, to grasp it, and to enjoy. The recollection of the brevity of life is a constant spur to him. Besides the good things which he possesses, he every instant fancies a thousand others which death will prevent him from trying if he does not try them soon. This thought fills him with anxiety, fear, and regret, and keeps his mind in ceaseless trepidation, which leads him perpetually to change his plans and his abode.

If in addition to the taste for physical well-being a social condition be superadded, in which the laws and customs make no condition permanent, here is a great additional stimulant to this restlessness of temper. Men will then be seen continually to change their track, for fear of missing the shortest cut to happiness.

It may readily be conceived, that if men, passionately bent upon physical gratifications, desire eagerly, they are also easily discouraged: as their ultimate object is to enjoy, the means to reach that object must be prompt and easy, or the trouble of acquiring the gratification would be greater than the gratification itself. Their prevailing frame of mind then is at once ardent and relaxed, violent and enervated. Death is often less dreaded than perseverance in continuous efforts to one end.

The equality of conditions leads by a still straighter road to several of the effects which I have here described. When all the privileges of birth and fortune are abolished, when all professions are accessible to all, and a man's own energies may place him at the top of any one of them, an easy and unbounded career seems open to his ambition, and he will readily persuade himself that he is born to no vulgar destinies. But this is an erroneous notion, which is corrected by daily experience. The same equality which allows every citizen to conceive these lofty hopes, renders all the citizens less able to realize them: it circumscribes their powers on every side, while it gives freer scope to their desires. Not only are they themselves powerless, but they are met at every step by immense obstacles, which they did not at first perceive. They have swept away the privileges of some of their fellow-creatures which stood in their way; but they have opened the door to universal competition: the barrier has changed its shape rather than its position. When men are nearly alike, and all follow the same track, it is very difficult for any one individual to walk quick and cleave a way through the dense throng which surrounds and presses him. This constant strife between the propensities springing from the equality of conditions and the means it supplies to satisfy them, harasses and wearies the mind.

It is possible to conceive men arrived at a degree of freedom which should completely content them; they would then enjoy their independence without anxiety and without impatience. But men will never establish any equality with which they can be contented. Whatever efforts a people may make, they will never succeed in reducing all the conditions of society to a perfect level; and even if they unhappily attained that absolute and complete depression, the inequality of minds would still remain, which, coming directly from the hand of God, will for ever escape the laws of man. However democratic then the social state and the political constitution of a people may be, it is certain that every member of the community will always find out several points about him which command his own position; and we may foresee that his looks will be doggedly fixed in that direction. When inequality of conditions is the common law of society, the most marked inequalities do not strike the eye; when everything is nearly on the same level, the slightest are marked enough to hurt it. Hence the desire of equality always becomes more insatiable in proportion as equality is more complete.

Among democratic nations men easily attain a certain equality of conditions: they can never attain the equality they desire. It perpetually retires from before them, yet without hiding itself from their sight, and in retiring draws them on. At every moment they think they are about to grasp it; it escapes at every moment from their hold. They are near enough to see its charms, but too far off to enjoy them; and before they have fully tasted its delights, they die.

To these causes must be attributed that strange melancholy which oftentimes will haunt the inhabitants of democratic countries in the midst of their abundance, and that disgust at life which sometimes seizes upon them in the midst of calm and easy circumstances. Complaints are made in France that the number of suicides increases; in America suicide is rare, but insanity is said to be more common than anywhere else. These are all different symptoms of the same disease. The Americans do not put an end to their lives, however disquieted they may be, because their religion forbids it; and among them materialism may be said hardly to exist, notwithstanding the general passion for physical gratification. The will resists—reason frequently gives way.

In democratic ages enjoyments are more intense than in the ages of aristocracy, and especially the number of those who partake in them is larger: but, on the other hand, it must be admitted that man's hopes and his desires are oftener blasted, the soul is more stricken and perturbed, and care itself more keen.

Chapter XIV.

TASTE FOR PHYSICAL GRATIFICATIONS UNITED IN AMERICA TO LOVE OF FREEDOM AND ATTENTION TO PUBLIC AFFAIRS.

When a democratic state turns to absolute monarchy, the activity which was before directed to public and to private affairs is all at once centred upon the latter: the immediate consequence is, for some time, great physical prosperity; but this impulse soon slackens, and the amount of productive industry is checked. I know not if a single trading or manufacturing people can be cited, from the Tyrians[1] down to the Florentines and the English, who were not a free people also. There is therefore a close bond and necessary relation between these two elements—freedom and productive industry.

This proposition is generally true of all nations, but especially of democratic nations. I have already shown that men who live in ages of equality continually require to form associations in order to procure the things they covet; and, on the other hand, I have shown how great political freedom improves and diffuses the art of association. Freedom, in these ages, is therefore especially favorable to the production of wealth; nor is it difficult to perceive, that despotism is especially adverse to the same result.

The nature of despotic power in democratic ages is not to be fierce or cruel, but minute and meddling. Despotism of this kind, though it does not trample on humanity, is directly opposed to the genius of commerce and the pursuits of industry.

Thus the men of democratic ages require to be free in order more readily to procure those physical enjoyments for which they are always longing. It sometimes happens, however, that the excessive taste they conceive for these same enjoyments abandons them to the first master who appears. The passion for worldly welfare then defeats itself, and, without perceiving it, throws the object of their desires to a greater distance.

There is, indeed, a most dangerous passage in the history of a democratic people. When the taste for physical gratifications among such a people has grown more rapidly than their education and their experience of free institutions, the time will come when men are carried away, and lose all self-restraint, at the sight of the new possessions they are about to lay hold upon. In their intense and exclusive anxiety to make a fortune, they lose sight of the close connexion which exists between the private fortune of each of them and the prosperity of all. It is not necessary to do violence to such a people in order to strip them of the rights they enjoy; they themselves willingly loosen their hold. The discharge of political duties appears to them to be a troublesome annoyance, which diverts them from their occupation and business. If they be required to elect representatives, to support the government by personal service, to meet on public business, they have no time—they cannot waste their precious time in useless engagements: such idle amusements are unsuited to serious men who are engaged with the more important interests of life. These people think they are following the principle of self-interest, but the idea they entertain of that principle is a very rude one; and the better to look after what they call their business, they neglect their chief business, which is to remain their own masters.

As the citizens who work do not care to attend to public business, and as the class which might devote its leisure to these duties has ceased to exist, the place of the Government is, as it were, unfilled. If at that critical moment some able and ambitious man grasps the supreme power, he will find the road to every kind or usurpation open before him. If he does but attend for some time to the material prosperity of the country, no more will be demanded of him. Above all he must ensure public tranquility: men who are possessed by the passion of physical gratification generally find out that the turmoil of freedom disturbs their welfare, before they discover how freedom itself serves to promote it. If the slightest rumor of public commotion intrudes into the petty pleasures of private life, they are roused and alarmed by it. The fear of anarchy perpetually haunts them, and they are always ready to fling away their freedom at the first disturbance.

I readily admit that public tranquility is a great good; but at the same time, I cannot forget that all nations have been enslaved by being kept in good order. Certainly it is not to be inferred that nations ought to despise public tranquility; but that state ought not to content them. A nation which asks nothing of its government but the maintenance of order is already a slave at heart—the slave of its own well-being, awaiting but the hand that will bind it.

By such a nation the despotism of faction is not less to be dreaded than the despotism of an individual. When the bulk of the community is engrossed by private concerns, the smallest parties need not despair of getting the upper hand in public affairs. At such times it is not rare to see upon the great stage of the world, as we see at our theatres, a multitude represented by a few players, who alone speak in the name of an absent or inattentive crowd: they alone are in action while all are stationary; they regulate everything by their own caprice; they change the laws, and tyrannize at will over the manners of the country; and then men wonder to see into how small a number of weak and worthless hands a great people may fall.

Hitherto the Americans have fortunately escaped all the perils which I have just pointed out; and in this respect they are really deserving of admiration. Perhaps there is no country in the world where fewer idle men are to be met with than in America, or where all who work are more eager to promote their own welfare. But if the passion of the Americans for physical gratifications is vehement, at least it is not indiscriminating; and reason, though unable to restrain it, still directs its course.

An American attends to his private concerns as if he were alone in the world, and the next minute he gives himself up to the common weal as if he had forgotten them. At one time he seems animated by the most selfish cupidity, at another by the most lively patriotism. The human heart cannot be thus divided. The inhabitants of the United States alternately display so strong and so similar a passion for their own welfare and for their freedom, that it may be supposed that these passions are united and mingled in some part of their character. And indeed the Americans believe their freedom to be the best instrument and surest safeguard of their welfare: they are attached to the one by the other. They by no means think that they are not called upon to take a part in the public weal; they believe, on the contrary, that their chief business is to secure for themselves a government which will allow them to acquire the things they covet, and which will not debar them from the peaceful enjoyment of those possessions which they have acquired.

Chapter XV.

THAT RELIGIOUS RELIEF SOMETIMES TURNS THE THOUGHTS OF THE AMERICANS TO IMMATERIAL PLEASURES.

In the United States, on the seventh day of every week, the trading and working life of the nation seems suspended; all noises cease; a deep tranquility, say rather the solemn calm of meditation, succeeds the turmoil of the week, and the soul resumes possession and contemplation of itself. Upon this day the marts of traffic are deserted; every member of the community, accompanied by his children, goes to church, where he listens to strange language which would seem unsuited to his ear. He is told of the countless evils caused by pride and covetousness: he is reminded of the necessity of checking his desires, of the finer pleasures which belong to virtue alone, and of the true happiness which attends it. On his return home, he does not turn to the ledgers of his calling, but he opens the book of Holy Scripture: there he meets with sublime or affecting descriptions of the greatness and goodness of the Creator, of the infinite magnificence of the handiwork of God, of the lofty destinies of man, of his duties, and of his immortal privileges.

Thus it is that the American at times steals an hour from himself; and laying aside for a while the petty passions which agitate his life, and the ephemeral interests which engross it, he strays at once into an ideal world, where all is great, eternal, and pure.

I have endeavoured to point out in another part of this work the causes to which the maintenance of the political institutions of the Americans is attributable, and religion appeared to be one of the most prominent among them. I am now treating of the Americans in an individual capacity, and I again observe that religion is not less useful to each citizen than to the whole State.

The Americans show, by their practice, that they feel the high necessity of imparting morality to democratic communities by means of religion. What they think of themselves in this respect is a truth of which every democratic nation ought to be thoroughly persuaded.

I do not doubt that the social and political constitution of a people predispose them to adopt a certain belief and certain tastes, which afterward flourish without difficulty among them; while the same causes may divert a people from certain opinions and propensities, without any voluntary effort, and, as it were, without any distinct consciousness, on their part. The whole art of the legislator is correctly to discern beforehand these natural inclinations of communities of men, in order to know whether they should be assisted, or whether it may not be necessary to check them. For the duties incumbent on the legislator differ at different times; the goal toward which the human race ought ever to be tending is alone stationary; the means of reaching it are perpetually to be varied.

If I had been born in an aristocratic age, in the midst of a nation where the hereditary wealth of some, and the irremediable penury of others, should equally divert men from the idea of bettering their condition, and hold the soul as it were in a state of torpor fixed on the contemplation of another world, I should then wish that it were possible for me to rouse that people to a sense of their wants; I should seek to discover more rapid and more easy means for satisfying the fresh desires which I might have awakened; and, directing the most strenuous efforts of the human mind to physical pursuits, I should endeavour to stimulate it to promote the well-being of man. If it happened that some men were immoderately incited to the pursuit of riches, and displayed an excessive liking for physical gratifications, I should not be alarmed; these peculiar symptoms would soon be absorbed in the general aspect of the people.

The attention of the legislators of democracies is called to other cares. Give democratic nations education and freedom, and leave them alone. They will soon learn to draw from this world all the benefits which it can afford; they will improve each of the useful arts, and will day by day render life more comfortable, more convenient, and more easy. Their social condition naturally urges them in this direction; I do not fear that they will slacken their course.

But while man takes delight in this honest and lawful pursuit of his well-being, it is to be apprehended that he may in the end lose the use of his sublimest faculties; and that while he is busied in improving all around him, he may at length degrade himself Here, and here only, does the peril lie. It should therefore be the unceasing object of the legislators of democracies, and of all the virtuous and enlightened men who live there, to raise the souls of their fellow-citizens, and keep them lifted up toward Heaven. It is necessary that all who feel an interest in the future destinies of democratic society should unite, and that all should make joint and continual efforts to diffuse the love of the infinite, a sense of greatness, and a love of pleasures not of earth. If among the opinions of a democratic people any of those pernicious theories exist which tend to inculcate that all perishes with the body, let the men by whom such theories are professed be marked as the natural foes of such a people.

The Materialists are offensive to me in many respects; their doctrines I hold to be pernicious, and I am disgusted at their arrogance. If their system could be of any utility to man, it would seem to be by giving him a modest opinion of himself. But these reasoners show that it is not so; and when they think they have said enough to establish that they are brutes, they show themselves as proud as if they had demonstrated that they are gods.

Materialism is, among all nations, a dangerous disease of the human mind; but it is more especially to be dreaded among a democratic people, because it readily amalgamates with that vice which is most familiar to the heart under such circumstances. Democracy encourages a taste for physical gratification: this taste, if it become excessive, soon disposes men to believe that all is matter only; and materialism, in turn, hurries them back with mad impatience to these same delights: such is the fatal circle within which democratic nations are driven round. It were well that they should see the danger and hold back.

Most religions are only general, simple, and practical means of teaching men the doctrine of the immortality of the soul. That is the greatest benefit which a democratic people derives from its belief, and hence belief is more necessary to such a people than to all others. When therefore any religion has struck its roots deep into a democracy, beware lest you disturb them; but rather watch it carefully, as the most precious bequest of aristocratic ages. Seek not to supersede the old religious opinions of men by new ones; lest in the passage from one faith to another, the soul being left for a while stripped of all belief, the love of physical gratifications should grow upon it and fill it wholly.

The doctrine of metempsychosis is assuredly not more rational than that of materialism; nevertheless if it were absolutely necessary that a democracy should choose one of the two, I should not hesitate to decide that the community would run less risk of being brutalized by believing that the soul of man will pass into the carcass of a hog, than by believing that the soul of man is nothing at all. The belief in a super-sensual and immortal principle, united for a time to matter, is so indispensable to man's greatness, that its effects are striking even when it is not united to the doctrine of future reward and punishment; and when it holds no more than that after death the divine principle contained in man is absorbed in the Deity, or transferred to animate the frame of some other creature. Men holding so imperfect a belief will still consider the body as the secondary and inferior portion of their nature, and they will despise it even while they yield to its influence; whereas they have a natural esteem and secret admiration for the immaterial part of man, even though they sometimes refuse to submit to its dominion. That is enough to give a lofty cast to their opinions and their tastes, and to bid them tend with no interested motive, and as it were by impulse, to pure feelings and elevated thoughts.

It is not certain that Socrates and his followers had very fixed opinions as to what would befall man hereafter; but the sole point of belief on which they were determined—that the soul has nothing in common with the body, and survives it—was enough to give the Platonic philosophy that sublime aspiration by which it is distinguished.

It is clear from the works of Plato, that many philosophical writers, his predecessors or contemporaries, professed materialism. These writers have not reached us, or have reached us in mere fragments. The same thing has happened in almost all ages; the greater part of the most famous minds in literature adhere to the doctrines of a super-sensual philosophy. The instinct and the taste of the human race maintain those doctrines; they save them oftentimes in spite of men themselves, and raise the names of their defenders above the tide of time. It must not then be supposed that at any period or under any political condition, the passion for physical gratifications, and the opinions which are superinduced by that passion, can ever content a whole people. The heart of man is of a larger mould; it can at once comprise a taste for the possessions of earth and the love of those of Heaven: at times it may seem to cling devotedly to the one, but it will never be long without thinking of the other.

If it be easy to see that it is more particularly important in democratic ages that spiritual opinions should prevail, it is not easy to say by what means those who govern democratic nations may make them predominate. I am no believer in the prosperity, any more than in the durability, of official philosophies; and as to state-religions, I have always held, that if they be sometimes of momentary service to the interests of political power, they always, sooner or later, become fatal to the church. Nor do I think with those who assert, that to raise religion in the eyes of the people, and to make them do honour to her spiritual doctrines, it is desirable indirectly to give her ministers a political influence which the laws deny them. I am so much alive to the almost inevitable dangers which beset religious belief whenever the clergy take part in public affairs, and I am so convinced that Christianity must be maintained at any cost in the bosom of modern democracies, that I had rather shut up the priesthood within the sanctuary than allow them to step beyond it.

What means then remain in the hands of constituted authorities to bring men back to spiritual opinions, or to hold them fast to the religion by which those opinions are suggested?

My answer will do me harm in the eyes of politicians. I believe that the sole effectual means which governments can employ in order to have the doctrine of the immortality of the soul duly respected, is ever to act as if they believed in it themselves; and I think that it is only by scrupulous conformity to religious morality in great affairs, that they can hope to teach the community at large to know, to love, and to observe it in the lesser concerns of life.

Chapter XVI.

THAT EXCESSIVE CARE OF WORLDLY WELFARE MAY IMPAIR THAT WELFARE.

There is a closer tie than is commonly supposed between the improvement of the soul and the amelioration of what belongs to the body. Man may leave these two things apart, and consider each of them alternately; but he cannot sever them entirely without at last losing sight of one and of the other.

The beasts have the same senses as ourselves, and very nearly the same appetites. We have no sensual passions which are not common to our race and theirs, and which are not to be found, at least in the germ, in a dog as well as in a man. Whence is it then that the animals can only provide for their first and lowest wants, whereas we can infinitely vary and endlessly increase our enjoyments?

We are superior to the beasts in this, that we use our souls to find out those material benefits to which they are only led by instinct. In man, the angel teaches the brute the art of contenting its desires. It is because man is capable of rising above the things of the body, and of contemning life itself, of which the beasts have not the least notion, that he can multiply these same things of the body to a degree which inferior races are equally unable to conceive.

Whatever elevates, enlarges, and expands the soul, renders it more capable of succeeding in those very undertakings which concern it not. Whatever, on the other hand, enervates or lowers it, weakens it for all purposes, the chiefest as well as the least, and threatens to render it almost equally impotent for the one and for the other. Hence the soul must remain great and strong, though it were only to devote its strength and greatness from time to time to the service of the body. If men were ever to content themselves with material objects, it is probable that they would lose by degrees the art of producing them; and they would enjoy them in the end, like the brutes, without discernment and without improvement.

Chapter XVII.

THAT IN TIMES MARKED BY EQUALITY OF CONDITIONS AND SCEPTICAL OPINIONS, IT IS IMPORTANT TO REMOVE TO A DISTANCE THE OBJECTS OF HUMAN ACTIONS.

In the ages of faith the final end of life is placed beyond life. The men of those ages therefore, naturally, and in a manner involuntarily, accustom themselves to fix their gaze for a long course of years on some immoveable object, toward which they are constantly tending; and they learn by insensible degrees to repress a multitude of petty passing desires, in order to be the better able to content that great and lasting desire which possesses them. When these same men engage in the affairs of this world, the same habits may be traced in their conduct. They are apt to set up some general and certain aim and end to their actions here below, toward which all their efforts are directed: they do not turn from day to day to chase some novel object of desire, but they have settled designs which they are never weary of pursuing.

This explains why religious nations have so often achieved such lasting results: for while they were thinking only of the other world, they had found out the great secret of success in this. Religions give men a general habit of conducting themselves with a view to futurity; in this respect they are not less useful to happiness in this life than to felicity hereafter; and this is one of their chief political characteristics.

But in proportion as the light of faith grows dim, the range of man's sight is circumscribed, as if the end and aim of human actions appeared every day to be more within his reach. When men have once allowed themselves to think no more of what is to befall them after life, they readily lapse into that complete and brutal indifference to futurity, which is but too conformable to some propensities of mankind. As soon as they have lost the habit of placing their chief hopes upon remote events, they naturally seek to gratify without delay their smallest desires; and no sooner do they despair of living for ever, than they are disposed to act as if they were to exist but for a single day. In sceptical ages it is always therefore to be feared that men may perpetually give way to their daily casual desires; and that, wholly renouncing whatever cannot be acquired without protracted effort, they may establish nothing great, permanent, and calm.

If the social condition of a people, under these circumstances, becomes democratic, the danger which I here point out is thereby increased. When every one is constantly striving to change his position—when an immense field for competition is thrown open to all—when wealth is amassed or dissipated in the shortest possible space of time amid the turmoil of democracy, visions of sudden and easy fortunes—of great possessions easily won and lost—of chance, under all its forms—haunt the mind. The instability of society itself fosters the natural instability of man's desires. In the midst of these perpetual fluctuations of his lot, the present grows upon his mind, until it conceals futurity from his sight, and his looks go no further than the morrow.

In those countries in which unhappily irreligion and democracy co-exist, the most important duty of philosophers and of those in power is to be always striving to place the objects of human actions far beyond man's immediate range. Circumscribed by the character of his country and his age, the moralist must learn to vindicate his principles in that position. He must constantly endeavour to show his contemporaries, that, even in the midst of the perpetual commotion around them, it is easier than they think to conceive and to execute protracted undertakings. He must teach them that, although the aspect of mankind may have changed, the methods by which men may provide for their prosperity in this world are still the same; and that among democratic nations, as well as elsewhere, it is only by resisting a thousand petty selfish passions of the hour, that the general and unquenchable passion for happiness can be satisfied.

The task of those in power is not less clearly marked out. At all times it is important that those who govern nations should act with a view to the future: but this is even more necessary in democratic and sceptical ages than in any others. By acting thus, the leading men of democracies not only make public affairs prosperous, but they also teach private individuals, by their example, the art of managing private concerns.

Above all they must strive as much as possible to banish chance from the sphere of politics. The sudden and undeserved promotion of a courtier produces only a transient impression in an aristocratic country, because the aggregate institutions and opinions of the nation habitually compel men to advance slowly in tracks, which they cannot get out of. But nothing is more pernicious than similar instances of favour exhibited to the eyes of a democratic people: they give the last impulse to the public mind in a direction where everything hurries it onward. At times of scepticism and equality more especially, the favour of the people or of the prince, which chance may confer or chance withhold, ought never to stand in lieu of attainments or services. It is desirable that every advancement should there appear to be the result of some effort; so that no greatness should be of too easy acquirement, and that ambition should be obliged to fix its gaze long upon an object before it is gratified.

Governments must apply themselves to restore to men that love of the future, with which religion and the state of society no longer inspire them; and, without saying so, they must practically teach the community day by day that wealth, fame, and power are the rewards of labour—that great success stands at the utmost range of long desires, and that nothing lasting is obtained but what is obtained by toil.

When men have accustomed themselves to foresee from afar what is likely to befal them in the world and to feed upon hopes, they can hardly confine their minds within the precise circumference of life, and they are ready to break the boundary and cast their looks beyond. I do not doubt that, by training the members of a community to think of their future condition in this world, they would be gradually and unconsciously brought nearer to religious convictions. Thus the means which allow men, up to a certain point, to go without religion, are perhaps after all the only means we still possess for bringing mankind back by a long and round about path to a state of faith.

Chapter XVIII.

THAT AMONG THE AMERICANS, ALL HONEST CALLINGS ARE HONOURABLE.

Among a democratic people, where there is no hereditary wealth, every man works to earn a living, or has worked, or is born of parents who have worked. The notion of labour is therefore presented to the mind on every side as the necessary, natural, and honest condition of human existence. Not only is labour not dishonourable among such a people, but it is held in honour: the prejudice is not against it, but in its favour. In the United States a wealthy man thinks that he owes it to public opinion to devote his leisure to some kind of industrial or commercial pursuit, or to public business. He would think himself in bad repute if he employed his life solely in living. It is for the purpose of escaping this obligation to work, that so many rich Americans come to Europe, where they find some scattered remains of aristocratic society, among which idleness is still held in honour.

Equality of conditions not only ennobles the notion of labour in men's estimation, but it raises the notion of labour as a source of profit.

In aristocracies it is not exactly labour that is despised, but labour with a view to profit. Labour is honorific in itself, when it is undertaken at the sole bidding of ambition or of virtue. Yet in aristocratic society it constantly happens that he who works for honour is not insensible to the attractions of profit. But these two desires only intermingle in the innermost depths of his soul: he carefully hides from every eye the point at which they join; he would fain conceal it from himself. In aristocratic countries there are few public officers who do not affect to serve their country without interested motives. Their salary is an incident of which they think but little, and of which they always affect not to think at all. Thus the notion of profit is kept distinct from that of labour; however they may be united in point of fact, they are not thought of together.

In democratic communities these two notions are on the contrary always palpably united. As the desire of well-being is universal—as fortunes are slender or fluctuating—as every one wants either to increase his own resources, or to provide fresh ones for his progeny—men clearly see that it is profit which, if not wholly at least partially, leads them to work. Even those who are principally actuated by the love of fame are necessarily made familiar with the thought that they are not exclusively actuated by that motive; and they discover that the desire of getting a living is mingled in their minds with the desire of making life illustrious.

As soon as, on the one hand, labour is held by the whole community to be an honourable necessity of man's condition—and on the other, as soon as labour is always ostensibly performed, wholly or in part, for the purpose of earning remuneration—the immense interval which separated different callings in aristocratic societies disappears. If all are not alike, all at least have one feature in common. No profession exists in which men do not work for money; and the remuneration which is common to them all, gives them all an air of resemblance.

This serves to explain the opinions which the Americans entertain with respect to different callings. In America no one is degraded because he works, for every one about him works also; nor is any one humiliated by the notion of receiving pay, for the President of the United States also works for pay. He is paid for commanding—other men for obeying orders. In the United States professions are more or less laborious, more or less profitable; but they are never either high or low: every honest calling is honourable.

Chapter XIX.

WHAT LEADS ALMOST ALL THE AMERICANS TO FOLLOW INDUSTRIAL CALLINGS.

Agriculture is, perhaps, of all the useful arts that which improves most slowly among democratic nations. Frequently, indeed, it would seem to be stationary, because other arts are making rapid strides toward perfection. On the other hand, almost all the tastes and habits which the equality of conditions engenders naturally lead men to commercial and industrial occupations.

Suppose an active, enlightened, and free man, enjoying a competency, but full of desires: he is too poor to live in idleness; he is rich enough to feel himself protected from the immediate fear of want, and he thinks how he can better his condition. This man has conceived a taste for physical gratifications, which thousands of his fellow-men indulge in around him; he has himself begun to enjoy these pleasures, and he is eager to increase his means of satisfying these tastes more completely. But life is slipping away, time is urgent—to what is he to turn? The cultivation of the ground promises an almost certain result to his exertions, but a slow one; men are not enriched by it without patience and toil. Agriculture is therefore only suited to those who have already large superfluous wealth, or to those whose penury bids them only seek a bare subsistence. The choice of such a man as we have supposed is soon made; he sells his plot of ground, leaves his dwelling, and embarks in some hazardous but lucrative calling.

Democratic communities abound in men of this kind; and in proportion as the equality of conditions becomes greater, their multitude increases. Thus democracy not only swells the number of working men, but it leads men to prefer one kind of labour to another; and while it diverts them from agriculture, it encourages their taste for commerce and manufactures.*

This spirit may be observed even among the richest members of the community. In democratic countries, however opulent a man is supposed to be, he is almost always discontented with his fortune, because he finds that he is less rich than his father was, and he fears that his sons will be less rich than himself. Most rich men in democracies are therefore constantly haunted by the desire of obtaining wealth, and they naturally turn their attention to trade and manufactures, which appear to offer the readiest and most powerful means of success. In this respect they share the instincts of the poor, without feeling the same necessities; say rather, they feel the most imperious of all necessities, that of not sinking in the world.

In aristocracies the rich are at the same time those who govern. The attention which they unceasingly devote to important public affairs diverts them from the lesser cares which trade and manufactures demand. If the will of an individual happens nevertheless to turn his attention to business, the will of the body to which he belongs will im-

---

* It has often been remarked that manufacturers and mercantile men are inordinately addicted to physical gratifications, and this has been attributed to commerce and manufactures; but that is, I apprehend, to take the effect for the cause. The taste for physical gratifications is not imparted to men by commerce or manufactures, but it is rather this taste which leads men to embark in commerce and manufactures, as a means by which they hope to satisfy themselves more promptly and more completely. If commerce and manufactures increase the desire of well-being, it is because every passion gathers strength in proportion as it is cultivated, and is increased by all the efforts made to satiate it. All the causes which make the love of worldly welfare predominate in the heart of man are favourable to the growth of commerce and manufactures. Equality of conditions is one of those causes; it encourages trade, not directly by giving men a taste for business, but indirectly by strengthening and expanding in their minds a taste for prosperity.

mediately debar him from pursuing it; for however men may declaim against the rule of numbers, they cannot wholly escape their sway; and even among those aristocratic bodies which most obstinately refuse to acknowledge the rights of the majority of the nation, a private majority is formed which governs the rest.*

In democratic countries, where money does not lead those who possess it to political power, but often removes them from it, the rich do not know how to spend their leisure. They are driven into active life by the inquietude and the greatness of their desires, by the extent of their resources, and by the taste for what is extraordinary, which is almost always felt by those who rise, by whatsoever means, above the crowd. Trade is the only road open to them. In democracies nothing is more great or more brilliant than commerce: it attracts the attention of the public, and fills the imagination of the multitude; all energetic passions are directed toward it. Neither their own prejudices, nor those of any body else, can prevent the rich from devoting themselves to it. The wealthy members of democracies never form a body which has manners and regulations of its own; the opinions peculiar to their class do not restrain them, and the common opinions of their country urge them on. Moreover, as all the large fortunes, which are to be met with in a democratic community, are of commercial growth, many generations must succeed each other before their possessors can have entirely laid aside their habits of business.

Circumscribed within the narrow space which politics leave them, rich men in democracies eagerly embark in commercial enterprise: there they can extend and employ their natural advantages; and indeed it is even by the boldness and the magnitude of their industrial speculations that we may measure the slight esteem in which productive industry would have been held by them, if they had been born amid an aristocracy.

A similar observation is likewise applicable to all men living in democracies, whether they be poor or rich. Those who live in the

---

* Some aristocracies, however, have devoted themselves eagerly to commerce, and have cultivated manufactures with success. The history of the world might furnish several conspicuous examples. But, generally speaking, it may be affirmed that the aristocratic principle is not favourable to the growth of trade and manufactures. Monied aristocracies are the only exception to the rule. Among such aristocracies there are hardly any desires which do not require wealth to satisfy them; the love of riches becomes, so to speak, the high road of human passions, which is crossed by or connected with all lesser tracks. The love of money and the thirst for that distinction which attaches to power, are then so closely intermixed in the same souls, that it becomes difficult to discover whether men grow covetous from ambition, or whether they are ambitious from covetousness. This is the case in England, where men seek to get rich in order to arrive at distinction, and seek distinctions as a manifestation of their wealth. The mind is then seized by both ends, and hurried into trade and manufactures, which are the shortest roads that lead to opulence.

This, however, strikes me as an exceptional and transitory circumstance. When wealth is become the only symbol of aristocracy, it is very difficult for the wealthy to maintain sole possession of political power, to the exclusion of all other men. The aristocracy of birth and pure democracy are at the two extremes of the social and political state of nations: between them monied aristocracy finds its place. The latter approximates to the aristocracy of birth by conferring great privileges on a small number of persons; it so far belongs to the democratic element, that these privileges may be successively acquired by all. It frequently forms a natural transition between these two conditions of society, and it is difficult to say whether it closes the reign of aristocratic institutions, or whether it already opens the new era of democracy.

midst of democratic fluctuations have always before their eyes the phantom of chance; and they end by liking all undertakings in which chance plays a part. They are therefore all led to engage in commerce, not only for the sake of the profit it holds out to them, but for the love of the constant excitement occasioned by that pursuit.

The United States of America have only been emancipated for half a century from the state of colonial dependance in which they stood to Great Britain: the number of large fortunes there is small, and capital is still scarce. Yet no people in the world has made such rapid progress in trade and manufactures as the Americans: they constitute at the present day the second maritime nation in the world; and although their manufactures have to struggle with almost insurmountable natural impediments, they are not prevented from making great and daily advances.

In the United States the greatest undertakings and speculations are executed without difficulty, because the whole population is engaged in productive industry, and because the poorest as well as the most opulent members of the commonwealth are ready to combine their efforts for these purposes. The consequence is, that a stranger is constantly amazed by the immense public works executed by a nation which contains, so to speak, no rich men. The Americans arrived but as yesterday on the territory which they inhabit, and they have already changed the whole order of nature for their own advantage. They have joined the Hudson to the Mississippi, and made the Atlantic Ocean communicate with the Gulf of Mexico, across a continent of more than five hundred leagues in extent which separates the two seas. The longest railroads which have been constructed up to the present time are in America.

But what most astonishes me in the United States, is not so much the marvellous grandeur of some undertakings, as the innumerable multitude of small ones. Almost all the farmers of the United States combine some trade with agriculture; most of them make agriculture itself a trade. It seldom happens that an American farmer settles for good upon the land which he occupies: especially in the districts of the far west he brings land into tillage in order to sell it again, and not to farm it: he builds a farm-house on the speculation, that, as the state of the country will soon be changed by the increase of population, a good price will be gotten for it.

Every year a swarm of the inhabitants of the North arrive in the Southern states, and settle in the parts where the cotton-plant and the sugar-cane grow. These men cultivate the soil in order to make it produce in a few years enough to enrich them; and they already look forward to the time when they may return home to enjoy the competency thus acquired. Thus the Americans carry their business-like qualities into agriculture; and their trading passions are displayed in that, as in their other pursuits.

The Americans make immense progress in productive industry, because they all devote themselves to it at once; and for this same reason they are exposed to very unexpected and formidable embarrassments.

As they are all engaged in commerce, their commercial affairs are affected by such various and complex causes, that it is impossible to foresee what difficulties may arise. As they are all more or less engaged in productive industry, at the least shock given to business all private fortunes are put in jeopardy at the same time, and the State is shaken. I believe that the return of these commercial panics is an endemic disease of the democratic nations of our age. It may be rendered less dangerous, but it cannot be cured; because it does not originate in accidental circumstances, but in the temperament of these nations.

Chapter XX.

THAT ARISTOCRACY MAY BE ENGENDERED BY MANUFACTURES.

I have shown that democracy is favourable to the growth of manufactures, and that it increases without limit the numbers of the manufacturing classes: we shall now see by what side-road manufactures may possibly in their turn bring men back to aristocracy.

It is acknowledged, that when a workman is engaged every day upon the same detail, the whole commodity is produced with greater ease, promptitude, and economy. It is likewise acknowledged, that the cost of the production of manufactured goods is diminished by the extent of the establishment in which they are made, and by the amount of capital employed or of credit. These truths had long been imperfectly discerned, but in our time they have been demonstrated. They have been already applied to many very important kinds of manufactures, and the humblest will gradually be governed by them. I know of nothing in politics which deserves to fix the attention of the legislator more closely than these two new axioms of the science of manufactures.

When a workman is unceasingly and exclusively engaged in the fabrication of one thing, he ultimately does his work with singular dexterity; but at the same time he loses the general faculty of applying his mind to the direction of the work. He every day becomes more adroit and less industrious; so that it may be said of him, that in proportion as the workman improves the man is degraded. What can be expected of a man who has spent twenty years of his life in making heads for pins? and to what can that mighty human intelligence, which has so often stirred the world, be applied in him, except it be to investigate the best method of making pins' heads? When a workman has spent a considerable portion of his existence in this manner, his thoughts are for ever set upon the object of his daily toil; his body has contracted certain fixed habits, which it can never shake off: in a word, he no longer belongs to himself, but to the calling which he has chosen. It is in vain that laws and manners have been at the pains to level all barriers round such a man, and to open to him on every side a thousand different paths to fortune; a theory of manufactures more powerful than manners and laws binds him to a craft, and frequently to a spot, which he cannot leave: it assigns to him a certain place in society, beyond which he cannot go: in the midst of universal movement, it has rendered him stationary.

In proportion as the principle of the division of labour is more extensively applied, the workman becomes more weak, more narrowminded and more dependant. The art advances, the artisan recedes. On the other hand, in proportion as it becomes more manifest that the productions of manufactures are by so much the cheaper and better as the manufacture is larger and the amount of capital employed more considerable, wealthy and educated men come forward to embark in manufactures which were heretofore abandoned to poor or ignorant handicraftsmen. The magnitude of the efforts required, and the importance of the results to be obtained, attract them. Thus at the very time at which the science of manufactures lowers the class of workmen, it raises the class of masters.

Whereas the workman concentrates his faculties more and more upon the study of a single detail, the master surveys a more extensive whole, and the mind of the latter is enlarged in proportion as that of the former is narrowed. In a short time the one will require nothing but physical strength without intelligence; the other stands in need of science, and almost of genius, to ensure success. This man resembles more and more the administrator of a vast empire—that man, a brute.

The master and the workman have then here no similarity, and their differences increase every day. They are only connected as the two rings at the extremities of a long chain. Each of them fills the station which is made for him, and out of which he does not get: the one is continually, closely, and necessarily dependant upon the other, and seems as much born to obey as that other is to command. What is this but aristocracy?

As the conditions of men constituting the nation become more and more equal, the demand for manufactured commodities becomes more general and more extensive; and the cheapness which places these objects within the reach of slender fortunes becomes a great element of success. Hence there are every day more men of great opulence and education who devote their wealth and knowledge to manufactures; and who seek, by opening large establishments, and by a strict division of labour, to meet the fresh demands which are made on all sides. Thus, in proportion as the mass of the nation turns to democracy, that particular class which is engaged in manufactures becomes more aristocratic. Men grow more alike in the one—more different in the other; and inequality increases in the less numerous class, in the same ratio in which it decreases in the community.

Hence it would appear, on searching to the bottom, that aristocracy should naturally spring out of the bosom of democracy.

But this kind of aristocracy by no means resembles those kinds which preceded it. It will be observed at once, that, as it applies exclusively to manufactures and to some manufacturing callings, it is a monstrous exception in the general aspect of society. The small aristocratic societies which are formed by some manufacturers in the midst

of the immense democracy of our age, contain, like the great aristocratic societies of former ages, some men who are very opulent, and a
multitude who are wretchedly poor. The poor have few means of escaping from their condition and becoming rich; but the rich are constantly becoming poor, or they give up business when they have
realized a fortune. Thus the elements of which the class of the poor is
composed, are fixed; but the elements of which the class of the rich is
composed are not so. To say the truth, though there are rich men, the
class of rich men does not exist; for these rich individuals have no
feelings or purposes in common, no mutual traditions or mutual
hopes: there are therefore members, but no body.

    Not only are the rich not compactly united among themselves, but
there is no real bond between them and the poor. Their relative position is not a permanent one; they are constantly drawn together or
separated by their interests. The workman is generally dependant on
the master, but not on any particular master; these two men meet in
the factory, but know not each other elsewhere; and while they come
into contact on one point, they stand very wide apart on all others.
The manufacturer asks nothing of the workman but his labour; the
workman expects nothing from him but his wages. The one contracts
no obligation to protect, nor the other to defend; and they are not permanently connected either by habit or by duty.

    The aristocracy created by business rarely settles in the midst of the
manufacturing population which it directs: the object is not to govern
that population, but to use it. An aristocracy thus constituted can have
no great hold upon those whom it employs; and even if it succeed in
retaining them at one moment, they escape the next: it knows not how
to will, and it cannot act.

    The territorial aristocracy of former ages was either bound by law, or
thought itself bound by usage, to come to the relief of its serving-men,
and to succour their distresses. But the manufacturing aristocracy of
our age first impoverishes and debases the men who serve it, and then
abandons them to be supported by the charity of the public. This is a
natural consequence of what has been said before. Between the workman and the master there are frequent relations, but no real partnership.

    I am of opinion, upon the whole, that the manufacturing aristocracy
which is growing up under our eyes, is one of the harshest which ever
existed in the world; but at the same time it is one of the most confined and least dangerous. Nevertheless the friends of democracy
should keep their eyes anxiously fixed in this direction; for if ever a
permanent inequality of conditions and aristocracy again penetrate
into the world, it may be predicted that this is the channel by which
they will enter.

THIRD BOOK.
INFLUENCE OF DEMOCRACY ON MANNERS, PROPERLY SO CALLED.

Chapter I.

THAT MANNERS ARE SOFTENED AS SOCIAL CONDITIONS BECOME MORE EQUAL.

We perceive that for several ages social conditions have tended to equality, and we discover that in the course of the same period the manners of society have been softened. Are these two things merely contemporaneous, or does any secret link exist between them, so that the one cannot go on without making the other advance? Several causes may concur to render the manners of a people less rude; but, of all these causes, the most powerful appears to me to be the equality of conditions. Equality of conditions and growing civility in manners are then, in my eyes, not only contemporaneous occurrences, but correlative facts.

When the fabulists seek to interest us in the actions of beasts, they invest them with human notions and passions; the poets who sing of spirits and angels do the same: there is no wretchedness so deep, nor any happiness so pure, as to fill the human mind and touch the heart, unless we are ourselves held up to our own eyes under other features.

This is strictly applicable to the subject upon which we are at present engaged. When all men are irrevocably marshalled in an aristocratic community, according to their professions, their property, and their birth, the members of each class, considering themselves as children of the same family, cherish a constant and lively sympathy toward each other, which can never be felt in an equal degree by the citizens of a democracy. But the same feeling does not exist between the several classes toward each other.

Among an aristocratic people each caste has its own opinions, feelings, rights, manners, and modes of living. Thus the men of whom each caste is composed do not resemble the mass of their fellow-citizens; they do not think or feel in the same manner, and they scarcely believe that they belong to the same human race. They cannot therefore thoroughly understand what others feel, nor judge of others by themselves. Yet they are sometimes eager to lend each other mutual aid; but this is not contrary to my previous observation.

These aristocratic institutions, which made the beings of one and the same race so different, nevertheless bound them to each other by close political ties. Although the serf had no natural interest in the fate of nobles, he did not the less think himself obliged to devote his person to the service of that noble who happened to be his lord: and although the noble held himself to be of a different nature from that of his serfs, he nevertheless held that his duty and his honor constrained him to defend, at the risk of his own life, those who dwelt upon his domains.

It is evident that these mutual obligations did not originate in the law of nature, but in the law of society; and that the claim of social duty was more stringent than that of mere humanity. These services were not supposed to be due from man to man, but to the vassal or to the lord. Feudal institutions awakened a lively sympathy for the sufferings of certain men, but none at all for the mysteries of mankind. They infused generosity rather than mildness into the manners of the time, and although they prompted men to great acts of self-devotion, they engendered no real sympathies; for real sympathies can only exist between those who are alike; and in aristocratic ages men acknowledge none but the members of their own caste to be like themselves.

When the chroniclers of the middle ages, who all belonged to the aristocracy by birth or education, relate the tragical end of a noble, their grief flows apace; whereas they tell you at a breath, and without wincing, of massacres and tortures inflicted on the common sort of people. Not that these writers felt habitual hatred or systematic disdain for the people; war between the several classes of the community was not yet declared. They were impelled by an instinct rather than by a passion; as they had formed no clear notion of a poor man's sufferings, they cared but little for his fate.

The same feelings animated the lower orders whenever the feudal tie was broken. The same ages which witnessed so many heroic acts of self-devotion on the part of vassals for their lords, were stained with atrocious barbarities, exercised from time to time by the lower classes on the higher.

It must not be supposed that this mutual insensibility arose solely from the absence of public order and education; for traces of it are to be found in the following centuries, which became tranquil and enlightened while they remained aristocratic.

In 1675 the lower classes in Brittany revolted at the imposition of a new tax. These disturbances were put down with unexampled atrocity. Observe the language in which Madame de Sévigné[1], a witness of these horrors, relates them to her daughter:

"AUX Rochers, 30 Octobre, 1675.

"Mon Dieu, ma fille, que votre lettre d'Aix est plaisante! Au moins relisez vos lettres avant que de les envoyer; laissez-vous surprendre à leur agrément, et consolez vous par ce plaisir de la peine que vous avez d'en tant écrire. Vous avez donc baisé toute la Provence? il n'y aurait pas satisfaction á baiser toute la Bretagne, à moins qu'on n'aumât à sentir le vin. . . . . . . Voulez-vous savoir des nouvelles de Rennes? On a fait une taxe de cent mille écus sur le bourgeois; et si on ne trouve point cette somme dans vingt-quatre heures, elle sera doublée et exigible par les soldats. On a chassé et banni toute une grande rue, et défendu de les recueillir sous peine de la vie; de sorte qu'on voyait tous ces misérables, vieillards, femmes accouchées, enfans, errer en pleurs au sortir de cette ville sans savior où aller. On roua avant-hier un violon, qui avait commencé la danse et la pillerie du papier timbré; il a été écartelé après sa mort, et ses quatre quartiers exposés aux quatre coins de la ville. On a pris soixante bourgeois, et on commence demain les punitions. Cette province est un bel exemple pour les autres, et surtout de respecter les gouverneurs et les gouvernantes, et de ne point jeter de pierres dans leur jardin.*

"Madame de Tarente était hier dans ces bois par un temps enchanté: il n'est question ni de chambre ni de collation; elle entre par la barrière et s'en retourne de même. . . . ."

In another letter she adds:—

"Vous me parlez bien plaisamment de nos misères; nous ne sommes plus si roués; un en huit jours, pour entretenir la justice. Il est vrai que la penderie me paraît maintenant un rafraîchissement. J'ai une tout autre idée de la justice, depuis que je suis en ce pays. Vos galériens me paraissent une société d'honnêtes gens qui se sont retires du monde pour mener une vie douce."

It would be a mistake to suppose that Madame de Sévigné, who wrote these lines, was a selfish or cruel person; she was passionately attached to her children, and very ready to sympathize in the sorrows of her friends; nay, her letters show that she treated her vassals and servants with kindness and indulgence. But Madame de Sévigné had no clear notion of suffering in any one who was not a person of quality.

In our time the harshest man writing to the most insensible person of his acquaintance would not venture wantonly to indulge in the cruel jocularity which I have quoted; and even if his own manners allowed him to do so, the manners of society at large would forbid it. Whence does this arise? Have we more sensibility than our forefathers? I know not that we have; but I am sure that our sensibility is extended to a far greater range of objects.

When all the ranks of a community are nearly equal, as all men think and feel in nearly the same manner, each of them may judge in a moment of the sensations of all the others: he casts a rapid glance upon himself, and that is enough. There is no wretchedness into which he cannot readily enter, and a secret instinct reveals to him its extent. It signifies not that strangers or foes be the sufferers; imagination puts him in their place: something like a personal feeling is mingled with his pity, and makes himself suffer while the body of his fellow-creature is in torture.

In democratic ages men rarely sacrifice themselves for one another; but they display general compassion for the members of the human

---

* To feel the point of this joke the reader should recollect that Madame de Grignan was Gouvernante de Provence.

race. They inflict no useless ills; and they are happy to relieve the griefs of others, when they can do so without much hurting themselves; they are not disinterested, but they are humane.

Although the Americans have in a manner reduced egotism to a social and philosophical theory, they are nevertheless extremely open to compassion. In no country is criminal justice administered with more mildness than in the United States. While the English seem disposed carefully to retain the bloody traces of the dark ages in their penal legislation, the Americans have almost expunged capital punishment from their codes. North America is, I think, the only country upon earth in which the life of no one citizen has been taken for a political offence in the course of the last fifty years.

The circumstance which conclusively shows that this singular mildness of the Americans arises chiefly from their social condition, is the manner in which they treat their slaves. Perhaps there is not, upon the whole, a single European colony in the New World in which the physical condition of the blacks is less severe than in the United States; yet the slaves still endure horrid sufferings there, and are constantly exposed to barbarous punishments. It is easy to perceive that the lot of these unhappy beings inspires their masters with but little compassion, and that they look upon slavery, not only as an institution which is profitable to them, but as an evil which does not affect them. Thus the same man who is full of humanity toward his fellow-creatures when they are at the same time his equals, becomes insensible to their afflictions as soon as that equality ceases. His mildness should therefore be attributed to the equality of conditions, rather than to civilization and education.

What I have here remarked of individuals is to a certain extent applicable to nations. When each nation has its distinct opinions, belief, laws and customs, it looks upon itself as the whole of mankind, and is moved by no sorrows but its own. Should war break out between two nations animated by this feeling, it is sure to be waged with great cruelty.

At the time of their highest culture, the Romans slaughtered the generals of their enemies, after having dragged them in triumph behind a car; and they flung their prisoners to the beasts of the Circus for the amusement of the people. Cicero,[2] who declaimed so vehemently at the notion of crucifying a Roman citizen, had not a word to say against these horrible abuses of victory. It is evident that in his eyes a barbarian did not belong to the same human race as a Roman.

On the contrary, in proportion as nations become more like each other, they become reciprocally more compassionate, and the law of nations is mitigated.

Chapter II.

THAT DEMOCRACY RENDERS THE HABITUAL INTERCOURSE OF THE AMERICANS SIMPLE AND EASY.

Democracy does not attach men strongly to each other; but it places their habitual intercourse upon an easier footing.

If two Englishmen chance to meet at the Antipodes, where they are surrounded by strangers whose language and manners are almost unknown to them, they will first stare at each other with much curiosity and a kind of secret uneasiness; they will then turn away, or, if one accosts the other, they will take care only to converse with a constrained and absent air upon very unimportant subjects. Yet there is no enmity between these men; they have never seen each other before, and each believes the other to be a respectable person. Why then should they stand so cautiously apart? We must go back to England to learn the reason.

When it is birth alone, independent of wealth, which classes men in society, every one knows exactly what his own position is upon the social scale; he does not seek to rise, he does not fear to sink. In a community thus organized, men of different castes communicate very little with each other; but if accident brings them together, they are ready to converse without hoping or fearing to lose their own position. Their intercourse is not upon a footing of equality, but it is not constrained.

When monied aristocracy succeeds to aristocracy of birth, the case is altered. The privileges of some are still extremely great, but the possibility of acquiring those privileges is open to all: whence it follows that those who possess them are constantly haunted by the apprehension of losing them, or of other men's sharing them; those who do not yet enjoy them, long to possess them at any cost, or, if they fail, to appear at least to possess them—which is not impossible. As the social importance of men is no longer ostensibly and permanently fixed by blood, and is infinitely varied by wealth, ranks still exist, but it is not easy clearly to distinguish at a glance those who respectively belong to them. Secret hostilities then arise in the community; one set of men endeavour by innumerable artifices to penetrate or to appear to penetrate, among those who are above them; another set are constantly in arms against these usurpers of their rights; or rather the same individual does both at once, and while he seeks to raise himself into a higher circle, he is always on the defensive against the intrusion of those below him.

Such is the condition of England at the present time; and I am of opinion that the peculiarity before adverted to is principally to be attributed to this cause. As aristocratic pride is still extremely great among the English, and as the limits of aristocracy are ill-defined, everybody lives in constant dread lest advantage should be taken of his familiarity. Unable to judge at once of the social position of those he meets, an Englishman prudently avoids all contact with them. Men are afraid lest some slight service rendered should draw them into an unsuitable acquaintance; they dread civilities, and they avoid the obtrusive gratitude of a stranger quite as much as his hatred.

Many people attribute these singular anti-social propensities, and the reserved and the taciturn bearing of the English, to purely physical causes. I may admit that there is something of it in their race, but much more of it is attributable to their social condition, as is proved by the contrast of the Americans.

In America, where the privileges of birth never existed, and where riches confer no peculiar rights on their possessors, men unacquainted with each other are very ready to frequent the same places, and find neither peril nor advantage in the free interchange of their thoughts. If they meet by accident they neither seek nor avoid intercourse; their manner is therefore natural, frank, and open: it is easy to see that they hardly expect or apprehend anything from each other, and that they do not care to display, any more than to conceal, their position in the world. If their demeanor is often cold and serious, it is never haughty or constrained; and if they do not converse, it is because they are not in a humour to talk, not because they think it their interest to be silent.

In a foreign country two Americans are at once friends, simply because they are Americans. They are repulsed by no prejudice; they are attracted by their common country. For two Englishmen the same blood is not enough; they must be brought together by the same rank. The Americans remark this unsociable mood of the English as much as the French do, and they are not less astonished by it. Yet the Americans are connected with England by their origin, their religion, their language, and partially by their manners: they only differ in their social condition. It may therefore be inferred, that the reserve of the English proceeds from the constitution of their country much more than from that of its inhabitants.

Chapter III.

WHY THE AMERICANS SHOW SO LITTLE SENSITIVENESS IN THEIR OWN COUNTRY, AND ARE SO SENSITIVE IN EUROPE.

The temper of the Americans is vindictive, like that of all serious and reflecting nations. They hardly ever forget an offence, but it is not easy to offend them; and their resentment is as slow to kindle as it is to abate.

In aristocratic communities, where a small number of persons manage everything, the outward intercourse of men is subject to settled conventional rules. Every one then thinks he knows exactly what marks of respect or of condescension he ought to display, and none are presumed to be ignorant of the science of etiquette. These usages of the first class in society afterward serve as a model to all the others; besides which, each of the latter lays down a code of its own, to which all its members are bound to conform. Thus the rules of politeness form a complex system of legislation, which it is difficult to be perfectly master of, but from which it is dangerous for any one to deviate; so that men are constantly exposed involuntarily to inflict or to receive bitter affronts.

But as the distinctions of rank are obliterated, as men differing in education and in birth meet and mingle in the same places of resort, it is almost impossible to agree upon the rules of good breeding. As its laws are uncertain, to disobey them is not a crime, even in the eyes of those who know what they are: men attach more importance to intentions than to forms, and they grow less civil, but at the same time less quarrelsome.

There are many little attentions which an American does not care about; he thinks they are not due to him, or he presumes that they are not known to be due: he therefore either does not perceive a rudeness, or he forgives it; his manners become less courteous, and his character more plain and masculine.

The mutual indulgence which the Americans display, and the manly confidence with which they treat each other, also result from another deeper and more general cause, which I have already adverted to in the preceding chapter. In the United States the distinctions of rank in civil society are slight, in political society they are null; an American, therefore, does not think himself bound to pay particular attentions to any of his fellow-citizens, nor does he require such attentions from them toward himself. As he does not see that it is his interest eagerly to seek the company of any of his countrymen, he is slow to fancy that his own company is declined: despising no one on account of station, he does not imagine that any one can despise him for that cause; and until he has clearly perceived an insult, he does not suppose that an affront was intended. The social condition of the Americans naturally accustoms them not to take offence in small matters; and, on the other hand, the domocratic freedom which they enjoy transfuses this same mildness of temper into the character of the nation.

The political institutions of the United States constantly bring citizens of all ranks into contact, and compel them to pursue great undertakings in concert. People thus engaged have scarcely time to attend to the details of etiquette, and they are besides too strongly interested in living harmoniously for them to stick at such things. They therefore soon acquire a habit of considering the feelings and opinions of those whom they meet more than their manners, and they do not allow themselves to be annoyed by trifles.

I have often remarked in the United States, that it is not easy to make a man understand that his presence may be dispensed with; hints will not always suffice to shake him off. I contradict an American at every word he says, to show him that his conversation bores me; he instantly labours with fresh pertinacity to convince me: I preserve a dogged silence, and he thinks I am meditating deeply on the truths which he is uttering: at last I rush from his company, and he supposes that some urgent business hurries me elsewhere. This man will never understand that he wearies me to extinction unless I tell him so; and the only way to get rid of him is to make him my enemy for life.

It appears surprising at first sight that the same man transported to Europe suddenly becomes so sensitive and captious, that I often find it as difficult to avoid offending him here as it was to put him out of countenance. These two opposite effects proceed from the same cause. Democratic institutions generally give men a lofty notion of their country and of themselves. An American leaves his country with a heart swollen with pride: on arriving in Europe he at once finds out that we are not so engrossed by the United States and the great people which inhabits them as he had supposed, and this begins to annoy him. He has been informed that the conditions of society are not equal in our part of the globe, and he observes that among the nations of Europe the traces of rank are not wholly obliterated; that wealth and birth still retain some indeterminate privileges, which force them-selves upon his notice while they elude definition. He is therefore pro-foundly ignorant of the place which he ought to occupy in this half-ruined scale of classes, which are sufficiently distinct to hate and despise each other, yet sufficiently alike for him to be always con-founding them. He is afraid of ranging himself too high—still more is he afraid of being ranged too low: this twofold peril keeps his mind constantly on the stretch, and embarrasses all he says and does.

He learns from tradition that in Europe ceremonial observances were infinitely varied according to different ranks; this recollection of former times completes his perplexity, and he is the more afraid of not obtaining those marks of respect which are due to him, as he does not exactly know in what they consist. He is like a man surrounded by traps: society is not a recreation for him, but a serious toil; he weighs your least actions, interrogates your looks, and scrutinizes all you say, lest there should be some hidden allusion to affront him. I doubt whether there was ever a provincial man of quality so punctilious in breeding as he is: he endeavours to attend to the slightest rules of eti-quette, and does not allow one of them to be waived toward himself: he is full of scruples, and at the same time of pretensions; he wishes to do enough, but fears to do too much; and as he does not very well know the limits of the one or of the other, he keeps up a haughty and embarrassed air of reserve.

But this is not all: here is yet another double of the human heart. An American is for ever talking of the admirable equality which pre-vails in the United States: aloud he makes it the boast of his country, but in secret he deplores it for himself; and he aspires to show that, for his part, he is an exception to the general state of things which he vaunts. There is hardly an American to be met with who does not claim same remote kindred with the first founders of the colonies; and as for the scions of the noble families of England, America seemed to me to be covered with them. When an opulent American arrives in Europe, his first care is to surround himself with all the luxuries of wealth: he is so afraid of being taken for the plain citizen of a democracy, that he adopts a hundred distorted ways of bringing some new instance of his wealth before you every day. His house will be in the most fashionable part of the town: he will always be surrounded by a host of servants. I have heard an American complain, that in the best houses of Paris the society was rather mixed; the taste which prevails there was not pure enough for him; and he ventured to hint that, in his opinion, there was a want of elegance of manner; he could not accustom himself to see wit concealed under such unpretending forms.

These contrasts ought not to surprise us. If the vestiges of former aristocratic distinctions, were not so completely effaced in the United States, the Americans would be less simple and less tolerant in their own country—they would require less, and be less fond of borrowed manners in ours.

Chapter IV.

CONSEQUENCES OF THE THREE PRECEDING CHAPTERS.

When men feel a natural compassion for their mutual sufferings— when they are brought together by easy and frequent intercourse, and no sensitive feelings keep them asunder, it may readily be supposed that they will lend assistance to one another whenever it is needed. When an American asks for the co-operation of his fellow-citizens it is seldom refused, and I have often seen it afforded spontaneously and with great good will. If an accident happens on the highway, everybody hastens to help the sufferer; if some great and sudden calamity befalls a family, the purses of a thousand strangers are at once willingly opened, and small but numerous donations pour in to relieve their distress.

It often happens among the most civilized nations of the globe, that a poor wretch is as friendless in the midst of a crowd as the savage in his wilds: this is hardly ever the case in the United States. The Americans, who are always cold and often coarse in their manners, seldom show insensibility; and if they do not proffer services eagerly, yet they do not refuse to render them.

All this is not in contradiction to what I have said before on the subject of individualism. The two things are so far from combating each other, that I can see how they agree. Equality of conditions, while it makes men feel their independence, shows them their own weakness: they are free, but exposed to a thousand accidents; and experience soon teaches them, that although they do not habitually require the assistance of others, a time almost always comes when they cannot do without it.

We constantly see in Europe that men of the same profession are ever ready to assist each other; they are all exposed to the same ills, and that is enough to teach them to seek mutual preservatives, however hard-hearted and selfish they may otherwise be. When one of them falls into danger, from which the others may save him by a slight transient sacrifice or a sudden effort, they do not fail to make the attempt. Not that they are deeply interested in his fate; for if, by chance, their exertions are unavailing, they immediately forget the object of them, and return to their own business; but a sort of tacit and almost involuntary agreement has been passed between them, by which each one owes to the others a temporary support which he may claim for himself in turn.

Extend to a people the remark here applied to a class, and you will understand my meaning. A similar covenant exists in fact between all the citizens of a democracy: they all feel themselves subject to the same weakness and the same dangers; and their interest, as well as their sympathy, makes it a rule with them to lend each other mutual assistance when required. The more equal social conditions become, the more do men display this reciprocal disposition to oblige each other. In democracies no great benefits are conferred, but good offices are constantly rendered: a man seldom displays self-devotion, but all men are ready to be of service to one another.

Chapter V.

HOW DEMOCRACY AFFECTS THE RELATION OF MASTERS AND SERVANTS.

An American who had travelled for a long time in Europe once said to me, "The English treat their servants with a stiffness and imperiousness of manner which surprise us; but on the other hand the French sometimes treat their attendants with a degree of familiarity or of politeness which we cannot conceive. It looks as if they were afraid to give orders: the posture of the superior and the inferior is ill-maintained."—The remark was a just one, and I have often made it myself. I have always considered England as the country in the world where, in our time, the bond of domestic service is drawn most tightly, and France as the country where it is most relaxed. Nowhere have I seen masters stand so high or so low as in these two countries. Between these two extremes the Americans are to be placed. Such is the fact as it appears upon the surface of things: to discover the causes of that fact, it is necessary to search the matter thoroughly.

No communities have ever yet existed in which social conditions have been so equal that there were neither rich nor poor, and consequently neither masters nor servants. Democracy does not prevent the existence of these two classes, but it changes their dispositions, and modifies their mutual relations.

Among aristocratic nations servants form a distinct class, not more variously composed than that of masters. A settled order is soon established; in the former as well as in the latter class a scale is formed, with numerous distinctions or marked gradations of rank, and generations succeed each other thus without any change of position. These two communities are superposed one above the other, always distinct, but regulated by analogous principles. This aristocratic constitution does not exert a less powerful influence on the notions and manners of servants than on those of masters; and, although the effects are different, the same cause may easily be traced.

Both classes constitute small communities in the heart of the nation, and certain permanent notions of right and wrong are ultimately engendered among them. The different acts of human life are viewed by one particular and unchanging light. In the society of servants as in that of masters, men exercise a great influence over each other; they acknowledge settled rules, and in the absence of law they are guided by a sort of public opinion; their habits are settled, and their conduct is placed under a certain control.

These men, whose destiny it is to obey, certainly do not understand fame, virtue, honesty, and honour in the same manner as their masters; but they have a pride, a virtue, and an honesty pertaining to their condition; and they have a notion, if I may use the expression, of a sort of servile honour.* Because a class is mean, it must not be supposed that all who belong to it are mean-hearted; to think so would be a great mistake. However lowly it may be, he who is foremost there, and who has no notion of quitting it, occupies an aristocratic position which inspires him with lofty feelings, pride, and self-respect, that fit him for the higher virtues and actions above the common.

Among aristocratic nations it was by no means rare to find men of noble and vigorous minds in the service of the great, who felt not the servitude they bore, and who submitted to the will of their masters without any fear of their displeasure.

But this was hardly ever the case among the inferior ranks of domestic servants. It may be imagined that he who occupies the lowest stage of the order of menials stands very low indeed. The French created a word on purpose to designate the servants of the aristocracy— they called them 'lacqueys.' This word lacquey served as the strongest expression, when all others were exhausted, to designate human meanness. Under the old French monarchy, to denote by a single expression a low-spirited contemptible fellow, it was usual to say that he had the *soul of a lacquey*; the term was enough to convey all that was intended.

The permanent inequality of conditions not only gives servants certain peculiar virtues and vices, but it places them in a peculiar relation with respect to their masters. Among aristocratic nations the poor man is familiarized from his childhood with the notion of being commanded; to whichever side he turns his eyes the graduated structure of society and the aspect of obedience meet his view. Hence in those

---

* If the principal opinions by which men are guided are examined closely and in detail, the analogy appears still more striking, and one is surprised to find among them, just as much as among the haughtiest scions of a feudal race, pride of birth, respect for their ancestry and their descendants, disdain of their inferiors, a dread of contact, a taste for etiquette, precedents, and antiquity.

countries the master readily obtains prompt, complete, respectful, and easy obedience from his servants, because they revere in him not only their master but the class of masters. He weighs down their will by the whole weight of the aristocracy. He orders their actions—to a certain extent he even directs their thoughts. In aristocracies the master often exercises, even without being aware of it, an amazing sway over the opinions, the habits and the manners of those who obey him, and his influence extends even further than his authority.

In aristocratic communities, there are not only hereditary families of servants as well as of masters, but the same families of servants ad-here for several generations to the same families of masters (like two parallel lines which neither meet nor separate); and this considerably modifies the mutual relations of these two classes of persons. Thus, al-though in aristocratic society the master and servant have no natural resemblance—although, on the contrary, they are placed at an im-mense distance on the scale of human beings by their fortune, educa-tion, and opinions—yet time ultimately binds them together. They are connected by a long series of common reminiscences, and however different they may be, they grow alike; while in democracies, where they are naturally almost alike, they always remain strangers to each other. Among an aristocratic people the master gets to look upon his servants as an inferior and secondary part of himself, and he often takes an interest in their lot by a last stretch of egotism.

Servants, on their part, are not averse to regard themselves in the same light; and they sometimes identify themselves with the person of the master, so that they become an appendage to him in their own eyes as well as in his. In aristocracies a servant fills a subordinate po-sition which he cannot get out of; above him is another man, holding a superior rank which he cannot lose. On one side are obscurity, poverty, obedience for life; on the other, and also for life, fame, wealth, and command. The two conditions are always distinct and al-ways in propinquity; the tie that connects them is as lasting as they are themselves.

In this predicament the servant ultimately detaches his notion of in-terest from his own person; he deserts himself as it were, or rather he transports himself into the character of his master, and thus assumes an imaginary personality. He complacently invests himself with the wealth of those who command him; he shares their fame, exalts him-self by their rank, and feeds his mind with borrowed greatness, to which he attaches more importance than those who fully and really possess it. There is something touching, and at the same time ridicu-lous, in this strange confusion of two different states of being. These passions of masters, when they pass into the souls of menials, assume the natural dimensions of the place they occupy—they are contracted and lowered. What was pride in the former becomes puerile vanity and paltry ostentation in the latter. The servants of a great man are commonly most punctilious as to the marks of respect due to him, and they attach more importance to his slightest privileges than he does himself. In France a few of these old servants of the aristocracy are still to be met with here and there; they have survived their race, which will soon disappear with them altogether.

In the United States I never saw any one at all like them. The Americans are not only unacquainted with the kind of man, but it is hardly possible to make them understand that such ever existed. It is scarcely less difficult for them to conceive it, than for us to form a correct notion of what a slave was among the Romans, or a serf in the middle ages. All these men were in fact, though in different degrees, results of the same cause: they are all retiring from our sight, and disappearing in the obscurity of the past, together with the social condition to which they owed their origin.

Equality of conditions turns servants and masters into new beings, and places them in new relative positions. When social conditions are nearly equal, men are constantly changing their situations in life: there is still a class of menials and a class of masters, but these classes are not always composed of the same individuals, still less of the same families; and those who command are not more secure of perpetuity than those who obey. As servants do not form a separate people, they have no habits, prejudices or manners peculiar to themselves: they are not remarkable for any particular turn of mind or moods of feeling. They know no vices or virtues of their condition, but they partake of the education, the opinions, the feelings, the virtues and the vices of their contemporaries; and they are honest men or scoundrels in the same way as their masters are.

The conditions of servants are not less equal than those of masters. As no marked ranks or fixed subordination are to be found among them, they will not display either the meanness or the greatness which characterize the aristocracy of menials as well as all other aristocracies. I never saw a man in the United States who reminded me of that class of confidential servants of which we still retain a reminiscence in Europe, neither did I ever meet with such a thing as a lacquey: all traces of the one and of the other have disappeared.

In democracies servants are not only equal among themselves, but it may be said that they are in some sort the equals of their masters. This requires explanation in order to be rightly understood. At any moment a servant may become a master, and he aspires to rise to that condition: the servant is therefore not a different man from the master. Why then has the former a right to command, and what compels the latter to obey?—the free and temporary consent of both their wills. Neither of them is by nature inferior to the other; they only become so for a time by covenant. Within the terms of this covenant, the one is a servant, the other a master; beyond it they are two citizens of the commonwealth—two men.

I beg the reader particularly to observe that this is not only the notion which servants themselves entertain of their own condition; domestic service is looked upon by masters in the same light; and the precise limits of authority and obedience are as clearly settled in the mind of the one as in that of the other.

When the greater part of the community have long attained a condition nearly alike, and when equality is an old and acknowledged fact, the public mind, which is never affected by exceptions, assigns certain general limits to the value of man, above or below which no man can long remain placed. It is in vain that wealth and poverty, authority and obedience, accidentally interpose great distances between two men; public opinion, founded upon the usual order of things, draws them to a common level, and creates a species of imaginary equality between them, in spite of the real inequality of their conditions. This all-powerful opinion penetrates at length even into the hearts of those, whose interest might arm them to resist it; it affects their judgement, while it subdues their will.

In their inmost convictions the master and the servant no longer perceive any deep-seated difference between them, and they neither hope nor fear to meet with any such at any time. They are therefore neither subject to disdain nor to anger, and they discern in each other neither humility nor pride. The master holds the contract of service to be the only source of his power, and the servant regards it as the only cause of his obedience. They do not quarrel about their reciprocal situations, but each knows his own and keeps it.

In the French army the common soldier is taken from nearly the same classes as the officer, and may hold the same commissions; out of the ranks he considers himself entirely equal to his military superiors, and in point of fact he is so; but when under arms he does not hesitate to obey, and his obedience is not the less prompt, precise, and ready, for being voluntary and defined. This example may give a notion of what takes place between masters and servants in democratic communities.

It would be preposterous to suppose that those warm and deep-seated affections, which are sometimes kindled in the domestic service of aristocracy, will ever spring up between these two men, or that they will exhibit strong instances of self-sacrifice. In aristocracies masters and servants live apart, and frequently their only intercourse is through a third person: yet they commonly stand firmly by one another. In democratic countries the master and the servant are close together: they are in daily personal contact, but their minds do not intermingle; they have common occupations, hardly ever common interests.

Among such a people the servant always considers himself as a sojourner in the dwelling of his masters. He knew nothing of their forefathers—he will see nothing of their descendants—he has nothing lasting to expect from their hand. Why then should he confound his life with theirs, and whence should so strange a surrender of himself proceed? The reciprocal position of the two men is changed—their mutual relations must be so too.

I would fain illustrate all these reflections by the example of the Americans; but for this purpose the distinctions of persons and places must be accurately traced.

In the south of the Union, slavery exists; all that I have just said is consequently inapplicable there. In the north, the majority of servants are either freed-men or the children of freed-men: these persons occupy a contested position in the public estimation; by the laws they are brought up to the level of their masters—by the manners of the country they are obstinately detruded from it. They do not themselves clearly know their proper place, and they are almost always either insolent or craven.

But in the northern States, especially in New England, there are a certain number of whites, who agree, for wages, to yield a temporary obedience to the will of their fellow-citizens. I have heard that these servants commonly perform the duties of their situation with punctuality and intelligence; and that, without thinking themselves naturally inferior to the person who orders them, they submit without reluctance to obey him.

They appeared to me to carry into service some of those manly habits which independence and equality engender. Having once selected a hard way of life, they do not seek to escape from it by indirect means; and they have sufficient respect for themselves, not to refuse to their masters that obedience which they have freely promised.

On their part, masters require nothing of their servants but the faithful and rigorous performance of the covenant: they do not ask for marks of respect, they do not claim their love or devoted attachment; it is enough that, as servants, they are exact and honest.

It would not then be true to assert, that, in democratic society, the relation of servants and masters is disorganized: it is organized on another footing; the rule is different, but there is a rule.

It is not my purpose to inquire whether the new state of things which I have just described is inferior to that which preceded it, or simply different. Enough for me that it is fixed and determined; for what is most important to meet with among men is not any given ordering, but order.

But what shall I say of those sad and troubled times at which equality is established in the midst of the tumult of revolution—when democracy, after having been introduced into the state of society, still struggles with difficulty against the prejudices and manners of the country? The laws, and partially public opinion, already declare that no natural or permanent inferiority exists between the servant and the master. But this new belief has not yet reached the innermost convictions of the latter, or rather his heart rejects it: in the secret persuasion of his mind the master thinks that he belongs to a peculiar and superior race; he dares not say so, but he shudders while he allows himself to be dragged to the same level. His authority over his servants becomes timid and at the same time harsh: he has already ceased to entertain for them the feelings of patronizing kindness which long uncontested power always engenders, and he is surprised that, being changed himself, his servant changes also. He wants his attendants to form regular and permanent habits, in a condition of domestic service which is only temporary; he requires that they should appear contented with and proud of a servile condition, which they will one day shake off—that they should sacrifice themselves to a man who can neither protect nor ruin them—and in short that they should contract an indissoluble engagement to a being like themselves, and one who will last no longer than they will.

Among aristocratic nations it often happens that the condition of domestic service does not degrade the character of those who enter upon it, because they neither know nor imagine any other; and the amazing inequality which is manifest between them and their master appears to be the necessary and unavoidable consequence of some hidden law of Providence.

In democracies the condition of domestic service does not degrade the character of those who enter upon it, because it is freely chosen, and adopted for a time only; because it is not stigmatized by public opinion, and creates no permanent inequality between the servant and the master.

But, while the transition from one social condition to another is going on, there is almost always a time when men's minds fluctuate between the aristocratic notion of subjection and the democratic notion of obedience. Obedience then loses its moral importance in the eyes of him who obeys; he no longer considers it as a species of divine obligation, and he does not yet view it under its purely human aspect: it has to him no character of sanctity or of justice, and he submits to it as to a degrading but profitable condition.

At that moment a confused and imperfect phantom of equality haunts the minds of servants; they do not at once perceive whether the equality to which they are entitled is to be found within or without the pale of domestic service; and they rebel in their hearts against a subordination to which they have subjected themselves, and from which they derive actual profit. They consent to serve, and they blush to obey: they like the advantages of service, but not the master; or rather, they are not sure that they ought not themselves to be masters, and they are inclined to consider him who orders them as an unjust usurper of their own rights.

Then it is that the dwelling of every citizen offers a spectacle somewhat analogous to the gloomy aspect of political society. A secret and intestine warfare is going on there between powers, ever rivals and suspicious of one another: the master is ill-natured and weak, the servant ill-natured and intractable; the one constantly attempts to evade by unfair restrictions his obligation to protect and to remunerate—the other his obligation to obey. The reins of domestic government dangle between them, to be snatched at by one or the other.

The lines which divide authority from oppression, liberty from license, and right from might, are to their eyes so jumbled together and confused, that no one knows exactly what he is, or what he may be, or what he ought to be. Such a condition is not democracy, but revolution.

Chapter VI.

THAT DEMOCRATIC INSTITUTIONS AND MANNERS TEND TO RAISE
RENTS AND SHORTEN THE TERMS OF LEASES.

What has been said of servants and masters is applicable, to a certain extent, to land-owners and farming tenants; but this subject deserves to be considered by itself.

In America there are, properly speaking, no farming tenants; every man owns the ground he tills. It must be admitted that democratic laws tend greatly to increase the number of land-owners, and to diminish that of farming tenants. Yet what takes place in the United States is much less attributable to the institutions of the country than to the country itself. In America land is cheap, and any one may easily become a land-owner; its returns are small, and its produce cannot well be divided between a land-owner and a farmer. America therefore stands alone in this as well as in many other respects, and it would be a mistake to take it as an example.

I believe that in democratic as well as in aristocratic countries there will be land-owners and tenants, but the connexion existing between them will be of a different kind. In aristocracies the hire of a farm is paid to the landlord, not only in rent, but in respect, regard, and duty: in democracies the whole is paid in cash. When estates are divided and passed from hand to hand, and the permanent connexion which existed between families and the soil is dissolved, the land-owner and the tenant are only casually brought into contact. They meet for a moment to settle the conditions of the agreement, and then lose sight of each other; they are two strangers brought together by a common interest, and who keenly talk over a matter of business, the sole object of which is to make money.

In proportion as property is subdivided and wealth distributed over the country, the community is filled with people whose former opulence is declining, and with others whose fortunes are of recent growth and whose wants increase more rapidly than their resources. For all such persons the smallest pecuniary profit is a matter of importance, and none of them feel disposed to waive any of their claims, or to lose any portion of their income.

As ranks are intermingled, and as very large as well as very scanty fortunes become more rare, every day brings the social condition of the land-owner nearer to that of the farmer: the one has not naturally any uncontested superiority over the other; between two men who are equal, and not at ease in their circumstances, the contract of hire is exclusively an affair of money.

A man whose estate extends over a whole district, and who owns an hundred farms, is well aware of the importance of gaining at the same time the affections of some thousands of men; this object appears to call for his exertions, and to attain it he will readily make considerable sacrifices. But he who owns a hundred acres is insensible to similar considerations, and he cares but little to win the private regard of his tenant.

An aristocracy does not expire like a man in a single day; the aristocratic principle is slowly undermined in men's opinion, before it is attacked in their laws. Long before open war is declared against it, the tie which had hitherto united the higher classes to the lower may be seen to be gradually relaxed. Indifference and contempt are betrayed by one class, jealousy and hatred by the others: the intercourse between rich and poor becomes less frequent and less kind, and rents are raised. This is not the consequence of a democratic revolution, but its certain harbinger: for an aristocracy which has lost the affections of the people, once and for ever, is like a tree dead at the root, which is the more easily torn up by the winds the higher its branches have spread.

In the course of the last fifty years the rents of farms have amazingly increased, not only in France but throughout the greater part of Europe. The remarkable improvements which have taken place in agriculture and manufactures within the same period do not suffice in my opinion to explain this fact: recourse must be had to another cause more powerful and more concealed. I believe that cause is to be found in the democratic institutions which several European nations have adopted, and in the democratic passions which more or less agitate all the rest.

I have frequently heard great English land-owners congratulate themselves that, at the present day, they derive a much larger income from their estates than their fathers did. They have perhaps good reason to be glad; but most assuredly they know not what they are glad of. They think they are making a clear gain, when it is in reality only an exchange: their influence is what they are parting with for cash; and what they gain in money will ere long be lost in power.

There is yet another sign by which it is easy to know that a great democratic revolution is going on or approaching. In the middle ages almost all lands were leased for lives, or for very long terms: the domestic economy of that period shows that leases for ninety-nine years were more frequent then than leases for twelve years are now. Men then believed that families were immortal; men's conditions seemed settled for ever, and the whole of society appeared to be so fixed, that it was not supposed that anything would ever be stirred or shaken in its structure. In ages of equality, the human mind takes a different bent: the prevailing notion is that nothing abides, and man is haunted by the thought of mutability. Under this impression the land-owner and the tenant himself are instinctively averse to protracted terms of obligation: they are afraid of being tied up to-morrow by the contract which benefits them to-day. They have vague anticipations of some sudden and unforeseen change in their conditions; they mistrust themselves; they fear lest their taste should change, and lest they should lament that they cannot rid themselves of what they coveted: nor are such fears unfounded, for in democratic ages that which is most fluctuating amid the fluctuation of all around is the heart of man.

Chapter VII.

INFLUENCE OF DEMOCRACY ON WAGES.

Most of the remarks which I have already made in speaking of servants and masters, may be applied to masters and workmen. As the gradations of the social scale come to be less observed, while the great sink the humble rise, and poverty as well as opulence ceases to be hereditary, the distance both in reality and in opinion, which heretofore separated the workman from the master, is lessened every day. The workman conceives a more lofty opinion of his rights, of his future, of himself; he is filled with new ambition and with new desires, he is harassed by new wants. Every instant he views with longing eyes the profits of his employer; and in order to share them, he strives to dispose of his labour at a higher rate, and he generally succeeds at length in the attempt.

In democratic countries, as well as elsewhere, most of the branches of productive industry are carried on at a small cost, by men little removed by their wealth or education above the level of those whom they employ. These manufacturing speculators are extremely numerous; their interests differ; they cannot therefore easily concert or combine their exertions. On the other hand the workmen have almost always some sure resources, which enable them to refuse to work when they cannot get what they conceive to be the fair price of their labour. In the constant struggle for wages which is going on between these two classes, their strength is divided, and success alternates from one to the other.

It is even probable that in the end the interest of the working class must prevail; for the high wages which they have already obtained make them every day less dependant on their masters; and as they grow more independent, they have greater facilities for obtaining a further increase of wages.

I shall take for example that branch of productive industry which is still at the present day the most generally followed in France, and in almost all the countries of the world—I mean the cultivation of the soil. In France most of those who labour for hire in agriculture, are themselves owners of certain plots of ground, which just enable them to subsist without working for any one else. When these labourers come to offer their services to a neighbouring land-owner or farmer, if he refuses them a certain rate of wages, they retire to their own small property and await another opportunity.

I think that, upon the whole, it may be asserted that a slow and gradual rise of wages is one of the general laws of democratic communities. In proportion as social conditions become more equal, wages rise; and as wages are higher, social conditions become more equal.

But a great and gloomy exception occurs in our own time. I have shown in a preceeding chapter that aristocracy, expelled from political society, has taken refuge in certain departments of productive industry, and has established its sway there under another form; this power-fully affects the rate of wages.

As a large capital is required to embark in the great manufacturing speculations to which I allude, the number of persons who enter upon them is exceedingly limited: as their number is small, they can easily concert together, and fix the rate of wages as they please.

Their workmen on the contrary are exceedingly numerous, and the number of them is always increasing; for, from time to time, an extraordinary run of business takes place, during which wages are in-ordinately high, and they attract the surrounding population to the factories. But when once men have embraced that line of life, we have already seen that they cannot quit it again, because they soon contract habits of body and mind which unfit them for any other sort of toil. These men have generally but little education and industry, with but few resources; they stand therefore almost at the mercy of the master.

When competition, or other fortuitous circumstances, lessen his profits, he can reduce the wages of his workmen almost at pleasure, and make from them what he loses by the chances of business. Should the workmen strike, the master, who is a rich man, can very well wait without being ruined until necessity brings them back to him; but they must work day by day or they die, for their only property is in their hands. They have long been impoverished by oppression, and the poorer they become the more easily may they be oppressed: they can never escape from this fatal circle of cause and consequence.

It is not then surprising that wages, after having sometimes sud-denly risen, are permanently lowered in this branch of industry; whereas in other callings the price of labour, which generally increases but little, is nevertheless constantly augmented.

This state of dependance and wretchedness, in which a part of the manufacturing population of our time lives, forms an exception to the general rule, contrary to the state of all the rest of the community; but, for this very reason, no circumstance is more important or more deserving of the especial consideration of the legislator; for when the whole of society is in motion, it is difficult to keep any one class sta-tionary; and when the greater number of men are opening new paths to fortune, it is no less difficult to make the few support in peace their wants and their desires.

Chapter VIII.

INFLUENCE OF DEMOCRACY ON KINDRED.

I have just examined the changes which the equality of conditions produces in the mutual relations of the several members of the com-munity among democratic nations, and among the Americans in par-ticular. I would now go deeper, and inquire into the closer ties of kindred: my object here is not to seek for new truths, but to show in what manner facts already known are connected with my subject.

It has been universally remarked, that in our time the several members of a family stand upon an entirely new footing toward each other; that the distance which formerly separated a father from his sons has been lessened; and that paternal authority, if not destroyed, is at least impaired.

Something analogous to this, but even more striking, may be observed in the United States. In America, the family, in the Roman and aristocratic signification of the word, does not exist. All that remains of it are a few vestiges in the first years of childhood, when the father exercises, without opposition, that absolute domestic authority, which the feebleness of his children renders necessary, and which their interest, as well as his own incontestable superiority, warrants. But as soon as the young American approaches manhood, the ties of filial obedience are relaxed day by day: master of his thoughts, he is soon master of his conduct. In America there is, strictly speaking, no adolescence: at the close of boyhood the man appears, and begins to trace out his own path.

It would be an error to suppose that this is preceded by a domestic struggle, in which the son has obtained by a sort of moral violence the liberty that his father refused him. The same habits, the same principles which impel the one to assert his independence, predispose the other to consider the use of that independence as an incontestable right. The former does not exhibit any of those rancorous or irregular passions which disturb men long after they have shaken off an established authority; the latter feels none of that bitter and angry regret which is apt to survive a by-gone power. The father foresees the limits of his authority long beforehand, and when the time arrives he surrenders it without a struggle: the son looks forward to the exact period at which he will be his own master; and he enters upon his freedom without precipitation and without effort, as a possession which is his own, and which no one seeks to wrest from him.*

It may perhaps not be without utility to show how these changes which take place in family relations, are closely connected with the social and political revolution which is approaching its consummation under our own observation.

---

* The Americans however have not yet thought fit to strip the parent, as has been done in France, of one of the chief elements of parental authority, by depriving him of the power of disposing of his property at his death. In the United States there are no restrictions on the powers of a testator.

In this respect, as in almost all others, it is easy to perceive, that if the political legislation of the Americans is much more democratic than that of the French, the civil legislation of the latter is infinitely more democratic than that of the former. This may easily be accounted for. The civil legislation of France was the work of a man who saw that it was his interest to satisfy the democratic passions of his contemporaries in all that was not directly and immediately hostile to his own power. He was willing to allow some popular principles to regulate the distribution of property and the government of families, provided they were not to be introduced into the administration of public affairs. While the torrent of democracy overwhelmed the civil laws of the country, he hoped to find an easy shelter behind its political institutions. This policy was at once both adroit and selfish: but a compromise of this kind could not last; for in the end political institutions never fail to become the image and expression of civil society; and in this sense it may be said that nothing is more political in a nation that its civil legislation.

There are certain great social principles, which a people either introduces everywhere, or tolerates nowhere. In countries which are aristocratically constituted with all the gradations of rank, the government never makes a direct appeal to the mass of the governed: as men are united together, it is enough to lead the foremost—the rest will follow. This is equally applicable to the family, as to all aristocracies which have a head.

Among aristocratic nations, social institutions recognise, in truth, no one in the family but the father; children are received by society at his hands; society governs him, he governs them. Thus the parent has not only a natural right, but he acquires a political right, to command them: he is the author and the support of his family; but he is also its constituted ruler.

In democracies, where the government picks out every individual singly from the mass, to make him subservient to the general laws of the community, no such intermediate person is required: a father is there, in the eye of the law, only a member of the community, older and richer than his sons.

When most of the conditions of life are extremely unequal, and the inequality of these conditions is permanent, the notion of a superior grows upon the imaginations of men: if the law invested him with no privileges, custom and public opinion would concede them. When, on the contrary, men differ but little from each other, and do not always remain in dissimilar conditions of life, the general notion of a superior becomes weaker and less distinct: it is vain for legislation to strive to place him who obeys very much beneath him who commands; the manners of the time bring the two men nearer to one another, and draw them daily toward the same level.

Although the legislation of an aristocratic people should grant no peculiar privileges to the heads of families, I shall not be the less convinced that their power is more respected and more extensive than in a democracy; for I know that, whatsoever the laws may be, superiors always appear higher and inferiors lower in aristocracies than among democratic nations.

When men live more for the remembrance of what has been than for the care of what is, and when they are more given to attend to what their ancestors thought than to think themselves, the father is the natural and necessary tie between the past and the present—the link by which the ends of these two chains are connected. In aristocracies, then, the father is not only the civil head of the family, but the oracle of its traditions, the expounder of its customs, the arbiter of its manners. He is listened to with deference, he is addressed with respect, and the love which is felt for him is always tempered with fear.

When the condition of society becomes democratic, and men adopt as their general principle that it is good and lawful to judge of all things for oneself, using former points of belief not as a rule of faith but simply as a means of information, the power which the opinions of a father exercise over those of his sons diminishes as well as his legal power.

Perhaps the subdivision of estates which democracy brings with it contributes more than any thing else to change the relations existing between a father and his children. When the property of the father of a family is scanty, his son and himself constantly live in the same place, and share the same occupations: habit and necessity bring them together, and force them to hold constant communication: the inevitable consequence is a sort of familiar intimacy, which renders authority less absolute, and which can ill be reconciled with the external forms of respect.

Now in democratic countries the class of those who are possessed of small fortunes is precisely that which gives strength to the notions, and a particular direction to the manners, of the community. That class makes its opinions preponderate as universally as its will, and even those who are most inclined to resist its commands are carried away in the end by its example. I have known eager opponents of democracy who allowed their children to address them with perfect colloquial equality.

Thus, at the same time that the power of aristocracy is declining, the austere, the conventional, and the legal part of parental authority vanishes, and a species of equality prevails around the domestic hearth. I know not, upon the whole, whether society loses by the change, but I am inclined to believe that man individually is a gainer by it. I think that, in proportion as manners and laws become more democratic, the relation of father and son becomes more intimate and more affectionate; rules and authority are less talked of; confidence and tenderness are oftentimes increased, and it would seem that the natural bond is drawn closer in proportion as the social bond is loosened.

In a democratic family the father exercises no other power than that with which men love to invest the affection and the experience of age: his orders would perhaps be disobeyed, but his advice is for the most part authoritative. Though he be not hedged in with ceremonial respect, his sons at least accost him with confidence; no settled form of speech is appropriated to the mode of addressing him, but they speak to him constantly and are ready to consult him day by day: the master and the constituted ruler have vanished—the father remains.

Nothing more is needed, in order to judge of the difference between the two states of society in this respect, than to peruse the family correspondence of aristocratic ages. The style is always correct, ceremonious, stiff, and so cold that the natural warmth of the heart can hardly be felt in the language. The language on the contrary addressed by a son to his father in democratic countries is always marked by mingled freedom, familiarity and affection, which at once show that new relations have sprung up in the bosom of the family.

A similar revolution takes place in the mutual relations of children. In aristocratic families, as well as in aristocratic society, every place is marked out beforehand. Not only does the father occupy a separate rank, in which he enjoys extensive privileges, but even the children are not equal among themselves. The age and sex of each irrevocably determine his rank, and secure to him certain privileges: most of these distinctions are abolished or diminished by democracy.

In aristocratic families the eldest son, inheriting the greater part of the property and almost all the rights of the family, becomes the chief, and to a certain extent the master, of his brothers. Greatness and power are for him—for them, mediocrity and dependance. Nevertheless it would be wrong to suppose that, among aristocratic nations, the privileges of the eldest son are advantageous to himself alone, or that they excite nothing but envy and hatred in those around him. The eldest son commonly endeavours to procure wealth and power for his brothers, because the general splendour of the house is reflected back on him who represents it; the younger sons seek to back the elder brother in all his undertakings, because the greatness and power of the head of the family better enable him to provide for all its branches. The different members of an aristocratic family are therefore very closely bound together; their interests are connected, their minds agree, but their hearts are seldom in harmony.

Democracy also binds brothers to each other, but by very different means. Under democratic laws all the children are perfectly equal, and consequently independent: nothing brings them forcibly together, but nothing keeps them apart; and as they have the same origin, as they are trained under the same roof, as they are treated with the same care, and as no peculiar privilege distinguishes or divides them, the affectionate and youthful intimacy of early years easily springs up between them. Scarcely any opportunities occur to break the tie thus formed at the outset of life; for their brotherhood brings them daily together, without embarrassing them. It is not then by interest, but by common associations and by the free sympathy of opinion and of taste, that democracy unites brothers to each other. It divides their inheritance, but it allows their hearts and minds to mingle together.

Such is the charm of these democratic manners, that even the partisans of aristocracy are caught by it; and after having experienced it for some time, they are by no means tempted to revert to the respectful and frigid observances of aristocratic families. They would be glad to retain the domestic habits of democracy, if they might throw off its social conditions and its laws; but these elements are indissolubly united, and it is impossible to enjoy the former without enduring the latter.

The remarks I have made on filial love and fraternal affection are applicable to all the passions which emanate spontaneously from human nature itself.

If a certain mode of thought or feeling is the result of some peculiar condition of life, when that condition is altered nothing whatever remains of the thought or feeling. Thus a law may bind two members of the community very closely to one another; but that law being abolished, they stand asunder. Nothing was more strict than the tie which united the vassal to the lord under the feudal system: at the present day the two men know not each other; the fear, the gratitude, and the affection which formerly connected them have vanished, and not a vestige of the tie remains.

Such, however, is not the case with those feelings which are natural to mankind. Whenever a law attempts to tutor these feelings in any particular manner, it seldom fails to weaken them; by attempting to add to their intensity, it robs them of some of their elements, for they are never stronger than when left to themselves.

Democracy, which destroys or obscures almost all the old conventional rules of society, and which prevents men from readily assenting to new ones, entirely effaces most of the feelings to which these conventional rules have given rise; but it only modifies some others, and frequently imparts to them a degree of energy and sweetness unknown before.

Perhaps it is not impossible to condense into a single proposition the whole meaning of this chapter, and of several others that preceded it. Democracy loosens social ties, but it draws the ties of nature more tight; it brings kindred more closely together, while it places the various members of the community more widely apart.

Chapter IX.

EDUCATION OF YOUNG WOMEN IN THE UNITED STATES.

No free communities ever existed without morals; and, as I observed in the former part of this work, morals are the work of woman. Consequently, whatever affects the condition of women, their habits and their opinions, has great political importance in my eyes.

Among almost all Protestant nations young women are far more the mistresses of their own actions than they are in Catholic countries. This independence is still greater in Protestant countries like England, which have retained or acquired the right of self-government; the spirit of freedom is then infused into the domestic circle by political habits and by religious opinions. In the United States the doctrines of Protestantism are combined with great political freedom and a most democratic state of society; and nowhere are young women surrendered so early or so completely to their own guidance.

Long before an American girl arrives at the age of marriage, her emancipation from maternal control begins: she has scarcely ceased to be a child, when she already thinks for herself, speaks with freedom, and acts on her own impulse. The great scene of the world is constantly open to her view; far from seeking concealment, it is every day disclosed to her more completely, and she is taught to survey it with a firm and calm gaze. Thus the vices and dangers of society are early revealed to her; as she sees them clearly, she views them without illusions, and braves them without fear; for she is full of reliance on her own strength, and her reliance seems to be shared by all who are about her.

An American girl scarcely ever displays that virginal bloom in the midst of young desires, or that innocent and ingenuous grace which usually attend the European woman in the transition from girlhood to youth. It is rarely that an American woman at any age displays childish timidity or ignorance. Like the young women of Europe, she seeks to please, but she knows precisely the cost of pleasing. If she does not abandon herself to evil, at least she knows that it exists; and she is remarkable rather for purity of manners than for chastity of mind.

I have been frequently surprised, and almost frightened, at the singular address and happy boldness with which young women in America contrive to manage their thoughts and their language, amid all the difficulties of stimulating conversation; a philosopher would have stumbled at every step along the narrow path which they trod without accidents and without effort. It is easy indeed to perceive that, even amid the independence of early youth, an American woman is always mistress of herself: she indulges in all permitted pleasures, without yielding herself up to any of them; and her reason never allows the reins of self-guidance to drop, though it often seems to hold them loosely.

In France, where remnants of every age are still so strangely mingled in the opinions and tastes of the people, women commonly receive a reserved, retired, and almost conventual education, as they did in aristocratic times; and then they are suddenly abandoned, without a guide and without assistance, in the midst of all the irregularities inseparable from democratic society.

The Americans are more consistent. They have found out that in a democracy the independence of individuals cannot fail to be very great, youth premature, tastes ill-restrained, customs fleeting, public opinion often unsettled and powerless, paternal authority weak, and marital authority contested. Under these circumstances, believing that they had little chance of repressing in woman the most vehement passions of the human heart, they held that the surer way was to teach her the art of combating those passions for herself. As they could not prevent her virtue from being exposed to frequent danger, they determined that she should know how best to defend it; and more reliance was placed on the free vigour of her will, than on safeguards which have been shaken or overthrown. Instead then of inculcating mistrust of herself, they constantly seek to enhance her confidence in her own strength of character. As it is neither possible nor desirable to keep a young woman in perpetual and complete ignorance, they hasten to give her a precocious knowledge on all subjects. Far from hiding the corruptions of the world from her, they prefer that she should see them at once and train herself to shun them; and they hold it of more importance to protect her conduct, than to be over-scrupulous of her innocence.

Although the Americans are a very religious people, they do not rely on religion alone to defend the virtue of woman; they seek to arm her reason also. In this they have followed the same method as in several other respects: they first make the most vigorous efforts to bring individual independence to exercise a proper control over itself, and they do not call in the aid of religion until they have reached the utmost limits of human strength.

I am aware that an education of this kind is not without danger; I am sensible that it tends to invigorate the judgement at the expense of the imagination, and to make cold and virtuous women instead of affectionate wives and agreeable companions to man. Society may be more tranquil and better regulated, but domestic life has often fewer charms. These however are secondary evils, which may be braved for the sake of higher interests. At the stage at which we are now arrived the time for choosing is no longer within our control; a democratic education is indispensable, to protect women from the dangers with which democratic institutions and manners surround them.

Chapter X.

THE YOUNG WOMAN IN THE CHARACTER OF A WIFE.

In America the independence of women is irrecoverably lost in the bonds of matrimony: if an unmarried woman is less constrained there than elsewhere, a wife is subjected to stricter obligations. The former makes her father's house an abode of freedom and of pleasure; the latter lives in the home of her husband as if it were a cloister. Yet these two different conditions of life are perhaps not so contrary as may be supposed, and it is natural that the American women should pass through the one to arrive at the other.

Religious people and trading nations entertain peculiarly serious notions of marriage: the former consider the regularity of woman's life as the best pledge and most certain sign of the purity of her morals; the latter regard it as the highest security for the order and prosperity of the household. The Americans are at the same time a puritanical people and a commercial nation: their religious opinions, as well as their trading habits, consequently lead them to require much abnegation on the part of women, and a constant sacrifice of her pleasures to her duties which is seldom demanded of her in Europe. Thus in the United States the inexorable opinion of the public carefully circumscribes woman within the narrow circle of domestic interests and duties, and forbids her to step beyond it.

Upon her entrance into the world a young American woman finds these notions firmly established; she sees the rules which are derived from them; she is not slow to perceive that she cannot depart for an instant from the established usages of her contemporaries, without putting in jeopardy her peace of mind, her honour, nay even her social existence; and she finds the energy required for such an act of submission in the firmness of her understanding and in the virile habits which her education has given her. It may be said that she has learned by the use of her independence, to surrender it without a struggle and without a murmur when the time comes for making the sacrifice.

But no American woman falls into the toils of matrimony as into a snare held out to her simplicity and ignorance. She has been taught beforehand what is expected of her, and voluntarily and freely does she enter upon this engagement. She supports her new condition with courage, because she chose it. As in America paternal discipline is very relaxed and the conjugal tie very strict, a young woman does not contract the latter without considerable circumspection and apprehension. Precocious marriages are rare. Thus American women do not marry until their understandings are exercised and ripened; whereas in other countries most women generally only begin to exercise and to ripen their understandings after marriage.

I by no means suppose, however, that the great change which takes place in all the habits of women in the United States, as soon as they are married, ought solely to be attributed to the constraint of public opinion; it is frequently imposed upon themselves by the sole effort of their own will. When the time for choosing a husband is arrived, that cold and stern reasoning power which has been educated and invigorated by the free observation of the world, teaches an American woman that a spirit of levity and independence in the bonds of marriage is a constant subject of annoyance, not of pleasure; it tells her that the amusements of the girl cannot become the recreations of the wife, and that the sources of a married woman's happiness are in the home of her husband. As she clearly discerns beforehand the only road which can lead to domestic happiness, she enters upon it at once, and follows it to the end without seeking to turn back.

The same strength of purpose which the young wives of America display, in bending themselves at once and without repining to the austere duties of their new condition, is no less manifest in all the great trials of their lives. In no country in the world are private fortunes more precarious than in the United States. It is not uncommon for the same man, in the course of his life, to rise and sink again through all the grades which lead from opulence to poverty. American women support these vicissitudes with calm and unquenchable energy: it would seem that their desires contract, as easily as they expand, with their fortunes.*

---

* I find in my travelling-journal a passage which may serve to convey a more complete notion of the trials to which the women of America, who consent to follow their husbands into the wilds, are often subjected. This description has nothing to recommend it to the reader but its strict accuracy.

. . . . ."From time to time we come to fresh clearings; all these places are alike: I shall describe the one at which we have halted to-night, for it will serve to remind me of all the others.

"The bell which the pioneers hang round the necks of their cattle, in order to find them again in the woods, announced our approach to a clearing, when we were yet a long way off; and we soon afterward heard the stroke of the hatchet, hewing down the trees of the forest. As we came nearer, traces of destruction marked the presence of civilized man: the road was strewn with shattered boughs; trunks of trees, half consumed by fire, or cleft by the wedge, were still standing in the track we were following. We continued to proceed till we reached a wood in which all the trees seemed to have been suddenly struck dead; in the height of summer their boughs were as leafless as in winter; and upon closer examination, we found that a deep circle had been cut round the bark, which, by stopping the circulation of the sap, soon kills the tree. We were informed that this is commonly the first thing a pioneer does; as he cannot, in the first year, cut down all the trees which cover his new parcel of land, he sows Indian corn under their branches, and puts the trees to death in order to prevent them from

The greater part of the adventurers who migrate every year to people the western wilds, belong, as I observed in the former part of this work, to the old Anglo-American race of the Northern States. Many of these men, who rush so boldly onward in pursuit of wealth, were already in the enjoyment of a competency in their own part of the coun-

---

injuring his crop. Beyond this field, at present imperfectly traced out, we suddenly came upon the cabin of its owner, situated in the centre of a plot of ground more carefully cultivated than the rest, but where man was still waging unequal warfare with the forest; there the trees were cut down, but their roots were not removed, and the trunks still encumbered the ground which they so recently shaded. Around these dry blocks, wheat, suckers of trees, and plants of every kind grow and intertwine in all the luxuriance of wild untutored nature. Amid this vigorous and various vegetation stands the house of the pioneer, or, as they call it, the log-house. Like the ground about it, this rustic dwelling bore marks of recent and hasty labour; its length seemed not to exceed thirty feet, its height fifteen; the walls as well as the roof were formed of rough trunks of trees, between which a little moss and clay had been inserted to keep out the cold and rain.

"As night was coming on, we determined to ask the master of the log-house for a lodging. At the sound of our footsteps, the children who were playing among the scattered branches sprang up and ran toward the house, as if they were frightened at the sight of man; while two large dogs, almost wild, with ears erect and outstretched nose, came growling out of their hut, to cover the retreat of their young masters. The pioneer himself made his appearance at the door of his dwelling; he looked at us with a rapid and inquisitive glance, made a sign to the dogs to go into the house, and set them the example, without betraying either curiosity or apprehension at our arrival.

"We entered the log-house: the inside is quite unlike that of the cottages of the peasantry of Europe: it contains more that is superfluous, less that is necessary. A single window with a muslin blind; on a hearth of trodden clay an immense fire, which lights the whole structure; above the hearth of good rifle, a deer's skin, and plumes of eagles' feathers; on the right hand of the chimney a map of the United States, raised and shaken by the wind through the crannies in the wall; near the map, upon a shelf formed of a roughly hewn plank, a few volumes of books—a bible, the six first books of Milton, and two of Shakspere's plays; along the wall, trunks instead of closets; in the centre of the room a rude table, with legs of green wood, and with the bark still upon them, looking as if they grew out of the ground on which they stood; but on this table a teapot of British ware, silver spoons, cracked teacups, and some newspapers.

"The master of this dwelling has the strong angular features and lank limbs peculiar to the native of New England. It is evident that this man was not born in the solitude in which we have met with him: his physical constitution suffices to show that his earlier years were spent in the midst of civilized society, and that he belongs to that restless, calculating and adventurous race of men, who do with the utmost coolness things only to be accounted for by the ardour of the passions, and who endure the life of savages for a time, in order to conquer and civilize the back-woods.

"When the pioneer perceived that we were crossing his threshold, he came to meet us and shake hands, as is their custom; but his face was quite unmoved; he opened the conversation by inquiring what was going on in the world; and when his curiosity was satisfied, he held his peace, as if he were tired by the noise and importunity of mankind. When we questioned him in our turn, he gave us all the information we required; he then attended sedulously, but without eagerness, to our personal wants. While he was engaged in providing thus kindly for us, how came it that in spite of ourselves we felt our gratitude die upon our lips? it is, that our host, while he performs the duties of hospitality, seems to be obeying an irksome necessity of his condition: he treats it as a duty imposed upon him by his situation, not as a pleasure.

"By the side of the hearth sits a woman with a baby on her lap: she nods to us, without disturbing herself. Like the pioneer, this woman is in the prime of life; her appearance would seem superior to her condition, and her apparel even betrays a lingering taste for dress; but her delicate limbs appear shrunken, her features are drawn in, her eye is mild and melancholy; her whole physiognomy bears marks of a degree of religious resignation, a deep quiet of all passions, and some sort of natural and tranquil firmness, ready to meet all the ills of life, without fearing and without braving them.

"Her children cluster about her, full of health, turbulence and energy: they are true children of the wilderness; their mother watches them from time to time with mingled melancholy and joy: to look at their strength and her languor, one might imagine that the life she has given them had exhausted her own, and still she regrets not what they have cost her.

"The house inhabited by these emigrants has no internal partition or loft. In the one chamber of which it consists the whole family is gathered for the night. The dwelling is itself a little world—an ark of civilization amid an ocean of foliage: a hundred steps beyond it the primeval forest spreads its shades, and solitude resumes its sway."

try. They take their wives along with them, and make them share the countless perils and privations which always attend the commencement of these expeditions. I have often met, even on the verge of the wilderness, with young women, who after having been brought up amid all the comforts of the large towns of New England, had passed, almost without any intermediate stage, from the wealthy abode of their parents to a comfortless hovel in a forest. Fever, solitude, and a tedious life had not broken the springs of their courage. Their features were impaired and faded, but their looks were firm: they appeared to be at once sad and resolute. I do not doubt that these young American women had amassed, in the education of their early years, that inward strength which they displayed under these circumstances. The early culture of the girl may still therefore be traced, in the United States, under the aspect of marriage: her part is changed, her habits are different, but her character is the same.

Chapter XI.

THAT THE EQUALITY OF CONDITIONS CONTRIBUTES TO THE MAINTENANCE OF GOOD MORALS IN AMERICA.

Some philosophers and historians have said, or have hinted, that the strictness of female morality was increased or diminished simply by the distance of a country from the equator. This solution of the difficulty was an easy one; and nothing was required but a globe and a pair of compasses to settle in an instant one of the most difficult problems in the condition of mankind. But I am not aware that this principle of the materialists is supported by facts. The same nations have been chaste or dissolute, at different periods of their history; the strictness or the laxity of their morals depended therefore on some variable cause, not only on the natural qualities of their country, which were invariable. I do not deny that in certain climates the passions which are occasioned by the mutual attraction of the sexes are peculiarly intense; but I am of opinion that this natural intensity may always be excited or restrained by the condition of society and by political institutions.

Although the travellers who have visited North America differ on a great number of points, they all agree in remarking that morals are far more strict there than elsewhere. It is evident that on this point the Americans are very superior to their progenitors the English. A superficial glance at the two nations will establish the fact.

In England, as in all other countries of Europe, public malice is constantly attacking the frailties of women. Philosophers and statesmen are heard to deplore that morals are not sufficiently strict, and the literary productions of the country constantly lead one to suppose so. In America all books, novels not excepted, suppose women to be chaste, and no one thinks of relating affairs of gallantry.

No doubt this great regularity of American morals originates partly in the country, in the race of the people, and in their religion: but all these causes, which operate elsewhere, do not suffice to account for it; recourse must be had to some special reason.

This reason appears to me to be the principle of equality and the institutions derived from it. Equality of conditions does not of itself engender regularity of morals, but it unquestionably facilitates and increases it.*

Among aristocratic nations birth and fortune frequently make two such different beings of man and woman, that they can never be united to each other. Their passions draw them together, but the condition of society, and the notions suggested by it, prevent them from contracting a permanent and ostensible tie. The necessary consequence is a great number of transient and clandestine connexions. Nature secretly avenges herself for the constraint imposed upon her by the laws of man.

This is not so much the case when the equality of conditions has swept away all the imaginary, or the real, barriers which separated man from woman. No girl then believes that she cannot become the wife of the man who loves her; and this renders all breaches of morality before marriage very uncommon: for, whatever be the credulity of the passions, a woman will hardly be able to persuade herself that she is beloved, when her lover is perfectly free to marry her and does not.

The same cause operates, though more indirectly, on married life. Nothing better serves to justify an illicit passion, either to the minds of those who have conceived it or to the world which looks on, than compulsory or accidental marriages.†

In a country in which a woman is always free to exercise her power of choosing, and in which education has prepared her to choose rightly, public opinion is inexorable to her faults. The rigour of the Americans arises in part from this cause. They consider marriage as a covenant which is often onerous, but every condition of which the parties are strictly bound to fulfil, because they knew all those conditions beforehand, and were perfectly free not to have contracted them.

The very circumstances which render matrimonial fidelity more obligatory also render it more easy.

* It is not the equality of conditions which makes men immoral and irreligious; but when men, being equal, are at the same time immoral and irreligious, the effects of immorality and irreligion easily manifest themselves outwardly, because men have but little influence upon each other, and no class exists which can undertake to keep society in order. Equality of conditions never engenders profligacy of morals, but it sometimes allows that profligacy to show itself.

† The literature of Europe sufficiently corroborates this remark. When a European author wishes to depict in a work of imagination any of those great catastrophes in matrimony which so frequently occur among us, he takes care to bespeak the compassion of the reader by bringing before him ill-assorted or compulsory marriages. Although habitual tolerance has long since relaxed our morals, an author could hardly succeed in interesting us in the misfortunes of his characters, if he did not first palliate their faults. This artifice seldom fails: the daily scenes we witness prepare us long beforehand to be indulgent. But American writers could never render these palliations probable to their readers; their customs and laws are opposed to it; and as they despair of rendering levity of conduct pleasing, they cease to depict it. This is one of the causes to which must be attributed the small number of novels published in the United States.

In aristocratic countries the object of marriage is rather to unite property than persons; hence the husband is sometimes at school and the wife at nurse when they are betrothed. It cannot be wondered at if the conjugal tie which holds the fortunes of the pair united allows their hearts to rove; this is the natural result of the nature of the contract. When, on the contrary, a man always chooses a wife for himself, without any external coercion or even guidance, it is generally a conformity of tastes and opinions which brings a man and a woman together, and this same conformity keeps and fixes them in close habits of intimacy.

Our forefathers had conceived a very strange notion on the subject of marriage: as they had remarked that the small number of love-matches which occurred in their time almost always turned out ill, they resolutely inferred that it was exceedingly dangerous to listen to the dictates of the heart on the subject. Accident appeared to them to be a better guide than choice.

Yet it was not very difficult to perceive that the examples which they witnessed did in fact prove nothing at all. For in the first place, if democratic nations leave a woman at liberty to choose her husband, they take care to give her mind sufficient knowledge, and her will sufficient strength, to make so important a choice: whereas the young women who, among aristocratic nations, furtively elope from the authority of their parents to throw themselves of their own accord into the arms of men whom they have had neither time to know, nor ability to judge of, are totally without those securities. It is not surprising that they make a bad use of their freedom of action the first time they avail themselves of it; nor that they fall into such cruel mistakes, when, not having received a democratic education, they choose to marry in conformity to democratic customs. But this is not all. When a man and woman are bent upon marriage in spite of the differences of an aristocratic state of society, the difficulties to be overcome are enormous. Having broken or relaxed the bonds of filial obedience, they have then to emancipate themselves by a final effort from the sway of custom and the tyranny of opinion; and when at length they have succeeded in this arduous task, they stand estranged from their natural friends and kinsmen: the prejudice they have crossed separates them from all and places them in a situation which soon breaks their courage and sours their hearts.

If, then, a couple married in this manner are first unhappy and afterward criminal, it ought not to be attributed to the freedom of their choice, but rather to their living in a community in which this freedom of choice is not admitted.

Moreover it should not be forgotten that the same effort which makes a man violently shake off a prevailing error, commonly impels him beyond the bounds of reason; that, to dare to declare war, in however just a cause, against the opinion of one's age and country, a violent and adventurous spirit is required, and that men of this character seldom arrive at happiness or virtue, whatever be the path they follow. And this, it may be observed by the way, is the reason why in the most necessary and righteous revolutions, it is so rare to meet with virtuous or moderate revolutionary characters. There is then no just grounds for surprise, if a man, who in an age of aristocracy chooses to consult nothing but his own opinion and his own taste in the choice of a wife, soon finds that infractions of morality and domestic wretchedness invade his household: but when this same line of action is in the natural and ordinary course of things, when it is sanctioned by parental authority and backed by public opinion, it cannot be doubted that the internal peace of families will be increased by it, and conjugal fidelity more rigidly observed.

Almost all men in democracies are engaged in public or professional life; and on the other hand the limited extent of common incomes obliges a wife to confine herself to the house, in order to watch in person and very closely over the details of domestic economy. All these distinct and compulsory occupations are so many natural barriers, which, by keeping the two sexes asunder, render the solicitations of the one less frequent and less ardent—the resistance of the other more easy.

Not indeed that the equality of conditions can ever succeed in making men chaste, but it may impart a less dangerous character to their breaches of morality. As no one has then either sufficient time or opportunity to assail a virtue armed in self-defence, there will be at the same time a great number of courtezans and a great number of virtuous women. This state of things causes lamentable cases of individual hardship, but it does not prevent the body of society from being strong and alert; it does not destroy family ties, or enervate the morals of the nation. Society is endangered not by the great profligacy of a few, but by laxity of morals among all. In the eyes of a legislator, prostitution is less to be dreaded than intrigue.

The tumultuous and constantly harassed life which equality makes men lead, not only distracts them from the passion of love, by denying them time to indulge in it, but it diverts them from it by another more secret but more certain road. All men who live in democratic ages more or less contract the ways of thinking of the manufacturing and trading classes; their minds take a serious, deliberate, and positive turn; they are apt to relinquish the ideal, in order to pursue some visible and proximate object, which appears to be the natural and necessary aim of their desires. Thus the principle of equality does not destroy the imagination, but lowers its flight to the level of the earth.

No men are less addicted to reverie than the citizens of a democracy; and few of them are ever known to give way to those idle and solitary meditations which commonly precede and produce the great emotions of the heart. It is true they attach great importance to procuring for themselves that sort of deep, regular, and quiet affection which constitutes the charm and safeguard of life, but they are not apt to run after those violent and capricious sources of excitement which disturb and abridge it.

I am aware that all this is only applicable in its full extent to America, and cannot at present be extended to Europe. In the course of the last half-century, while laws and customs have impelled several European nations with unexampled force toward democracy, we have not had occasion to observe that the relations of man and woman have become more orderly or more chaste. In some places the very reverse may be detected: some classes are more strict—the general morality of the people appears to be more lax. I do not hesitate to make the remark, for I am as little disposed to flatter my contemporaries as to malign them.

This fact must distress, but it ought not to surprise us. The propitious influence which a democratic state of society may exercise upon orderly habits, is one of those tendencies which can only be discovered after a time. If the equality of conditions is favourable to purity of morals, the social commotion by which conditions are rendered equal, is adverse to it. In the last fifty years, during which France has been undergoing this transformation, that country has rarely had freedom, always disturbance. Amid this universal confusion of notions and this general stir of opinions—amid this incoherent mixture of the just and the unjust, of truth and falsehood, of right and might—public virtue has become doubtful, and private morality wavering. But all revolutions, whatever may have been their object or their agents, have at first produced similar consequences; even those which have in the end drawn the bonds of morality more tightly began by loosening them. The violations of morality which the French frequently witness do not appear to me to have a permanent character; and this is already betokened by some curious signs of the times.

Nothing is more wretchedly corrupt than an aristocracy which retains its wealth when it has lost its power, and which still enjoys a vast deal of leisure after it is reduced to mere vulgar pastimes. The energetic passions and great conceptions which animated it heretofore, leave it then; and nothing remains to it but a host of petty consuming vices, which cling about it like worms upon a carcass.

No one denies that the French aristocracy of the last century was extremely dissolute; whereas established habits and ancient belief still preserved some respect for morality among the other classes of society. Nor will it be contested that at the present day the remnants of that same aristocracy exhibit a certain severity of morals; while laxity of morals appears to have spread among the middle and lower ranks. So that the same families which were most profligate fifty years ago are now-a-days the most exemplary, and democracy seems only to have strengthened the morality of the aristocratic classes. The French Revolution, by dividing the fortunes of the nobility, by forcing them to attend assiduously to their affairs and to their families, by making them live under the same roof with their children, and in short by giving a more rational and serious turn to their minds, has imparted to them, almost without their being aware of it, a reverence for religious belief, a love of order, of tranquil pleasures, of domestic endearments, and of comfort; whereas the rest of the nation, which had naturally these same tastes, was carried away into excesses by the effort which was required to overthrow the laws and political habits of the country. The old French aristocracy has undergone the consequences of the revolution, but it neither felt the revolutionary passions, nor shared in the anarchical excitement which produced that crisis: it may easily be conceived that this aristocracy feels the salutary influence of the revolution in its manners, before those who achieved it. It may therefore be said, though at first it seems paradoxical, that, at the present day, the most anti-democratic classes of the nation principally exhibit the kind of morality which may reasonably be anticipated from democracy. I cannot but think that when we shall have obtained all the effects of this democratic revolution, after having got rid of the tumult it has caused, the observations which are now only applicable to the few will gradually become true of the whole community.

Chapter XII.

HOW THE AMERICANS UNDERSTAND THE EQUALITY OF THE SEXES.

I have shown how democracy destroys or modifies the different inequalities which originate in society: but is this all? or does it not ultimately affect that great inequality of man and woman which has seemed, up to the present day, to be eternally based in human nature? I believe that the social changes which bring nearer to the same level the father and son, the master and servant, and superiors and inferiors generally speaking, will raise woman and make her more and more the equal of man. But here, more than ever, I feel the necessity of making myself clearly understood; for there is no subject on which the coarse and lawless fancies of our age have taken a freer range.

There are people in Europe who, confounding together the different characteristics of the sexes, would make of man and woman beings not only equal but alike. They would give to both the same functions, impose on both the same duties, and grant to both the same rights: they would mix them in all things—their occupations, their pleasures, their business. It may readily be conceived, that by thus attempting to make one sex equal to the other, both are degraded; and from so preposterous a medley of the works of nature, nothing could ever result but weak men and disorderly women.

It is not thus that the Americans understand that species of democratic equality which may be established between the sexes. They admit, that as nature has appointed such wide differences between the physical and moral constitutions of man and woman, her manifest design was to give a distinct employment to their various faculties; and they hold that improvement does not consist in making beings so dissimilar do pretty nearly the same things, but in getting each of them to fulfil their respective tasks in the best possible manner. The Americans have applied to the sexes the great principle of political economy which governs the manufactures of our age, by carefully dividing the duties of man from those of woman, in order that the great work of society may be the better carried on.

In no country has such constant care been taken as in America to trace two clearly distinct lines of action for the two sexes, and to make them keep pace one with the other, but in two pathways which are always different. American women never manage the outward concerns of the family, or conduct a business, or take a part in political life; nor are they, on the other hand, ever compelled to perform the rough labor of the fields, or to make any of those laborious exertions which demand the exertion of physical strength. No families are so poor as to form an exception to this rule. If on the one hand an American woman cannot escape from the quiet circle of domestic employments, on the other hand she is never forced to go beyond it. Hence it is that the women of America, who often exhibit a masculine strength of understanding and a manly energy, generally preserve great delicacy of personal appearance and always retain the manners of women, although they sometimes show that they have the hearts and minds of men.

Nor have the Americans ever supposed that one consequence of democratic principles is the subversion of marital power, or the confusion of the natural authorities in families. They hold that every association must have a head in order to accomplish its object, and that the natural head of the conjugal association is man. They do not therefore deny him the right of directing his partner; and they maintain, that in the smaller association of husband and wife, as well as in the great social community, the object of democracy is to regulate and legalize the powers which are necessary, not to subvert all power.

This opinion is not peculiar to one sex, and contested by the other: I never observed that the women of America consider conjugal authority as a fortunate usurpation of their rights, nor that they thought themselves degraded by submitting to it. It appeared to me, on the contrary, that they attach a sort of pride to the voluntary surrender of their own will, and make it their boast to bend themselves to the yoke, not to shake it off. Such at least is the feeling expressed by the most virtuous of their sex; the others are silent; and in the United States it is not the practice for a guilty wife to clamour for the rights of woman, while she is trampling on her holiest duties.

It has often been remarked that in Europe a certain degree of contempt lurks even in the flattery which men lavish upon women: although a European frequently affects to be the slave of woman, it may be seen that he never sincerely thinks her his equal. In the United States men seldom compliment women, but they daily show how much they esteem them. They constantly display an entire confidence in the understanding of a wife, and a profound respect for her freedom; they have decided that her mind is just as fitted as that of a man to discover the plain truth, and her heart as firm to embrace it; and they have never sought to place her virtue, any more than his, under the shelter of prejudice, ignorance, and fear.

It would seem that in Europe, where man so easily submits to the despotic sway of women, they are nevertheless curtailed of some of the greatest qualities of the human species, and considered as seductive but imperfect beings; and (what may well provoke astonishment) women ultimately look upon themselves in the same light, and almost consider it as a privilege that they are entitled to show themselves futile, feeble, and timid. The women of America claim no such privileges.

Again, it may be said, that in our morals we have reserved strange immunities to man; so that there is, as it were, one virtue for his use, and another for the guidance of his partner; and that, according to the opinion of the public, the very same act may be punished alternately as a crime or only as a fault. The Americans know not this iniquitous division of duties and rights; among them the seducer is as much dishonoured as his victim.

It is true that the Americans rarely lavish upon women those eager attentions which are commonly paid them in Europe; but their conduct to women always implies that they suppose them to be virtuous and refined; and such is the respect entertained for the moral freedom of the sex, that in the presence of a woman the most guarded language is used, lest her ear should be offended by an expression. In America a young unmarried woman may, alone and without fear, undertake a long journey.

The legislators of the United States, who have mitigated almost all the penalties of criminal law, still make rape a capital offence, and no crime, is visited with more inexorable severity by public opinion. This may be accounted for; as the Americans can conceive nothing more precious than a woman's honour, and nothing which ought so much to be respected as her independence, they hold that no punishment is too severe for the man who deprives her of them against her will. In France, where the same offence is visited with far milder penalties, it is frequently difficult to get a verdict from a jury against the prisoner. Is this a consequence of contempt of decency or contempt of woman? I cannot but believe that it is a contempt of one and of the other.

Thus the Americans do not think that man and woman have either the duty or the right to perform the same offices, but they show an equal regard for both their respective parts; and though their lot is different, they consider both of them as beings of equal value. They do not give to the courage of woman the same form or the same direction as to that of man; but they never doubt her courage: and if they hold that man and his partner ought not always to exercise their intellect and understanding in the same manner, they at least believe the understanding of the one to be as sound as that of the other, and her intellect to be as clear. Thus, then, while they have allowed the social inferiority of woman to subsist, they have done all they could to raise her morally and intellectually to the level of man; and in this respect they appear to me to have excellently understood the true principle of democratic improvement.

As for myself, I do not hesitate to avow, that, although the women of the United States are confined within the narrow circle of domestic life, and their situation is in some respects one of extreme dependance, I have nowhere seen women occupying a loftier position; and if

I were asked, now that I am drawing to the close of this work, in which I have spoken of so many important things done by the Americans, to what the singular prosperity and growing strength of that people ought mainly to be attributed, I should reply—to the superiority of their women.

Chapter XIII.

THAT THE PRINCIPLE OF EQUALITY NATURALLY DIVIDES THE AMERICANS INTO A NUMBER OF SMALL PRIVATE CIRCLES.

It may probably be supposed, that the final consequence and necessary effect of democratic institutions is to confound together all the members of the community in private as well as in public life, and to compel them all to live in common; but this would be to ascribe a very coarse and oppressive form to the equality which originates in democracy. No state of society or laws can render men so much alike, but that education, fortune, and tastes will interpose some differences between them; and, though different men may sometimes find it their interest to combine for the same purposes, they will never make it their pleasure. They will therefore always tend to evade the provisions of legislation, whatever they may be; and departing in some one respect from the circle within which they were to be bounded, they will set up, close by the great political community, small private circles, united together by the similitude of their conditions, habits, and manners.

In the United States the citizens have no sort of pre-eminence over each other; they owe each other no mutual obedience or respect; they all meet for the administration of justice, for the government of the State, and in general to treat of the affairs which concern their common welfare; but I never heard that attempts have been made to bring them all to follow the same diversions, or to amuse themselves promiscuously in the same places of recreation.

The Americans, who mingle so readily in their political assemblies and courts of justice, are wont on the contrary carefully to separate into small distinct circles, in order to indulge by themselves in the enjoyments of private life. Each of them is willing to acknowledge all his fellow-citizens as his equals, but he will only receive a very limited number of them among his friends or his guests. This appears to me to be very natural. In proportion as the circle of public society is extended, it may be anticipated that the sphere of private intercourse will be contracted; far from supposing that the members of modern society will ultimately live in common, I am afraid that they may end by forming nothing but small coteries.

Among aristocratic nations, the different classes are like vast chambers, out of which it is impossible to get, into which it is impossible to enter. These classes have no communication with each other, but within their pale men necessarily live in daily contact; even though they would not naturally suit, the general conformity of a similar condition brings them nearer together.

But when neither law nor custom professes to establish frequent and habitual relations between certain men, their intercourse originates in the accidental analogy of opinions and tastes; hence private society is infinitely varied. In democracies, where the members of the community never differ much from each other, and naturally stand in such propinquity that they may all at any time be confounded in one general mass, numerous artificial and arbitrary distinctions spring up, by means of which every man hopes to keep himself aloof, lest he should be carried away in the crowd against his will.

This can never fail to be the case; for human institutions may be changed, but not man: whatever may be the general endeavour of a community to render its members equal and alike, the personal pride of individuals will always seek to rise above the line, and to form somewhere an inequality to their own advantage.

In aristocracies men are separated from each other by lofty stationary barriers: in democracies they are divided by a number of small and almost invisible threads, which are constantly broken or moved from place to place. Thus, whatever may be the progress of equality, in democratic nations a great number of small private communities will always be formed within the general pale of political society; but none of them will bear any resemblance in its manners to the highest class in aristocracies.

Chapter XIV.

SOME REFLECTIONS ON AMERICAN MANNERS.

Nothing seems at first sight less important than the outward form of human actions, yet there is nothing upon which men set more store: they grow used to everything except to living in a society which has not their own manners. The influence of the social and political state of a country upon manners is therefore deserving of serious examination.

Manners are, generally, the product of the very basis of the character of a people, but they are also sometimes the result of an arbitrary convention between certain men; thus they are at once natural and acquired.

When certain men perceive that they are the foremost persons in society, without contestation and without effort—when they are constantly engaged on large objects, leaving the more minute details to others—and when they live in the enjoyment of wealth which they did not amass and which they do not fear to lose, it may be supposed that they feel a kind of haughty disdain of the petty interests and practical cares of life, and that their thoughts assume a natural greatness,

which their language and their manners denote. In democratic countries manners are generally devoid of dignity, because private life is
there extremely petty in its character; and they are frequently low, because the mind has few opportunities of rising above the engrossing
cares of domestic interests.

True dignity in manners consists in always taking one's proper station, neither too high nor too low; and this is as much within the
reach of a peasant as of a prince. In democracies all stations appear
doubtful; hence it is that the manners of democracies, though often
full of arrogance, are commonly wanting in dignity, and, moreover,
they are never either well-disciplined or accomplished.

The men who live in democracies are too fluctuating for a certain
number of them ever to succeed in laying down a code of good-
breeding, and in forcing people to follow it. Every man therefore be-
haves after his own fashion, and there is always a certain incoherence
in the manners of such times, because they are moulded upon the
feelings and notions of each individual, rather than upon an ideal
model proposed for general imitation. This, however, is much more
perceptible at the time when an aristocracy has just been overthrown
than after it has long been destroyed. New political institutions and
new social elements then bring to the same places of resort, and frequently compel to live in common, men whose education and habits
are still amazingly dissimilar, and this renders the motley composition
of society peculiarly visible. The existence of a former strict code of
good-breeding is still remembered, but what it contained or where it is
to be found is already forgotten. Men have lost the common law of
manners, and they have not yet made up their minds to do without it;
but every one endeavours to make to himself some sort of arbitrary
and variable rule, from the remnant of former usages; so that manners
have neither the regularity and the dignity which they often display
among aristocratic nations, nor the simplicity and freedom which they
sometimes assume in democracies; they are at once constrained and
without constraint.

This, however, is not the normal state of things. When the equality
of conditions is long established and complete, as all men entertain
nearly the same notions and do nearly the same things, they do not require to agree or to copy from one another in order to speak or act in
the same manner: their manners are constantly characterized by a
number of lesser diversities, but not by any great differences. They are
never perfectly alike, because they do not copy from the same pattern;
they are never very unlike, because their social condition is the same.
At first sight a traveller would observe that the manners of all the
Americans are exactly similar; it is only upon close examination that
the peculiarities in which they differ may be detected.

The English make game of the manners of the Americans; but it is
singular that most of the writers who have drawn these ludicrous delineations belonged themselves to the middle classes in England, to
whom the same delineations are exceedingly applicable: so that these
pitiless censors for the most part furnish an example of the very thing

they blame in the United States; they do not perceive that they are deriding themselves, to the great amusement of the aristocracy of their own country.

Nothing is more prejudicial to democracy than its outward forms of behaviour: many men would willingly endure its vices, who cannot support its manners. I cannot, however, admit that there is nothing commendable in the manners of a democratic people.

Among aristocratic nations, all who live within reach of the first class in society commonly strain to be like it, which gives rise to ridiculous and insipid imitations. As a democratic people does not possess any models of high-breeding, at least it escapes the daily necessity of seeing wretched copies of them. In democracies manners are never so refined as among aristocratic nations, but on the other hand they are never so coarse. Neither the coarse oaths of the populace, nor the elegant and choice expressions of the nobility, are to be heard there: the manners of such a people are often vulgar, but they are neither brutal nor mean.

I have already observed that in democracies no such thing as a regular code of good-breeding can be laid down; this has some inconveniences and some advantages. In aristocracies the rules of propriety impose the same demeanour on every one; they make all the members of the same class appear alike, in spite of their private inclinations; they adorn and they conceal the natural man. Among a democratic people manners are neither so tutored nor so uniform, but they are frequently more sincere. They form, as it were, a light and loosely-woven veil, through which the real feelings and private opinions of each individual are easily discernible. The form and the substance of human actions often therefore stand in closer relation; and if the great picture of human life be less embellished, it is more true. Thus it may be said, in one sense, that the effect of democracy is not exactly to give men any particular manners, but to prevent them from having manners at all.

The feelings, the passions, the virtues, and the vices of an aristocracy may sometimes re-appear in a democracy, but not its manners; they are lost, and vanish for ever, as soon as the democratic revolution is completed. It would seem that nothing is more lasting than the manners of an aristocratic class, for they are preserved by that class for some time after it has lost its wealth and its power—nor so fleeting, for no sooner have they disappeared, than not a trace of them is to be found; and it is scarcely possible to say what they have been, as soon as they have ceased to be. A change in the state of society works this miracle, and a few generations suffice to consummate it.

The principal characteristics of aristocracy are handed down by history after an aristocracy is destroyed, but the light and exquisite touches of manners are effaced from men's memories almost immediately after its fall. Men can no longer conceive what these manners were when they have ceased to witness them; they are gone, and their departure was unseen, unfelt; for in order to feel that refined enjoyment which is derived from choice and distinguished manners, habit and education must have prepared the heart, and the taste for them is lost almost as easily as the practice of them. Thus not only a democratic people cannot have aristocratic manners, but they neither comprehend nor desire them; and as they never have thought of them, it is to their minds as if such things had never been. Too much importance should not be attached to this loss, but it may well be regretted.

I am aware that it has not unfrequently happened that the same men have had very high-bred manners and very low-born feelings: the interior of courts has sufficiently shown what imposing externals may conceal the meanest hearts. But though the manners of aristocracy did not constitute virtue, they sometimes embellished virtue itself. It was no ordinary sight to see a numerous and powerful class of men, whose every outward action seemed constantly to be dictated by a natural elevation of thought and feeling, by delicacy and regularity of taste, and by urbanity of manners. Those manners threw a pleasing illusory charm over human nature; and though the picture was often a false one, it could not be viewed without a noble satisfaction.

Chapter XV.

OF THE GRAVITY OF THE AMERICANS, AND WHY IT DOES NOT PREVENT THEM FROM OFTEN COMMITTING INCONSIDERATE ACTIONS.

Men who live in democratic countries do not value the simple, turbulent, or coarse diversions in which the people indulge in aristocratic communities; such diversions are thought by them to be puerile or insipid. Nor have they a greater inclination for the intellectual and refined amusements of the aristocratic classes. They want something productive and substantial in their pleasures; they want to mix actual fruition with their joy.

In aristocratic communities the people readily give themselves up to bursts of tumultuous and boisterous gayety, which shake off at once the recollection of their privations: the natives of democracies are not fond of being thus violently broken in upon, and they never lose sight of their own selves without regret. They prefer to these frivolous delights those more serious and silent amusements which are like business, and which do not drive business wholly from their minds.

An American, instead of going in a leisure hour to dance merrily at some place of public resort, as the fellows of his calling continue to do throughout the greater part of Europe, shuts himself up at home to drink. He thus enjoys two pleasures; he can go on thinking of his business, and he can get drunk decently by his own fireside.

I thought that the English constituted the most serious nation on the face of the earth, but I have since seen the Americans and have changed my opinion. I do not mean to say that temperament has not a great deal to do with the character of the inhabitants of the United States, but I think that their political institutions are a still more influential cause.

I believe the seriousness of the Americans arises partly from their pride. In democratic countries even poor men entertain a lofty notion of their personal importance: they look upon themselves with complacency, and are apt to suppose that others are looking at them too. With this disposition, they watch their language and their actions with care, and do not lay themselves open so as to betray their deficiencies; to preserve their dignity, they think it necessary to retain their gravity.

But I detect another more deep-seated and powerful cause which instinctively produces among the Americans this astonishing gravity. Under a despotism communities give way at times to bursts of vehement joy; but they are generally gloomy and moody, because they are afraid. Under absolute monarchies tempered by the customs and manners of the country, their spirits are often cheerful and even, because, as they have some freedom and a good deal of security, they are exempted from the most important cares of life; but all free peoples are serious, because their minds are habitually absorbed by the contemplation of some dangerous or difficult purpose. This is more especially the case among those free nations which form democratic communities. Then there are in all classes a very large number of men constantly occupied with the serious affairs of the government; and those whose thoughts are not engaged in the direction of the commonwealth, are wholly engrossed by the acquisition of a private fortune. Among such a people a serious demeanour ceases to be peculiar to certain men, and becomes a habit of the nation.

We are told of small democracies in the days of antiquity, in which the citizens met upon the public places with garlands of roses, and spent almost all their time in dancing and theatrical amusements. I do not believe in such republics any more than in that of Plato: or, if the things we read of really happened, I do not hesitate to affirm that these supposed democracies were composed of very different elements from ours, and that they had nothing in common with the latter except their name.

But it must not be supposed that, in the midst of all their toils, the people who live in democracies think themselves to be pitied; the contrary is remarked to be the case. No men are fonder of their own condition. Life would have no relish for them if they were delivered from the anxieties which harass them, and they show more attachment to their cares than aristocratic nations to their pleasures.

I am next led to inquire how it is that these same democratic nations, which are so serious, sometimes act in so inconsiderate a manner. The Americans, who almost always preserve a staid demeanour and a frigid air, nevertheless frequently allow themselves to be borne away far beyond the bounds of reason by a sudden passion or a hasty opinion, and they sometimes gravely commit strange absurdities.

This contrast ought not to surprise us. There is one sort of ignorance which originates in extreme publicity. In despotic states men know not how to act, because they are told nothing: in democratic nations they often act at random, because nothing is to be left untold.

The former do not know—the latter forget; and the chief features of each picture are lost to them in a bewilderment of details.

It is astonishing what imprudent language a public man may sometimes use in free countries, and especially in democratic states, without being compromised; whereas in absolute monarchies, a few words dropped by accident are enough to unmask him for ever, and ruin him without hope of redemption. This is explained by what goes before. When a man speaks in the midst of a great crowd, many of his words are not heard, or are forthwith obliterated from the memories of those who hear them; but amid the silence of a mute and motionless throng, the slightest whisper strikes the ear.

In democracies men are never stationary; a thousand chances waft them to and fro, and their life is always the sport of unforeseen or (so to speak) extemporaneous circumstances. Thus they are often obliged to do things which they have imperfectly learned, to say things they imperfectly understand, and to devote themselves to work for which they are unprepared by long apprenticeship. In aristocracies every man has one sole object which he unceasingly pursues, but among democratic nations the existence of man is more complex; the same mind will almost always embrace several objects at the same time, and these objects are frequently wholly foreign to each other: as it cannot know them all well, the mind is readily satisfied with imperfect notions of each.

When the inhabitant of democracies is not urged by his wants, he is so at least by his desires; for of all the possessions which he sees around him, none are wholly beyond his reach. He therefore does everything in a hurry, he is always satisfied with "pretty well," and never pauses more than an instant to consider what he has been doing. His curiosity is at once insatiable and cheaply satisfied; for he cares more to know a great deal quickly, than to know anything well: he has no time and but little taste to search things to the bottom.

Thus then democratic peoples are grave, because their social and political condition constantly leads them to engage in serious occupations; and they act inconsiderately, because they give but little time and attention to each of these occupations.

The habit of inattention must be considered as the greatest bane of the democratic character.

Chapter XVI.

WHY THE NATIONAL VANITY OF THE AMERICANS IS MORE RESTLESS AND LESS CAPTIOUS THAN THAT OF THE ENGLISH.

All free nations are vainglorious, but national pride is not displayed by all in the same manner. The Americans in their intercourse with strangers appear impatient of the smallest censure and insatiable of praise. The most slender eulogium is acceptable to them, the most exalted seldom contents them; they unceasingly harass you to extort praise, and if you resist their entreaties they fall to praising themselves. It would seem as if, doubting their own merit, they wished to have it constantly exhibited before their eyes. Their vanity is not only greedy, but restless and jealous; it will grant nothing, while it demands everything, but is ready to beg and to quarrel at the same time.

If I say to an American that the country he lives in is a fine one, "Ay," he replies, "there is not its fellow in the world." If I applaud the freedom which its inhabitants enjoy, he answers, "Freedom is a fine thing, but few nations are worthy to enjoy it." If I remark the purity of morals which distinguishes the United States, "I can imagine," says he, "that a stranger who has been struck by the corruption of all other nations, is astonished at the difference." At length I leave him to the contemplation of himself; but he returns to the charge, and does not desist till he has got me to repeat all I had just been saying. It is impossible to conceive a more troublesome or more garrulous patriotism; it wearies even those who are disposed to respect it.*

Such is not the case with the English. An Englishman calmly enjoys the real or imaginary advantages which in his opinion his country possesses. If he grants nothing to other nations, neither does he solicit anything for his own. The censure of foreigners does not affect him, and their praise hardly flatters him; his position with regard to the rest of the world is one of disdainful and ignorant reserve: his pride requires no sustenance, it nourishes itself. It is remarkable that two nations, so recently sprung from the same stock, should be so opposite to one another in their manner of feeling and conversing.

In aristocratic countries the great possess immense privileges, upon which their pride rests, without seeking to rely upon the lesser advan-

---

* Setting aside all those who do not think at all, and those who dare not say what they think, the immense majority of the Americans will still be found to appear satisfied with the political institutions by which they are governed; and, I believe, really to be so. I look upon this state of public opinion as an indication, but not as a demonstration, of the absolute excellence of American laws. The pride of a nation, the gratification of certain ruling passions by the law, a concourse of circumstances, defects which escape notice, and more than all the rest, the influence of a majority which shuts the mouth of all cavillers, may long perpetuate the delusions of a people as well as those of a man.

Look at England throughout the eighteenth century. No nation was ever more prodigal of self-applause, no people was ever more self-satisfied; then every part of its constitution was right—everything, even to its most obvious defects, was irreproachable: at the present day a vast number of Englishmen seem to have nothing better to do than to prove that this constitution was faulty in many respects. Which was right?—the English people of the last century, or the English people of the present day?

The same thing has occurred in France. It is certain that during the reign of Louis XIV. the great bulk of the nation was devotedly attached to the form of government which, at that time, governed the community. But it is a vast error to suppose that there was anything degraded in the character of the French of that age. There might be some sort of servitude in France at that time, but assuredly there was no servile spirit among the people. The writers of that age felt a species of genuine enthusiasm in extolling the power of their king; and there was no peasant so obscure in his hovel as not to take a pride in the glory of his sovereign, and to die cheerfully with the cry "Vive le Roi" upon his lips. These very same forms of loyalty are now odious to the French people. Which are wrong?—the French of the age of Louis XIV., or their descendants of the present day?

Our judgement of the laws of a people must not then be founded exclusively upon its inclinations, since those inclinations change from age to age; but upon more elevated principles and a more general experience. The love which a people may show for its laws, proves only this:—that we should not be in too great a hurry to change them.

tages which accrue to them. As these privileges came to them by inheritance, they regard them in some sort as a portion of themselves, or at least as a natural right inherent in their own persons. They therefore entertain a calm sense of their superiority; they do not dream of vaunting privileges which every one perceives and no one contests, and these things are not sufficiently new to them to be made topics of conversation. They stand unmoved in their solitary greatness, well assured that they are seen of all the world without any effort to show themselves off, and that no one will attempt to drive them from that position. When an aristocracy carries on the public affairs, its national pride naturally assumes this reserved, indifferent, and haughty form, which is imitated by all the other classes of the nation.

When on the contrary social conditions differ but little, the slightest privileges are of some importance; as every man sees around himself a million of people enjoying precisely similar or analogous advantages, his pride becomes craving and jealous, he clings to mere trifles, and doggedly defends them. In democracies, as the conditions of life are very fluctuating, men have almost always recently acquired the advantages which they possess; the consequence is that they feel extreme pleasure in exhibiting them, to show others and convince themselves that they really enjoy them. As at any instant these same advantages may be lost, their possessors are constantly on the alert, and make a point of showing that they still retain them. Men living in democracies love their country just as they love themselves, and they transfer the habits of their private vanity to their vanity as a nation.

The restless and insatiable vanity of a democratic people originates so entirely in the equality and precariousness of social conditions, that the members of the haughtiest nobility display the very same passion in those lesser portions of their existence in which there is anything fluctuating or contested. An aristocratic class always differs greatly from the other classes of the nation, by the extent and perpetuity of its privileges; but it often happens that the only differences between the members who belong to it consist in small transient advantages, which may any day be lost or acquired.

The members of a powerful aristocracy, collected in a capital or a court, have been known to contest with virulence those frivolous privileges which depend on the caprice of fashion or the will of their master. These persons then displayed toward each other precisely the same puerile jealousies which animate the men of democracies, the same eagerness to snatch the smallest advantages which their equals contested, and the same desire to parade ostentatiously those of which they were in possession.

If national pride ever entered into the minds of courtiers, I do not question that they would display it in the same manner as the members of a democratic community.

Chapter XVII.

THAT THE ASPECT OF SOCIETY IN THE UNITED STATES IS AT ONCE EXCITED AND MONOTONOUS.

It would seem that nothing can be more adapted to stimulate and to feed curiosity than the aspect of the United States. Fortunes, opinions, and laws are there in ceaseless variation: it is as if immutable Nature herself were mutable, such are the changes worked upon her by the hand of man. Yet in the end the sight of this excited community becomes monotonous, and after having watched the moving pageant for a time the spectator is tired of it.

Among aristocratic nations every man is pretty nearly stationary in his own sphere; but men are astonishingly unlike each other—their passions, their notions, their habits, and their tastes are essentially different; nothing changes, but everything differs. In democracies, on the contrary, all men are alike and do things pretty nearly alike. It is true that they are subject to great and frequent vicissitudes; but as the same events of good or adverse fortune are continually recurring, the name of the actors only is changed, the piece is always the same. The aspect of American society is animated, because men and things are always changing; but it is monotonous, because all these changes are alike.

Men living in democratic ages have many passions, but most of their passions either end in the love of riches or proceed from it. The cause of this is, not that their souls are narrower, but that the importance of money is really greater at such times. When all the members of a community are independent of or indifferent to each other, the co-operation of each of them can only be obtained by paying for it: this infinitely multiplies the purposes to which wealth may be applied, and increases its value. When the reverence which belonged to what is old has vanished, birth, condition, and profession no longer distinguish men, or scarcely distinguish them at all: hardly anything but money remains to create strongly marked differences between them, and to raise some of them above the common level. The distinction originating in wealth is increased by the disappearance and diminution of all other distinctions. Among aristocratic nations money only reaches to a few points on the vast circle of man's desires—in democracies it seems to lead to all.

The love of wealth is therefore to be traced, either as a principal or an accessory motive, at the bottom of all that the Americans do: this gives to all their passions a sort of family likeness, and soon renders the survey of them exceedingly wearisome. This perpetual recurrence of the same passion is monotonous; the peculiar methods by which this passion seeks its own gratification are no less so.

In an orderly and constituted democracy like the United States, where men cannot enrich themselves by war, by public office, or by political confiscation, the love of wealth mainly drives them into business and manufactures. Although these pursuits often bring about great commotions and disasters, they cannot prosper without strictly regular habits and a long routine of petty uniform acts. The stronger the passion is, the more regular are these habits, and the more uniform are these acts. It may be said that it is the vehemence of their desires which makes the Americans so methodical; it perturbs their minds, but it disciplines their lives.

The remark I here apply to America may indeed be addressed to almost all our contemporaries. Variety is disappearing from the human race; the same ways of acting, thinking, and feeling are to be met with all over the world. This is not only because nations work more upon each other, and are more faithful in their mutual imitation; but as the men of each country relinquish more and more the peculiar opinions and feelings of a caste, a profession, or a family, they simultaneously arrive at something nearer to the constitution of Man, which is everywhere the same. Thus they become more alike, even without having imitated each other. Like travellers scattered about some large wood, which is intersected by paths converging to one point, if all of them keep their eyes fixed upon that point and advance toward it, they insensibly draw nearer together—though they seek not, though they see not, though they know not each other; and they will be surprised at length to find themselves all collected on the same spot. All the nations which take, not any particular man, but Man himself, as the object of their researches and their imitations, are tending in the end to a similar state of society, like these travellers converging to the central plot of the forest.

Chapter XVIII.

OF HONOUR* IN THE UNITED STATES AND IN DEMOCRATIC COMMUNITIES.

It would seem that men employ two very distinct methods in the public estimation of the actions of their fellow-men; at one time they judge them by those simple notions of right and wrong which are diffused all over the world; at another they refer their decision to a few very special notions which belong exclusively to some particular age and country. It often happens that these two rules differ; they sometimes conflict; but they are never either entirely identified or entirely annulled by one another.

Honour, at the periods of its greatest power, sways the will more than the belief of men; and even while they yield without hesitation and without a murmur to its dictates, they feel notwithstanding, by a dim but mighty instinct, the existence of a more general, more an-

---

* The word Honour is not always used in the same sense either in French or English. 1. It first signifies the dignity, glory, or reverence which a man receives from his kind; and in this sense a man is said to acquire honour. 2. Honour signifies the aggregate of those rules by the assistance of which this dignity, glory, or reverence is obtained. Thus we say that a man has always strictly obeyed the law's honour; or a man has violated his honour. In this chapter the word is always used in the latter sense.

cient, and more holy law, which they sometimes disobey although they cease not to acknowledge it. Some actions have been held to be at the same time virtuous and dishonourable—a refusal to fight a duel is a case in point.

I think these peculiarities may be otherwise explained than by the mere caprices of certain individuals and nations, as has hitherto been the customary mode of reasoning on the subject. Mankind is subject to general and lasting wants that have engendered moral laws, to the neglect of which men have ever and in all places attached the notion of censure and shame: to infringe them was *to do ill—to do well* was to conform to them.

Within the bosom of this vast association of the human race, lesser associations have been formed which are called nations; and amid these nations further subdivisions have assumed the names of classes or castes. Each of these associations forms, as it were, a separate species of the human race; and though it has no essential difference from the mass of mankind, to a certain extent it stands apart and has certain wants peculiar to itself. To these special wants must be attributed the modifications which affect in various degrees and in different countries the mode of considering human actions, and the estimate which ought to be formed of them. It is the general and permanent interest of mankind that men should not kill each other; but it may happen to be the peculiar and temporary interest of a people or a class to justify, or even to honour, homicide.

Honour is simply that peculiar rule, founded upon a peculiar state of society, by the application of which a people or a class allot praise or blame. Nothing is more unproductive to the mind than an abstract idea; I therefore hasten to call in the aid of facts and examples to illustrate my meaning.

I select the most extraordinary kind of honour which was ever known in the world, and that which we are best acquainted with, viz. aristocratic honour springing out of feudal society. I shall explain it by means of the principle already laid down, and I shall explain the principle by means of the illustration.

I am not here led to inquire when and how the aristocracy of the middle ages came into existence, why it was so deeply severed from the remainder of the nation, or what founded and consolidated its power. I take its existence as an established fact, and I am endeavouring to account for the peculiar view which it took of the greater part of human actions.

The first thing that strikes me is, that in the feudal world actions were not always praised or blamed with reference to their intrinsic worth, but that they were sometimes appreciated exclusively with reference to the person who was the actor or the object of them, which is repugnant to the general conscience of mankind. Thus some of the actions which were indifferent on the part of a man in humble life, dishonoured a noble; others changed their whole character according as the person aggrieved by them belonged or did not belong to the aristocracy.

When these different notions first arose, the nobility formed a distinct body amid the people, which it commanded from the inaccessible heights where it was ensconced. To maintain this peculiar position, which constituted its strength, it not only required political privileges, but it required a standard of right and wrong for its own especial use.

That some particular virtue or vice belonged to the nobility rather than to the humble classes—that certain actions were guiltless when they affected the villain, which were criminal when they touched the noble—these were often arbitrary matters; but that honour or shame should be attached to a man's actions according to his condition, was the result of the internal constitution of an aristocratic community. This has been actually the case in all the countries which have had an aristocracy; as long as a trace of the principle remains, these peculiarities will still exist: to debauch a woman of colour scarcely injures the reputation of an American—to marry her dishonours him.

In some cases feudal honour enjoined revenge and stigmatized the forgiveness of insults; in others it imperiously commanded men to conquer their own passions, and imposed forgetfulness of self. It did not make humanity or kindness its law, but it extolled generosity; it set more store on liberality than on benevolence; it allowed men to enrich themselves by gambling or by war, but not by labour; it preferred great crimes to small earnings; cupidity was less distasteful to it than avarice; violence it often sanctioned, but cunning and treachery it invariably reprobated as contemptible.

These fantastical notions did not proceed exclusively from the caprices of those who entertained them. A class which has succeeded in placing itself at the head of and above all others, and which makes perpetual exertions to maintain this lofty position, must especially honour those virtues which are conspicuous for their dignity and splendour, and which may be easily combined with pride and the love of power. Such men would not hesitate to invert the natural order of the conscience in order to give those virtues precedence before all others. It may even be conceived that some of the more bold and brilliant vices would readily be set above the quiet unpretending virtues. The very existence of such a class in society renders these things unavoidable.

The nobles of the middle ages placed military courage foremost among virtues, and in lieu of many of them. This was again a peculiar opinion which arose necessarily from the peculiarity of the state of society. Feudal aristocracy existed by war and for war; its power had been founded by arms, and by arms that power was maintained; it therefore required nothing more than military courage, and that quality was naturally exalted above all others; whatever denoted it, even at the expense of reason and humanity, was therefore approved and frequently enjoined by the manners of the time. Such was the main principle; the caprice of man was only to be traced in minuter details. That a man should regard a tap on the cheek as an unbearable insult, and should be obliged to kill in single combat the person who struck him thus lightly, is an arbitrary rule; but that a noble could not tranquilly receive an insult, and was dishonoured if he allowed himself to take a blow without fighting, were direct consequences of the fundamental principles and the wants of a military aristocracy.

Thus it was true to a certain extent to assert that the laws of honour were capricious; but these caprices of honour were always confined within certain necessary limits. The peculiar rule, which was called honour by our forefathers, is so far from being an arbitrary law in my eyes, that I would readily engage to ascribe its most incoherent and fantastical injunctions to a small number of fixed and invariable wants inherent in feudal society.

If I were to trace the notion of feudal honour into the domain of politics, I should not find it more difficult to explain its dictates. The state of society and the political institutions of the middle ages were such, that the supreme power of the nation never governed the community directly. That power did not exist in the eyes of the people: every man looked up to a certain individual whom he was bound to obey; by that intermediate personage he was connected with all the others. Thus in feudal society the whole system of the commonwealth rested upon the sentiment of fidelity to the person of the lord: to destroy that sentiment was to open the sluices of anarchy. Fidelity to a political superior was, moreover, a sentiment of which all the members of the aristocracy had constant opportunities of estimating the importance; for every one of them was a vassal as well as a lord, and had to command as well as to obey. To remain faithful to the lord, to sacrifice oneself for him if called upon, to share his good or evil fortunes, to stand by him in his undertakings whatever they might be— such were the first injunctions of feudal honour in relation to the political institutions of those times. The treachery of a vassal was branded with extraordinary severity by public opinion, and a name of peculiar infamy was invented for the offence which was called *felony*.

On the contrary, few traces are to be found in the middle ages of the passion which constituted the life of the nations of antiquity—I mean patriotism—the word itself is not of very ancient date in the language.* Feudal institutions concealed the country at large from men's sight, and rendered the love of it less necessary. The nation was forgotten in the passions which attached men to persons. Hence it was no part of the strict law of feudal honour to remain faithful to one's country. Not indeed that the love of their country did not exist in the hearts of our forefathers; but it constituted a dim and feeble instinct, which has grown more clear and strong in proportion as aristocratic classes have been abolished and the supreme power of the nation centralized.

This may be clearly seen from the contrary judgements which European nations have passed upon the various events of their histories, according to the generations by which such judgements have been formed. The circumstance which most dishonoured the Constable de Bourbon in the eyes of his contemporaries was that he bore arms against his king: that which most dishonours him in our eyes, is that

---

* Even the word *patrie* was not used by the French writers until the sixteenth century.

he made war against his country; we brand him as deeply as our forefathers did, but for different reasons.

I have chosen the honour of feudal times by way of illustration of my meaning, because its characteristics are more distinctly marked and more familiar to us than those of any other period; but I might have taken an example elsewhere, and I should have reached the same conclusion by a different road.

Although we are less perfectly acquainted with the Romans than with our own ancestors, yet we know that certain peculiar notions of glory and disgrace obtained among them, which were not solely derived from the general principles of right and wrong. Many human actions were judged differently, according as they affected a Roman citizen or a stranger, a freeman or a slave; certain vices were blazoned abroad, certain virtues were extolled above all others. "In that age," says Plutarch in the life of Coriolanus, "martial prowess was more honoured and prized in Rome than all the other virtues, insomuch that it was called *virtus*, the name of virtue itself, by applying the name of the kind to this particular species; so that virtue in Latin was as much as to say valour." Can any one fail to recognise the peculiar want of that singular community which was formed for the conquest of the world?

Any nation would furnish us with similar grounds of observation; for, as I have already remarked, whenever men collect together as a distinct community, the notion of honour instantly grows up among them; that is to say, a system of opinions peculiar to themselves as to what is blameable or commendable; and these peculiar rules always originate in the special habits and special interests of the community.

This is applicable to a certain extent to democratic communities as well as to others, as we shall now proceed to prove by the example of the Americans.*

Some loose notions of the old aristocratic honour of Europe are still to be found scattered among the opinions of the Americans; but these traditional opinions are few in number, they have but little root in the country, and but little power. They are like a religion which has still some temples left standing, though men have ceased to believe in it. But amid these half-obliterated notions of exotic honour, some new opinions have sprung up, which constitute what may be termed in our days American honour.

I have shown how the Americans are constantly driven to engage in commerce and industry. Their origin, their social condition, their political institutions, and even the spot they inhabit, urges them irresistibly in this direction. Their present condition is then that of an almost exclusively manufacturing and commercial association, placed in the midst of a new and boundless country, which their principal object is to explore for purposes of profit. This is the characteristic which most peculiarly distinguishes the American people from all others at the present time.

---

* I speak here of the Americans inhabiting those States where slavery does not exist; they alone can be said to present a complete picture of democratic society.

All those quiet virtues which tend to give a regular movement to the community, and to encourage business, will therefore be held in peculiar honour by that people, and to neglect those virtues will be to incur public contempt. All the more turbulent virtues, which often dazzle, but more frequently disturb society, will on the contrary occupy a subordinate rank in the estimation of this same people: they may be neglected without forfeiting the esteem of the community—to acquire them would perhaps be to run a risk of losing it.

The Americans make a no less arbitrary classification of men's vices. There are certain propensities which appear censurable to the general reason and the universal conscience of mankind, but which happen to agree with the peculiar and temporary wants of the American community: these propensities are lightly reproved, sometimes even encouraged; for instance, the love of wealth and the secondary propensities connected with it may be more particularly cited. To clear, to till, and to transform the vast uninhabited continent which is his domain, the American requires the daily support of an energetic passion; that passion can only be the love of wealth; the passion for wealth is therefore not reprobated in America, and provided it does not go beyond the bounds assigned to it for public security, it is held in honour. The American lauds as a noble and praiseworthy ambition what our own forefathers in the middle ages stigmatized as servile cupidity, just as he treats as a blind and barbarous frenzy that ardour of conquest and martial temper which bore them to battle.

In the United States fortunes are lost and regained without difficulty; the country is boundless, and its resources inexhaustible. The people have all the wants and cravings of a growing creature; and whatever be their efforts, they are always surrounded by more than they can appropriate. It is not the ruin of a few individuals which may be soon repaired, but the inactivity and sloth of the community at large which would be fatal to such a people. Boldness of enterprise is the foremost cause of its rapid progress, its strength, and its greatness. Commercial business is there like a vast lottery, by which a small number of men continually lose, but the State is always a gainer; such a people ought therefore to encourage and do honour to boldness in commercial speculations. But any bold speculation risks the fortune of the speculator and of all those who put their trust in him. The Americans, who make a virtue of commercial temerity, have no right in any case to brand with disgrace those who practise it. Hence arises the strange indulgence which is shown to bankrupts in the United States; their honour does not suffer by such an accident. In this respect the Americans differ, not only from the nations of Europe, but from all the commercial nations of our time, and accordingly they resemble none of them in their position or their wants.

In America all those vices which tend to impair the purity of morals, and to destroy the conjugal tie, are treated with a degree of severity which is unknown in the rest of the world. At first sight this seems strangely at variance with the tolerance shown there on other subjects, and one is surprised to meet with a morality so relaxed and so austere among the self-same people. But these things are less incoherent than they seem to be. Public opinion in the United States very gently represses that love of wealth which promotes the commercial greatness and the prosperity of the nation, and it especially condemns that laxity of morals which diverts the human mind from the pursuit of well-being, and disturbs the internal order of domestic life which is so necessary to success in business. To earn the esteem of their countrymen, the Americans are therefore constrained to adapt themselves to orderly habits, and it may be said in this sense that they make it a matter of honour to live chastely.

On one point American honour accords with the notions of honour acknowledged in Europe; it places courage as the highest virtue, and treats it as the greatest of the moral necessities of man; but the notion of courage itself assumes a different aspect. In the United States martial valour is but little prized; the courage which is best known and most esteemed is that which emboldens men to brave the dangers of the ocean, in order to arrive earlier in port—to support the privations of the wilderness without complaint, and solitude more cruel than privations—the courage which renders them almost insensible to the loss of a fortune laboriously acquired, and instantly prompts to fresh exertions to make another. Courage of this kind is peculiarly necessary to the maintenance and prosperity of the American communities, and it is held by them in peculiar honour and estimation; to betray a want of it is to incur certain disgrace.

I have yet another characteristic point which may serve to place the idea of this chapter in strong relief. In a democratic society like that of the United States, where fortunes are scanty and insecure, every body works, and work opens a way to every thing: this has changed the point of honour quite round, and has turned it against idleness. I have sometimes met in America with young men of wealth, personally disinclined to all laborious exertion, but who had been compelled to embrace a profession. Their disposition and their fortune allowed them to remain without employment; public opinion forbade it, too imperiously to be disobeyed. In the European countries, on the contrary, where aristocracy is still struggling with the flood which overwhelms it, I have often seen men, constantly spurred on by their wants and desires, remain in idleness, in order not to lose the esteem of their equals; and I have known them submit to ennui and privations rather than to work. No one can fail to perceive that these opposite obligations are two different rules of conduct, both nevertheless originating in the notion of honour.

What our forefathers designated as honour absolutely was in reality only one of its forms; they gave a generic name to what was only a species. Honour therefore is to be found in democratic as well as in aristocratic ages, but it will not be difficult to show that it assumes a different aspect in the former. Not only are its injunctions different, but we shall shortly see that they are less numerous, less precise, and that its dictates are less rigorously obeyed.

The position of a caste is always much more peculiar than that of a people. Nothing is so much out of the way of the world as a small community invariably composed of the same families, (as was for instance the aristocracy of the middle ages) whose object is to concentrate and to retain, exclusively and hereditarily, education, wealth, and power among its own members. But the more out of the way the position of a community happens to be, the more numerous are its special wants, and the more extensive are its notions of honour corresponding to those wants.

The rules of honour will therefore always be less numerous among a people not divided into castes than among any other. If ever any nations are constituted in which it may even be difficult to find any peculiar classes of society, the notion of honour will be confined to a small number of precepts, which will be more and more in accordance with the moral laws adopted by the mass of mankind.

Thus the laws of honour will be less peculiar and less multifarious among a democratic people than in an aristocracy. They will also be more obscure; and this is a necessary consequence of what goes before; for as the distinguishing marks of honour are less numerous and less peculiar, it must often be difficult to distinguish them. To this other reasons may be added. Among the aristocratic nations of the middle ages, generation succeeded generation in vain; each family was like a never-dying, ever-stationary man, and the state of opinions was hardly more changeable than that of conditions. Every one then had always the same objects always before his eyes, which he contemplated from the same point; his eyes gradually detected the smallest details, and his discernment could not fail to become in the end clear and accurate. Thus not only had the men of feudal times very extraordinary opinions in matters of honour, but each of those opinions was present to their minds under a clear and precise form.

This can never be the case in America, where all men are in constant motion; and where society, transformed daily by its own operations, changes its opinions together with its wants. In such a country men have glimpses of the rules of honour, but they have seldom time to fix attention upon them.

But even if society were motionless, it would still be difficult to determine the meaning which ought to be attached to the word honour. In the middle ages, as each class had its own honour, the same opinion was never received at the same time by a large number of men; and this rendered it possible to give it a determined and accurate form, which was the more easy, as all those by whom it was received, having a perfectly identical and most peculiar position, were naturally disposed to agree upon the points of a law which was made for themselves alone.

Thus the code of honour became a complete and detailed system, in which everything was anticipated and provided for beforehand, and a fixed and always palpable standard was applied to human actions. Among a democratic nation, like the Americans, in which ranks are identified, and the whole of society forms one single mass, composed of elements which are all analogous though not entirely similar, it is impossible ever to agree beforehand on what shall or shall not be allowed by the laws of honour.

Among that people, indeed, some national wants do exist which give rise to opinions common to the whole nation on points of honour: but these opinions never occur at the same time, in the same manner, or with the same intensity to the minds of the whole community; the law of honour exists, but it has no organs to promulgate it.

The confusion is far greater still in a democratic country like France, where the different classes of which the former fabric of society was composed, being brought together but not yet mingled, import day by day into each other's circles, various, and sometimes conflicting notions of honour—where every man, at his own will and pleasure, forsakes one portion of his forefather's creed, and retains another; so that, amid so many arbitrary measures, no common rule can ever be established, and it is almost impossible to predict which actions will be held in honour and which will be thought disgraceful. Such times are wretched, but they are of short duration.

As honour, among democratic nations, is imperfectly defined, its influence is of course less powerful; for it is difficult to apply with certainty and firmness a law which is not distinctly known. Public opinion, the natural and supreme interpreter of the laws of honour, not clearly discerning to which side censure or approval ought to lean, can only pronounce a hesitating judgement. Sometimes the opinion of the public may contradict itself; more frequently it does not act, and lets things pass.

The weakness of the sense of honour in democracies also arises from several other causes. In aristocratic countries, the same notions of honour are always entertained by only a few persons, always limited in number, often separated from the rest of their fellow-citizens. Honour is easily mingled and identified in their minds with the idea of all that distinguishes their own position; it appears to them as the chief characteristic of their own rank; they apply its different rules with all the warmth of personal interest, and they feel, (if I may use the expression,) a passion for complying with its dictates.

This truth is extremely obvious in the old black-letter law books on the subject of trial by battel. The nobles, in their disputes, were bound to use the lance and sword; whereas the villains used only sticks among themselves, "inasmuch as," to use the words of the old books, "villains have no honour." This did not mean, as it may be imagined at the present day, that these people were contemptible; but simply that their actions were not to be judged by the same rules which were applied to the actions of the aristocracy.

It is surprising, at first sight, that when the sense of honour is most predominant, its injunctions are usually most strange; so that the farther it is removed from common reason, the better it is obeyed; whence it has sometimes been inferred, that the laws of honour were strengthened by their own extravagance. The two things indeed originate from the same source, but the one is not derived from the other. Honour becomes fantastical in proportion to the peculiarity of the wants which it denotes, and the paucity of the men by whom those wants are felt; and it is because it denotes wants of this kind that its influence is great. Thus the notion of honour is not the stronger for being fantastical, but it is fantastical and strong from the self-same cause.

Farther, among aristocratic nations each rank is different, but all ranks are fixed; every man occupies a place in his own sphere which he cannot relinquish, and he lives there amid other men who are bound by the same ties. Among these nations no man can either hope or fear to escape being seen; no man is placed so low but that he has a stage of his own, and none can avoid censure or applause by his obscurity.

In democratic states on the contrary, where all the members of the community are mingled in the same crowd and in constant agitation, public opinion has no hold on men; they disappear at every instant, and elude its power. Consequently the dictates of honour will be there less imperious and less stringent; for honour acts solely for the public eye—differing in this respect from mere virtue, which lives upon itself contented with its own approval.

If the reader has distinctly apprehended all that goes before, he will understand that there is a close and necessary relations between the inequality of social conditions and what has here been styled honour—a relation which, if I am not mistaken, had not before been clearly pointed out. I shall therefore make one more attempt to illustrate it satisfactorily.

Suppose a nation stands apart from the rest of mankind: independently of certain general wants inherent in the human race, it will also have wants and interests peculiar to itself: certain opinions of censure or approbation forthwith arise in the community, which are peculiar to itself, and which are styled honour by the members of that community. Now suppose that in this same nation a caste arises, which, in its turn, stands apart from all the other classes, and contracts certain peculiar wants, which give rise in their turn to special opinions. The honour of this caste, composed of a medley of the peculiar notions of the nation, and the still more peculiar notions of the caste, will be as remote as it is possible to conceive from the simple and general opinions of men.

Having reached this extreme point of the argument, I now return.

When ranks are commingled and privileges abolished, the men of whom a nation is composed being once more equal and alike, their interests and wants become identical, and all the peculiar notions which each caste styled honour successively disappear: the notion of honour no longer proceeds from any other source than the wants peculiar to the nation at large, and it denotes the individual character of that nation to the world.

Lastly, if it be allowable to suppose that all the races of mankind should be commingled, and that all the peoples of earth should ultimately come to have the same interests, the same wants, undistinguished from each other by any characteristic peculiarities, no conventional value whatever would then be attached to men's actions; they would all be regarded by all in the same light; the general necessities of mankind, revealed by conscience to every man, would become the common standard. The simple and general notions of right and wrong only would then be recognized in the world, to which, by a natural and necessary tie, the idea of censure or approbation would be attached.

Thus, to comprise all my meaning in a single proposition, the dissimilarities and inequalities of men gave rise to the notion of honour; that notion is weakened in proportion as these differences are obliterated, and with them it would disappear.

Chapter XIX.

WHY SO MANY AMBITIOUS MEN, AND SO LITTLE LOFTY AMBITION, ARE TO BE FOUND IN THE UNITED STATES.

The first thing which strikes a traveller in the United States is the innumerable multitude of those who seek to throw off their original condition; and the second is the rarity of lofty ambition to be observed in the midst of the universally ambitious stir of society. No Americans are devoid of a yearning desire to rise; but hardly any appear to entertain hopes of great magnitude, or to drive at very lofty aims. All are constantly seeking to acquire property, power, and reputation—few contemplate these things upon a great scale; and this is the more surprising, as nothing is to be discerned in the manners or laws of America, to limit desire or to prevent it from spreading its impulses in every direction. It seems difficult to attribute this singular state of things to the equality of social conditions; for at the instant when that same equality was established in France, the flight of ambition became unbounded. Nevertheless I think that the principal cause which may be assigned to this fact is to be found in the social condition and democratic manners of the Americans.

All revolutions enlarge the ambition of men: this proposition is more peculiarly true of those revolutions which overthrow an aristocracy. When the former barriers which kept back the multitude from fame and power are suddenly thrown down, a violent and universal rise takes place toward that eminence so long coveted and at length to be enjoyed. In this first burst of triumph nothing seems impossible to any one: not only are desires boundless, but the power of satisfying them seems almost boundless too. Amid the general and sudden renewal of laws and customs, in this vast confusion of all men and all ordinances, the various members of the community rise and sink again with excessive rapidity, and power passes so quickly from hand to hand that none need despair of catching it in turn.

It must be recollected, moreover, that the people who destroy an aristocracy have lived under its laws; they have witnessed its splendour, and they have unconsciously imbibed the feelings and notions which it entertained. Thus at the moment when an aristocracy is dissolved, its spirit still pervades the mass of the community, and its tendencies are retained long after it has been defeated. Ambition is therefore always extremely great as long as a democratic revolution lasts, and it will remain so for some time after the revolution is consummated.

The reminiscence of the extraordinary events which men have witnessed is not obliterated from their memory in a day. The passions which a revolution has roused do not disappear at its close. A sense of instability remains in the midst of re-established order: a notion of easy success survives the strange vicissitudes which gave it birth; desires still remain extremely enlarged, when the means of satisfying them are diminished day by day. The taste for large fortunes subsists, though large fortunes are rare; and on every side we trace the ravages of inordinate and hapless ambition kindled in hearts which they consume in secret and in vain.

At length however the last vestiges of the struggle are effaced; the remains of aristocracy completely disappear; the great events by which its fall was attended are forgotten; peace succeeds to war, and the sway of order is restored in the new realm; desires are again adapted to the means by which they may be fulfilled; the wants, the opinions, and the feelings of men cohere once more; the level of the community is permanently determined, and democratic society established.

A democratic nation, arrived at this permanent and regular state of things, will present a very different spectacle from that which we have just described; and we may readily conclude that, if ambition becomes great while the conditions of society are growing equal, it loses that quality when they have grown so.

As wealth is subdivided and knowledge diffused, no one is entirely destitute of education or of property; the privileges and disqualifications of caste being abolished, and men having shattered the bonds which held them fixed, the notion of advancement suggests itself to every mind, the desire to rise swells in every heart, and all men want to mount above their station: ambition is the universal feeling.

But if the equality of conditions gives some resources to all the members of the community, it also prevents any of them from having resources of great extent; which necessarily circumscribes their desires within somewhat narrow limits. Thus among democratic nations ambition is ardent and continual, but its aim is not habitually lofty; and life is generally spent in eagerly coveting small objects which are within reach.

What chiefly diverts the men of democracies from lofty ambition is not the scantiness of their fortunes, but the vehemence of the exertions they daily make to improve them. They strain their faculties to the utmost to achieve paltry results, and this cannot fail speedily to limit their discernment and to circumscribe their powers. They might be much poorer and still be greater.

The small number of opulent citizens who are to be found amidst a democracy do not constitute an exception to this rule. A man who raises himself by degrees to wealth and power contracts, in the course of this protracted labour, habits of prudence and restraint which he cannot afterward shake off. A man cannot enlarge his mind as he would his house.

The same observation is applicable to the sons of such a man; they are born, it is true, in a lofty position, but their parents were humble; they have grown up amidst feelings and notions which they cannot afterward easily get rid of; and it may be presumed that they will inherit the propensities of their father as well as his wealth.

It may happen, on the contrary, that the poorest scion of a powerful aristocracy may display vast ambition, because the traditional opinions of his race and the general spirit of his order still buoy him up for some time above his fortune.

Another thing which prevents the men of democratic periods from easily indulging in the pursuit of lofty objects, is the lapse of time which they foresee must take place before they can be ready to approach them. "It is a great advantage," says Pascal, "to be a man of quality, since it brings one man as forward at eighteen or twenty as another man would be at fifty, which is a clear gain of thirty years." Those thirty years are commonly wanting to the ambitious characters of democracies. The principle of equality, which allows every man to arrive at everything, prevents all men from rapid advancement.

In a democratic society, as well as elsewhere, there are only a certain number of great fortunes to be made; and as the paths which lead to them are indiscriminately open to all, the progress of all must necessarily be slackened. As the candidates appear to be nearly alike, and as it is difficult to make a selection without infringing the principle of equality, which is the supreme law of democratic societies, the first idea which suggests itself is to make them all advance at the same rate and submit to the same probation. Thus in proportion as men become more alike, and the principle of equality is more peaceably and deeply infused into the institutions and manners of the country, the rules of advancement become more inflexible, advancement itself slower, the difficulty of arriving quickly at a certain height far greater. From hatred of privilege and from the embarrassment of choosing, all men are at last constrained, whatever may be their standard, to pass the same ordeal; all are indiscriminately subjected to a multitude of petty preliminary exercises, in which their youth is wasted and their imagination quenched; so that they despair of ever fully attaining what is held out to them; and when at length they are in a condition to perform any extraordinary acts, the taste for such things has forsaken them.

In China, where the equality of conditions is exceedingly great and very ancient, no man passes from one public office to another without undergoing a probationary trial. This probation occurs afresh at every stage of his career; and the notion is now so rooted in the manners of the people, that I remember to have read a Chinese novel, in which the hero, after numberless crosses, succeeds at length in touching the heart of his mistress by taking honours. A lofty ambition breathes with difficulty in such an atmosphere.

The remark I apply to politics extends to everything: equality everywhere produces the same effects; where the laws of a country do not regulate and retard the advancement of men by positive enactment, competition attains the same end.

In a well established democratic community great and rapid elevation is therefore rare; it forms an exception to the common rule; and it is the singularity of such occurrences that makes men forget how rarely they happen.

Men living in democracies ultimately discover these things; they find out at last that the laws of their country open a boundless field of action before them, but that no one can hope to hasten across it. Between them and the final object of their desires, they perceive a multitude of small intermediate impediments, which must be slowly surmounted: this prospect wearies and discourages their ambition at once. They therefore give up hopes so doubtful and remote, to search nearer to themselves for less lofty and more easy enjoyments. Their horizon is not bounded by the laws, but narrowed by themselves.

I have remarked that lofty ambitions are more rare in the ages of democracy than in times of aristocracy: I may add, that when, in spite of these natural obstacles, they do spring into existence, their character is different. In aristocracies the career of ambition is often wide, but its boundaries are determined. In democracies ambition commonly ranges in a narrower field, but, if once it gets beyond that, hardly any limits can be assigned to it. As men are individually weak—as they live asunder, and in constant motion—as precedents are of little authority and laws but of short duration, resistance to novelty is languid, and the fabric of society never appears perfectly erect or firmly consolidated. So that, when once an ambitious man has the power in his grasp, there is nothing he may not dare; and when it is gone from him, he meditates the overthrow of the State to regain it. This gives to great political ambition a character of revolutionary violence, which it seldom exhibits to an equal degree in aristocratic communities. The common aspect of democratic nations will present a great number of small and very rational objects of ambition, from among which a few ill-controlled desires of a larger growth will at intervals break out: but no such a thing as ambition conceived and contrived on a vast scale is to be met with there.

I have shown elsewhere by what secret influence the principle of equality makes the passion for physical gratifications and the exclusive love of the present predominate in the human heart: these different propensities mingle with the sentiment of ambition, and tinge it, as it were, with their hues.

I believe that ambitious men in democracies are less engrossed than any others with the interests and the judgment of posterity; the present moment alone engages and absorbs them. They are more apt to complete a number of undertakings with rapidity, than to raise lasting monuments of their achievements; and they care much more for success than for fame. What they most ask of men is obedience—what they most covet is empire. Their manners have in almost all cases remained below the height of their station; the consequence is that they frequently carry very low tastes into their extraordinary fortunes, and that they seem to have acquired the supreme power only to minister to their coarse or paltry pleasures.

I think that in our time it is very necessary to cleanse, to regulate, and to adapt the feeling of ambition, but that it would be extremely dangerous to seek to impoverish and to repress it over much. We should attempt to lay down certain extreme limits, which it should never be allowed to outstep; but its range within those established limits should not be too much checked.

I confess that I apprehend much less for democratic society from the boldness than from the mediocrity of desires. What appears to me most to be dreaded, is that, in the midst of the small incessant occupations of private life, ambition should lose its vigour and its greatness—that the passions of man should abate, but at the same time be lowered; so that the march of society should every day become more tranquil and less aspiring.

I think then that the leaders of modern society would be wrong to seek to lull the community by a state of too uniform and too peaceful happiness; and that it is well to expose it from time to time to matters of difficulty and danger, in order to raise ambition and to give it a field of action.

Moralists are constantly complaining that the ruling vice of the present time is pride. This is true in one sense, for indeed no one thinks that he is not better than his neighbour, or consents to obey his superior; but it is extremely false in another; for the same man who cannot endure subordination or equality, has so contemptible an opinion of himself that he thinks he is only born to indulge in vulgar pleasures. He willingly takes up with low desires, without daring to embark in lofty enterprises, of which he scarcely dreams.

Thus, far from thinking that humility ought to be preached to our contemporaries, I would have endeavours made to give them a more enlarged idea of themselves and of their kind. Humility is unwholesome to them; what they most want is, in my opinion, pride. I would willingly exchange several of our small virtues for this one vice.

Chapter XX.

THE TRADE OF PLACE-HUNTING IN CERTAIN DEMOCRATIC COUNTRIES.

In the United States as soon as a man has acquired some education and pecuniary resources, he either endeavours to get rich by commerce or industry, or he buys land in the bush and turns pioneer. All that he asks of the State is not to be disturbed in his toil, and to be secure of his earnings. Among the greater part of European nations, when a man begins to feel his strength and to extend his desires, the first thing that occurs to him is to get some public employment. These opposite effects, originating in the same cause, deserve our passing notice.

When public employments are few in number, ill-paid and precarious, while the different lines of business are numerous and lucrative, it is to business, and not to official duties, that the new and eager desires engendered by the principle of equality turn from every side. But if, while the ranks of society are becoming more equal, the education of the people remains incomplete, or their spirit the reverse of bold— if commerce and industry, checked in their growth, afford only slow and arduous means of making a fortune—the various members of the community, despairing of ameliorating their own condition, rush to the head of the State and demand its assistance. To relieve their own necessities at the cost of the public treasury appears to them to be the easiest and most open, if not the only way they have to rise above a condition which no longer contents them; place-hunting becomes the most generally followed of all trades.

This must especially be the case, in those great centralized monarchies in which the number of paid offices is immense, and the tenure of them tolerably secure, so that no one despairs of obtaining a place, and of enjoying it as undisturbedly as an hereditary fortune.

I shall not remark that the universal and inordinate desire for place is a great social evil; that it destroys the spirit of independence in the citizen, and diffuses a venal and servile humour throughout the frame of society; that it stifles the manlier virtues: nor shall I be at the pains to demonstrate that this kind of traffic only creates an unproductive activity, which agitates the country without adding to its resources: all these things are obvious.

But I would observe, that a government which encourages this tendency risks its own tranquility and places its very existence in great jeopardy.

I am aware, that at a time like our own, when the love and respect which formerly clung to authority are seen gradually to decline, it may appear necessary to those in power to lay a closer hold on every man by his own interest, and it may seem convenient to use his own passions to keep him in order and in silence; but this cannot be so long, and what may appear to be a source of strength for a certain time will assuredly become in the end a great cause of embarrassment and weakness.

Among democratic nations, as well as elsewhere, the number of official appointments has in the end some limits; but, among those nations, the number of aspirants is unlimited; it perpetually increases, with a gradual and irresistible rise, in proportion as social conditions become more equal, and is only checked by the limits of the population.

Thus, when public employments afford the only outlet for ambition, the government necessarily meets with a permanent opposition at last; for it is tasked to satisfy with limited means unlimited desires. It is very certain that of all people in the world the most difficult to restrain and to manage are a people of solicitants. Whatever endeavours are made by rulers, such a people can never be contented; and it is always to be apprehended that they will ultimately overturn the constitution of the country, and change the aspect of the state, for the sole purpose of making a clearance of places.

The sovereigns of the present age who strive to fix upon themselves alone all those novel desires which are aroused by equality, and to satisfy them, will repent in the end, if I am not mistaken, that ever they embarked in this policy: they will one day discover that they have hazarded their own power, by making it so necessary; and that the more safe and honest course would have been to teach their subjects the art of providing for themselves.

Chapter XXI.

WHY GREAT REVOLUTIONS WILL BECOME MORE RARE.

A people which has existed for centuries under a system of castes and classes can only arrive at a democratic state of society by passing through a long series of more or less critical transformations, accomplished by violent efforts, and after numerous vicissitudes; in the course of which, property, opinions, and power are rapidly transferred from one hand to another. Even after this great revolution is consummated, the revolutionary habits engendered by it may long be traced, and it will be followed by deep commotion. As all this takes place at the very time at which social conditions are becoming more equal, it is inferred that some concealed relation and secret tie exists between the principle of equality itself and revolution, insomuch that the one cannot exist without giving rise to the other.

On this point reasoning may seem to lead to the same result as experience. Among a people whose ranks are nearly equal, no ostensible bond connects men together, or keeps them settled in their station. None of them have either a permanent right or power to command—none are forced by their condition to obey; but every man, finding himself possessed of some education and some resources, may choose his own path, and proceed apart from all his fellow-men. The same causes which make the members of the community independent of each other, continually impel them to new and restless desires, and constantly spur them onward. It therefore seems natural that, in a democratic community, men, things and opinions should be for ever changing their form and place, and that democratic ages should be times of rapid and incessant transformation.

But is this really the case? does the equality of social conditions habitually and permanently lead men to revolution? does that slate of society contain some perturbing principle which prevents the community from ever subsiding into calm, and disposes the citizens to alter incessantly their laws, their principles, and their manners? I do not believe it; and as the subject is important, I beg for the reader's close attention.

Almost all the revolutions which have changed the aspect of nations have been made to consolidate or to destroy social inequality. Remove the secondary causes which have produced the great convulsions of the world, and you will almost always find the principle of inequality at the bottom. Either the poor have attempted to plunder the rich, or the rich to enslave the poor. If then a state of society can ever be founded in which every man shall have something to keep, and little to take from others, much will have been done for the peace of the world.

I am aware that among a great democratic people there will always be some members of the community in great poverty, and others in great opulence: but the poor, instead of forming the immense majority of the nation, as is always the case in aristocratic communities, are comparatively few in number, and the laws do not bind them together by the ties of irremediable and hereditary penury.

The wealthy, on their side, are scarce and powerless; they have no privileges which attract public observation; even their wealth, as it is no longer incorporated and bound up with the soil, is impalpable, and as it were invisible. As there is no longer a race of poor men, so there is no longer a race of rich men; the latter spring up daily from the multitude, and relapse into it again. Hence they do not form a distinct class, which may be easily marked out and plundered; and, moreover, as they are connected with the mass of their fellow-citizens by a thousand secret ties, the people cannot assail them without inflicting an injury upon itself.

Between these two extremes of democratic communities stand an innumerable multitude of men almost alike, who, without being exactly either rich or poor, are possessed of sufficient property to desire the maintenance of order, yet not enough to excite envy. Such men are the natural enemies of violent commotions: their stillness keeps all beneath them and above them still, and secures the balance of the fabric of society.

Not indeed that even these men are contented with what they have gotten, or that they feel a natural abhorrence for a revolution in which they might share the spoil without sharing the calamity; on the contrary, they desire, with unexampled ardour, to get rich, but the difficulty is to know from whom riches can be taken. The same state of society which constantly prompts these desires, restrains these desires within necessary limits: it gives men more liberty of changing and less interest in change.

Not only are the men of democracies not naturally desirous of revolutions, but they are afraid of them. All revolutions more or less threaten the tenure of property: but most of those who live in democratic countries are possessed of property—not only are they possessed of property, but they live in the condition of men who set the greatest store upon their property.

If we attentively consider each of the classes of which society is composed, it is easy to see that the passions engendered by property are keenest and most tenacious among the middle classes. The poor often care but little for what they possess, because they suffer much more from the want of what they have not, than they enjoy the little they have. The rich have many other passions besides that of riches to satisfy; and, besides, the long and arduous enjoyment of a great fortune sometimes makes them in the end insensible to its charms. But the men who have a competency, alike removed from opulence and from penury, attach an enormous value to their possessions. As they are still almost within the reach of poverty, they see its privations near at hand, and dread them; between poverty and themselves there is nothing but a scanty fortune, upon which they immediately fix their apprehensions and their hopes. Every day increases the interest they take in it, by the constant cares which it occasions; and they are more attached to it by their continual exertions to increase the amount. The notion of surrendering the smallest part of it is insupportable to them, and they consider its total loss as the worst of misfortunes.

Now these eager and apprehensive men of small property constitute the class which is constantly increased by the equality of conditions. Hence, in democratic communities, the majority of the people do not clearly see what they have to gain by a revolution, but they continually and in a thousand ways feel that they might lose by one.

I have shown in another part of this work that the equality of conditions naturally urges men to embark in commercial and industrial pursuits, and that it tends to increase and to distribute real property: I have also pointed out the means by which it inspires every man with an eager and constant desire to increase his welfare. Nothing is more opposed to revolutionary passions than these things. It may happen that the final result of a revolution is favourable to commerce and manufactures; but its first consequence will almost always be the ruin of manufactures and mercantile men, because it must always change at once the general principles of consumption, and temporarily upset the existing proportion between supply and demand.

I know of nothing more opposite to revolutionary manners than commercial manners. Commerce is naturally adverse to all the violent passions; it loves to temporize, takes delight in compromise, and studiously avoids irritation. It is patient, insinuating, flexible, and never has recourse to extreme measures until obliged by the most absolute necessity. Commerce renders men independent of each other, gives them a lofty notion of their personal importance, leads them to seek to conduct their own affairs, and teaches how to conduct them well; it therefore prepares men for freedom, but preserves them from revolutions.

In a revolution the owners of personal property have more to fear than all others; for on the one hand their property is often easy to seize, and on the other it may totally disappear at any moment—a subject of alarm to which the owners of real property are less exposed, since, although they may lose the income of their estates, they may hope to preserve the land itself through the greatest vicissitudes. Hence the former are much more alarmed at the symptoms of revolutionary commotion than the latter. Thus nations are less disposed to make revolutions in proportion as personal property is augmented and distributed among them, and as the number of those possessing it is increased.

Moreover, whatever profession men may embrace, and whatever species of property they may possess, one characteristic is common to them all. No one is fully contented with his present fortune—all are perpetually striving, in a thousand ways, to improve it. Consider any one of them at any period of his life, and he will be found engaged with some new project for the purpose of increasing what he has; talk not to him of the interests and the rights of mankind, this small domestic concern absorbs for the time all his thoughts, and inclines him to defer political excitement to some other season. This not only prevents men from making revolutions, but deters men from desiring them. Violent political passions have but little hold on those who have devoted all their faculties to the pursuit of their well-being. The ardour which they display in small matters calms their zeal for momentous undertakings.

From time to time, indeed, enterprising and ambitious men will arise in democratic communities, whose unbounded aspirations cannot be contented by following the beaten track. Such men like revolutions and hail their approach; but they have great difficulty in bringing them about, unless unwonted events come to their assistance. No man can struggle with advantage against the spirit of his age and country; and, however powerful he may be supposed to be, he will find it difficult to make his contemporaries share in feelings and opinions which are repugnant to all their feelings and desires.

It is a mistake to believe that, when once the equality of conditions has become the old and uncontested state of society, and has imparted its characteristics to the manners of a nation, men will easily allow themselves to be thrust into perilous risks by an imprudent leader or a bold innovator. Not indeed that they will resist him openly, by well-contrived schemes, or even by a premeditated plan of resistance. They will not struggle energetically against him, sometimes they will even applaud him—but they do not follow him. To his vehemence they secretly oppose their inertia—to his revolutionary tendencies their conservative interests—their homely tastes to his adventurous passions—their good sense to the flights of his genius—to his poetry their prose. With immense exertion he raises them for an instant, but they speedily escape from him, and fall back, as it were, by their own weight. He strains himself to rouse the indifferent and distracted multitude, and finds at last that he is reduced to impotence, not because he is conquered, but because he is alone.

I do not assert that men living in democratic communities are naturally stationary; I think, on the contrary, that a perpetual stir prevails in the bosom of those societies, and that rest is unknown there; but I think that men bestir themselves within certain limits beyond which they hardly ever go. They are for ever varying, altering, and restoring secondary matters; but they carefully abstain from touching what is fundamental. They love change, but they dread revolutions.

Although the Americans are constantly modifying or abrogating some of their laws, they by no means display revolutionary passions. It may be easily seen, from the promptitude with which they check and calm themselves when public excitement begins to grow alarming, and at the very moment when passions seem most roused, that they dread a revolution as the worst of misfortunes, and that every one of them is inwardly resolved to make great sacrifices to avoid such a catastrophe. In no country in the world is the love of property more active and more anxious than in the United States; nowhere does the majority display less inclination for those principles which threaten to alter, in whatever manner, the laws of property.

I have often remarked that theories which are of a revolutionary nature, since they cannot be put in practice without a complete and sometimes a sudden change in the state of property and persons, are much less favourably viewed in the United States than in the great monarchical countries of Europe: if some men profess them, the bulk of the people reject them with instinctive abhorrence. I do not hesitate to say that most of the maxims commonly called democratic in France would be proscribed by the democracy of the United States. This may easily be understood; in America men have the opinions and passions of democracy, in Europe we have still the passions and opinions of revolution.

If ever America undergoes great revolutions, they will be brought about by the presence of the black race on the soil of the United States—that is to say, they will owe their origin, not to the equality, but to the inequality, of conditions.

When social conditions are equal, every man is apt to live apart, centered in himself and forgetful of the public. If the rulers of democratic nations were either to neglect to correct this fatal tendency, or to encourage it from a notion that it weans men from political passions and thus wards off revolutions, they might eventually produce the evil they seek to avoid, and a time might come when the inordinate passions of a few men, aided by the unintelligent selfishness or the pusillanimity of the greater number, would ultimately compel society to pass through strange vicissitudes. In democratic communities revolutions are seldom desired except by a minority; but a minority may sometimes effect them.

I do not assert that democratic nations are secure from revolutions; I merely say that the state of society in those nations does not lead to revolutions, but rather wards them off. A democratic people left to itself will not easily embark in great hazards; it is only led to revolutions unawares; it may sometimes undergo them, but it does not make them: and I will add that, when such a people has been allowed to acquire sufficient knowledge and experience, it will not suffer them to be made.

I am well aware that in this respect public institutions may themselves do much; they may encourage or repress the tendencies which originate in the state of society. I therefore do not maintain, I repeat, that a people is secure from revolutions simply because conditions are equal in the community; but I think that, whatever the institutions of such a people may be, great revolutions will always be far less violent and less frequent than is supposed; and I can easily discern a state of polity, which, when combined with the principle of equality, would render society more stationary than it has ever been in our western part of the world.

The observations I have here made on events may also be applied in part to opinions. Two things are surprising in the United States—the mutability of the greater part of human actions, and the singular stability of certain principles. Men are in constant motion; the mind of man appears almost unmoved. When once an opinion has spread over the country and struck root there, it would seem that no power on earth is strong enough to eradicate it. In the United States, general principles in religion, philosophy, morality, and even politics, do not vary, or at least are only modified by a hidden and often an imperceptible process: even the grossest prejudices are obliterated with incredible slowness, amid the continual friction of men and things.

I hear it said that it is in the nature and the habits of democracies to be constantly changing their opinions and feelings. This may be true of small democratic nations, like those of the ancient world, in which the whole community could be assembled in a public place and then excited at will by an orator. But I saw nothing of the kind among the great democratic people which dwells upon the opposite shores of the Atlantic ocean. What struck me in the United States was the difficulty of shaking the majority in an opinion once conceived, or of drawing it off from a leader once adopted. Neither speaking nor writing can accomplish it; nothing but experience will avail, and even experience must be repeated.

This is surprising at first sight, but a more attentive investigation explains the fact. I do not think that it is as easy as is supposed to uproot the prejudices of a democratic people—to change its belief—to supersede principles once established, by new principles in religion, politics, and morals—in a word, to make great and frequent changes in men's minds. Not that the human mind is there at rest—it is in constant agitation; but it is engaged in infinitely varying the consequences of known principles, and in seeking for new consequences, rather than in seeking for new principles. Its motion is one of rapid circumvolution, rather than of straightforward impulse by rapid and direct effort; it extends its orbit by small continual and hasty movements, but it does not suddenly alter its position.

Men who are equal in rights, in education, in fortune, or, to comprise all in one word, in their social condition, have necessarily wants, habits and tastes which are hardly dissimilar. As they look at objects under the same aspect, their minds naturally tend to analogous conclusions; and, though each of them may deviate from his contemporaries and form opinions of his own, they will involuntarily and unconsciously concur in a certain number of received opinions. The more attentively I consider the effects of equality upon the mind, the more am I persuaded that the intellectual anarchy which we witness about us is not, as many men suppose, the natural state of democratic nations. I think it is rather to be regarded as an accident peculiar to their youth, and that it only breaks out at that period of transition when men have already snapped the former ties which bound them together, but are still amazingly different in origin, education, and manners; so that, having retained opinions, propensities and tastes of great diversity, nothing any longer prevents men from avowing them openly. The leading opinions of men become similar in proportion as their conditions assimilate; such appears to me to be the general and permanent law—the rest is casual and transient.

I believe that it will rarely happen to any man among a democratic community, suddenly to frame a system of notions very remote from that which his contemporaries have adopted; and if some such innovator appeared, I apprehend that he would have great difficulty in finding listeners, still more in finding believers. When the conditions of men are almost equal, they do not easily allow themselves to be persuaded by each other. As they all live in close intercourse, as they have learned the same things together, and as they lead the same life, they are not naturally disposed to take one of themselves for a guide, and to follow him implicitly. Men seldom take the opinion of their equal, or of a man like themselves, upon trust.

Not only is confidence in the superior attainments of certain individuals weakened among democratic nations, as I have elsewhere remarked, but the general notion of the intellectual superiority which any man whatsoever may acquire in relation to the rest of the community is soon overshadowed. As men grow more like each other, the doctrine of the equality of the intellect gradually infuses itself into their opinions; and it becomes more difficult for any innovator to acquire or to exert much influence over the minds of a people. In such communities sudden intellectual revolutions will therefore be rare; for, if we read aright the history of the world, we shall find that great and rapid changes in human opinions have been produced far less by the force of reasoning than by the authority of a name.

Observe, too, that as the men who live in democratic societies are not connected with each other by any tie, each of them must be convinced individually; while in aristocratic society it is enough to convince a few—the rest follow. If Luther had lived in an age of equality, and had not had princes and potentates for his audience, he would perhaps have found it more difficult to change the aspect of Europe.

Not indeed that the men of democracies are naturally strongly persuaded of the certainty of their opinions, or are unwavering in belief; they frequently entertain doubts which no one, in their eyes, can remove. It sometimes happens at such times, that the human mind would willingly change its position; but as nothing urges or guides it forward, it oscillates to and fro without progressive motion.*

* If I inquire what state of society is most favourable to the great revolutions of the mind, I find that it occurs somewhere between the complete equality of the whole community and the absolute separation of ranks. Under a system of castes generations succeed each other without altering men's positions: some have nothing more, others nothing better, to hope for.

Even when the reliance of a democratic people has been won, it is still no easy matter to gain their attention. It is extremely difficult to obtain a hearing from men living in democracies, unless it be to speak to them of themselves. They do not attend to the things said to them, because they are always fully engrossed with the things they are doing. For indeed few men are idle in democratic nations; life is passed in the midst of noise and excitement, and men are so engaged in acting that little time remains to them for thinking. I would especially remark that they are not only employed, but that they are passionately devoted to their employments. They are always in action, and each of their actions absorbs their faculties: the zeal which they display in business puts out the enthusiasm they might otherwise entertain for ideas.

I think that it is extremely difficult to excite the enthusiasm of a democratic people for any theory which has not a palpable, direct, and immediate connexion with the daily occupations of life: therefore they will not easily forsake their old opinions; for it is enthusiasm which flings the mind of men out of the beaten track, and effects the great revolutions of the intellect as well as the great revolutions of the political world.

Thus democratic nations have neither time nor taste to go in search of novel opinions. Even when those they possess become doubtful, they still retain them, because it would take too much time and inquiry to change them—they retain them, not as certain, but as established.

There are yet other and more cogent reasons which prevent any great change from being easily effected in the principles of a democratic people. I have already adverted to them at the commencement of the third volume.

If the influence of individuals is weak and hardly perceptible among such a people, the power exercised by the mass upon the mind of each individual is extremely great—I have already shown for what reasons. I would now observe that it is wrong to suppose that this depends solely upon the form of government, and that the majority would lose its intellectual supremacy if it were to lose its political power.

In aristocracies men have often much greatness and strength of their own: when they find themselves at variance with the greater number of their fellow-countrymen, they withdraw to their own circle, where they support and console themselves. Such is not the case in a democratic country; there, public favour seems as necessary as the air

---

The imagination slumbers amid this universal silence and stillness, and the very idea of change fades from the human mind.

When ranks have been abolished and social conditions are almost equalized, all men are in ceaseless excitement, but each of them stands alone, independent and weak. This latter state of things is excessively different from the former one; yet it has one point of analogy—great revolutions of the human mind seldom occur in it.

But between these two extremes of the history of nations is an intermediate period—a period as glorious as it is agitated—when the conditions of men are not sufficiently settled for the mind to be lulled in torpor, when they are sufficiently unequal for men to exercise a vast power on the minds of one another, and when some few may modify the convictions of all. It is at such times that great reformers start up, and new opinions suddenly change the face of the world.

we breath, and to live at variance with the multitude is, as it were, not to live. The multitude requires no laws to coerce those who think not like itself: public disapprobation is enough; a sense of their loneliness and impotence overtakes them and drives them to despair.

Whenever social conditions are equal, public opinion presses with enormous weight upon the minds of each individual; it surrounds, directs, and oppresses him; and this arises from the very constitution of society, much more than from its political laws. As men grow more alike, each man feels himself weaker in regard to all the rest; as he discerns nothing by which he is considerably raised above them, or distinguished from them, he mistrusts himself as soon as they assail him. Not only does he mistrust his strength, but he even doubts of his right; and he is very near acknowledging that he is in the wrong, when the greater number of his country-men assert that he is so. The majority do not need to constrain him—they convince him. In whatever way then the powers of a democratic community may be organized and balanced, it will always be extremely difficult to believe what the bulk of the people reject, or to profess what they condemn.

This circumstance is extraordinarily favourable to the stability of opinions. When an opinion has taken root among a democratic people, and established itself in the minds of the bulk of the community, it afterward subsists by itself and is maintained without effort, because no one attacks it. Those who at first rejected it as false, ultimately receive it as the general impression; and those who still dispute it in their hearts, conceal their dissent; they are careful not to engage in a dangerous and useless conflict.

It is true, that when the majority of a democratic people change their opinions, they may suddenly and arbitrarily effect strange revolutions in men's minds; but their opinions do not change without much difficulty, and it is almost as difficult to show that they are changed.

Time, events, or the unaided individual action of the mind, will sometimes undermine or destroy an opinion, without any outward sign of the change. It has not been openly assailed, no conspiracy has been formed to make war on it, but its followers one by one noiselessly secede—day by day a few of them abandon it, until at last it is only professed by a minority. In this state it will still continue to prevail. As its enemies remain mute, or only interchange their thoughts by stealth, they are themselves unaware for a long period that a great revolution has actually been effected; and in this state of uncertainty they take no steps—they observe each other, and are silent. The majority have ceased to believe what they believed before; but they still affect to believe, and this empty phantom of public opinion is strong enough to chill innovators, and to keep them silent and at a respectful distance.

We live at a time which has witnessed the most rapid changes of opinion in the minds of men; nevertheless it may be that the leading opinions of society will ere long be more settled than they have been for several centuries in our history: that time is not yet come, but it may perhaps be approaching. As I examine more closely the natural wants and tendencies of democratic nations, I grow persuaded that if ever social equality is generally and permanently established in the world, great intellectual and political revolutions will become more difficult and less frequent than is supposed. Because the men of democracies appear always excited, uncertain, eager, changeable in their wills and in their positions, it is imagined that they are suddenly to abrogate their laws, to adopt new opinions, and to assume new manners. But if the principle of equality predisposes men to change, it also suggests to them certain interests and tastes which cannot be satisfied without a settled order of things; equality urges them on, but at the same time it holds them back; it spurs them, but fastens them to earth;—it kindles their desires, but limits their powers.

This, however, is not perceived at first; the passions which tend to sever the citizens of a democracy are obvious enough; but the hidden force which restrains and unites them is not discernible at a glance.

Amid the ruins which surround me, shall I dare to say that revolutions are not what I most fear for coming generations? If men continue to shut themselves more closely within the narrow circle of domestic interests and to live upon that kind of excitement, it is to be apprehended that they may ultimately become inaccessible to those great and powerful public emotions which perturb nations—but which enlarge them and recruit them. When property becomes so fluctuating, and the love of property so restless and so ardent, I cannot but fear that men may arrive at such a state as to regard every new theory as a peril, every innovation as an irksome toil, every social improvement as a stepping-stone to revolution, and so refuse to move altogether for fear of being moved too far. I dread, and I confess it, lest they should at last so entirely give way to a cowardly love of present enjoyment, as to lose sight of the interests of their future selves and of those of their descendants; and to prefer to glide along the easy current of life, rather than to make, when it is necessary, a strong and sudden effort to a higher purpose.

It is believed by some that modern society will be ever changing its aspect; for myself, I fear that it will ultimately be too invariably fixed in the same institutions, the same prejudices, the same manners, so that mankind will be stopped and circumscribed; that the mind will swing backward and forward for ever, without begetting fresh ideas; that man will waste his strength in bootless and solitary trifling; and, though in continual motion, that humanity will cease to advance.

Chapter XXII.

WHY DEMOCRATIC NATIONS ARE NATURALLY DESIROUS OF PEACE, AND DEMOCRATIC ARMIES OF WAR.

The same interests, the same fears, the same passions which deter democratic nations from revolutions, deter them also from war; the spirit of military glory and the spirit of revolution are weakened at the same time and by the same causes. The ever-increasing numbers of men of property—lovers of peace, the growth of personal wealth which war so rapidly consumes, the mildness of manners, the gentleness of heart, those tendencies to pity which are engendered by the equality of conditions, that coolness of understanding which renders men comparatively insensible to the violent and poetical excitement of arms—all these causes concur to quench the military spirit. I think it may be admitted as a general and constant rule, that, among civilized nations, the warlike passions will become more rare and less intense in proportion as social conditions shall be more equal.

War is nevertheless an occurrence to which all nations are subject, democratic nations as well as others. Whatever taste they may have for peace, they must hold themselves in readiness to repel aggression, or in other words they must have an army.

Fortune, which has conferred so many peculiar benefits upon the inhabitants of the United States, has placed them in the midst of a wilderness, where they have, so to speak, no neighbours: a few thousand soldiers are sufficient for their wants; but this is peculiar to America, not to democracy.

The equality of conditions, and the manners as well as the institutions resulting from it, do not exempt a democratic people from the necessity of standing armies, and their armies always exercise a powerful influence over their fate. It is therefore of singular importance to inquire what are the natural propensities of the men of whom these armies are composed.

Among aristocratic nations, especially among those in which birth is the only source of rank, the same inequality exists in the army as in the nation; the officer is noble, the soldier is a serf; the one is naturally called upon to command, the other to obey. In aristocratic armies, the private soldier's ambition is therefore circumscribed within very narrow limits. Nor has the ambition of the officer an unlimited range. An aristocratic body not only forms a part of the scale of ranks in the nation, but it contains a scale of ranks within itself: the members of whom it is composed are placed one above another, in a particular and unvarying manner. Thus one man is born to the command of a regiment, another to that of a company; when once they have reached the utmost object of their hopes, they stop of their own accord, and remain contented with their lot.

There is, besides, a strong cause, which, in aristocracies, weakens the officer's desire of promotion. Among aristocratic nations, an officer, independently of his rank in the army, also occupies an elevated rank in society; the former is almost always in his eyes only an appendage to the latter. A nobleman who embraces the profession of arms follows it less from motives of ambition than from a sense of the duties imposed on him by his birth. He enters the army in order to find an honourable employment for the idle years of his youth, and to be able to bring back to his home and his peers some honourable recollections of military life; but his principal object is not to obtain by that profession either property, distinction, or power, for he possesses these advantages in his own right, and enjoys them without leaving his home.

In democratic armies all the soldiers may become officers, which makes the desire of promotion general, and immeasurably extends the bounds of military ambition.

The officer, on his part, sees nothing which naturally and necessarily stops him at one grade more than at another; and each grade has immense importance in his eyes, because his rank in society almost always depends on his rank in the army. Among democratic nations it often happens that an officer has no property but his pay, and no distinction but that of military honours: consequently as often as his duties change, his fortune changes, and he becomes, as it were, a new man. What was only an appendage to his position in aristocratic armies, has thus become the main point, the basis of his whole condition.

Under the old French monarchy officers were always called by their titles of nobility; they are now always called by the title of their military rank. This little change in the forms of language suffices to show that a great revolution has taken place in the constitution of society and in that of the army.

In democratic armies the desire of advancement is almost universal: it is ardent, tenacious, perpetual; it is strengthened by all other desires, and only extinguished with life itself. But it is easy to see, that of all armies in the world, those in which advancement must be slowest in time of peace are the armies of democratic countries. As the number of commissions is naturally limited, while the number of competitors is almost unlimited, and as the strict law of equality is over all alike, none can make rapid progress—many can make no progress at all. Thus the desire of advancement is greater, and the opportunities of advancement fewer, there than elsewhere. All the ambitious spirits of a democratic army are consequently ardently desirous of war, because war makes vacancies, and warrants the violation of that law of seniority which is the sole privilege natural to democracy.

We thus arrive at this singular consequence, that of all armies those most ardently desirous of war are democratic armies, and of all nations those most fond of peace are democratic nations: and, what makes these facts still more extraordinary, is that these contrary effects are produced at the same time by the principle of equality.

All the members of the community, being alike, constantly harbour the wish, and discover the possibility, of changing their condition and improving their welfare: this makes them fond of peace, which is favourable to industry, and allows every man to pursue his own little undertakings to their completion. On the other hand, this same equality makes soldiers dream of fields of battle, by increasing the value of military honours in the eyes of those who follow the profession of arms, and by rendering those honours accessible to all. In either case the inquietude of the heart is the same, the taste for enjoyment as insatiable, the ambition of success as great—the means of gratifying it are alone different.

These opposite tendencies of the nation and the army expose democratic communities to great dangers. When a military spirit forsakes a people, the profession of arms immediately ceases to be held in honour, and military men fall to the lowest rank of the public servants: they are little esteemed, and no longer understood. The reverse of what takes place in aristocratic ages then occurs; the men who enter the army are no longer those of the highest, but of the lowest rank. Military ambition is only indulged in when no other is possible. Hence arises a circle of cause and consequence from which it is difficult to escape: the best part of the nation shuns the military profession because that profession is not honoured, and the profession is not honoured because the best part of the nation has ceased to follow it.

It is then no matter of surprise that democratic armies are often restless, ill-tempered, and dissatisfied with their lot, although their physical condition is commonly far better, and their discipline less strict than in other countries. The soldier feels that he occupies an inferior position, and his wounded pride either stimulates his taste for hostilities which would render his services necessary, or gives him a turn for revolutions, during which he may hope to win by force of arms the political influence and personal importance now denied him.

The composition of democratic armies makes this last-mentioned danger much to be feared. In democratic communities almost every man has some property to preserve; but democratic armies are generally led by men without property, most of whom have little to lose in civil broils. The bulk of the nation is naturally much more afraid of revolutions than in the ages of aristocracy, but the leaders of the army much less so.

Moreover, as among democratic nations (to repeat what I have just remarked) the wealthiest, the best educated, and the most able men seldom adopt the military profession, the army, taken collectively, eventually forms a small nation by itself, where the mind is less enlarged, and habits are more rude than in the nation at large. Now, this small uncivilized nation has arms in its possession, and alone knows how to use them: for, indeed, the pacific temper of the community increases the danger to which a democratic people is exposed from the military and turbulent spirit of the army. Nothing is so dangerous as an army amid an unwarlike nation; the excessive love of the whole community for quiet continually puts its constitution at the mercy of the soldiery.

It may therefore be asserted, generally speaking, that if democratic nations are naturally prone to peace from their interests and their propensities, they are constantly drawn to war and revolutions by their armies. Military revolutions, which are scarcely ever to be apprehended in aristocracies, are always to be dreaded among democratic nations. These perils must be reckoned among the most formidable which beset their future fate, and the attention of statesmen should be sedulously applied to find a remedy for the evil.

When a nation perceives that it is inwardly affected by the restless ambition of its army, the first thought which occurs is to give this inconvenient ambition an object by going to war. I speak no ill of war: war almost always enlarges the mind of a people, and raises their character. In some cases it is the only check to the excessive growth of certain propensities which naturally spring out of the equality of conditions, and it must be considered as a necessary corrective to certain inveterate diseases to which democratic communities are liable.

War has great advantages, but we must not flatter ourselves that it can diminish the danger I have just pointed out. That peril is only suspended by it, to return more fiercely when the war is over; for armies are much more impatient of peace after having tasted military exploits. War could only be a remedy for a people which should always be athirst for military glory.

I foresee that all the military rulers who may rise up in great democratic nations, will find it easier to conquer with their armies, than to make their armies live at peace after conquest. There are two things which a democratic people will always find very difficult—to begin a war, and to end it.

Again, if war has some peculiar advantages for democratic nations, on the other hand it exposes them to certain dangers, which aristocracies have no cause to dread to an equal extent. I shall only point out two of these.

Although war gratifies the army, it embarrasses and often exasperates that countless multitude of men whose minor passions every day require peace in order to be satisfied. Thus there is some risk of its causing, under another form, the disturbance it is intended to prevent.

No protracted war can fail to endanger the freedom of a democratic country. Not indeed that after every victory it is to be apprehended that the victorious generals will possess themselves by force of the supreme power, after the manner of Sylla and Cæsar:[1] the danger is of another kind. War does not always give over democratic communities to military government, but it must invariably and immeasurably increase the powers of civil government; it must almost compulsorily concentrate the direction of all men and the management of all things in the hands of the administration. If it lead not to despotism by sudden violence, it prepares men for it more gently by their habits. All those who seek to destroy the liberties of a democratic nation ought to know that war is the surest and the shortest means to accomplish it. This is the first axiom of the science.

One remedy, which appears to be obvious when the ambition of soldiers and officers becomes the subject of alarm, is to augment the number of commissions to be distributed by increasing the army. This affords temporary relief, but it plunges the country into deeper difficulties at some future period. To increase the army may produce a lasting effect in an aristocratic community, because military ambition is there confined to one class of men, and the ambition of each individual stops, as it were, at a certain limit; so that it may be possible to satisfy all who feel its influence. But nothing is gained by increasing the army among a democratic people, because the number of aspirants always rises in exactly the same ratio as the army itself. Those whose claims have been satisfied by the creation of new commissions are instantly succeeded by a fresh multitude beyond all power of satisfaction; and even those who were but now satisfied soon begin to crave more advancement; for the same excitement prevails in the ranks of the army as in the civil classes of democratic society, and what men want is not to reach a certain grade, but to have constant promotion. Though these wants may not be very vast, they are perpetually recurring. Thus a democratic nation, by augmenting its army, only allays for a time the ambition of the military profession, which soon becomes even more formidable, because the number of those who feel it is increased.

I am of opinion that a restless and turbulent spirit is an evil inherent in the very constitution of democratic armies, and beyond hope of cure. The legislators of democracies must not expect to devise any military organization capable by its influence of calming and restraining the military profession: their efforts would exhaust their powers, before the object is attained.

The remedy for the vices of the army is not to be found in the army itself, but in the country. Democratic nations are naturally afraid of disturbance and of despotism; the object is to turn these natural instincts into well-digested, deliberate, and lasting tastes. When men have at last learned to make a peaceful and profitable use of freedom, and have felt its blessings—when they have conceived a manly love of order, and have freely submitted themselves to discipline—these same men, if they follow the profession of arms, bring into it, unconsciously and almost against their will, these same habits and manners. The general spirit of the nation being infused into the spirit peculiar to the army, tempers the opinions and desires engendered by military life, or represses them by the mighty force of public opinion. Teach but the citizens to be educated, orderly, firm, and free, the soldiers will be disciplined and obedient.

Any law which, in repressing the turbulent spirit of the army should tend to diminish the spirit of freedom in the nation, and to overshadow the notion of law and right, would defeat its object: it would do much more to favour, than to defeat, the establishment of military tyranny.

After all, and in spite of all precautions, a large army amid a democratic people will always be a source of great danger; the most effectual means of diminishing that danger would be to reduce the army, but this is a remedy which all nations have it not in their power to use.

Chapter XXIII.

WHICH IS THE MOST WARLIKE AND MOST REVOLUTIONARY CLASS IN
DEMOCRATIC ARMIES.

It is a part of the essence of a democratic army to be very numerous in proportion to the people to which it belongs, as I shall hereafter show. On the other hand, men living in democratic times seldom choose a military life. Democratic nations are therefore soon led to give up the system of voluntary recruiting for that of compulsory enlistment. The necessity of their social condition compels them to resort to the latter means, and it may easily be foreseen that they will all eventually adopt it.

When military service is compulsory, the burden is indiscriminately and equally borne by the whole community. This is another necessary consequence of the social condition of these nations, and of their notions. The government may do almost whatever it pleases, provided it appeals to the whole community at once: it is the unequal distribution of the weight, not the weight itself, which commonly occasions resistance.

But as military service is common to all the citizens, the evident consequence is, that each of them remains but for a few years on active duty. Thus it is in the nature of things that the soldier in democracies only passes through the army, while among most aristocratic nations the military profession is one which the soldier adopts, or which is imposed upon him, for life.

This has important consequences. Among the soldiers of a democratic army, some acquire a taste for military life, but the majority being enlisted against their will, and ever ready to go back to their homes, do not consider themselves as seriously engaged in the military profession, and are always thinking of quitting it. Such men do not contract the wants, and only half partake in the passions, which that mode of life engenders. They adapt themselves to their military duties, but their minds are still attached to the interests and the duties which engaged them in civil life. They do not therefore imbibe the spirit of the army—or rather, they infuse the spirit of the community at large into the army, and retain it there. Among democratic nations the private soldiers remain most like civilians: upon them the habits of the nation have the firmest hold, and public opinion most influence. It is by the instrumentality of the private soldiers especially that it may be possible to infuse into a democratic army the love of freedom and the respect of rights, if these principles have once been successfully inculcated on the people at large. The reverse happens among aristocratic nations, where the soldiery have eventually nothing in common with their fellow-citizens, and where they live among them as strangers, and often as enemies.

In aristocratic armies the officers are the conservative element, because the officers alone have retained a strict connexion with civil society, and never forego their purpose of resuming their place in it sooner or later: in democratic armies the private soldiers stand in this position, and from the same cause.

It often happens, on the contrary, that in these same democratic armies the officers contract tastes and wants wholly distinct from those of the nation—a fact which may be thus accounted for. Among democratic nations, the man who becomes an officer severs all the ties which bound him to civil life; he leaves it for ever; he has no interest to resume it. His true country is the army, since he owes all he has to the rank he has attained in it; he therefore follows the fortunes of the army, rises or sinks with it, and henceforward directs all his hopes to that quarter only. As the wants of an officer are distinct from those of the country, he may perhaps ardently desire war or labour to bring about a revolution, at the very moment when the nation is most desirous of stability and peace.

There are, nevertheless, some causes which allay this restless and warlike spirit. Though ambition is universal and continual among democratic nations, we have seen that it is seldom great. A man who, being born in the lower classes of the community, has risen from the ranks to be an officer, has already taken a prodigious step. He has gained a footing in a sphere above that which he filled in civil life, and he has acquired rights which most democratic nations will ever consider as inalienable.* He is willing to pause after so great an effort, and to enjoy what he has won. The fear of risking what he has already obtained, damps the desire of acquiring what he has not got. Having conquered the first and greatest impediment which opposed his advancement, he resigns himself with less impatience to the slowness of his progress. His ambition will be more and more cooled in proportion as the increasing distinction of his rank teaches him that he has more to put in jeopardy. If I am not mistaken, the least warlike, and also the least revolutionary part, of a democratic army, will always be its chief commanders.

But the remarks I have just made on officers and soldiers are not applicable to a numerous class which in all armies fills the intermediate space between them—I mean the class of noncommissioned officers. This class of noncommissioned officers which had never acted a part in history until the present century, is henceforward destined, I think, to play one of some importance. Like the officers, noncommissioned officers have broken, in their minds, all the ties which bound them to civil life; like the former, they devote themselves permanently to the service, and perhaps make it even more exclusively the object of all their desires: but noncommissioned officers are men who have not yet reached a firm and lofty post at which they may pause and breathe more freely, ere they can attain further promotion.

By the very nature of his duties, which is invariable, a noncommissioned officer is doomed to lead an obscure, confined, comfortless, and precarious existence; as yet he sees nothing of military life but its dangers; he knows nothing but its privations and its discipline—more difficult to support than dangers: he suffers the more from his present miseries, from knowing that the constitution of society and of the army allow him to rise above them; he may, indeed, at any time obtain his commission, and enter at once upon command, honours, independence, rights, and enjoyments. Not only does this object of his

---

* The position of officers is indeed much more secure among democratic nations than elsewhere; the lower the personal standing of the man, the greater is the comparative importance of his military grade, and the more just and necessary is it that the enjoyment of that rank should be secured by the laws.

hopes appear to him of immense importance, but he is never sure of reaching it till it is actually his own; the grade he fills is by no means irrevocable; he is always entirely abandoned to the arbitrary pleasure of his commanding officer, for this is imperiously required by the necessity of discipline: a slight fault, a whim, may always deprive him in an instant of the fruits of many years of toil and endeavour; until he has reached the grade to which he aspires he has accomplished nothing; not till he reaches that grade does his career seem to begin. A desperate ambition cannot fail to be kindled in a man thus incessantly goaded on by his youth, his wants, his passions, the spirit of his age, his hopes, and his fears.

Noncommissioned officers are therefore bent on war—on war always, and at any cost; but if war be denied them, then they desire revolutions, to suspend the authority of established regulations, and to enable them, aided by the general confusion and the political passions of the time, to get rid of their superior officers and to take their places. Nor is it impossible for them to bring about such a crisis, because their common origin and habits give them much influence over the soldiers, however different may be their passions and their desires.

It would be an error to suppose that these various characteristics of officers, noncommissioned officers, and men, belong to any particular time or country; they will always occur at all times, and among all democratic nations. In every democratic army the noncommissioned officers will be the worst representatives of the pacific and orderly spirit of the country, and the private soldiers will be the best. The latter will carry with them into military life the strength or weakness of the manners of the nation; they will display a faithful reflection of the community: if that community is ignorant and weak, they will allow themselves to be drawn by their leaders into disturbances, either unconsciously or against their will; if it is enlightened and energetic, the community will itself keep them within the bounds of order.

Chapter XXIV.

CAUSES WHICH RENDER DEMOCRATIC ARMIES WEAKER THAN OTHER ARMIES AT THE OUTSET OF A CAMPAIGN, AND MORE FORMIDABLE IN PROTRACTED WARFARE.

Any army is in danger of being conquered at the outset of a campaign, after a long peace; any army which has long been engaged in warfare has strong chances of victory: this truth is peculiarly applicable to democratic armies. In aristocracies the military profession, being a privileged career, is held in honour even in time of peace. Men of great talents, great attainments, and great ambition embrace it; the army is in all respects on a level with the nation, and frequently above it.

We have seen, on the contrary, that among a democratic people the choicer minds of the nation are gradually drawn away from the military profession, to seek by other paths, distinction, power, and especially wealth. After a long peace—and in democratic ages the periods of peace are long—the army is always inferior to the country itself. In this state it is called into active service; and until war has altered it, there is danger for the country as well as for the army.

I have shown that in democratic armies, and in time of peace, the rule of seniority is the supreme and inflexible law of advancement. This is not only a consequence, as I have before observed, of the constitution of these armies, but of the constitution of the people, and it will always occur.

Again, as among these nations the officer derives his position in the country solely from his position in the army, and as he draws all the distinction and the competency he enjoys from the same source, he does not retire from his profession, or is not superannuated, till toward the extreme close of life. The consequence of these two causes is, that when a democratic people goes to war after a long interval of peace all the leading officers of the army are old men. I speak not only of the generals, but of the noncommissioned officers, who have most of them been stationary, or have only advanced step by step. It may be remarked with surprise, that in a democratic army after a long peace all the soldiers are mere boys, and all the superior officers in declining years; so that the former are wanting in experience, the latter in vigour. This is a strong element of defeat, for the first condition of successful generalship is youth: I should not have ventured to say so if the greatest captain of modern times had not made the observation.

These two causes do not act in the same manner upon aristocratic armies: as men are promoted in them by right of birth much more than by right of seniority, there are in all ranks a certain number of young men, who bring to their profession all the early vigour of body and mind. Again, as the men who seek for military honours among an aristocratic people, enjoy a settled position in civil society, they seldom continue in the army until old age overtakes them. After having devoted the most vigorous years of youth to the career of arms, they voluntarily retire, and spend at home the remainder of their maturer years.

A long peace not only fills democratic armies with elderly officers, but it also gives to all the officers habits both of body and mind which render them unfit for actual service. The man who has long lived amid the calm and lukewarm atmosphere of democratic manners can at first ill adapt himself to the harder toils and sterner duties of warfare; and if he has not absolutely lost the taste for arms, at least he has assumed a mode of life which unfits him for conquest.*

---

* If the love of physical gratification and the taste for well-being, which are naturally suggested to men by a state of equality, were to get entire possession of the mind of a democratic people, and to fill it completely, the manners of the nation would become so totally opposed to military tastes, that perhaps even the army would eventually acquire a love of peace, in spite of the peculiar interest which leads it to desire war. Living in the midst of a state of general relaxation, the troops would ultimately think it better to rise without efforts, by the slow but commodious advancement of a peace-establishment, than to purchase more rapid promotion

Among aristocratic nations, the ease of civil life exercises less influence on the manners of the army, because among those nations the aristocracy commands the army: and an aristocracy, however plunged in luxurious pleasures, has always many other passions besides that of its own well-being, and to satisfy those passions more thoroughly its well-being will be readily sacrificed.

I have shown that in democratic armies, in time of peace, promotion is extremely slow. The officers at first support this state of things with impatience, they grow excited, restless, exasperated, but in the end most of them make up their minds to it. Those who have the largest share of ambition and of resources quit the army; others, adapting their tastes and their desires to their scanty fortunes, ultimately look upon the military profession in a civil point of view. The quality they value most in it is the competency and security which attend it; their whole notion of the future rests upon the certainty of this little provision, and all they require is peaceably to enjoy it. Thus not only does a long peace fill an army with old men, but it frequently imparts the views of old men to those who are still in the prime of life.

I have also shown that among democratic nations in time of peace the military profession is held in little honour and indifferently followed. This want of public favour is a heavy discouragement to the army; it weighs down the minds of the troops, and when war breaks out at last, they cannot immediately resume their spring and vigour. No similar cause of moral weakness occurs in aristocratic armies: there the officers are never lowered either in their own eyes or in those of their countrymen, because, independently of their military greatness, they are personally great. But even if the influence of peace operated on the two kinds of armies in the same manner, the results would still be different.

When the officers of an aristocratic army have lost their warlike spirit and the desire of raising themselves by service, they still retain a certain respect for the honour of their class, and an old habit of being foremost to set an example. But when the officers of a democratic army have no longer the love of war and the ambition of arms, nothing whatever remains to them.

I am therefore of opinion that, when a democratic people engages

---

at the cost of all the toils and privations of the field. With these feelings, they would take up arms without enthusiasm, and use them without energy; they would allow themselves to be led to meet the foe, instead of marching to attack him.

It must not be supposed that this pacific state of the army would render it averse to revolutions; for revolutions, and especially military revolutions, which are generally very rapid, are attended indeed with great dangers, but not with protracted toil; they gratify ambition at less cost than war; life only is at stake, and the men of democracies care less for their lives than for their comforts.

Nothing is more dangerous for the freedom and the tranquility of a people than an army afraid of war, because, as such an army no longer seeks to maintain its importance and its influence on the field of battle, it seeks to assert them elsewhere. Thus it might happen, that the men of whom a democratic army consists should lose the interests of citizens without acquiring the virtues of soldiers; and that the army should cease to be fit for war without ceasing to be turbulent. I shall here repeat what I have said in the text: the remedy for these dangers is not to be found in the army, but in the country: a democratic people which has preserved the manliness of its character will never be at a loss for military prowess in its soldiers.

in a war after a long peace, it incurs much more risk of defeat than any other nation; but it ought not easily to be cast down by its reverses, for the chances of success for such an army are increased by the duration of the war. When a war has at length, by its long continuance, roused the whole community from their peaceful occupations and ruined their minor undertakings, the same passions which made them attach so much importance to the maintenance of peace will be turned to arms. War, after it has destroyed all modes of speculation, becomes itself the great and sole speculation, to which all the ardent and ambitious desires which equality engenders are exclusively directed. Hence it is that the self-same democratic nations which are so reluctant to engage in hostilities, sometimes perform prodigious achievements when once they have taken the field.

As the war attracts more and more of public attention, and is seen to create high reputations and great fortunes in a short space of time, the choicest spirits of the nation enter the military profession: all the enterprising, proud, and martial minds, no longer of the aristocracy solely, but of the whole country, are drawn in this direction. As the number of competitors for military honours is immense, and war drives every man to his proper level, great generals are always sure to spring up. A long war produces upon a democratic army the same effects that a revolution produces upon a people; it breaks through regulations, and allows extraordinary men to rise above the common level. Those officers whose bodies and minds have grown old in peace, are removed, or superannuated, or they die. In their stead a host of young men are pressing on, whose frames are already hardened, whose desires are extended and inflamed by active service. They are bent on advancement at all hazards, and perpetual advancement; they are followed by others with the same passions and desires, and after these are others yet, unlimited by aught but the size of the army. The principle of equality opens the door of ambition to all, and death provides chances for ambition. Death is constantly thinning the ranks, making vacancies, closing and opening the career of arms.

There is moreover a secret connexion between the military character and the character of democracies, which war brings to light. The men of democracies are naturally passionately eager to acquire what they covet, and to enjoy it on easy conditions. They for the most part worship chance, and are much less afraid of death than of difficulty. This is the spirit which they bring to commerce and manufacturers: and this same spirit, carried with them to the field of battle, induces them willingly to expose their lives in order to secure in a moment the rewards of victory. No kind of greatness is more pleasing to the imagination of a democratic people than military greatness—a greatness of vivid and sudden lustre, obtained without toil, by nothing but the risk of life.

Thus, while the interest and the tastes of the members of a democratic community divert them from war, their habits of mind fit them for carrying on war well: they soon make good soldiers, when they are roused from their business and their enjoyments.

If peace is peculiarly hurtful to democratic armies, war secures to them advantages which no other armies ever possess; and these advantages, however little left at first, cannot fail in the end to give them the victory. An aristocratic nation, which in a contest with a democratic people does not succeed in ruining the latter at the outset of the war, always runs a great risk of being conquered by it.

Chapter XXV.

OF DISCIPLINE IN DEMOCRATIC ARMIES.

It is a very general opinion, especially in aristocratic countries, that the great social equality which prevails in democracies ultimately renders the private soldier independent of the officer, and thus destroys the bond of discipline. This is a mistake, for there are two kinds of discipline, which it is important not to confound.

When the officer is noble and the soldier a serf—one rich, the other poor—the former educated and strong, the latter ignorant and weak—the strictest bond of obedience may easily be established between the two men. The soldier is broken in to military discipline, as it were, before he enters the army; or rather, military discipline is nothing but an enhancement of social servitude. In aristocratic armies the soldier will soon become insensible to everything but the orders of his superior officers; he acts without reflection, triumphs without enthusiasm, and dies without complaint; in this state he is no longer a man, but he is still a most formidable animal trained for war.

A democratic people must despair of ever obtaining from soldiers that blind, minute, submissive, and invariable obedience which an aristocratic people may impose on them without difficulty. The state of society does not prepare them for it, and the nation might be in danger of losing its natural advantages if it sought artificially to acquire advantages of this particular kind. Among democratic communities, military discipline ought not to attempt to annihilate the free spring of the faculties; all that can be done by discipline is to direct it; the obedience thus inculcated is less exact, but it is more eager and more intelligent. It has its root in the will of him who obeys; it rests not only on his instinct, but on his reason; and consequently it will often spontaneously become more strict as danger requires it. The discipline of an aristocratic army is apt to be relaxed in war, because that discipline is founded upon habits, and war disturbs those habits. The discipline of a democratic army on the contrary is strengthened in sight of the enemy, because every soldier then clearly perceives that he must be silent and obedient in order to conquer.

The nations which have performed the greatest warlike achievements knew no other discipline than that which I speak of. Among the ancients none were admitted into the armies but freemen and citizens, who differed but little from one another, and were accustomed to treat each other as equals. In this respect it may be said that the armies of antiquity were democratic, although they came out of the bosom of aristocracy; the consequence was that in those armies a sort of fraternal familiarity prevailed between the officers and the men. Plutarch's lives of great commanders furnish convincing instances of the fact: the soldiers were in the constant habit of freely addressing their general, and the general listened to and answered whatever the soldiers had to say: they were kept in order by language and by example, far more than by constraint or punishment; the general was as much their companion as their chief. I know not whether the soldiers of Greece and Rome ever carried the minutiæ of military discipline to the same degree of perfection as the Russians have done; but this did not prevent Alexander from conquering Asia—and Rome, the world.

Chapter XXVI.

SOME CONSIDERATIONS ON WAR IN DEMOCRATIC COMMUNITIES.

When the principle of equality is in growth, not only among a single nation, but among several neighbouring nations at the same time, as is now the case in Europe, the inhabitants of these different countries, notwithstanding the dissimilarity of language, of customs, and of laws, nevertheless resemble each other in their equal dread of war and their common love of peace.* It is in vain that ambition or anger puts arms in the hands of princes; they are appeased in spite of themselves by a species of general apathy and good-will, which makes the sword drop from their grasp, and wars become more rare.

As the spread of equality, taking place in several countries at once, simultaneously impels their various inhabitants to follow manufactures and commerce, not only do their tastes grow alike but their interests are so mixed and entangled with one another, that no nation can inflict evils on other nations without those evils falling back upon itself; and all nations ultimately regard war as a calamity, almost as severe to the conqueror as to the conquered.

Thus, on the one hand, it is extremely difficult in democratic ages to draw nations into hostilities; but, on the other hand, it is almost impossible that any two of them should go to war without embroiling the rest. The interests of all are so interlaced, their opinions and their wants so much alike, that none can remain quiet when the others stir. Wars therefore become more rare, but when they break out they spread over a larger field.

Neighbouring democratic nations not only become alike in some re-

---

* It is scarcely necessary for me to observe that the dread of war displayed by the nations of Europe is not solely attributable to the progress made by the principle of equality among them; independently of this permanent cause several other accidental causes of great weight might be pointed out, and I may mention before all the rest the extreme lassitude which the wars of the Revolution and the Empire have left behind them.

spects, but they eventually grow to resemble each other in almost all.*
This similitude of nations has consequences of great importance in relation to war.

If I inquire why it is that the Helvetic Confederacy made the greatest and most powerful nations of Europe tremble in the fifteenth century, while at the present day the power of that country is exactly
proportioned to its population, I perceive that the Swiss are become
like all the surrounding communities, and those surrounding communities like the Swiss: so that as numerical strength now forms the only
difference between them, victory necessarily attends the largest army.
Thus one of the consequences of the democratic revolution which is
going on in Europe is to make numerical strength preponderate on all
fields of battle, and to constrain all small nations to incorporate themselves with large states or at least to adopt the policy of the latter.

As numbers are the determining cause of victory, each people ought
of course to strive by all the means in its power to bring the greatest
possible number of men into the field. When it was possible to enlist a
kind of troops superior to all others, such as the Swiss infantry or the
French horse of the sixteenth century, it was not thought necessary to
raise very large armies; but the case is altered when one soldier is as
efficient as another.

The same cause which begets this new want also supplies means of
satisfying it; for, as I have already observed, when men are all alike,
they are all weak, and the supreme power of the State is naturally
much stronger among democratic nations than elsewhere. Hence,
while these nations are desirous of enrolling the whole male population in the ranks of the army, they have the power of effecting this object: the consequence is, that in democratic ages armies seem to grow
larger in proportion as the love of war declines.

In the same ages too, the manner of carrying on war is likewise altered by the same causes. Machiavelli[1] observes in "The Prince," "that

---

* This is not only because these nations have the same social condition, but it arises from the
very nature of that social condition, which leads men to imitate and identify themselves with
each other.

   When the members of a community are divided into castes and classes, they not only differ
from one another, but they have no taste and no desire to be alike; on the contrary, every one
endeavours, more and more, to keep his own opinions undisturbed, to retain his own peculiar
habits, and to remain himself. The characteristics of individuals are very strongly marked.

   When the state of society among a people is democratic—that is to say, when there are no
longer any castes or classes in the community, and all its members are nearly equal in education and in property—the human mind follows the opposite direction. Men are much
alike, and they are annoyed, as it were, by any deviation from that likeness: far from seeking
to preserve their own distinguishing singularities, they endeavour to shake them off, in order
to identify themselves with the general mass of the people, which is the sole representative
of right and of might to their eyes. The characteristics of individuals are nearly obliterated.

   In the ages of aristocracy even those who are naturally alike strive to create imaginary differences between themselves: in the ages of democracy even those who are not alike seek
only to become so, and to copy each other—so strongly is the mind of every man always carried away by the general impulse of mankind.

   Something of the same kind may be observed between nations: two nations, having the
same aristocratic social condition, might remain thoroughly distinct and extremely different,
because the spirit of aristocracy is to retain strong individual characteristics; but if two
neighbouring nations have the same democratic social condition, they cannot fail to adopt
similar opinions and manners, because the spirit of democracy tends to assimilate men to
each other.

it is much more difficult to subdue a people which has a prince and its baron for its leaders, than a nation which is commanded by a prince and his slaves." To avoid offence, let us read public functionaries for slaves, and this important truth will be strictly applicable to our own time.

A great aristocratic people cannot either conquer its neighbours, or be conquered by them, without great difficulty. It cannot conquer them, because all its forces can never be collected and held together for a considerable period: it cannot be conquered, because an enemy meets at every step small centres of resistance by which invasion is arrested. War against an aristocracy may be compared to war in a mountainous country; the defeated party has constant opportunities of rallying its forces to make a stand in a new position.

Exactly the reverse occurs among democratic nations: they easily bring their whole disposable force into the field, and when the nation is wealthy and populous it soon becomes victorious; but if ever it is conquered, and its territory invaded, it has few resources at command; and if the enemy takes the capital, the nation is lost. This may very well be explained: as each member of the community is individually isolated and extremely powerless, no one of the whole body can either defend himself or present a rallying-point to others. Nothing is strong in a democratic country except the State; as the military strength of the State is destroyed by the destruction of the army, and its civil power paralysed by the capture of the chief city, all that remains is only a multitude without strength or government, unable to resist the organized power by which it is assailed. I am aware that this danger may be lessened by the creation of provincial liberties, and consequently of provincial powers, but this remedy will always be insufficient. For after such a catastrophe, not only is the population unable to carry on hostilities, but it may be apprehended that they will not be inclined to attempt it.

In accordance with the law of nations adopted in civilized countries, the object of wars is not to seize the property of private individuals, but simply to get possession of political power. The destruction of private property is only occasionally resorted to for the purpose of attaining the latter object.

When an aristocratic country is invaded after the defeat of its army, the nobles, although they are at the same time the wealthiest members of the community, will continue to defend themselves individually rather than submit; for if the conqueror remained master of the country, he would deprive them of their political power, to which they cling even more closely than to their property. They therefore prefer fighting to subjection, which is to them the greatest of all misfortunes; and they readily carry the people along with them, because the people has long been used to follow and obey them, and besides has but little to risk in the war.

Among a nation in which equality of conditions prevails, each citizen, on the contrary, has but a slender share of political power, and often has no share at all; on the other hand, all are independent, and all have something to lose; so that they are much less afraid of being conquered, and much more afraid of war, than an aristocratic people. It will always be extremely difficult to decide a democratic population to take up arms, when hostilities have reached its own territory. Hence the necessity of giving to such a people the rights and the political character which may impart to every citizen some of those interests that cause the nobles to act for the public welfare in aristocratic countries.

It should never be forgotten by the princes and other leaders of democratic nations, that nothing but the passion and the habit of freedom can maintain an advantageous contest with the passion and the habit of physical well-being. I can conceive nothing better prepared for subjection, in case of defeat, than a democratic people without free institutions.

Formerly it was customary to take the field with a small body of troops, to fight in small engagements, and to make long regular sieges: modern tactics consist in fighting decisive battles, and, as soon as a line of march is open before the army, in rushing upon the capital city, in order to terminate the war at a single blow. Napoleon, it is said, was the inventor of this new system; but the invention of such a system did not depend on any individual man, whoever he might be. The mode in which Napoleon carried on war was suggested to him by the state of society in his time; that mode was successful, because it was eminently adapted to that state of society, and because he was the first to employ it. Napoleon was the first commander who marched at the head of an army from capital to capital, but the road was opened for him by the ruin of feudal society. It may fairly be believed that, if that extraordinary man had been born three hundred years ago, he would not have derived the same results from his method of warfare, or, rather, that he would have had a different method.

I shall add but a few words on civil wars, for fear of exhausting the patience of the reader. Most of the remarks which I have made respecting foreign wars are applicable *a fortiori* to civil wars. Men living in democracies are not naturally prone to the military character; they sometimes assume it, when they have been dragged by compulsion to the field; but to rise in a body and voluntarily to expose themselves to the horrors of war, and especially of civil war, is a course which the men of democracies are not apt to adopt. None but the most adventurous members of the community consent to run into such risks; the bulk of the population remains motionless.

But even if the population were inclined to act, considerable obstacles would stand in their way; for they can resort to no old and well-established influence which they are willing to obey—no well-known leaders to rally the discontented, as well as to discipline and to lead them—no political powers subordinate to the supreme power of the nation, which afford an effectual support to the resistance directed against the government.

In democratic countries the moral power of the majority is immense, and the physical resources which it has at its command are out of all proportion to the physical resources which may be combined against it. Therefore the party which occupies the seat of the majority, which speaks in its name and wields its power, triumphs instantaneously and irresistibly over all private resistance; it does not even give such opposition time to exist, but nips it in the bud.

Those who in such nations seek to effect a revolution by force of arms have no other resource than suddenly to seize upon the whole engine of government as it stands, which can better be done by a single blow than by a war; for as soon as there is a regular war, the party which represents the State is always certain to conquer.

The only case in which a civil war could arise is, if the army should divide itself into two factions, the one raising the standard of rebellion, the other remaining true to its allegiance. An army constitutes a small community, very closely united together, endowed with great powers of vitality, and able to supply its own wants for some time. Such a war might be bloody, but it could not be long; for either the rebellious army would gain over the government by the sole display of its resources, or by its first victory, and then the war would be over; or the struggle would take place, and then that portion of the army which should not be supported by the organized powers of the State would speedily either disband itself or be destroyed. It may therefore be admitted as a general truth, that in ages of equality civil wars will become much less frequent and less protracted.*

FOURTH BOOK.

INFLUENCE OF DEMOCRATIC OPINIONS AND SENTIMENTS ON POLITICAL SOCIETY.

I should imperfectly fulfil the purpose of this book, if, after having shown what opinions and sentiments are suggested by the principle of equality, I did not point out, ere I conclude, the general influence which these same opinions and sentiments may exercise upon the government of human societies. To succeed in this object I shall frequently have to retrace my steps; but I trust the reader will not refuse to follow me through paths already known to him, which may lead to some new truth.

Chapter I.

THAT EQUALITY NATURALLY GIVES MEN A TASTE FOR FREE INSTITUTIONS.

The principle of equality, which makes men independent of each other, gives them a habit and a taste for following, in their private ac-

---

* It should be borne in mind that I speak here of sovereign and independent democratic nations, not of confederate democracies; in confederacies, as the prepondering power always resides, in spite of all political fictions, in the state governments, and not in the federal government, civil wars are in fact nothing but foreign wars in disguise.

tions, no other guide but their own will. This complete independence, which they constantly enjoy toward their equals and in the intercourse of private life, tends to make them look upon all, authority with a jealous eye, and speedily suggests to them the notion and the love of political freedom. Men living at such times have a natural bias to free institutions. Take any one of them at a venture, and search if you can his most deep-seated instincts; you will find that of all governments he will soonest conceive and most highly value that government, whose head he has himself elected, and whose administration he may control.

Of all the political effects produced by the equality of conditions, this love of independence is the first to strike the observing, and to alarm the timid; nor can it be said that their alarm is wholly misplaced, for anarchy has a more formidable aspect in democratic countries than elsewhere. As the citizens have no direct influence on each other, as soon as the supreme power of the nations fails, which kept them all in their several stations, it would seem that disorder must instantly reach its utmost pitch, and that, every man drawing aside in a different direction, the fabric of society must at once crumble away. I am however persuaded that anarchy is not the principal evil which democratic ages have to fear, but the least. For the principle of equality begets two tendencies; the one leads men straight to independence, and may suddenly drive them into anarchy; the other conducts them by a longer, more secret, but more certain road, to servitude. Nations readily discern the former tendency, and are prepared to resist it; they are led away by the latter, without perceiving its drift; hence it is peculiarly important to point it out.

For myself, I am so far from urging as a reproach to the principle of equality that it renders men untractable, that this very circumstance principally calls forth my approbation. I admire to see how it deposits in the mind and heart of man the dim conception and instinctive love of political independence, thus preparing the remedy for the evil which it engenders: it is on this very account that I am attached to it.

Chapter II.

THAT THE NOTIONS OF DEMOCRATIC NATIONS ON GOVERNMENT ARE NATURALLY FAVOURABLE TO THE CONCENTRATION OF POWER.

The notion of secondary powers, placed between the sovereign and his subjects, occurred naturally to the imagination of aristocratic nations, because those communities contained individuals or families raised above the common level, and apparently destined to command by their birth, their education, and their wealth. This same notion is naturally wanting in the minds of men in democratic ages, for converse reasons; it can only be introduced artificially, it can only be kept there with difficulty; whereas they conceive, as it were, without thinking upon the subject, the notion of a sole and central power which governs the whole community by its direct influence. Moreover in politics, as well as in philosophy and in religion, the intellect of democratic nations is peculiarly open to simple and general notions. Complicated systems are repugnant to it, and its favourite conception is that of a great nation composed of citizens all resembling the same pattern, and all governed by a single power.

The very next notion to that of a sole and central power, which presents itself to the minds of men in the ages of equality, is the notion of uniformity of legislation. As every man sees that he differs but little from those about him, he cannot understand why a rule which is applicable to one man should not be equally applicable to all others. Hence the slightest privileges are repugnant to his reason; the faintest dissimilarities in the political institutions of the same people offend him, and uniformity of legislation appears to him to be the first condition of good government.

I find, on the contrary, that this same notion of a uniform rule, equally binding on all the members of the community, was almost unknown to the human mind in aristocratic ages; it was either never entertained, or it was rejected.

These contrary tendencies of opinion ultimately turn on either side to such blind instincts and such ungovernable habits, that they still direct the actions of men, in spite of particular exceptions. Notwithstanding the immense variety of conditions in the middle ages, a certain number of persons existed at that period in precisely similar circumstances; but this did not prevent the laws then in force from assigning to each of them distinct duties and different rights. On the contrary, at the present time all the powers of government are exerted to impose the same customs and the same laws on populations which have as yet but few points of resemblance.

As the conditions of men become equal among a people, individuals seem of less importance, and society of greater dimensions; or rather, every citizen, being assimilated to all the rest, is lost in the crowd, and nothing stands conspicuous but the great and imposing image of the people at large. This naturally gives the men of democratic periods a lofty opinion of the privileges of society, and a very humble notion of the rights of individuals; they are ready to admit that the interests of the former are everything, and those of the latter nothing. They are willing to acknowledge that the power which represents the community has far more information and wisdom than any of the members of that community; and that it is the duty, as well as the right, of that power to guide as well as govern each private citizen.

If we closely scrutinize our contemporaries, and penetrate to the root of their political opinions, we shall detect some of the notions which I have just pointed out, and we shall perhaps be surprised to find so much accordance between men who are so often at variance.

The Americans hold, that in every state the supreme power ought to emanate from the people; but when once that power is constituted, they can conceive, as it were, no limits to it, and they are ready to admit that it has the right to do whatever it pleases. They have not the slightest notion of peculiar privileges granted to cities, families, or persons; their minds appear never to have foreseen that it might be possible not to apply with strict uniformity the same laws to every part, and to all the inhabitants.

These same opinions are more and more diffused in Europe; they even insinuate themselves among those nations which most vehemently reject the principle of the sovereignty of the people. Such nations assign a different origin to the supreme power, but they ascribe to that power the same characteristics. Among them all, the idea of intermediate powers is weakened and obliterated: the idea of rights inherent in certain individuals is rapidly disappearing from the minds of men; the idea of the omnipotence and sole authority of society at large rises to fill its place. These ideas take root and spread in proportion as social conditions become more equal, and men more alike; they are engendered by equality, and in turn they hasten the progress of equality.

In France, where the revolution of which I am speaking has gone further than in any other European country, these opinions have got complete hold of the public mind. If we listen attentively to the language of the various parties in France, we shall find that there is not one which has not adopted them. Most of these parties censure the conduct of the government, but they all hold that the government ought perpetually to act and interfere in everything that is done. Even those which are most at variance are nevertheless agreed upon this head. The unity, the ubiquity, the omnipotence of the supreme power, and the uniformity of its rules, constitute the principal characteristics of all the political systems which have been put forward in our age. They recur even in the wildest visions of political regeneration: the human mind pursues them in its dreams.

If these notions spontaneously arise in the minds of private individuals, they suggest themselves still more forcibly to the minds of princes. While the ancient fabric of European society is altered and dissolved, sovereigns acquire new conceptions of their opportunities and their duties; they learn for the first time that the central power which they represent may and ought to administer by its own agency, and on a uniform plan, all the concerns of the whole community. This opinion, which, I will venture to say, was never conceived before our time by the monarchs of Europe, now sinks deeply into the minds of kings, and abides there amid all the agitation of more unsettled thoughts.

Our contemporaries are therefore much less divided than is commonly supposed; they are constantly disputing as to the hands in which supremacy is to be vested, but they readily agree upon the duties and the rights of that supremacy. The notion they all form of government is that of a sole, simple, providential and creative power.

All secondary opinions in politics are unsettled; this one remains fixed, invariable, and consistent. It is adopted by statesmen and political philosophers; it is eagerly laid hold of by the multitude; those who govern and those who are governed agree to pursue it with equal ardour; it is the foremost notion of their minds, it seems conatural with their feelings. It originates therefore in no caprice of the human intellect, but it is a necessary condition of the present state of mankind.

Chapter III.

THAT THE SENTIMENTS OF DEMOCRATIC NATIONS ACCORD WITH THEIR OPINIONS IN LEADING THEM TO CONCENTRATE POLITICAL POWER.

If it be true that, in ages of equality, men readily adopt the notion of a great central power, it cannot be doubted on the other hand that their habits and sentiments predispose them to recognise such a power and to give it their support.* This may be demonstrated in a few words, as the greater part of the reasons, to which the fact may be attributed, have been previously stated.

As the men who inhabit democratic countries have no superiors, no inferiors, and no habitual or necessary partners in their undertakings, they readily fall back upon themselves and consider themselves as beings apart. I had occasion to point this out at considerable length in treating of individualism. Hence such men can never, without an effort, tear themselves from their private affairs to engage in public business; their natural bias leads them to abandon the latter to the sole visible and permanent representative of the interests of the community, that is to say, to the State. Not only are they naturally wanting in a taste for public business, but they have frequently no time to attend to it. Private life is so busy in democratic periods, so excited, so full of wishes and of work, that hardly any energy or leisure remains to each individual for public life. I am the last man to contend that these propensities are unconquerable, since my chief object in writing this book has been to combat them. I only maintain that at the present day a secret power is fostering them in the human heart, and that if they are not checked they will wholly overgrow it.

I have also had occasion to show how the increasing love of well-being, and the fluctuating character of property, cause democratic nations to dread all violent disturbance. The love of public tranquillity is frequently the only passion which these nations retain, and it becomes more active and powerful among them in proportion as all other passions droop and die. This naturally disposes the members of the community constantly to give or to surrender additional rights to the

---

* Men connect the greatness of their idea of unity with means, God with ends; hence this idea of greatness, as men conceive it, leads us into infinite littlenesses. To compel all men to follow the same course toward the same object is a human notion;—to introduce infinite variety of action, but so combined that all these acts lead by a multitude of different courses to the accomplishment of one great design, is a conception of the Deity.

The human idea of unity is almost always barren; the divine idea pregnant with abundant results. Men think they manifest their greatness by simplifying the means they use; but it is the purpose of God which is simple—his means are infinitely varied.

central power, which alone seems to be interested in defending them by the same means that it uses to defend itself.

As in ages of equality no man is compelled to lend his assistance to his fellow-men, and none has any right to expect much support from them, every one is at once independent and powerless. These two conditions, which must never be either separately considered or confounded together, inspire the citizen of a democratic country with very contrary propensities. His independence fills him with self-reliance and pride among his equals; his debility makes him feel from time to time the want of some outward assistance, which he cannot expect from any of them, because they are all impotent and unsympathizing. In this predicament he naturally turns his eyes to that imposing power which alone rises above the level of universal depression. Of that power his wants and especially his desires continually remind him, until he ultimately views it as the sole and neccssary support of his own weakness.*

This may more completely explain what frequently takes place in democratic countries, where the very men who are so impatient of superiors patiently submit to a master, exhibiting at once their pride and their servility.

The hatred which men bear to privilege increases in proportion as privileges become more scarce and less considerable, so that democratic passions would seem to burn most fiercely at the very time when they have least fuel. I have already given the reason of this phenomenon. When all conditions are unequal, no inequality is so great as to offend the eye; whereas the slightest dissimilarity is odious in the midst of general uniformity: the more complete is this uniformity, the more insupportable does the sight of such a diference become. Hence it is natural that the love of equality should constantly increase together with equality itself, and that it should grow by what it feeds upon.

This never-dying, ever-kindling hatred, which sets a democratic people against the smallest privileges, is peculiarly favourable to the

---

* In democratic communities nothing but the central power has any stability in its position or any permanence in its undertakings. All the members of society are in ceaseless stir and transformation. Now it is in the nature of all governments to seek constantly to enlarge their sphere of action: hence it is almost impossible that such a government should not ultimately succeed, because it acts with a fixed principle and a constant will, upon men, whose position, whose notions, and whose desires are in continual vacillation.

It frequently happens that the members of the community promote the influence of the central power without intending it. Democratic ages are periods of experiment, innovation, and adventure. At such times there are always a multitude of men engaged in difficult or novel undertakings, which they follow alone, without caring for their fellow-men. Such persons may be ready to admit, as a general principle, that the public authority ought not to interfere in private concerns; but, by an exception to that rule, each of them craves for its assistance in the particular concern on which he is engaged, and seeks to draw upon the influence of the government for his own benefit, though he would restrict it on all other occasions. If a large number of men apply this particular exception to a great variety of different purposes, the sphere of the central power extends insensibly in all directions, although each of them wishes it to be circumscribed.

Thus a democratic government increases its power simply by the fact of its permanence. Time is on its side; every incident befriends it; the passions of individuals unconsciously promote it; and it may be asserted, that the older a democratic community is, the more centralized will its government become.

gradual concentration of all political rights in the hands of the representative of the state alone. The sovereign, being necessarily and incontestably above all the citizens, excites not their envy, and each of them thinks that he strips his equals of the prerogative which he concedes to the crown.

The man of a democratic age is extremely reluctant to obey his neighbour who is his equal; he refuses to acknowledge in such a person ability superior to his own; he mistrusts his justice, and is jealous of his power; he fears and he contemns him; and he loves continually to remind him of the common dependence in which both of them stand to the same master.

Every central power which follows its natural tendencies courts and encourages the principle of equality; for equality singularly facilitates, extends, and secures the influence of a central power.

In like manner it may be said that every central government worships uniformity: uniformity relieves it from inquiry into an infinite number of small details which must be attended to if rules were to be adapted to men, instead of indiscriminately subjecting men to rules: thus the government likes what the citizens like, and naturally hates what they hate. These common sentiments, which, in democratic nations, constantly unite the sovereign and every member of the community in one and the same conviction, establish a secret and lasting sympathy between them. The faults of the government are pardoned for the sake of its tastes; public confidence is only reluctantly withdrawn in the midst even of its excesses and its errors, and it is restored at the first call. Democratic nations often hate those in whose hands the central power is vested; but they always love that power itself.

Thus, by two separate paths, I have reached the same conclusion. I have shown that the principle of equality suggests to men the notion of a sole, uniform, and strong government: I have now shown that the principle of equality imparts to them a taste for it. To governments of this kind the nations of our age are therefore tending. They are drawn thither by the natural inclination of mind and heart; and in order to reach that result, it is enough that they do not check themselves in their course.

I am of opinion, that, in the democratic ages which are opening upon us, individual independence and local liberties will ever be the produce of artificial contrivance; that centralization will be the natural form of government.*

---

* A democratic people is not only led by its own tastes to centralize its government, but the passions of all the men by whom it is governed constantly urge it in the same direction. It may easily be foreseen that almost all the able and ambitious members of a democratic community will labour without ceasing to extend the powers of government, because they all hope at some time or other to wield those powers. It is a waste of time to attempt to prove to them that extreme centralization may be injurious to the State, since they are centralizing for their own benefit. Among the public men of democracies there are hardly any but men of great disinterestedness or extreme mediocrity who seek to oppose the centralization of government: the former are scarce, the latter powerless.

Chapter IV.

OF CERTAIN PECULIAR AND ACCIDENTAL CAUSES WHICH EITHER LEAD A
PEOPLE TO COMPLETE CENTRALIZATION OF GOVERNMENT, OR WHICH
DIVERT THEM FROM IT.

If all democratic nations are instinctively led to the centralization of
government, they tend to this result in an unequal manner. This depends on the particular circumstances which may promote or prevent
the natural consequences of that state of society—circumstances
which are exceedingly numerous; but I shall only advert to a few of
them.

Among men who have lived free long before they became equal, the
tendencies derived from free institutions combat, to a certain extent,
the propensities superinduced by the principle of equality; and although the central power may increase its privileges among such a
people, the private members of such a community will never entirely
forfeit their independence. But when the equality of conditions grows
up among a people which has never known, or has long ceased to
know, what freedom is (and such is the case upon the continent of Europe,) as the former habits of the nation are suddenly combined, by
some sort of natural attraction, with the novel habits and principles
engendered by the state of society, all powers seem spontaneously to
rush to the centre. These powers accumulate there with astonishing
rapidity, and the state instantly attains the utmost limits of its
strength, while private persons allow themselves to sink as suddenly to
the lowest degree of weakness.

The English who emigrated three hundred years ago to found a
democratic commonwealth on the shores of the New World, had all
learned to take a part in public affairs in their mother country; they
were conversant with trial by jury; they were accustomed to liberty of
speech and of the press—to personal freedom, to the notion of rights
and the practice of asserting them. They carried with them to America
these free institutions and manly customs, and these institutions preserved them against the encroachments of the state. Thus among the
Americans it is freedom which is old—equality is of comparatively
modern date. The reverse is occurring in Europe, where equality,
introduced by absolute power and under the rule of kings, was already
infused into the habits of nations long before freedom had entered
into their conceptions.

I have said that among democratic nations the notion of government naturally presents itself to the mind under the form of a sole and
central power, and that the notion of intermediate powers is not familiar to them. This is peculiarly applicable to the democratic nations
which have witnessed the triumph of the principle of equality by
means of a violent revolution. As the classes which managed local affairs have been suddenly swept away by the storm, and as the confused mass which remains has as yet neither the organization nor the

habits which fit it to assume the administration of these same affairs, the state alone seems capable of taking upon itself all the details of government, and centralization becomes, as it were, the unavoidable state of the country.

Napoleon deserves neither praise nor censure for having centered in his own hands almost all the administrative power of France; for, after the abrupt disappearance of the nobility and the higher rank of the middle classes, these powers devolved on him of course: it would have been almost as difficult for him to reject as to assume them. But no necessity of this kind has ever been felt by the Americans, who, having passed through no revolution, and having governed themselves from the first, never had to call upon the state to act for a time as their guardian. Thus the progress of centralization among a democratic people depends not only on the progress of equality, but on the manner in which this equality has been established.

At the commencement of a great democratic revolution, when hostilities have but just broken out between the different classes of society, the people endeavours to centralize the public administration in the hands of the government, in order to wrest the management of local affairs from the aristocracy. Toward the close of such a revolution, on the contrary, it is usually the conquered aristocracy that endeavours to make over the management of all affairs to the state, because such an aristocracy dreads the tyranny of a people which has become its equal, and not unfrequently its master. Thus it is not always the same class of the community which strives to increase the prerogative of the government; but as long as the democratic revolution lasts, there is always one class in the nation, powerful in numbers or in wealth, which is induced, by peculiar passions or interests, to centralize the public administration, independently of that hatred of being governed by one's neighbour, which is a general and permanent feeling among democratic nations.

It may be remarked, that at the present day the lower orders in England are striving with all their might to destroy local independence, and to transfer the administration from all the points of the circumference to the centre; whereas the higher classes are endeavouring to retain this administration within its ancient boundaries. I venture to predict that a time will come when the very reverse will happen.

These observations explain why the supreme power is always stronger, and private individuals weaker, among a democratic people which has passed through a long and arduous struggle to reach a state of equality, than among a democratic community in which the citizens have been equal from the first. The example of the Americans completely demonstrates the fact. The inhabitants of the United States were never divided by any privileges; they have never known the mutual relation of master and inferior, and as they neither dread nor hate each other, they have never known the necessity of calling in the supreme power to manage their affairs. The lot of the Americans is singular: they have derived from the aristocracy of England the notion of private rights and the taste for local freedom; and they have been able to retain both the one and the other, because they have had no aristocracy to combat.

If at all times education enables men to defend their independence, this is most especially true in democratic ages. When all men are alike, it is easy to found a sole and all-powerful government, by the aid of mere instinct. But men require much intelligence, knowledge, and art to organize and to maintain secondary powers under similar circumstances, and to create amidst the independence and individual weakness of the citizens such free associations as may be in a condition to struggle against tyranny without destroying public order.

Hence the concentration of power and the subjection of individuals will increase among democratic nations, not only in the same proportion as their equality, but in the same proportion as their ignorance. It is true, that in ages of imperfect civilization the government is frequently as wanting in the knowledge required to impose a despotism upon the people, as the people are wanting in the knowledge required to shake it off; but the effect is not the same on both sides. However rude a democratic people may be, the central power which rules it is never completely devoid of cultivation, because it readily draws to its own uses what little cultivation is to be found in the country, and, if necessary, may seek assistance elsewhere. Hence, among a nation which is ignorant as well as democratic, an amazing difference cannot fail speedily to arise between the intellectual capacity of the ruler and that of each of his subjects. This completes the easy concentration of all power in his hands: the administrative function of the state is perpetually extended, because the state alone is competent to administer the affairs of the country.

Aristocratic nations, however unenlightened they may be, never afford the same spectacle, because in them instruction is nearly equally diffused between the monarch and the leading members of the community.

The Pacha, who now rules in Egypt, found the population of that country composed of men exceedingly ignorant and equal, and he has borrowed the science and ability of Europe to govern that people. As the personal attainments of the sovereign are thus combined with the ignorance and democratic weakness of his subjects, the utmost centralization has been established without impediment, and the Pacha has made the country his manufactory, and the inhabitants his workmen.

I think that extreme centralization of government ultimately enervates society, and thus after a length of time weakens the government itself; but I do not deny that a centralized social power may be able to execute great undertakings with facility in a given time and on a particular point. This is more especially true of war, in which success depends much more on the means of transferring all the resources of a nation to one single point, than on the extent of those resources. Hence it is chiefly in war that nations desire and frequently require to increase the powers of the central government. All men of military genius are fond of centralization, which increases their strength; and all men of centralizing genius are fond of war, which compels nations to combine all their powers in the hands of the government. Thus the democratic tendency which leads men unceasingly to multiply the privileges of the state, and to circumscribe the rights of private persons, is much more rapid and constant among those democratic nations which are exposed by their position to great and frequent wars, than among all others.

I have shown how the dread of disturbance and the love of well-being insensibly lead democratic nations to increase the functions of central government, as the only power which appears to be intrinsically sufficiently strong, enlightened, and secure, to protect them from anarchy. I would now add, that all the particular circumstances which tend to make the state of a democratic community agitated and precarious, enhance this general propensity, and lead private persons more and more to sacrifice their rights to their tranquility.

A people is therefore never so disposed to increase the functions of central government as at the close of a long and bloody revolution, which, after having wrested property from the hands of its former possessors, has shaken all belief, and filled the nation with fierce hatreds, conflicting interests, and contending factions. The love of public tranquility becomes at such times an indiscriminating passion, and the members of the community are apt to conceive a most inordinate devotion to order.

I have already examined several of the incidents which may concur to promote the centralization of power, but the principal cause still remains to be noticed. The foremost of the incidental causes which may draw the management of all affairs into the hands of the ruler in democratic countries, is the origin of that ruler himself, and his own propensities. Men who live in the ages of equality are naturally fond of central power, and are willing to extend its privileges; but if it happens that this same power faithfully represents their own interests, and exactly copies their own inclinations, the confidence they place in it knows no bounds, and they think that whatever they bestow upon it is bestowed upon themselves.

The attraction of administrative powers to the centre will always be less easy and less rapid under the reign of kings who are still in some way connected with the old aristocratic order, than under new princes, the children of their own achievements, whose birth, prejudices, propensities, and habits appear to bind them indissolubly to the cause of equality. I do not mean that princes of aristocratic origin who live in democratic ages do not attempt to centralize; I believe they apply themselves to that object as diligently as any others. For them, the sole advantages of equality lie in that direction; but their opportunities are less great, because the community, instead of volunteering compliance with their desires, frequently obeys them with reluctance. In democratic communities the rule is that centralization must increase in proportion as the sovereign is less aristocratic.

When an ancient race of kings stands at the head of an aristocracy, as the natural prejudices of the sovereign perfectly accord with the natural prejudices of the nobility, the vices inherent in aristocratic communities have a free course, and meet with no corrective. The reverse is the case when the scion of a feudal stock is placed at the head of a democratic people. The sovereign is constantly led, by his education, his habits, and his associations, to adopt sentiments suggested by the inequality of conditions, and the people tend as constantly, by their social condition, to those manners which are engendered by equality. At such times it often happens that the citizens seek to control the central power far less as a tyrannical than as an aristocratical power, and that they persist in the firm defence of their independence, not only because they would remain free, but especially because they are determined to remain equal.

A revolution which overthrows an ancient regal family, in order to place men of a more recent growth at the head of a democratic people, may temporarily weaken the central power; but however anarchical such a revolution may appear at first, we need not hesitate to predict that its final and certain consequence will be to extend and to secure the prerogatives of that power.

The foremost, or indeed the sole condition which is required in order to succeed in centralizing the supreme power in a democratic community, is to love equality, or to get men to believe you love it. Thus the science of despotism, which was once so complex, is simplified, and reduced as it were to a single principle.

Chapter V.

THAT AMONG THE EUROPEAN NATIONS OF OUR TIME THE POWER OF GOVERNMENTS IS INCREASING, ALTHOUGH THE PERSONS WHO GOVERN ARE LESS STABLE.

On reflecting upon what has already been said, the reader will be startled and alarmed to find that in Europe everything seems to conduce to the indefinite extension of the prerogatives of government, and to render all that enjoyed the rights of private independence more weak, more subordinate, and more precarious.

The democratic nations of Europe have all the general and permanent tendencies which urge the Americans to the centralization of government, and they are moreover exposed to a number of secondary and incidental causes with which the Americans are unacquainted. It would seem as if every step they make toward equality brings them nearer to despotism.

And indeed if we do but cast our looks around, we shall be convinced that such is the fact. During the aristocratic ages which preceded the present time, the sovereigns of Europe had been deprived of, or had relinquished, many of the rights inherent in their power. Not a hundred years ago, among the greater part of European nations, numerous private persons and corporations were sufficiently independent to administer justice, to raise and maintain troops, to levy taxes, and frequently even to make or interpret the law. The State has everywhere resumed to itself alone these natural attributes of sovereign power; in all matters of government the State tolerates no intermediate agent between itself and the people, and in general business it directs the people by its own immediate influence. I am far from blaming this concentration of power, I simply point it out.

At the same period a great number of secondary powers existed in Europe, which represented local interests and administered local affairs. Most of these local authorities have already disappeared; all are speedily tending to disappear, or to fall into the most complete dependance. From one end of Europe to the other the privileges of the nobility, the liberties of cities, and the powers of provincial bodies, are either destroyed or upon the verge of destruction.

Europe has endured, in the course of the last half century, many revolutions and counter-revolutions which have agitated it in opposite directions: but all these perturbations resemble each other in one respect—they have all shaken or destroyed the secondary powers of government. The local privileges which the French did not abolish in the countries they conquered, have finally succumbed to the policy of the princes who conquered the French. Those princes rejected all the innovations of the French revolution except centralization: that is the only principle they consented to receive from such a source.

My object is to remark, that all these various rights, which have been successively wrested, in our time, from classes, corporations, and individuals, have not served to raise new secondary powers on a more democratic basis, but have uniformly been concentrated in the hands of the sovereign. Everywhere the State acquires more and more direct control over the humblest members of the community, and a more exclusive power of governing each of them in his smallest concerns.*

Almost all the charitable establishments of Europe were formerly in the hands of private persons or of corporations; they are now almost all dependant on the supreme government, and in many countries are actually administered by that power. The State almost exclusively undertakes to supply bread to the hungry, assistance and shelter to the sick, work to the idle, and to act as the sole reliever of all kinds of misery.

Education, as well as charity, is become in most countries at the present day a national concern. The State receives, and often takes

---

* This gradual weakening of individuals in relation to society at large may be traced in a thousand ways. I shall select from among these examples one derived from the law of wills.

In aristocracies it is common to profess the greatest reverence for the last testamentary dispositions of a man; this feeling sometimes even became superstitious among the elder nations of Europe: the power of the State, far from interfering with the caprices of a dying man, gave full force to the very least of them, and insured to him a perpetual power.

When all living men are enfeebled, the will of the dead is less respected: it is circumscribed within a narrow range, beyond which it is annulled or checked by the supreme power of the laws. In the middle ages, testamentary power had, so to speak, no limits: among the French at the present day, a man cannot distribute his fortune among his children without the interference of the State: after having domineered over a whole life, the law insists upon regulating the very last act of it.

the child from the arms of the mother, to hand it over to official agents: the State undertakes to train the heart and to instruct the mind of each generation. Uniformity prevails in the courses of public instruction as in everything else; diversity, as well as freedom, are disappearing day by day.

Nor do I hesitate to affirm, that among almost all the Christian nations of our days, Catholic as well as Protestant, religion is in danger of falling into the hands of the government. Not that rulers are overjealous of the right of settling points of doctrine, but they get more and more hold upon the will of those by whom doctrines are expounded; they deprive the clergy of their property, and pay them by salaries; they divert to their own use the influence of the priesthood, they make them their own ministers—often their own servants—and by this alliance with religion they reach the inner depths of the soul of man.*

But this is as yet only one side of the picture. The authority of government has not only spread, as we have just seen, throughout the sphere of all existing powers, till that sphere can no longer contain it, but it goes further, and invades the domain heretofore reserved to private independence. A multitude of actions, which were formerly entirely beyond the control of the public administration, have been subjected to that control in our time, and the number of them is constantly increasing.

Among aristocratic nations the supreme government usually contented itself with managing and superintending the community in whatever directly and ostensibly concerned the national honour; but in all other respects the people were left to work out their own free will. Among these nations the government often seemed to forget that there is a point at which the faults and the sufferings of private persons involve the general prosperity, and that to prevent the ruin of a private individual must sometimes be a matter of public importance.

The democratic nations of our time lean to the opposite extreme. It is evident that most of our rulers will not content themselves with governing the people collectively; it would seem as if they thought themselves responsible for the actions and private condition of their subjects—as if they had undertaken to guide and to instruct each of them in the various incidents of life, and to secure their happiness quite independently of their own consent. On the other hand private individuals grow more and more apt to look upon the supreme power in the same light; they invoke its assistance in all their necessities, and they fix their eyes upon the administration as their mentor or their guide.

I assert that there is no country in Europe in which the public

---

* In proportion as the duties of the central power are augmented, the number of public officers by whom that power is represented must increase also. They form a nation in each nation; and as they share the stability of the government, they more and more fill up the place of an aristocracy.

In almost every part of Europe the government rules in two ways; it rules one portion of the community by the fear which they entertain of its agents, and the other by the hope they have of becoming its agents.

administration has not become, not only more centralized, but more inquisitive and more minute: it everywhere interferes in private concerns more than it did; it regulates more undertakings, and undertakings of a lesser kind; and it gains a firmer footing every day about, above, and around all private persons, to assist, to advise, and to coerce them.

Formerly a sovereign lived upon the income of his lands, or the revenue of his taxes; this is no longer the case now that his wants have increased as well as his power. Under the same circumstances which formerly compelled a prince to put on a new tax, he now has recourse to a loan. Thus the State gradually becomes the debtor of most of the wealthier members of the community, and centralizes the largest amounts of capital in its own hands.

Small capital is drawn into its keeping by another method. As men are intermingled and conditions become more equal, the poor have more resources, more education, and more desires; they conceive the notion of bettering their condition, and this teaches them to save. These savings are daily producing an infinite number of small capitals, the slow and gradual produce of labour, which are always increasing. But the greater part of this money would be unproductive if it remained scattered in the hands of its owners. This circumstance has given rise to a philanthropic institution, which will soon become, if I am not mistaken, one of our most important political institutions. Some charitable persons conceived the notion of collecting the savings of the poor and placing them out at interest. In some countries these benevolent associations are still completely distinct from the state; but in almost all they manifestly tend to identify themselves with the government; and in some of them the government has superseded them, taking upon itself the enormous task of centralizing in one place, and putting out at interest on its own responsibility, the daily savings of many millions of the working classes.

Thus the State draws to itself the wealth of the rich by loans, and has the poor man's mite at its disposal in the savings' banks. The wealth of the country is perpetually flowing around the government and passing through its hands; the accumulation increases in the same proportion as the equality of conditions; for in a democratic country the State alone inspires private individuals with confidence, because the State alone appears to be endowed with strength and durability.*

Thus the sovereign does not confine himself to the management of the public treasury; he interferes in private money-matters; he is the superior, and often the master, of all the members of the community; and, in addition to this, he assumes the part of their steward and paymaster.

---

* On the one hand the taste for worldly welfare is perpetually increasing, and on the other the government gets more and more complete possession of the sources of that welfare.

Thus men are following two separate roads to servitude: the taste for their own welfare withholds them from taking a part in the government, and their love of that welfare places them in closer dependance upon those who govern.

The central power not only fulfills of itself the whole of the duties formerly discharged by various authorities—extending those duties, and surpassing those authorities—but it performs them with more alertness, strength, and independence than it displayed before. All the governments of Europe have in our time singularly improved the science of administration: they do more things, and they do everything with more order, more celerity, and at less expense; they seem to be constantly enriched by all the experience of which they have stripped private persons. From day to day the princes of Europe hold their subordinate officers under stricter control, and they invent new methods for guiding them more closely, and inspecting them with less trouble. Not content with managing everything by their agents, they undertake to manage the conduct of their agents in everything: so that the public administration not only depends upon one and the same power, but it is more and more confined to one spot and concentrated in the same hands. The government centralizes its agency while it increases its prerogative—hence a two-fold increase of strength.

In examining the ancient constitution of the judicial power, among most European nations, two things strike the mind—the independence of that power, and the extent of its functions. "Not only did the courts of justice decide almost all differences between private persons, but in very many cases they acted as arbiters between private persons and the State.

I do not here allude to the political and administrative offices which courts of judicature had in some countries usurped, but to the judicial office common to them all. In most of the countries of Europe, there were, and there still are, many private rights, connected for the most part with the general right of property, which stood under the protection of the courts of justice, and which the State could not violate without their sanction. It was this semi-political power which mainly distinguished the European courts of judicature from all others; for all nations have had judges, but all have not invested their judges with the same privileges.

Upon examining what is now occurring among the democratic nations of Europe which are called free, as well as among the others, it will be observed that new and more dependant courts are everywhere springing up by the side of the old ones, for the express purpose of deciding, by an extraordinary jurisdiction, such litigated matters as may arise between the government and private persons. The elder judicial power retains its independence, but its jurisdiction is narrowed; and there is a growing tendency to reduce it to be exclusively the arbiter between private interests.

The number of these special courts of justice is continually increasing, and their functions increase likewise. Thus the government is more and more absolved from the necessity of subjecting its policy and its rights to the sanction of another power. As judges cannot be dispensed with, at least the State is to select them, and always to hold them under its control; so that, between the government and private individuals, they place the effigy of justice rather than justice itself.

The State is not satisfied with drawing all concerns to itself, but it acquires an ever-increasing power of deciding on them all without restriction and without appeal.*

There exists among the modern nations of Europe one great cause, independent of all those which have already been pointed out, which perpetually contributes to extend the agency or to strengthen the prerogative of the supreme power, though it has not been sufficiently attended to: I mean the growth of manufactures, which is fostered by the progress of social equality. Manufactures generally collect a multitude of men on the same spot, among whom new and complex relations spring up. These men are exposed by their calling to great and sudden alternations of plenty and want, during which public tranquility is endangered. It may also happen that these employments sacrifice the health, and even the life, of those who gain by them, or of those who live by them. Thus the manufacturing classes require more regulation, superintendence, and restraint than the other classes of society, and it is natural that the powers of government should increase in the same proportion as those classes.

This is a truth of general application; what follows more especially concerns the nations of Europe. In the centuries which preceded that in which we live, the aristocracy was in possession of the soil, and was competent to defend it: landed property was therefore surrounded by ample securities, and its possessors enjoyed great independence. This gave rise to laws and customs which have been perpetuated, notwithstanding the subdivision of lands and the ruin of the nobility; and, at the present time, land-owners and agriculturists are still those among the community who most easily escape from the control of the supreme power.

In these same aristocratic ages, in which all the sources of our history are to be traced, personal property was of small importance, and those who possessed it were despised and weak: the manufacturing class formed an exception in the midst of those aristocratic communities; as it had no certain patronage, it was not outwardly protected, and was often unable to protect itself. Hence a habit sprung up of considering manufacturing property as something of a peculiar nature, not entitled to the same deference, and not worthy of the same securities as property in general; and manufacturers were looked upon as a small class in the bulk of the people, whose independence was of small importance, and who might with propriety be abandoned to the disciplinary passions of princes. On glancing over the codes of the middle ages, one is surprised to see, in those periods of personal independence, with what incessant royal regulations manufactures were hampered, even in their smallest details: on this point centralization was as active and as minute as it can ever be.

---

* A strange sophism has been made on this head in France. When a suit arises between the government and a private person, it is not to be tried before an ordinary judge—in order, they say, not to mix the administrative and the judicial powers: as if it were not to mix those powers, and to mix them in the most dangerous and oppressive manner, to invest the government with the office of judging and administering at the same time.

Since that time a great revolution has taken place in the world: manufacturing property, which was then only in the germ, has spread till it covers Europe: the manufacturing class has been multiplied and enriched by the remnants of all other ranks; it has grown and is still perpetually growing in number, in importance, in wealth. Almost all those who do not belong to it are connected with it at least on some one point: after having been an exception in society, it threatens to become the chief, if not the only, class; nevertheless the notions and political precedents engendered by it of old still cling about it. These notions and these precedents remain unchanged, because they are old, and also because they happen to be in perfect accordance with the new notions and general habits of our contemporaries.

Manufacturing property then does not extend its rights in the same ratio as its importance. The manufacturing classes do not become less dependant, while they become more numerous; but, on the contrary, it would seem as if despotism lurked within them, and naturally grew with their growth.*

As a nation becomes more engaged in manufactures, the want of roads, canals, harbours and other works of a semi-public nature, which facilitate the acquisition of wealth, is more strongly felt; and as a nation becomes more democratic, private individuals are less able, and the State more able, to execute works of such magnitude. I do not hesitate to assert that the manifest tendency of all governments at the present time is to take upon themselves alone the execution of these undertakings; by which means they daily hold in closer dependance the population which they govern.

On the other hand, in proportion as the power of a state increases, and its necessities are augmented, the state consumption of manufactured produce is always growing larger, and these commodities are generally made in the arsenals or establishments of the government. Thus, in every kingdom, the ruler becomes the principal manufacturer: he collects and retains in his service a vast number of engineers, architects, mechanics, and handicraftsmen.

Not only is he the principal manufacturer, but he tends more and more to become the chief, or rather the master of all other manufacturers. As private persons become more powerless by becoming more

---

* I shall quote a few facts in corroboration of this remark:—

Mines are the natural sources of manufacturing wealth: as manufactures have grown up in Europe, as the produce of mines has become of more general importance, and good mining more difficult from the subdivision of property, which is a consequence of the equality of conditions, most governments have asserted a right of owning the soil in which the mines lie, and of inspecting the works; which has never been the case with any other kind of property.

Thus mines, which were private property, liable to the same obligations and sheltered by the same guarantees as all other landed property, have fallen under the control of the State. The State either works them or farms them; the owners of them are mere tenants, deriving their rights from the State; and, moreover, the State almost everywhere claims the power of directing their operations; it lays down rules, enforces the adoption of particular methods, subjects the mining adventurers to constant superintendence, and, if refractory, they are ousted by a government-court of justice, and the government transfers their contract to other hands; so that the government not only possesses the mines, but has all the adventurers in its power. Nevertheless, as manufacturers increase, the working of old mines increases also; new ones are opened; the mining population extends and grows up; day by day governments augment their subterranean dominions, and people them with their agents.

equal, they can effect nothing in manufacturers without combination; but the government naturally seeks to place these combinations under its own control.

It must be admitted that these collective beings, which are called combinations, are stronger and more formidable than a private individual can ever be, and that they have less of the responsibility of their own actions; whence it seems reasonable that they should not be allowed to retain so great an independence of the supreme government as might be conceded to a private individual.

Rulers are the more apt to follow this line of policy, as their own inclinations invite them to it. Among democratic nations it is only by association that the resistance of the people to the government can ever display itself: hence the latter always looks with ill-favour on those associations which are not in its own power; and it is well worthy of remark, that among democratic nations, the people themselves often entertain a secret feeling of fear and jealousy against these very associations, which prevents the citizens from defending the institutions of which they stand so much in need. The power and the duration of these small private bodies, in the midst of the weakness and instability of the whole community, astonish and alarm the people; and the free use which each association makes of its natural powers is almost regarded as a dangerous privilege. All the associations which spring up in our age are, moreover, new corporate powers, whose rights have not been sanctioned by time; they come into existence at a time when the notion of private rights is weak, and when the power of government is unbounded; hence it is not surprising that they lose their freedom at their birth.

Among all European nations there are some kinds of associations which cannot be formed until the State has examined their by-laws and authorized their existence. In several others, attempts are made to extend this rule to all associations; the consequences of such a policy, if it were successful, may easily be foreseen.

If once the sovereign had a general right of authorizing associations of all kinds upon certain conditions, he would not be long without claiming the right of superintending and managing them, in order to prevent them from departing from the rules laid down by himself. In this manner, the State, after having reduced all who are desirous of forming associations into dependance, would proceed to reduce into the same condition all who belong to associations already formed— that is to say almost all the men who are now in existence.

Governments thus appropriate to themselves, and convert to their own purposes, the greater part of this new power which manufacturing interests have in our time brought into the world. Manufactures govern us—they govern manufactures.

I attach so much importance to all that I have just been saying, that I am tormented by the fear of having impaired my meaning in seeking to render it more clear. If the reader thinks that the examples I have adduced to support my observations are insufficient or ill-chosen—if he imagines that I have anywhere exaggerated the encroachments of the supreme power, and, on the other hand, that I have underrated the extent of the sphere which still remains open to the exertions of individual independence, I entreat him to lay down the book for a moment, and to turn his mind to reflect for himself upon the subjects I have attempted to explain. Let him attentively examine what is taking place in France and in other countries—let him inquire of those about him—let him search himself, and I am much mistaken if he does not arrive, without my guidance, and by other paths, at the point to which I have sought to lead him.

He will perceive that for the last half century, centralization has everywhere been growing up in a thousand different ways. Wars, revolutions, conquests, have served to promote it; all men have laboured to increase it. In the course of the same period, during which men have succeeded each other with singular rapidity at the head of affairs, their notions, interests, and passions have been infinitely diversified; but all have by some means or other sought to centralize. This instinctive centralization has been the only settled point amidst the extreme mutability of their lives and of their thoughts.

If the reader, after having investigated these details of human affairs, will seek to survey the wide prospect as a whole, he will be struck by the result. On the one hand the most settled dynasties shaken or overthrown;—the people everywhere escaping by violence from the sway of their laws—abolishing or limiting the authority of their rulers or their princes;—the nations, which are not in open revolution, restless at least, and excited—all of them animated by the same spirit of revolt: and on the other hand, at this very period of anarchy, and among these untractable nations, the incessant increase of the prerogative of the supreme government, becoming more centralized, more adventurous, more absolute, more extensive:—the people perpetually falling under the control of the public administration—led insensibly to surrender to it some further portion of their individual independence, till the very men, who from time to time upset a throne and trample on a race of kings, bend more and more obsequiously to the slightest dictate of a clerk. Thus, two contrary revolutions appear, in our days, to be going on; the one continually weakening the supreme power, the other as continually strengthening it: at no other period in our history has it appeared so weak or so strong.

But upon a more attentive examination of the state of the world, it appears that these two revolutions are intimately connected together, that they originate in the same source, and that after having followed a separate course, they lead men at last to the same result.

I may venture once more to repeat what I have already said or implied in several parts of this book: great care must be taken not to confound the principle of equality itself, with the revolution which finally establishes that principle in the social condition and the laws of a nation: here lies the reason of almost all the phenomena which occasion our astonishment.

All the old political powers of Europe, the greatest as well as the least, were founded in ages of aristocracy, and they more or less represented or defended the principles of inequality and of privilege. To make the novel wants and interests, which the growing principle of equality introduced, preponderate in government, our contemporaries had to overturn or to coerce the established powers. This led them to make revolutions, and breathed into many of them, that fierce love of disturbance and independence, which all revolutions, whatever be their object, always engender.

I do not believe that there is a single country in Europe in which the progress of equality has not been preceded or followed by some violent changes in the state of property and persons; and almost all these have been attended with much anarchy and license, because they have been made by the least civilized portion of the nation against that which is most civilized.

Hence proceeded the twofold contrary tendencies which I have just pointed out. As long as the democratic revolution was glowing with heat, the men who were bent upon the destruction of old aristocratic powers hostile to that revolution, displayed a strong spirit of independence; but as the victory of the principle of equality became more complete, they gradually surrendered themselves to the propensities natural to that condition of equality, and they strengthened and centralized their governments. They had sought to be free in order to make themselves equal; but in proportion as equality was more established by the aid of freedom, freedom itself was thereby rendered of more difficult attainment.

These two states of a nation have sometimes been contemporaneous: the last generation in France showed how a people might organise a stupendous tyranny in the community; at the very time when they were baffling the authority of the nobility and braving the power of all kings—at once teaching the world the way to win freedom, and the way to lose it.

In our days men see that constituted powers are dilapidated on every side—they see all ancient authority gasping away, all ancient barriers tottering to their fall, and the judgment of the wisest is troubled at the sight: they attend only to the amazing revolution which is taking place before their eyes, and they imagine that mankind is about to fall into perpetual anarchy: if they looked to the final consequences of this revolution, their fears would perhaps assume a different shape. For myself, I confess that I put no trust in the spirit of freedom which appears to animate my contemporaries: I see well enough that the nations of this age are turbulent, but I do not clearly perceive that they are liberal; and I fear lest, at the close of those perturbations which rock the base of thrones, the domination of sovereigns may prove more powerful than it ever was before.

Chapter VI.

WHAT SORT OF DESPOTISM DEMOCRATIC NATIONS HAVE TO FEAR.

I had remarked during my stay in the United States, that a democratic state of society, similar to that of the Americans, might offer singular facilities for the establishment of despotism; and I perceived, upon my return to Europe, how much use had already been made by most of our rulers, of the notions, the sentiments, and the wants engendered by this same social condition, for the purpose of extending the circle of their power. This led me to think that the nations of Christendom would perhaps eventually undergo some sort of oppression like that which hung over several of the nations of the ancient world.

A more accurate examination of the subject, and five years of further meditations, have not diminished my apprehensions, but they have changed the object of them.

No sovereign ever lived in former ages so absolute or so powerful as to undertake to administer by his own agency, and without the assistance of intermediate powers, all the parts of a great empire: none ever attempted to subject all his subjects indiscriminately to strict uniformity of regulation, and personally to tutor and direct every member of the community. The notion of such an undertaking never occured to the human mind; and if any man had conceived it, the want of information, the imperfection of the administrative system, and above all, the natural obstacles caused by the inequality of conditions, would speedily have checked the execution of so vast a design.

When the Roman emperors were at the height of their power, the different nations of the empire still preserved manners and customs of great diversity; although they were subject to the same monarch, most of the provinces were separately administered; they abounded in powerful and active municipalities; and although the whole government of the empire was centered in the hands of the emperor alone, and he always remained, upon occasions, the supreme arbiter in all matters, yet the details of social life and private occupations lay for the most part beyond his control. The emperors possessed, it is true, an immense and unchecked power, which allowed them to gratify all their whimsical tastes, and to employ for that purpose the whole strength of the State. They frequently abused that power arbitrarily to deprive their subjects of property or of life: their tyranny was extremely onerous to the few, but it did not reach the greater number; it was fixed to some few main objects, and neglected the rest; it was violent, but its range was limited.

But it would seem that if despotism were to be established among the democratic nations of our days, it might assume a different character; it would be more extensive and more mild; it would degrade men without tormenting them. I do not question, that in an age of instruction and equality like our own, sovereigns might more easily succeed in collecting all political power into their own hands, and might interfere more habitually and decidedly within the circle of private interests, than any sovereign of antiquity could ever do. But this same principle of equality which facilitates despotism, tempers its rigour. We have seen how the manners of society become more humane and gentle in proportion as men become more equal and alike. When no member of the community has much power or much wealth, tyranny is, as it were, without opportunities and a field of action. As all fortunes are scanty, the passions of men are naturally circumscribed—their imagination limited, their pleasures simple. This universal moderation moderates the sovereign himself, and checks within certain limits the inordinate stretch of his desires.

Independently of these reasons drawn from the nature of the state of society itself, I might add many others arising from causes beyond my subject; but I shall keep within the limits I have laid down to myself.

Democratic governments may become violent and even cruel at certain periods of extreme effervescence or of great danger; but these crises will be rare and brief. When I consider the petty passions of our contemporaries, the mildness of their manners, the extent of their education, the purity of their religion, the gentleness of their morality, their regular and industrious habits, and the restraint which they almost all observe in their vices no less than in their virtues, I have no fear that they will meet with tyrants in their rulers, but rather guardians.*

I think then that the species of oppression by which democratic nations are menaced is unlike anything which ever before existed in the world: our contemporaries will find no prototype of it in their memories. I am trying myself to choose an expression which will accurately convey the whole of the idea I have formed of it, but in vain; the old words despotism and tyranny are inappropriate: the thing itself is new; and since I cannot name it, I must attempt to define it.

I seek to trace the novel features under which despotism may appear in the world. The first thing that strikes the observation is an innumerable multitude of men all equal and alike, incessantly endeavouring to procure the petty and paltry pleasures with which they glut their lives. Each of them, living apart, is as a stranger to the fate of all the rest—his children and his private friends constitute to him the whole of mankind; as for the rest of his fellow-citizens, he is close to

---

* I have often asked myself what would happen if, amid the relaxation of democratic manners, and as a consequence of the restless spirit of the army, a military government were ever to be founded among any of the nations of the present age. I think that even such a government would not differ very much from the outline I have drawn, and that it would retain none of the fierce characteristics of a military oligarchy. I am persuaded that, in such a case, a sort of fusion would take place between the habits of official men, and those of the military service. The administration would assume something of a military character, and the army some of the usages of the civil administration. The result would be a regular, clear, exact, and absolute system of government: the people would become the reflection of the army, and the community be drilled like a garrison.

them, but he sees them not;—he touches them, but he feels them not; he exists but in himself and for himself alone; and if his kindred still remain to him, he may be said at any rate to have lost his country.

Above this race of men stands an immense and tutelary power, which takes upon itself alone to secure their gratifications, and to watch over their fate. That power is absolute, minute, regular, provident, and mild. It would be like the authority of a parent, if, like that authority, its object was to prepare men for manhood; but it seeks on the contrary to keep them in perpetual childhood: it is well content that the people should rejoice, provided they think of nothing but rejoicing. For their happiness such a government willingly labours, but it chooses to be the sole agent and the only arbiter of that happiness: it provides for their security, foresees and supplies their necessities, facilitates their pleasures, manages their principal concerns, directs their industry, regulates the descent of property, and subdivides their inheritances—what remains, but to spare them all the care of thinking and all the trouble of living?

Thus it every day renders the exercise of the free agency of man less useful and less frequent; it circumscribes the will within a narrower range, and gradually robs a man of all the uses of himself. The principle of equality has prepared men for these things: it has predisposed men to endure them, and oftentimes to look on them as benefits.

After having thus successively taken each member of the community in its powerful grasp, and fashioned them at will, the supreme power then extends its arm over the whole community. It covers the surface of society with a net-work of small complicated rules, minute and uniform, through which the most original minds and the most energetic characters cannot penetrate, to rise above the crowd. The will of man is not shattered, but softened, bent, and guided: men are seldom forced by it to act, but they are constantly restrained from acting: such a power does not destroy, but it prevents existence; it does not tyrannize, but it compresses, enervates, extinguishes, and stupifies a people, till each nation is reduced to be nothing better than a flock of timid and industrious animals, of which the government is the shepherd.

I have always thought that servitude of the regular, quiet, and gentle kind which I have just described, might be combined more easily than is commonly believed with some of the outward forms of freedom; and that it might even establish itself under the wing of the sovereignty of the people.

Our contemporaries are constantly excited by two conflicting passions; they want to be led, and they wish to remain free: as they cannot destroy either one or the other of these contrary propensities, they strive to satisfy them both at once. They devise a sole, tutelary, and all-powerful form of government, but elected by the people. They combine the principle of centralization and that of popular sovereignty; this gives them a respite: they console themselves for being in tutelage by the reflection that they have chosen their own guardians. Every man allows himself to be put in leading-strings, because he sees that it is not a person or a class of persons, but the people at large that holds the end of his chain.

By this system the people shake off their state of dependance just long enough to select their master, and then relapse into it again. A great many persons at the present day are quite contented with this sort of compromise between administrative despotism and the sovereignty of the people; and they think they have done enough for the protection of individual freedom when they have surrendered it to the power of the nation at large. This does not satisfy me: the nature of him I am to obey signifies less to me than the fact of extorted obedience.

I do not however deny that a constitution of this kind appears to me to be infinitely preferable to one, which, after having concentrated all the powers of government, should vest them in the hands of an irresponsible person or body of persons. Of all the forms which democratic despotism could assume, the latter would assuredly be the worst.

When the sovereign is elective, or narrowly watched by a legislature which is really elective and independent, the oppression which he exercises over individuals is sometimes greater, but it is always less degrading; because every man, when he is oppressed and disarmed, may still imagine, that while he yields obedience it is to himself he yields it, and that it is to one of his own inclinations that all the rest give way. In like manner I can understand that when the sovereign represents the nation, and is dependant upon the people, the rights and the power of which every citizen is deprived, not only serve the head of the state, but the state itself; and that private persons derive some return from the sacrifice of their independence which they have made to the public. To create a representation of the people in a very centralized country is, therefore, to diminish the evil which extreme centralization may produce, but not to get rid of it.

I admit that by this means room is left for the intervention of individuals in the more important affairs; but it is not the less suppressed in the smaller and more private ones. It must not be forgotten that it is especially dangerous to enslave men in the minor details of life. For my own part, I should be inclined to think freedom less necessary in great things than in little ones, if it were possible to be secure of the one without possessing the other.

Subjection in minor affairs breaks out every day, and is felt by the whole community indiscriminately. It does not drive men to resistance, but it crosses them at every turn, till they are led to surrender the exercise of their will. Thus their spirit is gradually broken and their character enervated; whereas that obedience which is exacted on a few important but rare occasions, only exhibits servitude at certain intervals, and throws the burden of it upon a small number of men. It is vain to summon a people, which has been rendered so dependant on the central power, to choose from time to time the representatives of that power; this rare and brief exercise of their free choice, however important it may be, will not prevent them from gradually losing the faculties of thinking, feeling, and acting for themselves, and thus gradually falling below the level of humanity.*

I add that they will soon become incapable of exercising the great and only privilege which remains to them. The democratic nations which have introduced freedom into their political constitution, at the very time when they were augmenting the despotism of their administrative constitution, have been led into strange paradoxes. To manage those minor affairs in which good sense is all that is wanted—the people are held to be unequal to the task; but when the government of the country is at stake, the people are invested with immense powers; they are alternately made the play-things of their ruler, and his masters—more than kings, and less than men. After having exhausted all the different modes of election, without finding one to suit their purpose, they are still amazed, and still bent on seeking further; as if the evil they remark did not originate in the constitution of the country far more than in that of the electoral body.

It is, indeed, difficult to conceive how men who have entirely given up the habit of self-government should succeed in making a proper choice of those by whom they are to be governed; and no one will ever believe that a liberal, wise, and energetic government can spring from the suffrages of a subservient people.

A constitution, which should be republican in its head and ultra-monarchical in all its other parts, has ever appeared to me to be a short-lived monster. The vices of rulers and the ineptitude of the people would speedily bring about its ruin; and the nation, weary of its representatives and of itself, would create freer institutions, or soon return to stretch itself at the feet of a single master.

Chapter VII.

CONTINUATION OF THE PRECEDING CHAPTERS.

I believe that it is easier to establish an absolute and despotic government among a people in which the conditions of society are equal, than among any other; and I think that if such a government were once established among such a people, it would not only oppress men, but would eventually strip each of them of several of the highest qualities of humanity. Despotism therefore appears to me peculiarly to be

---

* It cannot be absolutely or generally affirmed that the greatest danger of the present age is license or tyranny, anarchy or despotism. Both are equally to be feared; and the one may as easily proceed as the other from the self-same cause, namely, that *general apathy*, which is the consequence of what I have termed Individualism: it is because this apathy exists, that the executive government, having mustered a few troops, is able to commit acts of oppression one day, and the next day a party, which has mustered some thirty men in its ranks, can also commit acts of oppression. Neither one nor the other can found anything to last; and the causes which enable them to succeed easily, prevent them from succeeding long: they rise because nothing opposes them, and they sink because nothing supports them. The proper object therefore of our most strenuous resistance, is far less either anarchy or despotism, than that apathy which may almost indifferently beget either the one or the other.

dreaded in democratic ages. I should have loved freedom, I believe, at all times, but in the time in which we live I am ready to worship it.

On the other hand, I am persuaded that all who shall attempt, in the ages upon which we are entering, to base freedom upon aristocratic privilege, will fail;—that all who shall attempt to draw and to retain authority within a single class, will fail. At the present day no ruler is skilful or strong enough to found a despotism, by reestablishing permanent distinctions of rank among his subjects: no legislator is wise or powerful enough to preserve free institutions, if he does not take equality for his first principle and his watchword. All those of our contemporaries who would establish or secure the independence and the dignity of their fellowmen, must show themselves the friends of equality; and the only worthy means of showing themselves as such, is to be so: upon this depends the success of their holy enterprise. Thus the question is not how to reconstruct aristocratic society, but how to make liberty proceed out of that democratic state of society in which God has placed us.

These two truths appear to me simple, clear, and fertile in consequences; and they naturally lead me to consider what kind of free government can be established among a people in which social conditions are equal.

It results from the very constitution of democratic nations and from their necessities, that the power of government among them must be more uniform, more centralized, more extensive, more searching, and more efficient than in other countries. Society at large is naturally stronger and more active, individuals more subordinate and weak; the former does more, the latter less; and this is inevitably the case.

It is not therefore to be expected that the range of private independence will ever be as extensive in democratic as in aristocratic countries;—nor is this to be desired; for, among aristocratic nations, the mass is often sacrificed to the individual, and the prosperity of the greater number to the greatness of the few. It is both necessary and desirable that the government of a democratic people should be active and powerful: and our object should not be to render it weak or indolent, but solely to prevent it from abusing its aptitude and its strength.

The circumstance which most contributed to secure the independence of private persons in aristocratic ages, was, that the supreme power did not affect to take upon itself alone the government and administration of the community; those functions were necessarily partially left to the members of the aristocracy: so that as the supreme power was always divided, it never weighed with its whole weight and in the same manner on each individual.

Not only did the government not perform everything by its immediate agency; but as most of the agents who discharged its duties derived their power not from the State, but from the circumstance of their birth, they were not perpetually under its control. The government could not make or unmake them in an instant, at pleasure, nor bend them in strict uniformity to its slightest caprice—this was an additional guarantee of private independence.

I readily admit that recourse cannot be had to the same means at the present time; but I discover certain democratic expedients which may be substituted for them. Instead of vesting in the government alone all the administrative powers of which corporations and nobles have been deprived, a portion of them may be entrusted to secondary public bodies, temporarily composed of private citizens: thus the liberty of private persons will be more secure, and their equality will not be diminished.

The Americans, who care less for words than the French, still designate by the name of County the largest of their administrative districts: but the duties of the count or lord-lieutenant are in part performed by a provincial assembly.

At a period of equality like our own it would be unjust and unreasonable to institute hereditary officers; but there is nothing to prevent us from substituting elective public officers to a certain extent. Election is a democratic expedient which ensures the independence of the public officer in relation to the government, as much and even more than hereditary rank can ensure it among aristocratic nations.

Aristocratic countries abound in wealthy and influential persons who are competent to provide for themselves, and who cannot be easily or secretly oppressed: such persons restrain a government within general habits of moderation and reserve. I am very well aware that democratic countries contain no such persons naturally; but something analogous to them may be created by artificial means. I firmly believe that an aristocracy cannot again be founded in the world; but I think that private citizens, by combining together, may constitute bodies of great wealth, influence, and strength, corresponding to the persons of an aristocracy. By this means many of the greatest political advantages of aristocracy would be obtained without its injustice or its dangers. An association for political, commercial, or manufacturing purposes, or even for those of science and literature, is a powerful and enlightened member of the community, which cannot be disposed of at pleasure or oppressed without remonstrance; and which, by defending its own rights against the encroachments of the government, saves the common liberties of the country.

In periods of aristocracy every man is always bound so closely to many of his fellow-citizens, that he cannot be assailed without their coming to his assistance. In ages of equality every man naturally stands alone; he has no hereditary friends whose co-operation he may demand—no class upon whose sympathies he may rely: he is easily got rid of, and he is trampled on with impunity. At the present time, an oppressed member of the community has therefore only one method of self-defence—he may appeal to the whole nation; and if the whole nation is deaf to his complaint, he may appeal to mankind: the only means he has of making this appeal is by the press. Thus the liberty of the press is infinitely more valuable among democratic nations than among all others; it is the only cure for the evils which equality may produce. Equality sets men apart and weakens them; but the press places a powerful weapon within every man's reach, which the weakest and loneliest of them all may use. Equality deprives a man of the support of his connexions; but the press enables him to summon all his fellow-countrymen and all his fellow-men to his assistance. Printing has accelerated the progress of equality, and it is also one of its best correctives.

I think that men living in aristocracies may, strictly speaking, do without the liberty of the press: but such is not the case with those who live in democratic countries. To protect their personal independence I trust not to great political assemblies, to parliamentary privilege, nor to the assertion of popular sovereignty. All these things may, to a certain extent, be reconciled with personal servitude—but that servitude cannot be complete if the press is free: the press is the chiefest democratic instrument of freedom.

Something analogous may be said of the judicial power. It is a part of the essence of judicial power to attend to private interests, and to fix itself with predilection on minute objects submitted to its observation: another essential quality of judicial power is never to volunteer its assistance to the oppressed, but always to be at the disposal of the humblest of those who solicit it; their complaint, however feeble they may themselves be, will force itself upon the ear of justice and claim redress, for this is inherent in the very constitution of the courts of justice.

A power of this kind is therefore peculiarly adapted to the wants of freedom, at a time when the eye and finger of the government are constantly intruding into the minutest details of human actions, and when private persons are at once too weak to protect themselves, and too much isolated for them to reckon upon the assistance of their fellows. The strength of the courts of law has ever been the greatest security which can be offered to personal independence; but this is more especially the case in democratic ages: private rights and interests are in constant danger, if the judicial power does not grow more extensive and more strong to keep pace with the growing equality of conditions.

Equality awakens in men several propensities extremely dangerous to freedom, to which the attention of the legislator ought constantly to be directed. I shall only remind the reader of the most important among them.

Men living in democratic ages do not readily comprehend the utility of forms: they feel an instinctive contempt for them—I have elsewhere shown for what reasons. Forms excite their contempt and often their hatred; as they commonly aspire to none but easy and present gratifications, they rush onward to the object of their desires, and the slightest delay exasperates them. This same temper, carried with them into political life, renders them hostile to forms, which perpetually retard or arrest them in some of their projects.

Yet this objection which the men of democracies make to forms is the very thing which renders forms so useful to freedom; for their chief merit is to serve as a barrier between the strong and the weak, the ruler and the people, to retard the one, and to give the other time to look about him. Forms become more necessary in proportion as the government becomes more active and more powerful, while private persons are becoming more indolent and more feeble. Thus democratic nations naturally stand more in need of forms than other nations, and they naturally respect them less. This deserves most serious attention.

Nothing is more pitiful than the arrogant disdain of most of our contemporaries for questions of form; for the smallest questions of form have acquired in our time an importance which they never had before: many of the greatest interests of mankind depend upon them. I think that if the statesmen of aristocratic ages could sometimes contemn forms with impunity, and frequently rise above them, the statesmen to whom the government of nations is now confided ought to treat the very least among them with respect, and not neglect them without imperious necessity. In aristocracies the observance of forms was superstitious; among us they ought to be kept with a deliberate and enlightened deference.

Another tendency, which is extremely natural to democratic nations and extremely dangerous, is that which leads them to despise and undervalue the rights of private persons. The attachment which men feel to a right, and the respect which they display for it, is generally proportioned to its importance, or to the length of time during which they have enjoyed it. The rights of private persons among democratic nations are commonly of small importance, of recent growth, and extremely precarious—the consequence is that they are often sacrificed without regret, and almost always violated without remorse.

But it happens that at the same period and among the same nations in which men conceive a natural contempt for the rights of private persons, the rights of society at large are naturally extended and consolidated: in other words, men become less attached to private rights at the very time at which it would be most necessary to retain and to defend what little remains of them. It is therefore most especially in the present democratic ages, that the true friends of the liberty and the greatness of man ought constantly to be on the alert to prevent the power of government from lightly sacrificing the private rights of individuals to the general execution of its designs. At such times no citizen is so obscure that it is not very dangerous to allow him to be oppressed—no private rights are so unimportant that they can be surrendered with impunity to the caprices of a government. The reason is plain:—if the private right of an individual is violated at a time when the human mind is fully impressed with the importance and the sanctity of such rights, the injury done is confined to the individual whose right is infringed; but to violate such a right, at the present day, is deeply to corrupt the manners of the nation and to put the whole community in jeopardy, because the very notion of this kind of right constantly tends among us to be impaired and lost.

There are certain habits, certain notions, and certain vices which are peculiar to a state of revolution, and which a protracted revolution cannot fail to engender and to propagate, whatever be, in other respects, its character, its purpose, and the scene on which it takes place. When any nation has, within a short space of time, repeatedly varied its rulers, its opinions, and its laws, the men of whom it is composed eventually contract a taste for change, and grow accustomed to see all changes effected by sudden violence. Thus they naturally conceive a contempt for forms which daily prove ineffectual; and they do not support without impatience the dominion of rules which they have so often seen infringed.

As the ordinary notions of equity and morality no longer suffice to explain and justify all the innovations daily begotten by a revolution, the principle of public utility is called in, the doctrine of political necessity is conjured up, and men accustom themselves to sacrifice private interests without scruple, and to trample on the rights of individuals in order more speedily to accomplish any public purpose.

These habits and notions, which I shall call revolutionary, because all revolutions produce them, occur in aristocracies just as much as among democratic nations; but among the former they are often less powerful and always less lasting, because there they meet with habits, notions, defects, and impediments, which counteract them: they consequently disappear as soon as the revolution is terminated, and the nation reverts to its former political courses. This is not always the case in democratic countries, in which it is ever to be feared that revolutionary tendencies, becoming more gentle and more regular, without entirely disappearing from society, will be gradually transformed into habits of subjection to the administrative authority of the government. I know of no countries in which revolutions are more dangerous than in democratic countries; because, independently of the accidental and transient evils which must always attend them, they may always create some evils which are permanent and unending.

I believe that there are such things as justifiable resistance and legitimate rebellion: I do not therefore assert, as an absolute proposition, that the men of democratic ages ought never to make revolutions; but I think that they have especial reason to hesitate before they embark in them, and that it is far better to endure many grievances in their present condition than to have recourse to so perilous a remedy.

I shall conclude by one general idea, which comprises not only all the particular ideas which have been expressed in the present chapter, but also most of those which it is the object of this book to treat of. In the ages of aristocracy which preceded our own, there were private persons of great power, and a social authority of extreme weakness. The outline of society itself was not easily discernible, and constantly confounded with the different powers by which the community was ruled. The principal efforts of the men of those times were required to strengthen, aggrandize, and secure the supreme power; and on the other hand, to circumscribe individual independence within narrower limits, and to subject private interests to the interests of the public. Other perils and other cares await the men of our age. Among the greater part of modern nations, the government, whatever may be its origin, its constitution, or its name, has become almost omnipotent, and private persons are falling, more and more, into the lowest stage of weakness and dependance.

In olden society everything was different: unity and uniformity were nowhere to be met with. In modern society everything threatens to become so much alike, that the peculiar characteristics of each individual will soon be entirely lost in the general aspect of the world. Our forefathers were ever prone to make an improper use of the notion, that private rights ought to be respected; and we are naturally prone on the other hand to exaggerate the idea that the interest of a private individual ought always to bend to the interest of the many.

The political world is metamorphosed: new remedies must henceforth be sought for new disorders. To lay down extensive, but distinct and settled limits, to the action of the government; to confer certain rights on private persons, and to secure to them the undisputed enjoyment of those rights; to enable individual man to maintain whatever independence, strength, and original power he still possesses; to raise him by the side of society at large, and uphold him in that position—these appear to me the main objects of legislators in the ages upon which we are now entering.

It would seem as if the rulers of our time sought only to use men in order to make things great; I wish that they would try a little more to make great men; that they would set less value on the work, and more upon the workman; that they would never forget that a nation cannot long remain strong when every man belonging to it is individually weak, and that no form or combination of social polity has yet been devised, to make an energetic people out of a community of pusillanimous and enfeebled citizens.

I trace among our contemporaries two contrary notions which are equally injurious. One set of men can perceive nothing in the principle of equality but the anarchical tendencies which it engenders: they dread their own free agency—they fear themselves. Other thinkers, less numerous but more enlightened, take a different view: beside that track which starts from the principle of equality to terminate in anarchy, they have at last discovered the road which seems to lead men to inevitable servitude. They shape their souls beforehand to this necessary condition; and, despairing of remaining free, they already do obeisance in their hearts to the master who is soon to appear. The former abandon freedom, because they think it dangerous; the latter, because they hold it to be impossible.

If I had entertained the latter conviction, I should not have written this book, but I should have confined myself to deploring in secret the destiny of mankind. I have sought to point out the dangers to which the principle of equality exposes the independence of man, because I firmly believe that these dangers are the most formidable, as well as the least foreseen, of all those which futurity holds in store; but I do think that they are insurmountable.

The men who live in the democratic ages upon which we are entering have naturally a taste for independence: they are naturally impatient of regulation, and they are wearied by the permanence even of the condition they themselves prefer. They are fond of power; but they are prone to despise and hate those who wield it, and they easily elude its grasp by their own mobility and insignificance.

These propensities will always manifest themselves, because they originate in the groundwork of society, which will undergo no change: for a long time they will prevent the establishment of any despotism, and they will furnish fresh weapons to each succeeding generation which shall struggle in favour of the liberty of mankind. Let us then look forward to the future with that salutary fear which makes men keep watch and ward for freedom, not with that faint and idle terror which depresses and enervates the heart.

Chapter VIII.

GENERAL SURVEY OF THE SUBJECT.

Before I close for ever the theme that has detained me so long, I would fain take a parting survey of all the various characteristics of modern society, and appreciate at last the general influence to be exercised by the principle of equality upon the fate of mankind; but I am stopped by the difficulty of the task, and in presence of so great an object my sight is troubled, and my reason fails.

The society of the modern world which I have sought to delineate, and which I seek to judge, has but just come into existence. Time has not yet shaped it into perfect form: the great revolution by which it has been created is not yet over; and amid the occurrences of our time, it is almost impossible to discern what will pass away with the revolution itself, and what will survive its close. The world which is rising into existence is still half encumbered by the remains of the world which is waning into decay; and amid the vast perplexity of human affairs, none can say how much of ancient institutions and former manners will remain, or how much will completely disappear.

Although the revolution which is taking place in the social condition, the laws, the opinions and the feelings of men, is still very far from being terminated, yet its results already admit of no comparison with anything that the world has ever before witnessed. I go back from age to age up to the remotest antiquity: but I find no parallel to what is occurring before my eyes: as the past has ceased to throw its light upon the future, the mind of man wanders in obscurity.

Nevertheless, in the midst of a prospect so wide, so novel, and so confused, some of the more prominent characteristics may already be discerned and pointed out. The good things and the evils of life are more equally distributed in the world: great wealth tends to disappear, the number of small fortunes to increase; desires and gratifications are multiplied, but extraordinary prosperity and irremediable penury are alike unknown. The sentiment of ambition is universal, but the scope of ambition is seldom vast. Each individual stands apart in solitary weakness; but society at large is active, provident, and powerful: the performances of private persons are insignificant, those of the State immense.

There is little energy of character; but manners are mild, and laws humane. If there be few instances of exalted heroism or of virtues of the highest, brightest, and purest temper, men's habits are regular, violence is rare, and cruelty almost unknown. Human existence becomes longer, and property more secure: life is not adorned with brilliant trophies, but it is extremely easy and tranquil. Few pleasures are either very refined or very coarse; and highly polished manners are as uncommon as great brutality of tastes. Neither men of great learning, nor extremely ignorant communities, are to be met with; genius becomes more rare, information more diffused. The human mind is impelled by the small efforts of all mankind combined together, not by the strenuous activity of certain men. There is less perfection, but more abundance, in all the productions of the arts. The ties of race, of rank, and of country are relaxed; the great bond of humanity is strengthened.

If I endeavour to find out the most general and the most prominent of all these different characteristics, I shall have occasion to perceive, that what is taking place in men's fortunes manifests itself under a thousand other forms. Almost all extremes are softened or blunted: all that was most prominent is superseded by some mean term, at once less lofty and less low, less brilliant and less obscure, than what before existed in the world.

When I survey this countless multitude of beings, shaped in each other's likeness, amidst whom nothing rises and nothing falls, the sight of such universal uniformity saddens and chills me, and I am tempted to regret that state of society which has ceased to be. When the world was full of men of great importance and extreme insignificance, of great wealth and extreme poverty, of great learning and extreme ignorance, I turned aside from the latter to fix my observation on the former alone, who gratified my sympathies. But I admit that this gratification arose from my own weakness: it is because I am unable to see at once all that is around me, that I am allowed thus to select and separate the objects of my predilection from among so many others. Such is not the case with that Almighty and Eternal Being, whose gaze necessarily includes the whole of created things, and who surveys distinctly, though at once, mankind and man.

We may naturally believe that it is not the singular prosperity of the few, but the greater well-being of all, which is most pleasing in the sight of the Creator and Preserver of men. What appears to me to be man's decline, is to His eye advancement; what afflicts me is acceptable to Him. A state of equality is perhaps less elevated, but it is more just; and its justice constitutes its greatness and its beauty. I would strive then to raise myself to this point of the Divine contemplation, and thence to view and to judge the concerns of men.

No man, upon the earth, can as yet affirm absolutely and generally, that the new state of the world is better than its former one; but it is already easy to perceive that this state is different. Some vices and some virtues were so inherent in the constitution of an aristocratic nation, and are so opposite to the character of a modern people, that they can never be infused into it; some good tendencies and some bad propensities which were unknown to the former, are natural to the latter; some ideas suggest themselves spontaneously to the imagination of the one, which are utterly repugnant to the mind of the other. They are like two distinct orders of human beings, each of which has its own merits and defects, its own advantages and its own evils. Care must therefore be taken not to judge the state of society, which is now coming into existence, by notions derived from a state of society which no longer exists; for as these states of society are exceedingly different in their structure, they cannot be submitted to a just or fair comparison.

It would be scarcely more reasonable to require of our own contemporaries the peculiar virtues which originated in the social condition of their forefathers, since that social condition is itself fallen, and has drawn into one promiscuous ruin the good and evil which belonged to it.

But as yet these things are imperfectly understood. I find that a great number of my contemporaries undertake to make a certain selection from among the institutions, the opinions, and the ideas which originated in the aristocratic constitution of society as it was: a portion of these elements they would willingly relinquish, but they would keep the remainder and transplant them into their new world. I apprehend that such men are wasting their time and their strength in virtuous but unprofitable efforts.

The object is not to retain the peculiar advantages which the inequality of conditions bestows upon mankind, but to secure the new benefits which equality may supply. We have not to seek to make ourselves like our progenitors, but to strive to work out that species of greatness and happiness which is our own.

For myself, who now look back from this extreme limit of my task, and discover from afar, but at once, the various objects which have attracted my more attentive investigation upon my way, I am full of apprehensions and of hopes. I perceive mighty dangers which it is possible to ward off—mighty evils which may be avoided or alleviated; and I cling with a firmer hold to the belief, that for democratic nations to be virtuous and prosperous they require but to will it.

I am aware that many of my contemporaries maintain that nations are never their own masters here below, and that they necessarily obey some insurmountable and unintelligent power, arising from anterior events, from their race, or from the soil and climate of their country. Such principles are false and cowardly; such principles can never produce aught but feeble men and pusillanimous nations. Providence has not created mankind entirely independent or entirely free. It is true that around every man a fatal circle is traced, beyond which he cannot pass; but within the wide verge of that circle he is powerful and free: as it is with man, so with communities. The nations of our time cannot prevent the conditions of men from becoming equal: but it depends upon themselves whether the principle of equality is to lead them to servitude or freedom, to knowledge or barbarism, to prosperity or to wretchedness.

Editor's Notes

Volume 1

INTRODUCTION

1. Kings of France (1461–83), (1643–1715), (1751–74).
2. Wars in the twelfth and thirteenth centuries between European Christians and those they considered religious enemies, most notably, Muslims in the Middle East. The idea of a religious crusade became a symbol of religious intolerance and fanaticism.
3. The "Hundred Years' War," between England and France from 1337 to 1453.
4. A "commoner." From the Old French roture, meaning newly cultivated land.

CHAPTER 2

1. The Tudors ruled England from Henry VII in 1485 until Elizabeth I in 1603.
2. The founders of Virginia in 1607.
3. King of Great Britain and Ireland from 1625 to 1649. His divine-right views led to civil war in 1640 and his execution in 1649.
4. The son of Charles I who ruled Great Britain and Ireland from 1660 until 1685.

CHAPTER 3

1. The independence struggle between the thirteen American colonies and the British crown begun in 1776.

CHAPTER 5

1. Benjamin Franklin (1706–1790) was a philosopher and scientist and one of America's "founding fathers."
2. The legislature assembled in 1792 which drafted a republican constitution for France.
3. Mohammed (570?–632) was the founder and principal prophet of Islam, whose revelations from God constitute the teachings of the Koran, the central text of the Muslim religion.
4. Charles Louis de Secondat, baron de Montesquieu (1689–1755) was the French Enlightenment author of Persian Letters (1721) and The Spirit of Laws (1748), whose theory of balanced government influenced the debates in the American constitutional convention.
5. The French Revolution of 1789 overturned the Bourbon monarchy that had governed France for centuries. It brought equally dramatic changes to French economic and cultural life, ending the inequities of feudalism.

CHAPTER 6

1. The principal governing body of France, created by Napoleon Bonaparte in 1799.

CHAPTER 8

1. Delaware, New York, New Jersey, Pennsylvania, Maryland, Virginia, North Carolina, South Carolina, Georgia, Connecticut, Rhode Island, New Hampshire, and Massachusetts declared themselves independent in 1776 as The United States.
2. The first American Constitution was The Articles of Confederation, signed in 1781, which remained in effect until 1789.
3. George Washington, commander of the Continental Army during the American Revolution (1775–83), became the first president of the United States (1789–97).
4. Thomas Jefferson, author of the Declaration of Independence (1776), also the third president of the United States (1801–09)
5. Parts of Northern France along the English Channel.

6. The Canton of Vaud is part of the Swiss Confederation on its western border. The Canton of Uri is in Central Switzerland.
7. A war between the United States and Great Britain begun in 1812 and ending in 1815.

CHAPTER 10

1. The party of Washington, Hamilton, and John Adams, which believed in a strong national government helpful to commercial interests.
2. The party formed in the 1790s led by Thomas Jefferson that opposed strong central authority and favored agrarian interests and states' rights. It soon became known at the Democratic Party.
3. Andrew Jackson, a military hero of the 1812 war, was the seventh president of the United States (1829–37).
4. President Jackson vetoed the bill to extend the charter of the Bank of the United States in 1832, claiming that the Bank benefited the privileged classes and monopoly capitalists.

CHAPTER 11

1. Tocqueville is referring to Blaise Pascal (1623–1662), a famous French mathematician, physicist, and religious philosopher, author of Lettres Provinciales in 1656 and the more famous Pensées in 1670.

CHAPTER 13

1. James Kent (1763–1847) was a famous American jurist best known for his Commentaries on American Law.
2. Louisiana, 1812; Mississippi, 1817; Alabama, 1819; Missouri, 1821; Arkansas, 1836.
3. Alexander Hamilton (1755–1804) was a principal author of the Federalist Papers and President Washington's secretary of the Treasury.
4. James Madison (1751–1836) the fourth president of the United States (1809–17) and the other principal author of the Federalist Papers.

CHAPTER 14

1. Man is a boy grown strong (Latin).

CHAPTER 15

1. Public executions as moral lessons in the Spanish Inquisition (Spanish).
2. Jean da La Bruyère (1645–1696) a French writer best known for Characters (1688).
3. Molière (1622–1673) was a witty, satiric seventeenth-century playwright, and one of France's greatest writers.
4. The Spanish Inquisition was begun by Pope Sixtus IV in 1478 to convert and persecute Jews, Muslims, and others the Church labeled heretics.

CHAPTER 16

1. Napoleon Bonaparte (1769–1821) overthrew the French republican government by staging a coup in 1799, then declaring himself emperor in 1804.

CHAPTER 17

1. The War of 1812 ended with the American victory over Britain in the 1815 Battle of New Orleans.
2. Pierre-Jean Cabanis (1757–1808) was a French physiologist and philosopher who believed that immaterial entities like the soul and consciousness were really material systems.
3. Robert Fulton (1765–1815) was the American inventor and entrepreneur responsible for the development of the steamboat.
4. Alabama, Louisiana, and Mississippi.
5. King of France from 1589 to 1610.

CHAPTER 18

1. William Penn (1644–1718) was the English Quaker and believer in religious freedom who founded the Commonwealth of Pennsylvania.
2. The Indian tribe that originally lived on the land that is now southeastern Mississippi.

3. Gaius Cornelius Tacitus (55–117 C.E.?) was a Roman historian who wrote *Germania* and *Historiae*, a history of the Roman Empire from 69–96 C.E.
4. Ethnic Muslims living in the Iberian Peninsula.
5. John C. Calhoun (1782–1850) from South Carolina was a senator and vice president of the United States. He was a vigorous defender of slavery and of states' rights.

Volume 2

First Book

CHAPTER 1

1. René Descartes (1596–1650) was a French philosopher and the author of *Discourse on Methods* and *Meditations on the First Philosophy*. He is often regarded as the father of modern philosophy.
2. Francis Bacon (1561–1626) was an English philosopher who introduced empirical scientific method with his *Novum Organum* and *Advancement of Learning*.
3. Martin Luther (1483–1546) was a German monk who questioned Catholicism and brought about the Protestant Reformation.
4. François-Marie Arouet (1694–1778) was an author and Enlightenment intellectual who passionately defended individual liberties and religious tolerance.

CHAPTER 4

1. The Assembly governed revolutionary France from 1789 to 1791 and drew up the Declaration of the Rights of Man and Citizen. The Convention met from 1792 to 1795 to draft a republican constitution for France.

CHAPTER 7

1. A doctrine that insists that God is in the natural universe, often associated with the Dutch rationalist Benedict Spinoza.

CHAPTER 9

1. Tocqueville here refers to Claude-Henri de Saint-Simon (1760–1825) and his followers, who were convinced of the progressive evolution of industrial society until a future "golden age."

CHAPTER 10

1. Archimedes (?287–212 B.C.E.) was a famous and influential Greek mathematician and inventor.
2. Plutarch (46–119 C.E.) was a Greek author and biographer whose most famous work, *Lives*, chronicled the lives of notable Greeks and Romans.
3. Tocqueville is referring to the steamboat, tested for the first time by the American John Finch in 1787 and subsequently developed commercially by Robert Fulton.

CHAPTER 11

1. Raphael (1483–1520) was a master painter of the Italian Renaissance who is famous for his paintings of the Madonna.
2. Jacques-Louis David (1748–1825) was a neoclassical artist who participated in the French Revolution as a planner of public festivals and ceremonies.

CHAPTER 12

1. A French town, northwest of Paris.
2. Hernán Cortés (1485–1547) was the Spanish military leader who led the conquest of the Aztec empire in 1521.

CHAPTER 16

1. Constantinople (now Istanbul) was conquered by the Ottomans in 1453; it was the capital of the Byzantine and Ottoman empires.

2. John Milton (1608–1674), the great English poet, is most remembered for his epic poem *Paradise Lost.*

CHAPTER 17

1. *Childe Harold's Pilgrimage* is Lord Byron's (1788–1824) autobiographical poem.
2. A novel (1805) written by Chateaubriand (1768–1848) about a melancholy hero.
3. A poem written by Lamartine (1790–1869) in 1836 about a fallen angel who has to choose between God and a woman.

CHAPTER 19

1. Jean-Baptiste Racine (1639–1699), author of *Britannicus,* was one of France's most noted dramatists.

CHAPTER 20

1. Marquis de Lafayette (1757–1834) was a French general revered in the United States for helping the Continental Army in the American Revolution.

Second Book

CHAPTER 8

1. Michel Eyquem de Montaigne (1533–1592) was a French writer whose *Essais* (1580) introduced a new literary form, the essay.

CHAPTER 12

1. Relating to Thebes, the ancient Egyptian city.
2. The philosophy founded on the teaching of Epicurus (341–270 B.C.E.), which regarded pleasure as the only good and pain the only evil.

CHAPTER 14

1. People from Tyre, an ancient Phoenician city.

Third Book

CHAPTER 1

1. Marie de Rabutin-Chantal, Marquise de Sévigné (1626–1696) was a French writer whose published letters about aristocratic society received extensive literary recognition.
2. Marcus Tullus Cicero (106–43 B.C.E.) was a Roman statesman and philosopher whose republican treatises have become part of the political theory canon.

CHAPTER 22

1. Lucius Cornelius Sylla (138–78 B.C.E.), triumphant in a civil war, ruled as a Roman dictator from 82–79 B.C.E. Julius Caesar (100?–44 B.C.E.), the Roman empire's most famous leader, also ruled as a dictator (46–44 B.C.E.) following victory in a civil war (49–46 B.C.E.)

CHAPTER 25

1. Alexander III, Alexander the Great (356–323 B.C.E.) was the king of Macedonia (336–323 B.C.E.) who conquered the Persian empire.

CHAPTER 26

1. Niccolò Machiavelli (1469–1527) was an Italian statesman, political theorist, and author of *The Prince* in 1509, which offered an amoral approach to princely leadership.

BACKGROUNDS

Tocqueville Letters

To Ernest de Chabrol, New York, 9 June 1831†

Imagine, my dear friend, if you can, a society formed of all the nations of the world: English, French, Germans . . . people having different languages, beliefs, opinions: in a word, a society without roots, without memories, without prejudices, without routines, without common ideas, without a national character, yet a hundred times happier than our own; more virtuous? I doubt it. That is the starting point: What serves as the link among such diverse elements? What makes all of this into one people? Interest. That is the secret. The private interest that breaks through at each moment, the interest that, moreover, appears openly and even proclaims itself as a social theory.

In this, we are quite far from the ancient republics, it must be admitted, and nonetheless this people is republican, and I do not doubt that it will be so for a long time yet. And for this people a republic is the best of governments.

I can explain this phenomenon only by thinking that America finds itself, for the present, in a physical situation so fortunate, that private interest is never contrary to the general interest, which is certainly not the case in Europe.

What generally inclines men to disturb the state? On the one hand, the desire to gain power; on the other, the difficulty of creating a happy existence for themselves by ordinary means.

Here, there is no public power, and, to tell the truth, there is no need for it. The territorial divisions are so limited; the states have no enemies, consequently no armies, no taxation, no central government; the executive power is nothing; it confers neither money nor power. As long as things remain this way, who will want to torment his life in order to attain power?

Now, looking at the other part of my assertion, one arrives at the same conclusion; because, if political careers are more or less closed, a thousand, ten thousand others are open to human activity. The whole world here seems a malleable material that man turns and fashions to his liking. An immense field, of which the smallest part has yet been traversed, is here open to industry. There is no man who cannot reasonably expect to attain the comforts of life: there is none who does not know that with love of work, his future is certain.

† Ernest de Chabrol (1803–1889) was a lawyer and lifelong friend whom Tocqueville met at Versailles in 1828. This and the 7 October 1831 letter to Chabrol are from *Alexis de Tocqueville: Selected Letters on Politics and Society*, edited by Roger Boesche, translated by James Toupin and Roger Boesche, copyright © 1986 by the Regents of the University of California. Reprinted by permission of the University of California Press.

Thus, in this fortunate country, nothing attracts the restlessness of the human spirit toward political passions; everything, on the contrary, draws it toward activity that poses no danger to the state. I would wish that all of those who, in the name of America, dream of a republic for France, could come see for themselves what it is like here.

This last reason that I just gave you, to my mind the prime reason, explains equally well the only two outstanding characteristics that distinguish this people: its industrial spirit and the instability of its character.

Nothing is easier than becoming rich in America; naturally, the human spirit, which needs a dominant passion, in the end turns all its thoughts toward gain. As a result, at first sight this people seems to be a company of merchants joined together for trade, and as one digs deeper into the national character of the Americans, one sees that they have sought the value of everything in this world only in the answer to this single question: how much money will it bring in?

As for the instability of character, it breaks through in a thousand places; an American takes up, quits and takes up again ten trades in his lifetime; he changes his residence ceaselessly and continually forms new enterprises. Less than any other man in the world he fears jeopardizing a fortune once he has acquired it, because he knows with what ease he can acquire a new one.

Besides, change seems to him the natural state of man, and how could it be otherwise? Everything is ceaselessly astir around him— laws, opinions, public officials, fortunes—the earth itself here changes its face every day. In the midst of the universal movement that surrounds him, the American could not stay still.

One must not look here either for that family spirit, or for those ancient traditions of honor and virtue, that distinguish so eminently several of our old societies of Europe. A people that seems to live only to enrich itself could not be a virtuous people in the strict meaning of the word; but it is *well ordered*. All of the trifles that cling to idle riches it does not have: its habits are regular, there is little or no time to devote to women, and they seem to be valued only as mothers of families and managers of households. Mores are pure; this is incontestable. The *roué* of Europe is absolutely unknown in America; the passion for making a fortune carries away and dominates all others.

To M. Louis de Kergolay, Yonkers, 20 June 1831†

In your last letter you ask me if this country has any *convictions*. I do not know the precise sense that you attach to that word. What strikes me is that the majority have certain opinions in common. Up to the present time, this is what I most envy in America. Thus I have not

---

† Count Louis de Kergolay (1804–1880) was a distant cousin and friend of Tocqueville's from childhood. This letter is found in *Memoir, Letters, and Remains of Alexis De Tocqueville*, vol. I (Boston: Ticknor & Fields, 1862).

heard a single person in any rank express a doubt as to a republic being the best possible form of government, or on the right of a nation to choose its own government. The greater number take republican principles in the most democratic sense. In a few you see peeping out an aristocratic tendency, which I shall presently try to explain. But that a republic is a good form of government, and that it is a form of government to which society naturally tends, are facts admitted by clergymen, by magistrates, by tradesmen, and by artisans. This opinion is so general and so seldom questioned, even in a country where there is entire freedom of speech, that it may almost be called a *conviction*.

Another idea is prevalent, apparently in an equal degree; a belief in the wisdom and good sense of mankind; the perfectibility of the human race is contradicted by few, if by any. No one denies that the majority may sometimes be mistaken; but they think that in the end it must be right; that it is not only the sole judge of its own interests, but even the safest, the nearest to infallibility. The result is the belief that education should be bestowed freely on the people; that they cannot be sufficiently enlightened. You remember how often in France we (among others) have puzzled our brains with the question, whether it were to be desired or feared that knowledge should penetrate every class of society. Though so difficult to solve in France, the doubt seems here never to have occurred. I have already propounded the question a hundred times to the most thoughtful men in this country. I saw by their summary method of dealing with it that they had never considered it; and that it should even be asked, struck them as shocking and absurd. The diffusion of intelligence, they said, is our only protection against the outbreaks of the mob.

These are what I should call the convictions of this people. They believe firmly in the excellence of their government; they believe in the wisdom of the masses, provided they be educated; and do not seem to be aware that there is a certain cultivation which can never be shared by the masses, but may yet be essential for the rulers of a state.

As for what we generally consider as making up the convictions of a nation, such as the moral standard, old traditions, recollections, of these I see as yet no traces. I even doubt whether religious opinions have as much influence as appears at first sight. The religious condition of this country is, perhaps, the most interesting subject of inquiry. I will try to tell you what I know about it when I resume my letter, which I am now forced to lay aside, perhaps for some days.

Calwell, forty-five miles from New York.

My mind has been so much excited since I began my letter to you this morning, that I feel obliged to take it up again, though I know not exactly what I shall say. I was speaking of religion. Sunday is rigorously observed. I have seen the streets barred in front of the churches during divine service. The law forbids labor; and opinion, which is much more powerful, obliges every one to appear in church, and to eschew amusement.

* * *

But to return to the present state of the public mind in America; you must not take what I have said in too positive a sense. I have spoken of tendencies not of facts that have already taken place. Christianity rests here on a firmer foundation than in any other country in the world which I know, and I have no doubt but that the religious element influences the political one. It induces morality and regularity; it restrains the eccentricities of the spirit of innovation; above all, it is almost fatal to the mental condition, so common with us in which men leap over every obstacle *per fas et nefas*[1] to gain their point. Any party, however anxious to obtain its object, would in the pursuit feel obliged to confine itself to means apparently legitimate, and not in open opposition to the maxims of religion, which are always more or less moral even when erroneous. . . .

I enter on another subject. I heard it said in Europe that there was an aristocratic tendency in America. It is a mistake; I am more sure of this than of most things. Democracy is rapidly advancing in some states, and fully developed in others. It is rooted in the habits, in the laws, and in the opinions of the majority. Its opposers hide their heads, and if they wish to rise are forced to borrow its colors. In New York, the beggars alone are without electoral rights. The effects of a democratic government are obvious—they are perpetual changes of men and of institutions, extreme external equality, manners without distinction, and ideas always commonplace.

We ourselves, my dear friend, are drifting towards complete democracy. I do not say that it is a good thing; what I see in this country convinces me that it will not suit France, but we are being driven on it by an irresistible force. No effort to stop its march will produce more than a halt. To refuse to admit these facts is weakness, and I cannot help believing that the Bourbons, instead of trying to fortify the aristocratic element, which is dying out with us, ought to have devoted all their energies to making it the interest of the democratic party to maintain order and stability.

In my opinion our parochial and municipal administration ought, from the first, to have attracted all their attention. Instead of living from day to day with the parochial institutions established by Napoleon, the Bourbons ought immediately to have modified them, to have gradually initiated and interested the people in the management of its own affairs; to have created local interests, and above all to have founded, if possible, the habit of submitting willingly to law, which, in my opinion, is the only counterpoise to democracy. These measures would, perhaps, have rendered the present movement less dangerous both to the state and to its rulers.

Democracy, in short, seems to me to be a fact which the government may hope in future to regulate, but not to reverse. I assure you that it was not without difficulty that I resigned myself to this idea. My view of this country does not prove to me that, even under the most favorable circumstances, and they existed here, the government of the

1. Through lawful or unlawful means (Latin) [*Editor's Note*].

people is a desirable event. All are pretty well agreed that in the early days of the republic, the statesmen and members of congress were much more distinguished men than they now are. They nearly all belonged to the class of country gentlemen, a race which diminishes every day. The country no longer selects so well. It chooses in general those who flatter its passions and descend to its level. This effect of democracy, joined to the extreme instability, the entire absence of coherence or permanence that one sees here, convinces me every day more and more, that the best government is not that in which all have share, but that which is directed by the class of the highest moral principle and intellectual cultivation.

However, it is impossible to deny that this country presents, on the whole, an admirable aspect. I frankly own, that it convinces me of the superiority of a free government over every other. I feel more certain than ever, that all nations are not fitted for the same amount of liberty, but also I am more inclined than ever to regret that such should be the case. It is impossible to give an idea of the universal satisfaction of this nation with the existing government. The lower classes are undeniably higher in the moral scale than with us; every man has a consciousness of his independent position and of his personal dignity which, without perhaps adding suavity to his manners, leads him to respect himself and others. The two things that I chiefly admire here are these:—First, the extraordinary respect entertained for law: standing alone, and unsupported by an armed force, it commands irresistibly. I believe, in fact, that the principal reason is, that they make it themselves and are able to repeal it. We see thieves who have violated all public laws obey those that they have made for themselves. I think that there is a similar feeling among nations. The second thing for which I envy these people is, the ease with which they do without being governed. Every man considers himself interested in maintaining the safety of the public and the exercise of the laws. Instead of depending on the police he depends on himself. The general result is that, without ever showing itself, a police is everywhere. You will scarcely credit the order kept by this people from the feeling that they themselves are the only safeguard against themselves.

You see that I give you as exact an account as I can of all my impressions. On the whole, they are more favorable to America than they were when I first arrived. There are many blots in the picture, but the general effect seizes the imagination. I fancy that it must act with irresistible power over minds that are at the same time reasoning and superficial, a combination which is not rare. The principles of the government are so simple, and the results are so sure, that if one is not on one's guard, one is carried away by the charm. One is forced to reflect, to struggle against one's impressions to discover that these simple and reasonable institutions would not suit a great nation, which must have a strong internal government, and a fixed foreign policy; that the government of this country is in its nature perishable; that a nation adopting it should long have been used to liberty and have reached a point of intellectual cultivation acquired seldom and by slow degrees. And after repeating all this to one's self, one still thinks that a free government is a grand institution, and that it is to be regretted that the moral and physical constitution of man should impede his enjoying it at all times and in all places.

To Ernest de Chabrol, Hartford, 7 October 1831

I have not yet received the letters of August 20, my dear friend. Consequently, I have nothing to say about what is happening in France, but I want to speak to you about myself.

Our stay in Boston was very useful for us; we discovered a great many distinguished men and precious documents there, but we are noticing again and again that the greatest obstacle to learning is not knowing.

On a multitude of points, we do not know what to ask, because we do not know what exists in France and because, without comparisons to make, the mind does not know how to proceed. It is therefore absolutely necessary for our friends in France to furnish us part of what we lack, if we are to gather some useful ideas here.

What is most striking to everyone who travels in this country, whether or not one bothers to reflect, is the spectacle of a society marching along all alone, without guide or support, by the sole fact of the cooperation of individual wills. In spite of anxiously searching for the government, one can find it nowhere, and the truth is that it does not, so to speak, exist at all.

You appreciate that to understand such a state of things, one must take apart the body social with great care, to examine each unit separately and then to see into what sphere of action these units need to go for the whole to form a nation. In order to make such a study fruitful, one would have had to reflect much more than I have on the principles that in general govern the administration of a people. But this is a subject to which I have never applied myself, not having had the time to do so.

I would at least like to know what *in fact* is the situation in France. The government, as I told you just now, is so small a thing here that I cannot conceive how it is so large in France. The Ministry of the Interior's 1,200 employees seem to me inexplicable. I know that you have never been any more occupied with administrative matters than I have, so I am not asking you about general principles, but perhaps you could obtain some precise practical information.

* * *

To the Countess de Tocqueville, On the Mississippi, 25 December 1831†

*** As we were thus debating on the bank, an infernal music resounded in the forest; it was a noise composed of drums, the neighing of horses, the barking of dogs. Finally a great troop of Indians, elderly people, women, children, baggage, all conducted by a European and heading toward the capital of our triangle. These Indians were the Chactas (or Choctaws), after the Indian pronunciation; with regard to this, I will tell you that M. de Chateaubriand was a little like La Fontaine's ape; he did not take the name of a port for the name of a man: but he gave to a man the name of a powerful nation in the south of America. Be that as it may, you undoubtedly wish to know why these Indians had arrived there, and how they could be of use to us; patience, I beg you, now that I have time and paper, I want nothing to hurry me. You will thus know that the Americans of the United States, rational and unprejudiced people, moreover, great philanthropists, supposed, like the Spanish, that God had given them the new world and its inhabitants as complete property.

They have discovered, moreover, that, as it was proved (listen to this well) that a square mile could support ten times more civilized men than savage men, reason indicated that wherever civilized men could settle, it was necessary that the savages cede the place. You see what a fine thing logic is. Consequently, when the Indians begin to find themselves a little too near their brothers the whites, the President of the United States sends them a messenger, who represents to them that in their interest, properly understood, it would be good to draw back ever so little toward the West. The lands they have inhabited for centuries belong to them, undoubtedly: no one refuses them this incontestable right; but these lands, after all, are uncultivated wilderness, woods, swamps, truly poor property. On the other side of the Mississippi, by contrast, are magnificent regions, where the game has never been troubled by the noise of the pioneer's axe, where the Europeans will *never* reach. They are separated from it by more than a hundred leagues. Add to that gifts of inestimable price, ready to reward their compliance; casks of brandy, glass necklaces, pendant earrings and mirrors; all supported by the insinuation that if they refuse, people will perhaps see themselves as constrained to force them to move. What to do? The poor Indians take their old parents in their arms; the women load their children on their shoulders; the nation finally puts itself on the march, carrying with it its greatest riches. It abandons forever the soil on which, perhaps for a thousand years, its fathers have lived, in order to go settle in a wilderness where the whites will not leave them ten years in peace. Do you observe the results of a high civilization? The Spanish, truly brutal, loose their dogs on the Indians

† The Countess de Tocqueville (1771–1836), also known as Louise Le Peletier de Rosanbo, was Alexis de Tocqueville's mother. This letter is from *Alexis de Tocqueville: Selected Letters on Politics and Society,* ed. Roger Boesche (University of California Press, 1985).

as on ferocious beasts; they kill, burn, massacre, pillage the new world as one would a city taken by assault, without pity as without discrimination. But one cannot destroy everything; fury has a limit. The rest of the Indian population ultimately becomes mixed with its conquerors, takes on their mores, their religion; it reigns today in several provinces over those who formerly conquered it. The Americans of the United States, more humane, more moderate, more respectful of law and legality, never bloodthirsty, are profoundly more destructive, and it is impossible to doubt that within a hundred years there will remain in North America, not a single nation, not even a single man belonging to the most remarkable of the Indian races. . . .

* * *

To Eugène Stoffels, Paris, 21 February 1835†

To return to the principal subject of your letters. I may say, dear friend, that the impression produced on you by my book, though in one respect stronger than I intended, is not of a kind that alarms or surprises me. This is the political object of the work:

I wished to show what in our days a democratic people really was; and by a rigorously accurate picture, to produce a double effect on the men of my day. To those who have fancied an ideal democracy, a brilliant and easily realized dream, I endeavored to show that they had clothed the picture in false colors; that the republican government which they extol, even though it may bestow substantial benefits on a people that can bear it, has none of the elevated features with which their imagination would endow it, and moreover, that such a government cannot be maintained without certain conditions of intelligence, of private morality, and of religious belief, that we, as a nation, have not reached, and that we must labor to attain before grasping their political results.

To those for whom the word democracy is synonymous with destruction, anarchy, spoliation, and murder, I have tried to show that under a democratic government the fortunes and the rights of society may be respected, liberty preserved, and religion honored; that though a republic may develop less than other governments some of the noblest powers of the human mind, it yet has a nobility of its own; and that after all it may be God's will to spread a moderate amount of happiness over all men, instead of heaping a large sum upon a few by allowing only a small minority to approach perfection. I attempted to prove to them that whatever their opinions might be, deliberation was no longer in their power; that society was tending every day more and more towards equality, and dragging them and every one else along with it; that the only choice lay between two inevitable evils; that the

† Eugène Stoffels (1805–1852) was a childhood friend and correspondent of Tocqueville. This letter is found in *Memoir, Letters, and Remains of Alexis De Tocqueville*, vol. 1 (Boston: Ticknor & Fields, 1862).

question had ceased to be whether they would have an aristocracy or a democracy, and now lay between a democracy without poetry or elevation indeed, but with order and morality; and an undisciplined and depraved democracy, subject to sudden frenzies, or to a yoke heavier than any that has galled mankind since the fall of the Roman Empire.

I wished to diminish the ardor of the Republican party, and without disheartening them, to point out their only wise course.

I have endeavored to abate the claims of the Aristocrats, and to make them bend to an irresistible future; so that the impulse in one quarter and resistance in the other being less violent, society may march on peaceably towards the fulfilment of its destiny. This is the dominant idea in the book—an idea which embraces all the others, and that you ought to have made out more clearly. Hitherto, however, few have discovered it. I please many persons of opposite opinions, not because they penetrate my meaning, but because, looking at only one side of my work, they think that they find in it arguments in favor of their own convictions. But I have faith in the future, and I hope that the day will come when all will see clearly what now only a few suspect. . . .

* * *

To Henry Reeve, Paris, 22 March 1837†

I received your letter with great pleasure, my dear Reeve; you give me good news of yourself and of your translation; I am much interested in both; I believe even that I am so unselfish as to prefer the prosperity of the former. Thank Heaven, both are going on well.

Before your letter came I received the speech of Sir Robert Peel and the pamphlet by an American citizen. I do not know if I am indebted to you for them. I should be much obliged if you would always let me see any publications of this description, if more should appear. Besides being seriously interested by the opinions which other people take the trouble of forming on me, I am amused at seeing the different characters that are ascribed to me according to the political views of the critic. I like to put them together as a series of portraits. Hitherto I have not found one that exactly represents the original.

My critics insist upon making me out a party-man; but I am not that. Passions are attributed to me where I have only opinions; or rather I have but one opinion, an enthusiasm for liberty and for the dignity of the human race. I consider all the forms of government only as so many more or less perfect means of satisfying this holy and legitimate craving. They ascribe to me alternately aristocratic and democratic prejudices. If I had been born in another period, or in another country, I might have had either the one or the other. But my birth, as

---

† Henry Reeve (1813–1895) was an English journalist and friend of Tocqueville's who translated *Democracy in America* into English. This letter is found in *Memoir, Letters, and Remains of Alexis de Tocqueville*, Volume II (Boston: Ticknor & Fields, 1862).

it happened, made it easy to me to guard against both. I came into the world at the end of a long revolution, which, after destroying ancient institutions, had created none that could last. When I entered life, aristocracy was dead and democracy as yet unborn. My instinct, therefore, could not lead me blindly either to the one or to the other. I lived in a country which for forty years had tried everything, and settled nothing. I was on my guard, therefore, against political illusions. Myself belonging to the ancient aristocracy of my country, I had no natural hatred or jealousy of the aristocracy; nor could I have any natural affection for it, since that aristocracy had ceased to exist, and one can be strongly attached only to the living. I was near enough to know it thoroughly, and far enough to judge dispassionately. I may say as much for the democratic element. It had done me, as an individual, neither good nor harm. I had no personal motive, apart from my public convictions, to love or to hate it. Balanced between the past and the future, with no natural instinctive attraction towards either, I could without an effort look quietly on each side of the question.

To John Quincy Adams, Paris, 4 December 1837†

* * * Your flattering comments on my work have touched me deeply, Sir; they could not but give me great pleasure, both in themselves and because of the person who admired them [sic]. My work is directed at people of a character and a lofty intellect such as yours, and their approval is invaluable to me.

The book you have read, moreover, is but the first part of a work on America I want to publish and which should comprise four volumes. I am currently working on the last two, which will deal with the customs [of American life] and with the influence that democratic institutions exert over them. I sincerely hope that this second part, which should appear, I think, in a year's time, will receive as favorable a review from you as the first part.

Even while working on the United States from a theoretical standpoint, I never cease to pay attention, as you might imagine, to the daily course of its affairs. I will not hide from you that I am sorely distressed by what has been happening in America these last years. The deplorable disturbances that have occurred in different parts of the Union with respect to the Blacks; the violent and illiberal principles expressed and supported by a large number of your statesmen on this occasion; the dispute between the President and the Bank, and finally the trade crisis from which you are only now emerging—all this has significantly diminished the moral power that the United States used to exercise in Europe. This is a regrettable consequence for all sincere

† John Quincy Adams (1767–1848) served as the sixth president of the United States of America from 1825 to 1829. Tocqueville was responding to a letter from Adams praising *Democracy in America*. The French text of Tocqueville's letter, translated here by Susan Tarrow and reprinted by permission, is from *Tocqueville, Lettres choisies, souvenirs, 1814–1859*, ed. F. Mélonio and L. Guellec (Paris: Gallimard, 2003). Original in Massachusetts Historical Society.

friends of humanity and liberty, while it delights all the partisans of despotism from one end of our continent to the other. Americans are not sufficiently aware of the world-wide repercussions of their errors and of the advantage that the enemies of freedom take of them in all parts of the globe. If they knew that, I believe they would exercise more self-restraint.

It is up to men like you, Sir, to educate your fellow citizens about the great power they hold and to teach them how to use it.

Please be assured, Sir, of my respect and esteem.

Reviews of *Democracy in America*

SAINTE-BEUVE

Le Temps, Paris, April 1835†

Studies of the United States of America have multiplied in France in recent times. In our current state of anxious uncertainty about the destiny of European society, we have been seeking guidance, reassuring or dire predictions, reasons for haste or for fear, from that great nation that has now seen sixty years of increasing prosperity under a political system almost unique in history. . . . One may no longer claim in response to examples drawn from the United States that they prove nothing when applied to ancient civilized peoples, coming as they do from a quite juvenile nation still in its elementary stages. Whatever the differences, both real and historical, that separate the civilization of the United States from that of Europe, we must now concede that the former [the United States] is very advanced, very developed, and quite capable in many cases of throwing light on the latter [Europe], to whom the United States may seem like a special case, both simplified and yet ahead of its time.

We now consider all this undeniable, particularly after reading the excellent work of M. de Tocqueville. . . . One particular quality that clearly distinguishes M. de Tocqueville's book from other works on the United States is that it is in no way either a plea or even a veiled promotion for or against this or that form of government; and yet M. de Tocqueville composed it with our Europe on his mind, with a lofty educational aim, and under the strong influence, as he himself confesses, of a kind of religious terror inspired by the inevitable progress of societies. He sees that all revolutions, wars and internal strife have had as their starting point or as their consequence the civil and political emancipation of the majority; he has noted that despite all the diversions, the daily misunderstandings and the absurdities that agitate the world stage, the gradual development of the equality of social status is slowly but surely gaining ground with each movement, taking advantage of every crisis, never retreating.

* * *

† Charles-Augustin Sainte-Beuve (1804–1869) was a poet, novelist, and literary critic who was elected to the Académie Française. Tocqueville responded cordially to this review, but relations between the two men soured in later years. This translation from the French is by Susan Tarrow and is reprinted by permission.

[M. de Tocqueville] follows the growth of democracy, and shows how with each decisive contest, it overturns everything in its path; but thus far, like a sturdy and undisciplined child, it has had no sense of direction or awareness of a specific goal. He shows how the rest of society, terrified by this spectacle and hostile to any unexpected endeavors, applies its knowledge only to conserve its own interests and well-being, and lacks that wise and positive energy that might rectify and temper blind energy. "I observe," he says, "calm and virtuous men whose pure morals, peaceful habits, wealth and education places them naturally at the head of the local population. Full of a sincere love of country, they are ready to make great sacrifices for her: however, civilization often finds them its adversaries; they confuse the abuses of civilization with its blessings, and in their mind the idea of evil is indissolubly linked with the idea of what is new."

This missing link between opinions and tastes, between actions and feelings, between the energy of desires and the soundness of views, this all too common divorce between remaining Christian convictions and the lure of the future, all this moral confusion saddens our young philosopher and seems to him a symptom without parallel in history. "So where are we?" he exclaims . . . "Has every other century resembled our own?" He is nevertheless heartened by the idea that there must be a law that governs these social destinies gone astray, and that European civilizations, so slow to be born, will enjoy a calm and settled future. "There is a country in the world," he says, "where the great social revolution seems to have reached its natural limits; it has taken place there quite simply, easily, or rather one might say that this country is seeing the results of the democratic revolution which is taking place amongst us here, without having gone through that revolution itself." So he takes us with him to America to study the major generative principle of modern societies, the equality of social status; to view it in this vast space where neither historical memories nor the ruins of ancient institutions have constrained it; to see it in action, invigorated by that moral purpose forged by the alliance of a spirit of religion and a zeal for hard work.

Once engaged with his topic, M. de Tocqueville sticks to it closely, and the eloquent general considerations of his Introduction give way to a learned and rigorous analysis, without any of those sentimental digressions that many of our young historians and publicists indulge in so easily. There is not a single chapter in the book that does not attest to one of the best and most steadfast minds, one of the most suited to political observations, in this profession which can claim so little brilliant or solid progress since the incomparable monument of Montesquieu.

The first volume of M. de Tocqueville's book is devoted to the study of American democracy in its institutions and written laws in the Township, the County, and the State; in the specific constitution of the different states, and in the federal constitution that unites them; and in the three branches of government, legislative, executive and judicial.

The second volume deals with this democracy and with the popular sovereignty which lies at its heart, in its continual influence and in its spirit outside of written law; here we find the customs, instincts, political and public passions of the governed and the governors; the good and the bad that ensue from this rule of the majority, the flaws and dangers it entails, as well as what moderates it. The scope and importance of the questions raised in the second volume, particularly in relation to Europe, are obvious; without ever claiming to have worked out in advance what the future may hold, the author has gathered all the elements of his experience and laid out the parameters for his most plausible speculations.

The basic natural element of democratic institutions seems to M. de Tocqueville to be the Township, and he describes its formation and existence in America, particularly in New England, in such as way as to transport us right away into the very heart of this society that governs itself. The great number of public offices in the Township, their many divisions of power, and the short tenure of office holders create within these small worlds a continual agitation, in which the desire for respect, the taste for fame and power operate alongside the ordinary intercourse of society. This very agitation of interests and passions around each little center contributes to the stability of the whole.

* * *

Everything else that M. de Tocqueville has to say on this interesting subject deserves further study, given his brilliance and eminence; it deals with his fundamental preoccupation, our future destinies in Europe. If it should come to pass in France that the monarchy or the republic (no matter which), . . . should repeatedly impose administrative regulation, whether gentle or harsh, on all levels of daily life in each part of the country; if we were unable to introduce and set up democratic institutions, with all the elemental animation essential to community life, M. de Tocqueville seems to fear that one natural outcome of this growing equality might one day, sooner or later, be the subjugation of all by one, once there was no prospect of self-government by all.

However, M. de Tocqueville does not push this ominous thought too far; governed by his philosophy of objectivity, he is content to point out one possible misfortune on the horizon, and he never indulges in any mood of discouragement or complaint. That is not his way. Indeed everything points to the fact that he has no great expectations, and that he in no way believes that our own opportunity to control and create our future has passed. But it is beneficial, in the midst of so many songs of praise that we ourselves have been singing about the infallibility and the delights of this unknown future, to hear a young and serious call to reality, to listen to a positive yet stern observer.

As an example of M. de Tocqueville's excellent method, at once experimental and philosophical, we draw your attention to what he says about the division of the legislature in the United States into two branches. In setting up two Chambers, the Americans did not want to create one hereditary assembly and another elected one; they did not aspire to make one an aristocratic body and the other a representative of democracy; to make one an adjunct of the powerful and the other an organ of the people. They wanted rather to divide the power of the legislature, to slow the movement of political Assemblies, and to create a court of appeal for the revision of laws. Pennsylvania had at first tried to establish a single Assembly, and Franklin, following a strict logic, had pressed for this measure. Experience soon forced him to return to two Chambers. "Thus," says M. de Tocqueville, "this theory (the necessity of dividing legislative action into several bodies), almost unknown in the ancient republics, was brought into the world almost by chance, like most great truths; at first unrecognized by several modern nations, it was finally accepted as an axiom of current political science."

This prudent and sound method of reasoning is a far cry from what some still imagine to be the inherent virtues of a Chamber of aristocrats and men of property that they would reconstitute artificially, and from what others find entirely logical in the simple unity of a sovereign Chamber or Convention that no collateral power would hold in check.

M. de Tocqueville, however preoccupied he may have been with Europe while he was writing about America, has no intention of applying conclusions from one to the other; he states this expressly, and the ideas running throughout the work prove it. He wanted to show through the example of America that laws, and above all customs, can allow a democratic nation to remain free. But he is far from believing that we should all follow this example and subject ourselves to these means. "For I am well aware," he says, "of the influence exercised by the nature and earlier history of a country on political constitutions, and I would consider it a great misfortune for the human race if liberty had to appear with the same features everywhere."

One of the first chapters focuses on what he calls "the point of departure," on the very origin of the different American states and the spirit that infused them from the start. His theory is that people can never cast off the circumstances of their birth and upbringing, however far away their subsequent lives may take them. Thus he shows us how the Puritans, and emigrants of different sects, especially in New England, who had fled persecution to seek asylum there, joined together in certain common needs, in certain fundamental rights, and except for a few inevitable errors and prejudices, immediately put into practice the union of the spirit of religion and the spirit of freedom. The entire moral code of democracy in America is derived from this initial union. As I was reading, I wondered if one had to leave one's homeland to accomplish such results; will there ever be a moment, in the heart of the old world, when all the vanquished, the wounded, the puritans of various opinions will set an example of a union on undisputed common ground, and will come to a sensible accord in the interest of a peaceful and secure freedom?

M. de Tocqueville's book, if one were to examine it in its entirety, would provide food for thought on all the major questions of modern politics; we wanted rather to characterize the book's general orientation and the mind that inspired it. In praising this most recent book, one is merely re-stating the well-informed opinion of all competent and serious individuals. The approbation of such luminaries as Chateaubriand, Royer-Collard and Lamartine has been expressed clearly enough for us to report it without fear of having been deceived by flattering appearances. We would have to go back a long way to find a book of scientific and political observation that has attracted and so rewarded the attention of our philosophers.

The style of M. de Tocqueville's book is simple, sober, measured with a kind of steady harmony, well suited to the subject. One might find it occasionally a little didactic and theoretical, with its abstract methods. Many facts and historical details, which have been relegated to the notes, could well have served to break up and enliven the text, as is the case with the great style of *L'Esprit des lois*.[1] Excellent from a philosophical point of view, and lacking only in its artistic qualities, M. de Tocqueville's style is direct and takes one straight to his deductions, thanks mostly to what he does not say; but in the first volume in particular, the reader has to turn frequently from the text to the notes that complement or modify it.

PELLEGRINO ROSSI

Revue des deux mondes, July–September 1840†

* * *

M. de Tocqueville has devoted himself wholeheartedly to the study of democracy. He began by observing all its developments, and its various manifestations. He neither loved nor hated it, but rather remained open to the different impressions it made on him: wounded one day, delighted the next, M. de Tocqueville, insofar as his restraint and reserve allow, has given us a glimpse of his sympathies as well as his distaste, of his hopes as well as his fears. Although he prefers to speak of the facts and ideas he has observed rather than of his own feelings, M. de Tocqueville has not made any pretense of impassivity, of an indifference that would be almost inconceivable in someone contemplating such a rich new lode of knowledge. He observed the facts before him as a man and a citizen, concealing nothing of the diverse impressions he encountered during the course of his work.

The writer's sincerity, a reflection not only of the workings of his mind but also of the sentiments of his soul, has prompted some peo-

---

1. Sainte-Beuve refers to Montesquieu's magisterial *The Spirit of the Laws* (1748) [*Editor's Note*].

† Pellegrino Rossi (1787–1848) was an Italian publicist and professor of political economy at the Collège de France who was appointed French ambassador to the Papal States in 1845. He was assassinated in November 1848 by a republican extremist. This translation from the French is by Susan Tarrow and is reprinted by permission.

ple to say that since the publication of his first book, the author changed his mind on the matter of democracy, that his work began and ended under the sway of two opposing sentiments. We cannot share this opinion; it is not the author who changes, it is democracy whose manifestations and impact remain in flux, like all things human.

The two parts of M. de Tocqueville's work, the one he published five years ago and this most recent one, complement each other and form a single work. In the first part, the author studied the influence of democracy on the laws, institutions and political customs of American society; in the second, he wants to introduce us to the changes that the spirit of democracy has brought to all other social relations, to the opinions and sentiments it has engendered; in short, the appearance of the civil society it has created.

This division of his subject is flawless in itself and complete, since social and political organization, the ends and the means, include all that civil society can offer to a philosopher's meditation; nevertheless it allows the introduction of notable differences between the two parts of the work. In the second part, we might search in vain for those perfectly defined outlines, those positive results, those irrefutable demonstrations that characterize the first part. M. de Tocqueville could not change the nature of things and accomplish the impossible. The political organization of a country is a clearly circumscribed topic; whatever it is like, good or bad, simple or complex, it is not very difficult to grasp its principles, or to assess its results. The political sciences have made so much progress that today's observer does not lack for instruments. If mediocre works or incomplete analyses of such subjects exist, one can justly claim that the authors have not brought the necessary attention and discernment to their research.

But when one undertakes the study of a whole society, in all its forms and manifestations, when one wants to probe all its depths, penetrate all its recesses to prove in each case the influence of a certain principle and the modifications it has caused, one takes on a fearsome task. It is an almost limitless field; and those limits are so uncertain and ill-determined that the precision and clarity of the work of even the most skilled observer is inevitably reduced.

A glance at the table of contents of the first and second parts of M. de Tocqueville's book will clearly illustrate our thinking. What did the first two volumes deal with essentially? With the principle of popular sovereignty in America, with the system of townships, with the three powers—legislative, executive and judiciary, with the federal constitution, parties, freedom of the press, universal suffrage, the rule of the majority in the United States, and so on; vast and important subjects, no doubt, but which are already familiar to us, well defined in both the ideas and the language. One may accept or reject the rule of the majority or the separation of powers; but there are no two ways of understanding these principles and these facts. Any educated person has a clear idea of the meaning of these expressions; on hearing them he understands neither more nor less than the next man.

In the second part M. de Tocqueville deals first with democracy's influence on the evolution of ideas, then with its influence on emotions; third, its influence on customs; in a final section he deals with the influence of democratic ideas and sentiments on political society. Can one say that these labels give the reader the concept of a clearly defined field, ideas as distinct as those suggested by the titles of the first part? Obviously not: the dividing line between intellectual movements and emotions, between emotions and customs, is no doubt real, but it is hard to grasp. Ask ten different people the details, chapter by chapter, of each of these sections, and you will probably get ten different interpretations. Ask ten different people about the sub-divisions of a treatise on the separation of powers, and you would probably find only slight differences of detail. Again, this diversity is in the very nature of things, and we certainly do not reproach M. de Tocqueville for any vagueness in the structure of his work.

Far from it; our remark had no aim other than to explain to readers the real reason behind a kind of disappointment they have felt on reading a book they had anticipated with a justifiable impatience and which they seized upon enthusiastically. They were seeking something that could not be there, I mean a real continuation, in both form and content, of the first work. In Part 1, the author applied Montesquieu's method to a totally new political organization. In the second part, he followed more closely the paths of Pascal or La Bruyère. In this vast tableau of passions and customs, of the strengths and weaknesses of democracy, there are portrayals that the author of *Les Caractères* would not have disavowed.

But in general M. de Tocqueville's book is the work of a thinker who is not afraid to tackle in a few lines the thorniest questions of philosophy, law, art, and political economy; the society he observes and analyzes provides him with the seed, or the development, or the application of all things.

The philosophical method, religious beliefs, eloquence, poetry, theater, education, *individualism*, the taste for material comfort, social relations, the family, the spirit of association, the question of salaries, armies and their discipline—all these are for M. de Tocqueville a subject for analysis and study, within the framework of identifying the influence of the spirit of democracy.

In this great variety of topics, opinions and judgments, it is probably impossible for all his readers to agree with the author on every issue; but no impartial reader can fail to admire on each page the purity of form, the subtle power of observation, the shrewd judgment, the ingenuity, the simple, lively style, both assured and gracious, all of which characterize M. de Tocqueville's writing. His workmanship is exquisite, perfect in all respects except perhaps for some carelessness here and there.

As for the content, the author had to struggle with immense difficulties in this second part of his work. We have tried to explain it. He had to know everything, so to speak; analyze, compare, and summarize everything. How else could he explain the influence of the democratic principle on all parts of such a varied, complex, and mobile entity as civil society? How could he know what is and what is not, what is old and what is new, what is the effect of a new cause or the result of pre-existing causes? How, in the study of effects, can one attribute the specific role of each cause, if one does not know exactly the extent of effects and the relative power of each cause? M. de Tocqueville has told us that in dealing with this immense subject, he was never satisfied. He should take comfort in the fact that no man would be equal to all the demands of such an endeavor; only lesser mortals might manage to be more easily satisfied.

* * *

M. de Tocqueville might have approached his task as a historian rather than as a philosopher; instead of these fine, ingenious, detailed analyses, which lead us to the very heart, to the furthest recesses of democratic society, he might have dealt with American society in large segments, described it in bold outlines, and thus added more animation, more richness, more diverse forms to his style. He would thus have avoided entirely some of the comments that we have heard about his book: There is nothing in the world, great or small, in which M. de Tocqueville does not implicate democracy; the form of the book is a little monotonous; as a result reading it cannot fail to be tedious.

We have not concealed how well founded the first comment may be; but it is only fair to add that it can be applied to only a few pages and to secondary points. Everywhere else M. de Tocqueville is right, and if some effects that he attributes to the influence of democracy may seem debatable at first glance, it is because the link between cause and effect in such cases is hard to grasp.

Thus we admit that M. de Tocqueville's book is not what people today are in the habit of reading. It requires not only one's eyes, but also one's thoughtful consideration. It is not an entertainment, it is hard work. It is extremely interesting, but it is not an amusing pastime.

This is to say that M. de Tocqueville has written the book he wanted to write, and we thank him for having produced a work of higher political philosophy, a profound and conscientious analysis of a very complex social state, and even more worthy of our study because the future of the world lies hidden in its depths.

Let there be no misunderstanding. We do not mean that sooner or later all the states in the old and new worlds will be tossed, so to speak, into the American mold. Far from it; we believe, on the contrary, that sooner or later the United States will undergo transformations that will make it more like our European societies. We meant only that the future of the world, in one form or another, is democracy, that is, the abolition of privilege and the establishment of civil equality.

We regret that we cannot go into all the details of the work here. In fact, we would be hard pressed to make a choice. The number of important and curious questions raised by M. de Tocqueville is so great that no sooner has one picked out one of them than one regrets not having chosen another.

Permit me to recall here a question that seems most pertinent for demonstrating the ingenuity, the curiosity even, of M. de Tocqueville's choice of research topics. This is the question: Why is the study of Greek and Latin literature especially useful in democratic societies? The solution the reader will find in Chap. XV of the first volume can be summarized thus: The writers of antiquity wrote only for connoisseurs; nothing in their works seems hurried or haphazard; the search for the ideal of beauty is evident everywhere. Democratic literatures, on the other hand, always teem (according to M. de Tocqueville) with authors who consider letters just an industry, and for every few great writers one finds a multitude of peddlers of ideas. All in all (he says elsewhere), the literature of the democratic age cannot offer the image of order, regularity, science and art that we found in the aristocratic age; artistic forms are usually neglected and even scorned. The style is often bizarre, incorrect, careless and woolly, and almost always bold and vehement. Authors are more concerned with the speed of production than with the perfection of detail. They seek to astonish rather than to please, and strive to seduce the passions rather than delight the sense of taste.

I do not want to ask the author where he came across all these judicious, witty observations on the literature of democratic peoples. Certainly not in America. "Strictly speaking, the inhabitants of the United States do not yet have a literature. The only American authors he recognizes are journalists." In several of his chapters, we might suspect M. de Tocqueville of having looked outside the confines of America. He proceeds less than one might think *a priori*, and by way of intuition. American democracy is not the only case providing colors to his palette. Thus we might easily say to certain Europeans, when certain chapters evoke a smile not quite devoid of malice: *de te fabula narratur* [this story is about you]. According to M. de Tocqueville, democratic literatures lack wisdom, taste, ideal beauty; the study of the masterworks of antiquity is the best way to contend with these literary flaws. This is an ingenious point of view, quite new; we recommend it to those idolaters of modern times who would snatch Homer and Virgil from our children's hands, and renew the solemn decree outlawing Greek and Latin that was once threatened by one of those ephemeral republics which blossomed in Italy after the French Revolution.

We fear nothing of the sort today. Thus it is not to reassure the friends of classical studies that we pointed out M. de Tocqueville's brilliant observation. We used it to introduce some general reflections that apply to the whole work, to its direction and its spirit.

M. de Tocqueville has concealed nothing about democracy, neither the good nor the bad which, as in all things human, are mingled, and have given rise to so many odes and satires, both equally far from the truth. With his noble soul, his lofty character, his exquisite taste, M. de Tocqueville does not resign himself easily to the vulgar, disorderly, excessively individualistic aspects of democracy; as a sincere and enlightened friend of the liberty and progress of humanity, he would certainly not want to restore privilege, or to purchase elegance, luxury, high intellectual culture, or the moral power of one caste at the expense of the poverty, ignorance, and enslavement of the masses, even if he had the power to do so. He accepts democracy, not only as a necessary reality, as the natural development of nations, but also as a form of progress, as a good, but as a mixed blessing that still leaves something to be desired.

Consequently, he has not just sought to inform us of the natural influence of democracy on intellectual developments, on feelings, customs and morals; he has not brought up the distressing consequences of certain democratic tendencies with an attitude of philosophical indifference, such as a naturalist might use to speak of the thorns and poisons of certain plants. Whenever he encountered a drawback, M. de Tocqueville carefully sought the corrective, either in democracy itself, or in other institutions which, far from being incompatible with democracy, might in fact be linked to it and modify it in a useful way.

Thus he calls on the study of the Classics to correct what is incorrect and vulgar in democracy's literary output.

He calls on political freedom to draw people away from their individual interests through broad institutions, to detach them every so often from their selfish viewpoint, to force them to forget themselves in some way and to think of others, if only for ambition's sake. "When the people govern, no man is unaware of the value of the people's good will, and he will try to attract it by winning the esteem and affection of those around him. Many of the passions that harden hearts and divide opinion are obliged to retreat into the depths of the soul and to remain hidden there. Pride is disguised, scorn dare not show its face; selfishness is afraid of itself."

He calls on newspapers to play a role in encouraging men who no longer enjoy the solid and permanent ties that bound aristocracies to come to an agreement and to work together. "The leading citizens in an aristocracy see each other from afar; if they want to join forces, they march towards each other, drawing multitudes in their wake." In democracies, "this can only happen regularly and easily with the help of a newspaper; only a newspaper can plant the same idea in a thousand minds at the same time. Thus newspapers become more necessary as men become more equal and individualism is more of a threat. We would diminish their importance if we thought that they only guaranteed liberty; in fact they sustain civilization."

In short, he asks that the spirit of association correct the incoherence and thus the weakness and impotence that *individualism* creates in democratic states. As he observes, "there is a necessary relationship between associations and newspapers: newspapers make the associations, associations make the newspapers; and if it were true to say that associations should multiply as social equality increases, it is even more certain that the number of newspapers increases as associations multiply."

This part of the work, where M. de Tocqueville tries to highlight anything that can attenuate or dispel the drawbacks of democracy, gives his book what I might call a high moral flavor, which attaches the reader to the writer in a remarkable way, as the reader becomes more and more convinced that the mind and the soul of the writer contributed to the work in equal measure.

Moreover, we declare openly that we do not share the fears that democracy seems to engender, even among several of its friends. We believe that these fears are due to a confusion between two ideas that M. de Tocqueville himself has perhaps not sufficiently distinguished and separated: I mean the ideas of civil equality and the equality of social rank.

It is civil equality, in other words the abolition of privilege and the establishment of common law, which constitutes true democracy, this is the principle which France has supported since the eighteenth century, and which, thanks to her, has been realized in a part of both worlds. That is the principle whose conquests are assured; it is the law that will sooner or later take over the universe; for civil equality is justice.

As for the equality of social status, actual equality, material equality (whatever you wish to call it), it does not exist anywhere, it has never existed, it will never exist, because it is contrary to human nature, and to the law: it is injustice.

The kind of injustice we oppose, that is to say, privilege, was able to endure so long because it had the advantage of external factors, of surface appearance, and we made the mistake of inferring entitlement from appearance. Aristotle himself made this mistake. But the equality of social status, if it were posed as a principle, would have in its favor neither practice nor law, neither reality nor the appearance of right.

Apart from that, most of the noted drawbacks of democracy are of little importance. Upon reflection, one might infer that these drawbacks need be feared only in a country where the land is not appropriated. Moreover, those who demand the abolition of private property are perfectly justified and consistent in their system.

With the inevitable inequality of social status and the appropriation of the land, democratic countries have nothing serious to fear from an excess of *individualism*. The fabric of society lacks neither a foundation nor cement to bind it.

On this point we continue to think that the United States presents the observer with facts that, when generalized, could lead to false inductions. As a new country, without forebears, without an earlier history, and set in quite unusual economic circumstances, America reconciles legal equality and actual equality in its own peculiar way, which does not exist and will never exist in our old societies, and which will cease to exist in America as the country matures; as the population gets more and more dense, when fertile plots of land are no longer available, and when a considerable number of Americans, gorged with wealth, become men of leisure, they will become aware of needs beyond the pursuit of money.

All this has long existed here in Europe, and we would be mistaken in thinking that it will disappear. Grown men do not return to childhood; rather it is the child who advances towards manhood. It is

America that is heading, in its own way, towards Europe; Europe cannot become American.

JOHN C. SPENCER

Preface to 1838 American Edition of
Democracy in America†

The following work of M. de Tocqueville has attracted great attention throughout Europe, where it is universally regarded as a sound, philosophical, impartial, and remarkably clear and distinct view of our political institutions, and of our manners, opinions, and habits, as influencing or influenced by those institutions. Writers, reviewers, and statesmen of all parties, have united in the highest commendations of its ability and integrity. The people, described by a work of such a character, should not be the only one in Christendom unacquainted with its contents. At least, so thought many of our most distinguished men, who have urged the publishers of this edition to reprint the work, and present it to the American public. They have done so in the hope of promoting among their countrymen a more through knowledge of their frames of government, and a more just appreciation of the great principles on which they are founded . . :

*** He has discussed many subjects on which very different opinions are entertained in the United States; but with an ability, a candour, and an evident devotion to the cause of truth, which will commend his views to those who most radically dissent from them. Indeed, renders of the most discordant opinions will find that he frequently agrees with both sides, and as frequently differs from them. As an instance, his remarks on slavery will not be found to coincide throughout with the opinions either of abolitionists or of slaveholders: but they will be found to present a masterly view of a most perplexing and interesting subject, which seems to cover the whole ground, and to lead to the melancholy conclusion of the utter impotency of human effort to eradicate this acknowledged evil. But on this, and on the various topics of the deepest interest which are discussed in this work, it was thought that the American readers would be fully competent to form their own opinions, and to detect any errors of the author, if such there are, without any attempt by the present editor to enlighten them. At all events, it is to be hoped that the citizens of the United States will patiently read, and candidly consider, the views of this accomplished foreigner, however hostile they may be to their own preconceived opinions or prejudices. He says: "There are certain truths which Americans can only learn from strangers, or from experience." Let us, then, at least listen to one who admires us and our institu-

---

† John C. Spencer (1788–1855) was a lawyer who served as secretary of war and secretary of the Treasury under President John Tyler. He met Tocqueville during his visit to America and wrote introductions to the first American editions of *Democracy in America*.

tions, and whose complaints, when he makes any, are, that we have not perfected our own glorious plans, and that there are some things yet to be amended. We shall thus furnish a practical proof, that public opinion in this country is not so intolerant as the author may be understood to represent it. However mistaken he may be, his manly appeal to our understandings and to our consciences, should at least be heard. "If ever," he says, "these lines are read in America, I am well assured of two things: in the first place, that all who peruse them will raise their voice to condemn me; and, in the second place, that very many of them will acquit me at the bottom of their consciences." He is writing on that very sore subject, the tyranny of public opinion in the United States.

Fully to comprehend the scope of the present work, the author's motive and object in preparing it should be distinctly kept in view. He has written, not for America, but for France. "It was not, then, merely to satisfy a legitimate curiosity," he says, "that I have examined America: my wish has been to find instruction, by which we might ourselves profit."—"I sought the image of democracy itself, with its inclinations, its character, its prejudices, and its passions, in order to learn what we have to hope or fear from its progress." He thinks that the principle of democracy has sprung into new life throughout Europe, and particularly in France, and that it is advancing with a firm and steady march to the control of all civilized governments. In his own country, he had seen a recent attempt to repress its energies within due bounds, and to prevent the consequences of its excesses. And it seems to be a main object with him, to ascertain whether these bounds can be relied upon; whether the dikes and embankments of human contrivance can keep within any appointed channel this mighty and majestic stream. Giving the fullest confidence to his declaration, that his book "is written to favour no particular views and with no design of serving or attacking any party," it is yet evident that his mind has been very open to receive impressions unfavourable to the admission into France of the unbounded and unlimited democracy which reigns in these United States. A knowledge of this inclination of his mind will necessarily induce some caution in his readers, while perusing those parts of the work which treat of the effects of our democracy upon the stability of our government and its administration. While the views of the author, respecting the application of the democratic principle, in the extent that it exists with us, to the institutions of France, or to any of the European nations, are of the utmost importance to the people and statesmen of those countries, they are scarcely less entitled to the attention of Americans. He has exhibited, with admirable skill, the causes and circumstances which prepared our forefathers, gradually, for the enjoyment of free institutions, and which enabled them to sustain, without abusing, the utmost liberty that was ever enjoyed by any people. In tracing these causes, in examining how far they continue to influence our conduct, manners, and opinions, and in searching for the means of preventing their decay or destruction, the intelligent American reader will find no better guide than M. de Tocqueville.

Fresh from the scenes of the "three days" revolution in France, the author came among us to observe, carefully and critically, the operation of the new principle on which the happiness of his country, and, as he seems to believe, the destinies of the civilized world, depend. Filled with the love of liberty, but remembering the atrocities which, in its name, had been committed under former dynasties at home, he sought to discover the means by which it was regulated in America, and reconciled with social order. By his laborious investigations, and minute observations of the history of the settlement of the country, and of its progress through the colonial state to independence, he found the object of his inquiry in the manners, habits, and opinions, of a people who had been gradually prepared, by a long course of peculiar circumstances, and by their local position, for self-government; and he has explained, with a pencil of light, the mystery that has baffled Europeans and perplexed Americans. He exhibits us, in our present condition, a new, and, to Europeans, a strange people. His views of our political institutions are more general, comprehensive, and philosophic, than have, been presented by any writer, domestic or foreign. He has traced them from their source, democracy—the power of the people—and has steadily pursued this foundation-principle in all its forms and modifications; in the frame of our governments, in their administration by the different executives, in our legislation, in the arrangement of our judiciary, in our manners, in religion, in the freedom and licentiousness of the press, in the influence of public opinion, and in various subtle recesses, where its existence was scarcely suspected. In all these, he analyzes and dissects the tendencies of democracy; heartily applauds where he can, and faithfully and independently gives warning of dangers that he foresees. No one can read the results of his observations, without better and clearer perceptions of the structure of our governments, of the great pillars on which they rest, and of the dangers to which they are exposed: nor without a more profound and more intelligent admiration of the harmony and beauty of their formation, and of the safeguards provided for preserving and transmitting them to a distant posterity. The more that general and indefinite notions of our own liberty, greatness, happiness, &c., are made to give place to precise and accurate knowledge of the true merits of our institutions, the peculiar objects they are calculated to attain or promote, and the means provided for that purpose, the better will every citizen be enabled to discharge his great political duty of guarding those means against the approach of corruption, and of sustaining them against the violence of party commotions. No foreigner has ever exhibited such a deep, clear, and correct insight of the machinery of our complicated systems of federal and state governments. The most intelligent Europeans are confounded with our *imperium in imperio*; and their constant wonder is, that these systems are not continually jostling each other. M. de Tocqueville has clearly perceived, and traced correctly and distinctly, the orbits in which they move, and has described, or rather defined, our federal government, with an accurate precision, unsurpassed even by an American pen. There is no citizen of this country who will not derive instruction from our author's account of our national government, or, at least, who will not find his own ideas systematized, and rendered more fixed and precise, by the perusal of that account.

Among other subjects discussed by the author, that of the *political influence* of the institution of trial by jury, is one of the most curious and interesting. He has certainly presented it in a light entirely new, and as important as it is new. It may be that he has exaggerated its influence as "a gratuitous public school": but if he has, the error will be readily forgiven.

His views of religion, as connected with patriotism, in other words, with the democratic principle, which he steadily keeps in view, are conceived in the noblest spirit of philanthropy, and cannot fail to confirm the principles already so thoroughly and universally entertained by the American people. And no one can read his observations on the union of "church and state," without a feeling of deep gratitude to the founders of our government, for saving us from such a prolific source of evil.

These allusions to topics that have interested the writer, are not intended as an enumeration of the various subjects which will arrest the attention of the American reader. They have been mentioned rather with a view of exciting an appetite for the whole feast, than as exhibiting the choice dainties which cover the board.

JOHN C. SPENCER

Preface to 1841 American Edition of
Democracy in America

The publishers of this edition of M. de Tocqueville's continuation of his *Views of Democracy in America*, applied to the editor who introduced the original work to the American public, to perform the same friendly office for this sequel. A desire to promote the circulation among his fellow-citizens, of a production upon subjects peculiarly interesting to them, has induced him to contribute for that purpose—all that his engagements would allow, and all, indeed, that seemed required—a brief introductory notice of the general scope and design of the work. Indeed, it affords scarcely any occasion for comment. The author is so copious and comprehensive in his discussion of the various topics which he has selected, that he has left nothing to be added. The few general facts upon which he reasons do not seem to require correction. We may think he exaggerates certain tendencies in the character of American citizens—that, for instance, of restless dissatisfaction with their condition individually—yet we must acknowledge that the circumstances under which he has formed his opinions, qualify him to be a better judge of us, than we can be of ourselves. The work is highly speculative; and yet, from it may be drawn practical results of the greatest importance. It presents the author's system, formed after minute and careful observation, and deep and intense consideration, with an evident democratic fellow-feeling, and with signal ability. It would be presumptuous and idle to attempt the correction of such a system. The author must speak for himself; and every reader must form his own conclusions respecting the accuracy of the views which are presented to him.

The very favorable opinion universally expressed of the discriminating judgement which distinguished the first part of "Democracy in America," will not be weakened by the perusal of this continuation. The former part treated of the influence of democracy upon our political institutions. The following books discuss the effects of the same cause upon the tastes, feelings, habits, and manners, of the Americans, and present a view of us in relations which have never occupied our own meditations.

The author's object is to trace the operations of political liberty and political equality. In his first book, he discusses the influence of democracy upon public opinion, upon individual thought, and upon religious belief; upon the cultivation of the arts, upon literature, and particularly language; treats of the inflated style of our orators and writers; and comments upon our parliamentary eloquence. The second book is devoted to the influence of democracy on our *feelings*; and in this individualism and association, as affected by political equality, are sketched with a masterly hand. He shows that there is a necessary and inevitable connexion between the principle of equality, when guarded by free institutions, and that of association; and thus accounts for the infinite variety and extent of associations in America. There are some who imagine companies of men formed for moral, intellectual, or industrial purposes, to be in their nature aristocratic and monopolizing, and hostile to freedom and equality. The remarks of our author will convince such of their mistake. He shows how legitimately associations spring from democracy, and are interwoven with it, and how impossible it would be to accomplish any useful purpose without them, in a country where political equality prevailed. "If men," he says, "are to remain civilized, or to become so, the art of associating together must grow and improve in the same ratio in which the equality of conditions is increased." He discusses our taste for physical well-being, and its effects; the cause of what he deems our restless spirit, and explains why all honest callings among us are honorable, and why almost all the Americans follow industrial pursuits.

In the third book he examines the influence of democracy upon *manners*; explains why it renders the intercourse of Americans simple and easy; the cause of our having so little sensitiveness in our personal intercourse at home, and so much when abroad; the relation of master and servant, the duration of leases, and the rate of wages, as affected by democracy, are discussed. The influence of the same cause upon kindred, upon the education of women, and upon good morals, forms the subject of what will probably be deemed the most interesting portion of the work. The author seems to have studied the character of our females with the greatest attention. His account of their position in society, his explanation of their peculiarities, and the reasons for their difference from the sex in Europe, are worthy the deepest consideration. It is a source of honest pride, to receive the testimony which such an observer bears to the fact, that our morals, so far as the intercourse of the sexes is concerned, are more pure than in any other country of the world, and that this is the natural and legitimate effect of democratic institutions.

M. de Tocqueville thinks that there is an undue proportion of ambitious men among us, and but little lofty ambition; and he seeks to explain the cause, and descants on the trade of place-hunting. The love of peace, and its influence on democratic armies, and the energy and effective power of such armies, form the subjects of some very interesting remarks.

The fourth book treats of the influence of democratic sentiments on political society; and is more connected with the subject of the former work. M. de Tocqueville thinks there is a tendency in democracies favorable to the concentration of power, but which may be controlled by peculiar and accidental causes; and such circumstances he thinks exist in America. He describes the kind of despotism which democratic nations have reason to apprehend, and which may exist in the midst of free institutions. The work terminates with a general survey of the whole subject.

This general survey confirms the remark made in the preface to the former part of the author's work, that "he has written, not for America, but for France." It is indeed obvious from the whole course of his remarks, that he anticipates the prevalence of democracy throughout Europe, if not the civilized world, and that he would learn the probable consequences of the change, from the results which have been produced in America. But he was desirous that the peculiar causes which controlled those results, and often gave them a new direction, quite different from what would occur in Europe, should be well understood. Hence the minuteness and care with which he analyzes our history, and examines our institutions, to discover the agencies that counteract the ordinary influences of democracy. This great object of the author should be borne in mind by his readers, to account for what would otherwise appear to be digressions from "a view of America." It was not his principal design to give an account of our political society, or of our manners, opinions, tastes, or feelings. Such an account was merely incidental to another and more general object before stated.

It is with great diffidence that the writer of this would venture to question the clearness and accuracy of our author's language. But it appears to him, that there is sometimes a want of precision in the use of the term democracy. It does not always indicate those free institutions which give to the people an ultimate control. It seems often to be used as merely expressing *equality* He frequently speaks of political equality, as something quite distinct from political liberty. The distinction may not at first appear sound; but it is certainly true that despotism may produce equality among its subjects.

The author is himself aware that he may have ascribed to democracy exclusively effects which resulted from other causes combined with that; but seems to think that he has ordinarily distinguished the other causes, and made suitable allowances for them. Whatever difference of opinion there may be upon this point, and it is apprehended there will be some, there is little danger of error from this source; for the discussions of the author are so ample as to lead the mind to the consideration of the influence of other causes and circumstances bearing upon the question, although he may not have taken them into the account, or allowed them sufficient weight. Still some caution should be used, in admitting all the consequences and influences of democracy, to the full extent which M. de Tocqueville claims.

It should be recollected that his object is to trace these influences and consequences, and not to censure or praise them. His work is a philosophical inquiry for political and moral truth; and he records whatever he finds. If the results are not always gratifying to our self-love, instead of condemning him who has developed them, we should endeavor to show the inaccuracy of his conclusions, or, what is better, strive to correct in ourselves, whatever is reflected back to us in this mirror. We have, at least, this consolation, that the evils of democracy are not exaggerated by a hostile pen, but are exhibited by one who is an ardent and intelligent friend of free institutions.

Upon the whole, it is believed that this part of the continuation of the author's views, will be found as useful, and more interesting, to the American reader, than its predecessor. The plan, object, and execution, of the whole work, are entirely new. America, or that portion of it consisting of the United States, is individualized, and here is its biography. Its social relations, its manners, opinions, feelings, and habits, are delineated; and they are accounted for by our territorial position; by the dispositions inherited from our ancestors; by the discipline of our preparatory education, as colonies, and by the operations of a new and ever-active principle, here, for the first time, allowed its full scope. The manner of conducting the inquiry which the author has instituted; the intimate acquaintance with all our institutions and relations everywhere evinced; the careful and profound thought; and, above all, the spirit of truth which animates and pervades the whole work; will not only commend it to the present generation, but will render it a monument of the age in which it is produced.

A work of such a character, relating to any other country, would challenge the attention of all who take any concern in the destiny of their race; but, treating as it does, of us and our institutions, it possesses an interest proportioned to our regard for our own welfare. In Europe, it has already taken its stand with Montesquieu, Bacon, Milton, and Locke. In America, it will be regarded, not only as a classic philosophical treatise of the highest order, but as indispensable in the education of every statesman, and of every citizen who desires thoroughly to comprehend the institutions of his country.

The North American Review, July 1836

* * *

*** M. de Tocqueville shows himself to be an original thinker, an acute observer, and an eloquent writer. We regard his work now before us, as by far the most philosophical, ingenious, and instructive, which has been produced in Europe on the subject of America. In the wide range of its topics, treated as they all are with boldness, there are, as might be anticipated, many things to which, as speculations, we cannot give our assent; there are several mistakes, as to matters of fact, some of considerable importance; there is occasionally a disposition shown, almost universal among intelligent original thinkers, to construct a theory, and then find the facts to support it. These, however, are slight defects in an excellent work. M. de Tocqueville shows, that he came to this country to study with impartiality its institutions, to ascertain its condition, and to trace the existing phenomena to their principles. There is no eulogy in it, and no detraction; but, throughout, a manly love of truth. M. de Tocqueville's observations uniformly discover a high degree of acuteness and discrimination. They show, that to observe accurately and profoundly requires a vigor of mind, as rarely perhaps to be met with, as the power of original invention. The number of men, who are able to lay aside the paltry prejudices of party,—who are not misled by superficial appearances,—who can separate what is permanent and essential from what is momentary—who can discern great principles under a thousand varying forms of development, is exceedingly small; and in no one effort perhaps is their talent more severely put to the test, than in writing a book of travels.

We take the greater satisfaction in the work of M. de Tocqueville, from a deep conviction that much mischief has been produced by works of a different character on the subject of America, which have of late years issued in great numbers from the European press. M. de Tocqueville speaks of the bitter hatred entertained by the Americans toward England. We consider that expression as too strong. The angry feelings excited by the wars between the two countries have yielded to time and other healing influences; and there is nothing to keep up the sort of animosity, which prevails, for instance, between the Turks and the Greeks, the Irish and English, the Russians and Poles, the Spaniards and Portuguese. Still, however, if not hatred, there is a very considerable soreness and sense of injury, existing on the part of America towards Great Britain, and almost exclusively produced by the publications of a portion of the British tourists in this country, and the countenance unadvisedly given to these publications by the most respectable literary journals in England. It is idle to talk of the peculiar irritability of the Americans. M. de Tocqueville, who falls into the vulgar error of foreigners, in imputing such an irritability to the people of this country, (or rather who, on this point, abandons his excellent habit of observing for himself, and adopts, without reflection, one of the stale, stereotyped sneers of the tourists,) explains himself the only circumstance, that gives a semblance of truth to the charge. A vastly greater portion of the community in this, than in any other country, are readers; and the novelties of the day, thrown into circulation, at a rate of almost incredible cheapness, may be said to be read by everybody. The scandal and gossip of the travellers in our own country, give their works an instantaneous circulation, on the same principle that gives zest to the columns of the most worthless journal, which deals in personalities and the abuse of contemporary characters. They are immediately read by almost all persons who read any thing; and those who escape the book itself, must encounter it, at second hand, in the reviews, magazines, and newspapers. These considerations account for the universality of the feeling, which the works in question excite. An American tourist in England might publish an equally offensive book, and not one in ten would hear of it of that class, which in America devours all the trash of every kind that issues from the press. But that the individual, in the two countries respectively, is differently affected by the perusal of works of this class, we have yet to learn. If an English gentleman, who had hospitably entertained an American, should find the confidence of his fire-side violated, and what was done and said in the unsuspicious frankness of the social board duly embalmed in the journal, and blazoned to the world, we are inclined to think he would express himself on the occasion, very much as an American gentleman does, when similarly situated. We did not observe, that the tone of the British critical press toward Prince Pückler Muscau was particularly characterized by a philosophical indifference toward the individual or personal detraction charged upon the pages of that eccentric writer; and the more recent instance of a countryman of our own furnishes an edifying comment on the atrocious violation of the decencies of life, which has marked the publications of many of the British tourists in America, and the unscrupulous countenance extended to them by the most respectable journals. John Bull's tremendous horn, long, hooked, and crumpled, has been for forty years buried deep in Jonathan's flank; and if the poor sufferer but winks under the discipline, Europe rings from side to side with his tetchiness. But when Jonathan, the other day, in a moment of indiscretion, showed a disposition, in a slight degree, to take a turn at the sport, all Albermarle Street was in commotion. For ourselves, we wholly reprobate this license, on whichever side of the water it is taken; and how gentlemen and ladies, English or American, can find in the mere fact, that they are foreign tourists, (in other words, that in the account of friendly offices, they must almost of necessity stand on the debtor's side,) a reason for liberating themselves from those restraints of good breeding, which would operate on a person travelling from city to city in his own country, we never have been able to conceive.

Much, however, as the violations of confidence and the ungrateful return for hospitality, to which we allude, are to be rebuked, there is a sin of a deeper dye at the door of some of the tourists. We mean that of undertaking the voyage expressly and for the avowed purpose of political effect at home, and consequently to find, and (what is the same thing, with such a purpose,) to make the materials for vilifying this country. These writers have done the greatest mischief; and have mainly contributed to produce that feeling, which M. de Tocqueville, overrating, we trust, its intensity, characterizes as hatred toward England. In the reign of Louis the Fourteenth, when the King was the State, an offensive device on a medal of doubtful authenticity was among the causes of the war with which he desolated Holland. Human nature is the same, in all ages, and on both sides of the Atlantic; and it would be underrating the vigor and efficiency of the British press to suppose, that, if its conductors and contributors, of all descriptions, desire to excite a bad temper between the two countries, they will fail of their object.

We have already intimated the opinion, that M. de Tocqueville's work exhibits more insight into our system than any European publication which we have seen, and we consider this circumstance as somewhat remarkable. Our institutions (to use a word which our English brethren profess not to understand, though in what its obscurity consists we do not perceive,) are modelled, to a considerable extent, on those of England. Our law in its frame-work, substance, and phraseology is English, and our constitutional forms generally are borrowed from those of the mother country. Between our legal and political system and that of France, there is, on the contrary, the greatest possible dissimilarity. And yet, while M. de Tocqueville has seized, with great accuracy and acuteness, the prominent points of our policy, both in matter of theory and practical operation, we do not recollect any English writer, who has comprehended either; certainly not Captain Hall or Colonel Hamilton, from whom, if from any of the British tourists, it might have been expected. No English writer on this country has discerned the important part sustained by our town and county organization in carrying on the government; or evinced any accurate knowledge of the relative limits of the National and State jurisdictions. We could almost think that the resemblance, which exists between the two countries, prevents a more accurate perception of the state of things, in points where the resemblance ceases, and the peculiarities and novelties commence. England lives under an organization, which may be compared to the solar system; every thing proceeds from or tends to the focus of central attraction. America possesses a much more complicated organization; like that of which the sun, with all its subject planets, is supposed to form a part in the heavens. The twenty-four independent States, each constituted substantially according to the political type of the mother country, compose a general system of government variously complicated with the separate systems, perpetually acting into them and reacted upon by them, both organically and sympathetically, forming in the general result, a highly artificial plan, whose main workings have been long ascertained by experience, but of which incidental properties and functions are continually unfolding themselves, beyond the range of any thing contemplated even by its founders. Now it is perhaps natural, that the Frenchman who approaches the subject as new in all its parts, and studies it in the existing phenomena, without being misled by previous associations, may attain a more accurate knowledge of it, than an Englishman who comes to America, expecting to find nothing but the English system, *mutatis mutandis*. The latter is not likely fully to comprehend to what extent the old names import new things; how far that which is wholly new, varies the action of that which is borrowed, and how far the absence of that which was not borrowed from England, changes the character of what was. Besides this, it is not to be disguised, that, with Englishmen of almost all classes, the American constitutions are regarded as the British, in a state of degeneracy. No man can comprehend a system against which he is prejudiced; the passions are on all subjects the great disturbers of perception and obstructers of knowledge. A Frenchman of the liberal school like M. de Tocqueville, is disposed to regard the representative republics of America, as a fair and natural attempt to carry the principles of the British constitution into their consequences. If he has no partiality for the experiment, he has at least no prejudice against it.

It would be underrating the importance of M. de Tocqueville's work to regard it merely as a book on America. It is a work of deep significance and startling import for Europe and for the modern civilized world. ***

* * *

*** He regards the government of this country, as founded on great ultimate principles, which lie deep in the nature of man; as a bold and noble experiment to develope and apply those principles. He farther considers the civilized world, which looks on, the spectator of the experiment, as itself profoundly interested in the result; nay more, that a similar experiment, in earlier stages and under other conditions, is proceeding at the same time in Europe; and that between the great experiments, going on in the two hemispheres, there is a constant action and reaction.

We conceive it of great importance to take these enlarged views of our politics. They elevate and purify the mind. They lift it out of the narrow sphere of contemporary intrigues; and they show the incalculable importance of the part which Providence has assigned us on the stage of life. In nothing has M. de Tocqueville more approved his sagacity, than in placing at the very head of his work, as the parent principle of our institutions, the "Equality of Conditions"; and it will be found, by a careful study of the genius of the various forms of government, at different times established in the world, that they differ mainly in this respect. This is essential, every thing else is accidental, in the constitution of political societies.

The fact of the equality of men is most curiously arranged in the providential order of human affairs; and it seems to us that the manner, in which the allotments of a Higher Wisdom have been obeyed and respected in the contrivances of our constitution, affords, more than any thing else, the proof of the almost inspired sagacity of our fathers. Religion teaches the moral equality of men, as the great foundation principle of our nature, which admits of no respect of persons with God. By the side of this moral equality, we perceive, nevertheless, the most extraordinary diversity of physical gifts and intellectual capacities; in the result of which, in every form of society that has ever been practically tried among men, from the most ancient patriarchal government, to the rudest simplicity of savage life on the one hand, and the most complicated and artificial constitution on the other, vast disparities of condition among individuals are continually presenting themselves. These inequalities of gifts and capacities are the basis, first, of wealth, influence, and power. The robust, healthy, intelligent, brave savage is found in the possession of a larger and more commodious wigwam, of a buffalo's skin more tastefully ornamented, of a finer horse, of a comelier squaw, and of superior influence, perhaps of a commanding lead in the tribe. The same elements, concentrated into military prowess, in a more artificial constitution of society, led to the formation of the various monarchical and aristocratical governments, which have at different times existed in the world, and which were so many political contrivances, devised by the self-perpetuating instinct of power, not to give effect to the moral equality, but to perpetuate the physical and intellectual inequality of men. This, in itself, was an abuse, because in a frame of government, organized on the true principles of the nature of man, the moral equality, which is eternal and universal, should have been the end, and the physical and intellectual diversity the modification of the system. But the evil did not stop here; the ancient governments, in seeking to perpetuate and organize the *diversity principle*, adopted institutions, which had the direct effect of still further impairing the *equality principle*. From this moment, the beautiful equilibrium of nature was disturbed, and enduring mischief was perpetrated. The fortunate general sought to transmit to his son that predominance in the state, which he had himself acquired by his valor. He was entitled to it for his personal qualities, and he wished to bequeath it to his son, who did not possess those personal qualities. Now and then the egregious absurdity, as well as injustice, of such a bequest peeps out. When Richard Cromwell, the good-natured, timid, smooth-visaged, English gentleman, tries to take up the mighty battle-axe with which his father Oliver, with a reeking hand and a brow ploughed and blackened by the thunder-bolts which staggered, but could not prostrate him, had hewed his way to power, the world looks on with derision, laughs awhile, and permits Richard, greatly hissed for his pains, to sink away to his hiding place. But the line of monarchs, from Nimrod down, has been principally the alternation of Oliver and Richard. Oliver gives an impulse to the system, which often lasts through a succession of Richards. And when mankind, disdaining at length the ignominious yoke of a feeble despotism, conspires to throw it off, and affairs fall into confusion, up starts Oliver again in the old line or a new one, and plies his iron flail, till they cry for mercy, and all again is quiet. This *rationale* of political history was well understood by the ancients, and happily illustrated in the annals of their sacred Majesties, King Log and King Stork.

As, in the transmission of power, the personal superiority strives to perpetuate itself at the expense of the general equality, so with the transmission of fortune. The very idea of property, that which makes it to be what it is, namely, *one's own*, authorizes the possessor to dispose of it at his pleasure, while he lives and at his death. Experience showed the convenience of strengthening transmitted power by an alliance with transmitted wealth. Hence the various devices, the entails, the substitutions, and the trusts, by which, in the language of the law, the accumulations of one generation are *committed to the faith* of the next, to be used, kept together, and handed down. But, as it is plain that the equality, on which all stood as candidates for power, in the first generation, is greatly disturbed in the second by the organization of society into permanent divisions of rank; so, for the acquisition of wealth, the equality principle is still more fatally impaired by all devices calculated to keep great accumulations together. In the first generation, all stand fairly in the competition, with no other inequality than that of the natural en-endowments. In the second, some start with great accumulations of inherited capital locked up against the vicissitudes of fortune. In this way, the natural constitution of society is subverted. The principle of equal rights is entirely lost sight of, a common interest ceases to exist, and every thing is reduced to force; with some considerable assistance from habit, patriotic pride, and superstition.

In this state the American Revolution found the world; and from this political and social condition the American constitutions seek to restore mankind. The plan was not excogitated in the philosopher's cell, nor proclaimed by the sound of the trumpet. It offered itself, as all mighty improvements must offer themselves, spontaneously, to men nearly unconscious of the great work of which they were the chosen instruments. Wise men proposed it; but they did not invent it, or create it. It grew out of the providential constitution of our race, and the heaven-controlled juncture of affairs. A child can drop an acorn into the ground, which will grow up into an oak; and all the academics in the universe, with all their chemistry, cannot compound a blade of grass. The time had come, the circumstances were favorable, the soil was mellow. The natural equality of man is embalmed in an elective system. *Detur digniori.* The impossibility of the actual intervention of each individual of a large nation is relieved by a representative government. The system in a moment is complete. It is an elective representative republic. As transmitted power sought the alliance of transmitted wealth, transmitted political equality demands a healthy circulation of property. This is effected by the statute of distributions, in virtue of which, at the end of the second generation in most cases, and invariably at the end of the third, the accumulation vanishes, and nature's noble upstarts are found at the head of affairs. No violence, no plunder, no invasion of the right of property. All is gradual, salutary, and life-giving, because all is done in conformity with the dictates of nature.

In this way, as far as theory goes, the individual diversity principle and the general equality principle are thoroughly harmonized; and the experiment of two hundred years (for the system in all its great features dates rather from the settlement of the country than the revolution) has fully tried it in practice. To say, that in no single instance it has failed; that no bad man has been raised to office; that no good man has lived in undervalued obscurity; that there has been no profligate wealth, and no wronged, heart-broken poverty, would, of course, be idle. But this may be truly said,—that all the evils which disfigure our system equally exist in all others. There are, and have been in all time, as many bad and incompetent rulers, as many worthless persons clothed with influence and fortune, in other countries as in this, and many monstrous oppressions elsewhere existing are here wholly unknown. This, also, may be said, that the evils which manifest themselves in the working of our system, are entirely analogous with those which are exhibited in the whole moral constitution of the universe, as far as we can comprehend it; which presents to our observation, alike in the intellectual and the physical world, the perpetual antithesis of a perfect theory and constantly recurring exceptions to its operation, an absolute nature thwarted in individual cases of development, a beneficent system struggling under the abuse of its most genial provisions.

But it is time to return from these speculations to the matter more immediately before us. No part of M. de Tocqueville's work has struck us as more masterly, than the manner in which, in his Introduction, he has traced the growth of the democratic principle in Europe.

* * *

Views like these are equally sound and cheering; they reconcile us to the fortunes of our race. When we contemplate the unsatisfactory progress of freedom; when we witness revolutions commencing under the most promising suspices, but soon plunging into seas of blood; when we see symptoms of degeneracy in the practical operation of the wisest systems of government; when we contemplate the leaden apathy of that ignorance and servitude, into which many of the nations have settled down, our hearts are apt to sink within us. We are ready to despair of the progress of man toward any substantial improvement of his condition, as a member of civil society. But a survey of broad tracts of history is sufficient to correct the impression. The dark annals of the middle ages furnish a source of cheerful hope. It is ground enough of consolation, that we do not live in the time of the crusades. The baronial castles, masses of tasteless ruins that lie in heaps on the hill-tops of Europe, and whisper from their crumbled battlements the tale of the private wars that desolated the nations for three centuries, are eloquent of encouragement. Arbitrary forms of government still subsist; but civilization, if not constitutions, has broken down much of their rigor. The fangs of the Inquisition are extracted, and nation after nation has risen up with their once enslaved children into the light of knowledge and Christianity. The crew of the ship may fall into unhappy dissensions, but she is ploughing her way onward before the breeze, and will yet reach the port. No doubt there is a mournful waste of energy, in the struggles of party against party and nation against nation, of those who have the same interests at stake and the same object at heart. No doubt there is a deplorable waste of innocent blood. Thousands and tens of thousands of intelligent men, in our own happy country, are constantly straining all their energies in worthless contests with each other for worthless objects; and hundreds of thousands throughout the civilized world annually fall a prey to the sword, to the diseases of the camp, and to the horrid reverses of fortune, that follow in the train of war. These evils we witness and feel, and they make us, perhaps, despond over the progress of mankind. But the age of Peter the Hermit, of the Guelfs and Ghibellines, of Louis the Eleventh and Henry the Eighth were worse. All the now existing evils existed in a tenfold degree. Abuses now unknown bore sway; and the great mass of men were actually brutalized in the depths of their ignorance and subjection. No brighter prospect need be desired for mankind than that religion, morals, government, literature, and the arts, in a word civilization and liberty, may, for ten centuries to come, make a progress equal to that, which has been made in the ten centuries past; and if we are authorized to hope, as we may without extravagance, that each newly discovered art, truth, and right will furnish in itself not merely a new blessing, but a new instrument of other discoveries and improvements in morals, government, and social existence, imagination itself must fail in the attempt to estimate the inheritance, which is in store for our children.

* * *

*** The views which are taken by the intelligent foreigner on all the subjects touched by him, are ingenious, often strongly stamped by originality, frequently both profound and correct. He is sometimes, as we have already observed, led away by a desire to generalize, and, occasionally, takes too readily for granted, that the existing phenomena justify theories, which he has formed rather in the exercise of his own power of combination and inference, than on the basis of previously collected facts. These however are by no means the characteristics of the work, which, as a whole, cannot be read either in Europe or America, without awaking new and profitable trains of thought. To the European it is replete with instruction.

There is one subject, which M. de Tocqueville has placed in an entirely new light. A favorite topic of reproachful comment with the British tourists and journalists has been the subject of religion in America. Some exaggerated pictures of the state of religious observances in the thinly settled frontier portions of the country, taken in connexion with the European prejudice, that religion can have no substantial foothold, where it is not supported by law, have produced among the class of writers to which we allude, an impression, which they take great pains to propagate in the reading world, that the people of the United States are an irreligious people. The testimony of a French traveller, so intelligent as M. de Tocqueville, of the liberal school of politics, but far from being a blind and indiscriminate admirer of America, and a professed Roman Catholic, will be heard with attention and respect on this subject. We pass over a section, in which the author discusses, with an ingenuity which has not carried conviction to our minds, the proposition that the Roman Catholic religion is not unfriendly to the genius of republican democracy. M. de Tocqueville ascribes the influence of religion to the multiplicity of sects, uncontrolled by an establishment, which leaves every man to the enjoyment of such a form of belief and worship as suits his peculiar temper; and to the entire abstinence of all the sects from an interference in politics, and a rigid adherence to moral influence alone. ***

* * *

M. de Tocqueville engages in a philosophical analysis of the idea of a separation of church and state, in the course of which we meet with several judicious and profound remarks.

> "As long," says he, "as a religion derives its power from the sentiments, the instincts, the passions, which are reproduced in the same manner in all periods of history, it braves the efforts of time, or at least it cannot be destroyed but by another religion. But when religion seeks to rest on the interests of this world, it becomes almost as frail as the powers of this earth. Alone, it may hope for immortality; connected with ephemeral powers, it follows their fortune, and falls often with the passions of the day which sustain it. In uniting itself to the different political powers, religion can but contract an onerous alliance. It has not need of their aid to live, and in serving them it may die."—p. 228.

But we have no time to pursue these extracts. The chapter is full of instruction, which our readers must seek in the volume of M. de Tocqueville himself. His remarks are made for the meridian of Europe and particularly of France; but they rest on a correct estimate of the facts of the case as existing in this country.

Perhaps there is nothing in which the guiding hand of a Superior Wisdom is more plainly traced in the affairs of this country, than in the general adoption and the unanimous approval of the principle, to which our author ascribes so much importance. One might have expected from the fathers of New England, at least, the foundation of an ecclesiastical establishment. Their notions of personal rights did not forbid it, the doctrine of toleration was not well understood by them, and their practice naturally, not to say necessarily, led for the time to the erection of one of the most rigid church systems ever known,—not so much a state religion as a theocracy. But many happy conspiring causes prevented its taking root in the state, and not the least curious was the relation of the colonies to the mother country, as a settlement of Dissenters watched with jealousy by the hierarchy at home, and compelled to purchase toleration by toleration. From the moment the colonies became important enough to attract the notice of the government of the mother country, every attempt to invest their own opinions with legal preference must have proved abortive. Meantime the austere fathers were compelled to fight the hard battles of liberty. They felt every day, that freedom was but one idea; that it must be embraced or repudiated; and that conscience could not be shackled and unrestrained at the same time. They were satisfied with a moral influence, in matters of faith, which was as absolute as they wished, and wisely forbore to grasp at a shadow of legal strength, which they could not have obtained, and the struggle for which would have sown bitterness among themselves. Thus the doctrine of liberty of conscience silently grew up and ripened, till, when the revolution conferred the power of creating a church establishment, a unanimous opinion was found existing, that it would be madness to attempt it.

The United States Democratic Review, October 1837

* * * In point of style alone, this is a work of uncommon merit. M. de Tocqueville's manner seems formed on that of Montesquieu, and he writes with great beauty, force and elegance; while, at the same time, he avoids entirely the inflated and rhetorical tone, which is the besetting sin of the best French writers of the present day. Apart from the mere choice of words and forms of language, the style of this work is also highly worthy of commendation for its uniform tone of dignity, seriousness, and good faith. In this, as in most other respects, it contrasts advantageously with that of the great majority of foreign works on this country, in which the gravest interests of society are habitually discussed with the flippancy of the worst newspapers. M. de Tocqueville has been led into errors, not always unimportant, in part by the prejudices of some of the circles of society into which he naturally fell—in part by the mere effect of the imperfect observation and hasty generalization, which, to a certain extent, are almost unavoidable in this kind of writing. But there are no faults in his book which are not entirely consistent with great powers of thought and language, the most upright intentions, and an uncommon freedom from the class of prejudice to which the race of travellers are more particularly liable.

The general object of M. de Tocqueville is to ascertain the results of the principle of *democracy*, as applied to practice in the United States, with a view to the instruction of other countries, and particularly his own. He remarks in his introduction that, on arriving in America, he was struck very forcibly with the general *equality* of conditions, and on farther observation and reflection, was fully satisfied that this is the substantial fact which lies at the bottom of our political institutions. * * *

* * * His tone is, on the whole, decidedly favorable to the cause of democracy. It is evident, however, that his views of persons and things were in some respects unfavorably modified by influences of which he was himself unconscious, and from which few European travellers among us can escape. In speaking of the character of political parties, M. de Tocqueville correctly remarks, that however various may be their origin, and apparent or immediate objects, they all resolve themselves ultimately into one or the other of the two great divisions of society, which have always existed in free countries, and which labor respectively to extend and diminish the influence of the government;

in other words, the *aristocracy* and the *democracy*. Now, in this country, the nucleus of the aristocratic party, by whatever name it may be temporarily known, will always be found in the monied men of the commercial cities. But this is precisely the class of persons among whom a well recommended traveller is naturally thrown on his first arrival in the country, and from whom he receives his first impressions, which cannot but give a general bias to his future observations. These circles of society he generally finds intelligent, polished, amiable, equal, probably, in all the elements of civilization, to the highest circles in the commercial and manufacturing cities of Europe. He is received among them with a marked attention, and listens in turn with a natural deference to their opinions. He finds them well-informed, candid, liberal, even, in their judgments of Europe; and, at the same time, expressing themselves with contempt and bitterness in regard to the political institutions and usages of their own country, and especially the character of men in office, who are of course generally taken from the 'democracy of numbers.' Not considering the strong partisan character of such remarks, he is apt to receive them with implicit faith, as the unwilling confessions of witnesses interested in favor of the country. In this way we account in part for the tone of disparagement in which our public functionaries and institutions are spoken of by most travellers, substantially liberal in their sentiments, and even to a certain extent by M. de Tocqueville. This gentleman, in fact, hints significantly that he has received important revelations of this description, in the confidence of private intercourse, which the persons making them would not like to proclaim upon the house-top, or even publicly in conversation;—but which they trust without reflection to the passing stranger! The weakness of the evidence, upon which M. de Tocqueville professes to found some of these unfavorable opinions, forms a singular contrast with the gravity of the charges, and serves of itself to prove that they rest substantially on such authority as we have just referred to—that is, that they are the opinions, not of M. de Tocqueville, but of the *aristocracy* among ourselves upon '*Democracy in the United States.*' We shall briefly notice some of these charges.

> "Many Americans," says M. de Tocqueville, "consider the instability of the laws as a necessary consequence of a system of which the general results are good. But there is nobody, I believe, in the United States, who pretends to deny that this instability exists, and who does not regard it as a great evil."

In support of this sweeping and unqualified assertion, M. de Tocqueville quotes a passage from the Federalist, in which Hamilton remarks that "the instability of the laws forms the greatest blemish on the character and genius of our Government;" a remark of Mr. Madison to the same effect in the same work; and a letter from Jefferson to Madison, dated December 20, 1787, in which he also gives the opinion that "the instability of the laws is really a very great inconvenience."

These remarks of Hamilton, Jefferson, and Madison, appear to be the only evidence upon which M. de Tocqueville has formed his opinion that the instability of the laws is a real and universally acknowledged feature in the political aspect of our country. It is only necessary to recollect the time when the remarks in question were made, to see that they allude to the unsettled state of things between the close of the war and the adoption of the Federal Constitution; and that, instead of being intended by their authors as objections to the now existing political institutions, they were used precisely as arguments in favor of their adoption.

Far from admitting the justice of the charge, of a too great proneness to frequent change in the laws, we have always considered the *stability* of our political institutions, in the midst of the "wreck of matter and the crush of worlds" that has been constantly going on around them ever since their establishment, as one of their most remarkable characteristics, and the strongest proof that could possibly be given of their substantial goodness. In fact, we have rather reason to regret that aversion even to improvement, which has hitherto so materially retarded the still progressive amelioration of our institutions. Being, as a mass, an actively industrious people, we are generally willing to make great concessions of convenience, and even sometimes of principle, for the sake of the tranquillity and regularity of the old habit; and it requires, indeed, a strong stimulus of great interests and principles at stake to overcome this moral *vis inertiæ*, and induce us to apply the hand of reform to any institution or system extensively connected with the general business of the country. The word "experiment" has been known to suffice, through more than an entire presidential contest, for the watch-word and rallying cry of a great party; and even when all sorts of previous plans have failed, we to the incautious statesman who shall be bold enough, instead of endeavouring to resuscitate the *corpus mortuum* of the prostrate failure, to dream of an "untried expedient,"—even though it be sanctioned by the clearest demonstration of its practicability, safety, and harmony with the true democratic principle, to say nothing of the general example of most civilized foreign nations! Wo to the impious reformer who would lay sacrilegious hand on renerable evils, consecrated by time, and by the 'vested interests' which never fail to vegetate most luxuriously from the most corrupt soil! We to him, we repeat; he will be denounced as a visionary theorist, a raving madman, an agrarian, a destructive, a *sans culottes*, and, the English language (beautifully rich as is the vocabulary of abuse which it can furnish at need) being exhausted, a new word,—fearfully compounded,—of uncouth sight and sound,—redolent of fire and brimstone,—and pregnant with monstrous but mysterious meaning, will be invented and fastened upon him, to frighten the whole community out of its propriety, as at the cry of 'mad dog.'

That a Frenchman, of all persons, should consider our laws and institutions as obnoxious to the charge of "instability," is really curious. Prince Metternich, in a recent conversation with one of our countrymen now travelling in Europe, made the remark, that during the four and twenty years, or thereabouts, since he came into power as prime minister of Austria, there had been in France about the same number of more or less complete revolutions, political or ministerial. "Sometimes," said he, "I have found myself two or three years ahead of them in the reckoning; but they soon contrived to bring up arrears, and in the main we are generally abreast." If M. de Tocqueville will compare the history of our government, during the fifty years of its existence, with the history of any which he may choose, for any fifty years in the whole 'tide of time,' and will produce an example of one that has suffered so little change of any kind, except in the tranquil and gradual growth of prosperity in the course of half a century, we will admit the correctness of his stricture. The fact undoubtedly is, that from the adoption of the constitution to the present day, the Government has suffered no change whatever, in any essential point—although the period *has*, in our opinion, *unquestionably arrived*, when the slow developement, during the course of half a century, of the different elements combined together as ingredients at the formation of the system, some for good and some for evil, requires some modifications in its forms, to adapt it to the evident progress of public opinion within that period. In points of minor importance, our laws are no doubt occasionally altered, though not more frequently than those of other nations. The tariff laws, for example, are changed at least as often in the commercial nations of Europe—England, France, Spain, Holland, and Prussia,—as in this country; and none of these countries has yet witnessed the spectacle of a system of tariff law confessedly unpopular in principle,—and pouring a pernicious deluge of surplus revenue upon the Government, almost crushing it beneath a weight of treasure,—which there was a general desire to get rid of and prevent, yet allowed to remain unchanged, from objection to disturbing an old, vague, *quasi* 'compromise!'

But what are alterations in the duties on imports, in the charter of a bank, in the mode of collecting the revenue, needed by an economical Government, in comparison with the tremendous convulsions that constantly agitate the kingdoms of the old world! Let M. de Tocqueville go back to the spring of 1789, when the first written constitution of France and the present constitution of the United States both went into operation. Let him then trace the successive reorganizations of the whole frame of the government that have since taken place in his own country: first the successive republican constitutions of the National Assembly, the Convention, and the Directory; then the successive usurpations of Napoleon, the consulate for ten years, the consulate for life, and the empire; afterwards the restoration; then, again, the hundred days, with the act in addition to the constitutions of the empire; the second restoration; the three days; and finally the accession of Louis Philippe. When he has surveyed this list, of itself sufficiently portentous, let him reckon up the number of unsuccessful attempts at violent changes which have interrupted the short intervals of tranquillity intervening between these successive convulsions; and then turn his eyes to this country, and see the Government pursuing its course in quiet majesty for more than half a century, undisturbed by revolutions, hardly agitated by a few transient storms, not to be compared in importance with the unsuccessful attempts at revolution in France, and remaining in substance, at the present day, precisely as it was at the outset; excepting that it has already acquired, by a successful experience of fifty years, for the good and democratic elements of its constitution, something of the *prestige* that belongs to venerable antiquity; while its bad and anti-popular elements have developed themselves to the degree of maturity at which they are already nearly ripe for reform, and ready to fall of their own accord.

Will it be said that the history of France, during this period, forms a sort of exception to the general course of events throughout the world, and is not to be taken as a proper text by which to judge of occurences in any other country? Let M. de Tocqueville recollect what has happened during the same time in the other parts of Europe—in Spain, Portugal, Italy, Holland, Germany; let him observe the boasted constitution of England herself, after breasting triumphantly the attack of the continent in arms for a quarter of a century, breaking down at last under the results of its own internal vices; let him look especially at the Spanish colonies on our continent, placed, as nearly as possible, in the same situation with the United States, yet thus far, as M. de Tocqueville himself correctly remarks, utterly unable to reach any solid basis, and foundering along from one revolution to another through a chaos of anarchy and wild uproar; let him go back, if he will, to the past history of the most celebrated nations of ancient or modern times, such as Rome, France, modern Italy, or England—at their brightest periods—and produce any one of fifty years, in the history of any of them, so free from internal change or convulsion as that of the United States for the last half century. If this comparative tranquility on our side proves nothing more, it at least absolves our institutions from the charge of "*instability.*"

In fact, M. de Tocqueville himself, although he assumes, as we have seen, and reasons, throughout his work, upon a supposed *instability* in our institutions, takes, in one of his concluding chapters, a more correct view of the subject, and one which varies but little from that which we have taken above; although he is still in error in thinking that changes of a secondary character are more frequent here than they are in other countries.

Another objection made by M. de Tocqueville to the political usages of this country is of a kindred character to the one just considered, and consists in a supposed constant fluctuation in the persons employed in the Government, and total want of method and order in all the public offices. We extract some of his remarks upon this head, which, if not correct, are at least curious:

> "As the persons employed in the administration come into power for a moment only, and are lost immediately after in a crowd which is itself constantly changing from day to day, it follows that the acts of the Government often leave behind them fewer traces than those of a more private family. The administra-

tion is, as it were, oral and traditional; hardly any thing is written, and the little that is, in fact, committed to paper is scattered abroad by the first wind, like the sybil's leaves, and disappears forever.

"The only historical documents in the United States are the newspapers. If a single paper is missing in a file of one of these, the chain of events is, as it were, broken—the present and the past cannot again be united. I am quite sure that fifty years hence it will be more difficult to collect materials for the history of the United States, during the present time, than for that of France during the middle ages. This instability, in every thing relating to the administration, has begun to extend itself to the habits of the people. I might almost say that it has already become a pretty general trait of character. No one troubles himself about what was done before him—no method is adopted—no collections are made—no documents are brought together, even when it might be done most easily—so value is set upon such papers by those who happen to possess them. I have myself original documents which were given me in some of the public offices, in answer to my inquiries for information."

As we cannot suspect the good faith of M. de Tocqueville, we are rather at a loss to conjecture on what ground he can have conceived views so entirely at variance with the truth as these. He has, perhaps, been led into error by attaching too much importance to the fact mentioned at the close of the above extract, which must have been, in one way or another, an exception to the general practice. We need hardly say that in this country public records are kept in nearly, if not quite all, the cases in which they are kept in Europe, and with equal regularity, particularly in the courts of justice, and in the various departments of the General and State Governments. Even the towns have their public records, as we are told by M. de Tocqueville himself; who, in speaking of the constitution of the municipalities, enumerates, among the other authorities, "the town clerk, who keeps a record of the proceedings at town meetings, and of other public acts." Some of these town records have been kept very regularly from the first settlement of the country, and are habitually consulted, with great profit, by those who are engaged in historical researches. It is scarcely necessary for us to advert to the numerous and valuable collections of papers, by eminent public men, known to exist, such as the Jefferson papers, (principally published,) the Washington papers, amounting to nearly a hundred large folio volumes, (purchased by the General Government,) the Madison papers, (likewise purchased,) the papers of the two Adams, (those of the former, to be published doubtless at some future day, are nearly as voluminous as those of Washington,) the immense diplomatic correspondence of the Government, of which the publication has been *commenced*, the papers of Franklin, (and here we will not omit a tribute to the excellent and indefatigable Sparks, to whom we owe so much in this department of learning,) the collection of

Wait, &c. &c. Nor will we make more than a passing allusion to the historical societies of the different States, which make it their precise object to collect, arrange, and, as far as their means permit, publish every thing which they can find of interest, respecting the country at large, and especially the State and vicinity in which they are seated. Some of these societies have been very active and successful in their researches. We have now before us three very curious volumes which have been recently issued by the Historical Society of Rhode Island, one of the last established, but not least industrious, of these institutions. The collections of the Historical Society of Massachusetts extend to upwards of twenty volumes, and are constantly increasing in interest. To this vast mass of documents, must be added the newspapers and other journals, which form a most valuable body of contemporary materials, and which, we need not say, exist in this country to an extent unknown in any other. In one point of view we may assent to M. de Tocqueville's stricture, namely, that our Government has not yet done half its duty with reference to the arrangement and publication of the vast mass of historical materials in its possession. It is also to be much regretted that we possess no good, digested, and *honest* historical register; which, as labor-saving machines, become, after the lapse of a few years, invaluable. But, on the whole, we cannot but smile at the apprehension expressed by M. de Tocqueville, of a deficiency of materials for the present period in our history. The historian will be much more likely to find himself laboring under the *embarras de richesses.* It will require indeed, we apprehend, the most untiring industry to master those multifurious treasures, and the highest talent and taste to digest their essence into a compact form. We rejoice to add, however, that the requisite qualifications for this great enterprise have already been brought to bear upon it, by a writer to whom we have alluded in the beginning of this article, and whose labors, if we may judge from the specimen in print, will leave but little to be done by others, or desired by the public, in reference to the period which he has taken for his subject.

Another trait in the political aspect of our community, which M. de Tocqueville signalises as one of the most injurious, is the supposed excessive influence of the declared opinion of a majority of the people. He treats this topic in two long chapters, occupying together more than fifty pages of the work, one of which is on 'the omnipotence of the majority in the United States, and its effects;' the other on 'the circumstances that limit (*tempérent*), in the United States, the tyranny of the majority.' These chapters have been noticed with great approbation by the foreign critics who have spoken of the book, especially in England. The London Quarterly Review, in particular, though somewhat at a loss how to treat a work of undoubted talent, and at the same time of a democratic tone, and highly favorable to our country, has contrived, by the help of these chapters, to draw from it the materials for an article written in the usual tone of that journal. Sir Robert Peel, again an active fellow-laborer with the London Quarterly in the cause of aristocracy—*et cantare pares, et respondere parati*[1]—in his recent speech at Glasgow, on his installation as Lord Rector of the university in that city, quotes these chapters with a high encomium, and represents the facts stated in them as sufficient of themselves to prove the vast inferiority of the American to the British constitution.

It would give us pleasure, did our limits permit, to lay these two chapters entire before our readers, that they might have an opportunity of judging for themselves of the truth of their opinions. For ourselves we are free to say, that after a repeated and diligent perusal of them, we have not been able to satisfy ourselves entirely as to what the author really means. The leading idea *seems* to be, that the influence of the declared opinions of a majority of the people is such as to preclude entirely all freedom, not merely of speech and action, but even of thought. Certain circumstances mentioned in the second of the two chapters alluded to, the most important of which is the weight of the legal profession, in some degree diminish this overwhelming power; but, on the whole, it is said to exist to such an extent as to justify the conclusion that there is less freedom of thought in this country than in any other. This conclusion has been, as we remarked, eagerly caught at by our English friends of the Conservative school, who exclaim, with one accord, that no Englishman would submit to such oppression, and that if this be the amount of our boasted liberty, they prefer to remain under the British constitution, 'monarchy and all.'

> "When we come to examine the modes of *thinking* in the United States," says M. de Tocqueville, "we first perceive distinctly how far the power of the majority exceeds any power with which we are acquainted in Europe.
>
> "Thought is an immaterial essence, which escapes the grasp of almost every kind of tyranny. In our day, the most absolute sovereigns in Europe cannot prevent certain opinions, hostile to their power, from circulating secretly among their subjects, and even at their courts. While the majority is doubtful, the discussion proceeds (*on parle*); but no sooner is the decision pronounced, than all is silent. Enemies and friends yoke themselves alike to the triumphant car of the majority."

These short paragraphs exhibit the concentrated essence of the author's doctrine. We are tempted to ask him, as we have said before, not what evidence he has in support of it, but what he really means by it. Are we to understand him as intending that when a public functionary—a President of the United States, for example—is elected by the decision of the majority, then all is silent, and the defeated minority yoke themselves to his triumphant car? M. de Tocqueville was in this country during the administration of Gen. Jackson, the successful candidate of an overwhelming majority; and he even quotes a violent passage from one of the *two-thirds* of the newspapers of the country

---

1. Both fit to sing and prepared to reply (Latin) [*Editor's Note*].

which opposed him through his two terms: does there need a further answer to the question?

Our author complains of the instability of our laws, and rapid successions of our public functionaries, implying, of course, corresponding changes of majorities; but how are these to be effected but by the resolute and persevering exertions of the defeated minorities, which so uniformly "*yoke themselves to the triumphant car of the majority?*" What, then, on his own showing, becomes of that supposed silent acquiescence of the minority—that immutability of the decisions of the majority—its omnipotence and its tyranny—its empire, not merely over action and speech, but over the mind! What, in short, does M. de Tocqueville (who is, after all, a generally clear and correct thinker) really mean in these two chapters, which have been considered in Europe, or rather in England, as the most important part of his work!

To these questions we are unable, as we have said, to furnish any satisfactory answer; and we respectfully recommend to M. de Tocqueville to avail himself of the opportunity afforded by some future edition of his work, to revise these chapters, and render them a little more clear in their import, and, if possible, a little more plausible and consistent.

In the mean time, however, we deem it not improbable that he has drawn an erroneous conclusion, from the state of public opinion, upon two or three subjects which habitually excite much controversy in Europe, but are very little, if at all, agitated in this country.

"The most absolute monarchs," he remarks, "cannot prevent the circulation of works, inculcating democratic doctrines, among their subjects, even at their courts. In the United States there is nothing published, either openly or secretly, in support of aristocratic and arbitrary principles of government. The inquisition has never been able to suppress the circulation, in Spain, of works opposed to religion. In the United States no such books are written. The governments of Europe are often compelled to punish severely the authors and publishers of immoral works. In the United States no such punishment takes place, because no one dreams of publishing a work of this description. Now," continues M. de Tocqueville, "it cannot be supposed that there are no persons in the United States who prefer the aristocratic or monarchical theory of government to the democratic; who are destitute of religious faith; who are inclined, by character, to licentiousness and immortality. There must be a certain number of persons of this description; who constitute, of course, a minority of the people. There is nothing to prevent them from expressing their opinions but their respect for the contrary opinion of the majority. *Donc*, consequently, the majority in the United States wield a power more absolute, more tyrannical, than all the inquisitions and despots of Europe; a power which is fatal to all freedom, not merely of action and speech, but even of thought. There is no liberty of mind in America. I know no country where there is less freedom of discussion, less real independence of mind, than in the United States."

These ideas it is easy to refute. This 'notion' of the real absence of moral independence of opinion amongst us, has been taken up by not a few foreigners, probably from some natural and unconscious disposition, provoked by the excess of national vanity too often exhibited by ourselves, to seek a flaw in that 'independence' which we make 'our boast'—certainly yielding a full and willing obedience to the precept given in our national anthem. The same string is sometimes harped on by some amongst ourselves, in defiance of the testimony of experience by which they are hourly surrounded, in the constant and warm discussions between majorities and minorities on a thousand subjects. We deny the fact *in toto*; and have no hesitation in insisting that the *reverse* is pre-eminently the case, comparatively with other nations.

If the premises were true, as here stated by M. de Tocqueville, of the universal silence of that partial opposition of opinion to the cause of republican principles, of religion, and of good morals, which he presumes must secretly exist to some extent, the inference thus drawn from two or three isolated instances, against the whole current of experience, would not be legitimate. They should be regarded but as exceptions to the general rule, and would probably, if properly examined, be found susceptible of explanation by accidental causes. Such would also be found, in a marked degree, the case with respect to the slavery question, if that had been similarly cited by our author.

But the truth is that M. de Tocqueville has not stated his facts quite correctly. The difference between the expression of public opinion on the subjects alluded to, in this country and in Europe, is not so great as he supposes it to be; and so far as it is real, it is easily accounted for by the difference in the state of society.

It is far from being correct, to say that there is no expression of opinion among us against religion, against morals, or against the republican theory of Government. Irreligious and immoral books circulate to a certain extent and are occasionally made the subjects of public prosecution. This, however, we rejoice to say, takes place to a much less extent than in Europe, and the difference is readily accounted for by a real difference in the state of society, which M. de Tocqueville himself is the first to acknowledge and even to insist upon as the basis of his reasoning on the subject of our political institutions. The almost universal respect for religion and purity of private morals are largely dwelt upon throughout the work, and justly described as the great security of our liberty. "If," says our author at the close of one of his chapters, "I have not succeeded in impressing upon my readers, in the course of this work, the importance which I ascribe to the practical experience of the Americans, to their habits, their opinions, in a word their *morals*, in maintaining their political institutions, I have failed in the principal object which I had in view." If, then, the moral and religious condition of society in this country be, as it is justly represented by our author, not affectedly, but really and substantially, different from what it is in Europe, why should it appear surprising that this difference should be indicated by a corresponding difference in the state of public opinion and its expression through the press, which are, after all, mere reflections of the state of society? In the same way we account for the absence, to a great extent, of any demonstration of opinion in opposition to republican theories of government. To say that no such opinion is ever expressed, would not be true. We might mention, as an example to the contrary, Fisher Ames, one of the finest writers our country has produced, who had contracted, from the peculiar circumstances in which he was placed, a strong distaste for democratic principles of Government, and expressed it, not only without hesitation, but with extraordinary power of eloquence. Governeur Morris took no pains to conceal his dislike of *democracy*. In fact, the political school to which both these gentlemen belonged, and of which Hamilton was the leader, considered *democracy* not, as M. de Tocqueville correctly represents it, as the *principle*, but as the *disease* of our political institutions. Far from concealing this opinion, they filled the newspapers with it for years, in discussion. And even at the present day, the number of respectable journals which openly avow strongly anti-democratic opinions, to an extent implying fully a preference for the "strong" forms of Government of aristocracy or monarchy, is not inconsiderable; journals which, in treating of foreign politics, freely give all their sympathies to the conservative parties of foreign countries; and denounce the reforming parties which, in the wildest excesses of democratic innovation proposed by them, never dream of going beyond the principles established as the A B C of our political alphabet. In fact, it would be an easy task for us to prove, by a collation of a few of their respective papers and speeches, the close analogy, if not entire identity in principle, between the "Whig" party of this country and the Tories of Great Britain. It is, however, undoubtedly true that the opposite opinion has been rapidly gaining ground since the time of the great federal leaders cited, and is now almost universal. It is at least so described by M. de Tocqueville himself. The general satisfaction of the people with the existing form of government—their conviction of its superiority over all others—their self-complacency at being able to reduce to practice so beautiful a theory, which had been previously regarded as visionary and impracticable, are pointed out by our author as remarkable traits in the national character. Miss Martineau describes the universal *contentment* of the people with the existing political institutions, as *sublime*. What wonder, then, that there should be but little expression of opinion to the contrary? If the people are all, not affectedly, but sincerely, enthusiastic in their attachment to republican principles, why resort to forced suppositions to account for the fact that they do not declare themselves openly in favor of aristocracy and monarchy! It is apparent that the state of public sentiment, and of its expression through the press, is in this case, as it necessarily must be in all, a more reflection of the actual condition of the society.

We submit those corrections to the consideration of M. de Tocqueville, and cannot but think that, on further reflection, he will agree with us in the views now expressed. The absence of any open opposition to religion, good morals, and republican government, is not owing, as our author supposes, to the omnipotence and tyranny of the majority, but correctly indicates the almost universal sentiment of the people on those subjects. Upon other matters on which opinion is divided, our minorities certainly express themselves with at least as much freedom as majorities, and not unfrequently with a violence in direct proportion to their weakness.

* * *

The Knickerbocker; or The New York Monthly Magazine, September 1838

M. de Tocqueville is a philosopher. He comprehends men, things, and even the Americans. We have hitherto been an enigma to all the world; but our author has at least partly solved it. He has put into the hands of the European public a key to our long-concealed mysteries; he has lifted more than one corner of the veil that was spread over us. His book carries on its face the marks of candor, cool and philosophic discernment, and probability, and will therefore work conviction abroad. He seems himself, however, to be in doubt whether it will work conviction among us: 'If ever these lines are read in America,' says he, 'I am well assured of two things: in the first place, that all who peruse them will raise their voices to condemn me; and in the second place, that very many of them will acquit me at the bottom of their consciences.' A conviction notwithstanding, though it may not stand confessed. Honestly, however, we believe he intends to apply this remark to his chapter on the tyranny of public opinion in America; for we see no reason why he should entertain such an apprehension as to the effects of his book, in general, on the people of this country. As a whole, he has not executed a work to bring a lasting blush over our face, though he has told some humiliating truths. He puts us down and sets us up alternately. With one dash of his pen he would seem to be sending us to Coventry; and with another, he restores us to good society, and confirms us in it. On one page, or part of a page, nay, by the sweep and power of a single sentence, a foreigner, who had no other means of acquaintance with the subject of the author's story, might be excused for losing all respect for us; anon, he will be put all aback by some sudden change of the winds, and be obliged to trim his sails and right his bark, to gain a favorable position and more easy course, from which he may gaze with admiration on that ship of state in the distance, which rides the mountain wave with a grace, and a dignity, and a skill, which insures a prosperous voyage, or which is well prepared to encounter a foe. According to M. de Tocqueville—and we must confess he appears more studious for truth than anxious to please—we might seem a people of contradictions, an agglomeration of anomalous accidents, yet to be assorted, and our social history yet to be explained, except so far as he himself has lifted the veil, and presented us to the eyes of the European public. A thousand and ten thousand things, of the nature of facts in our history, unknown before almost to ourselves, he has opened on the gaze of the world; and things, too, of a very mysterious, potential, and momentous character. He has analyzed our history, from the beginning and from the bottom, and *attempted* to show the effect and drift of the whole. But the latter task was too mighty even for him. For notwithstanding all his skill in combination and composition, he has left the field and the scene a chaos; a world in existence, but not a world reduced to order. The foreigner may see, in the glass which our author has put into his hands, many things in America to laugh at, but there will also be forced on his attention much to admire. In the consultation of his own acquired tastes and habits, if he is tolerably well off in his own country, he may feel for a moment that he would not desire to be a member of such a community as America, but his next thought will be, that America cannot be despised. He may discover a thousand little things, but he will always find them planted by the side of great things. He may see customs and manners which to him would be uncomfortable, but he will behold in the causes that have produced them, a sufficient quantum of redeeming influences to balance the account. He may find a sort of rampant freedom, and a bustle without any apparent order or object, but when he looks deeper, he will discover an indomitable respect for the laws, and a steady, all-ruling purpose in the aims and pursuits of these go-ahead republicans. From the violent political agitations of the community, and the apparent want of compactness and vigor in the body politic, he may imagine that the affairs of the country have brought it to the crisis of its existence; but he will afterward find that it has been in a state of crisis ever since it had any existence at all. In a word, he will be surprised, at every step, at some new development of redeeming qualities, to be set over against such faults, and of guiding, protecting powers, in the giddy whirl of such an active, bustling, and onward march of society. An enigma still the country and its institutions may be, sufficient to puzzle the politicians of the old world; but its characters are reflected from the dome of heaven, and he who would thoroughly understand them, must climb and tread among the stars. As M. de Tocqueville more than intimates, it was not man, but God, that made America. It is one of the results of a high and inscrutable Providence. Man opposes heaven, but heaven, in spite of man, rules over the earth. 'The powers that be,' and that have been, have armed themselves against the introduction and establishment of free governments; but God, from his throne, has decreed otherwise, and the whole state of the civilized world is rapidly and irresistibly tending to this result. Such seems to be the conviction of our author, and we are not disposed to dissent from him.

M. de Tocqueville has certainly bestowed on us some compliments—we may say, many. For all that he has done, we may respect ourselves, and shall be respected. Comparing all the faults he has found in us, with the excellencies he has awarded to us, we are still a great, and may be a proud, people. Our virtues we are accustomed to know, and perhaps sufficiently addicted to appreciate. But our author says: 'There are certain truths which the Americans can only learn from strangers or from experience.' Of course, they are the more unpleasant truths, in other words, our faults. Look at this: 'If great writers have not at present existed in America, the reason is very simply given in these facts: there can be no literary genius, without freedom of opinion; and freedom of opinion does not exist in America!' Surely, if this be a truth, we have first learned it from a stranger. But the particular and only application which he makes of it, is rather suspicious: 'There is no public organ of infidelity.' That is, the tyranny of public opinion is such, that infidelity cannot show its head, and front, and body, in an organized form. On this point, this simple statement may suffice for all the needful purposes of a reply. Nor would we suggest that M. de Tocqueville was himself an infidel, and grieved at this negative fact. We have on the whole set him down for a Christian. But it was rather a blunder, at least, that he should rest the truth, and hazard the influence, of his statement, on such a reference.

Again our author says: 'I know no country in which there is so little independence of mind, and freedom of discussion, as in America.' But observe, it is supported by the same reason, occult indeed, though allied to another that is cousin german: 'In any constitutional state of Europe, every sort of religious and political theory may be advocated and propagated abroad.' Mr. Spencer, in his notes to this work, has very properly qualified and rebuked our author's treatment of this subject. We think M. d. Tocqueville was led into error here, first by his theory, and next for lack of information as to its practical operation. Reckoning the majority as an unity, and assuming that men are the same in the aggregate as they are severally, he jumps to the conclusion, that the absolute sway of a majority is as dangerous as that of an individual: 'For these reasons,' he says, 'I can never willingly invest any number of my fellow creatures with that unlimited authority which I should refuse to any one of them.'

* * *

That a man who had observed so profoundly and correctly on other matters, and an author who had written so well, and discoursed so eloquently, upon them, could fall into this egregious blunder of theory and fact, excites our astonishment. Had we not other reasons for giving him credit for a christian belief, we should still apprehend that he had found some occasion in actual life to sympathize with the obloquy of an avowed and open infidel, laboring to propagate his sentiments, but defeated and borne down by public opinion, or with some other renegade to well-received and sacred opinions, who had dared to outrage the common feeling of the community. In our country, this description applies to no other case of fact. And yet our author appears to apply it to politics. ***

Doubtless there may have been some occasion for observing the tyranny of opinion in our country, when armed with the influence of the majority, both in the political and religious world, and in all other forms of the social state. But we are not aware, than any more perfect state of society has yet been invented, than the rule of the majority. And as our author appears to be an advocate of free governments, and in most respects an admirer of ours, we will just introduce the form he has suggested as a more perfect way: 'That the legislative power should be so constituted as to represent the majority, without necessarily being the slave of its passions; an executive, so as to retain a certain degree of uncontrolled authority; and a judiciary, so as to remain independent of the two other powers.' Very well. We know not but we would go for it, if it can be made practicable; though there seems to be so much of the indefinite in the whole, and so much of the nicety of detail to be settled, we fear there might be difficulties in the way.

Without descending to the minutire of criticism, which lie open to notice on the pages of the volume before us, we may say, in conclusion, that the author has executed a work for which the world ought to thank him—the European world, and the American world. He has shown us up to foreigners and to ourselves; and though he has found some fault in us, he has left us enough to be proud of. He has convinced us more than ever, that if just to ourselves, and true to our principles, we can yet become, if not the greatest, yet one of the greatest and happiest people on earth. We have indeed much to make us anxious, but much to hope for. M. de Tocqueville has demonstrated one thing—our positive and relative importance; and henceforth, so far as the influence of our author may go, and we predict it will not be small, the world will be constrained to acknowledge it. ***

JOHN STUART MILL

London Review, October 1835†

To depict accurately, and to estimate justly, the institutions of the United States, have been but secondary aims with the original and profound author of these volumes—secondary, we mean, in themselves, but indispensable to his main object. This object was, to inquire, what light is thrown, by the example of America, upon the question of democracy; which he considers as the great and paramount question of our age.

* * *

In America, therefore, if anywhere, we may expect to learn—first, what portion of human well-being is compatible with democracy in any form; and, next, what are the good and what the bad properties of democracy, and by what means the former may be strengthened, the latter controlled. We have it not in our power to choose between

---

† John Stuart Mill (1806–1873), the great English political writer and author of *On Liberty*, was a friend and correspondent of Tocqueville's.

democracy and aristocracy; necessity and Providence have decided that for us. But the choice we are still called upon to make is between a well and an ill-regulated democracy; and on that depends the future well-being of the human race.

When M. de Tocqueville says, that he studied America, not in order to disparage or to vindicate democracy, but in order to understand it, he makes no false claim to impartiality. Not a trace of a prejudice, or so much as a previous leaning either to the side of democracy or aristocracy, shows itself in his work. He is indeed anything but indifferent to the ends, to which all forms of government profess to be means. He manifests the deepest and steadiest concern for all the great interests, material and spiritual, of the human race. But between aristocracy and democracy he holds the balance straight, with all the impassibility of a mere scientific observer. He was indeed most favourably placed for looking upon both sides of that great contest with an unbiassed judgment; for the impressions of his early education were royalist, while among the influences of society and the age liberalism is predominant. He has renounced the impressions of his youth, but he looks back to them with no aversion. It is indifferent to him what value we set upon the good or evil of aristocracy, since that in his view is past and gone. The good and evil of democracy, be they what they may, are what we must now look to; and for us the questions are, how to make the best of democracy, and what that best amounts to.

We have stated the purposes of M. de Tocqueville's examination of America. We have now to add its result.

The conclusion at which he has arrived is, that this irresistible current, which cannot be stemmed, may be guided, and guided to a happy termination. The bad tendencies of democracy, in his opinion, admit of being mitigated; its good tendencies of being so strengthened as to be more than a compensation for the bad. It is his belief that a government, substantially a democracy, but constructed with the necessary precautions, may subsist in Europe, may be stable and durable, and may secure to the aggregate of the human beings living under it, a greater sum of happiness than has ever yet been enjoyed by any people. The universal aim, therefore, should be, so to prepare the way for democracy, that when it comes, it may come in this beneficial shape; not only for the sake of the good we have to expect from it, but because it is literally our only refuge from a despotism resembling not the tempered and regulated absolutism of modern times, but the tyranny of the Cæsars. For when the equality of conditions shall have reached the point which in America it has already attained, and there shall be no power intermediate between the monarch and the multitude; when there remains no individual and no class capable of separately offering any serious obstacle to the will of the government; then, unless the people are fit to rule, the monarch will be as perfectly autocratic as amidst the equality of an Asiatic despotism. Where all are equal, all must be alike free, or alike slaves.

The book, of which we have now described the plan and purpose, has been executed in a manner worthy of so noble a scheme. It has at once taken its rank among the most remarkable productions of our time; and is a book with which, both for its facts and its speculations, all who would understand, or who are called upon to exercise influence over their age, are bound to be familiar. It will contribute to give to the political speculations of our time a new character. Hitherto, aristocracy and democracy have been looked at chiefly in the mass, and applauded as good, or censured as bad, on the whole. But the time is now come for a narrower inspection, and a more discriminating judgment. M. de Tocqueville, among the first, has set the example of analysing democracy; of distinguishing one of its features, one of its tendencies, from another; of showing which of these tendencies is good, and which bad, in itself; how far each is necessarily connected with the rest, and to what extent any of them may be counteracted or modified, either by accident or foresight. He does this, with so noble a field as a great nation to demonstrate upon; which field he has commenced by minutely examining; selecting, with a discernment of which we have had no previous example, the material facts, and surveying these by the light of principles, drawn from no ordinary knowledge of human nature. We do not think his conclusions always just, but we think them always entitled to the most respectful attention, and never destitute of at least a large foundation of truth. The author's mind, except that it is of a soberer character, seems to us to resemble Montesquieu most among the great French writers. The book is such as Montesquieu might have written, if to his genius he had superadded good sense, and the lights which mankind have since gained from the experiences of a period in which they may be said to have lived centuries in fifty years.

We feel how impossible it is, in the space of an article, to exemplify all the features of a work, every page of which has nearly as great a claim to citation as any other. For M. de Tocqueville's ideas do not float thinly upon a sea of words; none of his propositions are unmeaning, none of his meanings superfluous; not a paragraph could have been omitted without diminishing the value of the work. We must endeavour to make a selection.

The first volume, the only one of which a translation has yet appeared, describes chiefly the institutions of the United States: the second, the state of society, which he represents to be the fruit of those institutions. We should have been glad to assume that the reader possessed a general acquaintance with the subject of the former volume, and to refer him, for details, to the work itself. But it so happens that in no one point has M. de Tocqueville rendered a greater service to the European public, than by actually giving them their first information of the very existence of some of the most important parts of the American constitution. We allude particularly to the municipal institutions; which, as our author shows, and as might have been expected, are the very fountain-head of American democracy, and one principal cause of all that is valuable in its influences; but of which English travellers, a race who have eyes and see not, ears and hear not, have not so much as perceived the existence.

In the New England States, the part of the Union in which the municipal system which generally prevails through the whole, has been brought to the greatest perfection, the following are its leading principles. The country is parcelled out into districts called townships, containing, on an average, from two to three thousand inhabitants. Each township manages its local concerns within itself; judicial business excepted, which, more wisely than their English brethren, the Americans appear to keep separate from all other functions. The remaining part—that is, the administrative part of the local business—is not only under the complete control of the people—but the people themselves, convened in general assembly, vote all local taxes, and decide on all new and important undertakings. While the deliberative part of the administration is thus conducted directly by the people, the executive part is in the hands of a variety of officers, annually elected by the people, and mostly paid. ***

M. de Tocqueville, though he is not sparing in pointing out the faults of the institutions of the United States, regards those institutions on the whole with no inconsiderable admiration. The federal constitution, in particular, (as distinguished from the various state constitutions,) he considers as a remarkable monument of foresight and sagacity. The great men by whom, during two years' deliberation, that constitution was constructed, discerned, according to him, with great wisdom, the vulnerable points both of democracy and of federal government, and did nearly everything which could have been done, in their circumstances, to strengthen the weak side of both.

Our space will not allow us to follow our author through the details of the American institutions; but we cannot pass without particular notice his remarks on one general principle which pervades them.

Two modes, says M. de Tocqueville, present themselves for keeping a government under restraint: one is to diminish its power; the other, to give power liberally, but to subdivide it among many hands. ***

The principle of sharing the powers of government among a great variety of functionaries, and keeping these independent of one another, is the mainspring of the American institutions. The various municipal officers are independent of each other, and of the general government of the state. The state governments, within their lawful sphere, are wholly independent of the federal government, and the federal government of them. Each of the state governments consists of two chambers and a governor; and the federal government consists of the House of Representatives, the Senate, and the President of the United States. Of each of these tripartite bodies the three branches are mutually independent, and may, and frequently do, place themselves in direct opposition to one another.

In what manner is harmony maintained among these jarring elements? How is so minute a division of the governing power rendered compatible with the existence of government? Since the concurrence of so many wills is necessary to the working of the machine, by what means is that concurrence obtained? The town-officers, for instance, are often the sole agency provided for executing the laws made or orders issued by the federal or by the state government; but those authorities can neither dismiss them if they disobey, nor promote them to a higher post in their department, for zealous service. How, then, is their obedience secured?

*** First, all those functionaries who are made independent of each other within their respective spheres, depend upon, for they are periodically elected by, a common superior—the People. No one, therefore, likes to venture upon a collision with any co-ordinate authority, unless he believes that, at the expiration of his office, his conduct will be approved by his constituents.

This check, however, cannot suffice for all cases; for, in the first place, the authorities may be accountable to different constituencies. In a dispute, for instance, between the officers of a township and the state government, or between the federal government and a state, the constituents of each party may support their representatives in the quarrel. Moreover, the check often operates too slowly, and is not of a sufficiently energetic character for the graver delinquencies.

The remedy provided for all such cases is the interference of the courts of justice. ***

In a general way, the following may be given as a summary of M. de Tocque-ville's opinion on the good and bad tendencies of democracy.

On the favourable side, he holds, that alone among all governments its systematic and perpetual end is the good of the immense majority. Were this its only merit, it is one, the absence of which could ill be compensated by all other merits put together. Secondly, no other government can reckon upon so willing an obedience, and so warm an attachment to it, on the part of the people at large. And, lastly, as it works not only *for* the people, but, much more extensively than any other government, *by means* of the people, it has a tendency which no other government has in the same degree, to call forth and sharpen the intelligence of the mass.

The disadvantages which our author ascribes to democracy are chiefly two:—First, that its policy is much more hasty and short-sighted than that of aristocracy. In compensation, however, he adds, that it is more ready to correct its errors, when experience has made them apparent. The second is, that the interest of the majority is not always identical with the interest of all; and hence the sovereignty of the majority creates a tendency on their part to abuse their power over all minorities.

To commence with the unfavourable side: we may remark, that the evils which M. de Tocqueville represents as incident to democracy, can only exist in so far as the people entertain an erroneous idea of what democracy ought to be. If the people entertained the right idea of democracy, the mischief of hasty and unskilful legislation would not exist; and the omnipotence of the majority would not be attended with any evils.

* * *

The interest of the people is, to choose for their rulers the most instructed and the ablest persons who can be found, and having done so, to allow them to exercise their knowledge and ability for the good of the people freely, or with the least possible control—as long as it *is* the good of the people, and not some private end, that they are aiming at. A democracy thus administered, would unite all the good qualities ever possessed by any government. Not only would its ends be good, but its means would be as well chosen as the wisdom of the age would allow; and the omnipotence of the majority would be exercised through the agency and at the discretion of an enlightened minority, accountable to the majority in the last resort.

But it is not possible that the constitution of the democracy itself should provide adequate security for its being understood and administered in this spirit, and not according to the erroneous notion of democracy. This rests with the good sense of the people themselves. If the people can remove their rulers for one thing, they can for another. That ultimate control, without which they cannot have security for good government, may, if they please, be made the means of themselves interfering in the government, and making their legislators mere delegates for carrying into execution the preconceived judgment of the majority. If the people do this, they mistake their interest; and such a government, though better than most aristocracies, is not the kind of democracy which wise men desire.

* * *

The substitution of delegation for representation is therefore the one and only danger of democracy. What is the amount of this danger?

In America, according to M. de Tocqueville, it is not only a great but a growing danger. "A custom," says he, "is spreading more and more in the United States, which tends ultimately to nullify the securities of representative government. It happens very frequently that the electors, in naming a representative, lay down a plan of conduct for him, and impose on him a certain number of positive injunctions, from which he is by no means to deviate. Tumult excepted, it is exactly as if the majority itself were to deliberate in general meeting."

The experience of America is, in our author's opinion, equally unfavourable to the expectation that the people in a democracy are likely to select as their rulers the ablest men.

* * *

The fact that the ablest men seldom offer themselves to the people's suffrages, is still more strongly stated by our author in another place, and is a point on which there is a striking concurrence of testimony. It may be said that they do not present themselves because they know that they would not be chosen; but a reason less discreditable to the American people was given to our author's fellow-traveller, M. de Beaumont, by an American: "Comment voulez-vous qu'un médecin se montre habile, si vous mettez entre ses mains un homme bien portant?" The truth is that great talents are not needed for carrying on, in ordinary times, the government of an already well-ordered society. In a country like America little government is required: the people are prosperous, and the machinery of the state works so smoothly, by the agency of the people themselves, that there is next to nothing for the government to do. When no great public end is to be compassed; when no great abuse calls for remedy, no national danger for resistance, the mere everyday business of politics is an occupation little worthy of any mind of first-rate powers, and very little alluring to it. In a settled state of things, the commanding intellects will always prefer to govern mankind from their closets, by means of literature and science, leaving the mechanical details of government to mechanical minds.

In national emergencies, which call out the men of first-rate talents, such men always step into their proper place. M. de Tocqueville admits, that during the struggle for independence, and the scarcely less difficult struggle which succeeded it, to keep the confederacy together, the choice of the people fell almost invariably upon the first men in the country. Such a body of men as composed the assembly which framed the federal constitution, never were brought together at any period of history. No wonder that, when compared with them, the present generation of public men appear like dwarfs.

* * *

But put these evils at their worst: let them be as great as it is possible they should be in a tolerably educated nation: suppose that the people do not choose the fittest men, and that whenever they have an opinion of their own, they compel their representatives, without the exercise of any discretion, merely to give execution to that opinion— thus adopting the false idea of democracy propagated by its enemies, and by some of its injudicious friends—the consequence would no doubt be abundance of unskilful legislation. But would the abundance, after all, be so much greater than in most aristocracies? In the English aristocracy there has surely been, at all periods, crude and ill-considered legislation enough. This is the character of all governments whose laws are made, and acts of administration performed, *impromptu*, not in pursuance of a general design, but from the pressure of some present occasion: of all governments, in which the ruling power is to any great extent exercised by persons not trained to government as a business.

* * *

When the governing body, whether it consist of the many or of a privileged class, is so numerous, that the large majority of it do not and cannot make the practice of government the main occupation of their lives, it is utterly impossible that there should be wisdom, foresight, and caution in the governing body itself. These qualities must be found, if found at all, not in the body, but in those whom the body trust. If the people in America, or the higher classes in England or France, make a practice of themselves dictating and prescribing the measures of government, it is impossible that those countries should be otherwise than ill administered. There has been ample proof of this in the government of England, where we have had, at all times, the clumsiness of an ill-regulated democracy, with a very small portion indeed of her good intentions.

In a numerous aristocracy, as well as in a democracy, the sole chance for considerate and wise government lies not in the wisdom of the democracy or of the aristocracy themselves, but in their willingness to place themselves under the guidance of the wisest among them. And it would be difficult for democracy to exhibit less of this willingness than has been shown by the English aristocracy in all periods of their history, or less than is shown by them at this moment.

But, while we do not share all the apprehensions of M. de Tocqueville from the unwillingness of the people to be guided by superior wisdom, and while this source of evil tells for very little with us in the comparison between democracy and aristocracy, we consider our author entitled to applause and gratitude for having probed this subject so unsparingly, and given us so striking a picture of his own impressions; and we are clearly of opinion that his fears, whether excessive or not, are in the right place. If democracy should disappoint any of the expectations of its more enlightened partisans, it will be from the substitution of delegation for representation; of the crude and necessarily superficial judgment of the people themselves, for the judgment of those whom the people, having confidence in their honesty, have selected as the wisest guardians whose services they could command. All the chances unfavourable to democracy lie here; and whether the danger be much or little, all who see it ought to unite their efforts to reduce it to the *minimum*.

We have no space to follow M. de Tocqueville into the consideration of any of the palliatives which may be found for this evil tendency. We pass to that which he regards as the most serious of the inconveniences of democracy, and that to which, if the American republic should perish, it will owe its fall. This is, the omnipotence of the majority.

M. de Tocqueville's fears from this source are not of the kind which haunt the imaginations of English alarmists. He finds, under the American democracy, no tendency on the part of the poor to oppress the rich—to molest them in their persons or in their property. That the security of person and property are the first social interests not only of the rich but of the poor, is obvious to common sense. And the degree of education which a well-constituted democracy ensures to all its citizens, renders common sense the general characteristic. Truths which are obvious, it may always be expected that the American democracy will see. It is true, no one need expect that, in a democracy, to keep up a class of rich people living in splendour and affluence will be treated as a national object, which legislation should be directed to promote, and which the rest of the community should be taxed for. But there has never been any complaint that property in general is not protected in America, or that large properties do not meet with every protection which is given to small ones. Not even in the mode of laying on taxes have we seen any complaint that favour is shown to the poor at the expense of the rich.

But when we put inequalities of property out of the question, it is not easy to see what sort of minority it can be, over which the majority can have any interest in tyrannizing. The only standing and or-

ganized minority which exists in any community, constituted as communities usually are, is the rich. All other minorities are fluctuating,
and he who is in the majority to-day is in the minority to-morrow: each
in his turn is liable to this kind of oppression; all, therefore, are interested in preventing it from having existence.

The only cases which we can think of, as forming possible exceptions to this rule, are cases of antipathy on the part of one portion of
the people towards another: the antipathies of religion, for example, or
of race. Where these exist, iniquity will be committed, under any form
of government, aristocratic or democratic, unless in a higher state of
moral and intellectual improvement than any community has hitherto
attained.

M. de Tocqueville's fears, however, are not so much for the security
and the ordinary worldly interests of individuals, as for the moral dignity and progressiveness of the race. It is a tyranny exercised over
opinions, more than over persons, which he is apprehensive of. He
dreads lest all individuality of character, and independence of thought
and sentiment, should be prostrated under the despotic yoke of public
opinion.

* * *

America is not only destitute of the very equivocal advantage so
strongly dwelt upon by our author, the existence of classes having a
private interest in protecting opinions contrary to those of the majority; she labours, also, under a much more serious deficiency. In America there is no highly instructed class; no numerous body raised
sufficiently above the common level, in education, knowledge, or refinement, to inspire the rest with any reverence for distinguished mental superiority, or any salutary sense of the insufficiency of their own
wisdom. Our author himself was struck with the general equality of
intelligence and mental cultivation in America. * * *

* * *

When all are in nearly the same pecuniary circumstances, all educated nearly alike, and all employed nearly alike, it is no wonder if all
think nearly alike; and where this is the case, it is but natural, that
when here and there a solitary individual thinks differently, nobody
minds him. These are exactly the circumstances in which public opinion is generally so unanimous, that it has most chance to be in reality,
and is sure to be in appearance, intolerant of the few who happen to
dissent from it.

M. de Tocqueville has himself told us, that there is no indisposition
in the Many of the United States to pay deference to the opinions of
an instructed class, where such a class exists, and where there are obvious signs by which it may be recognized. He tells us this, by what he
says of the extraordinary influence of the lawyers—in his opinion one
of the great causes which tend to restrain the abuse of the power of
the majority. We recommend especial attention to the section devoted
to this topic. (Tocqueville, Vol. II, p. 165.)

The faults incident to the character of a lawyer, in our author's
opinion, happily counterbalance those to which democracy is liable.

The lawyer is naturally a lover of precedent; his respect for established rules and established formalities is apt to be unreasonable; the spirit of his profession is everywhere a stationary spirit. He usually has in excess the qualities in which democracy is apt to be deficient. His influence, therefore, is naturally exerted to correct that deficiency.

If the minds of lawyers were not, both in England and America, almost universally perverted by the barbarous system of technicalities—the opprobrium of human reason—which their youth is passed in committing to memory, and their manhood in administering,—we think with our author that they are the class in whom superiority of instruction, produced by superior study, would most easily obtain the stamp of general recognition; and that they would be the natural leaders of a people destitute of a leisured class.

But in countries which, if in some respects worse, are in the other respects far more happily situated than America; in countries where there exist endowed institutions for education, and a numerous class possessed of hereditary leisure, there is a security, far greater than has ever existed in America, against the tyranny of public opinion over the individual mind. Even if the profession of opinions different from those of the mass were an exclusion from public employment—to a leisured class offices moderately paid, and without a particle of irresponsible authority, hold out little allurement, and the diminution of their chance of obtaining them would not be severely felt. A leisured class would always possess a power sufficient not only to protect in themselves, but to encourage in others, the enjoyment of individuality of thought; and would keep before the eyes of the many, what is of so much importance to them, the spectacle of a standard of mental cultivation superior to their own. Such a class, too, would be able, by means of combination, to force upon the rest of the public attention to their opinions. In America, all large minorities exercise this power; even, as in the case of the tariff, to the extent of electing a convention, composed of representatives from all parts of the country, which deliberates in public, and issues manifestoes in the name of its party. A class composed of all the most cultivated intellects in the country; of those who, from their powers and their virtues, would command the respect of the people, even in combating their prejudices—such a class would be almost irresistible in its action on public opinion. In the existence of a leisured class, we see the great and salutary corrective of all the inconveniences to which democracy is liable. We cannot, under any modification of the laws of England, look forward to a period when this grand security for the progressiveness of the human species will not exist.

While, therefore, we see in democracy, as in every other state of society or form of government, possibilities of evil, which it would ill serve the cause of democracy itself to dissemble or overlook; while we think that the world owes a deep debt to M. de Tocqueville for having warned it of these, for having studied the failings and weaknesses of democracy with the anxious attention with which a parent watches the faults of a child, or a careful seaman those of the vessel in which he embarks his property and his life; we see nothing in any of these tendencies, from which any serious evil need be apprehended, if the superior spirits would but join with each other in considering the instruction of the democracy, and not the patching of the old worn-out machinery of aristocracy, the proper object henceforth of all rational exertion. No doubt, the government which will be achieved will long be extremely imperfect, for mankind are as yet in a very early stage of improvement. But if half the exertions were made to prepare the minds of the majority for the place they are about to take in their own government, which are made for the chimerical purpose of preventing them from assuming that place, mankind would purchase at a cheap price safety from incalculable evils, and the benefit of a government indefinitely improveable; the only possible government which, to ensure the greatest good of the community subject to it, has only to take an enlightened view of its own.

* * *

JOHN STUART MILL

Edinburgh Review, October 1840

It has been the rare fortune of M. de Tocqueville's book to have achieved an easy triumph, both over the indifference of our at once busy and indolent public to profound speculation, and over the particular obstacles which oppose the reception of speculations from a foreign, and above all from a French source. ***

To this general neglect M. de Tocqueville's book forms, however, as we have already said, a brilliant exception. Its reputation was as sudden, and is as extensive, in this country as in France, and in that large part of Europe which receives its opinions from France. The progress of political dissatisfaction, and the comparisons made between the fruits of a popular constitution on one side of the Atlantic, and of a mixed government with a preponderating aristocratic element on the other, had made the working of American institutions a party question. For many years, every book of travels in America had been a party pamphlet, or had at least fallen among partisans, and been pressed into the service of one party or of the other. When, therefore, a new book, of a grave and imposing character, on Democracy in America, made its appearance even on the other side of the British Channel, it was not likely to be overlooked, or to escape an attempt to convert it to party purposes. If ever political writer had reason to believe that he had laboured successfully to render his book incapable of such a use, M. de Tocqueville was entitled to think so. But though his theories are of an impartiality without example, and his practical conclusions lean towards Radicalism, some of his phrases are susceptible of a Tory application. One of these is "the tyranny of the majority." This phrase was forthwith adopted into the Conservative dialect, and trumpeted by

Sir Robert Peel in his Tamworth oration, when, as booksellers' adver-tisements have since frequently reminded us, he "earnestly requested the perusal" of the book by all and each of his audience. And we be-lieve it has since been the opinion of the country gentlemen that M. de Tocqueville is one of the pillars of Conservatism, and his book a definitive demolition of America and of Democracy. The error has done more good than the truth would perhaps have done; since the re-sult is, that the English public now know and read the first philosoph-ical book ever written on Democracy, as it manifests itself in modern society; a book, the essential doctrines of which it is not likely that any future speculations will subvert, to whatever degree they may modify them; while its spirit, and the general mode in which it treats its sub-ject, constitute it the beginning of a new era in the scientific study of politics.

The importance of M. de Tocqueville's speculations is not to be es-timated by the opinions which he has adopted, be these true or false. The value of his work is less in the conclusions, than in the mode of arriving at them. He has applied to the greatest question in the art and science of government, those principles and methods of philosophiz-ing to which mankind are indebted for all the advances made by mod-ern times in the other branches of the study of nature. It is not risking too much to affirm of these volumes, that they contain the first analyt-ical inquiry into the influences of Democracy. For the first time, that phenomenon is treated of as something which, being a reality in na-ture, and no mere mathematical or metaphysical abstraction, mani-fests itself by innumerable properties, not by some one only; and must be looked at in many aspects before it can be made the subject even of that modest and conjectural judgment, which is alone attainable re-specting a fact at once so great and so new. Its consequences are by no means to be comprehended in one single description, nor in one sum-mary verdict of approval or condemnation. So complicated and end-less are their ramifications, that he who sees furthest into them will, in general, longest hesitate before finally pronouncing whether the good or the evil of its influence, on the whole, preponderates.

M. de Tocqueville has endeavoured to ascertain and discriminate the various properties and tendencies of Democracy; the separate rela-tions in which it stands towards the different interests of society, and the different moral and social requisites of human nature. In the in-vestigation he has of necessity left much undone, and much which will be better done by those who come after him, and build upon his foundations. But he has earned the double honour of being the first to make the attempt, and of having done more towards the success of it than probably will ever again be done by any one individual. His method is, as that of a philosopher on such a subject must be—a com-bination of deduction with induction: his evidences are, laws of hu-man nature, on the one hand; the example of America, and France, and other modern nations, so far as applicable, on the other. His con-clusions never rest on either species of evidence alone; whatever he classes as an effect of Democracy, he has both ascertained to exist in those countries in which the state of society is democratic, and has also succeeded in connecting with Democracy by deductions *à priori*, tending to show that such would naturally be its influences upon beings constituted as mankind are, and placed in a world such as we know ours to be. If this be not the true Baconian and Newtonian method applied to society and government; if any better, or even any other be possible, M. de Tocqueville would be the first to say, *candidus imperti*: if not, he is entitled to say to political theorists, whether calling themselves philosophers or practical men, *his utere mecum*.

That part of *Democracy in America* which was first published, professes to treat of the political effects of Democracy: the second is devoted to its influence on society in the widest sense; on the relations of private life, on intellect, morals, and the habits and modes of feeling which constitute national character. The last is both a newer and a more difficult subject of inquiry than the first; there are fewer who are competent, or who will even think themselves competent, to judge M. de Tocqueville's conclusions. But, we believe, no one, in the least entitled to an opinion, will refuse to him the praise of having probed the subject to a depth which had never before been sounded; of having carried forward the controversy into a wider and a loftier region of thought; and pointed out many questions essential to the subject which had not been before attended to: questions which he may or may not have solved, but of which, in any case, he has greatly facilitated the solution.

The comprehensiveness of M. de Tocqueville's views, and the impartiality of his feelings, have not led him into the common infirmity of those who see too many sides to a question—that of thinking them all equally important. He is able to arrive at a decided opinion. Nor has the more extensive range of considerations embraced in his Second Part, affected practically the general conclusions which resulted from his First. They may be stated as follows:—That Democracy, in the modern world, is inevitable; and that it is on the whole desirable; but desirable only under certain conditions, and those conditions capable, by human care and foresight, of being realized, but capable also of being missed. The progress and ultimate ascendancy of the democratic principle has in his eyes the character of a law of nature. He thinks it an inevitable result of the tendencies of a progressive civilization; by which expressions he by no means intends to imply either praise or censure. No human effort, no accident even, unless one which should throw back civilization itself, can avail, in his opinion, to defeat, or even very considerably to retard, this progress. But though the fact itself appears to him removed from human control, its salutary or baneful consequences do not. Like other great powers of nature, the tendency, though it cannot be counteracted, may be guided to good. Man cannot turn back the rivers to their source; but it rests with himself whether they shall fertilize or lay waste his fields. Left to its spontaneous course, with nothing done to prepare before it that set of circumstances under which it can exist with safety, and to fight against its worse by an apt employment of its better peculiarities, the probable effects of Democracy upon human well-being, and upon whatever is best and noblest in human character, appear to M. de Tocqueville extremely formidable. But with as much of wise effort devoted to the purpose as it is not irrational to hope for, most of what is mischievous in its tendencies may, in his opinion, be corrected, and its natural capacities of good so far strengthened and made use of, as to leave no cause for regret in the old state of society, and enable the new one to be contemplated with calm contentment, if without exultation.

It is necessary to observe that by Democracy M. de Tocqueville does not in general mean any particular form of government. He can conceive a Democracy under an absolute monarch. Nay, he entertains no small dread lest in some countries it should actually appear in that form. By Democracy, M. de Tocqueville understands equality of conditions; the absence of all aristocracy, whether constituted by political privileges, or by superiority in individual importance and social power. It is towards Democracy in this sense, towards equality between man and man, that he conceives society to be irresistibly tending. Towards Democracy in the other, and more common sense, it may or may not be travelling. Equality of conditions tends naturally to produce a popular government, but not necessarily. Equality may be equal freedom, or equal servitude. America is the type of the first; France, he thinks, is in danger of falling into the second. The latter country is in the condition which, of all that civilized societies are liable to, he regards with the greatest alarm—a democratic state of society without democratic institutions. For, in democratic institutions, M. de Tocqueville sees not an aggravation, but a corrective, of the most serious evils incident to a democratic state of society. No one is more opposed than he is to that species of democratic radicalism, which would admit at once to the highest of political franchises, untaught masses who have not yet been experimentally proved fit even for the lowest. But the ever-increasing intervention of the people, and of all classes of the people, in their own affairs, he regards as a cardinal maxim in the modern art of government: and he believes that the nations of civilized Europe, though not all equally advanced, are all advancing, towards a condition in which there will be no distinctions of political rights, no great or very permanent distinctions of hereditary wealth; when, as there will remain no classes nor individuals capable of making head against the government, unless all are, and are fit to be, alike citizens, all will ere long be equally slaves.

* * *

M. de Tocqueville sees the principal source and security of American freedom, not so much in the election of the President and Congress by popular suffrage, as in the administration of nearly all the business of society by the people themselves. This it is which, according to him, keeps up the habit of attending to the public interest, not in the gross merely, or on a few momentous occasions, but in its dry and troublesome details. This, too, it is which enlightens the people; which teaches them by experience how public affairs must be carried on. The dissemination of public business as widely as possible among the people, is, in his opinion, the only means by which they can be fitted for the exercise of any share of power over the legislature; and generally also the only means by which they can be led to desire it.

For the particulars of this education of the American people by means of political institutions, we must refer to the work itself; of which it is one of the minor recommendations, that it has never been equalled even as a mere statement and explanation of the institutions of the United States. The general principle to which M. de Tocqueville has given the sanction of his authority, merits more consideration than it has yet received from the professed labourers in the cause of national education. It has often been said, and requires to be repeated still oftener, that books and discourses alone are not education; that life is a problem, not a theorem; that action can only be learnt in action. A child learns to write its name only by a succession of trials; and is a man to be taught to use his mind and guide his conduct by mere precept? What can be learnt in schools is important, but not all-important. The main branch of the education of human beings is their habitual employment; which must be either their individual vocation, or some matter of general concern, in which they are called to take a part. The private money-getting occupation of almost every one is more or less a mechanical routine; it brings but few of his faculties into action, while its exclusive pursuit tends to fasten his attention and interest exclusively upon himself, and upon his family as an appendage of himself; making him indifferent to the public, to the more generous objects and the nobler interests, and, in his inordinate regard for his personal comforts, selfish and cowardly. Balance these tendencies by contrary ones; give him something to do for the public, whether as a vestryman, a juryman, or an elector; and, in that degree, his ideas and feelings are taken out of this narrow circle. He becomes acquainted with more varied business, and a larger range of considerations. He is made to feel that besides the interests which separate him from his fellow-citizens, he has interests which connect him with them; that not only the common weal is his weal, but that it partly depends upon his exertions. Whatever might be the case in some other constitutions of society, the spirit of a commercial people will be, we are persuaded, essentially mean and slavish, wherever public spirit is not cultivated by an extensive participation of the people in the business of government in detail; nor will the desideratum of a general diffusion of intelligence among either the middle or lower classes be realized, but by a corresponding dissemination of public functions and a voice in public affairs.

* * *

In estimating the effects of democratic government as distinguished from a democratic condition of society, M. de Tocqueville assumes the state of circumstances which exists in America—a popular government in the State, combined with popular local institutions. In such a government he sees great advantages, balanced by no inconsiderable evils.

Among the advantages, one which figures in the foremost rank is that of which we have just spoken, the diffusion of intelligence; the remarkable impulse given by democratic institutions to the active faculties of that portion of the community who in other circumstances are the most ignorant, passive, and apathetic. These are characteristics of America which strike all travellers. Activity, enterprise, and a respectable amount of information, are not the qualities of a few among the American citizens, nor even of many, but of all. There is no class of persons who are the slaves of habit and routine. Every American will carry on his manufacture, or cultivate his farm, by the newest and best methods applicable to the circumstances of the case. The poorest American understands and can explain the most intricate parts of his country's institutions; can discuss her interests, internal and foreign. Much of this may justly be attributed to the universality of easy circumstances, and to the education and habits which the first settlers in America brought with them; but our author is certainly not wrong in ascribing a certain portion of it to the perpetual exercise of the faculties of every man among the people, through the universal practice of submitting all public questions to his judgment.

* * *

The other great political advantage which our author ascribes to Democracy, requires less illustration, because it is more obvious, and has been oftener treated of; that the course of legislation and administration tends always in the direction of the interest of the greatest number. Although M. de Tocqueville is far from considering this quality of Democracy as the panacea in politics which it has sometimes been supposed to be, he expresses his sense of its importance, if in measured, in no undecided terms. America does not exhibit to us what we see in the best mixed constitutions—the class interests of small minorities wielding the powers of legislation, in opposition both to the general interest and to the general opinion of the community; still less does she exhibit what has been characteristic of most representative governments, and is only gradually ceasing to characterize our own—a standing league of class interests—a tacit compact among the various knots of men who profit by abuses, to stand by one another in resisting reform. Nothing can subsist in America that is not recommended by arguments which, in appearance at least, address themselves to the interest of the many. However frequently, therefore, that interest may be mistaken, the direction of legislation towards it is maintained in the midst of the mistakes; and if a community is so situated or so ordered that it can "support the transitory action of bad laws, and can await without destruction the result of the *general tendency* of the laws," that country, in the opinion of M. de Tocqueville, will prosper more under a democratic government than under any other. But in aristocratic governments, the interest, or at best the honour and glory, of the ruling class, is considered as the public interest; and all that is most valuable to the individuals composing the subordinate classes, is apt to be immolated to that public interest with all the rigour of antique patriotism.

* * *

These, then, are the advantages ascribed by our author to a democratic government. We are now to speak of its disadvantages.

According to the opinion which is prevalent among the more cultivated advocates of democracy, one of its greatest recommendations is
that by means of it the wisest and worthiest are brought to the head of
affairs. The people, it is said, have the strongest interest in selecting
the right men. It is presumed that they will be sensible of that interest;
and, subject to more or less liability of error, will in the main succeed
in placing a high, if not the highest, degree of worth and talent in the
highest situations.

M. de Tocqueville is of another opinion. He was forcibly struck with
the general want of merit in the members of the American legislatures,
and other public functionaries. He accounts for this, not solely by the
people's incapacity to discriminate merit, but partly also by their indifference to it. He thinks there is little preference for men of superior
intellect, little desire to obtain their services for the public; occasionally even a jealousy of them, especially if they be also rich. They, on
their part, have still less inclination to seek any such employment.
Public offices are little lucrative, confer little power, and offer no guarantee of permanency: almost any other career holds out better pecuniary prospects to a man of ability and enterprise; nor will instructed
men stoop to those mean arts, and those compromises of their private
opinions, to which their less distinguished competitors willingly resort. The depositaries of power, after being chosen with little regard to
merit, are, partly perhaps for that very reason, frequently changed.
The rapid return of elections, and even a taste for variety, M. de Tocqueville thinks, on the part of electors (a taste not unnatural wherever little regard is paid to qualifications), produces a rapid succession of new
men in the legislature, and in all public posts. Hence, on the one
hand, great instability in the laws—every new comer desiring to do
something in the short time he has before him, while, on the other
hand, there is no political *carrière*—statesmanship is not a profession.
There is no body of persons educated for public business, pursuing it
as their occupation, and who transmit from one to another the results
of their experience. There are no traditions, no science or art of public
affairs. A functionary knows little, and cares less, about the principles
on which his predecessor has acted; and his successor thinks as little
about his. Public transactions are therefore conducted with a reasonable share indeed of the common sense and common information
which are general in a democratic community, but with little benefit
from specific study and experience; without consistent system, long-
sighted views, or persevering pursuit of distant objects.

This is likely enough to be a true picture of the American Government, but can scarcely be said to be peculiar to it: there are now few
governments remaining, whether representative or absolute, of which
something of the same sort might not be said. In no country where the
real government resides in the minister, and where there are frequent
changes of ministry, are far-sighted views of policy likely to be acted
upon; whether the country be England or France, in the eighteenth
century or in the nineteenth. Crude and ill-considered legislation
is the character of all governments whose laws are made and acts of

administration performed *impromptu*, not in pursuance of a general design, but from the pressure of some present occasion; of all governments in which the ruling power is to any great extent exercised by persons not trained to government as a business. It is true that the governments which have been celebrated for their profound policy, have generally been aristocracies. But they have been very narrow aristocracies, consisting of so few members, that every member could personally participate in the business of administration. These are the governments which have a natural tendency to be administered steadily—that is, according to fixed principles. Every member of the governing body being trained to government as a profession, like other professions they respect precedent, transmit their experience from generation to generation, acquire and preserve a set of traditions, and all being competent judges of each other's merits, the ablest easily rises to his proper level. ***

In so far as it is true that there is a deficiency of remarkable merit in American public men (and our author allows that there is a large number of exceptions), the fact may perhaps admit of a less discreditable explanation. America needs very little government. She has no wars, no neighbours, no complicated international relations; no old society with its thousand abuses to reform; no half-fed and untaught millions in want of food and guidance. Society in America requires little but to be let alone. The current affairs which her government has to transact can seldom demand much more than average capacity; and it may be in the Americans a wise economy, not to pay the price of great talents when common ones will serve their purpose. We make these remarks by way of caution, not of controversy. Like many other parts of our author's doctrines, that of which we are now speaking affords work for a succession of thinkers and of accurate observers, and must in the main depend on future experience to confirm or refute it.

We now come to that one among the dangers of Democracy, respecting which so much has been said, and which our author designates as "the despotism of the majority."

It is perhaps the greatest defect of M. de Tocqueville's book, that from the scarcity of examples, his propositions, even when derived from observation, have the air of mere abstract speculations. He speaks of the tyranny of the majority in general phrases, but gives hardly any instances of it, nor much information as to the mode in which it is practically exemplified. The omission was in the present instance the more excusable, as the despotism complained of was, at that time, politically at least, an evil in apprehension more than in sufferance; and he was uneasy rather at the total absence of security against the tyranny of the majority, than at the frequency of its actual exertion.

Events, however, which have occurred since the publication of the First Part of M. de Tocqueville's work, give indication of the shape which tyranny is most likely to assume when exercised by a majority.

It is not easy to surmise any inducements of interest, by which, in a country like America, the greater number could be led to oppress the smaller. When the majority and the minority are spoken of as conflicting interests, the rich and the poor are generally meant; but where the rich are content with being rich, and do not claim as such any political privileges, their interest and that of the poor are generally the same: complete protection to property, and freedom in the disposal of it, are alike important to both. When, indeed, the poor are so poor that they can scarcely be worse off, respect on their part for rights of property which they cannot hope to share, is never safely to be calculated upon. But where all have property, either in enjoyment or in reasonable hope, and an appreciable chance of acquiring a large fortune; and where every man's way of life proceeds on the confident assurance that, by superior exertion, he will obtain a superior reward; the importance of inviolability of property is not likely to be lost sight of. It is not affirmed of the Americans that they make laws against the rich, or unduly press upon them in the imposition of taxes. If a labouring class, less happily circumstanced, could prematurely force themselves into influence over our own legislature, there might then be danger, not so much of violations of property, as of undue interference with contracts; unenlightened legislation for the supposed interest of the many; laws founded on mistakes in political economy. A minimum of wages, or a tax on machinery, might be attempted: as silly and as inefficacious attempts might be made to keep up wages by law, as were so long made by the British legislature to keep them down by the same means. We have no wish to see the experiment tried, but we are fully convinced that experience would correct the one error as it has corrected the other, and in the same way; namely, by complete practical failure.

It is not from the separate interests, real or imaginary, of the majority, that minorities are in danger; but from its antipathies of religion, political party, or race; and experience in America seems to confirm what theory rendered probable, that the tyranny of the majority would not take the shape of tyrannical laws, but that of a dispensing power over all laws. The people of Massachusetts passed no law prohibiting Roman Catholic schools, or exempting Protestants from the penalties of incendiarism; they contented themselves with burning the Ursuline convent to the ground, aware that no jury would be found to redress the injury. In the same reliance the people of New York and Philadelphia sacked and destroyed the houses of the Abolitionists, and the schools and churches of their black fellow-citizens, while numbers who took no share in the outrage amused themselves with the sight. The laws of Maryland still prohibit murder and burglary; but in 1812, a Baltimore mob, after destroying the printing office of a newspaper which had opposed the war with England, broke into the prison to which the editors had been conveyed for safety, murdered one of them, left the others for dead; and the criminals were tried and acquitted. In the same city, in 1835, a riot which lasted four days, and the foolish history of which is related in M. Chevalier's *Letters*, was occasioned by the fraudulent bankruptcy of the Maryland Bank. It is not so much the riots, in such instances, that are deplorable; these might have occurred in any country: it is the impossibility of obtaining aid from an executive dependent on the mob, or justice from juries which formed part of it: it is the apathetic cowardly truckling of disapproving lookers-on; almost a parallel to the passive imbecility of the people of Paris, when a handful of hired assassins perpetrated the massacres of September. For where the majority is the sole power, and a power issuing its mandates in the form of riots, it inspires a terror which the most arbitrary monarch often fails to excite. The silent sympathy of the majority may support on the scaffold the martyr of one man's tyranny; but if we would imagine the situation of a victim of the majority itself, we must look to the annals of religious persecution for a parallel.

Yet, neither ought we to forget that even this lawless violence is not so great, because not so lasting, an evil, as tyranny through the medium of the law. A tyrannical law remains; because, so long as it is submitted to, its existence does not weaken the general authority of the laws. But in America, tyranny will seldom use the instrument of law, because there is in general no permanent class to be tyrannized over. The subjects of oppression are casual objects of popular resentment, who cannot be reached by law, but only by occasional acts of lawless power; and to tolerate these, if they ever became frequent, would be consenting to live without law. Already, in the United States, the spirit of outrage has raised a spirit of resistance to outrage; of moral resistance first, as was to be wished and expected: if that fail, physical resistance will follow. The majority, like other despotic powers, will be taught by experience that it cannot enjoy both the advantages of civilized society, and the barbarian liberty of taking men's lives and property at its discretion. Let it once be generally understood that minorities will fight, and majorities will be shy of provoking them. The bad government of which there is any permanent danger under modern civilization, is in the form of bad laws and bad tribunals: government by the *sic volo* either of a king or a mob belongs to past ages, and can no more exist, for long together, out of the pale of Asiatic barbarism.

The despotism, therefore, of the majority within the limits of civil life, though a real evil, does not appear to us to be a formidable one. The tyranny which we fear, and which M. de Tocqueville principally dreads, is of another kind—a tyranny not over the body, but over the mind.

It is the complaint of M. de Tocqueville, as well as of other travellers in America, that in no country does there exist less independence of thought. In religion, indeed, the varieties of opinion which fortunately prevailed among those by whom the colonies were settled, have produced a toleration in law and in fact extending to the limits of Christianity. If by ill fortune there had happened to be a religion of the majority, the case would probably have been different. On every other subject, when the opinion of the majority is made up, hardly any one, it is affirmed, dares to be of any other opinion, or at least to profess it. The statements are not clear as to the nature or amount of the inconvenience that would be suffered by any one who presumed to question a received opinion. It seems certain, however, that scarcely any person has that courage; that when public opinion considers a question as settled, no further discussion of it takes place; and that not only nobody dares (what everybody may venture upon in Europe) to say anything disrespectful to the public, or derogatory to its opinions, but that its wisdom and virtue are perpetually celebrated with the most servile adulation and sycophancy.

These considerations, which were much dwelt on in the author's First Part, are intimately connected with the views promulgated in his Second, respecting the influence of Democracy on intellect.

The Americans, according to M. de Tocqueville, not only profess, but carry into practice, on all subjects except the fundamental doctrines of Christianity and Christian ethics, the habit of mind which has been so often inculcated as the one sufficient security against mental slavery—the rejection of authority, and the assertion of the right of private judgment. They regard the traditions of the past merely in the light of materials, and as "a useful study for doing otherwise and better." They are not accustomed to look for guidance either to the wisdom of ancestors, or to eminent cotemporary wisdom, but require that the grounds on which they act shall be made level to their own comprehension. And, as is natural to those who govern themselves by common-sense rather than by science, their cast of mind is altogether unpedantic and practical; they go straight to the end, without favour or prejudice towards any set of means, and aim at the substance of things, with something like a contempt for form.

From such habits and ways of thinking, the consequence which would be apprehended by some would be a most licentious abuse of individual independence of thought. The fact is the reverse. It is impossible, as our author truly remarks, that mankind in general should form all their opinions for themselves: an authority from which they mostly derive them may be rejected in theory, but it always exists in fact. That law above them, which older societies have found in the traditions of antiquity, or in the dogmas of priests or philosophers, the Americans find in the opinions of one another. All being nearly equal in circumstances, and all nearly alike in intelligence and knowledge, the only authority which commands an involuntary deference is that of numbers. The more perfectly each knows himself the equal of every single individual, the more insignificant and helpless he feels against the aggregate mass; and the more incredible it appears to him that the opinion of all the world can possibly be erroneous. "Faith in public opinion," says M. de Tocqueville, "becomes in such countries a species of religion, and the majority its prophet." The idea that the things which the multitude believe are still disputable, is no longer kept alive by dissentient voices; the right of private judgment, by being extended to the incompetent, ceases to be exercised even by the competent; and speculation becomes possible only within the limits traced, not as of old by the infallibility of Aristotle, but by that of "our free and enlightened citizens," or "our free and enlightened age."

On the influence of Democracy upon the cultivation of science and art, the opinions of M. de Tocqueville are highly worthy of attention. There are many who, partly from theoretic considerations, and partly from the marked absence in America of original efforts in literature, philosophy, or the fine arts, incline to believe that modern democracy is fatal to them, and that wherever its spirit spreads they will take flight. M. de Tocqueville is not of this opinion. The example of America, as he observes, is not to the purpose, because America is, intellectually speaking, a province of England; a province in which the great occupation of the inhabitants is making money, because for that they have peculiar facilities, and are therefore, like the people of Manchester or Birmingham, for the most part contented to receive the higher branches of knowledge ready-made from the capital. In a democratic nation, which is also free, and generally educated, our author is far from thinking that there will be no public to relish or remunerate the works of science and genius. Although there will be great shifting of fortunes, and no hereditary body of wealthy persons sufficient to form a class, there will be, he thinks, from the general activity and the absence of artificial barriers, combined with the inequality of human intelligence, a far greater number of rich individuals (*infiniment plus nombreux*) than in an aristocratic society. There will be, therefore, though not so complete a leisure, yet a leisure extending perhaps to more persons; while from the closer contact and greater mutual intercourse between classes, the love of intellectual pleasures and occupations will spread downward very widely among those who have not the same advantages of leisure. Moreover, talents and knowledge being in a democratic society the only means of rapid improvement in fortune, they will be, in the abstract at least, by no means undervalued; whatever measure of them any person is capable of appreciating, he will also be desirous of possessing. Instead, therefore, of any neglect of science and literature, the eager ambition which is universal in such a state of society takes that direction as well as others, and the number of those who cultivate these pursuits becomes "immense."

It is from this fact—from the more active competition in the products of intellect, and the more numerous public to which they are addressed—that M. de Tocqueville deduces the defects with which the products themselves will be chargeable. In the multiplication of their quantity he sees the deterioration of their quality. Distracted by so great a multitude, the public can bestow but a moment's attention on each; they will be adapted, therefore, chiefly for striking at the moment. Deliberate approval, and a duration beyond the hour, become more and more difficult of attainment. What is written for the judgment of a highly instructed few, amidst the abundance of writings may very probably never reach them; and their suffrage, which never gave riches, does not now confer even glory. But the multitude of buyers affords the possibility of great pecuniary success and momentary notoriety, for the work which is made up to please at once, and to please the many. Literature thus becomes not only a trade, but is carried on by the maxims usually adopted by other trades which live by the number, rather than by the quality, of their customers; that much pains need not be bestowed on commodities intended for the general market, and that what is saved in the workmanship may be more profitably expended in self-advertisement. There will thus be an immense mass of third and fourth-rate productions, and very few first-rate. Even the turmoil and bustle of a society in which every one is striving to get on, is in itself, our author observes, not favourable to meditation. "Il règne dans le sein de ces nations un petit mouvement incommode, une sorte de roulement incessant des hommes les uns sur les autres, qui trouble et distrait l'esprit sans l'animer et l'élever." Not to mention that the universal tendency to action, and to rapid action, directs the taste to applications rather than principles, and hasty approximations to truth rather than scientific accuracy in it.

Passing now from the province of intellect to that of sentiments and morals, M. de Tocqueville is of opinion that the general softening of manners, and the remarkable growth, in modern times, of humanity and philanthropy, are in great part the effect of the gradual progress of social equality. Where the different classes of mankind are divided by impassable barriers, each may have intense sympathies with his own class, more intense than it is almost possible to have with mankind in general; but those who are far below him in condition are so unlike himself, that he hardly considers them as human beings; and if they are refractory and troublesome, will be unable to feel for them even that kindly interest which he experiences for his more unresisting domestic cattle. Our author cites a well-known passage of Madame de Sévigné's Letters, in exemplification of the want of feeling exhibited even by good sort of persons towards those with whom they have no fellow-feeling. In America, except towards the slaves (an exception which proves the rule,) he finds the sentiments of philanthropy and compassion almost universal, accompanied by a general kindness of manner and obligingness of disposition, without much of ceremony and punctilio. As all feel that they are not above the possible need of the good-will and good offices of others, every one is ready to afford his own. The general equality penetrates also into the family relations: there is more intimacy, he thinks, than in Europe, between parents and children, but less, except in the earliest years, of paternal authority, and the filial respect which is founded on it. This, however, is among the topics which we must omit; as well as the connexion which our author attempts to trace between equality of conditions and strictness of domestic morals, and some other remarks on domestic society in America, which do not appear to us to be of any considerable value.

M. de Tocqueville is of opinion, that one of the tendencies of a democratic state of society is to make every one, in a manner, retire within himself, and concentrate his interests, wishes, and pursuits within his own business and household.

The members of a democratic community are like the sands of the sea-shore, each very minute, and no one adhering to any other. There are no permanent classes, and therefore no esprit de corps; few hereditary fortunes, and therefore few local attachments, or outward objects consecrated by family feeling. A man feels little connexion with his neighbours, little with his ancestors, little with his posterity. There are scarcely any ties to connect any two men together, except the common one of country. Now, the love of country is not, in large communities, a passion of spontaneous growth. When a man's country is his town, where his ancestors have lived for generations, of which he knows every inhabitant, and has recollections associated with every street and building—in which alone, of all places on the earth, he is not a stranger—which he is perpetually called upon to defend in the field, and in whose glory or shame he has an appreciable share, made sensible by the constant presence and rivalry of foreigners; in such a state of things patriotism is easy. It was easy in the ancient republics, or in modern Switzerland. But in great communities an intense interest in public affairs is scarcely natural, except to a member of an aristocracy, who alone has so conspicuous a position, and is so personally identified with the conduct of the government, that his credit and consequence are essentially connected with the glory and power of the nation he belongs to; its glory and power (observe,) not the well-being of the bulk of its inhabitants. It is difficult for an obscure person like the citizen of a democracy, who is in no way involved in the responsibility of public affairs, and cannot hope to exercise more than the minutest influence over them, to have the sentiment of patriotism as a living and earnest feeling. There being no intermediate objects for his attachments to fix upon, they fasten themselves on his own private affairs; and, according to national character and circumstances, it becomes his ruling passion either to improve his condition in life, or to take his ease and pleasure by the means which it already affords him.

As, therefore, the state of society becomes more democratic, it is more and more necessary to nourish patriotism by artificial means; and of these none are so efficacious as free institutions—a large and frequent intervention of the citizens in the management of public business. Nor does the love of country alone require this encouragement, but every feeling which connects men either by interest or sympathy with their neighbours and fellow-citizens. Popular institutions are the great means of rendering general in a people, and especially among the richer classes, the desire of being useful in their generation; useful to the public, or to their neighbours without distinction of rank; as well as courteous and unassuming in their habitual intercourse.

* * *

M. de Tocqueville considers a democratic state of society as eminently tending to give the strongest impulse to the desire of physical well-being. He ascribes this, not so much to the equality of conditions as to their mobility. In a country like America every one may acquire riches; no one, at least, is artificially impeded in acquiring them; and hardly any one is born to them. Now, these are the conditions under which the passions which attach themselves to wealth, and to what wealth can purchase, are the strongest. Those who are born in the midst of affluence are generally more or less *blasés* to its enjoyments.

They take the comfort or luxury to which they have always been accustomed, as they do the air they breathe. It is not *le but de la vie*, but *une manière de vivre*. An aristocracy, when put to the proof, has in general shown wonderful facility in enduring the loss of riches and of physical comforts. The very pride, nourished by the elevation which they owned to wealth, supports them under the privation of it. But to those who have chased riches laboriously for half their lives, to lose it is the loss of all; *une vie manquée*; a disappointment greater than can be endured. In a democracy, again, there is no contented poverty. No one being forced to remain poor; many who were poor daily becoming rich, and the comforts of life being apparently within the reach of all, the desire to appropriate them descends to the very lowest rank.

* * *

A regulated sensuality thus established itself—the parent of effeminacy rather than of debauchery; paying respect to the social rights of other people and to the opinion of the world; not "leading men away in search of forbidden enjoyments, but absorbing them in the pursuit of permitted ones. This spirit is frequently combined with a species of religious morality; men wish to be as well off as they can in this world, without foregoing their chance of another."

From the preternatural stimulus given to the desire of acquiring and of enjoying wealth, by the intense competition which necessarily exists where an entire population are the competitors, arises the restlessness so characteristic of American life.

* * *

And hence, according to M. de Tocqueville, while every one is devoured by ambition, hardly any one is ambitious on a large scale. Among so many competitors for but a few great prizes, none of the candidates starting from the vantage ground of an elevated social position, very few can hope to gain those prizes, and they not until late in life. Men in general, therefore, do not look so high. A vast energy of passion in a whole community is developed and squandered in the petty pursuit of petty advancements in fortune, and the hurried snatching of petty pleasures.

To sum up our author's opinion of the dangers to which mankind are liable as they advance towards equality of condition; his fear, both in government and in intellect and morals, is not of too great liberty, but of too ready submission; not of anarchy, but of servility; not of too rapid change, but of Chinese stationariness. As democracy advances, the opinions of mankind on most subjects of general interest will become, he believes, as compared with any former period, more rooted and more difficult to change; and mankind are more and more in danger of losing the moral courage and pride of independence, which make them deviate from the beaten path, either in speculation or in conduct. Even in politics, it is to be apprehended lest, feeling their personal insignificance, and conceiving a proportionally vast idea of the importance of society at large; being jealous, moreover, of one another, but not jealous of the central power which derives its origin from the majority, or which at least is the faithful representative of its desire to annihilate every intermediate power—they should allow that central government to assume more and more control, engross more and more of the business of society; and, on condition of making itself the organ of the general mode of feeling and thinking, should suffer it to relieve mankind from the care of their own interests, and keep them under a kind of tutelage; trampling meanwhile with considerable recklessness, as often as convenient, upon the rights of individuals, in the name of society and the public good.

Against these political evils the corrective to which our author looks is popular education, and, above all, the spirit of liberty, fostered by the extension and dissemination of political rights. Democratic institutions, therefore, are his remedy for the worst mischiefs to which a democratic state of society is exposed. As for those to which democratic institutions are themselves liable, these, he holds, society must struggle with, and bear with so much of them as it cannot find the means of conquering. For M. de Tocqueville is no believer in the reality of mixed governments. There is, he says, always and everywhere, a strongest power: in every government either the king, the aristocracy, or the people, have an effective predominance, and can carry any point on which they set their heart. "When a community really comes to have a mixed government, that is, to be equally divided between two adverse principles, it is either falling into a revolutionary state or into dissolution." M. de Tocqueville believes that the preponderant power, which must exist everywhere, is most rightly placed in the body of the people. But he thinks it most pernicious that this power, whether residing in the people or elsewhere, should be "checked by no obstacles which may retard its course, and force it to moderate its own vehemence." The difference, in his eyes, is great between one sort of democratic institutions and another. That form of democracy should be sought out and devised, and in every way endeavoured to be carried into practice, which, on the one hand, most exercises and cultivates the intelligence and mental activity of the majority; and, on the other, breaks the headlong impulses of popular opinion, by delay, rigour of forms, and adverse discussion. "The organization and the establishment of democracy" on these principles "is the great political problem of our time."

And when this problem is solved, there remains an equally serious one; to make head against the tendency of democracy towards bearing down individuality, and circumscribing the exercise of the human faculties within narrow limits. To sustain the higher pursuits of philosophy and art; to vindicate and protect the unfettered exercise of reason, and the moral freedom of the individual—these are purposes to which, under a democracy, the superior spirits, and the government so far as it is permitted, should devote their utmost energies.

* * *

If we were here to close this article, and leave these noble speculations to produce their effect without further comment, the reader probably would not blame us. Our recommendation is not needed in their behalf. That nothing on the whole comparable in profundity to them has yet been written on Democracy, will scarcely be disputed by any one who has read even our hasty abridgment of them. We must guard, at the same time, against attaching to these conclusions, or to any others that can result from such inquiries, a character of scientific certainty that can never belong to them. Democracy is too recent a phenomenon, and of too great magnitude, for any one who now lives to comprehend its consequences. A few of its more immediate tendencies may be perceived or surmised; what other tendencies, destined to overrule or to combine with these, lie behind, there are not grounds even to conjecture. * * *

It is not, therefore, without a deep sense of the uncertainty attaching to such predictions, that the wise would hazard an opinion as to the fate of mankind under the new democratic dispensation. But without pretending to judge confidently of remote tendencies, those immediate ones which are already developing themselves require to be dealt with as we treat any of the other circumstances in which we are placed;—by encouraging those which are salutary, and working out the means by which such as are hurtful may be counteracted. To exhort men to this, and to aid them in doing it, is the end for which M. de Tocqueville has written: and in the same spirit we will now venture to make one criticism upon him;—to point out one correction, of which we think his views stand in need; and for want of which they have occasionally an air of over-subtlety and false refinement, exciting the distrust of common readers, and making the opinions themselves appear less true, and less practically important, than, it seems to us, they really are.

M. de Tocqueville, then, has, at least apparently, confounded the effects of Democracy with the effects of Civilization. He has bound up in one abstract idea the whole of the tendencies of modern commercial society, and given them one name—Democracy; thereby letting it be supposed that he ascribes to equality of conditions, several of the effects naturally arising from the mere progress of national prosperity, in the form in which that progress manifests itself in modern times.

It is no doubt true, that among the tendencies of commercial civilization, a tendency to the equalization of conditions is one, and not the least conspicuous. When a nation is advancing in prosperity—when its industry is expanding, and its capital rapidly augmenting—the number also of those who possess capital increases in at least as great a proportion; and though the distance between the two extremes of society may not be much diminished, there is a rapid multiplication of those who occupy the intermediate positions. There may be princes at one end of the scale and paupers at the other; but between them there will be a respectable and well-paid class of artisans, and a middle class who combine property and industry. This may be called, and is, a tendency to equalization. But this growing equality is only one of the features of progressive civilization; one of the incidental effects of the progress of industry and wealth: a most important effect, and one which, as our author shows, re-acts in a hundred ways upon the other effects, but not therefore to be confounded with the cause.

So far is it, indeed, from being admissible, that *mere* equality of conditions is the mainspring of those moral and social phenomena which M. de Tocqueville has characterized, that when some unusual chance exhibits to us equality of conditions by itself, severed from that commercial state of society and that progress of industry of which it is the natural concomitant, it produces few or none of the moral effects ascribed to it. Consider, for instance, the French of Lower Canada. Equality of conditions is more universal there than in the United States; for the whole people, without exception, are in easy circumstances, and there are not even that considerable number of rich individuals who are to be found in all the great towns of the American Republic. Yet do we find in Canada that go-ahead spirit—that restless, impatient eagerness for improvement in circumstances—that mobility, that shifting and fluctuating, now up now down, now here now there—that absence of classes and class-spirit—that jealousy of superior attainments—that want of deference for authority and leadership—that habit of bringing things to the rule and square of each man's own understanding—which M. de Tocqueville imputes to the same cause in the United States? In all these respects the very contrary qualities prevail. We by no means deny that where the other circumstances which determine these effects exist, equality of conditions has a very perceptible effect in corroborating them. We think M. de Tocqueville has shown that it has. But that it is the exclusive, or even the principal cause, we think the example of Canada goes far to disprove.

For the reverse of this experiment, we have only to look at home. Of all countries in a state of progressive commercial civilization, Great Britain is that in which the equalization of conditions has made least progress. The extremes of wealth and poverty are wider apart, and there is a more numerous body of persons at each extreme, than in any other commercial community. From the habits of the population in regard to marriage, the poor have remained poor; from the laws which tend to keep large masses of property together, the rich have remained rich; and often, when they have lost the substance of riches, have retained its social advantages and outward trappings. Great fortunes are continually accumulated, and seldom redistributed. In this respect, therefore, England is the most complete contrast to the United States. But in commercial prosperity, in the rapid growth of industry and wealth, she is the next after America, and not very much inferior to her. Accordingly we appeal to all competent observers, whether, in nearly all the moral and intellectual features of American society, as represented by M. de Tocqueville, this country does not stand next to America? whether, with the single difference of our remaining respect for aristocracy, the American people, both in their good qualities and in their defects, resemble anything so much as an exaggeration of our own middle class? whether the spirit, which is gaining more and more the ascendant with us, is not in a very great degree American? and whether all the moral elements of an American state of society are not most rapidly growing up?

For example, that entire unfixedness in the social position of individuals—that treading upon the heels of one another—that habitual dissatisfaction of each with the position he occupies, and eager desire to push himself into the next above it—has not this become, and is it not becoming more and more, an English characteristic? In England, as well as in America, it appears to foreigners, and even to Englishmen recently returned from a foreign country, as if everybody had but one wish—to improve his condition, never to enjoy it; as if no Englishman cared to cultivate either the pleasures or the virtues corresponding to his station in society, but solely to get out of it as quickly as possible; or if that cannot be done, and until it is done, to seem to have got out of it. "The hypocrisy of luxury," as M. de Tocqueville calls the maintaining an appearance beyond one's real expenditure, he considers as a democratic peculiarity. It is surely an English one. The highest class of all, indeed, is, as might be expected, comparatively exempt from these bad peculiarities. But the very existence of such a class, whose immunities and political privileges are attainable by wealth, tends to aggravate the struggle of the other classes for the possession of that passport to all other importance; and it perhaps required the example of America to prove that the "sabbathless pursuit of wealth" could be as intensely prevalent, where there were no aristocratic distinctions to tempt to it.

Again, the mobility and fluctuating nature of individual relations—the absence of permanent ties, local or personal; how often has this been commented on as one of the organic changes by which the ancient structure of English society is becoming dissolved? Without reverting to the days of clanship, or to those in which the gentry led a patriarchal life among their tenantry and neighbours, the memory of man extends to a time when the same tenants remained attached to the same landlords, the same servants to the same household. But this, with other old customs, after progressively retiring to the remote corners of our island, has nearly taken flight altogether; and it may now be said that in all the relations of life, except those to which law and religion have given permanence, change has become the general rule, and constancy the exception.

The remainder of the tendencies which M. de Tocqueville has delineated, may mostly be brought under one general agency as their immediate cause; the growing insignificance of individuals in comparison with the mass. Now, it would be difficult to show any country in which this insignificance is more marked and conspicuous than in England, or any incompatibility between that tendency and aristocratic institutions. It is not because the individuals composing the mass are all equal, but because the mass itself has grown to so immense a size, that individuals are powerless in the face of it; and because the mass, having, by mechanical improvements, become capable of acting simultaneously, can compel not merely any individual, but any number of individuals, to bend before it. The House of Lords is the richest and most powerful collection of persons in Europe, yet they not only could not prevent, but were themselves compelled to pass, the Reform Bill. The daily actions of every peer and peeress are falling more and more under the yoke of *bourgeois* opinion; they feel every day a stronger necessity of showing an immaculate front to the world. When they do venture to disregard common opinion, it is in a body, and when supported by one another; whereas formerly every nobleman acted on his own notions, and dared be as eccentric as he pleased. No rank in society is now exempt from the fear of being peculiar, the unwillingness to be, or to be thought, in any respect original. Hardly anything now depends upon individuals, but all upon classes, and among classes mainly upon the middle class. That class is now the power in society, the arbiter of fortune and success. Ten times more money is made by supplying the wants, even the superfluous wants, of the middle, nay of the lower classes, than those of the higher. It is the middle class that now rewards even literature and art; the books by which most money is made are the cheap books; the greatest part of the profit of a picture is the profit of the engraving from it. Accordingly, all the intellectual effects which M. de Tocqueville ascribes to Democracy, are taking place under the democracy of the middle class. There is a greatly augmented number of moderate successes, fewer great literary and scientific reputations. Elementary and popular treatises are immensely multiplied, superficial information far more widely diffused; but there are fewer who devote themselves to thought for its own sake, and pursue in retirement those profounder researches, the results of which can only be appreciated by a few. Literary productions are seldom highly finished—they are got up to be read by many, and to be read but once. If the work sells for a day, the author's time and pains will be better laid out in writing a second, than in improving the first. And this is not because books are no longer written for the aristocracy: they never were so. The aristocracy (saving individual exceptions) never were a reading class. It is because books are now written for a numerous, and therefore an unlearned public; no longer principally for scholars and men of science, who have knowledge of their own, and are not imposed upon by half-knowledge—who have studied the great works of genius, and can make comparisons.

As for the decay of authority, and diminution of respect for traditional opinions, this could not well be so far advanced among an ancient people—all whose political notions rest on an historical basis, and whose institutions themselves are built on prescription, and not on ideas of expediency—as in America, where the whole edifice of government was constructed within the memory of man upon abstract principles. But surely this change also is taking place as fast as could be expected under the circumstances. And even this effect, though it has a more direct connexion with Democracy, has not an exclusive one. Respect for old opinions must diminish wherever science and knowledge are rapidly progressive. As the people in general become aware of the recent date of the most important physical discoveries, they are liable to form a rather contemptuous opinion of their ancestors. The mere visible fruits of scientific progress in a wealthy society, the mechanical improvements, the steam-engines, the railroads, carry the feeling of admiration for modern and disrespect for ancient times down even to the wholly uneducated classes. For that other mental characteristic which M. de Tocqueville finds in America—a positive, matter-of-fact spirit—a demand that all things shall be made clear to each man's understanding—an indifference to the subtler proofs which address themselves to more cultivated and systematically exercised intellects; for what may be called, in short, the dogmatism of common sense—we need not look beyond our own country. There needs no Democracy to account for this; there needs only the habit of energetic action, without a proportional development of the taste for speculation. Bonaparte was one of the most remarkable examples of it; and the diffusion of half-instruction, without any sufficient provision made by society for sustaining the higher cultivation, tends greatly to encourage its excess.

Nearly all those moral and social influences, therefore, which are the subject of M. de Tocqueville's second part, are shown to be in full operation in aristocratic England. What connexion they have with equality is with the growth of the middle class, not with the annihilation of the extremes. They are quite compatible with the existence of peers and *prolétaires*; nay, with the most abundant provision of both those varieties of human nature. If we were sure of retaining for ever our aristocratic institutions, society would no less have to struggle against all these tendencies; and perhaps even the loss of those institutions would not have so much effect as is supposed in accelerating their triumph.

The evil is not in the preponderance of a democratic class, but of any class. The defects which M. de Tocqueville points out in the American, and which we see in the modern English mind, are the ordinary ones of a commercial class. The portion of society which is predominant in America, and that which is attaining predominance here, the American Many, and our middle class, agree in being commercial classes. The one country is affording a complete, and the other a progressive exemplification, that whenever any variety of human nature becomes preponderant in a community, it imposes upon all the rest of society its own type; forcing all, either to submit to it or to imitate it.

* * *

It is not needful to go into a similar analysis of the tendencies of the other two classes—a leisured, and a learned class. The capabilities which they possess for controlling the excess of the commercial spirit by a contrary spirit, are at once apparent. We regard it as one of the greatest advantages of this country over America, that it possesses both these classes; and we believe that the interests of the time to come are greatly dependent upon preserving them; and upon their being rendered, as they much require to be, better and better qualified for their important functions.

If we believed that the national character of England, instead of reacting upon the American character and raising it, was gradually assimilating itself to those points of it which the best and wisest

Americans see with most uneasiness, it would be no consolation to us to think that we might possibly avoid the institutions of America; for we should have all the effects of her institutions, except those which are beneficial. The American Many are not essentially a different class from our ten-pound householders; and if the middle class are left to the mere habits and instincts of a commercial community, we shall have a "tyranny of the majority," not the less irksome because most of the tyrants may not be manual labourers. For it is a chimerical hope to overbear or outnumber the middle class; whatever modes of voting, whatever redistribution of the constituencies, are really necessary for placing the government in their hands, those, whether we like it or not, they will assuredly obtain.

The ascendancy of the commercial class in modern society and politics is inevitable, and, under due limitations, ought not to be regarded as an evil. That class is the most powerful; but it needs not therefore be all-powerful. Now, as ever, the great problem in government is to prevent the strongest from becoming the only power; and repress the natural tendency of the instincts and passions of the ruling body, to sweep away all barriers which are capable of resisting, even for a moment, their own tendencies. Any counterbalancing power can henceforth exist only by the sufferance of the commercial class; but that it should tolerate some such limitation, we deem as important as that it should not itself be held in vassalge.

INTERPRETATIONS

DAVID RIESMAN

Tocqueville as Ethnographer†

America in the first half of the nineteenth century was visited by a large number of articulate and often distinguished travelers from all the countries of Western Europe. British Tories came to confirm their prejudices against democracy and a few radicals came to confirm their symphaties. Many, like Dickens, were interested in the novel achievements of American philanthropy: the care of the poor, the unlettered, the mill hand, the prisoner. (It would be a rare inquirer who came to America today to look at our prisons!) But while we read Dickens or Mrs. Trollope now because of their eye for local color and the picture of American manners they present, we do not read them to understand our contemporary America. Those who criticized our bad manners or described our quaint customs amuse us more than they interest or annoy us. It is to Alexis de Tocqueville that we continue to turn for understanding, because the issues that preoccupied him were those he saw as portentous for France and for all of Europe, namely, the consequences for liberty of the growing equality of condition. Although he gathered and had sent to him a great stack of documents on juridical matters, and although his notebooks describe places and scenes to some extent, Tocqueville lived during his journeys in his moral imagination. No other visitor has to my knowledge been so little distracted by the accidental and so sensitive to implication. This was especially the case with his reflective second volume of *Democracy in America*, which he published five years after the first. As he wrote, "On leaving the ideas which American and French society presented me, *I wish to set out the general tendencies of democratic societies of which no complete example yet exists.*"[1]

Tocqueville had come to this country in 1831 at the age of twenty-six, along with his friend Beaumont, with whom he had secured a commission to look at American prisons and methods of penal reform. Although the young men did their duty by the prisons and wrote a report, this assignment proved a useful cover for their more important cultural mission—a mission complicated by the defensiveness of the Americans. As Tocqueville noted, ". . . to be on good terms with them, you have to praise them a great deal. I do it with all my heart, without its affecting my manner of seeing. The national pride induces them to do everything they can to fascinate our eyes and to show us

† David Riesman (1909–2002) was a professor in the department of social relations at Harvard University and the author of *The Lonely Crowd*. This essay appeared in *The American Scholar*, 30 (1961): 174–87. Reprinted by permission.
1. Quoted by J. P. Mayer, "Tocqueville's Influence," *History*, No. 3 (1960), Meridian, pp. 87–103, on p. 90.

only the fine side of things; but I hope we will manage to find out the truth."[2]

Tocqueville, an aristocrat and a Catholic, had not come to America in the hope of finding a brave new world. Rather, facing the legacies of the French Revolution which had been for him part of both his family biography and the nation's fate, he came in order to understand better what might be in store for his own country and what might be done by wise policy to make the coming age of democracy and equality less despotic and more free. He put this serious mission into the introduction of *Democracy in America*:

> I confess that in America I saw more than America; I saw there the image of democracy itself, with its inclinations, its character, its prejudices, and its passions, in order to learn what we have to fear or to hope from its progress.

Democracy in America is singularly free of detailed descriptions of people and places. (Beaumont, in contrast, kept a sketchbook and Pierson's book reprints many of his drawings.) As I have indicated, Tocqueville's book is a work not of observation but of interpretation, particularly so in the second volume where he discusses potential supports and hazards for liberty, arising less in the juridical and institutional spheres than in the psychological and cultural ones. In envisaging what an "ideal" (that is, complete) democracy would be like were it to go further in the American direction—further, that is, away from where Europe presently was, he imagined himself into the mind of a citizen of such a nonexistent land and pictured for himself how all aspects of life, from the image of the Deity to articles of commerce and fictions of the mind, would look to such a hypothetical person. He deployed his actual experiences in America to illustrate rather than to bound or limit his conception. He did not ask himself whether the sailor who told him that vessels were jerry-built because they would soon be made obsolete by the progress of invention was a typical American or not, for what he said fitted in with Tocqueville's vision. This inchoate "method," if we may use so formal a term, was fundamentally aristocratic in the sense that not everyone would be equally good at it. As a result, Tocqueville founded no school and the centenary of his death in 1959 was little celebrated.

The America to which Tocqueville and Beaumont came (they made a side journey, useful for comparative purposes, to Quebec) consisted of thirteen million people. And young, smart French visitors were sufficiently rare to give them access to anyone whom they wanted to see. Furthermore, the absence of a French colony in the United States protected them from filtering their own impressions through an already congealed ideology. However, as Pierson's book makes plain in providing us with the detailed trajectory of the nine months the young men spent

2. George Wilson Pierson, *Tocqueville and Beaumont in America*, Oxford University Press, 1938, pp. 73–74.

in this country, it is surprising how much Tocqueville transcended the prejudices of his informants, among whom were Hudson River patricians, embittered Federalist politicians, Catholic priests fearing the spread of Unitarianism, and men like Charles Carroll who regretted the passing of aristocratic forms. As scholars have pointed out, Tocqueville did go astray in some particulars (for instance, concerning the laws of inheritance), and Tocqueville left America with apparently little sense of the importance of President Jackson and what Marvin Meyers has called "the Jacksonian persuasion."[3] Yet Tocqueville liked America more than many of his conservative informants did and more perhaps than he had himself expected to: he liked the lack of servility, the freestanding quality of people who in his own country would be peasants, the self-reliant spirit and energy that he saw on all sides. For in the course of his travels he met innkeepers, traders, boatmen and such.

There is, inevitably, a bias in such encounters, unless one supplements them with a sample survey or knows already where to look for those whom one will not ordinarily meet. The Americans who were visible to Tocqueville and Beaumont were naturally the more active ones: the gregarious, the enterprising, the articulate, rather than the isolated and submerged. If they were farmers, they were more likely to be those up-and-coming ones who regarded their land as a property held for speculation than those withdrawn and secluded ones who regarded it as an inheritance to be conserved with a peasantlike tenacity. One finds in Tocqueville's pages neither the indolent, self-indulgent and shiftless frontiersmen whom Horace Greeley found in Kansas just before the Civil War, nor such groups as the pietistic Pennsylvania Dutch who even in today's America manage to seal themselves off in rural enclaves from currents of change. At the same time, the people Tocqueville did meet were precisely those who had more than a proportionate share in deciding what America was to be like. In that sense, the visitor's problem in discovering the typical was made easier by the dialectic his presence evoked.

There is evidence, however, that the image of America as a land of eager, enterprising, activist joiners and strivers has been overdone since the beginning. In frontier days, there were many who were isolated and unchurched, reached at most by an occasional revival. Today various researches show that the economic underdog and especially the older person is often entirely isolated: he may possibly be an inactive member of a trade union and an occasional churchgoer, but he is likely to have no other ties than this, beyond the pseudo-*Gemeinschaft* that television and the other mass media provide. (Church membership in terms of formal affiliation is much higher than in Tocqueville's day.) Granted these submerged exceptions, Tocqueville was nevertheless right to emphasize the difference between the mobile and fluid

---

3. See Marvin Meyers, *The Jacksonian Persuasion*, Stanford University Press, 1957, especially Chapter II. In Tocqueville's pages, one gets very little sense of the extent and inanity of snobbery, such as emerges from Francis J. Grund, *Aristocracy in America: From the Sketchbook of a German Nobleman*, Harper Torchbook edition, 1959.

organizational life of the average American and the usual French en-
capsulation in the ties of family and parish. Tocqueville, like other visitors, stressed what we might call the associational literacy of the
Americans, who on their own in a new country had learned how to
form a committee, how to advertise it in the newspapers and how to
go on then to the next job that needed doing.

One large group of silent Americans Tocqueville left largely to the
researches of his fellow ethnographer, Beaumont; I refer to the slaves.
Tocqueville was characteristically perceptive in seeing that the South
was different and that the issue of slavery might lead to an explosion,
and he was aware (as his later correspondence with Gobineau
showed) of the dangers of racism; in *Democracy in America* he rejects
racial and geographic explanations of national character. Beaumont's
work, however, made it possible for Tocqueville to concentrate on the
North and in this respect, too, on the American future. However, he
was here before the coming of the railways and before industrialism
had made any appreciable dent on the American landscape. Thus, he
confronted a largely commercial-agrarian but preindustrial culture
and was not distracted from his main task either by the slavery issue,
or by the colorful arguments over mechanization and industry: the factory system did not divert Tocqueville from the social system. Here,
too, he foresaw more than he could actually see: he described some of
the psychological reasons why mass production would appeal to the
American market; and he expressed his fear that the Americans might
succumb to a despotism of manufacturers facing laborers too handi-
capped by their dulling and constricting work to be free and mobile.
Considering the small scale of industrial development in 1831, this
glimpse of what America might look like in the age of the tycoon is
even more startling than Tocqueville's famous prediction that America
would have a population of one hundred and fifty million to face an
equally powerful Russia for the destiny of the world. Even though
Tocqueville continuously encountered American boasting (and its underlying defensiveness and vulnerability to criticism), it is doubtful
whether these images of the future were simple transpositions of what
his informants thought.

Tocqueville was protected against certain orders of mistake by being
an aristocrat with a country seat. We can get a sense of this by comparing *Democracy in America* with Dickens' *American Notes*. Dickens,
coming eleven years later, with a keen consciousness of the industrial
blight and urban slums of Britain, was an eager visitor to the Lowell
Mills, precursors of modern welfare state capitalism. He seems not to
have escaped a visit to a single charitable institution in Boston,
whether for orphans or for the insane or for what we would today call
juvenile delinquents—much as sentimental but uncritical visitors to
the Soviet Union in the 1930's were taken on tours of similar institutions. But on the other hand Dickens was terribly upset by American
crudity. He could not stand seeing ill-kempt men spitting on the car-
pets of the White House and lounging about without respect for the

authorities; spitting got in the way of his vision, as it did for Mrs. Trollope—just as other coarse parvenu traits obscured the vision of many travelers and residents in the early years of the Soviet Union. The author of *Great Expectations* could not generalize from his extraordinary psychological understanding of individuals to a whole society of Pips, not all of whom were ennobled by the vision of Estelle. The picture he gives of America is colorful and, in details, accurate, as in his comments on American gregariousness or love of comfort, but it remains superficial. In contrast Tocqueville, less threatened by grossness, observed that Americans lacked both great coarseness and great refinement. And his personal sense of the qualities of an aristocratic milieu was used constantly as an intellectual foil in developing his abstract conception of "democratic nations."

Democracy in America is addressed primarily to Tocqueville's aristocratic and conservative French friends. It is the plea of a man who feels that a romantic conservatism which rejects democracy and all the institutions of the modern world is doomed to end either in despotism or inanity, and that liberty—the principal value in life for which a man should care—would be best preserved by working with, rather than against, the grain of modernity, the long, slow, centuries-old march toward social equality. Tocqueville pleads that democracy, although it will never be elegant and although it may not give adequate place to excellence whether in workmanship or in art, could nevertheless be tamed and tempered. The remedy for the evils of democracy is not a hopeless quest for reaction. (John Lukacs argues in his introduction to Tocqueville's *The European Revolution and Correspondence with Gobineau* that Tocqueville today would be out of sympathy with the conservatives' fear of socialism.) Democracy could be kept from becoming despotic and the tyranny of the majority moderated by providing, on the one hand, political bulkheads such as the Founding Fathers had fashioned and, on the other, a cultural style invigorated by the individual experience of citizenship and chastened by the restraints of religion (which Tocqueville saw not in terms of individual salvation, but in terms of social cement). On so sober a platform, a Tory radical might unite with Matthew Arnold or with Tocqueville's friend, John Stuart Mill. It is a platform that attracts many Americans who want to surrender neither political democracy nor social equality, but who are afraid of revolutionary zeal, are not particularly aroused by injustice, and largely share the consensus Louis Hartz describes in *The Liberal Tradition in America*.

Tocqueville was impressed with the American separation of powers, as a therapy both for atomization and for excessive centralization—an attitude later strengthened by his work on *L'Ancien Régime*. He was also persuaded that the separation of Church and State strengthened religion, especially Catholicism, and was therefore a good thing for democracy. Indeed, the competing churches were for Tocqueville one example of what he regarded as the most efficacious and most characteristic American invention for the defense of political liberty, that is, the encouragement that liberty itself provided for forming decentralized associations. He saw political liberty as primarily an educational device that would teach men, reduced in individual stature by equality, to remain or become self-reliant and realistic. He regarded the town meeting as a principal school of this sort (not realizing from the accounts of his Whig friends the extent to which it had decayed). And, to his timorous and conservative compatriots, he emphasized the importance of America's bubbling associational life as increasing the distribution of political competence. Speaking of the democrat's "facility in prosecuting great undertakings in common," he declared:

> Political associations may therefore be considered as large free schools, where all members of the community go to learn the general theory of association. . . . Thus it is by the enjoyment of a dangerous freedom that the Americans learn the art of rendering the dangers of freedom less formidable.

Furthermore, Tocqueville insisted that the free press was essential as the organizational tool of associational life. By means of the press people learned that there were others of like mind with whom they could join when they could not know this automatically through membership in the same family or lifelong residence in a village. Accordingly, Tocqueville pictured Americans as busy with an infinite variety of associations, some private, some political, cannily making use of the newspapers as the basis for recruitment and excitement. (Curiously, he seems not to have reported the tremendous outcry against the Masonic order which was underway when he was here; his notebooks reveal his awareness of the kidnapping and murder of an ex-Mason that touched off this outcry, but Tocqueville gained little sense of what Edward Shils called "the torment of secrecy," the fear of being on the outside, the fear of conspiracy, that was in 1831 already a dark undercurrent in American life.) Tocqueville's attention, however, was focused less on the Masons and other lodges (whose role in American life today seems much attenuated, perhaps in part because formality no longer seems interesting or worthwhile) than on the associations Americans formed to organize a church (parishes not being given in the landscape), to found a hospital, to crusade for temperance, to build a college.

Above all, he was tremendously struck with the perfervid political activity of Americans which he seems to have taken as a regular feature of our national life and not as a periodic response to a leader and framer of issues such as Andrew Jackson. From his pages, one gets a picture of Americans marching forth from their domestic castles and from what he referred to as the dangerous solitude of the individual's own heart to learn the latest news of the courthouse, or to manifest their loyalties at a political rally—and to gain in this way a sense of confidence about what individuals when grouped together could accomplish, and a realistic awareness of the problems of the local and national life. Furthermore, he observed a kind of counterpoint between the easy gregariousness of politics and the exclusiveness of private life. Thus he wrote:

The Americans, who mingle so readily in their political assemblies and courts of justice, are wont on the contrary to carefully separate into small distinct circles, in order to indulge by themselves in the enjoyments of private life.

Tocqueville's view of civic activity as perhaps the chief affair of the civilized and educated man has an Athenian style (compare the eloquent discussion in Hannah Arendt's *The Human Condition*). For Tocqueville, political liberty was itself of value, something that made men manly as well as averted the evils of social equality. But, by the same token, Tocqueville feared American individualism (a term he himself brought into use, but that he regarded not as we do, but as similar to egocentricity or solipsism), a withdrawal into "virtuous materialism" from the great and ennobling affairs of the common life. So, too, he saw in the "small distinct circles" an effort to establish a status denied by the formal institutions of democracy.

Tocqueville was aware from the European despotic example that governments could forbid associations and he warned against this. He pointed out that aristocratic nations, such as France had been, were chambered by caste-like groupings; in such a society groups would be born, not made, just as men were born, not self-made. And since, as I have said, he believed such a form of social organization was doomed, he tried to persuade its residual cadres to welcome freedom of association as a guarantee of liberty.

Were Tocqueville to visit America now, he might well be alarmed at the ways in which individuals, called before governmental investigators, are asked to report on their ties with others and their informal as well as formal networks of association, so that the personal threatens to become political, and the political, personal. Tocqueville spoke of the bar as the most influential quasi aristocracy in America (he had in mind the practicing bar rather than the Supreme Court, being largely unaware of the significance of John Marshall's decisions). But the role of the bar in recent years in defending freedom of association has not been impressive. Many lawyers have feared to take the cases of men accused of subversive activities or associations, lest they themselves be thought sympathetic to their clients, leaving the work of defense either to a few older aristocrats of the bar like Lloyd Garrison, or to incompetents, or to Communist-dominated small fry. Thus, I have the impression that lawyers today are, if more professionalized than in Tocqueville's day, much less influential because of their reluctance to face popular distrust. The bar associations have done little to protect their individual members who take unpopular cases, and some have even gone so far as to attack the Supreme Court for those of its decisions which have sought to reinvigorate the freedoms both of speech and of association.

In fact, it is hard to see rising above the democratic plain any of the groups which Tocqueville thought might become potential aristocracies. Not, as I have just said, the lawyers, inspite of their numerical

preponderence in Congress and state legislatures. And not the manufacturers, that is, the owning class whom Tocqueville thought of as
possibly oppressing their workers and becoming an oligarchy. Something like this did happen after the Civil War, in the period of the rob-
ber barons and the formation of great combines and trusts, and one
could argue that in terms of discrepancies of wealth and power America between 1870 and 1900 differed both from the America Tocqueville saw and from the tamed managerial capitalism of today. In one
important respect, however, as Louis Hartz has observed, post–Civil
War Americans continued the movement toward equality, for by temporarily crushing the anti-industrial South they reduced all values to
dollar values, and every man in principle became every other man's
equal in the sense of having an equal opportunity to gain and to succeed. Certainly, men like Henry Adams felt that American life in the
era of Grant had no place for an Adams: lacking were even the remnants of gentility that had survived down to the Civil War—remnants
which had failed to impress Tocqueville because those who continued
this tradition already felt themselves defeated (much as American
businessmen today will tell all and sundry that it is impossible to make
a fortune in one's lifetime because of taxes, although this is not the
case). Thus, by eliminating the competing echelons of land and family
and cultivation, the post–Civil War oligarchy made in the end for a
still greater equalitarianism.

Tocqueville had, however, one other candidate for hegemony,
namely, certain groups of junior officers in the military establishment,
and what he had to say about them makes all too uncomfortable reading today. I cannot think of another American visitor in time of peace
and tiny armies who paid attention to this possibility. (Tocqueville was
probably alerted to it by the wars unleashed by the French Revolution.) The military, of course, was one of the few groups, and the only
influential one, having a code which played down the desire for material possessions. As Tocqueville wrote, the officer's "true country is the
Army, since he owes all he has to the rank he has attained in it; he
therefore follows the fortunes of the Army, rises or sinks with it, and
henceforth directs all his hopes to that quarter only." There have been
generals recently, notably General MacArthur, whose true country has
been the Army, but it is on the whole surprising how much respect
military men have for their civilian superiors in politics, and for their
monetary superiors in big business: far from regarding the latter as
vulgar men without honor and patriotism, the military in the absence
of feudal traditions have lacked a counterethos. Correspondingly, the
ambitions of individual officers for glory may be less important than
the corporate ambitions of their arm of the service, tied in as each arm
is with its defense contractors, its scientists, its friends on Congressional committees or on the Atomic Energy Commission. In the era of
the Cold War, Tocqueville's prophecies about the military direct our
attention in the right direction, but do not illuminate beyond that.

But in other respects and particularly in picturing the over-all psychology of what we have come to call mass society, Tocqueville's ex-

trapolation of an America he saw into one he foresaw was prescient. Equality has gone much further, facilitated in part by public education (something to which Tocqueville adverted in his journals but did not think important enough for his published book). The fear of the rich that the poor would envy or unseat them has become in our day not merely an influence on public relations, but the source of a kind of social osmosis upward as well as downward in which numerous sons of the well-to-do search out the values of the less privileged for fear of missing something important and emancipating in life. In Tocqueville's day, what Americans wanted were the rights and privileges and possessions of other Americans, but today's Americans seem to me less greedy, certainly less greedy for possessions *per se*. And while Tocqueville saw Americans as endlessly energetic, moving eagerly onward and upward in economic activity and political caucus, it is my impression that many Americans today are less compulsively gregarious and somewhat more passive politically: what they want out of life is less easily defined—and less easily attained.

By the same token, Tocqueville's isolated individuals seem to me a good deal more freestanding than many Americans of today. While Tocqueville spoke of every man striving "to keep himself aloof, lest he be carried away by the crowd against his will," today there would seem to be less aloofness, more going with the crowd unconsciously, and at the same time a more desperate search for nonconformity. It follows that the self-confidence of Americans which so struck Tocqueville has also become attenuated, even though in the West and South one can still find old-fashioned representatives of it. The "small distinct circles" of private life into which Americans retire are increasingly those of the suburban P.T.A. or other neighborhood groups that avoid the more intractable issues, either of the great metropolis or of the country as a whole. A great resurgence of the family, with people marrying at ever younger ages, has absorbed much of the leisure that Tocqueville thought would go into political and associational life. Contrary to what many think, the centralization of state power that Tocqueville feared has not come to pass in America: in many respects neither the several states, nor certainly the cities, nor even the federal government is strong enough for the burdens of making an affluent society also a civilized and humane one, even though our military and political leaders, in co-operative provocation with our enemies, may destroy the country and the world and en route oppress many individuals in the name of national loyalty.

Despite these dangers, American democracy remains a going, if threatened, concern, even though it violates many of the rules that Tocqueville's French conservative friends thought essential for civic order. But these rules were not of great importance for Tocqueville, who wanted to preserve from earlier times neither great refinement of taste nor feudal codes of honor (with their undercurrents of barbarity), but rather independence of mind and magnanimity of action. For the sake of a diminished servility and a wider ambiance of citizenship, he was willing to surrender many privileges from an earlier day. Moreover, he thought that the softening of manners that accompanied the growing equality of condition made men more human, for he did not share the attachment of romantic conservatives then and now for the chivalric styles of the older nobility. In an extraordinary passage, he spoke of the way in which casual cruelty had become *démodé* even before the French and American Revolutions, remarking on the way in which Mme. de Sévigné could express a callous pleasure in public executions that a generation later would be inconceivable. He seemed to feel that there was something in the human career, linked to Christianity, which was responsible for a long, slow and inevitable rise of equalitarianism, accompanied by a rise in sensitivity beyond the immediate enclaves of family and class. He did not delude himself that there were not losses in the democratic tide, for he was not entirely free of admiration for chivalry and punctilio, but he was quite willing to sacrifice these traditional virtues if the result would be an elevation of the mass of men and the disappearance of the abasement of the oppressed. What he feared was a new servility in which each man, respecting his neighbor no more than he respected himself, would respect only the serried and unranked mass of men. As he declared:

> Moralists are constantly complaining that the ruling vice of the present time is pride. This is true in one sense, for everybody thinks that he is better than his neighbor or refuses to obey his superior; but it is extremely false in another, for the same man who cannot endure subordination or equality has so contemptible an opinion of himself that he thinks he is born only to indulge in vulgar pleasures. He willingly takes up with low desires without daring to embark on lofty enterprises, of which he scarcely dreams. Thus, far from thinking that humility ought to be preached to our contemporaries, I would have endeavors made to give them a more enlarged idea of themselves and their kind.

Given the bombast and the big talk of many of the Americans he saw, Tocqueville drew here on his sense of the difference between the patrician ambition of those who are already in high place and the lesser vision of those who, motivated by envy, want merely to attain goals that are already there—in contemporary terms, the difference between Kennedy's personal pride and ambition for "his" country and Nixon's humble but even more egocentric drive to get to the top.

But such passages, in which Tocqueville extols what we today praise as individualism, must be set against his equally strong concern lest what *he* called individualism divide the nation into gangs of rapacious men pursuing an unenlightened self-interest. In the dialectic between individualism and solidarity, many intellectuals have tended (as has this writer) to stress the former—to the point where any eccentricity or idiosyncrasy, any rejection of the mass of men and their values, becomes praiseworthy, creating what Harold Rosenberg has dubbed "the herd of independent minds." An appropriately differentiated ethic for our own time barely exists and needs to be invented through experience; *Democracy in America* helps us to understand but not to solve our problem.

MAX LERNER

Tocqueville and American Civilization†

There is at once a spaciousness and subtlety in Tocqueville's view of freedom which ranks him with Milton, Mill, and Acton. As an inheritor of the French Revolution, but as a highly critical one, he took the first term of its trinitarian slogan with entire seriousness, where others were willing to see *Liberté* submerged by its sister terms *Egalité* and *Fraternité*. "I think that at all times I should have loved freedom," he writes in the second volume of his *Democracy*, "but, in the times in which we live, I am disposed to worship it." Perhaps the French were less concerned with freedom than with independence: the independence of the middle and lower classes from the power of the monarchy and aristocracy. But once independence and therefore a measure of equality were achieved in France, the scramble for power inside the new regime left little room for maintaining freedom. Tocqueville must have had this distinction in mind when he wrote that "the Revolution in the United States was caused by a mature and thoughtful taste for freedom, and not by some vague undefined instinct for independence." He was deeply impressed by the public spirit of the Americans, and their feeling for the authority of the law, which he did not find in Europe. American freedom, he pointed out, did not mean an absence of social obligation or an anarchic vacuum of social order, but a responsible assertion of individual autonomy within a social frame of equal rights and distributed powers.

This was not an easy concept for Tocqueville to hammer out in his day, any more than it is for us today. The path he had to traverse was difficult, sometimes even treacherous. He had some fixed conceptual points. I have noted his distinction between freedom and independence, and between anarchic and responsible freedom. He also had the problem of making these square with equality and individualism, both of which he saw as potential dangers to freedom, although historically, the pressure for all three of them had developed in recoil from a despotic order. Tocqueville sometimes used *equality* to mean only the abolition of hereditary class distinctions and privileges—not much more than an equality before the law. Sometimes he enlarged it to mean an equality of material conditions which enabled an individual to feel equal to others. But his characteristic use of the term was in the sense of the more extreme trend in democracy—the leveling and

† Max Lerner (1902–1992) was an educator, journalist, and writer on American civilization. This selection is from his *Tocqueville and American Civilization*, copyright © 1969. Reprinted by permission of Transaction Publishers.

corrosive trend, which he feared, rather than the equal participation of all in a common concern, which was for him the healthy phase of a democracy. He used *l'individualisme* (see the succession of chapters on that concept in his second volume) in the French sense of his time rather than in the present American sense. He meant by it, more than anything else, the loneliness of the individual and the atomization of the society, while we use the term to stress the self-reliant assertion of individual differences in talent and character. Today we see individualism as opposed to the leveling emphasis of egalitarianism; Tocqueville saw it as one of the consequences of egalitarianism. "In ages of equality," he wrote, "every man finds his beliefs within himself, and . . . all his feelings are turned in on himself."

Writing as a Frenchman about an American society that had presumably made freedom into a passion, Tocqueville nevertheless developed a theory of freedom which no American thinker has surpassed. On the issue of freedom and the state, there have been American anarchist thinkers, including Thoreau; there have been radical egalitarians; there has been the liberal tradition of freedom, starting with the Founding Fathers and stretching to the diverse liberal views of Justices Holmes, Learned Hand, Frankfurter and Black. The American tendency has been to see a freedom system as the kind that succeeds best in achieving a competition of ideas. Tocqueville's memorable sentence on freedom—"he who seeks in liberty anything more than liberty itself is destined for servitude"—must stand as abiding witness to his refusal to see freedom instrumentally. He saw it, as it were, existentially: it was a thing in itself, a subject, not a means or object. It was the condition which fulfills a man by the very fact of being the essence of his existence as himself, and not a creature or puppet of others.

As an heir of the European revolutionary tradition, Tocqueville was committed against arbitrary government by any aristocracy; but he was equally committed against oppressions by the new revolutionary majorities. In the American experience he saw a free people in the flush of their freedom, but he was concerned also about the increasing oppression of the nonconformist creative spirit by an oversimplifying majority given to stereotyped thinking. This was not a contradition in his thought nor a failure of commitment to freedom, but an effort to define the nature of that commitment. In fact, some critics have felt that his commitment to freedom was too absolute and "pure," and have scored him for his failure to recognize what the French Revolution was about: that coercion of some people is necessary to secure freedom for others, perhaps for the majority. Tocqueville very early saw that this could lead to a liberalism tainted by totalitarian passions. He sought to protect freedom not only from the aristocracy of birth and privilege, and from the new industrial and military aristocracies, but also from the coercions of the new mass society; he sought to protect it from tyranny in any form, whether from tyrannical minorities or tyrannical majorities.

His chapters "The Omnipotence of the Majority in the United States and Its Effects" and "What Tempers the Tyranny of the Majority in the United States" are the best known of the book. Tocqueville expected his American contemporaries to be angered by them, but they and the succeeding generations have embraced Tocqueville's thesis on majority tyranny—which should give us pause when he tells us how sensitive to praise and blame the Americans are as a nation. Both in wartime and in postwar periods Americans have known of the danger that national hysterias present to liberty of thought and expression. Periodically a great fear seems to sweep over America, not only during and after exhausting wars but in other crises of the national spirit. In this mood, sometimes of fear, sometimes of frustration, a wave of intolerance becomes impatient of minorities out of harmony with it and seeks to bring them into line. It is this pressure toward a general conformity of opinion which Tocqueville had in mind, and his prescience in foreseeing it has made him into something of a major prophet for American intellectuals, and has made even some of the Marxist-oriented among them forget the basic moderation of his thought, as they did for a time with Justice Holmes.

When he spoke of the tyranny of the majority, Tocqueville meant both an arrogance of power and a conformity of opinion. He was scornful of the idea that the people can do no wrong, and that the voice of the people is the voice of God. The notion that there is "no need to fear giving total power to the majority" is, he said, "the language of a slave." On this score, in good eighteenth-century natural-rights fashion, he appealed "from the sovereignty of the people to the sovereignty of the human race." But basically he was not talking of majority power as embodied in unjust laws, but of the even harsher majority power as embodied in mass opinion. What he feared in a democracy was the tyranny of narrow minds and mean spirits which would crush diversity and compel conformity. Even more than the external pressures on the minority he feared the internal censor operating in the mind of the majority which would inhibit individuality and stifle dissent from within. It was the first of these two strains in Tocqueville—that of majority pressures on the minority—which fascinated John Stuart Mill, evoking two remarkable essays on him. It influenced American liberals during the struggles of the McCarthy period in the early 1950's, giving a fillip to the study of political repression and to the political sociology of the "Radical Right." It gave the prevailing tone to the studies of American mass culture in the 1950's and 1960's. In a sense almost the whole of Tocqueville's second volume, written five years later, and stressing the mediocrity of opinion, belief, literature, the arts and the mores in a democracy, may be seen as an extended footnote to the seminal chapters in the first volume dealing with the moral tyranny of the majority and its constricted inner psychic universe.

Tocqueville's portrait of the role of the dissenter and intellectual in American life is a bleak one. He cites the "fury of the public" in Baltimore against a hapless fellow who dared oppose the War of 1812, the alienation (as we should now call it) of writers who oppose the prevailing opinion, the drastic punishment imposed on any who offend the sensibilities of the "power which dominates"—that is to say, the majority itself. In aristocracies, he points out, a writer may find shelter from the people with some patron or with the throne itself; he can find ways of eluding the censorship, and he can even slip antireligious books past an Inquisition. But America, which in theory allows him to write whatever he pleases, is in fact a naked society which holds no hiding place for him from the "irresistible power" of a people which, by ostracism and neglect, can impose a silence upon nonconformists more effective than any *auto-da-fé*.

It is a biting portrait of a mass society in action. Anyone who has studied the history of conformity in America will recognize its considerable measure of truth. Mill, in his second (1840) essay in the *Edinburgh Review*, noted that what Tocqueville ascribed to the despotism of the democratic principle was as true in England as in America, and that it was due less to the idea of majority rule than to the rise of industrial society and the triumph of the middle class. Tocqueville was not swayed from his analysis, although he did acknowledge that there were institutions which tempered the majority despotism: the absence of a strong central government, the jury trial (there would be many today who would wish he had been more critical of the jury system), the strength of the legal profession, the voluntary organizations that often joined in some reform cause or championed an unpopular one. But the important fact, as Tocqueville noted about the Americas, was that "freedom is not the chief and continued object of their desires; it is equality for which they feel and eternal love. . . . Nothing will satisfy them without equality, and they would rather die than lose it."

If one were to cite against him the long history of American reform movements and of the intellectual passion behind them, it would only play into his thesis: it is the movements embodying the passion for equality that succeed, and when they have succeeded they become themselves vested interests and vested ideas. More to the point would be the continual intervention of the American conscience, even at such low moments of the American story as the Mexican war, the slavery compromises, the imperialist adventures of the turn of the century, the "Red scares," and the McCarthy adventurism in the era of Communist espionage and spy trials. It is John P. Roche's contention that the deterioration story of American civil liberties has been overplayed, and that there is a more vigorous "quest for the dream" in American life today than ever, the "dream" being not only egalitarian but libertarian. But his is a minority viewpoint, although a close reading of history might bear him out. The drive among the American creative elite to be nonconformist, by underscoring the conformity of the American mass society, has itself threatened to become a new kind of intellectual group conformity. Perhaps this new trend bears out the Tocqueville thesis as strikingly as any in the past. Tocqueville was talking of "some mighty pressure of the mind of all upon the intelligence of each," and his insight could apply not only to American society as a whole but also to the particular groups within it. This gives point to Henry S. Commager's remark, that in our absorption with the tyranny of the majority we tend to forget about the tyranny of minorities. The pressure toward conformity within the "Radical Right," which itself laments the intolerance of the "conspiracy" of academic liberals, is so great that a moderate conservative is hard put to resist the urgencies of the extremists. The same may be said of the pressures within the militant Negro civil rights movement, or of the liberal and Leftist intellectuals who would lose their ingroup status if they cut against the grain of their fellows.

The disease that Tocqueville saw in America was the disease of a mass culture and the mediocrity it demands. But the conformity he saw applies not only to the pressures from the mass but to the pressures from the elites as well. James Fenimore Cooper, himself a Jacksonian, also uttered a cry of desolation in his novels at the falling-away of savor and distinction in the America that Tocqueville studied. It was not only a "tyranny" or "despotism" that both men—and many since then—have feared, but a deterioration of life style and a vacuum of values. Nor did religion help much, because the rigidity of its codes was calculated to "check the passion of innovation." For Tocqueville these pressures made for a certain flatness in the American national character. There is a tendency among the American social theorists today to attribute much of this flatness to recent changes in the society, whether toward the suburban housewife or toward her organization husband or their other-directed children. Tocqueville's book suggests that long before the suburbs, bureaucracies, automation, and status anxieties of today, what he called the "courtier spirit" of the American had already become a burden upon the culture. He faced the possibilities of this future with some nostalgia for the past: "The sight of such universal uniformity saddens and chills me," he wrote in the powerful concluding chapter of his second volume, "and I am tempted to regret that state of society which has ceased to be." It was less the tyranny than the bleakness of a mass culture that Tocqueville carried in his fears like a smoldering city. Yet when the reader goes on to finish the whole passage he finds that Tocqueville saw compensating qualities in a society of egalitarianism: "not the particular prosperity of the few, but the greater well-being of all. . . . Equality may be less elevated, but it is more just, and in its justice lies its greatness and beauty."

Such a portrait of unrelieved bleakness left little room for depicting the pluralism of American life. Tocqueville devoted a chapter to the "three races," but the ethnic pluralism of America developed much more rapidly after the great migrations of the turn of the century. While he gives us a magnificent descriptive overview of the face of America, in his early chapter on its "exterior form," there is little suggestion of the regional pluralism which was to form part of the diversity of the American character. Nor, despite his stress on religion in America, is there a vivid sense of the religious pluralism, nor of that fusion of religion, ethnic origin, speech, and even occupational diversity that were to form so many pockets to relieve the standardized flatness of the larger society. Curiously Tocqueville, who himself noted that democratic peoples have a way of personalizing the formless movements of mankind, did exactly that with the movements of opinion in American democracy. The American "majority" is usually a cluster of minorities whose diverse motivations happen to result in a similar stance. In his use of the term "the tyranny of the majority" Tocqueville turned what is pluralistic into something monolithic. True, the impact on the dissenting minority is the same, however diverse the groups are that compose the "majority," and Tocqueville was perceptive in seizing upon this impact. But as a political sociologist he overdid the simplicity of his "model" of American society, making it less complex in order to make it more compassable. Except for the "associations," he seemed to see little that could mediate between the monotony of the sprawling inorganic society and the loneliness of the atomized families and individuals.

He did not have a "class" approach to politics and society, as Madison tended to have. When he had to use a class division (as in his discussion of taxes and public finance) he used the three-class system of the wealthy, middle, and working classes. In his later writings, on the French Revolution, he dealt with the rhythm of the classes in a historical era, each coming up with a sense of its identity and power, and thrusting the others down. He wrote a sketch along these lines, on the state of French society before 1789, for Mill's *Westminster Review.* But in his book on America his attention was not on the division but on the tendency toward the abolition of the classes. He was impressed, as I have noted, with the way in which the laws of inheritance had largely done away with the old landed class, and he felt that the new businessmen—while they might someday form a dangerous aristocracy— were not yet a class in the accepted sense: their mobility was too great, men came into their ranks and left them too swiftly, and the pursuit of profit was rampant throughout the society instead of being restricted to them. There was moreover no proletariat in the European sense, no deep *ressentiment* (as Nietzsche was to call it) of the underlying population against the wealth and privileges of the upper orders: "Everyone having some possession to defend, recognizes the right to property in principle." Thus Tocqueville was perhaps the first great theorist of the modern era to recognize the classless society built into the American principle of equality—not a "permanent equality of property," for which "no other country" had a "stronger scorn," but the principle of an equal chance at life chances.

This principle of the abolition of classes cropped up later, as we know, in the Marxist canon, although in a different context. Marx said: the rich will get richer, the poor poorer, until the poor will overthrow the rich. Tocqueville said: the rich will get richer, but the poor will also get richer, until the divisions between them lose their old meaning. Marx said: the dialectic of history will abolish classes, and then man will at last be free. Tocqueville said: the logic of a democratic society is a classless logic, and its history moves toward the abolition of classes, but it will not bring freedom automatically; men will be free or unfree, depending upon what they do collectively in preventing either a despotism of laws or a despotism of opinion. Of the two, it was

Tocqueville who was the realist, and it was Marx who—for all his talk about "scientific" socialism—was following an abstraction.

Marx and Tocqueville never met; in the early 1840's, however, Marx and Proudhon met frequently, and Proudhon knew the Tocqueville volumes and may have told Marx about Tocqueville's idea of a classless society. Tocqueville was no revolutionary and did not mingle with the new group of Anarchists and Socialists on the fringes of French political-intellectual life. Along with a reference to Proudhon there is only one other reference to them in his *Souvenirs*, when he recounts meeting George Sand, who told the liberal aristocrats in Tocqueville's group of the ferment of the new radical energies under the crust of the old society, and warned them, "If it comes to a fight, believe me, you will all perish."

Whatever might happen to the democratic revolution in Europe, Tocqueville saw its American future more confidently. He had hopes about the future erosion of the white-Negro caste system, and saw some sort of impending showdown over slavery. In his mind it took the form of an internal conflict "between the Blacks and the Whites of the South of the Union," a danger "more or less distant, but inevitable," and "a nightmare constantly haunting American imagination." Thus while Tocqueville did not foresee the sectional form that the Civil War took, he had a foreboding of the nightmare years of the Reconstruction period afterward in the South. Nor did he have many illusions about what would follow abolition. "The Negroes might remain slaves for a long time without complaining; but as soon as they join the ranks of free men, they will be indignant at being deprived of almost all the rights of citizens; and being unable to become the equals of the Whites, they will not be slow to show themselves their enemies."

The apocalyptic vision of Tocqueville—"the most horrible of civil wars [Tocqueville meant inside the South] and perhaps the extermination of one or the other of the two races"—has happily not taken place. But America is caught in a protracted civil rights struggle in South and North alike, which Tocqueville foresaw, missing only its timing. The difference between the current civil rights revolution and the struggles of the past lies at least partly in the crisis of conscience which the whites have undergone, and which challenges the implied assumption in Tocqueville that the whites could not accept the Negroes as equals. But it lies even more in the new willingness of the Negroes to "show themselves their enemies" if they are not accepted as their equals. The reason why Tocqueville could uncannily call the turn on the current civil rights revolution lies in his insight into the dynamics of all passionate movements. It is the principle that every such movement "grows by what it gains" or (as Tocqueville sometimes put it) "grows by what it feeds on." This insight is so basic to Tocqueville's thinking, and so repeatedly applicable in every era, that one may think of it as the "Tocqueville effect."

What it amounts to, as Tocqueville notes in the *Ancien Régime*, is that once the passion of revolutionary claims and demands has seized hold of a movement, concessions and reforms must be seen not as ways of stopping or even of moderating it, but as steps toward its final fulfillment. This was true of the American Revolution, from the time when the intellectuals took up the cause of the people, and the King and nobles made the first concession to them. It was true of the French Revolution. Tocqueville noted in the *Ancien Régime* that the movement to sweep away the aristocracy "which started as a political revolution proceeded as a religious revolution." This tendency of intense social movements to become political religions gives them at once their effectiveness and their potential destructiveness, unless their own leaders can learn to channel and discipline them. Tocqueville is not necessarily happy with the operation of this "Tocqueville effect," for with all his passion he was not a revolutionary. But he faced unflinchingly the nature of social reality and the character of social movements as he saw them. One suspects that Tocqueville today would have little doubt about the ultimate and irresistible success of the movement for equal Negro civil rights, not only in law but in social actuality, in South and North alike. It has engaged the energies and imagination of men, and has developed a mystique against which it would be hard to find a counter-mystique. But one must also suspect that Tocqueville would make the same agonized appeal to its leaders that he makes to Americans and Europeans alike about the democratic revolution as a whole: an appeal to ride the whirlwind, to command the storm, and to tame the egalitarian energies of both to the purposes of humanist values.

ROBERT NISBET

Many Tocquevilles†

My interest here is, in almost equal parts, Alexis de Tocqueville's classic, *Democracy in America*, and the American intellectual scene, chiefly as we have known it since about 1940. Although some of Tocqueville's major insights form the substance of what follows, I shall consider them, not directly, much less systematically, but instead through the prisms that have been formed by successive American reactions to *Democracy in America*. The relation of a book to its public is always a matter of interest, especially when that public is the protagonist of the book.

Few books have ever been greeted with larger or more immediate applause than Part I of *Democracy in America* when it was published in Paris in 1835, four years after Tocqueville's and Beaumont's visit of nine months to the United States. Overnight the author was declared a major thinker, perhaps the foremost political philosopher since Montesquieu. There were scores of admiring reviews. When Part II

---

† Robert Nisbet (1913–1996) was a sociologist and the Albert Schweitzer Professor of the Humanities at Columbia University. This essay appeared in *The American Scholar* 46 (1976/77). Reprinted by permission of Caroline Nisbet.

appeared five years later, the applause was diminished, but Tocqueville's stature was unaffected. For three decades he remained lustrous as a political philosopher on both sides of the Atlantic. In France the book went through thirteen editions in the fifteen years following publication, and it did fully as well in the United States, where, early on, it was used in adapted form as a textbook in the public schools. The story was the same in England. John Stuart Mill described it as the best philosophical work ever written on democracy, and it was evidently regarded in this light not only by the reading public but by scholars and statesmen. In Germany, Dilthey, in later tribute, ranked Tocqueville among the first three minds of his age in Europe, calling him "the greatest analyst of the political world since Machiavelli and Aristotle." So it went.

Then the book fell upon hard times. From being widely read and quoted, by the 1870s it had become a text only occasionally studied and footnoted. In England, Dicey lamented that he could not interest students in a work that had been virtually the staple of his and his contemporaries' education. There were still, of course, occasional tributes: Bryce's, in his 1888 classic, *The American Commonwealth*; Woodrow Wilson's, H. B. Adams's, and a few others; but that was all. In this country just after the turn of the century, the book went out of print and, it is no injustice to add, out of mind. In France, Antoine Redier did publish, in 1925, the first detailed, thorough biography of Tocqueville, which bore the somewhat ironic title *Comme Disait M. de Tocqueville*. It received little notice, so far as I can tell, except among historians of the French Revolution, who had been continuously influenced by his 1854 *Old Regime and the French Revolution*.

In short, from the late 1860s until the late 1930s only an occasional monograph or article on Tocqueville appeared—nothing, really, that lifted him from the ranks of literally dozens of other French writers of the early nineteenth century. As a personal note I can attest that in the 1930s, during seven years of a better-than-average education, undergraduate and graduate, at Berkeley, I did not once hear the name Tocqueville in class or seminar. Others of my generation have assured me that my experience was not unique.

Nevertheless it was in the 1930s that matters began to change. The hundredth anniversary of Part I of *Democracy in America* produced a few notices, although I myself was unaware of them. More important, seeds planted then or earlier produced their yield during the next four or five years. George Pierson's fascinating *Tocqueville and Beaumont in America* appeared in 1938, though chiefly of interest to students of American history. In 1939 J. P. Mayer—preeminent Tocqueville scholar of our age—published his *Tocqueville: Prophet of the Mass Age*. There were a few other studies, all brief, in the late 1930s, among them two perceptive essays by Albert Salomon of the New School for Social Research. I recall coming upon a brief, penetrating reference to Tocqueville in one of Diana Trilling's earliest essays, around 1940.

Then came the deluge, slightly postponed by the impact of World War II. In 1945 Alfred A. Knopf, in one of his many services to Amer-

ican literacy, brought out the first new edition—the first reprinting indeed—of *Democracy in America*, with a splendid introduction by
Phillips Bradley, then of Queens College, New York. The book caught
on almost immediately, and by the late 1940s it was a rare month that
did not yield treatments of, or references to, Tocqueville in the little
magazines, the scholarly quarterlies, and a rising number of books.
Tocqueville's name began slowly to rival Marx's in literary and scholarly circles. This recovered eminence is by now three decades old, and
it shows no present sign of changing.

How do we account for the rise, then the fall, and then the rise
again of Tocqueville as an imposing prophet and analyst of democracy? What made *Democracy in America* popular during the three
decades or so that followed its publication? What brought about the
book's decline, in both intellectual and popular regard, by 1880? And
what, finally, restored it to the extraordinary importance it has had
since about 1940? Any answers to these questions will obviously say as
much about the changing character of the American mind as about
the book itself.

I take nothing from Tocqueville's well-recorded singleness of purpose and design when I say the book in its entirety is a composite—
one of extraordinarily diverse perceptions, reflections, and, far from
least, moods. Ostensibly rooted in the visit to America, the book is in
fact a collection of ideal types generated in Tocqueville's mind by the
tension he clearly and acknowledgedly experienced under the impact
of the revolution in Europe that had begun in 1789 and, in his judgment, had never ended, only grown wider and deeper. Himself the
child of aristocratic parents who had been jailed for months during
the Terror under the daily expectation of execution, himself unalter-
ably noble of manner as well as birth, Tocqueville was yet unable to
join those who sought to arrest or reverse democratic currents. Neither, however, could he bring himself to accept the implications of
that revolution of values which he saw as a providential fact and
which he refused to combat.

In a letter to his friend and translator, Henry Reeve, Tocqueville
wrote in 1837: "People ascribe to me alternately aristocratic and democratic prejudices. If I had been born in another period, or in another
country, I might have had either one or the other. But my birth, as it
happened, made it easy for me to guard against both. I came into the
world at the end of a long revolution, which, after destroying ancient
institutions, created none that could last. When I entered life, aristocracy was dead and democracy was yet unborn. My instinct, therefore,
could not lead me blindly either to the one or the other."

But if this division of mind is always present in Tocqueville's work, it
quite evidently manifests itself in varying proportions and intensities.
To the degree that the book is in fact about America, the spirit of optimism and affection for democracy is alive, with only occasional exceptions. But, as is well known to all Tocqueville readers, and has been
known since Part II was published in 1840, the book is only partly
about America, and, as a work of descriptive ethnography, somewhat

deficient. What the book most largely is devoted to is, by Tocqueville's own admission, "the image of democracy" and "what we have to fear or to hope from its progress." Paul Janet, who admired Tocqueville, wrote in 1840: "It is certain . . . that the problem that disturbed M. de Tocqueville and that brought him to the United States is the problem of European democracy. It is this very fact that gives the book its grandeur, I might also say its emotional quality, but which at the same time introduces a certain obscurity. Tocqueville describes America, but he thinks of Europe; hence those contradictory observations that cannot be applied at the same time to both."

Yet this very mixture—indeed confusion—of what, on the one hand, are direct observations drawn from the notebooks Tocqueville so assiduously kept while on his journey with Beaumont through America, and, on the other hand, intuitions, abstract reflections, and ideal types, has in no small degree kept *Democracy in America* an iridescent classic. It is not so much a book of prophecy, as it is often termed, as a book of many and diverse images to which time and circumstance lend mutability and variant evocation.

Which leads us to the signal difference between Part I and Part II. There are many ways of describing this difference, but certainly not the least among them is the difference in mood. In Part I the mood is, for the most part, buoyant, high-spirited, even optimistic. I do not say that the opposite of these qualities is altogether lacking. There are the ruminations on majority rule, on the power of public opinion, on the dangerous relation between whites and blacks. But overwhelmingly the mood of Part I is in celebration of American institutions, of local government, the judiciary, voluntary association, the ethic of work, legal pluralism, and the like.

We need only turn to the final chapter of Part I, titled "Future Prospects of the United States," to see how overriding are Tocqueville's optimism and admiration. Here America is pronounced a nation of the freest and the happiest people on earth, destined, he tells us (this in 1835!), to become the preeminent commercial nation of the world and, with this, the first naval power. Its expanse would, well before the end of the century, reach the Pacific. Its population would number more than one hundred and fifty million within a century. And, in a passage that has become celebrated, he prophesies that the future of the world will belong to two great nations, Russia and the United States. His words in this prophecy are worth reciting: "All other nations seem to have nearly reached their natural limits, and they have only to maintain their power; but these two are still in act of growth. . . . The American struggles against the obstacles which nature opposes to him; the adversaries of the Russian are men. The former combats the wilderness and savage life; the latter, civilization with all its arms. . . . The Anglo-American relies upon personal interest to accomplish ends, and gives free scope to the unguided strength and common sense of the people; the Russian centers all authority of society in a single arm. The principal interest of the former is freedom; of the latter, servitude. Their starting-point is different, and their courses are not the same; yet each of them seems marked out by the will of Heaven to sway the destinies of half the globe."

That this appreciation of American institutions lay deep in Tocqueville's mind is attested to by the preface he wrote to the twelfth French edition, a full thirteen years after initial publication. At that time he was tormented by the events of 1848 in France, events in which he played a major political role as elected deputy and as member of the Constitutional Commission. In the preface he declares flatly that all republics worthy of the name must be based upon American constitutional principles. To the end of his life, Tocqueville was best known as celebrant of American liberal democracy. Indeed, conservatives such as Frédéric Le Play criticized him precisely on this ground.

Needless to say, this mood of celebration of American institutions in Part I caught on in the United States after a slight hesitation by Americans, who were only too used to unflattering commentary by European visitors. This is the Tocqueville who for nearly three decades was a widely admired, widely read author in the United States. Rare was the article, book, or newspaper editorial on American political institutions written by an American that did not invoke the name of M. de Tocqueville. Substantial sections of *Democracy in America* were used in American schools.

We come now to the Fall. As Tocqueville had risen to eminence on both sides of the Atlantic by virtue of his celebration of American political progress, so now would he suffer decline (though not until after his death in 1859) from this selfsame celebration. If the cause of decline was the same on both sides of the Atlantic, the nature of the process was different. In Europe—where a kind of malaise had fallen upon those circles in which Tocqueville the philosopher of democracy had first won renown, where skepticism of progress and democracy was burgeoning—Tocqueville, identified as he was with both values, disappeared among the shades. True, the skeptics could have found rich food in Part II of *Democracy in America* had they looked, but they did not look, or if they looked they did not see.

Quite different is the story in the United States. Here, with rarest of exceptions, the spirit of progress remained ascendant at least down through World War I. In no other country in the world was the idea of progress so deeply, religiously held. There were few then who doubted American destiny. Ironically, it was this very intoxication with American progress, I believe, that led to Tocqueville's decline. Granted that he had helped generate it in the first place, it had now outreached him. He had praised American progress—but not recently! His place was taken by dozens, then hundreds, of Americans able themselves to praise the spirit from which all blessings flowed. Tocqueville's 1835 ode to American progress was now lost in the vast chorus that stretched from one ocean to the other.

If Tocqueville had sunk by his buoyancy, so to speak, he might now be said to have risen by his gravity—the sometimes foreboding gravity that exists only in patches of Part I but is the very warp of Part II of *Democracy in America*. By the 1940s it was not the progress of democracy and of equalitarianism that was most resplendent, either in Tocqueville's book or in the American intellectual mind, but, rather, what might be called the inversion of progress. We found ourselves beginning to suffer doubts concerning the very values of modernity we had for so long revered: the voice of the people, secularism, technology, political rationalism, and others. And this is, of course, the very character of Part II, with only the rarest relief—and indeed, as we were now beginning to see, even of Part I in a few places. As a boy Tocqueville had written in his daybook that the three greatest afflictions from which mankind suffers are disease, death, and doubt—in that order.

Doubt was the prevailing tone of the Tocqueville being read in the late 1930s and the 1940s. Who has failed to note the specters that hang over Part II—of moral decay caused from within, of erosion of community and authority, of collapsed honor, of spiritual restlessness unassuaged by the quest for material prosperity, of technology that diminishes the artisan even as it advances the art, and, most ominous, of the distinctive kind of despotism that democracy alone has the power of creating?

Yet what were the crucial circumstances surrounding Tocqueville's return to eminence by 1940? Not, certainly, those of the Great Depression. I have no recollection of any use of *Democracy in America* by those in this country—and their number was large—addressing themselves to the evils or insufficiencies of capitalism. In a way this is strange, given the fact of Tocqueville's revival. For well before Karl Marx had set down his animadversions to bourgeois commercialism, Tocqueville, chiefly in Part II, had offered some strikingly critical, even pessimistic, views on the economic institutions of democracy.

Commercialism, he tells us (and this was written, it has to be remembered, in the late 1830s, a full decade before the *Communist Manifesto* by Marx and Engels appeared), by its very nature must succumb to regular and increasingly devastating panics or crises. Further, although wages have tended to rise in the democracies, the increasing monopolization of capital is bound to depress this tendency. Conflict between "the aristocracy of manufacturers"—which Tocqueville calls the harshest in history—and the working class is unalterable and will only grow worse. Division of labor, so widely hailed by the friends of industrialism, makes the worker a mere victim; "the art advances, the artisan recedes." And in dour reference to Adam Smith's famous example, Tocqueville asks, "What can be expected of a man who has spent twenty years of his life making heads for pins?"

Nor is this all. Democratic passion for incessant buying and selling as the way to quick riches not only prevents a genuine landed or rural class from coming into existence in the United States, but the condition is set for what can only be a built-in tendency toward inflation. Finally—and here Tocqueville's eye is as much on Europe as the United States—there is the destructive power of money over both moral values and social stability. What the erosion of traditional social

classes has brought about is not any genuine equality of actual circumstances, but only the ascendancy of the wealthy. "I know of no
country," he writes of the United States, "where the love of money has
taken stronger hold on the affections of men and where a profounder
contempt is expressed for the theory of the permanent equality of
property."

These, then, are Tocqueville's views of what would later come to be
known as the capitalist system. Had we made our way to them in this
country in the 1930s, we should, obviously, have found much to support our indictments of capitalism. But we did not. And in any event,
the commanding presence of Marx would have prevented our assimilating Tocqueville the economist. Marx, after all, conveyed intellectual
certainty in religious intensity and was moreover identified with the
Church of the Soviet Union. It is in a way a high tribute to Tocqueville
that at no time has there been, or is there likely to be, anything called
Tocqueville*ism*. We must, in sum, look elsewhere for the crucial contexts in which Tocqueville's rebirth occurred.

Oddly, the first of the contexts in which American intellectuals
found their way to Tocqueville was European rather than American,
political rather than economic: a fact of both biographical and historical importance. As I observed above, one of the most common criticisms of Part II when it appeared in 1840 was that although
Tocqueville professed to be writing about the United States, his eye
was actually on Europe and the patterns of emerging power and affluence to be seen there. It was the France of Balzac rather than the
America of Emerson that Tocqueville was most deeply interested in.

Now, in the late 1930s, with the riveting of American intellectual
attention on European totalitarianism, especially Nazism, as this
new form of despotism was being interpreted to us by European philosophers and scholars in exile in this country, a seedbed came into
existence in which Tocquevillian ideas could take root. Through transplanted Europeans, American intellectuals were being made aware of
what Emil Lederer—in a book published in 1940, exactly a century after Part II of *Democracy in America*—called "the state of the masses,"
following Ortega y Gasset's earlier "revolt of the masses." And this, of
course, is exactly what Tocqueville had been writing about: the masses
as the source of despotism; the absence, rather than the presence, of
social class as the crucial factor in the rise of centralized, omnicompe-
tent political power.

I don't find much evidence that the problem of political power (of
centralization rooted in bureaucracy), in spreading social homogeneity
and loss of cultural diversity, had ever really interested American intellectuals before the 1930s. Economic power, yes; the kind of power
that went with big business, the trusts, the monopolies, what T.R. had
called "malefactors of great wealth," and F.D.R. was calling "economic
royalists." But not the kind of power, we were only later to discover,
that Nietzsche, Burckhardt, Taine, and Max Weber had written about.
Not the kind of power Tocqueville, even earlier, had foreseen and de-

scribed in a famous passage in Part II that I quote from only briefly, since it is well known by now:

> . . . that power is absolute, minute, regular, provident, and mild. It would be like the authority of a parent if, like that authority, its object was to prepare men for manhood; but it seeks, on the contrary, to keep them in perpetual childhood . . . . Thus it every day renders the exercise of the free agency of man less useful and less frequent; it circumscribes the will within a narrower range and gradually robs a man of all the uses of himself. The principle of equality has prepared men for these things; it has predisposed men to endure them and often to look on them as benefits. . . . Such a power does not destroy but it prevents existence; it does not tyrannize, but it compresses, enervates, extinguishes, and stupefies a people, till each nation is reduced to nothing better than a flock of timid and industrious animals of which the government is the shepherd.

Those, as is evident enough today, are words of prophecy as well as analysis. I am not likely myself to forget soon the thrill of their discovery when I first read *Democracy in America* in 1939. Of a sudden, a great deal about modern Western history and society took on new meaning for me. I found myself for the first time seeing social democracy, including the New Deal (of which I had been a fairly ardent admirer) in a different light. What was occurring in the Soviet Union, in Hitler's Germany, became freshly illuminated for me and also, as later became evident, for others as well. That absolute power could go with social humanitarianism, could be rooted in the mass rather than an upper class, could be given extension and penetration by the very political agencies that had been created in the name of the people to cope with their problems; that totalitarianism could be understood best, not as reversion to a dark past, but as a product, however corrupt, of democratic modernity—all this was new to American thinkers and, as I recall well, not immediately accepted.

It is important to stress that such insights did not really explain the actual rise of the Lenins, Stalins, and Hitlers. We could have learned more from Tocqueville about this in certain passages from his notable study of the French Revolution and from the notes he left behind (only later to be published) on Napoleon and the peculiar character of his dictatorship. There, rather more than in *Democracy in America*, we could have acquired prescient understanding of the use of terror, capture of democratic assemblies, flattery of the masses, and military might fused with large-scale governmental paternalism that were the vital elements in the Communist, Fascist, and Nazi despotisms.

Nevertheless, the vision of power I have just cited from *Democracy in America*, with its emphasis upon the network of bureaucracy and administrative penetration by government of the smallest recesses of human life, had a good deal of relevance to the new totalitarianisms. Quite apart from the crucial circumstances of their birth, these governments, once in existence, once in full command of their respective populations, did indeed seek, in Tocqueville's phrasing, to destroy all in society that was not of their own making: to compress, enervate, extinguish, and stupefy; to cover the surface of society with a network of small, complicated rules through which the most original minds could not penetrate.

Tocqueville's characterization of the distinctive kind of power that democracies of the future had most to fear, once it was widely read and grasped by intellectuals in this country in the 1940s, had a good deal to do with our belated discovery of the impact of bureaucracy upon society and individuals. I find it both interesting and illuminating that our rebirth of interest in Tocqueville coincided with our discovery of Max Weber and his systematic analysis of modern bureaucracy. No one has equaled Weber in his detailed grasp of the special kind of power that is lodged in bureaucracy, but a score of passages in *Democracy in America* attest to Tocqueville's earlier identification of this power and of its affinity with popular government. Totalitarianism to one side, democracy, as we have learned, can represent, through incessant development of administrative centralization, a very real form of despotism. And it was Tocqueville who first showed us the character of this despotism.

So much for the first context of Tocqueville's reappearance in contemporary thought, which was, as I have suggested, overwhelmingly political. The second set of circumstances within which Tocqueville became important to American intellectuals is to be found in the realm of the economic—more precisely, in the unprecedented affluence that arrived in Western societies, especially the United States, after World War II. Here too *Democracy in America* proved to be a brilliant beacon. For without doubt, capitalist wealth had fascinated Tocqueville on his visit to the United States; and it never ceased to fascinate, and also to repel, him during the course of his political and scholarly life thereafter. This is a dimension of *Democracy in America* that has been too little appreciated: the characteristics—moral, social, psychological, and cultural—that go with not just democracy alone, but substantial middle-class wealth. Tocqueville, it is evident to the attentive reader, is the anatomist of affluence. In this respect he takes rank with his contemporary, Balzac.

It was in the 1940s that we ourselves were beginning to become anatomists of affluent society in the United States. Nothing comparable to the prosperity generated by World War II had ever existed in the United States, or for that matter in the West as a whole. We were scarcely prepared for it intellectually. The roots of most intellectuals were largely populist or socialist. In the 1930s intellectuals had become students of depression and its varied stigmata, and they knew the answer for depression: prosperity! Now, a decade later, they were beginning to ask, what is the answer to prosperity?

Gone overnight, it now seems, were the accustomed specters of unemployment, depression, and poverty that had haunted the thinking and writing of American intellectuals. There were new specters—of social and psychological, rather than economic, insecurity; of loss of identity; of community. There was a new rhetoric in the fifties, with such phrases as "the lonely crowd," "the quest for community," "the eclipse of community," and "organization man," all given intensity by preoccupation with the master word of the postwar intellectual mind: *alienation*. These were hardly pressing matters for American intellectuals back in the nineteen-twenties and thirties. "Crisis" then referred to the capitalist economy, not to one's personal identity or to the intimacies of community. But in the fifties, the only perturbations, the only tensions, strains, and agonies that really mattered were those which could be seen in, or inferred from, the human spirit and its ties with culture.

And thus a new Tocqueville began to appear in American intellectual journals from 1950 on. I don't say the Tocqueville of totalitarianism and bureaucracy disappeared; not by any means. But the great interest of *Democracy in America* throughout the 1950s was much less political than it was social and cultural. The book became in substantial measure our guide to a suddenly perceived alienation and anomie in the midst of postwar American middle-class affluence.

Interestingly, a new Marx made his appearance at this time: the previously unknown or ignored Marx of the Paris essays, the Marx of alienation, the existentialist, the humanist Marx, so different from the Marx we had read and been moved by in the decade of the thirties. Marx, even the Paris Marx, is hardly the anatomist of affluence, but the fact remains that for the first time a kind of dialogue became possible between Marx and Tocqueville: hence another reason for the American Left's rising interest in Tocqueville during the 1950s.

Tocqueville had discovered, or believed he had, universal economic prosperity among middle-class Americans, and also among the European middle classes in the emerging democracies. Characteristically, he set himself to reflection, long before Lord Keynes, upon the social, cultural, and spiritual consequences of taking economic prosperity for granted. What Tocqueville perceived continues to make interesting and often persuasive reading.

He saw permanent inflation built into democracy—not only economic, but linguistic, rhetorical, moral, and cultural inflation—as the result of the constantly escalating expectations that a combination of equality and materialistic hedonism creates. A whole way of life, he thought, was founded, or would be founded, on this revolution of rising expectations. He saw other consequences or epiphenomena of affluence: a general weakening of the social bond; a decline in the sense of the reality and importance of society; a turning inward to the privacy of, first family, then self; a spread of egoism that he termed the rust of individualism; and, far from least, a diminished confidence of the individual in himself, a growing sense of isolation and of impotence in almost direct proportion to the democratization of the social order and to the increase in middle-class economic substance.

Gratification of material desires, he noted, is made easier and is ever more coveted; but such gratification, far from adding to the sum of middle-class happiness, seems to work in the opposite direction: to induce restlessness, even disquiet and melancholy. Alternations between passivity and a spiritualized fanaticism are common. "In democratic times, enjoyments are more intense than in the ages of aristocracy, and the number of those who partake in them is vastly larger, but it must be admitted that man's hopes and desires are oftener blasted, the soul is more stricken and perturbed, and care itself more keen." On the one hand, Tocqueville found in America "a kind of virtuous materialism," one that will not "corrupt but enervate the soul and noiselessly unbend its springs of action." But side by side with this materialism, he saw "in the midst of American society . . . men full of a fanatical, almost wild spiritualism." He continues: "The soul has wants which must be satisfied; and whatever pains are taken to divert it from itself, it soon grows weary, restless, and disquieted amid the enjoyments of sense."

Such perceptions did not go unnoticed in the United States in the 1950s when the full effects of postwar prosperity were so widely present in intellectual consciousness. No wonder affluent middle-class youth especially found itself preoccupied on a widening scale with this Tocqueville, as he was introduced into more and more college courses across the land. Those already predisposed to see conflict between material prosperity and virtue could, and did, find ample support from Tocqueville. His long chapter in Part II on honor and its inexorable decline as the consequence of democratic and commercial forces is a classic in itself, and as prescient as anything else to be found in *Democracy in America*. That men in high places and low would flout the coercions of honor under the temptations of modern power and affluence is only too clearly set forth in this chapter. It is no wonder, then, that the book came to attract the interest of the Left as well as the Right in this country. I have not forgotten how vital *Democracy in America* seemed to students of the New Left as well as to the New Conservatives in my classes at Berkeley when I first began to assign the book regularly. For here was a degree of detail in the limning of corruption of moral values that was not to be found in Marx or even the anarchists.

Almost equally prized by American intellectuals in this same decade of the 1950s were Tocqueville's ruminations on the decline in intellectual and cultural values under democracy. The lesson here was, to be sure, harder to accept. We had, after all, been nurtured by Jefferson and his long line of philosophical descendants. That democracy induced degradation of culture was not easily assimilated by American intellectuals. But they were attentive nevertheless to Tocqueville's treatment, in Part II, of the literary, scientific, and artistic characteristics of democracy set in commercialism. Cultural standards and "forms" diminish or else retreat to ever more private places. In literature a "trading spirit" is introduced, and "for some few great authors . . . you may reckon thousands of idea-mongers." Art ranges from the insignificant and banal to the emptily monumental; little intermediate ground is occupied. Science is overwhelmingly practical or applied; its vital philosophical and theoretical roots are untended, unheeded. Everywhere is to be seen adoration of the multitude, on the one hand, and anxious preoccupation with the puniness of the individual, on the other. Democracy cultivates regard for the entirety of a people and enjoins self-regard upon the individual; but all intermediate forms of community, whether moral, aesthetic, or social, tend to atrophy and, with them, individual self-confidence.

I needn't dwell any longer on this Tocqueville—the anatomist of affluence, its pleasures and profits, its pains and alienations. He was as real an eminence in the 1950s as an earlier Tocqueville, prophet of totalitarianism, had been in the 1940s and a much earlier Tocqueville, herald of American progress, had been a century earlier. How long this third Tocqueville would have survived in American intellectual consciousness had other things been held in abeyance, we can only guess. But, as is now a matter of vivid memory, other things did not remain the same. The Supreme Court decision of 1954 massively and permanently altered the American social and political landscape, although the implications of this decision were several years in reaching American life and thought. Suffice it to say that *Brown v. Board of Education* gave impetus and, in time, focus to what will surely prove to be the transcending moral and political issue of the second half of the twentieth century: *equality*.

Now another Tocqueville emerged gradually on the scene, a Tocqueville very much with us as I write. And here, I suggest, though with due regard for the authenticity of the other Tocquevilles I have described, we have the essential, the constitutive Tocqueville. For equality is the master concept in Tocqueville's writings, all of them: equality in its relations with power, freedom, and other major values. As many a reader has been forced to conclude, *equality*, not *democracy* with its several, variable connotations, should have been made the title of Part II of Tocqueville's classic. Where the *majority* is the brooding presence of Part I, *equality* succeeds to this eminence in the second part of the work. Tocqueville was quite literally tormented by the idea of equality. Countless letters and notes as well as passages in his books attest to this. He was also both ambiguous and ambivalent in his treatment of equality, just as many of us are at this moment.

For, although never doubting the omnipresent and inexorable character of equality as historical tendency, he is yet prone to its analysis, and quite often in this analysis indecision is the essence. Thus, through equality more men have become able to read and also to write books, but the quality of the books has diminished and, with rare interruptions, will continue to diminish. Language, having become the property of all or most, suffers inflation, becomes increasingly a means, ranging from the orotund to the primitive, of hiding or blurring meanings. Public monuments become more numerous but less and less important. Through equality ancient barriers are broken down, but money, rather than rank, becomes dominant and subjects man's spirit to its own torments. With inherited rank decreasingly important, the opportunity for competition is opened, but such competition for status becomes in its own way as tyrannical as anything before it. For the essence of competition, Tocqueville stresses, when it is fused with democratic equality, is to demand incessant proofs and demonstrations of merit, through examinations of one kind or other, and the creative spirit grows weak or becomes alienated altogether by the prospect of being forced constantly to prove itself through signs available to all. It is a great thing, he quotes Pascal as saying, to be born a man of intellectual quality; it is a clear gain of at least twenty years. But of what use is this if one must be perennially ready to prove it through means or symbols of the public's own choice, through wearying hurdles over which everyone must jump? There is also the sense of weakness generated in the individual by observation of the sea of equality. "The citizen of a democracy comparing himself with others feels proud of his equality with each. But when he compares himself with all his fellows, and measures himself against this vast entity, he is overwhelmed by the sense of his insignificance and weakness." Hence the decline of great ambition and its replacement by countless minuscule aspirations. The spirit of competition, he writes, overtakes and soon destroys the great ambition in an egalitarian age. Society is at once monotonous and agitated; the danger or prospect of genuine revolution is diminished, but with this the prospect also of genuine intellectual and cultural change.

But by far the greatest of tensions in Tocqueville's mind is that relating to freedom and equality. Others, beginning with Aristotle and continuing through Edmund Burke, noted the potential conflict between the two values, but Tocqueville was the first to construct a whole social and political philosophy around it, and ambivalence is its essence. Thus, in one passage he can write: "Personally, far from finding fault with equality because it inspires a spirit of independence, I praise it primarily for that very reason. I admire it because it lodges in the very depths of each man's heart and mind that indefinable feeling, the instinctive inclination for political independence, and thus prepares the remedy for the ill it engenders. It is precisely for this reason that I cling to it."

Only a few paragraphs below, however, Tocqueville can write in different key. All centralizing minds, he tells us, are fond of equality, and all egalitarian minds are attracted to centralization. "The foremost or indeed the sole condition required in order to succeed in centralizing the supreme power in a democratic community is to love equality or to get men to believe you love it. Thus the science of despotism, which was once so complex, is simplified, and reduced, as it were, to a single principle." Repeatedly, centralization of power and equality are made the separate variables in a single parametric equation.

Nor is this, in Tocqueville, invariably set in a hostile view. In his generally gloomy assessment of the Negro-white future in the United States—an assessment that comes toward the end of Part I but is picked up again in Part II and in many letters—we find centralization, even in despotic degree, seen by Tocqueville as perhaps the only means whereby black and white perceptions of their inequality can become dissolved in common subjection to a political will that equalizes even as it tyrannizes. Tocqueville loathed not only the slavery he saw in the South, but also the whole racist perspective in historical or sociological interpretation, as his fascinating correspondence with Gobineau makes incontestably clear. But he did not underestimate the sheer power of the black-white relation upon the American mind. If in Europe, he writes, centuries have been required for the marks of servitude to be erased from the faces of those who are, after all, members of the same race with those who were once their masters, how much longer will be required where color is involved? It is to American abolitionists that Tocqueville addresses the following warning: "I am obliged to confess that I do not regard the abolition of slavery as a means of warding off the struggle of the two races in the Southern states. The Negroes may long remain slaves without complaining; but if they are once raised to the level of freemen they will soon revolt at being deprived of almost all their civil rights, and if they cannot become the equals of the whites they will speedily show themselves as enemies."

He was as struck by the black freedman as by the slave, and what he saw depressed him. He writes: "If I were called upon to predict the future, I should say that the abolition of slavery in the South will, generally, increase the repugnance of the White population for the Black. I base this upon analogous observations I have made in the North. I have remarked that the White inhabitants of the North avoid the Blacks with increasing care in proportion as the legal barriers of separation are removed by the legislature." And in a note to himself he observes that whereas in the South the whites do not care how close physically the blacks come to them so long as they do not seek to rise in the social scale, in the North they do not care how high the blacks rise so long as they do not come too close.

Tocqueville's relevance to the present, and indeed possibly to the rest of this century, may very well be greater than it has been in any of his previous images in the American mind. For equality is, as Tocqueville in the introduction to his work declared it to be, a providential fact—by which he meant an irresistible, encompassing, and dominating fact or value. Who can doubt that, major war or other catastrophe aside, equality will be the point of reference for an ever-growing number of issues in social policy? Tocqueville himself was in no doubt whatever: "Would it be wise to imagine that a social movement the causes of which lie so far back can be checked by the efforts of one generation? Can it be believed that the equality which has overthrown the feudal system and vanquished kings will retreat before tradesmen and capitalists? Will it stop now that it is grown strong and its adversaries weak?"

Plainly Tocqueville did not think so, and if the prospect could on occasion sadden and depress him, he could yet, in the very final pages of *Democracy in America*, emphasize that what exhibited itself in his eyes as intellectual monotony, as a cultural desert brought on by the leveling of inequalities of talent, might well present itself differently to

God. "We may naturally believe," he writes, "that it is not the singular prosperity of the few, but the greater well-being of all that is most pleasing in the sight of the Creator and Preserver of men." We may so believe, but it is only too evident, taking Tocqueville in the full, that he did not himself believe—could not bring himself to believe—in this wise. The pursuit of equality, he writes in scores of contexts, the never-ending insistence upon equality, once the gates have been opened, must not only sterilize individuality and erode the authority of reason and of culture, but bring on a constantly augmenting feeling of personal impotence, of envy-inspired malice that will in the end almost certainly bring about power in unprecedented shape.

Yet I would be doing him an injustice if I left it at this. "Providence," he writes in the final three sentences of *Democracy in America*, "has not created man entirely dependent or entirely free. It is true that around every man a fatal circle is traced beyond which he cannot pass; but within the wide extent of that circle he is powerful and free; and as it is with man, so is it with communities. The nations of our time cannot prevent the conditions of men from becoming equal, but it depends upon themselves whether the principle of equality is to lead them to servitude or to freedom, to knowledge or barbarism, to prosperity or to wretchedness."

Was Tocqueville gifted, as some have said, with genuine prevision? Did he see things telescopically, as David Riesman has suggested, rather than through lenses designed for the scene immediately around him? Was he gifted—as a tiny few in history seem at times to be—with intuitions beyond the reach of ordinary analysis or method? It is tempting to believe that he was. I am mindful, though, of Tocqueville intuitions gone wrong, or at least yet unfulfilled. I would prefer to go back to my characterization of *Democracy in America* as a composite: a composite of genius, to be sure, but nevertheless a composite of many sometimes conflicting, rarely articulated, never systematized, ideal types or models. They spring, as these almost always do in talented minds, from combinations of perception and reflection, of observation and sheer brooding. Historical vicissitude gives them pertinence, ranging from visions of progress to foretellings of degeneration or disaster.

In the end, Tocqueville himself confessed impotence in prophecy, and also a certain weariness. A few years before his death he asked in his *Recollections*: "Shall we ever, as we are assured by other prophets, perhaps as delusive as their predecessors, shall we ever attain a more complete and far-reaching social transformation than our forefathers foresaw and desired, and that we ourselves are able to foresee; or are we not destined simply to end in a condition of intermittent anarchy, the well-known, chronic and incurable complaint of old nations? As for me, I am unable to say; I do not know when this long voyage will be ended; I am weary of seeing the shore in each successive mirage, and I often ask myself whether the *terra firma* we are seeking does really exist, and whether we are not doomed to rove upon the seas forever."

JAMES T. SCHLEIFER

From Egoism to Individualism†

The word *individualisme* first appeared in the early 1820s in the writings of Joseph de Maistre and other Frenchmen; after 1825, it could be found quite regularly in the works of the Saint-Simonians. René Rémond has even noted that by 1833 to 1835 certain journalists specifically applied *individualisme* to the American republic. So the term was not strictly speaking one of those new words to describe new things for which Tocqueville had issued so eloquent a call. But its use was still relatively rare enough, even in 1840, to cause Tocqueville to comment: "*Individualisme* is a word recently coined to express a new idea. Our fathers only knew about *égoïsme*."

Henry Reeve's translation of the 1840 *Democracy* saw the term's first appearance in English. Reeve felt obliged to add a personal note explaining his inability to offer any familiar English equivalent and apologizing for the neologism. Tocqueville's book, along with those of Michel Chevalier and Friedrich List, also introduced the word to America.

Curiously, in the United States (and to a lesser degree in England) the term would have a heavily positive connotation quite at odds with the typically pejorative use of *individualisme* by Tocqueville and most other Frenchmen. To Americans, especially as the nineteenth century progressed, the word would conjure up images of extensive political and economic freedoms. Tocqueville's own diary remarks about the "fundamental social principles" in the United States of self-reliance and of individual independence and responsibility had captured something of what Americans would later mean by "individualism." But Tocqueville's own understanding of the term would consistently be quite different.

In 1840 Tocqueville would begin his explanation by attempting carefully to distinguish *égoïsme* and *individualisme*.

"*Egoïsme* is a passionate and exaggerated love of self which leads a man to think of all things in terms of himself and to prefer himself to all.

"*Individualisme* is a calm and considered feeling which disposes each citizen to isolate himself from the mass of his fellows and withdraw into the circle of family and friends; with this little society formed to his taste, he gladly leaves the greater society to look after itself.

"*Egoïsme* springs from a blind instinct; *individualisme* is based on misguided judgment rather than depraved feeling. It is due more to inadequate understanding than to perversity of heart.

"*Egoïsme* sterilizes the seeds of every virtue; *individualisme* at first

† James T. Schleifer is a professor of American Studies at the College of New Rochelle and the author of *The Making of Tocqueville's Democracy in America* (Chapel Hill: The University of North Carolina Press, 1980), from which this selection is taken; reprinted by permission of the Liberty Fund. Footnotes have been deleted.

only dams the spring of public virtue, but in the long run it attacks and destroys all the others too and finally merges in *égoïsme*.

"*Egoïsme* is a vice as old as the world. It is not peculiar to one form of society more than another.

"*Individualisme* is of democratic origin and threatens to grow as conditions get more equal."

Key elements in this definition were the peaceful and reflective nature of individualism and Tocqueville's insistence that, despite apparent prudence, individualism arose from short-sighted and erroneous judgments. He also stressed that individualism was new, the result of advancing *démocratie*, and that, unlike *égoïsme* which largely fixed attention on the solitary "I," individualism stimulated the creation of a narrow, sacrosanct society of family and friends which then became the exclusive concern of each person.

Two letters between Tocqueville and Royer-Collard cast additional light upon certain features of this explanation. In the summer of 1838, Alexis and Marie arrived in Normandy where the husband hoped to find solitude and quiet for his writing and the wife hoped to supervise the undertaking of badly needed renovations of the old château. Alexis's loud complaints about the noise of workmen and the incessant interruptions by visiting local dignitaries soon demonstrated the magnitude of his miscalculations. In the midst of his troubles, Tocqueville could not help reflecting on the nature of these provincial visitors. "I have again found much good will and no end of attention here. I am attached to this population, without, all the same, concealing its faults which are great. These people here are honest, intelligent, religious enough, passably moral, very steady: but they have scarcely any disinterestedness. It is true that *égoïsme* in this region does not resemble that of Paris, so violent and often so cruel. It is a mild, calm, and tenacious love of private interests, which bit by bit absorbs all other sentiments of the heart and dries up nearly all sources of enthusiasm there. They join to this *égoïsme* a certain number of private virtues and domestic qualities which, as a whole, form respectable men and poor citizens. I would pardon them all the same for not being disinterested, if they sometimes wanted to believe in disinterestedness. But they do not want to do so, and that, in the midst of all the signs of their good will, makes me feel oppressed. Unfortunately only time can help me escape an oppression of this type, and I am not patient."

In reply the old Doctrinaire reminded Tocqueville that what he saw was not in any way peculiar to Normandy. "You are peeved about the country where you live; but your *Normans*, they are France, they are the world; this prudent and intelligent *égoïsme*, it is the *bonnêtes gens* of our time, trait for trait."

This "mild, calm, and tenacious love of private interests" which helps to form "respectable men and poor citizens," this *égoïsme* of 1838, closely paralleled Tocqueville's later description of *individualisme*. So aside from the implication that the good bourgeoisie of La Manche helped to shape Tocqueville's image of *individualisme*, these two letters raise a more significant question. Did Tocqueville's adoption by 1840 of the word *individualisme* signify that he had truly moved beyond this earlier notion of *égoïsme*? Or had he merely given a new name to a concept which he had already repeatedly defined?

Not only were many descriptions from 1835 and 1840 (and in between) similar, but also Tocqueville's 1840 list of essential remedies for *égoïsme* or *individualisme* would largely reiterate the prescriptions of 1835. It is also significant that Tocqueville would liberally and apparently indiscriminately sprinkle both the terms *égoïsme* and *individualisme* throughout his final 1840 text.

Yet despite great similarities and Tocqueville's habitually inexact use of key words, the *individualisme* of the 1840 *Democracy* would differ in certain significant ways from the *égoïsme* of 1835, or even 1838. In the second half of his book, Tocqueville would describe at length two additional causes of *individualisme*, would examine some new intellectual facets of the concept and, most important, would painstakingly expose its eventual political consequences.

Tocqueville had long recognized that the growth of *démocratie* and the gradual development of democratic social conditions favored the spread of selfishness and of a sense of individual helplessness in a society. But by 1840 he would also indict the *esprit révolutionnaire* as one of the forces that most exacerbated *individualisme*. In a summary of essential ideas about *égoïsme*, he declared:

"*Egoïsme*. How *démocratie* tends to develop the *égoïsme* natural to the human heart. When conditions are equal, when each person is more or less sufficient unto himself and has neither the duty to give nor to receive from anyone else, it is natural that he withdraws into himself and that for him society ends where his family ends.

"Only widespread enlightenment can then teach him the indirect utility that he can gain from the prosperity of all. Here, as in many other things, only democratic institutions can partially correct the evils which the democratic social state brings forth.

"What makes democratic nations selfish is not so much the large number of independent citizens which they contain as it is the large number of citizens who are constantly arriving at independence.

"That is a principal idea.

"Feeling of independence which, for the first time, grips a multitude of individuals and exalts them. This means that *égoïsme* must appear more open and less enlightened among people who are becoming democratic than among people who have been democratic for a long time.

"Considering everything, I do not believe that there is more *égoïsme* in France than in America. The only difference is that in America it is enlightened and in France it is not. The Americans know how to sacrifice a portion of their personal interests in order to save the rest. We want to keep everything and often everything escapes us.

"Danger if conditions equalize faster than enlightenment spreads. Here perhaps a transition to the doctrine of enlightened self-interest (*intérêt bien entendu*)."

This passage, probably dating from the early months of 1836, again underscored the link between *démocratie* and *égoïsme* and the importance of enlightened self-interest. It also repeated the definition of *égoïsme* as a feeling of individual detachment and exclusive concern for private interests and attempted to explain some significant differences between France and America. Tocqueville apparently believed that his own country suffered from a more virulent *égoïsme* because France had only recently undergone a democratic revolution (or was still in the midst of it); America, born in equality, had not required such an abrupt upheaval.

As the composition of his work went forward, Tocqueville became increasingly aware that an important difference existed between the changes caused by advancing *démocratie* and the effects of certain revolutionary forces which he sensed were still at work in France. "Idea to express probably in the Preface. All existing democratic peoples are more or less in a state of revolution. But the state of revolution is a particular condition which produces certain effects that must not be confused and that are unique to it. The difficulty is to recognize among democratic peoples what is *revolutionary* and what is *democratic*."

Elsewhere he reflected: "Idea to put well in the foreground. Effects of *démocratie*, and particularly harmful effects, that are exaggerated in the period of revolution in the midst of which the democratic social condition, *moeurs*, and laws are established . . . The great difficulty in the study of *démocratie* is to distinguish what is democratic from what is only revolutionary. This is very difficult because examples are lacking. There is no European people among which *démocratie* has completely settled in, and America is in an exceptional situation. The state of literature in France is not only democratic, but revolutionary. Public morality, the same. Religious and political opinions, the same."

In the "Rubish" of the final section on the political consequences of democracy, Tocqueville attempted yet another statement of the problem and a fuller definition.

"Separate with care the *ésprit Démocratique* and the *esprit Révolutionnaire*. . . . Definition of the *esprit révolutionnaire*:

Taste for rapid change; use of violence to bring them about.
Esprit tyrannique.
Scorn for forms.
Scorn for established rights.
Indifference for means, considering the ends [desired].
    Doctrine of the useful (*utile*).
Satisfaction given to brutal appetites.

"The *esprit révolutionnaire*, which is everywhere the greatest enemy of liberty, is so among democratic peoples above all; because there is a natural and secret link between it and *Démocratie*. A revolution can sometimes be just and necessary; it can establish liberty; but the *esprit révolutionnaire* is always detestable and can never lead anywhere except to tyranny."

So the revolutionary spirit, mentality, or attitude was responsible for some of the worst abuses during times of democratic advances. It was France's revolutionary heritage—rather than *démocratie* by itself—which helped to explain the severe dislocations and looming problems which so clearly faced that nation by the late 1830s. Repeatedly in the 1840 *Democracy* Tocqueville would resort to this explanation of what would otherwise have remained a baffling paradox. How did it happen that although America was the more thoroughly democratic nation, yet France more consistently witnessed the flaws and excesses of *démocratie*?

The second part of Tocqueville's book would argue that France should attempt to avoid some of the ills of *démocratie* by becoming more democratic. French political life had to be harmonized with the nation's increasingly democratic social condition; democracy had to be injected into politics. *Individualisme*, for instance, might be mitigated by local liberties and freedom of association. But his final volumes also often reminded readers of the recent and as yet incomplete nature of France's democratic revolution. That, too, helped to explain the intensity of French problems, especially the apparent epidemic of *individualisme*.

In 1835 Tocqueville had devoted only a few pages to the American desire for material well-being. But by 1840 he would place much more emphasis on the *goût du bien-être* and the love of material pleasures. A reason for this greater attention, in addition to his growing personal sensitivity to the materialism of the age, was probably a sharper awareness of the link between material desires and *individualisme*; each encouraged the other. The "democratic taste for material well-being," he stated in a draft, "leads men to become absorbed in its pursuit or enjoyment." *Individualisme* "causes each person to want to be occupied only with himself."

In the 1840 *Democracy*, Tocqueville exposed the preoccupation with material comfort which prevailed in democratic societies and then proceeded to explain his anxiety about such single-minded attachments. "The reproach I address to the principle of equality is not that it leads men away in the pursuit of forbidden enjoyments, but that it absorbs them wholly in quest of those which are allowed. By these means a kind of virtuous materialism may ultimately be established in the world, which would not corrupt, but enervate, the soul and noiselessly unbend its springs of action."

What he feared, in part, was the gradual fixation of men on their small, private material interests and their consequent failure to contribute time and energy to wider public concerns. So democratic materialism also hastened democratic *individualisme*; and the final result might well be the loss of liberty.

Tocqueville's formal definitions of *individualisme* (in manuscripts and text) usually stressed the withdrawal of individuals into petty private concerns and their indifference toward larger social issues. But his lengthy treatment in 1840 of democratic materialism added

ıough only implicitly) an additional feature to his definition: the re-
ιϲntless pursuit of physical ease for oneself and one's family. This single-minded striving for well-being diverted the talents and energies of
individuals from public life as effectively as any sense of isolation or
weakness. So *individualisme* actually had two faces: one passive—
helplessness and withdrawal; the other active—a passion for material
comfort.

In Tocqueville's broadening analysis of *individualisme*, the 1840
Democracy would not only disclose two major additional causes, the
revolutionary spirit and materialism, but would also explore the possible intellectual results of *individualisme*. On an undated page from the
1840 "Rubish," Tocqueville remarked that "There are in *individualisme* two kinds of effects that should be well distinguished so that they
can be dealt with separately. 1. *the moral effects*, hearts isolate themselves; 2. *the intellectual effects*, minds isolate themselves." And in a
sheet enclosed with the original working manuscript of the chapter
entitled "Concerning the Philosophical Approach of the Americans,"
he surveyed the development of what he would call "indépendance individuelle de la pensée."

"In the Middle Ages we saw that all opinions had to flow from authority; in those times philosophy itself, this natural antagonist to
authority, took the form of authority; it clothed itself in the characteristics of a religion. After having created certain opinions by the free
and individual force of certain minds, it imposed these opinions without discussion and compelled the [very] force that had given birth to
it.

"In the eighteenth century we arrived at the opposite extreme, that
is, we pretended to appeal all things only to individual reason and to
drive dogmatic beliefs away entirely. And just as in the Middle Ages we
gave philosophy the form and the style of a religion, so in the eighteenth century we gave religion the form and the style of philosophy.

"In our times, the movement still continues among minds of the
second rank, but the others [know?] and admit that received and discovered beliefs, authority and liberty, *individualisme* and social force
are all needed at the same time. The whole question is to sort out the
limits of these pairs.

"It is to that [question] that I must put all my mind."

In the margin, Tocqueville carefully (and luckily) penned the date:
"24 April 1837."

Here is the earliest dated use by Tocqueville of the term *individualisme* that has yet been uncovered in the voluminous drafts and manuscripts of the *Democracy*. But what is most intriguing about this first
dated instance is Tocqueville's relatively favorable or at least neutral
usage. Here he apparently grouped *individualisme* with liberty and intellectual discovery as opponents of authority and imposed belief.

Tocqueville would argue in the 1840 *Democracy* that the tendency
toward *individualisme* caused men in democratic ages to abandon traditional intellectual authorities and to rely on their own powers of rea-

son. His basic sympathy for a certain independence of mind would be evident, but he would worry first, that intellectual self-reliance might be pushed too far, and, second, that men would too quickly find a dangerous substitute for the authorities of old: the judgment of the public. The intellectual independence of individuals might thus succumb to the dictates of the mass.

Perhaps Tocqueville's relatively approving use of *individualisme* in the fragment above once again reflected the depth of his anxiety about a possible loss of freedom of ideas. Of all the ways in which the mass might stifle the individual, the suppression of personal thought and opinion struck him as the most terrible. So in democratic times, a fierce intellectual self-reliance, a stubborn defense of one's own mental independence apparently did not seem as potentially dangerous to Tocqueville as did other facets of *individualisme*. Only a profoundly rooted *raison individuelle indépendante* could possibly resist the enormous pressure of society as a whole.

The 1835 *Democracy* had predicted despotism as a result of the unequal struggle between "each citizen . . . equally impotent, poor, and isolated" and "the organized force of the government." But the 1840 volumes would now go beyond this to offer a detailed examination of the relationships among *individualisme*, centralization, and despotism.

The decline in individual energy and concern created a social and political vacuum into which the bureaucracy rushed. The "Rubish" of the large chapter entitled "How the Ideas and Feelings Suggested by Equality Influence the Political Constitution" offered a succinct but revealing description of the trend. "*Individualisme*—the habit of living isolated from one's fellows, of not concerning oneself with anything that is common business, of abandoning this care to the sole, clearly visible representative of common interests, which is the government. *Chacun chez soi; chacun pour soi.* That is the natural instinct which can be corrected."

Tocqueville also realized that, at the same time, the suffocating effects of a centralized and omnipresent government in turn further discouraged any private efforts. If unchecked, this relentless cycle of reinforcement would ultimately end in total "individual servitude," the hallmark of the New Despotism. So the final portion of his book would serve primarily to express his concern for the survival of *indépendance individuelle* in democratic times. "To lay down extensive but distinct and settled limits to the action of the government; to confer certain rights on private persons, and to secure to them the undisputed enjoyment of those rights; to enable individual man to maintain whatever independence, strength, and original power he still possesses; to raise him by the side of society at large, and uphold him in that position; these appear to me the main objects of legislators in the ages upon which we are now entering."

Often overlooked in Tocqueville's excellent analysis of the political effects of *démocratie* is his discussion of what he would call its liberal tendencies. His apprehensions about *individualisme*, centralization, and despotism would largely focus the last chapter of his book on the negative influences of advancing equality. His grim warnings divert attention from his praises for the encouragements which *démocratie* gave to liberty.

On an extra sheet in the working manuscript, he explicitly recognized certain redeeming democratic features:

The liberal tendencies of equality—
No respect.
No immobility.
Multitude and variety of desires.
Mobility of the political world.

In the published chapter, these ideas would first be explained and then be subsumed by the phrase "love of independence." Various drafts elaborated further on this democratic encouragement of independence and revealed Tocqueville's strong approval of this influence. In one version he declared: "Begin by establishing the first tendency of equality toward individual independence and liberty. Show that this tendency can go as far as anarchy. In general it is the democratic tendency that people fear the most; and it is the one that I consider the greatest element of salvation that equality leaves us. Finish by indicating that this is not, however, the strongest and most continuous tendency that equality suggests. How through phases of anarchy (because of *individualisme*) democratic peoples tend however in a continuous manner toward the centralization of power."

Another draft stated: "Two contrary tendencies, not equally sustained, not equally strong, but two tendencies. The one toward individual independence; the other toward the concentration of power. . . . As for me, I consider the taste for natural independence as the most precious gift which equality has given to men."

In 1840, the text would expand upon these ideas. And in his penultimate chapter Tocqueville would add: "The men who live in the democratic ages upon which we are entering have naturally a taste for independence; they are naturally impatient of regulation, and they are wearied by the permanence even of the condition they themselves prefer. They are fond of power, but they are prone to despise and hate those who wield it, and they easily elude its grasp by their own mobility and insignificance.

"These propensities will always manifest themselves, because they originate in the groundwork of society, which will undergo no change; for a long time they will prevent the establishment of any despotism, and they will furnish fresh weapons to each succeeding generation that struggles in favor of the liberty of mankind. Let us, then, look forward to the future with the salutary fear which makes men keep watch and ward for freedom, not with that faint and idle terror which depresses and enervates the heart."

So strong was Tocqueville's attachment to what was, in less noble terms, the cantankerous, free individual that he once again found himself at the brink of serious contradiction. In a draft he wrote: "I have shown . . . how, as equality became greater, each man, finding himself less dependent and more separated from his fellows, felt more inclined to consider himself apart and to live in isolation." In a note immediately following, he observed: "This implies a contradiction with what precedes on the idea of centralization."

In a passage in his working manuscript he declared that "during the centuries of equality, each man, living independent of all of his fellows, gets used to directing without constraint his private affairs. When these same men meet in common, they naturally have the taste and the idea of administering themselves by themselves. So equality carries men toward administrative decentralization; but at the same time it creates powerful instincts which lead them away from it."

Here was an idea directly contrary to the relationship between *démocratie* and centralization which Tocqueville had posited years earlier. In the margin of this fragment he suggested: "Perhaps keep this for the place where I will speak about the liberal instincts created by equality." Instead, however, he would simply strike these sentences from the final text. In 1840, the implied contradiction between the love of independence and the tendency toward centralization would remain for perceptive readers to ponder. Any explicit mention had been carefully deleted.

At the heart of Tocqueville's analysis of *égoïsme* or *individualisme* remained an abiding paradox that could be traced back at least as far as his references in 1830 to the struggle between *la force individuelle* and *la force sociale*. While condemning *individualisme*, Tocqueville consistently upheld the goal of *indépendance individuelle*. "In our times, those who fear an excess of *individualisme* are right, and those who fear the extreme dependence of the individual are also right. Idea to express somewhere *necessarily*."

He believed that individuals should not occupy themselves solely with their own affairs and ignore the needs of the wider society. Yet he was also persuaded that perhaps the highest purpose of a society was the fullest possible development of the dignity and freedom of the individual. He decried the tendency in democratic times for the individual to limit his efforts to a narrowly defined circle of concern. Yet he also deeply desired a secure and independent sphere of action for each person free from any unnecessary intrusions of public power. Democratic society must not be allowed to swallow up the individual, and yet each person must be led to a higher sense of his public responsibilities and to a healthy willingness to engage in common affairs. What America had taught him was some means of reconciling these private and public interests.

A statement of the essence of this paradox appeared in yet another of Tocqueville's drafts. "To sustain the individual in the face of whatever social power, to conserve something for his independence, his force, his originality; such must be the constant effort of all the friends of humanity in democratic times. Just as in democratic times it is necessary to elevate society and lower the individual."

In February 1840, a letter to Henry Reeve summarized Tocqueville's beliefs. "The great peril of democratic ages, you may be sure, is the destruction or the excessive weakening *of the parts* of the social body in the face of the *whole*. Everything that in our times raises up the idea of the individual is healthy. Everything that gives a separate existence to the species and enlarges the notion of the type is dangerous. The *esprit* of our contemporaries turns by itself in this direction. The doctrine of the realists, introduced to the political world, urges forward all the abuses of *Démocratie*; it is what facilitates despotism, centralization, contempt for individual rights, the doctrine of necessity, all the institutions and all the doctrines which permit the social body to trample men underfoot and which make the nation everything and the citizens nothing.

"That is one of my *fundamental* opinions to which many of my ideas lead. On this point I have reached an absolute conviction; and the principal object of my book has been to give this conviction to the reader."

This statement to Reeve underscored an additional peculiarity of Tocqueville's attachment to *indépendance individuelle*. To combat *individualisme*, to preserve the strength and the dignity of the individual, he assigned a predominant role to "the parts of the social body," to the *corps secondaires*, principally self-governing localities and associations of all sorts. In democratic times, *la force individuelle* required new means of sustenance. What Tocqueville proposed, in short, was to save the individual by encouraging the small group or the artificially created community. The individual would be buoyed up not by his own efforts or powers, but by the support of his fellows. Again we come face to face with paradox.

Concern for the integrity of the individual is one of the bedrocks of Tocqueville's book and outlook. At least as early as 1830, he had been alert to the tension between the individual and the society at large; and an acute awareness of that ancient struggle had informed the writing of his entire book. Whether Tocqueville labeled it *force individuelle* or *indépendance individuelle*, his desire for preserving the dignity of each human being remained at the core of the *Democracy*.

The fundamental solution to this ageless problem, Tocqueville argued, was to seek a deeper understanding of private and public interests and so to attempt the establishment of a new harmony between individual and social needs. This basic concept, which Tocqueville variously called *égoïsme intelligent* or *intérêt bien entendu*, had been among the many lessons of America. But it should also be noted that Tocqueville's anxiety about accelerating *individualisme*, like his interest in centralization, perhaps reflected more his concerns about the social and political conditions of France and French attitudes in the 1830s than his knowledge of American society. In fact, it might be said that on these matters, he kept forgetting America.

The 1840 volumes of the *Democracy* introduced a significant new reason for *individualisme*, the *esprit révolutionnaire*, and that cause served as yet another important analytic device throughout the last part of Tocqueville's book. It helped to explain not only the spread of *individualisme*, but also the increasing trend toward centralization, for example.

By the late 1830s, Tocqueville was increasingly persuaded that France's revolution had not ended in 1830, but was still proceeding and was perhaps even permanent. So a second fundamental historical force, *esprit révolutionnaire*, came to join *démocratie* in the second part of Tocqueville's work. Indeed, his attention during the 1840s and 1850s would be drawn more and more away from *démocratie* and toward revolution. (The latter along with the persistent theme of centralization would clearly come to the fore in Tocqueville's *L'Ancien Régime et la révolution*.) Even by the late 1830s, the trend toward *démocratie* was apparently facing increasing competition for Tocqueville's attention from the concept of *esprit révolutionnaire*.

In 1840 Tocqueville also specifically acknowledged and briefly discussed the significance of a third basic development, industrialization. So by the time the last section of his masterpiece was drafted, Tocqueville was writing about the conjunction of three great forces: *démocratie*, revolution, and industrialization. The focus of his work was still on *démocratie* and its influences and possibilities; but, as Tocqueville then recognized, the future of France and, more generally, of Western civilization ultimately hinged on the interplay of these three developments. Presumably one reason for the not uncommon opinion that the last is also the best and most profound portion of the *Democracy* is Tocqueville's masterful treatment of the complex interrelation of these forces. His work and thought had significantly broadened. Although that tendency presented certain well-recognized dangers of abstraction and lack of precision, it also allowed once again for great depth and insight.

So the 1840 volumes, more than the first two, presented a persistent problem of balance both for Tocqueville and his readers. Not only did he resort more frequently to double and triple comparisons of America, England, and France, but he also attempted, sometimes unsuccessfully, to distinguish clearly between what was American and what was democratic, or between what was democratic and what was revolutionary. When his growing recognition of industrialization is remembered, it becomes clear that, especially by the late 1830s, Tocqueville had become a sort of ambitious and sometimes highly skilled intellectual juggler, bravely attempting to keep a large number of key concepts simultaneously in motion.

We may go beyond this observation to suggest that Tocqueville liked to think in contraries. His penchants for learning by comparison and for making distinctions sometimes led him to (or even over) the brink of contradiction. But more often his mental inclinations simply caused him to see concepts as *pairs in tension*. Our examination of the making of the *Democracy* has suggested several significant examples of this intellectual trait. *Démocratie*, he wrote at various times, exhibited opposite tendencies: toward thinking for oneself and toward not thinking at all; toward suspicion of authority and toward the concentration of power; toward individual independence and toward conformity and submission to the crowd; toward a social and political activity so intense that it spilled over into intellectual and cultural pursuits and toward a pandering of mind and soul to reigning ideas and values. The major task for responsible and thoughtful persons in democratic times was, in one sense, to "sort out the limits of these pairs." The resulting inescapable tensions (and paradoxes) were a hallmark not only of periods of advancing equality, but also of Tocqueville's masterpiece itself.

Most of the major themes treated by Tocqueville in his book are so intricately linked that to grab hold of one is inevitably to pull many others along as well. This tightly knit character is especially apparent when the triple notions of centralization, despotism, and *individualisme* are involved. Particularly in the final section of the 1840 *Democracy*, the three ideas become virtually inextricable. To the extent that Tocqueville has an identifiable "doctrine," centralization, despotism, and *individualisme* (or their opposites: pluralism, liberty, and *indépendance individuelle*) are its Trinity; and *démocratie*, its One.

CATHERINE ZUCKERT

Not by Preaching: Tocqueville on the Role of Religion in American Democracy†

Both Jack Lively and Marvin Zetterbaum comment on the paradoxical character of Alexis de Tocqueville's teaching in *Democracy in America* with regard to the importance of religious belief in maintaining liberal democracy.[1] By concentrating on the political utility of religious belief to the point of indifference as to its content, they argue, Tocqueville undermines the very belief he finds necessary to the preservation of liberty. Moreover, how can the proponent of unrestrained freedom of the press and the enlightened rationalism of "self-interest rightly understood" advocate the creation of "social myths"? Both critics conclude that Tocqueville's position is untenable. I shall argue, on the contrary, that Tocqueville's argument is internally consistent. From a democratic perspective, Christianity represents an accidental historical heritage. By adapting to democratic conditions, Christianity can persist and even have important political effects, however. It provides an essential foundation for the individual and political self-restraint necessary to maintain liberal democracy, but it exercises its influence indirectly, through the wholly liberal means of public opinion in the context of a strict separation of church and state. Because Tocqueville sees a natural source for the simplified religious beliefs necessary to

† Catherine Zuckert is the Nancy Reeves Dreux Professor of Political Philosophy at the University of Notre Dame. This essay appeared in *The Review of Politics* 44 (1981): 259–80. Reprinted with permission of Cambridge University Press.
1. Jack Lively, *The Social and Political Thought of Alexis de Tocqueville* (Oxford, 1962), pp. 196–97; Marvin Zetterbaum, *Tocqueville and the Problem of Democracy* (Stanford, California, 1967), pp. 120–24, 147.

maintain a liberal democracy, he does not need to advocate the inculcation of myths." Popular faith alone does not secure the liberty of the
individual in the United States, but in the absence of widespread religious belief, neither economic "individualism" nor liberal political institutions would either.

Tocqueville explicitly directs his argument concerning the place of
religion in democracies to those in France who attack religion from
love of democracy.[2] Thus he begins by using the American experience
merely to show the compatibility of religion and democracy. Even the
Catholic church, so associated with the aristocratic past in Europe,
has strongly egalitarian aspects.

> In matters of dogma the Catholic faith places all intellects on the
> same level; the learned man and the ignorant, the genius and the
> common herd, must all subscribe to the same details of belief; rich
> and poor must follow the same observances, and it imposes the
> same austerities upon the strong and the weak; it makes no com-
> promise with any mortal, but applying the same standard to every
> human being, it mingles all classes of society at the foot of the
> same altar just as they are mingled in the sight of God. (p. 288)

Although Catholicism tends to produce obedience where Protestantism fosters independence, Tocqueville argues that "democratic nations show a more ardent and enduring love for equality than for
liberty" (p. 503). It is the egalitarian aspect of the Christian teaching
that makes it fundamentally compatible with democracy.[3] Beginning
his discussion of "Religion Considered as a Political Institution,"
Tocqueville observes:

> Every religion has some political opinion linked to it by affinity.
> The spirit of man, left to follow its bent, will regulate political so-
> ciety and the City of God in uniform fashion; it will, if I dare put
> it so, seek to *harmonize* earth with heaven. (p. 287)

Democratic men easily accept the thought of one God ruling all men
equally, because it coincides with their experience of rule on earth.
And in a simplified form, religious belief is natural.

> Alone among all created beings, man shows a natural disgust for
> existence and an immense longing to exist; he scorns life and

2. All citations are to the George Lawrence translation of *Democracy in America* (Garden City,
New York: Doubleday, 1969), here pp. 16–17, 300–301.
3. John C. Koritansky, "Two Forms of the Love of Equality in Tocqueville's Practical Teaching
for Democracy," *Polity*, 6, no. 4 (1974), 497n, suggests that Tocqueville's discussion constitutes an attack on the church *sub silentio*, presumably because of the contrast between the
independence of American Protestantism and the obedience required by Catholicism. Lively,
Social and Political Thought of Tocqueville, pp. 188–94, shows how Tocqueville's description
of the place of religion in democracy does in effect criticize certain aspects of the French
church's practice at the time. To go beyond this and argue that Tocqueville is attacking the
church simply and entirely, Koritansky would have to explain Tocqueville's prediction that
Americans would eventually divide into complete atheists and those who returned to the
church. He would also have difficulty with Tocqueville's conclusion to his chapter on "How
Religion in the United States Makes Use of Democratic Instincts": "By respecting all democratic instincts which are not against it and making use of many favorable ones, religion succeeds in struggling successfully with that spirit of individual independence which is its most
dangerous enemy" (p. 449).

fears annihilation. These different instincts constantly drive his soul toward contemplation of the next world, and it is religion that leads him thither. Religion, therefore, is only one particular form of hope, and it is as natural to the human heart as hope itself. (pp. 296–97)

Only when religion makes itself incredible and objectionable by lying itself to a changing secular order does it kill this natural hope. Tocqueville thus concludes that Christianity does not display the power in France that it retains in America for one primary reason, the close union there of politics and religion; he therefore urges his countrymen to establish a strict separation of church and state.

> Unbelievers in Europe attack Christians more as political than as religious enemies; they hate the faith as the opinion of a party much more than as a mistaken belief, and they reject the clergy less because they are the representatives of God than because they are the friends of authority. . . . I do not know what is to be done to give back to European Christianity the energy of youth. God alone could do that, but at least it depends on men to leave faith the use of all the strength it still retains. (pp. 300–301)

Because he thinks that the opposition to Christianity stems largely from political concerns, Tocqueville gives primarily political reasons for the critics to cease and desist in their attacks. He does not speak as a believer. On the contrary, he suggests that he has lost his faith:

> The unbeliever, no longer thinking religion true, still considers it useful. Paying attention to the human side of religious beliefs, he recognizes their sway over mores and their influence over laws. He understands their power to lead men to live in peace and gently to prepare them for death. (p. 299)

Tocqueville would not be concerned to establish the compatibility of Christianity and democracy if he did not think that religion was socially beneficial.[4] And from the perspective of social utility, the truth of religion is not so important.

> Though it is very important for man as an individual that his religion should be true, that is not the case for society. Society has nothing to fear or hope from another life; what is most important for it is not that all citizens should profess the true religion but that they should profess religion. (p. 290)

What is important is the moral effectiveness of religion; and Tocqueville observes, "All the sects in the United States belong to the great unity of Christendom, and Christian morality is everywhere the same" (pp. 290–91).

Tocqueville writes in a tradition emphasizing the importance of

4. Although Doris Goldstein, *Trial of Faith: Religion and Politics in Tocqueville's Thought* (New York, 1975), argues that Tocqueville has more personal commitment to Christianity than Lively or Zetterbaum allow, she, too, states, "The dominance of the functional posture in the *Democratie* is undeniable . . ." (p. 26). Cf. also Alfred Balitzer, "Some Thoughts about Civil Religion," *Journal of Church and State*, 16, no. 1 (Winter 1974), 31.

morality for democracies. The basic thought was that if men were not to be ruled by others or external forces, they would have to become masters of themselves. Applied to the individual, self-government meant self-restraint. Applied to the majority, self-restraint meant continued respect for the rights of minorities Montesquieu, for example, had taught that virtue was the principle of the ancient republics; if men were not forced to sacrifice themselves for the public good, they would have to be trained to do so. But he suggested that such stringent moral education would be neither necessary nor appropriate in the modern mixed regime, dedicated to liberty. In regimes such as England, government was limited by the balance of powers and individuals would be restrained by calculations of self-interest. Commerce would replace war as the dominant way of life; men would be less virtuous, but more pacific and tolerant.[5]

Jean Jacques Rousseau responded that true liberty only exists in conjunction with virtue or morality; and that both are products of the society established by the social contract. "We might add to the acquisitions of the civil state moral freedom, which alone remders man truly master of himself; for the impulse of mere appetite is slavery, while obedience to a self-prescribed law is liberty."[6] Rousseau argued that in order to be truly free men have to develop their reason. They have to be able to determine what they would really like to do and to exercise the self-control necessary to achieve it; by nature they merely follow their appetite. Men are not truly free in nature because their reason does not develop sufficiently until they have lived in society for a long time. The discovery of the foundations of a rational, just and free society thus presupposes much social experience. Although Rousseau believed that all men could understand the general principles of the just society after he pointed them out, they would need a man of exceptional practical wisdom to design a government capable of realizing these principles in their particular circumstances. Since his people would never possess understanding equal to his— it is too rare—the "legislator" would have to appeal to divine authority to get them to support the institutions and obey the laws he has established. But this dependence of civil authority on the divine raised further problems.

Rousseau states explicitly what Montesquieu only implied, that the complete subordination of religion to politics among the ancients made men good citizens, but bellicose and superstitious. Pagan religious institutions are no longer possible, moreover, because the sublimity of the doctrines of the Gospel makes the defects of earlier religion too clear. But Christianity makes men bad citizens by teaching them to care only for the afterlife; and the institution of the church divided both authority and allegiance. Thus Rousseau argues that a new kind of civil religion is needed. Since political authority is legitimately concerned only that men perform their duties in this world and not

---

5. Baron de Montesquieu, De L'Esprit des Loix, I: 2–8, 19–21; II: 24–25. See also Thomas Pangle, Montesquieu's Philosophy of Liberalism (Chicago, 1973), pp. 200–59.
6. Jean Jacques Rousseau, Du Contrat Social, I: 8; Lester Crocker, ed., The Social Contract and Discourse on the Origin of Inequality (New York, 1976), p. 23.

with their fate hereafter, the publicly enforced creed should be limited to the necessary foundations of morality: the existence of the Deity, the life to come, the happiness of the just, the suffering of the wicked, the sanctity of the social contract and the laws. All views as to the requirements of eternal salvation should be tolerated; and any church that argues it alone possesses the means to salvation will be banned.[7] Although Rousseau does not say as much, the toleration required for civic peace would seem to result in little religion beyond that the state approves.

In light of this tradition, the functions Tocqueville assigns religion in America appear rather modest. Unlike Montesquieu, Tocqueville does argue that religion is necessary to maintain liberty. But he does not speak so much of the way in which religion directly makes men better, more moral or virtuous as of the way it indirectly produces the habits and opinions, the "mores" that enable them to retain their liberty. And though he stresses the political functions of religion, he does not advocate the enforcement of a public dogma like Rousseau. On the contrary, Tocqueville urges the utility of a strict separation of church and state.

Because of the separation of church and state, the political influence of religion in the United States is largely indirect. It works through the opinions and attitudes of the people rather than directly in the government. It works on the people, moreover, not primarily by preaching the value of political and individual liberty as by supporting ideas and institutions which in turn enable men to continue to be free. Although religion did not give Americans the taste for liberty, according to Tocqueville, "it singularly facilitates their use thereof" (p. 292). "It is just when it is not speaking of freedom at all that [religion] best teaches Americans the art of being free" (p. 290).

Religion indirectly supports liberty in America in two ways. On the individual level, religion is one of the primary causes of the severity of mores or the self-control necessary for self-government. On the social level, religious beliefs underlie the notion that only constitutional or limited government is legitimate. Tocqueville's description of these two essential functions volume one is very brief. First, he refers to the private effect. By insisting upon the sanctity of the marriage tie, religious teachings help maintain civic peace by making domestic life orderly and quiet. A man who is content at home is not apt to foment public turmoil or to seek radical change. Rather, "as the regularity of life brings him happiness, he easily forms the habit of regulating his opinions as well as his tastes" (p. 291). The second indirect effect of religion is thus intellectual. By making everything in the moral sphere virtually unquestionable, the sway of Christianity in American public opinion confines the range of intellectual inquiry and political experimentation. "While the law allows the American people to do everything [they can amend the Constitution after all], there are things

7. *Du Contrat Social*, IV:8.

which religion prevents them from imagining and forbids them to dare" (p. 292). Widespread acceptance of general moral principles also supports public order by requiring, in effect, that all change take place on the basis of certain assumptions and through accepted procedures. Even the boldest leader is checked by the scruples of his would-be followers.

Government is limited and individuals retain their rights in America, Tocqueville argues, not because Constitutional checks and balances block the will of the majority, but because the majority does not imagine that government can do so much or, when told that it can, does not think it right. At most, the checks and balances slow the political process so that the majority is required to deliberate rather than merely react on the basis of passionate whim.[8] Something must make the majority accept the legitimacy of these restraints and accept the process; and that "something" is religion. "Religion, which never intervenes directly in the government of American society, should therefore be considered as the first of their political institutions" (p. 153).

The role of religion in the working of American democracy is thus absolutely fundamental, even if it is indirect. But Tocqueville does not describe either the content of American religious beliefs or the way they produce these political results very fully in his description of religion as a political institution in volume one of *Democracy in America*. When he describes American mores more fully in volume two, he shows that religion does not work alone to produce these politically desirable results.

The only concrete example that Tocqueville gives in volume one of religion producing individual self-restraint is its effect on women in maintaining the family. In his fuller description of the place of women and the nature of the American family in volume two, he reveals another source of their distinctive characteristics—economic interest.

> Religious people and industrial nations take a particularly serious view of marriage. The former consider the regularity of a woman's life the best guarantee and surest sign of the purity of her morals. The latter see in it the surest safeguard of the order and prosperity of the house. The Americans are both a Puritan and a trading nation. (p. 592)

Three pages later, he asserts, "No doubt this great strictness of American mores is due partly to the country, the race, and the religion. But all these causes, which can be found elsewhere, are still not enough to account for the matter" (p. 595). Tocqueville finds the true reasons for the strict interpretation of the marriage bond in America in the habitual way of life and characteristic ways of thought of a commercial people. "Almost all the men in a democracy either enter politics or practice some calling, whereas limited incomes oblige the wives to stay at home and watch in person very closely over the details of domestic economy" (p. 598). With the sexes busy and separated all day,

8. *Democracy*, I: 1: viii: 153.

there is little opportunity for philandering. Such practical individuals are apt, moreover, to pursue more prosaic, concrete objects rather than romantic escapades or illusions. With no class, family, or property restraints on marriage, it is difficult for a man to convince a woman that he loves her if he does not offer to marry her. Neither he nor she has much leisure to dream or to plan romantic rendezvous; unlike aristocrats living on family property, democratic people are fully occupied, even preoccupied, with earning a personal fortune.

Not religion, but calculations of self-interest prove to be the immediate and primary cause of individual self-restraint in America. The materialism of men living in democratic societies is too strong for any force to restrain completely.[9] Working in conjunction with calculations of self-interest, religion can prevent such calculations from destroying all notions of social obligation, however. But religion does this indirectly, by supporting the doctrine of "self-interest, properly understood" more than through direct moral suasion.

The materialism of modern men grows with their equality.

> No power on earth can prevent increasing equality from turning men's minds to look for the useful or disposing each citizen to get wrapped up in himself. One must therefore expect that private interest will more than ever become the chief if not the only driving force behind all behavior. But we have yet to see how each man will interpret his private interest. (p. 527)

In aristocracies, the place and power of each individual depend upon his family, and his family's position depends on the family's estate.[1] There is much talk of virtue and self-sacrifice, because self-interest is more hidden.[2] When notions of equality lead men to abolish primogeniture, individuals realize that they can amass more wealth and power through commercial ventures than by maintaining the family estate intact; their own identity and place in society no longer depend upon name or land, so they pursue their own self-interests and attach themselves only to their immediate family. Social distinction, power, and pleasure all come to rest on money, so it is rational for men to pursue it to the virtual exclusion of everything else.[3]

This tendency of modern men to devote themselves solely to their private concerns poses the most serious threat to the maintenance of liberty in democratic republics, Tocqueville argues. Men who do not take the time to govern themselves lose not only the opportunity but also the ability to do so.

> Intent only on getting rich, they do not notice the close connection between private fortunes and general prosperity. There is no need to drag their rights away from citizens of this type; they themselves voluntarily let them go. They find it a tiresome inconvenience to exercise political rights which distract them from

9. *Ibid.*, I: 2: ix: 291; II: 1: v: 448.
1. *Ibid.*, I: 1: iii: 52–3.
2. *Ibid.*, II: 2: viii: 525.
3. *Ibid.*, II: 3: xvii: 614–15.

industry. When required to elect representatives, to support authority by personal service, or to discuss public business together, they find they have no time. . . . Such folk think they are following the doctrine of self-interest, but they have a very crude idea thereof, and the better to guard their interests, they neglect the chief of them, that is, to remain their own masters. (p. 540)

Americans combat this "individualism" chiefly with free institutions. Although men may imagine that they are independent in civil or economic affairs, they quickly learn that they can achieve nothing in politics without the cooperation of others. But the existence of local government does not suffice to get men to participate. They need a reason; and the reason is supplied in America by the doctrine of "self-interest, properly understood."

Because modern men so openly calculate their own self-interest, Tocqueville observes, moralists take fright at the notion of suggesting self-sacrifice and seek to show instead the utility of virtue. Through the repetition of instances in which private and public advantage coincide, they enunciate a general doctrine that people serve their own interest in aiding their fellows; and this doctrine is sufficiently confirmed by experience in America to be generally held as true. Americans even do themselves injustice, by explaining acts of genuine charity and compassion as the products of calculation. The problem is that virtue is not always its own reward, if by reward one means the receipt of like services in exchange. The doctrine of "self-interest, properly understood," thus requires a religious foundation or extension if it is to supply an adequate foundation for a free political society.

If the doctrine of self-interest properly understood were concerned with this world only, that would not be nearly enough. For there are a great many sacrifices which can only be rewarded in the next. However hard one may try to prove that virtue is useful, it will always be difficult to make a man live well if he will not face death. (p. 528)

The religious belief necessary to support the doctrine of self-interest, properly understood, is minimal: there may be an after-life; we do not know. From this premise, men calculate; and they calculate on the basis of self-love. They would like to continue to exist; they would not like to suffer; and in the absence of certain knowledge, they decide à la Pascal to take no chances. They participate in religious exercises. The belief required is nothing more than an expression of that natural hope Tocqueville thinks all men feel unless particular political circumstances lead them to stifle it. Little explicit teaching or preaching is necessary to keep it alive. This is particularly true when the demands made by such a simple faith do not extend much further than the dictates of interest. If a man is going to contain his desires in order to build a nest egg, he might as well contain his desires in order to go to heaven. Tocqueville explicitly denies that Christianity can be reduced to a mere expression of human self-love; but he suggests "that interest is the chief means used by religions themselves to guide men, and [he has] no doubt that that is how they work on the crowd and become popular" (p. 529).

Lively and Zetterbaum are correct when they claim that calculations of self-interest are fundamental for Tocqueville. They err only in positing a necessary antagonism between calculations of self-interest and religious beliefs; that was precisely the position Tocqueville himself addressed.

But the role of religion in forming American "mores" is not confined to supporting individual self-restraint, according to Tocqueville. American religious beliefs also lead the people to think that only a limited government is legitimate. "Up till now no one in the United States has dared to profess the maxim that everything is allowed in the interests of society, an impious maxim apparently invented in an age of freedom in order to legitimize every future tyrant" (p. 292). However, the way religious beliefs indirectly produce social self-restraint is even more difficult to understand than the conjunction of calculation and faith in the operation of "self-interest, properly understood." It is difficult to see not only how Tocqueville can regard religiously based limitations on the imagination and intellectual inquiry as legitimate but also how he thinks that they can possibly survive the age of democratic freedom. He himself argues that freedom of speech is an essential element of liberal democracy and that there are only two feasible alternatives: complete freedom or complete suppression. Selective censorship will not work, because any attempt to enforce the law in court brings out and spreads the very doctrine the law seeks to contain.[4] If formal control does not work short of complete despotism, how can religion limit intellectual inquiry and yet preserve freedom?

Tocqueville's answer, briefly, is that democratic men will not tolerate enforced dogma; they think that they should decide for themselves. Nevertheless, democratic men will be as dogmatic as any before them, although they may not realize it in the absence of official censorship. Ironically, the very freedom of thought that seems to challenge all dogma in the long run makes men hold their fundamental beliefs all the more firmly. The question is not, then, whether men in democracies will hold fundamental beliefs or not, but what these beliefs will be. Will they continue to believe in the existence of a divine judge, to respect the value of the individual and to insist on a limited government; or will they gradually slide into the notion that anything is permissible in the interests of society?

Tocqueville does not damn democracy for being dogmatic. On the contrary, he argues that dogma is not only inevitable but also beneficial. No societies can exist without dogmatic beliefs; without common ideas, common action is impossible, and it is unlikely that men would agree on much if they all actually tried to think everything out for themselves. But in fact, no individual can think everything through; the greatest philosopher would barely make it out of bed if he actually

4. *Ibid.*, I: 2: iii: 180–86.

submitted every one of his ideas to rigorous analysis.[5] Tocqueville knows, of course, that the great philosophers of the past did not question literally everything. Rather they addressed the fundamental issues—the existence of God, the nature of man, his obligations to others. Since they have proved unable to agree on their answers, Tocqueville concludes that the questions, not the solutions, are eternal. Despair is no more grounded than hope: atheism no more "rational" than faith. Men simply do not know. What is certain is that, if the greatest philosophers could not agree on the answers to these questions, wage earners without the leisure to study and reflect surely cannot answer them satisfactorily on their own. They will either continue to believe; or, faced with questions they cannot answer, they will gradually begin to doubt. "Carried away by an imperceptible current against which they have not the courage to struggle but to which they yield with regret, they abandon the faith they love to follow the doubt that leads them to despair" (p. 299). Doubt about the existence of God or a natural order necessarily produces moral doubt. How does a man answer the question, what should I do, if he knows nothing of a higher power of the nature of man? Such moral doubt is debilitating, even paralyzing, because a man cannot act very successfully or decisively if he does not know what to do.[6] Unable to act, the individual feels his impotence; he sees that individuals do not and cannot make a difference. As an indirect result of his loss of faith in the divine, he also loses faith in himself and in the powers of the individual simply. The ability of both community and individual to act thus depends upon dogma, religious dogma.

Tocqueville sees that men enter democratic conditions thinking that all are equally valuable and, by right, free and independent; but he fears that the actual weakness of individuals in modern times will gradually lead most to conclude that men can do nothing on their own, that they are nothing without society. Institutions which enable individuals to act are therefore essential to the preservation of liberty, and religion is one such institution. Men who see individuals act on their own behalf continue to believe in the right and obligation of individuals to do so, where men who only see the incapacity of individuals will gradually come to regard individuality as a liability or fault. By giving them moral certainty religious beliefs help individuals act. But moral certainty does not suffice.

Tocqueville recognizes that the limitations of the powers of individuals in democracies are real and that they will become even greater in the future.[7] In order to have any control over their own lives, individuals have to associate with others. Thus Tocqueville praises the "decentralized administration" in the United States not so much because it

5. *Ibid.*, II: 1: ii: 433–34.
6. *Ibid.*, II: 1: v: 442–44.
7. *Ibid.*, II: 2: v: 515: "It is easy to see the time coming in which men will be less and less able to produce, by each alone, the commonest bare necessities of life. The tasks of government must therefore perpetually increase. . . . The more government takes the place of associations, the more will individuals lose the idea of forming associations and need the government to come to their help. That is a vicious circle of cause and effect."

enables the government to adapt policies to different local circumstances as because it teaches men to associate so that they can act to further and defend their own interests. There are, indeed, two "political effects" of the American experience with local government. Participation in community decisions not only teaches men the conjunction of individual and common interest, but it also gives the individuals involved confidence in their own powers to improve their condition.

> Each . . . conceive[s] an opinion of himself which is often exaggerated but almost always salutary. He trusts fearlessly in his own powers. . . . Suppose that an individual thinks of some enterprise . . . ; it does not come into his head to appeal to public authority for its help. He publishes his plan, offers to carry it out, summons other individuals to aid his efforts, and personally struggles against all obstacles. (p. 95)

Political association fosters purely civil association, moreover. And in volume two, Tocqueville suggests that association for moral and intellectual purposes may be even more important than it is in political and economic affairs, because the power of the majority to enforce conformity informally is greater even than its political power.[8] It is difficult for a man to stand up for his own opinion, even to think for himself in opposition to his peers. The support of others makes him more confident. Thus Tocqueville concludes, "In democratic countries knowledge of how to combine is the mother of all other forms of knowledge; on its progress depends that of all the others" (p. 517).

Institutions of self-government and the "knowledge of how to combine" are not enough to produce the proliferation of associations in the United States, however. Common religious beliefs are also necessary to provide the climate of trust needed to bring and keep people together. Associations based solely on the conjunction of a particular interest in the context of indifference or distrust are unlikely; they will certainly be of brief duration and limited effect. Common actions require common beliefs. Pure calculations of self-interest do not really suffice, because men do not willingly associate with complete egoists. To trust others, they must believe that the others share basically the same moral standards. Surely they will not tolerate differences or dissent if there is not a more fundamental source of trust in an agreement on standards of judgment.

Religion alone does not produce the self-confidence and energy that have characterized Americans. Nor does it uphold the value of the individual primarily by preaching. Religion does sustain the individual directly; but it supports him even more indirectly, in conjunction with the institutions of local government, by enabling him to act on his own behalf in association with others. And Americans continue to believe in the rights of individuals because they daily see them exercised.

Without a restraining belief in a higher authority and the limits of man, neither local government nor federal institutions could protect

8. *Ibid.*, II: 2: v: 517.

the individual from majority tyranny, particularly the tyranny of majority opinion. The small republic serves as a school for self-government, Tocqueville observes, but it can also provide the occasion for the pettiest and most obtrusive form of majority tyranny. He praises the federal institutions of the United States because they combine the advantages of small republics with the advantages of large empires, which include not only a stronger defensive posture but also a larger sphere for ambition and greater circulation of ideas.[9] Federal institutions help protect individuality by destroying some of the confines of the small community. But federal politics depend upon majority will as much as local politics do. The federal government has only two options either it enforces the will of the national majority or it leaves decisions to local majorities. There is no escape from majority rule. Constitutional "checks and balances" can prevent the majority from exercising its political power tyrannically, but laws and institutions cannot check the informal power of majority opinion. Only opinion itself or the "mores" can do that. This is the reason that Tocqueville says that "mores" are more fundamental than the laws or physical circumstances in preserving liberty in America.[1] Religion is not the sole source of these "mores" but it provides an essential element. It leads the majority to believe that it must restrain its own action through the conviction that man is not the final judge and that the will of the majority does not necessarily or always coincide with justice.

> Omnipotence in itself seems a bad and dangerous thing. I think that its exercise is beyond man's strength, whoever he be, and that only God can be omnipotent without danger because His wisdom and justice are always equal to His power. (p. 252)

Religion exercises its influence in America as part of public opinion; and the power of public opinion is as great as it is, Tocqueville argues, because it is not enforced. Democratic men would resist enforced dogma; equal men should be allowed to think issues out for themselves. But Tocqueville shows that this independence of thought is fleeting and deceptive. No man can in fact think most issues out for himself. Confronted with his own limitations, the individual looks to the opinions of others; and when they disagree, he comes to doubt his own. The others are, after all, his equals, and there are more of them. "Individual independence" gradually becomes conformity.

> The master no longer says: "Think like me or you die." He does say: "You are free not to think as I do; you can keep your life and property and all; but from this day you are a stranger among us. You can keep your privileges in the townships, but they will be useless to you, for if you solicit your fellow citizens' votes they will not give them to you." (p. 255)

9. *Ibid.*, I: 1: viii: 159–60.
1. *Ibid.*, I: 2: ix: 305–08: "If in the course of this book I have not succeeded in making the reader feel the importance I attach to the practical experience of the Americans, to their habits, opinions, and, in a word, their mores, in maintaining their laws, I have failed in the main object of my work."

Where there is no higher authority recognized than the majority, neither local government nor associations can protect the individual who disagrees, because no one will join with him. Nor can the institution of freedom of the press shake the dominance of settled majority opinion. Tocqueville admits that when free speech is initiated in a polity where discussion was formerly controlled, it does lead to widespread questioning of accepted dogma. Once all the alternatives have been canvassed and discussed, however, men do not easily change their minds. Thinking that they have decided the issues for themselves, they cling to their own judgment from pride as well as conviction. Even men who are not sure that their own opinions are right tend not to change their views. When they hear the "experts" disagree, they come to doubt whether any position is better grounded than their own, so they maintain their old familiar opinions and cease to pay any attention to a seemingly interminable debate. Only the individual's belief that his own opinion rests on an authority higher and firmer than the majority and the majority's respect for individuality can preserve individual differences. Whether the power of majority opinion operates despotically or not depends on its content.

In accord with his emphasis on the indirect character of religious influence in a liberal democracy, Tocqueville does not enumerate the articles of a necessary creed. The tenets of faith he finds that help preserve liberal democracy include a belief in the existence of God, the immortality of the soul or the possibility of an afterlife, and some version of the "golden rule." It is not necessary to propagate these simple beliefs as "social myths" because they already exist in public opinion as tenets of previously accepted Christian dogma. And these particular tenets are apt to endure, because they correspond to the experience and inclinations of men in democracies. Men who regard themselves as equal easily perceive the justice and desirability of one supreme judge. They feel their own limitations along with the desire to prolong their existence; and they learn the advantages of association with others from daily life. Most of all, they follow the majority. Thus Tocqueville can conclude that if the skeptics keep their questions to themselves, believers will proclaim their faith and

> With unbelievers hiding their incredulity and believers avowing their faith, a public opinion favorable to religion takes shape; religion is loved, supported, and honored, and only by looking into the depths of men's souls will one see what wounds it has suffered. (p. 300)

Tocqueville tends to minimize the changes required to adapt Christianity to democratic circumstances, although he does not deny that changes are necessary. Only in volume two does he state clearly that the separation of church and state will not suffice to perpetuate Christian beliefs. Doctrine and ritual must also be simplified. Men who believe that they should and can think things through for themselves are skeptical about the mysterious and impatient with formality. Churchmen must also take care to limit their pronouncements concerning the eternal to the afterlife.[2] If they tie the belief in God to the rapidly changing policies and personalities of democratic government, they will inevitably undermine popular belief in an eternal will.[3] The perpetuation of Christian faith thus requires self-restraint on the part of churchmen as well as skeptics. Ministers in America can and do address the worldly concerns of their congregations, Tocqueville observes, but they do so to celebrate the values and achievements the progress and prosperity of democracy. They do not and cannot oppose democratic materialism by praising ascetic virtues.

Anticipating the objection that such adaptations and dilutions of doctrine themselves destroy the faith, Tocqueville responds that religion must distinguish essential tenets of faith from externals. But, as Sanford Kessler points out, the opposition to Mammon is by no means external to Christianity. On the contrary, Jesus' saying that the chances of a rich man's going to heaven are as good as a camel's walking through the eye of a needle suggests that a faith which simply condoned gain would no longer be Christian.[4] The religion Tocqueville would preserve is indeed not simply Christian, although its historical origins are. There is, for example, no emphasis on redemption through Christ.[5] But Tocqueville has no reason to bring out the differences between Christianity and the democratic religion he defends, where he does have reason to understate them. Although he saw that there were sporadic reactions to the materialism dominant in America, he thought that the democratic commitment to individual judgment made it unlikely that a majority would accept a new religious teaching. He sought, therefore, only to establish conditions in which people retain the beliefs they already hold.

> When any religion has taken deep root in a democracy, be very careful not to shake it, but rather guard it as the most precious heritage from aristocratic times. Do not try to detach men from their old religious opinions in order to establish new ones for fear lest in the passage from one belief to another the soul may for a moment be found empty of faith and love of physical pleasures come and spread and fill it all. (p. 544)

His response might not satisfy a committed Christian. But Tocqueville warns that Christianity must either adapt itself to democratic conditions or religion itself will be destroyed. There are no other alternatives.

Lively and Zetterbaum agree that Tocqueville was concerned with the preservation of religious beliefs not from personal faith but for religion's beneficial political effects. They take note of Tocqueville's statement that religion cannot counteract the materialistic desires of

2. Ibid., II: 1: v: 449.
3. Ibid., I: 2: ix: 297.
4. Sanford Kessler, "Tocqueville on the Civic Religion and Liberal Democracy," Journal of Politics, 39 (February 1977), 140–41.
5. Robert Bellah points out that every president in his inaugural address has appealed to God as the final judge, although there are no specifically Christian references in Russell Richey and Donald Jones, ed., American Civil Religion (New York, 1974), pp. 21–37.

men under democratic conditions and trace his attempt to merge self-interest with religion. They also see that, according to Tocqueville, the power of religion in modern democracies is wholly dependent upon its incorporation into public opinion. But they conclude that Tocqueville's subordination of religion to politics destroys religion and that his indifference as to the content of the religious belief means in the end that he is simply advocating the propagation of socially useful myths. Careful analysis of Tocqueville's argument does not support these conclusions. Since the two major contemporary commentators come to this conclusion for somewhat different reasons, it is necessary to respond to their arguments separately.

Lively suggests that Tocqueville almost necessarily moved from praising the social effects of religion to advocating a social mythology.

> It is only a short move from emphasizing the importance of the persuasive effects of a theory to viewing it solely from the point of view of those effects, and only a short move again to advocating social myths on the grounds of their social benefits. It is impossible to deny that Tocqueville made these moves when discussing religion. (p. 197)

The question, of course, is whether Tocqueville actually made these moves. In fact, he very carefully distinguishes true faith from mere interest. In the chapter discussing "How the Americans Apply the Doctrine of Self-Interest Properly Understood to Religion," for example, Tocqueville observes:

> Christianity does, it is true, teach that we must prefer others to ourselves in order to gain heaven. But Christianity also teaches that we must do good to our fellows for love of God. That is a sublime utterance; man's mind filled with the understanding of God's thought he sees that order is God's plan, in freedom labors for this great design . . . expecting no other reward than the joy of contemplating it. Hence I do not think that interest is the only driving force behind men of religion. (p. 529)

Tocqueville certainly does not recommend the propagation of social mythology, because he does not think that any publicly propagated doctrine can withstand the resistance of democrats commitment to individual freedom of thought. He argues instead that freedom of speech will help maintain religious beliefs in democracies in the long run. He emphasizes the social utility of religion in order to persuade intellectual skeptics to cease their attacks, not to propagate or even to preserve religious beliefs in themselves.

Tocqueville distinguishes himself from earlier Enlightenment thinkers largely by his contention that democratic men are no more ruled by reason than those in the past; indeed, democrats promise to be more subject to the rule of opinion than their aristocratic ancestors. But recognizing the power of opinion in democracies does not lead him to advocate "myths." On the contrary, he endorses those opinions which reflect fundamental truths.[6] He grounds his hopes for the future of religion and, with it, liberal democracy on the nature of man, the particular attachment that each individual has to his own existence that produces the hope for an extension of that existence after death, and the limitations of human knowledge. He often links the rule of God, whose existence he does not claim to prove, to the natural order he thinks can be humanly perceived. And he argues that democratic opinions and institutions will gradually sweep away the old aristocratic order because democratic opinions reflect more of nature; they are not only less conventionally based but also closer to the truth.[7]

Zetterbaum recognizes that the function Tocqueville assigns to religion in liberal democracies extends beyond the inculcation of individual and social self-restraint to supporting individual enterprise and public association. But he argues that Tocqueville's attempted merger of self-interest and religion fails for three reasons. First, Tocqueville's complete subordination of religion to politics deprives religion of any independent power. Second, Tocqueville so minimizes the content of religion as to destroy it. Third, insofar as Tocqueville makes the power of religion depend upon public opinion, he puts that power on an inherently unstable

6. Lively, *Social and Political Thought of Tocqueville*, p. 199, argues that Tocqueville's tendency to advocate social myths comes to light even more clearly in his doctrine concerning the uses of "self-interest properly understood" than in his teaching concerning the place of religion in a democracy because Tocqueville urges the inculcation of the doctrine even though he doubted its truth, at least in its accepted form. What Tocqueville says, however, is that: "I do not think that the doctrine of self-interest as preached in America is in all respects self-evident. But it does contain many truths so clear that for men to see them it is enough to educate them" (p. 528). He never suggests that it is not truly in the self-interest of every man, literally "properly understood" to participate in politics. On the contrary, he urges that a man's most fundamental and dearest interest is to maintain his liberty and so his ability to rule himself (I: v: 93; II: ii: 15: 540). The problem is that men often lose sight of this truth in pursuing short-term economic gain, but Tocqueville argues that in America the doctrine of "self-interest, properly understood," helps counteract this characteristic failing of man's reason.

7. Zetterbaum considers the inevitable triumph of democracy to be the first and foremost of Tocqueville's salutary myths, partly because Tocqueville often expresses this thesis in providential terms. More fundamentally, Zetterbaum argues that the inevitability thesis must be a myth, because Tocqueville was not truly neutral as to the merits of aristocracy and democracy. The fact that Tocqueville thought that democracy was more natural and hence more just does not in itself mean that he did not also think that it would inevitably conquer feudal aristocracy. Zetterbaum also suggests that Tocqueville went so far as to deny the freedom of the will in an attempt to persuade aristocrats that opposition was useless. Tocqueville's observation in the preface to *Democracy in America* that many different past actions have all unintentionally furthered the progress of democracy does not entail a denial of free will, however; it merely acknowledges the limitations of our knowledge of the long term and cumulative effects of individual actions, a point that Tocqueville makes in the chapter on history as well as in his more private *Recollections*. (*Democracy*, II: i: 20: 494–95; Alexander Teixeira de Mattos, trans., *The Recollections of Alexis de Tocqueville* [New York, 1959], p. 64.) Tocqueville himself concludes *Democracy in America* by stating that "Providence did not make mankind entirely free or completely enslaved. Providence has, in truth, drawn a predestined circle around each man beyond which he cannot pass; but within those vast limits man is strong and free, and so are peoples" (p. 705). Tocqueville argues that intentional political actions can determine whether men will be free or not under democratic conditions. His expressions of uncertainty, both public and private, about the future do not contradict the inevitability thesis as Zetterbaum maintains, because Tocqueville explicitly holds out the possibility that democracy will become despotic. Over the long run, despotism might so change the character of a people that aristocrats could again establish themselves by force. He only asserts that it is impossible for aristocracy to withstand the rising democratic tide for the foreseeable future.

and transitory basis. Since the merger fails, he concluded, it must be considered to represent an ineffective attempt to propagate myth.[8]

As we have seen, Tocqueville does not think that religion can act independently to counter the defects of democracy, but he does not think that religion has ever acted independently of the social conditions. Christianity emerged on the egalitarian base laid by the Roman Empire, he observes, although it later adapted itself in feudal institutions.[9] Indeed, he argues that broad acceptance of any set of principles depends upon the conjunction of those principles with popular experience.[1] As a general rule, this seems hard to deny.

Zetterbaum cites the passage in which Tocqueville admits that if pressed into an extremely disagreeable choice, he would prefer even the doctrine of metempsychosis to materialism in order to show that Tocqueville's "primary concern with religion was not with the support it might give morality by promises of rewards or punishments in an afterlife, but rather with the support it would inevitably give a people's sense of continuity and futurity" (p. 19). Unfortunately Zetterbaum completely misses the point of Tocqueville's statement which does not refer to a "people" at all. Instead, Tocqueville stresses the indispensability of "the belief in an immaterial and immortal principle, for a time united to matter . . . to man's [de l'homme] greatness" (p. 544). That is, he indicates very precisely where the line must be drawn. The preservation of liberty under egalitarian conditions depends fundamentally upon the belief in the inviolability, the fundamental sanctity of the human being. This belief does not absolutely require a belief in an eternal afterlife or even the preservation of the individual soul in its present form. It only requires that men do not believe that everything is merely matter and so open to manipulation. Although Tocqueville does not state his contention in these terms, he clearly suggests that it is not the search for creature comforts that fundamentally threatens liberty or humanity so much as annihilism, the belief that nothing is sacred and that everything is therefore allowed.

Tocqueville certainly recognized that public opinion changes; indeed, the change in public opinion might be said to be his overriding theme. He thought, however, that under democratic conditions it was possible, although by no means necessary, to produce a certain conjunction of practice and belief that would prove to be exceptionally stable. If churchmen and democratic politicians would merely cease to attack each other, he argued, politics and religion could mutually reinforce each other's strength. Churchmen could, he acknowledged, continue to demand political power or to criticize modern materialistic goals, but he thought that they could do so only at the price of losing the greater part of their popular following. Likewise, liberal politicians could continue to attack faith, but only at the cost of eventual loss of freedom. Surely, he urged, the perpetuation of religious institutions

8. Zetterbaum, *Tocqueville and Problem of Democracy*, pp. 118–23, 147.
9. *Democracy*, II: 1: 5: 446.
1. *Ibid.*, II: 1: 1,3: 430–32, 438–39.

under democratic conditions depends upon the preservation of the freedom of individual conscience. But the preservation of the freedom of conscience depends upon the preservation of individual rights, which in turn requires the establishment of liberal political institutions. And the maintenance of liberal political institutions requires popular belief in the sanctity of individual rights, for which it is difficult to find a basis outside the loosely religiously based, practically reaffirmed public opinion that Tocqueville points to. Natural science does not provide a foundation for such a belief; nor does historicism. It is certainly not inconsistent or mythical for Tocqueville to appeal to the self-interest of both parties.

Ironically, Lively and Zetterbaum misconstrue Tocqueville because they do not read his political reduction of religion radically enough. He went far beyond the use of religious preaching to maintain political order; he was willing to reduce religion to belief in the sanctity of the individual human being or freedom of conscience. He sought thereby to preserve a truth, however, not to propagate a myth:

> It was not man who implanted in himself the taste for the infinite and love of what is immortal. These sublime instincts are not the offspring of some caprice of the will; their foundations are embedded in nature (p. 535).

Religion need not be reduced to this absolutely minimal belief but in order to maintain even the minimum, it had to cooperate with the spread and preservation of liberal political principles.

SHELDON S. WOLIN

Archaism and Modernity†

The text which serves as the basis for the reflections which follow is a single sentence from Tocqueville's Democracy in America: "A new science of politics is indispensable to a wholly new world."[1]

In a letter written to his English translator, Tocqueville attempted to explain how it had been possible for him to perceive American democracy in a different light from his predecessors. "It came into the world," he wrote, "when aristocracy was already dead . . . and democracy did not exist. . . . I was so nicely balanced between the past and the future that I was not naturally drawn to the one or to the other."[2] The binary opposites of aristocracy, dead and past, on the one hand, and, on the other, democracy and the future signified for Tocqueville that the political world was in reality two worlds. His masterpieces,

† Sheldon S. Wolin is a professor emeritus of politics at Princeton University, and the author of Politics and Vision: Continuity and Innovation in Western Political Thought. This essay appeared in The Tocqueville Review 7 (1985/1986): 77–88.
1. De la Démocratie en Amérique, 2 vols., Oeuvres complètes, ed. J.-P. Mayer (Paris: Gallimard, 1961), 1:5.
2. Letter to Reeve, 22 Mar. 1837, Correspondance Anglaise, ibid., 6:38.

Democracy in America and *The Old Regime and the French Revolution*, embody that division. The first deals with the New World of America, the second with the Old World. The concept of the "Old World" contained an ambiguity which importantly shaped Tocqueville's approach to the political realities associated with each of these worlds. The Old World referred both to Western Europe and to the prerevolutionary world of eighteenth-century France. Thus the Old World was itself divided by the consequences of the French Revolution of 1789. It was equivocally modern while the New World was simply modern.

From our present vantage point, one hundred fifty years after the appearance of the first volume of *Democracy in America*, those terms of reference, "old" and "new," seem strange, possibly because few if any old societies exist, or if they do, they are of greater interest to the anthropologist than to the political sociologist or political scientist. While for a brief moment, during the 1950s, the concept of "traditional society" was in vogue, that, too, proved as evanescent as the social conditions it attempted to characterize. The pace of change being experienced today by almost all societies seems to demand some category, partly temporal and partly cultural, that will furnish, if only illusorily, a point of reference or contrast so that we can better comprehend what is happening to us individually and collectively.

During the last decade the term *modern*, together with its cognates *premodern*, *modernizing*, and *modernization*, was supposed to provide a purchase on the cultural meaning of our rapid mode of temporality: from what and into what were we changing? The concept of the modern was our stab at stabilizing existence. The clear presumption was that science and technology had discovered the secret of perpetual progress. That guarantee made the modern appear as an ultima Thule, a historical stage with no beyond. How could one venture beyond modern science?

The increasing use of the word *postmodern* indicates that the modern is becoming problematic. The meaning of *postmodern* is not easy to pin down and it is probably useless to try. It means something different to the art historian than it does to the literary critic, to the social historian than to the music critic. But one thing can be said with some certainty, that the postmodern tendency in all intellectual endeavors is to insinuate a question mark after modern as a way of signifying scepticism and suspicion regarding the primary icons of modernity. The postmodern is doubtful about the objectivist view of scientific knowledge, indeed of all forms of knowledge; it accepts cultural and moral relativism and barely acknowledges solipsism as a problem; it tends to regard most academic disciplines as simply different ways of telling "stories" with no mode of discourse privileged; and in its preoccupation with language it displays advanced symptoms of an addiction to morphemes.

If we were to accept these temporal-cultural markers of pre- and postmodernity, and if, *pace* Tocqueville, we were to imagine ourselves situated between the modern and the postmodern worlds, between a world that is or has been and one that is or is becoming, would we want to claim, too, that a "new science of politics is needed for a new world"? I should like to explore that question by returning to Tocqueville to examine his notions about the "new" and the "old" and the ways in which they forward our theoretical understanding. My return to Tocqueville will be governed by two further questions, neither of which will seem to make much sense at this point but, I trust, will appear less opaque as my themes emerge. The first is: in *Democracy in America* what function has the modern and what is the premodern? The second is: regarding the political society of contemporary America, what is it that signifies the premodern and the modern and how do these stand to their counterparts in Tocqueville's work?

At first glance, there is nothing surprising about Tocqueville's juxtaposition of a "new science of politics" to a "new world." From the time of the first settlers to the most recent debates over American "exceptionalism," Americans and foreigners alike have taken to calling the United States a "new world" as though they were uttering yet another self-evident truth. This has helped to encourage the presumption that Tocqueville's new science was about America and for America and Americans. Such a presumption does not square with Tocqueville's professed intentions. There is a strong sense in which *Democracy in America* was not essentially about America at all. It was, as Tocqueville himself emphasized,[3] directed at the general phenomenon of democracy which had been gathering force for several centuries and had now revealed itself to be what Tocqueville called "a providential fact," that is, a universal, irresistible tendency which had often been facilitated by actors whose intentions were opposed to or ignorant of democracy.[4] Instead of being composed for the intellectual and political edification of Americans, which would have been to confine the significance of its theme, the work sought a less parochial plane, the plane of France. "My wish," Tocqueville confessed in his Introduction to *Democracy*, "has been to find instruction by which we [Frenchmen] may ourselves profit."[5] He was more candid in a letter to a friend: "I confess that I did not write a single page [of *Democracy*] without silent and perpetual reference to France."[6] Thus *Democracy in America* was about the New World, but it was for the Old.

Although, ironically, *Democracy* never acquired the status of classic in France as it soon did in America or attracted the scholarly attention of later generations of French political theorists and publicists as it has in America,[7] the fact that it was shaped for the Old World must

---

3. "I confess that in America I saw more than America; I sought the image of democracy itself" (*Démocratie*, 1:12).
4. Ibid., p. 4. The force of this passage is lost in the Lawrence translation, which renders *un fait providentiel* as "something fated." *Democracy in America*, ed. J.-P. Mayer, tr. George Lawrence (Garden City, N.Y.: Doubleday & Co., 1969), p. 12.
5. *Démocratie*, p. 11.
6. Letter to Kergorlay, 18 Oct. 1847, *Correspondance d'Alexis de Tocqueville et de Louis de Kergorlay*, 2 vols., *Oeuvres complètes*, ed. A. Jardin, 2:209.
7. This has been importantly rectified by the recent studies of François Furet, *Workshop of the Historian* (Chicago: University of Chicago Press, 1985).

have conditioned the structure of Tocqueville's theoretical perceptions such as to play off the temporal categories of New and Old to their mutual illumination of their respective worlds. How, then, did the new science seek to understand newness and what was the function of the Old in that understanding?

The short answer to the first part of the question is "with severe reservations." Certainly Tocqueville did not urge his readers to rush to embrace democracy, but rather to reconcile themselves to the inevitable. Embedded in that general attitude was, of course, a host of ideological assumptions: about the social groups and interests which needed to be reassured about democracy and about those, who really did not figure in Tocqueville's conception of audience, the working classes and elements of the petite bourgeoisie and peasantry who were likely to be less worried than hopeful about the alleged inevitability of egalitarian democracy. For the former groups, the bourgeoisie and the still significant aristocracy, *Democracy in America* was a cautionary tale, full of warnings about the dangerous tendencies of democracy: about its leveling impulse, the tyranny of majority opinion, the atomization effected by the equality of "social condition," and the obsession with individual self-interest. *Democracy in America* was also a book of remedies, of practices that would curb democratic excesses and blunt its drive toward uniformity.

Thus the new science was conceived, at least in part, as a book of counsel on how to combat the new.[8] It was intended as an antidemocratic science and disposed to be antimodern in its temper. It was not, however, a reactionary science. Tocqueville once described himself as "a liberal of a new kind," by which he meant that unlike Continental liberals he was not committed to carrying forward the antireligious and anticlerical values of the Enlightenment, and he was inclined toward an accommodation with democracy, although not at the expense of individual freedom or property rights. We might say that he was, in the strict sense, committed more to the liberalization of democracy than to the democratization of liberalism.

The association of a new science with antidemocracy was not an original idea of Tocqueville's, but one that he had borrowed from the authors of *The Federalist*, who had claimed that the new constitution embodied principles established by a "new science of politics."[9] Thanks to the careful scholarship of J. T. Schleifer, we are now able to trace the profound influence of *The Federalist* in shaping Tocqueville's understanding of the American constitutional system.[1] Tocqueville's analysis drew heavily on the antimajoritarianism of *The Federalist* and its distrust of the state legislatures which at the time of the contro-

---

8. In the history of political theory there is a continuous tradition of books of counsel. The most famous is Machiavelli's *Prince*. Henry Reeve, Tocqueville's translator, shrewdly observed that *Democracy in America* formed a modern parallel to *The Prince*, revealing the secrets of the people to the world as Machiavelli had revealed those of the princes (Letter to Tocqueville, 22 Feb. 1840, *Correspondance Anglaise*, 6:55).
9. See *The Federalist*, no. 9, by Hamilton.
1. J. T. Schleifer, *The Making of Tocqueville's "Democracy in America"* (Chapel Hill: University of North Carolina Press, 1982).

versy over the ratification of the constitution were significantly influenced by democratically oriented forces.[2]

There were, however, profound differences between *The Federalist* conception of a "new science" of politics and Tocqueville's. Both described the Americans as embarked upon a new "experiment." For Madison, writing in *Federalist* 14, the new constitution represented "the experiment of an extended republic." An extended republic would overcome the flaw which made democracy an unsuitable political form: it could be adapted to huge spaces and large populations. Part of the rhetorical strategy of the *Federalist* argument was to associate democracy with antiquity. Democracy was thus premodern.[3] Tocqueville, however, saw America as an experiment in democracy rather than as an alternative to it. He described it as "the great experiment . . . in the attempt to construct society upon a new basis." Theories hitherto unknown, or deemed impracticable, were to exhibit a spectacle for which the world had not been prepared by the history of the past.[4] For *The Federalist* the new science was embodied in the proposed constitution; for Tocqueville the new science would show that the constitution was only one element and that the success of the experiment depended on elements that could not have been designed in the way that constitutional provisions could be.

The nub of the matter was that *The Federalist* had been concerned to establish the idea of a strong national government which meant, inter alia, a more centralized system and a powerful executive. While Tocqueville was in no sense advocating a reversion to antifederalism, he believed that the states were the source of America's basic political principles and that America had "a spirit."[5] His famous discussion of voluntary associations was indicative of an outlook that was sympathetic to precisely what *The Federalist* had distrusted, an active citizenry with institutions through which they could govern their common affairs.

It has long been recognized that Tocqueville was deeply influenced by Montesquieu,[6] but, to my knowledge, no one has connected that influence to Tocqueville's call for "a new science of politics." My suggestion is that while Tocqueville borrowed the phrase, the actual substance of that science was not indebted to *The Federalist* but rather to Montesquieu's conception which in fundamental respects followed a rather different notion of science. Hasty readers have identified Montesquieu with a Newtonian view of constitutionalism, citing in support of that claim Book II, chapter 6, of *De L'Esprit des Lois* and its famous

2. *Démocratie*, pp. 54–55, 78, 119–20, 156–58, 257 ff.
3. See *The Federalist*, no. 10.
4. *Démocratie*, p. 25.
5. Ibid., p. 65.
6. See the comments of Melvin Richter, ed., *The Political Theory of Montesquieu* (Cambridge, Cambridge University Press: 1977), pp. 7 ff., and Jack Lively, *The Social and Political Thought of Alexis de Tocqueville* (Oxford, Clarendon Press:), p. 200. Royer-Collard was among the first of Tocqueville's contemporaries to emphasize the Montesquieu connection. See the comment by Cavour cited in J.-P. Mayer, *Alexis de Tocqueville*, tr. M. M. Bozman and C. Hahn (New York: Viking, 1940), p. 106.

discussion of the separation of powers. There is an undeniably Newtonian flavor to sections of that chapter and to a few other passages
elsewhere,[7] yet the theoretical point of De L'Esprit was diametrically
opposed to constitutional gadgeteering. It conceived of political societies as historical accretion, devised by no one founder, strongly
shaped by physical conditions (climate and geography), and consisting
of complex accommodations among religion, morality, customs, economy and civil and political laws. The main target of Montesquieu's
work was despotism: The Spirit of the Laws together with the Persian
Letters constitutes the most sustained meditation on that subject to be
found anywhere in modern political theory.

Montesquieu believed that despotism was the dominant tendency in
the monarchical state system of his day. He sought to counter it with a
theoretical construction which was deeply influenced by the practices
of feudalism and by the vestigial remnants of that system preserved in
the so-called intermediary bodies (les puissance intermédiaires).[8] These
consisted of provincial estates or assemblies, municipal governments,
and the judicial institutions of les parlements.[9] It was not any urge to restore feudalism that caught Montesquieu's attention but rather its imagery of a decentered political system in which power was dispersed
among many centers and thereby limited by natural rivalries.

The "feudal" element in Montesquieu's theory was decisive to
Tocqueville's "new science" and to its antimodern thrust. Its presence
in Tocqueville's theory resolves the logical paradox of how it is possible
to find a new language of theory for a New World which, for Europeans, was only now coming into existence. A truly New World would
be one without precedent and hence without a language appropriate
to it. What was, ultimately, most new about the New World was the
production of sameness. It could be described variously: as uniformity,
conformity, leveling, egalitarianism, or democracy, but it all came back
to the same striking point. Never before in human history had there
been a society where so many people thought alike, dressed alike, lived
alike, or occupied the same middling social station. To understand this
newness, that is, to be startled into an awareness of its radical novelty
requires the vantage point of the old, that is, a vantage point in which
variety, gradation, difference, and rarity were cherished with as much
passion as democratic man cherished equality. The theoretical understanding had to situate itself between the two worlds and move from
one to the other. The feudal element was decisive in Tocqueville's Old
World. That element was not simply old but importantly archaic. It
was not to be taken literally for it was, Tocqueville knew, dead beyond
recall, but if treated as a principle it might be useful in an entirely different political context, useful not only to the theoretical understanding of the new but also to an antimodern practice or pragmatics.

---

7. De L'Esprit des Lois, 2 vols., ed. Roger Caillois in the Pleiade edition of Montesquieu's Oeuvres complètes (Paris: Gallimard, 1951), 2:405.
8. Ibid., Bk. 2, ch. 4; Bk. 4, ch. 9.
9. In general see Fr. Olivier-Martin, L'Organisation corporative de la France d'ancien régime
(Paris, 1938), especially chap. 8.

More than a quarter century ago, Louis Hartz's classic work, *The Liberal Tradition in America*, retrieved and restated Tocqueville's fundamental interpretive principle. To understand America was to appreciate the fact that it had no feudal past.[1] What, then, can it mean politically not to have a feudal past? I would suggest the following interpretation of Hartz's thesis: to be without a feudal past is to experience politics as mythic. Myth is the plane of the eternal present where politics is freed of history. "Feudalism" represents a negative pole to the myth; it symbolizes historical politics. Historical politics inevitably brings inherited and unequal privileges and powers; a social space which is crowded with prior claims to ownership and status; and the transformation of a manifold of injustices from the dim past into vested rights of the present. Americans, in contrast, occupied a fresh land seemingly without limits or boundaries. Land was easily available and opportunities for wealth and higher status seemed limitless.

Accordingly, America's politics was "natural" rather than historical. The practices which it developed were written on the tabula rasa of nature, much as the contract theorists of the seventeenth century imagined men imposing an association upon the state of nature.[2] Inscribing its politics upon nature rather than history was the essence of what was modern about America. "History" does not stand for a narrative of events but for obstacles, the obstacles represented by vested interests, prescriptive powers, and settled expectations, in short, everything that has to be taken into account by political actors. To have no history is to face only natural obstacles and one's own limitations. Action is unimpeded. Such a vista is potentially dangerous, in Tocqueville's view. It is made to order for despotism or for centralized bureaucracy. The lack of traditions and customs allows the will to extend itself almost without limit. America, he believed, was spared that fate, at least temporarily, because central power remained undeveloped.

When Tocqueville remarks that America became democratic or egalitarian without having to pass through a destructive revolution, he is also recalling that the French had tried to establish democracy by overthrowing feudalism in the great revolution of 1789. France, in other words, had tried to accomplish by force what Americans inherited by accident, the destruction of history and the founding of natural politics. The lesson that Tocqueville's new science wants to impart is that although both societies are antifeudal, each should attempt to preserve archaic elements which derive from a feudal past, as in France, or are the functional equivalents of feudal institutions, as in America.

One of Tocqueville's favorite examples of archaism in America was the judiciary and the legal profession.[3] He regarded it as the insertion

---

1. Louis Hartz, *the Liberal Tradition in America* (New York: Harcourt, 1955).
2. Tocqueville's concept of "nature" has largely been neglected by commentators. Chapter 1 of *Democracy in America* presents a detailed physical description of America, a beginning point for any good Montesquieuean. Essential are the remarkable travel sketches which Tocqueville composed. These have been collected by J.-P. Mayer in vol. 5 of *OC*.
3. *Démocratie*, pp. 99 ff.

of an aristocratic principle into a political system which encouraged domination by the majority or the demagogic ambitions of a Jacksonian president. The principle of an independent judiciary, coupled with the high social esteem attached to bench and bar, operated to check the majority and to secure the property rights of the bourgeoisie and hence their loyalty. It represented, Tocqueville insisted, an elitist element which, strictly speaking, could not be justified by the logic of democracy. Its archaic character could be understood by analogy with the *noblesse de robe* and the *parlements* which represented a feudal element in the Old Regime. The *parlements* were law courts which had formed part of the privileges of a stratum of the prerevolutionary French nobility. Among their powers was the authority to grant or withhold registration of royal decrees and hence to deny them full legal authority. It could be invoked to block, at least temporarily, the efforts of monarchs to extend their powers. It could also be used to defend class privileges.[4] The point of the analogy was not to restore the *parlements* or class privileges but to teach democracy the value of protecting a counter-principle lodged at the center of its own system. But to do that, democracy had to think archaically, not simply indulge in self-distrust. For as the second installment of *Democracy in America* disclosed, democracy was a hegemonic political culture which settled its social categories upon an entire society and compelled the members to view the world through them. To grasp the implications of democracy, one had to get outside the new and view it from the vantage point of the old. The uses of archaism were a way of reinserting historicity into societies whose "natural" bent was to extirpate it.

Archaism takes on a new significance when the new nation which once was said to have no past now had one; and where it once had no feudal past has now acquired one. To put the matter this way may seem to be straining the Tocqueville-Hartz thesis beyond recognition. Yet the slightest familiarity with American history is enough to demonstrate that America has always had a past in which differentiated societies and complex cultures flourished before the colonists arrived early in the seventeenth century. At best one is only entitled to claim that before 1607 America did not have a European past. Tocqueville himself placed great importance upon the colonial heritage of English practices and theories and of biblical examples.[5] Yet these qualifications do not lessen Tocqueville's basic point, that America's newness, its vast spaces and natural resources, the egalitarianism favored by the availability of land, and the opportunities for social mobility, had conspired to make Americans appear eternally in movement, perpetually changing. Americans were continually changing laws, jobs, geographical locations, tastes, beliefs, and status, not once but several times. To be new was to accept instability and dislocation as normal features of existence. "The woof of time is every instant broken, and the track of generations effaced."[6]

4. Franklin L. Ford, *Robe and Sword, the Regrouping of the French Aristocracy* (New York: Harper, 1965), especially chap. 3.
5. *Démocratie*, pp. 26 ff.
6. Ibid., 2: p. 106.

Where Tocqueville looked upon change as the result of the uncoordinated strivings of largely autonomous, even isolated, individuals let loose upon a huge and empty social space, that spontaneous conception of change now appears anachronistic. The culture which contemporary science and technology have built under the bidding of corporate capitalism must, if it is to survive in an intensely competitive international economy, produce change as a matter of deliberate policy. The organization of scientific research and its subsidization by public and private funds signify the institutionalization of change. The intensification and rationalization of change, the continuous reproduction of the new and the simultaneous subversion of the old, may justify calling such a society postmodern, for there is no longer any old world to be transformed, only the changing of prior changes. Fashion, with its seasonal changes, may be more of a general emblem of society than a special case. A postmodern society produces its own archaeological strata at an almost daily rate as its members change cars, clothes, heroes, wives, sexual preferences, role models, and intellectual truths. Politicians complain of "volatile" electorates and seek ways of insulating party organizations from supporters who seem susceptible to short-term seizures or whimsies. To seek continuity between generations one must turn to computers which, we are reliably informed, are into their fourth or fifth "generations." They shall eat sour software . . .

One of the most striking changes turns Tocqueville on his head. It concerns the de-democratization of American political society. Today it is difficult to imagine that any respectable political scientist or political sociologist would write a book about the irresistible tide of democracy or its incarnation in America, except as parody. It is not that there have been no democratic gains during the past quarter century. Various movements—civil rights, students, women, and gays—have all contributed to the greater equalization of freedom in the society. Numerous social programs have eased the economic plight of the poor and the working classes generally. Yet none of these movements or developments can be said to have resulted in any significant restatement of democratic theory. Each of these movements was importantly a protest against antidemocratic practices being enforced by political and legal authorities who, for the most part, were formally elected by and accountable to the citizenry. Excepting the students, the others— racial minorities, women, and gays—can be treated in Tocquevillean terms as victims of "the tyranny of the majority."

It is possible to multiply the examples of majority tyranny: prayers in public schools, antibusing legislation, censorship of public library collections, and the efforts to replace evolutionist theory by creationism. The attitudes which underlie these proposals, especially when they emanate from fundamentalist religious groups, seem archaic—which they were in the sense being used here. Their historical roots are, however, closely intertwined with democratic traditions. Religious fundamentalism, "moralism," and racial and religious prejudice belong to the same historical culture as do traditions of local self-government, decentralized politics, participatory democracy, and egalitarianism.

I want to suggest that these traditions constitute our "feudalism." Like feudalism, they favor decentralization, local cultures, local prerogatives. They are suspicious of distant powers and centralized authority. Their prejudices appear as anachronisms, but then so does democracy itself. The reversal in the status of democracy, from being "modern" to being "archaic," is connected with another feature of America that astonished Tocqueville almost as much as its widespread equality. America seemed to lack the one political institution all European societies accepted as fundamental: it did not have a state. One looked in vain, Tocqueville reported, for an administrative apparatus which is the proof of the state's existence.[7]

The absence of the state in America meant that in a fundamental respect America was premodern. Virtually every historian, including Tocqueville himself in *The Old Regime*, has underscored the central role played by the state in promoting the transition to modernity. Yet America, the archetype of modern society, seemed to lack the crucial agent of modernization. It was not only a society without a feudal past but a society without an antifeudal past as well. It is, of course, true that Tocqueville and other commentators have underplayed the actual role of the state during the first half of the nineteenth century.[8] Nevertheless, it is roughly true that the concept of the state did not figure importantly in American political thought until the slavery debates were begun in earnest. Since the Civil War, however, and especially in the aftermath of the two world wars and economic depressions of the twentieth century, the American state has grown steadily more powerful until it is reckoned to be the major factor in our society as well as in world politics.[9] The triumph of the state, although late in coming to America, has repeated the European experience: it has come to its present power and dominance at the expense of America's version of feudalism, which is democracy. It is hostile to democratic participation, local autonomy, regional cultures, and the pluralism and variety nurtured by these forms. These are archaic elements which appear as anomalies to the state's bureaucratic apparatus whose penchant for government by uniform regulations signifies that the source of leveling does not emanate from a tyrannical majority but from the state. The rationalization of the state and the reduction of politics to management have, over the past half century, been the work of corporate and technocratic elites. Their political predominance is still another indication that time has reversed Tocqueville's prophecy of irreversible democratization. A fair case can be made that significant social, economic, and political inequalities have taken hold in America and that the discrepancies between social classes, if they are not slowly widening, are surely not diminishing. Inequality is as much a basic el-

7. Ibid., 1:214–15, 273–74.
8. See Jonathan R. T. Hughes, *The Governmental Habit: Economic Controls from Colonial Times to the Present* (New York: Basic Books, 1977).
9. See Stephen Skowronek, *Building a New American State: The Expansion of National Administrative Capacities* (Cambridge: Cambridge University Press, 1982).

ement of the American ideology as equality, and among younger groups it may be predominant. The dominating presence of the state, technocratic elitism, and the decline of the ideology of egalitarianism are all indications of a postmodern political form. Despite all of these signs suggestive of the attenuation of democracy there exists a highly flourishing archaic political culture that is democratic, participatory, localist, and, overall, more egalitarian than elitist in ideology. It is negligible as an influence in national politics and yet it occupies the energy, skills, and commitments of thousands of Americans every day. Sometime it involves the founding of new political association (e.g., to protest the electricity rates set by public utilities); other times it means politicizing certain services which were traditionally presented as the preserve of experts (medical clinics, schools, waste disposal). Like Tocqueville's feudal elements, these, too, are antistatist, antibureaucratic, and anomalous. Like Tocqueville's aristocracy, they are not unfailingly attractive: they can be bigoted, provincial, and myopic. Yet they represent the main political counter-thrust to *étatisme*. They may turn out to be the saving archaism in the postmodern world.

EDWARD C. BANFIELD

The Illiberal Tocqueville†

Democracy in America has been called the greatest book ever written about one country by a citizen of another. It is certainly the greatest book ever written by anyone about America. After 150 years there is hardly a page that does not open the reader's eyes to the larger implications of some familiar fact. It may appear perverse of me, then, to use this occasion to discuss not Tocqueville's illuminating view of America but rather his—as I think—unilluminating one of the nature and future of democracy. My excuse for doing so is not that this essay celebrates the Bicentennial of the Constitution (which is based on principles quite contrary to Tocqueville's). Rather, it is that Tocqueville considered the nature and future of democracy to be his real subject. "America," he wrote to J. S. Mill, "was only the frame, my picture was Democracy."[1]

In the memoir he wrote after Tocqueville's death, Beaumont listed the questions he said had filled Tocqueville's thoughts before they began their journey together—questions which brought Tocqueville to

† Edward C. Banfield (1916–1999) was a professor of government at Harvard University and the author of *The Moral Basis of a Backward Society* and *The Unheavenly City*. This essay, originally a lecture at the Claremont Institute in 1985, appeared in the volume *Interpreting Tocqueville's Democracy in America*. Reprinted by permission of Rowman and Littlefield Publishers.

1. *Memoir, Letters and Remains of Alexis de Tocqueville* (Boston: Ticknor & Fields, 1862), vol. II, p. 38. Hereinafter cited as *Memoir*. Tocqueville says essentially the same in his introductory chapter. Alexis de Tocqueville, *Democracy in America* (New York: Alfred A. Knopf, 1945), vol. I, p. 14. Hereinafter cited as *Democracy*.

the New World and which were to be the business of his life.[2] There were four:

How to reconcile equality, which separates and isolates men, with liberty? How to prevent a power, the offspring of democracy, from becoming absolute and tyrannical? Where to find a force able to contend against this power among a set of men, all equal, it is true, but all equally weak and impotent? Was the fate of modern society to be both democracy and despotism?

I shall discuss Tocqueville's reflections on these four questions, drawing mainly upon *Democracy in America* but also upon his other published writings, including letters.

I

Tocqueville writes as a French patriot, a member of the lesser nobility, who aspires to a career as a statesman and literary figure; who sees France in the turmoil of a social and political revolution likely to end in either anarchy or despotism; and who wants passionately to show the leaders of both right and left how they may guide events to an outcome which, although far from ideal, will nevertheless combine liberty with order and justice—a regime decent men will find tolerable. His purpose is frankly hortatory. He will paint a picture of democracy that will reassure extreme conservatives in France while at the same time dampening the enthusiasm of radical egalitarians.[3]

He finds it almost as difficult for a man to be inconsistent in his language as to be consistent in his conduct, but he himself uses his key concepts in at least two—usually vague—senses.[4] Thus "democracy" has two quite unrelated meanings: "general equality of social conditions" and "the absolute sovereignty of the majority."[5] In America, general equality of social conditions has developed farther than anywhere else: Indeed, it has approached its "natural limits."[6] Equality of social conditions does not necessarily imply popular government; thus Tocqueville can speak of a "democratic people ruled by a despot."[7] Although in both meanings "democracy" was more advanced in the United States than elsewhere, it was not likely that the nations of Europe could learn much from it. Tocqueville was well aware of this. He saw the United States as the unique product of its origins. The Puritan colonists of the seventeenth century, he writes, brought into an admirable combination two distinctive elements that hitherto had often been at war: the *"spirit of religion"* and the *"spirit of freedom"* (emphasis in the original).[8] The first Puritan carried with him the whole of the

---

2. *Memoir*, vol. I, pp. 19–20.
3. Ibid., pp. 376–78. This letter is reprinted in Roger Boesche, ed., *Alexis de Tocqueville: Selected Letters on Politics and Society* (Berkeley: University of California Press, 1985), pp. 98–99. Hereinafter cited as Boesche, *Selected Letters*.
4. *Democracy*, vol. I, p. 16; see also vol. II, p. 69.
5. Ibid., vol. I, pp. 3, 254.
6. Ibid., p. 13.
7. Ibid., vol. II, p. 26.
8. Ibid., vol. I, p. 43.

political future.[9] "There is not an opinion, not a custom, not a law, not even an event, that the origins of the Americans will not explain."[1] What is most important in the development of national character is not climate, law, or even institutions; rather, it is habits, opinions, usages, and beliefs.[2] New England, he points out, is very different from the West and the South.[3] Mexico, which has the same laws as the United States, is unable to govern itself democratically.[4]

If American democracy is unique, one wonders, what can be learned from it that will have any application elsewhere? What can France, for example, which never had a Puritan, learn from a country whose political tradition was decisively influenced by Puritanism? Tocqueville acknowledged the problem: A careful distinction must, he says, be made between the institutions of the United States and democratic institutions in general, adding that if human nature or social conditions are very different in America and Europe there is no possibility of making predictions about democracy in general on the basis of American experience.[5] Finally, he recognizes that what may be learned about democracy from American experience may not bear transplanting: A democracy, he says, can obtain truth only as a result of experience, meaning, presumably, *its own* experience.[6] Having acknowledged these methodological limitations, he proceeds as if they do not exist.

II

How to reconcile equality, which
separates and isolates men, with liberty?

All men at all times, Tocqueville says, have a passion for equality—one that is "ardent, insatiable, incessant, invincible."[7] Where conditions permit of rising in the world, there is universal competition to do so.[8] In Europe, over many centuries there has been a gradual but accelerating tendency to break down all forms of social hierarchy. The further advance of equality, that is, of democracy, constitutes a social revolution which cannot be stopped, although it may be guided and controlled.[9] Equality of social conditions, he writes in the first paragraph of *Democracy*, is "the fundamental fact from which all others seem to be derived. . . ."

By separating and isolating men, equality of social conditions gives rise to individualism, a state in which every man's feelings are turned toward himself alone. The individualist, with his family and friends,

9. Ibid., p. 290.
1. Ibid., p. 28.
2. Ibid., p. 322.
3. Ibid.
4. Ibid., p. 321.
5. Ibid., pp. 323–24.
6. Ibid., p. 231.
7. Ibid., vol. II, p. 97.
8. Ibid., vol. I, p. 201; vol. II, p. 138.
9. Ibid., vol. I, p. 7.

draws apart from others: He turns his back upon society, leaving it to take care of itself.

> As social conditions become more equal, the number of persons increases who, although they are neither rich nor powerful enough to exercise any great influence over their fellows, have nevertheless acquired or retained sufficient education and fortune to satisfy their own wants. They owe nothing to any man, they expect nothing from any man; they acquire the habit of always considering themselves as standing alone, and they are apt to imagine that their whole destiny is in their own hands.
>
> Thus not only does democracy make every man forget his ancestors, but it hides his descendants and separates his contemporaries from him; it throws him back forever upon himself alone and threatens in the end to confine him entirely within the solitude of his own heart.[1]

At first individualism attacks only the virtues of public life, but eventually it destroys all others as well. Equality is bound to spread and, with it, individualism. This being the case, how can liberty be maintained?

Clearly much depends upon how one conceives of liberty. Tocqueville has mutually antagonistic concepts of it.[2]

In an article written for a review edited by J. S. Mill, he defines it very much as Mill was to define it himself twenty years later:

> According to the modern, and democratic and, we venture to say, the only just notion of liberty, every man, being presumed to have received from nature the intelligence necessary for his own general guidance, is inherently entitled to be uncontrolled by his fellows in all that only concerns himself, and to regulate at his own will his own destiny.[3]

What Tocqueville here calls the "only just notion of liberty" sounds very much like what in the first volume of *Democracy* he describes as the "grand maxim" of American society; namely, that Providence has

---

1. Ibid., vol. II, p. 99.
2. In his account of the origins of the Americans, Tocqueville quotes the "fine definition" of liberty made by the Puritan leader John Winthrop in the seventeenth century (ibid., vol. I, p. 39). Civil or moral (as opposed to natural) liberty, Winthrop said, "is a liberty to do only that which is good, just, and honest"; such liberty, he added, "is exercised in subjection to authority." What Tocqueville finds admirable in this definition is the combination of the *spirit of religion* with the *spirit of liberty* (vol. I, p. 43). That the Puritans freely voted laws that were "fantastic and oppressive" he acknowledges, calling it an error "discreditable to human reason" (vol. I, pp. 39, 42; also vol. II, Appendix E). But of course it is precisely because men who are separated and isolated, acknowledging no principle of authority, are prone to error that the question of how to maintain liberty among them arises. Winthrop's notion of liberty is irrelevant to the kind of society with which Tocqueville is concerned.

   When addressing English readers, Tocqueville seems to use the word "liberty" differently than when addressing French ones. In a letter to J. S. Mill, he says he loves liberty "by taste" whereas he loves equality by "instinct and reason" (Boesche, *Selected Letters*, p. 100). Writing to his publisher, Henry Reeve, he says he has only one passion: "love of liberty and human dignity" (ibid., p. 115). To Madame Swetchine and to Beaumont, he takes a different tone. To the former he writes that liberty is "one of the most fertile sources of manly virtues and great actions" (ibid., p. 326), and to the latter it is "the necessary condition without which there has never been a truly great or virile nation" (ibid., p. 366).
3. *Memoir*, vol. I, p. 247.

given to every human being the degree of reason necessary to direct himself in the affairs that interest him exclusively.[4] This, however, is the principle of individualism, which he detests. A nation devoted to it, he says, must eventually slide into despotism.[5]

What Tocqueville meant by liberty was no more than the absence of despotism.[6] He was much mistaken when, writing Mill to thank him—before reading it—for a copy of On Liberty, he said that liberty "is a field in which we cannot but walk hand in hand."[7] But even by this weakest of definitions he contradicts himself. In The Old Regime and the French Revolution, he condemns as despotic the ideas of the Physiocrats, who, he says, believed the function of the state was not only to rule but also to shape the mentality of the population by instilling the ideas and sentiments they thought desirable.[8] But instilling ideas and sentiments was exactly what his own program for turning individuals into citizens entailed. In Democracy he proposes laying down "certain extreme limits which the state should never be allowed to overstep."[9] How, one must wonder, are "those who direct our [French] affairs" to keep within any limits while carrying out the duties Tocqueville says are imposed upon them:

> . . . to educate democracy, to reawaken, if possible, its religious beliefs: to purify its morals: to mold its actions: to substitute a knowledge of statecraft for its inexperience, and an awareness of its true interest for its blind instincts. . . .[1]

This list of reforms is lengthened in the second volume. The "leaders of modern society" should expose the community to difficulties and dangers "in order to raise ambition. . . ."[2] Government should do what it can to restore men to a love of the future.[3] A policy of giving democratic nations education and freedom and then leaving them alone will not suffice in the end, and it is likely to cause man "to lose the use of his sublimest faculties."[4]

III

> How to prevent a power, the offspring of democracy, from becoming absolute and tyrannical?

Tocqueville could answer this question in principle, but, alas, only in principle.

4. Democracy, vol. I, p. 418.
5. Ibid., p. 420.
6. See Joseph Hamburger, "Mill and Tocqueville on Liberty," ed. John M. Robson and Michael Laine, James and John Stuart Mill: Papers of the Centenary Conference (Toronto and Buffalo: University of Toronto Press, 1976), p. 124.
7. Memoir, vol. II, p. 428.
8. Alexis de Tocqueville, The Old Regime and the French Revolution, trans. Stuart Gilbert (Garden City, N.Y.: Doubleday, Anchor Books, 1955), pp. 158–64. Hereinafter cited as Old Regime.
9. Democracy, vol. II, p. 248.
1. Ibid., vol. I, p. 7.
2. Ibid., vol. II, p. 248.
3. Ibid., p. 151.
4. Ibid., p. 144.

The self-interested individual must be taught the ways of citizenship: He must learn to accept his share of responsibility for the welfare of the community. What is needed is a decentralization of government that will put the conduct of local affairs in local hands: The individual will then of necessity acquire the skills and habits of a citizen. American experience suggests a number of other "democratic expedients" having this tendency: among them the spread of associations for political and social ends, the jury system, a free press, and an independent judiciary.

Unfortunately, these "democratic expedients" would not be expedient in Europe, and the most important of them, local self-government, was rapidly ceasing to be so in the United States. Townships, Tocqueville remarks, must be "self-produced," and municipal freedom is "rarely created by others."[5] Developed societies, he says, are apt to be impatient with the blunders that result from local independence.[6] Moreover, both the interests of the politicians in power and the tastes of individuals are forces pressing for centralization.[7] It is far easier for a central government to destroy local independence than to create it.[8]

A somewhat more promising possibility lies in the American principle of self-interest rightly understood. Recognizing the futility of urging lofty ideas of man's duty upon self-interested individualists, American moralists content themselves with holding that it is to the individual's self-interest to serve others. This principle, Tocqueville points out, produces no great acts of self-sacrifice: It cannot make a man virtuous, but it does discipline men in habits of regularity, temperance, moderation, foresight, and self-command, and so it draws them in the direction of virtue.[9] If they could be drawn far enough, they would be good—no, fair—citizens.

Unfortunately they cannot be drawn far enough. "No power on earth," he says,

> can prevent the increasing equality of conditions from inclining the human mind to seek out what is useful or from leading every member of the community to be wrapped up in himself. It must therefore be expected that personal interest will become more than ever the principal if not the sole spring of men's actions. . . .[1]

If self-interest narrowly conceived comes to dominate, "freedom, public peace, and social order itself will not be able to exist. . . ."[2] Except as men take account of the public interest, "it is difficult to foresee to what pitch of stupid excesses their selfishness may lead them. . . ."[3]

The defining principle of democracy is the sovereignty of the major-

5. Ibid., vol. I, p. 60.
6. Ibid.
7. Ibid., vol. II, pp. 367–68.
8. Ibid., vol. I, p. 60.
9. Ibid., vol. II, p. 123.
1. Ibid., p. 124.
2. Ibid.
3. Ibid.

ity, but the majority, it appears, cannot be educated to citizenship. Moreover, that the people have a right to do anything they wish is an "impious and detestable maxim."[4] In America, Tocqueville finds, the principle of the sovereignty of the people has acquired "all the practical development that the imagination can conceive":[5] "The people reign in the American political world as the Deity does in the universe. They are the cause and aim of all things: Everything comes from them, and everything is absorbed in them."[6] The American Founders, he mistakenly thinks, carried the principle of popular sovereignty to its extreme by providing that the legislature be elected by the people *directly* and for *a very brief term* (the emphasis is his) in order to make it responsive not only to the convictions but "even to the daily passions" of the people.[7] (He was under the misapprehension that the national government was of little importance as compared to state governments.) The power of the majority in the United States, he concludes, "is harmful in itself and dangerous for the future."[8] The states, he thinks, must move toward indirect democracy or "risk perishing miserably among the shoals of democracy."[9]

The best government, Tocqueville wrote from America to a friend, "is not that in which all have a share, but that which is directed by the class of the highest moral principle and intellectual cultivation."[1] Democracy cannot be the best government since its very essence "consists in the absolute sovereignty of the majority. . . ."[2] But he wonders if in some country—France?—the people would consent to be ruled by their betters. Unmindful of American constitutional arrangements, Tocqueville speculates:

> Might not a democratic society be imagined in which the forces of the nation would be more centralized than they are in the United States; where the people would exercise a less direct influence upon public affairs, and yet every citizen, invested with certain rights, would participate, within his sphere, in the conduct of the government?[3]

Democratic institutions of this kind might be introduced elsewhere than in America, he thinks, if it were done gradually and without greatly disturbing the habits and opinions of the people.[4]

IV

Where to find a force able to contend against
this power among a set of men all equal,
it is true, but all equally weak and impotent?

4. Ibid., vol. I, p. 259.
5. Ibid., p. 57.
6. Ibid., p. 58.
7. Ibid., p. 254.
8. Ibid., p. 256.
9. Ibid., p. 205.
1. *Memoir*, vol. I, p. 297.
2. *Democracy*, vol. I, p. 254.
3. Ibid.
4. Ibid.

The "power" to which the question refers is that of an unenlightened majority. Tocqueville believes that two forces are able to contend against it: religion and patriotism. These, he says, are the only motives that can long urge all the people toward the same end.[5] Both are natural instincts, and both have been weakened by the effects of equality, especially excessive desire for physical gratifications and for the acquisition of wealth.

The compelling need is to direct men's attention away from the petty pleasures of the present and from theories of materialism and to point it toward distant objects. Legislators and all virtuous and enlightened men should endeavor to raise the souls of their fellow citizens and to keep them lifted up toward heaven.[6]

Religious belief should be awakened "if possible."[7] The purpose being a political one (Tocqueville says he is discussing religion "from a purely human point of view"),[8] it is not necessary that the awakening be to a true religion; any one will do, even one that is "false and dangerous"; indeed, even one that does not promise a personal immortality.[9]

Although he believes that man instinctively turns to religion, Tocqueville recognizes that the forces that have turned him from it—especially materialism—are not easily overcome. The only way by which rulers can get the doctrine of the immortality of the soul respected is to act *as if* they believe it themselves.[1] Will the rulers of an atheistic democracy act *as if* they believe? Tocqueville has his doubts. The American clergy, he notes, not wanting to be conspicuously out of step with public opinion, are far from vigorous in their efforts to turn attention from this world to the next.[2] How could it be otherwise? "The taste for well being," Tocqueville says, "is the prominent and indelible feature of democratic times."[3]

The other instinct able to unite men is patriotism. In a letter written late in his life, Tocqueville conjectures that nations were formed by God in order to show more clearly the ties by which individuals ought to be mutually attached.[4] (He adds that God's purpose was probably better served by giving men particular fatherlands than it would have been by trying to inflame their passion for all humanity!)[5] National pride is often puerile and absurd, he writes in another letter, but "with all its absurdities and weaknesses [it] is still the greatest sentiment that we [the French] have. . . ."[6] In the first of these two letters, Tocqueville goes on to say that he wishes the clergy would emphasize that a Christian belongs to his nation:

5. Ibid., p. 93.
6. Ibid., vol. II, p. 145.
7. Ibid., vol. I, p. 7.
8. Ibid., vol. II, p. 22.
9. Ibid.
1. Ibid., p. 147.
2. Ibid., p. 27.
3. Ibid., p. 26.
4. *Memoir*, vol. II, p. 333.
5. Ibid.
6. Boesche, *Selected Letters*, p. 144.

I wish the clergy to instill into their very souls that everyone belongs much more to this collective Being [the nation] than he does
to himself; that towards this Being no one ought to be indifferent,
much less, by treating such indifference as a sort of languid virtue,
to enervate many of our noblest instincts; that everyone is responsible for the fortunes of this collective Being; that everyone is bound
to work out its prosperity, and to watch that it be not governed except by respectable, beneficient, and legitimate authorities.[7]

This, Tocqueville recalls, was the teaching of his grandmother, a very
saintly woman who, after urging her young son to perform the duties
of private life, never failed to add: "And then, my child, never forget
that a man above all owes himself to his homeland; that there is no
sacrifice that he must not make for it. . . ."[8]

Tocqueville distinguishes categorically between public and private
virtue and exalts the former over the latter. Commerce he finds repel-
lent because the "paltry desires" and "vulgar pleasures" it engenders
distract men from "manly virtues and great actions," "lofty enterprises," "heroic deeds," and "altruistic sacrifices." He says that in a society consisting of good fathers, honest merchants, exemplary
landlords, and even good Christians, there cannot be a great citizen,
still less a great nation.[9] Why is it, he wonders, that in proportion as
private virtue increases, "the great family of the nation seems more
corrupt, more base, and more tottering."[1]

It is manly virtues that make a nation glorious. War is, of course,
the activity in which these virtues are most conspicuously displayed.
War "almost always enlarges the mind of a people and raises their
character."[2] Although he yields to no man in his hatred of the revolutionary spirit, Tocqueville writes to a friend in 1836 that he finds the
French revolutionaries' belief in man's innate virtue "admirable," the
basis of a new religion that freed them of "self-regarding emotions":
Indifferent to the petty amenities of life, unchecked by any scruples,
able to act with unprecedented ruthlessness, they were "the first of a
new race of men."[3] He has unstinting praise for the British record in
India: "Nothing under the sun is so wonderful as the conquest, and
still more the government, of India by the English."[4]

In the absence of the manly virtues that inspire lofty enterprises and
heroic deeds, Tocqueville concludes, "a nation can but relapse into a
servile state."[5]

7. *Memoir*, vol. II, p. 333.
8. Ibid., p. 329. This letter is included in Boesche, *Selected Letters*, p. 338.
9. *Old Regime*, p. xiv.
1. *Memoir*, vol. II, p. 317. In his famous address to the Chamber of Deputies of Jan. 27, 1848,
   Tocqueville condemns the idea that there are two moralities, a public and a private, a view
   which he later pressed upon Madame Swetchine (*Memoir*, vol. II, p. 328; see also Boesche,
   Selected Letters, p. 338). In his address he says that private mores affect public life, a matter
   "to cause disquiet and alarm to good citizens." His address to the Chamber is Appendix III
   of the George Lawrence translation of *Democracy in America*, ed. J.-P. Mayer (New York:
   Doubleday, 1969), pp. 750–51.
2. *Democracy*, vol. II, pp. 261–62.
3. *Memoir*, vol. I, p. 383.
4. Ibid., vol. II, p. 387.
5. Ibid., *Old Regime*.

All this is reminiscent of Robespierre, whose vision of political life, Stephen Holmes has written, was dominated by a dichotomy between base self-interest and noble virtue, for whom citizenship presupposed a preference for the public interest over all private interests, and for whom the first duty of a politician was to form and preserve public morality.[6]

V

Was the fate of modern society to be both democracy and despotism?

The answer to the question must be "yes" if one follows the logic of Tocqueville's argument. Here is the logic in summary:

1. All men at all times have an insatiable passion for equality; the movement toward equality of social conditions in all Christian countries is "a providential fact."[7]

2. Individualism, which spreads with equality, saps the virtues of both public and private life.[8]

3. Equality produces an excessive taste for small comforts[9] and, worse, for money-making, and—worse yet—materialism. These distract men from their public duties.[1]

4. Democratic tastes and habits lead to commerce and manufacturing, the tendency of which is to degrade the worker ("What can be expected of a man who has spent twenty years of his life making heads for pins?")[2] and to make the master an "aristocrat" who feels no responsibility for his workers.

5. The growth of commerce and manufacturing necessitates large governmental undertakings (roads, canals, etc.), and the principle of equality itself imparts a taste for strong, centralized government.[3]

6. Centralization of government eventuates in a new kind of tyranny. In former times it was impossible for a tyrant to administer strict and uniform regulations; now he can reach into every detail of everyone's life.[4]

Some of Tocqueville's most eloquent language describes the coming "democratic despotism":

> After having thus successively taken each member of the community in its powerful grasp and then fashioned him at will, the supreme power then extends its arm over the whole community. It covers the surface of society with a network of small complicated rules, minute and uniform, through which the most original minds and the most energetic characters cannot penetrate,

6. Stephen Holmes, *Benjamin Constant and the Making of Modern Liberalism* (New Haven, Conn.: Yale University Press, 1984), pp. 48–49.
7. *Democracy*, vol. I, p. 6.
8. Ibid., vol. II, p. 98.
9. Ibid., p. 128.
1. Ibid., pp. 133, 141.
2. Ibid., p. 158.
3. Ibid., pp. 296, 284; also app. Z.
4. Ibid., p. 318.

to rise above the crowd. The will of man is not shattered, but softened, bent, and guided; men are seldom forced by it to act, but they are constantly restrained from acting. Such a power does not destroy, but it prevents existence: it does not tyrannize, but it compresses, enervates, extinguishes, and stupifies a people, till each nation is reduced to nothing better than a flock of timid and industrious animals, of which the government is the shepherd.[5]

VI

Perhaps because his purpose was hortatory, Tocqueville chose not to follow where his logic led.[6] In the final paragraphs of *Democracy*, he says again that nations cannot prevent the conditions of men from becoming equal. But then, ignoring all that this "fundamental fact" entails, he asserts that for democratic nations to be virtuous and prosperous, they "require but to will it." His argument has been that they will *not* will it. But he passed over this in silence.

Brilliant as are his insights into so many aspects of life, Tocqueville's analysis fails utterly to explain the most massive facts of recent and current history. He foresees tyrannies that have not occured, while failing to see the ones that have. Centered as it is on the condition of equality, on individualism, the commercial mentality, and the displacement of national glory by petty pleasures and comforts, his analysis points in exactly the wrong directions. It is the values of his saintly grandmother, not those of the despised moneymaker, that supported the Nazi regime, that are exploited by the Soviet one, and that fire the fanaticism that is endemic in much of the Third World. In the commercial societies which Tocqueville considers doomed—and only in them—has freedom constantly been extended and combined with order and justice. It is to these societies that the world owes the relative material welfare of its many billions of people.

There are many reasons to fear for the future of modern society, but they are not Tocqueville's. By now we know enough about individualism and materialism to understand that they need not destroy private and public virtue. We know also that the pursuit of happiness, even when it leads to paltry pleasures, is compatible with the maintenance of freedom and justice. We know that the seamy side of a commercial society is only one of its many sides.

---

5. Ibid., p. 319; also vol. I, p. 329.
6. That Tocqueville saw the full implications of his argument is evident from recently published notes and chapter drafts. See James T. Schleifer, *The Making of Tocqueville's "Democracy in America"* (Chapel Hill: University of North Carolina Press, 1980), especially chap. 16, "Would Democracy Usher in a New Dark Ages?"

Richard Herr, after pointing out Tocqueville's failure to acknowledge the pessimism of his *Old Regime*, suggests that he was temperamentally incapable of stating a pessimistic conclusion explicitly. See his *Tocqueville and the Old Regime* (Princeton, N.J.: Princeton University Press, 1962), p. 91.

Tocqueville himself argued that to see events as determined is a "false and cowardly" doctrine of historians who live in democratic ages—one that, once it gets possession of the public mind, "will soon paralyze the activity of modern society and reduce Christians to the level of the Turks." *Democracy*, vol. II, p. 88.

A principal defect of Tocqueville's analysis, I think, is his assumption that only insofar as men are good can they produce a good society and that they will be good—or good enough—only if some central authority educates and guides them. The teaching of Mandeville and Adam Smith, that favorable outcomes often occur without anyone's intending them, was alien to his way of thinking.

Like the American Founders, Tocqueville believed that man is more a creature of passion than of reason and that his leading passion is self-interest—"the only immutable point in the human heart."[7] The Founders accepted the necessity of taking man as he was and endeavored to arrange institutions so that in the pursuit of happiness (paltry pleasures, most often), men would be distracted from socially more dangerous activities ("lofty enterprises," perhaps). Tocqueville thought—perhaps I should say wanted to believe—it possible for some authority to educate and guide men, if not to real public virtue, then at least to a more enlightened self-interest, at any rate, to something better than they were by nature. He could not bring himself to believe that if they were left alone the social outcome might be tolerable, let alone in some respects admirable.

It seems to me that the Founders had a much better understanding of things than did Tocqueville. If government can change the nature of man for the better, one would want it to do so right away. But it cannot. And therefore the best course—a perilous one, certainly—is to protect him from others in his pursuit of happiness, and to hope for the best.

DANIEL T. RODGERS

Of Prophets and Prophecy†

Democracy in America began as a piece of reportage, metamorphosed into a work in political philosophy, and became, at last, a book of prophecy. That is not the straightforward progression it may at first blush appear. The making of high theory out of reportage goes on every day, but prophecy is a rarer and more interesting phenomenon. Still more so is the canonization of prophets, the picking out of a handful of writers as gifted not merely with wisdom, or truth, or influence, but with prevision: the ability, not given to most mortals, to see in the tea leaves of their time a startlingly accurate picture of the future.

That status has been Tocqueville's for well over a generation now. We have read *Democracy in America* in many ways since the begin-

7. *Democracy*, vol. I, p. 246.
† Daniel T. Rodgers is the Henry Charles Lea Professor of History at Princeton University and is a historian of American ideas and culture. This essay first appeared in *Reconsidering Tocqueville's Democracy in America*, edited by Abraham S. Eisenstadt. Copyright © 1988 by Rutgers the State University. Reprinted by permission of Rutgers University Press.

nings of the modern Tocqueville revival in the 1940s, but in none more eagerly than the prophetic mode. We have cultivated the pleasures and pains of recognizing our twentieth-century selves, and the burdens of our modernity, in the America he described. We have granted that extraordinarily talented young Frenchman the prize of a tea-leaf reader *extraordinaire*. But in this quarrying of *Democracy in America* for its prevision of our contemporary dilemmas, we have rarely noticed how much that reading of *Democracy in America* diminished the book or stirred the tea leaves of history into confusion. What manner of prophet was Tocqueville? And what manner of readers have we ourselves been to insist so hard on the theme of prevision? To begin to read *Democracy in America* afresh demands some harder thought about prophecy.

Tocqueville did not not begin his reputation as a seer of the future, but rather as an observer and historian. The first American reviewers of *Democracy in America*, all but overwhelmed by the novelty of being taken so extraordinarily seriously, even admiringly, by a European writer, bestowed their praise on the book's descriptive sections, not on the orphic passages that would so rivet the attention of later readers. By the 1880s, James Bryce was interested enough in the prophetic side of *Democracy in America* to compile a checklist of Tocqueville's successful and unsuccessful predictions.[1] But Bryce was not profoundly impressed with Tocqueville's batting average, and in this he was not alone.

It was the Tocqueville revival of the 1940s and 1950s that stamped *Democracy in America* with the reputation of prevision, and it did so quickly, powerfully, and enduringly. In the postwar readers' guides to *Democracy in America*, the prophetic theme was everywhere. Here was a work of "prophetic insight," Phillips Bradley wrote in the Alfred A. Knopf edition of 1945 with which the resurgent postwar interest in Tocqueville began, so fertile "in confirmed perceptions that even a gleaning of the whole yields an abundant harvest of caution and counsel for our time." *Democracy in America* was "a tract for our times," Richard Heffner bolstered the point in his introduction to the Mentor edition of 1956, the cheap, mass-produced edition that stocked the bus stations and the neighborhood bookstores: the work of a "master prophet." Robert Nisbet, who has perhaps done more than any other modern social philosopher to boost Tocqueville's reputation as a thinker of the first rank, wrote in 1966 that sociological theory was best seen as a great magnetic field suspended between the nineteenth century's two master prophets, Tocqueville and Marx—of whom the victor, the more disturbingly accurate predictor, Nisbet claimed, was Tocqueville. Even now, in the best of all modern introductions to *Democracy in America*, Thomas Bender prepares student readers for the "premonitions of our modern condition" that they will find uncan-

---

1. James Bryce, "The Predictions of Hamilton and Tocqueville," *Johns Hopkins University Studies in Historical and Political Science* 5 (1887): 329–381.

nily prefigured in Tocqueville's pages. He has been a prophet of our modernity for over a generation now, and a powerful one.[2]

There was a side to Tocqueville, of course, which invited, indeed all but panted after that response. The second volume of *Democracy in America* was written in the orphic style of a man increasingly obsessed to read the future, to guess the shape of the "half buried" world rising under his feet. But there are many ways to admire Tocqueville's achievement other than as a tea-leaf reader for another century's discontents. Shaggily uneven, fraught with internal contradictions of mood and idea, *Democracy in America* was the work of a man doing what most of us are too timid to do—thinking deeply and furiously hard about his own, politically charged times. There is still no better way to read the book than that. Alternatively one may read it, jammed as it is with aphorisms and generalities, as the work of a provocateur and moralist, a work still capable of jolting us out of our easy mental tracks. One may read it, if one likes, as a classic in political theory. But we have not, I think, been content to rest our affections or our quarrels with *Democracy in America* on these grounds. For forty years now we have scoured the book for what it got right about modernity; we have pushed it on students as a book in which they can see the controlling features of their own America, revealed under the skin of Andrew Jackson's time. We have filled in the space between our America and Tocqueville's with the peculiar gasp of admiration we grant the prognosticator who somehow gets the future right.

But such a reading is not without its costs. One of the most important consequences of that focus has been to concentrate our reading of *Democracy in America* with intense narrowness on a handful of its particularly startling passages. I do not mean simply the trumping of such lucky guesses as Tocqueville's offhand prediction of a future great power rivalry between the United States and Russia. I mean, rather, that our preoccupation with the prophetic quality of *Democracy in America* has induced us over and again to condense the book into those small number of phrases that seem best to prefigure the urgencies of our present moment.

Those urgencies have taken two strikingly different forms since the beginning of the postwar Tocqueville revival. For Tocqueville's readers in the 1940s and 1950s, the heart of *Democracy in America* was the first volume's section on majority tyranny. To those chapters the editors guided their readers with a heavy, anxious hand. There, Phillips Bradley wrote in 1945, was to be found "the real *raison d'être* for the writing of the *Democracy*."[3] There, Richard Heffner concurred, Tocqueville's message for our times was concentrated. Through the course of the 1950s' agonized debate over mass culture and conformity, Tocqueville's name became virtually synonymous with the phrase

---

2. Alexis de Tocqueville, *Democracy in America*, ed. Phillips Bradley (New York, 1945), 2:486, 447; Tocqueville, *Democracy in America*, ed. Richard D. Heffner (New York, 1956), 9, 16; Robert Nisbet, *The Sociological Tradition* (New York, 1966); Tocqueville, *Democracy in America*, ed. Thomas Bender (New York, 1981), xl.
3. *Democracy* (Bradley ed.), 2:452.

"tyranny of the majority." David Riesman—although he was careful to note that the conformistic American Tocqueville had seen, holding his opinions in reserve lest he lose caste and business among his neighbors, was a figure radically different from the quicksilver manipulator of roles and interpersonal signals who seemed to Riesman to dominate the postwar American middle class—nonetheless ransacked *Democracy in America* for *The Lonely Crowd*'s epigrams.[4] Others were not so careful. In the tendencies of Jacksonian America, it was said, Tocqueville had had the gift to see the postwar man in the gray flannel suit: an emergent world of Levittowns, McCarthyism, and conformity, hidden in the potentials of early nineteenth-century democracy. This was, if my memory has not tricked me, the way Tocqueville was taught in the college curriculum when he came into vogue in American history and civilization courses. He was the seer of a public life grown moblike, over-charged with energy, rolling over the fragile, precious reserves of distinction and individuality.

When toward the end of the 1960s, that world of mass markets and cold war terrors dissolved into a startling new cacophony of politics and lifestyles, one might have expected a certain cautious reassessment of Tocqueville's prophetic abilities. Instead the bottom line of Tocqueville's prophecy was overhauled to suit the altered circumstances. *Democracy in America*'s first volume, controlled as it is by the specter of majority tyranny, student readers in the 1980s are now advised, will probably not compel their attention. It is the long-neglected second volume of 1840 where we now suddenly find Tocqueville's eye to have been keenest. Our prophetic Tocqueville's of the 1980s is the seer not of mass society's heavy, conformistic pressures but of enervation and withdrawal, of a public life in decay. The key to *Democracy in America* is now the spirit that Tocqueville called "individualism": the scurrying of men and women into the private, petty affairs of family and self, leaving the public sphere to the centralizers, the quiet horsemen of paternalism and bureaucratic power, who move in where public commitments fail. Here, in this bleak portrait of trivial affairs and private preoccupations are the sections of *Democracy in America* to which contemporary readers of the 1980s will now find themselves uncannily near, Thomas Bender writes. From roughly opposite poles of the political spectrum, Richard Sennett and Robert Nisbet have quarried the same lines of volume 2 for that common theme.[5]

The point is not simply that Tocqueville changed his mind—though, like most agile thinkers, he did. There was a side to Tocqueville reminiscent of Henry Adams: playing with alternative scenarios of disaster, unable to decide whether the world rising about him would end in fire or ice, in mob rule or entropic decay. The more important point, however, is that when Tocqueville's predictions of 1835 grew tattered, we

4. David Riesman et al., *The Lonely Crowd: A Study of the Changing American Character* (New Haven, 1950).
5. *Democracy* (Bender ed.), xl, xlvi; Richard Sennett, "What Tocqueville Feared," in *On the Making of Americans: Essays in Honor of David Riesman*, ed. Herbert J. Gans (Philadelphia, 1979); Robert Nisbet, "Many Tocquevilles," *American Scholar* 46 (1976): 64–71.

traded volume 1 in for volume 2, the specter of conformity for the specter of enervation and withdrawal, without doubting either prophetic reading of the book. We have hungered to see ourselves in his pages—not Jackson or Louis Philippe—but modernity.

In this eagerness we have rarely paused to ask what sort of prophet Tocqueville really was. For prophets come in three quite distinct molds, and they read the tea leaves of their moment in distinctly different ways. The oldest prophets did not so much predict as know. They were messengers of fate, mouthpieces of the Lord, to whom the strange dreams and burning bushes spoke with a clarity barred to others. In modern times, prophets of this sort have been eased out by those who only guess. The guessers themselves, however, fall into two fundamentally different camps: those who work by extrapolation, and those who work by something closer to intuition. The mark of the extrapolators is the density of their concern with present-day facts and their obsession with explanatory laws. Extrapolators tend to care deeply about the mechanics of change; they are drawn to the rhetoric of science; they think their way into the future, as it were, on straight lines and causal threads. One thinks in this regard of H. G. Wells, of Herman Kahn, and above all of the later Marx, deep in the fact-crammed bowels of the British Museum.[6]

The intuitional readers of the future tend to work in quite different ways. They think their way into the future, not along causal threads, but by the gift of seeing under the mundane surface of everyday life the half-concealed patterns of a world in birth. Their imaginations do not run toward explanatory laws but toward horizontal relationships, not toward facts but toward typologies and ideal types. *How* one gets from the world falling into ruins to the world about to be born is not their central question. Their preoccupation is to read the shape of the future, the chick in the thinned and cracking eggshell. They work not by extrapolation but by hunch and metaphor. One thinks of Comte, of Carlyle, of Weber. And of Tocqueville.

For to reread *Democracy in America* and its accompanying notebooks looking for the telltale signs of our modernity in the womb of Tocqueville's America is to realize with a start how bold a hunchmaker, how reckless a leaper between observations Tocqueville was. Take his fearful prediction of the impending tyranny of the majority. He made up most of it, it is clear, out of the frightened talk of the ex-Federalists and proto-Whigs, reeling from Jackson's victory, with whom he had conversed so much in America. He arrived in the United States just in time to see the final break-up of the deference politics of the eighteenth century: when Jackson's heavy-handed use of the power of patronage was still new and (to Jackson's opponents) deeply frightening, when the machinery of mass party mobilization was just beginning to be hammered into place, when on the radical flanks of Jackson's party

---

6. Cf. François Furet, "The Conceptual System of 'Democracy in America' " in his *In the Workshop of History* (Chicago, 1984), 193–196.

men were talking of popular, majoritarian sovereignty with an expansiveness that shivered the nerves of those still committed to the complex constitutional balances of an older, far less direct democracy. Tocqueville hardly spoke to a partisan of the new democratic order. "I have almost got proof that all the enlightened classes in America are opposed to General Jackson," he confided early to his notebook.[7] It was the American defenders of the *ancien régime* with whom he sensed a kindredness of spirit. They bent their young listener's ear with their dire, Madisonian fears of majoritarian democracy. Into the first volume of *Democracy in America* these fears poured, vivid and little changed.

To these conventional anti-Jackson prejudices, Tocqueville himself added a deeper and more novel worry: that what the political mob could not accomplish, the tyranny of public opinion might complete. Here his most vivid American informant was a Baltimore doctor, a bit of a freethinker it would appear, who told Tocqueville that in America the slightest hint of irregular religious opinions would instantly strip a professional man like himself of his clients. "Public opinion does with us what the Inquisition could never do," Dr. Stewart told Tocqueville in a phrase that worked its way virtually unaltered into Tocqueville's *Democracy*. In Baltimore, Tocqueville heard his first vivid description of a democratic, press-smashing mob. In Ohio, he had fallen in with a young reactionary lawyer, who confessed that he would never publicly admit to the antidemocratic opinions he was willing privately to confide to his French acquaintance.[8]

What drew the meager anecdotes into a pattern, however, was Tocqueville's own private surprise at the absence of so much of the cultural landscape familiar to him in Paris. The absence of an openly reactionary aristocracy, which made no secret of its loathing of the mob, and of a literary underground, seething with anticlerical sentiment and satire of bourgeois morality: this remained an enduring conundrum to him. Out of that surprise, together with an aristocrat's shock at the apparent sameness of conversations among the common and middling folk, flowed his famous conclusion that in no country he knew was there "less independence of mind and true freedom of discussion than in America."[9]

But it should not reflect particularly adversely on Tocqueville that that famous hunch was concocted largely out of preoccupations private to the peculiar sliver of Americans he talked to, and to Tocqueville himself. Jared Sparks, the Boston historian who had first offered Tocqueville the "tyranny by the majority" phrase, concluded upon reading *Democracy in America* that Tocqueville had "entirely mistaken" the point. The editors of the *Democratic Review*, pointing to the Democratic Party's uphill battle against a vigorously anti-Jackson

7. Alexis de Tocqueville, *Journey to America*, trans. George Lawrence, ed. J. P. Mayer (New Haven, 1960), 156.
8. Ibid., 80, 95, 159–160.
9. Alexis de Tocqueville, *Democracy in America*, trans. George Lawrence, ed. J. P. Mayer (Garden City, 1969), 254–255.

press, complained they had no idea what Tocqueville was talking about in adverting to the majority's monopoly over public opinion.[1] In 1830s England, Tocqueville's passages on the tyranny of the majority passed quickly into the shibboleths of those terrified that Chartism might break apart the cautious democratic reforms of 1832. In the United States, on the other hand, reviewers of all political stripes protested that Tocqueville had read far too much into the passing phenomenon of Jackson's early popularity.[2] Theirs was not simply the defensiveness of a generation hypersensitive to foreign criticism. Sixty years later, Daniel Coit Gilman noted that Tocqueville's "tyranny of the majority" chapters were impossible to connect to the America he knew—either to Gilman's America of the 1890s, split into a myriad of ethnic subcultures and still reverberating with Populist discontent, or the America in birth at the moment of Tocqueville's visit, just beginning to feel the explosive dissenting energies of abolitionism.[3]

Preoccupied by the spectacle of so politically timid an aristocracy, by the puzzle of a country without a genuinely reactionary party or a proper Bohemia, Tocqueville, in short, had not seen anything like the man in the gray flannel suit at all. His hunch that majoritarian democracy might make things hard for those who failed to think in step had precious little to do with Riesman's world of gladhanders and sales personnel, of mass fads, mass media, and pressing corporate loyalties. It was hardly Tocqueville's fault that even the language for this sort of polity escaped him, that he had to make do with Madisonian talk of better constitutional checks and balances.

As for the now-celebrated chapters on privatization, here it is quite clear that Tocqueville did not have democratic America in mind at all. There was much he could have seen to support the point, we now think, in Jacksonian America. The cultural revolution launched in the early years of the nineteenth century by middle-class Americans with new ideals of social discipline, temperance, and family order on their minds held within it tendencies both toward moral imperialism and toward quiet domestic retreat.[4] A particularly farsighted observer might have seen as much beneath the frenetic associational, do-gooding spirit with which Tocqueville was so impressed. But, in truth, Tocqueville does not seem to have seen it at all. It was not until he had returned to France—to narrow, provincial Normandy, to which he had transferred his writing project in 1838—that the term "individualism" (or as we would now call it, privatization) took shape in his vocabulary. To the theme of public enervation, America always seemed

1. Herbert B. Adams, "Jared Sparks and Alexis de Tocqueville," *Johns Hopkins University Studies in Historical and Political Science* 16 (1898): 605; Anon., "European Views of American Democracy: M. de Tocqueville," *United States Magazine and Democratic Review* 1 (1837): 102–107.
2. Alexis de Tocqueville, *Democracy in America, with an Original Preface and Notes by John C. Spencer* (New York, 1838), 1: 451–454; Anon., "Democracy in America," *American Quarterly Review* 19 (1836): 151–154.
3. Daniel C. Gilman, "Alexis de Tocqueville and His Book on America—Sixty Years After," *Century* 56 (1898): 712.
4. Mary P. Ryan, *Cradle of the Middle Class: The Family in Oneida County, New York, 1790–1865* (Cambridge, England, 1981).

to him the great exception. He readily granted that the language of American politics was poor in words for public life. The term "virtue," in its classic, republican sense, meant, he thought, nothing to the Americans. But in talk of "self-interest rightly understood," they had a way of talking about the common good serviceable enough to sustain a terrific, meddling, public-spirited energy.

It was barely democratized France that he had in mind when he wrote of men consumed in the "trivial, lonely, futile" activities of the self.[5] It was England he had in mind when he wrote of democracy's gravitational attraction toward centralized authority, in an oddly distorted and, as it turned out, an incorrect reading of the new Poor Law of 1834.[6] America in 1831–32 had seemed him full of startlingly centrifugal tendencies. Here "there is no, or at least there doesn't appear to be any government at all," he wrote his father soon after he reached New York. "All that is good in centralization seems to be as unknown as what is bad."[7] But by the time he wrote his arresting passages on bureaucratic power, Jackson's America had all but passed from his mind. It was Napoleon who haunted Tocqueville by the late 1830s: the specter of yet another round of Bonapartism, ushered in this time not by revolution but by the listless indifference of a bourgeoisie for whom liberty and honor had lost every shred of public meaning. In the short run, this was an acute prediction, weighted with tremendous import in Tocqueville's France. As a prevision of Reaganomics, jacuzzis, and yuppiedom, however, is it is hard to see that it was anywhere close to the mark.

It was, in short, out of thin stuff that Tocqueville made the predictive hunches for which we have so eagerly celebrated him. We allow as much in intuitional prophets. We do not ask diviners why their guesses work. If Tocqueville was acute enough to sense some of the shape of modern times, does it matter where he found it? He haunts us—even when we catch a glimpse of his rickety prognosticating machinery at work—with the timeless charges of an acute political moralist. Does it matter that the structures of his and our America are alike only on the wings of a loose and vague metaphor he called democracy?

The rub comes in Tocqueville's refusal to play the role of a merely intuitional prophet. The part he yearned for, clearly, was closer to that of the later Marx. He would not merely describe the world he sensed rushing into being. He would explain it, harness his phenomena to a causal engine. That engine, of course, was equality. It was the "nodal point" of his observations, he wrote at the outset of volume 1, the central historical fact from which all the others derived.[8] In America,

5. *Democracy* (Mayer ed.), 645.
6. Seymour Drescher, "Tocqueville's Two Democracies," *Journal of the History of Ideas* 25 (1964): 201–216.
7. James T. Schleifer, *The Making of Tocqueville's "Democracy in America"* (Chapel Hill, 1980), 122.
8. *Democracy* (Mayer ed.), 9.

equality had paved the way for democratic majoritarianism. Equality of condition fueled the tremendous associational energies of the Americans; it clamped on their minds the shackles of their neighbors' opinions. In Europe, by the same token, it was love of equality, he was convinced, on which the new model Bonapartes would ride. An homogenized citizenry absorbed in the gains of the self was no fodder for revolution, he thought. Where equality ruled, the demagogue "exhausts himself trying to animate [the] indifferent and preoccupied crowd."[9] But toward stealthily centralized bureaucracy, democracies went as silent sheep, without bleat or murmur.

Each of these points was but a variation on a common theme. The creed of equality—though at first blush it might seem to diffuse that spirit of independence in which liberty flourished—was as likely to lead, Tocqueville always suspected, through a secret back door, to novel and yet still stronger forms of tyranny. This has long been taken as the gist of the analytical Tocqueville: the historical law ratified by his uncannily predictive guesses. Between equality and the furious centralizing energies of modern nation-states, Robert Nisbet writes in a gloss on Tocqueville, there is "a fateful affinity." Hannah Arendt condensed the Tocqueville-derived point more simply: equality is a "danger to freedom."[1] And yet for Tocqueville this too was hardly a law, but hunch and metaphor.

Through what secret byways were democracies lured toward that hindering, restraining, enervating, stifling, stultifying bureaucratic despotism Tocqueville so vividly feared by 1840? His line of reasoning proceeded on two levels. The first—his insistence that in aristocratic families the claims of history pulled men out of their petty concerns and endowed them with a vigorous sense of public responsibility— strikes us now as a somewhat embarrassing piece of special pleading for Frenchmen of Tocqueville's own kind. Since Tocqueville's day, the lures of privatization have run at least as hard through the salons of the aristocracy as through the countinghouses of the bourgeoisie or the workshops of the masses. Tocqueville's second line of argument was the more powerful: that in a polity controlled by love of equality and resentment of aristocratic distinctions, the "ever-fiercer fire of endless hatred felt by democracies against the slightest privileges" beats against every privileged person except the state itself.[2] In the state, and only there, were democracies willing to bestow authority: wholesale and without reservation.

This was a powerfully haunting and yet—it seems to me—quite erroneous prediction: a hunch that hindsight hardly sustains. Centralized, liberty-extinguishing states we have had in abundance, but very few of them have sprung, as Tocqueville imagined they would, from equality. The first of the great modern, bureaucratically centralized

9. Ibid., 638.
1. Nisbet, *Sociological Tradition*, 121–122; Hannah Arendt, *On Revolution* (New York, 1963), 23.
2. *Democracy* (Mayer ed.), 673.

states, with a hand deep in the everyday affairs of its citizens, as Tocqueville himself knew well, was prerevolutionary France, riven with inequalities. The second—Weber's own iron cage—was Wilhelmine Germany, where war discipline and Junkerism, not egalitarian democracy, held the reins. At a time when the United States, so steeped in egalitarian talk that its immigrants boasted of eating white bread and meat like aristocrats, was struggling to establish the rudiments of a civil service, the war-nurtured states of turn-of-the-century Europe had already laid in place the apparatus of centralized state power Tocqueville so deeply feared. Even now, where the civilian employees of the United States Defense Department are eightfold as numerous as the employees of the Department of Health and Social Services, it is clear that war is the far better promoter of centralized, massively bureaucratized power than the flickering spirit of equality. There are Bonapartes abroad in the world, but, as always, they ride in, not on cries of equality, but of order and martial discipline.

It is true that where equality is so long resisted that it arrives only through the guns of revolution, the result has repeatedly been to funnel massive amounts of power into the central, revolution-consolidating apparatus of the state. But it was not this sort of revolution that Tocqueville had in mind in the haunting final passages of *Democracy in America*. These "great revolutions," springing out of deeply entrenched systems of caste and privilege, he thought (erroneously, as it turned out) would become more rare. The sort of despotism egalitarian societies had to fear was very different: a continual, barely noticed accretion of state authority, fueled by the accumulated resentments of its (almost) equal citizens, until they turned at last to sheep in the care of their absolute and despotic protectors. Midway through the age of Thatcher and Reagan, that hunch hardly seems a compelling item of prophecy. Tocqueville failed to foresee that democratic citizens might be at least as prickly about their rights as aristocratic ones. He failed to foresee that in democracies, the populace might take out the accumulated resentments of private life not on the privileges of private wealth but on the state itself, marching under the banner of tax revolts and anti-bureaucratic resentment. Our current political condition—marked not so much by political enervation as by a powerful rage to dismantle what shreds of public life we still possess—Tocqueville failed to foresee altogether.

Not only has history failed to attend overly well to Tocqueville's ventures in prophecy, but his hunches, fears, and premonitions fell themselves a good ways short of explanatory, predictive law. Tocqueville never thought, while in America, to take even the roughest factual measure of the equality that so absorbed him. He stirred together tendencies he felt in Jackson's America, elitist and commercial Britain, and centralized France into an ideal type that by the late 1830s floated increasingly free of any specific political referent. Under his keywords, as George Wilson Pierson wrote long ago, he tended to assimilate virtually every visible phenomenon of the world he sensed in birth.[3] His causal engine, equality, in short, was hardly a causal engine at all, but a big, accordion-like metaphor.

To get closer to the discontents of the twentieth century would have required a different language, one less beholden to classical politics, than the language Tocqueville possessed. The conformistic 1950s, beset by the terrors of exposure to a suddenly diminished and dangerously armed world, enraptured by agencies of persuasion the likes of which no one in the 1830s had the least presentiment, was a radically different society than Tocqueville foresaw. Our current scuttlings toward private pleasures likewise have their roots deep in phenomena of which Tocqueville had no inkling: the economics of a closed and pinching world system, the cyclical energies and exhaustions of modern politics, and the power of differential market advertising. John Stuart Mill came closer to the lineaments of our modernity in his objection that the great bulk of Tocqueville's phenomena were characteristic not of democratic societies but of "commercial" ones.[4] Tocqueville groped for that sort of language in Democracy in America; in his chapter on the dangers of a manufacturing aristocracy, he came closest to it. It was not entirely his fault that in the France of the 1830s and out of the circle of which he came he did not possess the words for it.

Does it diminish Tocqueville to acknowledge his deep flaws as a prophet? He was a diviner, a huncher, an extraordinarily acute observer of much that fell under his ken. If his picture of Jacksonian America was flawed, no other European saw it better. The timelessness of Democracy in America comes not from its prevision of the future of democracy, or from its occasional lucky guesses, but from its untarnished moral seriousness. As long as politics endure, there will be a need for Tocqueville's warnings against the mob, the Gleichschaltung of the mind, the bloated structures of state power, the erosion of public life and public commitments. Where the pleasures of private life triumph, the horsemen do not always ride in, but life surely decays. In that moral alone, in the example of a man thinking hard and engagedly about public life, there is more than enough in Democracy in America to sustain another century-and-half's reading.

But the world Tocqueville sensed in birth is not the modernity that besets us. In his farthest flights of prophecy, Tocqueville did not see the forces that have wrenched our world so far from his. He got a great deal wrong—not the least about the tendencies of equality. To think he had his eye on us has been for too long our private, oddly egocentric folly. It is time to stop reading Democracy in America as a book of prophecy; if we are to see the beasts in the eggshell of our times, we must do that, in different terms, ourselves.

3. George W. Pierson, Tocqueville in America (Garden City, 1959), 457–465.
4. John S. Mill, "De Tocqueville on Democracy in America [II]" in The Collected Works of John Stuart Mill (Toronto, 1963–), 18: 196.

ARTHUR SCHLESINGER JR.

Individualism and Apathy in Tocqueville's *Democracy*†

As Alexis de Tocqueville interpreted the modern world, history had confronted western civilization with a momentous choice. The revolution of equality, he believed, was irresistible. The question now was whether equality of legal conditions would lead on to free institutions or to despotism; whether the democratic revolution would end in liberty or in servitude. It was this underlying drama of choice that gives his vision of society its coherence and its troubled intensity.

Tocqueville's consuming passion was liberty; and the challenge before western man in his mind was to devise ways of securing liberty in the era of equality. He was vividly aware of perils in the new dispensation. It was no simple thing to reconcile liberty and equality. Still he could not accept, as he wrote in 1835, "that God has been pushing two or three million men for several centuries toward equality of conditions in order to have them end in the despotism of Tiberius and Claudius."[1] Within the fatal circle of necessity, men and communities retained a wide verge in which they could shape their own destiny—or at least this was the conviction that animated and inspired Tocqueville's message to his age.

In working out the means of salvation, Tocqueville drew much, but not all, from the social philosopher whom he had read longest and with the greatest sympathy—Montesquieu. For Montesquieu, virtue was the essential principle of republics, and virtue meant the renunciation of self for the sake of the public good. But Montesquieu's scheme did not quite fit Tocqueville's world. The republics Montesquieu had in mind were the ancient Greek city-states—polities limited in size and dedicated to husbandry and war. The pure principle of republican virtue seemed archaic among the bustling capitalist nation-states of the nineteenth century.

Montesquieu himself, however, had already somewhat modified that principle. For he was also the proponent of what Albert Hirschman calls the *"doux-commerce"* thesis—the contention that the rise of commerce would soften manners, tame passions, enlarge the mind, confer reciprocal benefits, reduce prejudice, and diffuse enlightenment.[2] The *doux-commerce* thesis thus qualified the commitment to republican virtue by providing an opening for self-interest. Commerce assumed a double aspect: on the one hand, it was the carrier of modern civilization; on the other, it remained, as it had been under the civic republican ethos, a potential source of luxury, egoism, and decay.

† Arthur Schlesinger Jr. (1917–2007) was an American historian and social critic who taught at Harvard University and the City University of New York. "Individualism and Apathy in Tocqueville's *Democracy*" by Arthur Schlesinger Jr. is from *Tocqueville and American Democracy, Michigan Quarterly Review* 25(3): 493–505 (Summer 1986). Copyright © 1988 by Arthur Schlesinger Jr. Reprinted by permission of the Wylie Agency, Inc.
1. Tocqueville to Louis de Kergolay, January 1835, Alexis de Tocqueville, *Selected Letters on Politics and Society*, ed. Roger Boesche (Berkeley, 1985), 94.
2. A. O. Hirschman, *The Passions and the Interests* (Princeton, 1977), 60–61.

The hope was that enough republican virtue could survive to check the excesses of self-interest and thereby gain the benefits of commerce without the risks of corruption.

According to Tocqueville, self-interest was inherent in democracy; perhaps in all societies. At one point he spoke of "private interest" as "the only immutable point in the human heart."[3] His American journey gave this immutable point new salience. Soon after his arrival in 1831, he asked himself what held together this dizzying miscellany of languages, beliefs, opinions mingled in a society without roots and without memories. "What serves as the link among such diverse elements? What makes all of this one people? Interest. That is the secret. . . In this, we are quite far from the ancient republics, it must be admitted, and nonetheless this people is republican."[4]

The American experiment, Tocqueville thought, demonstrated the possibility of reconciling public virtue and private interest, and therefore the possibility of reconciling liberty and equality. He first explained the reconciliation by claiming that "in a physical situation so fortunate . . . the private interest is never contrary to the general interest, which is certainly not the case in Europe."[5] As he elaborated his understanding, he began to revise and amend Montesquieu. "The Americans are not a virtuous people," he wrote in a note "Concerning Virtue in Republics," "and yet they are free. . . . It is not necessary to take Montesquieu's idea in a narrow sense. What this great man meant is that republics can survive only by the action of the society on itself. What he understood by virtue is the moral power that each individual exercises over himself and that prevents him from violating the rights of others." That power of self-discipline, when it results from the weakness of the temptation or from calculations of personal interest, may "not constitute virtue in the eyes of the moralist; but it is included in the idea of Montesquieu who spoke much more of the result than of the cause. In America it is not virtue which is great, it is temptation which is small, which amounts to the same thing. It is not disinterestedness which is great, it is interest which is rightly understood, which again almost amounts to the same thing."[6]

The great distinction, in short, between the classical republics and modern democracies lay in the insertion of the commercial motive. The city-state was founded on virtue, the nation-state on interest. The problem was to make private interest the moral equivalent of public virtue. This could be achieved through the disciplinary influence exerted by society on its members—an influence embodied in the mores and in laws and institutions. *Self-interest rightly understood:* this Tocqueville saw as the key to the balance between virtue and interest in commercial democracies.

In another note, indited at all places up the river at Sing-Sing, he

---

3. *Democracy in America*, ed. Phillips Bradley, 2 vols. (New York, 1945), 1, chap. 14.
4. Tocqueville to Ernest de Chabrol, 9 June 1831, *Selected Letters*, 38.
5. Ibid.
6. James T. Schleifer, *The Making of Tocqueville's Democracy in America* (Chapel Hill, 1980), 242–243.

enlarged on the difference between "the republics of antiquity," whose principle was to sacrifice private interests to the general good, and the United States, where the principle was "to make private interests harmonize with the general interest. A sort of refined and intelligent selfishness seems to be the pivot on which the whole machine turns." But the balance was precarious, and Tocqueville could not but wonder whether it could be maintained. "Up to what extent," he asked himself, "can the two principles of individual well-being and the general good in fact be merged? How far can a conscience, which one might say was based on reflection and calculation, master those political passions which are not yet born, but which certainly will be born? That is something which only the future can show."[7]

Looking at America in the 1835 *Democracy*, Tocqueville returned a rather hopeful answer. Religion, voluntary associations, local government, federalism, the free press, the machinery of justice, the traditions of the people, the absence both of feudal system to overthrow and a violent revolution to overthrow it—all held out the prospect of keeping private interest under social control.

Above all, he was impressed and reassured by the national ardor for civic participation. "In no country in the world," he remarked, "do the citizens make such exertions for the common weal."[8] Participation was both stimulated and guaranteed by political freedom. "Civic zeal," as Tocqueville put it, "seems to me to be inseparable from the exercise of political rights."[9]

Yet the balance between virtue and self-interest remained precarious, and he identified an array of dangers. Aggressive participation in the life of society, so valuable within limits, threatened if carried too far to enforce a tyranny of the majority—so heavy a pressure against the dissenter "that one must give up one's rights as a citizen and almost abjure one's qualities as a man if one intends to stray from the track" the majority prescribes.[1] Equally threatening to self-interest rightly understood was the "love of money." Tocqueville said he knew of no country where the acquisitive drive had "taken a stronger hold on the affections of men."[2] Still he left the United States reasonably optimistic about the American capacity to transmute private interest into a facsimile of public virtue and thereby to preserve the balance.

The 1840 *Democracy*, as we all know, presented a less cheering picture. Here Tocqueville introduced his theory of individualism. By individualism Tocqueville meant something very different from Emersonian self-reliance or Darwinian rugged individualism. He meant something close to the modern sociological concept of "privatization." For Tocqueville individualism meant not self-assertion but self-

7. *Journey to America*, ed. J. P. Mayer (New Haven, 1959), 210–211.
8. *Democracy in America*, 1, chap. 5. Unless otherwise indicated, all further references are to the *Democracy*.
9. *Democracy* (Bradley ed.) 1, chap. 14.
1. Ibid., 1: chap. 15.
2. Ibid., 1: chap. 3.

withdrawal—the disposition of each member of the community "to sever himself from the mass of his fellows, and to draw apart with his family and friends, so that after he has thus formed a little circle of his own, he willingly leaves society at large to itself."[3]

What was the source of this absorption in the democratic self? As Tocqueville explained it, individualism sprang from a "crude" interpretation of self-interest—that is, from self-interest wrongly understood.[4] This wrong understanding, he thought, resulted from the love of money and material gratification characteristic of democratic society. "The effort to satisfy the least wants of the body and to provide the conveniences of life," he wrote, "is uppermost in every mind."[5] This acquisitive compulsion, he feared, originated in the principle of equality itself; that principle "makes the passion for physical gratification and the exclusive love of the present predominate in the human heart."[6] As he put it more flatly a quarter century later in his foreword to The Old Regime and the French Revolution, when the aristocratic ties of family, of caste, of class, and of craft disappear, people tend "to think exclusively of their own interests, to become self-seekers practising a narrow individualism and caring nothing for the public good."[7]

Self-interest wrongly understood thereby upset the balance between virtue and interest. The outcome was "that general apathy which is the consequence of individualism."[8] By apathy, he meant civic apathy. Individualism fosters the isolation of people from one another, "saps the virtues of public life," and makes it "difficult to draw a man out of his own circle to interest him in the destiny of the state."[9] People begin to see their public obligations as a vexatious distraction from the scramble for money. Public purpose is displaced by private interest. People, their lives defined by the marketplace and the family, lose their concern for the long run. "The better to look after their own business, they neglect their chief business, which is to remain their own masters."[1]

In retrospect, one wonders whether Tocqueville did not go astray in linking civic apathy so definitively to the acquisitive drive. With the benefit of another century-and-a-half of history, we recognize that civic apathy is even more marked in nations that seek to abolish the acquisitive impulse than it is in capitalist nations. He would have done better to see his recessive individualism as a function of mass society in general than of capitalist society in particular.

Individualism, in any case, was bad news, though Tocqueville was never quite sure what form the dénouement would take. Apathy, he said at one point, could "almost indifferently" beget either anarchy or

3. Ibid., 2: second book, chap. 2.
4. Ibid., 2: second book, chap. 14.
5. Ibid., 2: second book, chap. 10.
6. Ibid., 2: third book, chap. 19.
7. The Old Regime and the French Revolution, trans. Stuart Gilbert (Garden City, N.Y., 1955), 13.
8. Democracy (Bradley ed.) 2: Appendix BB.
9. Ibid., 2: second book, chaps. 2, 4.
1. Ibid., 2: second book, chap. 14.

tyranny.[2] But, since anarchy was classically the prelude to tyranny, they amounted to the same thing in the end. If tyranny came, he no longer expected it in the guise of the specters haunting the 1835 *Democracy*—the uninstitutionalized tyranny of the majority, or the tyranny of legislative encroachment on the executive, or the tyranny of the Caesars. He anticipated rather the tyranny of the bureaucratic state—an "immense and tutelary power . . . absolute, regular, provident, and mild," covering society with "a network of small complicated rules" and reducing a nation to "a flock of timid and industrious animals, of which the government is the shepherd."[3]

Tyranny, in whatever form, would end in stagnation. When "men continue to shut themselves more closely within the narrow circle of domestic interests," when citizens grow "inaccessible to those great and powerful public emotions which perturb nations, but which develop them," then Tocqueville said, in a startlingly personal outburst:

> I cannot but fear that men may arrive at such a state as to regard every new theory as a peril, every innovation as an irksome toil, every social improvement as a stepping-stone to revolution, and so refuse to move altogether for fear of being moved too far: I dread, and I confess it, lest they should at last so entirely give way to a cowardly love of present enjoyment as to lose sight of the interests of their future selves and those of their descendants and prefer to glide along the easy current of life rather than to make, when it is necessary, a strong and sudden effort to a higher purpose.[4]

In a curious digression in the 1840 *Democracy*, Tocqueville warned against supposing that, because Rome fell under the barbarian onslaughts, civilization could perish in no other way. His mind drifted to China, which, he said, had "lost the power of change" for entirely internal reasons and had sunk into a "strange immobility." Egalitarian society, he suggested, might follow the course of China rather than that of Rome. "If the light by which we are guided is ever extinguished," he observed, "it will dwindle by degrees and expire of itself." Some nations "allow civilization to be torn from their grasp"; others "allow themselves to trample it underfoot."[5]

It is an instructive coincidence that, at the very time Tocqueville was penning such sentiments at his brother's chateau in Baugy, the only other nineteenth-century mind to rival him in the profundity of his meditations on democracy was pondering the threat to the American experiment in a similar spirit and language. "At what point," Abraham Lincoln asked the Young Men's Lyceum of Springfield, Illinois, in January 1838, "is the approach of danger to be expected? I answer, if it ever reach us, it must spring up amongst us, It cannot come from abroad. If destruction be our lot, we must ourselves be its author and

2. Ibid., 2: Appendix BB.
3. Ibid., 2: fourth book, chap. 6.
4. Ibid., 2: third book, chap. 21.
5. Ibid., 2: first book, chap. 10.

finisher. As a nation of freemen, we must live through all time, or die by suicide."[6]

The 1840 Democracy has a brooding, at times melancholy, cast; and ever since Seymour Drescher's notable essay twenty years ago,[7] commentators have wondered about the shift from the pervading optimism of 1835 to the pervading pessimism of 1840. Between the two works, the democratic distemper changes from mob rule to mass apathy, from activism to anomie. Plainly exposure to French politics after his return from America gave Tocqueville a new sense of the perils of privatization. He was struck by the "universal pettiness" of political life in his native land, by "the astonishing absence of disinterestedness," by the domination of "miserable day-to-day interests."[8] He began to fear that, once political liberty was "well established, and exercised in a peaceable milieu, it impels men to the practice and the taste of well-being, to the care and passion for making fortunes; and, as a repercussion, its tastes, its needs, its cares" extinguish political as well as religious passions.[9] His reentry into French politics thus persuaded him that self-interest could all too easily be wrongly understood.

At the same time, his visits in these years to England made him aware, as the American tour never had, of the potential impact of industrialism on democracy. He had taken from Montesquieu the idea that the spirit of commerce was favorable to liberty. But Montesquieu knew nothing of the spirit of industry; and this was another matter. Tocqueville's visit to Manchester left him with a horrified impression of the contrast between the "huge palaces of industry" and the homes "of vice and poverty . . . the last refuge a man might find between poverty and death . . . . Here is the slave, there the master; there the wealth of some, here the poverty of most; there the organised effort of thousands produce, to the profit of one man, what society has not yet learnt to give. Here the weakness of the individual seems more feeble and helpless even than in the middle of a wilderness; here the effect, there the causes."[1]

The forebodings generated by his visit to Manchester poured into his brilliant chapter in the 1840 Democracy on "How an Aristocracy May Be Created by Manufacturers." Where commerce was benign in its social effects, industry required a division of labor that divorced the worker from his product and deprived him of "the general faculty of applying his mind to the direction of the work. . . . What can be expected of a man who has spent twenty years of his life in making heads for pins?" At the same time that manufacturing degraded the class of workers, it elevated the class of masters. "This man," Tocqueville wrote, "resembles more and more the administrator of

6. "The Perpetuation of our Political Institutions," in Abraham Lincoln: Selected Speeches, Messages, and Letters, ed. T. Harry Williams (New York, 1957), 6.
7. Seymour Drescher, "Tocqueville's Two Democracies," Journal of the History of Ideas 25 (April–June 1964): 201–216.
8. Tocqueville to Pierre-Paul Royer-Collard, 20 August 1837, Selected Letters, 118.
9. Tocqueville to Louis de Kergolay, 18 October 1847, Selected Letters, 193.
1. From Journeys to England and Ireland in Alexis de Tocqueville on Democracy, Revolution, and Society, ed. John Stone and Stephen Mennell (Chicago, 1980), 305–306.

a vast empire; that man, a brute . . . and their differences increase every day."[2] Democratic freedom was compatible with a commercial destiny. But the *doux-commerce* thesis hardly applied to the industrial age.

Let us recapitulate the train of Tocqueville's thought. Where the republics of antiquity beloved by Montesquieu were founded on the principle of public virtue, modern democracy rested on private interest; and the hope for liberal institutions relied on a precarious balance between virtue and self-interest, rightly understood. But self-interest lends itself to being wrongly understood, especially after an established democracy begins to surrender to acquisitive passions and after commerce gives way to industry. Self-interest wrongly understood tilts the balance away from republican virtue and from public purpose. The individual withdraws from the public sphere, becomes isolated, weak, docile, powerless. Individualism in the Tocquevillian sense leads on to apathy, apathy to despotism, despotism to stagnation, stagnation to extinction. The light dwindles by degrees and expires of itself.

Now it is often asserted that Tocqueville, after writing about America in the 1835 *Democracy*, was really writing about Europe in the 1840 *Democracy*. Nor can anyone doubt that his confrontation with apathy in France and industrialism in England shaped the second treatise. Yet his ultimate concern was not to describe one side or the other of the Atlantic, but to set out the structural characteristics and tendencies of democracy as a new stage in the history of humanity. Although the time-frames might be different, although the law of uneven development might apply, America like France displayed a proclivity toward universal pettiness in public affairs; America, like England, was heading into the industrial age. The digression on China did not occur in the last third of the 1840 *Democracy*, where America was hardly mentioned; it occurred in the early chapter entitled "Why the Americans Are More Addicted to Practical than to Theoretical Science." Temporarily protected by geographic and political circumstance, America could not expect to remain forever immune to the maladies of egalitarian democracy.

Tocqueville saw the problem of reconciling equality and liberty as in a special sense a European problem. In meeting the problem, Americans had the advantage of having been born equal instead of having had to endure a democratic revolution. Nonetheless, it was an American problem too, and, as Tocqueville formulated it, a deeper and more subtle problem in 1840 than he had thought in 1836, rendered so by the discovery of individualism. In 1835 he had casually spoken of the irresistible movement of equality that "shatters and reduces to powder every obstacle, until we can no longer see anything but a moving and impalpable cloud of dust, which signals the coming of the Democracy."[3] But in 1835 he saw the cloud of dust seized and molded by

---

2. *Democracy* (Bradley ed.), 2: second book, chap. 20.
3. Ibid., 1: chap. 3.

powerful individuals and associations. By 1840, society itself appeared to be whirling away in the cloud of dust.

Individualism was the extension, at once logical and pernicious, of self-interest, even when rightly understood. How, Tocqueville asked in 1840, "to ward off a disorder at once so natural to the frame of democratic society and so fatal?"[4] He had at hand the pharmacopeia of institutional remedies prescribed in 1835—the collection of democratic expedients, from the town meeting through the free press to the jury system, which, he thought, could do the work done by intermediate powers in an aristocracy. But, more urgently than ever, he gave fundamental emphasis to civic participation and above all to direct participation in the political process. "In order to combat the evils which equality may produce," he wrote in the 1840 *Democracy*, "there is only one effectual remedy: namely political freedom."[5]

He had none of the patrician disdain for the political arena that he had encountered among the respectable conservatives he interviewed on the American journey. As scandal sheets seemed a not unreasonable price to pay for a free press, so party politics seemed a not unreasonable price to pay for political freedom. He briskly dismissed the objections "derived from electioneering intrigues, the meanness of candidates, and the calumnies of their opponents. . . . Such evils are doubtless great, but they are transient; whereas the benefits that attend them remain." Election quarrels might break up friendships; but "the electoral system brings a multitude of citizens permanently together who would otherwise always have remained unknown to one another. Freedom produces private animosities, but despotism gives birth to general indifference."[6]

His approval extended to political parties; for parties drew individuals out of their own circles. However much individuals might be kept apart by age, mind, and fortune, the party "places them nearer together and brings them into contact. Once met, they can always meet again." He likened the parties to "large free schools, where all the members of the community go to learn the general theory of association"; and the art of association, as he often said, was the "mother of action."[7]

Political participation and public action, he said, force individuals to recognize that they live not just for themselves but in society. "Men attend to the interests of the public, first by necessity, afterwards by choice; what was intentional becomes an instinct, and by dint of working for the good of one's fellow citizens, the habit and taste for serving them are at length acquired."[8] The object, he once told John Stuart Mill, was "to put the majority of citizens in a fit state for governing."[9] Politics, in short, was the great means of counteracting private inter-

4. Ibid., 2: second book, chap. 4.
5. Ibid., 2: second book, chap. 4.
6. Ibid., 2: second book, chap. 4.
7. Ibid., 2: second book, chap. 7.
8. Ibid., 2: second book, chap. 4.
9. Tocqueville to Mill [June 1835], *Selected Letters*, 101.

est, of reviving public virtue, and of overcoming the apathy that invited despotism. "Governments," Tocqueville concluded, "must apply themselves to restore to men that love of the future with which religion and the state of society no longer inspire them."[1]

Yet an anomaly still lingers in Tocqueville's portrait of democratic man. The essence in 1835, as we have noted, was activism—the ardent, committed citizen, establishing schools, repairing roads, forming associations, reading newspapers, electioneering, and voting. "To take a hand in the regulation of society and to discuss it," he wrote then, "is his biggest concern and, so to speak, the only pleasure an American knows. . . . If an American were condemned to confine his activity to his own affairs, he would be robbed of one half of his existence; he would feel an immense void in the life which he is accustomed to lead; and his wretchedness would be unbearable."[2]

By 1840, the essence was no longer activism, but apathy. Tocqueville's democratic man now confined his activity to his own affairs, not because he was condemned to do so and was wretched doing it, but because it was his dearest wish. The 1840 American could not wait to shuck off the public world and to withdraw into a circle of his own. What had happened? Tocqueville, having portrayed in successive volumes the American as activist and the American as solipsist, was puzzled. "An American," he wrote in 1840, "attends to his private concerns as if he were alone in the world, and the next minute he gives himself to the common welfare as if he had forgotten them. At one time he seems animated by the most selfish cupidity; at another, by the most lively patriotism." It was indeed a puzzle. "The human heart," Tocqueville thought, "cannot be thus divided"; and he rather lamely recurred to his early notion of the mysterious reconciliation of public virtue and private interest. Americans, he said, "alternately display so strong and so similar a passion for their own welfare and for their freedom that it may be supposed that these passions are united and mingled in some part of their character."[3]

With his marvelous antennae, Tocqueville perceived that American democracy comprehended both the public-spirited citizens of his first volume and the self-centered apathetic ones of his second. If he had reflected more on his own passing observation that Americans "alternately display" those contradictory qualities, he might have perceived further that public purpose and private interest succeed each other in cyclical sequences. He had perhaps too linear a view of the democratic process in America. Virtue and self-interest were not, as he sometimes seemed to think, in a condition of steady or unsteady balance. They were rather in dynamic equilibrium, first one prevailing, then the other, as the excesses of each phase regularly produced frustration, disenchantment, boredom, and the desire for change. It is an

---

1. *Democracy* (Bradley ed.), 2: second book, chap. 17.
2. Ibid., 1: chap. 14.
3. Ibid., 2: second book, chap. 14.

odd coincidence that Tocqueville saw democratic man as activist at the height of the age of Jackson and as apathetic in the year the voters terminated the Jacksonian phase and elected a Whig president.

Wise men have long remarked on patterns of alternation, of ebb and of flow, in human history. "The two parties which divide the state, the party of Conservatism and that of Innovation," wrote Emerson in 1841,

> are very old, and have disputed the possession of the world ever since it was made. . . . Now one, now the other gets the day, and still the fight renews itself as if for the first time, under new names and hot personalities. Innovation presses ever forward; Conservatism holds ever back. We are reformers spring and summer, in autumn and winter we stand by the old; reformers in the morning, conservers at night. Innovation is the salient energy; Conservatism the pause on the last movement.[4]

Half a century later, Henry Adams applied a more precise version of the cyclical thesis to the first years of the American republic. "Experience seemed to show," he wrote in the sixth volume of his great *History of the United States of America During the Administrations of Thomas Jefferson and James Madison*, "that a period of about twelve years measured the beat of the pendulum. After the Declaration of Independence, twelve years had been needed to create an efficient Constitution; another twelve years of energy brought a reaction against the government then created; a third period of twelve years was ending in a sweep toward still greater energy; and already a child could calculate the result of a few more such returns."[5]

Henry Adam's pendulum swung back and forth between the centralization and the diffusion of national energy. There have been subsequent interpretations of the cyclical phenomenon. My father half a century ago defined the swing as between conservatism and liberalism, between seasons of concern for the rights of the few and seasons of concern for the wrongs of the many. Albert Hirschman has recently reformulated the cycle in terms especially pertinent to the discussion of Tocqueville. In an extension of consumption theory to politics, Hirschman argued in *Shifting Involvements* (1982) that western society since the industrial revolution passes back and forth between times when citizens become wholly absorbed in the pursuit of private affairs and times of intense preoccupation with public issues; a regular alternation, in his words, between "private interest" and "public action."[6]

For people can be wholly fulfilled neither in the public nor in the private sphere. We try one, then the other, and the disappointments of the quest account for the shifts in involvement. Hirschman quotes

---

4. "The Conservative," in *The Portable Emerson*, ed. Mark van Doren (New York, 1946), 89–91.
5. *History of the United States*, 9 vols. (New York, 1889–1891), 6: 123.
6. A. O. Hirschman, *Shifting Involvements: Private Interest and Public Action* (Princeton, 1982).

Kant's remark to Karamzin, the Russian historian: "Give a man everything he desires and yet at this very moment he will feel that this *everything* is not *everything*." Tocqueville was aware of the strain of insatiability in modern man, though he tied it, too narrowly perhaps, to the search for equality. "They can never attain as much as they desire," he wrote in the 1840 *Democracy*. "It perpetually retires from before them, yet without hiding itself from their sight, and in retiring draws them on. At every moment they think they are about to grasp it; it escapes at every moment from their hold. They are near enough to see its charms, but too far off to enjoy them; and before they have fully tasted its delights, they die." This permanent frustration, Tocqueville thought, accounted for the perpetual restlessness of Americans, for the "strange melancholy" that haunted inhabitants of democratic countries in the midst of their abundance and the "disgust of life" that seized them in the midst of calm and easy circumstances.[7]

Also, in looking at the history of his own country, Tocqueville had a sense of the cyclical effect. "On several occasions during the period extending from the outbreak of the Revolution up to our time," he wrote in *The Old Regime and the French Revolution*, "we find the desire for freedom reviving, succumbing, then returning, only to die our once more and presently blaze up again."[8] The French dialectic, as he saw it, was between freedom and equality, but it could as easily have been, in the terms he inherited from Montesquieu, between public virtue and private interest. He arrived in New York only forty-two years and twelve days after George Washington's first inauguration, and his American experience was too brief to enable him to discern cyclical rhythms in the American democracy. Yet his observations support the cyclical hypothesis; and the cyclical context completes his diagnosis by resolving the apparent contradictions between 1835 and 1840, between involvement and individualism, between activism and apathy. The struggle between public purpose and private interest continues to be the essence of American democracy. It is likely that in the future, as in the past, this struggle will work itself out in the cyclical mode.

SEAN WILENTZ

Many Democracies: On Tocqueville and Jacksonian America†

What does *Democracy in America* have to tell us about American politics and society in the 1830s? The question may seem obvious, even impertinent. Since the Tocqueville revival of the late 1930s and 1940s, count-

7. *Democracy* (Bradley ed.) 2, second book, chap. 13.
8. *Old Regime*, 209.
† Sean Wilentz is the Dayton-Stockon Professor of History at Princeton University. This essay is from *Reconsidering Tocqueville's Democracy in America*, edited by Abraham S. Eisenstadt. Copyright © 1988 by Rutgers The State University. Reprinted by permission of Rutgers University Press.

less scholars have turned to *Democracy* as the single most insightful commentary on the Jacksonian era. Seemingly, there is nothing about Jacksonian politics, social relations, and culture about which Tocqueville was not an authoritative critic.[1] Nevertheless, it is time to reexamine *Democracy*'s historical significance. Over the last fifteen years, revisionist work on various subjects, much of it by social historians, has made it difficult to sustain many of Tocqueville's impressions of this country. A few historians have directly rebutted Tocqueville; many more have challenged what John Higham once called "the Tocquevillean idea that all Americans are basically alike."[2] Although attempts at synthesizing these findings into an intelligible whole have only just begun, we certainly have a far more comprehensive understanding of Jacksonian America than either Tocqueville or his later admirers down through the 1960s could have had. This understanding allows us to undertake a fresh and more critical appreciation of Tocqueville's masterpiece.

To cite recent scholarship—and *Democracy*'s many critics—is not to say that Tocqueville lacks for contemporary American disciples. A wide range of historians, political theorists, and sociologists still regard *Democracy* as a trustworthy entryway into the hearts and minds of Jacksonian Americans, with lasting relevance for our own time. Robert Bellah and his colleagues' study of the corrosive sociology of American individualism, *Habits of the Heart,* exemplifies *Democracy*'s abiding influence: A reviewer, summing up the book's frame of reference, aptly commented: "Once again the starting point is Tocqueville."[3] From very different perspectives, Richard Sennett, Thomas Bender, and John Diggins have all rooted historical analyses of current cultural and political problems in Tocqueville's description of the 1830s.[4] Andrew Jackson's most thorough modern biographer, Robert V. Remini, has concluded that "Tocqueville remains the surest and best key to unlocking the mysteries of Jacksonian America."[5] And various journalists, moonlighting academics, and other pundits have been unstinting in their praise of Tocqueville as the man who discovered the lineaments of modernity in Jackson's rural republic.[6]

1. Important critical appraisals of the Tocqueville revival and its aftermath include those by Max Beloff, "Tocqueville and the Americans" (1951), reprinted in idem., *The Great Powers: Essays in Twentieth Century Politics* (London, 1959); and Lynn L. Marshall and Seymour Drescher, "American Historians and Tocqueville's *Democracy*," *Journal of American History* 55, 3 (December 1968): 512–532. A full evaluation of more recent scholars' uses and abuses of Tocqueville remains to be written.

2. John Higham, *Writing American History: Essays on Modern Scholarship* (Bloomington, Ind., 1970), 159.

3. Robert Bellah et al., *Habits of the Heart: Individualism and Commitment in American Life* (Berkeley, 1985); Peter Steinfels, "Up from Individualism," *The New York Times Book Review,* 14 April 1985, 1.

4. Richard Sennett, *The Fall of Public Man* (New York, 1977); Alexis de Tocqueville, *Democracy in America,* ed., Thomas Bender (New York, 1981); John Patrick Diggins, *The Lost Soul of American Politics: Virtue, Self-Interest, and the Foundations of Liberalism* (New York, 1984).

5. Robert V. Remini, *Andrew Jackson and the Course of American Democracy, 1833–1845* (New York, 1984), 616.

6. Richard Reeves began the current round of Tocquevillian punditry with his *American Journey: Travelling with Tocqueville in Search of Democracy in America* (New York, 1982). More recently, James Reston has written that Tocqueville's observations "are still as fresh as this

Much of this writing glosses over *Democracy's* bad hunches, misinformed reporting, and ideological biases—shortcomings in *Democracy* that those who specialize in studying Tocqueville are now quick to point out.[7] There appear to be several reasons for this glossing over. Christopher Lasch has detected a political subtext in some neo-Tocquevillean writing, a tendency "to exalt bourgeois liberalism as the only civilized form of political life."[8] On a different tack, Daniel Rodgers points out elsewhere in this volume that many of Tocqueville's disciples have been too eager to read *Democracy* (or some portion of it) as prophecy, taking Tocqueville's own claims to prevision too seriously—and thereby misreading the present into the past that Tocqueville described. Just as troubling is the persistent slighting of so much important recent work about the past, work that should encourage a more distanced handling of *Democracy*.

Take, for example, what historians are now saying about one of Tocqueville's central themes, equality of condition in Jacksonian America. Tocqueville claimed that equality was the fundamental fact of a democratic order. By this he did not mean that an absolute material equality existed in the United States: Most of what he wrote about American conditions concerned not absolutes, but a relative equality, in contrast with the Old World. However, in asserting that American class differences existed within an egalitarian framework, Tocqueville made a variety of claims—about the rapid circulation of wealth, the plebeian origins of American fortunes, and the fluid structure of American opportunity—that now seem to have been dubious. Plainly, Tocqueville overestimated the proportion of the country's free population that was middle class—or, as he put it, "comfortably off"—while he slighted the opulence of the wealthy and the poverty of the poor.[9] Even more important, *Democracy's* treatment of democracy and equality seems at odds with another recent discovery—that over the same period during which American politics grew more democratic formally, inequalities of wealth and power declined hardly at all; if anything these inequalities became more severe.[1]

Likewise, recent historians have moved well beyond Tocqueville's

morning's newspaper" ("Democracy in America," *The New York Times*, 2 July 1986). A few weeks later, Arthur M. Schlesinger, Jr., remarked that "[t]he reader of Alexis de Tocqueville is constantly astonished to recognize the lineaments of modern America in his great work" ("The Challenge of Change," *The New York Times Magazine*, 27 July 1986, 20).

7. See, for example, James T. Schleifer's frequent comments about *Democracy's* shortcomings in his *The Making of Tocqueville's "Democracy in America"* (Chapel Hill, 1980). Schleifer's balanced evaluation is at once intensely admiring and painstakingly critical of Tocqueville's achievement. For an earlier critical appreciation of *Democracy*, see Jack Lively, *The Social and Political Thought of Alexis de Tocqueville* (New York, 1962).

8. Christopher Lasch, *The Culture of Narcissism: America in an Age of Diminished Expectations* (New York, 1978), 29–30.

9. Alexis de Tocqueville, *Democracy in America*, ed. J. P. Mayer (New York, 1969), 209. Unless otherwise noted, all subsequent citations of *Democracy* will be to this edition. The most sustained challenge to Tocqueville on these matters is Edward Pessen, *Riches, Class, and Power Before the Civil War* (Lexington, Mass., 1973).

1. In addition to Pessen's work, see Jeffrey G. Williamson and Peter H. Lindert, *American Inequality: A Macroeconomic History* (New York, 1980), esp. 36–46. Williamson and Lindert, drawing on several local studies, estimate that the concentration of wealth in America grew especially uneven from the 1820s to the 1840s.

treatment of another of his key topics, religion. Tocqueville was remarkably sensitive to the importance of religion to American political culture. His basic insight about how religion promoted social order in a democracy—"Despotism may be able to do without faith," he wrote, "but liberty cannot"—was profound.[2] More than ever, historians have come to agree with Tocqueville about the centrality of religion to American social life and social change in the 1830s and after. But as current work also suggests, Tocqueville never fully came to terms with the specifically evangelical Protestant character of the Second Great Awakening. Nor does *Democracy* elaborate the social processes (and conflicts) that helped produce the great religious revivals of the Jacksonian era. As Paul E. Johnson has written, Tocqueville treated religion as a form of personal rectitude and social control but he effectively ignored the question of who, in American society, was controlling whom.[3] It was precisely from the connections between transcendent religious experiences and shifting power relations—between employers and wage-earners, middle-class patriarchs and middle-class women, masters and slaves—that the religious passions of Jacksonian America gained so much of their force. In the northern states, evangelicalism became, among other things, a vehicle for promoting new forms of work discipline, public morality, and feminized family government.[4] In the south, masters adapted evangelical notions of stewardship to their emerging defense of slavery as a positive good, while slaves interpreted Christianity very differently, as a parable of endurance and deliverance.[5] Throughout the country, the sociology of American religion was more complex and conflict ridden than Tocqueville had appreciated.

Democracy was far more acute about another American institution, slavery. A great deal of current scholarship echoes Tocqueville's judgment that slavery fundamentally shaped the mores and social conditions of Jacksonian America in ways that distinguished the free states from the slave states. But Tocqueville also misjudged vital aspects of southern life, notably the cultural perseverence of the slave communities. In *Democracy* we read that "[t]he Negro has no family; for him a woman is no more than the passing companion of his pleasures, and from their birth his sons are his equals." Historians, to the contrary, have identified kin networks and family ties, along with slave religion, as some of the most powerful bonds among the antebellum slaves— extraordinary sources of dignity and mutuality, which helped fend off the worst social and psychological hardships of bondage.[6] Tocqueville,

2. *Democracy* (Mayer ed.), 294.
3. Paul E. Johnson, *A Shopkeeper's Millennium: Society and Revivals in Rochester, New York, 1815–1837* (New York, 1978), 136–137.
4. Johnson, *Shopkeeper's Millenium*; Mary P. Ryan, *Cradle of the Middle Class: The Family in Oneida County, New York, 1790–1865* (Cambridge, 1981); Carroll Smith Rosenberg, *Disorderly Conduct: Visions of Gender in Victorian America* (New York, 1985).
5. Donald Matthews, *Religion in the Old South* (Chicago, 1978); Eugene D. Genovese, *Roll, Jordan, Roll: The World the Slaves Made* (New York, 1974); Lawrence W. Levine, *Black Culture and Black Consciousness: Afro-American Folk Thought from Slavery to Freedom* (New York, 1977); Albert Raboteau, *Slave Religion* (New York, 1980).
6. *Democracy* (Mayer ed.), 317. On slave families, see especially Herbert G. Gutman, *The Black Family in Slavery and Freedom, 1750–1920* (New York, 1976).

it seems, too quickly deduced cultural disorder from the very real horrors of enslavement; his writings thus bypassed important features of both American slavery and an emerging Afro-American culture.

On women, family life, and gender, *Democracy* certainly raised themes of interest to recent historians. Although they were freed from the restraints of aristocratic authorities, Tocqueville observed, American women had lost their independence in the bonds of marriage— and had done so voluntarily.[7] Once confined to their dependent state, as wives and mothers, American women undertook their true vocation, to elevate the nation's moral tone by scrupulously attending to their private duties, following the canons of what historians now call "the cult of domesticity."[8] No less a promulgator of this cult than Catharine Beecher recognized in *Democracy* a near-perfect delineation of the advanced state of American women.[9] Yet Beecher (and Tocqueville) notwithstanding, *Democracy* contained at best a partial account of American womanhood. Quite apart from the female slaves, many women—women in small farming households, the women of the laboring poor—had neither the means nor the desire to live their lives in accord with emerging Victorian middle-class standards. At various flashpoints—notably between urban reformers and poor women— these differences exploded, as the champions of domesticity sought to remake "unruly" females and families in their own image, and the "unruly" resisted.[1]

More generally, Tocqueville appears to have slighted ideological differences and conflicts among free Americans, in and out of party politics. Not that he omitted discussion of these conflicts: "What strikes one most on arrival in the United States," he wrote, "is the kind of tumultuous agitation in which one finds political society."[2] In the end, though, Tocqueville was far more impressed by Americans' shared values, based on their common republicanism, individualism, and respect for the Constitution—"a tacit agreement and a sort of *consensus universalis*," which he thought precluded deep and lasting ideological divisions.[3] Today, historians are more wary. Closer examination of Americans' shared political vocabulary has revealed different versions of what these words meant; these clashing interpretations surfaced in bitter conflicts between Whigs and Democrats, labor unions and employers' associations, squatters and land speculators, abolitionists and slaveholders, and various other groups. In the 1980s, Americans can listen to Ronald Reagan and Coretta Scott King speak eloquently about the affirmation of equality and social justice without assuming that they mean anything like the same thing. So in the 1830s, behind Tocqueville's "tacit agreement," lurked far more powerful conflicts

7. *Democracy* (Mayer ed.), 600–603.
8. See Nancy F. Cott, *The Bonds of Womanhood: "Woman's Sphere" in New England, 1780–1830* (New Haven, 1977).
9. Catherine Beecher, *A Treatise on Domestic Economy* (Boston, 1842), 26–34.
1. On these conflicts, see especially Christine Stansell, *City of Women: The Female Laboring Poor in New York, 1789–1860* (New York, 1986).
2. *Democracy* (Mayer ed.), 398.
3. Ibid.

than *Democracy* captured—conflicts that would bring about (among
other things) the bloodiest civil upheaval in the history of the
nineteenth-century western world, an upheaval Tocqueville anticipated but thought the republic would avoid.[4]

All of this revisionism is, understandably, upsetting to those who
wish to regard Tocqueville as some sort of Olympian authority, the
surest and best key to Jacksonian America. Occasionally, *Democracy's*
admirers have struck back at the supposedly low-minded revisionists:
One historian has seen fit to label another historian's challenge to
Democracy as "a feeble effort to bury the noble Tocqueville in Brook-
lyn under a pile of tax receipts."[5] Put this way, the important historical
issues become personalized and therefore trivialized, as if the point is
to "prove" or "disprove" Tocqueville, or vote *Democracy* up or down.
Nothing that historians discover about Jacksonian America can rob
Democracy of its unique value as an ambitious attempt by an extremely perceptive man, thinking with all his might, to understand
democracy (and America) in the broadest possible terms. Certainly no
one can hold Tocqueville responsible for not knowing things that it
has taken scholars a century-and-a-half to learn. *Democracy* may be
regarded as a classic not because it is "right" or "accurate"—Tocqueville, himself, a compulsive self-doubter and reviser would almost certainly have conceded as much—but because of the breadth of its
author's moral and political concerns and the cogency of his questions. Revisionist efforts will have been wasted if they lead historians
merely to denigrate Tocqueville, or to neglect him, as historians before
the 1930s tended to do.[6] But Tocqueville's admirers serve neither the
man nor his work if they try to elevate them above subsequent research, or try to isolate Tocqueville's ideas from what we have learned
(and continue to learn) about their contexts. Instead, given all we now
know about Jacksonian America, it is time to reread *Democracy in
America* alongside current reinterpretations not as prophecy, nor as
some timeless diagnosis of modernity, but as a historical artifact.

Approached in this critical historical spirit, *Democracy in America*
loses some of its glamor, but retains considerable stature. *Democracy's*
great strength—indeed, its genius—was that it marked a breakthrough
in conservative thinking about property and mass democracy, a breakthrough that Tocqueville intuited, then elucidated earlier and far more
fully than his American friends and informants. The book's shortcomings, meanwhile, are instructive, because they point out the danger
of projecting a single ideal of democracy as the essence of Jacksonian
politics—and, for that matter, of our own politics. Tocqueville articulated a new conception of democracy in the 1830s, one that would become increasingly important (indeed, dominant) in the United States

4. See, for example, John Ashworth's sweeping analysis of conflicting party and factional ide-
ologies in his *"Agrarians" and "Aristocrats": Party Political Ideology in the United States,
1837–1846* (London, 1985).
5. Robert V. Remini approvingly repeats this remark as the opinion of "one wag" in *Jackson*,
613.
6. On the Progressive historians' neglect of Tocqueville, see Marshall and Drescher, "American
Historians," 513–515.

over the decades that followed. What he failed to comprehend was that this democracy was but one of several American democracies that had emerged out of the social tumults of his time.[7]

To understand the dimensions of Tocqueville's achievement, it is important to recognize that he visited, and then studied, an America in flux. Even if we concede that every historical moment is, in some sense, a moment of transition, there are ample grounds for describing the half-decade from 1828 to 1833—and even more specifically the period immediately surrounding Tocqueville's brief stay in 1831—as a turning point in American history. The sheer pace and drama of events, crowding in upon each other, reinforce that impression: The election of Andrew Jackson, the Virginia suffrage and slavery debates, the great Finneyite revivals in Rochester, the emergence of immediatist abolitionism, Nat Turner's rebellion, the bank war and then the nullification crisis, the rise of radical labor movements and trade unionism in the northeast, the drive for graduation and freeholds in the west, the gestation of this country's first mass democratic party system. In a matter of weeks (and sometimes days) Americans witnessed the fall of entire chunks of the gentry's old regime and the opening up of issues of section, class, and race that would dominate the nation's politics for decades to come.

Alexis de Tocqueville disembarked in New York City and stepped into the middle of this political maelstrom—unprepared. He and his friend de Beaumont had come to look at penitentiaries and to ponder the New World's lessons for the Old; crossing the ocean with his head full of Montesquieu and Guizot, he had expected to find a classical republic in the United States, where independent citizens exercised selfless civic virtue on behalf of the commonwealth. Such, after all, was what eighteenth-century political writers had said a republic was supposed to be; such was the kind of republic Americans boasted they had created.[8] It took Tocqueville less than a month, spent talking mainly with some of the leading men of New York City, for him to change his mind. It was not virtue that made the Americans a people; Tocqueville saw little enough of virtue. Individual *intérêt* was the secret of American politics.[9] For the rest of his visit, and then over the next nine years, Tocqueville puzzled over his discovery. Again and again, he asked himself the same question: How did the Americans, lacking virtue and the traditional forms of aristocratic authority, manage to maintain stability and order? From these ruminations—and with his attentions often fixed more on his native land than on the United

---

7. Several works have contributed to this reading of *Democracy*, including George W. Pierson, *Tocqueville and Beaumont in America* (New York, 1938); Louis Hartz, *The Liberal Tradition in America: An Interpretation of American Political Thought Since the Revolution* (New York, 1955); Schleifer, *Making*; Diggins, *Lost Soul*. Works of relevance to specific points are cited below.
8. By now, an enormous literature has explored the vicissitudes of republicanism in early America. For an introduction, see Robert Shalhope, "Republicanism in Early America," *William and Mary Quarterly* 38 (1982): 334–356.
9. Schleifer, *Making*, 235.

States—he constructed his grand themes, always claiming that in America he saw not simply America but an image of democracy itself.

It is hardly surprising that Tocqueville, immersed in so many different events, understood them in terms of a contrast between democratic America and aristocratic Europe: Such were the terms of intellectual inquiry he and his generation of educated Frenchmen had absorbed, above all from De l'Esprit des Lois. Nor is it surprising that, in explaining that contrast, Tocqueville fastened on the problems of virtue and self-interest, stability and order: Such were the preoccupations of enlightened aristocrats in France (and Britain) in the 1830s, alarmed by the specter of popular revolt and democratic reform. Tocqueville made no pretense about where his sympathies lay: Although inclined toward democratic institutions, he was an instinctual aristocrat who despised what he called "the mass." "I have a passionate love for liberty, law and respect for rights—but not for democracy," he wrote at one point. "There is the ultimate truth of my heart."[1]

Not quite so obvious is that Tocqueville's preoccupations haunted his American friends and informants as well—a point recent historical research has emphasized.[2] To be sure, upper-crust Americans, far more than even enlightened Old World aristocrats, had made their peace with republican principles; indeed, they were often insistent republicans, champions of the American Constitution. But no less than the young Tocqueville, the mainly ex-Federalist, soon-to-be Whigs from whom he learned so much were frightened by the seemingly irresistible democratic tide—a tide they feared would destroy the orderly American polity inaugurated in 1787 and bring to power either a lawless mob or an American Napoleon. Their world—a world of political deference, virtuous obligation, and elaborate checks and balances on the popular will—had been swept aside by the election of Andrew Jackson and the ascendancy of Martin Van Buren. The Jacksonians' consolidation of power only confirmed that, henceforth, party loyalty, the shameless pursuit of self-interest, and demagogic flattery of the electorate would be the cardinal American political virtues; some even saw Jackson as the much-feared military dictator. And on the horizon loomed even more dangerous mobocrats, men like the artisan radical, Thomas Skidmore, and women like the feminist agitator, Frances Wright, who supposedly would dissolve the moral bonds of civilization and destroy whatever checks on popular rule remained.

This was a conservative, self-serving, at times cranky view of American political culture in the 1830s, and it quickly became Tocqueville's. He expressed his fears (and his informants' fears) amply in the first volume of Democracy in America in his depictions of an irrational American people, goaded by semiliterate party hacks, destroying great institutions like the Second Bank of the United States for little more

<hr />

1. Tocqueville quoted in J. P. Mayer, Alexis de Tocqueville: A Biographical Study in Political Science (New York, 1960), 13.
2. See above all Linda K. Kerber, Federalists in Dissent: Imagery and Ideology in Jeffersonian America (Ithaca, 1970); and Daniel Walker Howe, The Political Culture of the American Whigs (Chicago, 1979).

reason than to see if the institutions would fall. Beyond that, Tocqueville discovered an even deeper problem, a singular timidity on the part of worthy gentlemen—the kinds of men who might be expected to understand and exercise civic virtue—in the face of majoritarian rule. In public, Tocqueville's wealthier friends actually lauded the democracy they so distrusted, "careful to avoid showing that [they were] hurt" by the state of things.[3] To do otherwise, Tocqueville reported, was to court utter marginality, or (even worse) physical attack.

It took no special gifts to collect these views and assemble them into a book. Had Tocqueville done only that, his writings would be nowhere near as interesting as they are. Had he gone on, as American conservatives like Rufus Choate did, to prescribe ways to institutionalize classical virtue in the United States, he might be as well known today as Rufus Choate.[4] Instead, Tocqueville scrutinized the peculiar American democrat more closely than his American friends had yet done—and he found that despite the potential tyranny of a democratic majority, there really wasn't so much to worry about after all. Perhaps, Tocqueville suggested, Madison and his successors had misjudged the American majority (and therefore misjudged democracy). Perhaps, in a democracy, popular self-interest could be turned into a kind of virtuousness, less exalted than the classical variety, but enough to shape an orderly, moral, public-spirited citizenry.

As John Diggins has pointed out, Tocqueville managed to transcend his fears and those of his American friends only by breaking with the prevailing modes of political inquiry. Instead of approaching democracy and democratic manners through a study of American laws and institutions, he tried to study democratic manners directly, to see how they affected politics. He did this not by taking any extensive surveys of American social structure—he hardly had the time or information for that—but by juxtaposing what he saw in America (eversymptomatic of democracy) with what he knew best, post–1830 France. He came to understand America, and democracy, in terms of a series of absences: The absence of a peasantry, the absence of a proletariat, the absence of an idle aristocracy. In America, all citizens worked and none lacked property or the means to obtain it; the pursuit of equality and material desires was universal. Out of that pursuit sprang a pride in work and achievement—as duties to the community as well as the means to self-gratification—which encouraged the public spirit, led to the creation of voluntary associations, and secured political stability.[5]

Contained in this analysis, quite apart from its shrewd discussion of the Jacksonian middle-class mentality, was a revolution in conservative thought about property and politics—a revolution that, in America, had begun in Jefferson's day, but was not yet completed when Tocque-

3. *Democracy* (Mayer ed.), 179.
4. On Choate, see Jean V. Matthews, *Rufus Choate: The Law and Civic Virtue* (Philadelphia, 1980).
5. *Democracy* (Mayer ed.), 525–528.

ville visited the United States.[6] From the framers onward, Americans preoccupied with order and stability had assumed that there was an inevitable conflict between the wealthy few and the poor (or property-less) many. Unless the many were held in check, they would use their majority power to despoil the few. Atop these gloomy assumptions, American conservatives, with one eye fixed on Europe, built their case for mixed government, the breaking up of popular sovereignty, and the elevation of virtuous men of property to political leadership. "We have no experience that teaches us that any other rights are safe where property is not safe," the young Federalist Daniel Webster warned during the Massachusetts constitutional convention of 1820.[7] Unfortunately, that convention, and subsequent developments elsewhere, portended the ascension of the self-interested many and an all-out assault on virtuous politics and property rights. All was lost unless some scheme could be devised that would submerge men's individual desires in what conservatives believed to be the rightful, orderly objects of government—but no such scheme seemed in the offing. "Montesquieu has somewhere a reflection to this purpose," an ironic, embittered Rufus King wrote to an associate in 1822, "but gives no hint in respect to the formation of so extraordinary a plan."[8]

Less than a decade later—and nearly half-a-century after the ratification of the Constitution—Tocqueville could see things differently. Not that the danger of majority tyranny had completely passed away: Tocqueville still found it in the American state legislatures as well as in the reign of public opinion. But contrary to the fears of founding fathers like Madison and John Adams (and of pessimistic Federalists like Webster and King), America had not become more and more like Europe, with its sharp distinctions between the few and the many. Democratic America had given rise to an exceptionally large middle class—an amorphous group of entrepreneurs, businessmen, shopkeepers, and commercial farmers, far larger than any comparable group in Europe. Tocqueville easily—all too easily—equated this class with the many. In America, Tocqueville observed, "everyone, having some possession to defend, recognizes the right to property in principle."[9] In this sense, America was a classless society, despite its manifest inequalities of wealth: The many, who either owned property or could reasonably expect to do so, would never strip the wealthy few of those property rights that they themselves held so dear. The framers' glorified notion of mixed government, which Tocqueville took to be a "chimera" anyway, was of little relevance in such a democratic republic; were it ever actually established, a truly mixed government—checking the power of the many with the privileges of the few—would

6. On earlier developments, see David Hackett Fischer, *The Revolution of American Conservatism: The Federalist Party in the Era of Jeffersonian Democracy* (New York, 1965).
7. Daniel Webster, "The Basis of the Senate," in *The Writings and Speeches of Daniel Webster* ed. Fletcher Webster, 18 vols. (Boston, 1903), 5:15.
8. Rufus King to Christopher Gore, 3 February 1822, quoted in Shaw Livermore, Jr., *The Twilight of Federalism: The Disintegration of the Federalist Party, 1815–1830* (Princeton, 1962), 124.
9. *Democracy* (Mayer ed.), 238.

only plunge the republic into revolution or anarchy.[1] Rather, in the politics of classless America—democracy in its most advanced state— the few could embrace both democracy and the people.

Tocqueville, in short, after nine months of travel and nine years of study, saw what it was taking his American friends a generation to see: In America, mass democracy did not necessarily endanger property; equality could mean the right to pursue both democracy and property. Once they did discover this truth for themselves, American conservatives proclaimed it to the rafters—and completed the Jacksonian revolution by helping to create in the Whig party a political counterweight to the Jacksonians and the radicals. There was not, Daniel Webster (now a Whig) announced in 1838, any "clear and well defined line, between capital and labor" in the United States, as there was in Europe.[2] America, Calvin Colton told the electorate six years later, was "a country of *self-made* men," where all were bound together in their individual pursuits by mutual dependence and an overarching harmony of interests.[3] The prattling of Democrats and other alehouse agitators about the few and the many, others asserted, were but attempts to foist Old World doctrines on an exceptional, democratic people.[4] Behind the petty squabbles of the day-to-day, the superficial violence of politics and the marketplace, was a greater democratic consensus promoting universal prosperity and upward mobility, which all right-thinking respectable Americans, rich and poor alike, understood and tried to exemplify.[5]

Here was a vision of politics that, unlike the eighteenth-century Whigs's view, could reconcile pessimistic American conservatives to mass democracy. Just as important, it could become a popular political philosophy in a country gripped by rapid commercial expansion and social transformation. Native-born craft workers, small shopkeepers, petty-capitalist farmers, and Southern planters all found ample reasons to rally behind the Whig democracy; by the late 1840s, many leading Democrats, as well as Whigs, had begun subscribing to its essentials.[6] Nowhere, however, did any American expound that vision and its logic more copiously or brilliantly than Alexis de Tocqueville. And no writer more fully explored this vision's possible implications for every aspect of American life, public and private.

Read this way, *Democracy* ends up saying a great deal about the 1830s, with significance far beyond the history of Jacksonian America. The book helps lay bare not simply an interpretation of American democracy, but a process whereby a particular set of assumptions about democracy emerged—assumptions congenial to those who had distrusted popular sovereignty, assumptions that were to become

1. Ibid., 251.
2. Webster quoted in Diggins, *Lost Soul*, 108.
3. Calvin Colton, *The Junius Papers: Number VII* (New York, 1844).
4. For further quotations, see Sean Wilentz, *Chants Democratic: New York City & the Rise of the American Working Class, 1788–1850* (New York, 1984).
5. For an overview, see Howe, *American Whigs.*
6. See Ashworth, *"Agrarians."*

prevalent in much of the world over the nineteenth and twentieth centuries. In this respect, Democracy in America is of singular importance to historians curious about the larger meaning of democratization in the United States and elsewhere. In the jargon of one important stream of current scholarship, Tocqueville captured, if not something so grand as "modernity," then a signal moment in the modernization of politics—the decline of deference and the emergence of political individualism. Or, if you prefer, Tocqueville helps us understand how certain hegemonic notions about democracy, property, and equality took shape in America in the second quarter of the nineteenth century.

Yet to notice these broader meanings is also to confront the limits of Tocqueville's analysis. If Democracy's sweeping antithesis opened up aspects of democracy that Americans were only beginning to understand in the 1830s, so too (as recent work suggests) Tocqueville reduced too much about Jacksonian America to a single conception of democracy. The turning point that gave rise to the Jacksonian political revolution—and the shift in conversative thinking that Democracy so nicely illustrates—also saw in this country the emergence of other, very different kinds of democracy.

Here lie Democracy's instructive shortcomings. Jacksonian America may not have been Europe, but it did have an increasingly reactionary and powerful landed elite, the elements of a republican working class, and a troubled yeomanry. Tocqueville observed the elite—the southern slaveholders—firsthand, and he wrote about them eloquently. The emerging working class and the yeomanry he barely saw or understood. All played important roles in the political crises of the 1830s and raised problems that were far graver and more complicated than Tocqueville imagined.

Few passages in Democracy are as arresting as Tocqueville's contrast between the north and the south:

> [The Northerner] with a greater degree of activity, common sense, information, and greater aptitude, has the characteristic good and evil qualities of the middle classes. [The Southerner] has the tastes, the prejudices, the weaknesses, and the magnanimity of all aristocracies.[7]

Slavery, as Tocqueville argued, was creating two civilizations within the United States, with different conceptions of labor, money, and leisure. If we now think that Tocqueville overlooked important things about the slave south, his intuitive grasp of the cultural divide between free labor and slavery remains extraordinary.

Where Tocqueville's analysis of democracy fell short was in its failure to probe the deeper paradoxes of slavery and freedom. Like other antislavery writers, Tocqueville found the peculiar institution an oppressive anomaly in democratic America, the cruelist kind of inequality: "Amid the democratic liberty and enlightenment of our age," he

---

7. In this instance, I have quoted the more felicitous translation in Alexis de Tocqueville, Democracy in America, ed., Phillips Bradley (New York, 1954), 1:412.

believed, slavery could not survive.[8] Yet he never adequately explained why it was that southerners, including slaveholders like Thomas Jefferson, had been among the leading advocates of democratic principles and natural rights from the mid-eighteenth century on. He did not grasp how slavery could have underwritten the expansion of democracy for southern whites in the 1820s and 1830s. Nor did he explore the paradox further to wonder why, at the very moment when he visited America, white southerners—planters and yeomen—began insisting with increasing urgency that their personal independence and democratic liberties would be threatened by any effort to interfere with the slaveholders' property. That an "aristocratic" elite and "democratic" populace could defend the enslavement of blacks—and, beginning in the 1830s, the denial of free speech to whites—on democratic grounds and in states which boasted some of the most democratic constitutions in the world was a terrible fact of Jacksonian democracy that Tocqueville never fully sorted out.[9] Failing in that, he underestimated how the growing cultural divisions between north and south fed a political crisis that cut through shared interests ideals—and stunted "middle-class" democracy in the south. Alongside the American democracy Tocqueville described, there was another very different theory and practice of democracy—the slaveholder's democracy.

Tocqueville likewise showed only passing interest in the meanings that the slaves and American free blacks might have attached to democracy. Better than other visitors, he did resist the blandishments of plantation paternalists about slavery's benefits to the slaves. He expected that if the masters did not grant emancipation, the slaves would take it for themselves, by any means necessary. He also understood how racism intensified the sufferings of free blacks, in both the north and south. Yet Tocqueville showed little curiosity about the possible implications of the eighteenth-century democratic revolutions for the enslaved men and women and the free blacks of the United States. A Frenchman might have been expected to have been more interested: Just as Toussaint L'Ouverture and the black Jacobins of Saint-Domingue had viewed the French Revolution as the signal for their own uprising, so slaves and free blacks in various parts of the United States absorbed the democratic message of the American Revolution as an unfulfilled promise. But while Tocqueville sensed the slaves' and the free blacks' restiveness, he did not ponder how they might have

8. *Democracy* (Mayer ed.), 363.
9. The classic works on these topics are Fletcher M. Green, *Constitutional Development in the South Atlantic States, 1776–1860: A Study in the Evolution of Democracy* (Chapel Hill, 1930), and idem., "Democracy in the Old South," *Journal of Southern History* 12 (1946): 3–23. These should be supplemented by some recent studies of the southern yeomanry and the second party system in the South: Steven Hahn, *The Roots of Southern Populism: Yeoman Farmers and the Transformation of the Georgia Upcountry, 1850–1890* (New York, 1983); J. Mills Thornton III, *Politics and Power in a Slave Society: Alabama, 1800–1860* (Baton Rouge, 1978); Harry Watson, *Jacksonian Politics and Community Conflict: The Emergence of the Second Party System in Cumberland County, North Carolina* (Baton Rouge, 1981). See also Watson's intelligent synthesis, "Conflict and Collaboration: Yeomen, Slaveholders, and Politics in the Antebellum South," *Social History* 10 (1983): 273–298. On the origins of these paradoxes, see Edmund S. Morgan, *American Slavery, American Freedom: The Ordeal of Colonial Virginia* (New York, 1975).

had their own definitions of democracy—and how, in time, these might have influenced their own struggles for emancipation and equality.[1]

Tocqueville had even more trouble with the free labor north and the political implications of its economic development. He easily grasped the rapidity of that development—occasioned by the rise of banks, internal improvements, and early corporations—and how it distinguished the north from the south.[2] He glimpsed the poverty that accompanied the transportation revolution, and noted in passing that the larger American cities had acquired "a rabble more dangerous even than that of European towns" (which he expected would eventually require the raising of a national standing army).[3] But when Tocqueville saw these crowds, he saw a traditional *canaille*. He could not see—as far less brilliant visitors like Thomas Hamilton could—that for these people, and for a growing number of other Americans all across the north, the line of demarcation between capital and labor was growing sharper and more permanent.[4]

Tocqueville's great friend and admirer, John Stuart Mill, helped account for *Democracy*'s oversights in these matters. While he praised *Democracy* lavishly, Mill also pointed out that much of what Tocqueville saw—and especially what he didn't like—was hardly peculiar to American democracy, or the result of democracy at all. In a sense, even though Tocqueville had taken a step beyond classical political theory, he remained too much the classicist, preoccupied with a limited set of questions about politics and society. Or, as Mill put it, Tocqueville "bound up in one abstract idea the whole tendencies of modern commercial society and [gave] them one name—Democracy." In fact, Mill argued, many of the defects that Tocqueville found special to the American democratic mind were "the ordinary ones of a commercial class."[5]

Tocqueville was too ambitious and careful an observer to miss completely what Mill was talking about. Buried in Tocqueville's unpublished papers at Yale University is a note referring to "the great difficulty in untangling what there is [about America] which is democratic, commercial, English, and puritan." ("To be discussed in introduction," Tocqueville added hopefully.)[6] He never really did untangle it all; still, toward the close of the first volume of *Democracy* and in the second volume, he looked for a language with which to describe the specifically "commercial" problems of the 1830s. At a few points he found it, especially in his trenchant, all-too-brief chapter on how

1. See Eugene D. Genovese, *From Rebellion to Revolution: Afro-American Slave Revolts in the Making of the Modern World* (Baton Rouge, 1979); Ira Berlin et al., eds., *Freedom: A Documentary History of Emancipation, 1861–1867*, series 1, vol. 1, *The Destruction of Slavery* (Cambridge, 1985).
2. On Tocqueville's appreciation of these matters, see Schleifer, *Making*, 168.
3. *Democracy* (Mayer ed.), 278, n. 1.
4. Thomas Hamilton, *Men and Manners in America*, 2 vols. (London, 1833), 1: 59ff.
5. John Stuart Mill, "M. de Tocqueville on Democracy in America," *Edinburgh Review* 72 (1840): 1.
6. Tocqueville quoted in Jean-Claude Lamberti, *Tocqueville et les Deux Démocraties* (Paris, 1983), 26.

an aristocracy might be created by manufactures.[7] But Tocqueville was too much a man of his class, his country, and his political education to make more of this language—or to make a single concrete reference to the labor movements and class conflicts of the Jacksonian north. He could not appreciate that the ideals of the working men's parties, the city central unions, the land reformers, and the radical wing of the Democratic party carried very different meanings than those of other groups of Americans. He could not comprehend that for these people, the cry for equality sprang not from irrational impulses or self-interest alone, but out of very real fears that exploitative businessmen and manufacturers were imposing new forms of power and dependency on the productive classes, destroying the democratic republic in the name of democracy and equal rights.[8] Beside the democracy Tocqueville did see, and the southern democracies he only began to understand, there was yet another democracy, a democracy of the wage-earning classes that came to life in the 1830s and would come into its own in later decades.

Finally, Tocqueville had practically nothing to say about the American yeomanry and its view of democracy. The oversight is understandable; in contrast to the French peasantry, America's freeholding rural small producers must have all seemed pretty much alike. But there were important divisions in the American countryside, between cash-crop producing commercial farmers and the relatively isolated, self-sufficient communities of yeomen. The former—particularly in the grain and dairy regions of the northwest—fit fairly easily within Tocqueville's conception of the individualist American democrat. The latter, however, pursued their self-interests according to intricate, customary rules of inheritance, household production, and barter exchange, in a balance of personal independence and local communalism quite unlike anything Tocqueville described. The transportation revolution and the commercialization of agriculture dealt severe blows to the northern yeomanry in the first half of the nineteenth century, but yeoman communities did persist in more remote areas with poorer soils; in the south, meanwhile, the majority of the white population consisted of yeomen and their families. In all areas, the yeomen equated democracy with the right to obtain and work their land—and to maintain their communal solidarities—without interference by absentee speculators, commercial developers, and meddlesome politicians. The yeomen mounted all sorts of local political efforts to defend themselves in the 1830s and 1840s, from squatters' clubs to antibank movements; these would culminate, fifty years later, in the rural insurgencies associated with Populism.[9]

7. *Democracy* (Mayer ed.), 555–558.
8. See, among other recent works, Alan Dawley, *Class and Community: The Industrial Revolution in Lynn* (Cambridge, Mass., 1976); Bruce Laurie, *Working People of Philadelphia, 1800–1850* (Philadelphia, 1980); Wilentz, *Chants Democratic*.
9. On the south, see Hahn, *Roots*; Watson, "Conflict and Collaboration"; as well as the various works Watson cites. On the north, see the classic works by Paul W. Gates, *The Farmer's Age: Agriculture, 1815–1860* (New York, 1951), and idem., *History of Public Land Law Development* (Washington, D.C., 1968), as well as John Mack Faragher, *Sugar Creek: Life on the*

Ultimately, the collisions among these different forms of American democracy would destroy the agrarian republic Tocqueville knew, not by the quiet action of society upon itself, but with considerable brutality and human suffering. By the 1880s, as James Bryce among others noted, the cumulative effects of civil war, emancipation, urbanization, immigration, and industrial capitalist growth had created entirely new structures of power, individualism, and commitment.[1] We are reminded of the transience of Tocqueville's time and place, of how the policy and social formations he analyzed carried the seeds of their own destruction.

But to leave it at that would be to miss all that lives in *Democracy*. For Tocqueville, it was only natural to see the great sameness of the Americans. Lacking the bold contrasts of Europe (by which he meant France)—Europe with its legitimist aristocrats and revolutionary workers—American political culture acquired a certain narrowness that seemed to ensure stability and public spirit despite the solitude of middle-class life. In this contrast, he saw the reasons why nineteenth-century conservatives could, at last, make their peace with democracy—first in America, eventually elsewhere. Yet where Tocqueville saw many things in Jacksonian America and called them one thing, there were in fact many democracies. Behind what he called the Americans' universal consensus there were fundamental differences about the first principles of democracy itself, born of the social changes that accompanied the democratic revolution. Over the decades that followed, these differences (and nothing so simple as *intérêt*) proved to be the central fact of American politics.

Of course, the specific vision of democracy that Tocqueville set down lived on long after the Jacksonian era. Although written in the 1830s, *Democracy in America* did at the very least anticipate what was to become the intertwining of capitalism and democracy, and suggest why so many Americans might come to understand democracy only in these terms. In recent years, there has been an extraordinary resurgence of this way of thinking, both at the centers of power and (to judge from the media) in the country at large. This leads to a final, more present-minded reflection.

Taking the long view, historians might well consider that while Tocqueville slighted the diversity of democracy in the 1830s, and while he failed to comprehend the social and political revolutions to come, the champions of middle-class democracy did ultimately triumph, smashing the slaveholders in the 1860s, marginalizing the more radical elements of working-class and rural unrest in the 1880s and 1890s, binding most Americans to what we now call capitalist democracy. Perhaps, after reexamining Tocqueville's historical significance, some of his old reputation as a prophet emerges intact. Per-

---

Illinois Prairie (New Haven, 1986). Allan Kulikoff's forthcoming study of the rise and fall of the American yeomanry promises to throw a great deal of additional light on this subject, particularly on the connections between economic change, family life, and gender relations in the countryside.

1. James Bryce, *The American Commonwealth*, 2 vols. (London and New York, 1888–1889).

haps, with a touch of perversity, one might even claim that *Democracy* presents a more accurate rendering of our own time than it does of Andrew Jackson's.

And yet one also wonders how much such a view misses about our own time and place. To look at contemporary America—with its warfare-welfare state, its extraordinary concentrations of private power, its place in world affairs—and then compare it to the age of Jackson is to be immediately reminded of how different we are from the America Tocqueville described. More important, it is also to be struck by the enormous disparities and contradictions between our social and political institutions and the hopeful vision of the middle-class American democracy that began to emerge in the 1830s. At other times in our past—the 1890s, the 1920s, the 1950s—that vision has appeared to be an all-encompassing, self-evident reality, only to be challenged by new and very different visions of democracy inspired by the gap between promise and actuality. We might expect that, as we wrestle with our own contradictions, new and different forms of democracy—possibly liberating, possibly not—have already begun taking shape without our fully realizing it. The portents are not especially good, now that public officials try to justify lying to the American people (and Congress) as essential to the national security and the future of democracy itself. But in addressing these matters, Tocqueville can only teach us so much. These are matters we must master on our own.

HENRY STEELE COMMAGER

Democracy and the Tyranny of the Majority†

Democracy, as it was being defined in nineteenth-century America and debated in Europe, had given a new dimension to the ancient problem of liberty. It presented on the one hand the promise of a larger, more encompassing, and more benevolent freedom, and on the other the threat of a new kind of tyranny, one for which the societies of the Old World were unprepared. For what now remains of those barriers that formerly arrested tyranny, Tocqueville asked, since religion has lost its empire over the souls of men, the most prominent boundary that divides good from evil is overthrown, and everything seems doubtful and indeterminate in the moral world? Kings and nations are guided by chance, and none can say where are the natural limits of despotism. Revolutions have forever destroyed the respect that surrounds rulers of the state, and since they have been relieved from the burden of public esteem, princes may henceforth surrender themselves without fear to the intoxication of arbitrary power. (For princes, you can of

† Henry Steele Commager (1902–1998) was an American historian and prolific author who taught history and American studies at Amherst College, Columbia University, and New York University. This selection is from *Commager on Tocqueville*. Copyright © 1993 by Henry and Mary Commager. Reprinted by permission of the University of Missouri Press.

course read führers or other leaders who took over in the twentieth century.)

Let us begin, then, with what is indubitably the most familiar and perhaps the most influential of Tocqueville's prognostications, that because in a democracy the majority will inevitably seek to tyrannize over minorities, democracy may prove incompatible with liberty. It was not a new idea, not even in America, nor is it one that has outlived its use; I do not say its usefulness. It was the very basis of the argument for checks and balances that John Adams elaborated in his ponderous defense of the constitutions of the United States. It runs like a black thread through the arguments of the state ratifying conventions of the 1780s by those whom Cecelia Kenyon has called "men of little faith." It was sound Federalist doctrine in Hamilton, Fisher Ames, and Gouverneur Morris, even though less ostentatiously in Justice John Marshall, and it was accepted by his ablest contemporary, Chancellor Kent of New York. The argument is almost too familiar to reiterate. A few samples will suffice.

Here is John Adams, who elaborated the theory more than any other, reminding his countrymen that "the experience of all ages has proved that the people constantly give away their liberties. The management of the executive and judicial powers together always corrupts them, and throws the whole power into the hands of the most profligate and abandoned among them." And he added that if the majority were ever to control the government, "debts would be abolished, taxes laid heavy on the rich and not at all on others, and the idle, the vicious, the intemperate would rush into the utmost extravagance of debauchery."

Here is Alexander Hamilton in his dramatic attack on the Virginia and New Jersey Plans of Union: "The voice of the people has been said to be the voice of God, however, generally this maxim has been outdated. It is not true to fact. Give therefore to the rich a distinct and permanent share of the government. They will check the unsteadiness of the second branch whose turbulence and uncontrollable disposition requires checks."

Or to paraphrase Chancellor Kent, resisting to the end the proposal to draw from the suffrage in New York State: "The extreme democratic principle when applied to the legislative and executive departments has been regarded with terror by the wise men of every age because in every European republic, ancient or modern, in which it has been tried, it has terminated disastrously, and been productive of corruption in justice, violence, and tyranny. Dare we flatter ourselves that we are a peculiar people, a question that has run down the corridors of our history and been answered by a resounding yes from one side and a querulous no from the other."

Fear of equality has always been with us, and fear of democracy too, and we could compile a depressing anthology of jeremiads from the early years of the Republic to the collapse of the southern Confederacy. To do so, however, would be an exercise in masochism. Captiousness of human depravity was, of course, deeply rooted in Puritanism, where it was, intellectually at least, respectable. It lingered on, long after its religious rationale had been dissipated, to find dubious justifications and misgivings about the impact of social equality upon a stable and comfortable society, a society that feared any undermining, any subversion of its prosperity, feared also political equality and the civility of the legal order, as well as the degeneration of Puritan morality into private irritability.

When we contemplate the objections that emerged in the early years of the Republic, we must agree with Henry Adams in that famous paragraph where he writes that the obstinacy of the race was never better shown than when, with the sunlight of the nineteenth century burst in upon them, those resolute sons of granite and ice turned their faces from the sight and smiled in their sardonic way at the folly and wickedness of men who would pretend to believe that the world improved because henceforth the ignorant and the vicious were to rule the United States and govern the churches and schools of New England.

In one form or another, this debate, launched at the very birth of the Republic, still persists; the debate between those who believe that government is safe only in the hands of those whom John Adams called the rich and the wellborn and the able, and those who ask rather the question Jefferson put in his first inaugural address: "Sometimes it is said that man cannot be trusted with the government of himself. Can he, then, be trusted with the government of others? Or have we found angels in the forms of kings to govern him?"

The persistence of this controversy is not surprising, for it centers on a paradox inherent in the philosophy and structure of our government and perhaps never is to be resolved. It is a paradox that has perplexed our wisest statesmen. Here is Jefferson, putting it almost unconsciously in that same first inaugural address: "All," he said, "will bear in mind this sacred principle, that though the will of the majority is in all cases to prevail, that will, to be rightful, must be reasonable." Sixty years later, Lincoln, himself a minority president, asserted that a majority held in restraint by constitutional checks and limitations is the only true sovereign of a free people. Whoever rejects it does of necessity fly into anarchy or despotism.

There it is. All Power inheres in the people, but the people, but the people may not exercise all power. The will of the majority must prevail, but only if it is righteous. The majority is a true sovereign, but only when held in check by balances and limitations. It is a dualism that might be expected to baffle, if not paralyze, a people less resourceful than the Americans. They not only took it in their stride but triumphantly institutionalized it in their constitutional structure, for as the American Constitution was the first in history to incorporate the principle that men make government and that all government derives its authority from consent, it was also the first to place effective limits on government.

No wonder Tocqueville was baffled. He saw that in America the people were sovereign and had all power, and he knew that all power corrupts. He was familiar with the complex system of checks and limits that Americans had constructed to restrain the misuse of power and acknowledged that these were effective. But he knew, too, that the temptations of tyranny were stronger than the attractions of self-restraint, and he suspected that they were irresistible and predicted therefore a new kind of tyranny, one that would operate within the framework of constitutionalism but would nevertheless be just as inimical to liberty as the older and more familiar forms of tyranny that had crushed liberty through the whole of history. He predicted the tyranny of opinion.

Listen to him as he designs variations on this argument: first the indictment, as it were, next the specification of the error, and finally the sober prediction of consequences. In the principle of equality he very clearly discerned two tendencies, one leading the mind of every man to untried thoughts, the other prohibiting him from thinking at all. Under the dominion of certain laws, democracy would extinguish that liberty of the mind in which the democratic social condition is favorable, so that after having broken all the bondage once imposed upon it by ranks or by men, the human mind would be closely fettered to the general will by the greatest number.

Along with this is a series of almost aphoristic accusations: "The power of the majority in America," he said, is "not only preponderant, but irresistible"; "No obstacles exist which can impede or so much as retard its progress, or which can induce it to heed the complaints of those whom it crushes upon its path"; "the power of the majority surpasses all the powers with which we are acquainted in Europe." These are disparate, unconnected observations, but they all say the same thing. "Freedom of opinion does not exist in America." "So long as a majority is still undecided, discussion is carried on; but as soon as its decision is irrevocably pronounced, a submissive silence is observed; and the friends, as well as the opponents of a measure, unite in assenting to its propriety."

What all this means is that in America, legislature is supreme, so said Tocqueville. It is under a legal despotism, it is indeed a legal despotism, and this favors too the arbitrary power of the magistrate. The majority, he concluded, therefore has absolute power both to make laws and to watch over their execution. The result is indeed sobering:

> I know of no country in which there is so little true independence of mind and freedom of discussion as in America. . . . The sovereign can no longer say, "You shall think as I do on pain of death"; but he says, "You are free to think differently from me, and to retain your life, your property, and all you possess; but if such be your determination, you are henceforth an alien among your people. You may retain your civil rights, but they will be useless to you. . . . You will remain among men, but you will be deprived of the rights of mankind. Your fellow-creatures will shun you like an impure being; and those who are most persuaded of your innocence will abandon you too, lest they should be shunned in turn."

This also proved a somber prediction of what happened in the Mc-Carthy era.

Following that conclusion came the ominous forecast: "If ever the free institutions of America are destroyed, that even may be attributed to the unlimited authority of the majority, which may at some future time urge minorities to desperation, and oblige them to have recourse to physical force. Anarchy will then be the result, but it will have been brought about by despotism."

That Tocqueville's argument, based as it was wholly upon deductive reasoning, his logic flawed and his facts erroneous, has nevertheless commanded respect down to our own day is a tribute to his genius for intuitive insights. For though Tocqueville does not submit a scintilla of evidence drawn from the America of his own day to support these allegations of majority tyranny, we are uncomfortably aware that the future was to provide evidence enough, evidence to give comfort to the enemies of democracy. Although majority tyranny triumphed only briefly and sporadically in the United States (outside of the South), we know that it did in other modern democracies, with consequences more tragic than even Tocqueville could have imagined, as he was concerned with democracy in Europe rather than the United States.

Let us follow Tocqueville as he deals with the American scene and in American terms. Here we stumble at the very threshold at his almost willful failure to define his terms *tyranny* and *majority*. As we have known it, tyranny is arbitrary power, oppression, despotism, the authority of the gallows and the faggot and the rack. What Tocqueville had in mind was not this tyranny, not the tyranny of St. Bartholomew's Eve or the revocation of the Edict of Nantes, of James II and Lord Chief Justice Jeffries, of Robespierre, who had sent Tocqueville's grandfather to the guillotine, or of Napoleon. Nor was it the tyranny that drove Roger Williams to Narragansett Bay or smothered Quakers to death in the Bay Colony, or even that lawless violence which Patriots visited upon hapless Loyalists. No, it was something new, something peculiar to democracy, the tyranny of public opinion. It was moral, it was intellectual, it was psychological. It was disapproval of, and hostility and ostracism toward, those who would not conform, and it affected chiefly those whose convictions were superficial or whose courage was weak or whose positions were vulnerable. Doubtless such a tyranny was pernicious, but it was after all less dangerous than the more overt tyrannies of the Old World.

What of the term *majority*? The United States of the 1830s was the one nation where the concept of majority was respectable, the one nation where it was most nearly realized in practice in the Western world. Yet not during Tocqueville's lifetime, not perhaps until our own time, has it been fairly tested. While suffrage was broader in the United States in Tocqueville's day than elsewhere on the globe, it still did not represent a majority of the population. Not remotely, for it was limited to white adult males who met whatever qualifications state constitutions might impose upon its exercise. Blacks who were slave or free were everywhere excluded from the suffrage. So were women, and of course, those under twenty-one. Of those who were entitled to vote, somewhat less than one-fourth of the population, only a minority, generally bothered to exercise the right, except in presidential elections and a few hotly contested local elections. Approximately forty percent of those entitled to vote actually did so in the election of 1832, somewhat over fifty percent in 1840, and as much as sixty percent in 1852, which is about where we have got now. This was spectacular by Old World standards, but it still did not constitute a majority, only a majority of a minority, and it furnished therefore a most dubious basis for generalizations about majority tyranny.

Had Tocqueville chosen to pursue this thesis of majority tyranny later in life, that is, in his own life, he might have made out almost an incontrovertible case in his own country. In December 1851, over 8 million Frenchmen representing an overwhelming majority of the adult males went to the polls and ratified Louis Napoleon's coup d'état by a vote of 7.5 million in favor and 650,000 against. It was a dusky vindication.

But if we look to our own history, as Tocqueville did not when he formulated his history of majority tyranny, we find only sporadic and local examples of anything approaching majority tyranny, whether in the realm of politics or even in the realm of opinion. It is easy enough to recount these, and if we were to string together every example of tyranny from the Alien and Sedition Acts to Lincoln's wartime infringements on the freedom of the press, from the Ku Klux Klan in the Reconstruction era to McCarthyism in the 1950s, the chain would be formidable. But we should keep in mind Jefferson's response to the hysterical fears excited by Shays's Rebellion, that one rebellion in thirteen states in the course of eleven years—he might have said in the course of a hundred—is but one in a century and a half. No country should be so long without one.

Perhaps the most interesting observation to make of the Alien and Sedition Acts is, after all, that they inspired the Kentucky and Virginia Resolutions and were wiped off the statute books within two years. There was tyranny of a sort early in the nineteenth century in Rhode Island, but it was tyranny of a minority over a majority, and tyranny that skulked behind an archaic constitution, namely, the original charter. It was a majority that agitated and almost fought for the right of manhood suffrage, and won it, too—I speak of course of Dorr's so-called Rebellion. It was tyranny, just the kind Tocqueville had in mind, in the persecution of the Mormons both in Illinois and in Missouri. But the Mormons found refuge in the West, set up their own commonwealth, and proceeded to establish a majoritarian rule of their own, which a good many gentiles regarded as tyranny.

Clearly, the major example of tyranny in America, and we have only one clear-cut example of tyranny by definition, is slavery. Let us observe, however, several interesting things there: first that, oddly enough, though Tocqueville devoted a chapter to slavery and races in the United States, he did not cite slavery as an example of tyranny in his general discussion of that subject. This was, as it turned out, rather wise, because what we had here was quite clearly a tyranny of a minority, not a majority, a minority of slaveholders among southerners and the minority of all the whites in the nation itself. We need not enter into anything as familiar as that. Where, as I recall, the number of slaveholders in the United States in 1860 was 352,000, the white population of the South, the slaveholding South, was perhaps 8 million. The total number of the slaveholders in the South themselves represented a distinct minority, which alone was committed to slavery; though that South did extend to Delaware and Maryland, it was certainly a minority section of the United States.

In another sense, perpetuation of white supremacy even after the legal end of slavery did vindicate Tocqueville's insight. For just as non-slaveholders in the South supported slavery and were prepared to fight for it to the bitter end at Appomattox, and to nullify emancipation or at least to nullify freedom afterward, so the majority of whites both North and South perpetuated the principle of white supremacy all through the nineteenth and well into the twentieth century.

Slavery is gone. Constitutionally, blacks are entitled to all the rights and privileges of others and to equal protection of the laws. Yet discrimination lingers on. This can probably not be labeled tyranny, but doubtless to its victims it seems much like that.

While Tocqueville saw no solution to the problem of slavery and predicted that it would eventually destroy the Union, and perhaps democracy as well, he was aware of those countervailing forces that might mitigate majority tyranny among Americans. Americans, he pointed out, had made great and successful efforts to counteract the imperfections of human nature and to correct the natural defects of democracy, and he referred to the township system in New England; the strength of local attachments everywhere; the closeness of representatives to those who chose them; the factors of annual or frequent elections, which foreshadowed the later referendum; the role of political parties, which drew their juices from the people; the shifting tides of party strength; and the experience of the people themselves in self-government. His conclusion was a tribute to the patent good sense, indeed the political genius, of the American people: "To evils which are common to all democratic peoples, they have applied remedies which none but themselves had ever thought of before, and although they were the first to make the experiment, they have succeeded in it. The manners and laws of Americans are not the only ones which may suit a democratic people; but the Americans have shown that it would be wrong to despair of regulating democracy by the aid of manners and of laws."

Tocqueville is prepared to recognize this, but not to build upon it. Perhaps nowhere else in his *Democracy in America* does he so stubbornly reject reality for speculation. In this, almost needless to say, he has had many and more reckless successors.

For in fact nothing was more impressive about American democracy than the passion and the ingenuity with which Americans had celebrated their newfound freedom by devising elaborate restraints upon it and upon government, the most elaborate restraints, indeed, known to history. The contrast here between the American and the French revolutions was dramatic and sobering. Written constitutions in America, state and national, separations of powers, bills of rights that protected not only procedural but substantive liberties, the supremacy of civil power over the military power, bicameral legislatures, intricate checks and balances within every governmental structure, a federal system that distributed authority among government, judicial review of legislative acts and of executive conduct, political parties and a two-party system that imposed compromise on all its members and elements, recurrence at frequent and exact intervals to the popular will, power to impeach or remove offending public servants: all these were some of the formal checks that were designed by Americans to make official tyranny almost impossible.

Alongside these, Americans developed and still retain informal limits on power, probably no less effective than the formal. There is the elementary fact of size, which, especially in the early years of the Republic, favored legal and religious diversity, and which implacably imposed upon the American people the habit of concession and compromise. The one time that failed, namely in 1860, the Union broke asunder. There was a safety valve of mobility, geographical mobility on a continental scale, social and economic mobility within the national social scale, which effectively discouraged the development anywhere of a class order. There was—Tocqueville was one of the first to perceive this—that habit of voluntary association, to which we shall return, which constantly and ubiquitously created new interest groups, new alignments, new counterbalancing elements in society. There was the principle of the open door for immigration, which introduced, indeed invited into the body politic, ever new and unknown elements, whose impact could not be foreseen by or regulated by government. And along with all this was a negative factor of immense significance, the absence in the New World of those deep and passionate attachments or commitments, religious, ideological, or class, which elsewhere nourished and presided over fanaticism.

Americans, almost alone of Western people, have never had genuine religious wars, or even religious persecution, nothing like the persecution of the Huguenots, nothing like the pogroms against the Jews in Russia and elsewhere. The American parties are not ideological but mostly innocent of ideas, and their objectives are not to change society but to change office, a very legitimate objective, by the way, perhaps much better than the objective of changing society.

We can indeed put the mater more positively. The record of that half century of democracy which Tocqueville was able to observe up to the Jacksonian era demonstrated that majorities, that is, majorities of the existing body politic, far from being instruments of tyranny, had everywhere, except in the South where slavery was the issue, supported and advanced the causes of democracy and of freedom. They have written and endorsed the state constitutions and insisted upon adding bills of rights eventually to all of them, and when the Federal

Constitution appeared without such a bill of rights, it was public opinion, skillfully organized by Jefferson and his followers, that forced the Congress to add one. After the inauguration of the Republic, almost every advance in what we now think of as liberal reform came from pressure by majorities insofar as we are able to distinguish them. It was the Federalists, under the leadership of those who most deeply distrusted the people, who wrote the Alien and Sedition Acts, and the Jeffersonian Democrats (who, as it turned out, were the majority) who erased these from the statute books. It was the majorities within the states that clamored for the reform of state constitutions, looking to broader suffrage, the end of property qualifications for officeholding, and the abolition of special privilege for favored denominations—in short, for broader political and religious freedom. It was the majority, too, who supported liberal immigration policy, the speedy admission of new western states, the broad suffrage, a generous western land policy, appropriations for public education, the abolition of imprisonment by debt, and many other reforms.

If once again we are assailed by the sobering suspicion that though Tocqueville did not always see clearly or justly what was before his eyes, no man of his generation had a surer vision for the distant future. Majority rule did not prove inimical to liberty or to justice during the nineteenth century, nor during the early years of the twentieth. In the Wilsonian era and with gathering force thereafter, the clouds drew across the bright horizons. I need not recapitulate what is familiar enough to most: the Espionage and Sedition Acts of the First World War; the petty reign of terror under Attorney General Palmer, the worst attorney general in American history until Mitchell; the gaggle of state laws designed to curb or outlaw subversive parties and subversive ideas; the misguided decisions of the Supreme Court, from *Abrams v. the United States* to *Dennis v. the United States* thirty years later, that so severely circumscribed the freedoms of the First Amendment; the tyrannies and atrocities committed by the Ku Klux Klan and many kindred organizations; Japanese relocation (the very euphemism is an affront); the antics of the un-American activities committees, state and federal alike; the Smith Act; the Mundt-Nixon Act; the McCarran Internal Security Act; the obscenities in the McCarthy crusade, supported by otherwise respectable men like Senator Taft; and perhaps the gravest threat to freedom and the integrity of the Republic since slavery itself, President Nixon's subversion of the Constitution and the Bill of Rights. Yet these same years saw the triumph and enactment of programs greatly enlarging the suffrage, liberating labor from the fetters of ancient common-law restrictions, ending child labor, underwriting lavish national support to elementary and higher education, to arts, and to science—in short, transforming a laissez-faire state into a welfare state, a revolution that went far toward making a government for the people, as earlier revolutions had made it a government by the people; and its ultimate design was a creation of that more just society which Tocqueville himself thought the special beauty of a democratic system. No one could doubt that the majority supported Wilson's New Freedom, and that Franklin Roosevelt's New Deal and Lyndon Johnson's Great Society were meant to enlarge the realm of liberty.

Though Tocqueville's analysis of the tyranny of the majority was profound, it was in its anticipation of the American scene misguided. Majorities did not, perhaps because they could not, impose either lasting or widespread conformity on the American mind or spirit, nor did they exercise tyranny over American opinion or conduct. Tocqueville knew, too, that when men turned to the state to enlarge democracy and enhance justice, they inevitably strengthened the centralized government and brought into being a giant bureaucracy. These, Tocqueville thought, were the implacable enemies of liberty.***

JAMES T. KLOPPENBERG

Life Everlasting: Tocqueville in America†

Democracy in America is not a classic text—at least if one accepts Mark Twain's definition of a classic as a book everyone wants to have read but no one wants to read. By that measure Locke's *Essay Concerning Human Understanding* might be a classic, or perhaps Hegel's *Phenomenology of Spirit* or James's *Principles of Psychology*. But by Twain's standard *Democracy in America* emphatically is not a classic, because it is a book that people continue to read and reread, a book that continues to engage readers and repay their efforts, a book cited and endorsed by both Newt Gingrich and Bill Clinton at their parties' National Conventions in the summer of 1996. It is also a book everyone wants to write about, judging from the hundreds of books and articles on Tocqueville and his ideas flowing from European and American writers in many different disciplines.

The topic of this essay, the status of Tocqueville in America, has generated so much attention that merely summarizing what has already been written on the subject could fill a short book.[1] Instead I will trace only in barest outline the shifting varieties of interpretation and levels of interest in Tocqueville among Americans, then hazard a tentative explanation of the current obsession with him, which may be the only thing Pat Buchanan and Hillary Clinton have in common.

Americans' continuing fascination with *Democracy in America* is easy to understand; Tocqueville himself was the first to explain it. In a letter to his friend Eugène Stoffels, made available to American read-

† James T. Kloppenberg is the David Woods Kemper '41 Professor of American History at Harvard University and the author of *The Virtues of Liberalism*. This essay appeared in *The Tocqueville Review* 17 (1996). Reprinted by permission of La Société Tocqueville.

1. Among the many overviews of this subject, the most valuable include Lynn Marshall and Seymour Drescher, "American Historians and Tocqueville's Democracy," *Journal of American History* 55 (1968): 512–532; Robert Nisbet, "Many Tocquevilles," *American Scholar* 46 (1976): 59–75; and Sean Wilentz, "Many Democracies: On Tocqueville and Jacksonian America," in Abraham S. Eisenstadt, ed., *Reconsidering Tocqueville's "Democracy in America"* (New Brunswick, N. J.: Rutgers University Press, 1988), pp. 207–228.

ers in John Bigelow's introduction to his 1899 edition of *Democracy in America*, Tocqueville stated his goal: he wanted to show his readers that the reality of popular government was neither so grand as its friend' estimates nor so awful as its enemies' fears. He sought to demonstrate, he wrote, that democracy has

> none of the elevated features with which [its champions'] imagination would endow it; and, moreover, that such a government can not be maintained without certain conditions of intelligence, of private morality, and of religious belief that we [French], as a nation, have not reached, and that we must labour to attain before grasping their political results. To those for whom the word democracy is synonymous with destruction, anarchy, spoliation, and murder, I have tried to show that under a democratic government the fortunes and rights of society may be respected, liberty preserved, and religion honoured; that though a republic may develop less than other governments some of the noblest powers of the human mind, it yet has a nobility of its own; and that, after all, it may be God's will to spread a moderate amount of happiness over all men, instead of heaping a large sum upon a few by allowing only a small minority to approach perfection.[2]

That passage, which echoes the concluding words of Tocqueville's second volume, signals the essential tension in *Democracy in America*, the ambivalence that gives Tocqueville's analysis its richness and makes possible the multiple readings offered by his many interpreters.

"I please many persons of opposite opinions," Tocqueville continued to Stoffels in a revealing admission, "not because they penetrate my meaning, but because, looking only to one side of my work, they think they find in it arguments in favour of their own convictions. But I have faith in the future, and I hope that the day will come when all will see clearly what now only a few suspect."[3] Whether or not that latter day has come, Tocqueville was right about the reasons for his enthusiastic initial reception in America. Many of the early reviewers of the book, like many of those with whom he spoke during his travels, were members of the American gentry about whom Daniel Walker Howe has written brilliantly in *The Political Culture of the American Whigs*. "Ordered liberty" was these ambivalent republicans' principal value.[4] Their complex combination of a longing for stability together with an appreciation of the republican principles of liberty and equality strongly resembled Tocqueville's own sensibility. Since these proto-

2. Tocqueville's February, 1835, letter to Eugene Stoffels in John Bigelow's introduction to his edition of *Democracy in America*, trans. Henry Reeve (New York: D. Appleton and Company, 1899), p. xiii.
3. *Ibid.*, p. xiv.
4. Daniel Walker Howe, *The Political Culture of the American Whigs* (Chicago: University of Chicago Press, 1979). See also the discussion of this theme in Howe's more wide-ranging study of self-discipline in American thought, *Virtue, Passion, and Politics: The Construction of the Self in American Thought, From Jonathan Edwards to Abraham Lincoln and Beyond* (Cambridge: Harvard University Press, forthcoming); and the discussion of "ordered freedom" in early New England in David Hackett Fischer, *Albion's Seed: Four British Folkways in America* (New York: Oxford University Press, 1979).

Whigs were among the most important of Tocqueville's sources, and since they were prominent among his reviewers, there is nothing surprising in the congruence between his account and their perceptions, which also accounts for the initial enthusiasm of his early American interpreters.

The first American edition of *Democracy in America* was published in 1838 with a preface written by the Whig attorney and New York state assemblyman John C. Spencer, who had discussed America with Tocqueville during his visit. Spencer emphasized the multidimensionality of Tocqueville's analysis and identified it as one of the two main sources of the immediate flurry of interest in the book in the United States. Tocqueville, Spencer wrote, "has discussed many subjects on which very different opinions are entertained in the United States; but with an ability, a candour, and an evident devotion to the cause of truth, which will commend his views to those who most radically dissent from them. Indeed, readers of the most discordant opinions will find that he frequently agrees with both sides, and as frequently differs from them."[5] If there was not always something in Tocqueville for everyone to like, there was at least something every American reader was likely to find intriguing.

The second reason for Americans' initial enthusiasm is more straightforward. Tocqueville's account was distinctive, as John Bigelow admitted candidly in his 1899 introduction, because "it was the first book written about the United States by any European of repute that was not conceived in a spirit of disparagement and detraction."[6] Frances Trollope, to cite only one prominent example, was disgusted by the fruits of democracy. She detested Americans' hypocrisy as slaveholders who proclaimed their love of liberty; their table manners, which made every trip to the dinner table a nightmare; and especially their proclamations of equality, which the most ignorant and untalented made with the greatest fervor.[7] In one of the most entertaining sections of his recent study of American democracy, *Self-Rule*, Robert Wiebe catalogs the numerous travellers' accounts of America written by Europeans in the early nineteenth century. He concludes that in the great chain of being, the typical portrait placed American citizens somewhere between pigs and dogs.[8] No wonder Tocqueville's account stood out. It was, in the words of the review published in *The United States Magazine and Democratic Review*, "decidedly the most remarkable and really valuable work that has yet appeared upon this country from the hand of a foreigner. . . The difference between M. Tocqueville and our common herd of travellers, is, that when he

5. John C. Spencer's Preface to *Democracy in America*, trans. Henry Reeve (New York: Dearborn, 1838), p. vii.
6. Bigelow's Introduction, p. xii.
7. Frances Trollope, *Domestic Manners of the Americans* (London, 1832). The best compilation of travelers' accounts remains the collection *Abroad in America: Visitors to the New Nation, 1776–1914*, ed. Marc Pachter and Frances Stevenson Wein (Reading, Mass.: Addison-Wesley, 1976); see especially Marcus Cunliffe's delightful essay on Trollope, pp. 33–42.
8. Robert H. Wiebe, *Self-Rule: A Cultural History of American Democracy* (Chicago: University of Chicago Press, 1995), pp. 61–85.

speaks of the principles of government he knows what he is talking of." In other words, Tocqueville alone could distinguish democratic activity in America from the behavior of barnyard animals.[9]

Democracy in America was wildly praised and widely adopted as a textbook in the schools popping up like mushrooms across America. But toward the turn of the twentieth century the book fell out of fashion—and out of print. Robert Nisbet has argued, and Wilfred McClay has recently concurred, that Tocqueville's account disappeared because his positive assessment of American democracy was drowned in a flood of equally enthusiastic celebrations.[1] I think that assessment misses the mark. It was instead the prevalence of conflict that submerged Tocqueville's Democracy. Conflict caused Americans to doubt the wisdom of Tocqueville's analysis, because they interpreted Democracy in America as stressing an underlying national consensus on basic values. By the end of the nineteenth century, the evidence of discord had become inescapable.

It is generally agreed that this interpretation of Tocqueville, which highlights his identification of what Americans had in common, accounted for his dramatic revival in the America of the 1940s and 1950s. It also accounts for the somewhat tiresome recitation by more recent American historians of all the conflicts in American society in the 1830s to which Tocqueville supposedly paid insufficient attention. In much the same way, the obvious breakdown of American consensus likewise explains the temporary disappearance of Tocqueville in the years from the outbreak of the Civil War until the outbreak of World War II.

This was a period marked by dramatic and violent disagreements among Americans on a wide variety of issues, including not only the questions of slavery and race relations that lay behind the Civil War and hovered over the post-war years, but also the destruction of American Indian cultures, the influx of immigration and the resulting controversy over religious and ethnic diversity, and the related struggles between labor and management, and between rural America and the emerging urban majority, over the economic as well as political meanings of democracy in America.

The almost complete lack of interest in Tocqueville among the most prominent progressive historians such as Frederick Jackson Turner and Charles Beard—historians struggling to make sense of their conflict-ridden nation—confirms this somewhat unconventional explanation of Tocqueville's eclipse. Confirmation of a different sort comes from noting that Henry Adams, arguably the least representative American historian writing at the end of the nineteenth century,

9. The anonymous assessment published in The United States Magazine and Democratic Review is quoted by Thomas Bender in an excellent introduction written for his recent edition of Democracy in America (New York: The Modern Library, 1981), p. xli. See also Bender's judicious article on Tocqueville in A Companion to American Thought, ed. Richard Wightman Fox and James T. Kloppenberg (Oxford: Blackwell Publishers, 1995), pp. 676–678.

1. Nisbet, "Many Tocquevilles"; Wilfred McClay, The Masterless: Self and Society in Modern America (Chapel Hill, N. C.: University of North Carolina Press, 1994), pp. 42ff., 235f., 252ff.

was almost alone in declaring himself a disciple of Tocqueville.[2] Although not quite a rule of American culture, it is nearly always true that wherever Henry Adams stood, at any stage of his life, scarcely anyone else could be found.

The resurgence of American interest in Tocqueville of course dates from the publication of George W. Pierson's landmark study *Tocqueville and Beaumont in America* in 1938 and the subsequent republication of several editions of *Democracy in America* in the mid- to late 1940s.[3] This wave crested twice, initially carrying the arguments of Tocqueville's first volume into American political discourse, then extending the subtler arguments of his second volume into broader and deeper assessments of American society and culture.

The first wave was launched by the emergence of what came to be called totalitarian governments in Europe. Americans in the 1930s and 1940s were searching for explanations of how European democracies such as Germany and Italy could have gone so wrong, and how the Soviet Union could have devolved so rapidly from a utopian experiment into a dangerous dystopia. *Democracy in America* seemed to offer a clue—or rather many clues. The first was Tocqueville's warning that the quest for equality could lead to the tyranny of the majority, in which the voices of dissent were stifled by an oppressive conformism, an all powerful centralized government, or a combination of the two that seemed ominously familiar in the 1940s, especially after European refugee intellectuals began arriving in America.

When Dwight MacDonald published his essay "A Theory of Mass Culture" in 1953, he brought into sharp focus the scattered anxieties that had been expressed in various writings by European and American social and cultural critics such as Erich Fromm, Hannah Arendt, Theodor Adorno, and Leo Lowenthal. Critiques of MacDonald, such as Daniel Bell's in *The End of Ideology*, tried to place the argument in a broader historical framework and to separate the critique of conformity from the often Marxist presuppositions—the ideology, to use Bell's term—behind it. Such analysts were turning away from the confident radicalism of the preceding decades toward something else. Whereas American thinkers in the first half of the twentieth century might have looked toward Jefferson or perhaps Marx for inspiration, a new generation of intellectuals looked instead to the less comforting but apparently more incisive wisdom of thinkers such as Max Weber,

2. Marshall and Drescher, "American Historians and Tocqueville's *Democracy*," p. 514 n. 7, point out that Adams drew heavily from Tocqueville in his *History of the United States during the Administrations of Thomas Jefferson and James Madison* (1891–98): " 'I have learned to think De Tocqueville my model,' wrote Adams in a letter of 1863, 'and I study his life and works as the Gospel of my private religion.' "
3. George Wilson Pierson, *Tocqueville and Beaumont in America* (New York: Oxford University Press, 1938). The first mass-market edition of *Democracy in America* appeared in 1945 with a revised translation and an extensive introduction by Phillips Bradley and a foreword by Harold Laski (New York: Knopf, 1945). A second, even less expensive abridged edition was published two years later with an introduction by Henry Steele Commager (New York: Oxford University Press, 1947). It is in this form, or in subsequent abridgements including that edited by Richard Heffner (New York: Mentor Books, 1956), that generations of students have encountered *Democracy in America* in its guise as, in Heffner's phrase, "a tract for our times" (p. 9).

who made his first appearance in translation in the 1940s, Karl Mannheim, who called in *Ideology and Utopia* for replacing faith in all-encompassing philosophical systems by reliance on the critical intelligence of independent intellectuals, and especially Tocqueville, who began making cameo appearances everywhere. The first President of the United States to quote Tocqueville was Dwight D. Eisenhower; since then his words have appeared in the speeches of every President.[4]

Tocqueville played starring roles in books such as Louis Hartz's *The Liberal Tradition in America*, published in 1955, and Marvin Meyers's *The Jacksonian Persuasion*, published in 1956. Sandwiched between those was political scientist Clinton Rossiter's apt (and typical) observation in 1955: "No book on an American subject is thought complete these days without a few insightful words from Alexis de Tocqueville," to which Rossiter then added a few insightful words from Tocqueville to nail down the point. Hartz's widely accepted notion of a liberal tradition could have been taken almost without modification from the opening pages of *Democracy in America* (although it could hardly have been sustained by a more careful reading of both volumes). Meyers brilliantly portrayed Jacksonian America as a land of "venturous conservatives" whose paradoxical invocations of the past and bold departures from it could best be explained through Tocqueville's nuanced and multi-dimensional analysis. In short, arguments drawn from *Democracy in America* were ubiquitous in the works of American social scientists during the 1950s. As the idea of American democracy emerged as a normative concept in both the critical and celebratory studies of American consensus produced in the early years of the Cold War, Tocqueville was everywhere.[5]

Perhaps Tocqueville's deepest impact registered in sociology, thanks

4. Dwight Macdonald's "A Theory of Mass Culture" was reprinted, along with a variety of post-WWII commentaries and earlier sources—including of course an excerpt from *Democracy in America*—in David Manning White and Bernard Rosenberg, eds., *Mass Culture: The Popular Arts in America* (New York: The Free Press, 1957). On Bell see *The End of Ideology*, revised edition with a new afterward (1962; Cambridge: Harvard University Press, 1988); and Howard Brick, *Daniel Bell and the Decline of Intellectual Radicalism: Social Theory and Political Reconciliation in the 1940s* (Madison: University of Wisconsin Press, 1986).
5. Clinton Rossiter, *The American Presidency* (New York, 1956), quoted by Marshall and Drescher, "American Historians and Tocqueville's *Democracy*," pp. 515–516; Louis Hartz, *The Liberal Tradition in America* (New York: Harcourt, Brace, and World, 1955); Marvin Meyers, *The Jacksonian Persuasion: Politics and Belief* (Stanford: Stanford University Press, 1957). On the normative status of American democracy in the post-WWII period, see especially Edward A. Purcell, Jr., *The Crisis of Democratic Theory: Scientific Naturalism and the Problem of Value* (Lexington: University Press of Kentucky, 1973). A still common misperception of Tocqueville's analysis of American democracy stems from an error contained in the epigraph to the original printing of Hartz's *Liberal Tradition in America*, an error whose survival, even after it was corrected in later editions of Hartz's book, underscores the power of the image of Tocqueville as a champion of individual freedom created in the 1940s and 1950s. Whereas Tocqueville wrote that "Americans have this great advantage, that they attained democracy without the sufferings of a democratic revolution and that they were born equal instead of becoming so," Hartz's epigraph read ". . . they are born free, instead of becoming so." [See *Democracy in America*, ed. J. P. Mayer, trans. George Lawrence (Garden City, N.Y.: Anchor Books, 1969), p. 509. All further quotations from *Democracy in America* are from this now-standard edition.] Illustrating the continuing vitality of this misunderstanding, John Patrick Diggins, in his widely read *The Lost Soul of American Politics: Virtue, Self-Interest, and the Foundations of Liberalism* (New York: Basic Books, 1984), pp. 35, 345, twice misquotes Tocqueville as having written that Americans were "born free."

initially to the dramatic success of David Riesman's argument in *The Lonely Crowd* (1953), hailed by academic specialists and the popular press alike as the key to understanding modern America. Riesman littered his book with quotations from Tocqueville, whose insights into the dangers lurking beneath prosperity framed and informed the book's analysis. Beyond the shift from nineteenth-century "inner directed" to post-WWII "other-directed" individuals, Riesman held out an ideal of "autonomy" for those strong enough, and far-seeing enough, to embrace the ironic sensibility he seemed to derive from, and to identify with, the wisdom of Tocqueville. The defense against mass culture, and the shield that protected America from the tyranny of the majority, could be found through careful study of *Democracy in America.*[6]

Throughout the 1950s and the long 1960s, which ended only in 1974 with the resignation of Richard Nixon and America's withdrawal from Vietnam, Tocqueville was a staple in the curriculum of American universities. For conservatives such as Robert Nisbet at Berkeley (or Vincent Starzinger at Dartmouth College, where I first encountered *Democracy in America* as a student), Tocqueville was a sober prophet who saw through the promise of material prosperity and egalitarian ideals to the hollowness at the core of modern democratic cultures that had lost touch with the values of tradition and authority. For members of the New Left, whom I also encountered at Dartmouth and as a graduate student at Stanford, Tocqueville was the scourge of conformism, a sober prophet who saw through the promise of material prosperity and egalitarian ideals to the invisible oppression that Herbert Marcuse was laying bare in books like *One-Dimensional Man* and *Essay on Liberation.*[7]

Tocqueville's odd stature as a sage revered by conservatives and radicals alike merely confirmed the accuracy of his own early assessment in the letter to Stoffels already quoted. He was still attractive to "many persons of opposite opinions," as he put it, because they were "looking only to one side" of his work and finding there "arguments in favour of their own convictions." That tendency has continued for a century and a half, and there is no reason to suspect that it will soon come to an end.

Tocqueville's eternal life in America is due partly to the *lack* of congruence between his ideas and those prevailing in American politics at any time, which makes possible his adoption by disparate guardians eager to embrace him for their own purposes. By his own admission he was neither simply a democrat nor simply an aristocrat. He fits only awkwardly into our categories of Hamiltonian or Jeffersonian, republi-

6. David Riesman et al., *The Lonely Crowd: A Study of the Changing American Character* (New Haven: Yale University Press, 1969). For an excellent discussion of Riesman and his use of Tocqueville in the context of post-WWII American social science, see McClay, *The Masterless,* pp. 226–268.
7. Vincent E. Starzinger, *Middlingness: Juste Milieu Theory in France and England, 1815–1848* (Charlottesville: University Press of Virginia, 1965); Herbert Marcuse, *One-Dimensional Man: Studies in the Ideology of Advanced Industrial Society* (Boston: Beacon Press, 1964); Marcuse, *An Essay on Liberation* (Boston: Beacon Press, 1969).

can or democrat, conservative or liberal. For that reason we characterize him, as Meyers did, as a "venturous conservative," or as Roger
Boesche has done recently, as a "strange liberal," or as Alan Kahan has
done even more recently, as an "aristocratic liberal."[8] But for reasons
Tocqueville himself made clear, such characterizations are inadequate:
recall his admission that he had "faith in the future" and his hope that
eventually "all will see clearly what now only a few suspect." Has that
day come?

At the considerable risk of appearing to pull a rabbit from a hat, in
my conclusion I will attempt to show clearly what only a few of
Tocqueville's interpreters have suspected. It is possible to see what
Tocqueville was driving at, to see both sides of his argument, by looking carefully at what remains constant in both of the quite different
volumes of his Democracy. It is by now a commonplace that these two
volumes differed considerably from one another in their tone, and
even in their arguments, largely because of developments in France
between Tocqueville's completion of volume one in 1835 and his completion of volume two in 1840. The first volume focuses on his fear
that majority tyranny will stifle dissent; the second that there will be
no dissent to stifle but only conformity. The first volume worries that
uncontrolled passions will lead to tyranny; the second that there will
be no passions to control but only torpor. The first volume registers no
concern with industrialization; the second expresses Tocqueville's
alarm (following his visit to England) about the dangers of a new industrial aristocracy, and so on.

Given those differences, what, if any, are the threads connecting the
two volumes? There are at least two. First, the characteristic of American democracy that has impressed commentators on Tocqueville from
the earliest to the most recent is the importance of voluntary associations. Participation in such associations prepares Americans for civic
life by prompting them to focus on solving concrete problems as members of community groups of all kinds, from the most benevolent
and/or ambitious to the most self-serving and/or trivial. Serving on juries leads them to imagine themselves in each other's shoes.[9] All of
these experiences prevent "self interest properly understood," to use
that crucial phrase of Tocqueville's, from degenerating into the old-
fashioned egoism that earlier moralists abhorred or the equally un-
attractive, new-fangled individualism that Tocqueville portrays as a
danger in volume two. Both egoism and individualism were inimical to
democracy.

Why did Tocqueville think voluntary associations, service on juries,
and all kinds of participation in public affairs mattered so much? He
certainly did not consider Americans uniquely virtuous. In fact, he re-

8. Meyers, The Jacksonian Persuasion, pp. 33–56; Roger Boesche, The Strange Liberalism of
Alexis de Tocqueville (Ithaca: Cornell University Press, 1988); Alan Kahan, Aristocratic Liberalism: The Social and Political Thought of Jacob Burckhardt, John Stuart Mill, and Alexis de
Tocqueville (New York: Oxford University Press, 1992).
9. For a Tocquevillean account of deliberation as the democratic means toward the end of
reaching unanimous verdicts, see Jeffrey Abramson, We, the Jury: The Jury System and the
Ideal of Democracy (New York: Free Press, 1994).

fused even to associate "self interest properly understood" with virtue, either in its republican or Christian forms.[1] But he did identify it closely with the practice of deliberation and the ethic of reciprocity, which he believed associational life fosters and which makes democracy work. The *experience* of associational life inclines Americans toward benevolence, or sympathy, whether they are virtuous or not. Even at the end of volume two, where Tocqueville confessed his anxiety about the threat of government centralization in democratic cultures lacking this practice of deliberation and the ethic of reciprocity that undergrids it—democratic nations such as France—he emphasized this feature of American democracy:

> It is through political associations that Americans of every station, outlook, and age day by day acquire a general taste for association and get familiar with the way to use the same. Through them large numbers see, speak, listen, and stimulate each other to carry out all sorts of undertakings in common. Then they carry these conceptions with them into the affairs of civil life and put them to a thousand uses (524).

In America, he wrote in the concluding pages of volume two, "interest as well as sympathy prompts a code of lending each other mutual assistance at need. The more similar conditions become, the more do people show this readiness of reciprocal obligation" (572).

This ideal of reciprocity, which underlay the exercise of deliberation in voluntary associations and in public life that was central to what Tocqueville meant by democracy, provides the thread of continuity between the two volumes of *Democracy in America*. It is reciprocity that prevents a tyrannical majority from stifling dissent through the decentralization of authority in volume one; it is reciprocity, or sympathy, that prevents the decline of "self interest properly understood" into egoism or selfish inwardness in volume two. Tocqueville valued associational life for the same reasons James Madison did, reasons seldom grasped by pluralists in the 1950s but now more sharply in focus thanks to the later work of Marvin Meyers and the work of Drew McCoy and Lance Banning. Madison, like Tocqueville, believed that as a result of participating in common projects, people learn something that transcends the simple clash of competing interests envisioned by political scientists writing about pluralism. Through the process of confronting and filtering different ideas, clashing interests, and divergent ideals, people in associations can learn to see things from other points of view. To translate this very old insight into the hip lexicon of contemporary cultural studies, encountering the other teaches people how to think dialogically, to appreciate the instabilities and complexi-

---

1. This remains a common misunderstanding of Tocqueville's assessment. At the conclusion of a film shown immediately before Bill Clinton's speech accepting his party's nomination for President at the Democratic Party Convention in Chicago on August 29, 1996, the President explained that his political career had helped him see again a truth he traced to Tocqueville: "America is great," Clinton proclaimed, "because America is good." Although familiar, and perhaps effective as election-year rhetoric, such claims are quite distant from Tocqueville's sober denial of Americans' superior civic or moral virtue.

LIFE EVERLASTING: TOCQUEVILLE IN AMERICA   843

ties of judgment. That hope underlay Madison's commitment to federalism, just as it underlay Tocqueville's stubborn refusal to dismiss the possibility that democracy in America might survive despite the dangers it faced.[2]

A similar hope animates the writings of a diverse group of contemporary thinkers who likewise do not fit comfortably into the standard categories of American politics. just as Tocqueville's analysis was attractive to readers of various persuasions but also somewhat unsettling—or "strange," to use Boesche's word again—so contemporaries who look to deliberation, and who embrace an ethic of reciprocity, do not fit our standard categories. Several of these writers, some of whom are called communitarians because they share Tocqueville's enthusiasm for the potential of association and his concerns for what happens to democracy when participation in community life vanishes and unbounded individualism triumphs, cluster around the journal *The Responsive Community*.

They include those associated with Robert Bellah in the project that became *Habits of the Heart*;[3] Harvard law professor Mary Ann Glendon, who has savaged the absurdities of *Rights Talk*, to use the title of her unclassifiable book;[4] historians such as Thomas Bender, whose studies of community and public life have helped keep alive Tocqueville's own insights into American democracy;[5] those political activists allied with Senator Bill Bradley who share the reasons for his dissatisfaction with both the Democratic and the Republican parties; and political theorists such as William Galston, who served for several years as a domestic advisor in the Clinton White House; Jane Mansbridge, who has shown the breadth of social scientists' dissatisfaction with the reductionist attribution of all human behavior to self-interest; and Jean Bethke Elshtain, who argues in her recent book *Democracy on Trial* that Americans' growing cynicism about politics, the absence of civic mindedness, and a destructive obsession with rights have sapped the mutual respect, empathy, and understanding that are necessary for the survival of a democratic community.[6] Such thinkers write in the

2. See Marvin Meyers, ed., *The Mind of the Founder: Sources of the Political Thought of James Madison* (Hanover, N.H.: University Press of New England, 1981); Drew R. McCoy, *The Elusive Republic: Political Economy in Jeffersonian America* (New York: Norton, 1980); and especially Lance Banning, *The Sacred Fire of Liberty: James Madison and the Founding of the Federal Republic* (Ithaca: Cornell University Press, 1995). I have discussed these issues in "The Virtues of Liberalism: Christianity, Republicanism, and Ethics in Early American Political Discourse," *The Journal of American History* 74 (1987): 9–33; and "The Republican Idea in American History and Historiography," *La Revue Tocqueville/The Tocqueville Review* 13 (1992): 119–136.
3. Robert Bellah et al., *Habits of the Heart: Individualism and Commitment in American Life* (Berkeley: University of California Press, 1985); and the later volume by Bellah et al., *The Good Society* (New York: Knopf, 1991). See also the work of William Sullivan, the member of the Bellah group most concerned with questions of philosophy and political theory, *Reconstructing Public Philosophy* (Berkeley: University of California Press, 1982).
4. Mary Ann Glendon, *Rights Talk: The Impoverishment of Political Discourse* (New York: Free Press, 1991).
5. Thomas Bender, *Toward an Urban Vision: Ideas and Institutions in Nineteenth-Century America* (Baltimore: Johns Hopkins University Press, 1975); Bender, *Community and Social Change in America* (New Brunswick, N. J.: Rutgers University Press, 1978).
6. William Galston, *Liberal Purposes: Goods, Virtues, and Diversity in the Liberal State* (Cambridge: Cambridge University Press, 1991); Jane Mansbridge, ed., *Beyond Self Interest*

spirit of Tocqueville, most of them explicitly acknowledge their debt to him, and all of them show that they have grasped both sides of his argument in *Democracy in America* because of the attention they pay to associational life and to the other common thread connecting both of Tocqueville's volumes, the importance of religious faith.

This dimension of Tocqueville's argument is more important than most American commentators in the last fifty years have appreciated. I will explain why indirectly, by turning to a phrase made familiar by the political scientist Robert Putnam in his widely read essay "Bowling Alone." Putnam, like the scholars and activists just mentioned, worries that America is losing the rich associational life that impressed Tocqueville. Such densely textured public life, according to Putnam's study of Italian politics over the last few centuries, *Making Democracy Work*, also explains the difference between the relatively stable cultures of Northern Italy and the chaos of the South. When Americans stop participating in voluntary associations such as little leagues, parent-teacher associations, Rotary clubs, and so on, civic life is impoverished. While the number of people bowling in America is rising, Putnam points out, the number of bowling leagues, and bowling teams, is falling. Thus we confront the haunting anomie of "bowling alone."[7]

But the associational life of such voluntary organizations is not always so warm and cuddly. When it became known that the primary suspect in the bombing of the federal building in Oklahoma City in the spring of 1994, Timothy McVeigh, and his friends, James and Terry Nichols, often went bowling together, it was clear American society would have been better off had each of them gone bowling alone. From that detour I return to the importance of religious faith for Tocqueville's analysis.

It is not clear that Tocqueville himself was religious; that vexed question may never be answered more thoroughly than it was by André Jardin in his biography of Tocqueville.[8] Nor is it clear that all of those identified as communitarians today are religious. But many of them endorse Tocqueville's judgment that nineteenth-century American democracy worked because of a shared commitment to the ethic of reciprocity and an orientation toward a future in which virtue would be rewarded and vice punished. From Tocqueville's perspective, the principal historical contribution of Christianity had been its revolutionary commitment to "the equality, the unity, the fraternity of all men," a commitment distinct from the prior acceptance of human inequality as inevitable. Moreover, Tocqueville insisted that even though some slave holders and their apologists professed a belief in Christianity, such ideas disgusted Christians who took seriously the brother-

(Chicago: University of Chicago Press, 1990); and Jean Bethke Elshtain, *Democracy on Trial* (New York: Basic Books, 1995).

7. See Robert D. Putnam, "Bowling Alone: America's Declining Social Capital," *Journal of Democracy*, January 1995; and Putnam, "Bowling Alone, Revisited," *The Responsive Community* 5 (1995): 18–33.

8. André Jardin, *Alexis de Tocqueville, 1805–1859* (Paris: Hachette, 1984), pp. 493–504.

hood of all races. Hypocrisy, however common, should not blind us to the ideals being mocked: "my heart rebels daily at seeing the little gentlemen who pass their time in clubs and wicked places, or great knaves who are capable of any base action as well as of, any act of violence, speak devoutly of *their holy religion*. I am always tempted to cry out to them: 'Be pagans with pure conduct, proud souls, and clean hands rather than Christians in this fashion.' "[9] Acknowledging the difference between Christian principles and the hypocrisy of some who call themselves Christians, as Tocqueville did, might make it possible to distinguish between murderous voluntary associations such as the Ku Klux Klan, the Mafia, and those wings of the militia movement currently attracting members like Timothy McVeigh, and associations committed to activities premised on an ethic of love rather than resentment.

Tocqueville argued in *Democracy* that the close connection between civic life and religious faith, which took various forms in the wildly diverse tapestry of America's ethnic communities, was possible in America only because the separation of church and state prevented an opposition from growing between individual liberty and religious institutions of the sort that an official state religion created in France and other European nations (289). In a democratic age, Tocqueville insisted, religion alone could draw people away from the materialism that might otherwise obsess them, thereby keeping alive the precious sense of mutual obligation that animated community life (445). "Despotism may be able to do without faith," Tocqueville reasoned, "but freedom cannot" (294).

In recent decades historians have underestimated the significance of this argument for the importance of religious faith, which Tocqueville advanced with reference to Pascal's wager. Historians have faulted Tocqueville for underestimating the importance of revivalism and for paying too much attention to the exceptional views of New England Unitarians.[1] That observation may be accurate. Yet it should not obscure the central importance of religion in Tocqueville's analysis. Religious faith was inextricably intertwined with associational life in the structure of his argument: as his emphasis on the Puritan concept of the covenant at the beginning of volume one makes clear, he believed that Americans' practice of association embodied the ethic of reciprocity that derived from their common Christian heritage. He also saw, as we should see just as clearly, that although such an ethic in principle elevates benevolence, in practice it could and did serve to justify slavery—or lynching, or assassination—activities driven by hatred instead of sympathy. Not by invocations of religiosity, then, but by the precise nature of the activities undertaken ostensibly under its in-

9. Tocqueville, *The European Revolution and Correspondences with Gobineau*, trans. John Lucacs (Gloucester, Mass.: Peter Smith, 1968), pp. 190f.; Tocqueville, *Selected Letters on Politics and Society*, ed. Roger Boesche, trans. James Toupin and Roger Boesche (Berkeley: University of California Press, 1985), pp. 342–344; and Joshua Mitchell, *The Fragility of Freedom: Tocqueville on Religion, Democracy, and the American Future* (Chicago: University of Chicago Press, 1995).
1. See for example Wilentz, "Many Democracies," pp. 209–210.

spiration, should the value of all forms of community organizing be judged.

I cannot claim too much originality for this argument. Indeed, my emphasis on the dual importance of voluntary associations and religious faith merely echoes Tocqueville's own, and that of his early American interpreters, as John Spencer pointed out in 1838 in his Preface to the first American edition of *Democracy in America*. Tocqueville's great achievement, Spencer concluded, derived from the connection between his "views of religion . . . [and] the democratic principle, which he steadily keeps in view." This insight, in Spencer's words, "cannot fail to confirm the principles already so thoroughly and universally entertained by the American people."[2] In other words, Tocqueville's sense of the mutual dependence of American democracy and American religiosity corresponded with Americans' understanding of themselves, a judgment I think most historians of nineteenth-century America now would share.[3]

The dual emphasis on voluntary associations and the civic value of religious faith, which enables us to bridge the gap between the first and second volumes of Tocqueville's *Democracy* and to see both sides of his argument, does help to account for the renewed intensity of engagement with Tocqueville that is apparent in much public debate in America today. Although that interest is hardly limited to those I have termed communitarians, their analyses are especially incisive because, like Tocqueville's, their ideas are less congruent with our rickety partisan categories of conservatism and liberalism than with the elusive and multi-dimensional realities of American democracy, which remain at least as complicated now as they were when Tocqueville first came to America.

Inasmuch as emphasizing the importance of reciprocity in *Democracy in America* helps focus attention on aspects of Tocqueville's analysis blurred by treatments that emphasized only his interest in individual freedom and voluntarism, it can serve to remind us of the delicate balance that characterizes his work and explains its perennial appeal. But exaggerating his emphasis on the ethic of reciprocity as the keystone of democracy would distort his arguments as much as ignoring that issue did several decades ago. If focusing on deliberation obscures the persistent realities of unequal wealth and power in America, for example, it will advance our understanding of one aspect of Tocqueville's argument only by blinding us to another: he emphasized not only the habits of the heart but also advanced a hard-headed assessment of the unsentimental calculations of self interest that such habits must struggle to restrain and redirect. Only within the relatively equal social and economic conditions of antebellum America could the practice of deliberation and the ideal of reciprocity flourish. Under

2. Spencer's Preface to *Democracy in America*, p. xi.
3. I have discussed these issues in greater detail in "Knowledge and Belief in American Public Life," in *Knowledge and Belief in America: Enlightenment Traditions and Modern Religious Thought*, ed. William M. Shea and Peter A. Huff (Cambridge: Cambridge University Press, 1995), pp. 27–51.

the more common conditions of inequality, Tocqueville feared, democratic behavior and democratic goals would wither.

The tendency to overlook this aspect of *Democracy in America* allows sentimental communitarians and supply siders alike to imagine that pockets of vibrant associational life can stand in for the egalitarian reality Tocqueville himself stressed. Thus New Gingrich, addressing the Republican Party National Convention in San Diego on August 13, 1996, praised the contributions of churches and neighborhood organizations and concluded that nothing less than "the moral case for lower taxes" is to be found in Tocqueville's *Democracy in America.* Simplification for simplification, that claim rivals the worst excesses of communitarians who imply that Tocqueville shows us how regular block parties can moderate the pathological violence of gangs.

Although only interpretations as multi-dimensional as Tocqueville's own can help us resist the persistent temptation to capture him and enlist his book for narrow partisan crusades, shrill and one-sided arguments attract more attention than such nuanced readings. Not only will competing American interpreters continue to champion various Tocquevilles for various purposes, new strains will no doubt also sprout from America's fertile soil. If the Tocqueville who warned us about the dangers of totalitarianism has died with the Cold War, for example, others in addition to the communitarians' partisan of deliberative democracy will doubtless take his place.

We need only remember that, at one end of our cultural spectrum, the President who quoted Tocqueville most frequently was Ronald Reagan, whose speech writers, like Gingrich, detached Tocqueville's emphasis on civil society from his emphasis on the ideal of reciprocity. At the opposite end, we are about to see the appearance of the first study arguing that Tocqueville, with his sensitivity to multiple causation, his tolerance for paradox, and his capacity to embrace conflicting values and hold in suspension contradictory ideas, should at last be recognized as an early postmodernist who has too long remained in shadow.[4] The life of Tocqueville in America, already reflecting the circuitous path of democratic theory and practice over a century and a half, seems destined to continue indefinitely. That interest persists, however, for reasons that owe more to Americans' irresistible urge to simplify Tocqueville's ideas than to a willingness to acknowledge his ambivalence or to keep in focus the multiple dimensions of his complex analysis of American democracy.

4. According to Allan Megill's comment at the symposium on Tocqueville at the University of Virginia on November 3, 1995, at which this essay was first discussed, in a forthcoming study of postmodernism and historiography Frank Ankersmit singles out Tocqueville's work as exemplifying the unresolved tensions of postmodernism.

TAMARA M. TEALE

Tocqueville and American Legal Studies: The Paradox of Liberty and Destruction†

In *Democracy in America*, Tocqueville's section entitled "The Present State and the Probable Future of the Indian Tribes Inhabiting the Territory of the Union" comes in the final chapter of the volumes published in 1835 and seems almost an afterthought. In fact, François Furet is sure Tocqueville had to "discard his analytical system" in order to write about Native North Americans (182). However, Tocqueville had stated that his main business was to describe "in what spirit and by the aid of what laws the Anglo-American confederation was formed" and thereby arrive at definitive statements about the "inferior position" of American Indians (316).¹ A close study of this "Indian Tribes" section reveals Tocqueville's contribution to the relatively new discipline of Native American legal studies. His extensive references to Congressional documents encourage us to focus on the specific juridical procedures and the White American *mœurs* which shaped the American Indian social and political situation.

Tocqueville recorded the contradiction between the unprecedented liberty for the European-become-American and the destruction of indigenous nations: "As the Indians have withdrawn and died, an immense nation is taking their place and constantly growing. Never has such a prodigious development been seen among the nations, nor a destruction so rapid" (321). With self-conscious irony, Tocqueville concluded that "the United States Americans" have both "exterminated" the First Nations and "prevented" them from "sharing their rights"; they have done so "with wonderful ease, quietly, legally, and philanthropically." Tocqueville added that "the conduct of the United States Americans toward the natives was inspired by the most chaste affection for legal formalities" (339). Tocqueville's achievement in Native American legal studies can best be approached by briefly looking at just a few of the numerous "legal" documents of destruction which he read.²

The primary point in analyzing the legal features of the destruction was Tocqueville's realization that the government structure which brought liberty to Whites, the separation of Federal and State govern-

† Tamara M. Teale is a professor of literature at the State University of New York at Stony Brook. This essay appeared in *The Tocqueville Review* 17.2 (1996). Reprinted by permission of La Société Tocqueville.

1. All page references to *Democracy in America* are for the George Lawrence translation. HarperPerennial, HarperCollins, New York, 1988.
2. James T. Schleifer provides indespensible insight into Tocqueville's sources in *The Making of Tocqueville's 'Democracy in America*, (Chapel Hill, 1980). See *Tocqueville and Beaumont in America*, page 727, for George Wilson Pierson's recounting of Tocqueville's acquisition of key texts including "legislative documents" supplied by Alexander Everett's brother, U.S. Representative from Massachusetts, Edward Everett. An anti-Removal advocate, Everett spoke in Congress May 19, 1830, against the Indian Removal Act; see *Speeches on the Passage of the Bill for the Removal of the Indians*, Kraus Reprint Company, Millwood, New York, 1973.

ments, actually worked toward the "complete expulsion" of Native Americans which was the "final objective" and the tacit end in mind (335). The major case which Tocqueville uses to illustrate the separation of State and Federal control is that of the Indian Removal Act of May 28, 1830, in which the Federal government finally fulfilled a pact with the State of Georgia dating from April 24, 1802. In 1802, Georgia had demanded that "the United States shall, at their own expense, extinguish, for the use of Georgia, as early as the same can be peaceably obtained, on reasonable terms, the Indian title" (United States Congress, *Laws of the Colonial and State Governments*, 190). The Federal government was very slow in finding a "peaceably obtained" time to satisfy the State of Georgia. As early as 1817, in a letter to President James Monroe, Major General Andrew Jackson stated that the complete removal of the Cherokee from Georgia was a national security issue linking the good of the State with the good of the nation.[3] Eventually, the Georgia legislature passed a Resolution, December 19, 1827, declaring the Cherokee Nation to be the "tenants at will" of the Georgians, what Tocqueville ironically called extending "the benefit" of their laws over the Cherokee Nation. The Monroe administration was slow to respond to Georgia's demands for compliance but finally, in 1830, two months after Andrew Jackson became President, he signed the Removal act as fulfillment of a campaign promise to Georgia and Tennessee.

In the following passage from *Democracy in America*, the central issues of State and Federal powers displayed in the Indian Removal Act, crystalize for Tocqueville:

> There is less of cupidity and violence in the Union's policy toward the Indians than in that of the individual states, but in both cases the governments are equally lacking in good faith.

> The states, in extending what they are pleased to call the benefit of their laws over the Indians, calculate that the latter will sooner depart than submit; and the central government, when it promises these unlucky people a permanent asylum in the West, is well aware of its inability to guarantee this.

> The states' tyranny forces the savages to flee, and the Union's promises make flight easy. Both are means to the same end. (337)

The State of Georgia, clamoring for Removal, is guilty of greed and tyranny, but the United States' government is only a little less guilty of "cupidity and violence." The "Union's promises" which "make flight easy" included the "philanthropic" gesture of an acre-for-acre exchange west of the Mississippi, guaranteed in the text of the Removal Act but never fulfilled.

For Tocqueville, the Indian Removal Act demonstrated that it didn't matter what the Cherokee had done to assimilate or acculturate to

---

3. In John Spencer Bassett's *Correspondence of Andrew Jackson*, Volume II, May 1, 1814 to December 31, 1819. New York: Kraus Reprint Co, 1969, 277–280.

White civilization, they still had to vacate the southeast: "In the little that they have done, these Indians have assuredly displayed as much natural genius as the European peoples in their greatest undertakings" (333), but "The tyranny of the government is usually added to the greed of the colonists" (334). The federal government was too weak to protect the Cherokee in their indigenous landbase, the "national spirit" was too expansionist.

Tocqueville cannot directly say everything about Indian policy that strikes him as crucial. With a footnote to the above passage, he directs us to further reading: "To form an exact idea of the policy of the individual states and of the Union toward the Indians" one should consult several documents, "[i]n particular that of March 30, 1802" (337). Tocqueville didn't provide the name of this document but it is the most important of the Indian Trade and Intercourse Acts of the Thomas Jefferson years. In this Act, the Jefferson administration connects trade and economic issues with land ownership and United States expansion. This Federal Act preceded the 1802 removal pact with Georgia by only one month and it is around this Trade and Intercourse Act that the issue of Federal control of Indian affairs crystalizes. In Section 12 of the act, only the United States can make a treaty with a Native nation for the purpose of "extinguishing" the Indian title. No "purchase, grant, lease, or other conveyance of lands," or any title or claim is lawful unless the treaty is made "pursuant to the constitution" and it shall be a "misdemeanor" for any persons not employed by the United States to negotiate such a treaty, "to treat with any such Indian nation, or tribe of Indians." However, agents of any State, in which the treaty is signed for title extinguishment, may be present at the treaty for the purpose of adjusting with the Indians the "compensation to be made" for land within that State (Prucha, 1990).[4] Jefferson sought an equitable blend of State and Federal interests in the highly sensitive issue of land acquisition.

Tocqueville's development of his interest in the Federal jurisdiction of American Indian affairs—"an exact idea of the policy of the individual states and of the Union"—stems in part from a conversation with the former Governor of Tennessee, expansionist Sam Houston, recorded in "Notebook E" of *Journey to America*. While traveling in the United States, Tocqueville may have had only an initial awareness of the 1802 Trade Act for he leaves only a superficial marginal note to the Houston conversation: "The United States does not recognize the Indians' right to alienate their land except in their capacity as a people, and when the purchaser is the United States itself" (243). One can imagine Tocqueville recording the Houston conversation for later

4. This particular Trade and Intercourse Act set the terms by which United States' agents could treat with Native nations for the purpose of "extinguishing" Indian title. This act sought to stringently regulate White interaction with Native nations and began the systematized policy of land acquisition that would form the basis of the Louisiana Purchase agreement of the following year, 1803. The Louisiana Purchase agreement was not a purchase of land *from* France, rather, the United States bought from France the right to be the sole imperial power to extinguish Indian title. The mechanism of extinguishment, treaty making, was later abolished in Congress on March 3, 1871 (Prucha, 1990).

use as evidence of the "chaste affection for legal formalities" and the "philanthropic" gloss of Indian Removal.[5] Though the 1802 Trade Act goes to great lengths to control White interaction within Native nations, Tocqueville saw, ironically, that "It is impossible to destroy men with more respect to the laws of humanity" (339).

Tocqueville had noticed that for Native nations it didn't matter which legislative body had superior power—the State or Washington, D.C.—the "end" was the same. Tocqueville saw that the State of Georgia's demands for Federal compliance with the 1802 pact were so strong that a State-Federal fight over control of Indian affairs had been inevitable; it only remained for a States' rights advocate, Andrew Jackson, to become president that the twenty-eight-year-old 1802 pact for removal would be honored to Georgia's liking. Additionally, while researching and writing *Democracy in America*, Tocqueville found the Clark-Cass report to Congress, a "curious record," which he frequently cites (325).[6] This report resulted in legislation during the Jackson administration, on June 30, 1834, that would bring all contact with Native nations under one systematic Federally-controlled policy also pleasing to the States.

In *The Making of Tocqueville's 'Democracy in America*, James Schleifer writes about Tocqueville's recognition that States' rights advocates worried about the "consolidation of sovereignty in the hands of the central government" (103). Though the Federal government had "ignominiously retreated" from a number of issues which it allowed the States to control (107), it was generally agreed that the central government controlled policies with Native nations. Schleifer cites a text which Tocqueville knew well and to which he often referred on U.S. Constitutional matters, Joseph Blunt's *A Historical Sketch of the Confederacy*, 1825. Schleifer writes that Blunt was "alarmed by the frequent charges of usurpation made against the national government because of its Indian and land policies" (106–7). However, Blunt clearly states that the Federal government dominates Native nations policy. Blunt maintained that *A Historical Sketch* "grew out of the controversy between the state of Georgia and the general government." Georgia's never ending "zeal" in States' rights is due to "the magnitude of their territorial claims" and "local aggrandizement" at the expense of the "general welfare" (6), that is, jeopardizing peaceful relations with the Cherokee and Choctaw Nations bordering Georgia. Blunt writes that "the regulation of all Indian affairs"—such as land cessioning—was "thought more peculiarly to belong to congress" (64). Furthermore, the Articles of Confederation show that "the general government exercised the then unquestioned

5. Tocqueville's note in *Journey* follows Houston's naïve statement about the Indian Removal Act of 1830. "The United States have bound themselves by the most solemn oaths never to sell the lands contained within those [Indian reservation] limits, and never in any form to allow the introduction of a while population there." Tocqueville's prediction was correct that American Indians would not be left in peace in their "permanent asylum." Oklahoma was opened to White settlement in the early 1880s.
6. House Document 117, 20th Congress, 2nd Session, Vol. 3, Serial Set 186, presented February 9, 1829; signed by William Clark and Lewis Cass, February 4.

prerogative, of defining the limits, guarantying the possessions, and establishing the condition of Indian tribes within the undisputed limits of a state" (66).[7]

Just two years before Blunt's publication, the Supreme Court case, *Johnson v. McIntosh* (8 Wheat. 543), determined that the Federal government's right to extinguish Indian title was "absolute" and Indian tribes and nations were "deemed incapable of transferring the absolute title to others" though they had natural or occupancy rights (Prucha, 1990, 36). There were two claimants to the same piece of land, one of whom had received the title directly from a Native nation, the other by a grant from the central government, then under the British crown (Prucha, 1962, 185). Chief Justice John Marshall delivered the majority opinion that the United States' central government inherited "the absolute title" directly from the British crown extending back to the earliest papal "line of demarcation" (Blunt, 3); thus, the federal grant was superior to an Indian-granted title. Blunt's work *in toto* can be read as an exegisis of the Supreme Court decision though he does not mention it directly. But another favorite reference work of Tocqueville's goes in depth on the *Johnson v. McIntosh* ruling. Also cited by James Schleifer, as helping Tocqueville to examine the "antagonism between the states and the Union" (92), was Joseph Story's *Commentaries on the Constitution of the United States*, 1833. Story says "one cannot do better than transcribe from the pages" of *Johnson v. McIntosh* (Vol. I, p. 7) and thus Tocqueville would have read in its entirety the text of Marshall's decision of absolute Federal control over Indian affairs. Tocqueville had concluded that "complete expulsion" is the objective of the "tyrannous measures" of the twin action of the State and Federal governments (335). Even so, Marshall's ruling had a "philanthropic" aspect, noticed by Tocqueville, when Marshall stated, "Humanity . . . acting on public opinion, has established, as a general rule, that the conquered shall not be wantonly oppressed" (Prucha, 36) and such may be the foundation of the United States' indigenous reservation policy. Nonetheless, Tocqueville agreed with the Cherokee delegation's petition to Congress, which he quotes, "our fathers never consented to a treaty whose result was to deprive them of their most sacred rights and to rob them of their country."[8] Tocqueville stated, "Such is the language of the Indians; what they say is true . . ." (338).

Tocqueville's unique contribution to American Indian legal studies has important implications today. His regular and systematic, though brief, work in the area of American Indian legal studies enables us to connect his analysis of Native nation legal standing to today's foremost

---

7. Today, the Indian Gaming Regulatory Act of October 17, 1988, is the new three-way battle for jurisdiction and sovereignty between Native nations, Washington, D.C., and the States. See "Supreme Court accepts Seminole gaming case." The Supreme Court "granted review in Seminole Tribe of Florida vs. the State of Florida—the first major test case involving the constitutionality of the federal Indian gaming law," in *Indian Country Today/Lakota Times,* January 26, 1995, Northern Plains Edition, p. A1.
8. The entirety of the Cherokee delegation petition to Congress, which Tocqueville quotes in part, can be found as *House of Representatives,* Report No. 331, (February 15, 1830) Vol. 3, Serial Set 201.

contemporary expert, Vine Deloria, Jr., a legal historian and philosopher of Lakota heritage. As Tocqueville briefly attempted in the 1830s, Vine Deloria, Jr., since the late 1960s, has committed himself to the study of the United States' Constitution and legal system as it relates to Native nations' sovereignty and juridical-political issues. Deloria writes that "The carefully designed system of checks and balances" which secured democracy and liberty for white Americans "simply did not function for American Indians" (288). Deloria's research shows that the judicial branch of government, the Supreme Court, had a determining influence in creating the atmosphere of the 1820s and shaping the belief in the Federal government's absolute title. He also analyzes the role of the President in American Indian political life which has effects well into the twentieth century. Certainly, Tocqueville's rendering of the American Indian social or "legal" position of the 1820s enables us to analyze current United States' policies toward government-to-government relations with sovereign Native nations.[9]

In conclusion, we must wonder at the singularity of the amount of time and space Tocqueville gave to American Indians. However marginal it may seem, he was unique in this. Though no one, including Tocqueville, understood that American Indians believed the earth could not be privately owned, he identified, to some degree, with the American Indian social position. Tocqueville knew that the Cherokee were an ancient people "established on the land where they now live before the arrival of the Europeans" (334). Their cultural pride was so great, and White ways of mass agri-business, profit, and accumulation so degrading to the small-scale farmers and hunters, that many Cherokee refused to be White. Tocqueville compared the Native person to the feudal noble in his castle refusing to take part in the new "social state" until "necessity sometimes drives them to it" (328). In the paradox of the twin birth of liberty and genocide, we can see Tocqueville's "appropriation of his inheritance," as a type of vanishing aristocrat, and his mapping of it onto the situation of American Indians. François Furet says that for the United States to be absorbed into the "ordinary flow of history," represented by the European model, America had to "lose its savages" (165). But Europe also had to "lose" its aristocrats to enter the flow of the increasingly bourgeois world. Furet elaborated that Tocqueville had a life-long "horrified fascination" with the near-extinction of his own family: "By the end of his adolescence, he had succeeded in transforming this family experience into an intellectual problem" (185). In a thunderstorm scene in his journal narrative, "Fortnight in the Wilds," Tocqueville identified with a young Anishanaabe (Chippewa) man, "un homme" like himself, who recognized in the thunder and "groans of the forest" a sign of the "final fate"

9. Examples of current issues include "U.S. Interior Secretary Bruce Babbitt declined during a visit to the Menominee reservation to take a stance on Indian gambling or the tribe's bid for broad hunting and fishing rights," *News from Indian Country*, late April 1995, p. 2; "Swift action by Indian nations to a potentially damaging Interior Department policy that could deprive numerous tribes of their sovereignty rights is getting Congressional response," *News from Indian Country*, mid-June 1994, p. 13.; and "Clinton signs law recognizing three Michigan Tribes," *News from Indian Country*, mid-Oct, 1994, p. 2.

of Native nations in the "unequal battle" against the leveling effects of industry and democracy (*Journey*, 374). If Tocqueville saw himself as part of a vanishing breed of aristocrat, so too did he see American Indians as making way for a European-American modernity; his melancholy in "Fortnight" is unmistakable.[1] Tocqueville wrote that in the United States "there is already some precedent for every act of tyranny, and every crime is following some example . . . nothing ancient remains which men are afraid to destroy" (*DA*, 314). Dare I suggest that as Tocqueville wrote the lines, "nothing ancient remains," he was thinking of his family extinction *as well as* the leveling effects of industry on Native Americans?

One thing is certain, Tocqueville provides us with a path for American Indian legal studies to enter mainstream debates on the definitions of democracy and culture. Those of us who follow him can pick up the path he left.

---

1. Tocqueville's belief in American Indians as vanishing was not necessarily a European metaphysics of manifest destiny. Furet says Tocqueville's "entire work can be regarded as an endless reflection on the nobility. . . . meditation begun in adolescence and focused on himself, his family, his life, the historical significance of what his parents had lived through . . ." Tocqueville's entire "intellectual process did involve a certain degree of fatalism . . ." (169–171).

Selected Bibliography

• indicates a work included or excerpted in this Norton Critical Edition.

Aron, Raymond. *Main Currents in Sociological Thought.* Vol. 1. New York: Basic Books, 1965.
• Banfield, Edward C. "The Illiberal Tocqueville." In *Interpreting Tocqueville's Democracy in America.* Ed. Ken Masugi. Savage, Md.: Rowman and Littlefield, 1991.
Boesche, Roger, ed. *Alexis de Tocqueville's Selected Letters on Politics and Society.* Berkeley: University of California Press, 1985.
• Commager, Henry Steele. *Commager on Tocqueville.* Columbia: University of Missouri Press, 1993.
Drescher, Seymour. *Tocqueville and England.* Cambridge, Mass.: Harvard University Press, 1964.
Eisenstadt, Abraham S. *Reconsidering Tocqueville's Democracy in America.* New Brunswick: Rutgers University Press, 1988.
Hadari, Saguiv A. *Theory in Practice: Tocqueville's New Science of Politics.* Stanford: Stanford University Press, 1989.
Hereth, Michael. *Alexis de Tocqueville: Threats to Freedom in Democracy.* Durham: Duke University Press, 1986.
Jardin, André. *Tocqueville: A Biography.* Baltimore: Johns Hopkins University Press, 1998.
Kammen, Michael. *Alexis de Tocqueville and Democracy in America.* Washington, D.C: Library of Congress, 1998.
Kessler, Sanford. *Tocqueville's Civil Religion.* Albany: State University of New York Press, 1994.
• Kloppenberg, James T. "Life Everlasting: Tocqueville in America. *The Tocqueville Review* 17 (1996): 19–36.
Koritansky, John C. *Alexis de Tocqueville and the New Science of Politics: An Interpretation of Democracy in America.* Durham: Carolina Academic Press, 1986.
Lawler, Peter A. *The Restless Mind: Alexis de Tocqueville on the Origin and Perpetuation of Human Liberty.* Lanham, Md.: Rowman and Littlefield, 1993.
Lawler, Peter A, and J. Alulis, ed. *Tocqueville's Defense of Human Liberty.* New York: Garland, 1993.
• Lerner, Max. *Tocqueville and American Civilization.* New York: Harper and Row, 1996.
Lively, Jack. *The Social and Political Thought of Alexis de Tocqueville.* Oxford: Clarendon Press, 1965.
Mancini, Mathew. *Alexis de Tocqueville.* New York: Twayne Publications, 1994.
Manent, Pierre. *Tocqueville and the Nature of Democracy.* Lanham, Md.: Rowman and Littlefield, 1996.
Mansfield, Harvey, Jr., and Delba Winthrop. Introduction. *Democracy in America.* Chicago: The University of Chicago Press, 2000.
Masugi, Ken, ed. *Interpreting Tocqueville's Democracy in America.* Savage, Md.: Rowman and Littlefield, 1991.
Mayer, J. P. *Alexis de Tocqueville, A Biographical Study.* New York: Viking Press, 1940.
Mélonio, Françoise. *Tocqueville and the French.* Charlottesville: University of Virginia Press, 1993.
Mélonio, Françoise, and F. Guellec, ed. *Tocqueville: Lettres Choisies, Souvenirs, 1814–1859.* Paris, Gallimard, 2003.
Mitchell, Joshua. *The Fragility of Freedom: Tocqueville on Religion, Democracy and the American Future.* Chicago: University of Chicago Press, 1995.
• Nisbet, Robert. "Many Tocquevilles." *The American Scholar* 46 (1976/1977): 59–75.
Pierson, George Wilson. *Tocqueville in America.* Baltimore: Johns Hopkins University Press, 1996.
• Riesman, David. "Tocqueville as Ethnographer." *The American Scholar* 30 (1961): 174–87.
de Robien, Gilles. *Alexis de Tocqueville.* Paris: Flammarion, 2000.
• Rodgers, Daniel T. "Of Prophets and Prophecy." In *Reconsidering Tocqueville's Democracy in America.* Ed. Abraham S. Eisenstadt. New Brunswick: Rutgers University Press, 1988.
• Schleifer, James T. *The Making of Tocqueville's Democracy in America.* Chapel Hill: University of North Carolina Press, 1980.
• Schlesinger, Arthur, Jr. "Individualism and Apathy in Tocqueville's *Democracy.*" In *Reconsidering Tocqueville's Democracy in America.* Ed. Abraham S. Eisenstadt. New Brunswick: Rutgers University Press, 1988.
Siedentop, Larry. *Tocqueville.* Oxford: Oxford University Press, 1994.
Taub, Richard, ed. *American Society in Tocqueville's Time and Today.* Chicago: Rand McNally College Publishing Co., 1974.

• Teale, Tamara M. "Tocqueville and American Legal Studies: The Paradox of Liberty and Destruction." *The Tocqueville Review* 17.2 (1996): 59–65.
• Wilentz, Sean. "Many Democracies: On Tocqueville and Jacksonian America." In *Reconsidering Tocqueville's Democracy in America*. Ed. Abraham S. Eisenstadt. New Brunswick: Rutgers University Press, 1988.
• Wolin, Sheldon *Tocqueville: Between Two Worlds*. Princeton, Princeton University Press, 2001.
  Zeitlin, Irving. *Liberty, Equality and Revolution in Alexis de Tocqueville*. Boston: Little Brown, 1971.
• Zuckert, Catherine. "Not by Preaching: Tocqueville on the Role of Religion in American Democracy." *The Review of Politics* 44 (1981): 259–83.